Baker's
Dictionary
of
Theology

Baker's Dictionary of Theology

Everett F. Harrison
Editor-in-chief

Geoffrey W. Bromiley
Associate Editor

Carl F. H. Henry
Consulting Editor

BAKER BOOK HOUSE
Grand Rapids, Michigan 49506

Paperback Edition
First printing, February 1985

ISBN: 0-8010-4289-5

Library of Congress Catalog Card Number: 60-7333

Printed in the United States of America

PREFACE

In recent years we have witnessed a resurgence of interest in biblical studies which continues unabated. It is fitting that a dictionary of theological and ecclesiastical terms should be added to the steadily increasing number of works designed to aid the student in acquiring a sound knowledge of the content of Scripture and of historical theology.

The articles are framed with a view to acquainting the reader with the tension points in theological discussion today in addition to providing a positive exposition of the biblical content in each case. Philosophical terms with a religious significance are included, as well as the various sects and movements which belong to the history of the church.

To serve the convenience of the reader as fully as possible, each term or concept is treated separately, as a rule. This avoids endless searching through long articles for a particular item of information.

The editors join the publisher in expressing the hope that the use of this volume will promote a richer understanding and appreciation of Christian truth.

LIST OF CONTRIBUTORS

Allis, Oswald T., B.D., Ph.D.
Retired

Archer, Gleason L., Jr., LL.B., B.D., Ph.D.
Professor of Biblical Languages, Fuller Theological Seminary

Babbage, Stuart B., Ph.D., Th.D.
Dean of St. Paul's Cathedral, Melbourne, Australia, and Principal of Ridley College

Barker, Glenn Wesley, A.M., Th.D.
Professor of New Testament, Gordon Divinity School

Beegle, Dewey M., B.S., B.D., Ph.D.
Associate Professor of Hebrew and Old Testament, The Biblical Seminary in New York

Boettner, Loraine, B.S., Th.M., D.D., Litt.D.
Theological writer

Booth, F. Carlton, A.B., Mus.D.
Associate Professor of Evangelism, Fuller Theological Seminary

Boyd, Robert Frederick, Th.D.
Professor of Bible, Presbyterian School of Christian Education

Brandon, Owen Rupert, A.L.C.D., A.M.
Tutor and Librarian, Lecturer in Theology and Psychology, London College of Divinity

Bromiley, Geoffrey W., Ph.D., Litt.D.
Professor of Church History and Historical Theology, Fuller Theological Seminary

Broomall, Wick, A.M., Th.M.
Minister, The Westminster Presbyterian Church, Augusta, Georgia

Bruce, Frederick Fyvie, A.M., D.D.
Rylands Professor of Biblical Criticism and Exegesis, University of Manchester, England

Buswell, J. Oliver, Jr., B.D., Ph.D.
Dean of Graduate Faculty, Covenant College and Seminary

Cameron, William John, B.D., A.M.
Professor of New Testament Language, Literature and Theology, Free Church of Scotland College, Edinburgh

Carlson, E. Leslie, Th.D.
Professor of Biblical Introduction, Old Testament, and Semitic Languages, Southwestern Baptist Theological Seminary

Carnell, Edward John, S.T.M., Th.D., Ph.D.
Professor of Apologetics, Fuller Theological Seminary

Cartledge, Samuel A., B.D., Ph.D.
Professor of New Testament, Dean of the Graduate Department, Columbia Theological Seminary

Clark, Gordon H., Ph.D.
Professor of Philosophy and Head of Department, Butler University

Clark, Robert Edward David, Ph.D.
Lecturer in Chemistry, Cambridgeshire Technical College and School of Art, Cambridge, England

Cleveland, Howard Z., Th.D.
Chairman of Language Department, Oak Hills Christian Training School.

Coates, Richard John, A.M.
Vicar of Christ Church, Weston-Super-Mare, Somerset, England, and Lecturer, Tyndale Hall, Bristol, England

Collins, George Norman MacLeod, B.D.
Minister, Free St. Columba's Church, Edinburgh, Scotland

Colquhoun, Frank, A.M., L.Th.
Vicar of Wallington, Surrey, England

Connell, J. Clement, A.M.
Director of Studies and Lecturer in Biblical Theology, London Bible College

Corlett, Lewis T., A.B.
President of Nazarene Theological Seminary

Craston, Richard Colin, A.B., B.D.
Vicar of St. Paul's Church, Deansgate, Bolton, England

Crum, Terrelle B., A.M., LL.D.
Dean of the College, Providence Barrington Bible College

Danker, Frederick W., A.B., B.D.
Assistant Professor in the Department of Exegetical Theology, Concordia Theological Seminary

Davis, Donald Gordon, B.D., Ph.D.
Professor of Church History, Talbot Theological Seminary

Duff-Forbes, Lawrence W. G., F.I.I.A., A.A.I.I., D.D., Litt.D., F.Pl.S.
President, Jewish Evangelical Witness

Earle, Ralph, Th.D.
Professor of New Testament, Nazarene Theological Seminary

Edman, V. Raymond, Ph.D.
President, Wheaton College

Ellis, E. Earle, B.S., B.D., Ph.D.
Associate Professor of New Testament Interpretation, Southern Baptist Theological Seminary

Ellison, Henry Leopold, A.B., B.D.
Supervisor in Old Testament, University of Cambridge, Cambridge, England

Farrer, Michael Robert Wedlake, A.M.
Tutor, Clifton Theological College, Bristol, England

Feinberg, Charles L., Th.D., Ph.D.
Professor of Semitics and Old Testament, and Director, Talbot Theological Seminary

Fisher, Fred Louis, Th.D.
Professor of New Testament, Golden Gate Baptist Theological Seminary

Free, Joseph Paul, Ph.D.
Director of Archaeological Studies and Professor of Archaeology, Wheaton College

Fuller, Daniel Payton, B.S., Th.D.
Associate Professor of English Bible, Fuller Theological Seminary

Gay, George Arthur, Th.M.
Vice-president of the Latin American Bible Seminary, San José, Costa Rica

Gerstner, John H., Th.M., Ph.D., D.D.
Professor of Church History and Government, Pittsburgh-Xenia Theological Seminary

Goddard, Burton L., S.M., S.T.M., Th.D.
Dean, Gordon Divinity School

Granberg, Lars I., B.S., Ph.D.
Dean of Students and Associate Professor of Pastoral Counseling and Psychology, Fuller Theological Seminary

Gribble, Robert F., A.B., B.D.
Professor of Old Testament Language and Exegesis, Austin Presbyterian Theological Seminary

Grider, J. Kenneth, Th.B., B.D., Ph.D.
Associate Professor of Theology, Nazarene Theological Seminary

Grounds, Vernon C., A.B., B.D.
President and Professor, Conservative Baptist Theological Seminary

Guthrie, Donald, Th.M.
Tutor for New Testament Language and Literature, London Bible College, London, England

Gwinn, Ralph, B.D., Ph.D.
Associate Professor of Religion, Knoxville College

Harris, R. Laird, B.S., Th.M., Ph.D.
Professor of Old Testament, Covenant College and Seminary

Harrison, Everett F., Th.D., Ph.D.
Professor of New Testament, Fuller Theological Seminary

Henry, Carl F. H., Th.D., Ph.D.
Editor, *Christianity Today*

Higginson, Richard Edwin, L.Th., B.D., A.M.
Vicar of Redland and Lecturer in Tyndale Hall, Bristol, England

Hodgman, Charles A., Jr., B.S., Th.M.
Candidate for Ph.D., Hartford Theological Seminary

Hubbard, David A., B.D., Ph.D.
Chairman of the Division of Biblical Studies and Philosophy, Westmont College

Hughes, Philip Edgcumbe, B.D., A.M., D.Litt.
Lecturer, Mortlake Parish Church, London, England

Jewett, Paul K., Th.M., Ph.D.
Associate Professor of Systematic Theology, Fuller Theological Seminary

Johnson, S. Lewis, A.B., Th.D.
Professor of New Testament Literature and Exegesis, Dallas Theological Seminary

Johnston, O. Raymond, A.M., Dip.Ed., Dip.Th.
Modern Languages Master at King Edward VII School, Sheffield, England

Kantzer, Kenneth S., S.T.M., Ph.D.
Chairman of the Division of Biblical Education, Wheaton College

Kelly, William, A.B.
Vicar of Flimby, Maryport, Cumberland, England

Kent, Homer A., Jr., Th.D.
Professor of New Testament and Greek, Grace Theological Seminary

Kerr, David W., A.B., Th.M.
Professor of Old Testament, Gordon Divinity School

Kerr, William Nigel, Th.D., Ph.D.
Professor of Church History, Gordon Divinity School

Kevan, Ernest F., Th.M.
Principal, London Bible College, London, England

Knox, David Broughton, Th.M., Ph.D.
Principal, Moore College, Newtown, New South Wales, Australia

Kromminga, Carl Gerhard, A.B., Th.B.
Associate Professor of Practical Theology, Calvin Theological Seminary

Kuhn, Harold B., S.T.M., Ph.D.
Professor of Philosophy of Religion, Asbury Theological Seminary

Ladd, George Eldon, Th.B., B.D., Ph.D.
Professor of Biblical Theology, Fuller Theological Seminary

Lamorte, André, Th.D., LL.D.
Aix-en-Provence, France

LaSor, William Sanford, Th.D., Ph.D.
Professor of Old Testament, Fuller Theological Seminary

Laurin, Robert B., Th.M., Ph.D.
Associate Professor of Old Testament, California Baptist Theological Seminary

Lewis, Jack Pearl, S.T.B., Ph.D.
Professor of Old Testament and New Testament, Harding College School of Bible and Religion

Lindquist, Stanley E., Ph.D.
Professor of Psychology, Fresno State College

Lindsell, Harold, B.S., Ph.D.
Dean of the Faculty and Professor of Missions, Fuller Theological Seminary

Marchant, George John Charles, A.M., Lic.Theol.
Vicar of St. Nicholas, Durham, England

Masselink, William, Th.D., Ph.D.
Teacher of Reformed Doctrine, Reformed Bible Institute

M'Callin, Albert Victor, A.B., B.D.
Vice-principal, London College of Divinity, London, England

McPheeters, Julian C., A.B.
President, Asbury Theological Seminary

Michelsen, A. Berkeley, B.D., Ph.D.
Associate Professor, New Testament Interpretation, Wheaton College Graduate School

Morris, Leon, B.Sc., Th.M., Ph.D.
Vice-principal, Ridley College, Melbourne, Australia

Motyer, John Alexander, B.D., A.M.
Vice-principal of Clifton Theological College, Stoke Hill, Bristol, England

Mounce, Robert H., Th.M., Ph.D.
Assistant Professor of Biblical Literature, Bethel College and Seminary

Mueller, J. Theodore, Th.D., Ph.D.
Professor of Doctrinal and Exegetical Theology, Concordia Theological Seminary

Murray, John, A.M., Th.M.
Professor of Systematic Theology, Westminster Theological Seminary

Nicole, Roger, Th.D., Ph.D.
Professor of Theology, Gordon Divinity School

Packer, James I., Ph.D.
Senior Tutor, Tyndale Hall, Bristol, England

Parker, Thomas Henry Louis, B.D., A.M.
Rector of Great and Little Ponton, Lincolnshire, England

Payne, J. Barton, A.M., Th.D.
Associate Professor of Old Testament, Wheaton College Graduate School of Theology

Pfeiffer, Charles F., B.D., Ph.D.
Associate Professor of Old Testament, Gordon Divinity School

Proctor, William Cecil Gibbon, B.D., A.M.
Rector, Harold's Cross Parish, and Lecturer in Divinity School, Trinity College, Dublin, Ireland

Purkiser, Westlake T., D.D., Ph.D.
Professor of Biblical Theology and English Bible, Nazarene Theological Seminary

Ramm, Bernard, B.D., Ph.D.
Professor of Theology and Apologetics, California Baptist Seminary

Rees, Paul S., A.B., D.D., Litt.D., L.H.D.
Vice President at Large, World Vision, Inc.

Rehwinkel, Alfred Martin, B.D., A.M.
Professor of Theology, Concordia Theological Seminary

Reid, William Stanford, Th.M., Ph.D.
Associate Professor of History, McGill University, Montreal, Canada

Renwick, Alexander MacDonald, D.D., D.Litt.
Professor of Church History, Free Church of Scotland College, Edinburgh, Scotland

Robinson, William Childs, A.M., Th.D.
Professor of Church History and Polity, Columbia Theological Seminary

Robinson, Donald W. B., A.M.
Vice-principal, Moore Theological College, Newtown, New South Wales, Australia

Roddy, Sherman, B.D., Ph.D.
Assistant Pastor, First Presbyterian Church, Aurora, Colorado

Ross, Alexander, A.M., D.D.
Professor Emeritus, New Testament Exegesis, Free Church College, Edinburgh, Scotland

Ross, Robert Winston, A.M.
Biblical and Educational Research Editor, Scripture Press Foundation

Rule, Andrew Kerr, B.D., Ph.D.
Professor of Apologetics, Louisville Presbyterian Theological Seminary

Ryrie, Charles C., Th.D., Ph.D.
President, Philadelphia College of Bible

Schmidt, Martin Anton, Th.D.
Associate Professor of Historical Theology, San Francisco Theological Seminary

Schultz, Arnold C., A.M., Th.D.
Professor of Old Testament, Northern Baptist Theological Seminary

Singer, C. Gregg, Ph.D.
Chairman, Department of History, Catawba College

Sivertsen, Eddie, A.M., Th.D.
Registrar, California Baptist Theological Seminary

Skilton, John H., Th.B., A.M.
Associate Dean, Associate Professor, Westminster Theological Seminary

Smith, Morton H., A.B., B.D.
Professor of Bible, Belhaven College

Smith, Wilbur M., D.D.
Professor of English Bible, Fuller Theological Seminary

Stanton, Gerald Barry, B.Sc., Th.D.
Professor of Systematic Theology, Talbot Theological Seminary, and Chairman, Doctrine Department, Biola College

Stephens-Hodge, Lionel E. H., A.M.
Tutor and Chaplain, London College of Divinity, London, England, and at St. John's Hall, Northwood, Middlesex, England

Tenney, Merrill C., Th.B., Ph.D.
Dean of Graduate School, Wheaton College

Thomson, J. G. S. S., B.D., Ph.D.
Professor of Hebrew and Old Testament, Columbia Theological Seminary

Tongue, Denis Harold, A.M.
Lecturer in New Testament, Tyndale Hall, Bristol, and Vicar of Locking, Somerset, England

Unger, Merrill F., Ph.D., Th.D.
Chairman of Old Testament Department, Dallas Theological Seminary

Unmack, Robert V., B.S., B.D., Th.D.
Professor of New Testament, Central Baptist Seminary

Van Horn, Leonard T., A.M., M.B.E.
Minister, First Presbyterian Church, Port Gibson, Mississippi

Van Til, Cornelius, Th.M., Ph.D.
Professor of Apologetics, Westminster Theological Seminary

Waetjen, Herman Charles, B.D., Th.D.
Assistant Professor, University of Southern California

Walker, George Stuart Murdoch, B.D., Ph.D.
Lecturer in Church History, University of Leeds, Yorks, England

Wallace, David H., Th.M., Ph.D.
Associate Professor of Biblical Theology, California Baptist Theological Seminary

Wallace, Ronald Stewart, B.Sc., Ph.D.
Minister, Lothian Road Church (Church of Scotland), Edinburgh, Scotland

Walls, Andrew Finlay, B.Litt., A.M.
Lecturer in Theology, Fourah Bay College, University of Durham, Sierra Leone, Africa

Walters, Dick H., A.B., Th.B.
President, Reformed Bible Institute

Walvoord, John F., A.M., Th.D.
President, Professor of Systematic Theology, Dallas Theological Seminary

Ward, Wayne E., A.B., Th.D.
Associate Professor of Theology, Southern Baptist Theological Seminary

Wessel, Walter W., Ph.D.
Professor of Bible, North American Baptist Seminary

Wheaton, David H., B.D., A.M.
Tutor at Oak Hill Theological College, and Curate of Christ Church, Cockfosters, London, England

Wilson, Carl W., A.B., Th.M.
Pastor, Presbyterian Church, U. S., Piney Flats, Tennessee

Wood, Arthur Skevington, A.B., Ph.D., F.R.Hist.S.
Minister of Southlands Methodist Church, York, England

Woolley, Paul, A.B., Th.M.
Professor of Church History, Westminster Theological Seminary

Woudstra, Marten H., Th.M.
Associate Professor of Old Testament, Calvin Theological Seminary

Wright, John Stafford, A.M.
Principal, Tyndale Hall, Bristol, England

Wyngaarden, Martin J., B.D., Ph.D.
Professor of Old Testament Interpretation, Calvin Theological Seminary

Young, Edward J., Th.M., Ph.D.
Professor of Old Testament, Westminster Theological Seminary

Young, G. Douglas, B.Sc., S.T.M., Ph.D.
Dean, Trinity Seminary of the Evangelical Free Church of America

Young, Warren C., B.D., Ph.D.
Professor of Christian Philosophy, Northern Baptist Theological Seminary

ABBREVIATIONS

AC — Adam Clarke's *Commentary*

Alf — Alford's *Greek Testament*

Arndt — Arndt-Gingrich, *Greek English Lexicon*

A-S — Abbott-Smith, *Manual Greek Lexicon of the NT*

ASV — American Standard Version

AThR — Anglican Theological Review

AV — Authorized Version

BA — Biblical Archaeologist

BCP — *Book of Common Prayer*

Beng — Bengel's *Gnomon*

BDB — Brown, Driver and Briggs, *Hebrew-English Lexicon of the OT*

BJRL — Bulletin of the John Rylands Library

Blunt — Blunt's *Dictionary of Doctrinal and Historical Theology*

BS — Bibliotheca Sacra

BTh — Biblical Theology

CB — *Companion to the Bible,* J. J. Von Allmen, ed.

CBQ — Catholic Biblical Quarterly

CDE — Century Dictionary and Encyclopaedia

CE — Catholic Encyclopaedia

CGT — Cambridge Greek Testament

CJT — Canadian Journal of Theology

CN — Coniectanea Neotestamentica (Lund)

ColEncy — Columbia Encyclopaedia

Corp Herm — Corpus Hermeticum

Crem — Cremer's *Biblico-Theological Lexicon of NT Greek*

DCA — Dictionary of Christian Antiquities

DCB — Dictionary of Christian Biography

DDB — Davis *Dictionary of the Bible*

DeissBS — Deissmann, Bible Studies

DeissLAE — Deissmann, Light from the Ancient East

EB — Encyclopaedia Biblica

EncyBrit — Encyclopaedia Britannica

EF — Enciclopedia Filosofica

EKL — Evangelisches Kirchenlexikon

EncSocSci — Encyclopaedia of the Social Sciences

EQ — Evangelical Quarterly

ER — An Encyclopaedia of Religion, Vergilius Ferm, ed.

ERV — English Revised Version (1881)

ETh — Evangelische Theologie

EVV — English Versions

Exp — The Expositor

ExpB — The Expositor's Bible

ExpGT — The Expositor's Greek Testament

ExpT — The Expository Times

GR — Gordon Review

HBD — Harper's Bible Dictionary

HBE — Harper's Bible Encyclopaedia

HDAC — Hastings' Dictionary of the Apostolic Church

HDB — Hastings' Dictionary of the Bible

HDCG — Hastings' Dictionary of Christ and the Gospels

HE — Historia Ecclesiastica (Eusebius)

HERE — Hastings' Encyclopaedia of Religion and Ethics

HJ — Hibbert Journal

HR — Hatch and Redpath, *Concordance to the Septuagint*

HTR — Harvard Theological Review

HZNT — Handbuch zum Neuen Testament (Lietzmann)

IB — Interpreter's Bible

ICC — International Critical Commentary

Interp — Interpretation

ISBE — International Standard Bible Encyclopaedia

JBL — Journal of Biblical Literature

JBR — Journal of Bible and Religion

JewEny — Jewish Encyclopaedia

Jos — Josephus

JQR — Jewish Quarterly Review

JTS — Journal of Theological Studies

JTVI — *Journal of the Transactions of the Victoria Institute*

KB — Koehler-Baumgartner, *Lexicon in Veteris Testamenti Libros*

KD — Keil and Delitzsch, *Commentary on the OT*

KeDo — *Kerygma und Dogma* (Goettingen)

LC — *Lutheran Cyclopaedia*

LSJ — Liddell, Scott, Jones, *Greek-English Lexicon*

LXX — Septuagint

MG — Moulton and Geden, *Concordance to the Greek Testament*

MM — Moulton and Milligan, *The Vocabulary of the Greek Testament*

MNT — *Moffatt's New Testament Commentary*

MSt — McClintock and Strong, *Cyclopaedia of Biblical, Theological and Ecclesiastical Literature*

NBC — *New Bible Commentary*, F. Davidson, ed.

Nestle — Nestle's *Novum Testamentum Graece*

NovTest — *Novum Testamentum*

NSBD — *New Standard Bible Dictionary* (Funk-Wagnalls)

NTS — *New Testament Studies*

ODCC — *The Oxford Dictionary of the Christian Church*

OS — *Oriental Studies* (London)

OTS — *Oudtestamentische Studiën*

PG — *Patrologia Graeca* (Migne)

PTR — *Princeton Theological Review*

RB — *Revue Biblique*

RGG — *Die Religion in Geschichte und Gegenwart*

RSV — Revised Standard Version

RTWB — *Richardson's Theological Word Book*

RV — Revised Version

SBD — *Standard Bible Dictionary*

SBK — *Kommentar zum Neuen Testament aus Talmud und Midrasch* (Strack and Billerbeck)

SHERK — *The New Schaff-Herzog Encyclopaedia of Religious Knowledge*

SJT — *Scottish Journal of Theology*

SmBD — *Smith Bible Dictionary*

ST — *Studia Theologica*

TCERK — *The Twentieth Century Encyclopaedia of Religious Knowledge*

ThLZ — *Theologische Literaturzeitung*

ThR — *Theologische Rundschau*

ThT — *Theology Today*

TQ — *Theologische Quartalschrift* (Tuebingen)

Trench — Trench's *Synonyms of the New Testament*

TS — *Theologische Studien*

TWNT — *Theologisches Woerterbuch zum Neuen Testament* (Kittel)

UJE — *Universal Jewish Encyclopaedia*

USR — *Union Seminary Review*

Vincent — *Word Studies in the NT*, by Marvin R. Vincent

VT — *Vetus Testamentum*

WC — *Westminster Commentaries*

WDB — *Westminster Dictionary of the Bible* (Davis-Gehman)

Wett — *Wettstein's Novum Testamentum Graecum*

WH — Westcott and Hort, *Text of the Greek NT*

WTJ — *Westminster Theological Journal*

ZAW — *Zeitschrift fuer die alttestamentliche Wissenschaft*

ZKG — *Zeitschrift fuer Kirchengeschichte*

ZNW — *Zeitschrift fuer die neuentestamentliche Wissenschaft*

ZThK — *Zeitschrift fuer Theologie und Kirche*

Baker's
DICTIONARY OF THEOLOGY

A

ABADDON. This is the name given to a satanic angel in Rev. 9:11, who appears as king of a horde of hellish locust-monsters sent to plague rebellious mankind. The Greek translation of the name is *ho Apollyōn,* "the Destroying One." In the OT *abaddōn* occurs several times as an epithet of Sheol or Hades and signifies literally "destruction" (from the root *ăbad* meaning "become lost, be destroyed"). It occurs, e.g., in Ps. 88:12: "Shall thy covenant-love be celebrated in the grave, thy faithfulness in (the place of) destruction [*abaddōn*]?" (Similarly Prov. 15:11; 27:20; Job 26:6; 28:22; 31:12).   G. L. ARCHER, JR.

ABBA. The word occurs three times in the NT. Mark uses it in Jesus' Gethsemane prayer (Mark 14:36). Paul employs it twice for the cry of the Spirit in the heart of a Christian (Rom. 8:15; Gal. 4:6). In every case it is accompanied by the Greek equivalent, *ho patēr.*

Abba is from the Aramaic *abba.* Dalman (*Words of Jesus,* T. & T. Clark, Edinburgh, 1909, p. 192) thinks it signifies "my father." It is not in the LXX. Perhaps Jesus said only "Abba" (*HDCG,* I, p. 2), but Sanday and Headlam think both the Aramaic and Greek terms were used (*ICC, Romans,* p. 203). Paul's usage suggests it may have become a quasi-liturgical formula.

See also FATHER, FATHERHOOD OF GOD.
RALPH EARLE

ABECEDARIANS. The Abecedarians were an extreme sect of the Reformation. They considered that the teaching of the Holy Spirit was all that was necessary. As a result they rejected all human teachings and even refused to learn to read or write. Hence, they were named for the A B C D they rejected.
SHERMAN RODDY

ABIDE, ABIDING. The Greek word for abide is *menō.* The papyri as well as the NT usage is best seen by dividing it with reference to place, time, and condition. With reference to place, it means to tarry as a guest, to lodge, to sojourn, maintain unbroken fellowship. With reference to time, it means to continue to be, to endure, to survive. With reference to condition, it means to remain as one is (see Arndt, MM, Grenfell and Hunt, *Oxyrhynchus Papyri*). When turning to the LXX, we find that no less than sixteen Hebrew words are used for the Greek *menō.* The principal ones are: (1) *yăšab;* meaning to live in, to dwell, to sit down; (2) *'āmad,* meaning to stand; (3) *qûm,* meaning to rise; and (4) *lîn,* meaning to lodge, tarry, dwell, spend the night. A few LXX examples will suffice: "let the maiden remain with us" (Gen. 24:55); "behold, the plague remains [stands or is checked] before him" (Lev. 13:5); "but the counsel of the Lord remains [stands or rises up] forever" (Prov. 19:21). Other OT usages are "to stand fast in battle" or "to abide by a conviction" (LSJ).

In the NT the verb is used both transitively and intransitively. The transitive usage means to await, be in store for, withstand or endure (cf. Jer. 10:10; Mal. 3:2; Acts 20:23; Heb. 13:14). The intransitive sense is to continue in a place or state in which one now is, to reside, to last, especially in the face of trial (cf. Luke 8:27; Acts 27:31; John 15:5; I Cor. 3:14). The word is used in composition with at least nine prepositions in the NT.

The examination of a concordance (MG) will show that *menō* is used around one hundred eighteen times, especially by the apostle John, where there are forty occurrences in the Gospel and twenty-six occurrences in the Epistles. With this preponderance of usage it is needful to examine the use of our word by the great apostle. It is crucial to the teaching in the fifteenth chapter of the Gospel of John. On the way to Gethsemane, Christ taught the disciples the imperative need of remaining in him by using the figure of the vine (q.v.) and branches. With the vine, the organic union with the trunk means life for the branches. This speaks of the essential union that must exist between Christ and believers. In 15:4 we have a divine imperative when Jesus said, "abide in me." Of course, there is a distinction between the natural order and the spiritual. The natural branch does not exercise its own will to choose whether or not to abide in the vine. It either remains in the vine or dies. But in the spiritual sense there is a definite act of the will on the disciple's part. The sense of urgency can be seen in the Saviour's imperative statement *meinate en emoi*. This immediately shows any disciple that there is responsibility on his part. Jesus' simple statement is true that in him there is fruitbearing but without him there is barrenness (15:5). This sense of dependency is found throughout the NT. Christ had taught earlier of a mutual responsibility which describes a true and genuine relationship (6:56; 15:4). The Master not only sustains life so as to produce fruitful branches, but he is also the very source and origin of life (1:3).

In the First Epistle of John the author speaks of this vital union with Christ by the words "in him remaining" (2:5). This expression is similar to Paul's thought *en Christō einai*. By the end of the first century, with the second coming so long delayed, this vital relationship of "abiding in Christ" needed to be interpreted in terms of long duration rather than tarrying for a short time. So today, this abiding is the pulse beat of the believer.

BIBLIOGRAPHY

Arndt; F. Godet, *Gospel of John*, Vol. II, pp. 292-305; R. H. Lightfoot, *St. John's Gospel*, pp. 282-85; ICC; J. H. Bernard, *Gospel According to St. John*, Vol. II, pp. 477-95; A. E. Brooke, *Johannine Epistles*, pp. 22-40.

ROBERT V. UNMACK

ABILITY. The word ability occurs seven times in the AV and ASV, rendering phrases which represent two ideas: (1) It may refer to physical, moral, or intellectual capacity (Dan. 1:4; Matt. 25:15; I Pet. 4:11; cf. Wisd. 13:19). The word *kōah*, in Greek represented by *dynamis* or *ischus*, in other con-

texts conveys the idea of "strength." (The RSV has rendered combinations of *hokmâ*, formerly rendered "wisdom," and *hayil*, formerly rendered "valor," by "ability" in fifteen additional instances.) (2) "Ability" may indicate material capacity, where "to give" is always mentally added (Neh. 5:8; Lev. 27:8; Ezra 2:69; Acts 11:29; cf. II Cor. 8:3, "means").

In later theology "ability" denotes man's power to do the will of God. Pelagius affirms the doctrine, while Augustine, Luther, and the Reformed creeds deny.   JACK P. LEWIS

ABLUTION. As a ceremonial act washing (*kibbēs, louein*, etc.) is a regular religious feature. There were three kinds of ablution recognized in biblical and rabbinic law. The first is the washing of the hands. As a means of cleansing this is not explicitly prescribed in the Bible but is to be inferred from Lev. 15:11. In the NT its significance has become largely social (Mark 7:3; Matt. 15:2). Feet were washed in the same way (Gen. 18:4; John 13:5). The second is the washing of both hands and feet with a view to the performance of priestly functions (Ex. 30:19; 40:31). In the tabernacle and temple a laver was provided for this purpose. The third is the immersion of the whole body as a symbolic cleansing of the entire man for admission or readmission to the sacred community or to the discharge of special functions within it, e.g., the high priest on the Day of Atonement (Lev. 16:24), Aaron and his sons before their consecration (Lev. 8:6). Lepers and those who had been in contact with an unclean person or thing were bathed (Lev. 14:8; 15:5-10, 19-27; Num. 19:19). So too were proselytes from the gentile world; this may be a prototype of Christian baptism. Vessels, houses, and clothes were also subjected to ritual cleansing (Mark 7:4; Lev. 14:52; 15:6-8; Ex. 19:14).

See also CLEAN, UNCLEAN.

L. E. H. STEPHENS-HODGE

ABOMINATION. "Abomination" (that which is to be abhorred) is the common Bible translation of *tó'ēḇâ* (Heb.) and *bdelygma* (Gk.), applying on the secular plane to certain contacts with and customs of foreigners. If performed by the wicked, that which is otherwise good is judged *by God* as abominable. He labels as abominations unethical practices: use of false weights and measures, dissemination of untrue information, false judging, bringing improper sacrifices. Repugnant to Jehovah are sexual abnormalities and heathen religious practices.

Other OT words, *piggûl* and *šeqeṣ*, have been translated "abomination," referring to that which was ceremonially unacceptable to God. The word *šiqqûṣ* was used particularly of the gods of Israel's neighbors. That *bdelygma* is the regular LXX translation of Hebrew words for the abominable supports the English version renderings of all these various words as "abomination."

BIBLIOGRAPHY
BDB; Arndt; W. Foerster in *TWNT*, I, pp. 598-600; S. Driver in *HDB*; G. Eager in *ISBE*.

BURTON L. GODDARD

ABOMINATION OF DESOLATION.

In this precise form these words are found in the AV in Matt. 24:15 and Mark 13:14, but there is an interpretative expression in Luke 21:20. The phrase is undoubtedly taken from Dan. 11:31 and 12:11, where the AV reads "the abomination that maketh desolate"; it is possible also that Dan. 8:13 and 9:27 contribute to the conception. Most expositors have been of the opinion that the passages in Daniel allude to the idolatrous desecration of the temple by Antiochus Epiphanes. On Dec. 15, 168 B.C., a pagan altar was built on the site of the great altar of burnt sacrifices, and ten days later heathen sacrifice was offered on it. The Alexandrian Jews interpreted Daniel's prophecy in this way. I Macc. 1:54 reads: *ōkodomēsan bdelygma erēmōseōs epi to thusiastērion.*

The altar was erected to Zeus Olympios, the Hebrew rendering of which name was *ba'al šamayim*. S. R. Driver points out that the title *ba'al šamayim* is often found in Phoenician and Aramaic inscriptions. By a change of the first word and a pun on the second this Aramaic title for "Lord of Heaven" was contemptuously reduced to *šiqqûṣ šōmēm*, meaning "abomination of horror" or "abomination of desecration." Moffatt renders it "appalling horror," but this seems to represent only one side of its significance. The term *šiqqûṣ* stands for that which is foul, disgusting, and hateful; *šômem* signifies that which desecrates or destroys what is good. The phrase therefore stands for that which utterly desecrates a holy thing or place. It can thus refer to the idolatrous image set up by Antiochus Epiphanes or to any other abhorrent object, person, or event which defiles that which is holy.

The passages in the NT are, of course, not exhausted by the historical fulfilment of the inter-testamental period, and they must be studied in their own right. The Greek phrase *bdelygma tēs erēmōseōs* may be rendered "a detestable thing that brings desolation." The emphasis appears to be more on the first word than on the last and draws attention to the objectionableness of the thing denoted. The word *bdelygma* refers to that which causes nausea and abhorrence: see the use of the word in Luke 16:15 and Rev. 17:4. It is a frequent LXX rendering of *šiqqûṣ* in the sense of an idol or false god, but it was not limited to that. Anything which outraged the religious feelings of the Jewish people might be so described (Swete).

The attempt to understand our Lord's allusion in the use of this expression seems partly involved in the view taken about the apocalyptic nature of the passage. If it is merely predictive and apocalyptic, then some idolatrous image may possibly be intended; but if our Lord's words are to be construed as prophetic in style, displaying that spiritual insight which belongs to true prophecy, then it may not be necessary to look for such an image but rather for something having a vital bearing on the behavior of the Jewish nation. Interpretative guidance is given in the record preserved by Luke, which reads: "When ye shall see Jerusalem compassed with armies, then know that the desolation thereof is nigh" (Luke 21:20). Writing for Gentiles, it would seem that Luke has replaced the obscure and mysterious word *bdelygma* by a term more intelligible to his readers. This is not, as some have said, to alter the Lord's meaning, but to explain it. On the principle of interpreting Scripture by Scripture, therefore, the "abomination of desolation" must mean the Roman troops. Matthew's reference to the abomination standing "in the holy place" does not require to be understood of the temple, but may equally indicate the holy "land." The historical fulfilment of the prophecy occurred first under Cestius (Gallus) in A.D. 66, then under Vespasian (A.D. 68), then under Titus (A.D. 70). It is possibly a superficial mistake to associate the abomination with the eagles of the Roman standards, for these had already been in the "land" long enough. It was the encirclement (*kukloumenēn*) of Jerusalem by besieging forces of the Roman army that constituted the sign. The participle is in the present tense and shows that the Christians were to flee when they saw the city "being compassed" with armies. The presence of the Roman army was thus a *bdelygma* of the worst kind and one that presaged coming ruin. The word *bdelygma* was not too strong an expression to describe this invasion, for it was detestable indeed that heathen feet should defile the holy land and that the ungodly should come into the heritage of the Lord. (The participle "standing" is masculine and possibly points away from the thought of an altar or image and might suggest "the abominable *one*.")

Alford rejects the view that the encirclement of Jerusalem with armies is identical with the *bdelygma* and argues that Matthew and Mark, writing for Jews, give the *inner* or domestic sign of the coming desolation, this being some desecration of the holy place by factious Jewish parties, and that Luke gives the *outward* state of things corresponding to this sign. Conceiving of the "abomination of desolation" as one thing and the encircling Roman armies as another, he nevertheless unites them in the event which occurred at the historical moment of which the Lord speaks. The question is an open one, of course, and Alford's view has much to commend it; but it seems preferable to take the simpler view, which explains the abomination in terms of the Roman army. It would appear that Jesus intends to foretell a desecration of the temple and city in a manner not unlike that brought about by Antiochus Epiphanes. The words of Daniel seemed to find a second fulfilment, and Rome has taken the place of Syria.

See also ANTICHRIST.

BIBLIOGRAPHY

A. B. Bruce in *ExpGT*, *Matthew*, *in loc*; Alf, *in loc*; A. T. Robertson, *Word Pictures in the New Testament*, Vol. I; S. R. Driver in *HDB*; Frank E. Hirsch in *ISBE*; H. W. Fulford in *HDCG*; H. B. Swete, *St. Mark*; G. R. Beasley-Murray, *Jesus and the Future*.

ERNEST FREDERICK KEVAN

ABRAHAM. God's promises to Abraham contain some of the first outlines of the covenant of grace, on the terms of which redemptive history is carried forward and consummated. Rather than stressing the conditions Abraham must meet in order to enjoy the promised blessings, the earlier statements of these promises stress what God will do in fulfilling his promises (note the repetition of "I will" in Gen. 12:1-3, 7; 13:14-17; 15:5-6, 18-20). When the covenant is formally estab-lished in Gen. 15:1-20, it is not Abraham but the theophany representing God who passes between the divided pieces of the animals to confirm the covenant. Hence this covenant must be understood not as a pact or contract between equals but rather as a disposition or testament in which God declares his gracious intentions for man (cf. Gal. 3:15, 17). The promises show that redemption will ultimately be universal in scope, because all nations will find blessing in Abraham's seed (Gen. 12:3; 18:18; 22:17-18).

Some thirteen years after the covenant of Gen. 15, God instituted the rite of circumcision, not as a condition for entry into covenantal blessings, but as a sign for Abraham, his household, and his posterity to indicate the claim that such blessings were already being enjoyed (Gen. 17:9-14). Thus Paul concludes that circumcision or any work by which men seek to distinguish themselves is of no value in gaining the blessings of the covenant of grace (Rom. 4:1-12). It therefore follows that the seed of Abraham to whom such blessings belong is not coextensive with Abraham's physical posterity who receive circumcision (Rom. 9:6-8) but rather with those who, whether circumcised or not, imitate Abraham's faith (Gal. 3:7). It is proper to term these "the seed of Abraham" because the faith they exhibit stems from their union with Christ, who, according to his human nature, was of Abraham's physical posterity (Gal. 3:16, 29).

The Genesis narrative shows how God worked to develop Abraham's faith to the extent that he became confident that God would fulfil his promises even though it meant over-coming the deadness of his and Sarah's bodies (Rom. 4:17-22) and the death decreed for Isaac (Heb. 11:17-19). Since the incarnation the elect have faith which is qualitatively the same as Abraham's in that they believe in God who raised up Jesus from the dead (Rom. 4:23-25). The works of love are a necessary concomitant to such faith (Gal. 5:6; James 2:14-26), and thus it is not surprising that, in the reiteration of the covenantal promises in the later parts of the Abraham narrative, the blessings are expressed as conditioned upon Abraham's obedience (Gen. 18:17-19; 22:15-18; cf. 26:3-5). Hence Abraham's life shows how the grace of God works to bring both the blessings of redemption and the fulfilment of the conditions necessary in order to receive these blessings.

BIBLIOGRAPHY
H. Bavinck, *Our Reasonable Faith*, pp. 73-78; J. Bear, *USR*, 52, pp. 351-74; J. Murray, *The Covenant of Grace*, pp. 1-12, 16-20; G. F. Oehler, *Old Testament Theology*, pp. 60-64; G. N. H. Peters, *The Theocratic Kingdom*, I, pp. 293-311; G. Vos, *Biblical Theology*, pp. 79-105; J. Walvoord, *BS*, 108, pp. 414-22, through 109, No. 4.

DANIEL P. FULLER

ABRAHAM'S BOSOM. In Luke 16:22 f. Lazarus is carried by the angels into Abraham's bosom. It is most natural and in keeping with NT thought elsewhere to think of the heavenly banquet to which Lazarus is now admitted. Reclining at table at Abraham's side (cf. John 13:23), Lazarus is thus enjoying the privileges of a guest of honor (cf. Matt. 8:11). Rabbinic Judaism used the expression also in a different sense, namely, that of rest from the toil and neediness of earthly life in intimate fellowship with the father of the race, who is still alive and blessed in death.

Hades and Abraham's bosom are distinct places, not two compartments of the same place. If Abraham's bosom was intended to have reference to one of the divisions of Hades, then the other division would have been mentioned with equal precision. Hades is mentioned in connection with Dives only; the other place is "afar off." Hades is associated with *being in torment;* the latter appears to be *the consequence of* being in Hades. If Hades were a neutral concept here, then the contrast with the rich man's former sumptuous state would not have been expressed.

BIBLIOGRAPHY
R. Meyer on *kolpos* in *TWNT*; SBK, II, pp. 225 ff.

MARTEN H. WOUDSTRA

ABSOLUTION. The word comes from the Latin, *absolvo,* "set free." It is used in theology to denote the forgiveness of sins, being specifically used by Roman Catholics of the remission given through or by the church. It is a suitable word in that the truly free man is one against whom no accusation of sin can be made.

I. The Bible teaches God's willingness to forgive human sin and his provision whereby justice and mercy are reconciled in the transaction. This study is properly made under the subject of the atonement (*q.v.*). Here we simply note the Bible teaching that all sin is sin against God ("Against thee, thee only, have I sinned," Ps. 51:4), and therefore sin can be forgiven only if it is forgiven by God. In the last analysis, then, absolution is the sole prerogative of God. This is basic in the whole conception of absolution.

But man's sin affects his fellow men as well as offending God, and in particular the sins of a Christian affect the whole church and his relationship with the church. We find this fact revealed in our Lord's teaching concerning forgiveness. He links the disciples' forgiveness of one another with God's forgiveness of them: "Forgive us our debts, as we also have forgiven our debtors." Several of his parables teach the same lesson (e.g., the unforgiving servant). And in our Lord's words (spoken first to Peter and afterwards to all the disciples), "Whatever you bind on earth shall be bound in heaven, and whatever you loose on earth shall be loosed in heaven" (Matt. 16:19, and 18:18), he clearly gives them their share in the matter of forgiveness of sins. Finally, the words spoken to the disciples in the upper room after the resurrection give unmistakable expression to the fact that the church has a part to play in conveying the sense of forgiveness to a penitent soul: "Jesus . . . said to them again, Peace be unto you: as the Father hath sent me, even so send I you. And when he had said this, he breathed on them, and saith unto them, Receive ye the Holy Spirit: whose soever sins ye forgive, they are forgiven unto them; whose soever sins ye retain, they are retained" (John 20:21-23).

Thus we conclude from Bible teaching that absolution comes from God alone; but, in that his church on earth is concerned with the sins of its members, it too has a ministry and commission in this matter, being given a special "inspiration" of the Holy Spirit for the purpose. How, then, has this been carried out by the church through history?

II. There is ample evidence to show that in the early church the practice was for the penitent to make public confession of his sin before the congregation, whereupon he was received back by the congregation as a whole with prayer and the imposition of the hands of the bishop. As time went on, a natural alternative to such public confession was for the penitent to confess before a minister of the church in private, the bishop or a presbyter. In both of these methods a prayer for absolution was used, asking God to forgive the sins so confessed and to restore the penitent "to the bosom of thy holy church" (from the *Apostolic Constitutions.*)

In the eighth century and later, when the

Eastern and Western Churches were beginning to fall apart, we find a development taking place in the Latin church whereby the presbyter (priest), hearing confessions, assumed more and more the position of a judge, inquiring into every department of the penitent's life and finally giving absolution in a declaratory form as distinct from the earlier precatory form. Thomas Aquinas (1227-74) was the first formally to defend this type of absolution, which is now used in the church of Rome as follows: *Ego te absolvo a peccatis tuis in nomine Patris et Filii et Spiritus Sancti.*

The Reformers of the sixteenth century sought to restore the matter to its scriptural teaching and early church usage. The confessional with its declaratory form of absolution was abolished by all the Protestant churches. Differences of procedure sprang up in the different denominations, but the same basic idea may be found in all, namely, to stir the conscience to an inner acknowledgment of sin, so that on confession to God it may be absolved directly by God himself. This stirring of the conscience is mainly effected by preaching and prayer, and if there is any declaration of forgiveness it has the form of a proclamation of the gospel promises. In most cases opportunity is given for a public confession in divine worship, whether representatively by the minister or corporately by the whole congregation.

Protestant thought in general, however, does not overlook the need sometimes for the confession of a sin which is burdening the conscience of an individual. In Anglicanism, provision is made for this by invitation to come to "a learned minister of God's Word"; and in other bodies, and often in evangelistic missions, opportunity is given for private consultation with a "counselor" or other Christian friend. In each case the Scriptures are the basis of instruction, and prayer is used to bring peace to the troubled mind and to kindle renewed faith in Christ.

To conclude, absolution is primarily identical with the divine remission. It is used especially of the declaration of forgiveness, i.e., the assuring of a penitent sinner that he is forgiven. It is received on the confession of sin to God, and its declaration is an integral part of the evangelical ministry of the church.

See also PENANCE.

BIBLIOGRAPHY
M. H. Seymour, *The Confessional.*

W. C. G. PROCTOR

ABSTINENCE. The word abstinence refers to a refraining from various external actions, such as drinking, eating, marriage, and participation in human society. In its wider meaning it includes the whole negative side of biblical spirituality and morality, but its usual sense involves abstinence from food or drink.

Many instances of both directed and voluntary abstinence are to be found in the OT, e.g., the prohibition of eating of the tree of the knowledge of good and evil (Gen. 2:17), of blood (Gen. 9:4), of unclean creatures (Lev. 11), and the fasting of Elijah (I Kings 19:8).

Although Jesus' entry upon his public ministry was preceded by forty days of fasting during the temptation in the wilderness, he cannot be viewed as an ascetic in either his practice or his teaching. He did not withdraw from society — weddings, feasts, etc. — nor subject himself to austere practices. He was accused by the meticulous Pharisees of being "gluttonous and a winebibber" (Matt. 11:18-19). The joyful inner attitude of devotion to Christ precluded mourning and fasting by Jesus' followers (Matt. 9:14-15).

In the early church, fasting of the Jewish type continued for a time (e.g., Acts 13:3; 14:23), but the Spirit-guided conscience came to be the determining factor in abstinence (Rom. 14:6), governed always, not by external regulations, but by concern for the weaker brother. Paul advised the Corinthians that food offered to idols was suitable for the Christian's use except when it offended the weak (I Cor. 8).

Various types of abstinence crept into the post-apostolic church as ascetic tendencies played their part in the development of the Catholic Church.

See also ASCETICISM, FAST.

BIBLIOGRAPHY
HDAC, I, pp. 6-11; MSt, I, pp. 38-39.

DONALD G. DAVIS

ABYSS. The word abyss is not found in the AV at all but it occurs nine times in the RV as the regular translation of the Greek word *abyssos.* The RSV uses it twice (Luke 8:31; Rom. 10:7). The AV translators rendered the word "deep" in Rom. 10:7 and Luke 8:31, and in the remaining places by "bottomless pit."

Plummer shows that *abyssos* in the classical Greek is always an adjective and means bottomless or boundless (A. Plummer, *A Critical and Exegetical Commentary of the Gospel of St. Luke,* p. 231). Its thirty-five occurrences in the LXX reveal that there it refers sometimes to the depth of the sea or earth while at other times it describes the abode of the dead (Ezek. 31:15).

The NT uses the word to describe the dwelling place of demons (Luke 8:31) as well as the place of torment (Rev. 9:1). Godet shows that Paul uses it in Rom. 10:7 to describe the abode of the dead. (F. Godet, *Commentary on Romans,* Vol. II, pp. 201-2).

HOWARD Z. CLEVELAND

ACCEPTANCE. Although the noun form is found only once in the AV (Isa. 60:7), the verb and adjective, representing a number of Hebrew and Greek words, occur often. Most frequently in both the OT and NT "acceptance" refers to the favor and approval of men by God. Under the old covenant the basis for this acceptance is sometimes ritualistic and ceremonial (Lev. 22:20) and sometimes ethical and moral (Prov. 21:3). The latter is particularly emphasized in the prophetical writings (cf. Isa. 1:12-15; Jer. 6:20; Mic. 5:21-24).

In the NT, acceptance by God is clearly revealed as resting squarely on the redemptive work of Christ (Eph. 1:6; I Pet. 2:5). This acceptance man does not merit; it is due entirely to God's grace. In both the OT and NT it was predicated on faith (Heb. 11). However, the regenerate man is exhorted to ethical living by the appeal to live his life "well pleasing" to God. Thus to present one's body as a living sacrifice (Rom. 12:1), to be careful not to place an occasion for stumbling before one's brother (Rom. 14:18), to care for a widowed mother (I Tim. 5:4), and to endure patiently undeserved suffering (I Pet. 2:20) are all instances of conduct acceptable to God. Such "'well pleasing" ethical living is perfectly exhibited in the life of our Lord, of whom the Father said, "This is my beloved son, in whom I am well pleased" (Matt. 3:17).

WALTER W. WESSEL

ACCESS. The English word access (found only in the NT in the AV) is the rendering of the Greek word *prosagōgē*, which occurs in only three places (Rom. 5:2; Eph. 2:18; 3:12). The related verb *prosagō*, meaning to bring forward (trans.) or to come near, approach (intrans.), is found in six places (Matt. 18:24; Luke 9:41; Acts 12:6; 16:20; 27:27; I Pet. 3:18). The Petrine use of the verb is its only use of doctrinal significance, but each of the uses of the noun is of interest.

The chief problem concerns the rendering of the Greek noun. Some give it the intransitive sense of access, while others prefer the transitive sense of introduction, which early was given it by Chrysostom. "The reference of all to Christ is further seen in the word inadequately rendered 'access': it describes not our act, but Christ's, not our coming, but His bringing us" (E. H. Gifford, *The Epistle of St. Paul to the Romans,* John Murray, London, 1886, p. 110). Gifford is followed in the transitive sense by Sanday and Headlam, Godet and others. On the whole the transitive sense of introduction is to be preferred, and I Pet. 3:18 affords further support.

The verb was used in the LXX of the bringing of sacrificial victims to God (Lev. 3:12; 4:4), of men to God to be ordained as priests (Ex. 29:4), and in secular Greek of the introduction of a speaker into the presence of the assembly, of the bringing of a person before a judge, or of the introduction of an individual into the presence of a king (Xenophon *Cyropaedia* 1:3.8; 3.2.12; 7.5.45). The general thought is that of introducing one into the presence of some higher authority and power. While it is impossible to prove that the NT writers had any of these figures in mind, they do, nevertheless, afford suggestive illustrations of the spiritual fact that believers in Christ have been brought into the presence of a royal and almighty Father by means of the cross.

BIBLIOGRAPHY
Arndt; William Barclay, *A New Testament Wordbook,* pp. 104-7; MM; J. O. F. Murray in HDB; W. Sanday and A. C. Headlam, *Epistle to the Romans* (ICC), p. 121.

S. LEWIS JOHNSON, JR.

ACCOMMODATION. The word accommodation as used in this article designates that characteristic of biblical literature which allows a writer, for purposes of simplification, to adjust his language to the limitations of his readers without compromising the truth in the process. Our concern will be to discriminate between the legitimate and the illegitimate application of this principle.

The following illustrations indicate the legitimate use of accommodation: (1) In the realm of theology proper God is often described as having physical properties (hands, eyes, etc.). This feature is called anthropomorphism (q.v.). It serves a useful purpose. (2) In the realm of cosmology the facts of nature (the sun sets, etc.) are often pictured in the language of appearance rather than in the language of exact science. This feature is called phenomenalism. It allows the Bible to speak in ordinary language. (3) In the realm of ethics a stronger brother may, in matters indifferent, accommodate himself to the scruples of a weaker brother (I Cor. 8; Gal. 2:3-5). (4) In the realm of didactics parabolic language may be employed to accommodate the deeper mysteries to the minds of the unenlightened (Matt. 13:10-17).

The following illustrations indicate the illegitimate use of accommodation. (1) The claim that Christ accommodated himself to the prejudices and erroneous views of the Jews is a false use of accommodation. The scholars who make this claim practically nullify Christ's authority on critical questions. (2) The claim that the early church invested OT prophecies with a meaning they cannot bear is another false use of accommodation. The scholars who advance this claim practically empty the OT of real messianic prophecy. (3) The claim that the writers of Scripture adopted ideas from pagan religions and then, after some purging, accommodated these ideas to the religion of Israel or to the theology of the nascent NT church is another erroneous use of accommodation. God's revelation cannot be intermingled with man's errors.

BIBLIOGRAPHY
Blunt; MSt; R. Hofman in *SHERK*; J. R. Willis in *HDCG*; L. M. Sweet in *ISBE*; G. T. Ladd, *The Doctrine of Holy Scripture*, I, pp. 27-74; W. Broomall, *Biblical Criticism*, pp. 30-33, 299-316.

WICK BROOMALL

ACCOUNTABILITY. This word does not actually appear in the formal English versions of the Scriptures, but its cognates are found in several places (e.g., Rom. 1:20; 14:12; Luke 16:2; Matt. 12:36; Heb. 4:13; 13:17; I Pet. 4:5).

The classic Scripture reference on the subject is Rom. 14:12, "So then each of us shall give to God an account about himself." Obviously this text implies that there is a supreme moral Ruler of the universe to whom all creatures are ultimately responsible and accountable. This same sentiment is expressed by the apostle in Rom. 2:12 where he indicates that

even those who knew not law are responsible; and they are to render an account to God since God has revealed himself to them in conscience.

Naturally those who live under the light of the gospel have a far greater responsibility; and hence on that day when all men render their account before God, their obligation will be greater and in direct proportion to their privileges. The Lord Jesus expressed the same sentiment when he said, "And that servant who knew his lord's will, and did not prepare himself or do according to his will, shall be beaten with many stripes; but the one who knew not, and did things deserving of stripes, shall be beaten with few stripes" (Luke 12:47-48a).

The Scriptures are rather outspokenly clear about accountability as far as individuals are concerned. The subject becomes vastly complicated, however, when we think of Scripture passages which speak of accountability of groups of persons or nations. Precisely what is the responsibility — hence accountability — that the individual has to society in general? To what extent does the individual incur guilt for the moral depravity of society? No one can say categorically what Paul's answer would be.

There is surely a responsibility somewhere in the actions of groups of people and of nations which are guilty of planning and executing moral outrages on the world. Any uncertainty about Paul's precise meaning in Rom. 5:12-21 is more than offset by the obvious gist of the whole section, namely, that sinful mankind (regardless of how it got that way) is now offered redemption full and free in Christ Jesus, the Lord. And now it is the responsibility of every man to repent and believe the gospel of Jesus Christ, before whom every single man will one day stand to render an account.

BIBLIOGRAPHY
HDAC.

ROBERT F. BOYD

ACCURSED. See ANATHEMA.

ADAM. The Hebrew word occurs about 560 times in the OT, nearly always meaning "man" or "mankind." However, in the opening chapters of the Bible it is plainly used as the proper name of the first man, who was created by God in his image, given dominion over the animals, placed in the Garden of Eden with the task of dressing it and commanded to multiply and fill the earth. Although like other animated creatures he is a living soul (*nepeš ḥayyâ*), because of his superior endowments he finds no real companionship with the animals but only with the woman who is bone of his bone and flesh of his flesh. This primal pair is put on probation by the Creator and their obedience tested through the instrumentality of the tree of the knowledge of good and evil. Under the duress of temptation, they fail to sustain the test, are overcome with a sense of guilt and shame, and hide from God their Maker. Having been found out, they are cursed to live a life of sorrow, pain, and hardship, which shall end on a tragic note as they return to the dust whence they were taken. It is, however, for our first parents a curse big with benediction, since it couches the promise of a Deliverer who shall crush the serpent's head. After they are cast out of the Garden, a brief account of their family life underscores the tragedy of their sin as Abel is murdered by his own brother Cain.

With Gen. 5:5 (in the canonical books of the OT) almost all allusion to the first man ceases, and it is not until we come to the Apocrypha, but especially the NT, that the theological significance of his transgression for the whole race is drawn out. A review of the NT data makes it very plain that the writers assumed Adam to have been an historical personality and that the record which we have just reviewed involved events in history. Luke 3:38 traces Jesus' ancestry up to Adam. In I Tim. 2:13, 14, Paul refers to the creation of man and woman in his argument for the subordination of woman to the man, making the statement that Adam was not beguiled. In Jude 14 we read of Enoch who was the seventh from Adam. The most significant passages, however, are Rom. 5:12-21 and I Cor. 15:22, 45. Here Paul institutes a contrast between Adam and Christ. Sin with all its dire consequences for the race as a whole is traced back to Adam. By the one man's disobedience the many are made sinners. In contrast to this principle of solidarity in evil is the principle of solidarity in life. By the obedience of the one man, Christ, the many are made righteous. Hence Paul can argue, "As in Adam all die, so also in Christ shall all be made alive." There are, to be sure, certain significant differences. We are by nature born in the first Adam; only by grace, through faith, are we engrafted into Christ. The "all" who are in

Adam is therefore a larger and more inclusive category than the "all" who are in Christ. Paul apparently assumed no one would infer universal salvation from his language in the light of his general teaching about sin and salvation. The point that he is making is that both alike acted in a representative capacity and he finds in the fall of all mankind through Adam's transgression an illustration of the way in which the sinner is justified by the righteousness outside himself and one that he cannot perfect by his own personal obedience.

A perennial question for the contemporary Christian man is how to understand this teaching of the Scripture in the light of modern science. In the older liberal tradition it was assumed that the narrative had no historical value and many regarded it simply as a composite of myths calculated to answer questions intriguing to the primitive mind, such as why snakes have no legs, why weeds grow, why women have pain in childbirth, why people wear clothes, and so on. Others argued that whereas the narrative was obviously mythological, yet it deeply probes those inward spiritual movements of man's being in order that he may discern the intrinsic nature of his spiritual heritage. Hence we have a parable in the form of simple narration. In keeping with a thoroughgoing evolutionary approach, it was frequently argued that we have in the story an account of how man matures from the childlike innocence of moral neutrality to the full-blown character of one whose spiritual sensitivity has been awakened by a responsible choice. This development of character was not without its risks, and the uprise of the spirit of man betrayed him (necessarily) into self-assertion in a way involving both good and evil as necessary corollaries. In keeping with the optimism of religious liberalism, it was assumed that the good in man and in human nature would ultimately triumph over the evil and that we have in Christ, the Second Adam, the high point in the evolution of the religious and moral consciousness of the race.

With the neo-orthodox reaction toward a serious attempt to interpret man's life in terms of the biblical doctrine of the fall and sin, the exegesis of the fall narrative becomes more wholesome. The neo-orthodox interpretation of the meaning and significance of the story of Adam is fundamentally Augustinian, in that the stress is laid properly upon the fact that man was created upright and fell from a state of integrity. The neo-orthodox school, however, has been plagued with the problem of how to take the narrative seriously in its theological import without being involved in what is considered a hopeless scientific obscurantism by acknowledging its historical character. It has been commonly argued that the loss of the historical form does not involve the loss of the theological teaching; this historical form is but the alphabet of the doctrine. No one who has sought seriously to interact with the evidences of modern science can fail to appreciate the problem. This solution, however, must be pronounced a failure, for a Christianity which is divorced from history becomes a Christianity of timeless ideas which is no Christianity. If we must believe that the Second Adam was crucified under Pontius Pilate — and the neo-orthodox party is emphatically convinced of this — then it would seem we must also believe that the first Adam fell not into history but in history. We can hardly existentialize the first Adam and at the same time insist on the historicity of the Second. In the reasoning of Paul, in Rom. 5 especially, the disobedience of the first man and the obedience of the Second Man constitute the two foci in the one elipse of salvation. If one be canceled out, Paul's entire structure falls to the ground. This is not to say that we must suppose that the events recorded in Gen. 1 through 5 transpired some 6,000 years ago. Neither the chronological data which are yielded by a literal interpretation of the text, nor even the cultural accoutrements of the narrative, are theologically significant to an understanding of the biblical view of Adam. But though he may have been a stone age man living in an antiquity much more remote than has been traditionally supposed, yet Adam must have been a complete man, possessed of all the moral and spiritual capacities and resources to have acted as a fully responsible agent and representative of the race.

It has been argued by many who thus take the narrative as both theologically and historically reliable, that we need not bother ourselves with the development of man on the empirical side, and that it may very well be that biological evolution along lines suggested by Darwin and his successors is the way in which the first man, the first human form, was created. All that is necessary is to suppose that God divinely superintended the development and that at the appropriate time the

human form, being sufficiently evolved, was informed with a human soul. Aside from the fact that there is no specific evidence which biological science offers that this was the case, it should also be noted that the narrative represents the Deity as shaping man out of the dust of the ground; that is to say, the clay from which he is formed is as it were manipulated by the hand of the Creator, so that there is a special divine intimacy even on the physical side implied in the creation of man. Whereas we read in the rest of the narrative, "God said, Let the earth sprout, let the seas swarm," etc., in the case of man it does not read, "Let the earth bring forth man." Rather, we read, "And God formed man out of the dust of the ground." It should be noted further that the divine inbreathing, which would be the point at which the human soul informed the body in the narrative in Genesis, seems to be simultaneous with the animation of the physical form. When God breathed in him the breath of life, then he became a *nepeš ḥayyâ*, that is, an "animated creature." It appears difficult to harmonize this point in the account with the view that man was already an animated creature, perhaps for long millennia of geological time prior to his receiving a distinctively human soul capable of rational and more particularly ethical and religious judgments.

See also MAN.

BIBLIOGRAPHY

K. Barth, *Christ and Adam*; J. F. Genung in *ISBE*; C. Hodge, *The Epistle to the Romans* (5:12-21); P. K. Jewett, *Emil Brunner's Concept of Revelation*, pp. 146-149.

PAUL K. JEWETT

ADIAPHORA. In Greek *adiaphoros* means indifferent. Adiaphorists may teach: (1) that certain *actions* are indifferent because they are neither commanded nor forbidden by God and can be done or not at pleasure; (2) that certain *rites and ceremonies* may be admitted to the church or not for the same reason; (3) that certain *doctrines* are of minor importance and may be taught or denied without injuring the foundations of faith.

In 1548 Emperor Charles V got three theologians to construct the Augsburg Interim, a creed for all Germany until a general council could come to final decisions. It taught the Roman view of transubstantiation, the seven sacraments, the Virgin Mary, the adoration of saints, medieval ceremonies, and the headship of the pope. It tried to appease the Lutherans by adopting a modified and vague doctrine of justification by faith, permitting the marriage of priests (with reservations), and permitting the cup to the laity. The Interim was enforced by authority but bitterly opposed by both Catholics and Protestants. In consultation with Melanchthon, Maurice of Saxony made the Leipzig Interim for his dominions, conserving certain Protestant essentials, but still strongly tinged with Romanism. These ordinances were vigorously opposed by Matthias Flacius, a professor at Wittenberg who removed to Magdeburg. He and the stricter Protestants strongly attacked the overpliant Adiaphorists, especially Melanchthon. The latter confessed his mistake, but much strife ensued between his followers and the "Flacianists." It is widely conceded that Flacius saved the Reformation. Adiaphorism was definitely contrary to the principles of the Reformed (or Calvinistic) church. Melanchthon and his friends deliberately veiled difficulties under vague expressions and treated the concessions to Rome as non-essential or indifferent (adiaphora).

BIBLIOGRAPHY
HERE; T. M. Lindsay, Reformation, Vol. II, p. 389; E. Schmid, Adiaphora; Ency. Brit, Vol. XVIII; J. K. L. Gieseler, Church History, Vol. IV.

ALEXANDER M. RENWICK

ADMONITION. The Greek word *nouthesia*, found three times in the NT (I Cor. 10:11; Eph. 6:4; Titus 3:10), denotes "a putting into the mind." Its verbal cognate, "to put in mind," appears four times (Rom. 15:14; Col. 3:16; I Thess. 5:12; II Thess. 3:15). In admonition what is put into another's mind is God's expectation. It can and often has degenerated into the church's expectation, assumed to be God's as well. In its formal sense admonition is a first-stage procedure in the disciplining of a church member. The intention is the individual's recovery. But the Pauline injunction was: "A man that is an heretic after the first and second admonition reject" (Titus 3:10). If the person's offense was private, the admonition was given privately; if public, it was done openly, before the church. But even if it was a private offense, Jesus taught that it was to go to the entire church if the offender would "hear" neither the one offended nor a committee consisting of the offended party and one or two witnesses (Matt. 18:15-17).

See also DISCIPLINE.   J. KENNETH GRIDER

ADOPTION. The Greek term is *huiothesia* and occurs five times in the NT (Rom. 8:15,

23; 9:4; Gal. 4:5; Eph. 1:5). In Gal. 4:5 it is used of the mature sonship secured for all believers (cf. 3:26) by the redeeming work of Christ and is contrasted with the nonage of Israel under the old covenant (cf. 4:3). That this contrast does not mean the exclusion of Israel from an adoptive relation to God is shown by Rom. 9:4, where "the adoption" is stated to be one of the privileges of Israel in accord with the witness of the OT (cf. Ex. 4:22; Deut. 14:1; Isa. 43:6; 63:16). The contrast of Gal. 4:3, 5 is comparative, not absolute. The difference is in line with the difference in general between the OT and the NT. The Old is preparatory, the New is consummatory. The grace of adoption in the NT appears in this, that by redemption accomplished and by faith in Christ all without distinction are introduced into the full blessing of sonship without the necessity of tutelary preparation corresponding to the pedagogical discipline of the OT period. (See COVENANT and TESTAMENT.) There is now no recapitulation in the individual sphere of what obtained in the realm of dispensational progression. In Rom. 8:15 and Eph. 1:5 nothing less than the mature status of Gal. 4:5 is in view. But it is not apparent that the contrast is reflected on as in Gal. 4:5. In Rom. 8:23 we have an eschatological use of the term to designate the grace bestowed at the resurrection; in Eph. 1:5 the same use may appear (cf. Rom. 8:29). This does not restrict the privilege of adoption to the future. Rom. 8:15 has a present privilege in view and Gal. 4:5 is even more explicit to this effect — the succeeding clause "because ye are sons" is equivalent to saying "because ye have received the adoption" (cf. also I John 3:1, 2). Rom. 8:23 indicates that consummated bliss is the full realization of the filial privilege (cf. the same use of the terms "redemption" and "salvation" in Luke 21:28; Eph. 1:14; 4:30; Rom. 13:11; Phil. 2:12; I Thess. 5:9; I Pet. 1:5).

Adoption is a specific act of God's grace distinct from calling, regeneration, and justification. It is that act by which we become sons of God, and the term in Greek clearly expresses this notion of instatement in the filial relation. The status is constituted by the bestowment of authority or right (John 1:12), a right belonging only to those who believe in Jesus' name. This action is specifically that of God the Father — "Behold what manner of love the Father hath bestowed upon us that we should be called children of God," and we are (I John 3:1; cf. also Eph. 1:5, where God the Father is the subject of the verb "predestinated"). (See FATHER, FATHERHOOD OF GOD.) As a result it is to God the Father that the filial relation is sustained. The evidence supporting this conclusion is copious (cf. John 20:17; Rom. 1:7; I Cor. 1:3; II Cor. 1:2; II Thess. 2:16, etc.).

The Spirit of adoption is the Holy Spirit (q.v.) (Rom. 8:15; Gal. 4:6). The act of adoption is necessary to the filial status, the Spirit of adoption to the cultivation of the privileges accruing from the status, particularly the confidence expressed in the cry, "Abba, Father."

The standard terms by which the adopted are designated are *huioi* and *tekna*. John uses *tekna* almost exclusively; only in Rev. 21:7 does *huios* occur. Paul uses both terms, and Rom. 8:14-17 is an example of the facility with which he can change from the one term to the other without any apparent distinction in respect of import. There is not sufficient evidence to indicate that *teknon*, because of its derivation, points to regeneration (q.v.) as the act of God by which we become the sons of God; and the considerations set forth above would indicate otherwise. Regeneration is closely related to adoption; it prepares for the new life in the family of God and for the exercise of the privileges of adoption. But it is by the distinct act of adoption that sonship is constituted. Adoption is the kind of action that has affinities with justification (q.v.) rather than with regeneration or sanctification (q.v.).

Adoption bestows the acme of privilege accorded to the people of God. By regeneration they are made members of God's kingdom (John 3:3, 5); by adoption, members of his family (Gal. 4:5-6). No other approach to God is characterized by the confidence and intimacy expressed in "Abba, Father." (See ABBA.) And the glory that awaits believers is the revelation of their sonship (Rom. 8:19), when they will be conformed to the image of God's own Son as the firstborn (q.v.) among many brethren (Rom. 8:29).

See also SON.

BIBLIOGRAPHY
T. J. Crawford, R. S. Candlish, J. S. Lidgett, *The Fatherhood of God*; J. Kennedy, *Man's Relations to God*; R. A. Webb, *The Reformed Doctrine of Adoption*; *TWNT*, V, pp. 981 ff.; Arndt, *ad huiothesia*.

JOHN MURRAY

ADOPTIONISM. Adoptionism was one of the christological errors that arose in the latter part of the second century. According to this view Christ was originally a man who, by a special decree of God, was born of a virgin and who, after having been thoroughly tested, was given supernatural powers by the Holy Spirit at the time of his baptism. As a reward for his sterling character and his achievements, he was raised from the dead and adopted into the sphere of the Godhead. He was thus a man who became God.

This doctrine was a rather crude attempt to explain the two natures of Christ to those who came into the Christian church from paganism. It sought to make allowance on the one hand for the human career of Christ and on the other for the miraculous powers and attributes of deity ascribed to him in the NT. Its tendency was to lead in the direction of Nestorianism, which also taught an abnormal separation between the human and the divine nature in Christ.

The most prominent advocate of adoptionism in the early church was Theodotus of Byzantium, although the doctrine appears to have been centered in Rome. Theodotus was excommunicated by Pope Victor (A.D. 190-98), and Adoptionism was condemned as a heresy. It later had a revival in Spain near the close of the eighth century, at which time it was put forward in an attempt to make Christianity more acceptable to Mohammedans, who placed strong emphasis on the unity of God. But it was again condemned in Rome in A.D. 800, after which it gradually disappeared.

BIBLIOGRAPHY
A. E. J. Rawlinson, *The New Testament Doctrine of the Christ*, pp. 265-69; CDE.

LORAINE BOETTNER

ADORATION. Such acts as bowing the head (Ex. 34:8), raising the hands (I Tim. 2:8), kneeling (I Kings 8:54), and prostration (Gen. 17:3; Rev. 1:17) manifest outwardly the soul's internal adoration of the Godhead.

In many of the Psalms (e.g., 93, 95-100) God is adored for his majesty and power, his providence and goodness, his righteousness and holiness.

Jesus received adoration at his birth (Matt. 2:11), during his ministry (Matt. 8:2; 9:18; 14:33; 15:25; 20:20), and after his resurrection (Matt. 28:9, 17). Men (John 9:38), angels (Heb. 1:6), and even demons (Mark 5:6) engaged in this adoration. Truly, there is no peril in worshiping Jesus, for he is God incarnate (Phil. 2:5-11).

The adoration of material objects is sternly forbidden (Ex. 20:1-6; Isa. 44:12-20). Adoration rendered to angels (Col. 2:18; Rev. 19:10), the man of sin (II Thess. 2:1-12; Rev. 13), or Satan (Luke 4:7 f.) is likewise condemned.

Heaven's holy citizens revel eternally in adoration (Rev. 4:8-11; 5:9-14; 7:11 f.).

BIBLIOGRAPHY
J. T. Marshall in HERE; D. M. Edwards in ISBE. . .

WICK BROOMALL

ADULTERY. In Scripture "adultery" denotes any voluntary cohabitation of a married person with any other than his lawful spouse. But at times the Bible designates this sin also by *porneia, "fornication"* (I Cor. 5:1), though this properly designates the offense of voluntary cohabitation between an unmarried person and one of the opposite sex. Where the two kinds of wrongdoing are to be distinguished, Scripture designates them by different terms: *pornoi,* "fornicators" and *moichoi,* — "adulterers" (I Cor. 6:9).

Adultery is forbidden in the Scriptures especially in the interest of the sanctity of the home and family (Ex. 20:14; Deut. 5:18). More specifically the sin is described in Lev. 18:20: "Thou shalt not lie carnally with thy neighbor's wife to defile thyself with her." The wrong is regarded as so great that its penalty was death (Lev. 20:10; John 8:5). While the law of Moses did not specify how this penalty was to be executed, it is explained in the NT as stoning: "Moses commanded us to stone such" (John 8:5). In Deut. 22:22 the mode of punishing an adulteress is not prescribed, though in Ezek. 16:40; 23:43-47 stoning is mentioned as the proper punishment. So also in Deut. 22:23 f. an adulterous young woman betrothed to a man, should be stoned together with her guilty partner. Various indications in Jewish tradition suggest that at times the punishment was inflicted by strangulation.

Since the death penalty could be inflicted only upon a person "taken in adultery, in the very act" (John 8:4), the woman suspected by her husband of having committed adultery had to undergo an ordeal to establish her innocence or be made manifest as a sinner by a divine judgment (Num. 5:11-31).

Though adultery was condemned in the divine law as a heinous crime (Job 31:9-11), it could not be rooted out, but both men and women were often found guilty of this grave offense (Job 24:15; 31:9; Prov. 2:16-19; 7:5-22). Even David became guilty of adultery and, as a result of this sin, of murder (II Sam. 11:2-5), of which, however, he earnestly repented (Ps. 51:1 ff.). Adultery filled the land especially through the influence of profane prophets and priests (Jer. 23:10-14; 29:23).

While the penal laws in the Scriptures consider only the actual transgression of the commandment of chastity, the moral law condemns also adulterous practices committed with the eye and the heart (Job 31:1, 7). Emphasis on this kind of transgression was urged especially by Christ in the Sermon on the Mount (Matt. 5:28), where he pronounced the person guilty of adultery who merely looked upon a woman to commit adultery with her, he having committed adultery with her already in his heart. Equally severe was our Lord's rebuke of the offensive hypocrites who condemned adultery while they themselves were guilty of unchastity (John 8:7). However, while he reproved the wicked accusers he did not condone the sin of the adulteress when he dismissed her with the command to go and sin no more (John 8:11). His words must be regarded rather as his solemn absolution of a sinner who was penitent.

When our Lord testified against the lax divorce practices of the Jews who followed the loose interpretation of Deut. 24:1-3 advocated by Hillel, he excepted adultery as the only cause justifying divorce (Matt. 5:12; 19:9), supporting in this the stricter school of Shammai, which likewise limited divorce to adultery. As a prevailing vice of perverted mankind, adultery will always be one of the continuing offenses among men. For this reason the NT so earnestly warns against it (I Cor. 6:9; Heb. 13:4; James 4:4). In view of the corruption of the human heart it behooves also every Christian daily to pray with great seriousness David's penitential prayer (Ps. 51:2, 10-12).

Paul does not contradict Christ, who in Matt. 5:32; 19:9 permits the putting away of the wife because of fornication, when in his directions on marriage in I Cor. 7:10-13 he commands the faithful Christian spouse to be at peace in case the unbelieving husband or wife should break the marriage union by malicious desertion. In vss. 10 and 11 he forbids Christians to break the marriage union, and that as a word of the Lord, the reference being very clearly to Matt. 5:32; 19:9, with Christ's express statement "except it be for fornication" clearly understood. In vss. 12 and 13 Paul addresses to Christians, joined in mixed marriages to unbelievers a new provision, which Christ had not considered when addressing Jews, namely, that if the unbelieving spouse desires to break the marriage bond by deserting the Christian, the latter is not bound, but is free to marry.

See also FORNICATION, DIVORCE.

BIBLIOGRAPHY
LC; ISBE; NSBD; SHERK; LSJ; WDB.

J. THEODORE MUELLER

ADVENT OF CHRIST. The word advent is derived from the Latin *adventus,* which in certain contexts corresponds to the Greek *parousia.* The latter term, however, occurs in the NT only with reference to the second advent. But in second century Christian literature it is applied to both comings of Christ. Thus Justin Martyr distinguishes between the first and second *parousia* in the *Dialogue against Trypho,* chaps. 52 and 121. A NT word used in connection with both advents is *epiphaneia,* which denotes the first advent in II Tim. 1:10. Two words referring to the first advent only are *eleusis* (Acts 7:5) and *eisodos* (Acts 13:24). The OT and the NT alike foster a forward gaze to an anticipated coming of the Lord. In this article we are concerned with the first advent alone.

The sources of our knowledge of the circumstances of the Saviour's entrance into the world are limited to the birth and infancy narratives in the first and third gospels. The whole NT witnesses to the fact of the incarnation, but only in Matt. 1:18 − 2:23 and Luke 1:5 − 2:39 are we told how and when it took place. The historicity of these passages has been challenged on several grounds since the beginning of the twentieth century, chiefly on account of the supernatural element which they include, the fact that no mention of the virgin birth appears in the second and fourth gospels, the lack of evidence from secular sources to support the description of the enrollment, and not least, the statement placing it within the period when Quirinius was Governor of Syria (Luke 2:1-5). It has been maintained that they formed no part of the Gospels in their original form or that they have

a midrashic character. To such objections it has been replied that textual and literary criticism do not lend support to theories of interpolation. Scientists are more hesitant now than formerly to rule out the possibility of miracle. Beginning his narrative where he does, Mark had no occasion to mention the birth of Jesus. John, who was probably acquainted with Luke's narrative, if not with Matthew's also, makes a general statement about the incarnation (John 1:14) which certainly does not stand in contradiction to either of these. No statement in the NT can be shown to be at variance with these Gospel stories of the manner of Christ's birth. On the other hand, if he came from God in a unique sense, there is nothing improbable in the view that he came also in a unique way. The repeated witness of the NT to his sinlessness is best accounted for by accepting the reliability of the story of the virgin birth (*q.v.*) The objections raised by Schuerer and others to Luke's account of the census have been largely met by the evidence adduced by Sir William M. Ramsay, Adolf Deissmann, and other scholars of repute. It is now known that a census was held every fourteen years in the first century, in Egypt at any rate, and that all absent from home were instructed to return for purposes of enrolment. Since Herod was only a vassal king and Augustus is known to have required an oath of allegiance from all Jews during the latter part of his vassal's reign, Schuerer's objection that his kingdom would have been exempt from the taxation order has no weight. Epigraphical evidence points to two periods of tenure of official office in Syria in the case of Quirinius. The earlier of these would appear to correspond with the last years of Herod's reign or the years immediately following his death in 4 B.C. If the latter be assumed, Luke may be understood to mean that a census begun in Herod's reign was brought to completion during the time when Quirinius held office. Vincent Taylor, while expressing the opinion that the difficulties of Luke's narrative have not yet been overcome, points to the vindication of his accuracy in the case of Lysanias (Luke 3:1) as a warning against too hastily concluding that Luke has erred in this matter (V. Taylor, *The Life and Ministry of Jesus,* Macmillan Publishing Co. Ltd., London, 1955, p. 43). It is safe to say that the substantial support provided by archaeological research for many Lukan passages formerly questioned makes strongly probable his reliability in the present instance.

The Contents of the birth narratives indicate that Jesus was born at Bethlehem in Judaea, of a virgin mother descended from David, in humble circumstances, in 4 B.C. Although the world at large and even the Jewish world was unaware of the event, it was not entirely unobserved nor unexpected. Angelic intimation, such as had preceded the birth of Isaac and Samson in OT times and John the Baptist in the NT era had been made some time previously, first to Mary and later to Joseph, to whom she was betrothed (Luke 1:26-38; Matt. 1:20-21). In both cases mention was made of the action of the Holy Spirit in the conception of the Child, the name to be given him, and the nature of his mission, but the language used was not identical, though not contradictory. Pious shepherds learned of the Saviour's birth from an angel who was joined by an angelic choir, praising God above the sheep pastures of Bethlehem (Luke 2:8-20). A brilliant star and the ancient prophecy of Micah guided a company of Magi to the place where they found the infant Saviour (Matt. 2:1-12; Mic. 5:2). The period was marked by a revival of prophetic song preceding and following the birth. The songs of Elizabeth, Mary, Zacharias, and Simeon reveal the close familiarity with the Scriptures and the reverent expectant piety that characterized the circles in which they originated (Luke 1:42-45, 46-55, 68-79; 2:29-33). The composers, along with the shepherds and Anna, represent a God-fearing minority at the time of the advent, whose attitude is variously described as "waiting for the consolation of Israel," and "looking for redemption in Jerusalem" (Luke 2:25, 38). They realized, more than most, the need for religious revival and prayerfully awaited the fulfilment of prophecy by which it would be met. In contrast to these pleasing evidences of sincere religious aspiration, the narratives provide a glimpse of the incredulous indifference of the official interpreters of the Scripture and a dark picture of the sinister hostility of King Herod.

In addition to the reference to the influence of Micah's prophecy in leading to the discovery of the Child Jesus by the Magi, Matthew points to several other prophecies which found fulfilment in the period of the advent (cf. Matt. 1:23; Isa. 7:14; Matt. 2:15; Hos. 11:1; Matt. 2:17-18; Jer. 31:15; Matt. 2:23; no single precise parallel). He also draws attention indirectly to the fulfilment of earlier promises when he traces the genealogy of Jesus from Abraham and David (Matt. 1:1). Harmonization of this genealogy and that given in Luke 3:23-38 is difficult. The most probable solution of the main problem appears to be found in assuming that Matthew provides the legal and royal descent in virtue of which Joseph, and Jesus as his adopted son, would have a claim to the throne if it were continued. Then Luke's genealogy will represent the natural line to which ultimately Joseph, as the husband of Mary, belonged.

The Time in the history of the world at which the advent took place is called by Paul "the fulness of times" (Gal. 4:4). This expression may have a twofold application, indicating on the one hand that it was the time foreordained by God, and implying on the other that prevailing world conditions rendered that time the most appropriate for the Saviour's coming. The history of the age serves to illustrate this.

Since 63 B.C. Palestine had been a part of the vast territory included in the Roman Empire, which united under a strong and single rule a larger proportion of the known world than had ever previously been so united. Wise distribution of armies, discreet adaptation of methods of provincial government to local circumstances, excellent roads linking Rome with the most distant lands governed by Caesar, and seas swept clear of piracy all helped to prolong the peace enjoyed by subject peoples and to facilitate the movements of troops, traders, and teachers. Recognizing that the Jews were a unique people, requiring special treatment, the Romans granted them exceptional concessions. Julius Caesar placed their religion in the category of those officially permitted; and, in 37 B.C., Herod, who, though Idumaean by birth, was a Jew by religion, was appointed to rule Judaea for Rome as a petty king.

Palestine at this time contained only a small fraction of the total number of Jews scattered throughout the empire. Dating from the fall of Jerusalem in 586 B.C., their dispersion had been extended through the colonizing policy of Alexander the Great and the Antiochene kings. They were to be found in considerable numbers in all the great centers of commerce, and wherever ten heads of families were resident a synagogue (q.v.) was usually built. There they gathered on the day appointed by God to hear the Scriptures read, and this practice, with the continued use of circumcision, became their bond and badge, securing their separate identity in the midst of many peoples. But in the providence of God the synagogue had come to serve a wider circle. The Greek language had assumed a common form in all the widely separated Greek-speaking communities. It had spread gradually over the eastern part of the empire and to a less extent in the west, becoming the language of the market place as well as of the study and university. This development was reflected in the translation of the OT Scriptures into Greek at Alexandria. Further, the long years of war and destruction preceding the reign of Augustus had produced much social unrest, moral disorder, and religious bankruptcy. To the last-mentioned result Greek philosophy had substantially contributed by undermining ancient beliefs. Adrift from their former moorings and conscious of a new unity, whether tending to hope or despair, multitudes were wistfully seeking some object of faith that would give meaning to life and peace to the mind. Some sought help by attaching themselves to a school of philosophy. Others became devotees of Oriental mystery cults. But not a few bewildered Gentiles were drawn to learn through the Scripture reading in the synagogue something of the unity and majesty of God, the moral rectitude required of man, and the hopes centered in the expected Saviour. Many of them even accompanied the Jews to observe the sacred festal seasons at Jerusalem and form a closer acquaintance with Judaism at its leading center. But a worldly, time-serving priesthood and a Pharisaic party, obsessed with the supposed value of external observances, yet blind to the inward demands of the divine law, were poor comforters for the spiritually oppressed in Palestine, not to say disconcerting examples of professed piety to the observant eye of the inquiring foreigner (Matt. 21:13; 23:15).

At such a time of widespread moral corruption, increasing pessimism, spiritual hunger, weakening of racial barriers, and enlarged interest in the Jewish Scriptures the Saviour was sent.

The Significance of the advent can scarcely be overestimated. It gave new lease of life to the race and made possible a new type of civilization. Religiously, it laid the foundation for all the evidence of the grace and goodness of God exhibited in the career of Jesus. It was preparatory to the atonement, the sole basis of forgiveness and of reconciliation to God. It demonstrated for all time the capacity of human nature for reflecting, within its own limits, the glory of the divine character.

BIBLIOGRAPHY

S. Angus, *Environment of Early Christianity*; K. S. Latourette, *History of the Expansion of Christianity*, I, pp. 8-44; J. G. Machen, *The Virgin Birth of Christ*, pp. 202-209.

WILLIAM J. CAMERON

ADVOCATE. The English word advocate is used only once (I John 2:1) in both the AV and RSV. It is a translation of the Greek *paraklētos*, which occurs four other times in the NT (John 14:16, 26; 15:26; 16:7).

Etymologically the word means "one who is called to the side of another," especially in a court of law. In the NT it has lost its passive sense and means simply "helper" or "intercessor." Thus in I John 2:1 Jesus Christ is called the advocate since he intercedes for the Christian who has fallen into sin. The efficacy of Christ's work as advocate rests on his propitiatory sacrifice (I John 2·2).

In John's Gospel *paraklētos* is a title given to the Holy Spirit. Although the Latin translators rendered the word *advocatus* even here, the AV translates it *"comforter"* in all four occurrences. This rendering goes back to Wycliffe, whose translation greatly influenced subsequent English versions. There is good reason, however, as evidenced by recent English versions, to translate *paraklētos* in its occurrences in John also by "advocate" or a synonym, such as "counselor," "helper," or "intercessor."

BIBLIOGRAPHY

Arndt; J. Behm in *TWNT*; E. Hoskyns and F. N. Davey, *The Fourth Gospel*, pp. 465-70; B. F. Westcott, *Gospel According to St. John*, II, pp. 188-91.

WALTER W. WESSEL

AFFECTIONS. This is an old English term for any bent, disposition, or emotion, good or evil. The AV uses it to translate *splagchnon* ("bowels," "compassionate feeling") in II Cor. 7:15; *phroneō* ("to mind," "think") in Col. 3:2; and *pathos* (feeling, passion) in Col. 3:5 and Rom. 1:26.

Any states of pronounced feeling may be called affections, although generally only those which incline the will to action (cf. Strong, *Systematic Theology*, I, p. 362). They are usually distinguished from passions as being less intense. Affections may be classified as "natural" or "spiritual" in accordance with their exciting cause.

The affective nature of man is regarded as one of the three fundamental aspects of consciousness, the others being cognition (knowledge) and conation (will). The older psychology tended to think of sensibilities or feelings as functioning apart from intellect and will. Rather, all three are closely related. The affections are "springs of action" and are an essential part of the religious life as the basis of love for God and man (Mark 12:30-31).

BIBLIOGRAPHY
Jonathan Edwards, "Treatise Concerning Religious Affections," *Works*, III, pp. 1-228; A. H. Strong, *Systematic Theology*, III, pp. 815 ff.; M. Baldwin in HERE.

WESTLAKE T. PURKISER

AFFLICTION. See SUFFER.

AGAPE. See LOVE FEAST.

AGE. I. THE OLD TESTAMENT USAGE.

The Hebrew word *'ôlām* means a long indefinite period of time, whether past or future, whose limits are determined only by the context or the nature of the thing spoken of.

A. *Undefined Past Time.* Amos 9:11 foresees the restoration of the tabernacle of David as in "days of antiquity." Events in past history are referred to in Isa. 63:9; Mic. 7:14; Mal. 3:4. Jer. 5:15 speaks of "a nation of antiquity," Isa. 58:12 of "ruins of antiquity," and Jer. 18:15 of "roads of antiquity." The expression "from antiquity" can refer to events in the indefinite past (Jer. 2:20; Josh. 24:2; Jer. 28:8). It can also include the whole sweep of human history (Joel 2:2; Isa. 64:4).

The word is used of God's acts and relationships to Israel in the undefined past (Isa. 63:16; Ps. 25:6). It can also refer to the totality of God's dealings with men (Isa. 63:19); and it can also designate merely an indefinite time (Isa. 42:14). In Prov. 8:23 it reaches to a point in time before the creation of the earth. The hills are called "everlasting" (Gen. 49:26). This refers to their antiquity and not to the eternity of matter.

These references show that the temporal determination of the word must be derived from its context. Therefore when it refers to God's existence, as in Ps. 93:2, "Thou art from everlasting," no point of beginning can be conceived, and the word takes on the idea of an eternity in the past. See "God of antiquity" in Gen. 21:33; Isa. 40:28; Jer. 10:10. When the idiom is applied to the messianic ruler in Mic. 5:2, linguistically it can mean either his

antiquity or his eternity. Context alone must decide.

B. *Indefinite Future Time.* The word *'ôlām* means an indefinite reach of future time, e.g., as long as a man will live (Deut. 15:17, I Kings 1:31; Ps. 61:7). The "eternity" of the earth (Ps. 104:5; 148:6) is only relative, for the earth is to be shaken in the final act of judgment and redemption (Hag. 2:6). An indeterminate future is seen in Isa. 32:14; I Sam. 13:13; Ezek. 25:15. Enduring without end are God's salvation (Isa. 51:6-8), his dwelling in Jerusalem (I Chron. 23:25), his covenants (Gen. 17:7; Isa. 55:3), the Mosaic institution (Ex. 27:21; 30:21; Lev. 3:17; 7:34; 10:9; Num. 10:8), the passover observance (Ex. 12:24), Solomon's temple (I Kings 9:3; II Kings 21:7), the Holy City (Ps. 125:1), and Messiah's rule (Ps. 45:6; Isa. 9:7). That some of these institutions have passed away illustrates again that the precise meaning of the phrase is to be derived from its context.

When the phrase is applied to the existence of God, the full idea of eternity emerges (Isa. 40:28; Deut. 32:40; Dan. 12:7).

The plural, "ages," is sometimes used to intensify the idea of an unending future: Isa. 45:17, "everlasting salvation" (salvation of ages); Dan. 9:24, "everlasting righteousness"; Isa. 26:4, "everlasting rock"; Ps. 145:13, "an everlasting kingdom" (a kingdom of all ages).

C. *Past and Future.* The indefinite past and future, "from antiquity and unto futurity," are brought together, referring to the existence of God (Ps. 90:2; 106:48); God's love (Ps. 103:17); praise to God (Neh. 9:5); the promise of the land of Israel (Jer. 7:7; 25:5).

II. THE NEW TESTAMENT USAGE.

A. *Aiōn as Indefinite Time.*

1. *In the Past.* The word *aiōn*, like *'ôlām*, is used to mean an indeterminate period of time. The age of the prophets is "from the age," i.e., from long ago (Luke 1:70; Acts 3:21). God's revelation to Israel was "from the age" (Acts 15:18). The phrase "from the age" in John 9:32 means from all past time. Jude 25 has a variant form, "before all the age," meaning before all time.

2. *In the Future.* The expression "unto the age" occurs twenty-seven times. The precise meaning must be determined from the context. In Matt. 21:19; Mark 3:29; John 13:8; I Cor. 8:13, it means "never." In other contexts, the

idea of a future eternity is apparent (John 6:51, 58; 10:22; 11:26; 12:34; 14:16; II Cor. 9:9; Heb. 5:6; 6:20; 7:17, 21; I Pet. 1:25; I John 2:17; II John 2; Jude 13).

The plural, "ages," is used to strengthen the idea of endlessness. (a) In the past: "before the ages" (I Cor. 2:7); "from the ages" (Col. 1:26; Eph. 3:9). In Eph. 3:11 we have the "purpose of the ages," i.e., God's eternal purpose. (b) In the future: "unto the ages" (Matt. 6:13; Luke 1:33; Rom. 1:25; 9:5; 11:36; II Cor. 11:31; Heb. 13:8). Jude 25 reads "unto all the ages." The parallelism of ages and generations in Col. 1:26 suggests that the plural form conceives of time as consisting of a succession of many ages or generations and this leads to the further thought that the ages are long but not unlimited periods of time.

The eternity of the future is further strengthened by doubling the form: (a) in the singular: "unto the age of the age" (Heb. 1:8); (b) in the plural: "unto the ages of the ages." This expression occurs twenty-one times, all in Paul or Revelation with the exception of Heb. 13:21; I Pet. 4:11; 5:11.

A number of variant expressions are Eph. 3:21, "unto all the generations of the age of the ages," and II Pet. 3:18, "unto the day of the age."

The lordship of God over all time is seen in the expression "king of the ages" (I Tim. 1:17; Rev. 15:3).

B. *Aiōn as a segment of time*. Theologically the most important usage of *aiōn* in the NT is that which designates two distinct periods of time: this age and the age to come. This structure provides the background for the eschatological character of the work of redemption. This idiom views redemptive history, not as a series of unending ages, but as two distinct and contrasting periods of time.

Several verses reflect this two-age structure without emphasizing it. Blasphemy against the Holy Spirit will never be forgiven in this age or in the age to come (Matt. 12:32). Christ is exalted above all authority both in this age and in the age to come (Eph. 1:21). Discipleship of Jesus, even though it brings its rewards, often involves the loss of possessions and family in this time, but it will mean eternal life in the age to come (Mark 10:29-30; Luke 18:28-30). This saying involves a slight variation in form: "time" (*kairos*) is sub-

stituted for "age" in the first member. This same idiom, "this time," is found in Rom. 3:26; 8:18; 11:5; II Cor. 8:13.

This age will come to its end with the *parousia* of Christ (Matt. 24:3). At the consummation of this age the Son of Man will send his angels to separate the wicked from the righteous (Matt. 13:39-42). The age to come will be the age of immortality in contrast to this age. "Those who are accounted worthy to attain to that age" will be "sons of the resurrection" and will be like the angels in one aspect: they will no longer be subject to death (Luke 20:34-35).

The age to come is the age of eternal life (Mark 10:30), when the righteous will "shine forth as the sun in the kingdom of their Father" (Matt. 13:43). Mark 10:24, 30 equate the age to come with both eternal life and the kingdom of God; and in Matt. 25:34, 46 the righteous inherit the kingdom of God and enter into eternal life when the Son of Man comes in his glory (Matt. 25:31) at the end of this age (Matt. 25:41).

The character of this age stands in sharp contrast to the coming age. It is evil (Gal. 1:4) because Satan is "the god of this age," holding men in darkness (II Cor. 4:4). This age stands in opposition to the kingdom of God; for, when the word of the kingdom is sown, "the care of the age" tends to choke it so that it does not become fruitful (Matt. 13:22). Love for this age caused Demas to forsake Paul (II Tim. 4:10). Paul describes those who live according to "the age of this world" in Eph. 2:1, 2 as dead in sins, sons of disobedience following a satanic leading, pursuing the passions of the flesh; therefore they are under God's wrath. This phrase "the age of this world" closely associates the temporal and the spatial words. Indeed, the expression "this world" is a parallel expression (John 8:23; 9:39; 11:9; 12:25; 13:1; 16:11; 18:36; I John 4:17; I Cor. 3:19; 5:10; 7:31). The debater of this age and the wisdom of this world are both folly to God (I Cor. 1:20; 2:6) for God can be known only by revelation, not by wisdom (I Cor. 2:6). The rulers of this age who in ignorance crucified the Lord of glory are doomed to pass away (I Cor. 2:6, 8). Some interpreters find in this verse a reference to the demonic hosts of "the god of this age," but this is not proved.

In brief, this age is the period of Satan's

activity, of human rebellion, of sin and death; the age to come, introduced by the *parousia* of Christ, will be the age of eternal life and righteousness, when Satan is destroyed and evil swept from the earth.

This dualistic structure is shared by the NT with contemporary Judaism (see IV Ezra 6:7-9; 7:20-31, etc.); but both are derived from elements implicit in the OT, which sees the world, the scene of human existence, in need of a miraculous transformation by the direct act of God before God's people can enjoy the fulness of the redemptive blessings (Isa. 65:17 ff.). However, at one important point the NT stands apart from its Jewish environment: in Christ the blessings of the age to come have entered into this evil age. Jesus, who will come in glory as the Son of Man to inaugurate the age to come, has already appeared on earth in humility to bring to men in the midst of this evil age the life of the age to come. We already taste the powers of the coming age (Heb. 6:5). Through the death of Christ we are now delivered from this present evil age (Gal. 1:4). We are no longer to be conformed to this age but are to be transformed by an inner power (Rom. 12:2). It is possible that, in I Cor. 10:11, "upon whom the ends of the ages are come" may refer to this overlapping of the two ages and mean that, while Christians live bodily in this age of sin and death, they live spiritually in the age of righteousness and life. This phrase, however, like Heb. 9:26, "the consummation of the ages," may mean that in Christ God's purpose in the ages of redemptive history has been fulfilled. In any case, the NT does teach an overlapping of the ages. Therefore, eternal life, which belongs to the age to come (Mark 10:30; Matt. 25:46; John 12:25; Rom 2:7), is a present possession (John 3:36; 6:47). Justification, which really means acquittal from guilt in the final judgment (Matt. 12:36, 37; Rom. 8:33 f.), is already accomplished (Rom. 3:24; 5:1). Salvation which belongs to the future (Rom. 13:11; I Pet. 1:5, 9) is also present (II Cor. 6:2; Eph. 2:8). The kingdom of God which belongs to the age to come (Matt. 25:34; I Cor. 15:50) has invaded this age, bringing to men its blessings in advance (Matt. 12:28; Luke 17:20; Col. 1:13; Rom. 14:17). In brief, the redemptive realities are eschatological; they are the blessings which belong to the age to come, but in Christ they have been given to believers who still live in this age. Christians live in two ages; they enjoy the powers of the age to come while living in the end of this age.

See also Eschatology and Kingdom of God.

C. *Aiōn as a Spatial Concept.* Sometimes *aiōn* refers not so much to a period of time as to that which fills the time period. The creation of the ages in Heb. 1:2 refers to all that fills the ages — the world. In Heb. 11:3 "the ages" are further described by the phrase "that which is seen" — the visible world which fills the ages of time.

Since *aiōn* can bear spatial connotations, it can be used interchangeably with *kosmos,* "world." See "the coming world" in Heb. 2:5 and "the coming age" in Heb. 6:5, "the wisdom of this world" (I Cor. 1:20; 3:19) and the "wisdom of this age" (I Cor. 2:6). Possibly the "care(s) of the age," in Mark 4:19 and Matt. 13:22, is synonymous with the care for the things of the world in I Cor. 7:33; and the assertion that God is the King of the ages (I Tim. 1:17) means not only that he is Lord of time but of all that fills time.

D. *Aiōn as a Person.* In hellenistic religion *aiōn* was used of semidivine beings standing between God and the world. Some scholars have found this meaning in the NT. Eph. 2:2 is said to be the *aiōn* who rules over this world; Col. 1:26 and Eph. 3:9 and 2:7 are said to refer to heavenly spirits from whom God concealed his redemptive purpose and over whom Christ is to triumph. This interpretation is highly improbable.

The biblical concept of "the ages" stands in contrast to the Greek idea of the time — eternity relationship, in which eternity is qualitatively other than time. Biblically, eternity is unending time. The future life has its setting in a new redeemed earth (Rom. 8:21; II Pet. 3:13) with resurrection bodies in the age to come. It is not deliverance from the realm of time and space but from sin and corruption. Rev. 10:6 does not mean that time is to end.

See also Eternity and Time.

BIBLIOGRAPHY

H. Sasse in *TWNT;* E. D. Burton, *The Epistle to the Galatians (ICC),* pp. 426-31; Oscar Cullmann, *Christ and Time;* G. Vos, *The Pauline Eschatology,* chaps. 1-2; G. E. Ladd, *ExpT,* 68:268-73.

GEORGE ELDON LADD

AGNOSTICISM. In the year 1869, at a meeting of the Metaphysical Society, Thomas Huxley (1825-95), invented the term *agnostic* as a play upon the ancient party name *gnostic,* The Gnostics *(q.v.)* in the ancient church claimed esoteric knowledge, *gnosis,* in matters not open to public investigation. By the term agnostic Huxley intended to cover the negative philosophical religious views which he shared with Herbert Spencer (1820-1903) and others.

Robert Flint's *Agnosticism* (C. Scribner's Sons, 1903) is an elaborate refutation. Flint strongly criticizes the lexicographical formation of the word, agnostic, which Huxley used loosely, and, it seems, somewhat playfully. Flint and others have pointed out that the ancient term skepticism would have been accurate and suitable.

The ancient Greek Skepticism of Pyrrho (365?-275? B.C.) and others was mainly directed against assumed knowledge of the physical world. The same was largely true of the Skepticism of Hume (1711-76). The more nearly contemporaneous Skepticism of Sir William Hamilton (1788-1856) and H. L. Mansel (1820-71) was pro-theistic. Hamilton's position was one of "denying that God can be known while affirming that God ought to be believed in" (Flint. *op. cit.,* p. 604). This is very similar to much that is found in contemporary Barthianism.

Spencer consciously adopted the negative side of the Skepticism of Hamilton and Mansel. Flint says, "His [Spencer's] agnosticism, as he has always candidly stated, was almost entirely derived from the teaching of Hamilton and Mansel" (*op. cit.,* p. 630). But Spencer's Agnosticism, like that of Huxley, was antitheistic. It is interesting to note that, whereas Huxley regarded the conservation of matter and of energy, and the law of the inverse square, as matters of positive knowledge, these are matters about which some modern physicists are very skeptical.

It must be remembered that the Agnosticism of Huxley and Spencer does not imply *"I do not know,"* but, *"One cannot know."* It is strictly a universal negative judgment, which would require universal knowledge for its verification.

See also UNBELIEF.

BIBLIOGRAPHY

Aside from the writings of Huxley and Spencer, and Flint's *Agnosticism* above referred to, and aside from articles on the subject in the larger encyclopaedias, the reader may consult the symposium by Henry Wace, Thomas Huxley, W. C. Magee, W. H. Mallock, and Mrs. Humphrey Ward, *Christianity and Agnosticism, a Controversy;* Paul Carus, *Kant and Spencer, a Study of the Fallacies of Agnosticism;* Clarence Darrow and Wallace Rice, *Infidels and Heretics, an Agnostic's Anthology* (short selections from many sources, a few from Darrow himself); R. C. Churchill, *English Literature and the Agnostics.*

J. OLIVER BUSWELL, JR.

AGONY. The word *agōnia* has three meanings: (1) contest or struggle for victory, (2) gymnastic exercise, and (3) when used of the mind, "anguish" (LSJ, p. 19). As with its cognate *agōn,* the idea of a contest or struggle is the most frequent meaning.

The word is found three times in the LXX (II Macc. 3:14, 16; 15:19).

Only in Luke 22:44 does it occur in the NT. Whether Luke 22:43-44 was in the text Luke originally wrote is questioned. Some scholars believe the scribes added it to the narrative as a scrap of historical tradition not found in any of the Gospels. The historicity of these verses is not in doubt — only their authenticity as part of Luke's original text.

Matt. 26:36-46 records that Christ prayed three times in Gethsemane. The first time he assumes that the cup can pass from him but adds "Not as I will but as you will." The second and third times he assumes that the cup cannot pass from him and adds again: "Let your will be done." The agony or anguish of Jesus during this time shows his inward struggle.

What does this experience of Jesus mean? Not that he feared death. When Herod Antipas wanted to kill him, he showed no fear, but a firm conviction that he would die in Jerusalem (Luke 13:31-35). To be sure, Jesus was keenly and fully conscious of his role as sin-bearer. For a sinless being to be "made sin" (II Cor. 5:21) would certainly involve an inward struggle. Stauffer suggests (*TWNT,* I, p. 140) that Jesus' agony lay in his deep concern for victory (compare Luke 22:44 with Luke 12:49-50). One thing is certain: the experience is more than human mind can fathom.

A. BERKELEY MICHELSON

ALBIGENSES. The Albigenses, inheritors of the dualistic heresies of the Bogomils and Paulicians, centered in Albi, a town in southern France. They flourished also in northern Spain and northern Italy during the twelfth century and were known also as the Cathari or Patarini.

The Cathari dualism taught a spiritual world made by a good power and a material creation made by an evil force. They rejected part of the OT, while emphasizing the Gospel of John. They formed an antisacerdotal protest against the evils of the medieval church.

The Albigenses were divided into two groups, the *perfecti* and the *credenti*. The latter were the lower order, who could marry, hold property, and share in the sacraments of the Roman church. These looked forward to the consolmentum which would provide full salvation for them. Many postponed experiencing the consolmentum until just before death. The *perfecti* were those who had experienced the consolmentum. They had been forgiven all their sins and hence must remain celibate or separate from their wives. They were prohibited from eating meat, milk, or eggs, since these resulted from sexual activity. They could not wage war or hold real estate.

Though protected by William IX, Duke of Aquitaine, Innocent III ordered the Cistercians to preach a crusade against them in 1209, but it failed. In 1229 the war ended with the Albigenses still in existence. The Inquisition of the fourteenth century succeeded in stamping them out.

BIBLIOGRAPHY

C. Schmidt, *Histoire de la secte des Cathares ou Albigeois;* H. J. Warner, *The Albigensian Heresy,* 2 vols.; H. Soederburg, *La religion des Cathari;* S. Runciman, *The Medieval Manicee.*

SHERMAN RODDY

ALEXANDRIA, SCHOOL OF.

It is probable that Christianity came to Alexandria in apostolic times, though the tradition that it was first brought by John Mark cannot be verified. The indications are that Christianity was well established in middle Egypt by A.D. 150. (H. I. Bell, *HTR* xxxvii, p. 204) and that Alexandria was its port of entry and supporting base.

Clement of Alexandria became head of the Catechetical School about 190. A philosopher throughout his life, Clement saw Greek philosophy as a preparation for Christ, even as a witness to divine truth. Plato was a cherished guide. Sin is grounded in man's free will. Enlightenment by the Logos brings man to knowledge. Knowledge results in right decisions. These draw a man towards God until he is assimilated to God (*Strom.* iv. 23). The Christian lives by love, free from passion. His life is a constant prayer. Clement set forth its pattern in minute detail in the *Paidagōgos.* He took an optimistic view of the future of all men, but knowledge would be rewarded in the world to come. An allegorical exegesis of Scripture supported these views.

Clement was succeeded in the Catechetical School (ca. 202) by the much abler Origen (ca. 186-ca. 255). A biblical student and exegete of great ability, Origen produced the *Hexapla* text of the OT. He wrote commentaries, scholia, or homilies on all the biblical books; but they were based on three senses of Scripture, the literal, moral, and allegorical. The Bible was inspired, useful, true in every letter, but the literal interpretation was not necessarily the correct one. Indebted, like Clement, to the Greeks, Origen was not as admiringly dependent upon them. His conception was of a great spiritual universe, presided over by a beneficent, wise, and personal being. Alexandrian Christology makes its beginnings with Origen. Through an eternal generation of the Son, the Logos (*q.v.*), God communicates himself from all eternity. There is a moral, volitional unity between the Father and the Son, but an essential unity is questionable. The world of sense provides the theater of redemption for fallen creatures who range from angels through men to demons. By the incarnation the Logos is the mediator of redemption. He took to himself a human soul in a union that was a *henōsis.* It was, therefore, proper to say that the Son of God was born an infant, that he died (*De princ.* II. vi. 2 f.). By teaching, by example, by offering himself a propitiatory victim to God, by paying the devil a ransom, Christ saves men. Men gradually free themselves from the earthy by meditation, by abstinence, by the vision of God. A purging fire may be needed in the process. Although this world is neither the first nor the last of a series, there will ultimately come the restoration of all things. Flesh, matter, will disappear, spirit only will remain, and God will be all in all. How long human freedom will retain the power of producing another catastrophe is not clear, but ultimately all will be confirmed in goodness by the power of God's love.

After Origen's departure from Alexandria his disciples diverged. One group tended to deny the eternal generation of the Logos. Dionysius, Bishop of Alexandria (247-265), sympathized with this party and declared the Logos to be a creation of the Father, but the future in Alexandria belonged to the opposite wing, which emphasized the divine attributes of the Logos. The Sabellian party was strong in Cyrenaica and Libya, and this influence affected Alexandria. When the presbyter Arius began, perhaps about 317, to proclaim that the Logos (q.v.) was a creation in time, differing from the Father in being, he attracted disciples, but Bishop Alexander opposed Arius. As Emperor Constantine found it impossible to restore harmony by exhortation and influence, he called for a general meeting of bishops. The resulting Council of Nicaea in 325 was attended by an Alexandrian delegation which included the deacon Athanasius. For the remaining years of his life Athanasius was to champion the Nicene conclusion that the Son was *homoousios* with the Father. The adoption of this term in spite of its chequered Gnostic and Sabellian background was a work of providential genius.

In 328 Athanasius succeeded Alexander as the Alexandrian bishop. In spite of some dictatorial tendencies, he possessed a superb combination of the talents of a successful administrator with great depths of theological insight. From this time on, Alexandria emphasized vigorously the identity in being of the Father and the Son. Athanasius presented, in his *On the Incarnation of the Logos,* the indispensability of the union of true God with true man for the Christian doctrine of salvation through the life and death of Christ. Wholly God and wholly man the Saviour must be. Through many false charges and five periods of exile Athanasius maintained his insistence upon one God, Father and Son of the same substance, the church the institute of salvation, not subject to the interference of the civil state. Athanasius also set forth the view that the Spirit is *homoousios* likewise with the Father and the Son, thus preparing the way for the formula *mia ousia, treis hypostaseis.*

That Christ need not be wholly divine and wholly human was a view which Apollinaris of Laodicea did not succeed in fastening upon Alexandria in spite of his efforts in that direction. His view that the *pneuma* of the Logos replaced the human spirit was rejected. His emphasis upon the unity of the personality of Christ, however, became increasingly an Alexandrian emphasis and was strongly stressed by Cyril, who became bishop in 412. The Logos took a full human nature upon himself, but the result was *henōsis physikē,* and Cyril loved the formula *mia physis,* one even though originally *ek duo.* The incarna-

tion was to the end of salvation. God became man that we might become God. Cyril supported this by allegorical exposition of the Scripture of both Testaments, especially those of the Pentateuch. The phenomenal allegory of the facts is designed to yield the noumenal meaning. His most famous writing is his series of twelve anathemas against Nestorius, attacking what appeared to him to be denials of the unity and full deity of Christ and of the crucifixion and resurrection of the Word. In 433 Cyril accepted, with the Antioch leaders, a profession of faith which declared that a unity of the two natures of Christ had come into existence (*henōsis gegone*) and used the term for which Cyril had so vigorously contended against Nestorius, *theotokos* (see MOTHER OF GOD) as a description of the Virgin Mary.

Dioscurus continued the Cyrillian emphasis on unity in the person of Christ but pushed it to an extreme. At the Council of Chalcedon (451) the Alexandrian radicals suffered defeat with the adoption in the *Definition* of the phrase *en duo physesin.* The final Alexandrian tendencies produced schism after Chalcedon. The great bulk of Egyptian Christendom rejected Chalcedon and became monophysite (see MONOPHYSITISM). Monothelitism (q.v.) proved to be only a temporary enthusiasm in Alexandria. The arrival of Islamic rule ended it.

The Alexandrian school with its Platonic emphasis was the popular school of its time. In its more moderate form it set the christological pattern for many centuries. The love of allegorical interpretation was characteristic. The intervention of the divine in the temporal was stressed, and the union of the natures of Christ with overriding emphasis on the divine component was dangerously accented.

See also CHRISTOLOGY.

BIBLIOGRAPHY

Edward R. Hardy, Jr., *Christian Egypt;* Einar Molland, *The Conception of the Gospel in the Alexandrian Theology* (Norske Videnskaps-Akademi Skrifter: II, Hist.-Filos. Klasse), Oslo, 1938; E. F. Osborn, *The Philosophy of Clement of Alexandria;* W. Schneemelcher, "Athanasius von Alexandrien als Theologe und als Kirchenpolitiker" in *ZNW,* XLIII, pp. 242-56; R. B. Tollinton, *Clement of Alexandria;* J. Danielou, *Origen;* Archibald Robertson, *Select Writings and Letters of Athanasius,* "Nicene and Post-Nicene Fathers," Second Series, IV; J. E. L. Oulton and H. Chadwick, eds., *Alexandrian Christianity,* "Library of Christian Classics," II, Philadelphia, 1954; Edward R. Hardy, ed., "Library of Christian Classics," III, Philadelphia, 1954; R. V. Sellers, *Two Ancient Christologies.*

PAUL WOOLLEY

ALLEGORY. An allegory, sometimes called a prolonged metaphor, is a rhetorical device which represents a sense higher than the literal. It differs from a metaphor in being longer and more detailed. Bunyan's *Pilgrim's Progress* is a classical religious allegory. Biblical examples include Ps. 80, which describes Israel as a vine, and Gal. 4:24, which Paul specifies as an allegory. Developed in the sixth century B.C. in Greece, this system of interpretation invaded biblical scholarship through Philo of Alexandria (20 B.C.-A.D. 42). Origen (182-251) postulated three levels of truth in Scripture: (1) the literal or fleshly sense; (2) the moral sense; and (3) the pneumatic sense. Allegory was widely employed in the Alexandrian school (See ALEXANDRIA, SCHOOL OF) to remove anthropomorphisms and crude literalisms which offended the Greek mind. Augustine adopted a modified allegorical system on the basis of II Cor. 3:6. Jerome is chiefly responsible for introducing allegory into the Roman church, and this subsequently became one of the great issues of the Reformation. Luther, Melanchthon, and Calvin rejected allegory because it is subjective and uncontrolled.

See also INTERPRETATION (BIBLICAL).

DAVID H. WALLACE

ALMIGHTY. See GOD.

ALMS, ALMSGIVING. The Mosaic law enjoined beneficence in both action and attitude toward the poor and afflicted (cf. Deut. 15:7; 24:13). It bestowed rights and privileges which included gleaning (Lev. 19:9, 10; Deut. 24:19, 21), sabbatical and jubilee year benefits (Ex. 23:11; Lev. 25:6, 25-30, 39-42, 47-54; Deut. 15:12-15), tithe portions (Deut. 14:28; 26:12, 13), prompt wage payment (Lev. 19:13), freedom from usury and retention of pledges (Lev. 25:35, 37; Ex. 22:25-27), and beneficial participation in joyous festivals (Deut. 16:11, 14; cf. Neh. 8:10). The ethical concept of ṣedaqâ is biblically associated with all who express the enjoined attitude and activity (Deut. 25:13). No single word in the English exactly conveys the meaning of ṣedaqâ, which is derived from a Hebrew root meaning justice, righteousness. The blend of ideas between almsgiving and righteousness is illustrated where the LXX translated the word as "alms" in Deut. 25:13 and Dan. 4:24 (27, AV). The same association is manifested at Matt. 6:1 where the Vulgate and some Greek manuscripts read *dikaiosynēn*, "righteousness," instead of *eleēmosynēn*, "alms." The latter word appears in the NT at least fourteen

times. From ṣedaqâ, the rabbis developed *gemîlaṭ ḥăsadîm*, "performing acts of loving-kindness" and declared such actions to be one of the three fundamentals of social economics (Aboth 1:2). Talmudic teaching interpreted "righteousness" by almsgiving in, e.g., Gen. 18:19; Ps. 17:15; Isa. 54:14. By expanding Prov. 10:2, the rabbis infused into almsgiving an intense religious connotation. The messianic era will be expedited by the universal practice of ṣedaqâ (Baba Bathra 10a). Systematic and even enforced almsgiving were developed in post-captivity times, even though pure motivation was recognized as of importance (Suk. 49b). The personality of the beneficiary must be respected, and the bestowal of charity should not be performed in such a way as to humiliate or embarrass the recipient. Ostentation in dispensing alms was deplored; but, being overzealous in religious performance, certain of the Pharisee sect yielded to this unbecoming manifestation (Matt. 6:2).

Born of the early association of charity and righteousness, noble Jewish institutions came into existence which made monetary loans free of interest and without tangible security, conducted burial services, and even provided dowries and trousseaux for poor girls. Care of the poor was a messianic injunction (Matt. 6:1-4; Luke 14:13) and a Christian practice (Gal. 2:10; Acts 11:27-30; Rom. 15:26; I Cor. 16:1-4).

BIBLIOGRAPHY
JewEnc; LXX.

LAWRENCE DUFF-FORBES

ALPHA AND OMEGA. The phrase, Alpha and Omega, is the rendering of the Greek expression *to alpha kai to ō,* which is found in three places in the NT (Rev. 1:8; 21:6; 22:13). It is also found in the Textus Receptus of Rev. 1:11, but modern scholarship largely regards it as not genuine in this place.

In this phrase there is probably a reference to the Jewish employment of the first and last letters of the Hebrew alphabet to indicate the totality of a thing. "The symbol *t'* was regarded as including the intermediate letters, and stood for totality; and thus it fitly represented the Shekinah . . ." (H. B. Swete, *The Apocalypse of St. John,* Eerdmans Publishing Company, Grand Rapids, Michigan, 1951, p. 10). It is a natural transition to the thought of eternity when the expression is related to time.

The expression is essentially the same as Isaiah's words, "I am the first, and I am the last; and beside me there is no God" (Isa. 44:6). Thus, it is a claim that the one to whom it refers is the Eternal One.

The expression in Rev. 1:8, due to the explanatory phrases that modify the subject, refers to the eternity and omnipotence of the Lord God. In 21:6 it is further defined by the words, "the beginning and the end," and in 22:13 by the words, "the first and the last." The thought conveyed in the second and third occurrences is the same.

In patristic and later literature the expression was referred to the Son. It seems clear, however, that the first two occurrences are to be referred to the Father (1:8; 21:6), while the third properly refers to the Son. On its last occurrence (22:13) Swete remarks, "The phrase is applicable in many senses, but perhaps it is used here with special reference to our Lord's place in human history. As creation owed its beginning to the Word of God, so in His incarnate glory He will bring it to its consummation by the Great Award" (op. cit., p. 307).

See also FIRST AND LAST.

BIBLIOGRAPHY
Arndt; Charles in HDB; H. B. Swete, *The Apocalypse of St. John*, pp. 10, 279-80, 307.

S. LEWIS JOHNSON, JR.

ALTAR. The Hebrew term for altar in the OT was *mizbēah* ("place of blood-sacrifice," derived from *zābah* "to slaughter" or "slay a victim"). Yet it was also used for the presentation of the bloodless meal-offering (*minhâ*) and the libations of oil and wine, as well as for burning sacrificial animals. Prior to the consecration of Moses' tabernacle, the altar usually consisted of one or more unhewn stones, and Ex. 20:24-26 allowed the continued erection of such "lay" altars in the holy land after the Israelite conquest. But the general rule after the inauguration of the tabernacle (Ex. 40) was that Israelite believers were to present their blood-sacrifices only upon the bronze altar installed before the door of the tabernacle itself. This was constructed according to the exact measurements (five cubits square and three cubits high) revealed to Moses on Mt. Sinai, and it was fashioned of acacia wood overlaid with bronze, and equipped with a horn at each of the four corners.

There was also a smaller (one cubit square and two cubits high) altar constructed of acacia wood and overlaid with gold. This "golden altar" (likewise called *mizbēah*) was distinguished from the "brazen altar" in that it was intended only for the offering up of incense (although blood might be smeared upon its horns). This stood right before the inner veil or curtain in such a position that the smoke of the incense might cover over the ark of the covenant inside the holiest place. The NT word for these altars was *thysiastērion* (from *thyō* "to sacrifice"). Only once is another word used for altar: *bōmos* in Acts 17:23, where a reference is made to a pagan altar.

G. L. ARCHER, JR.

AMAZEMENT. Expressions of amazement (*thambein*, Mark 1:27; *existanai*, Mark 2:12) and its related emotions, astonishment (*ekplēssesthai*, Mark 1:22), wonder (*thaumazein*, Mark 5:20) and fear (*phobeisthai*, Mark 4:41), appear frequently in the Synoptic Gospels as a description of the reaction of varied groups to the words and works of Jesus. Such words emphasize the revelatory character of these words and works.

Wonder is attributed to Jesus twice (Matt. 8:10; Mark 6:6). The word used, *thaumazein*, emphasizes a reaction not so much to the unexpected as to the extraordinary. In Mark's account of Gethsemane (Mark 14:33) Jesus' emotion is described with the word *ekthambeisthai* (only in Mark 9:15; 16:5, 6). In the light of the LXX use of this word and its cognates, which emphasizes dread or fear (see I Sam. 14:15; II Sam. 22:5), the source of the emotion is to be found in the awful awareness of the implications of the cross.

See also EMOTION.

CHARLES A. HODGMAN

AMBASSADOR. The word ambassador is the rendering of three Hebrew words in the OT: (1) *mal'āk*, meaning messenger, or angel (II Chron. 35:21); (2) *ṣîr*, meaning envoy, or messenger (Josh. 9:4); (3) *mēliṣ*, meaning interpreter, or ambassador, as a hiphil participle of *lûṣ* (II Chron. 32:31). Generally speaking, they were temporary officials chosen from court attendants to represent a king or government.

The chief interest of the word centers around the NT usage. It is the rendering of the Greek word *presbeuō*, which occurs in two places (II Cor. 5:20; Eph. 6:20). A related word, *presbeia*, meaning ambassage, occurs in Luke 14:32. The Greek words *presbeuō* and *presbeutēs* were used for the emperor's legate.

Paul's words, therefore, in II Cor. 5:20, "Now then we are ambassadors for Christ," set forth the Christian minister as a representative of the King of kings, delivering a message which is the very voice of God.

BIBLIOGRAPHY
Arndt; Deiss LAE, p. 374; MM.

S. LEWIS JOHNSON, JR.

AMEN. This Hebrew word originally was an adjective meaning "reliable, sure, true" or an adjectival verb, "It is reliable or true." The related verb *āman* meant "to support, sustain"; in the niphal stem: "prove oneself steady, reliable, loyal"; in the hiphil stem: "to regard someone as reliable, trustworthy or truthful," and hence, "to believe." *Āmēn* by itself was used as a formula ("Surely!" "In very truth!") at the end of (a) a doxology, such as: "Blessed be Jehovah forever" (where the *Amen* signifies: "Yes indeed!" or, "May it be so in very truth!") cf. Pss. 41:13; 72:19; 89:52; 106:48; also I Chron. 16:36 and Neh. 8:6, where the audience assents to and adopts their leader's praise of God; (b) a decree or expression of royal purpose, where the obedient listener indicates his hearty assent and cooperation (I Kings 1:36; Jer. 11:5). The one who prays or asseverates or joins in the prayer or asseveration of another, by the use of "Amen" puts himself into the statement with all earnestness of faith and intensity of desire. The usage is the same in the NT. Isa. 65:16 speaks of Jehovah as the God of Amen, meaning that he speaks the truth and carries out his word. The same is implied by the Lord Christ when he calls himself "The Amen" in Rev. 3:14.

G. L. ARCHER, JR.

'AM HĀ-ĀREṢ. The term *'am hā-āreṣ,* "people of the land," is used in the OT of: (1) the native inhabitants of Palestine in contrast to the Hebrews (Gen. 23:7, 12, 13; Num. 14:9); (2) the mixed population who resisted the resettlement of Palestine after the Exile (Ezra 9:1, 2; 10:2, 11; Neh. 10:28-31); (3) the Israelite people as a whole (II Kings 15:5; Ezek. 12:19; 33:2; 39:13); and (4) the common people distinguished from the king, princes, priests, and prophets (II Kings 11:14; Jer. 1:18; Ezek. 7:27; 22:29; 46:3, 9).

In all of the pre-exilic references the term carries with it the idea of possessing land and has sociological significance. In the rabbinic literature it becomes a purely religious term and refers to those who, because of poverty, distance from Jerusalem, or simply neglect, did not observe the laws of ritual purity. The *'am hā-āreṣ* were uninstructed in their religion and thus negligent in the performance of its obligations. The Pharisees sincerely believed that such folk were outside the pale of true religion. Hillel remarked: "A brutish man dreads not sin and the ignorant man (*'am hā-āreṣ*) cannot be pious" (*Aboth* 2:6).

Strack-Billerbeck attempts an identification of *'am hā-āreṣ* with the poor of Luke 6:20 and Matt. 5:3, but the fact that there were included in their number city dwellers and farmers, rich and poor, even kings (*SBK*, II, p. 495), makes this unlikely.

In all probability Jesus and his disciples were considered by the Pharisees to be *'am hā-āreṣ* because they ate with unwashed hands (Mark 7:1-15) and picked grain on the Sabbath (Luke 6:1-15). The Pharisees were undoubtedly referring to the *'am hā-āreṣ* in John 7:49: "This crowd, who do not know the law, are accursed."

The climax of the mutual bitterness between the Pharisees and the *'am hā-āreṣ* was reached in the early second century A.D. One rabbi taught that an *'am hā-āreṣ* could be killed on the Day of Atonement, even if it fell on the Sabbath! R. Akiba said of himself: "When I was an *'am hā-āreṣ* I used to say, I wish I had one of those scholars, and I would bite him like an ass" (*Pes.* 49b). After the Bar Kochba revolt (A.D. 132-35) these animosities disappeared.

BIBLIOGRAPHY
Montefiore, *Rabbinical Literature and Gospel Teachings,* pp. 3-15; I. Abrahams in Montefiore's *The Synoptic Gospels,* II, pp. 646-69; R. Meyer in TWNT; G. F. Moore in Jackson and Lake, *Beginnings,* I, pp. 439-45; *SBK,* I, pp. 190-92; II, pp. 494-500.

WALTER W. WESSEL

AMILLENNIALISM. See MILLENNIUM.

AMYRALDISM. The doctrine of "hypothetical universalism" held and taught by Moses Amyrald, Moyse Amyraut (1596-1664), at the French Reformed theological school in Saumur. A staunch defender of the Calvinist articles of the Synod of Dort (1618-19), Amyrald felt that a sort of Protestant scholasticism had emerged, and he desired to get back to the spirit of Calvin's *Institutes.*

Amyrald also feared that the Lutherans might be repelled by the Dort articles, feeling that they were being classed as Arminians along with the Dutch Remonstrants. Holding that the will always follows the intellect, he taught that God wills the salvation of all, but man's intellect is incapable of causing the will to believe apart from the operation of God in the elect.

Thus Amyrald explained double predestination while softening its harsher aspects. "Hypothetical universalism" is a confusing term, for it seems to favor Arminianism, which it actually condemns.

Amyrald was acquitted of heresy by two French Protestant synods, but the Swiss Reformed condemned his doctrine in the *Formula Consensus Helvetica* (1675), which denied universal atonement and the notion that God desires the salvation of all. Amyraldism lives on, however, in much of modern Calvinism.

BIBLIOGRAPHY
    HERE, I, pp. 404-6.

DONALD G. DAVIS

ANABAPTISTS. A religious group which appeared in Germany and other countries of Europe as an aftermath of the Lutheran Reformation but which was not an essential part of it. However, the fact that Luther shook the foundation of the political and ecclesiastical order in Germany made this movement possible. The seeds of economic and political revolt had been well planted in the German mind, and only an upheaval of major proportions was needed to bring them to life. The Anabaptist revolt, while essentially religious in nature, combined religious with social, economic, and political radicalism. The term itself designates the opposition of this group to the prevailing practice among the Lutherans and Roman Catholics of infant baptism and their own insistence upon adult immersion. Repudiating both the Roman Catholic and the Lutheran conception of the church and its government, the movement represented a distinct break in the church as an historic organism. Ritschl found its origin in the Spiritual Franciscans of the later Middle Ages while other scholars have felt that it can be traced back to the Waldensian movement. The Anabaptists were not a coherent group and represented various degrees of orthodoxy, ranging from the evangelical position of Conrad Grebel (1498-1528) to the much more radical thought of Balthasar Huebmaier (1485-1528), and Hans Denk (d. 1527). Their common denominator was their insistence on the necessity of adult baptism. The more radical element stressed the importance of the inner word rather than the

external word of the Scriptures. Denying such doctrines as the total depravity of man, original sin, election, and eternal damnation, they held that man possesses freedom of the will and is capable of a direct and mystic communion with God. Huebmaier and Denk preached a moderate communism along with a radical chiliasm, which brought upon them persecution by both the Roman Catholics and the Lutherans. Menno Simons became the leader of the Anabaptists after 1536 and brought them into the evangelical tradition of the Reformers.

BIBLIOGRAPHY
    J. Horsch, *The Mennonites in Europe*; R. H. Bainton, "The Left Wing of the Reformation," *Journal of Religion*, XXI, 1941; G. F. Hershberger, *The Recovery of the Anabaptist Vision*.

GREGG SINGER

ANALOGY. In logic, a form of inference. When an object resembles another in a certain number of points, it will probably resemble it in others. The Scholastics developed reasoning from the finite to the infinite by analogy to a precise science. Aquinas, using as his foundation the metaphysical scale of being, reasoned that if both creature and Creator are a part of the same scale of being, then there must be between them an analogy of proportion. Thus, if man has wisdom, by analogy God also has wisdom.

William of Occam pointed out the fallacy in reasoning thus by analogy from the known finite to the unknown infinite. So long as the differences between the creature and the Creator are indeterminable and infinite this type of reasoning can have very little meaning. This was ignored by later Protestant apologetes, such as Butler, who wrote his classic *Analogy of Religion,* in which he sought to make a reasonable use of reason to show that God probably exists.

The proper place of analogical reasoning is seen when it is recognized that God is the ultimate source of all truth. Thus when man discovers the truth in any realm of knowledge, he is thinking God's thoughts after him. His knowledge is analogical of God's. This fact is of basic importance for apologetics. All non-Christian systems assume that man reasons univocally, whereas only Christianity recognizes the fact that all our true reasoning is analogous.

MORTON H. SMITH

ANATHEMA. The Attic *anathēma* meant a thing laid by, specifically, a votive offering set apart to a god, which was hung in his temple or in a public place. The LXX employs it as the rendering for *ḥērem, and* in time it came to have the force of "anything devoted to destruction" (Lev. 27:29; Josh. 6:17 ASV). That which was "devoted" to God was forbidden for ordinary uses. In the NT the AV "accursed" in Rom. 9:3, I Cor. 12:3, and Gal. 1:8, 9 is *anathema.* It became a strong word of execration implying moral worthlessness. Ezra 10:8 is supposed to be the starting point of the theory that *anathema* could mean excommunication (*JewEnc*, I, p. 559). In the Talmud, *ḥērem* is undoubtedly used of excommunication. The Greek Fathers employed *anathema* also to denote excommunication (q.v.).

Rom. 9:3 cannot signify excommunication because of *apo tou Christou,* but rather separation (q.v.) from Christ and eternal bliss (Crem, p. 547). It was explained as excommunication by the Church Fathers because of a desire to avoid the appearance of profanity in the wish (*ICC, in loco*). Though convinced that nothing celestial nor terrestrial could separate him from Christ, Paul was moved to the desire because of voluntary self-sacrifice.

In I Cor. 12:3 Paul may have had in mind the days of his opposition to Christian truth (Acts 26:11). He now declares that no one can be motivated by the Spirit of God and still utter this execration. In later years during the persecutions of Christians they were put to this crucial test, that is, to blaspheme Christ.

Perhaps Gal. 1:8, 9 is the strongest use of the word. Paul places first himself, then even the angels, and lastly any man under a curse should any one of them presume to preach another (different) gospel than the one already delivered to the Galatians.

Anathema is joined with the Aramaic *Maranatha* ("Our Lord comes" or "Our Lord, come") in I Cor. 16:22. The use of the Aramaic has been explained as an expression in common use like our "Hallelujah" and "Amen." The usual interpretation is that he who loves not, even more, has not any affection for, our Lord Jesus Christ will be accursed at the coming of the Lord.

See also CURSE.

BIBLIOGRAPHY
Crem, p. 547; *EB*, I, pp. 468-70; *ISBE*, I, p. 130; *JewEnc*, I, pp. 559 ff.; Lange, *Romans*, pp. 302 ff.; LSJ; W. A. Sanday and A. C. Headlam (ICC), *Romans*; Thayer, p. 37; *WDB*, p. 28.

CHARLES L. FEINBERG

ANCHORITE. The English term is derived from the Greek *anachōreō,* to separate, withdraw, retire, and denotes one of the class of early ascetics who withdrew from the society of men, hoping to please God by living in solitary isolation while seeking victory over the flesh and the devil in meditation and prayer. Extreme ascetic practices characterized the anchorites, and they gave little evidence of a sense of mission to mankind.

Anthony of Egypt (250?-356?) became the first Christian anchorite, and he soon had many imitators. The Egyptian desert and the caves of the Middle East were favorite retreats. Western Europe produced few anchorites, probably because of the less favorable climate. Anchoritism did not prove to be a satisfactory way of life, and the communal type of monasticism was initiated by Pachomius (292?-349?), who had been disappointed in the solitary life.

BIBLIOGRAPHY
Herbert B. Workman, *The Evolution of the Monastic Ideal.*

DONALD G. DAVIS

ANGEL. The term *aggelos,* from which angel derives, is in itself a fairly colorless word, like its Hebrew equivalent, which can be used equally for human or heavenly messengers. But in the NT it is used almost exclusively for angelic beings in the latter sense, and the Vulgate rightly introduces a distinction between *angelus* and *nuntius* which has been maintained in modern renderings and usage.

The term which the Bible uses to describe angels gives us the clue to the function by which they are primarily to be known and understood. They are the ambassadors of God. They belong to his heavenly court and service. Their mission in heaven is to praise him (Rev. 4, 5) and to do his will (Ps. 103:20), and in this mission they behold his face (Matt. 18:10). But since heaven comes down to earth, they also have a mission to earth, accompanying God in his work of creation (Job 38:7), providence (Dan. 12:1), and especially reconciliation (Gen. 19:1 f. and *passim*). In fulfilment of this mission their task is to declare the word of God (e.g., Luke 1:26 f.) and to do his work (e.g., Matt. 28:2).

The function of angels is best seen from their part in the saving mission of Jesus Christ. It is natural that they should be present both when he came to earth and at his resurrection and ascension. They are also to accompany

him at his return in glory (Matt. 24:31).
They do not do the real work of reconciliation.
But they declare and accompany, and they
summon man to participate in their work of
praise. (cf. Luke 1:46). It is interesting that
between the nativity and the resurrection there
seem to be only two angelic appearances in
the ministry of Jesus, at the beginning of his
way to the cross in the temptation and at its
culmination in Gethsemane. This is perhaps
due to the fact that Jesus must tread this way
alone, and that in his humiliation he is made
a little lower than the angels (Heb. 2:9).

The Bible gives us only a few hints concerning the nature of angels. Belonging to the
sphere of heaven, they cannot be properly conceived in earthly terms. They are almost always described in relation to God, as "his angels" (e.g., Ps. 104:4). Even the two angelic
names Michael and Gabriel emphasize this relationship. In Heb. 1:14 they are described as
"ministering spirits," in a conflation of the two
parts of Ps. 104:4. Elsewhere, in Job and the
Psalms, they are called the "heavenly ones"
(Ps. 29:1), the "saints," i.e., set apart for
God's service, (Job 5:1), the "sons of God"
(Ps. 89:6) and even "gods" (Ps. 82:1). Since
Christians can also be called the "sons of God,"
we need not infer from the latter phrases, as
did some of the apologists (cf. Athenagoras
Leg. pro Christ. x and xxiv), that they are
lesser deities. Indeed the Bible clearly warns
us not to worship them (Col. 2:18).

Among the heavenly creatures mention is
made of the seraphim (Isa. 6:1), and more
frequently the cherubim (Gen. 3:24). Of the
angels named, Michael is described as "the
great prince" (Dan. 12:1), and in Rev. 12:7
the other angels seem to be led by him. Again,
we are told that the angel who appeared to
Joshua is the captain of the host of the Lord
(Josh. 5:14). Further distinctions seem to be
indicated in Rev. 4 and 5, with the references
to the beasts and elders, but the exact signification of these terms is disputed. (See LIVING
CREATURE).

From the various statements about the nature of angels, early and medieval theology
built up a complex speculative description of
the angelic world. Pseudo-Dionysius proved
already the most original and constructive
thinker in this field, arranging the angels in
three ascending or descending groups of nine
choirs each. Aquinas, the angelic doctor,
treated the question with great acuteness and

fulness. He, too, saw three hierarchies, but his
main interest was in the nature of angels as
individuals, spatial spiritual substances engaged
primarily in the work of enlightenment and
capable of rational demonstration (*S. c. Gent.*
ii. 91; *S. th.* i. 50-64).

As Calvin saw, the error in so much angelology was to treat the angels in abstraction
from the biblical witness. Even in respect of
the function of angels there was a tendency
to rationalize or a concentration of interest on
the idea of the guardian angel. The inevitable
result came in the age of the Enlightenment and
liberal Protestantism, when angels were either
dismissed as fantastic or subjected to a thoroughgoing process of neologization.

Yet there are perhaps certain legitimate deductions from the biblical evidence. The angels are non-corporeal. They form an ordered
unity. The fact that they are plural means
that they are multiple, and multiplicity entails
the existence of individuals within the totality,
with a possible gradation in function if not in
nature. They seem not to have an autonomous
will, but to give God the perfect service in
heaven for which we are to pray on earth
(Matt. 6:10). In relation to man, they have
the advantage of belonging to heaven and of
having the majesty and privileges of God's
ambassadors. But when man responds to the
saving work of God in Jesus Christ, he is
raised above them, enjoys their ministry (Heb.
1:14), and will finally judge them (I Cor.
6:3).

Two detailed problems call for brief mention. The first concerns the angel of the Lord,
who often, as in Judges 13:2 f., seems to be
identical with God himself. From the days of
the Fathers many have concluded that in the
OT at least the reference is to the preincarnate
Logos. Liberals explain it as the softening of
theophany to angelophany, though without
showing why this does not apply in other
cases. Another possible explanation is that
through the angel God speaks so clearly and
fully that he himself can be said to speak. At
any rate, the angel of the Lord in Luke 2:9
cannot be identified with Christ.

Second, the Bible speaks of the devil's angels as well as the angels of God, and seems
to suggest in verses like Jude 6 that there has
been a fall of angels. This was the deduction
of Irenaeus (*A.haer.* iv. 37.1) and many Fathers; and, while we cannot press too dogmatically a subject on which the Bible is so

reserved, we must reckon with the fact that in grotesque and finally impotent caricature of the angels there are real principalities and powers (q.v.) (Eph. 6:12) in a kingdom of evil. These angels and their leader were defeated at the cross (Col. 2:15) and will finally be brought to condemnation (Matt. 25:41).

BIBLIOGRAPHY
K. Barth, *Church Dogmatics*, Vol. III, part 3, § 51; H. Cremer, H. S. Nash, and B. Pick, *SHERK*, I, p. 174; A. B. Davidson, *HDB*, I, p. 93; G. Spinner, "Die Engel und Wir," *Kirchenblatt fuer die reformierte Schweiz*, pp. 18, 19.

GEOFFREY W. BROMILEY

ANGER. See WRATH.

ANGLO-CATHOLICISM. See TRACTARIANISM.

ANIMISM. This term is used to cover three varying conceptions: (1) that physical objects possess a life or spirit of their own (cf. children with their toys, and some primitives and occultists); (2) that physical objects are indwelt by spirits, which may survive if the objects are destroyed; and (3) that spirits manifest themselves sporadically through peoples, objects, or places, whether they be pure spirits (e.g., Jinns) or spirits of the departed (cf. ancestor worship; spiritualism). In (2) and (3) the spirits are personal and may be feared or venerated though they are less than gods. Generally a class of men or women can contact and control them (e.g., the Shaman, witchdoctor, or medium). Animistic peoples are found in many parts of the world. Their religion is largely one of fear. Some hold that all religions arose from animism, animism itself having arisen from dreams. See MONOTHEISM.

J. STAFFORD WRIGHT

ANNIHILATIONISM. The word is from the Latin *nihil*, "nothing" and expresses the position of those who hold that some, if not all, human souls will cease to exist after death. As observed by Warfield, (in *SHERK*, I, p. 183) this point of view may take three main forms: (a) that all men inevitably cease to exist altogether at death (materialism); (b) that, while man is naturally mortal, God imparts to the redeemed the gift of immortality and allows the rest of humanity to sink into nothingness (conditional immortality); (c) that man, being created immortal, fulfills his destiny in salvation, while the reprobates fall into non-existence either through a direct act

of God, or through the corrosive effect of evil (annihilationism proper). The distinction between conditionalism and annihilationism, as indicated above, is frequently not observed and these two terms are commonly used as practical synonyms. A fourth form of advocacy of the ultimate extinction of evil is the view that God will finally redeem all rational beings (universalism). Over against all the above positions, historic orthodoxy has always maintained both that human souls will eternally endure and that their destiny is irrevocably sealed at death.

The question whether or not man is naturally immortal pertains to the subject of *Immortality* (q.v.). In the present article we shall limit ourselves to stating and appraising very briefly the main evidence advanced in support of the cessation of the wicked.

1. God alone, it is urged, has immortality (I Tim. 6:16; 1:17). This argument, if it proves anything, proves too much. In fact, God who alone has immortality in himself may and does communicate it to some of his creatures.

2. Immortality, it is urged, is represented as a special gift connected with redemption in Jesus Christ (Rom. 2:7; I Cor. 15:53-54; II Tim. 1:10). The same may be said of life, or eternal life (John 10:28; Rom. 6:22-23; Gal. 6:8; etc.). It is freely granted that in all such passages life and immortality are represented as the privileged possession of the redeemed, but it is claimed that in these connections these terms do not represent merely continued existence, but rather connote existence in joyful fulfillment of man's high destiny in true fellowship with God (John 17:3).

3. Cessation of existence, it is urged, is implied in various scriptural terms applied to the destiny of the wicked, such as death (Rom. 6:23; James 5:20; Rev. 20:14; etc.), destruction (Matt. 7:13; 10:28; I Thess. 1:9, etc.), perishing (John 3:16, etc.). But these expressions do not so much imply annihilation as complete deprivation of some element essential to normal existence. Physical death (q.v.) does not mean that body or soul vanishes, but rather that an abnormal separation takes place which severs their natural relationship until God's appointed time. Spiritual death, or the "second death" (Rev. 20:14; 21:8), does not mean that the soul or personality lapses into nonbeing, but rather that it is ultimately and finally deprived of that presence of God and fellowship with him which is the chief end of man and the essential condition of worthwhile

existence. To be bereft of it is to perish, to be reduced to utter insignificance, to sink into abysmal futility. An automobile is said to be wrecked, ruined, destroyed, not only when its constituent parts have been melted or scattered away, but also when they have been so damaged and distorted that the car has become completely unserviceable.

4. It is inconsistent with God's love, it is urged, to allow any of his creatures to endure for ever in torment. Furthermore, the continuance of evil would spell some area of permanent defeat for the divine sovereignty, a dark corner marring perpetually the glory of his universe. These considerations are not without weight, and a complete answer may not be possible in the present state of our knowledge. They are not adjudged by traditional orthodoxy as sufficient to overthrow the substantial weight of scriptural evidence to the effect that the wicked will be consigned to endless conscious sorrow. This is apparent from the expressions "fire unquenchable" (Isa. 66:24; Matt. 3:12; Luke 3:17), or "that never shall be quenched" (Mark 9:43, 45), the worm that "dieth not" (Isa. 66:24; Mark 9:44, 46, 48), "the wrath of God *abideth* on him" (John 3:36), as well as from the use of "everlasting" or "forever," applying to chains, contempt, destruction, fire or burning, punishment, torment (Isa. 33:14; Jer. 17:4; Dan. 12:2; Matt. 18:8; 25:41, 46; II Thess. 1:9; Jude 6-7; Rev. 14:11; 19:3; 20:10). It is worthy of note that, in the biblical record, those who spoke most about future punishment in its irrevocable finality are Jesus and the apostle John, the very ones who also presented most glowingly the supreme glory of God's love and the unshakable certainty of his ultimate triumph.

For a discussion of the history of the doctrine of annihilationism, one may consult with profit the article of B. B. Warfield referred to above.

BIBLIOGRAPHY

B. B. Warfield in *SHERK*, reprinted in *Theological Studies*; G. C. Joyce in *HERE*. Both of these articles include helpful bibliographies. In addition to works mentioned there we may list: (a) in support of annihilationism: H. Constable, *The Duration and Nature of Future Punishment*; C. H. Hewitt, *A Classbook in Eschatology*; Eric Lewis, *Life and Immortality*; F. L. Piper, *Conditionalism*; (b) in opposition to annihilationism: H. Buis, *The Doctrine of Eternal Punishment*; R. Garrigou-Lagrange, *Life Everlasting*; W. G. T. Shedd, *Dogmatic Theology*, II, pp. 591-640, 667-754.

ROGER NICOLE

ANNUNCIATION. Three people receive an *annuntiatio* (euaggelismos) in the Gospels,

i.e., Zechariah (Luke 1:13), Joseph (Matt. 1:20), and Mary (Luke 1:26 ff.); but the term normally denotes the latter. Luke's information must derive originally from Mary, possibly through Joanna (see Sanday); his account shows a dignity and delicacy absent from parallel pagan myths (cf. Enoch 15:86). Luke relates the annunciation by Gabriel to Mary in her Nazareth home. Matthew gives an account of the announcement of the birth and name of Jesus to Joseph in a dream.

The message is threefold: (1) *Chaire kecharitōmenē*. This is translated *Ave, gratia plena* by the Vulgate, as if Mary were full of grace and dispensed gifts. But the context portrays Mary as merely a recipient of God's favor, "highly favoured," says Bengel, "not as mother of grace but daughter of grace." For vs. 28b (cf. Judg. 6:12) the RV rightly omits "Blessed art thou among women" which belongs to vs. 42. The unassuming Mary is much agitated but has recourse to meditation (cf. 2:19). (2) Vss. 30-33. "Fear not" (cf. Zechariah in vs. 13). The name Jesus (= Joshua), meaning "The Lord saves," was given frequently by parents hoping for a Messiah son; it is now given by God's command to him who fulfils Ps. 2:7 and Isa. 9:7. *Basileia* means "sovereignty." The old Latin MS "b" omits vs. 34; but Creed rejects the contention of Streeter that such slender evidence proves the virgin birth an interpolation. *Ginōskō* (Heb. *yāda'*) is used of sexual intercourse (cf. Gen. 19:8); but the tense is not future, as though Mary took oath of perpetual virginity, but present. (3) Vss. 35-37. The Gospel according to the Hebrews also ascribes the pregnancy to the Spirit. Jesus does not *become* the holy Son of God (cf. Luke 3:22) by the supernatural conception, but *is acknowledged* as such. The sign (cf. Isa. 7:14) is Elizabeth's pregnancy. Mary's submission is made in face of public disgrace and Joseph's dilemma.

The Feast of the Annunciation is a "red letter day" (March 25) in BCP, dated on the basis of December 25 for the Nativity, or in adaptation of the pagan festival of Cybele. Some claim an early origin from references in Athanasius or Gregory Thaumaturgus. The earliest certain mention is at the tenth Synod of Toledo (A.D. 656). In the Ethiopian Calendar it is called the "Conception of Christ."

BIBLIOGRAPHY

HDCG; N. Geldenhuys on Luke, pp. 74-80; ODCC; *Exp.*, April, 1903, p. 297.

DENIS H. TONGUE

ANOINTING. The practice of applying oil or perfumed oil upon persons or things. In the OT two roots are mainly used: *māšiah* and *sûk* (the latter only nine times); in the NT, *aleiphō* and *chriō* with its compounds (from which is derived the name Christ). The references are most common to the anointing of kings and priests. Olive oil was mainly used. Directions are given for compounding it with perfumes for holy use (Ex. 30:22-25).

The first mention of anointing is Gen. 31:13, where Jacob anointed the pillar commemorating the spot of his dream. In Exodus, Leviticus, and Numbers detailed instructions are given for anointing the tabernacle, its furnishings, and Aaron and his sons. They were thus sanctified, and the priests so set apart were not to profane themselves for the dead or in any other way.

In Samuel the anointing for the kingship is common (though it is referred to earlier, in Judg. 9:8 and I Sam. 2:10, 35). Samuel anointed Saul and the Spirit of the Lord came upon him. When Samuel later anointed David, the Spirit of the Lord came upon David, departing from Saul. From these circumstances the meaning of the anointing is clear. It symbolized the coming of the Holy Spirit upon God's servant for his work, be he priest, king, or prophet (I Kings 19:16). The Messiah in Isa. 61:1 is said to be anointed by the Spirit of the Lord; and, indeed, when Jesus entered upon his messianic ministry, the Spirit descended upon him visibly (Luke 3:22).

Following the establishment of the monarchy, references to the anointing of kings predominate. As messianic prophecies pointed ever more clearly to David's seed, "the anointed," *māšiah*, became first a description, then a title of the Messiah (*q.v.*) to come. Instances are seen in Ps. 45:7 and especially Dan. 9:25, 26. Whether the word *māšiah* here is a title or description ("the anointed") is perhaps less important than it is to realize that in either case it is a prophecy of the coming king of David's line (cf. John 4:25). The title is widespread in the intertestamental literature and Dead Sea material.

Oil was also used for anointing in non-religious contexts. Isa. 21:5 and probably II Sam. 1:21 speak of anointing a shield. The purpose is not stated. Perhaps it would serve as a preservative if the shield were of leather or iron. Anointing with oil or perfumed oil was also practiced for cosmetic purposes (Rev. 3:18; Dan. 10:3), which practice is associated with excess of luxury in Amos 6:6. This is the NT usage of *aleiphō* (Matt. 6:17). Jesus' feet were so anointed with myrrh (Luke 7:38), with nard (John 12:3). Anointing with oil was apparently a household remedy (cf. Mark 6:13; James 5:14; and Luke 10:34). Alford argues for a sacramental use of the oil in James 5:14. The Meyer commentary ascribes the healing to prayer, remarking that "James does not state" the purpose of the oil. The Roman Catholic use of this passage to support extreme unction is, as Alford shows, quite farfetched.

BIBLIOGRAPHY

B. B. Warfield, *Counterfeit Miracles*; Arndt, "Anoint" and "Messiah" in *DDB*; Alf on James; W. E. Biederwolf, *Whipping-post Theology*, pp. 97-108.

R. LAIRD HARRIS

ANTHROPOLOGY. See MAN.

ANTHROPOMORPHISM. The term (not found in the Bible — derived from Greek *anthrōpos*, man, and *morphē*, form) designates the view which conceives of God as having *human form* (Ex. 15:3; Num. 12:8) with *feet* (Gen. 3:8; Ex. 24:10), *hands* (Ex. 24:11; Josh. 4:24), *mouth* (Num. 12:8; Jer. 7:13), and *heart* (Hos. 11:8), but in a wider sense the term also includes *human attributes* and *emotions* (Gen. 2:2; 6:6; Ex. 20:5; Hos. 11:8).

This tendency toward anthropomorphism, common to all religions, found such full expression in Greek polytheism that the common man thought of the *gods as mortal men*. Xenophanes (about 570-480 B.C.) reacted strongly, accusing man of making the gods in his (man's) own image. Later developments in Greek thought considered *men as mortal gods* (an early form of humanism) or viewed God in the metaphysical sense of pure, absolute Being. The transcendentalism of the latter influenced the hellenistic Jews of Egypt so that the translators of the Greek OT, the Septuagint (LXX), made during the third and second centuries B.C., felt compelled to alter some of the anthropomorphisms. For example, where the Hebrew reads "they saw the God of Israel" (Ex. 24:10) the LXX has "they saw the place where the God of Israel stood"; and for "I will speak with him mouth to mouth" (Num. 12:8) the LXX translates "I will speak to him mouth to mouth apparently."

However, the OT, if read with empathy and understanding, reveals a spiritual development which is a corrective for either a crude, literalistic view of anthropomorphism or the equally false abhorrence of any anthropomorphic expressions. The "image of God" created in man (Gen. 1:27) was in the realm of personality, of spirit, not of human form. Because the Israelites "saw no form" (Deut. 4:12) at Sinai, they were prohibited images in any form: male or female, beast, bird, creeping thing, or fish (Deut. 4:15-19). The NT declaration of Jesus, "God is spirit, and those who worship him must worship in spirit and truth" (John 4:24), is anticipated by Job 9:32, Ps. 50:21, and Hos. 11:9.

The anthropomorphism of the Israelites was an attempt to express the non-rational aspects of religious experience (the *mysterium tremendum,* "aweful majesty," discussed by Rudolf Otto) in terms of the rational, and the early expressions of it were not as "crude" as so-called enlightened man would have one think. The human characteristics of Israel's God were always exalted, while the gods of their Near Eastern neighbors shared the vices of men. Whereas the representation of God in Israel never went beyond anthropomorphism, the gods of the other religions assumed forms of animals, trees, stars, or even a mixture of elements. Anthropomorphic concepts were "absolutely necessary if the God of Israel was to remain a God of the individual Israelite as well as of the people as a whole. . . . For the average worshipper . . . it is very essential that his god be a divinity who can sympathize with his human feelings and emotions, a being whom he can love and fear alternately, and to whom he can transfer the holiest emotions connected with memories of father and mother and friend" (William F. Albright, *From the Stone Age to Christianity,* 2d ed., 1946; Johns Hopkins Press, p. 202).

It is precisely in the area of the *personal* that theism, as expressed in Christianity, must ever think in anthropomorphic terms. To regard God solely as Absolute Being or The Great Unknown is to refer to *him* or *it,* but to think of God as literally personal, one with whom we can fellowship, is to say *Thou.* Some object to this view, calling it anthropomorphic, but they are at a loss to explain how the creatures of an impersonal force became personal human beings conscious of their personality.

"To say that God is completely different from us is as absurd as to say that He is completely like us" (D. Elton Trueblood, *Philosophy of Religion,* Harper, 1957, p. 270). Paradoxical as it may seem, there is a mediating position which finds the answer in the incarnation of Jesus the Christ, who said, "He who has seen me has seen the Father" (John 14:9). Finite man will ever cling to the anthropomorphism of the incarnation and the concept of God as Father (Matt. 7:11), but at the same time he will realize the impossibility of absolute, complete comprehension of God, for "my thoughts are not your thoughts, neither are your ways my ways, says the LORD" (Isa. 55:8).

BIBLIOGRAPHY

Blunt; Walther Eichrodt, *Theologie des Alten Testaments,* Vol. II, pp. 4-18; J. Hempel in ZAW, pp. 57, 75 ff.; G. Dawes Hicks, *The Philosophical Bases of Theism,* pp. 51 ff.; ISBE; Rudolf Otto, *The Idea of the Holy,* pp. 1-24, 72-86; H. H. Rowley, *The Faith of Israel,* pp. 60, 67, 70, 75, 76; SHERK; Henry B. Swete, *An Introduction to the Old Testament in Greek,* p. 327.

DEWEY M. BEEGLE

ANTICHRIST. Although the term antichrist occurs only in the Johannine letters, the conception of an archopponent of God and his Messiah is found in both testaments and in the intertestamental writings. Opposition is reflected in *anti,* which here probably means "against," not "instead of," although both ideas may be present: posing as Christ, Antichrist opposes Christ.

I. OLD TESTAMENT BACKGROUND. Because Christ is not fully revealed, the OT offers no complete portrait of Antichrist but furnishes materials for the picture in descriptions of personal or national opposition to God.

A. *Belial.* Certain individuals, infamous for wickedness, are called "sons of [or men of] Belial" (*beliyya'al,* probably "without worth," "useless"). Idolatry (Deut. 13:13), sodomy and rape (Judg. 19:22; 20:13), drunkenness (I Sam. 1:16), disregard of God (I Sam. 2:12), sacrilege (I Sam. 2:17, 22), disrespect for authority (I Sam. 10:27; II Chron. 13:7), lack of hospitality (I Sam. 25:17, 25), perjury (I Kings 21:10, 13), and evil speech (Prov. 6:12; 16:27) are among the sins of these "empty men" (II Chron. 13:7), whom the good shun (Ps. 101:3).

B. *Foreign Enemies.* Opposition to God's kingdom is opposition to him. The nations' vain plot against the Lord's anointed king in Ps. 2 may be a foreshadowing of the antichrist idea. Similarly, the taunt songs against the rulers of Babylon (Isa. 14) and Tyre (Ezek. 28) vividly describe the calamitous fall of monarchs who usurp divine prerogatives. Gog's defeat (Ezek. 39:1-20; Rev. 20:7-10) seems to culminate the fruitless struggle of nations to frustrate God's purposes by harassing his people.

C. *The Little Horn.* This rebellion is symbolized in Daniel's little horn. Chapter seven, the more eschatological, seems to depict the defeat of God's final enemy, while eight describes Antiochus IV Epiphanes (175-163 B.C.), the foreign ruler most hated by the Jews because of his personal wickedness and ruthless persecution of their religion.

The portrait of this "king of the north" (Dan. 11), the personification of evil, has helped significantly to shape the NT figure of Antichrist: (1) he abolished the continual burnt offering and erected the abomination of desolation (*q.v.*) in the temple (Dan. 11:31; Matt. 24:15; Mark 13:14; Rev. 13:14-15); (2) he exalted himself to the position of deity (Dan. 11:36-39; II Thess. 2:3-4); (3) his helpless death points to Christ's slaying of "the lawless one" (Dan. 11:45; II Thess. 2:8; Rev. 19:20). Whatever the antecedents of Daniel's beasts (W. Bousset, *Antichrist Legend,* holds that the battle of Antichrist and God stems from the Babylonian legend of Marduk's struggle with Tiamat), they are clearly nations opposing God and his people. The beast from the sea in Rev. 13:1 recalls Dan. 7:3, 7 and strengthens the link between Daniel's prophecy and the NT account of Antichrist.

II. INTERTESTAMENTAL ELABORATION. Two emphases appear in the Apocrypha and Pseudepigrapha: (1) Rome replaces Syria as the national enemy, and Pompey supplants Antiochus IV as the epitome of opposition to God; (2) Belial (Beliar) is personified as a satanic spirit.

The "lawless one" (II Thess. 2:8) has been connected with Beliar, which rabbinic tradition interpreted as *"without yoke"* (*b*e*li 'ol*), *i.e.,* refusing the law's yoke. This connection seems strengthened by the LXX translation of *belial* by *paranomos,* "lawbreaker" (Deut. 13:13, etc.). However, though Paul's description may partially reflect the Beliar tradition, he distinguishes Beliar from the lawless one: Beliar is a synonym of Satan (II Cor. 6:15), while Satan and the lawless one are differentiated (II Thess. 2:9).

III. NEW TESTAMENT DEVELOPMENT.

A. *The Gospels.* References to Christ's opponent are neither numerous nor specific. The disciples are warned that false Christs will attempt to deceive even the elect (Matt. 24:24; Mark 13:22). Similarly, Christ speaks of one who comes in his own name, whom the Jews receive (John 5:43). This may be a veiled reference to Antichrist or to any false Messiahs who present themselves to Judaism. Even the mention of the abomination of desolation (Matt. 24:15; Mark 13:14), recalling vividly Daniel's prophecy, is made with remarkable restraint. A single evil personality may be in view, but his portrait is not even sketched.

B. *II Thessalonians.* Paul gives a clearer picture of Christ's archenemy, whose outstanding characteristic is contempt of law. Two names — "man of lawlessness" (preferable to "man of sin") and "the lawless one" (II Thess. 2:3, 8-9) — stress this attitude, recalling Dan. 7:25, where the little horn tries to change the times and law. Furthermore, Antichrist makes exclusive claim to deity (II Thess. 2:4) in terms reminiscent of Dan. 7:25, 11:36. Paul does not picture a pseudo Messiah posing as God's messenger, but a pseudo God viciously opposing all other religion.

He deceives many by wonders (II Thess. 2:9-10). Christ worked miracles by God's power, and the Jews attributed them to Satan (Matt. 12:24 ff.); Antichrist will work miracles by satanic power, and many will worship him as God.

One of Antichrist's names — "son of perdition" (II Thess. 2:3; cf. John 17:12) — reveals his destiny: Christ will slay him by his breath and the brightness of his appearing (II Thess. 2:8; Rev. 19:15, 20; cf. Isa. 11:4).

Antichrist is the personal culmination of a principle of rebellion already working secretly — "the mystery of lawlessness" (II Thess. 2:7). When God's restraining hand which preserves law and order is withdrawn, this spirit of satanic lawlessness will become incarnate in "the lawless one."

C. *The Johannine Letters.* Though John recognized the expectation of a single antichrist, he turns his attention to the many antichrists who have come denying that Jesus is the Christ and thus denying the true nature of both Father and Son (I John 2:18, 22; 4:3). Contemporary Docetists discredited Christ's humanity (II John 7), claiming that he *seemed* to have human form. To John they were the embodiment of the antichrist spirit. Their view taught that man was divine apart from God in Christ and left God and the world ununited (Westcott, *Epistles of John*, p. 70).

John's account complements rather than contradicts Paul's. Following Daniel, Paul depicts a single archenemy, who claims the right to personal worship. John stresses the spiritual elements in these claims and the spiritual lie which made Antichrist seemingly strong.

D. *Revelation*. The Apocalyptist's beast (Rev. 13), dependent in spirit and detail on Daniel, combines the characteristics of all four OT beasts. Further, the NT beast has an authority belonging only to the little horn of Daniel's beast. John seemingly implies that the savage impiety of Antiochus will be embodied in a kingdom; for the beast, although he has some personal characteristics, is more than a person: his seven heads are seven kings (Rev. 17:10-12). The beast himself is an eighth king, springing from one of the seven. This complicated picture suggests that the beast symbolizes worldly power, the anti-God spirit of nationalistic ambition (in Daniel's prophecy personified in Antiochus and in John's day in Rome) which will become incarnate in one great demagogue — Antichrist.

To Paul's account John adds at least one important element — the false prophet, a second beast who works under the authority of Antichrist, as Antichrist gains his authority from the dragon, Satan (Rev. 13:2, 11-12). After directing Antichrist's political and religious enterprises, the false prophet shares his fate at Christ's advent (Rev. 19:20).

IV. CHRISTIAN INTERPRETATION. The Fathers generally believed in a personal antichrist. His identity hinged on whether the "mystery of lawlessness" was interpreted politically or religiously. Politically, the most likely candidate was Nero, who, legend held, would reappear in resurrected form *(redivivus)* to continue his terrible reign. This interpretation, propounded by Chrysostom and others, has gained prominence in this century through *preteristic* interpreters of Revelation like R. H. Charles and C. A. Scott. Irenaeus and others who held that Antichrist would emerge from a religious context traced him to Dan on the basis of Gen. 49:17; Deut. 33:22; Jer. 8:16 (cf. the omission of Dan in Rev. 7:5 ff.).

The reformers equated Antichrist with the papacy, as had some medieval theologians: (1) Gregory I (ca. A.D. 600), who taught that whoever assumed the title "universal priest" was Antichrist's forerunner; (2) Joachim of

Floris (ca. A.D. 1190); (3) Wycliffe (ca. A.D. 1360). Luther, Calvin, the translators of the AV, and the Westminster Confession concurred in this identification. Roman Catholic scholars retaliated, branding Rome's opponents Antichrist.

In the ideal or symbolic view, Antichrist is an ageless personification of evil, not identifiable with one nation, institution, or individual. This idea gains support from the Johannine letters and has value in emphasizing the constancy of the warfare between Satan's manifold forces and Christ's.

Futurists (e.g., Zahn, Seiss, Scofield) hold that idealists fail to stress sufficiently the culmination of this hostility in a personal adversary. They believe that Antichrist will usher in a period of great tribulation at history's close, in connection with a mighty empire like a revived Rome, and will dominate politics, religion, and commerce until Christ's advent.

See also ABOMINATION OF DESOLATION.

BIBLIOGRAPHY

S. J. Andrews, *Christianity and Antichristianity*; W. Bousset in *HERE*; G. G. Findlay, *Thessalonians in CGT*; G. Milligan, *Epistles to the Thessalonians*, pp. 158-73; H. H. Rowley, *Relevance of Apocalyptic*; G. Vos, *Pauline Eschatology*, pp. 94-135.

DAVID A. HUBBARD

ANTILEGOMENA. The ancient ecclesiastical term, apparently used first by Origen, for the disputed books claiming to be part of the NT. These Origen identified as Hebrews, II Peter, II and III John, James, Jude, Barnabas, Shepherd of Hermas, the Didache, and the Gospel of the Hebrews, and contrasted them with the *homologoumena*, the books universally accepted. Origen himself regarded as Scripture a number of the *antilegomena*. Eusebius divided the disputed books into two groups: (1) the books which he accepted, and (2) those which he considered spurious. In the former group were included James, Jude, II Peter and II and III John; in the latter the Acts of Paul, Shepherd of Hermas, Apocalypse of Peter, Barnabas, and the Didache.

WALTER W. WESSEL

ANTINOMIANISM. The word comes from the Greek *anti*, against, and *nomos*, law, and signifies opposition to law. It refers to the doctrine that the moral law is not binding upon Christians as a rule of life. In a wider sense it is applied to the views of fanatics who refuse to recognize any law but their own subjective ideas which they usually claim are from the Holy Spirit.

Antinomianism was so called by Luther when his old friend John Agricola (1492-1566) taught that Christians are entirely free from the law, i.e., the moral law as laid down by Moses. He argued that they are not required to keep the Ten Commandments. He took this ground for fear of works-righteousness, wrongly thinking that "justification by faith alone" demanded this. The Reformation teaching was: "Good works make not a good man, but a good man doeth good works." (Patrick Hamilton).

BIBLIOGRAPHY
HERE; SHERK.

ALEXANDER M. RENWICK

ANTIOCH, SCHOOL OF. The Book of Acts indicates that the term Christian was first used at Antioch and that there was a church there at the time of the early ministry of the Apostle Paul (11:26). It was from Antioch that Paul began his three missionary journeys. It might be called the nearest approach which he had to a headquarters base. The decisions of the Apostolic Council at Jerusalem were published there (Acts 15:30 f.).

The first monarchical bishop to secure notice was Ignatius of Antioch. He held the post in the early second century. In his seven epistles he shows himself to be a man eager to defend the full deity and full humanity of Christ. He particularly warns against docetism (q.v.), and here appears an emphasis which is increasingly to characterize the school of Antioch. God came into flesh, was born of the Virgin Mary. Christ died to deliver men from ignorance and from the devil. He rose again from the dead for us. The believer is not only in Christ, he is also *christophoros*. The Supper is the flesh and blood of Christ, though there is no suggestion of a substantial change. Brotherly love is a cardinal emphasis in Ignatius.

Theophilus of Antioch, in the latter part of the second century, developed the Logos (q.v.) doctrine, referring to the logos *prophorikos* brought forth to create. The word *trias* is used to apply to the Godhead first by Theophilus.

Three-quarters of a century later Paul of Samosata occupied the episcopal throne in Antioch. The emphasis on the human nature of Christ that was to characterize the later Antioch makes a clear appearance. With a monarchian (see MONARCHIANISM) stress, he found the Logos, a divine force, part of the mind of the Father, dwelling in Jesus from his birth, but apart from the Virgin. He manifested himself as *energeia*. Jesus was not to be worshiped though his enduement with the Logos was quantitatively unusual. His unity with God is one of purpose, of will, of love. While it is possible for Paul to speak of one *prosōpon* of God and the Logos, and to use the term *homoousios* of Christ and the Father, yet the Logos and the Son were not by any means identical. Paul was excommunicated and, after the Roman recapture of Antioch, wellnigh completely lost his influence. Paul's opponents did not approve the term *homoousios*, later to become a touchstone of orthodoxy.

Shortly after Paul's fall from power, a schoolmaster, Lucian, came to prominence in Antioch. Lucian conceived of Christ on a higher plane than did Paul. Whether he considered him as equal with the Father in his deity is questionable. His work on the text of the Greek Bible was extensive, and he favored the historical and critical interpretation of the Scriptures.

In the decades following the Council of Nicaea, Antioch exhibited wide differences of opinion on the Arian question (see ARIANISM), but in this atmosphere John Chrysostom grew to maturity with his extraordinary ability as a preacher. Emphasizing the moral values of Christianity, he continued the stress on historical exegesis. One of Chrysostom's teachers, the presbyter Diodorus, became, in due course, Bishop of Tarsus and was recognized as a "normal" theologian by the Council of Constantinople in 381. But he did not find an adequate expression for the relationship between the divine and human natures of Christ. There seemed almost to be a dual personality in his conception. Another presbyter, Theodore, later Bishop of Mopsuestia, developed historical criticism much farther. He failed to find the doctrine of the Trinity in the OT, and he minimized the messianic intimations in the Psalms. But he put heavy stress upon the importance of textual and historical study as a basis for exegesis. Theodore emphasized the difference between God and man. The Logos humbled himself and became man. The *prosōpon* of the man is complete and so is that of the Godhead. His disciple, the church historian Theodoret (d. 457), carried on his work. Theodoret's exegesis is in the best historical tradition, his apologetic writing clear and well organized. He stressed the infinite difference between God and man. His christological views were unquestionably influenced by his friend Nestorius, the most prominent representative of the Antiochan school. Impetuous, self-confident, full of energy, Nestorius was not a scholar. He emphasized the humanity of Jesus but it is reasonably clear that what he intended to express was not a view that is heretical. The union of Godhead and manhood in Christ is voluntary, but it can be said that there is one *prosōpon* of Jesus Christ. Nestorius campaigned against the term *theotokos* (see MOTHER OF GOD) as applied to the Virgin Mary, yet he agreed that, if properly understood, the term was unobjectionable. It was the violence of his emphases, with their stress on the separateness of the human and the divine in Christ, which was dangerous.

Justinian's Edict of the Three Chapters in 543 was unfair to the School of Antioch in its condemnations of the writings of Theodore of Mopsuestia and of Theodoret. The Council of Constantinople of 553, called the Fifth Ecumenical, condemned writings of the Antioch school, but on the basis of falsified and mutilated quotations.

The separation from the Imperial church of the bishops who led the Nestorian schism and the capture of Antioch in 637 by the rising power of Islam checked the further distinctive development of the school of Antioch. Its Aristotelian emphasis on rationality, on ethical quality, and on man's free agency was not popular. Yet it is to be valued for its stress on the genuine continuance in the Second Person of the properties of each nature and for its insistence upon the importance of grammatico-historical exegesis.

See also CHRISTOLOGY and INTERPRETATION, BIBLICAL.

BIBLIOGRAPHY

C. C. Richardson, *The Christianity of Ignatius of Antioch*; G. Bardy, *Paul de Samosate*; F. Loofs, *Paulus von Samosata*; H. de Riedmatten; *Les Actes du procès de Paul de Samosate*; G. Bardy, *Recherches sur saint Lucien d'Antioche et son école*; R. Devreesse, *Essai sur Theodore de Mopsueste*; J. F. Bethune-Baker, *Nestorius and His Teaching*; F. Loofs, *Nestorius and His Place in the History of Christian Doctrine*; A. R. Vine, *An Approach to Christology*; R. V. Sellers, *Two Ancient Christologies*.

PAUL WOOLLEY

ANTITYPE. The word, not used in the English Bible, is the Greek word translated "figure" in I Pet. 3:21 and Heb. 9:24. The word seems only to refer to an illustrative correspondence of meaning.

In common usage, certain OT items and practices are called types of NT truth. The NT realities are the antitypes. Thus Hebrews 3 and 4 draws the relation of type and antitype between the Canaan rest and the heavenly rest. As most divinely intended types of the OT point forward to Christ, he is the antitype of the tabernacle, its priests, and its offerings.

R. LAIRD HARRIS

ANXIETY. See CARE.

APOCALYPTIC, APOCALYPSE.

I. DEFINITION. The word apolcalypse (unveiling) is derived from Revelation 1:1, where it refers to the revelation to John by the ascended Jesus of the consummation of the age. The word has been applied by modern scholars to a group of Jewish books which contain similar literary and eschatological characteristics, not all of which are really apocalypses. An apocalypse is a book containing real or alleged revelations of heavenly secrets or of the events which will attend the end of the world and the inauguration of the kingdom of God.

II. HISTORICAL BACKGROUND. Many apocalypses were produced by unknown Jewish authors between 200 B.C. and A.D. 100 in imitation of the book of Daniel. (Daniel is often described as the first of such apocalypses, but numerous traits linking Daniel closely to the prophetic writings lead to the conclusion that Daniel stands between the prophetic and apolcalyptic types. There are also other reasons for dating Daniel earlier than Maccabean times.) The apocalypses arose out of an historical milieu involving an historical-theological problem consisting of three elements.

A. *The emergence of a "Righteous Remnant."* In the prophetic period Israel continually lapsed into idolatry, forsaking the law of God. After the restoration, there emerged circles of Jews who were loyal to the law. When Antiochus Epiphanes, in 168 B.C., attempted a forcible assimilation of the Jews to Greek culture and religion, these righteous, called Chasidim or Hasideans, refused to submit, choosing death rather than disobedience to the law. This spirit was preserved in their successors, the Pharisees. Another group, called the Qumran community, withdrew from the main stream of Jewish life to seek a monastic retreat in the desert, giving themselves in complete devotion to the study and observance of the law.

B. *The Problem of Evil.* The prophets promised that a repentant, restored Israel would inherit the kingdom. Now Israel was restored to the land and was faithful to the law. According to the Jewish definition of righteousness, the conditions laid down by the prophets were satisfied; but the kingdom did not come. Instead came unprecedented suffering. Antiochus Epiphanes (168 b.c.) attempted to destroy the Jewish faith, inflicting tortures and martyrdoms upon the faithful. The religious liberty won by the Maccabean rebellion did not bring the kingdom of God. Instead of God's rule came the rule of the secular, worldly Hasmoneans, and after 63 b.c. Rome's native puppets and procurators. A righteous Israel which merited the kingdom met only suffering and political bondage.

C. *The Cessation of Prophecy.* Throughout these times of unparallel evil, God did not speak to explain this historical enigma. The voice of prophecy was stilled. No prophet appeared to announce "Thus saith the Lord" and to interpret to the afflicted people of God the riddle of the suffering of the righteous.

The apocalypses arose out of this milieu to provide an explanation of the sufferings of the righteous and the delay of the kingdom of God.

III. Description. I Enoch or Ethiopic Enoch. A composite book of five parts consisting of Enoch's visions and journeys through the heavens. The Similitudes (chaps. 37-71, containing visions, etc.) are of outstanding importance because of the figure of the heavenly Son of Man. First two centuries b.c.

Jubilees. A revelation given to Moses of the history of the world from creation to his day. History is divided into Jubilee periods of forty-nine years each. Only a few portions of the book have to do with eschatology. Second century b.c.

The Testament of the Twelve Patriarchs is a book, not of apocalypses, but of imitations of prophetic writings. Each patriarch outlines his life and gives a moral exhortation and a prophecy of the future of his descendants. The book is thus eschatological but not apocalyptic. It has been heavily interpolated by Christian writers. Second century b.c.

The Psalms of Solomon. Eighteen Psalms written in imitation of the OT Psalms. They are not apocalypses, but the last two Psalms contain important eschatological materials. First century b.c.

Assumption of Moses. Moses' final charge to Joshua, in which he traces the course of history to the coming of the kingdom. The history can be followed down to the days of Herod the Great. First century a.d.

Sibylline Oracles. A composite apologetic work with both Jewish and Christian elements. Oracles are put into the mouth of the Greek Sibyl, and the book thus has the form of pagan prophecy. A few sections embody eschatological expectations of an apocalyptic sort.

Fourth Ezra (Second Esdras). Seven visions which Ezra saw in Babylon, after the fall of Jerusalem. The book reflects the despair of a devout Jew after the destruction of Jerusalem in a.d. 70. The most profound of the apocalypses, embodying much theology as well as apocalyptic eschatology. Late first century a.d.

The Apocalypse of Baruch. Revelations given to Baruch in the days of Jeconiah of the coming of God's kingdom. Important for theology. Late first century a.d.

Second Enoch or Slavonic Enoch. This is an apocalypse but is probably much later in date.

IV. Literary Characteristics.

Apocalyptic is a *genre* of literature which succeeded the prophetic. At some points apocalyptic is a development of elements in prophecy; at other points it departs from the prophetic character. No sharp line can be drawn between the two types; and characterizations of apocalyptic differ considerably.

A. *Revelations.* The prophets often received their message by revelation, but their main concern was "the word of the Lord." Often the word of God came to the prophets as an overwhelming inner conviction apart from visions or dreams. In the apocalypses, the word of the Lord has given way to revelations and visions. God does not speak by his Spirit to his servants. The seer must learn the solution to the problems of evil and the coming of the kingdom through dreams, visions, or heavenly journeys with angelic guides.

B. *Imitative Literary Character.* The prophets, out of experiences in which God disclosed his will, announced the divine will to the people. Scholars who reject any supernatural element admit real psychological experiences by the prophets. Possibly IV Ezra reflects real subjective experiences, but usually the revelations of the apocalyptists are only a literary form. The visions are literary fictions imitating the visions of the prophetic writings. Generally, therefore, prophecy was first spoken, while apocalypses were written.

C. *Pseudonymity*. The prophets spoke in the name of the Lord directly to the people. However, in the Maccabean period, the voice of prophecy was stilled and the apocalyptists attributed their revelations to OT saints as a means of validating their message to their own generation. In this matter, Daniel stands alone, for Daniel is unknown apart from his appearance in the apocalypse ascribed to him.

D. *Symbolism*. The prophets had often used symbols to convey the divine message. In the apocalypses, symbolism becomes the main stock in trade, particularly as a technique for outlining the course of history without employing historical names. This technique appears first in Daniel and was imitated with bizarre proliferation in later apocalypses.

E. *Rewritten History*. The prophets took their stand in their own historical situation and proclaimed the word of God to their generation against the background of the future kingdom of God. The apocalyptists sometimes took their stand at a point in the distant past and rewrote history as though it were prophecy down to their own day, at which time the coming of the kingdom is expected. In some instances apocalypses can be dated by the latest events reflected in the alleged prophecy.

V. RELIGIOUS CHARACTERISTICS.

The word apocalyptic is used also to describe the eschatology found in the apocalypses.

A. *Dualism*. Apocalyptic eschatology sees a contrast between the character of the present time of suffering and the future time of salvation which is so radical that it is finally described in terms of two ages: this age and the age to come. This age is characterized by evil; the age to come will see the kingdom of God. The transition from this age to the coming age can be accomplished only by a supernatural inbreaking of God. This dualism is not metaphysical or cosmic but historical and temporal. While this terminology of the two ages appears in the NT, it is found in the apocalyptic literature in fully developed form only in IV Ezra and the Apocalypse of Baruch.

Many critics attribute this development to the influence of Persian dualism; but it can also be explained as an historical development of ideas already implicit in the OT prophets. The prophetic expectation of the future kingdom includes a redeemed earth (Isa. 32:15-18,

11:6-9; 65:17; 66:22). This transformation will be accomplished only by a divine visitation, when God will shake the present order in judgment (Isa. 13:13; 34:4; 51:6; Hag. 2:7) and will cause a new order to emerge from the old.

Apocalyptic dualism is a development of this basic prophetic view of the world and redemption. The new order is usually described with Isaianic features of a new earth (Enoch 45:4 f.; 51:1-5). Assumption of Moses 10:1 looks forward to a manifestation of God's kingdom "in all his creation." Sometimes more "transcendental" terms are employed (Enoch 62:16).

Some OT passages describe the new order in terms very similar to the present order, while others (Isa. 65, 66) see a complete transformation involving new heavens and a new earth. Some apocalypses put together these two expectations and anticipate a temporal kingdom in this age followed by an eternal kingdom in the new order (IV Ezra 7:28, 29). The age to come in Baruch is pictured as a new earth (32:6). The language of IV Ezra is difficult to interpret (7:36, 113).

B. *Historical Perspective*. The prophets took their stand within a specific historical situation and addressed their message to their environment. On the horizon was God's kingdom, and the future stands in a constant tension with the present. Isa. 13 describes the historical judgment of Babylon against the background of the eschatological visitation as though they were one and the same day. Historical judgments are seen as realized eschatology.

The apocalyptists have lost this tension between history and eschatology. They do not view the present against the background of the future, but their viewpoint encompasses the entire sweep of history for the purpose of interpreting history theologically. The apocalypses are theological treatises rather than truly historical documents.

C. *Pessimism*. It is not correct ultimately to call the apocalyptists pessimists, for they never lost their confidence that God would finally triumph and bring his kingdom. However, they were pessimistic as to the present age. The problem of the suffering of the righteous had led to the conclusion that God had withdrawn his aid from his people in the present age and that salvation could be expected only in the age to come (Enoch 89:56-

75). IV Ezra sees the present age as hopelessly evil and the solution lying altogether in the future (4:26-32; 7:50; 8:1-3). The righteous can only patiently suffer while waiting a future salvation.

D. *Determinism.* The course of this evil age is predetermined and must run its course. The kingdom does not come even though the righteous deserve it, because fixed periods must intervene before the consummation. The kingdom must await its appointed time. God himself is pictured as waiting the passing of the times which he has decreed rather than bringing aid to the righteous (IV Ezra 4:36, 37). This idea often led to the dividing of the course of time into determined periods of weeks or years.

E. *Ethical Passivity.* The apocalyptists lack moral or evangelical urgency. Their problem rests in the very fact that there *is* a righteous remnant which is overwhelmed by undeserved evil. The prophets continually warned Israel of the penalty of faithlessness; the apocalyptists comfort the faithful who need no correction. Therefore there is very little ethical exhortation in most of the apocalyptic writings. Such books as *The Testament of the Twelve Patriarchs* and *Enoch*, 92-105, which have considerable ethical exhortation, are least apocalyptic in character.

VI. The New Testament Apocalypse.

The Revelation of John shares numerous traits with Jewish apocalypses but at other important points stands apart from them. Although the similarities are usually stressed, the differences will be here emphasized.

First, the author designates his book as a prophecy (1:3; 22:7, 10, 18, 19). The apocalyptic writings lost a prophetic self-consciousness; indeed they were written to fill the void caused by the absence of prophecy. Primitive Christianity witnessed a revival of the prophetic movement when God once more spoke directly through men. The Apocalypse, together with other NT books, is the product of the revival of the prophetic spirit. The visions given John were the means of conveying the word of God (1:2).

Second, John is not pseudonymous. The author merely signs his name: "John to the seven churches that are in Asia" (1:4). He appeals to no ancient saint for authority but writes out of the authority residing in him from the Spirit of God.

Third, John differs from the apocalyptic treatment of the future. The latter retraces history under the guise of prophecy. John takes his stand in his own environment, addresses his own contemporaries, and looks prophetically into the future to depict the eschatological consummation.

Fourth, John embodies the prophetic tension between history and eschatology. The beast is Rome and at the same time an eschatological Antichrist which cannot be fully equated with historical Rome. While the churches of Asia were facing persecution, there is no known persecution in the first century A.D. which fits that portrayed in the Apocalypse. The shadow of historical Rome is so outlined against the darker shadow of the eschatological Antichrist that it is difficult if not impossible to distinguish between the two. History is eschatologically interpreted; evil at the hands of Rome is realized eschatology.

Fifth, John shares the optimism of the gospel rather than the pessimism of apocalyptic thought. While John prophesies that the satanic evil of the age will descend in concentrated fury upon God's people in the end time, he does not see an age abandoned to evil. On the contrary, history has become the scene of the divine redemption. Only the slain Lamb is able to open the book and bring history to its eschatological denouement. The redemption which will be apocalyptically consummated is rooted in the event of Golgotha. Furthermore, it is probable that the first seal (6:2) represents the victorious mission of a conquering gospel in a world which is also the scene of war, famine, death, and martyrdom. God has not abandoned the age nor forsaken his people. The saints conquer the beast even in martyrdom and praise him who is the King of the ages (15:2, 3).

Finally, the Apocalypse possesses prophetic moral urgency. It does indeed promise a future salvation but not one which can be taken for granted. The seven letters strike a note of warning and a demand for repentance (2:5, 16, 21, 22; 3:3, 19). The outpourings of the divine wrath are not merely punitive but embody a merciful purpose whose intent is to bring men to repentance before it is too late (9:20; 16:9, 11). The Revelation draws to its close with an evangelical invitation (22:17). Thus the book as a whole has a great moral purpose: judgment will fall upon a lax sleeping church, and the door is held open for the wicked to turn to God.

In summary, there is a prophetic and a non-prophetic apocalypse, and the Apocalypse of the NT stands in the first type.

BIBLIOGRAPHY

Full bibliography will be found in H. H. Rowley, *The Relevance of Apocalyptic*, pp. 179-95. See especially Wm. Bousset, *SHERK*, I, pp. 208-10; R. H. Charles, *EB*, I, pp. 213-50; also *HDB*, I, pp. 741-49; J. B. Frey in Pirot's *Supplement au Dictionnaire de la Bible*, I, pp. 326-54; E. Lohmeyer in *RGG* (2 Aufl.), I, pp. 402-4.

GEORGE ELDON LADD

APOCRYPHA. The word apocrypha is from the Greek *ta apocrypha*, "the hidden things," although there is no strict sense in which these books are hidden. Some thirteen books comprise the Apocrypha: I and II Esdras, Tobit, Judith, The Rest of Esther, The Wisdom of Solomon, Ecclesiasticus which is also entitled The Wisdom of Jesus the Son of Sirach, Baruch, The Letter of Jeremiah, The Additions to Daniel, The Prayer of Manasses, and I and II Maccabees. Both the status of these books and the use of the term apocrypha have been in confusion since the early days of the church. In the restricted sense the word denotes the above-named books in contradistinction to the pseudepigrapha, or false writings; but in the broader sense the word refers to any extra-canonical scripture. Sometimes the term takes on a disparaging meaning, especially when used of the "apocryphal" gospels; this is to say they are spurious or heterodoxical. A further difficulty attending the restricted use of *apocrypha* is that some of the Apocrypha are pseudonymous, whereas some of the Pseudepigrapha are not pseudonymous. R. H. Charles broke the accepted order by including III Maccabees in the Apocrypha and transferring II Esdras to the Pseudepigrapha. The ancient rabbinic practice was to regard all such writings as "outside books," and this designation was continued by Cyril of Jerusalem, who used *Apocrypha* in the same sense, i.e., scriptures outside the canon. In modern times C. C. Torrey has revived this signification so that all such books, including the Pseudepigrapha, are called Apocrypha. Therefore to use the term Pseudepigrapha is a concession to an unhappy usage.

How did the Apocrypha secure a place in some of our English Bibles? The Jews uniformly denied canonical status to these books, and so they were not found in the Hebrew Bible; but the manuscripts of the LXX include them as an addendum to the canonical OT. In the second century A.D. the first Latin Bibles were translated from the Greek Bible, and so included the Apocrypha. Jerome's Vulgate distinguished between the *libri ecclesiastici* and the *libri canonici* with the result that the Apocrypha were accorded a secondary status. However, at the Council of Carthage (397), which Augustine attended, it was decided to accept the Apocrypha as suitable for reading despite Jerome's resistance to their inclusion in the Vulgate. In 1548 the Council of Trent recognized the Apocrypha, excepting I and II Esdras and The Prayer of Manasses, as having unqualified canonical status. Moreover, anyone who disputed this ecclesiastical decision was anathematized. The Reformers repudiated the Apocrypha as unworthy and contradictory to the doctrines of the uncontroverted canon; however, Luther did admit that they were "profitable and good to read." The Coverdale and Geneva Bibles included the Apocrypha but set them apart from the canonical books of the OT. After much debate, the British and Foreign Bible Society decided in 1827 to exclude the Apocrypha from its Bibles; soon afterwards the American branch concurred, and this action generally set the pattern for English Bibles thereafter. Among Protestant communions only the Anglican church makes much use of the Apocrypha today.

Many literary genres appear in the Apocrypha: popular narrative, religious history and philosophy, morality stories, poetic and didactic lyrics, wisdom literature, and apocalyptic. Most of these books were written in Palestine between 300 B.C. and A.D. 100, and the language of composition was either Hebrew or Aramaic, and occasionally Greek. They generally reflect the Jewish religious viewpoint of late OT times with certain additions which were emphasized. Almsgiving became an expression of good works meritorious to salvation; see Tobit 12:9. The Apocrypha, and to a greater extent the Pseudepigrapha, evince an amplified doctrine of the Messiah (*q.v.*) beyond what the OT reveals. Two types of messianic expectation predominate: the heavenly Son of Man, taken from Daniel and embellished by Enoch, and the earthly Davidic king described in the Psalms of Solomon. The doctrine of resurrection of the body, so seldom mentioned in the OT, is ubiquitous in the Apocrypha and shows an advance over the OT idea of Sheol. The hope for immortality was greatly influenced by Greek thought. Throughout the Apocrypha is a highly developed angelology which is a natural consequence of the impact of dualism upon Jewish religious thought after the Exile. The NT cites none of the books of the Apocrypha, although there are frequent parallels of thought and language as in the case of Eph. 6:13-17 and The Wisdom of Solomon 5:17-20, and Heb. 11 and Ecclus. 44. But to admit these parallels is not necessarily to admit dependence by NT authors upon the Apocrypha, and even if a clear case of dependence can be made, it does not follow that the NT author regarded these books as authoritative.

BIBLIOGRAPHY
R. H. Charles, *Apocrypha and Pseudepigrapha of the Old Testament*, Vol. I; B. M. Metzger, *An Introduction to the Apocrypha*; W. O. E. Oesterley, *The Books of the Apocrypha*; R. H. Pfeiffer, *A History of New Testament Times With an Introduction to the Apocrypha*.

DAVID H. WALLACE

APOLLINARIANISM. The doctrine held by Apollinaris the Younger, Bishop of Laodicea (310?-390?), and his followers during the christological controversies of the fourth century. A stalwart defender of Nicene orthodoxy, Apollinaris opposed both the Arian view of the mutability of the Logos and the complete union in Christ of full human and divine natures.

He maintained that in the incarnation "the Logos became flesh" (John 1:14) literally, the Logos thus taking the place of the rational human soul in the person of Christ. After several local synods had condemned Apollinarianism, it was declared heretical by the Second General Council at Constantinople in 381.

BIBLIOGRAPHY
H. Lietzmann, *Apollinaris von Laodicea und seine Schule*; J. F. Bethune-Baker, *Introduction to the Early History of Christian Doctrine*; G. L. Prestige, *Fathers and Heretics*; C. E. Raven, *Apollinarianism*.

DONALD G. DAVIS

APOLOGETICS. In that the subject matter of religion is God, the crucial issue of religion is whether or not it possesses a knowledge of God. It is the task of Christian apologetics to show on what grounds the Christian religion possesses such a knowledge of God. Since a knowledge of God is imparted by revelation, however defined, the concept of revelation is central to Christian apologetics.

Christian apologetics differs from an *apology*, which is a reply to a specific accusation; from a *theodicy*, which is an attempt to alleviate the problem of evil; and from *Christian evidences*, which attempts to show the supernatural imprimatur upon Christianity and its congruity with all types of facts.

There is no standard set of topics which comprises Christian apologetics, but *certain questions are fundamental to its discussion.*

1. *What Is the Character of Revelation?* Revelation may be stressed as absolutely unique and thereby excluding natural religion (Barth). Or the uniqueness of revelation may be stressed while admitting the validity of a natural theology only in the light of special revelation (Calvin). Or there may be a natural religion which gives rise to a natural theology, which forms the preamble to special revelation (Thomas).

2. *What Is the Relationship of Philosophy and Revelation?* This is usually and inappropriately put as the issue of faith and reason. However, faith is the reception of knowledge, and not its creator; and reason is not an unambiguous notion but is to be defined within an accepted philosophical position.

An apologist may consider philosophy the product of an unregenerate mind and thereby deny it any status in Christian theology (Tertullian). Or he may consider that there is a valid place for philosophy in scientific matters but not in the Christian religion (Pascal). Or he may believe that a philosophical criterion (or criteria) is possible for testing a revelation but that no philosophy as such apart from Christianity is possible. Or he may believe that a true philosophy may be achieved by the human reason, which, in turn, supports revealed religion (Thomas). Or he may believe that the Christian faith rests upon revelation but, in explicating that revelation, philosophy is a useful handmaiden (Augustine). Within this context is the debated issue whether a Christian philosophy as such does or does not exist.

Coupled with this problem is the task of assessing the damage done to the human mind by sin. Catholic and Arminian theologians (semi-Pelagian in doctrine of sin) do not admit a radical disturbance of the rational powers of man through sin, and are inclined to believe that the human reason can create a valid philosophical system, or at least can be adequately trusted in testing the truthfulness of a proposed religion. Some Calvinists believe that the doctrine of common grace (*q.v.*) sufficiently restores the radical disturbance of the human mind to the point where the theistic proofs are possible and valid and wherein

Christian evidences can establish Christianity as the true religion of God (Warfield). Other Calvinists emphasize the helplessness of the human mind in sin and emphasize the renewing power of the Holy Spirit (Kuyper, Van Til). The neo-orthodox school emphasizes the foolishness and the scandal of Christianity to the unregenerate mind, so that Christianity comes to it as a shock (Kierkegaard, Brunner, Barth).

3. *What Is the Status of the Theistic Proofs?* The empirical tradition accepts the validity of the *a posteriori* proofs as demonstrations (Thomas) or as credible evidences (Mullins, Hodge). The Pascal-Kierkegaard-Brunner tradition considers them as part of man's irreligion and rebellion against God. Others believe that the proofs are logically invalid, and still others accept the validity of the proofs based upon some inward property or possession of the human mind which usually turns out to be some form of the ontological (*a priori*) proof.

These three problems implicate each other, and are further implicated in the problem of religious knowledge or apologetic methodology. There are apologists who stress the self-validating character of Christian experience to carry the weight of the Christian apologetics, and, without using the term pejoratively, we might label them the *subjectivists* (Pascal). Others attempt to rest their apologetics in the uniqueness of Jesus Christ and may be called the *Christologists* (Fairbairn). Or an apologist may stress the uniqueness of revelation and assign to reason a ministerial function only (the *autopistics*). Others believe that Christianity is demonstrable on empirical grounds (*empiricists,* Thomas, Butler, and Paley). Others believe that the human reason still bears marks of the *imago Dei* and, while not able to create the truth out of itself, can test the truth of a revelation (*rationalists,* Augustine). Still others eschew all attempts at relating Christianity to philosophy and believe that the only apologetic is that of Christian evidences, and this may be called the *evidential school.*

Among the *problems which are of particular concern to contemporary apologists* the following may be noted.

1. *Natural Theology.* Some apologists, after Calvin, grant that there is a revelation in nature but that man in sin cannot deduce a theology from it, whereas others maintain that the revelation in nature demands the validity of a natural theology. Extremely critical here is the interpretation of Rom. 1 and Acts 17, and also the grounds upon which God holds men to be inexcusable. Also pertinent here is the Warfield-Kuyper debate, the latter teaching that the human logical faculty cannot be trusted in a sinner and therefore great emphasis must be laid upon the apologetic value of the inner witness of the Spirit, and the former (in the McCosh-Greene tradition) holding to the cogency of the human reason in constructing the theistic proofs and charging Kuyper with subjectivism.

2. *Faith.* What is pre-eminent in faith? The Christian intellectualist believes that faith resides in truth, and, since it is the function of the intellect to determine truth, we are necessarily committed to a robust Christian intellectualism. Others believe that there is in faith an indispensable, ethical, emotional or intuitional ("of the heart") ingredient of existential nature.

3. *Common Ground.* Those who believe in the cogency of the theistic proofs accept a common ground of argumentation between believer and unbeliever. Others believe that a common ground exists only in matters of fact and logic, but not in basic Christian presuppositions. Or an apologist may affirm that no common ground exists at any point between believers and unbelievers except that which God lovingly supplies by common grace. That is to say, this last school of apologists believes that all decisions of men that are not theistically inspired are sinful, i.e., that a sinner is incapable of an unprejudiced, unbiased, impartial act of the mind.

4. *Science.* Some apologists believe that scientific "knowledge" is so partial or transitory or imperfect that a theologian need not take it seriously, whereas others believe that in matters common to science and Scripture (or theology) the Christian interpreter and theologian ought to see if science can be of service to his interpretation or his theology. Still others believe that there are such anticipations of science in Scripture that they may be appealed to as proving the inspiration of Scripture.

5. *Miracle.* Christian apologists are divided over the nature of a miracle, (*q.v.*) some holding that it is a function of a higher law and so part of the law-abiding character of the universe, and others insisting that a miracle is a *de novo* creative act.

BIBLIOGRAPHY
Abraham Kuyper, *Principles of Sacred Theology;* E. J. Carnell, *Introduction to Christian Apologetics;* Bernard Ramm, *Types of Apologetic Systems;* C. Van Til, *The Defense of the Faith.*

BERNARD RAMM

APOSTASY. A word of increasing interest found twice in the NT (Acts 21:21; II Thess. 2:3). It comes from the Greek *apostasia,* a late form of *apostasis,* originally to desert a post or station in life. It is used by Plutarch of political revolt and is found in the OT in the sense of revolt against the Lord (Josh. 22:22). Antiochus Epiphanes enforced an *apostasia* from Judaism to Hellenism (I Macc. 2:15).

In the AV it is translated "falling away" in relation to the revelation of the man of sin, or Antichrist. In this sense the thought is of religious revolt. Cremer states that *apostasia* is used in the absolute sense of "passing over to unbelief," thus a dissolution of the "union with God subsisting through faith in Christ." Arndt adds rebellion or abandonment in the religious sense.

On the nature of apostasy there are lengthy articles in both the *JewEnc* and the *CE* developing an extensive doctrine of apostasy. A very full article is also found in the *EncSocSci* (see APOSTASY and HERESY).

In the NT, II Thess. 2:3 is a part of a prophetic passage of apocalyptic character. The "falling away" invites conjecture about whom and from what. The event seems future and thus related to Antichrist. The implication is that the apostates will welcome the man of sin.

BIBLIOGRAPHY
Arndt; CE.; Crem; James Denney, *Thessalonians; ExpGT; EncSocSci;* J. E. Frame, *Thessalonians, ICC;* HDAC; JewEnc; LSJ; MM.

ROBERT WINSTON ROSS

APOSTLE. The biblical use of this word is confined to the NT, where it occurs seventy-nine times: ten in the Gospels, twenty-eight in Acts, thirty-eight in the Epistles, and three in the Apocalypse. Our English word is a transliteration of the Greek *apostolos,* which is derived from *apostellein,* to send. Whereas several words for *send* are used in the NT, expressing such ideas as dispatch, release, or dismiss, *apostellein* emphasizes the elements of commission — authority of and responsibility to the sender. So an apostle is properly one sent on a definite mission, in which he acts with full authority on behalf of the sender and is accountable to him.

The noun occurs only once in the LXX. When the wife of Jeroboam came to Ahijah seeking information about the health of her son, the prophet answered, "I am sent unto thee with heavy tidings" (I Kings 14:6). Here *apostolos* renders the Hebrew *šālûaḥ,* which became a somewhat technical term in Judaism. A *šālûaḥ* could be one who led the synagogue congregation in worship and thus represented it, or a representative of the Sanhedrin sent on official business. The priesthood was included under this term also, and a few outstanding personalities of OT story who acted strikingly in God's behalf. But in no case did the *šālûaḥ* operate beyond the confines of the Jewish community. So there is no anticipation in the *šālûaḥ* of the missionary emphasis associated with the NT *apostolos.*

I. CHRIST. In Heb. 3:1 Jesus is called "the apostle . . . of our confession," in conscious contrast to Moses, to whom Judaism ascribed the term *šālûaḥ.* Jesus spoke more directly from God than Moses was able to do. Repeatedly he made the claim of being sent by the Father. When he declared that he was sending his chosen disciples into the world even as the Father had sent him, our Lord was bestowing on apostleship its highest dignity (John 17:18).

II. THE TWELVE. These men are most often called disciples in the Gospels, for their primary function during Christ's ministry was to be with him and learn of him. But they are also called apostles because Jesus imparted to them his authority to preach and to cast out demons (Mark 3:14-15; 6:30). Just because this activity was limited while Jesus was with them, the term apostle is rarely used. After Pentecost this situation was changed.

The number twelve recalls the twelve tribes of Israel, but the basis of leadership is no longer tribal, but personal and spiritual. Evidently the college of apostles was regarded as fixed in number, for Jesus spoke of twelve thrones in the coming age (Matt. 19:28; cf. Rev. 21:14). Judas was replaced by Matthias (Acts 1), but after that no effort was made to select men to succeed those who were taken by death (Acts 12:2).

Apostles receive first mention in the lists of spiritual gifts (I Cor. 12:28; Eph. 4:11). Since these gifts are bestowed by the risen Christ through the Spirit, it is probable that at the beginning of the apostolic age these men who had been appointed by Jesus and trained by him were now regarded as possessing a second investiture to mark the new and permanent phase of their work for which the earlier phase had been a preparation. They became the foundation of the church in a sense secondary only to that of Christ himself (Eph. 2:20).

The duties of the apostles were preaching, teaching, and administration. Their preaching rested on their association with Christ and the instruction received from him, and it included their witness to his resurrection (Acts 1:22). Their converts passed immediately under their instruction (Acts 2:42), which presumably consisted largely of their recollection of the teaching of Jesus, augmented by revelations of the Spirit (Eph. 3:5). In the area of administration their functions were varied. Broadly speaking, they were responsible for the life and welfare of the Christian community. Undoubtedly they took the lead in worship as the death of Christ was memorialized in the Lord's Supper. They administered the common fund to which believers contributed for the help of needy brethren (Acts 4:37), until this task became burdensome and was shifted to men specially chosen for this responsibility (Acts 6:1-6). Discipline was in their hands (Acts 5:1-11). As the church grew and spread abroad, the apostles devoted more and more attention to the oversight of these scattered groups of believers (Acts 8:14; 9:32). At times the gift of the Holy Spirit was mediated through them (Acts 8:15-17). The supernatural powers which they had exercised when the Lord was among them, such as the exorcism of demons and the healing of the sick, continued to be tokens of their divine authority (Acts 5:12; II Cor. 12:12). They took the lead in the determination of vexing problems which faced the church, associating the elders with themselves as an expression of democratic procedure (Acts 15:6; cf. 6:3).

III. PAUL. The distinctive features of his apostleship were direct appointment by Christ (Gal. 1:1) and the allocation of the gentile world to him as his sphere of labor (Rom. 1:5; Gal. 1:16; 2:8). His apostleship was recognized by the Jerusalem authorities in accordance with his own claim to rank with the original apostles. However, he never asserted membership in the Twelve (I Cor. 15:11), but rather stood on an independent basis. He was able to bear witness to the resurrection because his call came from the risen Christ (I

Cor. 9:1; Acts 26:16-18). Paul looked on his apostleship as a demonstration of divine grace and as a call to sacrificial labor rather than an occasion for glorying in the office (I Cor. 15:10).

IV. OTHERS. The most natural explanation of Gal. 1:19 is that Paul is declaring James, the Lord's brother, to be an apostle, agreeable to the recognition James received in the Jerusalem church. In line with this, in I Cor. 15:5-8, where James is mentioned, all the other individuals are apostles. Barnabas (along with Paul) is called an apostle (Acts 14:4, 14), but probably in a restricted sense only, as one sent forth by the Antioch church, to which he was obligated to report when his mission was completed (14:27). He was not regarded as an apostle at Jerusalem (Acts 9:27), though later on he was given the right hand of fellowship as well as Paul (Gal. 2:9). Andronicus and Junias are said to be of note among the apostles (Rom. 16:7). Silvanus and Timothy seem to be included as apostles in Paul's statement in I Thess. 2:6. The references in I Cor. 9:5 and 15:7 do not necessarily go beyond the Twelve.

It is reasonably clear that in addition to the Twelve Paul and James had the leading recognition as apostles. Others also might be so indicated under special circumstances. But warrant is lacking for making "apostle" the equivalent of "missionary." In the practice of the modern church, prominent pioneer missionaries are often called apostles, but this is only an accommodation of language. In the apostolic age one who held this rank was more than a preacher (II Tim. 1:11). All disciples were supposed to be preachers, but not all were apostles (I Cor. 12:29). Curiously, at one point in the church's life all were busy preaching except the apostles (Acts 8:4). Paul would not have needed to defend his apostleship with such vehemence if he were only defending his right to proclaim the gospel. Alongside the distinctive and more technical use of the word is the occasional employment of it in the sense of messenger (Phil. 2:25; II Cor. 8:23).

See also DISCIPLE, APOSTOLIC SUCCESSION.

BIBLIOGRAPHY

J. Y. Campbell in *RTWB*; Anton Fridrichsen, *The Apostle and His Message*; F. J. A. Hort, *The Christian Ecclesia*; K. Lake in *The Beginnings of Christianity*, V, pp. 37-59; J. B. Lightfoot, *St. Paul's Epistle to the Galatians*, pp. 92-101; T. W. Manson, *The Church's Ministry*, pp. 31-52; H. Mosbech, "Apostolos in the New Testament," *ST*, 1950, Vol. II, Fasc. 2, pp. 166-200; Johannes Munck, *Paulus und die Heilsgeschichte*, pp. 28-60; A. Plummer in *HDAC*; K. H. Rengstorf in *TWNT* (Eng. trans. by J. R. Coates in *Bible Key Words*).

EVERETT F. HARRISON

APOSTLES' CREED. See CREED, CREEDS.

APOSTOLIC CONSTITUTIONS AND CANONS. The Apostolic Constitutions, of which the Canons are a concluding section, form a corpus of ecclesiastical law, which by consensus of opinion is not apostolic, and is conjecturally dated from the latter half of the fourth century. The Trullan council (692) had the work under consideration but accepted only the Canons as authoritative because of the extent to which the Constitutions as a whole had been subject to unorthodox interpolations. The interpolator is thought by some to be a fourth century compiler, belonging either to the church at Antioch or to North Syria. The alleged Arianism of the documents is explained by some as being due to their having been written before the Council of Nicaea, 325, when theological precision was not essential.

The complete title of the Constitutions is "Ordinances of the Holy Apostles through Clement"; it comprises eight books. Books 1-6 resemble the Didascalia Apostolorum, a Syrian book of church order of the third century, and deal with: (1) Manners and habits of the laity, (2) Episcopacy and Worship, (3) Widows, the Clergy, Baptism, (4) Feeding of the poor, Virginity, (5) Martyrdom, (6) Schismatics. Of Book 7, Chaps. 1-32 are based on the Didache; 33-49 give details of liturgical practice. Of Book 8, Chaps. 1-2 concern spiritual gifts: Chaps. 3-27 present the Antiochene liturgy of St. John Chrysostom; Chaps. 28-46 are Canons, and Chap. 47, possibly a later addition, contains the eighty-five Apostolic Canons. Twenty of these appear to be based on the Canons of the Council of Antioch, 341. Dionysius Exiguus, a Scythian, translated the first fifty into Latin ca. 520, omitting the others, it is suggested, since they deviated from Roman practice. The omitted canons deal mostly with unseemly moral behavior. Through Dionysius' translation the Canons became part of the Western Canon Law and exercised great influence, e.g., with Gratian (*ca.* 1140), though their apostolicity was denied. These eighty-five canons are concerned mostly with the ordination, responsibilities and moral conduct of the clergy. Modern knowledge of the Constitutions dates from 1546 when a Venetian, Carolus Capellus, printed a Latin epitome of them.

BIBLIOGRAPHY
    PG; *Ante-Nicene Christian Library*, Edinburgh, 1864, Vol. xvii. pp. 257-69; ODCC.

M. R. W. FARRER

APOSTOLIC DECREE. The most critical problem of the primitive church was whether circumcision was necessary for salvation. The Judean church, by and large, held it to be indispensable, while the missionary church, represented by Antioch, considered it unnecessary. To deal with this problem which threatened to split the Christian movement, a council was called at Jerusalem. There it was decided that circumcision was neither a requirement for salvation nor a condition for social intercourse. However, it was thought advisable to ask the Gentile converts to abstain from certain practices which, because of idolatrous associations, would be especially abhorrent to the Jew and thus act as a barrier to fellowship. These prohibitions are known as the Apostolic Decree. They are set forth by James in Acts 15:20, written down in 15:29 and referred to in 21:25.

The main problem in connection with the Decree is a textual one. The Alexandrian text has four prohibitions. Gentiles are to abstain from (1) pollutions of idols, (2) unchastity, (3) what is strangled, and (4) blood. The Western text omits "what is strangled" and adds a negative Golden Rule ("Whatever you do not wish to happen to you, do not do to others"). This changes the Decree into a purely ethical one. Gentiles are to abstain from three cardinal sins — idolatry, fornication, and murder.

The Alexandrian text is to be preferred. *Alisgēmatōn tōn eidōlōn* (explained as *eidōlothuta* by 15:29 and 21:25) refer to meats left over from pagan sacrifices and not to idolatry itself. *Haimatos* is understood far more readily as combined with *pniktou* and referring to the eating of flesh with the blood still in it (an inevitable result of strangulation). To "abstain from blood" would be a curious equivalent for "Thou shalt not kill."

The Decree is best understood as a concession in the realm of Christian liberty for the purpose of effecting unity in life. It is not a summary of the Noachic precepts (Gen. 9) although it is not unrelated to them. It was not used by Paul in the case of the Corinthian liberals because he preferred to settle the problem on the basis of principle rather than external legislation.

BIBLIOGRAPHY
W. Sanday, *The Apostolic Decree.*

ROBERT H. MOUNCE

APOSTOLIC SUCCESSION. This theory of ministry in the church did not arise before A.D. 170-200. The Gnostics claimed to possess a *secret* tradition handed down to them from the apostles. As a counterclaim the Catholic church pointed to each bishop as a true successor to the apostle who had founded the see and therefore to the truth the apostles taught. The bishop, as an authoritative teacher, preserved the apostolic tradition. He was also a guardian of the apostolic Scriptures and the creed. In a generation when the last links with the apostles were fast dying out this emphasis on apostolic teaching and practice was natural. In the third century the emphasis changed from the *open* succession of teachers to the bishops as the *personal* successors of the apostles. This development owed much to the advocacy of Cyprian, Bishop of Carthage (248-58). Harnack regards this as a perversion rather than a development.

The terminology is not found in the NT. *Diadochē* is absent from the NT and the LXX. There is little evidence for the idea in the NT (cf. II Tim. 2:2). All early succession lists were compiled late in the second century.

There is also a difference between the Roman- and Anglo-Catholic viewpoint. The former is a centralized despotism with a papal succession traced back to Peter. The Tractarian teaches that all bishops alike, however insignificant the see, have equal power in a corporation. Thus an apostle transmitted to a bishop, through "the laying on of hands" and prayer, the authority which Christ had conferred on him. This theory of sacramental grace is a barrier to reunion in the Reformed churches, since the non-episcopal bodies are regarded as defective in their ministry.

The weakness of the argument of *The Apostolic Ministry* (edited by K. E. Kirk, 1946) was its failure to explain the absence of the idea in the first two centuries of the Christian era. Dr. Ehrhardt does not supply the defect by postulating a *priestly* succession derived from the Judaizing church of Jerusalem as it laid stress on the *new* Israel and the continuity of its priesthood. The idea was in the air in the second century (*The Apostolic Succession,* 1953).

Bishop Drury affirms that the apostles left behind them three things: their writings; the churches which they founded, instructed, and regulated; and the various orders of ministers for the ordering of these churches. There could be no more apostles in the original sense of that word. The real successor to the apostolate is the NT itself, since it continues their ministry within the church of God. Their office was incommunicable. Three kinds of succession are possible: *ecclesiastical* — a church which has continued from the beginning; *doctrinal* — the same teaching has continued throughout; *episcopal* — a line of bishops can be traced unbroken from early times. This does not necessarily mean that the episcopal office is the same as the apostolic.

See also ORDAIN, ORDINATION.

BIBLIOGRAPHY
Henry Bettenson, *Documents of the Christian Church;* Girdlestone, Moule, Drury, *English Church Teaching.*

RICHARD E. HIGGINSON

APOTHEOSIS. See DEIFICATION.

APPEARANCE. See RESURRECTION.

ARCANI DISCIPLINA. This is a seventeenth century term for the early Christian practice of concealing certain ceremonies and teachings from catechumens and pagans, through the desire to prevent misunderstanding or ridicule. Many ancient writers, both in East and West, mention the custom which slowly died out after the Edict of Milan. Theodoret, e.g., says, "We speak obscurely of the divine mysteries on account of the uninitiated, but when these have withdrawn we teach the initiated plainly." (*Quaest.* XV in Nu.). In speaking to pagans, the birth, death and resurrection of Jesus Christ were explained, but not Baptism, Holy Communion or the Trinity.

BIBLIOGRAPHY
DCA, ODCC.

M. R. W. FARRER

ARCHAEOLOGY. Archaeology provides a new open door to the study of ancient civilizations, which in turn helps us to understand better and interpret aright our ancient historical records, both secular and biblical. This archaeological investigation of ancient life includes the study of the monuments, inscriptions, language, literature, art, architecture, implements, houses, cities, and all other remains of man and his activities. Applied to biblical studies, every area of biblical research is illuminated and brought into sharp focus by the knowledge which comes from Near Eastern archaeology.

I. ARCHAEOLOGY AND BIBLE HISTORY. Our understanding of each major period of biblical history is broadened and deepened by archaeological discoveries. The era of the Patriarchs is illuminated by archaeological work at many cities of that time — Ai, Shechem, Bethel, Beersheba, Gerar, Dothan, Jerusalem — and by the discovery of actual literary texts bearing on the period — the Nuzi and Mari tablets. Smaller details of this era are clarified also. Why did Isaac not revoke his oral blessing on Jacob when he found it had not been given to Esau as he planned (Gen. 27:34-41)? The Nuzi tablets show that in patriarchal times an oral blessing was binding, even in a law court (Cyrus Gordon, BA, III, 1, p. 8). Why could Laban, with authority, point to his grandchildren and say, "These children are my children" (Gen. 31:43)? The Nuzi tablets show that in that day a grandfather exercised control over his grandchildren (ibid.).

As a summary of the abundant light shed on the kings of the Bible, we note that forty-one biblical kings are confirmed in archaeological discoveries (R. D. Wilson, A Scientific Investigation of the Old Testament, The Sunday School Times Co., Philadelphia, 1926, pp. 72-73).

II. ARCHAEOLOGY AS A COMMENTARY. For generations Bible students have gone to commentaries when they needed light on a biblical passage. In modern times archaeology has provided a vast new commentary. Bible students could guess at the meaning of the statement made three times in the Pentateuch, "Thou shalt not seethe a kid in its mother's milk" (Ex. 23:19; 34:26; Deut. 14:21), but it was not until the Ras Shamra tablets were excavated (1929) and studied (1930 to the present) that we knew for a certainty that this referred to a pagan ritual practice: one of the Ras Shamra tablets indicates that if one wishes to please a certain deity, he should boil a kid in milk. Ancient Israel was being warned not to backslide into the practices of the pagan people around them.

In summary, whole books have been written from the archaeological standpoint on various periods and areas of Bible study. One example

is John Garstang, Joshua, Judges, Constable, London, 1931.

III. ARCHAEOLOGY AND THE DATING OF BIBLICAL BOOKS. Certain critics have dated many of these books later than their internal evidence would imply. Wellhausen and his later disciples made the Pentateuch a late compilation (ninth to fifth centuries B.C.), a thousand years after the days of Abraham and several hundred years after the time of Moses. Archaeological discoveries such as the Nuzi tablets show, however, that the background of the Pentateuch is early and need not be downdated on the grounds of a late background.

Many of the Psalms have been downdated to the time of the Persian and Greek periods (sixth to third centuries B.C.) and even to Herodian times. Archaeological evidence from Ras Shamra has shown again and again that many Psalms which have been dated late by certain critics must be reassigned to an early date (W. F. Albright, The Archaeology of Palestine, Penguin, Baltimore, revised 1956, pp. 226-27). Other illustrations could be given of dates shifted to an earlier position in the light of archaeological evidence.

IV. ARCHAEOLOGY AND EVIDENCES. The apologetic value of archaeology is almost too well known to need illustration. In every period of biblical history we have confirmation both of broad areas and of minute details, whether the general accuracy of the patriarchal background (evidenced in Nuzi tablets, Mari tablets, and others), or specific details such as the confirmation of the existence of the once-doubted Hittites (evidence from Boghaz-Koi, cf. Free, Archaeology and Bible History, Scripture Press, Wheaton, Illinois, 5th ed., 1956, pp. 125-26), or once-mentioned individuals, as Sargon (Isa. 20:1; cf. discoveries at Khorsabad, ibid, pp. 200-201), or doubted narrative records, as Sennacherib's recorded failure to capture Jerusalem (II Kings 19:35-36; confirmed by Sennacherib's failure to boast that he captured the city — he could only say, "I shut up Hezekiah like a bird in a cage"). Examples of both general and specific confirmation of the historical reliability of the Bible can be multiplied many times over (Millar Burrows, What Mean Those Stones, American Schools of Oriental Research, New Haven, 1941, p. 281).

V. ARCHAEOLOGY AND EXEGESIS. Archaeology not only throws light on the general historical situation but frequently clears up for the exegete the meaning of particular words and phrases. The statement that Moses' "eye was not dim nor his natural force abated" (Deut. 34:7) has puzzled interpreters down through the centuries. The word translated natural force *(lē(a)ḥ)* is similar to the word for jaw in Hebrew, hence some translated it by extension as teeth (Jerome in the Vulgate). Objective light came with the discovery of the Ras Shamra tablets, where this same word occurs twice in the sense of manly vigor or natural force. Jerome and the Greek translators were wrong and the King James translators correct in their rendering natural force (Albright, *BASOR* 94). Many similar illustrations of light on words and phrases could be given, both for the OT and for the NT. In the latter a whole new area of study was opened up at the beginning of the century with the discovery of everyday Greek papyri texts in the excavations of Egypt.

VI. ARCHAEOLOGY AND HERMENEUTICS. The interpretation of a given passage often depends largely on a correct knowledge of the historical, geographical, and linguistic factors involved. As indicated previously, archaeology is a necessary adjunct in all of these. Furthermore, a correct translation is a prime requisite, and here the archaeological sources are a constant help. It is necessary, e.g., to know whether it was Moses' teeth or his natural force which was unimpaired to interpret correctly the passage in Deut. 34:7.

In the NT a great number of words have been amplified and some former interpretations definitely modified by the discovery of the non-literary papyri, whose significance was first pointedly brought to the attention of the world by Adolph Deissmann (*Light from the Ancient East,* Doran, New York, 1927).

VII. ARCHAEOLOGY AND THE HISTORICAL SETTING. For a correct comprehension of the Scriptures one needs a knowledge of the historical milieu in which these events took place. One is puzzled, for example, by Laban's pursuit of Jacob and Rachel to recover the family images (idols) which Rachel had stolen (Gen. 31:19-23). This puzzling action was clarified by the discovery of the Nuzi tablets, which showed that if one possessed the family images of the father he could lay claim to the family inheritance. In the light of this evidence one can easily understand the hurried flight of Laban to recover the images from Jacob, whom he did not want to inherit his estate.

A thousand years after the patriarchal period, Solomon is reported to have received the picturesque queen of Sheba, an account often regarded as unhistorical. The air of unreality ascribed by some to the record is removed in the light of Assyrian archaeological records which furnish factual details of the land of Sheba in the early first millennium B.C. and confirm its historical reality. As Professor James Montgomery of the University of Pennsylvania remarked in connection with the record of Solomon and the queen of Sheba, the biblical setting is "quite correct" (*Arabia and the Bible,* University of Pennsylvania Press, Philadelphia, 1934, p. 180).

VIII. ARCHAEOLOGY AND LITERARY CRITICISM. Literary criticism is concerned with the authorship, date, purpose, and integrity of the books of the Bible. The evident authorship of a book of the Bible is often denied on the ground that the book has a background too late for the time of the implied author. The Pentateuch, according to many critics, could not have been the work of Moses because of a supposedly late background. But in the twentieth century the discovery of the Nuzi tablets, the Mari tablets, and many others, reveals just the reverse — an early background, thus removing this objection to the Mosaicity of the Pentateuch. Many striking examples of similar help from archaeology on the question of date and authorship of other OT books could be given. Again and again hypercriticism fails to be supported (cf. W. F. Albright, *Archaeology of Palestine,* p. 225).

In the NT area also archaeological evidence supports early dating. For example, the supposed anachronistic use of "master" *(didaskalos)* as pointing to a late date for the Gospel of John is answered by the discovery of early ossuary inscriptions containing the same word (*ibid.,* p. 244).

IX. ARCHAEOLOGY AND THEOLOGY. The theologian comes to grips with such questions as the goodness of God. Puzzling are the commands of God to drive out the pagan Canaanites from the promised land (Deut. 7:1-5). How does this harmonize with the goodness of God? Concerning this very point the archaeological discoveries show that the Canaanites had a licentious and corrupt worship, as evidenced in the Ras Shamra tablets, which made it necessary to deal with them in judgment.

The systematic theologian works with a body of revealed truth. If this revelation is shown to be inaccurate, historically incorrect, filled with contradictions, what has the theologian to build on? The results of archaeological research show the firm support that exists for the revelation Christians accept and for the theology which derives from it.

BIBLIOGRAPHY

General works: W. F. Albright, *The Archaeology of Palestine* (1956); *The Archaeology of Palestine and the Bible* (1935); *Archaeology and the Religion of Israel; From the Stone Age to Christianity;* Millar Burrows, *What Mean These Stones;* Jack Finegan, *Light from the Ancient Past.*
Direct bearing of archaeology on the Bible: J. P. Free, *Archaeology and Bible History;* Merrill F. Unger, *Archaeology and the Old Testament.*
On the Dead Sea Scrolls: see art. in this Dictionary.
For summaries of current developments in biblical and Near Eastern archaeology: the quarterly publications *BA* and *BASOR.*

JOSEPH P. FREE

ARCHBISHOP. See OFFICES, ECCLESIASTICAL.

ARCHDEACON. See OFFICES, ECCLESIASTICAL.

ARCHPRIEST. See OFFICES, ECCLESIASTICAL.

ARIANISM. The Arian controversy arose in the diocese of Alexandria, Egypt, about the year A.D. 320, and was concerned primarily with the person of Christ. It took its name from Arius, a presbyter in Alexandria, who taught that there is a difference between God the Father and Christ the Son which makes the latter secondary. Arius maintained that God the Father alone is eternal, that Christ was created out of nothing as the first and greatest of all creatures, and that he in turn created the universe. Arius thus represented Christ as but the first and greatest of all creatures, God's intermediary agent through whom all other things were created. Yet, because of the power and honor delegated to him, he was to be looked upon as God and was to be worshipped. Most of the Arians also held that the Holy Spirit was the first and greatest of the creatures called into existence by the Son. This, therefore, meant a God who had a beginning and who might therefore have an end. In demanding worship for a created Christ, the Arians were in effect asserting the central principle of heathenism and idolatry, the worship of a creature. This controversy

continued longer and was more serious than any other that agitated the early church.

In the teaching of Arius it was assumed that deity could not appear substantially on the earth. Hence Christ was assumed to be a second essence which God had created, which came down to earth and took upon himself a human body. He was assumed to be not a "perfect man," for in his body the Logos took the place of the human intellect or spiritual principle.

This error arose because Arius and his followers misinterpreted certain Scripture statements relating to Christ's state of humiliation, that is, certain relationships which he assumed in order that he might accomplish the redemption of his people. The result was that they assumed that temporary subordination to the Father meant original and permanent inequality. But, because of the claims that Christ had made, the authority that he assumed, the miracles that he worked, and the glory that he displayed particularly in his resurrection and ascension, the great majority of Christians held that he was truly God.

In order to settle the controversy the Emperor Constantine called the first Christian council at Nicaea, in Asia Minor, in the year A.D. 325. It was hoped that a formula could be worked out which would be acceptable to the whole church. The council was attended by bishops and presbyters from practically all parts of the empire, and the controversy centered around the question as to whether Christ was to be considered as truly God or as only the first and greatest creature.

The leader of the orthodox forces was Alexander, Bishop of Alexandria. The teaching of Arius was condemned. Christ was held to be of the same substance with the Father, *homoousia*, not merely of similar substance, *homoiousia*, and was declared to be "God of God, Light of Light, very God of very God, being of one substance with the Father."

The defeat of Arianism, however, was only temporary. The Emperor Constantine was at first strongly inclined to enforce the decree of the council, but was persuaded to a more moderate course. Both views were tolerated in the church, with the result that Arianism rallied and for a considerable time became the dominant view. Alexander died soon after the council adjourned. He was succeeded by Athanasius, who contended strongly and skilfully for the orthodox doctrine, and to Athanasius belongs the primary credit for its eventual triumph. The controversy continued to agitate the church until the Council of Constantinople in A.D. 381, at which time the orthodox doctrine was reaffirmed. Even then the Arian view continued to be held by small groups, but finally disappeared about A.D. 650.

In denying the true deity of Christ while at the same time demanding worship for him, Arianism was opening the door to polytheism and destroying the basis for Christian Trinitarianism. Athanasius properly saw that only as the deity of Christ is maintained can there be established a firm basis for the Christian faith.

BIBLIOGRAPHY
F. J. Foakes-Jackson in *HERE*; "Arius" in *EncyBrit*, II, p. 360; *ColEncy*; L. Boettner, *Studies in Theology*, pp. 261-62.

LORAINE BOETTNER

ARK. See TABERNACLE.

ARMAGEDDON. This widely and variously-used word is defined in the *Oxford English Dictionary* as "the place of the last decisive battle at the day of judgment." It is found only once in the Bible, in the phrase "the place which is called in Hebrew, Har-Magedon" (Rev. 16:16 ASV). While in recent NT introductions the usually-given origin of the word, with specific reference, is denied, there is no reason for giving up the view of Alford, and most other conservative NT scholars, that the term itself means "the mountain of Megiddo." Megiddo is located on the southern side of the plain of Jezreel, and is often referred to in the OT as a military stronghold (Josh. 12:21; 17:11; Judges 1:27; 5:19; II Kings 9:27; 23:29, etc.).

Though the word itself occurs only in the one verse, the great, final battle of this age is recorded in detail in Rev. 19:11-21, and is referred to anticipatorily in 14:14-20; 16:13-16 and 17:8-17. The text clearly states that this battle will be on a gigantic scale, that it will involve the nations of the east, and that the kings going up to this battle, knowing it is to be waged against the Lamb, will be driven by demon powers. Several OT passages also speak of a great conflict at the end of the age (Joel 3:9-15; Jer. 51:27-36; Zeph. 3:8). This battle of Megiddo should not be confused with the overthrow of Israel's enemies in Ezekiel 37-39.

Here in Rev. 19:15 is the last reference to the wrath of God, and here, just before the battle begins, our Lord is designated "King of Kings, and Lord of Lords," for he is about to fulfil the title assigned to him at the beginning of this book, "the ruler of the kings of the earth" (1:5). In his commentary on the Apocalypse, Swete, writing at a time when the world seemed to be entering upon an era of universal peace (1906), well said, "Those who take note of the tendencies of modern civilization will not find it impossible to conceive that a time may come when throughout Christendom the spirit of Antichrist will, with the support of the state, make a final stand against a Christianity which is loyal to the person and teaching of Christ" (p. 257).

The word Armageddon is often used incorrectly, as when Theodore Roosevelt, candidating for President of the United States on the Bull Moose Party ticket, said, "We stand at Armageddon and we battle for the Lord."

BIBLIOGRAPHY
William Lee in *The Bible Commentary* (Heb. to Rev.) pp. 784-91; William Miller, *The Least of All Lands*, pp. 152-212; J. Seiss, *Lectures on the Apocalypse*, III, pp. 237-62; W. M. Smith, *World Crises and the Prophetic Scriptures*, pp. 131-61.

WILBUR M. SMITH

ARMINIANISM. Jacob Hermann, or in Latin Arminius, (1560-1609), was a Dutch theologian who, after receiving a strict Reformed training, conceived some doubts with respect to the Calvinistic tenets on the sovereign grace of God in salvation and related themes. His followers, called Arminians or Remonstrants, carried matters considerably further than Arminius had done in his writings, and set forth their views in a document called "Remonstrance" and consisting of five articles which may be briefly summarized as follows:

I. God elects or reproves on the basis of foreseen faith or unbelief.

II. Christ died for all men and for every man, although only believers are saved.

III. Man is so depraved that divine grace is necessary unto faith or any good deed.

IV. This grace may be resisted.

V. Whether all who are truly regenerate will certainly persevere in the faith is a point which needs further investigation.

After considerable discussion these views were condemned in the Synod of Dort (1618-19). They were maintained and developed in the Netherlands by H. Uytenbogaert (1557-1644), S. Episcopius (1583-1643), S. Curcellaeus (1586-1659), Hugo Grotius (1583-1645), Ph. a Limborch (1633-1712), and others. Under the leadership of these men Arminianism became characterized by increasing differences from the traditional Reformed faith. The following tenets are commonly held by Arminians:

1. God's knowledge of the future acts of free agents is mediate (*scientia media*).

2. God's decrees are based on his foreknowledge: election on foreseen faith and reprobation on foreseen resistance to grace.

3. The image of God in man consists in man's dominion over the lower creation.

4. Adam was created in innocency rather than in true holiness.

5. The covenant of works was abrogated after the Fall.

6. Sin consists in acts of the will.

7. Pollution is inherited from Adam, but his guilt is not imputed to any of his descendants.

8. Man's depravity as a result of the Fall should not be described as total.

9. Man has not lost the faculty of self-determination nor the ability to incline his will toward good ends.

10. The atonement was not absolutely necessary, but represents merely one way which God chose among many to manifest his love without prejudice to his righteousness.

11. The atonement is intended equally for all men and for every man, and it merely makes salvation possible. Salvation becomes effectual only when accepted by the repentant believer.

12. There is no common grace to be distinguished from special grace.

13. The external call of the gospel is accompanied by a universal sufficient grace which can be resisted.

14. Repentance and faith precede regeneration.

15. The human will is to be viewed as one of the causes of regeneration (synergism).

16. Faith is a good work of man and a ground of acceptance with God.

17. There is no imputation of Christ's righteousness to the believer.

18. The believer is able to attain in this life a state of such conformity to the divine will that he may be called perfect.

19. As long as a man lives he may fall away from grace and lose his salvation altogether.

Certain Arminians were led to profess further that:

20. Love is the supreme attribute of God, the very essence of his being.

21. The goal of creation is the happiness of the creatures (eudaemonism).

22. Man was created naturally mortal.

23. The atonement is not strictly substitutionary and penal, but it is a token performance designed to safeguard the interests of the moral government of God while opening the possibility of salvation on the ground of evangelical obedience (rectoral or governmental theory of the atonement).

24. Assurance of salvation is not possible in this life, except by a special personal revelation.

In the Netherlands Arminians, as well as many other movements, were profoundly affected by the rationalistic currents of the eighteenth century. The present-day Remonstrants still hold to Pelagian teachings and have lax views of inspiration and of the Trinity.

Outside of Holland Arminianism exercised considerable influence in France, Switzerland, Germany, and England, and hence throughout the world. In a number of cases this point of view gained the upper hand in spite of Calvinistic confessions of faith.

The Wesleyan branch of the Methodist movement embraced vigorously a revised form of Arminianism, sometimes called "evangelical Arminianism." It is characterized by a view of the themes touched upon in 3, 7, 8, and 9, which is slightly less distant from Calvinistic tenets.

BIBLIOGRAPHY

Beside the works of the authors mentioned above one might consult the collected works of John Goodwin, John Fletcher, John Wesley and D. Whitby, and the systematic theologies of W. Cooke, J. Miley, W. B. Pope, M. Raymond, T. O. Summers, R. Watson and H. O. Wiley. Able works against Arminianism have been produced by W. Ames, L. Boettner, P. Dumoulin, John Edwards, Jonathan Edwards, J. Gill, J. Owen, S. Rutherford, and many others. Helpful documentation may be found in W. A. Copinger, *A Treatise of Election, Predestination and Grace* (with bibliography of 235 pp.); W. Cunningham, *Historical Theology*, II pp. 371-513; J. L. Girardeau, *Calvinism and Evangelical Arminianism*; A. W. Harrison, *Arminianism; The Beginnings of Arminianism*; F. Platt in *HERE*; II. C. Rogge in *SHERK*; P. Schaff, *Creeds of Christendom*, I, pp. 508-23; III, pp. 544-49; D. D. Whedon, BS 19, 241-74.

ROGER NICOLE

ARMOR. For armor in general, *maddim* is used (I Sam. 17:38), also *kelî* (I Sam. 14:1 ASV); as military apparel, (*neseq*) (I Kings 10:25); Greek *hoplon*, with *pan*, thus *panoplia*, or "whole armor" only twice in the NT

(Luke 11:22; Eph. 6:11, 13). There are several other words translated "armor" in the OT, coming from roots not precisely related to arms or wars, such as from spoils, etc.

In the Bible the use of armor for military purposes is related to Israel and her enemies. In the battles which Israel fought, she learned from her enemies and adapted the armor and tactics of the enemy to her own use. That the armor of Israel was typical of the times can be demonstrated by comparing descriptions in I Sam. 17:8, II Chron. 26:14-15 and Jer. 46:3-4. In NT times the Pauline description of armor was typical of the Roman soldier, with whom he had every reason to be familiar. Paul adds the shoes and the girdle but does not mention the spear (Eph. 6:11-17).

Armor was designed for both offensive and defensive purposes. The most primitive offensive weapons were clubs, stones, staves and darts, all of which Israel used. Stones became deadly projectiles when propelled from the knitted or leather two-thonged sling. Such a weapon in the hands of David slew Goliath (I Sam. 17:40). The seven hundred Benjaminites, left-handed all, were noted for their accuracy with the sling (Judg. 20:16). In the conquest of Canaan the javelin and the sword were used. The phrase "edge of the sword" is almost a catch phrase in the book of Joshua. It seems to have fallen upon the Philistines to provide these weapons and to control a monopoly of keeping swords and tools sharpened. Such a factory and smelting furnace was found by Petrie at Gerar.

The bow and arrow were common weapons. Of several styles, the bow could be made of wood, copper, or bronze. It could also be a hunter's bow, a large battle bow, or a foot bow. The arrows might be tipped with stone or metal. The quiver was worn on the left side. If the bowmen went to battle in chariots, then the bow was slung on the side of the chariot.

The Hittites carried daggers, and the Philistines made knives with ivory inlaid handles. In the hands of the Philistines and the Greeks the two-edged sword was a deadly and much-feared weapon. The Greeks also effectively used the spear.

Solomon seems to have added the chariot (long used by others) to the offensive weapons of Israel. Several passages in the OT also mention the use of siege weapons such as the battering-ram.

Defensively, armor consisted of the helmet, which might be made of either metal or as a knitted cap; the shield which was in two styles: (1) the buckler, or small, round shield carried on the arm, and (2) the large shield of body length. The shield also could be of metal or of wood and leather or even of wicker. As a rule, metal helmets were worn by leaders and officers. These officers would also wear a coat of mail over the body, greaves over the shins, and leather boots on the feet. King Ahab was slain by an arrow that pierced between the joints of his coat of mail (I Kings 22:34). The armor of the Roman soldier was simply a more elegant and utilitarian adaptation of the above.

Metaphorically, the flaming circle of the sword barred Eden (Gen. 3:24); Gideon cried "the sword of Jehovah and of Gideon" into the ears of the Midianites (Judg. 7:20); the Psalmist spoke of the shield, buckler, etc. But the classic passage is the Roman soldier — Christian warrior metaphor of Ephesians. Paul's description compares with that of Polybius (vi. 23), but without the spear. Used in the war against sin and Satan, Paul speaks of the ". . . armor of God."

In this way also, the sword becomes a symbol of God's judgment; God's armor denotes his ability to conquer and to destroy and his all-sufficiency, and God is spoken of as putting on his armor (Isa. 59:17). The fire-tipped arrows of conquest become the "fiery darts" of Satan. As for the soldier, so for the Christian, his weapons and his armor are his life.

BIBLIOGRAPHY
Arndt; ExpGT; Gurnall, The Spiritual Warfare; or, The Christian in Complete Armor; ISBE; NSBD; HBD; HBE; Murray, Ephesians, CGT; RTWB.

ROBERT WINSTON ROSS

ARTICLE OF FAITH. A non-biblical term, though the terse creedal statements embedded in I Cor. 15:3, 4 and I Tim. 3:16 indicate the church's early preoccupation with concise formulations of Christian belief. Aquinas uses *articulus* to denote a revealed supernatural truth distinct in itself yet forming part of the organic whole of Christian teaching. The *Catechism of the Council of Trent* calls the truths of the Apostles' Creed "articles." The great confessions of Protestantism, which define the biblical faith of the Reformation in contradistinction both to Rome and to fanatical "enthusiasm," comprise individual dogmatic assertions usually styled "articles," e.g., the Thirty-nine Articles, the official doctrinal standard of the Church of England.

O. RAYMOND JOHNSTON

ASCENSION, THE. By the ascension is meant that act of the God-man by which he brought to an end his post-resurrection appearances to his disciples, was finally parted from them as to his physical presence, and passed into the other world, to remain there until his second advent (Acts 3:21). Luke describes this event in a word or two in Luke 24:51 and more fully in Acts 1:9. Even if the words "and he was carried up into heaven" are not part of the true text in Luke 24:51, we have good reason for saying, in the light of Luke's clear and unambiguous words in his second treatise, that the doubtful words in Luke 24:51 express what was in his mind. In accordance with the oral testimony of the apostles, he carries on his story of the life of Jesus as far as "the day that he was taken up" (Acts 1:22).

According to the Fourth Gospel, our Lord referred on three occasions to his ascending into heaven (John 3:13; 6:62; 20:17). Paul speaks of Christ ascending far above all heavens in order to permeate the whole universe with his presence and power (Eph. 4:10). Such phrases as "received up in glory" (I Tim. 3:16), "gone into heaven" (I Pet. 3:22), and "passed through the heavens" (Heb. 4:14) refer to the same event. Paul exhorts the Colossian believers to "seek the things that are above, where Christ is, seated on the right hand of God" (Col. 3:1, ERV), and the numerous references in the NT to the session at the right hand of God presuppose the ascension.

In Eph. 1:20 ff. Paul passes directly from the resurrection to the exaltation of Christ to the place of supreme power and authority in the universe. In passages like Rom. 8:34 and Col. 3:1 the session might seem to be thought of as the immediate result of the rising from the dead, thus leaving no room, as some have argued, for the ascension as a distinct event; but it is difficult to see that there is any force in any argument derived from Paul's silence in such passages when in Eph. 4:10 he states so emphatically his belief in the ascension. Our Lord's post-resurrection appearances had, no doubt, shown that he belonged already to the upper world of light and glory; but with the ascension his fleeting visits to his disciples from that world came to an end, and the heavens received him from their sight. Yet, through the indwelling Holy Spirit they were to come nearer to him than ever before, and he was to be with them forever (John 14:16-18).

To object to the account of the ascension of Christ into heaven as implying a childish and outmoded view of the universe is, more or less, solemn trifling. While we may agree with Westcott when he says that "the change which Christ revealed by the ascension was not a change of place, but a change of state, not local but spiritual" (Westcott, *The Revelation of the Risen Lord*, Macmillan & Co., London, 1898, p. 180), on the other hand, we are not unscientific when we think of the land where "the king in all His glory without a veil is seen" as the upper world of light and glory, high above us as good is above evil and blessedness above misery.

The Heidelberg Catechism suggests three great benefits that we receive from the ascension. (1) The exalted Lord in heaven is our Advocate in the presence of his Father (Rom. 8:34; I John 2:1; Heb. 7:25). As our High Priest he offered on the cross the one perfect and final sacrifice for sins for ever (Heb. 10:12), and now, having sat down on the right hand of God, he has entered on his priestly ministry in heaven. As our King-Priest he communicates, through the Holy Spirit, to all believers the gifts and blessings which he died to win for them. "Christ's intercession in heaven," said the old Scottish preacher, Traill, "is a kind and powerful remembrance of His people, and of all their concerns, managed with state and majesty; not as a suppliant at the footstool, but as a crowned prince on the throne, at the right hand of the Father." (2) We have our flesh in heaven, so that, as the subtle Scottish thinker, "Rabbi" Duncan, said: "The dust of the earth is on the throne of the majesty on high." In that, as the Heidelberg Catechism says, we have "a sure pledge that He, as our Head, will also take us, His members, up to Himself." (3) He sends us his Spirit, as the earnest of the promised inheritance.

That third benefit is of supreme importance. The Holy Spirit was not given, in the fulness of his gracious working in the souls of men, until Jesus was glorified (John 7:39). "Being by the right hand of God exalted, and having received of the Father the promise of the Holy Ghost, he hath poured forth this, which ye see and hear. For David ascended not into the heavens" (Acts 2:33, 34, ERV). Thus was it demonstrated to the universe that, as Zahn has put it, "the risen Lord lives in heavenly communion with His and our Father, and that He takes an active part in the working of the power as well as of the grace of God in this world" (Zahn, *The Apostles' Creed,* Eng. trans.; Hodder & Stoughton, London, 1899, p. 162). "There can be no doubt," James Denney wrote, "that in this passage Peter looks upon Jesus in His exaltation as forming with God His Father one Divine causality at work through the Spirit for the salvation of men" (Denney, *Jesus and the Gospel,* Hodder & Stoughton, London, 1913, p. 19).

The ascended Lord is with us in the struggle here (Mark 16:19-20), and we know that he has gone to heaven, "our entrance to secure, and our abode prepare" (John 14:2; Heb. 6:20).

BIBLIOGRAPHY

HDAC, HDB, HDCG; W. Milligan, *The Ascension and Heavenly Priesthood of Our Lord;* Swete and Zahn on *The Apostles' Creed;* A. M. Ramsey in *Studiorum Novi Testamenti Societas, Bulletin II* (1951).

ALEXANDER ROSS

ASCETICISM. From the Greek *askēsis* (exercise or training), asceticism denotes the practice of self-discipline, more particularly in relation to the body. It normally takes the form of renunciation, e.g., fasting, celibacy, but has sometimes been given a more active form in such excesses as self-flagellation. It is capable of extension to many spheres of life, especially the surrender of possessions or withdrawal from various aspects of intellectual or cultural life in the interests of spiritual edification or service.

The Bible allows a place for the right kind of asceticism. Thus Israel was to abstain from marital intercourse prior to the giving of the law (Ex. 19:15). The Nazaritic vow involved abstention from wine and strong drink and strictness in relation to unclean meats (Judg. 13:5). Elijah undertook a forty-day fast on his journey to Horeb (I Kings 19:8), and fasting in particular played an important part in penitential humiliation before God (Joel 2:15 ff.).

Nor is asceticism excluded by the NT. John the Baptist practiced great severity in respect of food and clothing (Matt. 3:4). Jesus entered on his ministry with a fast (Matt. 4:1 ff.) and had to forego the normal human rights of property, marriage, and even family relationships (Mark 3:33 f.) for the sake of his ministry. If he did not teach his disciples to fast, he indicated plainly that they must do so after his departure (Matt. 9:15) and obviously required that some should be celibate and renounce ordinary relationships for his sake (Matt. 19:12, 29). In the Epistles Paul sees a value in celibacy for the better pleasing of the Lord (I Cor. 7:32), and his own practice is one of rigorous self-discipline in order that he may be a good soldier and servant of Jesus Christ (I Cor. 9:27; II Tim. 2:3 f.).

The consistent biblical emphasis upon a proper asceticism is impressive, yet three points are to be carefully noted. First, there is no suggestion of anything intrinsically evil in that which is foregone, e.g., food, marriage, property, or ordinary relationships. Second, there is no universal or even permanent rule of asceticism in the majority of cases. Third, asceticism is not an end in itself but is undertaken with a view to something positive, e.g., repentance, hearing God's word, or, more particularly, service.

Ascetic witness was particularly valuable in the early pagan world with its lax standards of physical morality, and in measure most Christians had to accept a new level of abstemiousness, and many were prepared to go to greater extremes for the sake of their new life and witness. Hence it is not surprising to find the swift development of an eremitic and monastic movement designed to facilitate or foster ascetic practices. Nor is this wholly to be condemned. It accepted literally the biblical statements which far too often are evaded by spiritualization. It maintained a witness to higher standards than were achieved by the majority. And many of the early monks were foremost in the work of evangelism or practical service.

Unfortunately, however, the general tendency of the church has been to lose sight of the three distinctive and indispensable characteristics of genuine biblical asceticism. Under pagan influence, dominant especially in Gnosticism (*q.v.*), there has been a continuing suspicion that the physical is essentially evil and therefore to be necessarily renounced as such for the attainment of true sanctification and in full obedience to Christ. Again, attempts have been made to impose definite rules of asceticism as an indissoluble obligation, as in the Roman insistence upon celibate clergy or the permanent character of monastic vows. Third, it has been supposed that there is a merit in asceticism as such, the ascetic attaining to a higher level of Christian life and acquiring merit in the bid to escape purgatory. In this way the evils of dualism, ecclesiasticism, and legalism have perverted a true asceticism, avenging themselves either in a reversion to laxity on the one side (cf. clerical concubinage) or a self-centered Pharisaism on the other (Luke 18:11 f.). There could be no greater caricature of genuine asceticism than Simon Stylites on his pillar, the celibate priest with his "housekeeper," or the monk pursuing private edification in isolation from the world.

Yet the best antidote to perverted asceticism is the biblical and evangelical view. It rests on the fact that salvation is in Christ alone. It sees no superior merit or virtue in asceticism as such. It does not regard the physical as intrinsically evil. It cannot accept a binding or permanent rule of abnegation. But it is prepared for various measures of self-discipline and self-denial in obedience to the specific demands of Jesus Christ, out of overruling and singlehearted love for him and for the sake of greater effectiveness in the ministry of evangelism and edification.

See also FAST, CELIBACY.

BIBLIOGRAPHY
K. E. Kirk, *The Vision of God*; O. Zoeckler, in HERE.

WILLIAM KELLY

ASEITY. See ATTRIBUTES, DIVINE.

ASH WEDNESDAY. The first day of Lent, the traditional forty fast days before Easter. The title derives from the discipline in the ancient Roman Church of sprinkling ashes on the heads of penitents with a view to their being restored to Communion at Easter. The Sarum Missal contained a service for the blessing of the ashes, which were intended to be a mark of humiliation, contrition, and mourning (see, e.g., Isa. 61:3; Dan. 9:3; Matt. 11:21).

FRANK COLQUHOUN

ASHERAH. See GODS.

ASHEROTH. See GODS.

ASSUMPTION OF MARY. On Nov. 1, 1950, Pope Pius XII defined it as an article of the faith revealed by God, to deny which

would incur the wrath of Almighty God and the holy apostles, that the Blessed Virgin Mary, having completed her earthly life, was in body and soul assumed into heavenly glory. (*Munificentissimus Deus*, 1950, *Acta Apostolicae Sedis*, XLII). Before that date the belief was held as a pious and probable opinion. Benedict XIV declared in 1740 that the tradition is not of such a kind as to be sufficient for the elevation of this doctrine to the rank of an article of faith (*Opera*, Vol. X, p. 499, ed. 1751). Scripture is silent about the circumstances of the death of Mary, and the tradition of the assumption is unknown in the early church.

The story is first found in some apocryphal writings of the late fourth century bearing the titles *The Passing of Mary, The Obsequies of Mary*, and *The Book of the Passing of the Blessed Virgin*. The writings are condemned as spurious in the decretals attributed to Pope Gelasius at the end of the fifth or beginning of the sixth century (Migne, *Patrologiae Latinae*, pp. 59, 162). Gregory of Tours (d. 594) is the first orthodox writer who accepts them as authentic. A passage in *Concerning the Divine Names* (attributed to Dionysius the Areopagite but actually dating from the fifth to the sixth century) was taken by Andrew of Crete (d. 740) to imply that Dionysius had witnessed the assumption. John of Damascus (eighth century) presented the assumption as an ancient Catholic tradition. Since the sixteenth century, passages from a homily of his have provided some of the lessons used in the Roman Breviary during the Feast of the Assumption. Festivals observing the death of Mary, but not necessarily her bodily assumption, have been observed in the East from the Fifth Century and in the West from the end of the Seventh. The doctrine, it is said, is recommended by its intrinsic reasonableness. Our Lord would not permit the sacred body in which he himself dwelt to become a prey to corruption.

See also MARIOLATRY.

BIBLIOGRAPHY
Giovanne Miegge, *The Virgin Mary: the Roman Catholic Marian Doctrine*.

RICHARD J. COATES

ASSURANCE. The doctrine that those who are truly saved may know without a doubt that they are saved is often described as assurance (Col. 2:2; Heb. 6:11; 10:22). This certainty of salvation the Reformers referred to as *certitudo gratiae* or *certitudo salutis*, both of which terms imply the certainty or assurance of personal salvation.

The doctrine of assurance is predicated in the Westminster Confession of Faith (Chapter XVIII), which teaches that although believers may have the assurance of their redemption sorely tried and shaken, yet they are never utterly deprived of saving faith and hence have their assurance of salvation revived and re-established by the work of the Holy Spirit. Both Calvin and Luther held this position. The Arminian position would predicate certainty of salvation for the present only.

The NT word generally translated "assurance" is the Greek word *plērophoria*, which literally means "full conviction," and is used in such passages as Rom. 4:21; 14:5 (verb); and in I Thess. 1:5; Col. 2:2; Heb. 6:11 and 10:22 (noun).

The grounds of assurance are more objective than subjective; they are not so much within us as without us. Hence the basis of assurance must rest on sufficient objective evidence. The Bible provides the grounds of assurance: God's promise that those who come to him in Christ will not be cast out; the infinite and gratuitous love of God; the once for all and all-sufficient sacrifice of Christ for the sins of the world; the witness of the Holy Spirit that those who believe are children of God.

BIBLIOGRAPHY

LC; ER; L. S. Chafer, *Systematic Theology*, VII, pp. 21-24; T. Nicol in HDAC.

                                    ROBERT F. BOYD

ASTROLOGY. The doctrine that heavenly bodies foretell or reflect destinies of (a) individual men and/or (b) nations.

Scientifically, astrology of type (b) contains elements of truth. Shooting stars cause widespread rain (E. G. Bowen, 1957); disease shows peaks at sun-spot maxima and these, in turn, may be connected with the relative positions of Jupiter and Saturn (see R. E. de Lury, *Jour. Roy. Ast. Soc. Canada*, 1938, 32, 174), etc.

The Bible does not support astrology of type (a), though a few passages (Gen. 1:14; Job 38:31; Matt. 2) might be astrologically interpreted. It teaches, rather, that God is more to be feared than nature or mere stargazers (Isa. 47:13; Jer. 10:2-3). Paul (Rom. 8:39), choosing astrological terms, states that neither the *zenith* nor the *nadir* of the stars can separate believers from God. His point — fully up to date in our day — is that no known forces of nature can separate us from our Father's love.

BIBLIOGRAPHY

D. C. Allen, *The Star-Crossed Renaissance*; R. Eisler, *The Royal Art of Astrology*.

                                    R. E. D. CLARK

ATHANASIAN CREED. See CREED, CREEDS.

ATHEISM. The term atheism is frequently employed to designate a condition of being without the true God. Thus Paul says that gentile Christians had been "atheists" *atheoi* (Eph. 2:12) before their conversion. See also Rom. 1:28, "they did not see fit to acknowledge God." This usage obviously depends on the point of view of the speaker, for the early Christians themselves were called atheists by the pagans.

In its strictest definition, the term designates the denial of the existence of any god of any kind. Paul, doubtless referring to Dan. 11:36, says of "the man of sin" (II Thess. 2:3-4) that he "opposes and exalts himself above everything called a god or an object of worship." Yet this personage "sits in the temple of God, demonstrating that he himself is god" (author's translation).

The modern naturalists (i.e., pancosmists, antisupernaturalists) in their definitive volume, *Naturalism and the Human Spirit* (Y. Krikorian, ed., Columbia University Press, 1944, pp. 295 f.) in the words of Harry Todd Costello, have "at least one reductionist, or liquidationist thesis: there is no 'supernatural.' God and immortality are myths. William James speaks of the relief which we experience when at last we give up trying to be young or slender. We say, 'Thank God, those illusions are gone.' So the naturalist now looks up to the great white throne, where once sat great Jove himself, and exclaims, 'Thank God, that illusion is gone.' "

The book from which these words are taken might well be called the *Mein Kampf* of atheism. Yet John Dewey, one of the fifteen writers of the book, author of the first chapter, "Antinaturalism in Extremis," does not wish to be called an atheist. In *A Common Faith* (Yale University Press, 1934) he takes strong antisupernatural ground throughout. He even rejects Matthew Arnold's impersonal 'power not ourselves' as reminiscent of 'an external Jehovah' (p. 54). Rejecting all religions, and atheism also, he seeks to retain "religious values" (p. 28). He says, ". . . there are forces in nature and society that generate and support the ideals. . . . It is this *active* relation between ideal and actual to which I would give the name 'God.' I would not insist that the name *must* be given. . . . personally I think it fitting to use the word 'God' to denote . . . uniting of the ideal and the actual . . ." (pp. 51 f.).

Randall and Buchler (*Philosophy, an Introduction,* Barnes and Noble, 1942) very neatly *define* the supernatural out of court: ". . . 'event' is by definition 'natural event,' what test could possibly establish a given one as having 'supernatural' origin?" (p. 170). Nature is defined as "a term which represents all possibilities and all actualities . . ." (p. 177). Yet these philosophers would avoid the label "atheist." They frequently (see "God" and "Theism" in their index) refer to a concept of a god contained within nature.

The above data indicate the difficulty of identifying atheism under the strict definition. Even the explicit denial of every being traditionally called God or a god in western culture does not compel the acceptance of the label. That there are atheists who classify themselves as such in the strictest sense of the word cannot be denied. Robert Flint (*Anti-Theistic Theories,* Wm. Blackwood and Sons, 5th ed., 1894, chap. 1, *passim*) says, ". . . Feuerbach (1804-72) fully meant what he said when he wrote, 'There is no God . . .' " (p. 7). A group centering around Baron P. H. D. d'Holbach (1723-89) in France vigorously professed atheism. An American Association for the Advancement of Atheism was organized in New York in 1925. The second annual report of this association, 1927, is the latest report available in the Library of Congress. The League of Militant Atheists, communistic, was organized in 1929. *An Atheist Manifesto* by Joseph Lewis was published by the Free Thought Press Association, New York, in 1929. E. T. Weiant in *Sources of Modern Mass Atheism in Russia* (published by the author, 1953) calls attention to "a state which has been founded on the conscious premise that there is no God" and gives valuable historical background.

Atheism in theological and philosophical discussion has called forth an enormous literature. *HERE* gives seventeen quarto pages of double column fine print on the subject and includes materials from a variety of ancient and oriental, as well as western, sources.

See also NATURALISM.

J. OLIVER BUSWELL, JR.

ATONEMENT. The atonement is the center of gravity in Christian life and thought because it is the center of gravity in the NT, as a mere census of references immediately demonstrates. According to apostolic preaching and doctrine, the significance of Jesus Christ does not lie supremely in his person or ministry or teaching: it lies supremely in his death upon the cross. In the NT, to be sure, that event is never viewed in isolation from his person, his ministry, and his teaching; nor is it viewed apart from his resurrection (*q.v.*). His death exegetes his teaching, and together with his sin-free, miracle-working ministry of love, constitutes the active obedience of life (to use the Calvinistic formulation) without which the passive obedience of suffering would have been nugatory. Yet it is the event of Christ's death which the NT consistently underscores as all-important, and his death interpreted not as a martyrdom, brought to pass by a miscarriage of justice, but as the offering of a redemptive sacrifice *ephapax* (Heb. 10:1-14). This event, this saving deed, in the whole range of its results, is commonly called the atonement.

But precisely why was the atonement necessary? Precisely what were its effects upon God and man? Precisely how does the sacrifice of the cross avail for human redemption? Concerning the rationale of Christ's saving act there has been and continues to be the widest difference of belief. William J. Wolf's remark that today "there is great confusion about the place of the Cross" (*No Cross, No Crown: A Study of the Atonement,* New York, 1957, p. 17), can be applied retrospectively. The cross has always been central in Christian theology because it is central in the NT, yet the ground of its centrality has been fiercely debated. A survey of the theories which have proliferated across the centuries will show that the biblical data have been hammered into many conflicting shapes, often in forgetfulness of the mold which the word of God itself provides.

I. SOME HISTORIC THEORIES OF SOTERIOLOGY. How best to classify this theoretical proliferation is no trifling problem. Three rubrics may be set up, B. B. Warfield suggests, according to what is regarded as man's fundamental need: is it deliverance from ignorance or misery or sin? If ignorance, then, essentially, the demonstrative view of Abelard obtains; if misery, some modification of the rectoral idea of Grotius holds the field; if sin, then Anselm's satisfaction (q.v.) concept furnishes the ground motif. A fourth theory — Schleiermacher's mystical notion of a germ implanted by Christ which savingly leavens the mass of humanity — Warfield dismisses as a curious side-eddy in the main stream of theology ("Modern Theories of the Atonement," *Studies in Theology*, New York, 1932, pp. 283-5). In his study, *Christus Victor* (London, 1931), Gustaf Aulén also suggests three dominant interpretations. There is, first, the "dramatic" or, as he calls it, the "classic" theory which sees man's liberation from the tyrants of sin, law, death, wrath, and the devil, as the heart of Christ's work. Advocated by the early Fathers, it was stressed especially and originally by Irenaeus. This formulation, which can be denominated Greek or patristic, construes the atonement as a triumphant warfare against evil. There is, second, the "Latin" or "objective" concept; Latin is the preferable designation, however, since the Greek Fathers likewise recognized the objective nature of Jesus' redemptive deed. Stated initially and definitively by Anselm, it holds that Christ's death was a piacular sacrifice by which God's honor was satisfied and his holy judgment propitiated. There is, third, the "subjective" or "moral" concept eloquently advanced by Abelard, which considers the cross to be primarily a moving demonstration of forgiving love, magnetizing and eliciting man's love in response to God's agapaic self-oblation. In Aulén's opinion, under one of these three interpretations, with inevitable overlapping, of course, all other attempted constructs of the atonement may be subsumed. However, we prefer the temporal principle of classification, denoting the periods as Patristic, Medieval, Reformation, and Modern.

A. *The Patristic Period.* The speculations advanced by the Greek Fathers were indeed profound, though the metaphors they employed may impress us as grotesque and unfortunate. Irenaeus (*ca.* 130-*ca.* 200) in his two works, *Against Heresies* and *The Demonstration of the Apostolic Preaching*, taught that Jesus Christ as the second Adam recapitulated human experience, died as a ransom (q.v.) wrested man free from the grasp of the devil,

and so opened up the possibility of an incorruptible life for mortal sinners. "The ransom theory of Irenaeus," Hastings Rashdall tells us, "became, and for nearly a thousand years continued the dominant, orthodox, traditional theory on the subject" (*The Idea of Atonement in Christian Theology*, London, 1919, p. 247). Tertullian (*ca.* 160-*ca.* 220), Clement of Alexandria (150-215), and Origen (*ca.* 185-*ca.* 254) added nothing of particular value to what Irenaeus had set forth. The ransom provided by Christ was paid, Origen argued, not to God but to the devil. In his great defense of orthodox Christology, *On the Incarnation of the Word of God*, Athanasius (*ca.* 296-373) moved within the same general framework, emphasizing man's deliverance from ignorance and corruptibility by the triumph of the cross. Gregory of Nyssa (*ca.* 330-*ca.* 395) introduced some novel modifications, particularly the famous notion that our Lord's humanity (q.v.) was a sort of bait concealing the fishhook of his deity, a lure by which the devil was caught for our saving good and ultimately for his own as well. Gregory of Nazianzus (329-89) raised a strong protest against the accepted doctrine that Christ's death was a ransom paid to either God or the devil. Augustine (354-430) discussed the atonement in his *Enchiridion* and *On the Trinity*, incorporating all the traditional emphases (even venturing in his sermons to picture the cross as a mousetrap baited with the Saviour's blood!), but he stressed too the value of Christ's death as a satisfaction offered to God's justice, and he decisively influenced the vocabulary of Western Christendom by his free use of terms like the fall (q.v.), original sin (q.v.), and justification (q.v.). Cave points out that there are distinctive elements in Augustine's treatment of soteriology since he relates the work of our Lord to the church, argues that the cross was not the sole conceivable mode of redemption but the mode most congruous with the total human situation (an idea Thomas later appropriated), and fixed attention on the reality of Jesus' manhood which enabled him to function as Saviour (*op. cit.*, pp. 121-22). John of Damascus (*ca.* 675-*ca.* 749) summed up this whole era in his *Exposition of the Orthodox Faith* as he chronicled the old interpretations of Christ's death as a ransom to God, as a kind of fishing-expedition which snared the devil, and as a victory which destroyed death, liberated captive sinners, and brought to light life and immortality.

According to the Greek Fathers, whose overriding interest lies not so much in soteriology per se as in the cosmic issues of the incarnation (*q.v.*), Christ is Saviour not simply because he is Victor and Conqueror; he is Saviour because he is also Revealer, Benefactor, Physician, Victim, and Reconciler.

B. *The Medieval Period.* With respect to the atonement one man stands out in this epoch as a creative theologian, Anselm of Canterbury (1033-1109), whose *Cur Deus Homo* is a soteriological milestone. This work attempts by sheer ratiocination to establish the necessity of Christ's death. Man owes God complete obedience; when he fails to render this, he sinfully robs the sovereign Creator of the honor which is his due; because sin is an infinite affront to the divine glory which cannot be remitted simply by the exercise of mercy, God must vindicate himself in keeping with demands of his own holy nature; hence an adequate satisfaction must be offered. But an infinite affront necessitates an infinite satisfaction, and the satisfaction must be offered by the disobedient race. Thus the question, *Cur Deus Homo,* is answered with a logical coerciveness which Anselm considered overwhelming. His critics have stigmatized his logic as illusory, his concept of sin as quantitative, his view of the divine human relationship as impersonally mechanical, his isolation of our Lord's life and resurrection from his death as a misreading of the NT, and his slighting of God's love as an unChristian travesty of the gospel. Yet, even Anselm's critics recognize that his theory is fundamentally, even penetratingly biblical. It stresses the magnitude of sin (*"nondum considerasti quanti ponderis sit peccatum"*). It recognizes that either satisfaction or punishment is mandatory when sin has been committed. It seeks a rationale of the atonement in the very givenness of God's nature. Anselm's formulation has supplied the matrix for both Roman Catholic and Protestant orthodoxy and his satisfaction theory in its essentials continues to find staunch protagonists wherever Scripture is accepted as the authoritative word of God.

Antithetical to the Anselmic theory is that of Abelard (1079-1142), who in his *Epitome of Christian Theology* and his *Commentary on Romans,* advocates the view that our Lord's passion, exhibiting the great love of God, so

frees us from the fear of wrath that we may serve him in love. While Abelard retains the traditional concepts and speaks of Christ's death as a sacrifice offered to the Father, he subordinates everything to the controlling idea that the cross, by demonstrating God's love, draws out man's love almost automatically. Vital as this truth is, when magnified disproportionately it sentimentalizes that divine love which is indubitably the source of the atonement. Instead of holding fast to the NT insistence that the death of Christ changes potentially the relationship between God and man, a potentiality actualized by faith, Abelard reduces the saving event to a tragic martyrdom. A heart-rending spectacle, undoubtedly, the cross as interpreted by Abelard has no inexorable necessitatedness undergirding it. In the moral universe it is an epiphenomenon.

A fierce opponent of Abelard, Bernard of Clairvaux (1090-1153), revived the idea of the atonement as a means of ransoming man from the power of the devil. Thomas Aquinas (*ca.* 1225-74) in his *Summa Theologica* added little that was significant. Building on all his predecessors, he worked out a comprehensive synthesis which included the patristic component of release from bondage to the devil (excluding, however, the more questionable notions which carried Greek sanction), the Anselmic component of satisfaction (though Thomas held with Augustine that the death of Christ was the most suitable mode of redemption, not a mode intrinsically necessary), the Abelardian component of an ethical impact (not exaggerated of course to the point of untruth), and even a penal component, since Thomas held that as our Substitute Jesus Christ bore our punishment. Mere ripples on the river of Christian theology were the views of the medieval nominalists, Scotus (*ca.* 1264-1308), Occam (*ca.* 1300-*ca.* 1349) and Biel (*ca.* 1420-95). No rational vindication of the cross, they maintained, could be projected: God arbitrarily decreed his Son's death as the ground of forgiveness (*q.v.*). A few centuries later Bishop Butler adopted, with modifications, to be sure, the agnostic idea of a divine "acceptilation." Scripture plainly reveals that the death of Jesus saves; how it does so is not disclosed (cf. Wolf, *op. cit.*, pp. 133-34).

C. *The Reformation Period.* With some degree of validity Martin Luther (1483-1546) has been claimed as an exponent of the dramatic theory. Certainly his catechetical writings and his commentaries, notably that on Galatians, lend support to Aulén's interpretation. Yet Luther — unsystematic, paradoxical, antischolastic — regards the atonement as a propitiatory sacrifice. Unhesitatingly he speaks of the cross as placating both the law and the wrath of God and thus setting love at liberty to do its work. "Christ," he asserts, "is punished on our account (propter nos punitur)"; and typically, he asserts again: "The righteous and innocent man must tremble and fear as a poor damned sinner, and in His gentle and innocent heart feel God's wrath and judgment against sin, taste for us eternal death and damnation, and, in sum, suffer all what a damned sinner has earned and must suffer eternally" (cf. Cave op. cit., pp. 154-55). In brief, Luther assigns priority to God's justice rather than his love, an assignment which negates Aulén's claim. While defying neat categorization, Luther aligns himself with Anselm rather than with Irenaeus.

In the hands of Philip Melanchthon (1497-1560) Protestant soteriology begins to assume its characteristic shape. He explains in his Loci Communes that by Christ's death the just demands of the law (q.v.) have been met, the wrath of God has been appeased, and the soul of the sinner liberated from the curse. But it is John Calvin (1509-64), who with his remarkable logic and lucidity definitively formulates the Protestant doctrine in his Institutes of the Christian Religion. Agreeing with Anselm that the atonement is rooted in the nature of God, he contends that not the divine honor but the divine justice must be satisfied. If man is to be redeemed from the curse of sin and death, and more especially from the wrath of his Creator, a sacrifice must be offered. And the sacrifice has been offered! "Christ took upon himself and suffered the punishment which by the righteous judgment of God impended over all sinners, and by this expiation the Father has been satisfied and his wrath appeased" (Institutes of the Christian Religion Book II, chapter 16, Philadelphia, n.d.). In explicating the work of Christ Calvin avails himself of the three rubrics, Prophet, Priest and King. Jesus Christ saves us by performing on our behalf the functions proper to each of these offices (q.v.). As Priest, specifically, he appeases God by his self-oblation, and following his ascension, intercedes perpetually for his people. This, in stark abridgment, is the normative Reformation view, a view which has been continually assailed. It is charged that Calvin denies God's spontaneous love, apotheosizes the principle of retributive justice, and imprisons sovereign grace in a legalistic strait-jacket. But, persuasively espoused by modern Protestants like R. W. Dale, James Denney, Hermann Bavinck, B. B. Warfield, and Louis Berkhof, the satisfaction theory cannot be written off as anachronistic. Nor will it ever be possible to write off this theory as anachronistic until the Bible itself is so adjudged.

Theologizing a philosophy of law, Hugo Grotius (1583-1645) in his Defense of the Catholic Faith construed the atonement as an administrative necessity laid upon God if in his benevolence he would forgive human sin. As ruler of the moral universe, God must see to it that sin's pardon will not prompt man to think it a matter of indifference, a thing to be engaged in with impunity. So God had Jesus Christ die not to expiate his justice but rather to manifest it, furnishing a penal example which served prospectively as a deterrent from sin. Once the safety of the ethical order was thus assured, God could forgive sin on the ground of his clemency.

D. The Modern Period. In his magnum opus, The Christian Faith, Friedrich Schleiermacher (1768-1834) affirmed that Jesus redeems the members of the pistic community by arousing within them a God-consciousness which is the counterpart of his own. According to Albrecht Ritschl (1822-89), whose Justification and Reconciliation exerted an enormous influence, Jesus Christ suffered death in fidelity to his unique vocation as the Founder of God's kingdom. In so doing he took away man's guilt, which is essentially and simply mistrust of the divine love. Emil Brunner (1889-   ) in The Mediator and Karl Barth (1886-   ) in The Doctrine of Reconciliation, Volume IV of his Church Dogmatics, have broken with an immanental liberalism which shriveled the value of the atonement to a subjective influence. Pushing contemporary Protestantism in the direction of a theocentric Christianity, they have restored objective significance to the death of the cross; indeed, Brunner even interprets it as "the expiatory penal sacrifice of the Son of God" (The Mediator, p. 473). While historic orthodoxy takes issue with neo-orthodoxy (q.v.) at a number of crucial points, it is nevertheless grateful that some of the post-liberal theologians (cf., e.g., W. J. Wolf *op. cit.*) insist upon the indispensability of biblical categories for an understanding of the central event of the Bible.

In the recent past, works on the atonement have proliferated to such a degree that even a bare enumeration of titles is impossible here. T. H. Hughes has helpfully summarized most of the relevant literature, except from Continental sources, in *The Atonement: Modern Theories of the Doctrine* (London, 1949).

II. SOME POSTULATES OF NEW TESTAMENT SOTERIOLOGY. Debates between Calvinists and Arminians concerning the scope and application of our Lord's saving work are undoubtedly warranted, but in this context apology must supersede polemic. Let us therefore highlight those factors which are imperative if we are to interpret the atonement biblically.

1. The atonement cannot be interpreted biblically unless we are prepared to examine our own presuppositions and retain those which undergird the apostolic concept. Hence it is highly encouraging to witness among scholars a sustained attempt to go "Back to the Bible" in formulating their theories about the atonement. (Cf. T. H. Hughes, *op. cit.*, p. 164). For, if Scripture is the word of God, then once its teaching has been determined by a proper hermeneutic, we are faced with a choice between submission or disobedience. That teaching may seem irrational and unethical to the man who moves outside the revelational orbit; but precisely because of that he may be challenged to examine the validity of his own presuppositions. Of course, he may ignore so drastic a challenge. Thus Canon Vernon F. Storrs in *The Problem of the Cross* agrees with Hastings Rashdall that "it is impossible to get rid of the idea of substitution or of vicarious punishment from any faithful representation of St. Paul's doctrine"; yet Storrs immediately adds, "We are in no way bound to accept Paul's interpretation of Christ's death. I dismiss from my mind all ideas of substitution, or of the innocent paying the penalty of the guilty because these ideas offend my moral consciousness" (Hughes, *ibid.*, p. 61). But one who accepts the Scriptures in faith is bound to accept Paul's interpretation of Christ's death, submissively allowing his sin-distorted moral consciousness and mental functioning to be corrected by the divine norm. "Back to the Bible!" must be no empty shibboleth but rather an all-controlling

principle in our thinking about the atonement as well as about everything else.

2. Personal relationships constitute the essence and furnish the meaning of reality. These personal relationships include the I-Thou relationships between the Creator and his human creatures together with the I-Thou relationships among the members of the Trinity themselves. James Denney is therefore unimpeachably right when he contends that Christianity, "the highest form of religion," teaches "the existence of a personal God and of personal relations between God and man"; moreover, Denney says, "Christianity is unique in its doctrine of reconciliation through atonement," and "the heart of the reconciliation lies in the readjustment or the restoration of a true personal relation between God and the creature which has lapsed into its own act of alienation against Him; in other words, it consists in the forgiveness of sins" (*The Christian Doctrine of Reconciliation*, New York, 1918, pp. 5-6). If this is steadily remembered, biblical soteriology will be spared from the charge that it is sub-personal.

3. While God is loving, he is likewise holy: his self-integrity requires that he maintain and assert himself as self-derived, self-sufficient, and self-giving. And his glory lies in the creature's voluntary adoration of the Creator's holiness. Ultimately, then, it is God's intrinsic nature which explains the atonement. So, after quoting the statement in Matt. 16:21, "From that time forth began Jesus to shew unto his disciples, how that he must go unto Jerusalem, and suffer many things," W. J. Wolf comments, "It is in the mystery of that word 'must' that all subsequent Christian doctrines of the atonement are rooted" (*op. cit.*, p. 64). God's holiness alone accounts for the necessity of the cross.

4. Yet, while God is holy, he is also loving. And in his love he wills to bear the suffering which man's sin has produced. Consequently, far from negating the basic truth of divine love, the death of Jesus Christ discloses it. The death of Jesus Christ discloses that "The last reality is beyond sin. It is a love which submits to all that sin can do, yet does not deny itself, but loves the sinner through it all. It is a love which in Scripture language bears sin, yet receives and regenerates sinners" (James Denney, *op cit.*, p. 20). Thus, Denney avers, it is to the atonement that "we owe the very idea that God is love" (*ibid.*, p. 186).

(Cf. Leon Morris, *The Apostolic Preaching of the Cross,* Grand Rapids, Michigan, 1955, p. 180).

5. Man is a sinner, the creature who through the misuse of his love-bestowed freedom alienates himself from God and incurs both guilt and wrath. The human predicament created by sin is vividly set forth in the metaphors which the NT authors employ in describing the work of Jesus Christ. As a sinner, man is a slave who must be redeemed, an enemy who must be reconciled, a corpse which must be resurrected, a captive whose powerful oppressors must be overthrown, a criminal who must be justified. These metaphors, as Wolf remarks, are nothing less than "startling" (*op. cit.,* p. 82); taken together, they unveil the NT understanding of our human predicament no less than the amazing deed which our Lord has performed. For by the cross he has extricated man from this predicament. (Cf. on this point Leon Morris, *op. cit.;* Eric Wahlstrom, *The New Life in Christ,* Philadelphia, 1950; Adolph Deissmann, *Paul,* New York, 1926; *Light from the Ancient East,* New York, 1927.)

It is man's sin which poses God's dilemma: can he possibly be just to himself and yet justify his disobedient creature (Rom. 3:26)? Wolf phrases the problem strikingly: "How can a God of holy love accept sinners without destroying His holiness or sentimentalizing love into an immoral indifference to wrong? This question is the fundamental one for every theory of the atonement" (*op. cit.,* p. 84).

6. When the concepts of holiness and sin are brought together, they call irrepressibly for the concept of wrath (*q.v.*). The legitimacy of this concept has been hotly disputed, however. Lately, e.g., Anthony Tyrell Hanson has attempted to prove that in Paul's teaching references to divine wrath are merely the apostle's semantic equivalents for the impersonal process by which the consequences of human sin work themselves out in history (*The Wrath of the Lamb,* London, 1957). But this deistic notion can scarcely be squared with the NT which depicts divine wrath no less than divine mercy as a personal activity of God, an activity which springs from an attitude. Pertinent and devastating is H. Wheeler Robinson's judgment: "This wrath of God is not the blind and automatic working of abstract law — always a fiction, since 'law' is a conception, not an entity, till it finds expression through its instruments. The wrath of God is the wrath of divine personality" (*Redemption and Revelation,* London, 1942, p. 269).

We must purge from the concept of wrath all admixture of human limitation, sinful vindictiveness, and unethical pique. At the same time we must refuse to hide behind the smokescreen of anthropopathism. Wrath is no less anthropopathic than love. There is no irreconcilable antithesis between love and wrath. As Wolf points out, such an antithesis "springs from the poverty of our imagination" (*op. cit.,* p. 187). God's love is not akin to the mechanical gushing forth of a fountain. It is a personal attitude which is passionately concerned about genuine relationship. When love does not elicit love, there is, as even parental affection on the human level reveals, a reaction of pain, anger, and estrangement. Eliminate the possibility of wrath and God's love is flattened out into a sub-personal indifferentism. Retain this concept, on the other hand, and the grace (*q.v.*) of God has meaning. Emil Brunner for one perceives the involvement of love and wrath when he speaks of "the divine mystery of love in the midst of the reality of wrath" (*hilastērion*) (op. cit., p. 520).

7. In resolving what man sees as a dilemma and in rescuing man from his dire predicament, God by the death of Christ carries out an action which is bewilderingly vast and manysided, an action which has cosmic and eternal effects. Hence all the startling biblical metaphors are esssential, whether drawn from market place, slave trade, military campaign, temple sacrifice, or law court. But Warfield is incontestably correct when he maintains that the writers of the NT "enshrine at the center of this work its efficacy as a piacular sacrifice, securing the forgiveness of sin; that is to say, relieving its beneficiaries of 'the penal consequences which otherwise the curse of the broken law inevitably entails'" (*Atonement, op. cit.,* p. 262). Wolf is simply buttressing Warfield's position when he declares that Paul's "chief metaphor for atonement . . . is the law court, used by him in a very complex way" (*op. cit.,* p. 84). In other words, the piacular sacrifice of our Lord is interpreted by its greatest exegete in legal categories. Vehement objection has been leveled, as one might expect, against the apostolic teaching on this score. But the use of legal categories is not to be confounded with legalism; and the edge of this very common criticism is blunted once we

grasp, as Forsyth does, that "the holy law is not the creation of God but His nature" (*The Atonement and Modern Religious Thought: A Theological Symposium*, London, 1903, p. 69), and once we grasp, as E. A. Knox does, that lawlessness is "antagonism to that principle of law which is of the very essence of the nature of God" (*The Glad Tidings of Reconciliation, London,* 1916, p. 127n). With these insights securely grasped, we can insist that the concept of justification bears no legalistic taint.

But Wolf states that Paul uses legal categories such as justification solely to undercut them; he uses the language of the law court to show that God does what no good judge would think of doing as in grace he nullifies his own law. But does he? Abraham asked long before Paul, "Shall not the judge of all the earth do right?" (Gen. 18:25). And in justification God does right. God does what the supreme Judge ought to do. He refuses to waive the demands of the law. Rather than that, in love he himself meets the law's demand through the vicarious sacrifice of Jesus Christ. Thus instead of making void his law, God establishes it (Rom. 3:31). Justification certainly embodies paradoxical elements, but it is not quite the irrational paradox C. H. Dodd construes it to be (*Commentary on the Romans,* ed. J. Moffatt, London, 1932, p. 52).

8. Woven inextricably into the NT doctrine of the atonement is the fact of substitution. Here again objection has been raised. Bishop G. Bromley Oxnam protests in his *A Testament of the Faith,* "We hear much of the substitutionary theory of the atonement. This theory to me is immoral. If Jesus paid it all, or if He is the substitute for me, or if He is the sacrifice for all the sin of the world, then why discuss forgiveness? The books are closed. Another has paid the debt, borne the penalty. I owe nothing. I am absolved. I cannot see forgiveness as predicated upon the act of some one else. It is my sin. I must atone" (Boston, 1958, p. 144). This autosoteric criticism fails to appreciate that, according to the NT, Jesus Christ in love identified himself with us and we in faith identify ourselves with him.

9. If we are faithful to the NT data, we cannot deny that the atonement of Jesus Christ has a penal aspect. He became the object of retributive justice and hence bore our punishment. No doubt some formulations of this truth have been untruthfully distorted. No doubt, too, there are theologians who believe that any such theory implies a transfer of guiltiness both unethical and impossible (e.g., T. H. Hughes, *op. cit.,* pp. 69-70). But even Barth, who thinks the concept of a wrath-placating satisfaction foreign to the Bible, nevertheless declines to exclude the idea of substitutionary punishment from the NT, an idea which in his opinion rests back upon Isa. 53: "If Jesus Christ has followed our way as sinners to the end to which it leads, in outer darkness, then we can say with that passage from the Old Testament that He has suffered this punishment of ours" (*op. cit.,* p. 253). Leonard Hodgson likewise refuses to relinquish the penal aspect of the atonement, arguing that in Jesus Christ the punisher and the punished are one (*The Doctrine of the Atonement,* London, 1951, p. 142). James Denney also holds fast to this view (*op. cit.,* p. 273). And, if Hastings Rashdall may be quoted against himself, it is instructive to notice his comment on II Cor. 5:21: "This can hardly mean anything but that God treated the sinless Christ as if He were guilty, and inflicted upon Him the punishment which our sins had deserved; and that this infliction made it possible to treat the sinful as if they were actually righteous." To be sure, Rashdall adds that only a mere handful of such passages are discoverable in the Pauline corpus, yet almost ruefully he confesses, "There they are, and St. Paul's argument is unintelligible without them" (*op. cit.,* p. 94). With J. K. Mozley, then, "We need not shrink from saying that Christ bore penal suffering for us in our stead" (*The Doctrine of the Atonement,* London, 1947, p. 216).

10. The objectivity of the atonement is taken for granted in the NT. It is a work done outside man, wrought for him at a point in history and only after that applied to him, a work which possesses value for God and which reconciles him to man before it reconciles man to God. The atonement, to state it otherwise, is objective actually and subjective potentially. "Reduced to its simplest expression," Denney writes, "what an objective atonement means is that but for Christ and His Passion God would not *be* to us what He is. . . . The alternative is to say that quite independent of any value which Christ and His Passion have for God, God would still be to us what He is. But this is really to put Christ out of Christianity altogether, and needs no refutation" (*op. cit.,* p.

239). Though the atonement did not alter God's nature, it assuredly altered his relationship to his sinful creature. But in magnifying the Godward side of the atonement, the NT does :not minimize the manward side in the least. Granted that the apostolic authors are one with Vincent Taylor in their diffidence concerning "the psychology of man's response" (*Forgiveness and Reconciliation*, London, 1946, p. 108), yet that very response — made possible by sovereign grace, illumination, and power, a response of understanding, faith, gratitude, obedience, and love — looms large in their proclamation of the gospel. Nor does the NT ignore such factors as our union with the living Christ, our enablement by the indwelling Holy Spirit, and our incorporation into the church of which our Lord is the Head. And all these factors render biblical soteriology profoundly ethical.

11. When we have done our utmost to fathom the meaning of the cross, we must still confess that it embodies unfathomable mystery. Hence there is an element of truth in Alan Richardson's assertion: "The atonement in the New Testament is a mystery, not a problem. One can construct theories and offer them as solutions of problems, but one cannot theorize about the deep mystery of our redemption. The New Testament does not do so; it offers us not theories but vivid metaphors, which can, if we will let them operate in our imagination, make real to us the saving truth of our redemption by Christ's self-offering in our behalf" (*An Introduction to the Theology of the New Testament,* London, 1958, pp. 222-3). Yet in that statement there is also an element of untruth; for the NT does contain a theory in the sense of rational explanation, an interpretation which we must enter into imaginatively no doubt and which does not light up all the deep depths of mystery but which at any rate enables us in adoring love and wonder to sing:

Bearing shame and scoffing rude,
In my place condemned He stood;
Sealed my pardon with His blood:
Hallelujah! what a Saviour!

BIBLIOGRAPHY

In the works referred to in the body of this article—notably those by Cave, Warfield, Hughes, Morris, and Wolf—as well as in the standard theologies, expert guidance to the immense literature on the atonement from ancient and modern sources alike is available.

VERNON C. GROUNDS

ATTRIBUTES, THE DIVINE. The divine attributes are, in the language of ordinary conversation, simply the characteristics or qualities of God. As water is wet and fire hot, so God is eternal, immutable, omnipotent, just, holy, and so on. Perhaps these divine characteristics are quite numerous; but usually it is only the more comprehensive terms that are discussed.

Beneath this simplicity lurk some of the most intricate problems and some of the most futile discussions ever attempted by theology. Taking their start from Aristotle's confused theory of categories, theologians have analyzed God into an unknowable substratum, called his substance or essence, on the surface of which lay the knowable attributes, much like a visible coat of paint on a table-top that could never be seen or touched. Luther and Calvin made a great advance when they buried this scholastic rubbish, though it has been dug up more than once since.

ASEITY is a barbarous Latinism to indicate God's absolute independence. He depends *a se,* on himself. He is self-existent. Sometimes, on the assumption that every reality must have a cause, God has been said to be the cause of himself. In this case he would also have to be the effect of himself; but the terms *cause* and *effect* must be stretched beyond any ordinary meaning, if only a single reality is in view. It would be more intelligible to say that God is the necessary Being — a phrase used in the ontological argument for God's existence. In some imaginary polytheistic system there might be several self-existent beings and no creation *ex nihilo;* but in its biblical context the aseity of God and the doctrine of creation are inseparable. Certainly creation *ex nihilo* presupposes God's self-existence.

The ETERNITY of God also seems to be involved in his aseity. The two appear to be in reality the same thing. If God does not exist in virtue of some external cause, but is self-existent, he could not have come into being; for it is inconceivable that a pure nothing should suddenly generate a self-existent God. Furthermore, if time is a function of the created mind, as St. Augustine said, or a function of moving bodies, as Aristotle taught, and is therefore an aspect of the universe, it follows that God transcends temporal relationships.

IMMUTABILITY follows upon aseity and eternity. Time and change are together denied of God. "They shall be changed, but thou art the same" (Heb. 1:12). If self-existence should change, it would become dependent existence; eternity would become time; perfection imperfection; and therefore God would become not-God. Cf. Num. 23:19; Ps. 33:11; Mal. 3:6; James 1:17.

INFINITY is hardly different from the preceding. Infinite means unlimited. What is self-existent must be unlimited. Infinite has sometimes meant indefinite or imperfect, from which it has been concluded that an infinite God could not have the limitation or definiteness of personality. This ancient usage is not what is intended. God is not the vague "boundless" of Anaximander; he is thoroughly definite. Etymology to the contrary, his definite attributes are in-finite. Nothing limits his power, wisdom, justice, and so on.

OMNIPOTENCE means that God can do all things. See the entry on GOD. Sophistic objections are sometimes brought against divine omnipotence by raising pseudo-problems. Can God create a stone so heavy that he cannot lift it? Can God draw a square with only three sides? These questions involve self-contradictions, are therefore meaningless, and set no real problem. With omnipotence should be joined sovereignty. God is the Supreme Being.

OMNIPRESENCE, Ubiquity, and Immensity refer to God's relation to all space. To put it simply, God is everywhere. Cf. Ps. 139:7. Instead of saying God is everywhere in the world, it might be better to say that everywhere in the world is in God; for "in him we live and move, and have our being" (Acts 17:28). The difficulty is that God is not an extended, spatial being; God is a Spirit; and the preposition *in* cannot be used in its spatial sense. There are non-spatial senses: note the second *in* in the preceding sentence. Omnipresence therefore means that God knows and controls everything. It hardly differs from omnipotence.

OMNISCIENCE means that God knows all things. Why should he not? He made all things and decided their history. He works "all things after the counsel of his own will" (Eph. 1:11).

Theologians have argued whether these attributes are really distinct and different in God, or only seem different to us. Both positions have been defended. Some theologians have tried to straddle the question by saying that the attributes are not *really* different, nor merely *apparently* different to us, but are *virtually* different. It is hard to attach a meaning to such a vague expression. The short account above might suggest that the attributes are not only the same in God, but with a little thought they appear to be the same to us too.

Distinguished from these previous attributes, sometimes awkwardly named the natural attributes, is a second set called the moral attributes: WISDOM, JUSTICE, HOLINESS, GOODNESS, and the like. Neither group has a logical principle of derivation, and therefore there is no fixed number. The moral attributes are not too easily defined, but are better described by the scriptural passages that refer to them. With respect to wisdom one might cite: "The Lord is a God of knowledge" (I Sam. 2:3); and "His understanding is infinite" (Ps. 147:5). As for justice: "All his ways are judgment, a God of truth and without iniquity, just and right is he" (Deut. 32:4); and "to declare at this time his righteousness, that he might be just and the justifier of him which believeth in Jesus" (Rom. 3:26). Holiness is sometimes thought of as a synonym for justice and righteousness; it has also been given a root meaning of *separate,* from which the inference has been drawn that holiness is not an "attribute" but an effect of the attributes: the attributes separate God from all else.

At first sight these moral attributes seem more distinguishable among themselves than the natural attributes are, and still more distinguishable from the natural attributes. Yet justice is easily interpreted as a particular form of wisdom, and this merges with omniscience. Similarly righteousness is an expression of God's sovereignty in maintaining the divine legislation, and this is an exercise of power and knowledge. The unity of the attributes therefore is a thesis that cannot be thoughtlessly dismissed.

See also GOD, KNOWLEDGE.

GORDON H. CLARK

AUGSBURG CONFESSION. The first great Protestant symbol, or statement of belief, read in German before the Diet of Augsburg on June 25, 1530, by Christian Beyer, Vice-Chancellor of Saxony. The document was drafted by Melanchthon with the approval of Luther and signed by seven princes. The Confession is divided into two parts, the first containing twenty-one articles of faith and the second listing the seven principal abuses calling for reform. It was incorporated in the

Book of Concord in 1580 and is thus still authoritative for the Lutheran body. For text, see P. Schaff, *Creeds of Christendom*, III, pp. 3-73.

A. SKEVINGTON WOOD

AUGUSTINIANISM. A term applied to both the philosophy and the theology of Augustine (354-430), Bishop of Hippo.

Augustinianism as a philosophy has been regarded by some as a Christianized Platonism, an attempt to bring Plato into the stream of Christian thought by making certain necessary changes and by using Christianity as the means of answering the questions raised by classical philosophy against a Platonic background. By others the Augustinianism philosophy has been regarded as the greatest attempt in the history of the church to offer a Christian world and life view, a biblical philosophy which would clearly show the futility of all philosophic application apart from Christian doctrine. Augustinianism as a philosophy frequently used Platonic terms to set forth Christian concepts, and for this reason Augustine has been suspected of Platonic leanings. Its distinguishing characteristics were its emphasis upon the will rather than upon the intellect, and its doctrine of the divine enlightenment of the soul as the source of human knowledge. In his *De Civitate Dei* he brought forth the first Christian philosophy of history.

As a theology, Augustinianism represents the supreme achievement of the early church in the realm of theological advance. Augustine brought to completion the doctrinal achievements and aspirations of the first four centuries of Christian scholarship. He gave to the Western church, in his *De Trinitate,* a masterful exposition of the doctrine of the Trinity. In other writings he set forth, with clarity and a faithfulness to the Scriptures, the doctrines of the sovereignty of God, the total depravity of man, and election and predestination. In his emphasis on man's inability to achieve righteousness and the truth that man is saved by sovereign grace alone, Augustine made his greatest contribution to the church through the ages, and directly influenced Calvin, Luther, and the other Reformers, but his doctrine of the church and baptismal regeneration was a contributing factor, in the hands of late theologians, to the growth of the Roman Catholic conception of the church and its sacraments. However, in a very real sense, the Reformation was essentially the result of the revival of Augustinianism within the Roman Catholic Church of the later Middle Ages and the ensuing conflict with the decaying Scholasticism.

BIBLIOGRAPHY
Charles Norris Cochrane, *Christianity and Classical Culture;* B. B. Warfield, "Augustine" in *HERE;* Warfield, *Studies in Tertullian and Augustine.*

GREGG SINGER

AUTHENTICITY. As applied to a book of the Bible, authenticity indicates the state of possessing authority on the basis of being the production of its professed author. It is to be distinguished from genuineness, which denotes the quality of being uncorrupted from the original. An authentic document is one written by the hand from whom it professes to be (Jerome *Comm. in Ep. ad Titum* iii. 9), but a genuine writing is one whose received text is not corrupt. Thus the Epistle to the Romans is authentic since Paul wrote it, but Rom. 8:1b is not a genuine text because of the manuscript evidence against it.

WALTER W. WESSEL

AUTHORITY. The word *exousia,* usually translated "authority," or "power" in the sense of authority (*potestas*), is employed in many different references in the NT. It may indicate the power to forgive sins (Luke 5:24), the power to drive out spirits (Mark 6:7), the privilege of divine sonship (John 1:12), the authority of civil rulers (John 19:10), the control of possessions (I Cor. 9:4), marital rights or responsibilities (cf. I Cor. 7:4), apostolic privilege (I Cor. 9:6), the general kingship of Christ (Matt. 28:18), or, more specifically, the authority of the word and work of Christ (Matt. 7:29 and parallels) as compared with that of the scribes. The thoughts of right, privilege, and compulsive power are all gathered up in the concept.

The Bible makes it plain that the true source and seat of authority is in God. This is true even of civil power (Rom. 13:1), though on earth and especially in heaven there are usurped powers which God defeats and destroys (cf. Eph. 3:10; Col. 2:15). But it is even more true in relation to the spiritual sphere. God alone can forgive sins (Mark 2:7), reveal absolute truth, and speak with the note of absolute command (cf. Luke 7:8). No human authority can stand unless it derives from God and is subservient to him.

The divine authority, however, is exercised in and through the Son of God. If he resists the temptation to receive worldly honor from the devil, it is because he is already "the head of all principality and power" (Col. 2:10) and is destined to be exalted as such by God. Thus even civil government will finally revert to Christ as it derives from him. But he also has the power to forgive sins (Mark 2:10), to liberate from demonic forces (Matt. 9:8), to vanquish sickness and death (cf. John 10:18), and to teach and command with all the right and compulsion of God himself (Mark 1:22, 27). The divine authority itself is embodied in Jesus Christ, and it is by this absolute authority that every relative civil or ecclesiastical authority must be measured.

Yet Jesus Christ does not exercise his authority directly between his comings. Hence it is right and proper that there should be relative authorities with a valid claim to human obedience. The forces of law and order constitute such an authority in the civil sphere, and are thus to be honored not in virtue of their inherent validity but in virtue of their divinely given function and commission. A similar though less equivocal position is occupied in the ecclesiastical sphere by the apostles as the primary and authoritative witnesses to the word and work of Jesus Christ incarnate, crucified, and risen.

But how is apostolic authority exercised in the post-apostolic period? This is the critical issue in modern discussions of spiritual or ecclesiastical authority, which rest on the common assumption that absolute authority belongs to Christ alone and secondary authority to the apostles, but then see this authority exercised today in a variety of ways. Thus some argue that the apostles have transmitted their authority to episcopal successors, or that the church itself is authoritative, or that there is an authoritative apostolic tradition in addition to the written testimony of the NT, or that the first interpretations and decisions of the early church have a distinctive authority, so that there is at least a continual interplay of authorities in the church under the direction of the Holy Spirit.

Now it may be admitted that there are spheres of life in the church where the church itself, whether local or universal, has a certain right to take order, e.g., in the regulation of worship, the exercise of discipline, and even the closer definition of doctrine. It may also be allowed that what has been done by past ages in fulfilment of this right, e.g., in the

decisions and canons of early councils, is not without a certain weight. To this extent, proper account must be taken of the various claims to authority advanced in contemporary discussion.

In the Bible itself, however, there seems to be no clear warrant for assuming that the apostolic authority has now been inherited by others. The apostles alone are primary witnesses to Christ, and mediate authority is ascribed only to them. Hence, if the apostolic authority has not lapsed altogether, it is preserved in their writings as the inspired and normative testimony through which Christ himself still speaks and works by the Spirit. In other words, it is through the Bible that Jesus Christ now exercises his divine authority, imparting authoritative truth, issuing authoritative commands and imposing an authoritative norm by which all the arrangements or statements made by the church must be shaped and corrected.

BIBLIOGRAPHY
J. N. Geldenhuys, *Supreme Authority;* J. Gresham Machen, *The Christian Faith in the Modern World,* pp. 73-86; W. M. McPheeters in *HDCG;* F. L. Patton, *Fundamental Christianity,* pp. 96-173; A. Sabatier, *Religions of Authority and the Religion of the Spirit;* R. R. Williams, *Authority in the Apostolic Age.*

W. C. G. PROCTOR

AVARICE. See COVETOUSNESS.

AVENGE. While by Semitic custom it was the duty of the *gōēl* (next-of-kin) to avenge a relative's murder by procuring the slayer's death, justice concerned the whole clan (II Kings 9:26; Num. 31:2). Hebrew legislation sought to limit the vendetta to the actual criminal (Deut. 24:16), to provide asylum (Deut. 19:2-7), and to exempt accidental homicide. *Ekdikeō* is used of (a) procuring justice: e.g., for the widow in Luke 18:5; (b) divine vengeance for the blood of martyrs (Rev. 6:10) or at the last judgment (II Thess. 1:8; cf. *hēmerai ekdikeseōs,* Luke 21:22); and (c) avenging oneself (Rom. 12:19). (Although justice may be obtained from the authorities as God's avengers (Rom. 13:4), Christians are required to leave vengeance to God, who has become the ultimate *gōēl* in Rev. 19:2).

BIBLIOGRAPHY
Arndt; *HDB; HERE;* W. M. Thomson, *The Land and the Book,* pp. 289-92.

DENIS H. TONGUE

AWAKENING. The theological concept is based on passages likening spiritual death to sleep (I Thess. 5:6; Rom. 13:11; Eph. 5:14). The Shorter Oxford English Dictionary defines "awaken" in theological usage as "to arouse to a sense of sin" (1603), quoting Wesley: "Just awakening, and darkly feeling after God." It is the beginning of the divine work of conversion, whereby the sinner, previously indifferent and inactive towards God, is made aware of his condition and of God's claims upon him. Heb. 6:4-6 and 10:26 indicate that awakening is not yet full regeneration and the awakened person may subsequently reject God. An "awakening" in modern usage is a synonym for a mass spiritual revival.

J. CLEMENT CONNELL

AWE. See FEAR.

B

BAAL. See GODS.

BABYLON. Babylon, like Jerusalem, has a three-fold significance in Scripture — historic, prophetic, and symbolic (or typical). Historically, it may refer to the great city on the Euphrates River, to the kingdom of Babylon, or to the plain referred to as Babylonia. The empire of Babylon was used by God in the final defeat of Judah and the destruction of Jerusalem. Nebuchadnezzar begins the times of the Gentiles (Jer. 27:1-11; Dan. 2:37-38). The final and complete destruction of Babylon is foretold in the prophets (Isa. 13:17-22; Jer. 25:12-14). The city fell to the Medes in 539 B.C., but the vast desolation spoken of by the prophets has not yet come to pass.

Three primary passages (Isa. 13, 14, 47; Jer. 50, 51; Rev. 16:17 — 19:5) predict Babylon's ultimate destiny. The universal sweep, particularly in Isaiah's prophecy, exceeding the scope of Babylon even in the days of its greatest glory, suggests that many aspects of this prediction have not yet been fulfilled. God did not change the whole earth when Babylon fell; in fact, the city was not destroyed at that time.

Our chief concern is with the significance of Babylon in the Book of Revelation. The characteristics of the people of the land of Shinar — rebellion against God, self-sufficiency, lust for power and glory (Gen. 8:10; 11:1-9) — have marked the history of Babylon through the centuries and are basic in the Babylon passage of the Apocalypse.

The exact meaning of the term Babylon in the Revelation has been disputed from the times of the Church Fathers. Called a harlot repeatedly (17:1, 5, 15, 16), she is said to be seated on many waters, which are defined as peoples (vs. 15). She is also portrayed as sitting upon a scarlet colored beast, who represents worldly powers arrayed against the Lamb of God. The beast ultimately turns upon the harlot to destroy her. In Rev. 18 Babylon is given prominence as a commercial power.

What is the meaning of Babylon in these passages? The older commentators tended to make it a prophecy of the evil world. Others have insisted on a specific geographical reference, such as Jerusalem. But the mention of rivers and ships and extensive commercial activity does not fit the holy city. Others have identified Babylon with the city of Rome, basing the identification largely on the mention of seven hills (Rev. 17:9). The fundamental objection to this interpretation is that the persecution of the Christians by the Roman empire stopped at the advent of Constantine, whereas Rome was only taken by the barbarians a century later. Still another view refers the passage to literal Babylon on the Euphrates, which is now a heap of sand and ruins (so Seiss, Pember, et al). Others believe that the reference is symbolical, that Babylon is not to be defined geographically but ecclesiastically. Some in this group interpret Babylon of the papacy, which through the centuries has persecuted multitudes of the saints of God. The Reformers shared this view. Others of this group understand the passage as a description not so much of the Roman Church at the end of this age as of apostate Christendom as a whole. One may consult Auberlen, *The Prophecies of Daniel and the*

Revelation and the notes of Craven in the Lange Commentary.

Whatever be the final conclusion on the identity of Babylon, the following factors are clear: (1) at the end of this age two powerful forces, a federation of nations and an ecclesiastical apostate body, will unitedly exercise jurisdiction over the world; (2) there will be a persecution of the saints of God; (3) a godless, economic, commercial world-wide activity will hold sway; (4) a dual judgment will bring this condition of abomination to an end; (5) the ecclesiastical power will be torn to pieces by the federation of nations; and (6) the whole ungodly system, staggering in the drunkenness of Babylonian pride, power and wealth, will be destroyed by an act of God, which will bring rejoicing to the people of God (Rev. 18:20). If there is any chronological sequence in these last chapters of the Book of Revelation, this judgment on Babylon will soon be followed by the battle of Armageddon (*q.v.*).

WILBUR M. SMITH

BAPTISM. Deriving from the Greek *baptisma*, "baptism" denotes the action of washing or plunging in water, which from the earliest days (Acts 2:41) has been used as the rite of Christian initiation. Its origins have been variously traced to the OT purifications, the lustrations of Jewish sects and parallel pagan washings, but there can be no doubt that baptism as we know it begins with the baptism of John. Christ himself, both by precedent (Matt. 3:13) and precept (Matt. 28:19), gives us authority for its observance. On this basis it has been practiced by almost all Christians, though attempts have been made to replace it by a baptism of fire or the Spirit in terms of Matt. 3:11.

In essence the action is an extremely simple one, though pregnant with meaning. It consists in a going in or under the baptismal water in the name of Christ (Acts 19:5) or more commonly the Trinity (Matt. 28:19). Immersion was fairly certainly the original practice and continued in general use up to the Middle Ages. The Reformers agreed that this best brought out the meaning of baptism as a death and resurrection, but even the early Anabaptists did not think it essential so long as the subject goes under the water. The type of water and circumstances of administration are not important, though it seems necessary that there should be a preaching and confession of Christ as integral parts of the administration (cf. Acts 8:37). Other ceremonies may be used at discretion so long as they are not unscriptural and do not distract from the true action, like the complicated and rather superstitious ceremonial of the medieval and modern Roman Church.

Discussion has been raised concerning the proper ministers and subjects of the action. In the first instance there may be agreement with Augustine that Christ himself is the true minister ("he shall baptize you," Matt. 3:11). But Christ does not give the external baptism directly; he commits this to his disciples (John 4:2). This is taken to mean that baptism should be administered by those to whom there is entrusted by inward and outward calling the ministry of word and sacrament, though laymen have been allowed to baptize in the Roman Church (cf. LAY BAPTISM), and some early Baptists conceived the strange notion of baptizing themselves. Normally baptism belongs to the public ministry of the church.

As concerns the subjects, the main difference is between those who practice the baptism of the children of confessing Christians and those who insist upon a personal confession as a prerequisite. This point is considered in the two separate articles devoted to the two positions and need not detain us in this exposition of positive baptismal teaching. It may be noted, however, that adult baptisms continue in all churches, that confession is everywhere considered important, and that Baptists often feel impelled to an act of dedication of children. Among adults it has been a common practice to refuse baptism to those unwilling to leave doubtful callings, though the attempt of one sect to impose a minimum age of thirty years did not meet with common approval. In the case of children there has been misgiving concerning the infants of parents whose profession of Christian faith is very obviously nominal or insincere. The special case of the mentally defective demands sympathetic treatment, but there is no warrant for prenatal or forced baptisms, and even less for baptism of inanimate objects such as was practiced in the Middle Ages.

A clue to the meaning of "baptism" is given by three OT types: the Flood (I Pet. 3:19 f.), the Red Sea (I Cor. 10:1 f.) and circumcision (Col. 2:11 f.). These all refer in different ways to the divine covenant, to its provisional fulfilment in a divine act of judgment and grace, and to the coming and definitive fulfilment in the baptism of the cross. The conjunction of water with death and redemption is particularly apt in the case of the first two; the covenantal aspect is more particularly emphasized in the third.

When we come to the action itself, there are many different but interrelated associations which claim our attention. The most obvious is that of washing (Titus 3:5), the cleansing water being linked with the blood of Christ on the one side and the purifying action of the Spirit on the other (see I John 5:6, 8), so that we are brought at once to the divine work of reconciliation. A second is that of initiation, adoption, or, more especially, regeneration (John 3:5), the emphasis again being placed on the operation of the Spirit in virtue of the work of Christ.

These various themes find common focus in the primary thought of baptism (in the destructive, yet also life-giving, power of water) as a drowning and an emergence to new life, i.e., a death and resurrection (Rom. 6:3 f.). But here again the true witness of the action is to the work of God in the substitutionary death and resurrection of Christ. This identification with sinners in judgment and renewal is what Jesus accepts when he comes to the baptism of John and fulfils when he takes his place between two thieves on the cross (Luke 12:50). Here we have the real baptism of the NT, which makes possible the baptism of our identification with Christ and underlies and is attested by the outward sign. Like preaching and the Lord's Supper, "baptism" is an evangelical word telling us that Christ has died and risen again in our place, so that we are dead and alive again in him, with him, and through him (Rom. 6:4, 11).

Like all preaching, however, baptism carries with it the call to that which we should do in response or correspondence to what Christ has done for us. We, too, must make our movement of death and resurrection, not to add to what Christ has done, nor to complete it, nor to compete with it, but in grateful acceptance and application. We do this in three related ways constantly kept before us by our baptism: the initial response of repentance and faith (Gal. 2:20); the lifelong process of mortification and renewal (Eph. 4:22 f.); and the final dissolution and resurrection of the body (I Cor. 15). This rich signification of baptism, which is irrespective of the time or manner of baptism, is the primary theme which ought to occupy us in baptismal discussion and preaching. But it must be emphasized continually that this personal acceptance or entry is not independent of the once for all and substitutionary work of Christ, which is the true baptism.

It is forgetfulness of this point which leads to misunderstanding of the so-called grace of baptism. This may be by its virtual denial. Baptism has no grace apart from its psychological effects. It is primarily a sign of something that we do, and its value may be assessed only in explicable religious terms. The fact that spiritual gifts and even faith itself are true gifts of the Holy Spirit, with an element of the mysterious and incalculable, is thus denied.

On the other hand, it may be by distortion or exaggeration. Baptism means the almost automatic infusion of a mysterious substance which accomplishes a miraculous but not very obvious transformation. It is thus to be regarded with awe, and fulfilled as an action of absolute necessity to salvation except in very special cases. The true mystery of the Holy Spirit yields before ecclesiastical magic and theological sophistry.

But, when baptismal grace is brought into proper relationship to the work of God, we are helped on the way to a fruitful understanding. First, and above all, we remember that behind the external action there lies the true baptism which is that of the shed blood of Christ. Baptismal grace is the grace of this true reality of baptism, i.e., of the substitutionary work of Christ, or of Christ himself. Only in this sense can we legitimately speak of grace, but in this sense we can and must.

Second, we remember that behind the external action there lies the inward operation of the Spirit moving the recipient to faith in Christ's work, and accomplishing regeneration to the life of faith. Baptismal grace is the grace of this internal work of the Spirit, which cannot be presumed (for the Spirit is sovereign) but which we dare to believe where there is a true calling on the name of the Lord.

Third, the action itself is divinely ordained as a means of grace, i.e., a means to present Christ and therefore to fulfil the attesting work of the Spirit. It does not do this by the mere performance of the prescribed rite; it does it in and through its meaning. Nor does it do it alone; its function is primarily to seal and confirm, and therefore it does it in conjunction with the spoken and written word. It need not do it at the time of administration; for, under the gracious sovereignty of the Spirit, its fruition may come at a much later date. It does not do it automatically; for, whereas Christ is aways presented and his grace remains, there are those who respond neither to word nor sacrament and therefore miss the true and inward meaning and power.

When we think in these terms, we can see that there is and ought to be a real, though not a magical baptismal grace which is not affected greatly by the detailed time or mode of administration. The essentials are that we use it (1) to present Christ, (2) in prayer to the Holy Spirit, (3) in trustful dependence upon his sovereign work, and (4) in conjunction with the spoken word. Restored to this evangelical use, and freed especially from distorting and unhelpful controversy, baptism might quickly manifest again its power as a summons to live increasingly, or even to begin to live, the life which is ours in Christ crucified and risen for us.

BIBLIOGRAPHY

G. W. Bromiley, *Baptism and the Anglican Reformers;* J. Calvin, *Institutes,* IV, pp. 14-15; W. F. Flemington, *The New Testament Doctrine of Baptism; HERE,* "Baptism"; Reports on Baptism in the Church of Scotland, 1955 f.

GEOFFREY W. BROMILEY

BAPTISM, BELIEVERS'. Where the gospel is first preached, or Christian profession has lapsed, baptism is always administered on confession of penitence and faith. In this sense believers' baptism, i.e., the baptism of those who make a profession of faith, has been an accepted and persistent phenomenon in the church. Yet there are powerful groups amongst Christians who think that we should go further than this. Believers' baptism as they see it is not merely legitimate; it is the only true baptism according to the NT, especially, though not necessarily, in the form of immersion.

This is seen first from the precept which underlies its institution. When Jesus commanded the apostles to baptize, he told them first to make disciples and said nothing whatever about infants (Matt. 28:19). In other words, preaching must always precede baptism, for it is by the word and not the sacrament that disciples are first made. Baptism can be given only when the recipient has re-

sponded to the word in penitence and faith, and it is to be followed at once by a course of more detailed instruction.

That the apostles understood it in this way is evident from the precedents which have come down to us in Acts. On the day of Pentecost, for example, Peter told the conscience-stricken people to repent and be baptized, nor did he mention any special conditions for infants incapable of repentance (Acts 2:38). Again, when the Ethiopian eunuch desired baptism, he was told that there could be no hindrance so long as he believed, and it was on confession of faith that Philip baptized him (Acts 8:36 ff.). Even when whole households were baptized, we are normally told that they first heard the gospel preached and either believed or received an endowment of the Spirit (cf. Acts 10:45; 16:32 f.). In any case, no mention is made of any other type of baptism.

The meaning of baptism as developed by Paul in Rom. 6 supports this contention. It is in repentance and faith that we are identified with Jesus Christ in his death, burial, and resurrection. To infants who cannot hear the word and make the appropriate response, it thus seems to be meaningless and even misleading to speak of baptism into the death and resurrection of Christ. The confessing believer alone knows what this means and can work it out in his life. In baptism, confessing his penitence and faith, he has really turned his back on the old life and begun to live the new life in Christ. He alone can look back to a meaningful conversion or regeneration and thus receive the confirmation and accept the challenge which comes with baptism. To introduce any other form of baptism is to open the way to perversion or misconception.

To be sure, there is no direct prohibition of infant baptism in the NT. But in the absence of direction either way it is surely better to carry out the sacrament or ordinance as obviously commanded and practiced than to rely on exegetical or theological inference for a different administration. This is particularly the case in view of the weakness or irrelevance of many of the considerations advanced.

Christ's blessing of the children, for example, shows us that the gospel is for little ones, and that we have a duty to bring them to Christ, but it says nothing whatever about administering baptism contrary to the acknowledged rule (Mark 10:13 ff.). Again, the fact that certain characters may be filled with the Spirit from childhood (Luke 1:15) suggests that God may work in infants, but it gives us no warrant to suppose that he normally does so, or that he does so in any given case, or that baptism may be given before this work finds expression in individual repentance and faith. Again, the children of Christians enjoy privileges and perhaps even a status which cannot be ascribed to others. They are reckoned in some sense "holy" by God (I Cor. 7:14). But here too there is no express connection with baptism or the baptismal identification with Jesus Christ in death and resurrection.

Reference to the household baptisms of Acts is of no greater help. The probability may well be that some of these households included infants, yet this is by no means certain. Even if they did, it is unlikely that the infants were present when the word was preached, and there is no indication that any infants were actually baptized. At very best this could only be a hazardous inference, and the general drift of the narratives seems to be in a very different direction.

Nor does it serve to introduce the OT sign of circumcision. There is certainly a kinship between the signs. But there are also great differences. The fact that the one was given to infant boys on a fixed day is no argument for giving the other to all children some time in infancy. They belong, if not to different covenants, at least to different dispensations of the one covenant: the one to a preparatory stage, when a national people was singled out and its sons belonged naturally to the people of God; the other to the fulfilment, when the Israel of God is spiritual and children are added by spiritual rather than natural regeneration. In any case, God himself gave a clear command to circumcize the male descendants of Abraham; he has given no similar command to baptize the male and female descendants of Christians.

Theologically, the insistence upon believers' baptism in all cases seems better calculated to serve the true significance and benefit of baptism and to avoid the errors which so easily threaten it. Only when there is personal confession before baptism can it be seen that personal repentance and faith are necessary to salvation through Christ, and that these do not come magically but through hearing the word of God. With believers' baptism the ordinance achieves its significance as the mark of a step from darkness and death to light and life. The recipient is thus confirmed in the decision which he has taken, brought into the living company of the regenerate, which is the true church (see BAPTISTS), and encouraged to walk in the new life which he has begun.

This means that in believers' baptism faith is given its proper weight and sense. The need for faith is recognized, of course, in infant baptism. It is contended that infants may believe by a special work of the Spirit, or that their present or future faith is confessed by the parents or sponsors, or that the parents or sponsors exercise vicarious faith, or even that faith is given in, with, or under the administration. Some of these notions are manifestly unscriptural. In others there is a measure of truth. But none of them meets the requirement of a personal confession of personal faith as invariably fulfilled in believers' baptism.

Again, believers' baptism also carries with it a genuine, as opposed to a spurious, baptismal grace. The expression of repentance and faith in baptism gives conscious assurance of forgiveness and regeneration and carries with it an unmistakable summons to mortification and renewal. Properly understood, this may also be the case with infant baptism, as in the Reformed churches. But a good deal of embarrassed explanation is necessary to make this clear, and there is always the risk of a false understanding, as in the medieval and Romanist view of baptismal regeneration (q.v.). Baptism on profession of faith is the only effective safeguard against the dangerous notion that baptism itself can automatically transfer the graces which it represents.

To the exegetical and theological considerations there may also be added some less important but noteworthy historical arguments. First, there is no decisive evidence for a common Jewish practice of infant baptism in apostolic times. Second, the patristic statements linking infant baptism with the apostles are fragmentary and unconvincing in the earlier stages. Third, examples of believers' baptism are common in the first centuries and a continuing, if suppressed, witness has always been borne to this requirement. Fourth, the development of infant baptism seems to be linked with the incursion of pagan notions and practices. Finally, there is evidence of greater evangelistic incisiveness and evangelical purity of doctrine where this form of baptism is recognized to be the baptism of the NT.

BIBLIOGRAPHY

K. Barth, *The Teaching of the Church Regarding Baptism;* A. Booth, *Paedobaptism examined;* A. Carson, *Baptism in its Modes and Subjects;* J. Gill, *Body of Divinity,* Vol. III; *Infant Baptism To-day* (1948); J. Warns, *Baptism,* Eng. trans.

GEOFFREY W. BROMILEY

BAPTISM, INFANT. In a missionary situation, the first subjects of baptism are always converts. But throughout Christian history, as attested already by Irenaeus and Origen with a reference back to the apostles, it has also been given to the children of professing believers. This has not been solely on grounds of tradition, or in consequence of a perversion, but for what have been regarded as scriptural reasons.

To be sure, there is no direct command to baptize infants. But there is also no prohibition. Again, if we have no clear-cut example of an infant baptism in the NT, there may well have been such in the household baptisms of Acts, and there is also no instance of the child of Christians being baptized on profession of faith. In other words, no decisive guidance is given by direct precept or precedent.

Yet there are two lines of biblical study which are thought to give convincing reasons for the practice. The first is a consideration of detailed passages or statements from the Old and New Testaments. The second is a consideration of the whole underlying theology of baptism as it comes before us in the Bible.

To begin with the detailed passages, we naturally turn first to the types of baptism found in the OT. All these favor the view that God deals with families rather than individuals. When Noah is saved from the flood, his whole family is received with him into the ark (cf. I Pet. 3:20-21). When Abraham is given the covenant sign of circumcision, he is commanded to administer it to all the male members of his house (Gen. 17, and cf. Col. 2:11-12 for the connection between baptism and circumcision). At the Red Sea it is all Israel (men, women and children) which passes through the waters in the great act of redemption which foreshadows not only the sign of baptism but the work of God behind it (cf. I Cor. 10:1-2).

In the NT the ministry of our Lord is particularly rich in relevant statements. He himself becomes a child, and as such is conceived of the Holy Spirit. The Baptist, too, is filled with the Spirit from his mother's womb, so that he might have been a fit subject for baptism no less than circumcision very early in life. Later, Christ receives and blesses the little ones (Matt. 19:13 f.) and is angry when his disciples rebuff them (Mark 10:14). He says that the things of God are revealed to babes rather than the wise and prudent (Luke 10:21). He takes up the statement of Ps. 8:2 about the praise of sucklings (Matt. 21:16). He warns against the danger of offending against little ones that believe in him (Matt. 18:6), and in the same context says that to be Christians we have not to become adults but to become as children.

In the first preaching in Acts it is noticeable that Peter confirms the covenant procedure of the OT with the words: "The promise is unto you, and to your children." In the light of the OT background, and the similar procedure in proselyte baptisms, there is little reason to doubt that the household baptisms would include any children who might belong to the families concerned.

When we come to the Epistles, we find that children are particularly addressed in Ephesians, Colossians and probably I John. We also have the important statement in I Cor. 7:14 in which Paul speaks of the children of marriages which have become "mixed" by conversion as "holy." This cannot refer to their civil status, but can only mean that they belong to the covenant people, and therefore will obviously have a right to the covenant sign.

It will be noted that in different ways all these statements bring before us the covenant membership of the children of professing believers. They thus introduce us directly to the biblical understanding of baptism which provides the second line of support for baptizing infants.

As the Bible sees it, baptism is not primarily a sign of repentance and faith on the part of the baptized. It is not a sign of anything that we do at all. It is a covenant sign (like circumcision, but without blood-shedding), and therefore a sign of the work of God on our behalf which precedes and makes possible our own responsive movement.

It is a sign of the gracious election of the Father who plans and establishes the covenant. It is therefore a sign of God's calling. Abraham no less than his descendants was first

BAPTISM FOR THE DEAD

chosen and called by God (Gen. 12:1). Israel was separated to the Lord because he himself had said: "I will be your God, and ye shall be my people" (Jer. 7:23). Of all disciples it must be said: "Ye have not chosen me, but I have chosen you" (John 15:16). The elective will of God in Christ extends to those who are far off as well as nigh, and the sign of it may be extended not only to those who have responded, but to their children growing up in the sphere of the divine choice and calling.

But baptism is also a sign of the substitutionary work of the Son in which the covenant is fulfilled. As a witness of death and resurrection, it attests the death and resurrection of the One for the many without whose vicarious action no work even of repentance and faith can be of any avail. It preaches Christ himself as the One who is already dead and risen, so that all are dead and risen in him (II Cor. 5:14; Col. 3:1) even before the movements of repentance and faith which they are summoned to make in identification with him. This substitutionary work is not merely for those who have already believed. It may and must be preached to all, and the sign and seal given both to those who accept it and to the children who will be brought up with the knowledge of what God has already done for them once for all and all-sufficiently in Christ.

Finally, baptism is a sign of the regenerative work of the Holy Spirit by which individuals are brought into the covenant in the responsive movement of repentance and faith. But the Holy Spirit is sovereign (John 3:8). He works how and when and in whom he pleases. He laughs at human impossibilities (Luke 1:37). He is often present before his ministry is perceived, and his operation is not necessarily coextensive with our apprehension of it. He does not disdain the minds of the undeveloped as fit subjects for the beginning, or if he so disposes the completion, of his work. So long as there is prayer to the Spirit, and a readiness to preach the evangelical word when the opportunity comes, infants may be regarded as within the sphere of this life-giving work which it is the office of baptism to sign and seal.

Where infant baptism is practiced, it is right and necessary that those who grow to maturity should make their own confession of faith. But they do so with the clear witness that it is not this which saves them, but the work of God already done for them before they believed.

The possibility arises, of course, that they will not make this confession, or do so formally. But this cannot be avoided by a different mode of administration. It is a problem of preaching and teaching. And even if they do not believe, or do so nominally, their prior baptism as a sign of the work of God is a constant witness to call or finally to condemn them.

On the mission field adult baptism will naturally continue. In days of apostasy it can and will be common even in evangelized lands. Indeed, as a witness to the fact that our response is really demanded it is good for the church that there should always be a Baptist section within it. But once the gospel has gained an entry into a family or community, there is good scriptural and theological ground that infant baptism should be the normal practice.

BIBLIOGRAPHY
G. W. Bromiley, *The Baptism of Infants*; J. Calvin, *Instit.*, IV, 16, O. Cullman, *Baptism in the New Testament*; P. C. Marcel, *The Biblical Doctrine of Infant Baptism*; Reports on Baptism in the Church of Scotland, (1955 f.); W. Wall, *The History of Infant Baptism*.

GEOFFREY W. BROMILEY

BAPTISM FOR THE DEAD. The problem of baptism for the dead arises out of the question asked by Paul in I Cor. 15:29: "Else what shall they do which are baptized for the dead, if the dead rise not at all? Why are they then baptized for the dead?" Various interpretations have been suggested for this verse. Some take it that the Apostle refers to a practice of vicarious baptism as later reported among the Marcionites and Novationists. On this view, he is not necessarily approving it, but using it for the sake of the argument. The Cataphryges seem to have derived from it a baptizing of corpses. Others construe it as a baptism of the dying, or the administration of the sacrament "over dead men's graves." Most commentators try to avoid any connection with an actual practice, and there is again a wide range of suggestion. Baptism is to fill up the ranks left vacant by the dead, or under the inspiration of their witness, or with a view to death and resurrection in Christ, or more specifically in token that we are dead but may seek our new and true life in the Resurrected. Whatever the exact signification, the wider meaning is undoubtedly that baptism is a witness to the resurrection.

BIBLIOGRAPHY
H. A. W. Meyer, *I Corinthians*, II, p. 271 f.; A.

Plummer, *HDB*, I, p. 245; A. Robertson and A. Plummer, *ICC*, p. 359.

GEOFFREY W. BROMILEY

BAPTISMAL REGENERATION. Twice in the NT a connection is made between water, or washing in water, and regeneration. In John 3:3 we are told that a man must be born of water and of the Spirit to enter the kingdom of God. And in Titus 3:5 we read that we are saved "by the washing of regeneration, and renewing of the Holy Ghost." In view of these passages, of the interrelationship of baptism with Christ's resurrection, and of the fact that it is the sacrament of initiation, it is inevitable that there should be some equation between baptism and regeneration. This equation is most strongly made in the phrase "baptismal regeneration."

The phrase as such is not wholly objectionable so long as the following points are kept clearly in view. The new life of the Christian is in Christ born, crucified, and risen for us. Incorporation into Christ is the work of the Holy Spirit. The true baptism behind the sacramental rite is this saving action of Christ and the Holy Ghost. The rite itself, in conjunction with the word, attests this work and is a means used by the Holy Spirit to its outworking in the believer. Baptism is not regeneration, however, nor regeneration baptism, except in this deeper sense and context.

Unfortunately, medieval t h e o l o g y was tempted into a twofold isolation, that of the believer's regeneration from the substitutionary work of Christ, and that of the rite from baptism in its full and basic sense. In these circumstances the relationship between baptism and regeneration was necessarily misunderstood. "Regeneration" became the supernatural transformation of the believer and "baptism" a divinely appointed means of operation automatically efficacious so long as no bar (e.g., of insincerity) is opposed. The presuming of an absolute necessity of baptism, the emptying of regeneration of any true significance, and the whole problem of post-baptismal sin were evils which resulted from this perverted doctrine.

The Reformers clearly saw and rejected this perversion. But they did not make the mistake of breaking the relationship and treating baptism only as a symbolic rite with psychological effects. Rather, they tried to work back to the true and biblical understanding corrupted in the Romanist scheme. This certainly involves the danger of fresh misunderstanding, as emerges in the famous Gorham controversy in England. Hence the actual phrase "baptismal regeneration" is much better avoided. But in the long run the best antidote to perversion is the true and positive doctrine.

BIBLIOGRAPHY

G. W. Bromiley, *Baptism and the Anglican Reformers*, pp. 1 ff. and 168 ff.; J. B. Mozley, *The Baptismal Controversy*; J. C. S. Nias, *Gorham and the Bishop of Exeter.*

GEOFFREY W. BROMILEY

BAPTISTS. It is a popular misunderstanding about Baptists to think that their chief concern is with the administration of baptism. The convictions of Baptists are based primarily on the spiritual nature of the church, and the practice of believers' baptism arises only as a corollary of this and in the light of the NT teaching. The theological position taken up by Baptists may be presented as follows.

I. THE MEMBERSHIP OF THE CHURCH. According to the belief of Baptists, the church is composed of those who have been born again by the Holy Spirit and who have been brought to personal and saving faith in the Lord Jesus Christ. A living and direct acquaintance with Christ is, therefore, held to be basic to church membership. Negatively, this involves a rejection of the concept that equates a church with a nation. Membership of the church of Christ is not based on the accident or privilege of birth, either in a Christian country or in a Christian family. Baptists, therefore, repudiate the Anglican and Presbyterian view by deleting the phrase "together with their children" from the definition of the church. Positively, this view of church membership indicates that the church is entered voluntarily and that only believers may participate in its ordinances. All members are equal in status although they vary in gifts.

II. THE NATURE OF THE CHURCH. In distinction from churches of the institutional or territorial kind, the Baptist conviction is expressed in the concept of the "gathered church." The members of the church are joined together by God into a fellowship of life and service under the lordship of Christ. Its members are pledged to live together under his laws and to enter into the fellowship created and maintained by the Holy Spirit. The church conceived of in this way is perceived the most clearly in its local manifestation. Thus, although the church invisible consists of all the redeemed, in heaven and in earth, past, present, and future, it may be truly said that wherever believers are living together in the fellowship of the gospel and under the sovereignty of Christ there is the church.

III. The Government of the Church. Christ is the only Head of the church, and the early Baptist pioneers earnestly contended for what they called "the crown rights of the Redeemer." The local church is autonomous, and this principle of government is sometimes described as the "congregational order of the churches." Baptists believe in the competence of the local fellowship to govern its own affairs, and because of the theological importance of the local church in contradistinction to connectional systems (episcopal, presbyterian, or methodist) of church government, Baptists do not speak of the denomination as "the Baptist church," but as "the Baptist churches" in any given area. The congregational order of the churches, that is to say, the government of the church through the mind of the local congregation, is not to be equated with the humanistic concept of democracy. Democracy is too low and too small a word. The Baptist belief is that the church is to be governed, not by an order of priests, nor through higher or central courts, but through the voice of the Holy Spirit in the hearts of the members in each local assembly. Whereas in a strictly democratic order of church government there would be a government of the church *by* the church, the Baptist position makes recognition of Christ's rule in the church *through* the church. From the equality of status of every church member and the recognition of the diversity of gifts, two things follow. First of all, it is acknowledged that each member has a right and duty in the government of the local church, and secondly, that the church gladly accepts the guidance of its chosen leaders. Baptist churches are usually regarded as independent in their government, but they do not glory in independency for its own sake. The independence of a Baptist church relates to state control, and the Baptists of the seventeenth century in England were in the foremost rank of those who fought for this freedom. Baptists have always recognized the great value of association between churches, and associations of Baptist churches have been characteristic of Baptist life down the centuries. All such association is voluntary, however, and the mistake must not be made of assuming that the Baptist Union or the Baptist World Alliance is coextensive with the Baptist community.

IV. The Ordinances of the Church. These are normally spoken of as two, namely, believers' baptism and the Lord's Supper, though it would be more proper to speak of three and to include the ordinance of preaching. Baptists have normally preferred to use the word ordinance rather than sacrament because of certain sacerdotal ideas that the word sacrament has gathered to itself. The word ordinance points to the ordaining authority of Christ which lies behind the practice. Baptists regard the Lord's Supper somewhat after the Zwinglian manner. The bread and the wine are the divinely given tokens of the Lord's saving grace, "but the value of the service lies far more in the symbolism of the whole than in the actual elements" (Dakin). Henry Cook writes: "Being symbolic of facts that constitute the heart of the Gospel, they (the ordinances) arouse in the believing soul such feelings of awe and love and prayer that God is able by His Spirit to communicate Himself in a vitalising and enriching experience of His grace and power." Baptists acknowledge that the ordinances are thus a means of grace, but not otherwise than is also the preaching of the gospel. The position has been epitomized by saying that the ordinances are a special means of grace but not a means of special grace. It is also part of the Baptist position on this subject that believers' baptism and the Lord's Supper are church ordinances, that is to say, they are congregational rather than individual acts. Priestly mediation is abhorrent to Baptists and derogatory to the glory of Christ, who is the only Priest. For a detailed discussion of believers' baptism, see the article under that title.

V. The Ministry of the Church. The ministry is as broad as the fellowship of the church, yet for the purposes of leadership, the term ministry has been reserved for those who have the responsibility of oversight and instruction. Baptists do not believe in a ministerial order in the sense of a priestly caste. The Baptist minister has no "more" grace than the one who is not a minister: he does not stand any nearer to God by virtue of his official position than does the humblest member of the church. There are diverse gifts, however, and it is recognized that the gift of ministry is by the grace of God, as Paul himself intimated in Eph. 3:8. Pastors and deacons are chosen and appointed by the local church, though their appointment is frequently made in the wider context of the fellowship of Baptist churches. A Baptist minister becomes so by virtue of an inward call of God which, in turn, receives confirmation in the outward call of a church. Public acknowledgment of this call of God is given in a service of ordination, which ordination, it is held, does not confer any kind of superior or ministerial grace but merely recognizes and regularizes the ministry within the church itself. The importance of ordination lies in the fact that the church itself preaches through the minister; and, though ordination is not intended to imprison the activity of the Holy Spirit within the bounds of ecclesiastically ordained preachers, there is, nevertheless, considerable importance attached to the due authorization of those who are to speak in the name of the church.

VI. The Ecumenicity of the Church. The "Appeal to all Christian Believers" issued by the Lambeth Conference in 1920 was prayerfully considered by the Baptist churches. In 1926 these churches published a reply in the course of which the position of Baptists in relation to other denominations was expounded unequivocally. This reply, which was adopted by the Assembly of the Baptist Union at Leeds during that year, contains the following paragraphs.

"We associate ourselves with our Anglican brethren in longing and prayer for a larger unity among all who follow and serve our Lord and Saviour Jesus Christ. . . .

"We reverence and obey the Lord Jesus Christ, our God and Saviour, as the sole and absolute authority in all matters pertaining to faith and practice, as revealed in the Scriptures, and we hold that each church has liberty to interpret and administer His laws. We do not judge the conscience of those who take another view, but we believe that this principle of the freedom of the individual church under Christ has the sanction of Scripture and the justification of history, and therefore we cannot abandon it without being false to our trust. Moreover, it is plain to us that the headship and sole authority of our Lord in His Church excludes any such relations with the State as may impair its liberty.

"This view of the Church determines our attitude towards the special issues raised by the Lambeth Appeal. . . .

"Because we hold the Church to be a community of Christian believers, the ordinance of baptism is administered among us to those only who make a personal confession of repentance and faith. . . . In our judgment the baptism of infants incapable of offering a personal confession of faith subverts the conception of the Church as the fellowship of such believers. . . .

"The Lord's Supper is observed regularly and devoutly by our churches. Its value for us depends upon both the presence of our Lord and the faith with which we receive the bread and wine that show forth His redemptive sacrifice; but not upon the official position of a celebrant or upon any change in the elements due to words of consecration. It seems to us contrary to the simplicity that is in Christ that the full effect of the Lord's Supper as a means of grace should be held to depend on Episcopal ordination."

BIBLIOGRAPHY

A. C. Underwood, *History of English Baptists;* H. Wheeler-Robinson, *Baptist Principles;* Henry Cook, *What Baptists Stand For;* A. Dakin, *The Baptist View of the Church and Ministry.*

Ernest Frederick Kevan

BARBARIAN. *Barbaros* is an onomatopoeic word which originated by imitating the unintelligible sounds of people who spoke a language foreign to Greek. It thus became a designation for those who spoke in such a tongue or possessed a foreign culture.

The word is used in four different places in the NT: in Acts 28:2, 4 of the natives (so rendered in the RSV) of Malta without derogatory overtones; in Rom. 1:14 of Greeks to indicate the universality of Paul's apostleship; in I Cor. 14:11 of one who speaks an unintelligible language; and in Col. 3:11 in a bad sense as one of the social distinctions which finds no place in Christianity.

Walter W. Wessel

BATH QOL. See Voice.

BEAST. See Antichrist.

BEATIFIC VISION. A term used for the vision of God in himself. Our Lord taught: "Blessed are the pure in heart, for they shall see God." Absolute purity, that is, complete freedom from sin, is necessary in order that one may enjoy the presence of God. Roman Catholic theology makes this one reason for believing in purgatory (where sin is completely purged away). Evangelical theology, however, teaches that faith in Christ, as exhibited by the true believer, leads to acceptance by God, and being brought into his presence in Christ Jesus, who presents us "faultless before the presence of His glory" (Jude 24). The vision of God will be enjoyed in the final consummation of all things in Christ.

W. C. G. PROCTOR

BEATIFICATION. Beatification is the stage next to final canonization (*q.v.*) of a saint in the Roman Catholic Church. The process of canonization is governed by decrees of Pope Urban VIII in 1625, 1634, and 1642, and of succeeding popes since his time. The first mover in the cause for the beatification must be the bishop of the diocese to which the candidate belonged. The Congregation of Rites which conducts the examination must be assured that the deceased enjoys a reputation for sanctity and miracles and that no worship (*cultus*) has yet been paid to him. When beatification has been declared by the pope, which will not normally be for at least fifty years after death, the title of Blessed is accorded to the candidate, and his *cultus* is permitted in a specific diocese, religious order, or province.

RICHARD J. COATES

BEELZEBUB. In the OT the name is Beelzebub, "lord of flies" (II Kings 1:2 ff.), referring to a god of the Philistines. In NT times the Jews used it as an epithet for the prince of demons (Matt. 12:24). "It is a well-known phenomenon in the history of religions that the gods of one nation become the devils of its neighbors and enemies" (T. Rees in *ISBE*). Some of Jesus' contemporaries derogated our Lord by alleging that he was possessed by Beelzebub and thereby wrought miracles (Mark 3:22). Jesus was able to expose the baselessness of this charge and in so doing strongly assert that his works actually betokened the arrival of the kingdom of God (Luke 11:14-20).

EVERETT F. HARRISON

BEGINNING. The Greek word *archē* is frequently used in the NT to mark the initial point from which a series of events began. The most important of these uses are in reference to creation (Heb. 1:10; Matt. 19:4; II Pet. 3:4), to the ministry of Jesus (Luke 1:2; John 15:27; 16:4, I John 2:24; 3:11; II John 5, 6), to the point of entry into Christian salvation (II Thess. 2:13) and to the commencement of the devil's sin (I John 3:8; John 8:44).

Far-reaching theological significance attaches to John 1:1 and I John 1:1, in both of which the beginning is connected with the Logos. Its meaning in these contexts has been much discussed, but it seems reasonably certain that the reference must be determined by the $b^e r \bar{e} \check{s} \hat{\imath} t$ of Gen. 1:1, i.e., as a reference to the initial moment of creation. It does not of itself contain the notion of eternity, but this must be implied where it is used with the imperfect verb "was." This suggests that the Logos was already in existence at the time of the creation, and, as Godet remarks, "what is anterior to time must belong to the order of eternity" (*Commentary on John*, Vol. I, 1888, p. 330).

A significant change in the preposition can be observed when John 1:1 is compared with I John 1:1, for the *ap' archēs* of the latter points to what has already been operative in time although looking back to an initial point, whereas *en archē* in John 1:1 looks beyond time to that which was already existent when time began.

In I John 2:13 Christ is described as "him that is from the beginning," the center of the Christian revelation. Christian theology is always looking back to its beginning, and this in the Johannine sense must be sought in the pre-existent Word. This conception is an immeasurable advance on the contemporary Jewish Messianism. The pre-eminence of Christ is marked by the use of the same Greek word as a title in Col. 1:18.

BIBLIOGRAPHY

Arndt; G. Delling in TWNT; J. H. Bernard, *ICC* (*John*); B. F. Westcott, *Epistles of John*.

DONALD GUTHRIE

BEGOTTEN. This is a favorite Johannine term, commonly translated "born" and used metaphorically especially in the phrase "begotten of God" (*gennētheis ek tou Theou*), or usually, "born of God" (*gegennēmenos ek tou Theou*), the latter with reference to the new birth (John 3:5, 6), by which a person becomes a believer in Christ (John 1:12, 13). In general this new, spiritual birth (begetting) is ascribed to God (John 1:13; I John 3:9; 4:7; 5:1, 4, 18); in particular, to the Holy Spirit (John 3:5, 6) and, indirectly at least, to Christ as in I John 2:29, where the words "is born of him" (*ex autou gegennētai*) refer to our Lord, of whom vs. 28 speaks. This is in agreement with John's emphasis on the Trinity, especially on Christ's deity, and the oneness of the divine essence (John 10:30) and operation (John 5:19). In I John 5:18 the words: "He who was born of God" (RSV; cf. AV, "is begotten" are referred by some to the believer as parallel with: "He that is born of God" (*gegennēmenos ek tou Theou*) though the reference to Christ is preferable. The aorist *gennētheis* describes the action as once for all accomplished, while the perfects *gegennētai*, *gegennēmenos* designate continuance of the completed action, the believer abiding in the faith. The metaphorical use of the verb *gennaō*, however, is found also elsewhere in the NT. When in I Cor. 4:15 Paul writes *"dia tou euaggeliou egō humas egennēsa"* (cf. Philem. 10), he is speaking of the new, spiritual birth by God.

See also REGENERATION.

BIBLIOGRAPHY
Arndt; MM; Vincent; Meyer, *First Epistle of John*, pp. 437-625.

J. THEODORE MUELLER

BELIAL. See ANTICHRIST.

BELIEF. See FAITH.

BELOVED. The term *agapētos* occurs over sixty times in the NT. In the Synoptic Gospels it is six times applied to Christ as God's beloved Son, as also in II Peter 1:17. In each case the declaration was made by the voice from heaven in connection with Jesus' baptism or transfiguration (*q.v.*). Elsewhere — it is not found in John's Gospel — the adjective is applied to Christians. Occurring frequently in the plural in direct address, it might be translated "dear friends" (Arndt, p. 6). Eight times in his epistles John addresses his readers as "beloved." The same usage is prominent in II Peter (5 times) and Jude (3 times). In Paul's epistles it is frequently translated "dearly beloved" (AV). D. M. Pratt writes: "The beauty, unity, endearment of this love is historically unique, being peculiarly Christian" (*ISBE*, I, p. 432).

In the OT the word "beloved" is found in the Song of Solomon twenty-six times out of a total of forty-two. But in the NT it is used only of divine and Christian love (*q.v.*). Though *agapētos* inclines strongly toward "only beloved" (Arndt, p. 6), it is probably not to be taken as synonymous with "only begotten (*q.v.*).

RALPH EARLE

BENEDICTION. By this term is meant an act or pronouncement of blessing. The

Aaronic benediction was given to Aaron and his sons as a part of their ministry in God's behalf toward the people, and is epitomized as a putting of God's name upon them (Num. 6:22-27). The NT parallel is the apostolic benediction (II Cor. 13:14), which reflects the progress of revelation by its emphasis on the Trinity. Other passages, notably Eph. 3:20-21, Heb. 13:20-21, and Jude 24-25, are often treated as benedictions by members of the clergy. The question to be settled here is whether these are true benedictions or whether they are prayers. In the benediction the minister acts on behalf of God in pronouncing a blessing upon the congregation, whereas in a prayer he is the representative of the people, voicing a supplication to God on their behalf. It appears that in the strict application of the term there is only one benediction in the OT and one in the NT. Even more sharply is the benediction to be distinguished from the salutation, which is a common feature of the opening portion of the NT epistles (e.g., Gal. 1:3). Such salutations are the counterpart of the greetings found in the everyday letters of the hellenistic period, but they inject a spiritual flavor into the greeting which lifts it above the commonplace. It hardly need be said that the practice of inventing benedictions which are not framed in the language of Scripture is of doubtful propriety.

In Roman Catholic theory the virtue of the benediction which is regarded as quasi-automatic in its efficacy, increases with the rank of the one who pronounces it. "The higher the hierarchical position of him who bestows the blessing, the more powerful it is" (Achelis). It is common practice to "bless" objects also, giving them either a temporary or a permanent character of holiness. In modern times Romanism has introduced the Benediction of the Blessed Sacrament. The priest having taken the Host and placed it in the monstrance, then incenses the Blessed Sacrament. After appropriate singing and prayer, the priest makes the sign of the cross with the monstrance (still containing the Host) over the people. This benediction is given in silence.

BIBLIOGRAPHY
E. C. Achelis in *SHERK*; Blunt; W. H. Dolbeer, *The Benediction*; J. W. Kapp in *ISBE*.

EVERETT F. HARRISON

BETRAYAL. The word *paradidōmi* means to hand over or give up, as in reference to the arrest of Jesus and his deliverance to Jewish and Roman authorities.

The betrayal of Jesus plays a large part in the Gospel narratives. Jesus predicts it (Matt. 17:22; Mark 9:31; Luke 9:44; Matt. 20:19; Mark 10:33; Luke 18:32). Jesus knows Judas' character (John 6:46, 70-71). Judas conspires with the authorities (Matt. 26:14-16; Mark 14:10-11; Luke 22:3-6). Jesus shows that he knows one disciple will betray him (Matt. 26:21-25; Mark 14:18-21; Luke 22:21-23). In the experience itself Jesus' poise and act of mercy overshadows the treachery (Matt. 26:47-56; Mark 14:43-52; Luke 22:47-53; John 18:1-11).

Jesus' being given over to Pilate is much more strongly emphasized than his deliverance to Jewish authorities. It is Pilate who hands him over to death.

The betrayal has great theological significance. There is the guilt of the betrayer (John 19:11); his remorse (Matt. 27:2-3); his destiny (Acts 1:25), in spite of all his privileges and God's action towards him (John 15:16; 6:70; Acts 1:17; Matt. 26:24-25). How clearly this shows the sinfulness of the human heart.

A. BERKELEY MICKELSEN

BIBLE. The English word Bible is derived from the Greek *biblion,* "roll" or "book." (While *biblion* is really a diminutive of *biblos,* it has lost this sense in the NT. See Rev. 10:2 where *biblaridion* is used for a "little scroll.") More exactly, a *biblion* was a roll of papyrus or byblus — a reedlike plant whose inner bark was dried and fashioned into a writing material widely used in the ancient world.

The word Bible as we use it today, however, has a far more significant connotation than the Greek *biblion.* While *biblion* was somewhat neutral — it could be used to designate books of magic (Acts 19:19) or a bill of divorcement (Mark 10:4) as well as sacred books — the word Bible refers to *the Book par excellence,* the recognized record of divine revelation.

Although this meaning is ecclesiastical in origin, its roots go back into the OT. In Dan. 9:2 (LXX) *ta biblia* refers to the prophetic writings. In the Prologue to Sirach it refers generally to the OT Scriptures. This usage passed into the Christian church (II Clem. 14:2) and about the turn of the fifth century was extended to include the entire body of canonical writings as we now have them. The expression *ta biblia* passed into the vocabulary of the western church and in the thirteenth century, by what Westcott calls a "happy solecism" (*The Bible in the Church,* p. 5), the neuter plural came to be regarded as a feminine singular, and in this form the term passed into the languages of modern Europe. This significant change (from pl. to sing.) reflected the growing conception of the Bible as one utterance of God rather than a multitude of voices speaking for him.

The process by which the various books in the Bible were brought together and their value as sacred Scripture recognized is referred to as the history of the canon. Contrary to prevailing critical opinion, there existed, prior to the Exile, a large body of sacred literature. Moses wrote "all the words of the Lord" in the "book of the covenant" (Ex. 21 — 23; 24:4, 7). Joshua's farewell address was written "in the book of the law of God" (Josh. 24:26). Samuel spoke concerning the manner of the kingdom and "wrote it in a book" (I Sam. 10:25). "Thus saith the Lord" was the common preface to the utterances of the prophets.

This revelatory literature, although not reaching a fixed form until late in the second century, (B.C.) was nevertheless regarded from the very first as the revealed will of God and therefore binding upon the people. The "oracles of God" were held in highest esteem, and this attitude towards the Scriptures was quite naturally carried over into the early church. Few will deny that Jesus regarded the OT as an inspired record of God's self-revelation in history. He repeatedly appealed to the Scriptures as authoritative (Matt. 19:4; 22:29). The early church maintained this same attitude towards the OT, but alongside of it they began to place the words of the Lord. While the OT canon had been formally closed, the coming of Christ had, in a sense, opened it again. God was once again speaking. Since the cross was the central redemptive act of God in history, the NT became a logical necessity. Thus the voice of the apostles, and later their writings, were accepted as the divine commentary on the Christ event.

Viewed as a historical process, the formation of the NT canon occupied some 350 years. In the first century the various books were written and began to be circulated through the churches. The rise of heresy in the second century — especially in the form of

Gnosticism with its outstanding spokesman, Marcion — was a powerful impulse towards the formation of a definite canon. A sifting process began in which valid Scripture distinguished itself from Christian literature in general on the basis of such criteria as apostolic authorship, reception by the churches, and consistency of doctrine with what the church already possessed. The canon was ultimately certified at the Council of Carthage (397).

The claim of the Bible to divine origin is amply justified by its historical influence. Its MSS are numbered in the thousands. The NT had barely been put together before we find translations in Latin, Syriac, and Egyptian. Today there is not a language in the civilized world that does not have the word of God. No other book has been so carefully studied or had so much written on it. Its spiritual influence cannot be estimated. It is pre-eminently *the Book* — God's word in man's language.

BIBLIOGRAPHY

ISBE; F. F. Bruce, *The Books and the Parchments;* HERE; HDB; Westcott, *The Bible in the Church.*

ROBERT H. MOUNCE

BIBLICAL THEOLOGY. Although it is often used today in a more specialized sense, the phrase "biblical theology" is one which has more general meanings that call for notice. In the first instance, its primary reference should obviously be to the actual theology of the Old and New Testaments in the form of direct exposition. More generally, it may be said that any theology which draws its materials from the 'Bible and attempts to be faithful to the biblical norm is a biblical theology. To be a biblical theologian one does not have to take part in a particular movement which may adopt this title.

At the same time, we have to recognize that there is, in modern theology, a distinctive trend which, while it does not consist exclusively in exposition nor have any formal constitution as a school nor reject all others as non-biblical, is usually self-described as the Biblical Theology. It is this trend or movement which calls for particular evaluation.

Its origins are diverse. One of the most important contributory factors has been the developing concentration upon lexical studies, from experimental beginnings early in the century to the flood of detailed investigation which is producing such valuable works as Kittel's great *Theological Dictionary of the New Testament.* This is really a form of direct exegesis and exposition; and, quite apart from interpretation, the positive light shed on so many important biblical words and phrases is a great and lasting gain to every form of biblical theology.

Hand in hand with this patient, positive work there is the criticism and rejection of the liberal misunderstanding of the Bible, and especially the NT, which came to a head in the writings of Weiss and especially Schweitzer. No one can take seriously the extreme suggestions of the latter, but the startling form in which he put his criticism revealed the utter futility of pretending that the liberal Jesus was really the historical Jesus of the NT. Exposition was thus redirected to its true task of rediscovering, so far as possible, what Jesus and the apostles, and, indeed, the OT writers, really did say rather than what we think they said or ought to have said.

To do this, however, it has been seen that we must interpret the detailed sayings and books of the Bible in terms of their own background and presuppositions rather than those drawn from other sources. This is the point particularly made by Hoskyns and Davey in their pregnant book, *The Riddle of the New Testament,* and it has been followed up by such scholars as William Manson and Matthew Black in penetrating studies. But it has led to a new sense of the interrelationship of the Testaments, and of the books within them, so that the analytical studies of the past century are yielding to a richer synthetic approach as stated and attempted, for example, by A. M. Hunter.

The movement of exegetical and expository study is an essential and basic part of the new Biblical Theology. But it is accompanied by a theological reorientation directly linked in its origins and development with the work of Karl Barth. Barth, of course, makes extensive use of more directly biblical study, but he does so as a dogmatic theologian. In place of the older and fundamentally mistaken liberalism, he attempts a reconstruction of theology on genuinely biblical foundations both of content and method. And while the different theologians who have given themselves to pursue the newer Biblical Theology are far from agreed in their general or detailed conclusions, it may be said that they share with Barth this general approach and purpose.

A word must be said about the genuine gains which have accrued to all biblical and theological work in and through this general movement. We have referred already to the importance of lexical study, and this need not be labored. But all future exposition and theology must surely take into account the new understanding which has come through these detailed investigations.

Again, it is an obvious gain to have exposed the non-biblical assumptions which underlie so much of our reading of the Bible. To be really biblical in our theology, we must take the Bible as it really is. We must accept it on its own terms. We must see and study and state things on its own basis and from its own standpoint. We must not force it into an alien philosophical scheme. We must be genuinely historical, adopting its own approach and shaping our theology in accordance with the pattern which it imposes.

A further gain is the recapture of a sense of the unity of the Bible for all the diversity which it clearly displays. This sense is more fully present in some representatives of the new trend than others. The quest of a Pauline as opposed to a Johannine or Synoptic theology still has its attractions. But the pressure of the Bible itself is undoubtedly towards unity, and in the best exponents of Biblical Theology there is little or no sense of handling divergent traditions.

A final gain, for we cannot speak of individual insights, is the rediscovery of the relevance and power of great biblical theologies of the past such as those of the Fathers and the Reformers. Patristic and Reformation studies have contributed to the whole movement, but they have been able to do so only because they themselves have been understood in a way which was hardly possible in the eighteenth and nineteenth centuries. In other words, we have entered a new era of genuine theology, when there can be a proper evaluation and use of our whole theological heritage.

The movement of Biblical Theology is to be welcomed for these positive achievements. But there are certain less satisfactory features in the modern trend which call for caution and correction if its true aim is to be achieved. The more general of these may be briefly listed.

In the first place, it may be questioned whether the movement has attained a genuinely biblical view on the question of biblical inspiration. It is one thing to break free from traditional formulations, or to emphasize aspects which may have been neglected, but many of the expositions indicate plainly that there is an evasion at this point of the Bible's own claim for itself.

Again, there is confusion concerning the historical reliability of the Bible. It may be agreed that the Bible does not profess to write the kind of history attempted by some nineteenth century historians and that much of its material is poetical, etc. But too many writers of the new trend persist in judging the Bible by a non-biblical norm, and in varying degrees there is a questioning of the historicity of that which the Bible plainly intends to be regarded as real fact.

Third, there is a notable hesitation to accept what is obviously the biblical view on a question like miracles. The degree to which this is the case differs very widely; but it usually emerges in some way. It is obviously linked with the two preceding points, especially the latter. We cannot pursue genuinely biblical theology unless we really accept, e.g., the NT view that Christ was born of a virgin and that his tomb was empty. It is no good arranging spheres of influence between a scientific world of fact and a theological world of the incarnation and the resurrection. If the Word was made flesh, and if resurrection means the resurrection of the body, the saving work of God is a work in history. At this point, therefore, we have to choose between a materialistic and a biblical understanding. The reluctance to make this choice is one of the most discouraging features in so many who profess this way, and even when the camel is swallowed there seems to be a constant and rather futile straining at gnats.

True biblical theology cannot be mere description. Nor can it go hand in hand with a very different outlook on other things. It calls for uncompromising commitment in those who pursue it, both in the objective exegesis of Scripture in terms of itself and in the truly wholehearted readiness to accept its teaching. Failure in either or both of these respects explains why so much of what is called Biblical Theology stands under the continual threat of a desperate reversion such as that seen in Bultmann and his associates and disciples.

Is there a way forward to a genuinely biblical theology which can revitalize our thinking and action? It seems to lie in the following direction. All theologians must come together in the continuance and intensification of exegetical work. All must combine in the investigation of the Bible and its teaching as they are actually before us. All must combine in studies in historical theology. All must be prepared for the sifting and correction of their preconceptions in method, approach, outlook, subject matter, and formulation by what is actually there in Scripture. All must be ready to accept the teaching which is given as it is actually given, alien and difficult though it may sometimes appear.

There is much to learn from the modern movement as a contribution in this sphere. And the modern movement itself has much to learn. But on the common focus of the Bible, and in the common pursuit of a theology which is genuinely biblical, it is not impossible that, with humble and patient discussion and interaction, the true end may be attained.

GEOFFREY W. BROMILEY

BINDING AND LOOSING. These are technical terms for the exercise of disciplinary authority bestowed by Christ in conjunction with the keys of the kingdom, first to Peter in Matt. 16:19, then to all the disciples in 18:18. This does not mean that they are empowered to hand down decisions in matters of conduct; that is, in prohibiting or permitting specific duties or moral functions.

What is implied is the authority to exclude from, as well as to reinstate in, the community of believers. Although the equivalent Greek verbs *deō* and *lyō* do not bear this technical sense in themselves, they are translations from the Aramaic *'āsar* and *šerā'*, which represent the Jewish formula for excommunication and reinstatement. It is to be noted, however, that binding and loosing in Judaism also mean "to prohibit" and "to permit" in matters of casuistry.

Related to the Matthean sense of binding and loosing is John 20:23. Exclusion from the community is always due to some offense and, therefore, presupposes the retaining of sins; while readmission includes the forgiveness of sins.

This understanding of binding and loosing is found among the Church Fathers: Tertullian (*De Pud.* 21), Cyprian (73, 7 *ad Jub.*), Origen (*Com. in Mt.,* tom. XII). In the Reformation, Luther likewise interpreted this power as (1) that of retaining and remitting sins, and (2) granted to all Christians to be exercised in preaching and private absolution.

The Council of Trent recognized the former but declared that Matt. 18:18 applied only to bishops and priests.

BIBLIOGRAPHY
SBK, I, 738 ff.; J. K. Mozley in HERE.

HERMAN C. WAETJEN

BIRTH OF CHRIST. See ADVENT OF CHRIST.

BISHOP. "Bishop" is our translation of the Greek *episkopos,* which means overseer. It was generally used of secular officials, though one example at least is known of its application to religious functionaries. In the NT the bishop seems to be identical with the presbyter. Thus in Acts 20:17 Paul summons the presbyters of Ephesus; but, when they come, he calls them bishops (vs. 28). Again, in Phil. 1:1 bishops and deacons only are mentioned. Presbyters, forming as they did the staple of the local ministry, could not have been passed over in an official salutation, so they must be identical with the bishops. This is also the inference from I Tim. 3, where the qualifications of the deacon are given immediately after those for the bishop. So with Titus 1:5-7.

It is likely that the Christian presbyter was patterned on the synagogue model. Any ten Jewish men could form a synagogue, and the first Christian assemblies were simply Christian synagogues (see James 2:2, marg.), complete with presbyters. The functions of oversight discharged by these men were such that they might well be designated "bishops" in Greek. In course of time one presbyter in each church tended to become the leader, and "bishop" was restricted to him. The process was hastened by the need for a strong, centralized church organization to deal with heresies and persecutions. The bishop became the unchallenged head of the ecclesiastical unit. He was the official spokesman for his church. He was the pastor of the faithful. He was the guardian of the pure faith. Particular functions, notably ordination, could be carried out only by him. In the Catholic understanding of the church the bishop became the key figure, as the repository of all ordaining power. The evangelical sees him rather as the chief pastor of the diocese, responsible, in conjunction with the other ministers, for the spiritual welfare of the flock.

LEON MORRIS

BLASPHEMY. To speak evil of someone. The Greek *blasphemeō* is usually translated "blaspheme," but also "defame," "rail on," "speak evil of," etc. Five Hebrew roots are translated "blaspheme": *nāqab*, "curse," used only in Lev. 24:11-16; *gādēp*, "revile;" *hārap*, "reproach;" *nā'aṣ*, "contemn, spurn;" and *bārak*, which means either "bless" or, in sarcastic or overdone blessing, "curse" (so also in other Semitic languages). This latter word is used in the Naboth incident (I Kings 21:10-13).

The law of blasphemy of Lev. 24:11-16 prescribed death for the man in Israel who "cursed" (*qālal*) the name of the Lord or "blasphemed" (*nāqab*). It is not clear that this is a direct interpretation of the third commandment. The commandment is taken by many to refer, principally at least, to non-fulfilment of proper oaths taken in God's name. It is probably true that the death penalty obtained, not for thoughtless utterance of the divine name as in modern swearing (evil though that practice may be), but for a deliberate cursing of God involving a denial of his deity and attributes.

It should be remembered that Israel, being a theocracy, normally executed civil penalties for religious offenses. In the Christian era where separation of church and state obtains, blasphemy against God is as grave an offense as ever, but the punishment to be given by the church is only spiritual censure. Ultimate judgment is in the hands of God.

The Jews later perverted the laws against blasphemy and swearing and adopted the idea that the name of God was too sacred to pronounce. Instead of pronouncing the name of Jehovah (whose correct pronunciation for this reason is now uncertain) they substituted the word *'ādôn*, "Master." In the NT, this avoidance of the name of deity among Jews is observed (note Mark 14:61-62 and probably the phrase "kingdom of heaven" used in Matthew instead of kingdom of God). This tendency is found in the Dead Sea literature.

In the NT the English word blaspheme is used mainly concerning offenses against the Deity. Christ was repeatedly charged with blasphemy by those who rejected his claims to deity, and this was the final point in his trial before the Sanhedrin (Mark 14:64). The charge had been made often before (Mark 2:7; John 10:33).

The most discussed passage is the teaching on the unpardonable sin (Matt. 12:24-32; Mark 3:22-30; Luke 11:15-20; 12:10). Observe that, in Matthew and especially in Mark, the unpardonable sin of the Pharisees is associated with their charging that Christ was the agent of Satan. This evidently gives the key to the nature of blasphemy against the Holy Spirit. It was, in this case, a perverse declaration that Christ's deeds were of the devil when they could clearly be seen to be of God. For advantage, the Pharisees stifled conscience and denied evidence in attacking Jesus. They had sinned against light in the most determined way. The similarity to Num. 15:30 is usually pointed out. The soul that sins in ignorance is charged to bring a sin offering, but the soul that sins presumptuously (literally, with a high hand) is said to "reproach" (*gādēp*) the Lord and shall be cut off. Sinning seriously against clear knowledge of the truth is evidently blasphemy against the Holy Spirit (notice here the equivalence of God and the Holy Spirit), and this sin, by its nature, makes forgiveness impossible, for the only possible light is deliberately shut out. The thought of an unpardonable sin is not uncommon in the NT (see I John 5:16; II Tim. 3:8; Jude 13; Heb. 6:4-8 and 10:26-31).

The question is much discussed — whether the Hebrews 6 passage allows that Christians may thus blaspheme the Holy Ghost. It should be observed in any event that this passage allows of no repetition of the experience. Once that sin is done, there is no more hope. It therefore does not refer to any ups and downs of Christian experience. Much less would it allow the oscillation between a state of grace and of mortal sin which Roman Catholics allege. Those who hold to the security of the believer urge that Heb. 6:9 indicates that the preceding verses are only warnings for Christians, not actual experiences. Others say that verse 5 refers only to those of external profession. Similarly, on Heb. 10:26, Stibbs in *New Bible Commentary*, IVCF, Chicago, 1955, *in loco*, suggests that the reference is to an hypothetical case. Tender consciences should be encouraged on this subject. It is often said that those who worry about the unpardonable sin have not committed it. In Jesus' day, it was not the deep sinners of the street who were unforgivable. It was rather the apostate clerics who made unbelief their boast (John 7:48).

BIBLIOGRAPHY
    D. W. Amran in *JewEnc*; MSt; J. W. Melody in *CE*; J. Massie in *HDB*.

R. LAIRD HARRIS

BLESS, BLESSED, BLESSING.

I. Bless. The verbs so translated in the OT and the NT respectively are *bārak* and *eulogeō*. Both have the meaning to pronounce blessed, but the primary meaning of the former is to convey a gift by a potent utterance (Gen. 1:22, 28). When man is said to bless God, the reference is to praise and thanksgiving, such blessing being always preceded by some realization of the divine blessing which prompts it (Ps. 145:1-2; Neh. 9:5; Luke 1:64, RV; 24:53). In blessing man, God bestows good, at the time or later. It takes various forms, the direction of the blessing being sometimes indicated by a synonym (Gen. 12:2; Num. 6:23; Ps. 28:9). It includes both temporal and spiritual well-being in the OT (Gen. 26:12-13; I Chron. 4:10), but is more particularly associated with spiritual benefit in the NT (Acts 3:26; Eph. 1:3; Gal. 3:8-9).

In some passages, where the sense of the word is either to express a wish or to make a prophetic utterance, men are said to bless their fellows (Gen. 24:60; 27:4; 48:15). In a number of instances, such as the blessing of bread, thanksgiving is implied (Mark 6:41; 8:7; Matt. 26:26; I Cor. 14:16).

II. Blessed. *Bārûk* usually applies to God in the OT (Gen. 9:26; 24:27; I Sam. 25:32). Sometimes it describes men as blessed of God (Gen. 24:13; 26:29; I Sam. 15:13). *Eulogētos* is used only of God and Christ in the NT (Luke 1:68; II Cor. 1:2; Eph. 1:3). On the other hand, *'ašerê* and *makarios* always refer to men, or to a state. The former indicates earthly blessing (I Kings 10:18), a state in which blessing is possessed (Isa. 56:2) and is the result of God's gracious favor (Ps. 32:1, 2; 65:4; 94:12; 112:1). With few exceptions, the word stands for spiritual blessing in the NT. In addition to the eight beatitudes (Matt. 5:3-10), the frequent occurrence of single sayings in this form shows the prominence of the thought of blessedness in the teaching of Jesus (Matt. 11:6; 13:16; 16:17; Luke 11:28; 12:37; John 13:17, RV; 20:29).

III. Blessing. *Berākâ* is opposed to the divine curse (Deut. 23:5; 28:2; 33:23). Sometimes it represents the good ensured by God's favor (Gen. 28:4; 45:25; Ex. 32:29). *Eulogia*, the parallel term in the NT, generally means saving blessing (Eph. 1:3; I Pet. 3:9). Two exceptions occur in Hebrews (Heb. 6:7; 12:17). Both words may also express the word of blessing pronounced by men or the good designated (Gen. 27:12, 35, 36; II Chron. 5:1; James 3:10; Gen. 33:11; I Sam. 25:27; II Cor. 9:5).

WILLIAM J. CAMERON

BLOOD. Blood is used in both Old and New Testaments as the designation of the red fluid that flows in the veins of men and animals. It also has metaphorical uses, as when the moon is said to be "turned . . . into blood" (Joel 2:31). The most important of these is to denote death by violence, a use which is undoubted. In recent times the idea has grown up that blood is also used to denote life released from the flesh. The blood of sacrifice is then thought to denote life set free to be offered to God. The sacrifice of Christ on this view was essentially that of life, of a life lived in obedience to his Father. His death would accordingly not be the essence of the sacrifice, but no more than the supreme example of it. Obviously the evidence must be examined with care.

I. The *OT* employs the word *dam* 362 times. Of these, 203 refer to death with violence and 103 to the blood of sacrifices. There are seven passages connecting life and blood, with which, perhaps, we should link seventeen which refer to eating meat with blood. The remaining thirty-two examples represent miscellaneous uses not important for our present purpose.

Statistically the word is very closely linked with death (just as in our language). The strength of the case for linking life with blood is Lev. 17:11 and related passages: "For the life of the flesh is in the blood; and I have given it to you upon the altar to make atonement for your souls: for it is the blood that maketh atonement by reason of the life." Similarly Gen. 9:4 and Deut. 12:23 both tell us that "the blood is the life."

These passages are held to indicate that the Hebrews thought of life as somehow resident in the blood, so that, when an animal's blood was shed, its life remained in the blood. The ceremonial manipulation of blood in the sacrifices is then held to indicate that a pure life is being offered to God. It is unfortunate for the animal that this process involves death, but there is no other way for men to get the life in a form in which it may be presented to God. (Some who hold this theory differ in that they think the death is not unimportant, as indicating the penal consequences of sin, but they stress that the really significant thing is, not the death, but the presentation of life.)

No evidence seems to be adduced in favor of this view. It is held to be self-evident from passages like those cited and the widespread reverence among primitive peoples for blood. The latter may be discounted, for the men of the OT were far from being primitive savages. With respect to the former, the scriptural passages adduced are capable of other explanations than that offered. There is a close connection between life and blood: when the blood is shed, the life is ended. The ceremonial manipulation of the blood may well mean no more than the ritual presentation of the evidence that a death has taken place in obedience to the command of the Lord.

In favor of the view that blood points us to death is the statistical evidence. The term in an overwhelming majority of cases signifies death. The passages which link it with life are exceptional. There is also the universal OT view that sin is serious and invites the most serious punishment. This is crystallized in the dictum: "The soul that sinneth, it shall die" (Ezek. 18:20). The shedding of blood in the sacrifices is most naturally understood as being connected with this penalty. Indeed, most of the accounts of the sacrifices include some mention of the death of the victim while they say nothing about its life. Again, to speak of the life as continuing to exist after the slaying of the animal is to overlook the strong Hebrew connection of life with the body (so much so that man's life after death is linked with the resurrection of the body, not the continuing life of an immortal soul). Where atonement is not linked with blood it is never brought about by anything symbolic of life, though it may be brought about by death, as when Phinehas slew Zimri and Cozbi (Num. 25:13) or when David delivered seven descendants of Saul to be hanged (II Sam. 21:3 ff.)

The OT evidence clearly points to blood as indicating the infliction of death in the sacrifices as elsewhere.

II. The NT uses haima ninety-eight times in all. As in the case of the OT, the largest group is that indicating violent death (quite apart from references to the blood of Christ), there being twenty-five examples of this (e.g., Acts 22:20). On twelve occasions there are references to the blood of animal sacrifices, and, if our conclusions from the OT are valid, these will point to death. There are several

miscellaneous uses, and there are the important passages referring to the blood of Christ.

It is impossible to understand some of these passages as pointing to life. Thus Col. 1:20 refers to "the blood of his cross." Now a cross has no place in the sacrificial system, so this can only point to violent death. Again, Rom. 5:9 speaks of being "justified by his blood" and "saved from the wrath of God through him," which statements are parallel to "reconciled to God through the death of his Son" and "saved by his life" in verse 10. There are several references to death in the immediate context, and this seems to be the force of the term "blood" also. Other passages which indicate clearly the death of Christ are John 6:53 ff. (note the separation of flesh and blood); Acts 5:28; Eph. 2:13; I John 5:6; Rev. 1:5; 19:13. The passages where men are said to be redeemed by the blood of Christ (Acts 20:28; Eph. 1:7, etc.) possibly point in the same direction.

There are some passages where Christ's blood is mentioned in such a way as to show that a reference to the sacrifices is intended (e.g., Rom. 3:25 with its reference to hilastērion, and I Pet. 1:2 where "sprinkling of the blood" points to sacrificial ritual). But none of these passages disturbs our conclusion from the OT that the mention of blood in sacrifice is to draw attention to the infliction of death, and some reinforce it. Thus Heb. 9:14 f. refers to the sacrificial blood clearly enough, but there is explicit mention of "death" as having taken place. So in Heb. 12:24 the blood of Jesus is contrasted with that of Abel. In each case death is plainly meant.

The witness of Scripture then is clear. Only by taking isolated passages, and in their interpretation insisting upon one of the possibilities as the only meaning can a case be made out for thinking of blood as pointing to life. When the evidence is surveyed as a whole, there can be no reasonable doubt. Blood points not to life set free, but to life given up in death.

BIBLIOGRAPHY

Arndt; BDB; J. Behm in TWNT; F. J. Taylor in RTWB; H. C. Trumbull, The Blood Covenant; S. C. Gayford, Sacrifice and Priesthood; A. M. Stibbs, The Meaning of the Word "Blood" in Scripture; Leon Morris, The Apostolic Preaching of the Cross, chap. 3.

LEON MORRIS

BOASTING. The Bible regards boasting as misplaced confidence in power, success, possessions (Jer. 9:23; Ps. 52:1; 49:7; Deut. 8:11-18), which even human wisdom sees as false (I Kings 20:11), but which, above all, self-confidently rejects God's revealed providence (James 4:15, 16), the revealed knowledge of him (Jer. 9:24) and trust in his grace alone (Ps. 118:8 f.; I Cor. 1:31). It strongly condemns all boasting in spiritual privilege, either in the calling of Israel (Deut. 7:7, 8; 9:4) or under the grace of God in Christ (Titus 3:5; Eph. 2:9; I Cor. 1:26-29), and in the church (Rom. 11:18-20; I Cor. 4:6, 7). Yet the Hebrew terms for boasting (hālal, pā'ar) are cognate with those for praise of God, while the Greek (kauchaomai and derivatives) has both senses. The Christian's glory is in the cross (Gal. 6:14) and its fruits in experience (Rom. 5:1-3). So in II Corinthians Paul "glories" in Christian generosity (9:2, 3), in spiritual authority (10:8) and, because of the special circumstances, in his apostolic calling and labors (11:5, 16-30) and special experiences (12:1-10), yet he is always conscious that such boasting is dangerous (10:13, 15; 12:11).

See also PRIDE.

GEORGE J. C. MARCHANT

BODY. I. GENERAL USES. In the OT there is no single term to denote the human body. "Body" in the English versions represents different Hebrew words meaning, variously, belly or womb, back, bone, thigh, flesh, soul, etc. The most common Hebrew word is bāsār, "flesh," which in the LXX is generally translated sarx, "flesh," but sometimes sōma, "body."

In the NT, "body" is the translation of the single word sōma. (Ptōma in Matt. 24:28, Mark 6:29, and Rev. 11:8, 9 means a dead body, a carcase). Sōma is used variously: of the human body; of the bodies of animals (James 3:3; Heb. 13:11); of plants and the heavenly luminaries (I Cor. 15:35-44); in the plural, of slaves (Rev. 18:13) — a common usage at that period (MM, p. 621); and of the church as the body of Christ.

In some biblical passages "body" is used in contradistinction to the soul or spirit (e.g., Mic. 6:7; Matt. 10:28). In others the body is the instrument or vehicle of the life of the soul (Deut. 12:23; Isa. 53:12; II Cor. 5:10). Sometimes "body" is used to denote man as a person, the whole man: thus "Christ shall be magnified in my body" (Phil. 1:20) means "in me"; and "Present your bodies" (Rom.

12:1) may well mean present your selves (R. Bultmann, Theology of the New Testament, S. C. M. Press, London, 1952, pp. 194-95).

II. RELIGIOUS CONCEPTIONS. In the OT, physical and psychological functions are closely associated. Man is a psycho-physical organism. Yahweh is the giver of life, of which man partakes.

The rabbis taught that the body, being formed of dust, is frail and mortal, having life because the spirit of life was breathed into it; that man is created of two originally uncombined elements — soul, coming from the higher world, and body, from the lower; that the body is not impure, but that it is the soul's necessary agent, the one best suited to man's needs; that the body is the seat of the evil imagination (Gen. 6:5); and that the body decays but will rise again, the resurrection body being an exact reproduction of the body of this present life (Emil G. Hirsch, JewEnc., III, pp. 283-84).

Jesus taught that the body is of secondary importance in the life of man (Matt. 6:25-34), yet he healed men's bodies and commissioned his disciples to heal (Matt. 10:8).

Paul held lowly views of the body. He called it "the body of our humiliation" (Phil. 3:21) and urged discipline over the body (I Cor. 9:27; Rom. 8:13); yet he emphasized that "the body is . . . for the Lord" (I Cor. 6:13; cf. Rom. 12:1; I Thess. 5:23); and he looked for the transformation of the body at the resurrection (I Cor. 15:23-54).

In Heb. 10, it is said that, in his incarnate body, Christ fulfilled the will of God, and that, through the offering up of his body on behalf of men, believers are cleansed in their own heart, conscience, and body.

Brunner points out that in Christian doctrine there is no special theology of the body. He sums up Christian teaching thus: "Body and mind belong equally to the nature of man, neither is to be deduced from the other, the spirit is 'from above' and the body 'from below' — and, this is the most important, they are both destined for each other, and in a definite way adapted to one another. . . . The body as well as the mind is God's good creation, although at the same time the body is that which is intended to distinguish the being of the creature from the Being of the Creator, unto all eternity" (Emil Brunner, Man in Revolt: A Christian Anthropology, Lutterworth Press, London, 1939, pp. 373-75).

III. The Church as the Body of Christ.

The most prominent theological use of the NT term *sōma* is in relation to the doctrine of the church. The church is called "the body of Christ" (Rom. 12:5; I Cor. 10:16, 17; 12:12-27; Eph. 1:23; 2:16; 4:4, 12, 16; 5:23, 30; Col. 1:18, 24; 2:19; 3:15). Some interpret the phrase "body of Christ" literally. On this view, the church is "the extension of the incarnation," the "larger incarnation of Christ." In the main, this is the view of most Catholic writers. To them the term "body of Christ" is more than metaphor. As once Christ manifested himself through a human body (i.e., in his incarnate life), so now he manifests himself through his body the church, and especially in its sacraments. Most evangelical writers tend to interpret the phrase less strictly, in terms of fellowship. As the human body is one but with many members, and as it lives by the co-ordination of all its members, so believers, as members of Christ, are also members one of another. On this view, the church is the body of Christ analogically but not by strict equation. Christ is manifested to the world by the lives and service of his people; under his leadership, and with the power of his indwelling Spirit, they do his work and thus manifest him to the world (see John 17, esp. vss. 18 ff.)

Through the imagery of the term "body" the dependence of the church on Christ the Head and the concept of symmetrical growth are readily conveyed.

IV. Paul's Use of *sōma*. The word *sōma* holds a central place in Pauline theology. Robinson declares that it is the keystone of Paul's doctrine, knitting together all his great themes. We are delivered from the body of sin, saved through the body of Christ on the cross, incorporated into his body the church, sustained by his body in the Eucharist; his new life is manifested in our body; we are destined to a resurrection body like unto his glorified body. Thus in this term *sōma* are represented the doctrines of man, sin, the incarnation and atonement, the church, the sacraments, sanctification, and eschatology (J. A. T. Robinson, *The Body: A Study of Pauline Theology*, S.C.M. Press, London, 1952, p. 9).

BIBLIOGRAPHY

Arndt; A-S; BDB; Ernest Best, *One Body in Christ*; HDB; JewEnc; Aubrey R. Johnson, *The Vitality of the Individual in the Thought of Ancient Israel*; E. L. Mascall, *Christ, The Christian and the Church*; MM; RTWB; H. Wheeler Robinson, *The Christian Doctrine of Man*; Sanday and Headlam, *Romans*, ICC; W. D. Stacey, *The Pauline View of Man*, pp. 181-93; Thayer-Grimm, *Greek-English Lexicon*; L. S. Thornton, *The Common Life in the Body of Christ*; L. S. Thornton, "The Body of Christ," in *The Apostolic Ministry*, ed. by K. E. Kirk.

OWEN R. BRANDON

BODY OF CHRIST. See Body, III.

BOLDNESS. In the OT this word is the rendering of the Hebrew word *'ōz*, meaning strength (Eccl. 8:1), its only occurrence. The words bold and boldly also occur once in the AV, being the renderings of *bāṭah* (Prov. 28:1) and *beṭah* (Gen. 34:25) respectively. The verb *bāṭah* means to trust.

In the NT the word is the rendering of the Greek word *parrēsia* in nine of its thirty-one occurrences (Acts 4:13, 29, 31; II Cor. 7:4; Eph. 3:12; Phil. 1:20; I Tim. 3:13; Heb. 10:19; I John 4:17). The word means outspokenness, frankness of speech, openness to the public, or boldness. It is used of boldness of speech before men usually, but it may also be used of the boldness of believers before God (Eph. 3:12; Heb. 10:19; I John 4:17). This boldness is secured by faith in Christ.

S. LEWIS JOHNSON, JR.

BONDAGE. The physical bondage of the Israelites is vividly brought into focus in two important periods of their history. The slave conditions in Egypt with loss of independent action and the forfeiture of normal human rights were a constant reminder of the state of affairs out of which they had been redeemed (see Ex. 1:14; 13:3, 14; 20:2; Deut. 5:6). The word "bondage" was similarly used to describe the depressed conditions existing during the Exile (cf. Ezra 9:8; Neh. 5:18).

These periods of bondage supplied a natural metaphor for Christian development in a spiritual sense. Those under the law are described as under a "yoke of bondage" (Gal. 5:1, cf. 4:3, 9, 24, 25). Formalism was exercising a power over them comparable to that which enslaved their Hebrew ancestors. In Rom. 8:21 the word "bondage" (*douleia*) is used of the subjection of creation to physical decay in strong contrast to the liberty of the glory of God's children. Again, the Christian has not received the spirit of bondage, which can result only in fear, particularly the fear of death, which sometimes enslaves throughout life (Heb. 2:15), but the Spirit of adoption (Rom. 8:15). The paradox of bondage to libertinism is one of the marks of those deceived by the false teachers of II Pet. 2:19.

DONALD GUTHRIE

BOW, RAINBOW. The rainbow was God's bow, as the lightnings were his arrows (Hab. 3:3-11). In Gen. 9 God's bow set in the cloud is the token of his covenant not again to destroy the earth by a flood. For the bow as a covenant token see also I Sam. 18:3, 4. When the rainbow reappears in Ezek. 1:28 and Rev. 4:3, if not simply representing "the outskirts of his ways" (Job 26:14), it perhaps recalls the mercy of God against his decree of judgment.

DONALD W. B. ROBINSON

BOWELS. See COMPASSION.

BRANCH. The translation of over twenty Hebrew and Greek words, the more important of which are as follows. Hebrew: z*emōrâh*, especially "branch of grapevine;" *yôneqeṭ*, "suckling, twig;" *nēṣer*, "sprout, shoot;" *'ānēp*, "bough or branch" of tree or vine; *ṣemaḥ*, "bud, growth;" *qāneh*, "reed, cane;" Greek: *klados*, "branch" of tree; *klēma*, "branch," especially of grapevine. Most of these are self-explanatory in their contexts, referring to various kinds of branches and shoots of different trees, vines, or herbs.

The words calling for special mention are *nēṣer* and *ṣemaḥ* of messianic import. *Nēṣer* is used literally of branches in Isa. 14:19 and 60:21; figuratively, of a royal scion in Isa. 11:1 and Dan. 11:7. In Isa. 11:1 the parallel phrase seems to refer to a humble stump of the line of Jesse, from which root a sprout will grow. The awful invasions of the Assyrians in the days of Ahaz and Hezekiah had brought the Davidic house very low. It is impossible to divorce Isa. 11:1 from the messianic hope of a wonderful child of David's line who would bring miraculous deliverance. The child was called Immanuel in Isa. 7:14, 8:8, 10:8, given a fivefold divine name in 9:6, and promised the throne of David in 9:7. This could not be Hezekiah as he was already a grown boy when Ahaz took the throne. The following passage of Isa. 11:2-16 also is clearly messianic and is so referred to in Rom. 15:12. The similarity of *nēṣer* to Nazareth is doubtless alluded to in Matt. 2:23. There is no relation to the word nazarite (*q.v.*). It may be questioned whether Matthew urges a derivation of Nazareth from *nēṣer* or is only giving a play on words. The derivation of Nazareth is uncertain (Arndt). The town is not mentioned in the OT. The derivation of the word Nazarene (*q.v.*) from Nazareth is defended philologically by W. F. Albright, *JBL* 65 (1946), pp. 397-401.

Ṣemaḥ is used seven times of a bud or growth. The messianic usages are in Isa. 4:2, Jer. 23:5, 33:15, and Zech. 3:8, 6:12. Apparently these Messianic references become more clear as revelation progresses. The context of Isa. 4:2 is rather general, not even attaching the Branch of the Lord to the Davidic dynasty. It foretells a time of blessing for Jerusalem. Jer. 23:5 is more specific. A righteous Branch shall be to David. He shall reign and prosper (the same word translated "deal wisely" in the messianic passage of Isa. 52:13). His name is the Lord our Righteousness. His days shall be the time of final deliverance for Israel. Jer. 33:15 is very similar. Indeed, if an old vocalization be adopted which is witnessed to in Ugaritic and elsewhere, Jer. 33:15 may also be translated "and this is the name they shall call him, the Lord our Righteousness." Both passages thus foretell the messianic King.

In Zech. 3:8 and 6:12 this messianic title is significantly fastened upon Joshua the son of Josedech the high priest. Not of David's line, Joshua is not himself to be the Branch, but he and his fellows were "men wondered at" (Hebrew: "men of a sign"). Their crowns were to be given, then removed for future days. The prophecy speaks, not of Joshua, but of the future messianic King-Priest in line with the messianic Ps. 110.

Remark should further be made of the passage in John 15 in which Christ calls his followers to an intimate vital union with himself, typified as the union of the branch with the vine. An overliteralness has found in John 15:2 a teaching against security. Rather the point of the simile is to emphasize the necessity of abiding in him.

In Rom. 11 Israel is likened to an olive branch cast off during this age while the gentile church is grafted in. There is added a promise that the natural branch, Israel, will be grafted in again in the day when the Redeemer will come out of Zion (Rom. 11:26).

BIBLIOGRAPHY
E. W. G. Masterman in *ISBE*; W. E. Biederwolf, *The Millennium Bible (in loco.)*

R. LAIRD HARRIS

BREAD. The words *lehem,* appearing more than 200 times in the OT and *artos,* found about 100 times in the NT, both mean either bread, or other food prepared from grain, such as wheat or barley. Bread is a gift of God

(Ruth 1:6; Ps. 104:15); but, because of sin, it must be won from the earth by wearying toil (Gen. 3:19). Jesus taught his disciples to pray for daily bread (Matt. 6:11). At the same time, it is normal Christian duty to earn one's bread (II Thess. 3:8, 12). Examples of metaphorical usage are: bread of affliction (I Kings 22:27), of tears (Ps. 80:5), of wickedness (Prov. 4:17), of idleness (Prov. 31:27), of adversity (Isa. 30:30). Manna is called "bread from heaven" (Ex. 16:4, 22). Referring to this, Jesus described himself as the true bread from heaven (John 6:32-33). Bread used at the Passover and in worship generally was unleavened, leaven being commonly symbolical of evil, though not so in Jesus' parable (Ex. 12:15; 23:18; Matt. 13:33). In certain cases, however, leavened bread was permissible (Lev. 7:13; 23:17). Twelve loaves of "presence bread," representing the sufficiency of God's temporal and spiritual provision for his people, were placed each Sabbath on the golden table in the holy place (Lev. 24:5-9). The father of a household customarily opened a meal by taking a loaf, giving thanks, and distributing it. Jesus followed this form in the miraculous feedings and in the institution of the Lord's Supper (Jer. 16:7; Matt. 14:19; 15:36; 26:26). Paul thinks of the sacramental loaf, partaken of by all communicants, as a symbol of the unity of the church (I Cor. 10:17).

WILLIAM J. CAMERON

BREAKING OF BREAD. The precise phrase *klasis tou artou* is found only in Luke 24:35 and Acts 2:42. The verbal form occurs in Mark 8:6, 19; Matt. 14:19 and 15:36 at the feedings of the multitude; Mark 14:22 (cf. Matt. 26:26 and Luke 22:19) at the Last Supper; Luke 24:30 (Emmaus); Acts 2:46, 20:7 and 11, 27:35; I Cor. 10:16, and 11:24 of the Eucharist; and rarely, in the LXX (see Jer. 16:7, *klasthê artos*, at funeral in memory of dead). In Hebrew, *pāras* ("to break") is used of opening a meal, sometimes without the word for bread, and is linked with blessing. The bread was made from wheat or barley, or from fine flour for ritual offerings, unleavened cakes (*maṣṣôt*) being used during Passover. The Qumran Manual orders the priest to stretch forth his hands upon the bread and wine in communal blessing before the banquet. The Didache contains a thanksgiving

for the broken bread which symbolizes the in-gathering of the church.

In feeding the multitude, Christ used a peasant boy's customary lunch of barley loaves and fish (John 6:9). The seating in groups by hundreds and fifties (Mark 6:40) may be modeled on the ranks of the Qumran banquet (see Allegro, *D. S. Scrolls*, p. 115). The meal was perhaps regarded by Jesus as an anticipation of the messianic banquet. or of the Eucharist (if John 6:53 ff. is taken sacramentally).

An ordinary meal is envisaged in Luke 24:35 (see Zahn and Plummer) embodying a characteristic action of Jesus. In Acts, breaking of bread can mean (1) a Eucharist or Agape, (2) a common meal. The first is unlikely in 27:35, possible in 20:7, and probable in 2:42 with the article; Peshitta here renders, "The breaking of the Eucharist." The second gives a reasonable sense in all the Acts passages and accounts for the absence of references to the cup.

In I Cor. 10:16 Christian bread-breaking is called *koinōnia tou sōmatos tou Christou*. It is compared to Jewish ritual meals which involve a relationship with the altar and amounts to participation in the body of Christ, the community of many members. In I Cor. 11:17-34 a community meal is described *en ekklēsia*, during which a Eucharist is held and bread broken in remembrance of Christ's death until he comes. By quoting Christ's word, "This is my body which is for you," Paul seems to recall I Cor. 10:16, adding the theme of the church as the society of the new covenant in vs. 25.

BIBLIOGRAPHY
    HDB; Foakes-Jackson & Lake, *The Beginnings of Christianity*, Vol. IV, p. 28; *HERE*; C. H. Dodd, *Interpretation of the Fourth Gospel*, pp. 333-45.

DENIS H. TONGUE

BRIDE, BRIDEGROOM. The prophets often use the analogy of the bridegroom and the bride in describing the relation between God and Israel (Isa. 62:5; 54:5; Hos. 2:19-20; Ezek. 16). Israel's unfaithfulness is harlotry (Ex. 34:15; Ps. 73:27; Hos. 4:12; Jer. 3:1). Divorce and widowhood have been the consequences (Hos. 2:2; Isa. 54:4). The appeal to Israel to return in repentance is an appeal to forsake false lovers and to deck herself in bridal attire for what is nothing less than a remarriage (Isa. 49:18; 69:10). The grace of God in receiving back his people is to be dimly pictured in the husband who goes to the slave market to buy back and remarry the former wife who has sold herself to bondage in her iniquity (Hos. 3).

Other OT passages describing the earthly love and nuptials of bride and bridegroom, without any direct reference to the love of God for his people, have been traditionally regarded as having this allegorical meaning (Ps. 45; S. of Sol.).

In the NT, John the Baptist refers to Jesus as the Bridegroom, he himself being the "bridegroom's friend" who arranges the wedding and rejoices when, after standing before the bridal chamber, he hears the bridegroom's voice announcing his coming (John 3:29). Jesus identifies himself with the divine Bridegroom in explaining why his disciples need not fast when he is with them for they are his wedding party (Matt. 9:13-14). He uses the same analogy in the parables (Matt. 25:1-13; 22:1-14). Paul describes his ministry as the task of preparing the church for the final espousal at the second advent (II Cor. 11:2). Baptism is the bridal ablution. Marriage is a true analogy of the relationship between Christ and his church which is seen most vividly in the Lord's Supper (Eph. 5:22-32). In the Book of Revelation the bride is not so much the church on earth as the heavenly Jerusalem (Rev. 19:7 ff.; 21:2, 9) finally perfected in fulfilment of prophecy (Isa. 61:10; 62:4-5). But possibly in Rev. 22:17 the reference is to the ministry of the church on earth.

The analogy Bridegroom-bride is used of Christ and the church, not of Christ and the individual soul. The use of the analogy is strongly ethical, stress being laid on the need for the cleansing of the church from compromise and heresy. The mystery of the marriage union between Christ and his church can help to sanctify the natural relationship which is a sign of it.

BIBLIOGRAPHY
    A. Plummer, HDB, I, p. 327; J. Jeremias, TWNT, IV, pp. 1092-99; J. G. Davies, The Spirit, the Church and the Sacraments, pp. 65-71, 98-104, 119-22.

RONALD S. WALLACE

BROTHER, BRETHREN. In the OT the word occurs hundreds of times, nearly always as a translation of 'āh. The NT word is adelphos, which means from the same womb.

I. USE IN THE OT. Most common is the ordinary meaning of blood brother, as in Gen. 4:2. By a natural extension, it came to express the notion of broader blood relationship. Abraham spoke of himself and Lot as brethren (Gen. 13:8). With the emergence of the nation Israel, the term came to mean fellow countryman, a member of the same people (Ex. 2:11). Occasionally it denoted one of the same tribe (Deut. 18:7). It occurs also as a synonym for neighbor (Lev. 19:17). Apparently it was not used of the stranger dwelling in the land, although the Israelite was enjoined to love him. In one passage (Gen. 29:4) there appears to be a conventional use, similar to our "fellows" in direct address which aims at a show of familiarity toward strangers. Nothing is said about a natural brotherhood of all men, even though it is recognized that all come from one Creator. Sin had rendered the bond of a common humanity insecure. Fratricide in the very first family advertized the need for a stronger tie, which the gospel eventually provided.

II. NT USAGE. In part, this is similar to that of the OT. The word denotes a member of the same family (Mark 1:16); a neighbor (Matt. 7:3); a fellow countryman (Rom. 9:3). But the most significant use assigns it to men who are called brethren because of their membership in the Christian Group. They may be Jews or Gentiles. The requirement is not the tie of blood or of acquaintance or of nationality; it is purely spiritual.

It may be that the term "brethren" in ancient Israel, as used by the more pious segment of the people, contained the seeds of this NT use, for the covenant relationship of the chosen nation made the bond between fellow Israelites religious as well as natural. In the interbiblical period the term attains special significance in connection with the Pharisees, who called one another Ḥăbērîm ("brethren") in distinction from the rank and file of Israel and particularly in distinction from the 'Am Hā-Āreṣ. They were pledged to strict observance of the law, with paramount concern for tithing and the honoring of vows. Likewise, the members of the Qumran community used the term for one another as bound by the New Covenant. They were conscious of being a fellowship within the larger entity of the national Israel, so the term is quasi-esoteric. Yet, one detects in these instances an exclusivism and detachment from the common life of men which Christianity, with its breadth of outlook and evangelistic aggressiveness, was able to avoid.

Jesus magnified two basic criteria. If one were prepared to do the will of God, he would be recognized as a brother by the Lord (Mark 3:34-35). This tie was more meaningful to him than the bond of natural kinship, as the context shows. Again, all those who recognize in Jesus their Leader and Teacher become brethren by that acknowledgment (Matt. 23:8). Some interpreters have seen in Jesus' use of the word in Matt. 25:40 a national reference (his brethren the children of Israel); but, if this be so, it is the sole instance of this usage on the lips of Jesus. Such a passage must be distinguished from others in which Jesus used "brother" with reference to the relation of his hearers to one another (e.g., Matt. 5:22).

It is clear from the Book of Acts and from the Epistles that "brethren" was the common mode of designation for fellow believers. It expressed manward what "saints" expressed Godward. Most frequently the term is used absolutely, but we read also of brethren in the Lord (Phil. 1:14); holy brethren (I Thess. 5:27); beloved brethren (Phil. 4:1); faithful brethren (Col. 1:2), etc. James is fond of the phrase "my brethren." The word is found in direct address in the singular also, as by Ananias when he came in to see Saul of Tarsus (Acts 9:17). One can fairly feel in this one word the communication of sympathy and love toward one who had come bent on persecution, only to be suddenly transformed. Onesimus the slave, because he is now a son of God through faith in Christ, is to be welcomed as a brother beloved, even by his master (Philem. 16).

Appeal is made from time to time to the fact of brotherhood as a regulating force for conduct. One may be compelled to go to law with an unbeliever, but to do so with a brother is reprehensible, a virtual denial of the bond of fellowship and love (I Cor. 6:8). The whole relationship is so intimately bound up with the higher relationship to Christ that to sin against a brother is to sin against the Lord himself (I Cor. 8:12). Love is the distinctive token of the Christian brotherhood (John 13:34-35; I Pet. 2:17). A special term for this love, *philadelphia*, occurs five times in the NT. It denotes an affection for the saints as distinct from that which is due all men (II Pet. 1:7).

Alongside the typical use of the word for fellow believers one notes that at the inception of the Christian movement Jewish believers felt no inhibition in the use of the term for fellow Jews who were not followers of Jesus (Acts 3:17). Near the end of his life Paul still continued this practice (Acts 28:17). His copious use of the word when defending himself before the Jews (Acts 22:1, 5; 23:1, 5, 6) is understandable. He was seeking to establish rapport in every legitimate way.

This double use of the word (for believers and for unconverted Jews) finds its rationale in Rom. 9:3. While Paul is careful to guard his language here — the brethren in this instance are his kinsmen according to the flesh — he is desirous of emphasizing that the blessings received in the past by Israel from the hand of God lead naturally to the supreme gift of the Christ. It was at this point that believing and non-believing Jews found their ways parting, but they had much in common up to this point. The passage breathes the poignancy of desire to see these countrymen embrace Jesus as the promised Messiah, making it possible to receive them as brethren in the Lord, brethren in the highest sense.

III. LATER USAGE. The word is common in the Apostolic Fathers, especially Clement, Ignatius, and the Didache, used in the specific Christian sense. By the close of the third century it was passing out of currency (A. Harnack, *The Expansion of Christianity*, II, p. 10), but it appeared again in the Middle Ages (Brethren of the Common Life) and has been adopted as part of the name of several groups in the modern church.

IV. BRETHREN OF THE LORD. On this much-discussed question, whether these were half brothers (sons of Mary) or stepbrothers (sons of Joseph by a former marriage) or cousins, see the article by J. B. Mayor in *HDB*. It is possible that the reference in Acts 1:14 includes the sisters. See Arndt, *adelphos*, 1.

BIBLIOGRAPHY
Arndt; H. von Soden in TWNT; C. H. Watkins in *HDAC*; J. H. Farmer, "Brotherhood," *HDCG*.

EVERETT F. HARRISON

BROTHERHOOD. See BROTHER.

BUILDING. The idea of the church (*q.v.*) as a building goes back to the words of Jesus himself. In Matthew 16:18 he declared, "Upon this rock I will build my church." The verb is *oikodomeō*, from *oikos*, "house." It is used literally of erecting a building.

In all three Synoptic Gospels Jesus is recorded as quoting Ps. 118:22: "The stone which the builders rejected, the same was made the head of the corner." It is not clear whether this means the cornice or the corner-stone (q.v.). But in either case Jesus is the key-stone that holds the building together (cf. I Pet. 2:7).

Paul wrote to the Corinthians, "Ye are God's building" (I Cor. 3:9). Jesus Christ is the only foundation (q.v.) (I Cor. 3:11). This shows that the church is not built on Peter (q.v.), as Matthew 16:18 is sometimes inter-preted as teaching, except in the sense of Eph. 2:20. Peter was one of the "living stones," built together into a "spiritual house" (I Pet. 2:5). The word oikodomē is often translated "edifying" or "edification" (q.v.).

RALPH EARLE

BULL (PAPAL). An apostolic letter bear-ing in its superscription the title of the pope as Episcopus, Servus servorum Dei in which the pope speaks to the church ex cathedra in matters pertaining to faith and morals and thus infallibly according to Roman Catholic doc-trine. It is so named because of the leaden seal (Lat., bulla, seal) by which papal documents were authenticated during the Middle Ages. The term was at first applied to all kinds of official documents which emanated from the papal chancery, but a much more precise defi-nition has existed since the fifteenth century. These pronouncements cover a wide range of subjects and may be declaratory or directive in character, specific or general in application.

GREGG SINGER

BURIAL. This was the accepted method for disposing of dead bodies among Hebrews and early Christians. The practice is first re-ferred to in the case of Sarah (Gen. 23:4 — Hebrew, qābar; LXX, thaptō). Mention is there made of sepulchers: natural or artificial caves where the dead were laid to rest (He-brew, qeber; LXX and NT, mnēmeion — e.g., Gen. 50:13). This custom continued through-out Bible times (e.g., I Kings 13:31; John 19:41). Bodies were sometimes buried in the earth (Gen. 35:8, 19).

To dishonor a body it was left unburied (Deut. 21:23; II Sam. 21:12-14; II Kings 9:10), and disposal by burning was unusual (I Sam. 31:12; Amos 6:10), sometimes em-ployed as a climax of the death penalty (Josh. 7:25). Where possible, interment was in fam-ily burial places (Gen. 49:29; II Sam. 19:37; II Chron. 21:20), and from earliest times Christians shared "places of rest," koimētēria. (Koimaō, I sleep; so cemetery means dormi-tory — see I Thess. 4:14-15.)

The simple ceremony was carried out the same day (John 11:17, 39; Acts 5:6, 10; cf. Num. 19:11-14). The body was washed (Acts 9:37), anointed (II Chron. 16:14; Matt. 26:12), and wrapped in linen (John 19:39-40), and mourners accompanied it to the sepulcher (Luke 7:12; Acts 8:2).

Paul mentions the burial of Christ as part of the gospel (I Cor. 15:4), since it attested the reality both of the death which preceded and of the resurrection which followed. It has its place also in the Apostles' Creed from earliest times.

For the symbolism behind burial see John 12:24; I Cor. 15:35-38, 42-49; Rom. 6:4-6.

BIBLIOGRAPHY

HDB on "Burial" and "Sepulchre"; HERE on "Death" and "Disposal of the Dead"; ISBE; SHERK; A. Edersheim, Life and Times of Jesus the Messiah, II, pp. 316-20.

DAVID H. WHEATON

BURNT OFFERING. One of the five main offerings of the Levitical law. The He-brew name ʿōlâ, "going up," probably refers to the fact that the whole sacrifice was con-sumed. It is also called a kālîl, "complete," or holocaust offering.

The offering, described in Lev. 1 and 6:8-13, could be made of either a bullock, ram, goat, or (for the poor) a turtledove. The of-ferer placed his hand on the animal's head, picturing transfer of guilt (see Lev. 16:21), then the animal was killed and the blood sprinkled to make an atonement. Anyone might bring a burnt offering, but a regular morning and evening sacrifice were required with extra offerings on sabbaths and special feast days (Num. 28:2 — 29:39).

The Greek equivalent holokautōma is used only in the NT in Mark 12:33 and Heb. 10:6, 8. In the Hebrews passage, quoted from Ps. 40, the offering of Christ is cited as the antitype to all the OT sacrifices.

The word for the atonement effected is often translated "cover," from an Arabic cog-nate. But the Hebrew verb kippēr seems rather a denominative from the noun kōper, "ran-som," and means give a ransom, propitiate. The "mercy seat," (kappōreṭ) is thus the place of pro-pitiation — Greek, hilastērion, propitiation (Rom. 3:25; Heb. 9:5).

R. LAIRD HARRIS

C

CALENDAR. See CHRISTIAN YEAR.

CALL, CALLED, CALLING. The developed biblical idea of God's calling is of God summoning men by his word, and laying hold of them by his power, to play a part in and enjoy the benefits of his gracious redemptive purposes. This concept is derived from the ordinary secular meaning of the word (LXX and NT, *kaleō*) — i.e., summon, invite (see Matt. 2:7; 22:3-9) — by the addition of that quality of sovereign effectiveness which Scripture ascribes to the words of God, as such. Divine utterance is creative, causing to exist the state of affairs which it declares to be intended (cf. Isa. 55:10 f.; Gen. 1:3; Heb. 11:3). The thought in this case is of an act of summoning which effectively evokes from those addressed the response which it invites. The concept passes through various stages of growth before it reaches its final form in the NT Epistles.

Throughout the OT, Israel regards itself as a family which God had called first from heathendom, in the person of its ancestor (Isa. 51:2), and then from Egyptian bondage (Hos. 11:1), to be his own people (Isa. 43:1), serving him and enjoying his free favor for ever. This conviction is most fully stated in Isa. 40-55. Here, the central thought (developed in reference to the coming return from captivity) is that God's gracious once for all act of calling sinful Israel into an unbreakable covenant relation with himself guarantees to the nation the eventual everlasting enjoyment of all the kindnesses that omnipotent love can bestow (Isa. 48:12 ff.; 54:6 ff.; etc.). The calling of individuals receives mention only in connection with Israel's corporate destiny, either as the prototype of it (Abraham, Isa. 51:2), or as a summons to further it and bring the Gentiles to share it (Cyrus, Isa. 46:11; 48:15; the Servant, 42:6; 49:1). The essence of the thought here is not verbal address (indeed, Cyrus, though called "by name" — i.e., announced as God's "shepherd" and "anointed" — does not know God's voice, Isa. 45:4; cf. 5:26 ff.; 7:18 ff.); "calling" signifies rather a disposition of events and destinies whereby God executes his purposes. The prophet's argument rests entirely on the assumption that God's callings express determinations which are unconditional, irreversible and incapable of frustration (cf. Rom. 11:29). He views God's callings as sovereign acts, the temporal execution of eternal intentions.

In the NT, the thought of calling has to do with God's approach to the individual. In the Synoptics and Acts, the term denotes God's verbal summons, spoken by Christ or in his name, to repentance, faith, salvation, and service (Mark 2:17 = Luke 5:32; Mark 1:20; Acts 2:39). The "called" (*klētoi*) in Matt. 22:14 are the recipients of this summons, as such; they form a larger company than the "chosen" (*eklektoi*), those who respond. In the Epistles and Revelation, however, the concept is broadened, in accordance with the Isaianic development noted above, to embrace God's sovereign action in securing a response to his summons. The verb "call," and the noun "calling" (*klēsis*), now refer to the effective evocation of faith through the gospel by the secret operation of the Holy Spirit, who unites men to Christ according to God's gracious purpose in election (Rom. 8:30; I Cor. 1:9; Gal. 1:15; II Thess. 2:13 f.; II Tim. 1:9; Heb. 9:15; I Pet. 2:9; II Pet. 1:3, etc). The "called" are those who have been the subjects of this work, i.e., elect believers (Rom. 1:6 f.; 8:28; Jude 1; Rev. 17:14, etc.). This is the "effectual calling" of classical Reformed theology, the first act in the *ordo salutis* whereby the benefits of redemption are conveyed to those for whom they were intended (see Rom. 9:23-26). This "upward," "heavenly" calling to freedom and felicity (Phil. 3:14 RSV; Heb. 3:1; Gal. 5:13; I Cor. 7:22 RSV; I Thess. 2:12; I Pet. 5:10) has ethical implications: it demands a worthy walk (Eph. 4:1) in holiness, patience and peace (I Thess. 4:7; I Pet. 1:15; 2:21; I Cor. 7:15; Col. 3:15), and sustained moral exertion (Phil. 3:14; I Tim. 6:12).

The terminology of calling has two subordinate applications in the NT: (1) to God's summons and designation of individuals to particular functions and offices in his redemptive plan (apostleship, Rom. 1:1; missionary preaching, Acts 13:2; 16:10; high priesthood, Heb. 5:4; cf. the calling of Cyrus above mentioned, and of Bezaleel (Ex. 31:2; (2) to the external circumstances and state of life in which a man's effectual calling took place (I Cor. 1:26; 7:20). This is not quite the sense of "occupation" or "trade" which the Reformers supposed that it bore in the latter verse; but their revaluation of secular employment as a true "vocation" to God's service has too broad a biblical foundation to be invalidated by the detection of this slight inaccuracy.

BIBLIOGRAPHY
Arndt; Schmidt in *TWNT*; J. P. Thornton-Duesbery in *RTWB*; R. Macpherson in *HDCG*; T. Nicol in *HDAC*; systematic theologies of C. Hodge (II. pp. 639-732), L. Berkhof (IV. v-vi: pp. 454-72).

JAMES I. PACKER

CALVINISM. According to Benjamin Breckenridge Warfield, Calvinism is theism and evangelicalism come to its own. A Calvinist describes his position as follows.

Calvinism seeks, first and above all, to take its "system of truth" from the Scriptures of the Old and New Testaments as the self-authenticating revelation of God in Christ. If it is to be called a "system" at all, then this system must be seen to be open to the Scriptures. The doctrines of Calvinism are not deduced in *a priori* fashion from one major principle such as the sovereignty of God. On the contrary, whatever can, by sober exegesis, be found to be taught in Scripture, that, and only that, constitutes part of the "system" of Calvinism.

With true evangelical zeal Calvinism therefore presents the unrestricted, universal offer of the gospel. Human responsibility is a basic teaching of Scripture. But the meaning of human responsibility must be taken from Scripture itself, not deduced from a supposed "experience of freedom" taken from non-scriptural philosophy. Accordingly, Calvinism relates human responsibility to the all-inclusive plan of God. Human responsibility does not take place within a vacuum. It takes place within history which is under the ultimate disposition of God. Man is therefore responsible as the *creature* of God.

It was only as a creature of God, made in his image, that man could sin. So, when a sinner, and as such "dead in trespasses," unable of himself even to stretch forth his hand to receive salvation, Scripture continues to deal with him as a responsible being. He is called to faith and repentance. Yet faith is a gift of God. Lazarus lay in the tomb. He was dead. Yet Jesus told him to come forth. And he did come forth. Thus Calvinism seeks to be truly evangelical in stressing the free offer of the gospel. But this true evangelicalism is enforced rather than denied by relating it to the sovereign grace of God. Without this relation there can be no true evangelicalism. Without this relation to the sovereign counsel of God there would be no human responsibility, for man, granted he could then have internal coherence, would then not be responsible to God.

BIBLIOGRAPHY
Girardeau, *Calvinism and Evangelical Arminianism*; B. B. Warfield, *Calvin and Calvinism*; Abraham Kuyper, *Calvinism*; L. Van der Linde, *De Leer van den Heiligen Geest by Calvyn*; G. Brillenburg Wurth, *Het Calvinisme Vandaag*; John T. McNeill, *The History and Character of Calvinism*; H. Henry Meeter, *In God-Centered Living*.

CORNELIUS VAN TIL

CANON. See BIBLE.

CANON. See OFFICES, ECCLESIASTICAL.

CANON LAW. Canon law may be simply defined as the rules of the church for purposes of order, ministry and discipline. At first these consisted of *ad hoc* pronouncements by leaders or councils in a local setting. Particularly important were those which came from the greater centers, and especially the canons adopted at Nicaea (A.D. 325). Indeed, it was not long before canons were put out under the name of the apostles or great figures of the first centuries, and a necessary process of collection and codification continued through the Dark Ages, with much standardization in the West under Charlemagne. Gratian was the man who brought this process to a virtual culmination in the Roman communion with his famous *Decretum* (A.D. 1140) which under lies the developed study of canon law in the Middle Ages and is the basis of the modern *Corpus iuris canonici*. The Protestant churches have naturally disowned this whole body of legislation and generally avoid the terms canon or canon law, but in so far as any church must make rules for the ordering of its life and work various forms of canon law are naturally found in all churches.

GEOFFREY W. BROMILEY

CANONIZATION (of saints). An ecclesiastical decree regarding the public or ecclesiastical veneration of an individual. The Roman Catholic Church claims authority for this practice in the writings of St. Augustine, and affirms that it has its origin in the worship of the saints. At first canonization was given only to those who were martyrs of the faith; later, to those who were noted for their holy living and working of miracles. It requires a sufficient number of verified miracles and can only be granted by the Papacy after the death of the recipient.

See also BEATIFICATION.

GREGG SINGER

CANTICLE. The word is derived from the Latin *canticulum,* the diminutive of *canticum,* a "song." As used by such writers as Jerome and Augustine, the word denoted that which was sung unaccompanied, in contrast with the Psalms, which were sung to an instrumental accompaniment. Liturgically, however, the term is confined to sacred songs or prayers (other than the Psalms) taken from the Bible and used in the daily offices.

In the early church, both of the East and of the West, the canticles chiefly employed were the following: the two songs of Moses (Ex. 15:1-19; Deut. 32:1-43), the thanksgiving of Hannah (I Sam. 2:1-10), the prayers of Habakkuk (chap. 3), Isaiah (chap. 12), and Jonah (chap. 2); and from the NT the songs of the Virgin Mary, Zacharias, and Simeon, still known by their Latin titles as (respectively) the *Magnificat,* the *Benedictus,* and the *Nunc Dimittis.*

These three canticles are in common use in the worship of the Reformed churches. The *Magnificat* (Luke 1:46-55) has been sung at evening worship since the sixth century, being the canticle of Vespers in the Western church. It has certain obvious points of resemblance to the song of Hannah (I Sam. 2), though it rises to a loftier spiritual level. The *Nunc Dimittis,* or song of Simeon (Luke 2:29-32), is also an evening canticle and has been so used in the daily prayers of the church since the fourth century. In the Roman Breviary it formed part of the service of Compline. The song of thanksgiving of Zacharias known as the *Benedictus* (Luke 1:68-79) became associated with the church's morning worship and was incorporated into the Western service of Lauds.

The noble hymn of praise known as the *Te Deum,* while not strictly speaking a canticle in that it is not derived from the Bible, has been used in liturgical worship since the sixth century. Its origin is obscure. A song of praise

of another kind is the *Benedicite,* or hymn of Creation. This is an apocryphal addition to the book of Daniel, being found in the LXX between verses 23 and 24 of the third chapter. Its use in Christian worship dates from early times.

BIBLIOGRAPHY

G. Harford, M. Stevenson, J. W. Tyrer, *The Prayer Book Dictionary;* C. Neill, J. M. Willoughby, *The Tutorial Prayer Book;* A. Barry, *The Teacher's Prayer Book.*

FRANK COLQUHOUN

CAPTAIN OF SALVATION. The expression "captain of salvation" is found in Heb. 2:10 (AV, "captain of their salvation") and is the rendering of the Greek *ho archēgos tēs sōtērias.* The word *archēgos* is also found in Acts 3:15; 5:31; Heb. 12:2. The general sense appears to be that of originator. The Son was the originator, or pioneer, of salvation in the sense that he in his sufferings opened the way for "many sons" to enter glory.

S. LEWIS JOHNSON, JR.

CARDINAL. See OFFICES, ECCLESIASTICAL.

CARE (ANXIETY). In the OT the words translated "care" include *dāag* (Ezek. 4:16; Jer. 17:8), i.e., anxious foreboding; *hārēd* (II Kings 4:13) i.e., solicitude towards another; and *beṭah,* implying childlike trust (Judg. 18:7) and also an ill-grounded sense of security (Isa. 32:9). "Care" is mainly expressed in the NT as *melei* (Mark 4:38) i.e., interest in; *epimeloumai* (Luke 10:34 f.), i.e., taking care of someone; and *merimna* or *merimnaō* (Matt. 13:22), i.e., anxious concern.

The word is frequently found in warnings against the spirit of anxious care (Matt. 6:25-34; Phil. 4:6; 1 Pet. 5:7) and its correlative, a falsely based sense of security; for these foes of the spiritual life are common responses to the experience of anxiety.

Anxiety is defined as "the apprehension cued off by a threat to some value which the individual holds essential to his existence as a personality" (Rollo May, *The Meaning of Anxiety,* Ronald Press, New York: 1950, p. 191). It is grounded in the spiritual nature of man; for it involves man's capacity for creative aspiration, moral decision, the experience of guilt and the capacity to anticipate death. Some have maintained that anxiety is a result of man's fall into sin and its consequent breach of fellowship with God. Anxiety appears to be more closely tied to the broken relationship than the fact of original sin; for Christ, whose nature was unaffected by original sin, apparently experienced acute anxiety in the garden of Gethsemane as he faced the prospect of being forsaken of God while he who knew no sin was being made sin for us (II Cor. 5:21). His anxiety lends credence to the suggestion that anxiety inheres in the tension between freedom and finitude. It is the "internal description of the state of temptation" and as such the *precondition* for sin, although it is not itself sinful (Reinhold Niebuhr, *The Nature and Destiny of Man*, Scribners, New York: 1941, I, pp. 168, 182 f.). However, because man is in bondage to original sin, he mishandles the tension between freedom and finitude either by pridefully seeking to usurp God's supremacy by seeking to overreach his limitations, or by fearfully turning away from the creative potentialities present in the state of anxiety in an effort to gain immediate and absolute security from some finite source.

Psychotherapy has learned to distinguish two forms of anxiety. Normal (existential) anxiety is grounded in the tension between possibility and finitude. It has creative as well as destructive potential. It leads to creativity and growth when the anxious person finds courage to face the risk of destruction in the interest of responsible moral decision, i.e., is willing to lose his life, thereby saving it. The Bible teaches that man's only adequate source of courage is a childlike trust in God.

Neurotic (pathological) anxiety results when the person cannot muster the courage to face the painful consequences that may result from decision. He seeks to detach himself from the anxiety-inducing demand by eliminating it from awareness through ego-defense measures. He may invoke such means as alcohol or compulsive sociability or isolating himself from others in his effort to gain an absolute sense of security. His aim is to feel comfortable rather than to come to a wise decision. In this way anxiety becomes detached from its source. Its consequent "free floating" character only arouses greater dread. This causes greater involvement in defensive activity; and, if corrective measures are not sought, leads to serious personality breakdown.

The Bible teaches that the only way anxiety can be a source of creativity rather than sin is by experiencing it within the context of an abiding relationship of trust in God's loving concern. It is therefore imperative that the character of God, as revealed at Calvary, be clearly understood.

LARS I. GRANBERG

CARNAL. See FLESH, FLESHLY.

CASUISTRY. Derived from the Latin *casus*, meaning "case," casuistry denotes the application of general principles of morality to particular cases of conduct and conscience. With the possible exception of Acts 15:20, no casuistry is to be found in the NT. Subsequent church history, however, is marked by its exercise and influence.

In common parlance the word has come to be associated with mishandling of principle in order to justify a position or a line of conduct.

See also PROBABILISM, ACCOMMODATION.

BIBLIOGRAPHY
R. M. Wenley in *HERE*.

HERMAN C. WAETJEN

CATECHUMEN. A word derived from the Greek *katēchoumenos*, the passive participle of *katēchein*, "to sound over or through, to instruct," and thus in the passive "to be instructed." In the NT the word occurs seven times (Luke 1:4; Acts 18:25; 21:21, 24; Rom. 2:18; I Cor. 14:19; Gal. 6:6) and always refers to instruction in religious matters. "Catechumen" early became a technical word for one receiving instruction in the Christian religion with a view to being admitted into the church through baptism. This practice in Christianity grew out of the church's heritage in Judaism which emphasized the thorough indoctrination of its proselytes.

Although the earliest known occurrence of *katēchein* in the technical sense of catechizing is in II Clement 17:1, the researches of P. Carrington (*The Primitive Christian Catechism*, University Press, Cambridge, 1940) and E. G. Selwyn (*The First Epistle of St. Peter*, 2nd ed., Macmillan, London, 1947), have shown that there is much common catechetical material in the NT Epistles, which suggests the early existence of a catechumenate.

WALTER W. WESSEL

CATHOLIC. A transliteration of the Greek *katholikos*, "throughout the whole," "general," this word has been used in a variety of senses during the history of the church. In the earlier patristic period it had the denotation of universal. This is its meaning in the first occurrence in a Christian setting — "Wherever Jesus Christ is, there is the catholic church" (Ignatius *ad Smyrn.* viii. 2). Here the contrast with the local congregation makes the meaning "universal" mandatory. Justin Martyr could speak of the "catholic" resurrection, which he explains as meaning the resurrection of all men (*Dial.* lxxxi). When the term begins to appear in the Apostles' Creed — "the holy catholic church" (*ca.* 450) as it had earlier appeared in the Nicene — "one holy catholic and apostolic church," it retains the sense of universality and thus accents the unity of the church in spite of its wide diffusion. The Catholic Epistles of the NT were so designated by Origen, Eusebius, *et al.*, to indicate that they were intended for the whole church rather than a local congregation.

A second meaning emerges toward the end of the second century, when heresy had become a menace. Catholic becomes the equivalent of orthodox. The Muratorian Canon (*ca.* 170) refers to certain writings "which cannot be received in the catholic church, for gall cannot be mixed with honey." For the logical connection between this meaning and the former, see Lightfoot on Col. 1:6. Vincent of Lérins (*Commonitorium,* A.D. 434) in his famous maxim, "What all men have at all times and everywhere believed must be regarded as true," combines the ideas of universality and orthodoxy.

In Reformation times the word became a badge of those churches which adhered to the papacy in contrast to those groups which identified themselves with the Protestant cause. The designation Roman Catholic emerged in connection with the controversy between Rome and the Anglican Church, which insisted on its right to use the term catholic as linking it with the ancient apostolic church. Rome, on the other hand, put forth its claim as the true church because of organizational continuity. Churches could not be regarded as properly "Catholic" unless they submitted to the government of the Roman hierarchy.

Two modern uses should be noted. One is the designation of an individual as a Catholic, a member of the Roman Catholic Church. The word is sometimes employed also to indicate a breadth of spirit or outlook in contrast to that which is regarded as rigidly narrow. This vague use of the word, at times quite latitudinarian, is completely different from the ancient significance, where universality was coupled with precision of Christian belief.

Historians refer to the Old Catholic church as that phase of the development of Christianity which followed the apostolic and preceded the Roman Catholic.

BIBLIOGRAPHY
CE; HERE; J. B. Lightfoot, *The Apostolic Fathers,* 2nd ed., Part II, Vol. II, pp. 310-12; J. Pearson, *An Expositon of the Creed,* pp. 501-8; SHERK; H. E. W. Turner, *The Pattern of Christian Truth.*

EVERETT F. HARRISON

CELIBACY. The English term is derived from the Latin *caelebs,* "unmarried," and refers to the abstinence from marriage on the part of the clergy and monastic orders of the Roman Catholic Church. The latter recognizes that until about the time of the Council of Nicaea (325) the clergy were free to marry (*CE,* III, p. 483), in accordance with the practice of the apostolic church (I Tim. 3:1-12). Toward the close of this period, however, a double standard of spirituality crept into the church. Notice was taken of Jesus' words concerning some who "have made themselves eunuchs for the kingdom of heaven's sake" (Matt. 19:12). His conclusion, "He that is able to receive it, let him receive it," seemed to imply celibacy as a higher voluntary standard.

Paul, due to the exigencies of the day, advised the Corinthians (I Cor. 7:32-35) that one might serve the Lord more fully in the unmarried state. The increasing sacerdotalism of the early centuries transformed the exceptional situation into the preferable. The *Apostolic Constitutions* (*ca.* 400) form the basis of Eastern Orthodox canon law and allow the clergy and bishops one marriage contracted before ordination. The Council of Trullo (692) provided that a bishop must be celibate or separate from his wife upon consecration, still the rule in the East.

From the fourth to the tenth centuries in the Roman Catholic Church various local usages were determined by local synods favoring clerical celibacy, from requiring married candidates to put away their wives to allowing them to live with their partners, in some cases as husband and wife, in others platonically.

Pope Gregory VII in 1075 initiated sweeping reform requiring complete celibacy of deacons, priests, and bishops, which was confirmed by the Fourth Lateran Council (1215) and the Council of Trent (1563). The Protestant Reformation of the sixteenth century vigorously rejected enforced celibacy of the clergy in favor of a return to apostolic freedom.

See also ASCETICISM.

BIBLIOGRAPHY
H. C. Lea, *History of Sacerdotal Celibacy in the Christian Church*, 2 vols.; CE, III, pp. 481-88.

DONALD G. DAVIS

CENOBITE. One who shares the life of a religious community under a rule and a superior (Greek *koinos*, "common," and *bios*, "way of life"). The word first appears in use in Egypt, third or fourth century A.D., where some hermits desired the protection and regulation of a communal life.

M. R. W. FARRER

CERINTHIANS. Followers of Cerinthus, a Jewish heretic (*ca.* A.D. 100). His system, a mixture of Ebionite and Egyptian Gnosticism, taught that matter was evil; that a Demiurge made the world; and that Christ, a divine power, descended on Jesus, an ordinary mortal, at baptism, leaving him before his crucifixion.

BIBLIOGRAPHY
DCB, ODCC.

M. R. W. FARRER

CHARISMATA. See SPIRITUAL GIFTS.

CHARITY. See LOVE.

CHASTEN, CHASTISE. The Hebrew *yāsar* (substantive *mûsār*) is the principal word rendered "chasten, chastise" in the OT. Its basic meaning is "the learning or teaching of a lesson. . . . The lesson may be learned in three different ways, through the experience of suffering (Jer. 10:24), through the acceptance of verbal instruction (Ps. 16:7) . . . and through observing a given situation (Jer. 2:30)." (J. A. Sanders, *Suffering as Divine Discipline in the Old Testament and Post-Biblical Judaism*, Colgate Rochester Divinity School Bulletin, Special Edition, Nov. 1955, p. 41).

The NT word is *paideuein* (noun *paideia*) which properly means to instruct, train, educate physically and mentally (Acts 7:22) Through its use in the LXX to translate *yāsar*, it came to have the added sense of moral instruction, discipline, correction through suffering. In the NT the chastening is mostly that of God upon his own people (I Cor. 11:32; II Cor. 6:9; and especially Heb. 12:5-11),

but human fathers also chasten their sons (Heb. 12:7, 10a), and beneficial discipline can even be effected through Satan (I Tim. 1:20). The NT insists that God chastens his people for their own spiritual good. The word *paideuein* is never used of God's dealing with the unbeliever.

See also DISCIPLINE.

BIBLIOGRAPHY
Arndt; G. Bertram in *TWNT*; J. Sanders, *Suffering as Divine Discipline in the Old Testament and Post-Biblical Judaism*, pp. 6-45.

WALTER W. WESSEL

CHASTITY. Chastity, or moral purity, for the Jews in general, was consistence with marriage. This also obtained for the NT writers. For although *hagnos*, for "chaste," is used of virgins (II Cor. 11:2), it is used of married women also (Titus 2:5; I Pet. 3:2). But adultery and fornication were not consistent with chastity, which breaches of moral purity gave the church no little trouble.

J. KENNETH GRIDER

CHERUB, CHERUBIM. Hebrew *kᵉrûb*, derivation uncertain. Cherubim were placed at Eden's entrance after the expulsion of man (Gen. 3:24). Poetically they are viewed as Yahweh's chariot at his descent from heaven (Ps. 18:10), but note the parallelism! Two gold cherub-figures adorned the ark (Ex. 25:17-22) and two huge replicas were made for Solomon's temple (I Kings 6:23-28); hence the expression *yōšēb hakkᵉrûbîm*, "enthroned above the cherubim", used of Yahweh (I Sam. 4:4; Ps. 80:1). Ezekiel's elaborate description is full of symbolism and based on visionary experience (cf. Ezek. 1:10 with 9:3; 10:15-22). This argues against a mythological connection. The cherubim used in the decorative art of temple and tabernacle must have aided the worshiper rather than terrified him. Had they resembled the hybrid figures of mythology their function in worship would be doubtful. Cherubim are ministering spirits in God's immediate presence, whose invisible presence they manifest and whose action they symbolize. Their human appearance predominates (Ezek. 1:5) but symbolical traits are added to emphasize spiritual excellence. Some parallel features in Assyro-Babylonian thought may be explained from common paradise-traditions.

BIBLIOGRAPHY
P. Van Imschoot, *Theologie de l'Ancien Testament*, pp. 127-29; W. F. Albright, BA 1, 1938; J. Pedersen, *Israel*, III-IV, pp. 691 f.

MARTEN H. WOUDSTRA

CHILD, CHILDREN. The word child is represented in Hebrew by *yeled* and *na'ar,* either word being used for a baby or little child, though *na'ar* can also mean a youth. Samuel is called a *na'ar* when a baby (I Sam. 1:22) and at each mention of his childhood until and including God's call to him (I Sam. 3:8), so that the particular word is no guide to his age on that occasion. *Tap* is used only of little children. The very common word *bēn* indicates offspring in general and is often used to name a tribe or race, "the children of Benjamin," "of Israel," "of Ammon," etc.

Since a child's character follows that of his father, Hebrew developed the use of *bēn* in the plural, "the children of" or "the sons of" to describe leading traits of character, especially "children (sons) of Belial" (Deut. 13:13, etc.), or "children of iniquity" (Hos. 10:9). This idiom is not always apparent in the English translation, e.g., "valiant" in I Sam. 18:17 is literally "child of valor."

In the NT, apart from the variety of words expressing the stages of normal childhood, this Hebraic idiom is sometimes found, e.g., "obedient children" in I Pet. 1:14 is "children of obedience," but Alford's note *in loco* asserts that the comparable phrase in Eph. 5:6 "children of disobedience" involves a far deeper meaning than a mere Hebraistic equivalent of "disobedient children." He quotes Winer: "Children of disobedience belong to *apeitheia* . . . as a child to its mother, to whom disobedience is become a nature, a ruling disposition." On the other hand "children of wrath" (Eph. 2:3) does not describe their character as wrathful: it denotes their subjection to wrath, being the objects of wrath; for being sinful by nature they are inevitably under the wrath of God. An OT parallel for this use is Deut. 25:2, where "worthy to be beaten" is a "son of stripes" and the English would more accurately be "subject to stripes." Compare II Pet. 2:14, "cursed children," i.e., subject to the curse.

In such phrases there is no difference of meaning between *teknon* used in Eph. 2:3; 5:8; I Pet. 1:14; II Pet. 2:14 and *huios* in Eph. 2:2; 5:6; Col. 3:6; I Thess. 5:5, but for the concept "children of God" Westcott's comment on I John 3:1 defines *teknon* as marking "community of nature (i.e., with God) with the prospect of development" but *huios* as "the position of privilege." The emphasis in John's Gospel and Epistles reveals

the imparting of divine life through new birth to those who trust in the Son of God, a sharing in the life of the Father. John therefore uses *teknon,* but Paul writes rather of the status and privilege of those who have received the adoption of sons (*huiothesia,* Rom. 8:15) and thus become heirs of God, and accordingly he uses *huios* for this relation (Gal. 3:26; 4:6; Rom. 8:14). A similar use of *huios* for status and privilege appears in the Gospels, as "children of God" (Matt. 5:9), "of your Father" (Matt. 5:45), or "of the bride-chamber" (Luke 5:34).

See also ADOPTION, SON.

BIBLIOGRAPHY
Arndt, s. v. *teknon* and *huios*; B. F. Westcott, *Epistles of John,* pp. 122-24; S. W. Green in HDB (one volume edition).

J. CLEMENT CONNELL

CHILIASM. See MILLENNIUM.

CHOOSE, CHOSEN. See ELECT, ELECTION.

CHRIST. See MESSIAH AND CHRISTOLOGY.

CHRISTIAN. The word Christian comes from the Greek word *Christianos,* an adjective made from the noun *Christos,* "the Christ," or "the anointed one." A Christian, then, is a person related in some way to the Christ. The word comes into usage first in Acts 11:26 — "The disciples were first called Christians in Antioch." It is not known whether the term was invented by the Christians themselves or their enemies. But even if it was first used as a term of derision, the church began to use it proudly. The word was used only twice more in the NT, in Acts 26:28 and I Pet. 4:16, so it seems to have taken hold rather slowly. Other terms were in more common use, such as "disciples," "brethren," and "those of the way."

It is impossible to give an exact definition of the word. In the strictest sense it would be applied to one who has a true, saving faith in Christ, but only God himself has a certain knowledge as to who the true believers are. The word is often used of members of the church; this would lead to debate about what bodies should be included in the concept of the church. It is often used laxly in the sense of "Christlike," applicable to persons who make no pretense of being believers in Christ in a religious sense but who admire and try to copy some features of his character. Then it is applied to things which are appropriate to such persons, with the rather vague meaning of decent, gentle, or charitable.

SAMUEL A. CARTLEDGE

CHRISTIAN YEAR. The Christian Year has been described as "an arrangement by which special days and seasons of the year are set aside for the commemoration of particular aspects of the Christian faith" (A. A. Fleming, *The Christian Year,* Iona Community Publishing Dept., p. 8). Its adoption was of gradual development in the Christian church. It followed the pattern set by the Jewish church, with its ordered round of high festivals and solemn days of remembrance, such as the Passover, the Day of Atonement, the Day of Pentecost, and so on. Some of these were taken over by the Christian church and adapted for its own use.

Origin. The purpose of the Christian year is to celebrate progressively the great acts of God in the redemption of the world by our Lord Jesus Christ, and to stress the corresponding duties incumbent upon the church in response to what God has done. Since the two focal points in the divine plan of salvation are the incarnation and the atonement, the first part of the year is based on the two great festivals of Christmas and Easter. Each of these is preceded by a suitable period of spiritual preparation, viz., Advent and Lent. Whitsunday, which marks the crown and climax of the Christian revelation in the pentecostal gift of the Spirit, concludes this first part of the year. The second part, consisting of the Sundays after Whitsun, and extending (according to the date of Easter) from twenty-one to twenty-seven weeks, is concerned with the practical application of the Christian faith to the daily life of the church and its members.

Easter was, naturally enough, the first annual festival to be observed by the primitive church, linking up historically with the Jewish feast of the Passover. Closely associated with this was the feast of Pentecost, which followed forty-nine days later. In the minds of the early believers, with their Jewish background, these annual festivals could not fail to recall the mighty acts which God had wrought for their salvation in the cross, the empty tomb, and the coming of the Comforter.

The celebration of the anniversary of the birth of Christ, now known as Christmas, did not become general until the fourth century.

Before that time the Eastern Church kept the feast on January 6th (now the feast of the Epiphany); but later the Western practice of observing December 25th began to prevail, the Nativity being separated from the Epiphany. It has been remarked that "the controversies of the fourth to sixth centuries on the incarnation and the person of Christ doubtless contributed to the growth in importance of the feast" (F. L. Cross, *Oxford Dictionary of the Christian Church,* Oxford Univ. Press, 1957, p. 277).

Order and Meaning. The Christian Year begins on the first Sunday in Advent, which is the fourth Sunday before Christmas Day. The Advent season bears witness to the "coming" of Christ, both in his humiliation at Bethlehem and in his final glory as the Judge of Mankind. Christmas Day celebrates the nativity of our Lord. The thirteenth day afterwards (Jan. 6th) is the feast of the Epiphany — "The manifestation of Christ to the Gentiles." The Epiphany season, which links up particularly with the story of the wise men (Matt. 2:1-12), emphasizes the world-wide character of the Christian revelation. Next follows the season of Lent, which opens on Ash Wednesday (q.v.) and covers the six Sundays before Easter Day. The forty days of Lent (excluding the Sundays) are a penitential preparation for the great Easter festival. The fifth Sunday in Lent is commonly known as Passion Sunday and the sixth as Palm Sunday. This latter ushers us into Holy Week, in which we move day by day through the events of the last week of our Lord's earthly life. Good Friday marks the day of Christ's passion, and Easter Sunday celebrates his glorious resurrection. The forty days of the Easter season (see Acts 1:3) conclude with Ascension Day, which commemorates the Lord's exaltation to the right hand of God and testifies to his kingship. Ten days later comes the feast of Pentecost, or Whitsunday, with its definite stress upon the ministry of the Holy Spirit in the church. This ends the first half of the Christian Year.

The second half consists of the Trinity season, beginning with Trinity Sunday, which bears witness to the Christian doctrine of God as Father, Son, and Holy Spirit. The Sundays "after Trinity" (or "after Pentecost," as in the Roman Catholic Church) are concerned with the practical outworking of the great facts and events remembered from Advent to Pentecost. As it has been said, the first half of the year answers the question, "What does a Christian believe?"; the second half answers the question, "What ought a Christian to do?"

Value. The spiritual value of observing the liturgical year is receiving increasing recognition on the part of the non-liturgical churches in all parts of the world. It is an undoubted aid in holding the fullness of the Christian faith and in maintaining the primary doctrines in due proportion. It places the emphasis, as the NT does, upon God's revelation of himself in our Lord Jesus Christ and upon those "once for all" events by which man's redemption was accomplished. Its comprehensive character leaves no aspect of Christian faith and life untouched and so meets man's entire spiritual need. In this way it is also an antidote to modern heresies and "isms," which arise all too often from a neglect or understressing of specific elements in the Christian gospel. For the pastor, the Christian Year provides a tested framework for maintaining a balanced, all-inclusive teaching program and saves him from becoming ·one-sided; for the congregation, it offers an overall picture of faith and life in which can be seen the proportions of any particular doctrine or duty.

BIBLIOGRAPHY

F. L. Cross in *ODCC*; A. A. McArthur, *The Evolution of the Christian Year*; A. Barry, *The Teacher's Prayer Book*; G. Harford, M. Stevenson, J. W. Tyrer (edd.), *The Prayer Book Dictionary*.

FRANK COLQUHOUN

CHRISTIANITY. Though the term Christian (*q.v.*) appears three times in the NT, the time was not yet ripe for its companion word, which came into use in the second century as a designation for the religion which centers in Jesus Christ. It is found first in the writings of Ignatius, where it retains in one passage the NT flavor of the word Christian — opposed and hated by the world (Rom. iii). Twice it is contrasted with Judaism (Magn. x; Phila. vi). Once it is mentioned as a system of truth calling for a corresponding mode of life (Magn. x).

The Christian movement began on Jewish soil and made its first converts among the sons of Israel. Those who adhered to the new faith differed from their fellow Jews in that they believed that Jesus of Nazareth was the Messiah and that God had vindicated his claim by raising him from the dead. The ties with Judaism were not completely cut, but persecution drove an ever deepening wedge between the two groups. Before Judaic Christianity dwindled into comparative insignificance, it passed on its heritage to the Gentiles, who were reached through Greek-speaking Jews such as Barnabas and Paul.

Christianity has certain distinctives. It is historically grounded in the sense that its founder was an actual personage in history, who lived at a certain period in the land of Palestine. In this it differs from religions which are built around mythological figures and emphasize ideas rather than facts which are historically verifiable as well as religiously important.

It is also supernatural in character, for it frankly depends upon revelation. Man is no longer feeling out after God but is resting on the divine self-disclosure in Christ. God has become incarnate in his Son, who confirmed the revelation in the OT and added to it by his teaching and by personal impact. To see him was to see the Father. The miraculous element in Christianity is agreeable to its supernatural nature. History ceases to be a riddle. Eternity has dipped into time. Divine nature has taken human form in order to reveal itself fully and to lift man into fellowship with God.

To accomplish this latter goal, a plan of redemption was necessary. This is crucial to the Christian faith. Christ came to save sinners by the sacrifice of himself. Salvation is by grace through faith. Works are excluded as a ground for acceptance with God (Eph. 2:8-10).

Christianity is trinitarian, acknowledging God the Father, Son, and Holy Spirit. In this it is distinguished from the other monotheistic religions.

The Christian faith is also exclusive. It does not grant that men are saved by any other means than the gospel of Christ. It derives this conviction from the teaching of Scripture, and not from partisan feeling or narrowness of outlook. It does not deny good in other religions, nor does it claim to have all truth. Rather, it rejoices in the truth which God has been pleased to reveal, which is sufficient for salvation. Exclusivism only becomes offensive when it ceases to be missionary.

Christianity may be viewed as a creed, but behind its confession is a personal relation to the Saviour. It may vary from place to place in its form of government, but it everywhere acknowledges the lordship of Christ. Its forms of worship may differ from church to church, but its aim is to glorify God and to make known his saving grace.

BIBLIOGRAPHY

G. G. Findlay, *Christian Doctrine and Morals*; Adolph Harnack, *What is Christianity?*; J. Gresham Machen, *Christianity and Liberalism*; Sverre Norborg, *What is Christianity?*; Francis L. Patton, *Fundamental Christianity*; B. B. Warfield, *Christology and Criticism*, pp. 313-67; 393-444; HERE; SHERK.

EVERETT F. HARRISON

CHRISTMAS. The early Christians did not observe the festival of Christ's birth, to which they did not attach the importance ascribed to his death and resurrection. In the East, and later in the West, Christ's birthday was observed on January 6th in connection with his baptism, a day on which the pagan world celebrated the feast of Dionysus, associated with the lengthening of the days. The night of January 5th-6th was devoted to the feast of Christ's birth and the day of January 6th to his baptism. A fourth century papyrus contains the oldest Christmas liturgy in existence. The nativity festival was separated from the early Christian Epiphany feast and given its own day, December 25th, between the years 325 and 354. In Rome, December 25th is attested as the day of Christ's birth in 336. It was introduced perhaps by Constantine the Great who evidently chose the day because of the popular pagan feast of the sun. Gregory Nazianzen and Chrysostom popularized the new festival in Constantinople. But opposition to the new feast was stubborn throughout the East, especially in Syria (Antioch). Egypt did not receive it till 431, Armenia never.

See also CHRISTIAN YEAR.

BIBLIOGRAPHY

O. Cullmann, *The Early Church*, pp. 21-36; LC.

J. THEODORE MUELLER

CHRISTOLOGY. I. NEW TESTAMENT CHRISTOLOGY. In the NT, the writers indicate who Jesus is by describing the significance of the work he came to do, and the office he came to fulfill. Amidst the varied descriptions of his work and office, always mainly in terms of the OT, there is a unified blending of one aspect with another, and a development that means an enrichment, without any cancellation of earlier tradition.

A. *Jesus in the Gospels.* His humanity (*q.v.*) is taken for granted in the Synoptic Gospels, as if it could not possibly occur to anyone to question it. We see him lying in the cradle, growing, learning, subject to hunger, anxiety, doubt and disappointment, surprise, etc. (Luke 2:40; Mark 2:15; 14:33; 15:34; Luke 7:9) and finally to death and burial. But elsewhere his true humanity is specifically witnessed to, as if it might be called in question (Gal. 4:4; John 1:14), or its significance neglected (Heb. 2:9, 17; 4:15; 5:7-8; 12:2).

Besides this emphasis on his true humanity, there is nevertheless always an emphasis on the fact that even in his humanity he is sinless and also utterly different from other men and that his significance must not be sought by ranking him alongside the greatest or wisest or holiest of all other men. The virgin birth and the resurrection are signs that here we have something quite unique in the realm of humanity. Who or what he is can be discovered only by contrasting him with others, and it shines out most clearly when all others are against him. The event of his coming to suffer and triumph as man in our midst is absolutely decisive for every individual he encounters, and for the destiny of the whole world (John 3:16-18; 10:27-28; 12:31; 16:11; I John 3:8). In his coming the kingdom of God has come (Mark 1:15). His miracles are signs that this is so (Luke 11:20). Woe, therefore, to those who misinterpret them (Mark 3:22-29). He acts and speaks with heavenly regal authority. He can challenge men to lay down their lives for his own sake (Matt. 10:39). The kingdom is indeed his own kingdom (Matt. 16:28; Luke 22:30). He is the One who, in uttering what is simply his own mind, at the same time utters the eternal and decisive word of God. (Matt. 5:22, 28; 24:35). His word effects what it proclaims (Matt. 8:3; Mark 11:21) as God's word does. He has the authority and power even to forgive sins (Mark 2:1-12).

B. *Christ.* His true significance can be understood only when his relationship to the people in whose midst he was born is understood. In the events that are set in motion in his earthly career, God's purpose and covenant with Israel is fulfilled. He is the One who comes to do what neither the people of the OT, nor their anointed representatives — the prophets, priests and kings — could do. But they had been promised that One who would rise up in their own midst would yet make good what all of them had utterly failed to make good. In this sense Jesus of Nazareth is the One anointed with the Spirit and power (Acts 10:38) to be the true Messiah (*q.v.*) or Christ (John 1:41; Rom. 9:5) of his people.

He is the true Prophet (Mark 9:7; Luke 13:33; John 1:21; 6:14), Priest (John 17; Epistle to Hebrews), and King (Matt. 2:2; 21:5; 27:11), as e.g., his baptism (Matt. 3:13 ff.) and his use of Isa. 61 (Luke 4:16-22) indicate. In receiving this anointing and fulfilling this messianic purpose, he receives from his contemporaries the titles Christ (Mark 8:29) and Son of David (Matt. 9:27; 12:23; 15:22; cf. Luke 1:32; Rom. 1:3; Rev. 5:5).

But he gives himself and receives also many other titles which help to illuminate the office he fulfilled and which are even more decisive in indicating who he is. A comparison of the current messianic ideas of Judaism with both the teaching of Jesus himself and the witness of the NT, shows that Jesus selected certain features of messianic tradition which he emphasized and allowed to crystallize round his own person. Certain messianic titles are used by him and of him in preference to others, and are themselves reinterpreted in the use he makes of them and in the relationship he gives them to himself and to one another. This is partly the reason for his "messianic reserve" (Matt. 8:4; 16:20; John 10:24; etc.).

C. *Son of man.* Jesus used the title, "Son of man," of himself more than any other. There are passages in the OT where the phrase means simply "man" (e.g., Ps. 8:5) and at times Jesus' use of it corresponds to this meaning (cf. Matt. 8:20). But the majority of contexts indicate that in using this title Jesus is thinking of Dan. 7:13, where the "Son of man" is a heavenly figure, both an individual and at the same time the ideal representative of the people of God. In the Jewish apocalyptic tradition this Son of man is regarded as a pre-existent one who will come at the end of the ages as Judge, and as a light to the Gentiles (cf. Mark 14:62). Jesus sometimes uses this title when he emphasizes his authority and power (Mark 2:10; 2:28; Luke 12:19). At other times he uses it when he is emphasizing his humility and incognito (Mark 10:45; 14:21; Luke 19:10; 9:58). In the Gospel of John the title is used in contexts which emphasize his pre-existence, his descent into the world in a humiliation which both conceals and manifests his glory (John 3:13 f.; 6:62 f.; 8:6 ff.), his role of uniting heaven and earth (John 1:51), his coming to judge men and hold the messianic banquet (John 5:27; 6:27).

Though "Son of man" is used only by Jesus of himself, what it signified is otherwise expressed, especially in Rom. 5 and I Cor. 15, where Christ is described as the "man from heaven" or the "second Adam." Paul here takes up hints in the Synoptic Gospels that in the coming of Christ there is a new creation (Matt. 19:38) in which his part is to be related to and contrasted with that of Adam in the first creation (cf., e.g., Mark 1:13; Luke 3:38). Both Adam and Christ have the representative relationship to the whole of mankind that is involved in the conception "Son of man." But Christ is regarded as One whose identification with all mankind is far more deep and complete than that of Adam. In his redeeming action salvation is provided for all mankind. By faith in him all men can participate in a salvation already accomplished in him. He is also the image and glory of God (II Cor. 4:4, 6; Col. 1:15) which man was made to reflect (I Cor. 11:7) and which Christians are meant to put on in participating in the new creation (Col. 3:10).

D. *Servant.* Jesus' self-identification with men is brought out in passages that recall the suffering servant of Isaiah (Matt. 12:18; Mark 10:45; Luke 24:26). It is in his baptismal experience that he enters this role (cf. Matt. 3:17 and Isa. 42:1) of suffering as the One in whom all his people are represented and who is offered for the sins of the world (John 1:29; Isa. 53). Jesus is explicitly called the "Servant" in the early preaching of the church (Acts 3:13, 26; 4:27, 30), and the thought of him as such was also in Paul's mind (cf. Rom. 4:25; 5:19; II Cor. 5:21).

In the humiliation of his self-identification with our humanity (Heb. 2:17; 4:15; 5:7; 2:9; 12:2) he fulfils the part, not only of victim, but also of High Priest offering himself once for all (Heb. 7:27; 9:12; 10:10) in a self-offering that brings about for ever a new relationship between God and man. His "baptism," the fulfilment of which he accomplishes in his earthly career culminating in his cross (cf. Luke 12:50), is his self-sanctification to his eternal priesthood, and in and through this self-sanctification his people are sanctified for ever (John 17:19; Heb. 10:14).

E. *Son of God.* The title "Son of God" is not used by Jesus himself to the same extent as "Son of man" (though cf. e.g., Mark 12:6), but it is the name given to him (cf. Luke 1:35) by the heavenly voice at his baptism and transfiguration (Mark 1:11; 9:7), by

Peter in his moment of illumination (Matt. 16:16), by the demons (Mark 5:7) and the centurion (Mark 15:39).

This title "Son of God" is messianic. In the OT, Israel is the "son" (Ex. 4:22; Hos. 11:1). The king (Ps. 2:7; II Sam. 7:14) and possibly the priests (Mal. 1:6) are also given this title. Jesus, therefore, in using and acknowledging this title is assuming the name of One in whom the true destiny of Israel is to be fulfilled.

But the title also reflects the unique filial consciousness of Jesus in the midst of such a messianic task (cf. Matt. 11:27; Mark 13:32; 14:36; Ps. 2:7). This has the profoundest christological implications. He is not simply *a* son but *the* Son (John 20:17). This consciousness, which is revealed at high points in the Synoptic Gospels, is regarded in John as forming the continuous conscious background of Jesus' life. The Son and the Father are one (John 5:19, 30; 16:32) in will (4:34; 6:38; 7:28; 8:42; 13:3) and activity (14:10) and in giving eternal life (10:30). The Son is in the Father and the Father in the Son (10:38; 14:10). The Son, like the Father, has life and quickening power in himself (5:26). The Father loves the Son (3:35; 10:17; 17:23 f.) and commits all things into his hands (5:35), giving him authority to judge (5:22). The title also implies a unity of being and nature with the Father, uniqueness of origin and preexistence (John 3:16; Heb. 1:2).

F. *Lord.* Though Paul also uses the title "Son of God," he most frequently refers to Jesus as "Lord" (*q.v.*). This term did not originate with Paul. Jesus is addressed and referred to in the Gospels as Lord (Matt. 7:21; Mark 11:3; Luke 6:46). Here the title can refer primarily to his teaching authority (Luke 11:1; 12:41), but it can also have a deeper significance (Matt. 8:25; Luke 5:8). Though it is most frequently given to him after his exaltation, he himself quoted Ps. 110:1, and prepared for this use (Mark 12:35; 14:62).

His lordship extends over the course of history and all the powers of evil (Col. 2:15; I Cor. 2:6-8; 8:5; 15:24) and must be the ruling concern in the life of the church (Eph. 6:7; I Cor. 7:10, 25). As Lord he will come to judge (II Thess. 1:7).

Though his work in his humiliation is also the exercise of lordship, it was after the resurrection and ascension that the title of Lord was most spontaneously conferred on Jesus (Acts 2:32 ff., Phil. 2:1-11) by the early church. They prayed to him as they would pray to God (Acts 7:59 f.; I Cor. 1:2; cf. Rev. 9:14, 21; 22:16). His name as Lord is linked in the closest association with that of God himself (I Cor. 1:3; II Cor. 1:2; cf. Rev. 17:14; 19:16; and Deut. 10:17). To him are referred the promises and attributes of the "Lord" God (*Kyrios,* LXX) in the OT (cf. Acts 2:21 and 38; Rom. 10:3 and Joel 2:32; I Thess. 5:2 and Amos 5:18; Phil. 2:10 f., and Isa. 45:23). To him are freely applied the language and formulae which are used of God himself, so that it is difficult to decide in e.g., a passage like Rom. 9:5 whether it is the Father or the Son to whom reference is made. In John 1:1; 1:18; 20:28; II Thess. 1:12; I Tim. 3:16; Tit. 2:13 and II Pet. 1:1, Jesus is confessed as "God."

G. *Word.* The statement, "The Word became flesh" (John 1:14), relates Jesus both to the Wisdom of God in the OT (which has a personal character, Prov. 8) and to the law of God (Deut. 30:11-14, Isa. 2:3) as these are revealed and declared in the going forth of the Word (*q.v.*) by which God creates, reveals himself, and fulfils his will in history (Ps. 33:6; Isa. 55:10 f.; 11:4; Rev. 1:16). There is here a close relationship between word and event. In the NT it becomes clearer that the Word is not merely a message proclaimed but is Christ himself (cf. Eph. 3:17 and Col. 3:16; I Pet. 1:3 and 23; John 8:31 and 15:17). What Paul expresses in Col. 1, John expresses in his prologue. In both passages (and in Heb. 1:1-14) the place of Christ as the One who in the beginning was the agent of God's creative activity is asserted. In bearing witness to these aspects of Jesus Christ, it is inevitable that the NT should witness to his pre-existence. He was "in the beginning" (John 1:1-3; Heb. 1:2-10). His very coming (Luke 12:49; Mark 1:24; 2:17) involves him in deep self-abasement (II Cor. 8:9; Phil. 2:5-7) in fulfilment of a purpose ordained for him from the foundation of the world (Rev. 13:8). In the Gospel of John, he gives this testimony in his own words (John 8:58; 17:5, 24).

Yet while his coming from the Father involves no diminution of his Godhead, there is nevertheless a subordination of the incarnate Son to the Father in the relationship of love and equality which subsists between the Father and the Son (John 14:28). For it is the Father who sends and the Son who is sent

(John 10:36), the Father who gives and the Son who receives (John 5:26), the Father who ordains and the Son who fulfils (John 10:18). Christ belongs to God who is the Head (I Cor. 3:23; 11:13) and in the end will subject all things to him (I Cor. 15:28).

II. PATRISTIC CHRISTOLOGY. In the period immediately following the NT, the Apostolic Fathers (A.D. 90-140) can speak highly of Christ. We have a sermon beginning: "Brethren, we ought so to think of Jesus Christ, as of God, as the Judge of the quick and the dead" (II Clem.). Ignatius with his emphasis on both the true deity and humanity of Christ can refer to the "blood of God." Even if their witness falls short of this, there is a real attempt to combat both Ebionitism (q.v.), which looked on Christ as a man born naturally, on whom the Holy Spirit came at his baptism, and also Docetism (q.v.) which asserted that the humanity and sufferings of Christ were apparent rather than real.

The Apologists (e.g., Justin ca. 100-165, and Theophilus of Antioch) of the next generation sought to commend the gospel to the educated and to defend it in face of attacks by pagans and Jews. Their conception of the place of Christ was determined, however, rather by current philosophical ideas of the logos than by the historic revelation given in the gospel, and for them Christianity tends to become a new law or philosophy and Christ another God inferior to the highest God.

Melito of Sardis at this time, however, spoke clearly of Christ as both God and man, and Irenaeus (ca. 140-200), in meeting the challenge of Gnosticism, returned also to a more biblical standpoint, viewing the person of Christ always in close connection with his work of redemption and revelation, in fulfilment of which "he became what we are, in order that he might make us to become even what he is himself." He thus became the new Head of our race and recovered what had been lost in Adam, saving us through a process of "recapitulation." In thus identifying himself with us he is both true God and true man. Tertullian (ca. 160-220) also made his contribution to Christology in combating Gnosticism (q.v.) and the various forms of what came to be known as Monarchianism (Dynamism, Modalism, Sabellianism) which had reacted in different ways against the apparent worship of Christ as a second God beside the Father. He was the first to teach that the Father and

Son are of "one substance," and spoke of three persons in the Godhead.

Origen (ca. 185-254) had a decisive influence in the development of Christology in the East. He taught the eternal generation of the Son from the Father and used the term homoousios. Yet at the same time his complicated doctrine included a view of Christ as an intermediate being, spanning the distance between the utterly transcendent being of God and this created world. Both sides in the later Arian controversy which began ca. 318 show influences which may be traced to Origen. (See ORIGENISM).

Arius (ca. 265-336) denied the possibility of any divine emanation, or contact with the world, or of any distinction within the Godhead. Therefore the Word is made out of nothing before time. Though called God, he is not very God. Arius denied to Christ a human soul. The council of Nicaea ca. 325 condemned Arius by insisting that the Son was not simply the "first born of all creation" but was indeed "of one essence with the Father." In his long struggle against Arianism (q.v.), Athanasius (298-373) sought to uphold the unity of essence of the Father and Son by basing his argument not on a philosophical doctrine of the nature of the Logos, but on the nature of the redemption accomplished by the Word in the flesh. Only God himself, taking on human flesh and dying and rising in our flesh, can effect a redemption which consists in being saved from sin and corruption and death, and in being raised to share the nature of God himself.

After Nicaea the question was raised: If Jesus Christ be truly God, how can he be at the same time truly man? Apollinaris (310-90) tried to safeguard the unity of the person of the God-man by denying that he had complete manhood. He assumed that man was composed of three parts: body; irrational or animal soul; and rational soul or intellect (nous). In Jesus the human nous was displaced by the divine Logos. But this denied the true reality of Christ's humanity and indeed of the incarnation itself and therefore of the salvation. The most cogent objection to it was expressed by Gregory of Nazianzus: "The unassumed is the unhealed." Christ must be true man as well as true God. Apollinaris was condemned at Constantinople, 381.

How, then, can God and man be united in one person? The controversy became focused on Nestorius, Bishop of Constantinople (d. 451), who refused to approve the use of the phrase "mother of God" (theotokos) as applied to Mary, who, he asserted, bore not the Godhead but "a man who was the organ of the Godhead." In spite of the fact that Nestorius (see NESTORIANISM) clearly asserted that the God-man was one person, he seemed to think of the two natures as existing side by side and so sharply distinguished that the suffering of the humanity could not be attributed to the Godhead. This separation was condemned, and Nestorius' deposition at the Council of Ephesus (431) was brought about largely by the influence of Cyril in reasserting a unity of the two natures in Christ's person so complete that the impassible Word can be said to have suffered death. Cyril sought to avoid Apollinarianism (q.v.) by asserting that the humanity of Christ was complete and entire but had no independent subsistence (anhypostasis).

A controversy arose over one of Cyril's followers, Eutyches, who asserted that in the incarnate Christ the two natures coalesced in one. This implied a docetic view of Christ's human nature and called in question his consubstantiality with us. Eutychianism and Nestorianism were finally condemned at the Council of Chalcedon (451) which taught: One Christ in two natures united in one person or hypostasis, yet remaining "without confusion, without conversion, without division, without separation."

Further controversies were yet to arise before the mind of the church could be made up as to how the human nature could indeed retain its complete humanity and yet be without independent subsistence. It was Leontius of Byzantium who advanced the formula that enabled the majority to agree on an interpretation of the Chalcedonian formula. The human nature of Christ, he taught, was not an independent hypostasis (anhypostatic), but it was enhypostatic, i.e., it had its subsistence in and through the Logos.

A further controversy arose as to whether two natures meant that Christ had two wills or centers of volition. A formula was first devised to suit the Monothelites who asserted that the God-man, though in two natures, worked by one divine-human energy. But finally, in spite of the preference of Honorius, Bishop of Rome for a formula asserting "one will" in Christ, the Western church in 649 decreed that there were "two natural wills" in

Christ, and this was made the decision of the whole church at the sixth Ecumenical Council at Constantinople in 680, the views of Pope Honorius I being condemned as heresy.

III. FURTHER DEVELOPMENT. The theologians of the Middle Ages accepted the authority of patristic Christology and allowed their thought and experience to be enriched by Augustine's (354-430) stress on the real humanity of Christ in his atoning work, on his importance as our example in humility, and on mystical experience. But this emphasis on the humanity of Christ tended to be made only when he was presented in his passion as the One who mediates between man and a distant and terrible God. In their more abstract discussion of the person of Christ, there was a tendency to present One who has little share in our real humanity. The humanity of Jesus, however, became the focus of mystical devotion in St. Bernard of Clairvaux (1091-1153) who stressed the union of the soul with the Bridegroom.

At the Reformation, Luther's Christology was based on Christ as true God and true man in inseparable unity. He spoke of the "wondrous exchange" by which through the union of Christ with human nature, his righteousness becomes ours, and our sins become his. He refused to tolerate any thinking which might lead to speculation about the God-man divorced either from the historical person of Jesus himself or from the work he came to do and the office he came to fulfil in redeeming us. But Luther taught that the doctrine of the "communication of attributes" (communicatio idiomatum) meant that there was a mutual transference of qualities or attributes between the divine and human natures in Christ, and developed this to mean a mutual interpenetration of divine and human qualities or properties, verging on the very commingling of natures which Chalcedonian Christology had avoided. In Lutheran orthodoxy this led to a later controversy as to how far the manhood of the Son of God shared in and exercised such attributes of divine majesty, how far it was capable of doing so, and how far Jesus used or renounced these attributes during his human life.

Calvin also approved of the orthodox Christological statements of the church councils. He taught that when the Word became incarnate he did not suspend nor alter his normal function of upholding the universe. He found the extreme statements of Lutheran Christology guilty of a tendency towards the heresy of Eutyches, and insisted that the two natures in Christ are distinct though never separate. Yet in the unity of person in Christ, one nature is so closely involved in the activities and events which concern the other, that the human nature can be spoken of as if it partook of divine attributes. Salvation is accomplished not only by the divine nature working through the human but is indeed the accomplishment of the human Jesus who worked out a perfect obedience and sanctification for all men in his own person (the humanity being not only the instrument but the "material cause" of salvation). This salvation is worked out in fulfilment of the threefold office of Prophet, Priest and King.

There is here a divergence between the Lutheran and Reformed teaching. The Lutherans laid the stress upon a union of two natures in a communion in which the human nature is assumed into the divine nature. The Reformed theologians refused to think of an assumption of the human nature into the divine, but rather of an assumption of the human nature into the divine person of the Son in whom there was a direct union between the two natures. Thus, while keeping to the patristic conception of the *communicatio idiomatum,* they developed the concept of the *communicatio operationum,* (i.e., that the properties of the two natures coincide in the one person) in order to speak of an active communion between the natures without teaching a doctrine of mutual interpenetration. The importance of the *communicatio operationum* (which also came to be taken up by Lutherans) is that it corrects the rather static way of speaking of the hypostatic union in patristic theology, by seeing the person and the work of Christ in inseparable unity, and so asserted a dynamic communion between the divine and human natures of Christ in terms of his atoning and reconciling work. It stresses the union of two natures for his mediatorial operations in such a way that this work proceeds from the one person of the God-man by the distinctive effectiveness of both natures. In this light the hypostatic union is seen as the ontological side of the dynamic action of reconciliation, and so incarnation and atonement are essentially complementary.

Since the early nineteenth century the tendency has been to try to depart from the Chalcedonian doctrine of the two natures on the ground that this could not be related to the human Jesus portrayed in the Gospels, and that it made use of terms which were alien both to Holy Scripture and to current modes of expression. Schleiermacher built up a Christology on the basis of finding in Christ a unique and archetypal consciousness of utter filial dependence on the Father. In Lutheran Christology there was a further important development, the attributes of the humanity of Jesus being regarded as limiting those of his deity, according to the "Kenotic" theory of Thomasius. On this view, the Word, in the incarnation, deprived himself of his "external" attributes of omnipotence, omnipresence, and omniscience, yet still retained the "essential" moral attributes. Though always remaining God, he ceased to exist in the form of God. Even his self-consciousness as God was absorbed in the single awakening and growing consciousness of the God-man. Ritschl, too, stressed the importance of the ethical attributes of the person of Christ, and of refusing to speculate beyond the revelation of God found in the historic Jesus who must have for us the value of God and whose perfect moral nature is both human and divine. Since the beginning of the twentieth century, modern conceptions of personality and scientific and philosophical doctrines of evolution have enabled theologians to produce further variations in the development of nineteenth century Christology.

In more recent discussion there has been a return to the use of the Chalcedonian doctrine of the two natures, particularly as interpreted in the Reformed tradition, and a realization that this apparently paradoxical formula is meant to point towards the mystery of the unique relationship of grace set up here between the divine and human in the person and work of the God-man. This mystery must not be thought of apart from atonement, for it is perfected and worked out in history through the whole work of Christ crucified and risen and ascended. To share in this mystery of the new unity of God and man in Christ in some measure is also given to the church through the Spirit. This means that our Christology is decisive in determining our doctrine of the church and of the word of sacraments as used in the church. Our Christology must indeed indicate the direction in which we seek to solve all theological problems where we are dealing with the relation of a human event or reality to the grace of God in Christ. In this christological pattern the whole of our theological system should find its coherence and unity.

Nor must this mystery be thought of in abstraction from the person of Jesus shown to us in the Gospels in the historical context of the life of Israel. The human life and teaching of the historical Jesus have to be given full place in his saving work as essential and not incidental or merely instrumental in his atoning reconciliation. Here we must give due weight to modern biblical study in helping us to realize both what kind of a man Jesus was and yet also to see this Jesus of history as the Christ of faith, the Lord, the Son of God. Through the study of his office and work we come to understand how his humanity is not only truly individual but is also truly representative.

See also IMAGE; ALEXANDRIA, SCHOOL OF; ANTIOCH, SCHOOL OF.

BIBLIOGRAPHY
H. R. Mackintosh, *The Person of Christ*; J. L. M. Haire, "On Behalf of Chalcedon" in *Essays in Christology for Karl Barth* (edited by T. H. L. Parker); D. M. Baillie, *God was in Christ*; O. Cullmann, *Die Christologie des Neuen Testaments*; E. Brunner, *The Mediator*; L. B. Smedes, *The Incarnation, Trends in Modern Anglican Thought*; H. Relton, *A Study in Christology*; J. N. D. Kelly, *Early Christian Doctrines*; K. Barth, *Church Dogmatics* IV, 1 and IV, 2; RGG, 3rd ed., Art. *Christologie* I, pp. 1745-89; T. F. Torrance, "Atonement and the Oneness of the Church," SJT, Vol. 7, pp. 245-69.

RONALD S. WALLACE

CHURCH. Our word church, like its cognate forms, *kirche, kerk, kirk,* comes from the Greek adjective, *to kuriakon,* used first of the house of the Lord, then of his people. The NT word, *ekklēsia,* is used of a public assemblage summoned by a herald (Acts 19:32, 39, 40). In the LXX, however, it means the assembly or congregation of the Israelites, especially when gathered before the Lord for religious purposes. Accordingly, it is used in the NT for the congregation which the living God assembles about his Messiah Jesus. Thus the church is the spiritual family of God, the Christian fellowship created by the Holy Spirit through the testimony to the mighty acts of God in Christ Jesus. Wherever the Holy Spirit unites worshiping souls to Christ and to each other there is the mystery of the church.

The Definition of the Church. More fully stated, the one church of God is not an institutional but a supernatural entity which is in process of growth towards the world to come.

It is the sphere of the action of the risen and ascended Lord. All its members are in Christ and are knit together by a supernatural kinship. All their gifts and activities continue the work of Christ by the power of the Holy Spirit, originate from Christ, and are co-ordinated by him to the final goal. Then the church will appear in the age to come as the one people of God united in one congregation before the throne, as the one celestial city — the new Jerusalem.

The Marks of the Church. The Lord brings and keeps his people in covenant fellowship with himself by his Spirit and his Word (Isa. 59:21). His voice is heard in the proclamation of his Word and his acts are seen in the administration of his sacraments. Accordingly, these with prayer and praise are the marks of the visible church, the means the Holy Spirit uses to bring individuals to personal faith and to nourish believers in the corporate worship of the Christian community. As they receive God's promises, he forgives the sins of his people and seals them with his sacraments for the world to come.

The Biblical History of the Church. The existence of the church is a revelation of the gracious heart of God. The Father chose his eternal Son to become the Saviour of sinners, the Messiah of the whole Israel of God. In him God chose the people for his own possession and called individuals into this fellowship. This one people of God includes the patriarchs, the congregation of ancient Israel, Jesus and his disciples, the primitive community of his resurrection, and the Christian church.

For the people of God, the OT period was the dispensation of promise, the NT that of fulfilment. Jesus Christ revealed not a new God, but a new way of worshiping the same God. In the OT it is "the whole assembly of the congregation of Israel" (Deut. 31:30) who hear the law (Deut. 4:10; 9:10; 18:16; Acts 7:38), who sacrifice the passover lamb (Ex. 12), whom God redeems from Egypt (Ex. 15:13, 16; Ps. 77:15; 74:2; Acts 20:28), with whom God makes the covenant at Sinai (Ex. 33-35), for whose sins expiatory sacrifices are provided (Lev. 4 and 16), who are a holy nation to praise God (Ex. 19:6; Hos. 2:23; Ps. 22:22; cf. Heb. 2:12; I Pet. 2:9-10). Other NT passages also recognize a unity with the OT people of God (Matt. 8:11; Rom. 11:16-28; I Cor. 10:1-4). The messianic expectation of the OT includes the formation of a faithful new Israel. In Christ the God of the OT speaks so that the NT church is the fulfilment of the OT congregation.

The several steps in the formation of the new Israel of God include the calling of the disciples to gather as sheep about their shepherd, the confession of Peter, the Last Supper, the cross and the resurrection, Pentecost and the sending out of the apostles as eyewitnesses of the resurrection. Jesus bound the disciples not to the Torah of the rabbis nor to the ideas of a Socrates, but to himself. To this fellowship gathered around God's saving self-revelation in the Messiah, Jesus gave the *kerygma,* the Lord's prayer, the sacraments with common praise following ·the Last Supper, a distinct code with special teachings on such matters as divorce, authoritative teachers, a common purse and treasurer.

God's dealings with men are marked first by a narrowing of the channel that the stream of revelation may be deepened and then thereafter that the blessing may become world-wide. Thus he dealt first with the human race, then with the nation of Israel, later with the remnant thereof, further with the few pious families from which John, Jesus and the first disciples came. When the Good Shepherd was taken, all the disciples forsook him and fled so that the Israel of God was one person, the Saviour who died on Calvary for the sins of the world. But God raised up from the dead our Lord Jesus Christ and sent that Great Shepherd of the sheep to gather again the flock. At the appointed mountain over five hundred met him at one time, three thousand were converted at Pentecost, and the Lord continued to add together daily those who were being saved.

On the basis of the OT and the gospel preparation Christ poured forth the Holy Spirit at Pentecost to constitute the assembled fellowship the church of God. The Spirit anointed, christened, sealed every member of the gathering. From the exalted Christ, he came to be the life and guide of the church until the return of her Lord. In bringing the gospel to the gentile world, God established a new missionary center, Antioch, called a new voice, the Apostle Paul, and approved a new name for his people, Christian.

The Nature of the Church. The Apostle Paul speaks of the whole and of each local group as "the church" even as he uses this term for a household of believers as well as for larger gatherings. Thus it is not the addition of churches which makes the whole church, nor is the whole church divided into separate congregations. But wherever the church meets she exists as a whole, she is the church in that place. The particular congregation represents the universal church, and, through participation in the redemption of Christ, mystically comprehends the whole of which it is the local manifestation.

The terms "the church of God," "the churches in Christ" reach their full expression in "the churches of God . . . in Christ Jesus," (I Thess. 2:14). This phraseology indicates that the significant features of the church are her relationship to God and to Jesus Christ.

As to the former, the church is a fact established by God. It is his supernatural act. According to the consentient testimony of the Old and of the New Testaments, this is not a man-made myth but a God-given fact. The same God who spoke the word of promise to ancient Israel speaks the word of fulfilment to the Christian congregation. As the Father reveals the Son, the Messiah builds his church (Matt. 16:17-18; 11:25-30). At Pentecost the three miracles manifest the direct action of God establishing his church. The NT speaks of the church as God's building, his planting, his vineyard, his temple, his household, his olive tree, his city, and his people. It describes her ministers as the gifts of God (I Cor. 12:28), of the ascended Christ (Eph. 4:11), or of the Holy Spirit (Acts 20:28). Paul recognized the priority of the Jerusalem church not because of the personal importance of the individuals who composed it, but because this fellowship of men and women was the assembly of God in Christ. That is, he recognized the fact of God's action and did not treat it as a matter of human speculation which was at his disposal.

As the church is a fact established by God, so is she the place where God acts for our salvation. Here the risen Lord encounters men, changes them from rebels against their Maker into children of their heavenly Father, brings them from enmity into peace. It pleases God by the foolishness of the *kerygma* to save those who believe (I Cor. 1:21). The gospel is the power of God who saved us and called us to faith (Rom. 1:16; 15:16 f.; II Tim. 1:8). As we observe the outward functioning of the Word and the sacraments with the bodily senses, it is not less important that we contemplate the activity of God in the church with the ear and the eye of faith. Preaching becomes more effective as it calls men more often to behold God working for them than when it scolds men for not working better for God. "God, the Creator of heaven and earth, speaks with thee through His preachers, baptizes, catechises, absolves thee through the ministry of His own sacraments" (Luther). As the sacrament is administered, Christ is not less busy giving himself and his blessings to the believer than the minister is in distributing the bread and the cup to the communicants. The Reformers speak of the Sabbath as the day in which we are to rest from our labors that *God may work* in us. As God generates believers by the preaching of the Word of Christ, and nourishes them by the sacraments of his grace, faith beholds the face of the Lord in the form of the church of the living God.

God's acts in the church are in Christ Jesus. An adequate recognition of Jesus as the Messiah and of the mighty acts of God in him establishes the integral relation of the church to her Lord. The King-Messiah and the people of God belong together. As the shepherd implies the flock, as the hen gathers her chickens under her wings, as the vine has many branches, the body its several members, as the foundation supports its building, as the Servant justifies many, as the Son of Man stands for the saints of the Most High, as the King implies the kingdom, so the Messiah has his twelve and the Lord his church. Jesus spoke of "my church" and of "my flock," and these two are linked together in Acts 20:28. The several lines of parallel thoughts support the infrequent use by Jesus of the word church (Matt. 16:18; 18:17). Following his exaltation, by the one Holy Spirit we are all baptized into the one body of Christ and each is given a special function in his body. Christ is the church herself in that she is the body of Christ, and yet Christ is distinct from the church in that while she is the body he is her Head, and at the same time her Lord, her Judge, her Bridegroom. Her life, her holiness and her unity are in him.

The heavenly church is the bride awaiting Christ her Bridegroom (Mark 2:19, 20; II Cor. 11:2; Rom. 7:1-6 and especially Ephesians and Rev. 19-21). Christ loved the church and gave himself up for her. Having cleansed the church by the washing of water with the Word, he is now sanctifying her in order that he may present her spotless for the marriage feast of the Lamb. Thus, within the heart of Christ's bride there should ever be a great longing for the hour when all the shadows shall flee before the flaming of his advent feet.

The Ministry of the Church. The one essential ministry of the church is, therefore, the ministry of her Lord and Saviour Jesus Christ. Hebrews and Revelation reveal the Lamb in the midst of the throne, the High Priest ever interceding at the heavenly altar of prayer as the focus of Christian worship. By his heavenly ministration all of God's people have access to the throne of grace. In the NT church there is no chancel separating the clergy from the laity. All of the flock are God's heritage (clergy), a royal priesthood, a people (laity) for God's own possession (I Pet. 2:9; 5:2-3).

As under-shepherds, Christ appointed first of all the apostles who had companied with him through his ministry and who were eyewitnesses of his resurrection. By the apostolic *kerygma,* God brought those who had not seen Jesus into a like precious faith with the apostles. As they directly represent Christ and speak with the authority he has conferred, so there is no way to him which detours around the apostolic witness to Christ. They preached Christ Jesus as Lord and themselves servants for Christ's sake (II Cor. 4:5). While the church belongs to Christ, the apostles belong to the church, not the church to them (I Cor. 3:22). Lest any one would think they baptized in their own name, it was their custom to have baptism performed by their associates (Acts 10:47 f.; I Cor. 1:13-17).

Following the apostles were the prophets who brought words from God for the practical problems of life and were responsible to the church. Then there were evangelists gifted in presenting the gospel to win men to Christ and teachers to instruct them in Christian living. In the local congregations there was a plurality of officers: elders to oversee the work and conduct of the church, and deacons to distribute to the necessities of saints. In this latter service, ministering women ably assisted.

The Mission of the Church. Our Lord Jesus Christ is the sun about which the whole mission of the church revolves. Public worship is the encounter of the risen Redeemer with his people; evangelism is calling men to the Saviour; publishing the law of God is proclaiming his lordship; Christian nurture is feeding his lambs and disciplining his flock; ministering to the needs of men is continuing the work of the Great Physician.

In the whole work and witness of the church, Jesus Christ is to be recognized as Lord, the only King in Zion. Her business is to obey his will, to proclaim not her own but his reign. For God has established him upon that throne of which David's was a type (Isa. 9:6-7; Luke 1:26-35; Acts 2:25-36). He has been enthroned with all authority that he may give repentance and remission of sins (Matt. 28:18; Acts 5:31). Thanks to his intercession, his people have access to the throne of grace for mercy and help in every time of need. Every mercy received from Christ, every comfort of the Spirit, every assurance of the Father's love is a testimony to the praise of the glory of God's grace. And the church is this witness, the concrete evidence of the grace of the Lord Jesus Christ, the love of God and the communion of the Holy Spirit.

BIBLIOGRAPHY

Arndt; K. L. Schmidt "Ekklesia" in *TWNT*; pamphlet 92 of World Conference on Faith and Order, 1939; *The Nature of the Church*, American Theol. Committee, Chicago, 1945; F. J. A. Hort, *The Christian Ecclesia*; R. N. Flew, *Jesus and His Church*; Geo. Jonnston, *The Doctrine of the Church in the NT*; G. Aulen, *The Universal Church in God's Design*; A. Nygren, *Christ and His Church*; A. Schlatter, *The Church in the NT Period*; W. G. Kuemmel, *Kirchenbegriff und geschichtsbewusstsein in der urgemeinde und bei Jesus*; J. Knox, *The Early Church and the Coming Great Church*; S. deDietrich, *The Witnessing Community*; W. A. Visser'T Hooft, *The Kingship of Christ*; and *The Renewal of the Church*.

Articles include: E. Schlink, "Christus und die Kirche," *KeDo* I (1955), pp. 1-27; N. A. Dahl, "Christ, Creation and the Church" in (Dodd) *Background of the NT* (1955), pp. 422-43; K. Barth, "Die Kirche die lebendige Gemeinde des lebendigen Herrn Jesus Christus" *TS* heft 22 (1947), pp. 21-44; E. L. Allen, "The Jewish Christian Church in the Fourth Gospel," *JBL*, LXXIV (1955), pp. 175-87; R. L. Hicks, "Jesus and His Church," *ATR*, XXXIV (1952), pp. 85-93; E. Fascher, "Jesus der Lehrer. Ein Beitrag zur Frage nach dem Quellort der Kirchen idee," ThLZ 80 (1955), pp. 325-42; R. Bultmann, "The Transformation of the Idea of the Church in the History of Early Christianity," CJT (1955), pp. 73-81; O. Kuss, "Jesus und die Kirche im NT," *TQ* 135 (1955), pp. 18-33; B. Metzger, E. Brunner, C. Norborg, "The Church" *ThT* (1947), pp. 316-45.

WILLIAM CHILDS ROBINSON

CHURCH GOVERNMENT. Basically there are three types of church government, the episcopal, the presbyterian, and the congregational. Probably none of these exists in a pure form without admixture of the others. Episcopalianism, for example, finds a large place for presbyters in its synods and elsewhere, and its congregations have many functions of their own. Presbyterian congregations also play their part, while the appearance of moderators attests a movement towards episcopal supervision. The very existence of such groupings as Congregational and Baptist Unions, with their presidents, shows that churches with a basically congregational polity are yet alive to the place of other elements in the Christian tradition. Yet the generalization we have stated does apply, and we shall examine these systems in turn.

I. EPISCOPACY is the system in which the chief ministers of the church are bishops, others being presbyters (or priests) and deacons. All of these are mentioned in the NT, although there bishops and presbyters seem to be identical (see EPISCOPACY). Those who see an episcopal system in the NT point to the function of the apostles (which some feel was passed on to the bishops they ordained), to the position of James of Jerusalem (which is not unlike that of the later bishop), to the function of Timothy and Titus as revealed in the Pastoral Epistles (which seems to indicate a status intermediate between those of the apostles and the bishops of later times). There are also the facts that the apostles practiced ordination by the laying on of hands (Acts 6:6; I Tim. 4:14), and that they appointed elders in the churches they founded (Acts 14:23), presumably with the laying on of hands. On this view the apostles were the supreme ministers of the early church, and they took care that suitable men were ordained to the ministry. To some of them they entrusted the power to ordain, and so provided for the continuance of the ministry in succeeding generations.

It is further alleged that the organization of the church subsequent to NT days supports this view. In the time of Ignatius the threefold ministry was clearly in existence in Asia Minor. By the end of the second century it is attested for Gaul and Africa by the writings of Irenaeus and Tertullian. Nowhere is there evidence of a violent struggle (as would be natural if a divinely ordained congregationalism or presbyterianism were overthrown), and the same threefold ministry appeared universally. The conclusion that is drawn is that episcopacy is the primitive and rightful form of church government.

But there are objections. For example, there is no evidence that bishops differed from presbyters in NT days. It is going too far to say that all the ministry of those times was of apostolic origin. What was the case with churches not of apostolic foundation like

Colosse? Again some of the early church orders, like the *Didache,* are congregational in outlook. The case is not proved.

II. PRESBYTERIANISM does not usually hold that only its polity is to be found in the NT. At the Reformation the Presbyterian leaders thought that they were restoring the original form of church government, but this would not be vigorously defended by many Presbyterians today. It is recognized that there has been much development, but it is held that this took place under the guidance of the Spirit, and that the essentials of the presbyterian system are scriptural. In the NT it is beyond question that the presbyters occupy an important place. They are identical with the bishops, and form the principal local ministry. In each place there appears to have been a number of presbyters who formed a kind of college or committee which was in charge of local church affairs. That is the natural conclusion to which exhortations like Heb. 13:17; I Thess. 5:12 f., etc., point. From the account of the Council of Jerusalem in Acts 15 we see that the presbyters occupied an important place at the very highest levels of the early church. In the subapostolic age the bishop developed at the expense of the presbyters. This was due to such circumstances as the need for a strong leader in times of persecution and in the controversies against heretics, and perhaps to the prestige attaching to the minister who regularly conducted the service of Holy Communion.

There is much that is convincing here. Against it, as a complete understanding of the NT and the early church, are the considerations we have adduced under EPISCOPACY, and those to follow under the next heading.

III. CONGREGATIONALISM, as the name implies, puts the chief stress on the place of the congregation. Perhaps it would not be unfair to say that the chief scriptural buttresses of this position are the thoughts that Christ is the Head of his church (Col. 1:18, etc.), and that of the priesthood of all believers (I Pet. 2:9). It is fundamental to NT teaching that Christ has not left his church. He is the living Lord among his people. Where but two or three are gathered together in his name, he is in the midst. Nor is it any less fundamental that the way into the very holiest of all is open to the humblest believer (Heb. 10:19 f.). Other religions of the first century required the interposition of a priestly caste if

a man would approach God, but the Christians would have none of this. Christ's priestly work has done away with the necessity of any earthly priest if a man would approach God. Added to this is the emphasis on the local congregation in the NT. There, it is maintained, we see autonomous congregations, not subject to episcopal or presbyterian control. The apostles, it is true, exercise a certain authority, but it is the authority of founders of churches, and of the Lord's apostles. After their death there was no divinely instituted apostolate to take their place. Instead the local congregations were still self-governing, as we see from local church orders like the *Didache.* Appeal is also made to the democratic principle. The NT makes it clear that Christians are all one in Christ, and there is no room for any absolute authority.

A consideration of all this evidence, then, leaves us with the conclusion that it is impossible to read back any of our modern systems into the apostolic age. If we are determined to shut our eyes to all that conflicts with our own system, then we may find it there, but hardly otherwise. It is better to recognize that in the NT church there were elements that were capable of being developed into the episcopal, presbyterian and congregational systems, and which, in point of fact, have so developed. But, while there is no reason why any modern Christian should not hold fast to his particular church polity and rejoice in the values it secures to him, that does not give him license to unchurch others whose reading of the evidence is different.

BIBLIOGRAPHY

J. B. Lightfoot, *Commentary on Philippians,* pp. 181-269; E. Hatch, *The Organization of the Early Christian Churches;* H. B. Swete, ed., *Essays on the Early History of the Church and Ministry;* B. H. Streeter, *The Primitive Church;* T. W. Manson, *The Church's Ministry;* K. E. Kirk, ed., *The Apostolic Ministry;* R. W. Dale, *Manual of Congregational Principles;* J. Moffatt, *The Presbyterian Church.*

LEON MORRIS

CIRCUMCISION. An operation performed on the male organ of propagation for the removal of the foreskin. Although practiced also among other nations, within Israel circumcision has a distinct meaning. As a sign of the covenant with Abraham (Gen. 17:11) it partakes of the characteristics of this covenant. It appears capable of a progressive deepening of import and teaches ethical and spiritual truth. The external rite, whose observance is strictly enjoined (Gen. 17:12 ff.; Ex. 4:24 ff.; Josh. 5:2 ff.), ought to be the sign of an internal change, effected by God (Deut. 10:16; 30:6). The uncircumcised as well as the unclean are barred from the "holy city" (Isa. 52:1; cf. Ezek. 44:7, 9). Humility and acceptance of God's punishment are to take the place of the uncircumcised heart before God will restore his covenant (Lev. 26:41).

The NT echoes this teaching and brings it to its completion. Circumcision being a sign of the righteousness of faith (Rom. 4:10 f.) and having lost its relevance for justification through Christ's coming (Gal. 5:6), no NT believer can be compelled to submit to it (Acts 15:3-21; cf. Gal. 2:3). In the light of this NT fulfilment the term circumcision now applies equally to Jewish and gentile Christians alike (Phil. 3:3) since in the "circumcision of Christ" all those who are baptized have put off the body of the flesh (Col. 2:11 f.).

BIBLIOGRAPHY
Rudolf Meyer on *peritemno* in *TWNT*; G. Vos, *Biblical Theology*, pp. 103-05; F. Sierksma, *OTS*, 9, pp. 136-69; Joh. DeGroot, *OTS*, 2, pp. 10-17.

MARTEN H. WOUDSTRA

CITIZENSHIP. The word citizenship is not used in the AV, but it is used by the ASV and the RSV in Acts 22:28 and the ASV in Phil. 3:20. "Citizen" and "fellow-citizen" are used by all three versions in Luke 15:15; 19:14; Acts 21:39 and Eph. 2:19. The same Greek root is used in a few other passages with various translations. The RSV often translates *Rōmaios* "Roman citizen," and in Judg. 9 translates "citizens of Shechem" where the other versions have "men of Shechem."

Roman citizenship was highly prized because of its privileges and advantages, such as exemption from degrading punishment, the right of trial before Roman courts with their administration of the famed Roman justice, and the right of appeal to Caesar himself as the supreme court. Citizenship could be inherited by birth, could be granted to individuals, or bestowed upon those living in certain cities or districts.

The Christian has his citizenship in the kingdom of God. That fact should make us aware both of our glorious blessings and our corresponding obligations.

SAMUEL A. CARTLEDGE

CITY. The term *polis* (Heb. *'îr*) was applied in biblical times to places of quite modest proportions (e.g., Lachish covered fifteen acres) to distinguish them from villages and countryside (Mark 6:56). The Hebrew city occupied a defensive hill site (Josh. 11:13) near a water supply, and contained a citadel (Judg. 9:51), walls, gates, narrow streets, market place (Matt. 11:16), cisterns and a sanctuary. Particular quarters housed special crafts; control was vested in elders (Deut. 19:12), judges and watchmen (Isa. 62:6). The Greek free city state embraced citizens beyond its walls, was administered by *ekklēsia* (citizen-assembly) and *boulē* (council), and acknowledged its *Tychē* or goddess (cf. Roman genius).

Jerusalem was regarded as the holy city (Isa. 52:1 = Matt. 4:5) of the great King (Ps. 48:2 = Matt. 5:35) while it contained God's temple. The concept of a restored Jerusalem appears in Ezek. 40 ff.; Zech. 2; Hag. 2:6-9, Pss. Sol. 17:33 and I Enoch 90:28, and leads Paul to envisage a free city of Jerusalem above as the mother (II Sam. 20:19) of Christians (Gal. 4:26). Revelation, viewing the present world order as corrupt, teaches that the holy city must be established either in the millennial age (Rev. 21:9 ff.) or as the final habitation of redeemed humanity in the eternal state (Rev. 21:1-2). The city is the church, Christ's bride, and the new Israel of twelve gates, founded on the *kerygma* of the twelve apostles. It lies foursquare like the holy of holies, but being sanctified by God's presence throughout its infinite extent needs no local temple. By allusion to Gen. 2:10 and Ezek. 47:7 the seer depicts the city's ideal water supply and security. It was by depicting Christian society as the City of God that Augustine fostered the medieval conviction that the empirical Catholic Church was the kingdom of God.

BIBLIOGRAPHY
Arndt; *HDB*; *HERE*; Sir Charles Marston, *The Bible Comes Alive*, pp. 78-118; *MNT*, Martin-Kiddle on Rev. 21.

DENIS H. TONGUE

CLEAN, UNCLEAN. The Hebrew *ṭāhôr* and the Greek *katharos* chiefly represent the idea expressed by "clean;" whereas the Hebrew *ṭāmē'* and the Greek *akathartos* (and *akatharsia*) chiefly represent the idea expressed by "unclean."

The OT presents four clean-unclean categories: (1) Sex — the uncleanness of parturition (Lev. 12), menstruation (Lev. 15:19-24), unlawful copulation (Lev. 20:10-21) and seminal emission (Lev. 15:16-18). (2) Food

— the uncleanness of certain creatures for food (Lev. 11). Blood is likewise forbidden as human diet (Gen. 9:3 f.). (4) Disease — the defilement of leprosy (Lev. 13, 14). (5) Death — the pollution of the corpse (Lev. 11:24-40; Hag. 2:13).

These distinctions may be justified on the following grounds: (1) the natural stigma attached to certain things (serpents, death, etc.) because of their association with human sin (Gen. 3). (2) The hygienic cleanliness of the people as preservatives of health (Deut. 23:9-14). (3) The ceremonial use of certain things in worship (such as blood for atonement), thus making them "unclean" for other uses (Lev. 17:10-14; Deut. 12:15 f.). (4) The covenant relationship of Israel as a holy (uncontaminated) people (Lev. 20:7, 22-26). (5) The typical significance of ceremonialism as symbols of a spiritually "clean" heart (Ps. 24:3 f.; 51:7, 10).

The NT revelation sets forth eight levels: (1) the natural impurity of evil spirits (Mark 1:26 f.) and the unregenerate (Rom. 1:24). (2) The legal observance (Gal. 4:4) of ceremonial distinctions in Jesus' life (Luke 2:21-24; 5:14). (3) The implicit abrogation of Jewish ceremonialism in Jesus' teaching (Matt. 15:3-20). (4) The complete repudiation of ceremonial distinctions in apostolic practice (Acts 11:1-12) and teaching (Rom. 14:14, 20; Titus 1:15). (5) The explicit retention of the concept of the "clean" with reference to children of a believing parent (I Cor. 7:14; cf. Acts 15:20,.29). (6) The retrogression to ceremonialism in nascent Gnosticism (Col. 2:16, 20-22). (7) The resurgence of ceremonial distinctions in the predicted apostasy (I Tim. 4:1-5). (8) The eternal separation of the "clean" (the saved) and the "unclean" (the lost) in the world to come (Rev. 22:14 f.).

BIBLIOGRAPHY
J. Hastings in HDB; S. Smith in HDAC; P. W. Crannell in ISBE.

WICK BROOMALL

CLERGY. The word is derived from the Greek *klēros,* "a lot," which may point to a method of choosing something like that in Acts 1:26 (cf. also Acts 1:17 where "part" translates *klēros*). As early as Jerome it was pointed out that the use of the term is ambiguous. It may denote those who are chosen out to belong in a special sense to the Lord, or it may signify those whose lot or portion is

the Lord. In the NT the word is not used of a restricted class. It denotes either a lot or a heritage, and in I Pet. 5:3 the plural is used of God's people as a whole. But by the time of Tertullian we find it used of the class of ordained office-bearers in the church. It was applied to the threefold ministry of bishops, priests and deacons. Later on the word extended its meaning to include the minor orders, and sometimes, it would seem, members of religious orders or even educated people generally. Then it reverted to an earlier use and now denotes regular members of the ministry of the church (without respect to denomination) as distinct from lay people generally.

LEON MORRIS

CLOUD. See GLORY AND SHEKINAH.

COLLECT. From the Latin *collecta,* denoting the "gathering together" of the prayers of the congregation into a short compass. Brevity is thus the essence of a collect. In construction it consists of three elements: (a) an invocation, which is usually based on some particular attribute of the Godhead; (b) the petition, with which is commonly linked some spiritual objective; (c) the termination, pleading the name and merits of Jesus Christ or ascribing glory to the triune God. Most of the collects in current liturgical use are ancient, being derived from the Latin Sacramentaries of Leo I (fifth cent.), Gelasius (492), or Gregory (590). Of the more modern collects to be found in the Anglican Book of Common Prayer, some date from the Reformation and were the work of Cranmer (e.g., Advent I and II), while others were added in 1662 (e.g., Advent III, Epiphany VI).

FRANK COLQUHOUN

COLLECTION (for the Saints). The word *logeia,* which often occurs in the Koine for collections with a religious purpose, is used by Paul in I Cor. 16:1 to describe the collection for the poverty-stricken Jewish Christians at Jerusalem. Paul also uses *leitourgia* for the same idea in II Cor. 9:12 to set forth this charity as a religious service commendable to God. The plan, although organized by Paul, was sponsored by the Jerusalem "pillar apostles" (Gal. 2:10). Paul himself seems to have regarded it as the climax of his work in Galatia, Asia, Macedonia and Achaia (Acts 24:17; Rom. 15:25, 26; II Cor. 8:1 ff.), and the importance he attached to it can be seen in his careful planning (note the explicit directions in I Cor. 16:2), his own determination to deliver it personally if at all possible, and his appointment of delegates to accompany him (cf. G. S. Duncan, *St. Paul's Ephesian Ministry*, 1929).

DONALD GUTHRIE

COMFORT. *Nehāmā* and *tanhûmim* are variously rendered by the words "comfort," "consolation," "exhortation," "encouragement," and the usual Greek equivalent is *paraklēsis*. From the Hebrew root come the proper names Nahum (comfort) and Nehemiah (God comforts). The Greek word has a personal form *paraklētos* which is a descriptive title of the Holy Spirit (Comforter, Paraclete) and means "one called alongside (to help)."

The Hebrew verb "covers a large sphere of action; its reflexive use denotes man's sorrowing for the past whereas the intensive form applies to active consolation" (Ulrich Simon, *A Theology of Salvation*, p. 28). When God comforts, he does so by reversing human situations and turning sorrow into joy. On the national scale this was seen particularly in the deliverance of Israel from the exile (Isa. 40:1; 49:13; 51:3; etc).

In the NT, although a national application is found in Luke 2:25, *paraklēsis* is used in a more personal sense. Comfort is promised to those who mourn (Matt. 5:4). All three persons of the Godhead are associated in the ministry of consolation (II Cor. 1:3, 5; Phil. 2:1; Acts 9:31). Christ by his incarnation is well fitted to be our Comforter, having fully shared our sorrows and temptations (Luke 7:13; Heb. 2:18).

Barnabas means "son of consolation" (Acts 4:36); the Epistle to the Hebrews is described as a "word of consolation" (Heb. 13:22); II Corinthians is pre-eminently the epistle of consolation (*paraklēsis* in each case). Readiness to support one another in griefs and trials should always be characteristic of the Christian fellowship (see I Thess. 2:11; Rom. 1:12; Col. 4:11).

BIBLIOGRAPHY

Arndt; A-S; HDB; HDCG; H. H. Farmer, *The Healing Cross*, p. 133; N. Snaith, *Distinctive Ideas of the Old Testament*, p. 180.

L. E. H. STEPHENS-HODGE

COMFORTER. See HOLY SPIRIT.

COMMAND, COMMANDMENT. These are the words most frequently used to express authority, whether divine or human. They are the rendering of several Hebrew and Greek words which occur as nouns or verbs about nine hundred times in Scripture. The first word of God to man was a command: "The Lord God commanded the man saying" (Gen. 2:16). Man's disobedience to that command was the fall. The commandments of God are his law which in its fullest sense covers everything which God has commanded. Ps. 119 uses ten different words nearly two hundred times to express this idea: the most frequent are law, word, judgment, testimony, commandment, statute, precept, saying. In a narrow and specific sense, the reference is to the Decalogue or ten commandments (*q.v.*).

OSWALD T. ALLIS

COMMISSION, THE GREAT. Jesus' command to the Eleven to preach the gospel on a world-wide basis is confined to the post-resurrection period. This is not to say that intimations of the divine purpose are lacking prior to this time (e.g. Mark 14:9). But there is an undeniable fitness in withholding precise directions until the events which constitute the basis of the gospel have occurred.

Each of the Gospels has its own statement of the Commission, which was doubtless repeated in somewhat varying form by our Lord on several occasions. Mark's account, found in the disputed ending of his Gospel (16:15), emphasizes the obligation to go to every creature with the message. Luke's statement stresses the evangelization of the nations as the fulfilment of God's purpose set forth in the OT Scriptures. It is a part of the divine program as definitely as the death and resurrection of the promised Christ (Luke 24:46-48). In John the words of Jesus impart dignity to this task. As the Father has sent him, so does the Saviour send the apostles. The mention of the Spirit suggests the source of needed power for this mission, and the word about forgiveness of sins points to the effectiveness of the application of the gospel to the needs of sinful men (John 20:21-23).

The peculiarity of Acts 1:8 lies in its specification of the areas in which the witness is to be given. Galilee is omitted, perhaps on the assumption that the disciples, being Galileans, will not neglect their own section. Each of the places mentioned has its own reason for emphasis. Jerusalem must not be avoided because of antipathy for those who there crucified the

Lord. Such people advertise their need for the gospel. Judea is the probable home of the betrayer, but it must not suffer neglect on this account. Samaria conjures up feelings of animosity, but this must not deter the apostles from ministry there. Jesus himself had pointed the way (John 4). The uttermost part of the earth suggests the masses of paganism with their idolatry and immorality. These must be reached, and without the complaint that the Master confined his labors to the Jews.

In Matthew 28:19 the emphatic word is not *go* but *make disciples*. This means to make converts, as in Acts 14:21. Evangelism must be followed by *baptizing* and *teaching*. The command is grounded in Jesus' universal authority (v. 18) and is implemented by his promise of unfailing presence and support (v. 20).

EVERETT F. HARRISON

COMMON. The Jewish concept of "common" as "unclean" is reflected in Acts 10:14, 28; 11:8, in connection with Peter's vision on the housetop. There the two terms are synonymous. The word *koinos* is even translated "defiled" in Mark 7:2, "unclean" in Rom. 14:14 (three times), and "unholy" in Hebrews 10:29 (AV). The cognate verb *koinoō* is rendered "defile" in eleven of its fifteen occurrences in the NT (AV). This reveals the strong Jewish emphasis on ceremonial cleanness and uncleanness.

But in the NT *koinos* also has its original meaning of "belonging to the group." Thus we read of "the common faith" (Titus 1:4) and "the common salvation" (Jude 3). It is stated that the early disciples in Jerusalem "had all things common" (Acts 2:44; 4:32) (see COMMUNITY OF GOODS). A careful study of the Greek tenses, however, shows that when special needs arose these were met by some believer selling property and donating the proceeds. Private property was not abolished.

RALPH EARLE

COMMON GRACE. The doctrine of common grace, says Herman Bavinck, enables one to recognize and appreciate all that is good and beautiful in the world while at the same time holding unreservedly to the absolute character of the Christian religion. Whereas special grace regenerates the hearts of men, common grace: (1) restrains the destructive process of sin within mankind in general and (2) en-

ables men, though not born again, to develop the latent forces of the universe and thus make a positive contribution to the fulfilment of the cultural mandate given to men through the first man, Adam, in paradise.

Recent criticism of this general idea centers around the person of the Reverend Herman Hoeksema. He holds the view that common grace is an unavoidable stepping-stone toward the Arminian view that God desires to save all men.

In the face of such criticism the Synod of the Christian Reformed Church of North America in 1924 reaffirmed the idea of common grace under three heads: (1) a favorable attitude on the part of God toward mankind in general; (2) the restraint of sin in the life of individual men and in society; and (3) the performance of civic righteousness by the unregenerate.

Going beyond these "three points" William Masselink, following Valentine Hepp, sets forth a point of view which leads back toward a Romanist notion of natural theology.

Avoiding the extreme views of Hoeksema and Masselink others would think of common grace as a limiting concept supplementing the basic concept of the full sovereignty of God and the genuine significance of human responsibility. Thus viewed, common grace does not tone down but supports even as it supplements the view of the total depravity of man. Those who hold this position maintain that particularly when thus viewed, there can be a true and full appreciation of all that is "true and good" anywhere on the part of those who greatly stress the idea of saving grace as of God alone.

BIBLIOGRAPHY
    H. Bavinck, *De Algemeene Genade*; A. Kuyper, *De Gemeene Gratie*; H. Kuiper, *Calvin on Common Grace*; H. Danhof and H. Hoeksema, *Of Sin and Grace*; H. Hoeksema, *The Heidelberg Catechism*; W. Masselink, *General Revelation and Common Grace*; K. Schilder, *Christ and Culture*.

CORNELIUS VAN TIL

COMMUNION, HOLY. See LORD'S SUPPER.

COMMUNION OF SAINTS. *Sanctorum Communionem*, the second clause of the ninth article of the Apostles' Creed, traceable to the text of Nicetas of Aquileia in the fifth century, is probably the latest addition to the Roman symbol, but is of uncertain origin and implication. Communion implies a sharing, but from the earliest times there has been confusion over what is shared. (1) The acts of the council of Nimes, Aquinas, and Abelard treat *sanctorum* as neuter gender and understand it to affirm participation in the sacraments. (2) Others, as Nicetas, treat *sanctorum* as masculine, representing an expansion of the preceding phrase, "holy catholic church." It is fellowship of believers with each other that was understood by the Reformers and many modern interpreters. There is debate, however, over whether the communion is limited to those on earth, or, as some Catholic theologians insist, is with saints in heaven, on earth, and in purgatory. (3) Others like Barth affirm a combination of these first two views. (4) Still others, like Faustus of Reiz, have understood a communion of saints and angels in heaven to be enjoyed after death.

BIBLIOGRAPHY
F. J. Badcock, *JTS* 21, pp. 106-26; K. Barth, *Dogmatics in Outline*, p. 144; J. Koestlin, *SHERK* 3, pp. 181-82; A. C. McGiffert, *The Apostles' Creed*, pp. 200-04; J. F. Sollier, *CE*, 4, pp. 171-74; H. B. Swete, *The Holy Catholic Church*.

JACK P. LEWIS

COMMUNITY OF GOODS. The primitive *koinōnia* is confined to Acts 2:42-46; 4:32 — 5:4, but see also terms *koinōnos* = partner (Luke 5:10), *koinōnein* = to share (Rom. 12:13), *koinōnikos* (I Tim. 6:18), and *koinōnia* = communion (I Cor. 10:16) and *yahad*, "fellowship." Heb. *yahad* (= *koinōnia*) often occurs in Manual of Dead Sea Sect, which practiced total community of goods and banished the fraudulent. Philo praises the Essene *koinōnia* which included sharing of houses, clothes, food and wages (Q.O.P.L. par. 84, 91). Josephus says it obtained from city to city.

Jesus fed the multitudes communally, sanctioned a common purse (John 12:6), and accepted the *diakonia* of many women (Luke 8:3). Peter organized the *koinōnia* (Acts 2:42) for the 3,000 Jerusalem converts to offset ostracism and excommunication from synagogues (John 9:22). Believers had all things common, but based the system on the sale of capital, not on daily labor as at Qumran; hence its swift collapse. From Acts 4:33 — 5:4 the "communism" appears voluntary, proceeds being at Ananias's disposal after sale. Many, like Barnabas, sold possessions to relieve the needy, anticipating an early Parousia.

The *koinōnia* soon disappeared, to be replaced by an organized *diakonia* (Acts 6:1, 2). In gentile churches Paul urged converts to share in the *diakonia* and relieve the poverty of Jerusalem saints. In II Cor. 8:4 he uses the remarkable phrase *tēn koinōnian tēs diakonias tous hagious*.

BIBLIOGRAPHY
HDB; HERE; A. Dupont-Sommer, *Jewish Sect of Qumran*, pp. 64-67, 90; Foakes-Jackson and Lake, *Beginnings of Christianity*, Acts 4:36. Addit. note 12.

DENIS H. TONGUE

COMPARATIVE RELIGION. This is the study of the various religions of the world in their relationships of similarity and dissimilarity. It is obviously legitimate in itself, and to the extent that Christianity has the external features of religion it may rightly be included in this type of investigation. Indeed, a higher legitimation may be found in the fact that with varying degrees of corruption all religions derive originally from natural revelation (*q.v.*). On the other hand, certain dangers are to be noted. First, comparative religion is often applied to the explaining away of all religion and therefore of Christianity. Second, it has the result of making religion a purely human phenomenon and thus subjectivizing it. Third, it entails a relativizing of Christianity as perhaps the best religion, yet only one among many others. Finally, it obscures the proper work of Christian theology, substituting historical investigation for biblical exposition and dogmatics. It has thus to be realized that comparative religion can teach us only the less important things concerning the *form* of the divine revelation in Jesus Christ and our response to it. If this is firmly grasped, and it is given only a minor role in theology, it is not without a certain interest and value. But if not, it denies from the very outset the basic factor of God's own Word and work, and in the hands of friends and foes alike its results are necessarily mischievous.

GEOFFREY W. BROMILEY

COMPASSION. Denoting by its derivation "suffering with another," compassion may be described as pity touched with loving concern. The principal scriptural terms are the Hebrew *raḥămîm*, related to "womb," and the Greek *splagchna*, "bowels." Used metaphorically, they carry the thought of yearning over another with great feeling. The Bible shows a preference for the use of the verb form rather than the noun. Our Lord felt compassion for the neglected multitudes (Matt. 9:36) and also for the suffering and sorrowing individual (Luke 7:13). The prominence given to this trait in his parabolic teaching (Luke 10:33; Matt. 18:27; Luke 15:20) reflects the degree to which it was dominant in his own character. By constantly exemplifying it, he gave to the OT representation of God as a pitying father (Ps. 103:13) a real (rather than a merely illustrative) significance. Though he showed such great compassion for others, Jesus sought none for himself, even in the agony of the garden and the pain of the cross. He was a stranger to self-pity.

When Christ is enthroned in the hearts of his people, the appeal to be compassionate toward one another is both natural and practicable (Phil. 2:1; I Pet. 3:8).

Whereas compassion has a strong emotional coloring, its synonym mercy (q.v.) more often is connected with positive measures for relief (Rom. 12:8).

EVERETT F. HARRISON

CONCEPTUALISM. A solution to the philosophic problem of universals first set forth by Peter Abelard and reaffirmed by St. Thomas Aquinas. Avoiding the errors of the extreme realism of William of Champeaux on the one hand, and those of nominalism on the other, it affirmed that universals exist *in re*.

See also REALISM AND NOMINALISM.

GREGG SINGER

CONCISION. Paul uses the term once (Phil. 3:2) in a play on words with circumcision, to stigmatize the "cutting" party which sought to force circumcision upon Gentile believers. In the OT this word *katatomē* is used of lacerations inflicted on the body, as in the case of the prophets of Baal (I Kings 18:28). Since in Christ outward circumcision is nothing (Gal. 6:15), the imposition of it on the believer is meaningless mutilation, seeing that he already has the circumcision of Christ which sets him apart unto God (Phil. 3:3; Col. 2:11).

EVERETT F. HARRISON

CONCOMITANCE. This is a technical term used in the eucharistic theology of Roman Catholicism to describe the presence of both the body and blood of Christ in each of the species of bread and wine, and thus to afford a theological justification for the denial of the cup to the laity. More widely, it denotes the presence of the whole Christ, i.e., his human soul and Godhead, together with the body and blood in virtue of the hypostatic union. It is

sometimes linked with grace to describe the divine operation which accompanies the human as distinct from the prevenient grace which precedes.

GEOFFREY W. BROMILEY

CONCORDAT. A treaty or legal agreement between the Roman Catholic Church and a secular state having to do with religious matters of concern to the church within that particular state. Usually such agreements are negotiated in the interests of the Papacy when its properties and standing are threatened. The existence of a concordat supposes a diplomatic victory for the church. When states or rulers work closely with the church to maintain its position or primacy there is no need for an agreement, but when the church has been deprived of what it considers to be its rights or privileges then the concordat guarantees to the church whatever rights and privileges may be negotiated.

One of the most important treaties signed was that between Napoleon Bonaparte and the church known as the Concordat of 1801.

HAROLD LINDSELL

CONCUPISCENCE. Concupiscence is the equivalent of the Greek *epithumia* usually translated "lust" but occasionally "concupiscence" and, in a good sense, "desire." It signifies for the most part the wrongful inclination of the sinner which characterizes his nature and leads to sinful acts. While allowing that it is sinful in the unregenerate, medieval and Romanist theologians argue that it is only the testing scar and combustible material of sin in the baptized, in whom original sin is supposed to be abolished. But Reformation theology does not accept this distinction or its presupposition. Although not imputed, original sin remains in believers, and therefore concupiscence may and must be said to have "of itself the (true and proper) nature of sin."

GEOFFREY W. BROMILEY

CONCURSUS. This term denotes God's continuous action on the creation in conjunction with the action of his creatures. His providential control may be said to embrace the preservation of all things and also their direction so as to insure that they will fulfil his will. The concursus is necessarily of divine provision and continues to operate according to his good pleasure. As applied to human life, it involves the problem of divine sovereignty in relation to human freedom. Among the Schoolmen, Aquinas gave to concursus its most extensive elaboration.

See also FREEDOM, PROVIDENCE, WILL OF MAN.

BIBLIOGRAPHY
G. J. Stokes in HERE; J. Koestlin in SHERK; ODCC.

EVERETT F. HARRISON

CONDEMN, CONDEMNATION. The verb is used in a typically forensic setting in Deut. 25:1, where the judges are to "justify the righteous, and condemn the wicked." From this a regular use arises for the condemnation of one man by another. The more important use of the verb however, and the regular use of the noun, is for condemnation by God. The teaching of the Bible on this subject is summed up in two passages in John. Men's condemnation lies in this, "that the light is come into the world, and men loved the darkness rather than the light; for their works were evil" (John 3:19). The other passage says: "He that heareth my word, and believeth him that sent me, hath eternal life, and cometh not into judgment (i.e., condemnation), but hath passed out of death into life" (John 5:24). That is to say, there is a very real and a very serious condemnation. Men who choose the lesser way, the love of darkness rather than light, come under nothing less serious than God's condemnation with all that that implies. But the work of Christ is to deliver men from condemnation. "There is therefore now no condemnation to them that are in Christ Jesus" (Rom. 8:1).

LEON MORRIS

CONDITIONAL IMMORTALITY. On this view, first advanced by Arnobius, condemned at the Lateran Council in 1513, but much favored today, immortality is a divine gift only to believers, the wicked being subject to annihilation. Supporters of this teaching argue that the Bible does not proclaim the Greek view of immortality, that death as the penalty of sin entails destruction, and that the eternity of punishment refers to its finality rather than its duration. They try to maintain harmony with Scripture by agreeing that all are raised at the last judgment but presuming that unbelievers then fall under the condemnation of the second death. In this way they hope to avoid what are thought to be the more repugnant elements in the doctrine of eternal punishment without making any concessions

to a weak universalism. From the biblical standpoint, however, they fail to do justice to such passages as Isa. 66:24 (cf. Mark 9:44, 46, 48); Matt. 22:13 and 25:46; John 3:36; Acts 1:25 and Rev. 20:10. Again, while eternal or everlasting is not to be construed merely in terms of temporal duration, its sense is surely more than that of termination. Finally, while the Bible speaks of the overthrow of death and hell (Rev. 20:14), it is difficult to think of a total extinction of being as distinct from exclusion from the divine presence (II Thess. 1:9) and therefore from real life (cf. S. D. F. Salmond, *The Christian Doctrine of Immortality*).

See also ANNIHILATIONISM.

WILLIAM KELLY

CONFESSION OF CHRIST. The word confession (*homologia*) means acknowledgment of something along with other people, or agreement as to the facts. In the technical sense of an acknowledgment of Christ it is used mainly in the verb form *homologeō*. Believers confessed that Jesus was the Messiah (John 9:22); that he was the Son of God (I John 4:15); that he had become incarnate (I John 4:2); and that he was Lord, chiefly on the basis of his resurrection (Rom. 10:9; Phil. 2:11). Jesus taught the necessity of confessing him before men if one would be acknowledged by him before the Father in heaven (Matt. 10:32). Failure to confess him in these ways is attributed to theological error (II John 7) or to craven fear (John 12:42).

In view of the variety of predicates assigned to Christ in these statements, it is improbable that confession was limited to the occasion of baptism.

Since confession is not inevitably linked with the mention of faith as a condition of salvation, the implication is that true faith will issue in confession, even as repentance is understood as a necessary condition, along with faith, even though it is not always mentioned.

BIBLIOGRAPHY
A. E. Burn in HDAC; J. Y. Campbell in RTWB; O. Michel in TWNT.

EVERETT F. HARRISON

CONFESSION OF FAITH. A declaration of religious belief, an acknowledgment made publicly before witnesses (I Tim. 6:12, 13). Occasionally the phrase is used to describe the creeds of the early church, but more particularly the formal statements made by the

Protestant churches at the time of the Reformation and afterwards. The main Evangelical (Lutheran) confessions are the Confession of Augsburg, 1530, the work of Melanchthon, approved by Luther; Articles of Smalkald, 1573; Formula, 1577; and Book of Concord, 1580. Reformed (Calvinist) confessions number nearly thirty of which the most important are: the Helvetic Confession, 1536 and 1566; the Scottish, 1560; the Heidelberg Catechism, 1563; The Canons of the Synod of Dort, 1618; and the Westminster Confession, 1646, the work of the Westminster Assembly, a synod appointed by the Long Parliament in 1642 to revise the Thirty-Nine Articles of the Church of England. This latter confession has been used by the Church of Scotland since 1647, and was approved by Parliament in 1648.

M. R. W. FARRER

CONFESSION OF SINS. The confession of sins is part of the confession or acknowledgment (Greek *homologia*) of the sovereignty of God (Isa. 45:23; Rom. 3:19). It is the admission of guilt when confronted with the revealed character and will of God, whether or not forgiveness follows (Lev. 26:40; Josh. 7:19; Matt. 27:4). Confession is consequently a test of repentance and belief in the gospel, as Mark 1:1-5 illustrates, and by God's grace is a condition of forgiveness (Ps. 32:5; I John 1:9) and of effectual prayer (I Kings 8:33; Neh. 1:6; Ps. 66:18; Dan. 9:4; Luke 18:9-14). The Levitical law required confession (with restitution where possible) before remission of either individual or corporate trespasses (Lev. 5:5; Num. 5:7; Lev. 16:21).

While confession of sins is primarily before God (Ps. 51:3-4; Rom. 14:10-12), it may on occasion involve some sort of open communication, as in a general confession of the church to God either collectively or by the mouth of a representative (Ezra 9:6), or in confession by individuals, in the presence of the church, of their sins against God (Acts 19:18; James 5:16). The latter is not a public disclosure of secret sins (which might be unedifying and scandalous: Eph. 5:12) but an admission of guilt in matters of general concern where the conscience of the church might be aggrieved; it is not for the benefit of the confessor. II Cor. 2:5-7 and Gal. 6:1 imply such confession. But there is no suggestion of private confession of sins to an individual presbyter or

even to the whole body of presbyters. In James 5:16 confession is mutual among church members, as is the prayer for one another.

It is a corollary of confession to God that acknowledgment of sins against a brother should be made to the offended person. Matt. 5:21 implies this. Such a private offense may, on occasion, also come to be confessed in the presence of the whole church (Matt. 18:17).

DONALD W. B. ROBINSON

CONFESSOR. (a) A name first applied to early Christians who confessed the faith in times of persecution, and were exposed to possible dangers and suffering, but who did not actually suffer martyrdom. Later the name was applied more loosely to those who had not been exposed to dangers but who were known to have led holy lives. After the fourth century the church publicly honored confessors even though they had not suffered martyrdom. (b) The priest who hears confessions in the Roman Church (in the sacrament of penance). This generally means private confessions to those who have been appointed for this purpose.

HAROLD LINDSELL

CONFIDENCE. The word confidence in the OT is primarily the rendering of the Hebrew word *bāṭaḥ,* meaning to trust, and its derivatives. In the NT it is primarily the rendering of the Greek words *parrēsia,* meaning boldness (Acts 28:31; Heb. 3:6; 10:35; I John 2:28; 3:21; 5:14), and *peithō* with its derivative *pepoithēsis,* meaning to put confidence in (2 pf.) and confidence respectively (II Cor. 1:15; 2:3; 8:22; 10:2; Gal. 5:10; Eph. 3:12; Phil. 1:25; 3:3, 4; II Thess. 3:4; Philem. 21). The word frequently refers to trust or confidence in men (II Cor. 1:15). Its most striking use is in connection with the confident access that the believer has toward God due to faith in Christ (Eph. 3:12).

S. LEWIS JOHNSON, JR.

CONFIRMATION. One of the seven sacraments of both the Roman Catholic and Eastern Orthodox Church. The Roman Church teaches that it was instituted by Christ, through his disciples, for the church. Its early history is somewhat uncertain and only gradually did it receive recognition as a sacrament. It was given a sacramental status by Peter Lombard in the twelfth century, and by Thomas Aquinas in the thirteenth century;

finally, by the Council of Trent in the sixteenth century. One of the two sacraments administered by a bishop in the Roman Catholic Church, its purpose is to make those who have been baptized in the faith strong soldiers of Jesus Christ. It is administered to children before they receive their first communion, generally at about the age of twelve. Concerning it St. Thomas Aquinas wrote: "Confirmation is to baptism what growth is to generation." It is administered according to this form: "I sign thee with the sign of the Cross and confirm thee with the chrism of salvation." Since it confers an indelible character upon the recipient, it is administered but once. According to Roman Catholic theology, sanctifying grace is increased in the soul and a special sacramental grace consisting of the seven gifts of the Holy Spirit is conferred upon the recipient. In the Lutheran Church confirmation is a rite rather than a sacrament and the recipient offers it as a confirmation in his own heart of those baptismal vows which his parents assumed in his behalf. It is administered but once at about thirteen or fourteen years of age and admits the recipient to the communion. In the Protestant Episcopal Church it is a sacramental rite completing baptism.

BIBLIOGRAPHY

H. J. D. Denzinger, *Sources of Catholic Dogma;* G. W. Bromiley, *Sacramental Teaching and Practice in the Reformation Churches.*

GREGG SINGER

CONFORMITY. From the verb "to conform" ("to become or be like," or "to follow the pattern of"), conformity indicates an internal or external adherence to an accepted norm. In the NT, the Christian is not to be conformed to this world (Rom. 12:2) but is predestinated to be conformed to the image of the Son of God (Rom. 8:29). Hence there must always be marks of both nonconformity and conformity in Christian life. In historical usage the term denotes acceptance of the common standard, either of belief or more specifically of modes of worship, government and conduct.

GEOFFREY W. BROMILEY

CONSCIENCE. The word conscience is derived from the Latin *conscientia* which is a compound of the preposition *con* and *scio* meaning "to know together," "joint knowledge with others," "the knowledge we share with another." It stems from the same root as con-

sciousness which means "awareness of." Conscience is an awareness but restricted to the moral sphere. It is a moral awareness. The Greek equivalent in the NT is *syneidēsis,* a compound of *syn* "together" and *eidenai* "to know," that is, to know together with, to have common knowledge together with someone. The German *Gewissen* has the same meaning. The prefix *ge* expresses a collective idea, the "together with," and *wissen* is "to know."

The word conscience does not appear in the OT. However, the idea is well known and is expressed by the term heart. It appears at the very dawn of human history as a sense of guilt with Adam and Eve after the fall. We read of David that his heart smote him (II Sam. 24:10). Job says: "My heart shall not reproach me" (Job 27:6). And Ps. 32:1-5 and 51:1-9 are the cries of anguish of an aroused conscience.

The Babylonians, like the Hebrews, identified conscience with the heart. The Egyptians had no specific word for conscience but recognized its authority, as is evident from the Book of the Dead. The early Greeks and Romans personified conscience and depicted it as fiendish female demons called Erinyes and Furies respectively.

The word *syneidēsis* or "conscience" appears thirty times in the NT — nineteen times in the writings of Paul, five times in Hebrews, three times in the letters of Peter, twice in Acts, and once in the Gospel of John, although the correctness of the latter reading (8:9) has been questioned.

Definition. Conscience is that faculty in man by which he distinguishes between the morally right and wrong, which urges him to do that which he recognizes to be right and restrains him from doing that which he recognizes to be wrong, which passes judgment on his acts and executes that judgment within his soul. Webster defines conscience as the sense or consciousness of right and wrong. Kant speaks of it as a consciousness of a court within man's being or the categorical imperative. Others have defined conscience as the ethical sense organ in man.

Conscience is innate. According to Rom. 2:14-15 conscience is innate and universal. It is not the product of environment, training, habit, race impression, or education, though it is influenced by all of these factors.

As to function, conscience is threefold. (1) Obligatory. It urges man to do that which he regards as right and restrains him from doing that which he regards as wrong. (2) Judicial. Conscience passes judgment upon man's decision and acts. (3) Executive. Conscience executes its judgment in the heart of man. It condemns his action when in conflict with his conviction by causing an inward disquietude, distress, shame, or remorse. It commends when man has acted in conformity with his convictions.

Erring conscience. This is a misnomer. Conscience does not err, but the standard on the basis of which conscience acts might be in error.

The morbid, perverted or narrow conscience. By this is meant a conscience out of proper balance, narrow, fanatic, bigoted.

Pathological and neurotic conscience. This has its origin in a psychic disorder or in a neurosis related to phobias, obsessions, fixed ideas, and compulsions.

Doubting conscience. One who acts in uncertainty. Rom. 14:23 declares such action to be sinful.

Dulled, calloused, or a dead conscience. This is a condition wherein conscience ceases to function because of repeated disregard of its warning voice. Paul speaks of it as a seared conscience (I Tim. 4:2).

Good conscience. When man acts in conformity with his convictions, he is said to have a good conscience. "Faith cannot exist and abide with and alongside of a wicked intention to sin and to act against conscience" (*Formula of Concord*, Epitome IV, Triglotta, p. 795, Concordia Publishing House, St. Louis, Mo.).

Social conscience. The merging of the individual moral consciousness into a group moral consciousness results in the social conscience.

Freedom of conscience. The freedom to believe, practice, and propagate any religion whatsoever or none at all is referred to as freedom of conscience.

Conscience is a wonderful gift of God. It is a guardian of morality, justice, and decency in the world. It is an irrefutable testimony to the existence of God.

BIBLIOGRAPHY
A. M. Rehwinkel, *The Voice of Conscience*; C. A. Pierce, *Conscience in the New Testament*.

ALFRED M. REHWINKEL

CONSECRATE, CONSECRATION. In the AV these terms are used some forty times

to translate a number of Hebrew words: On *qādēš* see below. On *ḥāram* (Mic. 4:13, "devote") see CURSE. *Nēzer* signifies a pagan religious dedication (Hos. 9:10 RSV) as well as the Nazarites' act and status of *separation to God.* (Num. 6:7, 9, 12; Num. 6:18 f. RSV; cf. Lev. 21:12 RSV). Cf. Judg. 13:5 LXX-A (*naziraion*) and Matt. 2:23. *Millē' yād,* "to fill the hand," is a technical phrase used primarily of a priest's installation (Ex. 28:41; Lev. 21:10 RSV) and, as a substantive, *millu'im,* of the installation offerings (Ex. 29:22). The idiom reflects an ordination ceremony in which a portion of the sacrifice was placed in the priest's hand symbolizing his future duties and rights.

In the RSV the hundred odd occurrences usually stand for *qādēš* and its Greek equivalent, *hagiazō,* "to dedicate, to set apart to God." See SANCTIFY, SANCTIFICATION, HOLY. They are applied to the priests, people, temple, sacrifices, money (Ex. 19:10; 29:33, 36; 40:9 f.; Judg. 17:3); and, in the NT, to Christ, Christians, and food (John 17:19; I Tim. 4:5).

Teleioō (and its cognates), usually translated "make perfect," "perfection," is a cultic term in the Greek mystery religions meaning "to consecrate, to initiate, the initiate." Similarly, the patristic writers use it of the act of baptism and of the baptized person. The death of a martyr is expressed also by this word (Eusebius HE III. 35; VII. 15; cf. IV Macc. 7:15; Heb. 12:23, Rev. 6:9). The LXX sometimes so translates *millē', millu'im,* with reference to the priest's installation and the installation sacrifice (e.g. Ex. 29:9, 22; cf. Philo, *de vita Mosis* II. 149).

This technical usage may carry over into some NT passages which speak of Christ as "consecrated" or "made perfect" (*teleioō*) by death (Heb. 2:10; 5:9; 7:28). That is, Christ's sacrifice involves a final consecration through which he is installed (in his resurrection) into his high priestly function (Luke 13:32) and in which believers also are consecrated (John 17:23; Heb. 10:14). This act of consecration likewise sanctifies (*hagiazō*) and glorifies (*doxazō*) both Christ (John 17:19; 12:23; 13:31 f.; 17:5) and believers (Heb. 2:10 f.; John 17:10). The relationship of these terms is of some soteriological significance.

BIBLIOGRAPHY
Arndt; MM; KD on Lev. 7:37; O. Michel, *Der Brief an die Hebraeer*, pp. 76 f, 137 f; B. F. Westcott, *Epistle*

to the Hebrews, p. 63 f. H. A. A. Kennedy, St. Paul and
the Mystery Religions, p. 130 ff.

E. EARLE ELLIS

CONSISTORY. The consistory was formerly the antechamber of the imperial palace.
Here the emperor sat on a tribunal to dispense
justice, with others standing around him (con-
sistentes). The term was taken over at a later
date by the church, mostly in connection with
the administration of ecclesiastical law. Thus,
in certain Presbyterian churches the church
sessions are known as consistories. In the
Church of England the bishop's court for the
administering of canon law is in most cases
known as the consistory court. In Roman
Catholicism the term is used for an assembly
of the cardinals in the presence of the Pope
and may take one of three forms, a public, a
semi-public and a private.

GEOFFREY W. BROMILEY

CONSOLATION. See COMFORT.

CONSUBSTANTIATION. A technical
term of Scholastic origin commonly applied to
the Lutheran doctrine of the Lord's Supper.
Consubstantiatio carries several possible senses:
(1) a commixture of two substances, (2) an
inclusion of one substance in another, (3) a
simultaneous coexistence of two substances.
Only (3) may properly be identified with orthodox Lutheran teaching; (1) is a fiction
which appears only by misrepresentation; (2)
is more accurately styled impanation. In Luther's own language, the actual body and blood
of Christ exist "in, with, or under" the elements of bread and wine. No permanent association is postulated: the relationship is confined to the sacramental action. The transformation is effected by the Word of God, not
by priestly consecration. Luther was less concerned with metaphysical speculation than
with the affirmation of what he believed to be
theological truth. His doctrine of Holy Communion is integral with his Christology
(Works, Philadelphia Edition, II, 187-94).

A. SKEVINGTON WOOD

CONTENTMENT. A steady restfulness of
spirit, a freedom from care — based on satisfaction with one's situation. If its basis is the
suppression of desire for the Oriental, and
wisdom for the ancient Greek, it is the result
of faith in God for the Judeo-Christian tradition. Since the Lord is the psalmist's shepherd,
he will not want (Ps. 23:1). The Lord could

give, and take away, but Job would still say,
"Blessed be the name of the Lord" (1:21).
Jesus enhanced the concept of God as an interested Father, and thereby helped men to
cease from their anxieties (Matt. 6:24-34).
Paul did it by urging faith in Christ and belief in immortality. And for him "godliness
with contentment (autarkeia) is great gain"
(I Tim. 6:6).

J. KENNETH GRIDER

CONTRITION. Contrition is sorrow for
sin because it is displeasing to God. When we
analyze the meaning of repentance (q.v.), we
realize that a person may repent of sin for two
reasons: (a) the fear of punishment; (b) because he has offended a just and holy God.
The term "attrition" is used in Roman Catholic
theology (from the Middle Ages) to denote
the first, and "contrition" the second. Obviously the first reason for repentance is not because
sin is an evil thing, but because of possible
unpleasant consequences to oneself. Such an
attitude does not constitute penitence in the
true sense (cf. II Cor. 7:9-10). The second
is the proper attitude, and indicates real love
of God and desire to please him. Even Roman
Catholic theologians, though teaching the necessity of confession to a priest to receive absolution, allow that a true "act of contrition,"
without the presence of the priest, receives absolution from God. Evangelical theology and
practice seeks to equate repentance with contrition, and always to stir up contrition in the
heart of sinners.

W. C. G. Proctor

CONTROVERSY. It is generally agreed
that controversy for the sake of controversy is
an evil. For that reason most Christians have a
desire to avoid it as far as possible. But we live
in a world in which truth and error are in
deadly conflict and it is often impossible to
remain silent. Jude exhorts us to "contend
earnestly for the faith which was once for all
delivered unto the saints" (Jude 3).

Controversy that is carried on with candor
and moderation and in a spirit of honest inquiry can result in much good. Repeatedly
throughout the course of church history erroneous beliefs have appeared and it has been
necessary to refute them. The rise of such beliefs has often stimulated a more detailed study
of the doctrine in question, and has forced the
orthodox leaders to present reasoned statements
for their faith. The fact is that most of our

creedal advances have come about in that way. Doctrinal controversies are the focal points at which truth and error come into conflict, with the result that further study substantiates the truth and exposes the error. In all realms the advance of knowledge has taken a zigzag course, first to one side then to the other as demonstrated errors have forced it back to the path of truth. In the theological realm, as in that of politics, economics, history, etc., most of us, if indeed not all of us, have some erroneous ideas, and an intelligent opponent can point those out and reveal new truth.

BIBLIOGRAPHY
M. Campbell Smith in *HERE*.

LORAINE BOETTNER

CONVENTICLE. The main usage of this term has been in relation to groups meeting together for religious worship outside and in opposition to the established order in the church. Thus some of the early Puritans in post-Reformation England formed conventicles when they associated for free worship, particularly after the passing of the 1604 canons. Whenever five or more persons gathered in a house in addition to the family, and took part in some form of worship, this constituted an illegal conventicle as defined in the later legislation. The acts against conventicles were repealed in 1689 with the toleration and licensing of dissenting bodies.

GEOFFREY W. BROMILEY

CONVERSATION. In the AV the word has two meanings: (1) the modern sense of talking together (*synomileō*) as in Acts 10:27, and (2) the archaic sense of behavior, manner or course of life (*anastrophē*). This idea comes from the Vulgate, *conversamini*, "the whole course of life." The *ISBE* develops the modern use; Moule, *Ephesians, CGT,* gives the older usage, (Acts 23:1; Phil. 1:27).

Modern translations stress the concept of deportment (see Heb. 13:5, RV). Many times the word is translated "manner of life" in the ASV and the RV, whether *anastrophē, tropos* or *politeuomai*. See also *politeuma,* "citizenship." Confusion can be avoided by remembering to emphasize the idea of conduct in all these cases.

ROBERT WINSTON ROSS

CONVERSION. The act of conversion is represented by the Hebrew verb *šûḇ* and the Greek verb *epistrephō* — both meaning to turn or to return (either physically or spiritually). The following survey is based on the usage of these words.

Conversion is described in the OT as a turning from evil (Jer. 18:8) unto the Lord (Mal. 3:7). Because of man's evil nature (Hos. 5:4), this change is resisted (II Chron. 36:13). God is the primary mover (Jer. 31:18), although man appears to have a subordinate part (Jer. 24:7). Individuals (II Kings 23:25) and nations (Jonah 3:10) are subjects of conversion. God uses the prophets as secondary agents in effectuating conversion (Neh. 9:26; Zech. 1:4). Those who refuse to turn to the Lord are punished with such evils as chastisement (Amos 4:6-12), captivity (Hos. 11:5), destruction (I Kings 9:6-9), death (Ezek. 33:9, 11); those who return to the Lord receive such blessings as forgiveness (Isa. 55:7), freedom from punishment (Jonah 3:9 f.), fruitfulness of service (Ps. 51:13; Hos. 14:4-8), life (Ezek. 33:14 f.). The conversion of large multitudes is anticipated at the Messiah's advent (Deut. 4:30; Hos. 3:5; Mic. 5:3; Mal. 4:5 f.).

The NT harmonizes exactly with the OT description of conversion. Apostolic preaching insists (Acts 26:20) that men must turn from evil to God (Acts 14:15; I Thess. 1:9). Such an act translates them from Satan's power to God's kingdom (Acts 26:18). True conversion involves faith and repentance; it issues in the forgiveness of our sins (Acts 3:19; 26:18). Israelites (Luke 1:16 f.; II Cor. 3:16), Gentiles (Acts 15:19) and Christians (Luke 22:32; James 5:19 f.) are subjects of conversion. Paul is the outstanding example (Acts 9:1-18). The apostles were instrumental in the conversion of large multitudes (Acts 9:35; 11:21). Only converted men can bring about results in this blessed ministry (Luke 22:32; James 5:19 f.).

Such problems as (1) the relation of conversion to predestination (cf. Isa. 6:10; John 12:39 f.), (2) the future conversion of Israel (cf. Deut. 4:30; Isa. 59:20; Rom. 11:26 f.) and (3) the relation of conversion to free agency (cf. Matt. 18:3) constitute some of the most debated questions of theology.

BIBLIOGRAPHY
Arndt; James Strachan in *HERE;* W. F. Lofthouse in *HDAC.*

WICK BROOMALL

CONVICT, CONVICTION. The words convict or conviction, common in any Christian's vocabulary, never occur in the AV. Convicted occurs only in John 8:9. The RSV uses convict once and convicts and conviction twice each. Convict is found three times in the RV. Convicted occurs twice. Convicteth and conviction each occur once. *Elegcho* is the most common Greek word involved, found fifty times in the LXX and eighteen times in the NT. The AV variously translates the word by "reprove," "tell," "rebuke," etc.

The NT uses this word to describe the work of the Holy Spirit by which the satanic blindness is lifted from men's eyes, and they are enabled to see themselves as they are in God's sight — guilty, defiled, and totally unable to save themselves. Sin is thus brought to the conscience. John 16:7-11 is the fullest treatment on this subject in the NT. While this is a neglected theme it is well handled by Chafer and Hendriksen (L. S. Chafer, *Systematic Theology*, Vol. VII, pp. 94-96; William Hendriksen, *The New Testament Commentary: Exposition of the Gospel According to John*, Vol. II, pp. 324-27).

HOWARD Z. CLEVELAND

CONVOCATION. As used in the OT, more specifically in Lev. 23, a holy convocation is a solemn assembling of God's people on the sabbath or on the occasion of the various festivals. Hence it is sometimes used to denote the gathering together of Christians for purposes of worship or mutual edification. A specific application of the term is found in the Church of England, in which for many centuries it has described the official gatherings of the clergy to consider matters of particular relevance to the church. In the Middle Ages the main business was the voting of taxes and the making or revising of canons. After the Reformation the importance of convocation declined, and the gatherings were purely formal throughout the eighteenth and nineteenth centuries, but more recently convocation has been given new powers in conjunction with a house of laity, and again has the initiative in church affairs.

See also CONVENTICLE.

GEOFFREY W. BROMILEY

CORBAN. The word corban, from the Hebrew word meaning "offering," is used only once in the Bible (Mark 7:11). The Hebrew word is used in Lev. 1:2, 3; 2:1; 3:1 and Num. 7:12-17 in reference to sacrifices. In the Markan passage Jesus is referring to the despicable practice of children refusing to help needy parents on the pretense that money that might have been used for that purpose had already been dedicated as a gift to God and his service. This casuistry was allowed by the scribal tradition of Jesus' day; later scribal authorities modified it, as they were able to see its clear misuse.

SAMUEL A CARTLEDGE

CORNERSTONE. In the NT the people of God are viewed as a spiritual temple in which Jesus Christ is the cornerstone, *eben pinnâ, akrogōniaios* (Isa. 28:16; Eph. 2:20; I Pet. 2:6). The theological significance of the term arises from this usage. The word appears to be practically the equivalent of the phrase, "head of the corner," *rō'š pinnâ, kephalē gōnia* (Ps. 118:22; Matt. 21:42 and parallels; Acts 4:11; I Pet. 2:7). For example, in Ps. 118:22 the latter phrase is rendered *akrogōniaios* by Symmachus and, in turn, Isa. 28:16 is translated by the Peshitta as "head of the wall." There is a difference of opinion, however, regarding its precise connotation. Generally, it has been considered the first laid cornerstone above the foundation level of the building and, hence, the stone by which the other stones were measured or beveled and to which the design of the building conformed. KD (on Ps. 118:22 and Zech. 4:7) view *rō'š pinnâ* as designating the final topstone of the temple. Similarly, J. Jeremias, in *TWNT* (see bibliography), argues that *akrogōniaios* is the capstone (*Abschlussstein*) which completes the building and which is placed at the summit or (probably) over the entrance. This use of the term occurs in some extra-canonical Jewish literature and in IV Kings 25:17 (Symmachus) where the crown or capital of a column is so rendered. In either case the "cornerstone" signifies a keystone in which "the whole structure is welded together" (Eph. 2:21 Moffatt).

The "temple typology," of which the cornerstone is a part, expresses a basic theological concept in the NT (cf. E. E. Ellis, *Paul's Use of the Old Testament*, Wm. B. Eerdmans Publishing Company, Grand Rapids, 1957, pp. 87-92). The true temple of God, "not made with hands," is superior to the material temple (Mark 14:58; Acts 7:48; 17:24; cf. Matt. 12:6). It is a spiritual house of which Christ is the builder (Mark 14:58; cf. Matt. 16:18), the cornerstone, and the high priest (Heb.

9:11). In fact, Christ's body is the very essence of the temple (John 2:21), and Christians, who are the "body" of Christ, are the "living stones" (I Pet. 2:5) of the temple. It is no little thing, therefore, that the Jewish "builders" should reject the stone which God has destined to be "head of the corner." The result is the rejection of the builders themselves. It is within this context that the Lord quotes Ps. 118:22 in which Israel, the stone, is rejected by the gentile builders. The NT, typically, views Jesus Christ as "Israel" and unbelieving Jews as "Gentiles" and so applies the passage.

The "cornerstone" is a part of what Austin Farrer has called the great images of the NT. The concept is no less real for being in the language of imagery; rather, we may believe that in just this fashion it is best conveyed.

BIBLIOGRAPHY
Arndt; MM; E. G. Selwyn, *The First Epistle of St. Peter*, p. 163; TWNT, I, pp. 79 f; IV, pp. 275 ff.

E. EARLE ELLIS

CORRECTION. "Correction" must be considered along with "chastisement, chastening, instruction," all used to translate *mûsār* and its equivalent in the LXX and the NT, *paideia*. "Correction" is less frequent than the other words in the English versions. *Tôkaḥaṭ* is also used (Prov. 3:11), being rendered "correction" (AV), "reproof" (RV). Generally, the thought of discipline and improvement through chastisement is conveyed, and this represents the Hebrew concept of child-training. Hence, Jehovah's "chastisement" of his own people was corrective and prompted by loving concern for their welfare (Prov. 3:11, 12). In Isa. 53:5, however, *mûsār* carries no thought of correction, but of chastisement vicariously received.

In the NT *paideia* always implies corrective discipline, chastisement or chastening being the usual rendering. Correction is often by means of adverse circumstances (I Cor. 11:30-32; Heb. 12:5, 6, 11). But in II Tim. 3:16 *paideia* and *epanorthōsis*, which is found only here in the NT and also means correction or amendment, are received through the Scriptures, according to God's purpose.

R. COLIN CRASTON

CORRUPTION. In the OT the substantives rendered "corruption" are principally *mišḥat*, *mošḥat* and *mašḥît*: all three signify physical degeneration and decay (Isa. 52:14; Lev. 22:25; Dan. 10:8). In addition *šaḥaṭ* is so translated in the AV, although its meaning is place of corruption, pit. The cognate verb *šaḥaṭ* indicates the act of corrupting or of becoming corrupt morally through sin (Gen. 6:12; Ex. 32:7; Hos. 9:9).

In the NT *diaphthora* and *phthora* are rendered "corruption." The former occurs six times (Acts 7:27, 31; 13:34, 35, 36, 37) and consistently denotes the decomposition or decay of the body. The latter has this meaning also (I Cor. 15:42, 50), but in addition signifies the decomposition of the material world and the world of nature (Rom. 8:21; Col. 2:22; II Pet. 2:12a); religious and moral corruption (II Pet. 1:4; 2:19); and eschatological destruction (Gal. 6:8 where *phthora* is contrasted with *zōē aiōnios*, "eternal life;" II Pet. 2:12b). No indication is to be found in the word *phthora* itself of the precise nature or duration of this eschatological ruin.

BIBLIOGRAPHY
Arndt; H. Windisch, *Die Katholischen Briefe*, HZNT, p. 95.

WALTER W. WESSEL

COUNCIL. An assembly, from the Latin *consilium*, a collection of people, of persons for the purpose of deliberation, consultation, or decision. In the NT the word is commonly used to translate *synedrion*, "seated together." Ecclesiastically, councils and synods are assemblies of Christian leaders for the purpose of discussion and decision in matters of doctrine and administration. The synod, from the Greek *synodia*, "a company," is usually more local in character.

The assembly of the apostles in Jerusalem (Acts 15) during the apostolic period is sometimes referred to as the first Christian council. The regional synods of the second century were loosely organized; they met to decide local issues, and their authority seems not to have been binding upon individual congregations.

The general or ecumenical councils are numbered from the first, called by Constantine at Nicaea in 325. The decisions of the general councils, composed of bishops of the whole church, but in practice representing largely the East, were binding, both in ecclesiastical and imperial law. Both Eastern and Western churches consider the first seven general councils as authoritative. After 754 so-called general councils were held independently in the East and West.

BIBLIOGRAPHY

C. J. von Hefele, *History of the Councils of the Church; Nicene and Post-Nicene Fathers*, 2nd series, XIV.

DONALD G. DAVIS

COUNSEL. The Hebrew *'ēṣâ* and the Greek *boulē* and *symboulion* chiefly represent the idea expressed by the English "counsel." This word indicates the deliberative process whereby presumably wise decisions are rendered.

The following contrasts represent some of the manifold ramifications of counsel: (1) human (Isa. 30:1; Jer. 49:30) and divine (Jer. 50:45); (2) good (I Kings 1:12-40) and evil (I Kings 12:8; Ps. 1:1; 83:3; Ezek. 11:2); (3) accomplished (Ps. 20:4; Prov. 19:21) and unaccomplished (Neh. 4:15; Esth. 9:25; Ps. 33:10; Isa. 47:13-15); (4) received (Ezra 10:3-8; Prov. 12:15) and rejected (II Chron. 25:14-17; Prov. 1:25, 30); (5) wise (Acts 5:38-40) and foolish (Job 38:2; 42:3 ff; Acts 27:42 f.); (6) peaceful (Ps. 55:14; Prov. 27:9) and rebellious (Ps. 106:43; 107:11; Ezek. 11:2); (7) upheld by the Lord (Isa. 44:26; 46:10; John 11:49-53; 18:14) and rejected by the Lord (Isa. 19:3; Jer. 18:18-23; 19:7).

God's counsels are eternal (Ps. 33:11), immutable (Prov. 19:21; Heb. 6:17), all-comprehensive (Acts 4:28; Eph. 1:11), directive (Ps. 73:24), wonderful (Isa. 28:29), faithful (Isa. 25:1), great (Jer. 32:19) and consistent with man's free agency (Prov. 19:21; Acts 2:23). God clothed the Messiah with counsel (Prov. 8:14; Isa. 11:2; Zech. 6:13).

WICK BROOMALL

COURAGE. Although among the four cardinal virtues (Wisdom 8:7), the word "courage," *tharsos,* occurs only once in the NT (Acts 28:15). Yet, the idea of courage, born of faith in God (Ps. 56:3; Matt. 8:26), is common. Chief Hebrew words are *ḥāzaq* (Num. 13:20; I Chron. 19:13), and *'āmaṣ* (Deut. 31:6, 7, 23; Josh. 1:6, 9, 18). The LXX uses *andrizomai,* "play the man," for both (cf. I Cor. 16:13). Heart and spirit are also translated courage.

R. COLIN CRASTON

COVENANT. The OT word is *bᵉrît;* the NT *diathēkē.* Basically, it denotes a compact or agreement between two parties binding them mutually to undertakings on each other's behalf. Theologically (used of relations between God and man) it denotes a gracious undertaking entered into by God for the benefit and blessing of man, and specifically of those men who by faith receive the promises and commit themselves to the obligations which this undertaking involves.

I. COVENANT IN THE OT. Uniformly the word used to express the covenant concept is the Hebrew *bᵉrît.* The original meaning of this word was probably "fetter" or "obligation," coming from a root *bārâ,* "to bind." This root does not occur as a verb in Hebrew, but it does occur in Akkadian as *bārû,* "to bind," and appears as a noun in the Akkadian *birîtu,* which means "bond" or "fetter." Thus a *bᵉrît* would originally signify a relationship between two parties wherein each bound himself to perform a certain service or duty for the other. But some scholars prefer to derive this noun from the verb *bārâ* "to eat," which occurs in II Sam. 13:6; 12:17, etc., and thus interpret it as "a meal" or "food," with reference to the sacrificial meal which the contracting parties often ate together when ratifying their agreement before the deity who was invoked as protector and guarantor of the covenant. So E. Meyer, B. Luther, L. Koehler. Still others, like E. Koenig and H. Zimmern, trace it from a *bārâ,* meaning "to perceive" or "to determine"; hence *bᵉrît* would involve the basic idea of "vision." But neither of these explanations commends itself as being so fitting or appropriate to the basic character of a covenant as the idea of "bond" preferred by the majority of scholars — including G. Quell in *TWNT.*

A general characteristic of the OT *bᵉrît* is its unalterable and permanently binding character. The parties to a covenant obligated themselves to carry out their respective commitments under the penalty of divine retribution should they later attempt to avoid them. Usually, although not necessarily, the promise of each was supported by some sort of legal consideration or *quid pro quo.* But where the one party to the agreement was greatly superior to the other in power or authority, the situation was a bit different: the ruler or man of authority would in the enactment of the *bᵉrît* simply announce his governmental decree or constitution which he thought best to impose upon those under him, and they for their part expressed their acceptance and readiness to conform to what he had ordained. Doubtless it was true even in this type of covenant that the ruler impliedly committed himself to rule for the best interests of his people and to contrive for their protection against their foes.

But in the case of the promulgation of a covenant by God with his chosen people, this one-sided aspect of the transaction was even more apparent, since the contracting parties stood upon an entirely different level. In this case the covenant constituted a divine announcement of God's holy will to extend the benefits of his unmerited grace to men who were willing by faith to receive them, and who by entering into a personal commitment to God bound themselves to him by ties of absolute obligation. The characteristic statement of this relationship occurs in the formula "I will be their God and they shall be my people" (cf. Jer. 11:4; 24:7; 30:22; 32:38; Ezek. 11:20; 14:11; 36:28; 37:23; Zech. 8:8, etc.) This signifies that God unreservedly gives himself to his people and that they in turn give themselves to him and belong to him. Thus they are his "peculiar treasure" (sᵉgullâ — Ex. 19:5; Deut. 7:6; 14:2; 26:18; Ps. 135:4; Mal. 3:17). His motive in adopting them as his own covenant-children is stated to be "lovingkindness" or "covenant-love" (ḥesed), a term with which bᵉrîṭ is often associated (cf. Deut. 7:9; I Kings 8:23; Dan. 9:4). (Compare also I Sam. 20:8, where Jonathan is said to exercise ḥesed when he enters into his covenant-relationship with David.) This presents a remarkable contrast to the motivation attributed by the heathen Semites to their gods, who were uniformly depicted as entering into covenant-relations with their devotees for the purpose of extracting service and nourishment from their altars, more or less like the feudal lords of human society who extract their support from the labor of their vassals.

One very important element in God's covenant-relations with Israel lay in the dual aspect of conditionality and unconditionality. Were his solemn promises, which partook of the nature of a binding oath (cf. Deut. 7:8), to be understood as capable of non-fulfilment, in case of the failure of man to live up to his obligations towards God? Or was there a sense in which God's covenant-undertakings were absolutely sure of fulfilment, regardless of the unfaithfulness of man? The answer to this much-debated question seems to be: (a) that the promises made by Jehovah in the covenant of grace represent decrees which he will surely bring to pass, when conditions are ripe for their fulfilment; (b) that the personal benefit — and especially the spiritual and eternal benefit — of the divine promise will accrue only to those individuals of the covenant people of God who manifest a true and living faith (demonstrated by a godly life). Thus the first aspect is brought out by the initial form of the covenant with Abram in Gen. 12:1-3; there is no shadow of doubt but what God will truly make of Abram a great nation, and make his name great, and shall bless all the nations of earth through him and his posterity (cf. Gal. 3:8). This is set forth as God's plan from the very beginning; nothing shall frustrate it. On the other hand, the individual children of Abraham are to receive personal benefit only as they manifest the faith and obedience of Abraham; thus: Ex. 19:5 ("Now therefore if ye will obey my voice indeed, and keep my covenant, then ye shall be a peculiar treasure unto me. . . . And ye shall be unto me a kingdom of priests and a holy nation"). In other words, God will see to it his plan of redemption will be carried out in history, but he will also see to it that none partake of the eternal benefits of the covenant in violation of the demands of holiness. No child of the covenant who presents to him a faithless and insincere heart shall be included in its blessings.

This triumphantly enduring quality of the covenant of grace is especially set forth by the prophets in the form of the "New Covenant." In the classic passage on this theme (Jer. 31:31-37) the earliest phase of the covenant (that entered into at Sinai) is shown to have been temporary and provisional because of the flagrant violation of it by the Israelite nation as a whole, and because of their failure to know or acknowledge God as their personal Lord and Saviour. But there is a time coming, says Jehovah, when he will put his holy law into their very hearts, so that their cordial inclination and desire will be to live according to his holy standard. Moreover he shall beget within them a sense of sonship towards himself, so that they shall have a personal knowledge and love of him that will not require artificial human teaching. Furthermore the carrying out of this redeeming purpose is stated to be as sure as the continued existence of sun, moon and stars, or even of the foundations of heaven itself.

II. COVENANT IN THE NT. The term for

covenant employed in the NT is *diathēkē,* the word used constantly in the LXX for *bᵉrîṭ.* Since the ordinary Greek word for "contract" or "compact" *(synthēkē)* implied equality on the part of the contracting parties, the Greek-speaking Jews preferred *diathēkē* (coming from *diatithemai* "to make a disposition of one's own property") in the sense of "a unilateral enactment." In secular Greek this word usually meant "will" or "testament," but even classical authors like Aristophanes (*Birds* 439) occasionally used it of a covenant wherein one of the two parties had an overwhelming superiority over the other and could dictate his own terms. Hence the biblical *diathēkē* signified (in a way much more specific than did *bᵉrîṭ*) an arrangement made by one party with plenary power, which the other party may accept or reject but cannot alter. Johannes Behm (in Kittel's *TWNT* ii, p. 137) defines it as: "The decree *(Verfuegung)* of God, the powerful disclosure of the sovereign will of God in history whereby he constitutes the relationship, the authoritative divine ordinance (institution), which introduces a corresponding order of affairs." There is just one passage in which the more usual secular significance of "will" or "testament" appears along with the covenantal idea: Heb. 9:15-17. A legal analogy is drawn from the fact that a testator must die before his will can take effect; so also in the enactment of the Mosaic covenant there was slain a sacrificial animal, representing the atonement of Christ, and it was the blood of that victim which was sprinkled upon the people and the covenantal document itself. But even here the predominant notion in *diathēkē* is "covenant" rather than "testament."

BIBLIOGRAPHY
J. Behm in *TWNT,* ii, pp. 127-37; G. Berry in *ISBE,* pp. 727-29; A. B. Davidson, *The Theology of the OT;* W. Eichrodt, *Theologie des AT;* D. Estes in *ISBE,* p. 729; G. E. Mendenhall, *Law and Covenant in Israel and the Ancient Near East;* G. Oehler, *Theology of the OT,* pp. 175 ff.; G. Quell in Kittel's *TWNT,* ii, pp. 107-27; W. Oesterley and T. H. Robinson, *Hebrew Religion,* pp. 156-59; G. Vos, *Biblical Theology.*

G. L. ARCHER, JR.

COVENANT THEOLOGY. The theology of the Reformed churches, in the place which it gives to the covenants, has its prototype in patristic theology as systematized by Augustine of Hippo. It represents the whole of Scripture as being covered by two covenants: (1) the covenant of works, and (2) the covenant of grace. The *parties* to the former covenant were God and Adam. The *promise* of the covenant

was life. The *proviso* was perfect obedience by Adam. And the *penalty* of failure was death. To save man from the penalty of his disobedience, a second covenant, made from all eternity, came into operation, namely, the covenant of grace. Throughout the OT period there were successive proclamations of this covenant. We find it in the *protevangelium* of Gen. 3:15. Certain of its provisions were later revealed to Noah (Gen. 9). It was then established with Abraham (Gen. 12), and with his descendants after him, thus becoming a national covenant. Although in the NT this covenant is described as *new,* such passages as Rom. 4 and Gal. 3 show that it is essentially one with the covenant under which believers lived in OT times. Salvation was shown to be of grace and not of merit, for the OT sacrifices were prefigurative of the atoning death of Christ. But although the same covenant, it is described as a *better* covenant under the NT dispensation, because it is now administered not by Moses, a servant, but by Christ the Son (Heb. 3:5, 6).

The covenant of grace is treated under two aspects. The first is a Godward aspect, under which it is sometimes called the covenant of redemption. The *parties,* under this aspect, are God and Christ; the *proviso* is the Son's perfect obedience even to his suffering the penalty of man's disobedience, namely, death; and the *promise* is the salvation of all believers. The second is a manward aspect, in which the *parties* are God and the believer; the *promise* eternal life; and the *proviso* faith in Jesus Christ as the only "work" required of the believer (John 6:29).

BIBLIOGRAPHY
H. Witsius, *On the Covenants;* A. A. Hodge, *Outlines of Theology,* pp. 309-14, 367-77; Charles Hodge, *Systematic Theology,* ii; pp. 117-22, 354-76; L. Berkhof, *Manual of Reformed Doctrine,* pp. 130-64.

GEORGE N. M. COLLINS

COVENANTERS. The Covenanters were those who, in Scotland, resolutely contended for religious freedom from 1637 to 1688 against Stuart absolutism in church and state. The name is particularly applied to the "suffering remnant" persecuted from 1660 onwards. Many bonds or covenants had been signed for the defence of the Reformed religion. The most important was the National Covenant of 1638, signed in Greyfriars Church, Edinburgh, by most of the nobles and vast numbers of commoners.

Years before, the court had suppressed Presbyterianism and established Prelacy against the wishes of the nation. The church was in chains. A crisis was precipitated by the introduction of a new Book of Canons and a new Liturgy on High Church lines. The king bowed temporarily before the storm, and permitted a General Assembly in 1638. This Assembly abolished Prelacy. War ensued, in which the Scots were successful. The king gave solemn guarantees of religious liberty but soon broke them. In 1643, the Scots entered into the Solemn League and Covenant with the English Parliament. In the Civil War the Parliamentary party triumphed and Charles I was executed. At the Restoration in 1660, although Charles II had sworn to defend the Covenants, there began a shameful oppression of the Covenanters. Argyle, Sir Archibald Johnston of Warriston, and other eminent men, were hurried to the scaffold. Three hundred and fifty ministers were driven from their churches. Then began the conventicles on the hills and moorlands of southern Scotland. In twenty-eight years, 18,000 suffered from the ruthless persecution — many thousands banished or imprisoned, 498 executed without process of law, and 362 after formal process. Nothing could break the spirit of the more resolute. Finally, their principles triumphed in the Revolution of 1688 under William of Orange.

BIBLIOGRAPHY
Alexander Smellie, *Men of the Covenant*; King Hewison, *The Covenanters*.

ALEXANDER M. RENWICK

COVETOUSNESS. Covetousness means primarily "inordinate desire." It has come to mean a desire for anything which is inordinate in degree, or a desire for that which rightfully belongs to another, especially in the realm of material things. In a general sense it means all inordinate desire for worldly possessions such as honors, gold, etc. In a more restricted sense, it is a desire for the increasing of one's substance by appropriating that of others.

The shades of meaning vary according to the particular word used and the context. The following are some of the uses: *beṣaʿ*, "dishonest gain" (Ex. 18:21); *pleonexia*, "the desire to have more than one possesses" (Luke 12:15), "an intense love or lust for gain" (Rom. 1:29), "greed" (II Pet. 2:14 RSV); *philarguria*, "an inordinate love of money" (I Tim. 6:10).

Covetousness is a grave sin. It is labeled idolatry (Col. 3:5), for intensity of desire and worship are closely related. Its heinousness doubtless is accounted for by its being, in a very real sense, the root of many forms of sin. This is the reason Jesus warned against it so sternly (Luke 12:15).

BIBLIOGRAPHY
Andrew K. Rule in *TCERK*; William Evans in *ISBE*, II, p. 733; MSt, II, p. 546; AC.

LEWIS T. CORLETT

CREATION. The doctrine of the origin of the universe by the creative power of God and not from previously existing material, is found only in monotheistic religion. Since there is only one monotheistic tradition in all of human culture, the Hebrew tradition — Judaism, Christianity and Mohammedanism, the only monotheistic religions, consciously deriving their monotheism from the Hebrew sources — there is only one source of the doctrine of creation out of nothing, and that is found in the Bible.

The biblical cosmogony, the doctrine of the creation of the cosmic order out of nothing, including the human order as a culmination, is given explicitly in Genesis 1:1 — 2:25, but it is also declared or assumed in many other passages.

John 1:3. To consider first certain Scriptures outside of the Genesis account, let us note the doctrine of creation in the prologue to the Fourth Gospel. The first postulate is God and the Logos, who is God and with God. In other words, the first postulate is the eternal God, whose personal being is complex. The second postulate is the creation of the finite cosmos by God. The common English version reads, "All things were made by him, and without him was not any thing made that was made." But the word "made" translates, not a form of *poieō*, to make, but of *ginomai*, to come to pass or to come into being. Literally, "Everything came into being through him, and without him not one thing came into being which has come into being."

We need not try to argue that John 1:3 amounts to a categorical declaration of creation *ex nihilo*. Had there been such a declaration in the most literal terms, the modern mystics and existentialists generally would have sought to argue that the nothing was something. It is a fact of history that John 1:3 has been a source and cause of the doctrine of theistic cosmogony.

It is in John 1:3, Col. 1:16, and Heb. 1:2, that the second person of the Trinity is said to have been the special divine agent in creation.

Hebrews 11:3. The author of the Epistle to the Hebrews alludes to creation in 1:2, 10 and 4:3. In 11:3 the doctrine is expressed in striking terms. The following suggestions may help toward a more explicit interpretation than the common version gives: (1) "Faith" in this chapter is not subjective but objective, not our act of believing, but what we believe, i.e., the content of the gospel. (2) The word of God, as in other Scriptures (cf. Ps. 33:6-9), is taken as the sole and sufficient cause of creation. (3) "Things which are seen," or more correctly "that which is seen," is a simple reference to the visible material universe. (4) "Things which do appear," *phainomenōn,* seems to refer to things which, though sometimes invisible, do come into view. The following expanded paraphrase is thus suggested: "By what we believe in the gospel, we can understand the doctrine of creation, namely, that by the word of God as a sole and sufficient cause the worlds were set in order, so that the visible universe did not come into being out of previously existing things which come into view."

Granted that this is an expansion and not a strict translation, nevertheless the strictest possible rendering must admit the probability that . . . *rhēmati theou . . . mē ek phainomenōn to blepomenon gegonenai* was intended as an assertion of creation out of nothing.

Colossians 1:15-17. The "founding of the world" and similar phrases recur in the NT (cf. John. 17:24; Eph. 1:4; 3:9; I Pet. 1:20; Rev. 13:8; 17:8). The vigorous insistence in Col. 1:16-17 that everything without exception was made by Christ, and that he is "before all things," and in him all things "consist," leaves no room for previously existing material. Creation *ex nihilo* is certainly assumed here.

Space does not allow for the examination of many other Scriptures referring to creation. See especially Rom. 1:18-23; Acts 14:15-17; 17:22-29; Ps. 33:6-9; 148:1-5; Prov. 3:19; 8:22-31; Job 26:7b; 38; Isa. 37:16; 40:26; Amos 4:13; 5:8; Zech. 12:1. The Apocrypha naturally reflect the scriptural attitude (cf. Ecclus. 16:26 — 17:9. Although Wisd. 11:17 shows extraneous influence, ". . . created the world out of formless matter, *ex amorphou hylēs,*" II Macc. 7:28 teaches a strict theistic cosmogony, ". . . made them not of things that were, *ouk ex ontōn."*

Genesis 1 and 2. It should be clear from what has been said that the biblical doctrine of creation *ex nihilo* is not dependent upon the meaning of the word *bārā'* in the first chapter of Genesis. Indeed (with the exception of the *piel* stem, in which the word means to cut down or cut out) the word *bārā'* always means to create something new, and God is always the one who does the creating. But the word itself does not exclude previously existing materials. Rather, it has about the breadth of meaning of the English word "create." The doctrine of creation out of nothing is implied rather (1) in the words "In the beginning," (2) in the total absence of any suggestion of any thing uncreated upon which God worked, (3) in the references to the divine *fiat* as causative, and (4) in the way in which the record was understood by the later writers of Scripture. For the different interpretations of the Genesis account, see Ramm's work listed below.

Beginning with 2:5 we have a literary phenomenon sometimes called a "recurrence." That is, the author goes back to a previous point in the narrative to bring up the threads in detail. In this instance the author goes back to a point in the second "day" and tells how rain came, and then how, and in what condition, the human race began.

Theological importance of great weight attaches to the biblical cosmogony. If God is not the creator of absolutely everything but himself, with no exceptions, then he is not completely sovereign. If the substance of which the universe is made is not created by God, then it is co-eternal with God. Then God, in making the universe, was limited to the possibilities of the substance with which he had to work. Then he is not omnipotent in creation, nor in providence, nor in redemption, for we had to be made out of the substance which God found on hand.

If, on the other hand, God created the universe out of his own substance, as some have held, then we have stark pantheism. Then the substance of God is physically divisible and finitely extended in space. Then the substance of God is the substance of every sinner and of every instrument of crime and shame.

The God whose attributes are delineated on

virtually every page of the Bible is the creator, the absolute originator, of everything.

BIBLIOGRAPHY

For the older writers, C. Hodge, *Systematic Theology*, I, pp. 550-74; J. Orr, *The Christian View of God and the World*, 3rd ed., 1897; for recent literature, Bernard Ramm, *The Christian View of Science and Scripture*; current popular works on the physical history of the universe are *The Birth of the Sun* and *Biography of the Earth* by George Gamow, and *The Nature of the Universe*, and *Frontiers of Astronomy* by Fred Hoyle. A University of Chicago Ph. D. dissertation on "The Idea of Creation" (1909) by William Caldwell, while assuming the higher criticism current at the time, yet takes the position that, "The idea of creation . . . out of nothing by a supramundane God . . . in so far as it expresses the unconditional sovereignty of God . . . is indispensable to Christianity."

J. OLIVER BUSWELL, JR.

CREATIONISM. Creationism is one of three theories found in the Christian tradition whereby the origin of the soul of man is explained. The other two are traducianism (*q.v.*) and pre-existence (*q.v.*). According to the creationist theory, God makes the soul *de novo* at the moment of conception or birth and immediately unites it with the body. The foetus or the newly born child is polluted and therefore guilty (mediate imputation) or guilty and therefore polluted (immediate imputation) because of the first sin of the parent of the human race. Thus, the soul is sinful not because the creation of it is in some manner defective, but because of its immediate contact with inherited pollution and guilt. Some of the principal Scripture passages on which creationists base their belief are: Zech. 12:1; Isa. 42:5; Num. 16:22; Heb. 12:9. This view is common among Protestants, especially the Reformed; traducianism is associated especially with the Roman Church.

BIBLIOGRAPHY

H. Heppe, *Reformed Dogmatics*; Heinrich Denzinger, *Enchiridion Symbolorum*, 26th ed., 1946; Charles Hodge, *Systematic Theology*.

JOHN H. GERSTNER

CREED, CREEDS. The term creed derives from the Latin *credo* ("I believe"), and as used in the Christian church signifies a confession of faith. The form of the ancient creeds makes it plain that primarily a creed is not a mere statement of beliefs or acceptance of divine revelation, though these are also involved. It is an acknowledgment of personal trust in God. Hence we do not merely say: *Credo Deum (esse)*: "I believe that God exists"; or *Credo Deo*: "I believe what God says"; but: *Credo in Deum*: "I believe, or trust, or have faith, in God."

The historical derivation of our present creeds will always be something of a mystery.

There seems little doubt, however, that they grew out of the rudimentary forms of confession which we find in the NT (cf. Acts 8:36 ff.; Rom. 10:9; I Cor. 12:3; I Pet. 3:18 ff.) and which were probably used not only at baptism but also for purposes of worship and instruction. In some cases these express faith in Jesus Christ alone, but in others the Father is also included and the baptismal formula in Matt. 28:19 (cf. II Cor. 1:21 f.; I Pet. 1:2) shows us that trinitarian as well as binitarian and purely christological forms were already in use in the NT period.

The main development of creeds in the centuries which followed was almost certainly within the context of the catechumenate and baptism, with a consequent emphasis upon the original element of confession. Two main problems have engaged the interest of scholars: first, whether the creeds are an expansion of the purely christological formula of Acts (cf. 8:16; 19:5) or of the trinitarian formula of Matt. 28:19; and second, whether their original use was declaratory (as in the later baptismal orders and fairly certainly in catechetical instruction) or more strictly interrogatory, as seems to be suggested in some of the earlier writers (e.g., Tertullian, Hippolytus). The probability is that we do not have to make a simple choice in these matters, but that various complementary forces were at work. In any case, however, there can be no doubt as to the confessional character of the earliest creeds.

Yet the use of creeds for instructional purposes inevitably carried with it an emphasis upon the substance of what is confessed. This is not wrong in itself. To believe in God necessarily and quite rightly means to believe that God is, and to believe that which he tells us about himself. It is not surprising, therefore, that certain of the more important biblical truths or facts concerning God and his work should come to have a part in the primary confession of faith in Jesus Christ or the triune God, nor can the process be described as illegitimate so long as "the faith" is kept in the primary context of faith.

With the development of heretical teaching, however, there was a natural tendency to use the creeds as a test of catholic orthodoxy. This is the most likely explanation of the use of the Latin term *symbolum* for a creed. It is a token by which the true Christian can be known from the infidel or heretic. The genuine Christian does not merely express faith in Jesus Christ and therefore in the Father and the Holy Ghost. He states this faith and certain of its basic implications in a particular way. We cannot be certain, of course, that this is the real reason for the use of the word "symbol," but it seems to harmonize best both with the detailed evidence and the general development.

Instances of this new emphasis and application are perhaps to be seen even in a brief and simple statement like the later Apostles' Creed. Thus the confession that God is the Creator excludes the Gnostic idea of a Demiurge, and the stress on the death of Christ is an answer to Docetism. But the emergence of new heresies, especially in the field of Christology (q.v.), necessitated continuing elaboration in creedal definition and even the introduction of terminology for which there is no direct scriptural precedent. This is reflected in the so-called Nicene Creed and more particularly the complicated Athanasian.

Up to a point this might seem to be a natural and justifiable development. Yet it carried with it four serious dangers. First, the element of genuine confession of faith in Christ was very largely lost in that of assent to theological orthodoxy. Second, the creed became an instrument of division rather than unity. Third, the highly intellectual content made it impossible for the average man to understand the statements and therefore he was required to accept a good deal on trust, with all the associated evils of implicit faith. Fourth, it became difficult to stop the process of elaboration, and the continuing requirement of this or that new dogma on pain of eternal damnation could only enhance the power of the church, weaken true faith and its confession, and call forth from protesting or reforming groups opposing statements which had also to be given some measure of symbolical significance.

In typical reaction against over-emphasis on the creedal content, liberal Protestantism has ascribed a new and false importance to the confessing subject and thus given a distinctive nuance to the term creed. "My" creed is that which I now happen to believe concerning God, the world and myself, the important thing being, not that it is my response to the divine word and work in Jesus Christ, but that it is the non-obligatory and variable product of my own thinking, fantasy or experience.

In its basic sense of confession, the creed must always have a place as the profession of justifying faith in Jesus Christ and therefore in the Father and the Holy Ghost. For baptismal and liturgical purposes, the Apostles' Creed offers a short and biblical statement which under Scripture may well remain in continued use in the churches. Liturgical and instructional value may also be found in the other two primary creeds, though they can hardly be imposed or used in the same sense and must always be subjected to the scriptural norm. More detailed confessions have a legitimate place in expressing the mind of the churches on disputed issues and therefore helping forward the work of exposition and theology. But these again cannot be regarded as absolutely binding or final, and care must always be taken that they do not bind either the church or the Bible on the one side or on the other subjugate the true nature and use of confession to the search for detailed orthodoxy.

BIBLIOGRAPHY
HERE; F. J. Badcock, *The History of the Creeds*; O. Cullmann, *The Earliest Christian Confessions*; J. N. D. Kelly, *Early Christian Creeds*; H. B. Swete, *The Apostles' Creed*.

WILLIAM KELLY

CRITICISM, NEW TESTAMENT. The aspect of criticism with which this article deals is frequently called higher criticism to distinguish it from lower criticism which has for its province the Greek Text. It deals with questions of authorship, time of writing, literary structure and contents. The study of such questions may prove of great value for the better understanding of Scripture, if it is controlled by balanced judgment and due recognition of the fact that if the sacred writings are the works of men employing contemporary literary forms and modes of expression, they are at the same time much more, being also records of supernatural revelation and giving evidence of divine supervision of their composition.

I. DEVELOPMENT OF CRITICISM. The beginnings of criticism as applied to separate books of the NT may be seen in the early centuries of the Christian era, notably in the comments of Origen and Dionysius. It was not, however, until the late eighteenth century that it developed so as to exert an influence upon the interpretation of the NT as a whole. At that time a reaction was beginning to make itself felt against a wave of rationalism which had promoted skepticism on matters of religious faith. But the influence of the Cartesian philosophy and the Newtonian conception of the universe still tended to produce an attitude of mind relying strongly on subjective judgment and unfavorably disposed to belief in supernatural activity in the world. The way was thus prepared for regarding the books of the NT as purely human works. The miraculous was suspect. It was freely assumed that a heightening of Christology and modification in accordance with the developing thought of the Church was discernible in the NT writings. Consequently, books of earlier date were thought to be more reliable than those of later date and sources behind the Gospels more accurate than the Gospels themselves. Literary questions and the quest of the "Jesus of History" became the center of scholarly interest. It was hoped that with the discovery of the "real Jesus," who was believed to have been a merely human prophet, leading a blameless life and teaching the fatherhood of God, the brotherhood of man and the nearness of the kingdom of heaven, enough would be salvaged to prevent the Christian faith from being overwhelmed by rationalism.

II. THE TUEBINGEN SCHOOL. The first critical introduction to the NT was issued in 1804 by Eichhorn who had already written a critical introduction to the OT. But, about a quarter of a century later, works of far greater importance began to appear. Their author, F. C. Baur of Tuebingen, became the leader of an influential critical school. He approached the NT documents from the historical viewpoint and showed the value of relating the books to their original setting and considering the circumstances and motives of their writers. But by applying the principles of the Hegelian philosophy to the interpretation of the contents of the NT he arrived at extreme and misleading conclusions. He supposed that the chief clue to the date and character of the various books was their relation to the antagonism between the Petrine and Pauline schools. Those which gave clearest evidence of the opposition between the parties were early and those which showed conciliatory tendencies, or made little reference to it, were later. This method of classification led to the hypothesis that Paul wrote only Galatians, I and II Corinthians and Romans 1-14. A number of books were placed in the second century, the writings of Luke being among them. Late writings were considered tendentious and untrustworthy. Today this hypothesis is a matter of history. Comparatively little is heard of it. The present century has witnessed the dating of most, if not all, of the books within the second half of the first century. The Epistles bearing Paul's name have been restored to him, with the exception of Ephesians and the Pastoral Epistles which are still questioned by certain critics, although leading scholars, conservatively or otherwise inclined, have given strong reasons for regarding them all as Pauline. The archaeological researches of Sir William Ramsay, the works of James Smith, Hobart and, more recently, F. F. Bruce, have done much to restore confidence in the authenticity, unity and historicity of the Lukan books.

III. SOURCE CRITICISM. In 1835 Synoptic criticism received considerable impetus from Lachmann's theory of the priority of Mark, based on the belief that Matthew and Luke, when covering common ground with him, never agree against him. It now came to be accepted by many scholars that the other Synoptists used Mark's Gospel as one source. In course of time, the material which they have in common in addition to what they owe to Mark, was held to be derived from a source written or unwritten, denoted by Q, from the German *Quelle* (source). Some scholars inclined to identify it with the *logia* which Papias attributed to Matthew the apostle. This two-document source theory was later elaborated to become a four-document hypothesis in order to account for matter peculiar to each of Matthew and Luke. These further hypothetical sources are known as M and L respectively. The theory that Mark existed in an earlier form, called by critics Ur Markus, is rejected by Vincent Taylor. Canon Streeter supports a Proto-Luke hypothesis, on the assumption that Q and L were combined before Luke came upon Mark's Gospel, and together represented comparatively early tradition. Opinion on the merits of this theory varies.

IV. JOHN AND PAUL. The Fourth Gospel was commonly held to be of late date and little historical value. Its ideas represented the influence of developing theology and hellenistic conceptions upon primitive tradition. Critics generally regarded it as non-apostolic. Recent tendency has been to date it in the last decade of the first century, to allow that it has at least apostolic authority behind it and that the apparent differences between it and the Synoptic Gospels are less inexplicable than was formerly believed. The Dead Sea Scrolls have revealed that certain Johannine ideas, once confidently thought to be hellenistic, may well have been current in Palestine when Jesus taught. The early opinion of Dionysius that on literary grounds the author of the Fourth Gospel could not have written the Apocalypse has persisted, but even R. H. Charles admits some connection between Revelation and the Fourth Gospel.

The keen interest in the "Jesus of History," already mentioned, had as one of its consequences a reaction against Paulinism. Liberal scholars maintained that Paul's Christ was the creation of a writer who paid little attention to historical fact, and borrowed largely from current Judaism and mystery religions. Outstanding advocates of these views were Wrede and Reitzenstein. But many scholars joined in research to examine the foundations of these daring hypotheses and among those who helped to vindicate Paul's claim to be a true witness to Jesus may be mentioned, H. A. A. Kennedy, Anderson Scott and J. Gresham Machen.

V. ESCHATOLOGY AND FORM CRITICISM. An epoch-making book, published in Germany in 1906, had two important effects. It was translated into English under the title *The Quest of the Historical Jesus*. The author, Albert Schweitzer, reviewed the course of criticism in the nineteenth century and claimed that the emphasis of the original gospel was eschatological. In certain respects views expressed in Schweitzer's book are open to grave objection. But the book raised the question of the apologetic value of the supposed "Jesus of History" and also turned the attention of scholars to the eschatological teaching of the Gospels.

Some years earlier, Wrede had published a work entitled *The Messianic Secret in the Gospels*. Its thesis that Mark had superimposed upon tradition a series of messianic claims based on post-resurrection belief met with strong opposition in Germany and England. But it was used by the Form Historical critics, who came into prominence after World War I, to discredit the Markan framework on the ground of artificiality. This school, professing disappointment with the meager results of source criticism, concentrated on the period when tradition was forming. They assumed that it would follow patterns familiar from

other kinds of tradition. On this basis, Dibelius and Bultmann, among others, classified the whole material of the Gospels, dividing it into groups of supposedly varying historical value. While drawing attention to some things which were, perhaps, little noticed previously, they made serious mistakes. They exaggerated the length of time between the ascension and the earliest written records. They misjudged the extent and character of the influence of the life and thought of the church upon tradition. They gave too large a place to subjective opinion.

Much criticism is thus seen to have yielded destructive or negative results. But all scholarly labor in this direction was not in vain. Error stimulated fresh study in order to refute it and so one way or another work of lasting value was produced.

BIBLIOGRAPHY
Collins, *The New Testament Problem*; W. F. Howard, *The Fourth Gospel in Recent Criticism*; E. B. Redlich, *Form Criticism*; C. H. Dodd, *History and the Gospel*; J. Gresham Machen, *The Origin of Paul's Religion*.

WILLIAM J. CAMERON

CRITICISM, OLD TESTAMENT. OT criticism may be defined as the serious and scholarly study of the OT. It is generally divided into the two categories of lower and higher criticism. Lower criticism deals with the text of the OT, its transmission and condition. Higher criticism on the other hand occupies itself with the study of the date, authorship, place and circumstances of composition as well as the purpose and nature of the individual biblical books. In popular parlance, however, the term "higher criticism" has come to designate an approach to the OT which discards its absolute trustworthiness and in the study of the above mentioned questions feels free to set itself in conflict with express statements of the Bible.

During the early Christian centuries, particularly among groups which were outside the pale of the orthodox church, hostile criticism of the OT made its appearance. This was the case among certain Gnostic groups, Marcion, Celsus, Porphyry and others. These latter were hostile opponents of Christianity and opposed the OT from a heathen philosophical standpoint. Among the Jews there were some who attacked certain statements in the OT, and one or two denied the latter chapters of Isaiah to that prophet.

Spinoza (1632-77) has been termed the "father of higher criticism." He denied the

Mosaic authorship of the Pentateuch, and thought that it might have been the work of Ezra. A German scholar, H. B. Witter (1711) thought that there were two parallel accounts of creation in Genesis, distinguished by the use of different divine names. Jean Astruc (1753) also used the divine names as criteria for the identification of documents and carried his analysis throughout Genesis, finding in all some twelve different documents.

The principle of documentary analysis was adopted by Eichhorn (1780-83), although, unlike Astruc, he denied that Moses was the compiler of Genesis. He designated the documents J and E after the divine names Jehovah and Elohim. The next stage in the development of this negative criticism (negative, because it ran counter to the positive statements of Scripture) is found in the work of K. D. Ilgen who believed that E really consisted of two documents, E^1 and E^2. The order thus stood E^1, E^2, J and D (Deuteronomy). This arrangement is known as the Earlier Documentary Hypothesis.

During the nineteenth century other views also appeared, the most important of which was known as the supplementary hypothesis. This view maintained that there was one basic document to which supplements or additions had been made.

An important step in the history of the documentary hypothesis is associated with the name of Herman Hupfeld (1853) who, even more clearly than Ilgen, distinguished between 1st and 2nd E. He labeled his documents E or P, E^2, J, and D, regarding P (priestly) as the earliest and D as the latest.

Largely due to the influence of K. H. Graf (1866) P was now considered the latest document and J the earliest, giving the order J E D and P. This position was maintained in connection with a particular theory (known as the development hypothesis and popularized by Julius Wellhausen, 1876) of the origin of Israel's religious institutions. According to the development hypothesis the religion of Israel was not a special revelation but arose from natural impulses in man. The patriarchs were not historical figures and Genesis was said not to present an accurate picture of patriarchal times. It was not until the Deuteronomic reform in 622 B.C. under Josiah that worship at a single sanctuary was required. The Levitical system was thought to be even later.

Advocates of the development hypothesis of Israel's religion denied also the Davidic authorship of those psalms which are attributed to him, as well as the unity and Isaianic authorship of Isaiah and the Danielic authorship of Daniel. During the early part of this present century the development hypothesis was truly regnant. At the present, however, it has largely been discarded, although some form of documentary hypothesis is generally held by those who refuse to accept the trustworthiness of the Bible. The reasons why the development hypothesis has now become almost obsolete are to be found principally in the discoveries of archaeology and the world wars which shattered the evolutionary conception of man that underlay much of this theory. The inherent weaknesses of the position itself also led to its decline.

Under the influence of Hermann Gunkel and Hugo Gressmann a school of study arose which sought to determine the life situation which gave rise to each bit of OT material, poetry, oracle or narrative. These units were then classified and categorized. According to Martin Noth (1943) the first four books of the Bible (the Tetrateuch) consist of ancient traditions which reach back into ancient times. Noth's position is in reality based upon the earlier work of Gunkel and Gressmann. Noth's views have influenced modern Scandinavian scholars, notably Ivan Engnell, who maintains that most of the OT was transmitted orally until it was finally written down at the time of the exile. Engnell lays great stress upon the importance of oral transmission.

Adherents of the documentary hypothesis for the most part held a low view of the Massoretic text and its reliability, often preferring the readings of the LXX. Largely as a result of the discovery of the Dead Sea Scrolls a greater respect for the Massoretic text has arisen. There was a time when scholars were quite free in suggesting emendations of the OT Hebrew text. Such a time has passed, however, and at present a more cautious attitude is prevalent.

Side by side with the critical movement whose history has just been sketched there has also existed a reverent scholarship which has regarded the Scriptures as authoritative and infallible. Adherents of this movement have produced valuable commentaries and have published and continue to publish scholarly biblical studies. This group engages in scholarly, critical study of the OT, but endeavors to be guided in its research by the authority of the Scriptures. In this group some of the greatest names in OT study are to be found, e.g., E. W. Hengstenberg, K. F. Keil and William Henry Green.

It is of course impossible to tell what direction future studies in the field of OT will take. Without a doubt the discoveries of archaeology have brought about a more conservative frame of mind, and this is probably a good thing. The OT scholar, however, needs more than a conservative frame of mind. He must be a man who is regenerate and who possesses the necessary scholarly equipment. It is upon such men that the future of true OT scholarship rests.

BIBLIOGRAPHY

E. M. Gray, *Old Testament Criticism;* Emil G. Kraeling, *The Old Testament Since the Reformation;* H. J. Kraus, *Geschichte der historisch-kritischen Erforschung des Alten Testaments;* Edward J. Young, *Introduction to the Old Testament.*

EDWARD J. YOUNG

CROSS. The Greek word for "cross" is *stauros* and lit. means an upright, pointed stake or pale; piles driven in to serve as a foundation. The verb means to make a fence with stakes, to palisade, to crucify. The Latin *crux* ("cross") and *palus* ("stake") are background expressions for our English word. In the NT the noun is used twenty-eight times and the verb forty-six. The use of the cross as a form of punishment was adopted by the Greeks and Romans from the Phoenicians, Persians and Carthaginians. In pre-Christian days, besides the upright post, there were primarily two types of crosses. The *crux commissa* or St. Anthony's cross was shaped like the capital "T", consisting of an upright post with a cross-bar on top. Vine maintains that this came from the symbol of the god Tammuz and the *tau* became the initial of his name (Vine, *An Expository Dictionary,* Westwood, N. J., Fleming H. Revell Company, 1956, p. 256). The other type was the Latin cross or *crux immissa* with the cross-bar lowered about a third of the way on the upright post. Not only does tradition bear witness to the latter but also the four Gospels (Matt. 27:37; Mark 15:26; Luke 28:38; John 19:19-22) in stating that a title was nailed to the cross of Christ. Josephus records that two thousand were crucified after the death of Herod the Great by Varus (*Ant.* XVII. x. 10). Titus, in A.D. 70, also carried out mass crucifixion. The Jews never killed by crucifying but they did hang dead bodies

on a cross to symbolize a curse (cf. Deut. 21:22; Josh. 10:26; II Sam. 4:12). An exception to this was by the Jewish ruler Alexander Jannaeus (104-78 B.C.) when in raging anger he ordered eight hundred deserters to be crucified and the throats of their children and wives to be cut before their eyes (Jos. *Ant.* XIII. xiv. 2). The public use of the cross was adopted by the Christians as a symbol at the time of Constantine.

For the early Christians, surrounded by crucifixion as a grim fact of common experience, there was no danger of beautifying the cross by sentiment. Its grimness remained as the epitome of the sufferings of Christ and the very heart of discipleship. It ceased to be an embarrassment in the light of the resurrection. At the cross salvation was achieved and the doom of hostile powers was sealed (I Pet. 2:24; 3:18; Col. 2:15).

BIBLIOGRAPHY

Arndt; HDB; J. J. Collins in CBQ, April 1939, pp. 154-59; Crem.

ROBERT V. UNMACK

CROWN. In the NT there are two Greek words for "crown" — *diadēma* and *stephanos.* The former is found only in Revelation (12:3; 13:1; 19:12). Originally it meant "the sign of royalty among the Persians, a blue band trimmed with white, on the tiara" (Arndt, p. 181). So the term suggests a symbol of royalty.

On the other hand, *stephanos* (also used as a proper name, Stephen) meant "the wreath . . . given as a prize for victory, as a festal ornament, or as a public honor for distinguished service or personal worth" (A-S, p. 27). It was used for the laurel wreath presented to the victor in an athletic contest (cf. I Cor. 9:25). It means "prize" or "reward" (Arndt, p. 775).

This gives added poignancy to its use for the "crown of thorns" placed on Jesus' brow (Matt. 27:29; Mark 15:17; John 19:2, 5). The reward he received from those to whom he had ministered in loving compassion was a cruel crown of thorns.

The expression "crown of life" occurs twice (James 1:12; Rev. 2:10). In both cases the idea of reward for faithfulness is the prominent feature. "Of life" is probably the genitive of definition; i.e., "the crown which consists in life eternal" (J. B. Mayor, *The Epistle of St. James,* Zondervan Publishing House, Grand Rapids, Mich., n.d., p. 49).

Trench (p. 78) insists that while *diadēma*

signifies a crown of royalty, *stephanos* always means a crown of victory. It is "always the conquerer's, and not the king's" (*ibid.,* p. 79). Yet he admits that the crown of thorns suggested mock royalty (*ibid.,* p. 81).

An inscription relating to a second century athlete, in the theater at Ephesus, reads: "He fought three fights, and twice was crowned" (Deiss LAE, p. 309). Another inscription, from the second century B.C., honors a man for public service "with a golden crown" (*ibid.,* p. 312). In both cases *stephanos* is used.

BIBLIOGRAPHY
Arndt; A-S; Deiss LAE; Mayor; *Trench.*

RALPH EARLE

CUP. This word is used in three ways: literally, literal-metaphorically, and metaphorically.

Literally it is used of the cup of cold water given in Christ's name (Matt. 10:42; Mark 9:41) and of the attention given to cups by the Pharisees (Matt. 23:25; Luke 11:39; Mark 7:4).

The literal-metaphorical usages involve a literal cup but the contents have a metaphorical meaning. In the institution of the Lord's Supper (Matt. 26:27; Mark 14:23; Luke 22:17, 30; I Cor. 11:25) and in its practice by the church (I Cor. 10:16, 21; 11:26, 27, 28) we have an actual cup but its material contents depict the atoning death of Christ.

The metaphorical usages are profound and worthy of careful study. The cup symbolizes the suffering and death of Christ (Matt. 20:22; Mark 10:38; Matt. 26:39; Mark 14:36; Luke 22:42; John 18:11). This symbol of a violent death is also applied to James and John (Matt. 20:23; Mark 10:39). The cup also stands for the wrath of God to be poured out upon sinful men at the end of this age (Rev. 14:10; 16:19). In interpreting these metaphors, stress should be put upon the symbolic nature of the cup and its contents.

A. BERKELEY MICKELSEN

CURATE. See OFFICES, ECCLESIASTICAL.

CURSE. The Scriptures employ the term "curse" (OT noun forms, *qᵉlālâ* and *ḥērem;* verb, *'ārar et al.;* NT noun forms, *katara* and *anathema; verb, kataraomai et al.*) in certain well-defined significations. In general usage a curse is an imprecation or an expressed wish for evil. If it be directed against God, it is blasphemy (Job 1:5, 11; 2:5, 9). It may be a

desire uttered to God against another person or thing. A curse was considered to have an innate power to carry itself into effect (Zech. 5:1-3, where the curse inevitably found its victim). Curses among the heathen were supposed to be possessed of the power of self-realization (Num. 22-24 with Balaam). In Scripture a curse was invariably related to sin (Gen. 3) and disobedience (Prov. 26:2). In certain cases the concept of oath suffices to convey the meaning (Judg. 17:2; Isa. 65:15).

In its specific usage the curse was an act of dedicating or devoting to God. Things or persons thus devoted could not be used for private purposes (Lev. 27:28). In time of war a city was devoted to the Lord. This included the slaying of men and animals (Deut. 20:12-14; Josh. 6:26); the redeeming of children and virgins (Deut. 21:11-12); the burning of combustibles (Deut. 7:25); the placing of metals in the temple (Josh. 6:24); and the imposition of the ban on those who violated these provisions (Josh. 6:18). How literally the last named ban was carried out may be seen from the tragic history of Achan and his family, and the experience of Hiel the Bethelite (Josh. 7:1 ff. and I Kings 16:34). The Canaanites as a nation were set apart for this kind of destruction (Josh. 2:10; 6:17).

In its higher significance the curse indicates a thing devoted to an exclusively sacred use. It amounts then to a vow. Compare the consecration of John the Baptist (Luke 1:15; 7:33), and the misuse of the vow among the people of Israel by an evasion instituted by their religious leaders (Mark 7:11 ff.). It denotes, as seen, the ban of extermination and occurs frequently in the OT, but there is no clear instance of this in the NT. The ban of annihilation was replaced at times by the discipline of excommunication (John 9:22; 12:42; 16:2; Matt. 18:17). Ezra 10:8 is understood to approximate the later rabbinic practice of excommunication (Matt. 18:17; Luke 6:22). Admittedly, the Lukan reference may have a wider application.

One regular use of the word is in contrast to blessing. When the term is so employed, there are no sacred associations, and the word runs the gamut from divine to satanic. Before the people of Israel entered Canaan they were given the choice of obedience and God's blessing or disobedience and the curse. The curse was placed symbolically on Mount Ebal, while the blessings were attached to Mount Gerizim

(Deut. 27:13-26). The rarity of the curse in the NT is in keeping with the spirit of the new age (Matt. 21:19 ff.; Mark 11:12 ff.).

The curse has a definite christological reference. Paul states that Christ became a curse for us (Gal. 3:13) by bearing the penalty of the law (Deut. 21:23). The curse of the law (Deut. 27:26) fell upon him by the manner of his death as well as the fact of it. It was a criminal's death and so under the curse.

BIBLIOGRAPHY

EB, I, p. 591; HDB, I, p. 534 f.; HDCG, I, p. 404; ISBE, II, p. 767; LSJ; SBD, p. 162.

CHARLES L. FEINBERG

CUSTOM, CUSTOMS. The word custom(s) reflects the meaning of the Greek *ethos* or the Latin *mores*. A custom is any norm of voluntary action that has been developed in a national or tribal community. It has a place in the growing awareness of the moral ideal. With primitive man, custom is the great guide of life.

Custom is allied to both habit and law. Habit is more individualistic, while custom is more social. Law is more universal in its scope than custom.

As man emerges from savagery he tends to regulate his conduct in society by the generally accepted standards of the tribe. His attitude is not due to deep reflection; it is mere conformity to what is usually practiced. The integration of morality and religion with tribal customs is for primitive man the attempt to preserve the identity and the unity of his clan in the struggle for survival.

As moral ideas develop, customs are seen to be inadequate or even harmful as standards. The abominable customs of the heathen were forbidden to Israel (Lev. 18:30). Even Israel's traditions are seen to be harmful in the light of growing ethical awareness. The word of God was being rendered of none effect by clinging to outmoded traditions. The customs of Moses tended to stifle the universality and freedom of the gospel. Paul was arraigned on charges of changing the customs which Moses commanded (Acts 6:14; 16:21). The law needed to be fulfilled.

BIBLIOGRAPHY

W. Wundt, Ethics, VI. chap. 3; J. S. Mackenzie, Manual of Ethics, pp. 97 ff; L. H. Gray in HERE.

ALBERT VICTOR M'CALLIN

D

DARKNESS. Beyond the literal meaning of the Hebrew *ḥōšek*, *'ōpel*, and the Greek, *skotia, skotos, zophos,* there is a wealth of metaphor. Concerning man, darkness means ignorance (Job 37:19), calamity (Ps. 107:10), death (Ps. 88:12), wickedness (Prov. 2:13; John 3:19), damnation (Matt. 22:13). These metaphors are grounded in the truth that God is light (I John 1:5) and in creation and redemption (II Cor. 4:6) he has conquered darkness, the forces which oppose his rule (Luke 22:53; Eph. 6:12). Darkness is associated with divine interventions, firstly, as in Deut. 4:11, because God is hidden except he reveal himself; secondly, because the light of revelation (Isa. 60:2) becomes darkness and condemnation to those who refuse it (Amos 5:18; Zeph. 1:15).

JOHN ALEXANDER MOTYER

DAVID. The son of Jesse, musician, warrior, poet, prophet, king, is one of the most prominent figures in OT history. Some sixty chapters in the historical books deal with his many-sided career. In them we are given the *biography* of David. We read of the shepherd lad, secretly anointed by Samuel; of the harp player whose music soothed the troubled spirit of Saul; of the youthful warrior who slew Goliath, became the friend of Jonathan, and the hero of the people; of the fugitive from the murderous hate of Saul, resorting to lying, treachery and cruelty to save his life; of the king who reigned first at Hebron and then at Jerusalem over all Israel; of his successful wars which delivered Israel from her enemies; of the bringing up of the ark, of the ungranted desire to build the temple, and of the messianic promise of II Sam. 7; of the great sin and its terrible consequences: the murder of Amnon, the rebellion of Absalom, the slaying of Amasa, fulfilling the word of the prophet, "The sword shall not depart from thine house forever"; of the preparation in material things for the building of the temple and in spiritual ways by the ordering of the worship, especially the service of song; of the crowning of Solomon to succeed him and of the death of David. This, in brief, is the history. It reveals David as the men of his own day knew him, a great man, capable of the noblest acts, but alas also of very ignoble deeds.

The autobiography of David is given largely in the Book of Psalms. Seventy-three are assigned to him by the headings; and it is in these Psalms that the heart of David is revealed to us. In Ps. 23 we meet the youth who fought with Goliath, in Ps. 18 the warrior king who triumphed over all his enemies, in Ps. 51 the penitent sinner seeking and rejoicing in the forgiveness of God, in Pss. 8, 19, 103 and 139 the man after God's own heart, the man of profound piety and love. The greatest thing in David's life was the messianic promise made through Nathan (II Sam. 7), which has its echo in Pss. 2, 89, and 110 (cf. Ps. 72); and these promises regarding David's house, which are so gloriously fulfilled in Christ, are the "sure mercies of David" of which Isaiah spoke (55:3) and which Paul proclaimed in his first sermon addressed to gentile ears (Acts 13). In Ps. 22 the afflicted David prefigures the Sufferer of Calvary; and in Ps. 16 we read one of the clearest predictions of the resurrection. In Ps. 32 the forgiveness of David's sin reveals the absolute character of justification.

The Psalter, of which so much was written by David, has been called "the song book of the second temple." Much of it was undoubtedly intended to be the song book of the first temple. In it we learn what was the true faith and life of the Israel of old under the covenant of Sinai. For David is a true representative of that Israel which, as the people of God, learned, often by bitter experience, to worship the God of Abraham and of Moses in spirit and in truth.

The truly amazing thing is that the psalms of David are not only the songs of the first and of the second temple, they are the songs of the Christian church. The sweet singer of Israel has struck the chords to which the hearts of men of every age have responded and will respond until the end of time.

OSWALD T. ALLIS

DAY. I. NATURAL MEANINGS. The greatest number of uses of day (*yōm; hēmera*) refers to natural time units; but in the progress of revelation its theological use increases to such an extent that in the Synoptic Gospels almost one-third of all uses of *hēmera* is eschatological.

A. *Hours of Daylight* on any given day between dawn and dusk (Gen. 1:5, 16, 18). The Lord Jesus spoke of a day of twelve hours, assuredly of light since man does not stumble (John 11:9). Day is used to indicate the dawn (Josh. 6:15; II Pet. 1:19), midday (I Sam. 11:11; Acts 26:13), late afternoon or evening hour (Judg. 19:9; Luke 9:12). A large number of references speak of day as opposed to night (Isa. 27:3; Mark 5:5; Luke 18:7; I Tim. 5:5).

B. *Legal or Civil Day*, a period of twenty-four hours' duration. The sabbath is from dusk to dusk (Lev. 23:32). There are six days and a sabbath in a week (Luke 13:14). The Lord's resurrection is after three days (Mark 8:31; Luke 24:46). The period between the resurrection and the ascension is forty legal days (Acts 1:3). The legal day is contrasted with the hour and month and year in Rev. 9:15.

C. *A Longer Period.* Although day is used in the singular to designate long periods of time, as the "day" of Christ (John 8:56), or the day of salvation (Isa. 49:8; II Cor. 6:2), yet it is more generally used in this respect in the plural in such expressions as "the days of Adam" (Gen. 5:4), "the days of Abraham" (Gen. 26:18), "the days of Noah" (Matt. 24:37), "the days of the Son of man" (Luke 17:26). Christ's presence is "always" (lit. "all the days") with those who go out to preach his word (Matt. 28:20).

II. THEOLOGICAL MEANINGS. A. *General.* The antithesis of day and night in the literal sphere is seen in the description of believers as children of the day and unbelievers as children of the night (I Thess. 5:5-8). The Lord Jesus indicates that the day is the time of opportunity for service which will end with the coming night (John 9:4). Paul, however, teaches that the period up to the time of eschatological salvation is the night and this will issue in the glorious day of Christ (Rom. 13:11-13).

B. *Eschatological.* In the records of man's earliest history the word day came to be associated with special days set aside as belonging to Jehovah (Gen. 2:3; Ex. 20:8-11; 12:14, 16; Lev. 16:29-31). In the total OT concept they were designed for judgment of sin in nations or individuals (Isa. 2:12; 13:9, 11; Ezek. 7:6-8; Zeph. 1:14-18; Obad. 15), but they also had the purpose of salvation, vindication, or restoration of God's chosen ones (Gen. 7:10-13, 23; Mic. 2:12; Isa. 4:3-6). The local days of Jehovah visited on Israel and Judah (Ezek. 7:4-8) or upon pagan nations (Isa. 13:9) were just a foretaste of one climactic *dies irae* to come upon the whole world (Joel 2:31; Mal. 4:5; Isa. 2:12; Jer. 25:15). Immediately following this supernatural intervention on the plane of history God would set up his eternal kingdom (Dan. 2:28, 44) in which he alone would be sovereign and exalted (Isa. 2:11).

In the NT the day of Jehovah, or final day of reckoning, is designated by various phrases (I Thess. 5:4; John 6:39; Matt. 10:15; I Pet. 2:12), principally in combinations with the name of Jesus Christ (Phil. 1:6, 10; I Cor. 1:8; 5:5; Acts 2:20; II Pet. 3:10), but they contain the same basic concepts as in the OT, i.e., God's judgment, salvation, sovereignty, and exaltation.

The phrase, "the last days" (Acts 2:17; Heb. 1:2; II Tim. 3:1; II Pet. 3:3, 4), seems to include, in its greatest extension, the whole period from the cross to the Second Advent. More specifically, day in its plural form is used to designate that final terrible period immediately before the *parousia*, including the Great Tribulation (Matt. 24:19-22; Luke 17:26-30; cf. Rev. 4-11). In the singular form it designates the *parousia itself* (Matt. 24:30, 31, 36; II Thess. 2:1, 2) and also the post-*parousia* period up to the creation of the new heavens and earth (II Pet. 3:8-13).

The theological connotations of day do not rob it of its literalness when referring to the *parousia*. Rather, God's choice of the term "day" only serves to emphasize its literal reality. When the Lord himself makes his second appearance on earth, then will begin what Peter in the last verse of his second epistle calls "the day of eternity" (II Pet. 3:18, Greek).

BIBLIOGRAPHY

Arndt; A-S; BDB; Thayer; articles "Day," "Eschatology," and "Day of the Lord" in *CE, HDB, HERE, ISBE, JewEnc, SHERK;* "Time" in *RTWB;* O. Cullmann, *Christ and Time;* W. G. Kuemmel, *Promise and Ful-*

filment; H. W. Robinson, *Inspiration and Revelation in the Old Testament;* H. H. Rowley, *The Faith of Israel.*

GEORGE A. GAY

DAY OF ATONEMENT. A full description of its ritual is given in Lev. 16 (cf. 23:27-32; 25:9; Num. 29:7-11). It was held on the tenth of Tishri (October-November) and underlined by its elaborate symbolism the *universal* need for atonement. The people, the high priest and his house and even the sanctuary shared in this need. Typically it points forward to Christ's atonement (Heb. 9).

Two main elements of the ritual are the sprinkling of blood at the mercy seat, not otherwise accessible, and the ceremony of the two male goats, one of which was sent into the wilderness for Azazel, probably a demon thought to be residing there, and the other to be slain. Together these two animals symbolized the expiation and removal of sin (cf. for a similar rite of removal Lev. 14:4-7, 49-51 and Zech. 5:5-10).

The prominent place given to sanctuary and mercy seat in this ritual ill suits an assumed exilic or post-exilic origin of the day.

BIBLIOGRAPHY

Th. C. Vriezen in *OTS* 7, pp. 201-35; G. B. Gray, *Sacrifice in the OT,* pp. 310-22; W. H. Gispen, *Leviticus,* pp. 238-54.

MARTEN H. WOUDSTRA

DAY OF THE LORD, GOD, CHRIST. See ESCHATOLOGY.

DAYSPRING. (Luke 1:78, *anatolē*) "the rising of the sun"; here "the dawn," elsewhere in NT "the east." *SBK* II, p. 113 points out it is the LXX rendering for *semah,* i.e., branch, in Jer. 23:5, Zech. 3:8, 6:12, and interprets it here in this sense as a messianic title; see also Arndt, p. 62a; Edersheim, *Life and Times,* p. 158.

H. L. ELLISON

DEACON. From Phil. 1:1, an official salutation, we gather that deacons (the word means "servant") were one of the two main orders of ministry in the apostolic church. Some hold that the institution of the diaconate is seen in Acts 6, though this is never said. More likely we have there a temporary measure to meet a particular situation. But the officers proved of value, and in due course settled into an established order. The qualifications of a deacon are given in I Tim. 3:8-13. Sound character and a good grasp of the faith are required, but there is no mention of teaching or the like. The functions of these officials may well have been administrative and financial.

LEON MORRIS

DEAD SEA SCROLLS. I. QUMRAN. The most important manuscripts among those discovered since 1947 on the NW shores of the Dead Sea are those found in eleven caves in the Wadi Qumran — apparently the remnants of the library of a community which had its headquarters at Khirbet Qumran between *ca.* 100 B.C. and A.D. 68 (with a thirty years' break *ca.* 34-4 B.C.). This community, founded by a leader called the Teacher of Righteousness, regarded itself as the righteous remnant of Israel, and withdrew to the wilderness of Judea to prepare for the cataclysmic events which would terminate the "epoch of wickedness" and introduce the kingdom of God. By diligent study and practice of the law they hoped to win acceptance for themselves and expiate the errors of their fellow-Israelites; they also expected to be the executors of divine judgment on the ungodly at the end-time. The end-time would coincide with the rise of three figures foretold in OT prophecy — a prophet like Moses, a warrior-prince of David's line and a great priest of Aaronic descent. This priest would be head of the state in the new commonwealth, taking precedence over the Davidic Messiah. They refused to recognize the priesthood of the "epoch of wickedness" partly because it did not belong to the family of Zadok and partly because of its moral unfitness for the sacred office. In their own ranks they preserved the framework of worthy priests and Levites, ready to resume a pure sacrificial worship in the temple of the new Jerusalem.

Their library, of which over 400 scrolls have been identified (most in very fragmentary state), included biblical and non-biblical writings. About 100 scrolls are biblical, all the OT books (except Esther) being represented, some of them several times over. These biblical scrolls date from the last few centuries B.C. and the first century A.D. and attest at least three distinct textual traditions of Hebrew Scripture — not only the text (of Babylonian provenience) underlying the later Massoretic recension, but the text underlying the Septuagint version (of Egyptian provenience) and a text akin to the Samaritan Pentateuch (of Palestinian provenience). The discovery of these manuscripts has reduced the gap separating the autographs from the oldest extant copies by 1000 years, and is immensely important for the textual history of the OT.

The non-biblical scrolls, along with the archaeological evidence furnished by the excavation of Khirbet Qumran, give us a picture of the beliefs and practices of this community, which almost certainly was an Essene group. They practiced ceremonial ablutions, they held fellowship meals, they followed the calendar of the Book of Jubilees, they cherished apocalyptic hopes, they interpreted prophetic Scripture in terms of persons and events of their own days and the days immediately to follow. Some of the most interesting of these documents are commentaries (*pesharim*) on biblical books, from which we may learn their ideas of biblical interpretation. The prophets, they believed, knew by revelation what God was going to do at the end-time, but they were not told when the end-time would come; this revelation was reserved for the Teacher of Righteousness, who imparted it to his followers. They accordingly regarded themselves as men whom God had favored by initiating them into his wonderful mysteries. Their system of interpretation presents striking points of resemblance and contrast with the interpretation of the OT found in the NT.

The expectations of the Qumran sect were not realized; they were dispersed, and their headquarters destroyed, by Vespasian's forces in A.D. 68.

The Qumran sect has been compared to the early church in its eschatological outlook and its remnant mentality, as well as in its biblical exegesis. But the decisive difference between the two lies in the person and work of Jesus. The Teacher of Righteousness was exactly what his title suggests; he was no Messiah or Saviour. Jesus was to the early Christians all that the Teacher was to the men of Qumran, but he was more. As Messiah, he was prophet and priest and king in one; and he fulfilled his messianic mission in terms of the portrayal of the Suffering Servant which the Qumran community endeavored to fulfil corporately. If (as appears possible) refugees from Qumran after A.D. 68 made common cause with the refugee church of Jerusalem, they learned at last how Jesus fulfilled the hopes which had not been fulfilled in the way of their expectation.

II. MURABBA'AT. In caves in Wadi Murabba'at, about eleven miles south of Qumran, manuscripts were discovered around 1952, the most significant belonging to the period when Murabba'at was occupied by a garrison of Bar-kokhba, leader of the second Jewish revolt against Rome (A.D. 132-35). From some of the documents (including two letters from the leader himself) it appeared that his proper patronymic was Ben-Kosebah. Many fragments of biblical manuscripts of this period were found, all of them exhibiting a "proto-Massoretic" text. From neighboring caves further manuscripts of the same period came to light, including not only biblical manuscripts in Hebrew but an important Septuagint fragment of the Minor Prophets.

III. Khirbet Mird. Another collection of manuscripts was unearthed at Khirbet Mird, north of the Wadi en-Nar (Kidron valley), midway between Qumran and Murabba'at. This collection dates between the fifth and eighth centuries A.D., is of Christian provenience, and contains several biblical texts in Greek (including fragments of uncial codices of Wisdom, Mark, John' and Acts) and in Palestinian Syriac (including fragments of Joshua, Luke, John, Acts and Colossians).

BIBLIOGRAPHY

Millar Burrows, ed., *The Dead Sea Scrolls of St. Mark's Monastery*; Elazar Lipa Sukenik, ed., *The Dead Sea Scrolls of the Hebrew University*; D. Barthélemy and Jozef T. Milik, edd., *Discoveries in the Judaean Desert*, I; Nahman Avigad and Yigael Yadin, edd., *A Genesis Apocryphon*; Krister Stendahl, ed., *The Scrolls and the New Testament*; Frank Moore Cross, Jr., *The Ancient Library of Qumran and Modern Biblical Studies*; Charles F. Pfeiffer, *The Dead Sea Scrolls*; F. F. Bruce, *Second Thoughts on the Dead Sea Scrolls*.

FREDERICK FYVIE BRUCE

DEAN. See Offices, Ecclesiastical.

DEATH. Under normal conditions, death is a universally lamented event in human experience. It is a phenomenon which cannot be regarded as wholly natural, but as a mystery which calls for explanation. If man is truly the crown of the divine handiwork, why should he have a shorter existence than some forms of plant and animal life? One may go further and ask why, if man is made in the image of the eternal God, he should perish at all. The answer which Scripture provides is that man's involvement in transgression of God's will and law has brought death as a penalty (Gen. 2:17). This does not mean that death, whether as to its timing or its manner, is directly related in each case to some personal sin (Luke 13:1-4). It does mean that by reason of the very universality of sin, death is present as a necessary consequence (Rom. 5:12-14).

In the OT, death is set forth in various ways. It was sometimes described as a gathering to one's fathers (II Kings 22:20). More often it was stated as a going down into Sheol, a cheerless abode where no work could be continued and where no communion was possible (Eccl. 9:10; Ps. 6:5). But brighter expressions appear here and there, breathing an expectation of continued fellowship with God (Ps. 73:24). An influence in this direction may well have been the inequalities in earthly existence — the suffering of the righteous and the prosperity of the wicked. Justice would be meted out in the life after death.

Because of the connection between sin and death, Christ's redemptive mission entailed his own death (I Cor. 15:3; Rom. 4:25; I Pet. 3:18). By submitting to death he triumphed over it, abolishing it and bringing life and immortality to light (II Tim. 1:10). The believer in Christ, despite the impartation to him of spiritual life, is subject to physical death, for this is the last enemy to be overcome (I Cor. 15:26). It will be banished at the return of Christ, when the Christian dead shall be raised incorruptible (I Cor. 15:52; Phil. 3:20-21). In view of the future bodily resurrection of the saints, death can be described as a sleep. (I Thess. 4:15). The animation of the body in its perfected state following upon its motionless condition in death finds its analogue in the stirring of the inactive frame after a night of slumber. The fear of death is overcome for the Christian because he no longer has to cope with sin when he stands in the presence of God — sin which is the sting of death (I Cor. 15:56). Christ has removed the sting by his atoning death. To depart this life is positive gain (Phil. 1:21). It brings a betterment of the condition of the believer, even a sharing of the glorified presence of the Son of God (Phil. 1:23; II Cor. 5:8). Death has no power to effect separation from Christ (Rom. 8:38).

In the teaching of Paul, so intimate and effective is the union between Christ and his own that the believer is regarded as having died to sin together with Christ. For this reason he is under no obligation to serve sin any longer (Rom. 6:1-4; Col. 3:1-3). Death may also denote the moral inability of human nature (Rom. 7:24).

The unbeliever is dead because of his sins, unresponsive to God (Eph. 2:1; Col. 2:13). This strain of teaching is found in John also

(5:24). Jude describes apostates as twice dead (Jude 12). The deadness of their natural state is matched by the deadness of their professedly Christian experience. When the wicked are finally punished, their doom of separation from God is called the second death (Rev. 21:8).

See also IMMORTALITY, RESURRECTION.

BIBLIOGRAPHY
H. Bavinck in *ISBE*; J. C. Lambert, *"Life and Death"* in *HDAC*; Leon Morris, *The Wages of Sin*; L. Muirhead, *The Terms Life and Death in the Old and New Testaments*, pp. 3-30; A. Richardson in *RTWB*; J. J. Von Allmen in *CB*.

EVERETT F. HARRISON

DEATH OF CHRIST. See ATONEMENT.

DEBTOR. References are few in the OT because of the spirit of brotherhood and mutual helpfulness fostered by the Mosiac law. No provision was made for the recovery of debt, but non-payment was severely condemned (cf. Ps. 37:21; Deut. 15:1; I Sam. 22:2; II Kings 4:1; Neh. 5:5). Occasionally poverty led to slavery, but the creditor's power was limited (cf. Lev. 25:39; Deut. 24:6). In Roman law imprisonment was inflicted on the debtor (Matt. 5:25).

In NT times, due to Roman commercial practice, the moneylender was a familiar figure. Two striking parables were used by Jesus Christ to express the indebtedness of all men to God. This vital relationship cannot be placed on a business footing, since man is spiritually bankrupt (Matt. 18:27).

The word debtor is a favorite description of Paul for his position as an apostle. The divine impulse in his evangelistic work was kindled by his sense of debt to Christ, and to mankind (Rom. 1:1, 14).

All kinds of obligations, moral as well as financial, are covered by it. Taxes are to be paid in full as a duty owing to the State (Rom. 13:6). Domestic harmony is fostered by the rendering of what is due from husband to wife, and vice versa (I Cor. 7:3). Law keeping is futile as a means of salvation (Rom. 4:14; Gal. 5:3). Christians owe more than they can ever repay even to their brethren (Rom. 13:8). Gentile Christians were deeply indebted to their Jewish brethren for the gospel (Acts 11:29; II Cor. 9:1; Rom. 15:26). The same idea is found in "bondservant." The Christian is purchased by Christ, is his property and is delivered from bondage to all else.

RICHARD E. HIGGINSON

DECALOGUE. This word does not occur in the Bible. But the "ten words" from which this Greek word is derived appear in Ex. 34:28 and Deut. 10:4. The usual biblical name is "testimony." The testimony was placed in the ark (Ex. 25:16, 21) which is consequently often called "the ark of the testimony" (25:22), and so also the tabernacle where the ark dwelt is called "the tabernacle of testimony" (Num. 1:50). It is God's testimony to Israel because it represents his will for Israel; and above the ark is the mercy seat where once a year the high priest makes atonement for the children of Israel for all their sins against his holy law (Lev. 16:33 f.).

That there are ten commandments is clearly stated. But they are not numbered; and this has led to difference of opinion regarding them. The grouping adopted by the Reformed churches regards vss. 4-6 as the second commandment and vs. 17 as the tenth. The Jews treat vs. 2 as the first commandment and unite vs. 3 with vss. 4-6 as the second. The Lutherans treat vss. 3-6 as the first and divide vs. 17 into two, the ninth and tenth.

The ten commandments are on two tables (Ex. 31:18). It is natural to assume that the first states man's duty toward God. It is the first and great commandment, summarized in Deut. 6:4-5. Cf. Matt. 22:36 f. The second table defines man's duty to his fellow men and is summed up in Lev. 19:18.

That the Decalogue is a declaration of ethical monotheism can hardly be denied. For while the first command, "Thou shalt have no other gods before [or beside] me" might seem to recognize the existence of other gods, and therefore to require only monolatry and not monotheism, the emphatic prohibition of idolatry in the second and the declaration in the fourth that "Jehovah made heaven and earth, the sea and all that in them is" excludes such an inference. Idolatry was practiced by all the nations with which the Israelites came in contact. The importance of the Decalogue and its permanent authority is indicated by Jesus' words: "On these two commandments hang all the law and the prophets" (Matt. 22:40). That the Decalogue is binding upon the Christian is generally recognized. It is for this reason that an exposition of the Ten Commandments and their meaning for the Christian (Matt. 5:17) has been made an integral part of such well-known catechisms as Luther's, the Heidelberg, and the Westminster. For the freedom of the Christian from the law (Rom. 6:14) is not lawlessness. The Christian keeps the moral law as a son obeys his father, not out of constraint but of love. In this sense love is the fulfilling of the law (Rom. 13:10; Gal. 5:16-26).

For many years it has been maintained in "critical" circles that the Decalogue of Ex. 20 is not Mosaic, that the ethical monotheism (*q.v.*) of which it is the expression was not attained until about the eighth century B.C. Insofar as this is argued from Scripture and not from a theory of naturalistic development imposed upon Scripture it is based on the fact that the OT so often represents the people of Israel as living on a far lower plane than that required by the Decalogue. It is claimed that such a code of laws could not have existed in the days of the Judges or even much later. This claim ignores or rejects the fact that the Bible declares the Decalogue to have been given at Sinai and represents idolatry and similar sins as apostasy. Hence the date of the Decalogue is important to the vital question whether the religion of Israel is a divine revelation or a natural evolution.

See also COMMAND.

OSWALD T. ALLIS

DECEIT. A deliberate concealing or perverting of the truth, especially in moral and spiritual matters, with the intention of misleading another. One of several words for it in the OT, *mirmâ*, appears twenty times. In the NT deceit, *dolos*, is a specific kind of act, since it is differentiated from several others in Mark 7:22 and Rom. 1:29. Its being mentioned alongside of murder, etc., suggests its seriousness. To guile, or to use a bait, is suggested by *dolioō* in Rom. 3:13. Paul's exhortation was "not of deceit" (I Thess. 2:3), meaning that he did not lead the people astray. It is a broader term than fraud, the latter referring particularly to financial contracts.

J. KENNETH GRIDER

DECREES, ETERNAL. The Reformed confessions are at one in teaching that all that happens is by the eternal decree of God. The Arminians, indeed, have modified the Reformed view in the respect that where they do recognize the existence of the divine decree they base it upon God's foreknowledge of events. The Reformed view goes further. It regards God's decrees as in no wise based upon his foreknowledge of events, and teaches that

events happen because God has decreed them. This doctrine is taken as rooted in the very nature of God. As sovereign, nothing is outside his dominion; chance is eliminated. Eternal and immutable himself, his purposes are likewise timeless and changeless. When men change their plans, they do so either because they have lost the ability to fulfil them, or because greater wisdom has led them to plan differently. But because of God's perfections, his plans never require revision; his decrees shall never be revoked. Evil actions as well as good are covered by his decrees, but never in such a way as to involve him in the evil. When evil things happen they do so by what the Reformers call his *permissive* decree, as distinct from his express enactment. But the evil event is so overruled as to fall in with the great purpose of his eternal decree, namely, his own glory. In this connection, Acts 2:23 is often cited. The "determinate counsel of God" operated even in the crucifixion of his Son by "wicked hands." And yet, in executing his purpose God did not violate the moral freedom of the agents through whom his permissive decree took effect in the death of his Son.

The doctrine of God's eternal decrees inevitably raises the question, Why does God permit sin? The above-mentioned Arminian modification of the doctrine does not remove the difficulty. The problem is to us insoluble because, as A. A. Hodge puts it, "it is grounded in the inscrutable relations of the eternal to the temporal, of the infinite to the finite."

BIBLIOGRAPHY
W. G. T. Shedd, *Dogmatic Theology* i, pp. 391-462; L. Boettner, *The Reformed Doctrine of Predestination*, pp. 228-353.

GEORGE N. M. COLLINS

DECRETALS, FALSE. A collection of ecclesiastical laws supposedly authored by Isidor of Seville (d. A.D. 636). The book is properly divided into three sections. The first part contains sixty forged decretals of Ante-Nicene popes and fifty Apostolical Canons from the collection of Dionysius. The second part contains the forged Donation of Constantine and a collection of canons of councils. The latter are mainly genuine. The third part includes a large collection of letters of the popes from Sylvester (d. 335) to Gregory II (d. 731). Thirty-five of these decretals are forged.

The Isidorian Decretals were regarded as

genuine during the middle ages. However, the Italian humanist, Lorenzo Valla (*ca.* 1406-57) demonstrated the non-genuine character of the Donation of Constantine in *De Falso Credita et Ementita Constantini Donatione Declamatio* (1440). Now, both Protestant and Roman Catholic historians are all agreed that the Decretals are false. The true authorship is uncertain although they were of French origin. The date popularly assigned for their composition lies between A.D. 847 and 865.

BIBLIOGRAPHY
P. Hinschius, *Decretales Pseudo-Isidorianae et Capitula Angilramni*; Text in J. P. Migne, *Patrologia Latina*, cxxx; H. C. Lea, *Studies in Church History*, pp. 43-102. P. Schaff, *History of the Christian Church*, Vol. IV, pp. 266-73.

HAROLD LINDSELL

DEIFICATION. The biblical insistence on the separation of man as creature, and as fallen, from his Creator, and on the uniqueness of Christ the God-man leaves little place for the conferring of divinity upon a man.

Deification of the king held an acknowledged place in the cultus of the nations surrounding Israel; but the covenant between Jehovah and the head of the Davidic house was a standing protest against assimilation to the common pattern.

For Greeks, deification followed easily from both the anthropomorphism of the myths, which emptied the concept of godhead of much numinous content, and the philosophico-religious belief in immortality and the divine affinities of the soul. Heroes and benefactors received quasi-divine honors, and at least from the fifth century B.C. divine honors were paid to living men. Alexander received worship in the Oriental lands he conquered: with his successors and kings and kinglets thereafter it became a commonplace. This might be Oriental flattery, like that dearly bought by Herod Agrippa (Acts 12:20 ff.); but it might be intensely serious, as when Antiochus IV Epiphanes, opponent of devout Jews and their God, identified himself with Zeus and called himself "God" on coins; and it might have deep associations as in Egypt, where sacred kingship was traditional, and the Ptolemaic family, living and dead, were worshiped officially.

From Julius Caesar onward deification was a carefully regulated part of Roman policy. Traditional Roman sentiment was inimical and Caesar worship was always restrained in Rome: but in the empire local communities frequently outran official pronouncements. Julius received worship in his conquests. Augustus promoted the worship of "Divus Julius," but moderated the worship proffered to himself. He and most of his successors were *officially* deified at death (hence Vespasian's deathbed joke, "I think I'm becoming a god"). Unbalanced Emperors — Caligula, Nero, Domitian — insisted on divine honors during life. Relatives, even favorites, of Emperors received consecration. With Diocletian and the anti-Christian movement of the late third century the cult of the reigning Emperor reached its peak. The Christian empire ended it, but consecration and the title *Divus* remained in use for many years.

When the Emperors were still regularly consecrated only at death, an oath by the Emperor's "genius," perhaps conjoined with his consecrated predecessors, became a test of the loyalty of citizens. Christians regarded this oath as inconsistent with their exclusive allegiance to Christ: and suffered (cf. e.g., Pliny to Trajan, *Ep.* 96; *Mart. Polycarpi*).

Some Asian cities were noted for Caesar worship as "the seven churches," especially Pergamum, well knew (Rev. 2:10, 13).

There was no coherent theology of deification. Imperial cult was not exclusive, and local consecrations of celebrities continued.

Hellenistic mysticism, as expressed most fully in the mystery religions, but observably even in the Jewish Philo, tended to seek identification of the soul with the divinity to which it was kin. This passed into some forms of Christian mysticism; the Christian's adoptive status was neglected; "partakers of the divine nature" (II Pet. 1:4) came to express an essential, rather than a moral transformation.

BIBLIOGRAPHY
E. R. Bevan in *HERE*; *House of Seleucus*; J. Schaefer, "Consecratio II" in *Reallexikon fuer Antike und Christentum*; A. D. Nock, *Conversion*, pp. 103 ff; A. R. George, *Communion with God in the New Testament*.

ANDREW F. WALLS

DEISM. The term deism, as distinguished from theism, polytheism, pantheism, etc., designates no well defined doctrine or system of doctrine. Strictly, the term denotes a certain movement of rationalistic thought which was manifested chiefly in England from the mid-seventeenth to the mid-eighteenth century.

Affirmatively, the chief doctrines generally held by those who called themselves deists were (1) the existence of a personal God, Creator and Ruler of the universe; (2) the obligation of divine worship; (3) the obligation of ethical conduct; (4) the necessity of repentance from sins; and (5) divine rewards and punishments, here, and in the life of the soul after death. These five points were stated by Lord Herbert of Cherbury (1583-1648), called the father of deism.

Negatively, the deists generally denied any direct intervention in the natural order on the part of God. Though they professed faith in personal Providence, they denied the Trinity, the incarnation, the divine authority of the Bible, the atonement, miracles, any particular elect people such as Israel or the church, or any supernatural redemptive act in history.

The deists' attitude is anticipated in II Pet. 3:4. "Where is the promise of . . . (any supernatural intervention) . . . all things continue as they were from the beginning of the creation."

The rationalism of the deists was of the common sense variety, *quod semper quod ubique quod ab omnibus.* Their ethic was based upon the stoic notion of natural law. Denying revelation and affirming natural theology only, they yet generally claimed to be within the Christian tradition.

An unsigned article on deism in the eleventh edition of *Ency. Brit.* significantly points out that the most important ten of the deists, except Lord Herbert himself, were all born between 1654 and 1679, and that "by far the greater part of the literary activity of the deists, as well as of their voluminous opponents, falls within the same half century." The greatest contemporaneous writing against deism was Bishop Joseph Butler's *Analogy of Religion, Natural and Revealed, to the Course of Nature,* published in 1736 and used as a college textbook in courses in philosophy of religion for more than two hundred years.

BIBLIOGRAPHY (RECENT)

S. G. Hefelbower, *Relation of John Locke to English Deism,* 1918; N. L. Torrey, *Voltaire and the English Deists,* 1930; H. M. Morais, Edited by Faculty of Political Science, Columbia University, *Deism in Eighteenth Century America,* 1934; John Orr, *English Deism, Its Roots and its Fruits,* 1934; D. R. McKee, *Simon Tissot de Patot and the Seventeenth Century Background of Critical Deism,* 1941; A. O. Aldridge, *Shaftesbury and the Deist Manifesto,* 1951; Dorothy B. Schlegel, *Shaftesbury and the French Deists,* 1956.

J. OLIVER BUSWELL, JR.

DELIVER. This verb is used in two meanings: to deliver from, translating (mainly) the Hebrew *nāṣal, pālaṭ,* and Greek *exaireō,* *rhuomai;* and to deliver up, translating *nātan,* and *paradidōmi.*

I. THE OLD TESTAMENT. Both *nāṣal* and *pālaṭ* are used characteristically of acts of God. Out of a total of two hundred and eleven instances, *nāṣal* has God as its subject in one hundred and three; and nineteen out of twenty-two cases where *pālaṭ* means to make to escape likewise refer to acts of God. With the possible exceptions of Ps. 39:8; 51:14; and 79:9, both words refer to temporal deliverances granted by God to his people. The use of *nāṣal,* however, in connection with the Exodus (Ex. 6:6; 18:10) establishes its close relation with the redemption concept. Examination of the use of *nāṣal, pālaṭ* and *nātan* (to give, hence to give over to) shows that they reveal God as sovereign, redemptive, and righteous. As Lord of history, he is able to intervene to deliver (Ps. 106:23) his own; and his deliverances are his saving acts (Ps. 7:1), ultimately in a spiritual sense. Thus the OT safeguards the historical basis of salvation. However, God is not mocked, and when his people sin they experience the other side of his power, for he takes the initiative against them, and delivers them into the hand of their enemies (Jer. 29:18-21) that they may learn his righteousness.

II. Without forgetting God's temporal providences, THE NEW TESTAMENT is concerned with spiritual deliverance. *Exaireō* means to deliver from danger (Acts 12:11; 26:17), but also to deliver from sin (Gal. 1:4); *rhuomai* (to rescue) has its temporal side (II Cor. 1:10), but also its eternal, which in fact preponderates (Col. 1:13; I Thess. 1:10); *paradidōmi* is much used of the delivering of Jesus to his enemies (Luke 24:7; Rom. 4:25) — thus God vindicates his righteousness upon the substitute of his apostate people.

JOHN ALEXANDER MOTYER

DEMIURGE. A Greek word for "craftsman." Plato uses it for the divine being whose inferior deities form the world (*Timaeus* 40:C; *Republic* 530:A). According to Irenaeus, a majority of Gnostic writers (e.g., Simon, Menander, Saturninus and Carpocrates) taught that angels made the world. Two systems suppose a single creator, those of Marcion and Valentinus. The latter alone names the Creator the Demiurge. He probably borrowed Plato's usage, which through him obtained wide currency. In Valentinian cosmology Demiurge is born of the mingling of Wisdom, herself a fallen spirit, and Matter. He creates the visible world, orders its course, and is identified with Jehovah, the author of Judaism and of false notions in Christianity. From Demiurge spring three classes corresponding to the Supreme God, Demiurge himself, and matter: namely, spiritual men, i.e., Gnostics; psychical, that is, orthodox Christians; and hylic (fleshly) men who are beyond redemption.

BIBLIOGRAPHY
DCA.

M. R. W. FARRER

DEMON. Among the Greeks a demon was originally, as in Homer, a god or deity, and the word is used once in this sense in the NT (Acts 17:18). However, from Homer down to NT times the term *daimōn*, which Plato derives from *daēmōn*, an adjective formed from *daō* and signifying "knowing" or "intelligent" (*Cratylus* I:398), the sense of this word and its derivative *daimonion* increased gradually in inferiority to *theion*, "divinity," "deity."

In post-Homeric usage the term demon came to denote an intermediary between the gods and men (Plato, *Symposium* 202, 3) and demons were viewed as morally imperfect beings, both good and bad. By NT times the expression had reached its precise meaning of an "evil spirit," a "messenger and minister of the devil." In the LXX the word demon was employed to translate Hebrew *šēdîm*, "lords," or *'ĕlîlîm*, "idols" since the Hebrews very early regarded idolatrous images as mere visible symbols of invisible demons (Deut. 32:17; Ps. 96:5; LXX 95:5; Bar. 4:7; Ps. 106:37, 38).

The LXX also rendered the *se'îrîm*, (AV "he goats," RSV "satyrs") as *daimonia* (Lev. 17:7). Isaiah portrays these "hairy creatures" (demon-satyrs) as dancing in the ruins of Babylon (Isa. 13:21; 34:14).

In the NT demons afflict men with mental, moral, and physical distempers (Mark 1:21, etc.). They enter into men and control them in demon-possession (Mark 5:1-21), instigate "doctrines of demons" (I Tim. 4:1), exercise power in the government of the satanic world system (Eph. 6:12; cf. Dan. 10:13), energize idolatry, immorality and human wickedness (I Cor. 10:20; Rev. 9:20, 21), inspire false teachers (I John 4:1, 2), and in general assist Satan (*q.v.*) in his program of opposition to the word and will of God.

BIBLIOGRAPHY
Edward Langton, *Essentials of Demonology*; S. Vernon McCasland, *By the Finger of God*; Merrill F. Unger, *Biblical Demonology*.

MERRILL F. UNGER

DENIAL. *Arnēsis* is rare (*Martyrdom of Polycarp* 2, 4) but derives from the biblical verbs *arneomai* and *aparneomai*. Both are used (1) to repudiate a person or belief. Joshua warns Israel of this danger (Josh. 24:27), but the ultimate denial is perpetrated before Pilate (Acts 3:13). Jesus warns his disciples as the new Israel not to repudiate him (Matt. 10:33) and incur divine repudiation. He probably equates himself here as Son of Man with his saints or church and deplores apostasy (Luke 9:26). Peter thrice denies "before them all" (Matt. 26:70, cf. 10:33) any acquaintance with the man Jesus, and calls down curses on himself if he is lying; but he scarcely repudiates the collective Son of Man or church, as Judas does; he remains in the group and on repentance is restored (John 21:15). The heretics in II Pet. 2:1 and Titus 1:16 may by word profess to know Christ, but repudiate God by antinomian conduct. Those in I John 2:22 (cf. 4:2) are docetic teachers who dissociate the man Jesus from the divine Christ. The repudiation of the faith or name in the Apocalypse (Rev. 2:13; 3:8) covers any apostasy in persecution; in I Tim. 5:8 it is uncharitable behavior, and evokes reciprocal denial in II Tim. 2:12 and Luke 12:9. Further meanings are (2) to deny a fact or refuse to admit one (Luke 8:45; Acts 4:16); (3) to deny oneself (a) by acting in wholly unselfish manner and renouncing worldly interests daily (Luke 9:23, and for an extreme statement cf. Luke 14:26) or (b) by being untrue to oneself, as God cannot (II Tim. 2:13); (4) to deny by formal orthodoxy the power of the Gospel (II Tim. 3:5); and (5) to refuse as a man of faith to associate with the heathen (Heb. 11:24).

Specific denials in the NT are made by the Sadducees, who say there is no resurrection and reject popular angelology (Acts 23:8), and by the false teachers in Jude 4 who deny the *Kyrios* title to Jesus.

BIBLIOGRAPHY
Arndt; M. Goguel, "Did Peter Deny his Lord?" HTR 25, 1932, pp. 1-27; H. Riesenfeld, CN, pp. 11, 47, 207-19; Vincent Taylor, St. Mark, pp. 572-77.

DENIS H. TONGUE

DENOMINATION. A class, kind, or sort designated by a specific name; ecclesiastically, a body or sect holding peculiar distinctives. From the sixteenth century to recent times a tendency toward the multiplication of denominations has been a characteristic of Protestantism. Values in danger of being obscured or lost were thus preserved through periods of transition. Without a central controlling human authority the distinctives thus conserved by religious bodies have not all been of equal value, and the current trend is in the direction of consolidating denominations holding basically the same doctrines and practices.

See also ECUMENICAL.

DONALD G. DAVIS

DEPRAVITY, TOTAL. Total depravity is a theological term used to denote the unmeritoriousness of man in the sight of God. Negatively, the concept does not mean (1) that every man has exhibited his depravity as thoroughly as he could; (2) that sinners do not have conscience or "naive induction" concerning God; (3) that sinners will indulge in every form of sin; or (4) that depraved man does not perform actions that are good in the sight of man. Positively, total depravity means (1) that corruption extends to every part of man's nature, including all the faculties of his being; and (2) that there is nothing in man that can commend him to a righteous God. Calvinists trace depravity to an inherent corruption of nature inherited from Adam. Until the time of Augustine this idea of original sin was relatively undeveloped by the Fathers, and the semi-Pelagian reaction to the teachings of Augustine finds its successor today in Arminianism which denies *total* depravity, the guilt of original sin, and the loss of free will, and which affirms involvement in the sin of Adam to the extent of giving mankind a tendency toward sin but not a sinful nature (cf. John Miley, *Systematic Theology*, I, pp. 441-533; L. Berkhof, *Systematic Theology*, pp. 244-50; L. S. Chafer, *Systematic Theology*, II, pp. 218-19).

See also SIN.

CHARLES C. RYRIE

DESCENT INTO HELL. The words, "He descended into hell," were not in the Old Roman form of the Apostles' Creed, but were included in the form given by Rufinus about A.D. 400. He derived them from the creed of the church at Aquileia in Italy. Occurring there as *descendit ad inferna*, they appear in the later so-called Athanasian Creed as *descendit ad inferos* — "he descended to the underworld." It is probable that this item was added in order to combat docetic views of the person of Christ.

Many Christian writers of the second century taught that Christ went to Hades after his death. Paul had affirmed Christ's descent into the lower parts of the earth as the counterpart of the ascension (Rom. 10:6-8; Eph. 4:8-10). Closely connected with this teaching is the OT prophetic announcement cited by Peter in Acts 2:31. The reality of Christ's humanity demanded that he share man's lot in death, as in life.

Varied views have been held as to the purpose of the *descensus*. The Roman Catholic position is that Christ descended to the *limbus patrum* to manifest his glorious power and deliver the souls of the righteous dead, bearing them to heaven. The Eastern Church limits the work to OT saints who believed in the Messiah. The Formula of Concord (Lutheran) states: "For it ought to be enough for us to know that Christ descended into hell, that he destroyed hell for all believers, and that we through him have been snatched from the power of death and Satan, from eternal damnation, and even from the jaws of hell." Calvin taught that in this experience Christ, for the benefit of believers, "suffered in his soul the dreadful torments of a person condemned and irretrievably lost." The modern period has witnessed the rise of the notion (based largely on I Pet. 3:19) that the preaching of Christ in Hades opens the possibility of salvation after death for those who lacked opportunity to hear the message in this life.

BIBLIOGRAPHY

J. N. D. Kelly, *Early Christian Creeds*, pp. 378-83; F. Loofs in HERE; H. B. Swete, *The Apostles' Creed*, pp. 56-63.

EVERETT F. HARRISON

DESIRE. The question of desire was much discussed in Greek ethics, but did not command a dominant interest in the NT. The noun *epithumia* is occasionally translated by "desire," but more often by "lust." In the RSV, "desire" replaces "lust" in eight passages. Numerous words are used to express the same general idea. They possess no necessary moral connotation (as e.g., in Luke 20:46; 15:16; 10:24), but because of the sinful nature of man they came generally to describe wrong desire. In Matt. 5:28 *epithumeō* is used specifically of sexual desire, understood as contravention of the law. In the NT Epistles the noun has become fixed as a description of lust.

DONALD GUTHRIE

DESTRUCTION. The idea of temporal calamity dominates the wide range of OT words on this topic, but of the twenty-two instances of *apōleia*, *olethros* and *kathairesis* in the NT only five concern temporal distress; the rest refer to eternal loss. Where the truth of eternal life shines fully, it illumines the truth of eternal destruction (see HADES).

The exceptions to the general OT notion are found in the word *'ăbaddôn*. This word occurs in parallelism with *š^eôl* (see HELL), *māwet* (death), *qeḇer* (grave) and *hošek* (darkness). The suggestion of reference here to the state after death is borne out by examination of instances (though, as with Sheol, the teaching is nebulous and scanty). Thus, while Job 26:6 refers to Sheol and Abaddon in proof of God's power, Prov. 15:11 does so in proof of his moral discernment. This notion that moral distinctions are made hereafter is enforced by Job 31:12 where Abaddon is the ultimate destiny of the adulterer. Finally, in Ps. 88, the Psalmist, in temporal distress, depicts himself as one who, already in Sheol (identified in vs. 11 with Abaddon), is under pressure of God's wrath (v. 7) and cut off from God's fellowship (vss. 10-12).

The bridge between this unformulated OT doctrine and the full NT teaching is Rev. 9:11 where Abaddon (*q.v.*) is the name of the "angel of the abyss" also called Apollyon (cf. "son of *apōleia*," John 17:12; II Thess. 2:3). Destruction meets those who have chosen the broad road (Matt. 7:13), oppose the cross (Phil. 3:19; II Pet. 2:1), are ungodly (II Pet. 3:7), pervert Scripture (II Pet. 3:16) and are unready for Christ's return (I Thess. 5:3). Destruction is the opposite of life (Matt. 7:13), and salvation (Phil. 1:28; Heb. 10:39); is swift, personally merited (II Pet. 2:13), inescapable (I Thess. 5:3) and by fire (II Thess. 1:8, 9; II Pet. 3:7); and results in eternal separation from God (II Thess. 1:9). The justice of this condemnation is guaranteed by the unimpeachable will of God (Rom. 9:22).

JOHN ALEXANDER MOTYER

DETERMINE, DETERMINATE. As a biblical and theological term the verb *horizein* is associated particularly with the sovereign de-

crees of God whereby he determines or ordains circumstances and events in accordance with his will and purpose. It occurs eight times in the NT. The periods of human history and the bounds of human habitation are determined by God (Acts 17:26); so also God is spoken of as determining a certain day (Heb. 4:7); the way of the cross was determined for Christ by God (Luke 22:22); he was delivered up by the determinate (*hōrismenē*) counsel and foreknowledge of God (Acts 2:23; cf. Acts 4:28, where the use of the verb *proorizein*, "to foreordain," in a similar context confirms the close connection of our verb with the doctrine of foreordination); by his resurrection from the dead Jesus has been marked off by God as the Son of God (Rom. 1:4); and it is he whom God has ordained to be the Judge of both living and dead (Acts 10:42; 17:31).

The doctrine implied by these terms is characteristic of the OT as well as the NT; see, for example, Deut. 32:8; Job 14:5; Isa. 19:17; Dan. 9:24; 11:36; Zeph. 3:8.

PHILIP EDGCUMBE HUGHES

DEVIL. See SATAN.

DEVOTE. See CURSE.

DIALECTIC. This term has a long history stretching from the pre-Socratics to neo-orthodoxy, and its meaning has changed from century to century. In medieval theology it was a tool of the theologians which reached its acme in the *Summa Theologica* of Thomas in which he stated an opinion of a Father, then gave a counter opinion, and then gave a reconciling exposition of the problem. Use of the term in recent theology stems from Kant. He used the term to denote pseudo-philosophizing, i.e., the postulation of metaphysical systems beyond the limits of experience. Hegel, taking a cue from Fichte, reversed Kant and used the term to describe the true process of philosophical thought. Kant stated that certain contrarieties in human thought (antinomies and paralogisms) were symptomatic of the limitations of the human reason. Hegel felt that these contrarieties were the stuff of philosophical thought. Following Fichte he stated that a thesis (being) gave rise to its anti-thesis (nothing), and the two were "reconciled" in a synthesis (becoming). This triadic dialectic was (according to Hegel) the structure of the progress of all branches of human culture which in turn were the divers manifestations of the Absolute Spirit.

Soeren Kierkegaard, who was familiar with the Hegelian dialectic, recast it for his own purposes. He affirmed that theological assertions were paradoxical in character, and denied a synthesis of the two contrarieties. The mind was to hold the members of the paradox in opposition, and their reconciliation was accomplished in faith (defined as man's highest emotion) or subjectivity. The acceptance of the paradox, while exciting man's subjectivity to its highest intensity, appears to the mind as a leap or a risk.

Neo-orthodoxy, (q.v.) deeply influenced by Kierkegaard, has made much of a two-term dialectic of paradox and so has been called dialectical theology. Revelation coming from above to man in the contradiction of sin and within the limitations of finitude can only appear to the human mind as a series of paradoxes. Barth's *Epistle to the Romans* (2nd edition, Munich. Chr. Kaiser, 1922) is the modern landmark of dialectical·theology. Although Barth has moved away from the strong dialecticism of his earlier years, paradoxical modes of thought reinforced by existentialism widely pervade much contemporary theology.

BIBLIOGRAPHY
"Dialektik," *Woerterbuch der philosophischen Begriffe* (edited by R. Eisler), I, pp. 268-72.

BERNARD RAMM

DICHOTOMY. This term, which signifies a division into two parts (Greek *dicha,* in two; *temnein,* cut), is applied in theology to that view of human nature which holds that man has two fundamental parts to his being: body and soul. Usually the two are sharply contrasted, considered to have different origins and independent existence. Thus, the actual relationship between body and soul becomes the crucial question.

Plato taught that the body was perishable matter, but the soul existed in the heavenly world of pure form or idea before its incarnation in the human body. The soul was therefore uncreated and immortal — a part of deity. The body is the prison house of the soul; the soul is locked in the body like an oyster in its shell. At death the soul leaves the body to return to the heavenly world or to be reincarnated in some other body.

Aristotle's adaptation of Plato by dividing the soul into its animal and rational aspects was further developed in Roman Catholic doctrine through Thomas Aquinas, who taught that the soul was created in heaven and placed in the forming body, probably at the time of "quickening" in the mother's womb. The new philosophy after Descartes affirmed the independent origin of body and soul, supposing that the apparent unity of them in the human personality is due to the coincidental correlation which occurs momentarily, as when the penduli of separate clocks happen to swing together. Contemporary theology usually rejects this view, holding to the body-soul unity of man as set forth in Hebrew thought: ". . . and man became a living soul" (Gen. 2:7).

BIBLIOGRAPHY
R. Bultmann, *New Testament Theology,* Vol. I; G. P. Klubertanz, *The Philosophy of Human Nature;* R. Niebuhr, *The Nature and Destiny of Man;* H. W. Robinson, *The Christian Doctrine of Man;* E. C. Rust, *Nature and Man in Biblical Thought.*

WAYNE E. WARD

DISCIPLE. The English term is derived from the Latin *discipulus,* meaning pupil or learner, an exact equivalent of the Greek word *mathētēs.* Curiously, LXX has no certain examples of the use of *mathētēs,* though the root is found in Isaiah 8:16 and I Chronicles 25:8. In Greek literature the word is common as a designation for a philosopher's understudy. Occasionally it is found in the sense of apprentice.

Chief interest centers upon its use in the Gospels. We read of Moses' disciples (John 9:28) and of John the Baptist's (Mark 2:18). The Pharisees had them also (Matt. 22:16). Because of Jesus' inspiring teaching and beneficent works, many flocked to him and attached themselves in varying degrees of conviction and loyalty. A broad and a narrow use of the term is discernible in the Gospels and is seen to best advantage in connection with the choice of the Twelve. This latter group was chosen from a larger company of disciples and by virtue of this selection became the disciples *par excellence* (Luke 6:12-18).

For the most part Jesus' followers are designated as "his disciples" in the Gospels, thus preserving the genuine flavor of contemporaneous description. They had not been with him a sufficiently long time to make "the disciples" a self-explanatory term. By contrast, in Acts the word is practically always used absolutely, no further description being needed. It was an accepted description of adherents to the Christian movement. That a disciple might be exceedingly limited in understanding and achievement is obvious from Acts 19:1 ff. No example of the word is to be found in the Epistles.

Early in the second century Ignatius used it of himself as the equivalent of martyr. Death would prove his true discipleship. See Lightfoot's note on Ignatius' Ephesian Epistle 1:2.

In summary, disciple may mean: (1) a believer, as in Acts 11:26, (2) a learner in the school of Christ, (3) one who is committed to a sacrificial life for his sake, as in Luke 14:26, 27, 33, (4) one who acts to fulfil the climactic obligation of discipleship, namely, to make disciples of others (Matt. 28:19).

BIBLIOGRAPHY
Arndt; K. H. Rengstorf in *TWNT*; J. Y. Campbell in *RTWB*.

EVERETT F. HARRISON

DISCIPLINE. Discipline implies instruction and correction, the training which improves, molds, strengthens, and perfects character. It is the moral education obtained by the enforcement of obedience through supervision and control. Usually the concept is translated chastening, chastisement, and instruction (Heb. *yāsar, mûsar;* Gr. *paideuō, paideia*). The discipline of the believer on the part of the heavenly Father is frequently illustrated by the correction made by the human father. "As a man chasteneth (*yāsar*) his son, so the Lord thy God chasteneth thee" (Deut. 8:5; Ps. 6:1; 38:1). He is taught not to despise the chastening, *mûsar,* of the Almighty (Job 5:17; Prov. 3:11). The value of discipline by a human father is stressed in Prov. 19:18.

The OT teaching is amplified in the New, especially in Heb. 12:3-12, by considering carefully the suffering endured by the Saviour (vs. 3). The Christian is reminded to value the discipline of the Almighty (*paideia*), vss. 5, 7, 11. The discipline is a sure evidence of sonship (vss. 7, 8); and of God's love (vs. 6). Lack of chastening is an evidence of hatred rather than of love (Prov. 13:24). Furthermore, the end result of discipline which for the moment is grievous is the ultimate good of that one who is thereby instructed (Heb. 12:10, 11).

Discipline may be severe but not disastrous "as chastened, and not killed" (II Cor. 6:9; Ps. 118:18); and such chastening delivers from condemnation with the world (I Cor. 11:33). Discipline is often by pain, sorrow, and loss (Job 33:19, *yākah*) whereby the Christian shares Paul's assurance of God's comfort (II

Cor. 1:3-11; 12:7-10). There is self-chastening (Dan. 10:10, *hithpael* of *'ānâ*). The consequent fumbling and suffering are designed to deliver from temporal consideration (I Pet. 4:1, 2; II Cor. 5:15; I John 2:15-17).

The purpose of discipline is the correction, the improvement, the obedience, the faith, and the faithfulness of God's child. The outcome is a happiness, a blessedness (Job 5:17; Ps. 94:12; and assurance of Rev. 3:19: "as many as I love, I rebuke and chasten. . . .").

While there is no special term for discipline by the church upon erring believers, there is clear teaching of the subject (cf. I Cor. 5:1-13; II Cor. 2:4-11). It appears that only public sins are subject to ecclesiastical censure; while other wrongs are to be confessed, first to God (I John 1:9) and then to one's fellow Christian (James 5:16). If private conference, confession, and attempted corrections fail, then the matter should be taken to the church (Matt. 18:15; I Thess. 5:14).

The lazy, irresponsible busybodies in the affairs of others were to be rebuked; and if necessary, separated from the assembly of believers (II Thess. 3:6-15).

Discipline upon the flagrant offender was to be inflicted in open assembly of the church membership (I Cor. 5:4). Censure suitable to the offense was to be placed upon the sinning Christian; even to the extent that he be delivered unto Satan (vs. 5). Such open rebuke and condemnation will bring fear and reverence on the part of others (I Tim. 5:20; Acts 5:11). All fellowship with the "wicked" person was to be cut off (vs. 13; Rom. 16:17; II John 10). Upon true repentance the erring brother was to be restored, forgiven, and comforted lest he be "swallowed up with his overmuch sorrow. . . ." (II Cor. 2:7-10). The result of church discipline properly administered in the light of the Scriptures (II Tim. 3:16), in the love of Christ, and under the guidance of the Holy Spirit was a clean church, wholesome, wholehearted (I Cor. 5:7, 8).

BIBLIOGRAPHY
HDAC, I, pp. 303-4; *ISBE,* II, p. 852; *CE,* V, pp. 30-32.

V. R. EDMAN

DISPENSATION. The English word dispensation translates the Greek *oikonomia* and occurs in I Cor. 9:17; Eph. 1:10; 3:2, 9 (corrected Greek text) and Col. 1:25. *Oikonomia* also occurs in Luke 16:2, 3, 4, where it is rendered "stewardship," and in the best Greek texts of I Tim. 1:4, where in the AV the translators have followed the text with *oikodomēn* and so rendered it by the word "edifying." Charles Hodge points out the double use of the word: (1) with respect to one in authority, it means a plan or scheme; (2) with respect to one under authority, it means a stewardship or administration. The theological interest of the term belongs to the former of these uses. When God is the Dispenser the term dispensation refers to the purpose he has in view and the way he intends to execute it. God's covenanted purpose with sinful man has ever been one of grace; but the covenant of grace was based on a double plan, or, to use scriptural terminology, was revealed in two dispensations. The first of these was the Mosaic dispensation sometimes called the "Old Covenant," and the second is the Christian dispensation, usually called the "New Covenant." Strictly, the covenant (*q.v.*) is one and the same covenant of grace all through (see Paul's discussion of the relation of law to grace in Gal. 3), and it would be more proper to speak of the old dispensation and the new. What has become known in recent days as "dispensationalism" finds many more "dispensations" in the Bible. Scofield, for example, discovers no less than seven, namely, the dispensation of innocence, of conscience, of civil government, of promise, of law, of grace, of the kingdom. Dispensationalism claims to be a method of "rightly dividing the word of truth" in relation to dispensations. According to this view a dispensation is "a period of time during which man is tested in respect of obedience to some *specific* revelation of the will of God" (Scofield Reference Bible, p. 5). If the use of the word is to be kept strictly biblical, however, it will be found that it is used in the Scriptures to make only one distinction, that is, the distinction between the way the grace of God was made known before the coming of Christ and the way it was manifested after his redeeming work had been accomplished. This is the Pauline sense of the word when he speaks of God's "dispensation" in Eph. 1:10; 3:2, 9; Col. 1:25. It is the plan that belongs to "the fulness of times." That is to say, it is God's manner of presenting his grace which belongs to his revelation in the Lord Jesus Christ. The "mystery" to which Paul refers in this connection is not the calling of the Gentiles, as some infer, but the redemption which is effected by Christ. The sugges-

tion that a dispensation is "a period of time" is quite outside the scope of the meaning of the word and is but incidental to the fact that the two plans of God — the Mosaic and the Christian — were consecutive in their administration.

Under the Mosaic or "old" dispensation the gospel was presented in types and shadows, and the Epistle to the Hebrews shows the relation between this former dispensation and that of the gospel. In the form of priest, altar, sacrifice, tabernacle and mercy seat were exhibited the way in which God was purposing man's salvation. Faith in these provisions of God's grace, which in turn expressed itself in conformity to the demands of his holy law, was the plan by which God not only prefigured the saving work of Christ but by which also he truly accepted and justified the penitent saints of OT times. But "he taketh away the first, that he may establish the second" (Heb. 10:9), and in the new or "second" dispensation the "figures of the true" (Heb. 9:24) are removed, and Christ, not by the blood of goats and calves, "but by his own blood he entered in once into the holy place, having obtained eternal redemption for us" (Heb. 9:12).

ERNEST FREDERICK KEVAN

DISPERSION. This is a technical term to denote Jews who were scattered abroad throughout the world beyond the borders of Palestine. Originally the dispersal was the penalty for disobedience to the law (cf. Deut. 4:27, etc.) . This prediction was largely fulfilled in the captivity of the ten tribes in 721 B.C., and later of the two in 586 B.C. (Jer. 25:34). Under Alexander the Great emigrations took place to Syria and Egypt (cf. Ps. 146:2 [LXX]; II Macc. 1:27). In the Roman empire there were numerous settlements, so that Agrippa in a letter to Caligula, preserved by Philo, says that "Jerusalem is the capital, not alone of Judaea but, by means of colonies, of most other lands also" (cf. Acts 15:21). Three chief centers existed in Babylonia, Syria, and Egypt, but Jerusalem was the common religious center, and liberal offerings were sent to the temple by them. Each colony had its representative synagogue also in Jerusalem (cf. Acts 2:5, 11; 6:9).

When we turn to the NT we find that the great highroads of the Dispersion were followed by the apostles, and well-nigh every apostolic church grew out of a Jewish synagogue (*q.v.*) of the Dispersion. The movement thus appears to be of the clearest providential order to act as a bridge between Israel and the Gentile world (cf. Acts 15:21).

In the NT period the word has gained a distinctive meaning, yet the apostles are not afraid to use it for their own purpose. In James 1:1 its use is figurative and prophetic. The letter is addressed to Jewish Christians in Palestine and Syria apart from the mother church at Jerusalem. In I Pet. 1:1 the sense appears to be that of gentile Christians, constituting the new Israel, who as pilgrims in this world (1:17; 2:11) are yet removed from their heavenly home.

BIBLIOGRAPHY

J. Juster, *Les juifs dans l'empire romain;* C. Guignebert, *The Jewish World in the Time of Jesus;* pp. 211-37; E. Schuerer, art. "Diaspora" in *HDB,* V.

RICHARD E. HIGGINSON

DIVINATION. Divination is a phenomenon of paganism and involves the art of obtaining clandestine knowledge, especially that of the future. Two main types of divination exist — artificial and inspirational. The artificial variety is augury, and consists in interpreting certain signs called omens, such as examination of the liver of animals, consulting the teraphim, or observing the way arrows fall (Ezek. 21:21). Inspirational divination involves the medium's coming under the immediate influence or control of evil spirits or demons, who enable him to utter oracles involving superhuman knowledge.

The early Church Fathers were correct in describing the divination of heathenism as demonically inspired and a satanic imitation of prophecy. As the Holy Spirit inspires the true prophets of God, demons inspire the false prophets of idolatrous religions. For this reason divination is denounced in the Bible as incompatible with the knowledge of the one true God (Deut. 18:10-14). Balaam (Num. 22-24) is a case of a diviner who reached the status of a true prophet of God, but lapsed back into corrupt paganism.

The demon-inspired girl at Philippi (Acts 16:16) had actual powers of oracular utterance, as did the ancient diviners at Delphi and other shrines of paganism. Ancient necromancy, essentially the same as modern spiritualism (spiritism) involves the medium's coming under demon influence and consulting not the spirits of the departed dead, but evil spirits, who have superphysical knowledge. Such traffic is once for all condemned in the Bible in the case of Saul and the spiritistic medium at Endor (I Sam. 28).

See also SPIRITISM.

BIBLIOGRAPHY

T. K. Oesterreich, *Possession, Demoniacal and Other Among Primitive Races in Antiquity, the Middle Ages, and Modern Times;* M. F. Unger, *Biblical Demonology,* pp. 119-64; E. Schneweiss, *Angels and Demons According to Lactantius.*

MERRILL F. UNGER

DIVINITY OF CHRIST. See CHRISTOLOGY.

DIVISION. See SCHISM.

DIVORCE. The OT provisions are given in Deut. 24:1-4. In this passage vss. 1-3 form the protasis and vs. 4 the apodosis. This construction shows that divorce was not mandatory in the case of the unseemly thing mentioned in vs. 1 nor does the passage approve of divorce in the circumstances mentioned; it simply provides that, if a man puts away his wife and she marries another, the former husband cannot under any conditions take her again to be his wife. Divorce was, however, permitted or tolerated to the extent that no civil or ecclesiastical penalty was imposed. It was practiced in terms of this permission (cf. Lev. 21:7, 14; 22:13; Num. 30:9 (10); Deut. 22:19, 29; Isa. 50:1; Jer. 3:1; Ezek. 44:22). It is not certain what the unseemly thing was. It was not adultery — death was the penalty for such (cf. Lev. 20:10; Deut. 22:22-27). Nor could it be adultery suspected but not proven (cf. Num. 5:11-31). Other provisions can be found in Deut. 22:13-29.

In the NT the question of divorce is dealt with in our Lord's teaching (Matt. 5:31, 32; 19:3-9; Mark 10:2-12; Luke 16:18). These passages make it plain that the only reason for which a man may put away his wife is adultery on her part. The one exception, mentioned in Matt. 5:32; 19:9, underlines the illegitimacy of any other reason. Mark 10:12 implies that the right to put away for adultery belongs also to the woman when she is the innocent party and that the same restriction applies to her also.

Other considerations derived from these passages should also be appreciated. (1) The person put away for any other cause than adultery is not at liberty to remarry (Matt. 5:32b) — this would be adultery. The bond of the marriage has not been dissolved, and the divorce is not valid in the sight of God. (2) The person who puts away (divorces) for any other cause is not at liberty to remarry (Matt. 19:9; Mark 10:11, 12; Luke 16:18). (3) Our Lord did *authorize* divorce for adultery. He did not make it mandatory. What course of action is to be followed by the innocent is to be decided by other considerations. Sometimes it may be mandatory. (4) Mark 10:12 implies that not only may the man sue for divorce in the case of adultery but it is also the right of the woman when her husband commits adultery. (5) By implication, our Lord abrogated the OT penalty for adultery. (6) He likewise repealed the permission, allowed by Deut. 24:1-4, to put away for cause other than that of adultery. (7) Matt. 19:8 confirms the interpretation of Deut. 24:1-4 — the Mosaic provision was sufferance but not approval.

The most disputed question concerns Matt. 19:9 in relation to Mark 10:11, 12; Luke 16:18. The former allows the person who puts away for adultery to remarry; the two latter mention no such exception. One way adopted for the harmonizing of this apparent discrepancy is to say that in Matt. 19:9 all that is permitted is to put away for adultery but not to remarry — the exception applies only to divorce from bed and board. This is a forced interpretation. There is no warrant for such a restriction of the exception stated; syntactical as well as other considerations are against this construction. And, although there is a textual variant which would support this type of solution, the evidence favors the text followed by our standard versions. The most acceptable solution is to note that in all three passages the burden of emphasis falls upon abrogation of the Mosaic permission. In respect of this permission the annulment is absolute in all three accounts. And Mark and Luke focus attention upon that one fact without additional information. Matthew, on the other hand, provides us with the information respecting two additional reservations made by our Lord in this connection, that a man may put away his wife for adultery and that when he does this he may marry another. Mark and Luke say nothing about the right to put away for adultery. Hence they could not mention what right belongs to the innocent spouse in this event. The conclusion is, therefore, that there is no contradiction and that Matt. 19:9 accords to the innocent spouse the right of remarriage.

In the NT elsewhere the most significant passages are Pauline. In Rom. 7:1-3 and I Cor. 7:39 the principle is plainly asserted that the death of one spouse dissolves the marriage, and the surviving partner is at liberty to marry again. The permanency of the marital bond is here also unequivocally established. But these passages are not to be interpreted as excluding the right of dissolution in the abnormal circumstance of the marital infidelity mentioned above. It would not have been germane to the apostle's purpose to introduce in these passages this special and exceptional contingency.

The passage in Paul most relevant to our topic is I Cor. 7:10-15. Here it is all-important to note the distinction between the situation contemplated is vss. 10, 11 and that viewed in vss. 12-15.

In the former Paul appeals to the teaching of Christ in the days of his flesh and enunciates two principles binding upon spouses. They are not to be separated from each other. But, if there is actual separation, they are to remain unmarried or be reconciled. Dissolution of the marital bond is rigidly forbidden. It is assumed, by reason of the distinction expressed in vs. 12, that both spouses profess the Christian faith.

In vss. 12-15 an eventuality is dealt with that did not come within the purview of our Lord's teaching — "I say, not the Lord." The case is that of a mixed marriage — one spouse is a believer, the other is not. Several considerations should be noted. (1) The believer is not to put away the unbeliever (vss. 12, 13). (2) The reason is that the unbeliever as well as the offspring are sanctified in the believer and hence no defilement arises for the believer or the children (vs. 14). (3) Unbelief or disavowal of the Christian faith is not a legitimate ground of divorce. (4) If the unbeliever wilfully departs, the believer is not obliged to discharge marital obligations to the deserting spouse. These are usually spoken of as the obligations of bed and board — in respect of these the believer is free. There is no room for doubt as to these conclusions.

The question that occasions difficulty is the force of the expression "is not bound" in vs. 15. Does it mean merely freedom from the debts of bed and board? Or does it also imply freedom from the bond of marriage, with the result that the marriage may be dissolved and the believer free to marry another? There is widespread disagreement. Much can be pleaded in favor of both interpretations. It should be understood, however, that, if the latter alternative is adopted, this does not necessarily conflict with the principle that only for adultery may a spouse *put away*. In this case of desertion the believer does not *put away* — the unbeliever has wilfully and wantonly deserted. And the conspicuous difference between the terms of vs. 12 (where no dissolution is allowed) and vs. 15 lends considerable support to the second alternative. If this view is adopted, however, it should be clearly understood that the liberty applies only to a believer wilfully deserted by an unbeliever.

BIBLIOGRAPHY
F. L. Cirlot, *Christ and Divorce*; C. Gore, *The Question of Divorce*; G. H. Box, *Divorce in the New Testament*; R. H. Charles, *The Teaching of the New Testament on Divorce*; "Divorce" in *The Catholic Encyclopedia*; A. Devine, *The Law of Christian Marriage*; J. Murray, *Divorce*; F. A. Adams, *Divorce*; Arndt *ad apoluo*, 2.a.

JOHN MURRAY

DOCETISM. A theological term derived from the Greek verb *dokeō*, "to seem." Docetism was the doctrine that Christ did not actually become flesh, but merely seemed to be a man. It was one of the first theological errors to appear in the history of the church, for it is probably the target of the warning in I John 4:2, 3: "Every spirit that confesseth that Jesus Christ is come in the flesh is of God: and every spirit that confesseth not that Jesus Christ is come in the flesh is not of God: and this is that spirit of antichrist, whereof ye have heard that it should come: and even now already it is in the world."

The first known advocate of this doctrine was Cerinthus, (ca. A.D. 85) traditionally an Alexandrian, who was a pupil of Philo. He held that Jesus differed from other men only in that he was better and wiser than they, and that the divine Christ descended upon him at the baptism and left him at the cross. The effect of this reasoning was to make the incarnation an illusion. Either there was no human Jesus at all, but only an apparition, or else the real Son of God was simply using the human Jesus as a vehicle of expression, but was not in real union with him.

Marcion in the middle and latter part of the second century was willing to concede the reality of the suffering of Christ, but not the reality of his birth. In his version of the Gospel of Luke he asserts that Christ simply appeared in the reign of Tiberius, by which we understand that he descended from heaven.

Docetism was attacked by Ignatius and Irenaeus, who dealt extensively with its varied forms, and by Tertullian, who wrote five books against Marcion. The essence of this heresy which influenced Mohammed has survived in some of the doctrines of Islam concerning Jesus, and in the modern cults which regard matter as evil.

BIBLIOGRAPHY
Harnack, *History of Dogma*, I, pp. 194, 258; II, pp. 276 ff., 370; Smith and Wace, *Dictionary of Christian Biography*, I, pp. 865-70.

MERRILL C. TENNEY

DOCTRINE. Occurring infrequently in the OT, the word there translates terms denoting what is received or heard. In the NT *didachē* and *didaskalia* derive from the root, "to teach," and may mean the act of teaching or the content of what is taught.

Doctrine is the teaching of Scripture on theological themes. It differs from dogma (*q.v.*) in that it does not connote an authoritative ecclesiastical affirmation but is rather the raw material of the word of God which councils use in formulating theological truth in definitive and sometimes polemical forms.

In current discussions, doctrine is sometimes used in contrast to spiritual life. However, an antithetical use here is unfortunate, for these two elements are complementary. When Paul speaks of "sound [healthy] doctrine" (I Tim. 1:10; Titus 2:1) he seems to affirm that true doctrine is life-giving.

EVERETT F. HARRISON

DOGMA. Derived from the Greek *dogma*, from *dokein*, "think, seem, seem good," the word designates a tenet of doctrine authoritatively pronounced. In the LXX *dogma* appears in Esth. 3:9; Dan. 2:13 and 6:8 for a decree issued by the king. In Luke 2:1 it is the decree of Caesar Augustus, in Acts 16:4 the decrees laid down by the apostles, in Col. 2:14 and Eph. 2:15 the judgments of the law against sinners, which Jesus triumphed over in the cross.

In Greek philosophy, especially Stoicism, it referred to axiomatic principles considered settled forever, beyond all doubt. Josephus (*Contra Apion.* i. 8) calls the Jewish sacred books *Theou dogmata*, "decrees of God." Ignatius (*Ad Magnes.* 13), Origen (*De Principiis* iv. 156), and Clement of Alexandria (*Stromateis* vii. 763) all apply the term to the Christian revelation. Now it designates those propositions of religious truth believed to have originated from divine revelation and set forth as a part of a comprehensive doctrinal system by a duly constituted religious authority.

WAYNE E. WARD

DOMINION. The Hebrew verbs *bāʻal, māšal* and *rādâ* (and their noun forms) and the Greek nouns *kratos* and *kuriotēs* (and its verbal form *kurieuō*) are the chief words expressing dominion. The larger aspects of the subject involve man, Satan and Christ.

Man's dominion may be categorized as creature — over other creatures (Gen. 1:26 ff.); head — over woman (Gen. 3:16); ruler — over nations (Matt. 20:25); sinner — under the law (Rom. 7:1) and under sin (Rom. 7:14, 23); believer — co-dominion with Christ (II Tim. 2:12; Rev. 3:21).

Satan's dominion was secured by rebellion (Isa. 14:12-16). It was proffered to Christ (Luke 4:6), who restricted it (Mark 3:27). It will be revived during the reign of Antichrist (II Thess. 2:1-12; Rev. 13); but Christ's return will terminate it (II Thess. 2:8).

Christ's dominion was predicted in the OT (Isa. 11:1-10); promised at the nativity (Luke 1:32 f.); proved in his conquests over the devil (I John 3:8), demons (Mark 5:1-15) and death (Heb. 2:14 f.); proclaimed at the ascension (Acts 2:34 ff.; cf. Ps. 24); and perfected at the second advent (I Cor. 15:24-28).

WICK BROOMALL

DONATISTS. A schismatic reform party of the fourth and fifth centuries taking its name from Donatus, a north African bishop. The protest arose when Bishop Felix, a *traditor,* presided over the ordination of the bishop of Carthage. The party soon to be called Donatists objected and separated themselves from the major church group, declaring it to be apostate and its baptism invalid. They were noted for their severe discipline, insistence on separation of church and state, and high standards for the ministry. They held to baptismal regeneration and infant baptism. Unfortunately their conscientious separationism degenerated into bigotry and extremism. The party was combatted by Augustine in the early fifth century but Donatism was not destroyed until the invasions by the Arian Vandals in A.D. 428 and Islam in the seventh century. Significantly the laws enacted against Donatist rebaptism were used by Romanists during the Reformation to inflict capital punishment on the Anabaptists.

BIBLIOGRAPHY

W. H. C. Frend, *The Donatist Church;* S. L. Greenslade, *Schism in the Early Church;* G. G. Willis, *St. Augustine and the Donatist Controversy.*

WILLIAM NIGEL KERR

DOOR. In the OT there are two main Hebrew words for *door:* (1) *petaḥ,* meaning opening, doorway; (2) *delet,* "door," i.e., the object which closes the opening. In the NT *thyra* does service for both of these meanings (e.g., Matt. 6:6; 27:60). A competent description of the construction of doors in the Near East is found in *HDCG. Thyra* is also employed figuratively in several ways: first, signifying nearness, *at the door* (Matt. 24:33; Mark 13:29; James 5:9); secondly, describing the entrance to the kingdom of God, *the narrow door* (Luke 13:24); thirdly, symbolizing opportunity or feasibility, *an open door* (Acts 14:27; I Cor. 16:9; II Cor. 2:12; Col. 4:3; Rev. 3:8; cf. Hos. 2:15, *a door of hope,* which may be the seedplot of this meaning); fourthly, depicting Christ, *the door to the sheep* (John 10:7) and *the door for the sheep* (John 10:9); lastly, portraying the persistent and loving invitation of Christ to men (Rev. 3:20).

BIBLIOGRAPHY

Arndt; B. R. Downer in *ISBE;* G. B. Eager in *HDCG;* B. F. Westcott, *The Revelation of the Father,* pp. 63-74.

DAVID A. HUBBARD

DOUBT. The term denotes a state of uncertainty with respect to some cause, person or event. In the NT it is usually employed in one of two ways. It may indicate a state of being at a loss to comprehend some situation (John 13:22; Acts 2:12, 10:17; Gal. 4:20). It implies hesitancy to act, and may or may not be sinful.

Used in the second sense, it signifies positive wavering of judgment, and issues in lack of conviction, and in many cases disbelief and skepticism (Mark 6:6; Rom. 14:23). Doubt may be resolved by further thought and action; or it may remain unresolved, and as such it may become positively sinful.

Doubt and moral unwillingness are closely related. II Thess. 2:10-12 embeds the principle, that much doubt stems from refusal to accept the mandates of revealed truth. Volitional doubt may become the pattern of one who rejects divine revelation and its claims. *ISBE,* II, pp. 870 f.

HAROLD B. KUHN

DOVE. The dove's docile nature is sometimes a simile for foolish trust (Hos. 7:11) or defenselessness (Ps. 74:19), but it is also used to denote lack of guile. So Jesus enjoins the disciples to be "innocent as doves" (Matt. 10:16), that is, be pure and open in motive and action. This quality of perfect purity then becomes an apt emblem of the Holy Spirit (Matt. 3:16; cf. Heb. 7:26; bHag. 15a; Targ. S. of Sol. 2:12). The dove is also a term of endearment (S. of Sol. 2:14; 5:2) and a symbol of beauty (S. of Sol. 1:15; 4:1), and thus stands occasionally in Jewish literature for marital felicity (bErub. 100b; bBaba Kamma 93a). Sometimes the mournful cooing of the dove, although in reality a sign of happiness, is used to signify suffering (Ezek. 7:16; cf. S. of Sol. Rabba 1:15).

The dove, along with the pigeon, was used in general purificatory offerings (Lev. 12:6; 14:4-8), especially if brought by the poor (Lev. 12:8; Luke 2:24). However, it was never involved in any sacrificial meal, nor is there any evidence that the dove was ever part of the Hebrew diet. Perhaps this is related to the sacrosanct character of the dove in other parts of the ancient Near East (cf. W. Robertson Smith, *The Religion of the Semites,* Adam & Charles Black, London, 1894 (2nd ed.), pp. 219 (note 2), 225, 294).

ROBERT B. LAURIN

DOXOLOGY. The term, which is derived from the Greek *doxa* (glory), denotes an ascription of praise to the three persons of the Blessed Trinity. In its commonest form, known as the *Gloria Patri* or "Lesser Doxology," it is rendered: "Glory be to the Father, and to the Son, and to the Holy Ghost: As it was in the beginning, is now, and ever shall be, world without end. Amen." Its use at the end of the Psalms, as directed e.g., in the Book of Common Prayer, dates from the fourth century. It is thus a symbol of the duty of Christianizing the Psalms and serves at the same time "to connect the Unity of the Godhead as known to the Jews with the Trinity as known to Christians" (*Tutorial Prayer Book,* Harrison Trust, London, p. 101).

The so-called "Greater Doxology" is the *Gloria in Excelsis,* "Glory be to God on high." On account of its opening words, taken directly from Luke 2:14, it is sometimes known as the Angelic Hymn. This doxology is of Greek origin (fourth century) and was used at first as a morning canticle. Later it became incorporated into the Latin Mass, where it occupied a place at the beginning of the service. In the English Communion Service of 1552 the Reformers transferred the hymn to the end of the office, no doubt in accordance with the usage at the first eucharist: "When they had sung an hymn, they went out" (Matt. 26:30). In this position it forms a fitting conclusion to the Christian sacrifice of praise and thanksgiving.

It is now generally agreed that the doxology at the end of the Lord's Prayer is not part of the original text of Matt. 6:9-13. It may be regarded as an ancient liturgical addition to the prayer, which was adopted by the Greek church, but not by the Latin.

FRANK COLQUHOUN

DREAM. The Bible assigns to involuntary dreams a legitimate place in revealing future events. This is true in dispensations of God's dealings with men in which there was an absence of regularly constituted prophets or little or no written revelation, as in the patriarchal period (Gen. 31:10-14; 37:5-9) and in the time of the Judges (Judg. 7:9-14), or for very special occasions (Matt. 1:20; 2:13). Such guidance may be divinely induced in any age. But in the era of an outpoured Spirit and a full written revelation to guide, we walk by faith, and normally have little need for such unusual methods of guidance (II Cor. 5:7). Yet, even now, should God choose to lead in this extraordinary way, there would be nothing in it inconsistent with his holiness, or smack of the divinatory taint of heathenism.

The case is quite different, however, with voluntary or humanly (demoniacally) induced dreams, definitely divinatory in character. In this category occur dreams induced by "incubation" or sleeping in some shrine where the patron deity is believed to reveal his secrets to the sleeper. Herodotus cites the occurrence of this practice among an Egyptian sect known as the Nasamonians (*Herod. IV,* p. 172, ed. by A. D. Godley).

The Bible denounces this heathen custom as a corruption to which God's people yielded. They are described as those who "sit among the graves and lodge in the secret places [vaults]" (Isa. 65:4). King Solomon's famous dream at the high place of Gibeon (I Kings 3:1-15), although it came to him at a shrine with pagan associations, was nevertheless God-given, involuntary on the monarch's part, and not an instance of incubation.

BIBLIOGRAPHY
Cutten, *The Psychological Phenomena of Christianity*.

MERRILL F. UNGER

DRUNKENNESS. The excessive drinking of intoxicants was a common vice among the ancient Jews and other early peoples. But since intoxicants were so expensive, it was particularly a practice of the rich (Amos 6:6; 4:1; 2:8). Jesus condemns it only once (Luke 21:34); probably since he had been sent to the poor, and intoxicants were still costly. Paul frequently urged temperance (Gal. 5:21; Eph. 5:18).

Although intemperance is consistently condemned in both the OT and the NT, total abstinence for all is not explicitly required in either. Nazarites vowed to refrain (Num. 6:3 f.); Daniel and his friends elected to do so (Dan. 1:8-16); and priests were required to abstain while on duty in the sanctuary (Lev. 10:9). But although abstinence is never a universal requirement, such instances of a total refraining imply that it is a higher ethic than mere temperance. Also, there are abstinence implications, as in Matt. 16:24 f., Rom. 14:13-21, and I Cor. 8:8-13.

J. KENNETH GRIDER

DUALISM. A theory in interpretation which explains a given situation or domain in terms of two opposing factors or principles. In general, dualisms are twofold classifications which admit of no intermediate degrees. There are three major types: (a) metaphysical, (b) epistemological or epistemic, and (c) ethical or ethico-religious.

Metaphysical dualism asserts that the facts of the universe are best explained in terms of mutually irreducible elements. These are often considered to be mind and matter, or as by Descartes, thought and extension. Mind is usually conceived as conscious experience, matter as occupying space and being in motion. They are thus two qualitatively different orders of reality.

Epistemological dualism is an analysis of the knowing situation which holds that the idea or object of judgment is radically other than the real object. The "object" of knowledge is held to be known only through the mediation of "ideas." This type of thinking raises the important question of the manner in which knowledge can bridge the gap between the idea of an object and the object itself.

Ethical or ethico-religious dualism asserts that there are two mutually hostile forces or beings in the world, the one being the source of all good, the other the source of all evil. The most clear-cut type of ethico-religious dualism is that of the ancient Iranian religion, usually associated with the name of Zoroaster, in which Ahura Mazda and Ahriman represent the projection into cosmology, respectively, of the forces of good and evil. The universe becomes the battle-ground for these opposing beings, identified respectively with light and darkness. More moderate forms of dualism pervade most religions, expressed, for example, by the distinction between "sacred" and "profane," or by the analysis of reality in terms of *yang* and *yin* in Chinese thought. Christian theology generally accepts a modified moral dualism, recognizing God as supremely good, and Satan as a deteriorated creature bent everywhere upon the intrusion of evil. This, however, is not dualism in the sense of its usual definition, since Christian theology does not consider Satan to be ultimate or original, and sees him ultimately excluded from the universe.

BIBLIOGRAPHY
SHERK, IV, p. 15; Dagobert Runes, *Dictionary of Philosophy*, pp. 84 f.

HAROLD B. KUHN

DUTY. The verb *opheilō* signifies moral obligation; what is due by or to someone. This is more often expressed by the impersonal verb *dei*. Shades of meaning in the NT are: (1) payment of financial debt (Matt. 18:28), (2) be obligated (Luke 17:10), (3) bound (by oath) (Matt. 23:16, 18).

Always there is the idea of compulsion of some kind; of fate, or law or inner necessity. Sin is sometimes represented as debt. Kant regarded duty for duty's sake as the true motive of moral action. This is formal and abstract. Jesus regarded love for both God and man as the true moral motive.

See also ETHICS.

ALBERT VICTOR M'CALLIN

E

EARNEST. The Greek *arrabōn* occurs in II Cor. 1:22; 2:5; Eph. 1:14 (RSV, "guarantee"). and its Hebrew equivalent in Gen. 28:17, 18, 20. A commercial term of Phoenician origin, it is used in the papyri of an engagement ring, a down payment on a cow, an advance payment to dancing girls ("as earnest money to be reckoned in the price" MM). It may, then, designate a *pledge* which is later returned (Gen. 38:17 ff.), a *down payment* which validates a contract, or a *first installment* which secures (and partakes of the nature of) a further performance. It is always an act which binds one to a future action. In patristic literature, the Letter of Polycarp 8:1 speaks of the death of Christ as "the *earnest* of our righteousness." In the NT occurrences the Holy Spirit is given to the Christian as God's *arrabōn* — his guarantee and/or first installment (Rom. 8:23) of a promised future redemption. Significantly, II Cor. 1:21 f. uses the words *arrabōn* and *bebaioun* ("establish") together (see also SEAL); the latter also is a commercial contractual term meaning "to make legally binding." Their combined usage reinforces Paul's concept which represents "the relation of God to believers under the image of a legally indisputable relation" (A. Deissmann, *Bible Studies*, T and T Clark, Edinburgh, 1903, p. 108 f.).

E. EARLE ELLIS

EASTER. The annual festival of our Lord's resurrection, as Sunday is the weekly commemoration of the same. It is at once the oldest and greatest festival of the Christian church, having been observed from very early times. The importance of the feast derives from the centrality of the resurrection in the church's faith and preaching.

The festival is preceded by the forty days of Lent (*q.v.*) and extends for forty days afterwards, viz., until Ascension Day. In the primitive church Easter was one of the special occasions for the baptism of catechumens and also for the restoration of penitents to the Holy Communion.

During the first three centuries there was a difference of opinion between the churches of Alexandria and Rome as to the method of calculating the date of Easter; but since the Council of Nicaea (A.D. 325) the date has been determined by the Jewish Passover and falls on the Sunday nearest to the 14th Nisan. This means that the extreme limits of the feast are from March 21 to April 25.

According to Bede, the name Easter is derived from *Eostre,* an Anglo-Saxon goddess whose festival was held in the spring. The original title given to the feast, both in the East and the West, was *Pascha*, on account of its association with the Jewish Passover.

FRANK COLQUHOUN

EAT. The word eat (OT *'ākal* and others; NT *esthiō, et al.*) is employed in a variety of meanings. The first test of the human race centered about a prohibition to eat (Gen. 2:16, 17). Since Adam and Eve had been graciously supplied by God with every good, this was the best test of their obedience. The fall became a historical actuality through Adam's eating the forbidden fruit (Gen. 3:6; Rom. 5:12). In Noah's day there was the proscription of eating blood (Gen. 9:4 and Acts 15:19-20). Forbidden foods were instituted in order to impress upon Israel her separate position among the nations, that she might be kept from idolatrous practices to be a clean channel for the coming Messiah (Lev. 11 and Deut. 14). It is well known how rabbinical Judaism enlarged these injunctions to make a burdensome load upon the people of Israel (Mark 7:1-8; Acts 15:10). Meticulous regulations were set forth for the eating of the Passover meal (Ex. 12:4 ff.).

Eating and drinking express man's ordinary life (Matt. 11:19; Luke 7:34) as in the days of Noah (Luke 17:27). The moral aspects of this activity are contained in a number of prescriptions and prohibitions on the manner, time, and articles of eating.

Eating together meant either adoption (II Sam. 9:7; Jer. 52:33) or entrance into covenant relationship (Jer. 41:1). Exodus 24:11 reveals that the concept of covenant relationship underlay the sacrificial meal. It was perfidy and treason of the worst sort to break a

175

covenant made through eating together (Ps. 41:9; John 13:18).

When eating was not related to the spiritual life, it was unsatisfying (Ezek. 12:18; Mic. 6:14). To "eat up" meant to destroy (Ps. 53:4). Excess in eating is condemned throughout the Bible (Eccl. 10:16, 17; Isa. 5:11, 12; I Cor. 6:13; Phil. 3:19). Careless self-indulgence is also condemned (Matt. 24:49; Luke 12:19). Anxiety over the provision of food is prohibited (Matt. 6:24-34; Luke 12:22-34).

Of the Synoptic accounts of the institution of the Lord's Supper only Matthew (26:26-28) has the command to eat, although I Cor. 11:26 mentions the eating without enjoining it by an imperative. The bread which symbolizes Christ's body given vicariously for sinful man, must be received and eaten by the communicant. Although the drinking of the cup was withheld by the Roman hierarchy from the laity during the Middle Ages, eating the bread was always an indispensable part of the celebration of the Eucharist. The followers of Christ will eat with him in his kingdom (Luke 22:30).

In John 6:35-50 Christ points to himself as the bread of life. He is the spiritual food of believers through his redemptive work in his death. Whether it is warranted to see here a reference to the Lord's Supper or not, communion with and appropriation by faith of Christ in his redemptive work are indicated. There is life-sustaining power in communion with Christ.

A perusal of the Book of Acts reveals the importance of eating for fellowship in the early Christian church, whether in regular communal meals or *agapē* feasts (Acts 2:42; I Cor. 11:20, 21), and in the commemoration of the Lord's Supper (I Cor. 11:28). As significant as these gatherings were at first in the assembly of Jewish believers, they were all the more vital later for the cementing of the bond between Jewish and gentile believers. It was thus not without reason that Paul was gravely concerned over the conduct of Peter at Antioch (Gal. 2:11-13).

The matter of Christian liberty is taken up and thoroughly expounded on the subject of eating either things sacrificed to idols (I Cor. 8:10) or foods which may be repugnant to other believers (Rom. 14).

The appropriation of truth is sometimes illustrated by the "eating" of the message to be conveyed or preached (Ezek. 2:8; 3:3; Rev. 10:10).

BIBLIOGRAPHY

HDCG, I, p. 504; H. A. W. Meyer, *Commentary on the Gospel of John*, p. 215; A. Plummer, *Gospel of John* (Cambridge Series), pp. 160 ff; SBD, p. 194; M. C. Tenney, *John: The Gospel of Belief*, p. 122; A. Tholuck, *Commentary on the Gospel of John*, pp. 180 ff.

CHARLES L. FEINBERG

EBIONITE. The name is derived from the Hebrew. In the OT the word poor implied humility, suffering for righteousness' sake. The sect was a logical development from the Judaizers of Paul's day. It kept the entire Mosaic law with special attention to circumcision and Sabbath, and revered Jerusalem as if it were the abode of God. Jesus was regarded as the last and greatest of the prophets, the natural son of Joseph and Mary, but not the eternal Son of God. "After his baptism Christ descended upon him in the form of a dove," but departed from him before the crucifixion. Jesus died and rose again, but Christ remained impassible, being by nature spiritual (Irenaeus *Adv. haer.* I, xxvi, 1, 2). Only the Gospel of Matthew was used, and Paul was rejected as an apostate from the law (Eusebius iii. 27).

The destruction of the temple in A.D. 70 was a fatal blow to all Jewish Christians. They ceased to wield any influence because they were removed from the main centers of activity which were exclusively gentile. They lingered for a long time and the remnants were absorbed by Islam. Their imperfect conception of Christ has reappeared from time to time in Christian history.

Some scholars maintain that the Qumran Community consisted of Jewish Christians of the Ebionite type.

BIBLIOGRAPHY

H. J. Schonfield, *Secrets of the Dead Sea Scrolls*; F. F. Bruce, *Second Thoughts on the Dead Sea Scrolls*; A. Dupont Sommer, *The Jewish Sect of Qumran and the Essenes*; Charles F. Pfeiffer, *The Dead Sea Scrolls*.

RICHARD E. HIGGINSON

ECUMENICAL. The word *oikoumenē* was used in the classical Greek, caught up in the NT, applied throughout history by Eastern, Latin, and Evangelical churches, but has taken on a special meaning and importance in the twentieth century non-Roman communions. A brief consideration of these items constitutes this article.

The basic, original meaning of the word was geographical. According to Herodotus, Demosthenes and Aristotle it carried the connotation of "inhabited world." Since, however, Greece represented the tutored and refined versus the "barbarian," the word acquired a cultural implication superimposed on its fundamental geographical significance.

The NT uses the word fifteen times, usually in the geographical sense, but generally without conveying any cultural implications. There is a little carryover of the proud Greek usage, now in the form of the proud Roman usage (cf. Luke 2:1; Acts 11:28; 19:27; 24:5) but this is alien to the NT viewpoint itself. In it the word reverts to its basic etymology and designates the entire inhabited world. The gospel is to be preached in the *oikoumenē* (Matt. 24:14); the *oikoumenē* is to be judged by Jesus Christ (Acts 17:31; cf. Luke 21:26); the kingdoms of the *oikoumenē* are shown to Jesus by Satan (Luke 4:5). Other occurrences (Acts 17:6; Rom. 10:18; Heb. 1:6; 2:5; Rev. 3:10; 12:9; 16:14) repeat, combine or develop the above significations.

The various branches of the Christian church since apostolic times have employed this term. Thus the Eastern Church has had "ecumenical" synods and theologians. The Roman Church calls its councils "ecumenical." Evangelical churches speak of the Apostles', Nicene, Athanasian and others as "ecumenical creeds."

The fissiparousness of the non-Roman churches has called into being a powerful modern counter-tendency and its label is "ecumenical." One of its chief exponents, W. A. Visser t'Hooft, associates two current meanings with the term: unity and universality. These are expressed in the various inter-church movements which bear the designation "ecumenical." Some indication of the scope of ecumenism in the twentieth century is seen not only in the large number of councils formed, the most significant being the World Council of Churches, but in the numerous actual denominational unions.

The ecumenical movement has tended to handle the divergent theologies of cooperating groups gingerly and unrealistically, in order to prevent the occurrence of ruptures. However, one writer has said that the ecumenical "honeymoon" is over and the real questions involved in living together must now be faced.

Leadership in the ecumenical movement has often been in the hands of those less concerned theologically, but Evangelicals have been far from uninterested. A recent volume typical of their thinking is Marcellus Kik's *Ecumenism*

and the Evangelical. The new ecumenical evangelical magazine, *Christianity Today*, devotes much space to the question of Christian unity.

BIBLIOGRAPHY

G. K. A. Bell, *Documents on Christian Unity*; R. C. Bilheimer, *The Quest for Christian Unity*; Cajus Fabricius, *Ecumenical Handbook of the Churches of Christ*; O. Michel in *TWNT*; J. Kaerst, *Die Antike Idee der Oekumene in ihrer politischen und kulturellen Bedeutung*; E. L. Mascall, *Recovery of Unity*; J. R. Nelson, *One Lord, One Church*.

JOHN H. GERSTNER

EDIFICATION. "Edification" is used in the AV in Rom. 15:2; I Cor. 14:3; II Cor. 10:8 and 13:10 to translate the Greek *oikodomē*. The same Greek word is also translated "edifying" several times in I and II Corinthians and Ephesians; in Rom. 14:19 it is used in a phrase, "things wherewith one may edify." The same root is used in I Tim. 1:4, where *oikodomia* is translated "building up." The corresponding verb form is used several times in Acts and the Pauline epistles. The ASV and RSV are similar but not identical.

The Greek word literally means "building a house." Paul uses both the noun and verb forms to impress upon the Christian the importance of development in the Christian life. A person becomes a Christian at the moment of the expression of a true, saving faith, when the foundation of faith in Christ is laid. Then throughout the rest of his life he must build a house upon that foundation. Each Christian should build up his own Christian life and also help others build up theirs — provoking them to good works.

SAMUEL A. CARTLEDGE

EGYPT. Although this country was no promised land for the patriarchs and was forbidden as a refuge in famine (Gen. 26:2; cf. 12:10-20), it nevertheless served as a haven for Jacob and his posterity (Gen. 46:3; cf. 15:13-16), who, as pilgrims and strangers, never ceased to look on Canaan as their home (Gen. 47:30; 50:24-25). Compared to the wilderness, Egypt offered creature comforts which brought nostalgia to many Israelites (Num. 11:4-6). Their experience of sojourn there was intended by God to teach them compassion toward the strangers in their own midst (Ex. 23:9), and their deliverance from helpless servitude by God's mighty power was held before the nation as a reminder of his redemptive purpose (Deut. 4:34; Ps. 78:52).

Pharaoh becomes representative of those who

fulfil God's will despite their stubborn resistance to him (Ex. 14:17; Rom. 9:17-18). The theology of the Exodus includes judgment upon false gods (Ex. 12:12). Egypt was sensual (Ex. 23:19-21) and marked by pride which merited divine punishment (Ezek. 29:3 ff.). Judah's contemplated alliance with her is stigmatized as a covenant with death and an agreement with Sheol (Isa. 28:15). Egypt appears consistently as a symbol of worldly, anti-God power (Rev. 11:8). This makes all the more remarkable the promise of God's favor upon her in the latter days (Isa. 19:25).

EVERETT F. HARRISON

ELDER. "The elders of the people" or the "elders of Israel" are frequently associated with Moses in his dealings with the people (Ex. 3:16; 4:29; 17:5; 18:12; 19:17; 24:1, 11; Num. 11:16). They later administer local government (Judg. 8:14; Josh. 20:4; Ruth 4:2) and have a hand in national affairs (I Sam. 4:3) even after the institution of the monarchy (I Sam. 8:4; 30:26; II Sam. 3:17; 5:3; I Kings 21:8). They achieve fresh prominence during the exile (Jer. 29:1; Ezek. 7:1; 14:1; 20:1) and after the return are associated both with the governor in his functions (Ezra 5:9 ff.; 6:7) and with local administration (Ezra 10:14). They have by themselves certain juridical functions (Deut. 22:15; 25:7 ff.) and are associated with the judges, who are probably appointed from their number, in the administration and execution of justice (Deut. 16:18; 21:2 ff.; Ezra 7:25; 10:14). They are also associated with Moses and Aaron in conveying the word of God to the people (Ex. 3:14; 4:29; 19:7) and in representing the people before God (Ex. 17:5; 24:1; Num. 11:16) on great occasions. They see to the Passover arrangements (Ex. 12:21).

Other nations had elders (cf. Gen. 50:7; Num. 22:7), the right to the title being due to age, or to the esteem in which an individual is held, or to the holding of a definite office in the community (cf. Saxon *alderman,* Roman *senator,* Greek *gerousia*). The elder in Israel no doubt at first derived his authority and status as well as his name by reason of his age and experience.

In the Maccabean period the title "elders of Israel" is used of the members of the Jewish Sanhedrin which was regarded as being set up by Moses in his appointment of the seventy elders in Num. 11:16 ff. At the local level a community of 120 (cf. Acts 1:15) or more could appoint seven elders (*Mishna,* Sanhedrin 1:6). These were called the "seven of a city," and it is possible that the seven appointed in Acts 6 were regarded as such elders (cf. D. Daube, *The New Testament and Rabbinic Judaism,* p. 237). In the Gospels the elders are associated with the scribes and chief priests as those at whose hands Jesus (Matt. 16:21; 27:1) and the apostles (Acts 6:12) suffered.

In the NT, elders or "presbyters" (*presbyteroi*) appear early in the life of the church, taking their place along with the apostles, prophets and teachers. At Jerusalem they are associated with James in the government of the local church after the manner of the synagogue (Acts 11:30; 21:18), but in association with the apostles they also share in the wider, or more sanhedral, government of the whole church (Acts 15:2, 6, 23; 16:4). An apostle can be a presbyter (I Pet. 5:1).

Presbyters do not appear at Antioch during Paul's stay there (Acts 13:1), nor are they mentioned in Paul's earlier epistles. Possibly government was then a matter of minor importance. But Paul and Barnabas on their first missionary journey had presbyters appointed in all the churches they founded (Acts 14:23).

The presbyters whom Paul addressed at Ephesus (Acts 20:17 ff.) and those addressed in I Peter and Titus have a decisive place in church life. Besides their function of humble pastoral oversight, on them largely depends the stability and purity of the flock in the approaching temptation and crisis. They are in such a position of authority and privilege as can be abused. They share in the ministry of Christ towards the flock (I Pet. 5:1-4; Acts 20:28; cf. Eph. 4:11).

It is often asserted that in the gentile churches the name *episcopos* is used as a substitute for *presbyteros* with identical meaning. The words seem to be interchangeable in Acts 20:17; 20:28; and Titus 1:5-9. But though all *episcopoi* are undoubtedly *presbyteroi,* it is not clear whether the reverse is always true. The word *presbyteros* denotes rather the status of eldership while *episcopos* denotes the function of at least some elders. But there may have been elders who were not *episcopoi.*

In I Tim. 5:17 teaching as well as oversight is regarded as a desirable function of the presbyter. It is likely that when the apostles and teachers and prophets ceased to be able to minister to the whole church in their travels, the function of teaching and preaching would fall on the local presbyters and thus the office and the qualifications of those holding it would develop. This, again, may have led to distinction within the presbyterate. The president of the body of presbyters, both in the ordering of the congregation and the celebration of the Lord's Supper, would tend to become a permanent office held by one man.

The "elder" in II and III John refers merely to some one highly esteemed within the church. The twenty-four elders who appear so frequently in the visions of the Book of Revelation are examples of how all authority should humbly adore God and the Lamb (Rev. 4:10; 5:8-10; 19:4). It is to be noted that even these presbyters seem to minister in heaven to the church on earth (Rev. 5:5; 5:8; 7:13).

At the time of the Reformation, Calvin found that the office of elder was one of the four "orders or offices" which Christ had instituted for the ordinary government of the church, the others being pastors, doctors (teachers) and deacons. The elders, as representatives of the people, along with pastors or bishops, were responsible for discipline. In Scotland the elder was later ordained for life, without the laying on of hands, and was given the duty of examining communicants and visiting the sick. He was encouraged to teach. The theory arose, through I Tim. 5:17, that ministers and elders were both presbyters of the same order, the former being the teaching elder, the latter the ruling elder. But, as a whole, the Presbyterian Church has held that there is a distinction between ordination to the ministry and that to the eldership, ordination being determined by the end to which it is directed. The elder has been regarded as a representative of the people (though not appointed by or responsible to the people) in the ordering of church affairs, and has fulfilled many of the functions appropriate to the diaconate in the NT. The pattern of the elder's work within the church corresponds closely to that of the OT "elder of the people."

BIBLIOGRAPHY

T. M. Lindsay, *The Church and Ministry in the Early Centuries*; B. H. Streeter, *The Primitive Church*; G. Bornkamm in *TWNT*; G. D. Henderson, *The Scottish Ruling Elder*; J. M. Ross, *What is an Elder?* (Presbyterian Church of England); A. A. Hodge, *What is Presbyterianism?*

RONALD S. WALLACE

ELECT, ELECTION. The term elect may be a verb of action or it may identify the person who is the object of this action. It is thus synonymous with "choose" and "chosen" respectively. In Scripture it is frequently applied to the action of God in reference to men and to the category in which men are placed as a result of this action. The term election likewise may reflect on the action of God or on the resulting status of men. The terms always imply differentiation whether viewed as action on God's part or as privilege on the part of men.

In the OT this concept appears in God's choice of Israel from among all the nations of the earth to be his people in the possession of covenant privilege and blessing (cf. Deut. 4:37; 7:6, 7; I Kings 3:8; Isa. 44:1-2). It is also used with reference to the Messiah (Isa. 42:1) and this is reiterated in the NT (Luke 23:35; I Pet. 2:4, 6). In reference to Christ the differentiation implied points to the unique and distinctive office with which he is invested and to the peculiar delight which God the Father takes in him.

As the election which applies to Christ has respect to the offices which he executes in the accomplishment of salvation and the securing of its ends, so election as it concerns men is pre-eminently that which pertains to their salvation in Christ. Election on the part of God in eternity is the source from which the process of salvation springs and it is the ultimate reason for the salvation of men — they are chosen by God unto salvation (II Thess. 2:13). The fruits which accompany salvation supply to us men the proof of God's election (cf. I Thess. 1:3, 4). This election took place in Christ before the foundation of the world and was to the end that the elect should be holy and without blame (Eph. 1:4).

As election is eternal, so is it sovereign. No passage shows this more clearly than Rom. 9:11 where the differentiation between Esau and Jacob finds its explanation in, and is directed to the vindication of, "the purpose of God according to election." It is futile to appeal to the foreknowledge of God as in any way abridging or modifying the sovereign character of election. Rom. 8:29 shows that the term "foreknow" is itself differentiating and cannot mean the foresight of faith but refers to that distinguishing knowledge of God by which he loved the persons concerned from eternity. Rom. 8:29 is similar to Eph. 1:5, that in love God predestinated his people unto adoption. Foreknowledge is the synonym of "forelove" and so "whom he foreknew" (Rom. 8:29) is equivalent to election in Christ (Eph. 1:4).

As salvation in possession is the proof of election, so election is the guarantee of all that salvation implies. We are therefore enjoined to make sure that it is a fact (II Pet. 1:10) and in this assurance we have the certainty of divine vindication (Rom. 8:33). But election offers no ground for presumption or license. It is in our identity as "elect of God" that we are to put on "bowels of mercies, kindness, humbleness of mind, meekness, longsuffering" (Col. 3:12). The pure sovereignty of God's grace, when apprehended, constrains the amazement which humbles and the gratitude which sanctifies.

BIBLIOGRAPHY
Abraham Booth, *The Reign of Grace*, pp. 53-97; G. C. Berkouwer, *De Verkiezing Gods*; G. Schrenk in *TWNT*, IV, pp. 181-97; B. B. Warfield, *Biblical Doctrines*, pp. 3-67; *Biblical and Theological Studies*, pp. 270-333.

JOHN MURRAY

ELEMENTS OF THE WORLD, THE.

The expression *ta stoicheia tou kosmou* is found only in Gal. 4:3 and Col. 2:8, 20 (cf. the *Sib. Or.* 2.206: *ta asthenē kai ptōcha stoicheia* Gal. 4:9). *Stoicheion* is used by Greek writers from Plato onwards for: (1) alphabet letters or elements of learning; (2) the four elements, earth, water, air, fire: so Stoics, Philo, *Sib. Or.* 2.206; (3) the principles of knowledge or mathematics; (4) the stars and their physical elements: so Justin Martyr; (5) angel-spirits: so II Enoch 16:7 and Tatian. *Kosmos* is used of the earth, firmament, humanity and sinful humanity.

For *ta stoicheia tou kosmou* there are four possible meanings: (1) the physical elements of the universe (Wisdom 7:17), favored by Zahn because Jewish festivals were fixed by movements of the heavenly bodies; (2) the heavenly bodies worshipped by the Galatians before conversion (cf. Deut. 4:19), advocated by Justin Martyr and Theodoret, who thought acceptance of the Jewish calendar would renew bondage to these elements (Gal. 4:9); (3) the angels associated with these elements who gave the law on Sinai: so Ritschl, Bauer, Dibelius and RSV, who regard the Colossian heresy as a syncretistic cult including angel worship; (4) elements of religious knowledge common to Jews and Gentiles before Christ (Tertullian) and superseded by Christian revelation: so Burton (ICC) and Goodspeed.

Against (3) Burton argues that there is no evidence to link *stoicheia* with deities in Paul's day, and that heavenly bodies cannot be described as *asthenē* and *ptōcha*. There would be a good case for (2) if the Colossian heresy were Essenism (Lightfoot): the Qumran Manual stresses calendar festivals. Radford favors (3) on the ground that the Colossians regarded Christian salvation as liberation from sin but not from the need to conciliate the planetary angels.

The term *stoicheia* is used again in II Pet. 3:10 of the basic elements of which the natural world is composed and which will disappear in the world conflagration at the end of time; also in Heb. 5:12 of the elementary truths of God's word.

BIBLIOGRAPHY
Arndt; E. Burton, ICC, pp. 510-18; L. B. Radford, WC on Colossians; *HDB*; M. Dibelius, *Geisterwelt*, pp. 78 ff., 228 ff.

DENIS H. TONGUE

ELIJAH.

In the OT Elijah is given a twofold role: (1) as the voice of denunciation against social oppression and the amoral worship of Baal during the days of Ahab of Israel (I Kings 17, etc.), and (2) as the voice of preparation resurrected during eschatological days to proclaim the imminent appearance of the "day of the Lord" (Mal. 4:5).

When the apostate, idolatrous worship of Israel had reached its lowest ebb during the reign of Ahab (I Kings 16:30), Elijah suddenly appeared to predict a drought of indefinite length as a penalty for Israel's rejection of the Lord (I Kings 17:1). This was lifted when the people acknowledged the Lord as God following the successful contest on Mt. Carmel between Elijah and the prophets of Baal (I Kings 18). But Elijah, fearful of the wrath of Jezebel at his victory over the Baalistic worship, fled to Mt. Horeb for forty days and nights. There God appeared to him, rebuked him, and sent him back to continue his role of being the national conscience, and to anoint Elisha as his successor (I Kings 19:21; II Kings 1). The ministry of Elijah concluded when he was taken up alive to heaven in a whirlwind (II Kings 2). However he was to return during the last days to prepare men's hearts for the advent of world judgment (Mal. 3:1; 4:6).

The NT and later Judaism reflect the eschatological role of Elijah. The common pharisaic teaching was that before the advent of the Messiah "Elijah must first come" (Mark 9:11). Indeed Jesus announced that John the Baptist was the fulfilment of this prophecy (Matt. 11:7-15). Throughout the rabbinic literature Elijah is expected to reappear in the last days to deal with all those legal problems and difficulties which Israel had been unable to solve through the years. The common phrase is "until Elijah comes" (cf. bMenaḥoth 63a; bBekhoroth 24a; mEduyoth 8:7; I Macc. 4:41-47; 14:41). It is possible that one of the Dead Sea Scrolls also reflects this tradition (1QS 9:11). A final aspect of Elijah's preparatory role was at the transfiguration when Moses and he, representing the law and the prophets, appeared with Jesus to symbolize their fulfilment in him (Matt. 17:3; Mark 9:4).

BIBLIOGRAPHY

J. Jeremias in *TWNT;* H. S. Gehman in *WDB;* Julian Morgenstern in *UJE.*

ROBERT B. LAURIN

ELKESAITES. A syncretistic sect of early Jewish Christianity which flourished east of the Dead Sea from about the beginning of the second century and contributed to the origin of Islam. The derivation of the name is in doubt. Perhaps the Greek *ēlchasai* is derived from the Aramaic ḥêl kᵉsê, hidden power, referring to the Holy Spirit. A secret book with the same Greek title, reputed to have been brought down from heaven by an angel, and central to the system, was known to Origen and Hippolytus.

The Elkesaites took their rise from the Ebionites, and, theosophical as they were, are considered by some as a class of that Jewish sect. Among their practices were Jewish legalism and circumcision, two Christian baptisms, the Lord's supper observed with bread and salt, and pagan ablutions and astrology (*q.v.*). Christ was viewed as a mere man and the Holy Spirit as female. Basically Gnostic, Elkesaism formed the basis of the Pseudo-Clementine system, which spread even to Rome.

DONALD G. DAVIS

EMANATION. Derived from Latin, meaning to flow out, this is a common term in Gnosticism (second century A.D.). It there plays an important part in the attempted solution of the problem of evil. The material world was considered evil in itself. The Supreme Being had to be separated from such a degrading connection. A series of emanations (or aeons) thus became interposed between him and the creator of the material universe, called the Demiurge, or god of the OT. The term is also used by the medieval mystics of those states of mind which were like ladders of ascent to God. Such graduated scales of virtues were the products of imagination.

RICHARD E. HIGGINSON

EMOTION. The word emotion is derived from the Latin verb *emovere* (*e*, "out" and *movere*, "to move, to stir up"). The emotions are an aspect of the mind. They are experienced within the soul but have physical manifestations. Anger, for example, affects the adrenal glands, worry the digestive glands, sorrow the tear glands, fear the circulatory system, etc. Different emotions affect the organism in different ways. Fear may increase physical strength, prolong the power of endurance, cause insensitivity to pain, but may also paralyze. Emotions may interfere with normal processes of body and mind, may cause physical or mental ailments or even death. Emotions, like sensations, elude precise definition. As the idea of sweetness, sourness, or bitterness can be conveyed only by reference to an object which possesses these qualities, so the meaning of a specific emotion can be communicated to another only by a reference to that emotion. Everyone knows what is meant by love, fear, anger, worry, etc. But it is most difficult to convey the meaning of any one of these emotions by an attempted definition. However, all emotions have in common the general idea of being stirred up, excited, perturbed. They are a part of the inherited equipment of the child but are developed or modified by maturation and training. They are important factors in motivating human behavior. People are influenced more by their feelings than by reason. Emotions are more tenacious than ideas. Hence we say, "I am convinced but not persuaded." Emotions are means of communication. A gloomy person spreads gloom, a cheerful person good cheer, and an angry person anger. The emotions give color and richness to life and value to our possessions. They give rise to the noblest deeds of men but also may change him into a savage fiend. They make an individual attractive or repulsive, reasonable or irrational, saintly or ignoble. Emotions are an important factor in man's religious life. God so loved the world (John 3:16) is the essence of the gospel. To love God with all your heart, soul, and mind and your neighbor as yourself is the fulfilment of the whole law (Matt. 22:37-39). He that hateth his brother is a murderer (I John 3:15). He that hath pity upon the poor lendeth unto the Lord (Prov. 19:17). Fear not them which are able to kill the body (Matt. 10:28). The emotions enrich Christian worship. Church architecture, music, art windows, subdued light, liturgies, vestments, symbolism, incense, candles, etc. all appeal to the emotions. Christian faith sanctifies and purifies our emotions.

ALFRED M. REHWINKEL

EMPEROR-WORSHIP. See DEIFICATION.

ENCRATITES. Encratites was a term used, not for any particular sect, but for those who in the early church lived a life of strict discipline (Greek *egkrateis*, Latin *continentes*, hence the alternative name Continents). The main point of their asceticism seems to have been in respect of wine and flesh, though celibacy was also practiced. The apologist Tatian had Encratite connections, and though it was quite possible for Encratites to be strictly orthodox there was undoubtedly a Gnostic and docetic tendency in many such circles. It was in this milieu that much of the NT apocryphal literature originated (cf. *HERE*).

WILLIAM KELLY

ENCYCLICAL. A circular letter (Greek *egkuklios*). It is confined in modern times almost exclusively to papal documents, although the term has been applied to the letters sent out by the bishops of the Lambeth Conference to churches of the Anglican communion. An encyclical varies from a Bull (a solemn mandate with the Pope's seal, *bulla*) and a Brief (a less formal papal letter sealed with the Pope's signet ring). There is no particular form by which to identify an encyclical, though some definitely use the name in the opening words. Recent popes have adopted the encyclical as the means of making many important utterances on questions theological and social. The Pope's authority does not constitute an encyclical an infallible utterance.

RICHARD J. COATES

END. See ESCHATOLOGY, AGE.

ENDURANCE. The word endurance is derived from the Latin verb *indurare* meaning "to make hard." Endurance is the capacity to endure, the power to be hard or strong in the face of suffering, persecution or pain, to bear up in sorrow, to be longsuffering, patient and tolerant with others, to be firm and steadfast in trials and temptation, to be unmovable in the faith. He that endureth to the end shall be saved (Matt. 10:22; 24:13). To continue in the faith (Col. 1:23; I Cor. 9:24), to remain firm in temptation (James 1:12), to remain steadfast (James 5:11), to stand fast in confidence (Heb. 3:6, 14) — these are manifestations of endurance.

ALFRED M. REHWINKEL

ENEMY. In the OT the enemy of Israel (or of the godly) was *ipso facto* the enemy of God. The imprecatory Psalms and the attitude toward gentile nations must, therefore, be understood in this religio-political sense: God's attitude toward evil itself is expressed in his attitude toward "the enemy." The NT term is applied to Satan (Matt. 13:39), evil powers (I Cor. 15:25 f.), unregenerate men (Col. 1:21), and personal enemies (Matt. 5:43 f.). But the OT connotation is not absent (Luke 1:74), and "true Israel" underlies the meaning virtually throughout. See *TWNT*.

E. EARLE ELLIS

ENLIGHTENMENT, THE. The Enlightenment (Aufklaerung), was a most important rationalistic movement in German theology, philosophy and literature, headed by Lessing, Nicolai and Moses Mendelssohn in the middle of the eighteenth century. Carrying the rationalistic principle further, it revolted against the existing Wolffian compromise which had built a superstructure of revelation on the basis of rational truth, and insisted that even the documents and truths of Christianity must be subjected to rational analysis. While he avoided the excesses of Voltaire, Lessing pressed this analysis to the doubting of the historical reliability of the NT in his publication and defense of the *Wolffenbuettel Fragments* by Reimarus. He himself found certain truths of reason underlying the Bible, and thought the Bible a useful means of conveying them to the ignorant. This was an extremer form of the neologising by means of which the more advanced theologians tried to meet the challenge of the Enlightenment, giving to all the Christian doctrines an attenuated, rational significance. The philosophical basis of the Enlightenment was virtually destroyed by

Kant, and its theology superseded by that of Schleiermacher, but its influence remained in the higher critical movement and the neological impulses of the following century.

BIBLIOGRAPHY

K. Aner, *Die Theologie der Lessingszeit*; E. Cassirer, *The Philosophy of the Enlightenment*; H. Chadwick, *Lessing's Theological Writings*; H. B. Garland, *Lessing.*

GEOFFREY W. BROMILEY

ENOCH. Genesis 5 is the prime source in the OT for information about the patriarch Enoch. He was assumed into heaven, and because of this an extensive Jewish lore grew up around his name (see L. Ginzberg, *The Legends of the Jews,* Jewish Publication Society, Philadelphia, 1946, Vol. VII, pp. 137, 138). Luke 3:37 mentions him, and in Heb. 11:5 he is cited as one of the heroes of the faith.

Three Jewish pseudepigraphical books bear his name. First in date and importance is "Ethiopic Enoch," an edited collection of writings treating a common general apocalyptic theme, and dating from the last two centuries B.C. The name "Ethiopic" points to the language of the extant version, although originally the book was composed in either Hebrew or Aramaic. Ethiopic Enoch may be divided into five sections: (1) chaps. 1-36 are a discussion of angels and the universe; (2) chaps. 37-71, the "Similitudes of Enoch," constitute apocalyptic descriptions of the end time; (3) chaps. 72-82 are called "The Book of the Heavenly Luminaries"; (4) chaps. 83-90 contain two visions; and (5) chaps. 91-104 include the well-known "Apocalypse of Weeks" which divides human history into ten parts, seven past (from the author's standpoint), and three to come. Much debate has been prompted by Enoch's use of the term "Son of Man" (46:2, 3 ff.), especially concerning its origin, its meaning in Enoch and its significance for Jesus' use of the title. There is no doubt that it is a messianic appellation, and some (e.g., R. Otto) hold that Jesus borrowed it from Enoch. The better case may be made for Dan. 7:14 as the source of Jesus' usage. Jude 14, 15 cites Enoch to enforce his discussion about future judgment upon the ungodly.

A second book bearing Enoch's name is "Slavonic Enoch," sometimes also called "The Book of the Secrets of Enoch." Once thought to have been written in the first century A.D., it is now quite commonly agreed to be of later date, possibly as late as the seventh century A.D. It was written originally in Greek, and betrays a typical apocalyptic genre, treating of visions, angels, heaven, hell, sun, moon, stars and divisions of future time. Last is "Third Enoch" which is also post-Christian. It is of minor importance because of its late date and fragmentary character.

DAVID H. WALLACE

ENVY. In the OT *qānā', qin'â* (derived from the blush of emotion) are translated "jealousy," "zeal," or "envy" according to sense. Envy is always bad, jealousy and zeal are frequently good. Similarly "to eye" (I Sam. 18:9) and "the evil eye" (Ecclus. 14:8, 10; Matt. 20:15; Mark 7:22) express envy. In the NT *zēlos* ("jealousy," "zeal," seldom "envy") can be good or bad; *phthonos* ("envy") is always evil (except James 4:5; R. V. G. Tasker, *The General Epistle of James,* Tyndale Press, London, 1956, pp. 90, 91, 105). Trench discriminates between envy as passively and jealousy as actively antagonistic towards another's good. *HDCG* ("Envy") relates envy to desire for another's possession and jealousy to rivalry for a common objective. But envy (e.g., Joseph's brethren, Saul towards David and the chief priests towards Christ) has reference to an inalienable possession (paternal love, victorious honors or spiritual greatness), while jealousy and zeal, good and bad (Gal. 4:17, 18), relate to alterable circumstances. Envy is essentially devilish (Wisd. 2:24; I John 3:12; see I Clem. 3) and a work of the flesh (Gal. 5:21), and was a "deadly sin" in later moral theology.

GEORGE J. C. MARCHANT

EPICUREANS. Adherents of the Greek philosopher Epicurus (341-270 B.C.). He founded a community in Athens, condemned excess, and commanded a simple mode of life. He discouraged ambition and counselled retirement from the world. The gods were not supernatural beings, controlling nature from without. The soul is a corporal substance. Happiness and the avoidance of pain are the chief ends in life. Feelings are the touchstone of conduct (cf. I Cor. 15:32). Rabbinic Judaism used the name as a stock synonym for a materialist or infidel. Bentham's Hedonism is a modern version of Epicurean teaching.

RICHARD E. HIGGINSON

EPIPHANY. The feast of the Epiphany takes place on the twelfth day after Christmas, viz., Jan. 6. The name is derived from the Greek *epiphaneia* ("manifestation"), and the

festival is accordingly of Eastern origin. It celebrated on the one day the nativity of our Lord,
his baptism in the Jordan, and the manifestation of his glory at Cana's wedding feast (John
2:11). When in the fourth century the Greek
Church adopted the Roman usage as to Christmas (Dec. 25), the Epiphany began to be observed in the West as a separate festival and
became associated with the manifestation of
Christ to the Gentiles in the persons of the
wise men (Matt. 2:1-11). The day is now
closely connected with Christmas, marking the
close of the festivities in honor of our Lord's
birth. In the Greek Church the Epiphany still
retains its character as a feast of the baptism
of Christ.

FRANK COLQUHOUN

EPISCOPACY, EPISCOPAL. These
terms are derived from the Greek *episcopos,*
meaning "bishop." They refer accordingly to
that system of church government in which
the principal officer is the bishop. In recent
times there have appeared Methodist Episco-
pals, with bishops as their chief officers, but
with no connection with the "historic" ministry, i.e., with that ministry which goes back to
a remote antiquity in a direct line of ordinations from bishop to bishop. They do not accordingly come within episcopacy in the traditional sense.

The antiquity of episcopacy is disputed.
Some hold it to be the primitive form of
church government, and that it is to be discerned in the NT. The evidence for this, however, is not convincing. But it had certainly
made its appearance by the second century,
and in time it became practically universal.

Characteristic of episcopacy is the presence
of one bishop (though he may have assistants
called suffragans or coadjutors) in each diocese. He is the supreme officer, but is expected
not to govern without taking note of the special functions of the other orders. He is not a
despot. The bishop is the ordaining officer.
He officiates at all ordinations, though presbyters also join with him in ordinations to the
presbyterate. The actual work of a bishop has
varied considerably through history. At one
time he was apparently very much like our
parish minister, then we may discern the
evangelist or missionary, the royal counselor,
the feudal noble, the politician of Whig and
Tory times, the administrator of modern days,
and others. But his essential function is that

of pastor of his flock. He is the supervisor of
his diocese. He is a "father in God" to his
people. He performs rites like confirmation
and ordination. It is in this, and not in anything else that the essence of episcopacy consists.

LEON MORRIS

EPISTEMOLOGY. Epistemology is the
science of the nature and possibility of knowledge; religious epistemology, the science of religious knowledge. The relation of the concepts
of thought to the religious Reality, and of religious knowledge to knowledge in general,
are pressing issues of contemporary theology
and philosophy. Such questions are at stake
as: In what sense is theology a science? Is the
Christian knowledge of God a form of knowledge in general (albeit a special form), or does
it have a validity all its own? Is there a unique
source and avenue, and/or a unique criterion,
of Christian knowledge? These questions turn
on the definition of knowledge, on the right
of religion to claim knowledge-status for its affirmations, and on the validity of the Christian
claim to a distinctive knowledge of God over
against other world religions.

I. BIBLICAL TERMS. The Bible does not
systematically present a theory of knowledge,
yet it excludes many theories and implies one
of its own. Its approach is not abstract and
speculative, but ethico-religious (cf. Gen. 2:17;
John 8:32). Its frame of reference is God as
Truth (cf. John 1:1, where the Logos is
identified with Deity), the universe as a rational creation (cf. Gen. 1-2), and man as the
unique bearer of the divine image (Gen.
1:26). The Logos is the source of all knowledge, not simply of the knowledge of God
(John 1:4, 9). All knowledge, therefore, in
some sense has the character of revelation.
Human reason is a divinely fashioned instrument for its apprehension.

Man stands in perpetual relation to God, to
other selves, and to the world. His natural
knowledge of God springs from an immediate
relationship through conscience, not simply by
inference from nature and history in which
the Creator is also revealed (Ps. 19, Rom.
1-2).

The problem of knowledge is never raised
in Scripture simply through an analysis of
human cognition. Man the knower is a self,
conditioned by will and emotions as well as by
thought. As truth and goodness are united in

the divine nature, so knowledge exists for the sake of spiritual and moral obedience. The Scriptures enforce this point by a turn of phrase that seems strange to modern readers because of Greek philosophical influence upon the West. They speak not simply of knowing the truth, but of *doing* truth (cf. John 3:21; Gal. 3:1; I John 1:6, 7, 2:8-11; II John 4; III John 3). Man was fashioned by divine creation for spiritual fellowship and obedience.

Although immediately related to God through conscience, and confronted continually in nature and history with the revelation of God's existence, fallen man seeks constantly to suppress this awareness of God (Rom. 1:18 ff.) and distorts it for his own comfort and convenience in sin. Scripture does not teach that man as sinner attains a trustworthy knowledge of God on the basis of general revelation alone; rather, although emphasizing the fact of general divine revelation, it stresses man's blindness in sin and the reality of the special redemptive revelation addressed to him. In view of man's moral revolt against the Creator and his predicament in sin, his restoration to the true knowledge of and fellowship with God is a work of divine grace. The scriptural revelation of redemptive love objectively discloses the nature and purposes of God, simultaneously holding out the prospect of the remission of sins. Ontologically, the high point of that special revelation is Jesus of Nazareth; epistemologically, the sacred Scriptures.

In a striking turn of vocabulary, the Bible employs the term "to know" (Hebrew, *yāda'*; Greek, *ginōskō*) of the most intimate personal relationship between human beings, sexual intercourse between man and wife (Gen. 4:1, 17, 23; Matt. 1:25) and also of personal communion with God available to the redeemed sinner (John 14:7; 17:3).

II. RELATED ISSUES. The *imago Dei,* broken by sin but not destroyed, survives in every human life as a point of contact for the gospel, the God of creation and of redemption being one (John 1:3, 14). But man's revolt against God becomes more pronounced as the interpretation of life and existence is formalized from the standpoint of sin and revolt. As systems of thought, the great religions and philosophies must be viewed not simply as inadequate but false. The emphasis on Christianity as true religion gives point to the fact that Platonism, Aristotelianism, Hegelianism, and so forth, as systems of thought, delineate

false gods. Yet in some respects even secular views seem inevitably to borrow facets of the biblical ideology (even in the distorted pagan expositions the living God is not "without a witness,". cf. Acts 17:28), although as speculative systems they proceed on first principles antithetical to the Christian revelation. Yet as persons men retain a point-of-contact with the gospel in the broken *imago Dei.*

Contemporary theology suffers still from the influence of Kant's critical philosophy, which excludes cognitive knowledge of the supernatural world, and derives the content of knowledge exclusively from sensation. While Kant insists that the forms of reason are innate, he arbitrarily dismisses the view that they are divinely created, hence that man as bearer of the *imago Dei* is especially endowed for knowledge of God and his works. Man is indeed not passive in the knowledge situation but, if biblical theism be true, he is not ultimately creative, but is fashioned to think God's thoughts after him.

Assuming some genuine knowledge to be possible to man, we face the question whether the peculiar religious claim to knowledge is valid. As an experience of the whole self, knowledge may involve overtones of volition and feeling, but the cognitive element discriminates it as intellectual. What lies outside our conceptual grasp also lies outside the possibility of effective transmission to others; communicable knowledge consists of judgments that satisfy the law of non-contradiction. While a distinction is necessary between religious knowledge and knowledge in general, an absolute distinction is unwarranted. Knowledge is one; it must meet the test of logical consistency and coherence, or it is not knowledge. Christianity is a religion (cf. James 1:27: "pure religion") and is not in all respects to be contrasted with religion (cf. Calvin's *The Institutes of the Christian Religion*), although it is peculiarly a religion of special historical revelation. Christianity involves a unique avenue of knowledge therefore: special divine disclosure based on the initiative of the living God. It has, moreover, its own conditions — repentance and faith — for living access to this way of knowledge. Yet neither the instrument of knowledge (cognition) nor the test or criterion of knowledge (consistency and coherence) are unique. For that reason, although Christian revelation communicates a higher knowledge, both as dealing with supernatural realities and as conveying what is otherwise beyond man's ken, the content of revelation has a genuine knowledge-status. The validity of knowledge is one in kind, although its sources and methods may be multiple.

The relation of the religious Object and the God-concept, as well as the relation of religious knowledge to general knowledge, remain fundamental issues in contemporary thought. Influential representations are: (1) Religious knowledge is a species of knowledge in general, but Hebrew-Christian religion involves a special historical disclosure of God implying a special method and avenue of knowledge (Augustine, Calvin). (2) Religious knowledge is a species of knowledge in general, involving no distinctive way of truth and no distinctive methodology (D. C. Macintosh). (3) Religious knowledge is not a species of knowledge in general (Kant). (4) Christian knowledge is not a species of knowledge in general; it involves not only a special avenue and method, but special criteria, being non-conceptual and self-validating (Barth). Inherent in the views asserting the existence of the religious Reality independently of the knowing mind, yet denying an epistemological overlapping of human concepts and the religious Object, is a dual difficulty: that of avoiding religious agnosticism, and that of preserving the ultimate unity of knowledge.

See also TRUTH, KNOW, KNOWLEDGE.

BIBLIOGRAPHY

Karl Barth, *The Doctrine of the Word of God;* Emil Brunner, *Revelation and Reason;* Gordon H. Clark, *Thales to Dewey;* Calvin, *Institutes;* Carl F. H. Henry, *The Drift of Western Thought;* J. Gresham Machen, *What Is Faith?;* D. C. Macintosh, *The Problem of Religious Knowledge;* C. Van Til, *The New Modernism;* B. B. Warfield, *Studies in Theology.*

CARL F. H. HENRY

EPISTLE. The word comes directly from the Greek word *epistolē.* It is the regular word for a letter (*q.v.*), and it is used often in Acts and the Pauline Epistles and twice in II Peter. In the AV and ASV it is translated "epistle" or "letter" with almost equal frequency; the RSV uses "letter" only.

A distinction is often made between a letter and an epistle. A letter is actually written from one person or group to another person or group, whereas an epistle is in the form of a letter but is meant for general circulation. If this distinction is made, we should call the NT "epistles" letters. All the books called epistles and all the epistles mentioned in the NT are letters in the fullest sense. Usually we know the very names of the persons who wrote them and also the persons or groups to whom they were written. They were written for specific purposes to meet definite needs.

In interpreting an epistle or letter, then, we should strive to discover all we possibly can about the author, the person or persons to whom the letter was written, the place and time of writing, and as much as possible about the conditions of both the author and the recipient. After we have discovered what messages the author intended to convey to his original readers, we can then apply those messages to our own needs today, as our needs may be similar to those of the original readers.

It is customary to divide the NT Epistles into the Pauline and the catholic, or general, Epistles, though these divisions are not too exact. The Epistles are very important for giving us insight at first hand into the life and thought of the early Christian church.

SAMUEL A. CARTLEDGE

ERASTIANISM. Erastianism takes its name from Thomas Erastus (1524-83) who was born at Baden, studied theology at Basel, and later medicine, becoming Professor of Medicine at Heidelberg. He was the friend of Beza and Bullinger and was a Zwinglian.

A controversy arose in Heidelberg as to the powers of the presbytery. Erastus emphasized strongly the right of the state (*q.v.*) to intervene in ecclesiastical matters. He held that the church has no scriptural authority to excommunicate any of its members. As God has entrusted to the civil magistrate (i.e., the state) the sum total of the visible government, the church in a Christian country has no power of repression distinct from the state. To have two visible authorities in a country would be absurd. The church can merely warn or censure offenders. Punitive action belongs to the civil magistrate alone. The church has no right to withhold the sacraments from offenders.

In practice, the term Erastianism is somewhat elastic. Figgis calls it: "the theory that religion is the creature of the state." Generally, it signifies that the state is supreme in ecclesiastical causes, but Erastus dealt only with the disciplinary powers of the church. When the Roman emperors became Christian the relations of civil and ecclesiastical rulers became a real problem. It became universally accepted until modern times that the state could punish heretics or put them to death.

The name Erastian emerged in England in the Westminster Assembly (1643) when outstanding men like Selden and Whitelocke advocated the supremacy of the state over the church. The Assembly rejected this view and decided that church and state have their separate but co-ordinate spheres, each supreme in its own province but bound to co-operate with one another for the glory of God.

BIBLIOGRAPHY
HERE; EncyBrit; W. Cunningham, Historical Theology, pp. 396 ff.

ALEXANDER M. RENWICK

ERROR. The words error and err (derived from Latin erro, "to wander") are used in Scripture chiefly to translate words from two OT roots, šāgâ or šāgâg and tārâ, and one basic NT word, planaomai, planē. These words suggest the idea of straying or wandering.

Error is, first of all, a wandering from the truth and is not merely the absence of truth but the presence of a positive conviction of the truth of what is really false (knowledge, falsely so called I Tim. 6:20-21; see also II Tim. 2:18) or of the falsity of what is really true (saying there is no resurrection, Mark 12:18, 27).

More frequently, in Scripture, error represents a departure from right conduct (Num. 15:22; Ps. 119:21; Jude 11, etc). In either case, the emphasis is upon the unpremeditated character of the act. It is arrived at by "wandering" rather than by deliberate plan. At this point it is to be distinguished from heresy or sect (hairesis), which suggests both voluntary choice and self-conscious commitment and which is not necessarily bad (though almost always so in the NT except possibly for Acts 26:5).

Error and heresy are often distinguished by degree of importance. Error suggests minor deviations of faith or conduct, heresy a departure from the truth so grievous as to impair the structure of the faith as a whole. Errors may be permitted within the Christian fellowship, heresy passes beyond the permissible bounds of fellowship.

This does not quite point up the NT distinction between these two words, however. It is true that heresy is a commitment outside the bounds of what is legitimately Christian. Error is a much broader word. It indicates divergence in conduct as well as thought and

may refer to less serious departures (Lev. 5:18; Ps. 19:12; James 1:16) or, on the other hand, to departures from right faith and conduct so serious as to destroy any possible fellowship (I John 4:6; James 5:19; Rom. 1:27).

For the correction of error, whether venial or mortal, whether of thought or of conduct, man must apply to the Holy Scriptures and to the power of God, which are able to correct the thought and to cleanse the conduct (Matt. 22:29; Ps. 19:7-12. See also I John 4:6).

BIBLIOGRAPHY
Arndt; H. Schlier in TWNT; KB.

KENNETH S. KANTZER

ESCHATOLOGY. Eschatology is traditionally defined as the doctrine of the "last things" (Greek eschata) — in relation either to the individual human being (in which case they comprise death, resurrection, judgment and the afterlife) or to the world. In this latter respect, some would confine "eschatology" to the absolute end of the world, thus excluding much that commonly falls within its scope. Such a restriction is not warranted by biblical usage. Hebrew be'aḥărît hayyāmîm, rendered in the LXX en tais eschatais hēmerais ("in the last — or latter — days"), may mean the end of the present order or even, more generally, "hereafter." It is therefore best to define eschatology fairly broadly. The biblical conception of time is not cyclical (like the Greek conception, in which eschatology at best could refer only to the completion of a cycle) nor purely linear (in which case eschatology could refer only to the terminal point of the line); it presents us rather with a pattern in which divine judgment and redemption combine in a rhythm which "finds characteristic expression in terms of death and resurrection" (Charles Harold Dodd, According to the Scriptures, Nisbet, London, 1952, p. 129). This being so, the term may be used "to designate the consummation of God's redemptive purpose whether or not an 'end of history' or of the world is anticipated" (George Eldon Ladd, EQ, 30, 1958, p. 140), whether the consummation is the absolutely final one, or a "springing and germinant accomplishment" revealed in the unfolding rhythm of God's purpose.

I. INDIVIDUAL ESCHATOLOGY IN THE OT. The ideas about existence after death (q.v.) expressed in much of the OT are very shadowy. As Jesus told the Pharisees, deeper truths were implicit in men's relation to God:

the God who calls himself the God of Abraham, Isaac and Jacob (Ex. 3:6) "is not God of the dead, but of the living; for all live unto him" (Luke 20:38). But these implications were not generally realized in OT times. It may have been partly in reaction against Canaanite cults of the dead that the OT lays such little emphasis upon the afterlife. *She'ol* is viewed as a vast underworld region where the dead dwell together as shades; their former status and character are of little account there. The praises of God, which engaged so much of a pious man's activity in life, remained unsung in *She'ol* (Ps. 88:10 ff.; Isa. 39:18); in popular thought *She'ol* was outside Yahweh's jurisdiction. Only occasionally do we find a more hopeful note. The writers of Pss. 73 and 139 know that a man who walks with God in life cannot be deprived of his companionship in death: "If I make my bed in Sheol, thou art there!" (Ps. 139:8). Job and his friends mostly discount the possibility that a man will live again after he dies (Job 14:10 ff.); they do not suppose that the comforts of a future existence can compensate for the sufferings of the present. Only in one moment of upleaping faith does Job assert that, if not in this life, then after death he will find one to vindicate his cause, and that this one will be God himself (Job 19:25 ff.).

A more explicit expectation of a life to come is bound up with the hope of a national resurrection. In Ezekiel's vision of the valley of dry bones the dead warriors receive new life when the divine breath enters them; but the interpretation of the vision points not to an individual but to a national resurrection: "these bones are the whole house of Israel" (Ezek. 37:11). In the Isaiah-apocalypse there is a further promise of resurrection — "Thy dead shall live, their bodies shall rise" (Isa. 26:19) — but even here it is arguable that national restoration is intended. Individual resurrection first becomes explicit in Dan. 12:2: "Many of those who sleep in the dust of the earth shall awake, some to everlasting life, and some to shame and everlasting contempt."

Henceforth the belief in the future resurrection of the dead came to be part of Jewish orthodoxy except among the Sadducees, who in this regard looked on themselves as the champions of the old-time religion against Pharisaic innovations. The belief received a tremendous impetus from the persecution of the martyrs under Antiochus Epiphanes in the years following 168 B.C.

With the new emphasis on resurrection (*q.v.*) goes a tendency to distinguish more sharply between the fortunes of the righteous and the wicked in the world to come, in Paradise and Gehenna respectively, and even in the intermediate state between death and resurrection (cf. Dives and Lazarus in Luke 16:19 ff.).

But in biblical teaching it is supremely Christ who, by his death and resurrection, has begotten his people anew to a living hope (I Pet. 1:3), because he has "abolished death and brought life and immortality to light through the gospel" (II Tim. 1:10).

II. WORLD ESCHATOLOGY IN THE OT. OT eschatology is closely linked with the concept of "the day of the LORD." In the earliest significant occurrence of this phrase (Amos 5:18-20), Amos rebukes his fellow countrymen for desiring this day so eagerly, assuring them that when it comes it will bring not light (as they hope) but darkness, not rejoicing but mourning. From the context it is evident that this was the day when Yahweh was expected to vindicate himself and his people against the ungodly. But Amos insists that, since Yahweh is so utterly righteous, his intervention to vindicate his own cause will involve his judgment on unrighteousness wherever it appears, and especially if it appears among his chosen people, because they had better opportunities of knowing his will than the other nations had.

Perhaps the Israelites' idea of the day of Yahweh was associated with an annual autumnal festival at which they celebrated the kingship of Yahweh. If the so-called "enthronement psalms" (e.g., Ps. 93; 95-100) can be used as evidence for this festival, we may infer that Yahweh's kingship was celebrated in a number of ways. He was sovereign over creation; he was sovereign in his seasonal gifts of fertility and harvest; he was sovereign in his redemptive dealings with his people Israel; he was sovereign in his dealings with other nations too. His sovereignty in all those spheres would be fully manifested on a universal scale on the day when he came to "judge the world with righteousness" (Pss. 9:8; 96:13; 98:9). The psalmists and prophets recognized that, while Yahweh's kingship was already exercised in so many ways, the reality which they saw fell far short of what they knew to be the ideal. Yahweh's sovereignty did not receive due acknowledgment even in Israel, not to speak of those nations which had never known him. This disparity between the actual and the ideal would not endure for ever; on the day of Yahweh his righteous kingship would be universally acknowledged, and the earth would be filled with "the knowledge of the LORD" (Isa. 11:9; cf. Hab. 2:14). On that day, said a later prophet, "the LORD will become king over all the earth; on that day the LORD will be one and his name one" (Zech. 14:9). The day of Yahweh, here and in several other places, is the occasion of a theophany; in Zech. 14:3 f. Yahweh leads the attack upon his people's assailants and plants his feet victoriously on Mount Olivet.

One factor which emphasized the contrast between what was and what ought to be was the decline of the Davidic monarchy. The house of David represented the divine kingship on earth; but when disruption, social injustice and foreign invasion had reduced its pristine grandeur, its capacity to be a worthy representative of God's sovereignty was impaired. But, as the fortunes of David's house sink lower and lower, we find emerging with increasing clarity the figure of a coming king of David's line in whom God would fulfil all the bright promises which he had made to David, a king who would restore and surpass the vanished glories of earlier days (cf. Isa. 7:13 ff.; 9:6 f.; 11:1 ff.; 32:1 ff.; Mic. 5:2 ff.; Jer. 23:5 f.; 33:14 ff.).

Much of later Jewish eschatology is dominated by this hope of a Davidic Messiah — a Messiah who would inaugurate the new age by vanquishing his people's enemies and ascending the throne as God's permanent vicegerent. At times, however, the Davidic prince is overshadowed by the priesthood in portrayals of the coming age; this is evident, for example, in Ezekiel's program for the new commonwealth in the age of restoration when Yahweh would take up his abode amid his people. A later instance of the same form of expectation is found in the Qumran literature, where the Davidic Messiah is plainly envisaged as subordinate to the chief priest, who will be head of the state in the age to come.

In the Book of Daniel another form of the eschatological hope appears. Although the Hebrew monarchy is no more, the Most High has not abdicated his kingship; he continues to rule in the kingdoms of men and the various pagan rulers in their successive empires attain power by his will and hold it only so long as he permits. The epoch of pagan dominion is limited; when the last pagan empire has fallen, the God of heaven will set up a kingdom which will endure for ever. In the vision of the day of judgment described in Dan. 7, this eternal and universal dominion is given at the time of the end to "one like a son of man" (vs. 13), who is associated, if not equated, in the interpretation of the vision with "the saints of the Most High" (vss. 18, 22, 27).

As time went on, the day of the LORD was increasingly portrayed in apocalyptic language (cf. Isa. 24:1 ff.; Joel 2:30; 3:9 ff.; Mal. 3:16 — 4:6) — although such language is found even in the pre-exilic prophets (cf. Jer. 4:23-26, with its picture of "Chaos come again"; Zeph. 1:2 ff.). And not only the pictorial language of apocalyptic, but the very idea of the day of the LORD, as his active intervention and not simply as an inevitable development from the current situation, is present in the prophets, although it receives sharpened emphasis in the apocalyptists.

Some apocalyptic literature also betrays the influence of Zoroastrianism, in which there was a well-defined conception of a day of ultimate reckoning, separation and regeneration, when evil would be burned up in purifying fire and the "desired dominion" of good would be established.

One interesting sample of eschatological expectation at the end of the pre-Christian era is provided by the Qumran literature, mentioned above (see also DEAD SEA SCROLLS).

III. NT ESCHATOLOGY: JESUS AND THE KINGDOM OF GOD. In passing from the OT to the NT, we mark a change in eschatological emphasis. OT eschatology is forward-looking; its dominant notes are those of hope and promise. While these are present in the NT too, the dominant note here is that of fulfilment — in Jesus. This is apparent even in NT books which otherwise differ considerably. Thus, no two books are more diverse in literary form than John's Gospel and the Revelation, but when we get behind the form to the substance, we hear in both of them one whose name is "The Word of God" saying to his followers: "In the world you have tribulation; but be of good cheer, I have overcome the world" (John 16:33; cf. Rev. 5:5; 19:13).

With the ministry of Jesus biblical eschatology reaches its decisive moment. His Galilean ministry, as summarized in Mark 1:15 ("The time is fulfilled, and the kingdom of God is at hand; repent, and believe in the gospel"), proclaims the fulfilment of Daniel's vision: "The time came when the saints received the kingdom" (Dan. 7:22). In one sense the kingdom of God was already present in Jesus' ministry: "If it is by the finger of God that I cast out demons, then the kingdom of God has come upon you" (Luke 11:20; cf. Matt. 12:28). But in another sense the kingdom of God (q.v.) was something yet future, for which he taught his disciples to pray: "Thy kingdom come" (Luke 11:2). This was the sense in which it would come "with power" (Mark 9:1) — an event associated with the *parousia* ("advent") of the Son of Man "in clouds with great power and glory" (Mark 13:26).

This figure of the Son of Man, who plays such a prominent part in Jesus' teaching about the kingdom of God, especially after Peter's confession at Caesarea Philippi (Mark 8:29), goes back to the "one like a son of man" whom Daniel saw in his vision of judgment (Dan. 7:13 f.). In Jesus' teaching it becomes increasingly plain that he himself is to fulfil this role. But while he does on occasion echo Daniel's language and speak of the Son of Man as "coming with the clouds of heaven" (Mark 14:62), he more often speaks of the Son of Man as destined to suffer, using language strongly reminiscent of the portrayal of the obedient and suffering Servant of Yahweh in Isa. 52:15 — 53:12. This practical identification of the Son of Man with the Servant may not have been a complete innovation (Daniel's "one like a son of man" is perhaps one of the earliest, if not indeed the earliest, of the many interpretations of the Servant); but Jesus' way of speaking about the Son of Man in terms of the Servant is quite distinctive, for not only did he identify these two figures with each other, but he presented himself as the one who would fulfil them both at once in his own person. As Daniel's "one like a son of man" receives the kingdom from the Ancient of Days, so in the Gospels Jesus receives the kingdom from his Father. But as in Dan. 7:18 ff. "the saints of the Most High" receive the kingdom, so Jesus shares the kingdom with his disciples, his "little flock" (Luke 12:32; 22:29 f.). It is clear from his teaching, however, that the fulness of the kingdom — its coming "with power" — must await the suffering of the Son of Man.

Occasionally Jesus uses the term "life" — more fully, "eternal life" (the life of the age

to come) — as a synonym of "the kingdom of God"; to enter into the kingdom is to enter into life. This accords with the view then current, that the kingdom of God would be established in the new age, when the righteous would be brought back from death to enjoy without end resurrection life.

In the apostolic teaching (which here makes explicit what was implicit in Jesus' own words) this eternal life is something which may be enjoyed in the present, although its full flowering may await a consummation yet to come. For the death and resurrection of Christ have introduced a new phase of the kingdom of God, so that those who believe in Christ already share his resurrection life, even while they live on earth in a mortal body. There is an interval (be it shorter or longer) between the resurrection of Christ and his *parousia,* and during this interval ("the last hour") the age to come overlaps the present age (q.v.). Christians live spiritually in "that age" while they live temporally in "this age"; they possess eternal life before the resurrection of the body has taken place.

This outlook, which is specially characteristic of the writings of Paul and John, has been called "realized eschatology." But the "realized eschatology" of the NT, unlike much that goes by that name today, does not exclude an eschatological consummation in the future.

IV. "Realized Eschatology." What is the *eschaton,* the "last thing," which is the proper object of eschatological hope? If it came in the ministry, passion and triumph of Jesus, then it cannot be the absolute end of time (q.v.), for time has continued to flow on since then. Perhaps we should say that the NT reveals the "last thing" to be really the "Last One" — the *Eschatos* (masculine) rather than the *eschaton* (neuter). (We may compare Jesus' title "The First and the Last" in Rev. 1:17; 2:8; 22:13.) That is to say, Jesus is himself the fulfilment of the hope of the people of God, the "Amen" to all God's promises.

A generation or two ago the most significant name in this field of study was Albert Schweitzer, with his "thorough-going eschatology." According to him, Jesus, who believed himself to be Israel's Messiah of the end time, found that the consummation did not arrive when he expected it, and embraced death in order that thus his *parousia* as the promised "Anointed One" would be forcibly brought to pass. Since the wheel of world history would not respond to his hand and turn round to complete its last revolution, he threw himself upon it and was broken by it. "The wheel rolls onward, and the mangled body of the one immeasurably great Man, who was strong enough to think of Himself as the spiritual ruler of mankind and to bend history to his purpose, is hanging upon it still. That is His victory and His reign" (*The Quest of the Historical Jesus*, Black, London, 1911, p. 369). The thought and message of Jesus, that is to say, was basically eschatological, and eschatological in the sense exemplified by the crudest apocalypticism of his day. His ethical teaching was designed only for the brief interim-period between his ministry and his imminent *parousia*. Later, when his death was seen to have destroyed the eschatological conditions instead of bringing them in, the proclamation of the kingdom was replaced by the teaching of the church.

While Schweitzer's interpretation of the message of Jesus was in its way a healthy reaction to the liberal interpretation which he rejected, it was equally one-sided and exaggerated in its selection from the Gospel data. One may acknowledge the value of his contribution to the debate without accepting his interpretation.

More recently C. H. Dodd, with his "realized eschatology," has become possibly the most significant name in this field (especially in Britain). In his *Parables of the Kingdom* (Nisbet, London, 1935), he interprets Jesus' parables in terms of the challenge to decision with which men are confronted as he proclaims the gospel of the kingdom. In *The Apostolic Preaching and its Developments* (Hodder and Stoughton, London, 1936), "the kingdom of God is conceived as coming in the events of the life, death and resurrection of Jesus, and to proclaim these facts, in their proper setting, is to preach the Gospel of the Kingdom of God" (pp. 46 f.). Here no reference is made to a future coming of Jesus. The historic events of the gospel constitute an eschatological process, "a decisive manifestation of the mighty acts of God for the salvation of man"; and the later concentration on a "last thing" yet to come was the result of a relapse into Jewish eschatology which had the effect of relegating to a secondary place just those elements of the gospel which are most distinctive of Christianity. In a later work, however — *The Com-*

ing of Christ (Cambridge University Press, 1951) — Dodd appears to allow a future consummation associated with the person of Christ: what came to earth with Christ's incarnation "was final and decisive for the whole meaning and purpose of human existence, and we shall meet it again when history has been wound up . . . At the last frontier-post we shall encounter God in Christ" (p. 58).

A similar position to Dodd's is taken up by Joachim Jeremias in *The Parables of Jesus* (S.C.M., London, 1954); indeed, Jeremias acknowledges his indebtedness to Dodd. According to Jeremias, the parables of Jesus express an eschatology "that is in process of realization"; they proclaim that "the hour of fulfilment is come" and compel hearers to make up their minds about the person and mission of Jesus (p. 159).

There is no more stimulating thinker of this school than John Arthur Thomas Robinson. His *In the End, God* . . . (Clarke, London, 1950) interprets the *parousia* of Christ not as a literal event of the future but as a symbolical or mythological presentation of "what must happen, and is happening already, whenever the Christ comes in love and power, wherever are to be traced the signs of His presence, wherever to be seen the marks of His cross. Judgment Day is a dramatized, idealized picture of every day" (p. 69). In a later work, *Jesus and His Coming* (S.C.M., London, 1957), he faces the crucial question: Did Jesus ever use language which suggested that he would return to earth from heaven? A critical examination of the data leads him to answer "No." Jesus' sayings on the subject really express the twin themes of vindication and visitation, e.g., his reply to the high priest's question whether or not he was the Messiah (Mark 14:62 f.): "I am; and you will see the Son of man sitting at the right hand of Power, and coming with the clouds of heaven." In Matt. 26:64 and Luke 22:69 a word or phrase meaning "from now on" or "henceforth" is inserted before "you will see"; this Robinson takes to be a genuine part of the reply. These words of Jesus, based mainly on Ps. 110:1 and Dan. 7:13, declare that the Son of Man, though condemned by his earthly judges, will be vindicated in the court of God. And if here the coming of the Son of Man betokens vindication, there are other sayings of Jesus in the Gospels where the coming of the Son of Man betokens a visitation in judgment which will be set in motion by his rejection (e.g., Luke 12:40; Matt. 10:23; Luke 18:8). This visitation in judgment will take place "from now on" as surely as the vindication. Robinson, instead of speaking of "realized eschatology," speaks of an "inaugurated eschatology" — an eschatology inaugurated by Jesus' death and resurrection. For his death and resurrection did not exhaust his messianic activity; on the contrary, they "would but release and initiate that reign of God in which *henceforth* the Father's redeeming work could be brought to the fulfilment which hitherto it was denied" (p. 81). To Jesus' ministry before his death and resurrection Robinson applies the term "proleptic eschatology" (p. 101), because in his words and deeds the signs of the messianic age were to be seen by anticipation.

At an early period in church history, he believes, the perspective was changed. While Christians continued to think of Jesus' *vindication* as following immediately upon his death and resurrection, they postponed his *visitation* to a future day.

V. THE SECOND ADVENT. Plainly Jesus' reply to the high priest must be examined more closely to determine whether or not he implied a coming of the Son of Man to earth. In Dan. 7:13 (the OT passage on which the description of his coming with the clouds of heaven is based) the "one like a son of man" comes *to the Ancient of Days,* and it has been inferred from this that Jesus thought of the Son of Man as coming with the clouds of heaven into the presence of God, and not to earth. But how in that case would the Sanhedrin see the Son of Man? And where in fact is the Ancient of Days located in Dan. 7:13? The thrones of Dan. 7:9 are placed on earth rather than in heaven; it is apparently on earth that the Ancient of Days occupies his judgment-seat, bestows dominion upon the Son of Man, and gives judgment for the saints of the Most High.

In Mark 13:26, another passage where Jesus speaks of men seeing "the Son of man coming in clouds with great power and glory," there is little doubt that a coming to earth is meant, for it is men on earth who see him, and he proceeds to "send out the angels, and gather his elect from the four winds, from the ends of the earth to the ends of heaven" (vs. 27). But it is widely held that the discourse of Mark 13 in its present form is not the unaltered teaching of Jesus, and that vss. 24-27

in particular are secondary, the product of that changed perspective in the early church which is reflected also, e.g., in II Thess. 1:6-10.

The argument from Mark 13, however, cannot be so quickly dismissed. Quite probably Jesus' discourse in this chapter did have a history of its own before it was incorporated in Mark's Gospel, and it may have been preserved in a disjointed condition. Certainly vss. 24-27 draw upon the OT prophets in their portrayal of the day of the LORD; but what could be more natural? "When God steps forth for salvation the universe pales before him" (George Raymond Beasley-Murray, *A Commentary on Mark Thirteen,* Macmillan, London, 1957, p. 67). And against this background of a darkened heaven the Son of Man comes with clouds — to earth. A similar interpretation of Mark 14:62 seems most reasonable, although the contrary interpretation of this verse "is becoming almost a new orthodoxy in Britain" (Beasley-Murray, op. cit., p. 91). Yet the "new orthodoxy" has not been accepted universally; Joseph Edward Fison adduces Mark 14:62 as the one sure text which unambiguously proves that Jesus did speak of his return to earth (*The Christian Hope,* Longmans, London, 1954, p. 194).

If Jesus indeed envisaged such a return to earth, we may inquire if he envisaged an interval between the completion of his ministry and that second coming. In seeking the answer to this question we become aware of a tension between the idea of the kingdom of God as present in the life and work of Jesus and the idea of its future consummation — a tension apparent in the thought and teaching of Jesus himself as well as in the thought and teaching of the early church. We fail to do justice to this tension when we interpret the NT evidence in terms of an exclusively realized or an exclusively future eschatology. That Jesus did think of an interval separating his passion from his *parousia* seems clear from a saying like Mark 13:10 ("the gospel must first be preached to all nations") — certainly a genuine saying of Jesus referring to the period before the final consummation, whether it originally belonged to its present context or not. The final consummation is vitally related to what happened when Jesus came the first time. For he both fulfilled the kingdom, and promised it. His promise of it is confirmed by his fulfilment of it in life and death; his fulfilment of it in life and death will be vindicated when his promise of it comes true.

The implications of this tension are expounded by Werner Georg Kuemmel in *Promise and Fulfilment* (S.C.M., London, 1957). Oscar Cullmann, who acknowledges his indebtedness to Kuemmel, has also treated the subject illuminatingly (cf. "The Return of Christ" in *The Early Church*, S.C.M., London, 1956, pp. 141 ff.). He has caught the imagination of many by his happy analogy of D-Day and V-Day (Victory Day) to illustrate the relation between what Christ did at his first coming and what he will do when he comes again. Once the decisive battle of a war has been won, the final outcome is assured; the interval elapsing before the ultimate manifestation and celebration of victory is of uncertain duration and relative unimportance. So Jesus' *parousia* is not the decisive event of the gospel; it is rather the inevitable sequel of the decisive event, which took place with his death and resurrection. The time of its occurrence does not matter so much as the fact that its occurrence is assured.

With the work accomplished by Jesus at his first coming the eschatological epoch has been inaugurated. The slaughtered Lamb (*q.v.*) has vindicated his title to be the Lord of history: this is the lesson of Rev. 5:5 ff. The consummation of the eschatological epoch is as closely bound up with his person as the inauguration was; it is called in II Thess. 2:8 the "epiphany of his parousia" (literally the "manifestation of his presence"). He has been vindicated by God, although that vindication has yet to be universally revealed and acknowledged. But the believer who lives now "between the times" and awaits the "manifestation of his presence" experiences already the assurance of his presence, his coming, his abiding as Victor and Deliverer. The NT writing which dwells in greatest detail on the present vindication and exaltation of Christ admits that as yet we do not see all things put under him, but teaches us to rest content so long as we see Jesus glorified (Heb. 2:8 f.); this is guarantee enough that the Coming One will come (Heb. 10:37).

The *parousia* of Christ is closely associated in the NT with the resurrection of his people (and more generally with the resurrection of mankind) and with the judgment of the world. While the people of Christ experience the resurrection life here and now, while those who refuse him are "condemned already" (John 3:18), this "realized" aspect of resurrection and judgment does not exclude their future consummation. The Gospel which most distinctively emphasizes that the judgment of the world coincided with the incarnation and passion of Christ (John 12:31), and that believers in him already possess eternal life (John 3:36), also speaks plainly of a resurrection to be effected by Christ at the last day (John 6:39 f.), when "all who are in the tombs will hear his voice and come forth, those who have done good, to the resurrection of life, and those who have done evil, to the resurrection of judgment" (John 5:28 f.).

Some minor questions actively canvassed in connection with the *parousia*, especially among evangelical people — such as its time-relation to the thousand years of Rev. 20:2 ff., or with the great distress of Mark 13:19, etc. — belong more to the detailed exegesis of individual Scriptures than to the general survey of biblical eschatology. What is of the essence of the gospel is the sure expectation of the time when the cosmic effects of Christ's redemptive work will be accomplished and "the creation itself will be set free from its bondage to decay and obtain the glorious liberty of the children of God" (Rom. 8:21).

BIBLIOGRAPHY

R. H. Charles, *A Critical History of the Doctrine of a Future Life*; S. D. F. Salmond, *The Christian Doctrine of Immortality*; H. A. A. Kennedy, *St. Paul's Conceptions of the Last Things*; M. J. Wyngaarden, *The Future of the Kingdom*; R. Otto, *The Kingdom of God and the Son of Man*; T. F. Glasson, *The Second Advent* and *His Appearing and His Kingdom*; E. F. Sutcliffe, *The Old Testament and the Future Life*; H. N. Ridderbos, *De Komst van het Koninkrijk*; O. Cullmann, *Christ and Time*; G. Vos, *The Teaching of Jesus concerning the Kingdom and the Church* and *The Pauline Eschatology*; G. E. Ladd, *Crucial Questions about the Kingdom of God* and *The Blessed Hope*; G. R. Beasley-Murray, *Jesus and the Future*; H. Quistorp, *Calvin's Doctrine of the Last Things*; D. Daube and W. D. Davies, editors, *The Background of the NT and its Eschatology*.

FREDERICK FYVIE BRUCE

ESSENES. An ascetic Jewish group. The derivation of the name is obscure.

Philo paints an idyll of an agricultural community, (elsewhere he speaks of city-dwelling Essenes), voluntarily poor, devoted to theological and moral instruction and solemnly observing the sabbath in corporate worship; with common purse, table and wardrobe, deprecating marriage as threatening unity.

Pliny the Elder, a pagan, refers to the Essene tribe without money or women, maintaining its numbers by almost daily accessions of the disillusioned. He locates it (if rightly understood) north of Engedi near the Dead Sea. Josephus often refers, not always perspicuously, to the Essenes. He has firsthand knowledge, but is out to impress gentile readers. He speaks enthusiastically, outlining their austere discipline, with the awful fate of excommunicates; their worship and daily lustrations (the sunworship which some find, undoubtedly arises from misunderstanding); their dread of ceremonial defilement; their initiation, with its three year preparation (with purificatory lustration after one year); and their secrecy about their books.

In an obscure passage Josephus seems to mean that they sent offerings to the temple, but were excluded from the common court since they refused regular priestly ministrations. They were noted for herbal lore and predictions, arising both from prescience and study of the OT.

He numbers them at about 4,000. Some were butchered in the Roman-Jewish War. They differed on marriage; to maintain their numbers, some adopted children, others practiced trial marriage.

Hippolytus, the early third century heresiologist, probably follows the same source as, rather than reproduces Josephus, and is occasionally more helpful, e.g., on the Essene belief in resurrection.

It is generally, though not universally, agreed that the Qumran discoveries (see DEAD SEA SCROLLS) relate to an Essene settlement. The site recalls Pliny's description, and many observations about the Essenes — from initiation and excommunication to details like the horror of spitting — are illustrated by the scrolls. A clue is thus offered to the fate of the Essenes and their books. An Essene origin for *Enoch, Jubilees, Testaments of the Twelve Patriarchs* and other works is not unlikely.

At present it is probably best to regard the Essenes as including, but not restricted to, the Qumran group. Like "Nonconformist" in England, "Essene" doubtless had different manifestations which from certain viewpoints presented a broad unity. Essene celibacy and quietism attracted general notice: but some (including, apparently, Qumran) were clearly not celibate; while Josephus and Hippolytus mention separate striking departures from pacifism.

The question of an organic connection between the Essenes and early Christianity has been variously raised. Essene antecedents have been attributed to John the Baptist (*q.v.*) and even Jesus, and a few think the Qumran sectaries Christians. Relations between the Qumran group and Jewish Christians after A.D. 70 are not impossible (though obscure); but the differences between normative NT Christianity and Essenism are radical. Essenism, however, helps in understanding such pietistic legalism as afflicted the Colossians.

BIBLIOGRAPHY

Philo, *Quod omnis probus liber* 12-13, and in Eusebius, X *Prep. Evang.* viii. 11; Jos, *Bell. Jud.* ii. 8.2; *Antiq.* xviii. 1.5; Pliny, *Hist Nat.* v. 17; Hippolytus, *Ref. Omn. Haer.* ix. 13-23; For older literature see E. Schuerer, *History of the Jewish People* (Eng. Trans.) Div. II, Vol. II, pp. 188-218; J. Moffatt in *HERE.* For literature since 1947 see under Dead Sea Scrolls. J. Strugnell, *JBL* 77, 106-15.

ANDREW F. WALLS

ETERNAL GENERATION. This is the phrase used to denote the intertrinitarian relationship between the Father and the Son as this is taught by the Bible. *Generation* makes it plain that there is a divine sonship prior to the incarnation (cf. John 1:18; I John 4:9), that there is thus a distinction of persons within the one Godhead (John 5:26), and that between these persons there is a superiority and subordination of order (cf. John 5:19; 8:28). *Eternal* reinforces the fact that the generation is not merely economic (i.e., for the purpose of human salvation as in the incarnation, cf. Luke 1:35), but essential, and that as such it cannot be construed in the categories of natural or human generation. Thus it does not imply a time when the Son was not, as Arianism argued. Nor is there to be expected a final absorption of the Son. Nor does the fact that the Son is a distinct person mean that he is separate in essence. Nor does his subordination imply inferiority. In virtue and not in spite of the eternal generation, the Father and the Son are one (John 10:30). Objections have been lodged against the phrase on the ground that it is rhetorical, meaningless and ultimately self-contradictory. Yet it corresponds to what God has shown us of himself in his own eternal being, and, if it carries an element of mystery (as is only to be expected), it has rightly been described by O. A. Curtis (*The Christian Faith*, p. 228) as "not only conceivable" but "also one of the most fruitful conceptions in all Christian thinking." It finds creedal expression in the phrases "begotten of his Father before all worlds" (Nicene) and "begotten before the worlds" (Athanasian).

See also ONLY BEGOTTEN.

GEOFFREY W. BROMILEY

ETERNAL LIFE. Though anticipated in the OT, the concept of eternal life seems to be largely a NT revelation. The common translation, "eternal life" or "everlasting life," is the translation of *zōē* (life) and *aiōnion* (eternal), an expression found throughout the NT, but especially in the Gospel of John and I John. *Zōē* is found 134 times, translated "life" in every instance in the AV except one (Luke 16:25). The verb form *zaō* is found 143 times and is similar in meaning. *Aiōnion* appears 78 times, usually translated "eternal" (42 times in AV), but also "everlasting" (25) and once "for ever."

Both the terms *eternal* and *life* are difficult to define except descriptively. *Zōē* is used in many shades of meaning in Scripture, sometimes little different than *bios* which occurs only eleven times in the NT and refers to earthly life only. *Zōē* is found in the following meanings: (1) life principle, or that which makes one alive physically (John 10:11, 15, 17; 13:37); (2) life time, or duration of man's life — similar to *bios* (Heb. 7:3; James 4:14); (3) the sum of all activities comprising life (I Cor. 6:3-4; I Tim. 2:2; 4:8); (4) happiness or state of enjoying life (I Thess. 3:8, verb form; cf. John 10:10); (5) as a mode of existence given by God, whether physical or spiritual (Acts 17:25); (6) spiritual or eternal life, a state of regeneration or renewal in holiness and fellowship with God (John 3:15-16, 36; 5:24; 6:47); the life which is in Christ and God — divine life itself (John 1:4; I John 1:1-2; 5:11).

Though *zōē* is sometimes used without adjective to denote eternal life (I John 5:12), in many instances *aiōnios* is used to distinguish eternal life from ordinary physical life. The adjective *aiōnios* corresponds to the noun *aiōn* which refers to life in general, or the age (*q.v.*) in which a life is lived. The idea of eternity seems to be derived from the fact that eternity is a future age which eclipses in importance all other ages, and thus is the age pre-eminent. Hence, eternal life or age-life is that which anticipates and assures fellowship with God in eternity as well as having promise of entering into that eternal fellowship in time.

The Scriptures describe but do not formally define eternal life. The nearest approach to a definition is given in John 17:3 where Christ stated: "This is life eternal, that they might know thee the only true God, and Jesus Christ, whom thou hast sent." Eternal life is described in its experimental aspect of knowing God and having fellowship with God through his Son, Jesus Christ.

Eternal life is contrasted in Scripture with ordinary physical life. Though human life is endless in its duration, it does not possess inherently the qualities which enter into eternal life. Hence, one having physical life without eternal life is described as "dead in trespasses and sins" (Eph. 2:1). The lack of eternal life is equated with the state of being unsaved, condemned, or lost, in contrast to those who have eternal life who are declared to be saved, and promised that they shall never perish (John 3:15-16, 18, 36; 5:24; 10:9).

Even in the case of the elect, eternal life is not possessed until faith in Christ is exercised (Eph. 2:1, 5). Eternal life is not to be confused with efficacious grace, or that bestowal of grace which is antecedent to faith. Nor is it to be confused with the indwelling of the Holy Spirit or of Jesus Christ, though this accompanies and manifests eternal life. Eternal life is to be identified with regeneration and is received in the new birth. It is resultant rather than causative of salvation, but is related to conversion or the manifestation of the new life in Christ.

Eternal life is given by the work of the Holy Spirit at the moment of faith in Christ. As in the case of the incarnation of Christ, however, the Trinity is related to the impartation of life. According to James 1:17-18, the Father is said to beget his spiritual children. The life which is bestowed upon the believer is identified with the life which is in Christ (John 5:21; II Cor. 5:17; I John 5:12). In other passages, the Holy Spirit is declared to be the one who regenerates (John 3:3-7; Titus 3:5).

The impartation of eternal life is embodied in three principal figures in the Scripture. (1) Regeneration is described first as a new birth, being "born . . . of God" (John 1:13), or "born again" (John 3:3). The bestowal of eternal life therefore relates the believer to God in a father and son relationship. (2) The new life in Christ is described as a spiritual resurrection. Not only is the believer "raised together with Christ" (Col. 3:1) but is "alive from the dead" (Rom. 6:13). Christ anticipated this in his prophecy: "The hour cometh, and now is, when the dead shall hear the voice of the Son of God; and they that hear shall live" (John 5:25). (3) The bestowal of new life is compared to the act of creation. As Adam became a living soul by the breath of God, so the believer becomes a new creation (II Cor. 5:17). The possessor of eternal life is declared to be "created in Christ Jesus unto good works" (Eph. 2:10). The concept of a new creation carries with it not only the possession of eternal life, but involves a new nature which corresponds to the life, "old things are passed away; behold, they are become new" (II Cor. 5:17 ASV).

See also LIFE.

BIBLIOGRAPHY

Articles on "Life" and "Eternal Life" in *HDB, ISBE, Unger's Bible Dictionary*; L. Berkhof, *Systematic Theology*, pp. 465-79; L. S. Chafer, *Systematic Theology* IV, pp. 24-26, 389, 400-1; VII, pp. 142, 227; A. H. Strong, *Systematic Theology*, pp. 809-29; J. F. Walvoord, *The Holy Spirit*, pp. 128-37.

JOHN F. WALVOORD

ETERNAL PUNISHMENT. It is plain from the Bible that sin will be punished (Dan. 12:2; Matt. 10:15; John 5:28 f.; Rom. 5:12 ff., etc.). Orthodox Christianity has always understood this to signify that eternal punishment is the lot of the finally impenitent. In recent times, however, this has been disputed from two directions. Some hold that eventually all will be saved. While this might, perhaps, be deduced from a few scriptural passages taken in isolation, it cannot be maintained that it accords with the general tenor of Bible teaching. Others think that man is no more than potentially immortal. If he puts his trust in Christ and enters into salvation, he attains immortal life. If he fails to do so, he simply dies, and that is the end of him. This might accord with those passages which speak of "death" or "destruction" as the lot of the wicked, but not with those referring to Gehenna or the like.

The usual NT way of speaking of eternal punishment is by the use of *aiōn* or one of its derivatives. This word means "an age," but its application to the never ending "age to come" gave it the significance "eternal." Thus we read of "the King eternal" (I Tim. 1:17), glory is ascribed to God "for ever" (Rom. 11:36), and God is blessed "for evermore" (II Cor. 11:31). A. A. Hodge can say: "The Greek language possesses no more emphatic terms with which to express the idea of endless duration than these" (*Outlines of Theology*, T. Nelson & Sons, London, 1873, p. 469). The use of these terms for the eternity of God shows conclusively that they cannot be held to imply a limited duration.

Now the same terminology is used of "eternal" punishment as of "eternal" life (Matt. 25:46 has both in the same verse). The implication of this is that the punishment is just as "eternal" as the life. The one is no more limited than the other.

Then there are expressions which do not use the term "eternal." Jesus said: "It is good for thee to enter into life maimed, rather than having thy two hands to go into hell, into the unquenchable fire" (Mark 9:43; cf. Luke 3:17). He referred to "hell; where their worm dieth not, and the fire is not quenched" (Mark 9:47 f.). He spoke of fearing God because he, "after he hath killed hath power to cast into hell" (Luke 12:5). He said there is a sin which "shall not be forgiven . . . neither in this world, nor in that which is to come" (Matt. 12:32). Similarly John writes: "He that obeyeth (mg. believeth) not the Son shall not see life, but the wrath of God abideth on him" (John 3:36). Then there is the awful finality of Christ's warnings. He spoke of the door being shut (Matt. 25:10), of being cast "into the outer darkness" (Matt. 8:12; Luke 13:28, etc.), of an impassable gulf (Luke 16:26). Nowhere is there a hint of any possible reversal of the last judgment.

More could be cited. It is clear that there is a strong body of NT evidence pointing in the direction of a continuing punishment. Against it we cannot put one saying which speaks plainly of an end to the punishment of the finally impenitent. As Orr says, "It adds to the terribleness of these sayings that, as before remarked, there is nothing to put against them; no hint or indication of a termination of the doom. Why did Jesus not safeguard His words from misapprehension, if behind them there lay an assurance of restoration and mercy? One may ask with Oxenham, in a reply to Jukes, whether if Christ had intended to teach the doctrine of eternal punishment, He could possibly have taught it in plainer terms" (*ISBE* iv, p. 2502).

In the light of the cross we can be sure that the mercy of God reaches as far as mercy can reach. God does all that can be done for man's salvation. Beyond that, and the teaching of the permanence of the doom of the wicked, we cannot go. It may be that the dread reality is other than men have usually pictured it, as C. S. Lewis suggests. It must be borne in mind that Scripture uses symbolic terms of necessity to refer to realities beyond the grave. We must not press statements about "fire," "death," and the like. But neither must we yield to a sentimental demand that they be watered down. That there is a dread reality Scripture leaves us in no doubt.

BIBLIOGRAPHY
C. S. Lewis, *The Great Divorce;* J. Orr, *"Punishment"* in *ISBE;* A. Richardson, *"Hell"* in *RTWB;* S. D. F. Salmond, *The Christian Doctrine of Immortality;* Harry Buis, *The Doctrine of Eternal Punishment.*

LEON MORRIS

ETERNAL SIN. See ETERNAL PUNISHMENT, BLASPHEMY.

ETERNITY. The word eternity suggests transcendence of the temporal and is employed in various senses: durability (cf. "the eternal hills"); time without end (cf. "passing to his eternal reward"); time without beginning (cf. speculative conceptions of the universe as "an eternal process"); infinite time (cf. the ascription of temporality to the nature of God). Beyond this, the term traditionally has been used by theology and philosophy to designate God's infinity in relation to time, that is, to designate the divine perfection whereby God transcends temporal limitations of duration and succession and possesses his existence in one indivisible present.

In Greek philosophy the eternity of divine being simultaneously implied the shadow-reality and insignificance of the temporal, a speculative view contradictive of biblical theism with its emphasis on redemptive revelation in time (*q.v.*) and place. Parmenides already had shaped the Greek prejudice: only the unchanging and permanent is real, all else is illusory. By another route Plato and Aristotle reached the same conclusion: genuine significance pertains only to eternal realities, never to the temporal.

Biblical theology and philosophy, however, affirmed the unique eternity of God without ruling out the created and conditional reality of the time-space order and its momentous significance. The doctrines of creation, preservation, providence, incarnation and atonement, all involved a strategic role for the world of time and history.

Prompted by Hegel, modern philosophy lodged time (and the universe) in the very nature of the Absolute. The immanental speculations conceived the whole of reality as temporal, as the Absolute in process of logical evolution. Thus the idea of an insignificant temporal order was subverted, but so also was the conception of the self-sufficient God. Hegel indeed distinguished the Absolute's indivisible timeless inner unity from the Absolute's temporal differentiation as nature and spirit. But this ambiguity led post-Hegelian thinkers in two directions. F. H. Bradley declared temporal distinctions unreal in the Absolute's experience, while most post-Hegelian scholars rejected divine timelessness. Josiah Royce proposed a mediating position. While affirming the temporality of all experience, he asserted that the Absolute knows all events in a single time-span, a unitary act of consciousness, in contrast with the long successions of time-spans involved in our finite knowledge. But Royce's formula transcended the duality of eternity and time only verbally, since on his theory time would not exist for the Absolute in the same sense as for its parts, nor would events as known by finite selves carry absolute significance. Edgar S. Brightman vigorously asserted the divine temporality of his finite god. As naturalism more and more displaced idealism as the influential modern philosophy, its exponents affirmed the ultimacy of time (cf. Samuel Alexander's *Space, Time and Deity*).

In reaction to the modern temporalizing of deity, neo-orthodox theology stresses the "infinite qualitative difference" between eternity and time. It emphasizes not only the ontological transcendence of God as Creator, and his moral transcendence of man as sinner, however, but sketches his epistemological transcendence in such a way that, in the exposition of the *imago Dei,* it curtails the role of cognition and the significance of the forms of logic in the human reception of divine revelation (see EPISTEMOLOGY). It minimizes the historical aspect of redemptive revelation, moreover, by assigning God's disclosure a superhistorical locus in man's encounter with deity. Later writings of Barth and Brunner somewhat moderate their more extreme early statements; nonetheless, although now emphasizing the created reality of time and the crucial importance of the incarnation and atonement, they evade the direct identification of history at any point with divine revelation.

To repair this gulf between the temporal order and the Deity, some recent theologians in turn discard the definition of eternity as pure timelessness or non-temporality. While thus avoiding Hegel's identification of the temporal order with God's direct self-manifestation, they lodge time in the very nature of God instead of viewing it as in created dependency. Oscar Cullmann drops the whole idea of time-lessness with reference to the eternal. He maintains that eternity is simply infinitely extended time: the former, boundless time; the latter, bound by creation at the one end and by eschatological events at the other.

Here the philosophical and theological repudiation of non-temporal eternity meet, though the philosophical motives are avowedly speculative, while Cullmann's are professedly biblical and exegetical. From the NT use of *aiōn* for a period of time, both defined and undefined in duration, alongside its use of this term for eternity, Cullmann argues that eternity is not timeless but rather is unending time. Since the same term is applied both to this age and to the next, the temporal and eternal worlds are presumably not qualitatively distinguishable in respect to time. The eschatological drama, moreover, requires the idea of time progression. Hence the qualitative disjunction of eternity and time is dismissed as Greek rather than biblical in outlook. Instead of binding time to the creation alone, Cullmann affirms that time falls into three eras: pre-creation; from creation to "the end of the world"; and post-eschatological. The first is unbegun, the last unending (cf. *Christ and Time*).

No objection can be taken to Cullmann's aim, which is to preserve the absolute significance of redemptive history, and to prevent a dissolution of the Christ-event as the decisive center of history from which both time and eternity are to be understood. His detection of docetic and hellenic influences in the theology of Kierkegaard, Barth, Brunner and Bultmann, moreover, gains its point from their excessive formulations of divine transcendence. But the repudiation of the unique eternity or non-temporality of God is not required to preserve the reality and significance of historical revelation and redemption; indeed, the temporalizing of the Eternal poses theological problems all its own.

Admittedly many biblical representations suggest nothing beyond an exaltation of God above all temporal limitations of the universe (John 17:24; Eph. 1:4; II Tim. 1:9). Recourse to Ex. 3:14, "I am who I am," where the French render the name of Jehovah as The Eternal, is unavailing, for the comfort of the oppressed Israelites in Egypt must surely have sprung from an assurance that God intervenes redemptively in fallen history, and not especially from his non-temporality.

But the non-temporality of God nonetheless can be firmly supported. The constant use of *aiōn* for the spatial world (cosmos) suggests the concomitance of time and space; hence not simply the temporality but also the spatiality of God — an assumption objectionable to biblical theists — would seem to be implied by a one-sided reliance on *aiōn*. From this circumstance the conviction gains support that time and space belong to the created order as distinct from the divine essence, and that eternity is an incommunicable divine attribute. Moreover, the biblical contrast of divine and temporal duration frequently looks beyond a quantitative or proportional to a qualitative contrast. Temporal categories are viewed as inapplicable to Jehovah (cf. Ps. 90:2) and the word *'ōlām* gains theological significance. This qualitative connotation is more fully carried by the later use of *'ōlām* in plural form for God's eternity, a turn of phrase required by the absence of alternatives in Hebrew vocabulary to express a qualitative differentiation. "The plural cannot mean the literal addition of a number of indefinite, unbounded temporal durations: it can only be read as a poetic emphasis by which a quantitative plural is a symbol for a qualitative difference" (John Marsh, *Theological Word Book of the Bible*, Alan Richardson, ed.: "Time," p. 266b). The NT translation of *'ōlām* by *aiōn* and *aiōnios* is instructive, moreover. The primary thrust of the familiar terms "eternal life" and "eternal death" is qualitative, and not simply quantitative. The former phrase depicts a quality of life fit for eternity, in which the believer *already* participates through regeneration (John 5:24), although it does not, of course, imply non-temporality; the latter, eternal death, is spiritual death which, in the case of the impenitent unbeliever, is transmuted at physical death into an irrevocable condition. Finally, the attribute of eternity cannot be disjoined from God's other attributes. The biblical emphasis on divine omniscience supports the view of his supertemporal eternity. If God's knowledge is an inference from a succession of ideas in the divine mind, he cannot be omniscient. Divine omniscience implies that God knows all things in a single whole, independent of a temporal succession of ideas.

BIBLIOGRAPHY

Oscar Cullmann, *Christ and Time*; C. F. H. Henry,

Notes on the Doctrine of God, pp. 124-36; John Marsh, "Time," in *RTWB*.

CARL F. H. HENRY

ETHICS. Ethics is the science of conduct. It is a systematic attempt to consider the purposeful actions of mankind, to determine their rightness or wrongness, their tendency to good or evil. The variety of terms in ethical usage testifies to the complexity of the problem of determining the nature of morality. Such terms include good, right, duty, ought, goodwill, virtue and motive.

What kind of a science is ethics? It has to do with the mind but is not an exact science as are mathematics and logic. It is not merely descriptive. It is normative, as it is concerned with an ideal or standard of conduct. Good (*q.v.*) is a conception that cannot be accurately defined. It has been equated with happiness. Pleasure has been regarded as the good by many. So too, has duty and also knowledge. No doubt all these are ingredients in the good, but none of them singly is the highest good.

I. SYSTEMS OF ETHICS. The Greek philosophers Socrates, Plato and Aristotle were among the first to formulate ethical theories. For Socrates, virtue and knowledge are one. He tried to identify practical excellence of character with intellectual insight into the true nature of actions.

Plato treated the subject for the most part as a quest for justice. For him, morals was a branch of politics. What obtains in the good state is true also for the individuals who compose it. Justice is a harmony in which wisdom rules over the spirited emotions and appetites. The just man allows wisdom to control him. Plato's system has the permanent value of putting the highest good in the realm of spirit. The good is spiritual in its nature. It resembles the sun in the physical world, giving light and life to all things. So the idea of the good reveals itself in everything that truly exists. It is the source of all truth, knowledge, beauty, and moral goodness.

Aristotle was more down to earth in his treatment of the subject. He saw man as a social being in his essence. Morality arises out of this. In social contacts, moral actions are determined. They are the result of deliberate habitual good actions. He defines virtue as "a state of deliberate moral purpose consisting in a mean that is relative to ourselves, the mean being determined by reason, or as a prudent man would determine it" (Aristotle, *Ethics*,

Bk. 2, Chap. 6). Instinctive moral intuition determines the moral mean between extremes, partly innate and partly the result of constantly seeking the right path.

Against the intellectualism of these systems of ethics the Stoics and Epicureans reacted. Stoics found the good life in suppressing the emotions. Virtue was fortitude. For Epicureans it was pleasure. In one form or another these ethical ideas have traveled down through the history of thought.

Augustine was deeply impressed by Plato. He taught that the *Summum Bonum* is the love of God, in which all man's faculties reach their highest perfection and his desires are completely satisfied.

Aquinas was influenced by Aristotle. The highest good is the knowledge of God. Reason and faith, though distinct, are harmonious, for each comes from the one source of truth.

II. OBLIGATION. The Greeks rarely raised the question of moral obligation, i.e., why anyone should pursue the good. They thought that knowledge of it was sufficient to supply the motive to desire it. The specific nature of the ought tends to be lost sight of in such systems of thought. We can seek to explain the sense of moral obligation roughly along one of two ways. On the one hand we may hold that it develops naturally, or on the other hand that we see the obligation by intuition.

Naturalism in all its forms misses the point of obligation. Such theories may serve as a history or a description of ethics but the real point of why some course of action is right or wrong or why we ought to pursue the right and combat the wrong is glossed over.

Intuitionism at least sees the issue raised by the sense of obligation. Bishop Butler showed that conscience has a supremacy of moral authority, over pleasure and self-love, in determining motives and actions.

Kant separated obligation and self-love on rationalist principles. He assumed that every rational being has the conception of obligation; the moral law is unconditionally binding on all rational beings as such. It is categorically imperative, admitting of no exceptions. The moral agent should only act on the maxim that what he wills should become a universal law. Nothing is good absolutely but the good will. Duty for duty's sake is the moral motive.

Utilitarianism as expounded by J. S. Mill with its determining principle of "the greatest good of the greatest number" founders on this rock of absolute moral obligation. Evolutional naturalism similarly fails. "Being more complex" or "having the ability to endure" is not what we mean by being right.

The organism as it evolves, develops mind, whose characteristic is free thinking ideas.

To be able to reflect on itself and to criticize its ideas shows that the thinking personality cannot be explained on naturalistic grounds. If naturalistic explanation will not suffice we have to fall back on intuition, i.e., insight into the truth of things moral.

III. CHRISTIAN ETHICS. Insight into moral obligation is given by the indwelling of the Holy Spirit of God. The Holy Spirit not only gives enlightenment into what is good and true and beautiful, but also the desire and the power to follow them.

Conscience (q.v.) is the power of moral judgment informed by the Holy Spirit. It is capable of being educated and enlightened more and more as the indwelling is maintained in experience and behavior.

The highest good of man is union with God. This union of human spirit with the Holy Spirit purifies the motive of inordinate self-love and gives instead *agapē* — the disinterested love of man, as a child of God.

BIBLIOGRAPHY

J. S. Mackenzie, *Ethics*; R. A. Rogers, *History of Ethics*; W. D. Ross, *Foundations of Ethics*; E. P. Garrett, *Theory of Morals*; L. Dewar, *Christian Morals*.

ALBERT VICTOR M'CALLIN

EUCHARIST. See LORD'S SUPPER, SACRAMENTS.

EUNOMIANISM. A short-lived system of extreme Arian doctrine associated with Eunomius, Bishop of Cyzicus (*ca.* 395). He taught that the Godhead was one substance without distinction or properties, and derived from Aetius the "Anomoean" doctrine that the Son was unlike (Greek *anomoios*) the Father in essence, and had been generated outside his nature. The writings of Eunomius which survive reveal a logical, anti-sacramental and anti-mystical mind.

BIBLIOGRAPHY

Eunomius, *PG*, 30:835-68; Socrates, Church History, 4:7; Basil, *PG*, 39:497-774; Gregory Nyssa, *Contra Eunomium*; DCB; ODCC.

M. R. W. FARRER

EUTYCHIANISM. Named after Eutyches, archimandrite of a large monastery near Constantinople and a man of great influence, this is a view of the person of Christ which confounds the divine and human natures, denying Christ's consubstantiality with us and thus overthrowing any genuine work of atonement. Eutyches, who advanced his teaching in opposition to Nestorianism (*q.v.*), was condemned and deposed in A.D. 448. He gained temporary support at the Robber Council of Ephesus in 449, but was finally condemned and exiled at Chalcedon in 451, when the balanced teaching of Leo in his *Tome* was adopted in the famous Definition. Eutychianism, however, was not destroyed, but re-emerged in the powerful Monophysite heresy.

See also CHRISTOLOGY.

GEOFFREY W. BROMILEY

EVANGELICAL. The evangelical Christian faith is the "good news" or the "glad tidings" that God has provided redemption for man. It affirms that salvation from sin is obtained through the grace of God, not that it is earned by good works or given because of merit on the part of man. It sets forth the basic Christian doctrines, such as: the Trinity, the deity of Christ, the personality of the Holy Spirit, the plenary inspiration of the Scriptures, miracles, the substitutionary or vicarious suffering and death of Christ as an atonement for the sins of his people, his resurrection from the grave, his ascension into heaven, his personal and glorious coming again, the resurrection and judgment of all men, heaven and hell. See also CHRISTIANITY.

The most important issue between evangelicals and others is that of biblical authority (*q.v.*). The evangelical insists that Scripture is the word of God written, and that it is therefore infallible in its original autographs. When this tenet is granted the other doctrines of the evangelical faith follow as a matter of course.

Two special uses of the word evangelical should be noted. In patristic literature the Gospel records are sometimes referred to as "the evangelical instrument," or "the evangelical voice." In our own time, in Europe, the word may be used as the equivalent of Protestant, or still more narrowly, as meaning Lutheran.

BIBLIOGRAPHY

James M. Gray in *ISBE*; HDB.

LORAINE BOETTNER

EVANGELIST. The word comes directly into the English from the Latin *evangelista* which is derived from the Greek *euaggelistēs*, meaning a bringer of the gospel, i.e., one who announces good tidings. It is the same root as *euaggelion,* meaning gospel and *euaggelizomai,* meaning to herald good news. It occurs three times in the NT: (1) referring to Philip the Evangelist (Acts 21:8), (2) evangelists as gifts to the church (Eph. 4:11), (3) Timothy the pastor who was called to do the work of an evangelist (II Tim. 4:5). Hence in the early church an evangelist was one who brought the first news of the gospel message, paving the way for the more systematic work of settled church officers. Evangelists today are regarded as itinerants traveling from place to place preaching with a view to winning converts to the Christian faith. Not to be overlooked however is the blending of evangelistic fervor with pastoral fidelity in the parish work of the pastoral evangelist. See also MINISTER.

In the ancient church the writers of the Four Gospels were also called evangelists. Since this custom begins to emerge at the end of the second century, shortly after the individual Gospels begin to be referred to by name, it is probable that the term evangelist, being of the same Greek root as Gospel, was felt to be appropriate as a designation for the men who composed them.

F. CARLTON BOOTH

EVE. The suggested derivations of this name, given by Adam to his wife after the fall (Gen. 3:20), are many (Koehler's *Lexicon* mentions nine possibilities). Apart from exact linguistic precision the biblical connection between Eve (Hebrew *hawwâ*) and "living" (Hebrew *hayyâ*) correctly indicates the rich symbolism implied (cf. Gen. 3:15). Eve's creation out of Adam's rib (Gen. 2:21, 22) suggests intimate unity between man and woman (Gen. 2:23). It also teaches woman's duty of submissiveness to man (I Tim. 2:12, 13). By yielding to the tempter's suggestion Eve virtually put him in the place of God and then became the instrument of Adam's fall (Gen. 3:1-7). The divine verdict upon her was adapted to her womanhood. Its severity was mitigated by the privilege of childbirth. In the ensuing redemptive process she and her "seed" (community, people) will be involved in a God-imposed enmity with the serpent and his "seed" (Gen. 3:15). The symbolical names Eve gave her children may suggest an incipient insight based on faith in the promise.

MARTEN H. WOUDSTRA

EVIL. Evil is the bad (moral evil) or the harmful (natural evil). Natural evil, although distinct from moral evil, is not separate from it.

According to the Bible, natural evil is the consequence of moral evil. At first, while still sinless, man is placed in an idyllic garden, where he lives in a happy relationship with his Creator, his wife and his animals. There is the possibility of eternal life. The "day" that he disobeys God, i.e., commits moral evil, he is covered with shame, confusion and anxiety, is condemned by God and ejected from the garden. The man must bring forth the fruit of the earth, the woman the fruit of the womb, in agony (Gen. 3).

This view prevails throughout the OT (Deut. 27:14 f.; Ps. 1; Prov. 14:31; Mal. 4:1-6). Although Job was convinced for a time that natural suffering had come upon him without his deserving, at the end he humbles himself under the divine rebuke (Job 42:1-6). The prophets predict the Messiah's advent, whose righteous role shall return the natural order to the Edenic state (Isa. 11:1-9; Hos. 2:18). The experience of Job presents in biographical form what the 91st Psalm states didactically: that catastrophe "shall not come nigh thy soul," that is, though natural evil exists in this sinful world, it shall not be able to harm the soul of the godly person.

This same theme is caught up in the teaching of Christ, whose doctrine may be summarily stated in five points. First, sin and punishment are interrelated. His revelation of hell is most pertinent here (Matt. 10:28; 23:33; Luke 16:23). The Galileans, on whom the tower fell (Luke 13:1 f.), although no more sinful than others, were assumed to have been sinful and therefore serve to warn the rest of sinful mankind. Second, the cancellation of sin removes punishment. This is especially clear in the healing of the paralytic (Mark 2:3 f.). Third, faith is necessary to receive this forgiveness and deliverance (Matt. 9:22; Mark 6:56; Luke 8:48; 17:19). Fourth, the purpose of some suffering is benign. This is revealed especially in the case of the man born blind (John 9:1 ff.), particular affliction coming upon him that its healing might be an occasion for the revelation of the glory of God in Christ. Fifth, the resurrection of the bodies of the righteous and the wicked is in order that each group should be placed in the natural state appropriate to its moral state (John 5:29).

The rest of the NT, especially Paul, maintains the same doctrine. "The wrath of God" is revealed against all unrighteousness (Rom. 1:18). "The wages of sin is death" (Rom. 6:23). The death here mentioned represents not only the ultimate natural evil of temporal life, but also of eternal existence, for it is set in contrast to the eternal life which is through Christ. John closes the NT (Rev. 22:14, 15) with an apocalyptic vision of the world to come in which there will be a place filled with nothing but moral evil and natural evil or suffering (hell) and a place filled with nothing but moral good and natural good or blessedness (heaven). Thus the Bible represents God as permitting moral evil and its consequent, natural evil (cf. especially Rom. 8:22 f.), and restoring some persons to a state of moral goodness and natural blessedness. According to Paul, all this is with a view to revealing his power in vessels of wrath (q.v.), no less than his grace in vessels of mercy (Rom. 9:22-23).

The extra-biblical development shows considerable variety. Augustine echoes the theodicy of Paul (City of God, especially XI) as do Aquinas and Calvin. While the Pauline-Augustinian tradition sees this twofold purpose of evil, a tradition from Origen to Karl Barth sees only a benign purpose. The evil of men is interpreted as functional to the good; and the wrath of God is an aspect of his love (cf. article on UNIVERSALISM). This optimistic universalism, shared approximately by the philosopher Leibniz, is in stark opposition to the pessimism of Schopenhauer and von Hartmann, who find evil to be ultimate. The other philosophy of evil is embodied in the dualism of Zoroastrianism (q.v.) wherein, however, the good principle conquers in the end-time.

Those who deny the realism of the Bible, the optimism of universalism or the pessimism of Schopenhauer are faced with irreducible "surd" evil. One group sacrifices God's goodness to his power; the other, his power to his goodness. The one affirms that God is certainly powerful and since he does not prevent evil he must not be altogether good. The other says, God is certainly good and since he does not prevent evil he must not be altogether powerful. He wants to eliminate evil and he is partly successful in overcoming it, but not completely. Plato found a recalcitrant matter outside of God which prevented the full expression of the highest Idea or the Good. E. S. Brightman internalized the recalcitrant element which he called the "given" and saw a "finite God" struggling with himself. But whether it be a dualist like Plato, a mystic like Boehme, a pragmatist like William James, or limited theists, such as Brightman and Berdyaev, they all solve the problem of evil by yielding belief in some of the attributes of God.

See also GOD, THEODICY.

BIBLIOGRAPHY

Augustine, City of God and Enchiridion; J. S. Candlish, The Biblical Doctrine of Sin; J. Edwards, The Great Christian Doctrine of Original Sin; G. W. Leibniz, Théodicée; C. S. Lewis, The Problem of Pain; Julius Mueller, The Christian Doctrine of Sin; R. A. Tsanoff, Nature of Evil.

JOHN H. GERSTNER

EVOLUTION. Etymologically "evolution" (Latin evolutio = an unrolling of a scroll) refers to processes involving the appearance of hitherto concealed features. In biology it may refer to the development of (a) the embryo (older use of word) or (b) the race (modern usage).

Today it is often claimed that in evolution (modern usage) true novelty arises de novo. But when and how does it arise? The word evolution is now usually confused with one or more of the various possible answers to these questions. Thus evolution may mean: (1) "descent with modification" (Darwin) as a mere process of change; (2) descent with modification as a creative process, simple forms of life spontaneously becoming more complex; (3) as in (2) but with the implication that the process occurs in a particular manner (e.g., by the "survival of the fittest"); (4) as in (2) with the addition that lifeless matter also spontaneously became alive; (5) as in (2) and possibly (4), not as a result of a force residing within matter but as a result of frequent or continuous intervention by God (Theistic evolution) or some other power (cf. "evolution" of the motor car).

Further possibilities arise if the parts of man are distinguished. Thus some hold that it may be that man's body and soul evolved but God implanted spirit or psychic powers.

It will readily be seen that to speak of belief or disbelief in evolution is highly ambiguous.

I. BIBLICAL TEACHING. Scripture gives no clear answer to the questions raised. In Gen. 1 and 2 two words are used — "created" and "made." "Created" is generally assumed to mean "created from nothing," though this is sometimes disputed. God is said to have "created" (bārā') heaven and earth, creatures that swim, birds and man; and to have "made" ('āśâ) the firmament, the beasts of the earth, every creeping thing and, once again, man. In the Genesis story conspicuous life on land is mentioned first: "God said, Let the earth put forth vegetation . . . And it was so." Here the language is similar in form to: "Let the waters. . . . be gathered . . . And it was so." In this last event, at least, natural forces were at work. Could they have been responsible for plant life too? The question is left open.

There is the view that the passage deals with early pre-history from the standpoint of an imaginary observer. This would explain why sun, moon and stars are said to be "made" when the sky (firmament) clears sufficiently for them to become visible. Likewise it would explain why the very small forms of life are omitted from the story and sea-monsters are mentioned before smaller fish because they are more conspicuous.

Genesis speaks of two creative acts in connection with man: his body was made of the dust and the breath of life was then implanted. One interpretation is that, through long ages, God prepared a sub-human creature called man, the most noble of the beasts of the field, and that one day, by an act of miracle, he made man in his own image, implanting in him a measure of his own nature. In a similar way Gen. 2:21 is regarded as a symbolical picture of how, without the knowledge of Adam, the first man, his own God-given nature was implanted in woman also.

The traditional view that, according to the Bible, man was anatomically as well as spiritually a new creation, is equally possible. Even so, some see in the Genesis narrative an implication that the beasts of the field included man-like creatures, since otherwise the possibility of Adam finding a helpmeet amongst them could hardly have been envisaged (Gen. 2:20; cf. 4:14).

The variety of possible interpretations serves to underline the fact that God did not intend to enlighten us on points of science. Yet we do know that in many matters of detail Genesis is scientifically sound; quite remarkably so.

II. SCIENTIFIC EVIDENCE. We may summarize this as follows.

(1) At one time there was no life on earth. When life arrived the smaller and *apparently* simpler forms came first followed by *apparently* more complex, larger and more specialized forms.

(2) Evidence that early life was, in fact, simpler than later life is lacking. Biologists have long been impressed by the resemblance between evolution and development from the egg ("ontology repeats phylogeny"). Sex cells (like all cells) possess enormous complexity. These unfold in growth and cells become specialized. Similarly evolution may consist only of the unfolding of what was there before. God may have created cells which, over the years, have unfolded into the present forms of life. This view explains many puzzling features of evolution (J. L. Baldwin, *New Answer to Darwinism*, 1957, M. Baldwin, Manhattan Bldg., Chicago, 5.).

(3) Scientifically the notion that lifeless matter became living bristles with difficulties. True, radiation produces amino-acids in *micrograms* from ammonia, carbon dioxide etc. but it destroys them too and would be highly destructive of lower forms of life once produced. The "lowest" forms of life involve unsuspected complexity, suggestive of immense ingenuity. A creative act for the beginning of life seems called for.

(4) It is exceedingly difficult to suppose that, in evolution, radically new mechanisms of great intricacy can arise spontaneously. Natural selection cannot function unless each stage is advantageous; it can be virtually proved that this is not always so. In the last analysis all scientific laws are based upon the spontaneous disordering of matter, a fact hard to reconcile with "creative" evolution.

It is often suggested that matter, dead or alive, possesses subtle properties which enable it to create organization under rare conditions or over immense periods. Such a view merely postulates the unobservable. If we must invoke the unobservable in any case, the chief objection to the view that God intervened in creation disappears.

Science undoubtedly suggests that intelligence has been at work in creation. This is also the teaching of Genesis.

III. MAN. Anatomically man is, in many respects, like the beasts — though significant differences exist and must not be forgotten. Archaeology shows that creatures which were anatomically man-like existed 100,000 years ago — perhaps earlier.

The Bible dates man at, probably, 5-10,000

EXAMPLE 204

B.C. and places him in Mesopotamia. It tells us that after his arrival there was a welter of technological invention. If attention is paid, not to man's anatomy, but to his mental endowment, then archaeology confirms both the biblical date and, probably, place: civilization started relatively suddenly and spread rapidly. When God made man in his own image the face of the world was changed and history commenced.

See also CREATION.

ROBERT E. D. CLARK

EXAMPLE. With the exception of I Pet. 2:21 (hypogrammon) the word is in translation of hypodeigma and typos or, occasionally, their cognates. Once used together (I Tim. 1:16), typos more frequently is found in conjunction with mimeomai, "to imitate," and usually signifies an ethical or spiritual model or pattern (Vorbild) to be followed (Phil. 3:17; I Thess. 1:7; II Thess. 3:9; I Tim. 4:12; I Pet. 5:3; cf. Acts 7:44; Heb. 8:5; Rom. 6:17; Titus 2:7). Hypodeigma is likewise so used (John 13:15; James 5:10). Both also refer to patterns to be avoided, i.e., warning examples or exhibitions of God's judgment and wrath (I Cor. 10:6, 11; Heb. 4:11; II Pet. 2:6).

In the typology of Hebrews a further significance appears, although this is not absent in the usage elsewhere (cf. Rom. 5:14; I Cor. 10:11; II Pet. 2:4-6; Jude 7). In Hebrews the OT cultus and Heilsgeschichte are viewed as a copy, a Nachbild (hypodeigma) and shadow (skia) of a heavenly prototype (typos: this is a peculiar usage due, perhaps, to the fact that it is a quotation; Heb. 8:5). Contrariwise, "the NT is not merely a reproduction of the Heavenly Reality but its actual substance, the Reality itself come down from heaven, the autē eikōn," i.e., the very archetype; cf. Heb. 10:1 (G. Vos, The Teaching of the Epistle to the Hebrews, Wm. B. Eerdmans Publishing Company, Grand Rapids, 1956, p. 58). The Old Covenant compares to the New as a shadow to reality. A preview of a film, though to the viewer chronologically prior, is actually a subsequent copy which is meaningful only in the light of the film itself. So OT patterns or examples have, temporally, a Vorbild character — models illustrating a plan of future (New Covenant) redemption and judgment and, thereby, giving a pattern to follow or avoid. But they are significant as Vorbild only when recognized as essentially Nachbild —

copies and "previews" of a prior Heavenly Reality whose substance is made visible only in the messianic age (cf. TWNT on hypodeigma). OT examples are patterns to follow or avoid precisely because they give insight into the nature and ways of God in redemption and in judgment. See TYPE.

E. EARLE ELLIS

EXCOMMUNICATION. The idea of disciplinary suspension of members from the fellowship of the church is found in only a few NT statements, but in later times it became an established ecclesiastical procedure. Its roots go back to the OT ban (ḥērem) applied to those who violated the Mosaic law and consequently placed themselves outside the covenant relationship (Ex. 30:22-38; Lev. 17:4). It was also imposed on lepers (Lev. 13:46). Judaism modified this ban by using degrees of excommunication, the more lenient nidduy imposing restrictions on social behavior lasting from thirty to sixty days, while the officially pronounced ḥērem involved ejection from the community.

The pronouncement of Jesus against any offender who refuses to hear the church (Matt. 18:17) does not consist of formal excommunication, although it suggests some severance of fellowship. In I Cor. 5:1-8 Paul urges a corporate act of ecclesiastical discipline against a serious offender and describes such action as a delivery to Satan, a term also used in I Tim. 1:20, where the apostle personally pronounces sentence upon Hymenaeus and Alexander. In the former case the offence was moral, but in the latter doctrinal. Another example of community discipline is found in II Cor. 2:5-11, where the harshness of the Corinthians' own decision leads Paul to plead for moderation. That at an early stage this procedure could be abused is strikingly seen in the action of Diotrephes (III John 10).

DONALD GUTHRIE

EXEGESIS. The term is derived by transliteration from the Greek exēgēsis, meaning narration or explanation. Although the noun does not occur in the NT (it appears once in the B text of Judg. 7:15), the verb is found several times with the former sense, and once with the latter (John 1:18). As the term suggests, exegesis is the science of interpretation. It is closely related to hermeneutics (q.v.). Whereas hermeneutics seeks to establish the ruling principles of biblical interpretation, exegesis seeks to fix the meaning of individual statements and passages.

This branch of study is basic to biblical theology even as biblical theology is basic to systematic theology. Exegesis, in turn, rests on the study of language, for translations, however serviceable, are not able to convey all the niceties of meaning which the Hebrew and Greek originals afford. The ingredients of this linguistic study are morphology, or the structure of the language; lexicography, or the meanings of the words; and syntax, or the functions of the various parts of speech. When these factors have been marshaled and utilized, it may still be necessary to appeal to the author's peculiarities of usage and to the demands of thought in the immediate context and even of the wider range of biblical teaching as a whole.

Exegesis is predicated on two fundamentals. First, it assumes that thought can be accurately conveyed in words, each of which, at least originally, had its own shade of meaning. Second, it assumes that the content of Scripture is of such superlative importance for man as to warrant the most painstaking effort to discover exactly what God seeks to impart through his word.

See also INTERPRETATION.

BIBLIOGRAPHY

E. C. Blackman, *Biblical Interpretation;* "The Task of Exegesis," in *The Background of the NT and its Eschatology* (ed. by W. D. Davies and D. Daube), pp. 3-26; O. Cullmann, "Le nécessité et la fonction de l' exégèse philologique et historique de la Bible," in *La Problème Biblique dans le Protestantisme,* pp. 131-47; H. Cunliffe-Jones, "The Problems of Biblical Exposition" in *ExpT* 65:4-7; O. Piper, "Modern Problems of NT Exegesis," in *Princeton Seminary Bulletin,* Aug. 1942, 3-14; J. N. Sanders, "The Problem of Exegesis," in *Theology* 43:324-32.

EVERETT F. HARRISON

EXHORTATION. The word usually translated "exhortation" is *paraklēsis* (verb, *parakaleō*). Originally it indicates a calling for, or near, with the same root as comforter (AV) or advocate (RV mg) in John 14:16. In the LXX and sometimes in the NT (Luke 2:25; 6:24; II Thess. 2:16, etc.) the meaning is consolation or comfort. More frequently, however, the word is translated "exhortation" (Acts 13:15; Rom. 12:8; I Tim. 4:13; Heb. 12:5; 13:22, etc.). Doubtless, the sense of consolation or strengthening is present even here. I Cor. 14:3 has "exhortation" (AV) or "comfort" (RV). Though incumbent on all (Heb. 10:25), *exhortation* is a particular responsibility of pastors and is to be exercised in the public exposition of Scripture (I Tim. 4:13).

R. COLIN CRASTON

EXISTENTIAL, EXISTENTIALISM. Existential is a term used by neo-orthodoxy (*q.v.*) to designate the place of personal commitment in an act of faith. Existential faith believes with inward passion; it is concerned with the relation between the self and the object of belief; it chooses from within the center of moral freedom. Cheap faith believes too easily; it does not count the cost.

Kierkegaard formulated the case for existentialism. He was greatly disturbed by the dead orthodoxy in the church of Denmark. He found that Christians were substituting symbols of the faith — baptism, confirmation, and general doctrine — for faith itself. The Christians recited the Apostles' Creed, but they took no account of the relation between what they recited and the state of their own lives.

Kierkegaard illustrated the peril of faith by Abraham's offering of Isaac. Cheap faith reads the account and sighs, "Yes, yes." It then turns to other affairs. Existential faith is troubled by the account because it must be personally responsible for what it believes. How can a holy God commend a human sacrifice? And how can a sinner love God so perfectly that his affection for his own son is transcended? Existential faith admires what it cannot believe; and when it does believe, it believes with fear and trembling.

Speculation is the opposite of existential faith, and the most relevant illustration of fitting speculation is science. The scientist is able to pursue it because he divorces himself from any personal involvement in his experiment. He assumes a detached attitude; he seeks objectivity, prediction, and control.

Existential faith cannot assume the role of spectator for it must unite itself with the object of faith in spiritual commitment. God is a person, and a person is known only in and through an act of self-surrender. Fellowship is the blending of life with life; it is a sharing of essence.

Although the term "existential" properly denotes neo-orthodox interests, it signifies a concept which has always been precious to Christians everywhere. Scripture distinguishes between general and vital faith. General faith is cheap faith; it is the faith of demons. Vital faith is cordial trust; it is a whole-souled act of personal commitment. Vital faith is transformed by the relation between the self and that which is believed.

BIBLIOGRAPHY
E. L. Allen, *Existentialism from Within*; Marjorie Grene, *Dreadful Freedom*; S. Kierkegaard, *Fear and Trembling*; Helmut Kuhn, "Existentialism — Christian and Anti-Christian" in *ThT* 6, 311-23.

EDWARD JOHN CARNELL

EXODUS. The English word is from the LXX title (Greek *exodos* "a way out") of the second book of the OT, but it refers more specifically to the crucial event of that book — God's redemption of his people Israel from Egypt. This divine act in human history, recounted from generation to generation, was never lost sight of, even in the NT (Acts 7:36). Psalmists, prophets, and historical writers were continually pointing back to this miraculous event.

It served as a point of reference (Judg. 19:30; Jer. 7:25) and dating (I Kings 6:1); it was the basis for God's command to keep the sabbath day (Deut. 5:15); it was the essence of Israelite epistemology, for by this expression of God's power all were to *know* that there was only one God and him they were to obey (Deut. 4:37-40). Of even greater significance, the might manifested in the Exodus was the motivation and source of power for living a holy life (Lev. 11:45).

The Exodus, as God's deliverance of his "first-born son" (Ex. 4:22-23) from an "iron furnace" (Deut. 4:20; Jer. 11:4) and from a "house of bondage" (Ex. 13:3; Deut. 5:6), typifies God's gracious redemptive act in the lives of all men of faith, "the assembly (church) of the first-born who are enrolled in heaven" (Heb. 12:23). The passover lamb, slain the night before the Exodus (Ex. 12:21, 28), becomes the symbol for Jesus Christ, the Paschal Lamb "who takes away the sin of the world" (John 1:29). The celebration of the Lord's Supper, initiated at the Passover season, becomes not only an occasion for "proclaiming the Lord's death" (I Cor. 11:26), but also a time for remembering the powerful, loving God of the Exodus who, by sending his only Son, made possible for the "Israel of God" (Gal. 6:16) "a way out" of sin and oppression. For special NT uses of *exodos*, see Luke 9:31; II Pet. 1:15.

See also PASSOVER.

BIBLIOGRAPHY
Patrick Fairbairn, *The Typology of Scripture*, Vol. II, pp. 30-50.

DEWEY M. BEEGLE

EXORCISM. Exorcism is the act of expelling evil spirits in order to deliver the afflicted from their malign influence. Incantations, magical charms, and formulae for this purpose appear in Egyptian and Babylonian literature. Jews of the Persian Empire used incantation bowls bearing formulae containing various names of the God of Israel, other deities, angels, King Solomon, and an illustrious rabbi (Joshua ben Perahya) deemed potent in insuring protection from evil spirits.

The NT describes two professional exorcists. Simon Magus (Acts 8:9 ff.) looked upon the gospel as a kind of superior magic and desired to add it to his repertoire. Bar Jesus (Acts 13:6 ff.) is described as a "sorcerer" and "false prophet."

Healing the body and casting out demons are frequently associated in the ministry of Jesus (cf. Mark 1:21-34). Power was delegated to the disciples to cast out evil spirits and to heal (Luke 9:1).

In the development of the liturgy for baptism a form of exorcism was introduced. The pre-baptismal state was looked upon as one of bondage to Satan, hence the formula: "Depart from him, foul spirit, and give place to the Holy Spirit, the Paraclete."

Toward the end of the third century an order of exorcists was established which continues as one of the minor orders of the Roman Church.

CHARLES F. PFEIFFER

EXPEDIENCY. Expediency is the character of an act in which any predetermined goal is sought by whatever means will enable one to achieve the goal most directly and advantageously without regard to the moral implications of these means.

The relationship between expediency and moral values may be set forth in different ways. According to utilitarians the two areas coalesce; what is really expedient constitutes the right.

According to the Stoics (*q.v.*) and Kant the two areas overlap. The good must always be followed for the sake of duty (*q.v.*) alone; but where no moral standard for conduct is applicable, expediency becomes the only sensible path to follow.

A third type of relationship between expediency and moral principles sets them apart as mutually exclusive guides to conduct and as usually in conflict. The expedient, therefore, must never be followed because it is expedient, but every act must be morally determined.

Christians generally have followed the second view and argued for an area of *adiaphora* (*q.v.*) where expediency has a place, but some have tended to hold to the third view. All Christians have insisted that, however inexpedient the right course of action may sometimes appear to be, in the overruling providence (*q.v.*) of God the believer may know that the morally good always works out *ultimately* to his best advantage (Rom. 8:28).

KENNETH S. KANTZER

EXPERIENCE. In the broad sense, this term includes all of our conscious processes. Thus defined, it involves sense perceptions, feelings, memory, recollections, knowledge, prejudices, illusions, hopes, fears, beliefs, etc. The common denominator for these is the sense of personal awareness, an awareness residing in the subjective life of a person.

A systematic development of the emphasis upon experience is the methodology of empiricism, which holds that all knowledge comes through experience. Empiricists have usually limited experience to sense-experience, and maintained that the only valid knowledge is either (a) that which is acquired through the five senses, or (b) that which is referable to the five senses for verification.

Empiricism has for several decades had the last word in most questions. Hence it is to be expected that its possibilities have been explored in the area of religion. Religious empiricists hold that all religious ideas issue from experience, however defined. They hold that belief in God results from "witness theology" as distinct from speculative theology.

Some thinkers have been willing to expand the definition of experience to include such experiences as the mystic claims for himself; others have allowed moral experience as a source of religious ideas. The religious romanticists sought to explain the origin of religion in terms of man's experience of specialized types of feeling: e.g., the feeling of dependence (Schleiermacher) or the feeling of awe in the presence of the "numinous" quality of the universe (Otto).

Historic Christianity has understood the term "Christian experience" to mean the conscious reception of the ministry of divine grace in the life of the soul. The study of Christian experience has most frequently involved the investigation of the phenomenon of conversion.

BIBLIOGRAPHY
HERE, V, pp. 630-35; L. W. Beck, *Philosophic Inquiry*, pp. 55-59; Dagobert Runes, *Dictionary of Philosophy*, p. 103; John Wild, *Challenge of Existentialism*, pp. 188, 219.

HAROLD B. KUHN

EXPIATION. See ATONEMENT, SACRIFICE.

EXTREME UNCTION. An anointing with oil of the sick used as a sacrament in the Roman Catholic Church. "Extreme" may refer to the fact that the unction is the last of the three sacramental unctions, the former at baptism and confirmation, or to the fact that it is administered when the patient is *in extremis*. The Council of Trent states that it was instituted by Christ. No reference is given, but it is said to be implied in Mark. Its sacramental status and effects are based on an interpretation of James 5:14, 15. Oil, consecrated by the bishop, is the matter; unction with prayer by the priests the sign; the grace given on condition of repentance and faith is forgiveness of sins, renewed health and strength of soul, and also of body if God sees fit. Our Lord used varied means in healing the sick, but there is no actual record of his use of oil, unless we infer it from apostolic practice in Mark 6:13. Was the use of oil medicinal or symbolical? The Roman Church makes the oil symbolical of the Holy Spirit. Prayer for the blessing of oil for the sick is found in the Apostolic Tradition of Hippolytus (*ca.* A.D. 225) and in the Euchologion of Serapion (*ca.* A.D. 365). From the fifth century references to anointing are more frequent. The rite was included among the seven sacraments in the thirteenth century, and its doctrine defined at Trent.

RICHARD J. COATES

EYE. The OT word is '*ayin*, while the NT most often uses *ophthalmos* and twice *omma* (Matt. 20:34; Mark 8:23).

The most frequent use is in the ordinary literal sense. As such the eye is considered of great value. This is revealed by the custom of putting out the eyes of one's enemies (Judg. 16:21; I Sam. 11:2), and by such a statement as Gal. 4:15. The eye also was considered the main channel of temptation (Gen. 3:6; cf. I John 2:16).

The most interesting uses are figurative. In

this sense the eye usually stands for mental or spiritual understanding. Thus to know Christ is to have the eyes of one's understanding enlightened (Eph. 1:18) and to keep the commandments of the Lord enlightens the eyes (Ps. 19:8).

The figurative use of the eye in the Bible discloses the close relationship between the state of the soul and the physical self in Hebrew thought, e.g., a person with an "evil eye" is envious (Deut. 28:54), a "bountiful eye" is generous (Prov. 22:9), a "high eye" is proud (Ps. 18:27; cf. Isa. 10:12).

WALTER W. WESSEL

F

FACE. The Hebrew *'ap,* "nostril;" *'ayin,* "eye;" *pānim,* "face" ("presence," "sight," "countenance," etc.); and the Greek *prosōpon,* "face" (person, presence, etc.) are all rendered by face.

Literally, face designates the front, surface, or essential part of man (Ezek. 10:14), animals (Gen. 30:40), the earth (Gen. 1:29), the sky (Luke 12:56), water (Gen. 7:18), etc.

Figuratively and idiomatically, face is used in the following meaningful combinations: hiding the face — expressing disapproval (Deut. 31:17 f.), unconcern (Ps. 10:11; 13:1), forgiveness (Ps. 51:9), shame (Isa. 53:3), fear (Rev. 6:16); falling upon the face — symbolizing prostration before man (Gen. 50:18; II Sam. 9:6; Ruth 2:10) or God (Gen. 17:3; Num. 16:22; Josh. 5:14; Judg. 13:20); setting the face — signifying determination (II Kings 12:17; Isa. 50:7; Jer. 42:15; Luke 9:51) or opposition (Lev. 17:10; Ezek. 14:8); covering the face — signalizing mourning (II Sam. 19:4), reverence (Ex. 3:6; Isa. 6:2), or doom (Esth. 7:8; Mark 14:65); looking another in the face — implying challenging boldness (II Kings 14:8, 11; Gal. 2:11); turning the face — illustrating disapproval (II Chron. 30:9) or rejection (Ps. 143:7; Ezek. 7:22); spitting in the face — displaying utter contempt (Num. 12:14; Deut. 25:9; Job 30:10; Matt. 26:67); disfiguring the face — portraying paganism (Lev. 19:28; 21:5) or feigned religiosity (Matt. 6:16); knowing or beholding another's face — denoting intimate relationship (Deut. 34:10; Ps. 17:15; Matt. 18:10; I Cor. 13:12); causing the face to shine upon another — giving or beseeching a blessing or benediction (Num. 6:25; Ps. 31:16; 67:1; 80:3, 7; 119:135).

The faces of Moses (Ex. 34:30-35; II Cor. 3:7, 13), Christ (Isa. 52:14; Matt. 17:2), Stephen (Acts 6:15), believers (II Cor. 3:18), a mighty angel (Rev. 10:1) and God (Ex. 33:20, 23; Rev. 22:4) have special significance.

See also PRESENCE, DIVINE.

WICK BROOMALL

FAITH. Noun corresponding to the verb "believe," for which the Hebrew is *he'ĕmîn,* the hiphil form of *'āman,* and the Greek (LXX and NT) *pisteuō.* The latter is a key word in the NT, being the term regularly used to denote the many-sided religious relationship into which the gospel calls men — that of trust in God through Christ. The complexity of this idea is reflected in the variety of constructions used with the verb (a *hoti*-clause, or accusative and infinitive, expressing truth believed; *en* and *epi* with the dative, denoting restful reliance on that to which, or him to whom, credit is given; *eis* and, occasionally, *epi* with the accusative — the most common, characteristic and original NT usage, scarcely present in the LXX and not at all in classical Greek — conveying the thought of a movement of trust going out to, and laying hold of, the object of its confidence). The Hebrew noun corresponding to *'āman* (*'ĕmûnâ,* rendered *pistis* in the LXX), regularly denotes faithfulness in the sense of trustworthiness, and *pistis* occasionally bears this sense in the NT (Rom. 3:3, of God; Matt. 23:23; Gal. 5:22; Titus 2:10, of man). The word *'ĕmûnâ* normally refers to the faithfulness of God, and only in Hab. 2:4 is it used to signify man's religious response to God. There, however, the contrast in the context between the temper of the righteous and the proud self-sufficiency of the Chaldeans seems to demand for it a broader sense than "faithfulness" alone — the sense, namely, of self-renouncing, trustful reliance upon God, the attitude of heart of which faithfulness in life is the natural expression. This is certainly the sense in which the apostolic writers quote the text (Rom. 1:17; Gal. 3:11; Heb. 10:38), and the sense which *pistis,* like *pisteuō,* regularly carries in the NT, where both words are used virtually as technical terms (John preferring the verb, Paul the noun) to express the complex thought of unqualified acceptance of, and exclusive dependence on, the mediation of the Son as alone securing the mercy of the Father. Both normally bear this whole weight of meaning, whether their grammatical object is God, Christ, the gospel, a truth, a promise, or is not expressed at all. Both signify commitment as following from conviction, even in contexts where faith is defined in terms of the latter only (e.g., compare Heb. 11:1 with the rest of the chapter). The nature of faith, according to the NT, is to live by the truth it receives; faith, resting on God's promise, gives thanks for God's grace by working for God's glory.

Some occasional contractions of this broad idea should be noticed:

(1) James, alone of NT writers, uses both noun and verb to denote bare intellectual assent to truth (James 2:14-26). But here he is explicitly mimicking the usage of those whom he seeks to correct — Jewish converts, who may well have inherited their notion of faith from contemporary Jewish sources — and there is no reason to suppose that this usage was normal or natural to him (his reference to faith in 5:15, for instance, clearly carries a fuller meaning). In any case, the point he makes, namely, that a merely intellectual "faith," such as the demons have, is inadequate, is wholly in line with the rest of the NT. For example, when James says: "faith without works is dead" (2:26), he is saying the same as Paul, who says in essence, "faith without works is not faith at all, but its opposite" (cf. Gal. 5:6; I Tim. 5:8).

(2) Occasionally, by a natural transition, "the faith" denotes the body of truths believed (e.g., Jude 3; Rom. 1:5(?); Gal. 1:23; I Tim. 4:1, 6). This became standard usage in the second century.

(3) From Christ himself derives a narrower use of "faith" for an exercise of trust which works miracles (Matt. 17:20 f.; I Cor. 12:9; 13:2), or prompts the working of miracles (Matt. 9:28 f.; 15:28; Acts 14:9). Saving faith is not always accompanied by "miracle-faith," however (I Cor. 12:9); nor vice versa (cf. Matt. 7:22 f.).

I. GENERAL CONCEPTION. Three points must be noted for the circumscribing of the biblical idea of faith:

A. *Faith in God involves right belief about God.* The word faith in ordinary speech covers both credence of propositions ("beliefs") and confidence in persons or things. In the latter case, some belief about the object trusted is the logical and psychological presupposition of the act of trust itself, for trust in a thing reflects a positive expectation about its behavior, and rational expectation is impossible if the thing's capacities for behavior are wholly unknown. Throughout the Bible, trust in God is made to rest on belief of what he has revealed concerning his character and purposes. In the NT, where faith in God is defined as trust in Christ, the acknowledgment of Jesus as the expected Messiah and the incarnate Son of God is regarded as basic to it. The writers allow that faith in some form can exist where as yet information about Jesus is incomplete (Acts 19:1 ff.), but not where his divine identity and Christhood are consciously denied (I John 2:22 f.; II John 7-9); all that is possible then is idolatry (I John 5:21), the worship of a man-made unreality. The frequency with which the Epistles depict faith as knowing, believing and obeying "the truth" (Titus 1:1; II Thess. 2:13; I Pet. 1:22, etc.) show that their authors regarded orthodoxy as faith's fundamental ingredient (cf. Gal. 1:8-9).

B. *Faith rests on divine testimony.* Beliefs, as such, are convictions held on grounds, not of self-evidence, but of testimony. Whether particular beliefs should be treated as known certainties or doubtful opinions will depend on the worth of the testimony on which they are based. The Bible views faith's convictions as certainties and equates them with knowledge (I John 3:2; 5:18-20, etc.), not because they spring from supposedly self-authenticating mystical experience, but because they rest on the testimony of a God who "cannot lie" (Titus 1:2) and is therefore utterly trustworthy. The testimony of Christ to heavenly things (John 3:11, 31 f.), and of the prophets and apostles to Christ (Acts 10:39-43), is the testimony of God himself (I John 5:9 ff.); this God-inspired witness is God's own witness (cf. I Cor. 2:10-13; I Thess. 2:13), in such a sense that to receive it is to certify that God is true (John 3:33), and to reject it is to make God a liar (I John 5:10). Christian faith rests on the recognition of apostolic and biblical testimony as God's own testimony to his Son.

C. *Faith is a supernatural divine gift.* Sin and Satan have so blinded fallen men (Eph. 4:18; II Cor. 4:4), that they cannot discern dominical and apostolic witness to be God's word, nor "see" and comprehend the realities of which it speaks (John 3:3; I Cor. 2:14), nor "come" in self-renouncing trust to Christ (John 6:44, 65), till the Holy Spirit has enlightened them (cf. II Cor. 4:6). Only the recipients of this divine "teaching," "drawing" and "anointing" come to Christ and abide in him (John 6:44-45; I John 2:20, 27). God is thus the author of all saving faith (Eph. 2:8; Phil. 1:29: see CALL, REGENERATION).

II. BIBLICAL PRESENTATION. Throughout Scripture, God's people live by faith; but the idea of faith develops as God's revelation of grace and truth, on which faith rests, enlarges. The OT variously defines faith as resting, trusting and hoping in the Lord, cleaving to him, waiting for him, making him our shield and tower, taking refuge in him, etc. Psalmists and prophets, speaking in individual and national terms respectively, present faith as unwavering trust in God to save his servants from their foes and fulfil his declared purpose of blessing them. Isaiah, particularly, denounces reliance on human aid as inconsistent with such trust (Isa. 30:1-18, etc.). The NT regards the self-despairing hope, world-renouncing obedience and heroic tenacity by which OT believers manifested their faith as a pattern which Christians must reproduce (Rom. 4:11-25; Heb. 10:39 — 12:2). Continuity is avowed here, but also novelty; for faith, receiving God's new utterance in the words and deeds of Christ (Heb. 1:1 f.), has become a knowledge of present salvation. Faith, so regarded, says Paul, first "came" with Christ (Gal. 3:23-25). The Gospels show Christ demanding trust in himself as bearing the messianic salvation. John is fullest on this, emphasizing (1) that faith ("believing on," "coming to," and "receiving" Christ) involves acknowledging Jesus, not merely as a God-sent teacher and miracle worker (this is insufficient, John 2:23 f.), but as God incarnate (John 20:28), whose atoning death is the sole means of salvation (John 3:14 f.; 6:51-58); (2) that faith in Christ secures present enjoyment of "eternal life" in fellowship with God (John 5:24; 17:3). The Epistles echo this, and present faith in various further relationships. Paul shows that faith in Christ is the only way to a right relationship with God, which human works cannot gain (see Romans and Galatians); Hebrews and I Peter present faith as the dynamic of hope and endurance under persecution.

III. HISTORY OF DISCUSSION. The church grasped from the first that assent to apostolic testimony is the fundamental element in Christian faith; hence the concern of both sides in the Gnostic controversy to show that their tenets were genuinely apostolic. During the Patristic period, however, the idea of faith was so narrowed that this assent came to be regarded as the whole of it. Four factors together caused this: first, the insistence of the anti-Gnostic fathers, particularly Tertullian, that the faithful are those who believe "the faith" as stated in the "rule of faith" (*regula fidei*), i.e., the Creed; second, the intellectualism of Clement and Origen, to whom *pistis* (assent on authority) was just an inferior substitute for, and steppingstone to, *gnōsis* (demonstrative knowledge) of spiritual things; third, the assimilation of biblical morality to Stoic moralism, an ethic, not of grateful dependence, but of resolute self-reliance; fourth, the clothing of the biblical doctrine of communion with God in Neo-Platonic dress, which made it appear as a mystical ascent to the supersensible achieved by aspiring love, having no link with the ordinary exercise of faith at all. Also, since the doctrine of justification (*q.v.*) was not understood, the soteriological significance of faith was misconceived, and faith (understood as orthodoxy) was regarded simply as the passport to baptism (remitting all past sins), and to a lifelong probation in the church (giving the baptized opportunity to make themselves worthy of glory by their good works). The Scholastics refined this view. They reproduced the equation of faith with credence, distinguishing between *fides informis* ("unformed" faith, bare orthodoxy) and *fides caritate formata* (credence "formed" into a working principle by the supernatural addition to it of the distinct grace of love). Both sorts of faith, they held, are meritorious works, though the quality of merit attaching to the first is merely *congruent* (rendering divine reward fit, though not obligatory), and only the second gains *condign* merit (making divine reward due as a matter of justice). Rome still formally identifies faith with credence, and has added a further refinement by distinguishing between "explicit" faith (belief which knows its object) and "implicit" faith (uncomprehending assent to whatever it may be that the church holds). Only the latter (which is evidently no more than a vote of confidence in the teaching church, and may consist with complete ignorance of Christianity) is held to be required of laymen for salvation. But a mere docile disposition of this sort is poles apart from the biblical concept of saving faith.

The Reformers restored biblical perspectives by insisting that faith is more than orthodoxy — not *fides* merely, but *fiducia*, personal trust and confidence in God's mercy through Christ; that it is not a meritorious work, one facet of human righteousness, but rather an appropriating instrument, an empty hand outstretched to receive the free gift of God's righteousness in Christ; that faith is God-given, and is itself the animating principle from which love and good works spontaneously spring; and that communion with God means, not an exotic rapture of mystical ecstasy, but just faith's everyday commerce with the Saviour. Confessional Protestantism has always maintained these positions. In Arminianism, there resides a tendency to depict faith as the human work upon which the pardon of sin is suspended — as, in fact, man's contribution to his own salvation. This would be in effect a Protestant revival of the doctrine of human merit.

Liberalism radically psychologized faith, reducing it to a sense of contented harmony with the Infinite through Christ (Schleiermacher), or a fixed resolve to follow Christ's teaching (Ritschl), or both together. Liberal influence is reflected in the now widespread supposition that "faith," understood as an optimistic confidence in the friendliness of the universe, divorced from any specific credal tenets, is a distinctively religious state of mind. Neo-supernaturalist and existentialist theologians, reacting against this psychologism, stress the supernatural origin and character of faith. They describe it as an active commitment of mind and will, man's repeated "yes" to the repeated summons to decision issued by God's word in Christ; but the elusiveness of their account of the content of that word makes it hard sometimes to see what the believer is thought to say "yes" to.

Clearly, each theologian's view of the nature and saving significance of faith will depend on the views he holds of the Scriptures, and of God, man, and of their mutual relations.

BIBLIOGRAPHY
Arndt; MM; E. D. Burton, *Galatians* (ICC), pp. 475-86; B. B. Warfield in *HDB*, s.v., and *Biblical and Theological Studies*, pp. 375-444; G. H. Box in *HDCG*; J. G. Machen, *What is Faith?*; B. Citron, *New Birth*, pp. 86-94; systematic theologies of C. Hodge (III, pp. 41-113) and L. Berkhof (IV, viii: pp. 493-509).

JAMES I. PACKER

FAITHFUL, FAITHFULNESS. God's faithfulness in the OT has a twofold emphasis. First, he is absolutely reliable, firmly constant, and not given to arbitrariness or fickleness. His faithfulness is great (Lam. 3:23), extensive (Ps. 36:5), and enduring (Ps. 100:5). Two words are used to depict this attribute: *'emet* (usually translated in the AV "truth," i.e., that which is reliable, and "faithfulness" in the RSV) and *'emûnâ* (commonly rendered "faithfulness"), both derived from *'mn* which denotes "firmness," "fixity." The name Rock (Deut. 32:4, 15; Ps. 19:14, etc.) depicts this firmness.

Second, God's faithfulness is revealed in his covenant-loyalty (Deut. 7:9), his steadfast, loyal love (*hesed*, usually "mercy" or "kindness" in the AV). The frequent combination of *hesed* and *'emet* (Gen. 24:27, 49; Ex. 34:6; Ps. 40:11, etc.) indicates that *hesed* connotes a determined, almost stubborn, steadfastness toward his people and covenant (cf. Ps. 136).

Faithful men fulfil responsibilities steadfastly (Prov. 13:17); their word is dependable (Prov. 14:5). By relying on God, the righteous man gains the reliability and firmness which he does not have in himself (cf. Hab. 2:4, where the AV translates *'emûnâ* by faith).

The NT builds upon the OT in affirming God's faithfulness (*pistis*, in a passive sense), which can never be nullified by man's faithlessness. The faithful (*pistos*) God guarantees his sons' entry into glory (I Cor. 1:9; I Thess. 5:24), fulfils his promises (II Cor. 1:18; Heb. 10:23; 11:11), brings triumph to sufferers (I Pet. 4:19), forgives confessed sins (I John 1:9). Divine faithfulness is not conditioned by *external* standards: God must be faithful; he cannot deny himself (II Tim. 2:13).

In the NT a faithful man does his duty diligently, as a servant (Matt. 25:21, 23), steward (Luke 12:42; I Cor. 4:2), or witness (Rev. 2:13). Several apostolic companions were deemed faithful: Timothy (I Cor. 4:17), Tychicus (Eph. 6:21; Col. 4:7), Onesimus (Col. 4:9), Silas (I Pet. 5:12). Paul viewed his divine commission as a proof of his faithfulness (I Cor. 7:25; I Tim. 1:12) and affirmed, near his death, his complete loyalty (II Tim. 4:7). NT faithfulness has both its incentive and dynamic: Christ's sterling example (Heb. 2:17; 3:2; Rev. 1:5; 3:14; 19:11) and the Spirit's fruitfulness (Gal. 5:22, where the passive force of *pistis* accords with the other virtues).

In the Pastorals five declarations are called *faithful* because they are completely reliable (I Tim. 1:15; 3:1; 4:9; II Tim. 2:11; Titus 3:8). Compare the "faithful and true" words of Rev. 21:5; 22:6. This combination recalls the OT relationship between *faithfulness* and *truth*. Occasionally (cf. Rom. 3:7; 15:8; I Cor. 5:8; II Cor. 7:14; Eph. 5:9), "truth" (*alētheia*) seems to reflect a Hebrew antecedent and could be translated "trustworthiness," "dependability."

BIBLIOGRAPHY
Arndt; C. W. Hodge in *ISBE*; H. H. Rowley, *Faith of Israel*, pp. 66-67; N. H. Snaith, *Distinctive Ideas of the OT*, pp. 98-106.

DAVID A. HUBBARD

FAITH-HEALING. This term describes healings that occur contrary to normal medical expectation, wrought by virtue of a special spiritual gift (I Cor. 12:28). Biblical miracles of this kind are regarded as coming through direct divine action, in response to the faith of the sick person (Matt. 9:22, 29), or of someone else on his behalf (Matt. 9:2; Mark 9:24; John 4:50). Jesus Christ miraculously healed all types of disease, and also cast out demons. During his earthly ministry he gave his disciples power to heal diseases and to cast out demons (Matt. 10:1), and this power was also exercised after Pentecost, when again the need of faith is mentioned (Acts 14:9), and more specifically faith in Christ (Acts 3:16).

Paul says that some have the gift of healing from the Holy Spirit, though this gift is not for everyone (I Cor. 12:9, 30). In James 5:14, 15 probably no one is available with the gift of healing; then the elders are to anoint the sick man, and pray over him: again faith is emphasized; "the prayer of faith shall save the sick." Commentators differ over whether this is medical treatment (oil) with prayer, or whether the anointing is a symbolic act of faith like the laying on of hands (cf. Mark 6:13). In no way, however, does this passage, which deals with healing, support the Roman idea of the sacrament of Extreme Unction as a preparation for death. In the NT we note: (1) Christians were not always healed (II Tim. 4:20); (2) all recorded faith-healings were virtually instantaneous, and patients did not need after-treatment.

All down the ages, and today, miracles of healing have been claimed, not only by orthodox Christians, but by followers of various cults. Christian Scientists claim healing through the denial of the existence of disease. Spiritualist healers usually claim to be guided by some deceased spirit-doctor. Roman Catholics claim many cures at Lourdes through the influence of the Virgin Mary, though only a tiny proportion of these are officially put forward as miracles. Pentecostalists and others often conduct "healing missions." Many Christians have experiences of cases that appear to have been healed miraculously in answer to prayer when doctors had given up hope.

It is noteworthy that almost all these cures are either gradual, or necessitate further treatment, whether medical or further laying on of hands. Are they of the same order as NT divine healings? In assessing modern cases we note: (1) the amazing effect of mind over body (e.g., in hypnotism); (2) the psychic power that some possess, which makes them vehicles of healing; (3) the willingness of God to answer believing prayer that is according to his will. It would seem that he normally answers prayer for healing by a gradual process that may include the use of medicines, though sometimes it is against normal medical expectation; but that, as in NT times, he does not will to heal all Christians.

BIBLIOGRAPHY
B. B. Warfield, *Miracles: Yesterday and Today*; J. Stafford Wright, "Man in the Process of Time," in *What is Man?*, Chap. viii.

J. STAFFORD WRIGHT

FALL, THE. Genesis confines its attention to events and their consequences, usually not even stating the connection, but allowing facts to speak for themselves. Furthermore, the total biblical revelation must be allowed to teach the importance and implications of any event. We cannot, therefore, treat of Genesis 3 in isolation, or as if the rest of the Bible did not, explicitly and implicitly, point back to it as the explanation of the dislocated and frustrated life of man. We will first survey the central NT passage and then proceed to Genesis 3.

In Rom. 5:12-21, Paul compares Adam and Christ. (1) The terms of the comparison — the "one man," Adam, counterpoises the "one man," Jesus — demand that we think of Adam as a veritable, historical person, federal head of mankind, as Jesus, in his place, is federal head of the redeemed. Hodges (*Romans*, Edinburgh, 1864, p. 179) quotes Turretin on this last point. The union of mankind with Adam is "1. Natural, as he is the father and we are the children, and 2. Political and forensic, as he was the representative head and chief of the whole human race." (2) Adam's sin is *hamartia*, "a missing of the mark;" *parabasis*, "transgression of a known law" (cf. I Tim. 2:14, where Adam's awareness of his sin's implications is pointed out); and *paraptōma*, "a blunder." Adam's probation was genuine, not fictional. He possessed all facts and capacities to maintain his unfallen state and was surrounded by every inducement to do so; yet he fell. (3) The result was that death and condemnation passed on to the whole race, by virtue of God's imputation of Adam's sin and guilt.

In Genesis 3 we not only find nothing inconsistent with, but everything pointing to, Rom. 5:12 ff. (1) The origin of the impulse to sin was both external, in the tempter, and internal, in the consent of the will (cf. James 1:14; 3:6). (2) The nature of the temptation was to query God's word (vss. 2-4a), suspect God's character and good will (4b-5), and exalt ambition, sensuality, and selfishness above loyalty to God in his word (5-6). "Man, therefore, when carried away by the blasphemies of Satan, did his very utmost to annihilate the whole glory of God" (Calvin, *Institutes*, II, 1, 4). (3) The result was death, banishment, dislocation of the whole natural order, and the begetting of an evil progeny. Except for the first mentioned of these results, they hardly need comment. The Bible teaches clearly that sin banishes from God's presence (Isa. 6:4-5), disrupts nature (Deut. 28), and is transmitted by natural generation (Ps. 51:5). But what of death? The narrative affirms that death (*q.v.*) physical and spiritual, is not native to man, but a penalty on his sin.

In Paradise he lived under the twofold direction that he should eat the Tree of Life and live, but not eat the Tree of Knowledge lest he die. When he disobeyed, God removed him from the proximity of the Tree of Life, thus confirming upon man, judicially and in effect, the sentence of death, which remained in operation until Christ brought life and immortality to light in the gospel.

JOHN ALEXANDER MOTYER

FALSE CHRISTS. The expression false Christs, formed on the analogy of "false apostles" (II Cor. 11:13) and "false brothers" (II Cor. 11:26), is derived from the Greek *pseudochristoi*, and is used in Matt. 24:24 and Mark 13:22 to denominate those who falsely claim to be Israel's deliverer. Gamaliel alludes to a revolt (A.D. 6) led by a Judas of Galilee and to a certain Theudas who perished with four hundred followers (Acts 5:36-37). The military tribune (Acts 21:38) mentions a certain Egyptian who led four thousand daggermen (*sikarioi*) to the Mt. of Olives and bade them wait until, at his command, the walls fell flat. When the attack failed the Egyptian conveniently hid himself. The tribune erroneously thought that the Jewish leaders had identified Paul as the Egyptian and were exacting vengeance for his self-imposed exile. During the revolt against Rome John of Giscala, leader of the Zealots, and Simon bar Gioras (i.e., son of the proselyte) opposed one another with ruinous consequences terminating in the debacle of A.D. 70. The last of the false Christs in the early Christian eras was Simon bar Cochba (A.D. 131-135) to whom R. Aqiba referred Num. 24:17.

In its broader application, as the phrase "in my name" (Matt. 24:5) suggests, the term false Christs suggests a problem prompted by consideration of the apparent contradiction between Jesus' claims to lordship and the disappointing evidence of his sovereignty inside history. The temptation is to have the chasm bridged by more patent demonstrations of Jesus' sovereignty rather than to live in constant faith that Jesus Christ's purposes ripen fully not within but outside history.

BIBLIOGRAPHY
Arndt; G. R. Beasley-Murray, *A Commentary on Mark Thirteen*, pp. 83-85; HDCG, s.v. "False Christs"; E. Schuerer, *Geschichte des Juedischen Volkes*[3], I, pp. 600 ff.

FREDERICK W. DANKER

FAMILY. The family is historically the first social group to emerge among men and contains in its primitive form the germs of both state and church. It is both a good in itself and a means for promoting further good. Its purpose is (1) physical — to beget children and (2) moral — to train individuals to sink their individuality in a higher unity. Thus "education is not primarily the concern of the school, or even of the state, but of the family" (E. Brunner, *The Divine Imperative*, p. 512).

The Hebrew *mišpāhâ*, "a family connection of individuals," comes to mean also clan, tribe or nation (Num. 3:15; Judg. 13:2; Amos 3:1-2). In Judg. 6:15 "family" is *elep*, i.e., thousand (as in I Sam. 10:19; Mic. 5:2). The usual NT equivalent is *patria* (from *patēr*, "father"), occasionally translated "lineage" (Luke 2:4 AV, RSV) or "kindred" (Acts 3:25 AV). In Acts 7:13 RSV "family" is *genos* (AV has "kindred," ERV "race").

In ancient Israel the family was an important social and administrative unit. Law and worship remained in the hands of the "elders," i.e., heads of families, long after the settlement in Canaan. A woman (*q.v.*) was regarded as the absolute possession of her husband, hence the *mōhar*, "purchase-price," paid to her father (Ex. 22:17). She was valued chiefly for the bearing of sons; failure led to the practice of polygamy and divorce. A nobler conception of marriage appears in the creation story where Eve is Adam's "helper, matching him," (Gen. 2:18). Monogamy is implied too in Gen. 2:24 and in the prophetic insistence (e.g., Hosea) that Israel is Yahweh's wife to the exclusion of all others.

Christ seems to relegate the family to a secondary place in Matt. 10:36 f.; Luke 14:26; but for him too it was "a training ground for larger sympathies and duties" (E. F. Scott) and he regarded it as a pattern for his new order as the "Our Father" shows. All true family life stems from God (Eph. 3:15).

See also MARRIAGE.

BIBLIOGRAPHY
Arndt; A-S; D. S. Adam, *Handbook of Christian Ethics*, par. 218-32; W. F. Lofthouse, *Family and State*; E. F. Scott, *Man and Society in the New Testament*, pp. 73-75.

L. E. H. STEPHENS-HODGE

FAST, FASTING. Fasting (Heb. *ṣôm*, Gk. *nēsteia*) signifies deprivation of food, normally as deliberately undertaken for a religious purpose. There are many instances of fasts in both the Old and the New Testament. The Israelites fasted when the ark was restored by the Philistines (I Sam. 7:6). Nehemiah fasted when he heard of the sorry state of Jerusalem (Neh. 1:4). Joel summoned the people to return to the Lord with fasting (Joel 2:12). Cornelius was engaged in a fast when he was told to send for Peter (Acts 10:30), who himself may well have been fasting in his period of intercession (Acts 10:10). There was fasting when Paul and Barnabas were commissioned for the first missionary journey (Acts 13:3), and Paul speaks of his own frequent fastings (II Cor. 6:5; 11:27) and can see a place for times of continence, prayer and fasting within the legitimate marriage relationship (I Cor. 7:5). Jesus himself fasted (Matt. 4:2) and while he did not require his disciples to do so he stated plainly that after his ascension the days would come when they should accept this discipline (Mark 2:20).

The proper use of fasting may be easily gathered from the Bible. It is particularly linked with self-humiliation in repentance (I Kings 21:27; Ps. 35:13). But it is also brought into a close connection with prayer (Matt. 17:21; Acts 13:3), especially in the pursuance of Christian work or the seeking of God (cf. Acts 10:30). The undertaking of a definite commission for God (Ezra 8:23; Acts 13:3) is an occasion for fasting. This is supremely illustrated in the case of the Lord himself, whose baptism is followed at once by the forty days of fasting in the wilderness (Matt. 4:2; cf. Paul's withdrawal to Arabia). In this connection, it is to be noted that the fast is also a time of temptation and therefore of testing (Matt. 4:1, 3 ff.) with a view to the greater strength and constancy in the future ministry.

As with any religious practice, there are dangers in fasting which are clearly noted in Scripture. The fast may be regarded as a means of getting things from God (Isa. 58:3). It may be substituted for the genuine repentance which issues in amendment of life (Isa. 58:5 ff.). It may become a mere convention and therefore an end in itself (Zech. 7:5). It may become an occasion for a parade of religion (Matt. 6:16) and thus finally lead to the self righteousness which is the very opposite of true repentance and therefore of justification before God (Luke 18:12). The imposition of set days of fasting is perhaps a mistake in this connection, since it leads to the formality which empties fasting of its true significance.

In spite of these warnings, Christian history gives ample evidence of the abuse as well as the proper use of fasting. From an early period legalism invaded this biblical and intrinsically valuable practice, special days and periods being imposed and distinctions made between what might or might not be eaten. In reaction against this perversion, the evangelical churches have been tempted to remedy the abuse by discontinuing the practice altogether rather than restoring it to its proper use in individual and congregational life. Yet fasting itself is obviously a biblical practice capable of a profitable use. In face of corruption, the true aim should be to restore it to its evangelical setting and purpose.

See also ASCETICISM.

WILLIAM KELLY

FATALISM. The common meaning of fatalism is that events happen inexorably, following a blind (i.e., non-rational) cosmic process. In this sense fatalism has no place in Christianity, but is commonly encountered in Oriental religions. The doctrine of providence (*q.v.*) is not to be confused with fatalism, for it teaches that the will of God by which events are controlled is good and rational.

Westerners who reject Christianity often, almost unwittingly, become fatalists. Hitler frequently alluded to fate. In wars soldiers speak of bullets inscribed with their names. But sometimes fate is used euphemistically for God.

As a philosophy fatalism is dangerous in that it is a doctrine of despair and saps individual responsibility.

ROBERT E. D. CLARK

FATHERHOOD OF GOD. There is nothing in the Bible to support the heathen notion of a literal divine fatherhood of clans or nations. Several passages of Scripture imply that God is the Father of angels and men as their Creator (Job 1:6; 2:1; 38:7; Ps. 86:6; Luke 3:38). But it is chiefly in connection with Israel, the Davidic king and Messiah that references to the fatherhood of God occur in the OT. By the historical event of deliverance from Egypt, God created the nation of Israel and subsequently cared for them, establishing a special relationship with them. Allusions to his fatherly regard for them look back to this crisis as the time of the nation's origin. Their emancipation marked them off from other peoples as his adopted children. His care for them is frequently compared to that of a father (Hos. 11:1; Deut. 14:1; II Sam. 7:14; Ps. 2:7; 89:26; Deut. 1:31; 8:5; Isa. 1:2). On the other hand, a response of filial love expressed in obedience was required from them (Jer. 3:9; Mal. 1:6), and since it was so often refused, a more restricted conception of the fatherhood of God resulted. According to this deeper view, he is the Father of the God-fearing among the nation rather than of the nation as a whole (Ps. 103:13; Mal. 3:17). This later mode of thought finds expression also in the literature of the intertestamental period (Jub. 1:24; Ps. Sol. 13:8; 17:30; Eccl. 23:1, 4), and is endorsed by the teaching of Jesus. He gave largely increased prominence to the doctrine of the fatherhood of God. The number of instances of the word *Father* as applied to God in the Gospels is more than double the number found in the remaining books of the NT. In the Gospel by John alone 107 occur. Two points in connection with Jesus' use of this title are of special interest. (1) He never joins his disciples with himself in allusions to his relationship with the Father, in such a way as to suggest that their relationship to God is of the same kind. He was aware of standing in an intimate and unparalleled relation. He claimed to be the pre-existent eternal Son, equal with the Father, who became incarnate for the fulfilment of his purpose of salvation, being appointed by him sole Mediator between God and men (Matt. 11:27; John 8:58; 10:30, 38; 14:9; 16:28; 3:25; 5:22). (2) When he speaks of God as the Father of others he almost always refers to his disciples. While accepting the teaching of the OT that all men are children of God by creation and receive his providential kindness (Matt. 5:45), he also taught that sin has brought about a change in men, necessitating rebirth and reconciliation to God (John 3:3; 8:42; 14:6). In accordance with this, the apostles teach that men become children of God by faith in Christ and thus receive the Spirit of adoption (John 1:12; Gal. 3:16; Rom. 8:15; Gal. 4:5). Sonship leads to likeness and inheritance (Matt. 5:16; Rom. 8:29; I John 3:2; Rom. 8:17). The Father is revealed as sovereign, holy, righteous and merciful. Prayer may confidently be offered to him in Jesus' name (Matt. 6:32; John 17:11, 25; 14:14).

WILLIAM J. CAMERON

FATHERS. Ecclesiastically, the fathers are those who have preceded us in the faith, and are thus able to instruct us in it. In this sense, ministers and particularly bishops are often referred to as fathers. More particularly, however, the term has come to be applied to the first Christian writers of acknowledged eminence. Already in the fourth century it was used in this way of the teachers of the preceding epoch, and later all the outstanding theologians of at least the first six centuries have come to be regarded as fathers. This is the normal usage of the term today, although sometimes the patristic era is extended and Protestants may also speak of the Reformation fathers.

The question arises how a given author may be classified as a Father. The mere survival of his work is not enough, for many heretical writings have come down to us, together with others of doubtful value. Four main characteristics have been suggested as necessary qualifications: first, substantial orthodoxy; second, holiness of life; third, widespread approval; and fourth, antiquity. It is allowed that Fathers may be in error on individual points, as necessitated by the many disagreements, but they can still be counted and read as Fathers so long as they satisfy these general requirements (cf. especially the cases of Origen and Tertullian).

Various answers may be given to the question of patristic authority. From the Roman Catholic standpoint, the Fathers are infallible where they display unanimous consent. Otherwise, they may err, but are always to be read with respect. Protestants naturally insist that the Fathers too are subject to the supreme norm of Scripture, so that their statements or interpretations may call for rejection, correction or amplification. On the other hand, they deserve serious consideration as those who have preceded us in faith and made a serious attempt to express biblical and apostolic truth. Their support is thus valuable, their opinions demand careful study, they are to be set aside only for good reason, and their work constitutes no less a challenge to us than ours to them.

To list the Fathers is hardly possible in so brief a compass, nor is it easy to classify them except perhaps in terms of the broad distinction between Greek and Latin. Mention may be made of the immediate post-apostolic Fathers who have given us our earliest Christian

literature outside the NT. The Alexandrian school (Clement and Origen) at the end of the second and early in the third century deserves notice, as do such writers as Irenaeus, Tertullian, Hippolytus and Cyprian. The fourth century, which was already referring to the Fathers, provides us with some of the greatest of all in men like Athanasius, Hilary, Basil, Gregory of Nyssa, Gregory of Nazianzus, Ambrose, Augustine, Chrysostom and Jerome. Among others who may be mentioned are the Cyrils, Theodoret, the two popes Leo I and Gregory I, and at the every end of the patristic period John of Damascus and Isidore of Seville. But these are only a selection from the great company of writers who over a wide and complex front gave to the church its earliest magnificent attempt in theology.

See also ALEXANDRIA, SCHOOL OF, and ANTIOCH, SCHOOL OF.

GEOFFREY W. BROMILEY

FEAR. The first mention of fear in the Bible is in connection with Adam's disobedience. Sin was followed by awareness of God's displeasure and fear of his judgment (Gen. 3:10). Fear is itself part of sin's punishment (Lev. 26:17; Deut. 28:25, 66). Selfish fear unfits for duty (Josh. 2:11) and quickly affects others (Deut. 20:8). The man in the parable who received one talent failed to use it because he was afraid (Matt. 25:25). The fearful are among those excluded from the heavenly city (Rev. 21:8). The need for courage in the service of God is repeatedly emphasized (Josh. 1:7, 9; Jer. 1:8; Ezek. 2:6). Fear is conquered by faith (Ps. 46:2; 112:7). By far the most characteristic use of the term fear, when associated with God, is to denote reverential awe. The "fear of God" is, in fact, a definition of true religion in the OT. It is the beginning of wisdom (Ps. 111:10), the secret of uprightness (Prov. 8:13), brings about the keeping of God's commandments (Eccl. 12:13) and distinguishes the people in whom God takes pleasure (Ps. 147:11). It is a gift bestowed by the Spirit upon the Branch of Jesse (Isa. 11:2, 3). In the NT, although a contrast is drawn between the spirit of bondage and of adoption (Rom. 8:15; Eph. 3:12), this fear of God is not absent. It controls the walk of the Christian, conscious of the comfort of the Holy Spirit (Acts 9:21); it stimulates honest service (Col. 3:2) and effort after holiness (II Cor. 7:1). Nor do reverential awe and adoration, arising from the apprehension of God as holy love, exclude the fear which is the fitting reaction to a consciousness of his displeasure. Jesus counseled his disciples to fear him who has power to inflict ultimate punishment on sin (Luke 12:4, 5). Paul also exhorts that salvation be worked out and service rendered with anxious concern to avoid evil and to be acceptable to God (Phil. 2:12; Eph. 6:5-6).

WILLIAM J. CAMERON

FEASTS. Universally man has celebrated the uniformities and seasons of nature. These in their Palestinian form were taken up by the Mosaic law, but apart from the minor feast of the New Moon (Num. 28:11) they celebrate God's grace in salvation as well. This is well seen in the Sabbath, though its rhythm is not that of the lunar month (cf. Ex. 20:11 with Deut. 5:15). This is true even of the Feast of Weeks (cf. Deut. 16:2). We must distinguish between the pilgrim feasts (ḥag): Passover — Unleavened Bread, Weeks and Tabernacles, and the Sabbath and New Moon, celebrated at home. To the latter were added Purim (Esth. 9:20 ff.) and the Feast of the Dedication (ḥănukkâ — I Macc. 4:59, II Macc. 10:8; Jos. Ant. XII. vii. 7). After the Babylonian exile the New Year was moved from Nisan (Abib, Ex. 12:2) to Tishri, the seventh month, so conforming to the natural rather than to the soteriological pattern.

Occasional fasts were frequent under the monarchy, but only the Day of Atonement was commanded by the law. This was a major sanctuary occasion, but in spite of the description in the Mishnah tractate *Yoma* it had little impact on the people as a whole until after A.D. 70; hence its non-mention in the historical books of the OT and a mere passing reference (Acts 27:9) in those of the NT.

Jewish Christians continued observing the Jewish feasts, doubtless with a Christian meaning, but except for Passover and Pentecost they soon faded out, the more so as their nature aspect dimmed with transplantation to Europe.

H. L. ELLISON

FEDERAL THEOLOGY. The name of Johannes Cocceius (1603-69) stands in the closest association with Federal Theology because of the prominence into which he brought it in the theological schools. But Federal Theology finds clear exposition in I Cor. 15 and Rom. 5. "As in Adam all die," writes Paul, "even so in Christ shall all be made alive" (I Cor. 15:22). Adam, as the first man, was the natural head of the race, and represented all mankind as the human party to the covenant of works into which God entered with him. As the natural head, he stood in a federal (*foedus*, Latin "covenant") relationship to all posterity. His obedience, had it been maintained, would have transmitted an entail of blessedness to them; his disobedience involved them with him in the curse which God pronounced upon the transgressors of his law. This argument is developed in Rom. 5:15-21. The entire human race is summarized in the two Adams. The first Adam was the federal head of the race under the covenant of works; the second Adam, the Lord Jesus Christ, is the federal head of all believers under the covenant of grace. Thus as the sin of Adam was legally and effectively *our* sin, so the obedience of Christ is legally and effectively the righteousness of all believers. The federal relationship in which Adam (*q.v.*) stood to the race was the ground of the imputation of his guilt to them, and the judicial cause of their condemnation. And the law which condemned them could not justify them unless an adequate reparation should be made for the wrong done, a reparation which they were incapable of making because of the corruption which they inherited from Adam as their natural and federal head. In order to their salvation, the needed reparation had to be made by another who was not of federal connection with Adam, and therefore was free from the imputation of his guilt. The Federal Theology represents these requirements as being met in Christ, the second Adam, in whom a new race begins. God had entered into covenant with him, promising him the salvation of all believers as the reward of his obedience. But the obedience required of him as the Federal Head of his people was more than the mere equivalent of that required of Adam. His representative obedience must include a penal death. And thus his resurrection victory is also the victory of the new humanity which has its source in him.

The various theological schools differ with regard to the implications of the imputation of Adam's guilt to his posterity. Pelagius (late fourth and early fifth century) denied that there was any necessary connection between the sin of Adam and that of his descendants.

Cocceius himself did not found his Federal Theology on the doctrine of predestination, after the manner of Calvin. The earlier Arminians held that man has inherited his natural corruption through Adam, but that he is not implicated in the guilt of Adam's first transgression. The later Arminians, however, particularly those of the Wesleyan following, admitted that man's inborn corruption also involves guilt. Yet notwithstanding these and other modifications, there is a broad agreement between the Roman, Lutheran and Reformed theologies that man's loss of original righteousness is the consequence of Adam's first sin as the covenant head of the race. "Nothing remains," writes Augustine, "but to conclude that in the first man all are understood to have sinned, whereby sin is brought in with birth and not removed save by the new birth." Any other view tends to break the analogy that is so clearly set forth in Rom. 5:19: "For as by one man's disobedience many were made sinners, so by the obedience of one shall many be made righteous." A real imputation of the righteousness of Christ as federal Head of his people requires a real imputation of the guilt of Adam to his posterity. For, as Calvin argues against the Pelagian view, if the imputation of Adam's sin means no more than that Adam became our example in sin, then the strict application of Paul's analogy of the two Adams would mean no more than that Christ became the example of his people in righteousness, and not the *cause* of their righteousness. Their vital union with Christ is the cause of their righteousness and also the guarantee of their growth in personal sanctification.

BIBLIOGRAPHY
Cocceius, *Summa Doctrinae de Foedere et Testamentis Dei*; Calvin, *Commentary on Romans*, pp. 134-46; C. Hodge, *Commentary on I Corinthians*, pp. 324-26; A. A. Hodge, *Outlines of Theology*, pp. 348-66; L. Berkhof, *Manual of Reformed Doctrine*, pp. 143-50, 262-64.

GEORGE N. M. COLLINS

FEET-WASHING. Feet-washing ranked high among Eastern hospitality rites. Open sandals on hot, dusty or muddy roads made feet-washing on arrival at the tent or house of a friend a necessity, for which facilities were provided. A slave, or the guest himself, performed the act (Gen. 18:4; 19:2; 24:32; 43:24; Judg. 19:21). If the host wished to honor his guest and demonstrate affection and humility, he could personally perform the act (I Sam. 25:41). Thus the failure of Simon (Luke 7:36-50) even to provide facilities for

Christ to wash his own feet marks not only pride and lack of respect for him, but also discourtesy and unfriendliness.

Despite its place in rites of hospitality (*q.v.*), feet-washing never became the ritual observance in the Jewish religion that hand-washing did. Only priests, in preparation for approach to God, observed such a rite (Ex. 30:18-21; 40:30-32).

The feet-washing in John 13:1-17 invested the hospitality rite with deeper meaning. The utensils were there, the servants were absent, but no disciple would humble himself to perform the act. Quarreling, arising from pride, had created tension (Luke 22:24). Christ's action, in addition to breaking their pride and antagonism, taught that the mark of greatness is service (*q.v.*), that frequent spiritual cleansing is needed even of his own, and that service must be humbly received from Christ before it can be given to him (see Wm. Temple, *Readings in St. John's Gospel*, MacMillan and Co., London, 1950, pp. 209-10).

Is the command of John 13:14, 15 to be taken literally? I Tim. 5:10 might suggest a literal observance in the early church, although hospitality in a general sense is probably indicated. Some sects took the command literally. Some sections of the church (from the fourth century) observed the Pedilavium ceremony for the newly baptized, and some observed it on Maundy Thursday. Bernard of Clairvaux advocated feet-washing as a sacrament, but the church as a whole has understood the command in a symbolic sense.

BIBLIOGRAPHY
G. A. Frank Knight in *HERE*; F. L. Anderson in *ISBE*.

R. COLIN CRASTON

FELLOWSHIP. I. WORDS INVOLVED. The Greek words *koinōnia* and *metochē* (and their cognates) are the principal terms expressing "fellowship" in NT literature. Both in classical and biblical usage these terms express joint participation in a person or project and secondarily association or mutuality of spirit.

II. FELLOWSHIP DEFINED. No specific definition is found in the NT. However, this term can be said to designate that social relationship existing between Christians who are regenerated members of the family of God and their cooperation in the work of the Lord. Fellowship posits as its prerequisite a likeness of nature that transcends external and temporary differences. True fellowship can exist only among true believers.

III. NEGATIVE FACTORS. Certain relationships are described as incompatible with Christian fellowship. (1) A Christian cannot have real fellowship with an unbeliever (II Cor. 6:14-16). Their natures are radically different: one is a child of God; the other a child of the devil (I John 3:10-12). (2) A Christian must not participate in pagan rites and ceremonies (I Cor. 10:20-22). Such things belong to demonism. (3) A Christian must "have no fellowship with the unfruitful works of darkness" (Eph. 5:11). Light and darkness have no affinity. The believer is a child of the light; the unbeliever dwells in darkness (I Thess. 5:4-8; cf. Rom. 13:11-14; I Pet. 2:9-12; 4:3 f.). (4) A Christian must not participate in the sins of another person (I Tim. 5:22). Such participation brought judgment upon the Gentile and the Jew (Rom. 1:32 — 2:2); it will bring similar judgment upon the Christian (Eph. 5:3-14; I Pet. 4:14-18). (5) A Christian cannot have fellowship with God while walking in darkness (I John 1:5 ff.). This darkness is identified as hatred of a Christian brother (I John 2:9-11; 3:15). (6) A Christian must not fellowship with a person who walks contrary to the teaching of Christ (II John 9-11). Error and truth cannot coexist in the same fellowship: sometimes the errorists depart (Acts 20:29 f.; I John 2:18 f.); sometimes Christians must leave the external fellowship (II Cor. 6:14-18; Rev. 18:4).

IV. POSITIVE FACTORS. There is a foundational unity among true believers as evidenced by the following particulars: (1) Christians partake of the divine nature (II Pet. 1:4). The divine seed planted in them at the new birth makes them new creatures (II Cor. 5:17; I John 3:9). (2) Christians partake of Christ (Heb. 3:14). The "new man" (Eph. 4:24) is "created in Christ Jesus" (Eph. 2:10). (3) Christians partake of the Holy Spirit (Heb. 6:4). They are the temple in which the Spirit dwells (I Cor. 3:16; 6:19). (4) Christians partake of a heavenly calling (Heb. 3:1). Their real citizenship is in heaven (Phil. 3:20); they are pilgrims and strangers here (I Pet. 2:11). (5) Christians partake of the Father's chastisement (Heb. 12:8). All of God's sons have some of God's chastening hand applied to them. (6) Christians partake of

Christ's suffering (Phil. 3:10; Heb. 10:33; I Pet. 4:13). In some mystical way believers enter into the meaning of the suffering of their Lord. (7) Christians partake of the future glory (II Cor. 1:7; I Pet. 5:1). They will share in the glory of their Lord's return (II Thess. 1:10).

V. SIGNS OF FELLOWSHIP. Certain signs always characterize true fellowship. (1) Mutual love. Christ made the "new commandment" of love the test of Christian discipleship (John 13:34 f.; 15:12). In opposition to the dissension in the Corinthian church Paul wrote his hymn of love (I Cor. 13). (2) Bearing another's burdens (Gal. 6:2). The stronger Christian must always help to bear the burdens of the weaker brother (Rom. 14; I Cor. 8). (3) Unity of faith. There is a "common salvation" (Jude 3) and a "common faith" (Titus 1:4; cf. Eph. 4:3-6, 13) that instinctively unites all true Christians.

VI. EXPRESSIONS OF CHRISTIAN FELLOWSHIP. Many are the ways, tangible and specific, in which fellowship is expressed among Christians. The following list is merely typical: (1) a student shares in the material needs of his teacher (Gal. 6:6). (2) A church supports its minister (Phil. 1:5; 4:15 f.). (3) Ministers recognize the cooperation of others in the work of God's kingdom (II Cor. 8:23; Gal. 2:9; Philem. 17; III John 5-8). (4) Churches unitedly help a needy church (Rom. 15:26; II Cor. 8:4; 9:13). (5) Christians spontaneously share their wealth with other Christians (Acts 2:44-45; 4:32). (6) Christians assemble regularly for worship and edification (Acts 2:42; Heb. 10:25). (7) They pray for one another (Eph. 6:18).

VII. THE DEEPER DEPTHS OF FELLOWSHIP. The child of God has fellowship with each person of the Trinity. (1) Fellowship with the Father (I John 1:3, 6). A Christian must walk in the light to enjoy this fellowship. (2) Fellowship with the Son. Christians are called to this fellowship (I Cor. 1:9). In the inner sanctuary of the soul this fellowship is realized in the Lord's Supper (I Cor. 10:16 f., 21). Christians desire to enter into the deeper meaning of their Lord's suffering (Phil. 3:10). (3) Fellowship with the Spirit. As a blessing given in the benediction (II Cor. 13:14) and realized in Christian experience (Phil. 2:1), Christians participate in this blessed fellowship. The eternal fellowship will be consummated in heaven's glory (Eph. 2:21 f.; Rev. 21:1-4).

BIBLIOGRAPHY
Arndt; F. A. Falconer in *HDCG*; E. von Dobschuetz in *HDAC*.

WICK BROOMALL

FESTIVALS. In the Christian church Sunday (*q.v.*) has been observed from apostolic times as the weekly festival of the Lord's resurrection, and as a special day of worship; but it was not until 321 that the Emperor Constantine decreed that Sunday should be a general holiday.

The annual ecclesiastical festivals may be divided into two classes: (a) the movable feasts, of which the two most important are Easter and Whitsunday, the dates of which vary according to the Jewish feasts of Passover and Pentecost; and (b) the immovable feasts, of which the most important are Christmas (Dec. 25) and Epiphany (Jan. 6). The dates of these were fixed in the fourth century. Other immovable feasts include the various saints' days and holy days to be found in the church calendar.

See CHRISTIAN YEAR, CHRISTMAS, EPIPHANY, EASTER, and WHITSUNDAY.

FRANK COLQUHOUN

FIG TREE. The fig tree (OT *te'ēna*; NT *sykē*) is native to western Asia. Canaan is described as a land of fig trees (Deut. 8:8). The first ripe fruit matures in June and sometimes earlier (Isa. 28:4 ASV). Late figs are ripe from August on, growing on the spring shoots. Summer foliage is abundant and exceeds that of other trees of its size (John 1:48, 50). The tree was valued and is mentioned with the vine (Ps. 105:33; Jer. 5:17; Joel 1:12). Sitting under the vine and fig tree is symbolic of peace and prosperity (I Kings 4:25; Mic. 4:4). The barren fig tree (Luke 13:6-9), the budding fig tree (Matt. 24:32-35 and parallels), and the cursed fig tree (Matt. 21:18-22) are taken to mean the Jewish nation. The cursing of the fig tree by our Lord is best understood as condemnation upon appearance without reality. Having leaves, it should have had some fruit; the condemnation was not for barrenness but for falsity of profession (Trench, *Notes on the Miracles*, p. 349).

BIBLIOGRAPHY
EB, II, pp. 1519 ff.; HDB, II, pp. 5 f.; HDCG, I, p. 592; ISBE. II. pp. 1108 f.; Plummer (ICC) *Luke*, pp. 339 ff.; R. C. Trench, *Notes on the Miracles*, pp. 343 ff.; *WDB*, p. 183.

CHARLES L. FEINBERG

FILIOQUE. The term means "and from the Son," and refers to the sentence in our Western versions of the Nicene creed which speaks of the proceeding of the Holy Spirit from the Father and from the Son. Originally this was not contained in the confessions agreed at Nicaea (A.D. 325) and Constantinople (A.D. 381). It seems to have been first inserted at the local Council of Toledo (A.D. 589) and gradually to have made its way into the usage of the West. It was denounced, however, by Photius of Constantinople in the ninth century, and formed a main doctrinal issue in the rupture between East and West in A.D. 1054. On the Eastern side two points may be made, first, that the relevant verse in John's Gospel (15:26) speaks only of the proceeding of the Spirit from the Father, and second, that the addition to the creed was never decided ecumenically. In favor of the addition two points may also be made. The first is that the term safeguards the vital Nicene truth that the Son is of one substance with the Father. The second is that, since the Son no less than the Father sends the Spirit according to John 15:26, we may legitimately infer by analogy from this relationship in respect of us that the Holy Spirit proceeds both from the Father and from the Son within the intra-trinitarian relationship. To say otherwise is ultimately to divorce the Son from the Spirit in direct contradiction to the passages which speak of him as the Spirit of Christ (cf. Rom. 8:9; Gal. 4:6).

GEOFFREY W. BROMILEY

FIRE. The Hebrew *'ēš* and the Greek *pyr* chiefly represent the English fire. The word is frequently used both literally and figuratively.

Fire designates the divine (1) presence (Ex. 3:2), (2) persons (the Father, Heb. 12:29; the Son, Rev. 1:14; 19:12; the Spirit, Acts 2:3; Rev. 4:5), (3) perfections (holiness, Isa. 6:4-7), (4) passions (jealousy, Deut. 4:24; fury and indignation, Isa. 30:27; 66:15), (5) punishments (Gen. 19:24; Num. 11:1 ff.; 16:1-35; Rev. 18:8), (6) purification (Zech. 13:9; Mal. 3:2 f.; Rev. 3:18), (7) protection (Ex. 14:24 f.; Zech. 2:5; Rev. 11:5), (8) predictions (Amos 2:2, 5; Joel 2:30), (9) power (Jer. 5:14; 23:29), (10) proclamation (I Kings 18:23 f., 30-39; Amos 7:4 f.).

Fire is used to represent human passions (Prov. 6:27; 16:27; I Cor. 7:9; James 3:5 f.).

Fire is used eschatologically (1) to signalize the return of Christ (II Thess. 1:8; cf. Rev. 20:9), (2) to atomize the present world (II Pet. 3:7, 12), (3) to purify the believer's works (I Cor. 3:13, 15), (4) to punish the wicked (Matt. 3:12; 13:40, 42, 50; 25:41; Luke 16:24; Jude 7; Rev. 20:9-15), (5) to visualize the abode of God (Ezek. 1:4, 13, 26-28; Dan. 7:9 f.; Rev. 8:5; 15:2).

Neither the fires of trials now (Isa. 43:2) nor the fires of judgment later (II Pet. 3:7-14) can overcome the believer.

WICK BROOMALL

FIRST AND LAST. This expression is apparently derived from several OT passages (Isa. 41:4; 44:6; 48:12) referring to the God of Israel. It refers to the eternity and supremacy of the Father.

In the NT the expression occurs three times (Rev. 1:17; 2:8; 22:13), and in each occurrence it is referred to the Son. There can be little question of its meaning. In the first two occurrences it is linked with the resurrection of Christ, while in the third it is grouped with other phrases which suggest the eternity and supremacy of the Son. It is evident that John accords the Son a place of equality with the Father. He has the prerogatives of God, the titles of God, and passages referring to the God of Israel are applied to him.

It is fitting that the Son be called the first and the last in the Book of Revelation. The stream of God's revelation finds its consummation here, as it found its inception in Genesis. The Son as the Word of God is responsible for the creation and also for its consummation. He is supreme in human history, as he said, "I am Alpha and Omega, the beginning and the end, the first and the last" (Rev. 22:13, AV).

See also ALPHA AND OMEGA.

S. LEWIS JOHNSON, JR.

FIRST-BORN. Primogeniture, the exclusive right of inheritance belonging to the first-born, is traceable back to patriarchal times. Ishmael, though the eldest son of Abraham, was not accounted a first-born because his mother was a slave (Gen. 21:10). Esau bartered his birthright and thereby opened himself to the charge of profanity, for he had spurned his right of inheritance (Gen. 25:33).

The idea of first-born in the NT is indicated

by *prōtotokos*, which occurs eight times, most of them referring to Christ, sometimes historically, sometimes figuratively. That the term is a messianic title is suggested by the Greek of Ps. 89:27. The NT alludes to Christ as the first-born in three aspects. In Col. 1:15 he is said to be the "first-born of all creation," and Heb. 1:6 also describes him by this word. The Arians used these passages as evidence that our Lord was a created being, but the proper understanding is implied by the context in Colossians, viz., that it refers to the pre-incarnate Christ. Moreover, the term declares Christ to be the Lord of creation for as the first-born he is the heir of the created order. Secondly, Col. 1:18 and Rev. 1:5 use first-born in a sense similar to the first fruits (*q.v.*) of I Cor. 15:20. Christ is the first-born from the dead because he was the first to be raised. Thirdly, Rom. 8:29 teaches that Christ is the "first-born among many brethren," which affirms that believers have joined the family of which Christ is the eldest Son. Heb. 12:23 projects the idea so that all who believe are given the status of first-born sons and therefore heirs of God.

DAVID H. WALLACE

FIRST FRUITS. Hebrew *rē'šit* ("first"); *bikkûrîm* ("first ripe"); Greek *aparchē* ("beginning"). First fruits as required in the law of Moses were an acknowledgment that the land and all its fruits were a gift of God. Just as the first-born of man and beast was claimed by God (Ex. 13:2), so the first fruits of the land were to be presented to God (Ex. 22:29). The offerings were generally products of the soil in the natural state such as grain, fruit, grapes, honey, and wool, described as that which is "first ripe" (*bikkûrîm*) (Ex. 22:29; 23:16, 19; 34:26; Deut. 18:4; II Chron. 31:5). First fruits included products of man's labor such as flour, oil, wine, dough, and bread (Ex. 34:18, 22; Lev. 23:16-20; II Chron. 31:5). The distinction between the "first ripe" (*bikkûrîm*) as natural products and products of human labor (*rē'šit*) is not maintained in all passages.

In general, the first fruits were offerings of various kinds, especially of products of the soil and prepared foods, a portion of which was offered to the priest as the divine representative and, except for a small portion offered on the altar, were for the priest's use.

The law of the first fruits is recorded in

Ex. 23:16, 19 where it is called "the feast of harvest, the firstfruits of thy labours" (vs. 16), and is mentioned as one of the three principal feasts to be observed by the entire nation. In Lev. 23:9-14 additional instruction is given concerning the first fruits offered at the time of harvest. Further details are given in Deut. 26:1-11, where an elaborate ritual is prescribed. The offerer is commanded to take "the first of all the fruit of the ground" (vs. 2) and place it in a basket and bring it to the priest, confessing that the Lord had brought him to the land, that God had brought Israel out of Egypt by his power, and had given them this "land flowing with milk and honey" (vs. 9). The offering of the first fruit is followed by instructions to tithe all the increase (vss. 12-19).

In the history of Israel in the OT, the observance of offering of first fruits seems to have been neglected after Solomon, but was revived by Hezekiah (II Chron. 31:5) and Nehemiah (Neh. 10:35, 37; 12:44). Elisha in the time of Israel's apostasy received "bread of the firstfruits" as well as grain which was miraculously multiplied to feed one hundred men (II Kings 4:42-44).

In its figurative use in Scripture, Israel is designated "the firstfruits of his increase," i.e., as holy to the Lord (Jer. 2:3). Frequent use of the figure is found in the NT. First converts in an area were designated "firstfruits" (Rom. 16:5; I Cor. 16:15). Christians generally are described as "a kind of firstfruits of his creatures," i.e., a first fruit of created beings (James 1:18). In both James and Revelation the implication is that those described as first fruits are by this description made holy to God. So also, the 144,000 of Rev. 14:1-5 are described as "firstfruits" (vs. 4). The work of the Spirit in Christians now, in contrast to their ultimate perfection, is described as "the firstfruits of the Spirit" (Rom. 8:23), i.e., tokens of the harvest to come, the resurrection of the body and complete deliverance from the world.

One of the most important figurative uses of first fruits in the NT is in reference to Christ who is described as "the firstfruits of them that are asleep" (I Cor. 15:20; cf. 15:23), i.e., the first who rose from the dead as the promise of the full harvest, the resurrection of all the saints.

BIBLIOGRAPHY

Articles on "First Fruits" in *ISBE, SHERK, Unger's Bible Dictionary*; L. S. Chafer, *Systematic Theology* VII, pp. 153-55.

JOHN F. WALVOORD

FLESH, FLESHLY. It will be well to commence the study of this very complex notion by indicating briefly certain obvious meanings, literal and figurative, expressed throughout the Bible by the word "flesh." In the first place, the words *še'ēr* and *bāśār* in the OT, and *sarx* in the New, describe the vehicle and circumstances of man's physical life in this world. Thus, in Phil. 1:22-24, Paul contrasts abiding "in the flesh" with departing to be "with Christ." Regularly, "flesh" is used along with "bones," "blood," or "body" (e.g., Prov. 5:11; I Cor. 15:50) to isolate for inspection the physical aspect of man's nature. From its use for the outer covering of the body (Gen. 2:21), there arose a figurative sense of "outward appearance," "worldly standards" (I Cor. 1:26; Eph. 2:11). More important is the recognition of the contrast between two modes of being signified by the words "flesh" and "spirit" (Isa. 31:3; Jer. 17:5; John 1:13). By comparison with God, mankind is seen as sharing in a common flesh, and the expression "all flesh" customarily acknowledges the solidarity of the race (Gen. 6:12; Matt. 24:22; I Pet. 1:24). It is no distance from this to the use of "flesh" to mean "next of kin" (Lev. 18:12) or, more remotely, "human ancestry" (Rom. 4:1).

Turning more particularly to the OT, the first thing which becomes clear from its use of the word "flesh" is its outright opposition to anything that savors of Gnosticism. While there is general recognition that man is psychical as well as physical — Ps. 63:1 shows man, in both aspects, longing for God — there is total absence of any suggestion that these are separable as far as a doctrine of human nature is concerned, or that "flesh" is lower in the scale of personality than "spirit." In fact, man's psychical capacities are, more often than not, instanced by reference to physical organs. Thus, Ps. 73:26 speaks of the end of earthly life and hope as the failing of "flesh" and "heart," and the corresponding use of "reins" or "bowels" is too well known to need exemplification. The unity of human personality in its psycho-physical nature could not be seen more clearly than by recalling that, according to the Bible, the act of sexual intercourse is spoken of as "knowing" (Gen. 4:1), and the result of that act is that "they shall be one flesh" (Gen. 2:24; Matt. 19:5; I Cor. 6:16). "To know" is not here used euphemistically but literally. Marriage (q.v.), in God's plan, is intended to bring two people into the deepest and most intimate knowledge of each other. This ultimate interpenetration of personalities is called becoming "one flesh." While there is nothing in the OT corresponding to the NT view of the "flesh" as the central and dynamic principle of fallen humanity, yet we can see that the OT, with its emphasis on man's "flesh-personality," offers the background against which the NT can paint its picture of human nature held in thrall by a dynamism which has captured the citadel of its essential unity. This, in turn, illuminates the constantly fleshly terms in which the holy life is expressed. In Gen. 17:13 God says that his covenant is "in your flesh," and the prophets (e.g., Jer. 4:4) use the same symbol of circumcision to express a consecrated return to God. There can be no salvation of man which is not a salvation of his "flesh," and when Ezekiel looks forward to God's act of regeneration, he declares that God will "take away the stony heart out of your flesh, and will give you an heart of flesh" (36:26). Herein he implies what Paul states: that the flesh has become perverted, and that God plans for man that which we have learned to call the "resurrection of the body."

The NT doctrine of the flesh is chiefly but not exclusively Pauline. The "flesh" is a dynamic principle of sinfulness (Gal. 5:17; Jude 23). The unregenerate are "sinful flesh" (Rom. 8:3); they are "after the flesh" (Rom. 8:5). In them the flesh, with its "passions and lusts" (Gal. 5:24), works "death" (Rom. 7:5). The flesh, producing "works" (Gal. 5:19) in those who live "after the flesh" (Rom. 8:12), is characterized by "lust" (I John 2:16; Gal. 5:16; I Pet. 4:2; II Pet. 2:10), which enslaves the bodily members and also dominates the mind (Eph. 2:3), so that there is a complete mental affiliation called "the mind of the flesh" (Rom. 8:5, 7). Under these circumstances, life is given to fleshly satisfactions (Col. 2:23) and is described as "sowing unto the flesh," whence is reaped a harvest of fleshly corruption (Gal. 6:8). Such people are dominated by "sinful passions" (Rom. 7:5); unable to obey God's law (Rom. 8:3) or to please God (Rom. 8:8). Even their religious practice is astray from God's will because of fleshly thinking (Col. 2:18). They are "chil-

dren of wrath" (Eph. 2:3). Very different are those who have experienced God's regeneration. They remain "in" the flesh, but they are no longer "after" the flesh (II Cor. 10:3; Gal. 2:20). They need to be watchful. For the fact of the flesh means dullness of spiritual perception (Rom. 6:19), and though the Christian need pay none of the claims of the flesh (Rom. 8:12), yet he must remember that in his flesh there is nothing good (Rom. 7:18), and that if he should repose his trust there again (Phil. 3:3; Gal. 3:3) he would lapse into bondage (Rom. 7:25). He has become the recipient of a new principle of life sufficient to oust the old principle of death (Rom. 8:4, 9, 13; Gal. 5:16-17), "the life of Christ" in his "death-bound body" (II Cor. 4:10, 11).

We have thus traced the notion of the flesh from its pure conception in the Creator's plan to the depths of its self-wrought corruption, and to the recreation in Christ. It remains to show how the work of Christ is expressed in the same terminology. Here also Christ redeemed us from the curse by becoming the curse himself: "The Word became flesh" (John 1:14). The sinlessness of Jesus is preserved by the careful statement that God sent his Son "in the likeness of sinful flesh" (Rom. 8:3; cf., Heb. 4:15), and the blessed truth is declared that the Son became one with us at the point of our need (Heb. 2:14) in order to deal with sin at the point of its strength (see Rom. 8:3, ERV). "Flesh" is constantly used to teach the genuine manhood of the Saviour (Rom. 1:4; 9:5; I Tim. 3:16; Heb. 5:7). Yet it is not his flesh as displayed in its perfection, but his flesh as "given" (John 6:51-56) which avails for the life of the world. It was by his being made "an offering for sin" that he condemned sin in his flesh (Rom. 8:3, ERV). The flesh is the sphere and instrument of his redeeming work (Col. 1:22; I Pet. 3:18; 4:1). This was the sublime purpose of the incarnation (Heb. 10:5-20). He took flesh in order that in and by his flesh he might loose us from the bondage of "the flesh" and fulfil the prophecy by making us "epistles of Christ . . . written not with ink, but with the Spirit of the living God; not in tables of stone, but in tables that are hearts of flesh" (II Cor. 3:3; Ezek. 36:26).

BIBLIOGRAPHY

Oscar Cullmann, Immortality of the Soul or Resurrection of the Dead? pp. 28-39; H. Cremer in SHERK;

W. D. Davies, *Paul and Rabbinic Judaism*, pp. 17-35; W. P. Dickson, *St. Paul's Use of the Terms Flesh and Spirit*.

JOHN ALEXANDER MOTYER

FOLLOWING CHRIST. This phrase is best understood by noticing how the meaning becomes increasingly intensive and how easily it passes from the literal to the metaphorical.

In the least intensive sense of simply going to see and hear him, great multitudes followed Jesus (Matt. 4:25; 8:1; 12:15; 19:2; 20:29, etc.). More intensive is Jesus' use of "Follow me" to invite men to become disciples (Mark 1:17; 2:14; 8:34, etc.). "It was not only the practice of the Rabbis, but regarded as one of the most sacred duties for a Master to gather around him a circle of disciples" (Edersheim, *Life and Times of Jesus the Messiah*, vol. 1, p. 474). This transition in meaning is made clear by comparing John 1:37 ff., where following implies a short walk and visit, with Mark 1:17 ff., where it means for the same men quitting their occupation and becoming apprentices to Jesus for the new work of fishing for men.

Because following Christ becomes synonymous with discipleship this phrase gains distinctive meanings from the teachings and example of Jesus. From among the many followers Jesus chose twelve to live with him and to represent him (Mark 3:7-15). For these, discipleship now meant receiving instruction (Sermon on the Mount, parables of the kingdom and conduct), announcing the gospel message (the Twelve sent out, later the Seventy), casting out demons, healing the sick and performing water baptism (John 4:2). However, some outside the Twelve also cast out demons in Jesus' name and were approved by him (Mark 9:38-41).

After Peter's confession Jesus spoke plainly of his coming sufferings and death (Matt. 16:21). He now said, "If any man will come after me let him deny himself and take up his cross daily and follow me" (Luke 9:23), meaning literally a daily readiness to travel with him up to a hostile Jerusalem (Mark 10:32-34) and to suffer death when necessary for his sake (cf. Luke 9:24-26 with Mark 10:38-39 and Phil. 3:10). The following of Jesus by dying for him was Peter's premature profession (John 10:37-38), Jesus' subsequent prediction (John 21:18-22) and Peter's actual experience years later according to tradition (e.g., in *Quo Vadis*). But note also that Peter makes it clear (I Pet. 2:19-25) that following Jesus in martyrdom does nothing to procure forgiveness of sins for us or for another; only Jesus bore the sins of others in his own body on the tree. Often this limitation is forgotten: our following Jesus in suffering and death benefits others and brings us reward here and hereafter, but it secures no one's forgiveness as did Jesus' death. Countless individuals in the early Christian centuries consciously followed Jesus by dying for him (e.g., Ignatius, Polycarp) and during the Middle Ages, it was believed, many experienced his death mystically through the nail and thorn prints of Christ (stigmata) in their flesh (see IMITATION, etc.).

The three cases in Luke 9:57-62 indicate that to follow Jesus in daily discipleship implies: (1) utter self-denial and voluntary homelessness in this world, (2) immediate obedience in giving Jesus' program priority over family duties, and (3) undivided allegiance. The rewards of following Christ are illustrated in John 8:12 (daily guidance), in Mark 10:28-31 (spiritual kinsfolk and possessions with persecutions) and in Rom. 8:17-18 (eternal glory). See also DISCIPLE.

BIBLIOGRAPHY
Arndt; *HDB*; *HDCG*.

TERRELLE B. CRUM

FOOL, FOOLISHNESS. The Hebrew words *'ĕwîl*, *kᵉsîl* and *nābāl* represent the ideas expressed by fool and foolishness. In the NT negative terms are used: *anoētos*, "unmindful"; *aphrōn*, "senseless"; *asophos*, "unwise"; *asynetos*, "unintelligent." *Mōros* generally means "foolish" or a "fool."

Foolishness is defined in Eccl. 7:25; a fool, in Isa. 32:6. Nabal (I Sam. 25:25) and the rich fool (Luke 12:20) illustrate a fool's philosophy.

A fool is often contrasted with a wise man (Prov. 3:35; 10:8). A fool's moral obliquity is far more evident in his heart than in his head (Ps. 14:1). His spiritual depravity vitiates his mental processes.

Among many traits, a fool may be described as a lustful (Prov. 7:22; 9:13), loquacious (Prov. 10:8; 15:2; Eccl. 10:14), litigious (Prov. 20:3; 29:9, 11), listless (Eccl. 10:15), libelous (Prov. 10:18) loggerhead.

The term is so pregnant with sinister connotations that its promiscuous use is sternly forbidden (Matt. 5:22). The preaching of the cross is foolishness to the world (I Cor. 1:18,

21, 23, 25). Christians may sometimes act foolishly (Gal. 3:1, 3). Even Paul, ironically, acted "as a fool" to chide the Corinthian church (II Cor. 11:16, 19; 12:6, 11). Preachers must become "fools for Christ's sake" (I Cor. 4:10; cf. Acts 26:24). Any foolishness that *is* foolishness must be scrupulously avoided by Christians (Eph. 5:4).

BIBLIOGRAPHY
Arndt; G. Vos in HDB; H. Bulcock in HDAC; W. L. Walker in ISBE.

WICK BROOMALL

FOOTSTOOL. The word is used literally on two occasions: (1) Of the accessory to the throne of Solomon (II Chron. 9:18). It was made of gold, emblematic of the magnificence of his empire. (2) Of an article of furniture in a Christian synagogue, expressive of condescension toward a poor visitor (James 2:3).

Several figurative uses are noted: (1) The earth (Isa. 66:1; Matt. 5:35). The lesson to be gathered is that of the majesty of the Almighty, with a suggestion of omnipresence. (2) The sanctuary in Jerusalem, the center of worship for Israel (Isa. 60:13; Ps. 99:5). (3) The mercy seat, where God manifested his holy presence (I Chron. 28:2). (4) Messiah's enemies (Ps. 110:1, quoted several times in the NT).

EVERETT F. HARRISON

FORBEARANCE. See LONGSUFFERING.

FOREIGNER. See STRANGER.

FOREKNOWLEDGE. In theological language the word foreknowledge designates the prescience or foresight of God concerning the entire course of future events. The constant representation in Scripture is that God knows all things, actual or possible, past, present and future. Whereas human knowledge is very limited, and is derived from observation and from a process of reasoning, divine foreknowledge is unlimited and is intuitive, innate, and immediate. It involves first of all a knowledge of God himself in all his relations, and secondly a knowledge of all the things that are included in his eternal plan. It thus provides the basis for prophecy.

That which we term "past," "present," and "future," is all "present" in the divine mind. It can best be described as an eternal "now." Isaiah describes God as "the high and lofty one who inhabiteth eternity" (Isa. 57:15); and the Psalmist says, "A thousand years in thy sight are but as yesterday when it is past, and as a watch in the night" (Ps. 90:4). Hence the events which we see coming to pass in time are those which God appointed and set before himself from eternity. Time (*q.v.*) is thus a property of the finite creation and is objective to God. He is above it and sees it, but he is not conditioned by it.

Scripture teaches very explicitly that God acts according to a plan. And, knowing that plan, he knows the future. "The counsel of Jehovah standeth fast forever, the thoughts of his heart to all generations" (Ps. 33:11). "I am God and there is none like me; declaring the end from the beginning, and from ancient times things that are not yet done" (Isa. 46:9, 10).

Probably the most difficult problem in regard to foreknowledge relates to the free agency and moral responsibility of men. The Bible teaches both the sovereignty of God, in which he is represented as foreordaining and controlling all events, and it also teaches the free agency of man, in which he makes his own choices and is morally responsible (Acts 4:27, 28, Eph. 1:11; Rom. 8:29, 30; Ps. 33:11; Isa. 14:14; Luke 22:22; Dan. 4:35; Job 43:2). No attempt is made to give a full explanation of this mystery. Calvinistic theology emphasizes the doctrine of the sovereignty of God while at the same time insisting that man is free within the limits of his nature and that he is morally responsible. Arminianism (*q.v.*), on the other hand, substitutes foreknowledge for predestination. Some acknowledge that God foreknows all things. Others say that he foreknows all events that are knowable, but that the acts of free agents by their very nature are uncertain. But this does not solve the problem. For if God's foreknowledge of all things is acknowledged the acts of men then become as certain as if foreordained. But if God's foreknowledge is limited, he is then represented as ignorant of much of the future and as gaining vast amounts of knowledge every day, and his plans are then subject to change to meet the changing circumstances.

BIBLIOGRAPHY
C. W. Hodge in ISBE; A. Stewart in HDB.

LORAINE BOETTNER

FOREORDINATION. See PREDESTINATION.

FORERUNNER. The word *prodromos* ("one who goes before") is found only in Heb. 6:20 in biblical Greek. Christ precedes believers into heaven (cf. John 14:2 f.).

John the Baptist is commonly designated as "the forerunner of the Messiah." His ministry illustrates the features of a true forerunner: (1) authorization and prediction (Mal. 3:1; 4:5); (2) specific mission and definite message (Mal. 4:6; Luke 1:76-79); (3) performance of a necessary preliminary work (Matt. 3:1-17); (4) identification of the person he precedes (John 1:19-34).

A forerunner may be a person (as Noah) or an event (as signs preceding the second advent); it may be constructive or destructive in intention and execution.

WICK BROOMALL

FORGIVENESS. There are seven words in Scripture which denote the idea of forgiveness: three in the Hebrew and four in the Greek. In the Hebrew OT they are *kāpar,* "to cover"; *nāśā',* "to bear" — "take away" (guilt); and *sālah,* "to pardon." *Nāśā* is used of both divine and human forgiveness. The other two, *kāpar* and *sālah,* are used only of divine forgiveness. In the Greek NT the words for forgiveness are *apolyein, charizesthai, aphesis,* and *paresis. Apolyein* is found numerous times as "to put away," e.g., a wife (Matt. 5:31); but only once to signify forgiveness (Luke 6:37). *Paresis* is also found only once (Rom. 3:25), and suggests "disregarding," but without any suggestion of indifference. *Charizesthai* is used only by Luke and Paul, and only by the latter in the sense of "to forgive sins" (II Cor. 2:7; Eph. 4:32; Col. 2:13; 3:13, etc.). It specially expresses the graciousness of God's forgiveness.

The most common NT word for forgiveness is *aphesis.* It conveys the idea of "sending away" or "letting go." The noun occurs fifteen times. The verb with the same meaning is used about forty times.

No book of religion except the Bible teaches that God completely forgives sin. But in it we read, "I will heal their backslidings, I will love them freely" (Hos. 14:4); "God for Christ's sake hath forgiven you (*echarisato,* graciously forgiven)" (Eph. 4:32); and "Their sins and iniquities will I remember no more" (Heb. 10:17). The initiative in this forgiveness, too, is with God, especially in Paul's use of *charizesthai* (II Cor. 12:13; Col. 2:13). It is a

ready forgiveness as is shown in the prodigal son or "Gracious Father" parable (Luke 15:11-32).

There is only one sin for which the Father does not promise forgiveness: blasphemy against the Holy Ghost (Mark 3:28; Matt. 12:32). The contexts suggest this to be the sin of attributing to unclean spirits the work of the Holy Spirit, but many interpreters (including Augustine) have understood it to include a deliberate persistence in such evil. This sin is also considered by some to be the unforgiving spirit (see Matt. 18:34-35). It might be the "sin unto death" of I John 5:16 (see Westcott; cf. Heb. 6:4-6).

There are to be no limitations whatever to forgiveness of one's fellows. In Luke 17:4 it is to be "seven times in a day," and until "seventy times seven" in Matt. 18:22, both of which signify limitlessness. It is to be an attitude of mind even before the offending party asks for pardon, as is implied by Jesus, "if ye forgive not every one his brother from your hearts" (Matt. 18:35).

For man to receive forgiveness, repentance is necessary (Luke 17:3-4). For the holy God to extend forgiveness, the shedding of blood (Heb. 9:22) until no life is left (Lev. 17:11) is prerequisite — ultimately, the once-for-all (Heb. 9:26) spilling of Christ's blood and his rising again (Rom. 4:25).

BIBLIOGRAPHY

Bruder, *Greek Concordance*; W. C. Morro in *ISBE*; Paul Lehmann, *Forgiveness*; H. R. Mackintosh, *The Christian Experience of Forgiveness*; E. B. Redlich, *The Forgiveness of Sins*; Vincent Taylor, *Forgiveness and Reconciliation.*

JOSEPH KENNETH GRIDER

FORM, LIKENESS. The Hebrew words in this group are scarcely distinguishable in significance: *selem* (probable root "to cut (out)"); *demût* ("to resemble"); *tabnit* ("to build"); and *temûnâ* (related to "kind," or "species," suggesting resemblance by kinship). It does not seem possible that some of these refer to material, and the others to immaterial, likeness, as suggested for *selem* and *demût* respectively in Gen. 1:26, because in Dan. 3:19 *selem* means "outward appearance revealing inner character" and in II Kings 16:10 *demût* parallels *tabnit* in a material sense. Deut. 4:16 identifies *tabnit* with *temûnâ.* The OT, therefore, stresses visible form, material likeness.

Phil. 2:6-8 associates *morphē* ("form"), *homoiōma* ("likeness") and *schēma* ("fashion"). E. H. Gifford (*The Incarnation*, Hodder and Stoughton, London, 1897, p. 22 ff.) says: "*Morphē* is . . . the Divine Nature actually and inseparably subsisting in the Person of Christ." Lightfoot urges that *homoiōma* speaks of relation to others of the same kind, and that "the *morphē* is contrasted with the *schēma*, as that which is intrinsic and essential with that which is accidental and outward." Other important words are *eikōn*, signifying correspondence with prototype (Matt. 22:20; Col. 1:15), and *eidos*, stressing visibility (Luke 3:22).

How are form and likeness used of God? There is a visible "form" proper to God. Moses (Num. 12:8; cf. Ps. 17:15) sees the *t͞emûnâ* of the Lord. Israel saw no *t͞emûnâ*, for this cannot be granted to those who might debase the Godhead to visible representation (Deut. 4:12). This helps to explain the creation of man in the likeness of God. Redeemed man is to be "renewed after the *eikōn* of him that created him" (Col. 3:10), inwardly (Eph. 4:24), outwardly (Phil. 3:21), as Christ is "formed" (*morphoun*) in him (Gal. 4:19). Jesus is the *eikōn* of God (II Cor. 4:4) from which man fell (see FALL); and "in the likeness (*homoiōma*) of sinful flesh" (Rom. 8:3) he came to recreate man into his image (II Cor. 3:18).

JOHN ALEXANDER MOTYER

FORM CRITICISM. Form Criticism (German *Formgeschichte*, "form history") is a method of approach which has been applied to biblical and non-biblical literature alike; within the Bible it has been applied to both Testaments (e.g., in OT, to the Pentateuch and Psalter), but pre-eminently to the Gospels. It endeavors to get behind the written Gospels and their literary sources to the oral stage of the Gospel tradition, and to classify and examine the various "forms" or types of story, utterance, etc., represented in that oral tradition.

The pioneer of this method was Martin Dibelius, whose *Die Formgeschichte des Evangeliums* appeared in 1919, followed in 1921 by Rudolf Bultmann's independent study *Die Geschichte der synoptischen Tradition*.

I. CLASSIFICATION. The main division in form-classification of the Gospel material is that between narratives and sayings. Narratives have been subdivided into (a) pronouncement stories, (b) miracle stories, (c) stories about Jesus; sayings into (a) wisdom sayings, (b) prophetic and apocalyptic sayings, (c) law-pronounce-

ments and community-rules, (d) sayings introduced by "I," (e) parables.

Pronouncement stories (as Vincent Taylor calls them) partake of the character of both narratives and sayings. In them a particular situation gives rise to a pointed saying of Jesus (an "apophthegm," in Bultmann's terminology), for the sake of which the incident was remembered and recorded. Frequently the situation is controversial; something done by Jesus or his disciples is criticized, and Jesus replies to the criticism with a decisive pronouncement, e.g., "The sabbath was made for man, not man for the sabbath" (Mark 2:27). Dibelius called these narratives "paradigms" because they served as illustrations in early Christian preaching.

Pronouncement stories sometimes overlap other subdivisions, e.g., the incident of the paralytic of Capernaum (Mark 2:1-12) is a pronouncement story because it leads up to the saying "the Son of man has authority on earth to forgive sins" (Mark 2:10), but it might also be classified as a miracle story, more specifically a healing story. Healing stories can be readily recognized; all over the world they follow a recurrent form which stresses the intractability of the disease, the completeness of the cure, the effect on the spectators. But the fact that a story reproduces this stereotyped form tells us nothing about its historicity. This should be remembered not only in healing and other miracle stories, but in those other "stories about Jesus" (like the baptism, the temptation, the transfiguration, the resurrection appearances) sometimes called "myths" or "legends." The ascription of these designations to the Gospel stories may obscure the fact that form criticism makes a judgment about *form*, not about *substance*.

Similarly, the classification of sayings of Jesus according to form can throw little light on their authenticity; much more depends on the individual form critic's view of the person of Jesus.

II. FRAMEWORK. Many form critics envisage the Synoptic tradition as consisting of unrelated incidents and sayings, woven into a continuous narrative by means of editorial summaries devoid of independent historical value. (It is allowed, however, that the passion narrative existed as a continuous record from earliest days, being repeated at every eucharistic meal, according to I Cor. 11:26.) But Charles Harold Dodd ("The Framework of the

Gospel Narrative," *ExpT* 43, 1931-32, 396 ff.) showed that the "editorial summaries" elsewhere in Mark, when put together, constitute a separate outline of the Gospel story, comparable to those outlines which can be reconstructed from the speeches in Acts and passages in the Epistles.

III. LIFE-SETTING. Again, many form critics explain the various elements in the Gospels as arising out of situations in the experience of the early church; e.g., the mission charge of Matt. 10:1 ff. reflects the methods adopted by Jewish Christians who preached the gospel throughout Palestine between A.D. 30 and 66, or the controversial incidents reflect disputes between legalist and liberal groups in the early Palestinian church, or between Christian and non-Christian Jews. But why then was this practice not carried out more widely and usefully? Why has the circumcision question, which bulked so largely in Christian debate around A.D. 50, not left a more distinct mark in the Gospels?

Early Christians, in fact, made a clear distinction between actual pronouncements of Jesus and their own judgments on disputed points (cf. I Cor. 7:10, 12, 25). After all, for three or four decades after A.D. 30 many people could still remember what Jesus had said and could have protested against the ascription to him of views which he had not expressed. There is justice in Vincent Taylor's observation: "If the Form-Critics are right, the disciples must have been translated to heaven immediately after the Resurrection" (*The Formation of the Gospel Tradition*, London, 1933, p. 41). This consideration holds good outside the church as well as within it: a strong point in early apostolic preaching is the appeal to the hearers' knowledge of the story of Jesus (Acts 2:22; 10:36).

No doubt a life-setting in the early church — in preaching, in fellowship meetings, in debate — explains why many sayings and incidents in the Gospels were put on record. When a question arose about divorce, for example, or paying the temple tax, it was natural to recall what Jesus had said on the subject; but such a setting in the life of the early church does not exclude an earlier setting in the life of Jesus.

IV. CONCLUSION. The radical positions to which form criticism often seems to lead are the positions of certain form critics and not necessarily those of form criticism. Form criticism is of value not only because it provides a fresh classification for the study of our Gospel material, but also because it underlines (a) the inadequacy of documentary hypotheses alone to account for the composition of the Gospels, (b) the universal tendency in antiquity to stereotype the forms in which religious instruction was given, and (c) the fact that no discernible stratum of Gospel tradition knows any Jesus but the Messiah, the Son of God.

BIBLIOGRAPHY

Martin Dibelius, *From Tradition to Gospel*; F. C. Grant, ed., *Form Criticism*; R. H. Lightfoot, *History and Interpretation in the Gospels*; E. B. Redlich, *Form Criticism*; E. F. Scott, *The Validity of the Gospel Record*; Vincent Taylor, *The Formation of the Gospel Tradition*.

FREDERICK FYVIE BRUCE

FORNICATION. In its more restricted sense fornication denotes voluntary sexual communion between an unmarried person and one of the opposite sex. In this sense the fornicators (*pornoi*) are distinguished from the adulterers (*moichoi*) as in I Cor. 6:9. In a wider sense *porneia* signifies unlawful cohabitation of either sex with a married person. In this meaning it is used interchangeably with *moicheia*, as in Matt. 5:32, where Christ says that anyone who divorces his wife except for *porneia* causes her to become the object of adultery (*moicheuthēnai*) since he who marries her commits adultery (*moichātai*). The same use of *porneia* in the sense of adultery (*moichātai*) is found in Matt. 19:9. In its widest sense *porneia* denotes immorality in general, or every kind of sexual transgression. In I Cor. 5:1 *porneia* is rightly translated in the RSV by *immorality*, which term it properly uses also in I Cor. 5:11, where the word stands without any further modification (cf. 6:18). The plural *fornications* (*dia tas porneias*) is best taken in the sense of "temptations to immorality" (I Cor. 7:2; cf. RSV). While other sins must be overcome by spiritual crucifixion of the flesh (Gal. 5:24), the sin of immorality (*porneia*) is one from which the Christian must flee in order to keep pure (I Cor. 6:18). Since God's close relation to his people is regarded as a marriage bond (Eph. 5:23-27), all forms of apostasy are designated in Scripture as adultery, and this indeed very fittingly as the pagan cults were usually connected with immorality (Hos. 6:10; Jer. 3:2, 9; Rev. 2:21; 19:2). The use of the verb *porneuein* and of the noun *pornos* (and *pornē*) is similar to that of the abstract *porneia*. It proves the greatness of divine grace in Christ Jesus that our Lord permitted Rahab (Heb. 11:31; Matt. 1:5) and other fornicators to be numbered in his genealogy.

See also ADULTERY.

BIBLIOGRAPHY

Arndt; ISBE; JewEnc.

J. THEODORE MUELLER

FOUNDATION. The English term is usually a translation of some form of the Hebrew *yāsaḏ* and the Greek *katabolē* and *themelios*. The usage may be summarized as follows:

I. LITERAL. That part of a structure which supports the rest is its foundation. That which is supported may be mountains (Deut. 32:22), the temple (I Kings 6:37), walls (Ezra 4:12), a house (Luke 6:48), etc.

II. FIGURATIVE. The following may here be cited as illustrative uses: (1) the foundation or beginning of the world (Matt. 13:35; 25:34; Luke 11:50; John 17:24; Eph. 1:4; Heb. 4:3; 9:26; I Pet. 1:20; Rev. 13:8; 17:8); (2) Christ as the foundation of the church (I Cor. 3:11; cf. Isa. 28:16; Matt. 16:18); (3) the prophets and apostles as foundations of the church, with Christ as the cornerstone (Eph. 2:20; cf. Rev. 21:14, 19 f.); (4) one's ministry (Rom. 15:20; I Cor. 3:10); (5) the security of God's seal (II Tim. 2:19).

In addition to the uses cited above, the word foundation is often used in theological literature in different connotations. Sometimes, for example, it is used for "foundational studies" (that is, Apologetics); sometimes for the "fundamentals" (that is, the basic beliefs of Christianity); sometimes for "foundation-passages" (that is, the passages of the Gospels accepted by modern criticism as absolutely reliable); and in many other ways.

WICK BROOMALL

FREEDOM, FREE WILL. The ordinary idea of freedom as the happy state of not being a slave is common throughout the Bible. The unique biblical development of it sprang from reflection on the unique privileges of Israel. God, in sovereign mercy, had brought the Israelites out of bondage, made them his people, given them his covenant, settled them in the promised land, and undertaken to maintain them there in political independence and economic prosperity as long as they eschewed idolatry and kept his laws. This meant that Israel's freedom would depend, not on human effort or achievement, either military or political, but on the quality of Israel's obedience to God. Freedom was a supernatural blessing, God's gracious gift to his own people, unmerited and, apart from God, unattainable in the first instance, and now maintained only through God's continued favor. Disobedience, whether in the form of religious impiety or social injustice, would mean the loss of freedom; divine judgment would take the form of national disaster and subjugation, and ultimately of deportation into a land in which no token of God's favor could be expected (see Deut. 28:15 ff.; Amos 5; II Kings 17:6-23). The theological idea of freedom thus comes to mean, on the one hand, deliverance from all created forces that would prevent men from serving and enjoying their Creator, and, on the other, the positive happiness of living in fellowship with God in the place where he is pleased to bless. It is a free gift of grace, bestowed on those who serve God according to his covenant. The condition of freedom from bondage to the created is therefore bondage to the Creator. Freedom is God's gift to his own slaves. This is the essence of the biblical concept.

This concept was given its Christian reference, in outline at least, by Christ himself, who opened his public ministry by announcing himself as the fulfilment of Isa. 61:1: ". . . he hath anointed me . . . to preach deliverance to the captives. . ." (Luke 4:16 ff.). Ignoring Zealot hankerings after national deliverance from Rome, Christ declared that he had come to liberate the slaves of sin and Satan (John 8:34-36, 41-44); to overthrow the "prince of this world," the "strong man"; and to release his prisoners (John 12:31-32; Mark 3:27; Luke 10:18). Exorcisms (Mark 3:22 ff.) and healings (Luke 13:16) were part of this work of dispossession.

Paul expands the thought that Christ liberates believers, here and now, from destructive influences to which they were previously in bondage: from sin, the tyrant whose wages for services rendered is death (Rom. 6:18-23); from the "power of darkness" (Col. 1:13); from polytheistic superstition (I Cor. 10:29; Gal. 4:8 f.); from the law as a system of salvation (Gal. 4:21 ff.; 5:1; Rom. 7:6); and from the burden of Jewish ceremonialism (Gal. 2:4). To all this, freedom from physical corruption and death will be added in due course (Rom. 8:18-21). This comprehensive freedom is the gift of Christ, who bought his people out of bondage (I Cor. 6:20; 7:22-23), just as, by a legal fiction, Greek deities "bought" slaves for their manumission. It is creatively conveyed to believers by the indwelling Spirit of Christ (Rom. 8:2; II Cor. 3:17). It is the royal freedom of God's adopted sons, to whom accordingly the Spirit witnesses as a Spirit, not of bondage, but of adoption (Rom. 8:15-16; Gal. 4:6-7). The obverse of Christ's gift of freedom (*eleutheria*) is the Christian's freely accepted bondservice (*douleia*) to God (Rom. 6:22), to Christ (I Cor. 7:22), to righteousness (Rom. 6:18), and to all men for the sake of the gospel (I Cor. 9:19-23) and of the Saviour (II Cor. 4:5). The "law of liberty" (James 1:25; 2:12), which is the "law of Christ" (Gal. 6:2; cf. I Cor. 9:21) for his free servants, is the law of love (Gal. 5:13-14), the principle of voluntary self-sacrifice without limit for the good of men (I Cor. 9:1-23; 10:23-33) and the glory of God (I Cor. 10:31). This is the essential NT ethic; a life of love is the response of gratitude which the gospel of grace both requires and evokes. Christian liberty is precisely freedom to love and serve, and is therefore abused when it is made an excuse for loveless license (Gal. 5:13; cf. I Pet. 2:16; II Pet. 2:19) or inconsiderateness (I Cor. 8:9-12).

The historic controversy about "free will" is connected with the biblical concept of freedom only indirectly. It concerns the question whether fallen man's slavery to sin is so radical and complete as to make him wholly unable to perform spiritual good or to avoid sinning, or to repent and put faith in Christ. Reformed theology follows Augustine in affirming, on the basis of such passages as Rom. 8:5-8; Eph. 2:1-10; John 6:44; 15:4-5, that man's will is not in fact free for obedience and faith till freed from sin's dominion by regenerating grace. Only on this basis, it is claimed, can human merit be excluded and God's sovereignty acknowledged in the matter of salvation, and justice be done to the biblical insistence that we are saved by faith alone (without works, Rom. 3:28), through grace alone (not human effort, Rom. 9:16), and for God's glory alone (not man's, I Cor. 1:28-31). Any alternative view, it is said, makes man a decisive contributor to his own salvation, and so in effect his own Saviour.

BIBLIOGRAPHY
Arndt; MM; H. Schlier in *TWNT*; J. P. Thornton-Duesbery in *RTWB*; *Deiss LAE*, pp. 326 ff.; H. Wedell in *AThR* 32, pp. 204-16.

JAMES I. PACKER

FRIEND. The English word is derived from the Saxon *freond*, meaning one loved or freed. Its Greek counterpart, *philos*, bears this idea in its use in the NT, especially in John. There the friend is one who has been freed (John 8:31-36) by the knowledge Jesus has imparted (15:15). The disciples are henceforth no longer slaves but friends who now share in Christ's glory (17:22).

Of importance is the phrase "friend of God," serving as a title of distinction (e.g., Abraham in Isa. 41:8; adopted by Christianity, as in James 2:23, and Islam). Judaism conferred this honor upon Moses (Ex. 33:11) and Israel. Philo (*Mig.* 45) included the prophets in this category, but in the Greek sense of every *sophos* being a "friend of God."

Among Alexandrian Christians "friend of God" was ascribed to martyrs and monks, gradually receiving a mystical significance which was expanded in the mysticism of the Middle Ages.

BIBLIOGRAPHY
E. Peterson, "Der Gottesfreund," *ZKG* (1923), 161-202.

HERMAN C. WAETJEN

FRUIT. In a literal sense "fruit" occurs many times in the OT, less frequently in the NT. In Gen. 1:11 the Hebrew classification of vegetation as grasses, plants or herbs and fruit-bearing trees first appears. See full treatment in Moldenke, *Plants of the Bible*, Chronica Botanica Co., Waltham, Mass., 1952. This entry treats particularly figurative uses of sixteen Hebrew and three Greek words translated fruit and their theological significance.

Typical examples of fruit used metonymously are: fruit of the ground or land for agricultural products generally (Gen. 4:3; Lev. 25:19; Ps. 72:16; Jer. 7:20); fruit of the womb, loins or body for children or descendants (Gen. 30:2; 49:22; II Kings 19:30; Ps. 21:10; Lam. 2:20; Luke 1:42 — in this case, Christ; Acts 2:30; Mic. 6:7; Rev. 18:14 figurative children); fruit of cattle or serpent for their offspring (Gen. 1:22, 28; 8:17; 9:1; Deut. 28:4, 11; Isa. 14:29); fruit of the vineyard or vine for grapes or wine (Deut. 22:9; II Kings 19:29; Isa. 65:21; Matt. 26:29).

Samples of metaphorical use are: fruit of the table for food (Mal. 1:12); fruit of the lips or mouth for speech (Prov. 13:2; 18:20,

21; Isa. 57:19; Heb. 13:15); fruit of the stout heart for boasting (Isa. 10:12); fruit of lies or evil thoughts for God's just punishments (Hos. 10:13; Jer. 6:19); fruit of one's hands for handmade articles or monetary gain (Prov. 31:16, 31); fruit of God's works for his creation (Ps. 104:13); fruit in season for true prosperity (Ps. 1:3; 92:14; Jer. 17:8); fruit for seeming prosperity of the wicked (Jer. 12:2); fruits of righteousness (Matt. 21:43; Phil. 1:11) or of repentance for good deeds (Matt. 3:8; contrast Amos 6:12); eating the fruits of one's doings for experiencing the consequences (Prov. 1:31; Isa. 3:10; Jer. 17:10; Mic. 7:13). The full fruit of the removal of Jacob's sin will be the exile, an expiating judgment according to Isa. 27:9. The wicked are fruitless trees (Jude 12).

Fruit is used for a charitable contribution in Rom. 15:28; II Cor. 9:11; in Dan. 4:12-21 for Nebuchadnezzar's generous provision for his subjects.

In Eden God forbade man to eat the fruit of the tree of the knowledge of good and evil (Gen. 2:9 ff.) to test his obedience. A literal tree is implied by the physically edible fruit (whether fig, apple, poisonous or whatever is unknown), but its significance is symbolic, suggesting the inevitable experience of evil mixed with good as the penalty of disobedience to God's command. The tree of life (Gen 2:9; 3:22 ff.) must likewise have been a literal tree with edible fruit and in this case symbolic of the everlasting life to which man was denied access after Adam's sin except by way of repentance and sacrifice. In Prov. 11:30 the idea of "righteous" would include observing Mosaic sacrifices. In Rev. 22:2 the tree of life again appears, bearing leaves of healing and fruit for each month to symbolize the eternal sustenance of God's people in the holy city. Many Reformed Church theologians regard the tree of life as a sacrament of the covenant of works, and analogous to the bread and wine used by Melchizedek (Gen. 14:18) and to the Christian Eucharist (Matt. 26:29) in the covenant of grace.

The fig tree which was withered by Jesus' curse because it was fruitless is probably meant to suggest the nation Israel, its failure to repent, to confess Jesus as Messiah, and to bring forth truly righteous rule of the people (Mark 11:14). Similarly Luke 13:6-19. Israel is represented by a once fruitful olive tree in Jer. 11:16 and Rom. 11:17-24; a fruitful cedar in Ezek. 17:23; a once fruitful vine in Ezek. 19:10-14 and Hos. 9:10 and 10:1, still to be fruitful in Isa. 27:6.

Most commonly theologians use fruit in the context of Jesus' usage and Paul's writings. Jesus taught that good and bad trees (teachers) are distinguished by their fruit (Matt. 7:16-20, 12:33), that is, by teaching of truth or deceit. The word of God is seed sown in the human heart bringing forth fruit in proportion to our way of receiving it (Matt. 13:8, 23). By abiding in Christ, the vine, the believer as a branch produces fruit (cf. Hos. 14:8), which is a steadfast Christlike life in words and deeds, issuing normally in converting others to Christ (John 15:1-16; cf. Rom. 1:13). In Pauline terms the Holy Spirit produces fruit in us (Col. 1:6, 10) a possibility for every Christian (Phil. 1:8-11) in contrast to the gifts of the Spirit which are to be coveted (I Cor. 12:31) but are distributed to particular individuals by God in sovereign will (I Cor. 12:11). Paul lists (Gal. 5:22-23) the fruit(s) of the Spirit (nine virtues as a single cluster, but love is the fruit pre-eminent). Note Paul's contrasting of unfruitful work of darkness with the fruit of light (Eph. 5:9-11), or fruits of flesh (Phil. 1:22; Rom. 6:20) with fruit unto holiness (Rom. 6:22; Phil. 1:11), and fruit unto death with fruit unto God (Rom. 7:4-5).

BIBLIOGRAPHY

MSt; HDCG; M. S. and J. L. Miller, Ency. of Bible Life, pp. 198-219.

TERRELLE B. CRUM

FULFIL, FULFILMENT. These words appear in the English versions of the Bible as translations of the Hebrew *mālē'* and the Greek *plēroō* and *plērōma*. The root *mālē'* is used with various significations. It may (1) have the connotation to fill, e.g., Gen. 1:22 ("fill the waters in the seas," LXX, *plērōsate*); to fill something with something else, e.g., I Kings 18:33 ("fill four barrels with water," *Qal*, LXX *labete*), I Sam. 16:1 ("fill thine horn with oil," *Pi'ēl*). The root is also used in the *Pi'ēl* in the sense to fill a person with something. Thus, Ex. 28:3, ". . . whom I have filled with the spirit of wisdom" (LXX, *eneplēsa*).

(2) Prominent in the OT also are the stative and passive forms of the verb, as, for example, in II Kings 4:6, "when the vessels were full." The stative is also employed with reference to days, and is apparently based on

an Akkadian idiom, *ûme imlu* ("the days filled"). Thus, it is said of Rachel, "And when her days to be delivered were fulfilled" (Gen. 25:24a). The thought is that the days had become full so that there were no more of them. When one day had become full that day was regarded as completed and consequently as past. This thought is also expressed by the passive, as in Ex. 7:25 (LXX, *aneplērō-thēsan*). Cf. also Gen. 6:11, II Kings 10:21.

(3) The stative form of *mālē'* is also employed to express the thought that something may be filled with something else, e.g., ". . . the earth is filled with violence through them . . ." (Gen. 6:13b). The earth is here represented as a container which holds and is completely filled with violence. To paraphrase: "the earth is in the condition of being filled full of violence." Similar in import are Ex. 8:17 and Deut. 34:9.

(4) In the Pi'ēl stem *'mālē'* may also be rendered to fulfil, as in Gen. 29:27a, "fulfil her week." This is actually the converse of (2) above. Jacob is to fill the week full, and then it will be regarded as accomplished. Somewhat similar is the thought of fulfilling a promise, as found, e.g., in Jer. 44:25 (LXX 51:25, *eplērōsate*). In this passage the word fulfil is the equivalent of "to accomplish." Cf. also Ps. 20:6, where the reference is to the fulfilment, i.e., the performance or accomplishment of a petition. A slight variation of this connotation is found in I Kings 1:14 where AV renders "confirm."

A number of passages do not actually fit into the above categories and probably represent idiomatic usages of the verb. In most of these, however, it is possible to perceive how the idiomatic connotation was obtained. We may note Isa. 40:2, "her warfare is accomplished," i.e., is filled full (LXX *eplēsthē*). Of particular interest are Josh. 3:15, "for Jordan overfloweth all his banks . . ." (lit., "is full upon his banks"); Num. 14:24b, "and hath followed me fully" (lit., "and he filled after me"). Cf. also Num. 32:11, and I Sam. 18:27, "and they gave them in full tale," (lit., "and they filled them"). Of interest too is the expression translated "gather the shields" AV, (lit., "fill the shields") in Jer. 51:11. The following also should be noted, "consecrate yourselves today" (lit., "fill your hand today"), Ex. 32:29; "and consecrate them" (lit., "and thou shalt fill their hands"), Ex. 28:41; also Ezek. 43:26, "the heart of the sons of men

is fully set in them" (lit., "the heart — is filled in them"), Eccl. 8:11; "And Jehu drew a bow with his full strength" (lit., "and Jehu filled his hand and the bow"), II Kings 9:24a.

The usage in the NT is on the whole similar to that of the Old. The verb *plēroō* is also used in the sense "to fill," "to be filled" as in Acts 2:2; 13:32 and Rom. 15:13. It is also employed with the connotation "to bring to completion" as in Rom. 15:19; II Cor. 10:6 (passive) and Phil. 2:2; "to bring to an end," as in Acts 12:25. One usage, prominent in the NT, and based upon OT passages such as Jer. 44:25, has reference to the fulfilment of OT prophecy, e.g., Matt. 1:21, where certain events are said to have occurred in order to fulfil prophecy. The thought is that the thing spoken in prophecy has now been accomplished, and in such passages the word "fulfil" is a practical equivalent of "accomplish," "complete." We may also note the usage of the noun *plērōma* in Gal. 4:4, rendered "fulness of the time" AV. Here the noun is equivalent to "the state of being full." Time had been filled full, i.e., the necessary time had passed, so that God might send forth his Son.

Revelation is progressive. The revelations of the OT, although genuine, nevertheless were partial and incomplete. In the NT they received their enrichment and completion, as the type gave way to antitype, the partial to the complete, the preparatory to the final. This concept of progressive revelation lies at the heart of biblical theology.

BIBLIOGRAPHY
Arndt; KB; W. G. Kuemmel, *Promise and Fulfilment*; R. V. G. Tasker, *The Old Testament in the New Testament*.

EDWARD J. YOUNG

FULNESS. The Greek word *plērōma* denotes that which fills, fulfils or completes. In classical and hellenistic Greek it may mean the entire contents, or sum-total. It is used, e.g., of the full strength of a military corps, or of a ship's complement. Philo applies it to the collection of animals in Noah's ark; he also describes a soul as having a full cargo (*plērōma*) of virtues.

I. NON-THEOLOGICAL OCCURRENCES IN THE NT. Of the seventeen instances of *plērōma* in the NT, eleven have no technical sense; they may be classified as follows. The word is used (a) of the patch put in to "fill up" the rent in an old garment (Matt. 9:16 = Mark 2:21); (b) of the leftover fragments which "filled" several baskets after the miraculous feedings (Mark 6:43; 8:20); (c) of the earth's contents, in a quotation from Ps. 24:1 (LXX 23:1), representing Heb. *m^elō'* (I Cor. 10:26); (d) of the final sum-total of believing Jews and Gentiles respectively (Rom. 11:12, 25); (e) of love as the "fulfilment" of the law (Rom. 13:10); (f) of the "fulness" of Christ's blessing which Paul hopes to bring to Rome (Rom. 15:29); (g) of the completion of an appointed period of time (Gal. 4:4).

II. THEOLOGICAL OCCURRENCES IN THE NT. The remaining six instances have the following connotations:

(a) The "fulness" of Christ (John 1:16), i.e., the inexhaustible resources of his grace ("grace upon grace") on which his people may freely draw.

(b) The "fulness" of Christ (Eph. 4:13), i.e., that spiritual maturity to which believers attain as members of his body.

(c) The "fulness" of God (Eph. 3:19), i.e., the full realization in believers of that eternal purpose towards which God is working.

(d) The "fulness" which by God's decree resides in Christ (Col. 1:19), i.e., the "fulness" of deity which is embodied in him (Col. 2:9). In Colossians Paul refutes an incipient Gnosticism which evidently used *plērōma* as a technical term, denoting the plenitude of the divine nature as distributed among several emanations, intermediaries between God and the world. Paul insists that Christ, the one Mediator between God and men, embodies the fulness of the Godhead, and in addition imparts his fulness to his people. Without him they remain incomplete fragments; incorporated in him they share a common life in which he and they complement each other as the head does the body and the body the head.

(e) This last thought probably underlies the use of *plērōma* in Eph. 1:23, where the church, the body of Christ, is called "the *fulness* of him who fills all in all" — or (as others translate) "the *complement* of him who is being perpetually filled" (with the fulness of deity). Whether the verb is middle ("fills") or passive ("is being filled"), "fulness" is probably in apposition with "body." Another view treats the clause "which is his body" as parenthetical and takes "fulness" in apposition with "him" (vs. 22), making Christ the Father's *plērōma* or "complement." So, according to Charles John Vaughan, *plērōma* in Eph. 1:23 "seems very likely to refer to *Christ —*

'gave him, Christ, I say, as the fulness of him who is filled with (*or* in respect of) all things' — or middle, 'who fills the universe with all things.' 'The fulness of him,' i.e., the fulness of God, is what Christ is here said to be. This view seems supported by Col. 1:18" (Derek D. W. Mowbray, C. J. *Vaughan [1816-1897]: Bible Expositor,* unpublished Ph.D. thesis, University of Sheffield, 1958, Vol. II [Appendix], p. 216). For the same view cf. A. E. N. Hitchcock, *ExpT* 22, 1910-11, p. 91; Charles F. D. Moule, *ExpT* 60, 1948-9, p. 53. It involves unnecessary awkwardness in construing the text.

III. GNOSTIC USAGE. In Valentinianism *plērōma* denotes the totality of the divine attributes. These attributes are expressed mythologically as thirty "aeons" emanating from God, but distinct from him and from the material world. They correspond to the Platonic "ideas"; sometimes each aeon is called a *plērōma* by contrast with the defectiveness of its earthly copies. Again, an individual's spirit-counterpart is called his *plērōma;* in this sense Heracleon on John 4:16 says that the Samaritan woman was told to fetch her *plērōma.* Each of the aeons imparted its peculiar excellence to Jesus, so that he appeared on earth as "the perfect beauty and star of the *plērōma"* (Irenaeus, *Heresies* i.14.2). In the Valentinian *Gospel of Truth* the Word comes forth from the *plērōma,* which is its place of repose.

BIBLIOGRAPHY

Arndt; G. Delling in *TWNT;* MM; J. B. Lightfoot, *Colossians and Philemon,* pp. 257 ff.; J. A. Robinson, *Ephesians,* pp. 255 ff.; C. A. A. Scott, *Christianity according to St. Paul,* pp. 266 f.; F. C. Burkitt, *Church and Gnosis,* pp. 41 ff.; E. Percy, *Probleme der Kolosser- und Epheserbriefe,* pp. 76 f.; P. Benoit, "Corps, tête et plérôme dans les Épitres de la Captivité," *RB* 63, (1956), pp. 5 ff.; C. F. D. Moule, *Colossians and Philemon,* pp. 164 ff.; E. K. Simpson and F. F. Bruce, *Ephesians and Colossians,* pp. 42 ff., 206 f., 232 f.

FREDERICK FYVIE BRUCE

FULNESS OF TIME. See ADVENT OF CHRIST.

FUNDAMENTALISM. The term denotes a movement in theology in recent decades designed to conserve the principles which lie at the foundation of the Christian system, and to resist what were considered dangerous theological tendencies in the movement calling itself Modernism. Its tenets are not those distinctive of any Protestant denomination, but comprise the verities essential to the Christian gospel as inherited from all branches of the Reformation.

The movement found literary expression in and received its name from the publication, between 1910 and 1912, of *The Fundamentals: A Testimony to the Truth.* The authors of this series of twelve volumes sought to enumerate and expound the verities which are essential to Protestant orthodoxy.

Organizationally, Fundamentalism took shape as a consequence of the World Conference in Christian Fundamentals which convened at Philadelphia in May of 1919. Taking the name, The World's Christian Fundamentals Association, the organization required of its members adherence to nine points of doctrine, namely: (1) the inspiration and inerrancy of Scripture, (2) the Trinity, (3) the deity and virgin birth of Christ, (4) the creation and fall of man, (5) a substitutionary atonement, (6) the bodily resurrection and ascension of Christ, (7) the regeneration of believers, (8) the personal and imminent return of Christ, and (9) the resurrection and final assignment of all men to eternal blessedness or eternal woe. W. B. Riley was president of the Association until 1930, Paul W. Rood from 1930 to 1952, at which time it merged with the Slavic Gospel Association.

BIBLIOGRAPHY

SHERK, IV, pp. 411 f.; V. Ferm, *Encyclopedia of Religion*, pp. 291 f.; *Encyclopedia Britannica* IX, pp. 291 f.; S. G. Cole, *History of Fundamentalism*; J. I. Packer, *"Fundamentalism" and the Word of God.*

HAROLD B. KUHN

G

GALLICANISM. The name given to an ecclesiastical movement in France which since the thirteenth century has consistently resisted the infringement of liberties by the See of Rome. The term is now more broadly applied to a similarly independent attitude on the part of any national church. The promulgation of the Gallican articles on March 19, 1682, was precipitated by the action of Louis XIV in exercising his right of *Regalia* in the matter of episcopal appointments. The Declaration merely served to codify the insistences of Philip IV, the Councils of Constance and Basel and the Pragmatic Sanction of Bourges.

A. SKEVINGTON WOOD

GARMENT. The garment was first used in the Garden of Eden where the girdle (*hăgôrâ*) of fig leaves was an attempt to hide the nakedness of the original parents. This use of clothing as a means of concealment finds its expression in such a passage as Matt. 7:15, where the false prophets are described as appearing "in sheep's clothing, but inwardly are ravenous wolves"; that is, they conceal their real purposes by a lamblike exterior (cf. Gen. 20:16; Isa. 50:3).

The garment is also used as indicative of close relationship, just as clothing clings to the body. Thus it is figurative of a wife (Mal. 2:16), and of the Lord as taking possession of a person (Judg. 6:34; cf. Job 38:9). This idea is given greater meaning by the special use of '*ēzôr*, "waist-cloth," to describe the relationship of Judah and Israel to the Lord. Since the waist-cloth was always worn next to the skin, it emphasizes the closest possible position (Jer. 13:1 ff.).

Dominant characteristics of a person are often designated by the use of garments, as things which are worn in everyday life. The messianic king will be characterized by faithfulness and righteousness because these things will be his "girdle" (Isa. 11:5; cf. 59:17; 61:10; Job 29:14; Eph. 6:14 ff.). Paul, indeed, sees one's whole nature as something which clothes a person (Col. 3:7-10; cf. I Cor. 15:53 ff.). And when one rends his garments it is a sign of deep mourning (Gen. 37:29; Isa. 36:22) or of indignation (Matt. 26:65).

According to Mosaic regulations the outer garment (*śimlâ;* NT, *himation*), if taken in pawn, was to be returned before sunset so as to give covering for sleep (Ex. 22:27). But Jesus taught that his followers must be prepared to give up even that garment which the law allowed as an expression of Christian love (Matt. 5:40; cf. I Cor. 6:7).

ROBERT B. LAURIN

GEHENNA. See HELL.

GENERATION. The word "generation" (or "generations") occurs in the AV over 200 times. It is used to translate the Hebrew words *dôr* (also translated "age" and "posterity") and *tôledôt* (in one place translated "birth"), and the Greek words *genea* (meaning a begetting, birth, clan), *genesis* (source, origin, birth, creation), *genos* (race, family, stock), and *gennēma* (progeny, offspring, that which is begotten or born). Basically, therefore, generation has to do with creation, the act of begetting; but it has variant applied uses in both Testaments. For example: (1) it is used in relation to the time process, to denote an age or successive ages (so Gen. 9:12; Ex. 30:10; Ps. 102:24); (2) in Matt. 24:34; Mark 13:30; Luke 21:32, it might mean the race, or those living at one time — either the time when the words were spoken, or when the signs begin; (3) it is used in the sense of offspring, descendants from the same stock (so Acts 2:40; I Pet. 2:9).

In dogmatic theology generation (*gennēsis*) is used of the Son's relation to the Father in the Godhead. The terms *unbegotten, begotten,* and *proceeding* are applied to the nature of the being of the Father, Son and Holy Spirit respectively. The Nicene formula is: "We believe . . . in one Lord Jesus Christ the Son of God, begotten (*gennēthenta*) of the Father, only-begotten (*monogenē*) . . . of one substance (*homoousion*) with the Father."

See also ONLY BEGOTTEN.

BIBLIOGRAPHY

Arndt; A-S; BDB; HDB; MM; R. L. Ottley, *The Doctrine of the Incarnation*, pp. 286 f., 357, 581 f.; G. L. Prestige, *God in Patristic Thought*; J. W. C. Wand, *Four Great Heresies; The Four Councils*.

OWEN R. BRANDON

GENTILES. The Hebrew *gôyim* designates non-Jewish peoples, rendered by the AV as "nations" or "heathen," by the RV frequently as "Gentiles." The "people," *'am,* is usually confined to Israel. The LXX makes a similar distinction between *ethnos* and *laos* (Luke 2:32). The Suffering Servant of the Lord includes both groups in his mission of salvation (Isa. 42:6; 49:6; 56:6-7).

Israel as the people of God developed a strict exclusiveness from other peoples at the time of the restoration from captivity. This attitude gave great offence to the gentile world, but was really a safeguard against the influence of gentile ways. For a Jew to enter the house of a Gentile, or eat with him, involved uncleanness (Acts 10:28; 11:3; John 18:28). Yet proselytes (*q.v.*) were made by the Jews from among the Gentiles, and a court was provided for them in the temple. One of the bitterest struggles in the early church was over the question of the inclusion of gentile converts to Christianity. Were they to be admitted via the portal of Judaism, or directly into the fold? The verdict of the apostles in conference with the church at Jerusalem was in favor of Paul (Acts 15:19). No Jewish rites were demanded except the admonition to eat clean food and abstain from moral impurities.

The mystery of Jewish unbelief and the admission of the Gentiles to the church of God is treated in Romans 9-11, where the figure of an olive tree is used (cf. Jer. 11:16; Hos. 14:6). Some of its branches have been broken off because of unbelief. Shoots from the wild olive have been grafted to the root. This is a picture of Jew and Gentile. Dr. Ramsay has shown that when an olive tree ceased to bear fruit, cuttings from the wild olive were grafted to the stock. The Gentiles stood by faith. There was no place for boasting, but a solemn obligation to communicate the gospel to the wide world and especially to the Jew.

Paul called himself "the apostle of the Gentiles" (Rom. 11:13; Eph. 3:3; Acts 22:21). Yet the day of gentile opportunity is limited in the purpose of God (Luke 21:24).

RICHARD E. HIGGINSON

GENTLENESS. "Gentle," "gentleness" are used in the English versions for several words. The AV, RV and RSV translate *epieikēs* thus, the meaning of which is dealt with under MODERATION. Moffatt and the RSV (on occasions) translate *praotēs* similarly, although "meekness" (*q.v.*) is more usual.

In the OT, "gentleness" occurs only once (II Sam. 22:36 = Ps. 18:35). The RV mg. renders "condescension," which more accurately gives the sense, the thought being of Almighty God condescending to visit the lowly (cf. Isa. 57:15).

A NT word for which "gentle" is clearly right is *ēpios* (I Thess. 2:7; II Tim. 2:24). The tenderness of "a nurse among trying children or a teacher with refractory pupils" (J. Denney in *HDB*) is indicated.

In Gal. 5:22, one of the fruits of the Spirit is *chrēstotēs* "gentleness" (AV), "kindness" (RV). It occurs in eight places (only in Pauline writings), usually being translated "kindness." Gentleness, therefore, signifies a patient and kind condescension, but the distinctive qualities of *epieikēs* and *praotēs* should be noted.

R. Colin Craston

GIFTS. See Spiritual Gifts.

GIRDLE. See Armor.

GLORY. The principal word in the Hebrew for this concept is *kābôd,* and in the Greek *doxa,* which is derived from *dokeō,* "to think" or "to seem." These two meanings account for the two main lines of significance in classical Greek, where *doxa* means opinion (what one thinks for himself) and reputation (what others think about him), which may shade into fame or honor or praise.

I. OT usage. Since *kābôd* derives from *kābēd,* "to be heavy," it lends itself to the idea that the one possessing glory is laden with riches (Gen. 31:1), power (Isa. 8:7), position (Gen. 45:13), etc. To the translators of the LXX it seemed that *doxa* was the most suitable word for rendering *kābôd,* since it carried the notion of reputation or honor which was present in the use of *kābôd.* But *kābôd* also denoted the manifestation of light by which God revealed himself, whether in the lightning flash or in the blinding splendor which often accompanied theophanies. Of the same nature was the disclosure of the divine presence in the cloud which led Israel through the wilderness and became localized in the tabernacle. So *doxa,* as a translation of *kābôd,* gained a nuance of meaning which it did not possess before. At times *kābôd* had a deeper penetration, denoting the person or self. When Moses made the request of God, "Show me thy glory" (Ex. 33:18) he was not speaking of the light-cloud, which he had already seen, but he was seeking a special manifestation of God which would leave nothing to be desired (cf. John 14:8). Moses had a craving to come to grips with God as he was in himself. In reply, God emphasized his goodness (Ex. 33:19). The word might be rendered in this instance "moral beauty." Apart from this the eternity of God as a subject of human contemplation might be depressing. This incident involving Moses is the seed plot for the idea that God's glory is not confined to some outward sign which appeals to the senses, but is that which expresses his inherent majesty, which may or may not have some visible token. Isaiah's vision

of him (6:1 ff.) included both the perception of sensible features and the nature of God, particularly his holiness (cf. John 12:41). The intrinsic worth of God, his ineffable majesty, constitutes the basis of warnings not to glory in riches, wisdom or might (Jer. 9:23) but in the God who has given all these and is greater than his gifts. In the prophets the word glory is often used to set forth the excellence of the messianic kingdom in contrast to the limitations of the present order (Isa. 60:1-3).

II. NT usage. In general *doxa* follows rather closely the pattern established in the LXX. It is used of honor in the sense of recognition or acclaim (Luke 14:10), and of the vocalized reverence of the creature for the Creator and Judge (Rev. 14:7). With reference to God, it denotes his majesty (Rom. 1:23) and his perfection, especially in relation to righteousness (Rom. 3:23). He is called the Father of glory (Eph. 1:17). The manifestation of his presence in terms of light is an occasional phenomenon, as in the OT (Luke 2:9), but in the main this feature is transferred to the Son. The transfiguration is the sole instance during the earthly ministry, but later manifestations include the revelation to Saul at the time of his conversion (Acts 9:3 ff.) and to John on the Isle of Patmos (Rev. 1:12 ff.). The fact that Paul is able to speak of God's glory in terms of riches (Eph. 1:18; 3:16) and might (Col. 1:11) suggests the influence of the OT upon his thinking. The display of God's power in raising his Son from the dead is labeled glory (Rom. 6:4).

Christ is the effulgence of the divine glory (Heb. 1:3). By means of him the perfection of the nature of God is made known to men. When James speaks of him as the Lord of glory (2:1) his thought seems to move along the lines of the revelation of God in the tabernacle. There the divine presence was a gracious condescension but also an ever-present reminder of God's readiness to mark the sins of his people and to visit them with judgment. So the readers of James' epistle are admonished to beware of partiality. The Lord is in the midst of his people as of yore.

The glory of Christ as the image of God, the Son of the Father, was veiled from sinful eyes during the days of his flesh but was apparent to the men of faith who gathered around him (John 1:14).

Even as the pre-incarnate Son had dwelt with the Father in a state of glory (with no sin to mar the perfection of the divine mode of life and intercourse), according to his own consciousness (John 17:5), so his return to the Father can properly be called an entrance into glory (Luke 24:26). But more seems to be involved here than a sharing with the Father of what he had enjoyed in ages past. God now gives him glory (I Pet. 1:21), in some sense as a reward for the faithful, full completion of the Father's will in relation to the work of salvation (Phil. 2:9-11; Acts 3:13). So it is that both the taking up of Christ from the earth (I Tim. 3:16) and his return (Col. 3:4; Titus 2:13), and the representations of his presence and activity as the future judge and king (Matt. 25:31) are also associated with a majesty and radiance which are largely lacking in the portrayals of Jesus in the days of his humiliation.

While the contrast is valid, therefore, between the sufferings of Christ and the glory (literally, the glories) to follow (I Pet. 1:11), John's Gospel reveals a further development, namely, that the sufferings themselves can be viewed as a glorification. Jesus was aware of this and expressed himself accordingly. "The hour is come that the Son of man should be glorified" (John 12:23). This word hour in the fourth Gospel points regularly to the death of Christ. Jesus was not seeking to invest the cross with an aura of splendor which it did not have, in order to conjure up a psychological antidote to its pain and shame. Rather, glory properly belongs to the finishing of the work which the Father had given him to do, since that work represented the perfect will of God.

Eschatological glory is the hope of the Christian (Rom. 5:2). In this future state he will have a new body patterned after Christ's glorified body (Phil. 3:21), an instrument superior to that with which he is presently endowed (I Cor. 15:43). Christ within the believer is the hope of glory (Col. 1:27). He is also the chief ornament of heaven (Rev. 21:23).

The word glory is found in the plural to denote dignitaries (Jude 8). It is not easy to determine whether the reference is to angels or men of honor and repute in the Christian community.

A somewhat specialized use of the word is that which it has in the doxologies, which are ascriptions of praise to God for his worth and works (e.g., Rom. 11:36).

On several occasions glory is used as a verb (kauchaomai) where the meaning is to boast, as in Gal. 6:14.

BIBLIOGRAPHY
I. Abrahams, *The Glory of God*; A. von Gall, *Die Herrlichkeit Gottes*; G. B. Gray and J. Massie in *HDB*; G. Kittel and G. von Rad in *TWNT*, II, pp. 235-58; H. Kittel, *Die Herrlichkeit Gottes*; E. C. E. Owen, "Doxa and Cognate Words" in *JTS* 33: 132-50, 265-79; A. M. Ramsey, *The Glory of God and the Transfiguration of Christ*; J. Schneider, *DOXA*.

EVERETT F. HARRISON

GNOSTICISM. A very dangerous heresy which came into the church like a flood in the second century. By the beginning of the third century nearly all the more intellectual Christian congregations in the Roman Empire were markedly affected by it. Its errors are clearly referred to in the NT, e.g., I John 2:22; 4:2-3, where reference is made to those who denied that Christ had "come in the flesh." The system was eclectic and its materials were drawn from many quarters such as the mythologies of Greece, Egypt, Persia, and India, and from the philosophies and theosophies of these lands. Many of its leading ideas had existed before the Christian era but its votaries felt that in the Christian religion were valuable elements which could be worked into their scheme of things. Their aim was to reduce Christianity to a philosophy and relate it to various pagan teachings as well as to the OT which they distorted.

The term Gnostic comes from the Greek word *gnosis* which means "knowledge." The Gnostic claimed special esoteric or secret knowledge. It could be possessed only by that section of humanity which was "pneumatic," or spiritual. They alone were inevitably led back to the realm of light of the Supreme God. There was a second class of men, those who were only "psychic" and could not get beyond faith. The prophets and other good Hebrews belonged to this class but they must be eternally in a sphere much inferior to that occupied by those who had "gnosis." A third class represented the overwhelming mass of human kind. They were merely "hylic" (i.e., subject to matter) and their case was utterly hopeless for they were in endless bondage to Satan and their own lusts, and their end was to be completely destroyed. Here was one of the worst features of Gnosticism, the elevating of a limited number into a specially privileged class, and the consigning of the vast majority of mankind to unredeemable destruction. This was totally contrary to the teachings of Christianity.

We encounter several very distinct schools of thought among the Gnostics. It is exceedingly difficult to make a satisfactory classification of these. They have been divided into ascetic and licentious; monistic and dualistic; Syrian and Alexandrian. H. M. Gwatkin (*Early Church History*, Vol. II, p. 20) provisionally describes Gnosticism as "a number of schools of philosophy, Oriental in general character, but taking in the idea of a redemption through Christ, and further modified in different sects by a third element which may be Judaism, Hellenism, or Christianity." The classification of the Gnostic sects in this way is as good as any, but not entirely satisfactory.

In general, all the varied schools taught that matter was utterly and irretrievably evil. They agreed that the God of the Jews, the Creator of the world, was not the Supreme Being but a very inferior being whom they called the Demiurge. The Supreme Being, the Absolute, is the unknown and ineffable one of whom nothing can be predicated. He is Bythos, dwelling infinitely remote from the world, in the spiritual light of the Pleroma which is the fulness of God. The problem was to explain how this ineffably pure Being could have originated a material world, seeing that matter is essentially evil. The difficulty was surmounted by postulating a series of thirty emanations (or "aeons") from Bythos, each of these originating the next in order. The aeons were attributes thought of as personal, and took the place of the abstract ideas of Greek philosophy. When one of these aeons was sufficiently remote from the Supreme God, and was on the borderland of light and darkness, he created the world and did it badly. This was the Demiurge or God of the OT. Sometimes he was regarded as actively hostile to the Supreme God, and in every case was regarded as the producer of a very evil material world. It contained, however, certain germs of a higher life, rays of immortal life from the glorious light of the Pleroma above. These were ever struggling to be free. Thus there was a constant struggle between good and evil, life and death, matter and spirit. Here we have Eastern dualism. Some had infinitely more of this divine life than others. They were those who had "gnosis."

The historical Christ was a mere man, but he was taken possession of by the heavenly Christ who was the brightest of all aeons. This heavenly Christ acted in the man Jesus but was never incarnate. He could not be, because matter was so evil. The heavenly Christ returned to heaven before the crucifixion, so it was only a man who died on the cross. Another version was that the heavenly Christ only had the semblance of a body.

The two greatest Gnostics intellectually were Valentinus and Basilides, both of Alexandria, and both hellenic in outlook. The former was at the zenith of his fame about A.D. 150. He lived in Rome A.D. 138-61. Basilides was at his height about A.D. 130. He differed from Valentinus in that he taught that every development of God and the world was brought about from below upwards, and not by emanations from above. The great Syrian section of Gnosticism was founded by Saturninus at Antioch. He flourished about A.D. 125. One of the earliest Gnostics was Cerinthus, a contemporary of St. John at Ephesus. He was half Ebionite. Marcion of Sinope (*ca.* 140) was one of the most Christian Gnostics, yet he mutilated the Scriptures wholesale, and rejected all the apostles except Paul.

The Ophites were a Gnostic sect which venerated the serpent. They taught that God was bad and the serpent good. One school of thought turned the Scriptures upside down, teaching that Pharaoh and Ahab were saints while Moses and Elijah were sinners. Altogether, Gnosticism was a deadly peril in the church for about 150 years.

BIBLIOGRAPHY
Moffatt in *HERE*; J. F. Bethune-Baker, *Early Christian Doctrine*; H. M. Gwatkin, *Early Church History*, Vol. II.

ALEXANDER M. RENWICK

GOD. Since the topic *God* is unmanageably immense, this article will simplify matters by a division between the biblical data and the philosophical problems they raise. Of course, this division is slightly arbitrary. Biblical theology must systematize its material to some degree; and systematic theology, if definitely Christian, constantly appeals to the text of Scripture. Nevertheless there is a difference. Biblical theology stays closer to the text in its chronological development and is easier to understand; systematic theology follows a logical order, draws out implications, and can become highly technical.

I. BIBLICAL THEOLOGY.

A. *The Names of God.* The first word for God in the OT is *Elohim*. It is also the most general and least specific in significance. Thus it would correspond to *Theos* in Greek and to *God* or *Deity* in English. Unlike *Jehovah,* explained below, Elohim can be used for pagan gods (Gen. 31:30; Ex. 12:12).

Since it is so used and since it is a plural noun, some critics have seen in it an indication of an original polytheism. This theory is not well founded because the singular form, *Eloah,* is poetic and rare. In prose the plural has to be used, whether polytheistically or monotheistically, because there is no other suitable word. Therefore its use cannot prove an underlying polytheism in biblical religion.

On the other hand, some Christians have explained the plural as an anticipation of the Trinity. But again, without a commonly used singular no one in OT times could have developed trinitarian ideas from the word alone. The plural would suggest polytheism more readily than trinitarianism were it not for hints other than the word itself being used with a singular verb. This is not to say that material in the OT cannot hint at some distinctions within the Godhead.

The plural form is better understood as indicating a plenitude of power. Though the etymology is obscure, the word may have come from a root meaning *strong.* Its poetic singular, *Eloah,* seems to mean an object of terror. In any case, this name is used chiefly in connection with God's governance of the world and mankind in general.

Another word, *El,* which is not related directly to Elohim, occurs more than 200 times, chiefly in Job, Psalms, and Isaiah. It is often accompanied by some descriptive term or in such combinations as *El-Shaddai,* God Almighty, or *El-Elyon,* God Most High.

In contrast with this most general name of God there stands *Jehovah,* the most specific. Jehovah is an artificial English word put together from the four Hebrew consonants JHVH and the vowels of the Hebrew word *Adonai,* or Lord. Before the time of Christ the Jews developed a superstitious dread of pronouncing JHVH; when they came to it in the text, they pronounced Adonai instead; then later the vowels of Adonai were written into the manuscripts, and in modern times people have been saying Jehovah. The original pronunciation was probably Yahveh.

A basic explanation of the name is given in Ex. 3:13-15: "I am that I am," or, better, "I will be what I will be." The hellenistic Jews wrongly identified JHVH with the Pure

Being of Greek philosophy. Quite the reverse, whereas Elohim designates God's universal action, JHVH is the name used in connection with God's choice of, revelation to, and special care for his covenant people. It is the term almost always used in theophanies, and almost always revelation is "the word of JHVH." Or, more briefly, JHVH is the redemptive name of God.

Higher criticism has often tried to maintain that one author could not possibly have used both names for God, and that therefore the first chapter of Genesis was written by one man and the second by another. The theory of two authors is not needed to explain the use of these two names. The first chapter tells of God's general relation to the world, and then the second begins to relate his special care for men who by Adam's fall soon were in need of redemption. God in his wisdom furnished these two names as a convenient method of summarizing what the Scriptures teach about God: *Elohim,* his work of creation; and *Jehovah,* his work of redemption.

B. *God as Creator.* The Bible opens with the account of God's creating the universe. The first chapter of Genesis gives the impression that, aside from God himself, everything that exists has been created. God alone is self-existent. Nothing else exists of its own right, independently, or without beginning. This initial impression is corroborated by many later passages. Neh. 9:6 states, "Thou, even thou, art Lord alone; thou hast made heaven, the heaven of heavens, with all their host, the earth, and all things that are therein, the seas, and all that is therein, and thou preservest them all; and the host of heaven worshippeth thee." Cf. Ex. 20:11; Isa. 42:5; John 1:3; Heb. 3:4, *et al.*

The expressions of Scripture as to the extent of God's creative act are so comprehensive that we say God created all things *ex nihilo,* out of nothing. Before any natural processes began, God created absolutely. He made no use of prior existing material to fashion the universe as a sculptor makes a beautiful statue out of an ugly block of stone; but "By the word of the Lord were the heavens made, and all the host of them by the breath of his mouth" (Ps. 33:6); and "God said, Let there be light, and there was light" (Gen. 1:3), "for he spake, and it was done" (Ps. 33:9). This is usually called *fiat* creation (*q.v.*). This is not to say that after bringing the universe into existence, God did not use previously created substance in completing his creation. The Bible specifically states, for example, that "God formed man of the dust of the ground."

Since speaking and creating are voluntary actions, the first chapter of Genesis teaches the personality of God. God is not a physical, inanimate, mechanical First Cause. Nor is he a descriptive principle abstracted from the phenomena of nature. He arranges the parts of the universe for a purpose (Gen. 1:14, 16, 26, 28). Intelligence and volition are personal.

Most religions have preserved some notion of a personal God. In modern times even pantheists, like Spinoza and Hegel, though they deny creation and identify God and the universe, consider their All or Absolute a living being. In antiquity Aristotle taught that the First Mover thinks. All these views show a trace of personality, but only a trace. Spinoza denied that God had a will, and Aristotle denied that God knew history. In fact, the polytheists often seem to have a better appreciation of personality, even if their divine persons are more limited and human than divine. It may also be said that a universal creation presupposes, not polytheism, but the unity of the Godhead.

There are levels or degrees of heathen idolatry. The Ephesians (Acts 19:35) believed that Diana herself lived above. Jupiter was supposed to have thrown down to earth a wooden image of Diana. In Paul's day the Ephesian silversmiths had developed a lucrative trade making small replicas of this image. Thus the Ephesians clearly distinguished between the goddess and the images. But in other cases the depravity of the idolatrous mind was such that, though its psychology is an enigma to us, the distinction between the inanimate idol and the god or goddess became blurred. Somehow or other the two were practically identified. If and when this identification was made, the Psalmist's sarcasm would be exceptionally biting when he says, "Their idols . . . have mouths but they speak not; eyes have they, but they see not; . . . they that make them are like unto them" (Ps. 115:4-8). Cf. Isa. 44:17; 45:20; 46:7. See also GODS.

In contrast with both ancient paganism and modern pantheism, the Scriptures ascribe to God a full and complete personality. Not only did he create all things, not only does he control the universe, not only does he think and know, not only does he hear the prayers of his people, but most particularly and in a manner impossible in the systems of Spinoza and Hegel, he speaks to man. We learn the nature and attributes of God, not by a scientific study of nature, but by a verbal revelation (q.v.). The idea of revelation or divine communication of knowledge, as well as the righteousness and love by which that revelation so sharply distinguishes God from the imaginations of the heathen, comes to clearest expression in the works of providence and redemption. For the moment, however, the implications of creation require further development.

If God has created all things of nothing, simply by his word, his fiat, his command, it follows that he is omnipotent. Neither a greater power nor a more impossible task is conceivable. The biblical concept of God Almighty differs radically from paganism and idolatry. Where there are many gods, each limits the others. Since no one of them is the creator of all, no one of them is in complete control.

The Lord God Almighty, who created the heavens and the earth, has a power and control that is universal in extent and total in depth. Omnipotence, first seen in creation, is stated and exemplified throughout the Bible. All the miracles come to mind. When Abraham despaired of having a son by his wife Sarah, God introduced his promise by saying, "I am the Almighty God"; and, "Is anything too hard for the Lord" (Gen. 17:1; 18:14). Because Abraham believed this, he was willing later to sacrifice Isaac, "accounting that God was able to raise him up, even from the dead" (Heb. 11:19). After Abraham there were Moses' dealings with Pharaoh, the water in the wilderness, the capture of Jericho, the works of Elijah, Hezekiah's shadow, and the miracles of Christ and the apostles. Conversely the attacks on miracles by secular authors are uniformly, though not always explicitly, based on a prior rejection of omnipotence.

In addition to these examples of omnipotence there are many doctrinal or abstract statements of it. "I know that thou canst do all things, and that no purpose of thine can be restrained" (Job 42:2, ASV). "Whatsoever the Lord pleased, that did he in heaven and in the earth" (Ps. 135:6). "He doeth according to his will in the army of heaven and among the inhabitants of the earth: and none can stay his hand or say unto him, What doest thou?" (Dan. 4:35). "Who worketh all things after the counsel of his own will" (Eph.

1:11). Cf. Deut. 32:39; I Chron. 29:12; Ps. 62:11; Isa. 45:5-7; Jer. 32:27; Matt. 19:26; Rom. 9:18-24; et al.

Omniscience, as well as omnipotence, is involved in creation. The one cannot be separated from the other. At the very least, if an omnipotent God could be thought to be ignorant of something, he still would be able to learn it; otherwise there would be something he could not do. But even a momentary ignorance would be a momentary limitation upon omnipotence. Therefore the two attributes are inseparable.

Omniscience is more particularly related to creation in that the works of creation and providence follow a plan eternally existent in the divine mind. Control of all things presupposes knowledge of all things. "Known unto God are all his works from the beginning of the world" (Acts 15:18). This knowledge includes the minutest details: "The very hairs of your head are all numbered" (Matt. 10:30). Volitional and purposeful action (Eph. 1:11), since it initiates a series of concatenated events, requires a knowledge of the future. Isaiah speaks of God as "declaring the end from the beginning" (46:10). Apart from knowledge and control of all future details there could be no trustworthy prophecy. Hence all the predictions in Scripture exemplify this point. A few other statements of omniscience are: "All things are naked and opened unto the eyes of him with whom we have to do" (Heb. 4:13). "He that planted the ear, shall he not hear? He that formed the eye, shall he not see?" (Ps. 94:9). "The eyes of the Lord are in every place, beholding the evil and the good" (Prov. 15:3). Cf. Ps. 139:1-6, 12; 147:5; Prov. 15:11; I John 3:20.

Creation exemplifies another of God's prerogatives. Actually it is an aspect of omnipotence, though not usually thought of as such. In the Genesis account God is presented not only as creator of the physical universe, but also as the creator of moral distinctions. When God created Adam and Eve and placed them in the garden, he made certain demands upon them. Adam was to cultivate the garden; with one exception Adam and Eve were to eat of the fruit of the trees; and they were to reproduce and populate the earth. This "covenant of works," including the threat of penalty for disobedience, is the original moral legislation.

The prohibition to eat of the tree of the knowledge of good and evil displays the inmost essence of moral obligation. It was a test of pure obedience to divine authority. Had God commanded Adam not to murder Eve, he might have obeyed because she was so fair, or he might have disobeyed because she was a shrew. In either case his action would have had mixed motives. But the tree was as indifferent as an object can be. No motive could be involved except that of obedience to the Creator. The rightness and the wrongness were purely a matter of divine legislation. There was nothing in the tree itself to make the eating wrong. God could as well have chosen another tree. Similarly the Mosaic ritual became obligatory by divine legislation. The appointments of the tabernacle and the details of the sacrifices could have been quite different. They were what they were, and they were to be observed, only because of their divine imposition.

Devout Christians who have been brought up in the nurture and admonition of the Lord, imbued with the principles of monogamy, honesty, and truth, sometimes think that these obligations are independent of the divine will. They suppose that God could not have created a race for which polygamy would have been beneficial; it escapes their attention that God might have made men like the angels, without marriage, so that the fifth and seventh commandments would be null and void. Yet non-Christians today remind us that God might have approved of destroying the ill and aged, and might not have approved of private property. We must remind them in return that although God might have done so, actually he did not. The commandments for this world are established.

To view morality as fixed independently of God's will is inconsistent with the concept of omnipotence. Plato and Leibniz attempted to conceive God as subordinate to independent moral principles. Thus they limited God by a reality external to him. No such view is countenanced in the Bible. The highest norm of morality is the law of God. It is God's command that makes an act right or wrong. This is substantiated throughout the Scripture by the threat of punishment, as in the case of Adam, by the promise of reward, as in the case of Abraham and many others; and by the constant insistence on obedience to God's precepts.

For this reason secular philosophies fail to solve the problem of ethics by their appeals to a categorical imperative, to the greatest good of the greatest number, or to values allegedly discovered in experience.

C. *God as Redeemer.* Thus far God has been considered only as Creator. Biblical theology reveals much more about God as Redeemer. Naturally the two activities often exhibit the same divine attributes. For example, the biblical plan of redemption would necessarily presuppose the personality of God; some conceivable plans even though they involved future events might not necessarily require omniscience and omnipotence; but there is no question but that the biblical plan does. At the same time, redemption reveals much more than these particular attributes.

There is one factor, obvious but only implicit in the account of creation, which, though explicit and emphasized in the plan of redemption, is not always so obvious to sinful minds. It is divine sovereignty over all — absolute sovereignty. As no external force compelled or motivated God to create, so also the initiation of redemption is God's choice alone. When Adam violated the covenant of works, God with perfect justice could have executed the full penalty immediately. No obligation rested upon him to talk to Adam again. Nor did Adam seek God and beg for a visit. On the contrary, Adam tried to avoid the meeting. "There is none that seeketh after God . . . no, not one" (Ps. 14:2; 53:2; Rom. 3:11-12). The initiative is God's alone.

Abraham is another example. God called the idolatrous Abram; Abram did not seek God. God might have called some other citizen of Ur; or he might have called an Egyptian. The initiative and choice was entirely God's. "Blessed is the man whom thou choosest and causest to approach unto thee" (Ps. 65:4). "Ye have not chosen me, but I have chosen you" (John 15:16).

This initiative is love, a divine attribute pervasively emphasized in both the OT and NT. This love is unmotivated by any worth in its object. God does not love anyone because of what he is, but in spite of what he is. The merits of man are "as filthy rags" (Isa. 64:6). Man is an enemy of God (Col. 1:21); but yet while "we were enemies, we were reconciled to God" (Rom. 5:10). "God commendeth his love toward us, in that, while we were yet sinners, Christ died for us" (Rom. 5:8).

Whoever draws an antithesis between a wrathful God of the OT and a different loving God of the NT, evinces a blindness to the actual words of Scripture. Divine love and choice are combined with human unworthiness in the verses: "The Lord thy God hath chosen thee to be a special people . . . The Lord did not set his love upon you, nor choose you, because ye were more in number . . . but because the Lord loved you . . ." (Deut. 7:6-8). "In his love and pity he redeemed them" (Isa. 63:9). "When Israel was a child, then I loved him . . . I drew them with cords of a man, with bands of love" (Hos. 11:1, 4). "Yea, I have loved thee with an everlasting love" (Jer. 31:3). And the loving-kindnesses and tender mercies set forth in the Psalms are too numerous to mention. They are all summed up in the statement, "God is love" (I John 4:8).

In both the OT and the NT the love of God is depicted under two figures of speech. Sometimes God is called the father of his children; sometimes the husband of a wife.

The fatherhood of God (*q.v.*) is a most important idea. It exhibits God's love for his children. Jesus taught his disciples to pray, "Our Father . . ." (Matt. 6:6, 8, 9). The fowls of the air neither sow nor reap, but "your heavenly Father feedeth them . . . for your heavenly Father knoweth that ye have need of all these things" (Matt. 6:26, 32). "If ye then being evil know how to give good gifts to your children, how much more shall your Father which is in heaven give good things to them that ask him?" (Matt. 7:11). Cf. Matt. 10:20, 29; 13:43; 18:14; 23:9.

Like all important biblical concepts the fatherhood of God has been distorted. First, God has been regarded as the Father of all men. This misinterpretation confuses the relation between Creator and creature with the relation between God as redeemer and the elect. Since the gospel requires men to be born again, natural birth is clearly not sufficient for entrance into the family of God. The Epistles make use also of the idea of adoption (*q.v.*). "They which are the children of the flesh, these are not the children of God" (Rom. 9:8). "For as many as are led by the Spirit of God, they are the sons of God; for . . . ye have received the Spirit of adoption, whereby we cry, Abba, Father" (Rom. 8:15). Cf. Rom. 9:4; Gal. 4:5; Eph. 1:5. Then, too, Jesus rebuked the unbelieving Jews, "Ye are of your father the devil" (John 8:44). The idea of a universal fatherhood of God is thus inconsistent with the Scripture and is destructive of grace and redemption.

A second misunderstanding of the fatherhood of God occurs when it is made a new idea first enunciated in the NT by Jesus. On the contrary, the fatherhood of God is an OT idea, and the essential identity of the message of both Testaments should not be broken. "He shall cry unto me, Thou art my Father" (Ps. 89:26). "Thou art our Father" (Isa. 63:16; 64:8). "Yet shall call me, My Father" (Jer. 3:19). Cf. II Sam. 7:14; I Chron. 29:10; Mal. 1:6.

Usually the fatherhood of God relates to the redeemed individually and distributively; but when the people or the church is conceived collectively, God is pictured as a husband or bridegroom. This figure of the marriage relationship is a particular application of the pervasive notion of the covenant (q.v.). God made a covenant with Noah, Abraham, David and with their seed after them. When this posterity is thought of as a nation, God is pictured as the husband, the nation as the wife, and the individuals as the children. The interpretation of the covenant as a marriage bond is especially prominent in Hosea; but it also occurs in Isa. 54:1; 62:5; Jer. 31:32; Ezek. 16:8. Yet it is not a late invention of the prophetic age. Implicitly it underlies the condemnation of idolatry as "going a-whoring after other gods" (Ex. 34:15, 16; Lev. 17:7; Num. 15:39; Deut. 31:16). For this reason strange worship, like adultery, is a violation of the law. The terms of the contract have been broken (Hos. 4:1; 8:1; Amos 2:4).

All this sharpens the concept of God as a jealous God. Strange as it often appears to modern minds, jealousy is one of the attributes the Bible ascribes to God. Ex. 34:15, 16, referred to above, is introduced by the command, "Thou shalt worship no other god: for the Lord, whose name is Jealous, is a jealous God" (Ex. 34:14). This idea, of course, is embedded in the Decalogue (Ex. 20:5). Cf. Deut. 4:24; Nah. 1:2. This concept of jealousy is consistent with the sovereignty of God. Any ascription of divine prerogatives to another is a violation of the first and basic commandment. "I am the Lord . . . and my glory will I not give to another" (Isa. 42:8).

In the NT the covenant idea retains the same importance (Gal. 3:6 ff.), but its appearance in the form of a marriage vow is not so prominent. However, the church is said to be the bride of Christ (II Cor. 11:2; Rev. 21:2; 22:17). Not quite so explicit are Matt. 25:1-13; John 3:29; Gal. 4:26-28; Eph. 5:23-25.

The covenant interpreted as a marriage contract emphasizes another aspect of God's nature. The marriage contract, however much it may reflect the love of the parties, is at the same time a legal obligation. Violation results in liability to punishment. Beyond the covenant relation as well, man is subject to God's laws, and their infraction carries with it a penalty. Thus the Scriptures represent man as being under the wrath and curse of a righteous God. The Christian concept of God, the plan of redemption, and even the love of God, cannot be understood apart from the attribute of righteousness. God therefore is not of a character simply to forgive and forget. Forgiveness alone could be unrighteous. And when a human judge frees a guilty criminal, the act of mercy may in some sense be justified by extenuating circumstances, but the strictness of the law has been ignored.

Since God is righteous, his plan of redemption must maintain the majesty of the law. Righteousness and a bare disregard for sin are incompatible. Therefore the penalty must be executed. An atonement (q.v.) or satisfaction must be made. This was the teaching of the Mosaic ritual; this ritual also taught that God provides a substitute to suffer the penalty. The Atonement therefore is an expression both of love and of righteousness. For the purpose of redemption God set forth Jesus Christ to be a propitiatory sacrifice in order to declare, publish, and exemplify his righteousness, so that God, when he justifies a sinner, might remain just in doing so (Rom. 3:25-26; 5:8; II Cor. 5:21; I Peter 1:18-19; I John 2:2 et al.).

The crucifixion of Christ as a sacrifice of the Lamb of God to satisfy the justice of the Father brings out one further feature of deity. At the beginning the personality of God was pointed out. Now it is evident that God is not one Person, but more than one. If the Son is sent from heaven, while the Father is not sent; if the Father loves the Son and the Son loves the Father; if the Son sacrifices himself or pays a ransom to the Father; it follows that the Father and the Son are different Persons. Thus, with the other biblical material on the Holy Spirit, the concept of God is the concept of a Trinity (q.v.).

Some dim anticipation of the Trinity can be found in the appearances of the Angel of the Lord to the patriarchs. Since the definite article is used, this Angel must in some way be different from other angels. When the Angel appeared to Hagar, she called him the Lord and spoke of him as God (Gen. 16:7-13). In an appearance to Abraham the Angel calls himself the Lord (Gen. 22:11, 15). When the Angel spoke to Jacob, he again called himself God (Gen. 31:11). The passages indicate a unity of and a difference between the Angel and the God who sends him. Neither these passages nor later ones concerning a coming King, a Messiah, a suffering Servant, were explicit enough to produce the trinitarian concept in the minds of the Israelites. The NT clarifies the obscurities of the OT. All the passages that teach the deity of Christ bear on the doctrine of the Trinity (Matt. 11:25-27; John 1:1, 14; Rom. 9:5; Phil. 2:6; Col. 1:13-19; 2:9 et al.). The well-known benediction also (II Cor. 13:14) would be incongruous unless these three Persons were equal in power and glory in the one Godhead.

II. PHILOSOPHICAL THEOLOGY.

A. *Theology Proper.* The first half of this article has been a brief summary of what the Bible says about God. Its statements are deceptively simple in form; the ideas are profound and their implications have puzzled many minds, both devout and irreligious. Therefore the descriptive method of biblical theology must give way to a more systematic and philosophic analysis. But, again, as the descriptive summary was brief, so too this second half can barely indicate the labor of centuries on these problems. Only three types of problem will be mentioned: theology proper, science, and ethics.

Since the Bible everywhere asserts the existence of God, the first question of systematic or philosophic theology concerns the proof of this assertion. Does our belief in God's existence depend solely on scriptural authority, or does it depend on some sort of proof? If the latter, is the "proof" a direct mystical experience of God, or is it a syllogistic process that starts with observation of nature?

The Thomistic philosophy of the Roman Catholic Church, derived from Aristotle, begins with sensory experience of bodies in motion and by an intricate series of arguments concludes with the existence of an Unmoved Mover, God. The language of Thomas Aquinas

indicates that he thought the whole argument to be formally valid and that the conclusion necessarily follows from the premises. The philosophers David Hume and Immanuel Kant contended that the "cosmological argument" was a fallacy. Some Protestant theologians seem to accept the argument, while others admit that it is not "mathematical" (strictly logical), but that it is of some value. The present writer believes that the argument is worthless because (1) it is circular, in that the existence of God is itself used to disprove an infinite series of causes, which disproof is necessary to prove the existence of God; (2) its premises use the term existence in a spatial and temporal sense, while the conclusion uses the term in a different sense; and (3) an argument from effect to cause can assign to the cause only sufficient attributes to account for the effect by which alone it is known, and this would give us a God who is neither omnipotent, omniscient, nor perfectly righteous.

St. Anselm at the beginning of the twelfth century constructed the "ontological argument" for God's existence. It is not based on an observation of nature but on an analysis of the concept of God. As a man who would deny that a triangle contains 180 degrees simply does not understand the meaning of triangle, so one who denies the existence of God has not grasped the concept of God. God, as the being than whom a greater cannot be conceived, cannot be conceived not to exist; for if God could be conceived not to exist, it would be possible to conceive of an existing being greater than God; but to conceive of a being greater than the being than whom a greater cannot be conceived is a self-contradiction.

Immanuel Kant did not like the ontological argument either, but his underlying prejudice that God is beyond the grasp of human concepts is itself highly vulnerable.

A mystical assurance of God's existence is difficult to discuss, for mysticism is a very ambiguous term. Loosely it could refer to jumping to a conclusion by a hunch; in the strictest meaning of a non-rational trance, it has nothing intelligible to communicate.

If then rational arguments do not demonstrate the existence of God (as one demonstrates a theorem of geometry by valid inferences from axioms), then we must accept God's existence solely on scriptural authority, or we must take it as the first and therefore indemonstrable principle of our thought; and these two may be the same thing.

Some philosophers virtually imply that the existence of God is not such an important issue as is commonly thought. Spinoza and other pantheists identify the universe as God. We grant that the universe exists. Professor H. N. Wieman has defined God as "that character of events to which man must adjust himself in order to attain the greatest good and avoid the greatest ills." We grant again that events have characters. And so, by a sort of ontological argument, i.e. by definition, God must exist. Atheism has become impossible.

The important question therefore is not, Is there a God? Of course there is. But the important question is, What is God? And this returns us to the description of biblical theology.

Although the proofs of God's existence have been prominent in theological discussion, they are but part of a more general problem: Can God be known? Some secular philosophers, e.g., Kant and Spencer, have asserted the existence of unknowable entities. A philosophic Absolute may be thought to be so transcendent as to be beyond thought. Or, as in Thomas Aquinas, the human mind, taking its rise from sensory experience, may be essentially incapacitated to know much if anything of an eternal Being. Or, more popularly, the finite mind cannot grasp the infinite God, simply because the finite cannot grasp the infinite.

Those who assert the existence of unknowable objects seem to contradict themselves, for if the object were quite unknowable, one could not know either that it existed or that it was unknowable. Then too this type of philosophy is usually suspected of making all knowledge impossible, even knowledge of arithmetic and the weather. Skepticism is thus self-destructive.

Those who, like Thomas Aquinas, base knowledge on sensory experience find it necessary to assign an important role to mental pictures or visual images. Some philosophers have taught that all knowledge consists of sensory images. If so, man could never have a concept of God because God is not a sense object and no image of him is possible. Either then a believer in God must reject empiricism and find some a priori basis of knowledge, or he must struggle, as Thomas did (with such little success) to bridge the chasm between concepts abstracted from sensation and a knowledge of the timeless and spaceless Spirit.

The impossibility of knowing what God is has also been argued from a theory of definition. When an apple tree or a squirrel is defined, it is placed in a genus. An apple tree is a species of rose, and a squirrel is a species of rodent. But God is not a species of any genus. "To whom then will ye liken me, or shall I be equal? saith the Holy One" (Isa. 40:18, 25). Since knowledge of what a thing is, is its definition, it follows that God cannot be known. The theist, to avoid this conclusion, must produce a different theory of definition; and its desirability may be emphasized by pointing out that if species only can be defined and known, genera, especially the highest genera or genus, remain unknown.

But can the finite hope to grasp the infinite? The negative assertion flies in the face of ordinary mathematics. Infinite series are perfectly well understood; their infinity does not prevent us from knowing the law of their construction, their sum or limit when they have a limit, "and many other cheerful facts about the square of the hypotenuse." Whatever else may be the case, it is not God's infinity that keeps us from knowing him.

Plato and Hegel constructed theories of knowledge which, if pressed to their logical extreme, imply that man must be either omniscient or completely ignorant. If every item of knowledge is so intimately connected with every other that its true nature cannot be seen except in its relation to all, then either we know all or we know nothing. Plato and Hegel both had a hard time escaping this dilemma.

Now Moses said, "The secret things belong unto the Lord our God; but those things which are revealed belong unto us and to our children forever" (Deut. 29:29). The Bible, therefore, both here and everywhere, assumes that we can know some truths without knowing all truths. Accordingly it is incumbent upon us to develop an epistemology in which the relationships are not such as to limit us to the disjunction of total ignorance or omniscience.

This epistemology may follow Augustine's view that Christ is the light of every man: that is, mankind possesses as an a priori endowment at least the rudiments of knowledge, so that whenever anyone knows anything he is in contact with God, who is truth. Or, the epistemology required may be more skeptical as to geometry and science and simply insist that God, being omnipotent, can by a verbal revelation make his truths understandable to me. See also EPISTEMOLOGY.

For a dictionary article of this type these subjects are too technical to pursue further. The aim here can be merely to call attention to some of the more important issues.

In the twentieth century the discussion concerning our knowledge of God has assumed a different form; and because of its timeliness some special mention of it will not be out of place.

Reaction against the ambitious rationalism of Hegel and later disillusionment with the superficial optimism of modernistic theology have in these days produced the so-called school of neo-orthodoxy (q.v.). Barth and Brunner teach that rational language expresses abstract knowledge about things, while there is another sort of knowledge not rationally grasped in concepts. This is direct confrontation with a person. Therefore biblical concepts, apart from any historical errors that destructive critics may allege, cannot be knowledge of God. Intellectual concepts can be only pointers — they cannot be the real truth. When we talk *about* God, we are not talking about *God.*

Barth in particular holds that all religious expression is figurative or symbolic. Logic and mathematics are merely human constructions, and perhaps this allows of literal meaning; but all language about God is a parable. Since an interpretation of the parable would itself be a parable (for this too would be religious language), or, in other words, since the explanation of a symbol would itself be symbolic, does it not follow that a literal knowledge of God is impossible? Not only so, but if there is no literal norm by which to test the adequacy of parables and symbols, the Koran would seem to be as satisfactory as the Bible.

The Hegelian system, with its completely knowable Absolute and its prior rejection of the idea of creation, is a form of pantheism. The divine principle is not outside the universe. No doubt the universe depends on it, but also it depends on the universe, as a tree depends on its leaves and its leaves depend on the tree. Thus the Absolute (or God) is an immanent and not a transcendent principle.

Opposing this pantheism as destructive of true religion and humble worship, as blind to the reality of evil in human nature, and as disdainful of free grace, the neo-orthodox stress the transcendence of God and deny his immanence. At one time some of them were designating God as the Wholly-Other. But this takes God completely out of the world, negates the image of God in which man was created, and reduces the whole religious problem to an insoluble paradox (q.v.).

Orthodox Christianity sees no conflict between immanence and transcendence. The sovereignty of the creative fiat is evidence of transcendence; and because of creation God's power extends everywhere. This is his immanence. In fact, instead of saying that God is in the world, it is better to say that the world is in God, for in him we live and move and have our being.

Let this suffice for an example of the problems of theology proper. The Trinity and other subjects are discussed under separate headings.

B. *Science.* The next type of problem is scientific. With the rise of modern mechanistic science in the seventeenth century the possibility of miracles was called into question, and with the popular acceptance of evolution (q.v.) since the middle of the nineteenth century the whole theistic world-view has been subjected to a massive attack. What had previously been a naturalistic speculation was now presented as an assured result of infallible science.

A Christian might reply that the evolutionists have produced no empirical evidence that life spontaneously arose from inanimate matter. He might also remark that operationalism no longer looks on science as infallible or as descriptive of antecedent reality. At the same time he might humbly admit that he was mistaken in supposing the fixed species of Linnaeus to be the special creations of Genesis. And finally he might very well claim that as the opponents covertly assume the falsity of theism in order to undermine creation and miracles (and thus beg the question), these latter points cannot be profitably discussed until all the presuppositions are brought into the open.

C. *Ethics.* In addition to theology proper and science a third area in which problems arise for theism is that of morality and evil.

The biblical concept of God as sovereign Creator and in some instances all concepts of God have been repudiated because of the manifest evil in the world. Early in Christian history the objection was stated: either God wants to but cannot eradicate evil, or he can but does not want to; in the first case he is good but not omnipotent and in the second he may be omnipotent but he cannot be good. In modern history John Stuart Mill, even more than David Hume, vigorously attacked Christianity on this score.

Roman Catholics and some Protestants have made feeble replies by trying to account for evil as the result of the free will of Satan or of Adam. This of course does not answer the objection, for if God be omnipotent he still could eradicate the evil if he wanted to — in fact, he could have prevented it in the first place by creating a different type of world or even none at all.

The problem is so vexing that many Christians decide not to think about it in hopes that their opponents will not bring it up.

The paradox of God's goodness and the manifest evil, with the aggravation of the pains of hell forever, is partly the result of a theme taken from pagan nature religions. Primitive heathenism generally looks upon God as a God of nature. Sometimes God is identified with nature. Therefore when reflection has proceeded a little distance and some notion of nature's regularity is grasped, it is concluded that God must treat everyone alike. Nature is everywhere uniform. Then if goodness is attributed to God, it follows that God must be good to all.

This divine impartiality not only conflicts with the idea of grace, but more fundamentally it denies divine sovereignty by implying that creatures impose a moral obligation on the Creator.

The Scriptures, however, teach that God is the potter, who, from the very same lump of clay, can fashion one vessel for honor and another for dishonor. "Behold therefore the goodness and severity of God" (Rom. 11:22).

Now, finally, the problem of evil (q.v.), so far as human conduct is concerned, centers in the identification of right and wrong. It was shown in the first part of this article that right is what God commands and that sin is any want of conformity unto or transgression of the law of God.

If some phases of philosophic theology are embarrassing when we confront modern unbelief, this is one where the enemy is soon put to rout.

When modernism, following its founder Schleiermacher, repudiated the Scriptures to base its theology on experience, it believed that it could still preserve Christian values. In the development the crucial point became the identification of the values. Can many articles of the creed be discarded as the husks and historical trappings of Christianity, while Schleiermacher's feeling of absolute dependence preserves what is essential? Or must this early modernist value give place to the later ideal of integration of personality? Should the Trinity be abandoned and God be defined as "that character of events to which man must adjust himself in order to attain the greatest goods and avoid the greatest ills"?

Humanism developed out of modernism because modernism did not consistently base its ideals on experience. Modernism had an inconsistent attachment to Jesus. Rejecting this irrationality, humanism concluded that Jesus had no appreciation of intelligence or of science, that he had no political theory, and his view of labor relations was positively bad! Honesty requires us to accept other ideals. The Christian life is at best a semi-moral life.

Humanism claims that its ideals (a collectivistic society, independence of an imaginary God, materialistic security, etc.) are found in experience. Yet even humanists admit that ideals change from age to age. There are no absolute norms, no fixed truths, no universal principles. Ethics, and therefore economics and sociology, are relativistic.

In actual history this reduces to the simple question as to whose ideals will dominate a given age and society. Dictators answer this in concreto.

Socialistic destruction of political liberty with the brutality that totalitarian governments have always exercised forces attention on a point that humanists hardly consider. Regardless of which set of ideals an individual or society may accept, is it worth the trouble trying to realize them? Or, in other words, is life worth living?

In times of relative peace, prosperity, and freedom the question is set aside as silly or perverse. Life is pleasant. But in ethical theory it is basic. The mere fact that several people or a great many find life pleasant does not make it universally worthwhile. This is merely personal preference, not normative theory. On the humanistic position why should I not shoot my best friends to end their futile exertions and then commit suicide?

To this humanism has no answer. The only theory which guarantees value to life itself and makes suicide immoral is a theory in which God has forbidden murder and punishes disobedience in a future life. Normative ethics depends on sovereign legislation and omnipotent sanctions.

If other phases of theology, philosophy, and science are sometimes hard to work out, here at least biblical theism is easily vindicated.

See also ATTRIBUTES, THE DIVINE.

BIBLIOGRAPHY
S. Harris, *The Self-Revelation of God; God the Creator and Lord of All;* Carl F. H. Henry, *Notes on the Doctrine of God;* C. Hodge, *Systematic Theology,* I, pp. 191-441; F. L. Patton, *Fundamental Christianity,* pp. 1-95; J. Orr, *The Christian View of God and the World,* pp. 73-115; A. Seth Pringle-Pattison, *The Idea of God;* W. G. T. Shedd, *Dogmatic Theology,* I, pp. 151-546; G. Vos, *Biblical Theology.*

GORDON H. CLARK

GODLINESS. The noun *eusebeia* is characteristic of the Pastoral Epistles and occurs elsewhere in the NT only in Acts 3:12 (Peter's speech) and II Pet. 1:3, 6, 7; 3:11. *Theosebeia* is used in I Tim. 2:10. Godliness is not used in the OT, but occurs in the Apocrypha (e.g., II Macc. 12:45).

In general *eusebeia* means piety, reverence, whether towards men or God, but Christian *eusebeia*, like *theosebeia*, is restricted to the Godward use. Alford on Acts 3:12 claims that *eusebeia* "bears in it the idea of operative, cultive, piety, rather than of inherent character," and here renders it "meritorious efficacy," but the AV "holiness" and the RSV "piety." Eusebius (*Praep. Evang.* i. p. 3) defines it as "looking up to the one . . . God and life appropriate to him." These definitions give due weight to both elements in godliness, right attitude towards God and right conduct appropriate thereto. E. F. Scott regards it as right belief coupled with right mode of action, but godliness is devotion rather than belief and the action is not coupled with, but springing from that devotion, generated by an inner power (II Tim. 3:5; II Pet. 1:3).

The spiritual depth of *eusebeia* appears in I Tim. 3:16, "the mystery of godliness," where both Arndt and the RSV have "the mystery of our religion." The translation "religion" is unsatisfactory here and for *theosebeia* in I Tim. 1:10, for it suggests our way of belief, but I Tim. 3:16 indicates "the implied comparison between the practical godliness previously enjoined on church officers and the inner character of its revealed secret (*mystērion*) described here" (D. Guthrie, *The Pastoral Epistles,* The Tyndale Press, London, 1957, p. 89). The outward activity of godliness is emphasized by

the Greek plural in II Pet. 3:11, godly acts. Godliness also is the standard by which teaching is tested (I Tim. 6:3; Titus 1:1).

BIBLIOGRAPHY
A. E. Garvie in *HDB;* Arndt s. v. eusebeia.

J. CLEMENT CONNELL

GODS. The biblical world had a multitude of gods, as many as men could invent. In the ancient world, there was only one religion with similar characteristics (H. Frankfort, *Ancient Egyptian Religion,* Columbia University Press, New York, N. Y., 1948, p. 3). Originally, religion was monotheistic, but became debased through idolatrous worship, and the true God and his attributes came to be represented by idols, cult objects, and fetishes. Because God was unseen and transcendent, men set up idols as a materialistic expression of him. Soon the created thing was worshiped as a god instead of the Creator. Thus, each nation had its chief god and as many more as they felt were necessary. Not only were idols used, but also various forms of nature as the heavenly bodies, mountains, seas, rivers, insects, birds, and animals.

I. EGYPT. In Egypt, the supreme god was worshiped by different names depending upon the religious center. At Heliopolis, he was called Aten-Re-Khepri (sun god); at Elephantine, Khnum-Re; at Thebes, Amon-Re (king of the gods); and at Tel el Amarna, Atun-Re, the solar disc. The beetle, Khepera or Khepri, was accepted generally as a form of Re, the supreme god. The most commonly found idol is that of the beetle, known as the scarab, which kept its sacred meaning though used for other purposes.

The supreme god was the head of a triad or trinity as Ptah and Sekhmet and Nefer Tem, i.e., father, mother, and son; Amen-Re and Mut (mother goddess), Khensu (moon god), father, mother, and son; and also that of Osiris (god of the dead), Isis (his wife), and their son, Horus (the sky god). The thought of a trinity forming a family relationship was an ancient conception with the Egyptians.

There are lesser gods that should be noted as: Apis or Serapis, the deified bull of Memphis who was the god that the children of Israel worshiped as a golden calf (Ex. 32; I Kings 12:25-33); Hapi, the Nile god; Hathor, the goddess of love and beauty; Maat, the goddess of right and order; Sothis, the dog star; Sekor, the god of the underworld; Shu, the god of air; Thoth, the scribe of the gods, besides a host of sacred animals and birds. In all, the number of gods mentioned in the Pyramid Texts are over two hundred while in the Book of the Dead and other writings about twelve hundred. Since Pharaoh was the descendant and successor to the supreme god, he was considered divine and entitled to receive worship.

II. MESOPOTAMIA. In Mesopotamia (which land includes the Sumerians, Babylonians, and Assyrians), the inhabitants worshiped a host of gods. Over seven hundred have been listed in Babylonia. It is to be noted that as the land was conquered, the conquerors accepted the gods they found, adding them to their own pantheon. In some instances, the same god would have a Sumerian name and a Babylonian name. Here, as in Egypt, the same general conception of a creator was maintained. The concept of monotheism is not as apparent for there was a succession of great gods, worshiped sometimes conjunctively in the same city. They had the same creative power and were given credit for the creation of the universe, the earth, and man, as well as the lesser gods.

The first great god is Anu (the god of the heavens), of whom there is no pictorial representation. He is called "Father and King of the gods." His wife was Antu and their children are numbered among the lesser underworld gods. Antu was later superseded by Ishtar, the goddess of love. Anu's chief center of worship was Lagash.

The second great god was Enlil (god of the earth), who was later superseded by Marduk. Enlil's chief center of worship was Eridu. His wife was Damkina and their son was Marduk. This latter group formed a trinity of father, mother, and son. When Babylon rose to the supremacy, the earlier great gods were superseded by the Semitic named god, Marduk. There was a confusion as to the creative acts of these chief gods. Other gods and goddesses shared with them. The mother goddess Ninmack or Aruru was associated with Ea in the creation of man. Ashur became the chief god of Assyria, taking the place of Ea.

Three other great gods, which were Semitic, are to be noted. They were Sin (or Nannar, under his Sumerian name), the moon god; Shamash, the sun god, and son of Sin; and Adad or Hadad, the storm god. The wife of Sin was Ningal and mother of the sun god, Shamash. His chief cities were Ur and Haran.

The goddess, Ishtar, is associated also with these three deities. She is earlier designated by her Sumerian name, Innina. She became the chief female goddess superseding the wives of the six great gods. Yet, closely connected with her is Tammuz (Sumerian name, Dumuzi), the god of plants and vegetation, as her husband. The descent of Isthar into the underworld to search for him and their return to earth is the story of the death of vegetation in the winter and the rebirth of new vegetation in the spring. As a fertility goddess as well as of love, her descent to the underworld prevented the begetting of offspring during her absence. She is the most important of all the goddesses and her relationship to the six great gods and Tammuz shows the low conception of moral standards. The worship of Tammuz was practiced in Israel even at a late date (Ezek. 7:14).

Other important gods and goddesses were: the goddess Ereshkigal (Semitic Allatu), ruler of the underworld; Namtar, the herald god of death with his train of sixty diseases; Irra, the plague god; Kingsu, goddess of Chaos; and her husband, Apsu, the god of the underworld ocean; Nabu, the patron god of science and learning; and Nusku, the god of fire. The confusion in the Mesopotamian pantheon is no doubt due to the conquest of the land by diverse invaders — the Sumerians being Hamitic and the Assyro-Babylonians being Semitic.

In addition to Tammuz, the following Mesopotamian gods are mentioned: Adrammelech, god of Sepharvaim (Sippar), was perhaps Adad-Milki (II Kings 17:31); Anammelech, also a god of Sepharvaim (Sippar), was perhaps Anu-Melik (II Kings 17:31); Bel, mentioned in Jer. 51:44, and in Jer. 50:2 found in association with Merodach (Marduk) and in Isa. 46:1 with Nebo; Merodach (Babylonian, Marduk) as above noted in Jer. 50:2; Nebo (Nabu), mentioned in Isa. 46:1 (a mountain in the Abarim range east of the north end of the Dead Sea bears his name); Nergal, patron god of Gutha (II Kings 17:30), found compounded in the name of the Babylonian general Nergal-Sharezer (Jer. 30:3, 13); Nisroch, an Assyrian god who was so important that there was a temple to him in Nineveh (II Kings 19:37); Succoth-Benoth, a god of the men of Babylon, who has yet to be identified (II Kings 17:30); and Tartak, a god of Avva, yet to be identified (II Kings 17:31).

III. PALESTINE AND SYRIA. In Palestine and Syria, only Yahweh (Jehovah) makes the claim of exclusive Creator of the universe, heaven, and man. The gods of the neighboring nations of the Hebrews were not in the rank of the gods of Egypt, Mesopotamia, and other world powers. They all seem to be of a national level and as has been noted, these nations also worshiped gods of the larger powers, together with their own. Yahweh stands aloof and superior, with his lofty claims and holy spiritual nature with highest moral demands of his worshipers.

The gods of Syria were also known and worshiped by the people of Palestine so that they will be discussed together.

The pantheon of Ugarit shows El as the supreme god who was later superseded by his son Baal, the storm and vegetation god. After winning triumph over the god Mat, the lord of the sea, he established his right to reign over all the gods as their king. This supremacy was evidently acknowledged by most of the people of Syria and Palestine (Num. 22:41; I Kings 18; II Kings 17:16; Hos. 11:2; Rom. 11:4; and fifty-eight other references in the OT). In Tyre he was supreme, and during the reign of Ahab he was the chief god of Israel. His name was coupled with that of the Palestine Baalzebub, god of the flies; Baal of the lightning; Aleyan Baal, the storm god, and Baal Sapuna in Ugarit. Towns as centers of his worship coupled Baal with their name, as Baal-peor in Moab (Hos. 9:10; Ps. 106:28). This was the center of worship of the chief god, Chemosh of Moab. Since Baal, meaning "lord," was so applicable to other gods, it shows that he became a composite deity combining a number of important activities. Even the plural form, Baalim, is used in the OT with reference to him in his various forms. His sister was Asherah, the goddess of Tyre, who also was worshiped in Samaria by the Israelites. (I Kings 15:13, 18, 19; II Kings 21:7; 23:4). In the AV and the LXX the name of Asherah was translated "groves," but inscriptions found more recently have proven her to be a goddess. The goddess Anat was her sister and was worshiped in Syria, especially in Ugarit. There were many goddesses, as Qadesh, called the "lady of the skies and mistress of all the gods in Syria;" the Syrian goddess Min; Hepa, a goddess whose idol was found in Ugarit that could have been Hurrian; Ashtoreth, also known as Ishtar (Egypt), Astarte (Greece and Phoenicia), and Venus (Rome), queen of heaven (Jer. 7:18; 44:17-19, 25), and also goddess of fertility. She is known throughout Bible lands by the above names (Judg. 2:13; 10:6; I Kings 11:5, 33; II Kings 23:13). The goddess "Lady of Byblos" whose idol wears the head dress of Hathor, the goddess of love, shows Egyptian influence. Besides these above mentioned there have been found in Ugarit several unknown goddesses showing their vile fertility worship.

Among the male gods are: Dagon, the half fish and half man god, a supreme god among the Philistines who held that Baal was the son of Dagon (Josh. 15:41; Judg. 16:23; I Sam. 5:1-7); Ashima, the god of Hamath who was deported to Samaria by Sargon II of Assyria (II Kings 17:30); Chium, a planetary god, named for Saturn and mentioned in Amos 5:26 AV; Acts 7:43; Gad, a god of fortune that was worshiped by the Israelites (Isa. 65:11), his name being found as a god in Phoenician, Assyrian, and Aramaic; Men, perhaps of Egyptian origin (Menu), the god of destiny and good luck, possibly an astral god, one of the Pleiades or representing that entire group of stars, named with Gad in Isa. 65:11; Mekal, the chief god of Bethshean, shown holding the "ankh," Egyptian symbol of life, which shows Egyptian influences; Milcom, the "abomination" of the Ammonites (I Kings 11:5, 33; II Kings 23:13), their god and perhaps the same as Moloch (Moloch or Molech was the god who was designated "Melek" [king] whose worship demanded human sacrifice burned with fire, Lev. 18:21; 20:1-5); Rimmon (Rammon, Thunderer), the chief god of Damascus (II Kings 5:18) akin to the Mesopotamian god Adad (Hadad); Resheph, the Syrian war god, not only accepted by Syria-Palestine, but found sculptured in Egypt holding the "ankh," the Egyptian emblem of life.

Besides all these gods, there were sun images; snake worship as seen in "Nehushtan," the brazen serpent, which was worshiped by the Hebrews (II Kings 18:4); sacred trees or groves as the terebinth and the tamarisk trees; the host of heaven (II Kings 17:16), and the teraphim, which were household gods of every sort (Gen. 31:19; Judg. 17:5).

IV. CRETE. In Crete, the chief object of worship was a mother goddess who was evidently Cybele, the great mother of the gods. Her worship is thought to have originated in

Asia Minor and one of her places of abode and worship was Mount Ida, the highest mountain of Crete. Virgil in his "Aeneid" held that Cybele originally came from Crete. Cybele is identified with Rhea, the mother goddess of Greece and mother of Zeus. In the Mediterranean religions she is the embodiment of the earth's fertility. This is in accord with the Cretan belief, as she has as many aspects as nature itself. She was so associated in art with the heavenly bodies, vegetation and rocks, of earth, with reptiles, birds, and animals, besides the weapons and dress of man, that she seems to have taken over all the functions of the other gods. If the Philistines came originally from Crete and the other Mediterranean islands (H. R. Hall, *Cambridge Ancient History*, Cambridge Univ. Press, Cambridge, England), the transition was natural to adopt the Semitic gods they found in Palestine.

V. PHILISTINE, HITTITE. Astarte was a fertility goddess even as Cybele or Rhea, and her consort was Dagon, the chief god of the Philistines. The Hittites came into Palestine during the nineteenth century B.C. and brought with them their gods. These, even their chief gods such as Teshup, the weather god, and Khepa, the sun god, are not mentioned. It is to be noted that the Hittite pantheon contained among their thousand gods those of their neighbors — Semitic, Hamitic, and Indo-European. Thus in Palestine, they worshiped the Semitic gods in their pantheon.

VI. GRAECO-ROMAN. The Graeco-Roman religion was an anthropomorphic polytheism whose gods had the form and mind of man. Ideals and desires were deified in the person of the various gods. They were worshiped wherever Greece and Rome ruled. The chief god was Zeus (Roman Jupiter or Jove) who became the main god of popular belief, almost monotheistic. He was the creator of the universe and father of both the gods and men. Homer recognized him as a god of pity and mercy. Associated with him as his consort and wife was Hera (Roman Juno). She was called the queen of heaven and goddess of marriage. To her also was ascribed the title of goddess of air, earth, and moon. Hermes (Roman Mercury) was the god of fertility, the protector of cattle and sheep as well as patron of music. When the Romans adopted him he became their god of merchants and merchandise, and speaker for the gods (Acts 14:12).

Athena, the virgin goddess of counsel, war,

female arts, and industries was called by the Romans Minerva. She was emphasized as the goddess of war. With her the Romans worshiped the god Mars, their god of war and agriculture. Apollo was the artist god, poet, musician, and especially the god of prophecy. The Romans later worshiped him as the god of light and heaven. Adonis was the god of love and linked with the Semitic god Tammuz. Aphrodite (Roman Venus) is but the Greek name of Ishtar or Astarte. She was the goddess of love and beauty, and like her Semitic counterparts, the goddess of vegetation and fruitfulness. As among their Egyptian and Semitic neighbors, the sun was worshiped in the person of Helios, the sun god. To him a colossal statue was erected over the harbor entrance of Rhodes. The goddess Artemis (Roman Diana) was the goddess of chastity and the hunt as well as of agriculture. In Ephesus, she was worshiped as the goddess of productivity and of all nourishing mothers (Acts 19:23 ff.). Ceres was accepted both by the Greeks and Romans as the goddess of the growth of food plants. Dionysus (Roman Bacchus) was a nature god of wine and also of fruitfulness. His worship led to extreme debauchery and drunken orgies. Janus was the Roman two-faced god of entrances and beginnings. His idol was placed at doors and entrances of buildings and thought of as the beginning of periods of time, e.g., the first month of the Roman year was named after him.

Aesculapius (Roman Asklepius) was worshiped as the god of medicine and healing. Associated with him and encircling his staff was a serpent. Associated with him either as his wife or sister was Hygeia, the goddess of health. The twin gods, Castor and Pollux, children of Zeus and Leda (the swan goddess) were the gods of sailors (Acts 28:11).

With the death of Julius Caesar, emperor worship had its beginning. In his death, he was deified and thereafter it became mandatory to worship the living emperors of Rome.

It is to be noted that, "For the Greeks, Christianity had been in a certain way continuous with paganism. It might be said that the old deities and heroes who had protected their cities were still their guardians, under the new forms of saints (sometimes imaginary) and archangels and performed for them the same kind of miracles. Pagan idolatry was replaced by Christian image worship, which by the Christians of many parts of Asia Minor, as well as by the Mohammedans, was regarded as simply polytheism" (*EncyBrit,* Encyclopedia Britannica, Inc., Chicago, Ill., 1954, Vol. 19, p. 438).

VII. The Israelites and Idolatry. The question is asked, Why did the Israelites want to follow after the idols of their neighbors when they had the true God? What were the reasons that they should be thus allured to polytheistic worship? We name seven reasons: (1) It offered them a definite materialistic and tangible object of and for faith. (2) The elaborate ritual and colorful ceremonies and costumes appealed to their aesthetic natures. (3) The idea of the mother goddess, playing on the family idea, e.g. the triad of father, mother, and son, transferred this idea of family to that of gods and the mother goddess who was mother of gods and man. (4) Sex appeal and extreme immoral orgies appealed to the animalistic nature in the worshipers. (5) The deification of the attributes and functions of the supreme God did away with his transcendence. (6) There was the appeal to the mysterious by use of secret initiations and ceremonies. (7) The stress of need for abundant crops, cattle, sheep, and other necessities made attractive the gods of crops, weather, fertility, and productivity.

The ten commandments given by God at Sinai stress that he is a jealous God and brooks no interference as to loyalty, love, and worship of himself (Ex. 20:3-5; Deut. 5:7-9). To turn from him and worship idols was stressed by the prophets as spiritual adultery. God spoke through his prophets and they, moved by his Holy Spirit, demonstrated by word and deed his attitude. This was shown in the severe punishment of the Israelites when Moses found them worshiping the golden calf (Ex. 32:25); the zeal of Phinehas in slaying the man of Israel and the Midianitish woman, besides the twenty-four thousand that died of the plague at Baal-peor (Num. 25:1-9). Judgments came upon individuals by punishment, by illness, persecution by enemies, enslavement, and death. Nationally, the Israelites were made captives of their enemies to serve as slaves in foreign lands. Besides, many were tortured or slain, their homes, lands, and crops plundered or destroyed, their cities pillaged and left in smoking ruins, their crops destroyed by drought, insects (Joel 1:4-20), fire, floods, and storms. It seems that every kind of punishment came as judgment upon

them. Every true prophet from Moses to Malachi preached with all the vehemence and power he possessed to turn the people from the worship of idols.

"Yet, the more the prophets called them, the more they went from them" (Hos. 11:2). Both Israel and Judah went into exile as the last great punishment because they went after other gods (II Kings 22:17). It took this terrible judgment to wean them from idolatry and it had its desired result. When they returned from captivity to their land under Zerubbabel they never again as a nation returned to the worship of other gods.

BIBLIOGRAPHY

A. Wallis Budge, *Cook's Handbook for Egypt and the Sudan,* pp. 641-62; Leonard Cottrell, *The Bull of Minos,* pp. 120-43; H. Frankfort, *Ancient Egyptian Religion,* pp. 3-29; John Garstang, *The Heritage of Solomon,* pp. 55-57, 68-78, 82-86, 156-63; O. R. Gurney, *The Hittites,* pp. 132-69; S. H. Hooke, *Babylonian and Assyrian Religion,* pp. 23-46; E. O. James, *Myth and Ritual in the Ancient Near East,* pp. 37-278; James B. Pritchard, *The Ancient Near East in Pictures,* pp. 303-18.

E. Leslie Carlson

GOEL. This word is the active participle of a verb meaning to recover or redeem. It is found in several senses:

(1) It is used of the regaining possession of a property which has been sold for debt (Lev. 25:25).

(2) It is used of the restoring or preserving of the name of one who has died without offspring: his brother is then to take his wife (levirate marriage), and raise up seed to him, that his name be not forgotten in Israel (Deut. 25:5; cf. Gen. 38:8). Boaz is the most familiar example of this (Ruth 3-4). As such the *goel* is called the kinsman.

(3) Since murder means the cutting off of a man from his earthly kin and possessions, it was the duty of his relatives to avenge him. The *goel* is then the revenger or avenger of blood (Num. 35:12-34; Deut. 19:1-3).

(4) In its highest sense *Goel* is used of God, who is the author of life and whose prerogative it is to redeem from death, both physical and spiritual. "Redeemer" occurs most frequently in Isa. 40-66. Job 9:25, "I know that my redeemer liveth" is a very familiar instance.

Oswald T. Allis

GOOD, THE GOOD, GOODNESS. In the OT "good" renders the Hebrew word *tôb.* Its germ meaning is pleasant. Only derivatively has it an ethical connotation. Good, in the sense of moral goodness, emerges progressively in the Bible. God is love, is the culmination of the self-disclosure of God in Jesus Christ.

A great variety of usages attend the word good in Holy Scripture. God's work in creation is seen to be good (Gen. 1). A more ethical meaning makes it equivalent to right (Deut. 6:18). It has the meaning of benefits in Job 2:10. In the NT the Greek words *agathos* and *kalos* are rendered by "good." In none of these usages has it its full ethical content.

In contrast to Greek ethics the Bible centers goodness on God. It is true that both Plato and Aristotle make "the good" central in their systems of thought. "The essential Form of the Good is the highest object of science" (Plato, *Republic,* Bk. VI). "If it is true that in the sphere of action there is an end which we wish for its own sake, and for the sake of which we wish everything else — it is clear that this will be the good or the supreme good" (Aristotle, *Ethics,* Bk. I). Noble as these ideas are of the nature of the *Summum Bonum* they do not lead to a living personal God as the ground of the good. In the Bible, however, God is declared to be good because of his acts of redeeming love. This is not a conclusion arrived at by conceptual thinking, but by personal religious insight on the part of those who have been enlightened and uplifted by the grace of God mediated through Christ.

I. Goodness and Values. Beauty, truth and goodness are often referred to as the three ultimate values. Many Christian theologians consider this triad is reducible to one fundamental value, viz, goodness. Doubts arise as to the value of some truths. They may be trivial or worthless or harmful. Not every beautiful thing ought necessarily to exist. But goodness is, in the fullest sense, an absolute value. "What constitutes any of these values is precisely the goodness they share in common" (F. R. Barry, *Relevance of Christianity,* Nisbet, London, 1936, p. 172).

II. God and Goodness. Moral goodness can only exist for personal minds. The ideal of absolute goodness can only exist in a mind from which all reality is derived. Goodness cannot be explained on naturalistic or evolutionist grounds. It is distinct from the useful and the pleasant. Even though we do not always follow the good, we acknowledge its absolute claim upon us.

When we say God is good, we mean that he is good in the same sense in which we use this word of men, only in the highest degree. God's goodness always actively promotes truth and righteousness. Some severity is necessary to make sinful men good.

BIBLIOGRAPHY

Plato, *Republic*; H. E. C. Welldon, *Ethics of Aristotle*; G. E. Moore, *Principia Ethica*; A. C. Ewing, *Ethics*; P. H. Nowell Smith, *Ethics*; Sir W. David Ross, *Foundations of Ethics*.

ALBERT VICTOR M'CALLIN

GOOD WORKS. A good work, theologically speaking, is any activity of a moral agent which proceeds from a right motive (love), is in accord with a proper moral standard (law), and aims at the glory of a worthy object (God). The first and the third qualifications tend to run closely together: the love motive and the love object each, in the ultimate sense, being divine. That is, according to Christian theology, "we love because he (Christ or God) first loved us" (I John 4:19; cf. Rom. 5:6). In other words, it is God in the soul who is the source of the motive of love and this, in turn, directs the soul back to God as the object. The other qualification, law, must be from the Creator if it be valid for the creature; however, this is external, or objective. We may, therefore, think of a good work as an activity of a moral being which is good, or God-produced, in its internal (or subjective) and external (or objective) aspects.

An activity of a moral agent may conceivably be sound internally and defective in its outward expression. That is, it may proceed from love of and to God, but still be misdirected or contrary to the law of God. If a loving person were misinformed about the law of God his love would lead him to act accordingly, that is, according to his misinformation. Therefore, he would unintentionally disobey the law. It is out of the reach of this brief article to consider whether a moral agent with perfect love to God could ever be capable of misunderstanding the will of God (we think not); but it is apparent that such an agent with some love of God, but not a perfect love, could be capable of misunderstanding the law of God.

Consequently, a man could, with at least a partially good motive, perform an outwardly bad act. Such an activity we would call a good bad work (that is, good with respect to intention; bad in expression). On the other hand, a moral agent with an evil motive is, conceivably, capable of performing an outwardly good work, that is, something which externally corresponds to the law of God. "Ye then being evil know how to give good gifts . . ." (Matt. 7:11). Such an activity we would call a bad good work. This is because the good (in the with respect to expression). With reference to the doer, the good bad work is a truly good work; while the bad good work is not a truly good work. This is because the good (in the good bad work) belongs to the doer (that is, it is his true motive or desire); but the bad (in the good bad work) does not truly belong to the doer (it is not his intention or doing at all).

Men can observe the outward acts of others but not their inner motives. Consequently they cannot be infallible judges of morality, so far as the doer is concerned. God, on the other hand, not only can discern the thoughts and intents of the heart but glories in his ability to do so. He makes the secrets of men manifest in the day of judgment so that other creatures may see the basis of his judgment (Rom. 2:11).

According to Protestant doctrine, justification (*q.v.*) is by faith alone without any merit deriving from any good work of the recipient either before or after justification. Justification is on the basis of good works — the good works of Jesus Christ. But the benefits of his redemptive work are received by the believer who has no merit of his own to contribute. Nothing which he ever does, even after justification, merits anything; because nothing which he does is ever perfectly good. That is, nothing which he does proceeds from a perfectly good motive, is directed perfectly according to the good standard, and is aimed perfectly at the glory of God. Nothing short of this is truly good. Since no justified person, in this life, ever does anything which meets such standards he does no meritorious good work. Therefore, he never has any merit to claim which in any way supplements the merit of Christ. This was the crux of the Reformation difference with Roman Catholicism, which regards good works done before faith as having "merit of congruency" and good works done after justification as having "merit of condignity."

Good works are enjoined on the believer as ordained of God (Eph. 2:10; Titus 2:14) and useful to those who benefit from them (Titus 3:8-9). They are the proper fruit of the right use of Scripture (II Tim. 3:17). Because of

them men may be led to glorify God (Matt. 5:16). With reference to them the Lord will dispense rewards (I Cor. 3:14; Rev. 22:12).

Pragmatism is the doctrine that truth is determined by good works. That is, that which leads to good works is true. While Christianity teaches that "by their fruits you shall know them" (Matt. 7:20) it is not "pragmatic." In such a statement it does not mean to say that we determine what truth is by the way a person behaves, but simply that one determines what a person really believes to be true by how he behaves. If he behaves wickedly, this verse implies, he believes wickedly, that is, erroneously. Truth, according to Christianity, is determined by revelation (natural and supernatural). Deeds are then judged by their correspondence to the revealed standard of truth. Summarily speaking, pragmatism judges truth by works, Christianity judges works by truth.

The criticism of the pragmatic theory is this: If one does not have an initial definition of truth, he cannot say whether a given behavior "works" or not. For example, if a certain theory, being believed by a certain person, leads him to commit murder, one cannot conclude from that, that the theory is wrong — unless he knows, to begin with, that murder is not good. But this evaluation is not determined by the commission of the deed but by ethical judgments made independently. If you do know in advance, as is usually assumed by pragmatists (contrary to their own avowed principles) that murder is wrong, you may conclude that a theory which leads to it is untrue. If you did not know, in advance, the sinfulness of murder, you could not learn anything about the theory from the fact that it led to murder.

BIBLIOGRAPHY

Joseph Butler, *Works*; Heinrich Denzinger, *Enchiridion Symbolorum,*, 26th ed., (1946); William James, *Pragmatism*; John Murray, *Principles of Conduct*.

JOHN H. GERSTNER

GOSPEL. The English word "gospel" (from the Anglo-Saxon *god-spell*, i.e., God-story) is the usual NT translation of the Greek *euaggelion*. According to Tyndale, the renowned English Reformer and Bible translator, it signified "good, mery,. glad and ioyfull tydinge, that maketh a mannes hert glad, and maketh hym synge, daunce, and leepe for ioye" (*Prologue to NT*). While his definition is more experiential than explicative, it has touched that inner quality which brings the word to life. The gospel is the joyous proclamation of God's redemptive activity in Christ Jesus on behalf of man enslaved by sin.

I. ORIGIN. *Euaggelion* (neut. sing.) is rarely found in the sense of "good tidings" outside of early Christian literature. As used by Homer it referred not to the message but to the reward given to the messenger (e.g., *Od.* xiv. 152). In Attic Greek it always occurred in the plural and generally referred to sacrifices or thank offerings made in behalf of good tidings. Even in the LXX *euaggelion* is found for sure but once (II Kings 4:10: Eng. versions, II Sam.) and there it has the classical meaning of a reward given for good tidings. (In II Kings 18:22, 25, *euaggelion* should undoubtedly be taken as fem. sing. in harmony with verses 20 and 27 where this form is certain.) *Euaggelion* in the sense of the good news itself belongs to a later period. Outside of Christian literature the neuter singular first appears with this meaning in a papyrus letter from an Egyptian official of the third century A.D. (Deiss *LAE,* pp. 366 ff. In the plural it is found in a calendar inscription from Priene about 9 B.C.). It is not until the writings of the Apostolic Fathers (e.g., *Didache* 8:2; *II Clem.* 8:5) that we sense a transition to the later Christian usage of *euaggelion* as referring to a book which sets forth the life and teaching of Jesus (Justin *Apol.* i. 66).

Against this background, the frequency with which *euaggelion* occurs in the NT (more than 75 times) with the specific connotation of "good news," is highly informative. It suggests that *euaggelion* is quite distinctively a NT word. Its true significance is therefore found, not by probing its linguistic background, but by observing its specific Christian usage.

This is not to deny, of course, that the basic concept has its rightful origin in the religious aspirations of the nation Israel. Some seven centuries before Christ the prophet Isaiah had delivered a series of prophetic utterances. With vivid imagery he portrayed the coming deliverance of Israel from captivity in Babylon. A Redeemer shall come to Zion preaching good tidings unto the meek and liberty to the captives (Isa. 60:1, 2). "How beautiful upon the mountains are the feet of him who brings good tidings" (Isa. 52:7). Jerusalem itself is pictured as a herald whose message is good tidings (Isa. 40:9).

Jesus saw in these prophecies a description of his own mission (Luke 4:18-21; 7:22). They expressed that same sense of liberation and exultation which was the true characteristic of his messianic proclamation. What was at first simply a literary allusion came easily to represent the actual message which was being proclaimed. *Euaggelion* was the natural result of the LXX's *euaggelizein.* Thus Mark could write that Jesus came into Galilee "heralding the *euaggelion* of God" (Mark 1:14).

II. EUAGGELION IN THE GOSPELS. Upon examining the four Gospels we find that the word *euaggelion* is used only by Matthew and Mark. The concept, however, is not foreign to Luke. He uses the verb form twenty-six times in Luke-Acts, and the noun twice in the latter book. In the Fourth Gospel there is no trace of either verb or noun.

In all but one instance, Matthew further describes *euaggelion* as the gospel "of the kingdom." This gospel is not to be distinguished from what Mark calls the "gospel of God" (many MSS read "the gospel of the kingdom of God") and summarizes in the words, "the time is fulfilled, and the kingdom of God is at hand" (Mark 1:14, 15). On the other occasion Matthew writes *"this* gospel" (Matt. 26:13) — the context indicating that Jesus is alluding to his coming death. The phrase, "preaching the gospel of the kingdom," is twice used in summary statements of the ministry of Jesus (Matt. 4:23; 9:35). This gospel is to be preached throughout the entire world prior to the consummation of the age (Matt. 24:14; cf. Mark 13:10).

The way in which Mark uses *euaggelion* is suggested by his opening words, "The beginning of the gospel of Jesus Christ, the Son of God." Here *euaggelion* is a semi-technical term meaning "the glad news which tells about Jesus Christ." Where Luke writes, "for the sake of the kingdom of God" (Luke 18:29), the Markan parallel is, "for my sake and for the gospel" (Mark 10:29). This gospel is of such tremendous import that for its sake a man must be willing to enter upon a life of complete self-denial (Mark 8:35). In the long ending of Mark, Christ commands his disciples to "preach the gospel to the whole creation" (Mark 16:15).

III. THE GOSPEL ACCORDING TO PAUL. Over against the six occasions (discounting parallels) on which *euaggelion* is used by the Gospel writers, it is found a total of sixty times in the writings of Paul. *Euaggelion* is a favorite Pauline term. It is evenly distributed throughout his epistles, missing only in his note to Titus.

Paul's ministry was distinctively that of the propagation of the gospel. Unto this gospel he was set apart (Rom. 1:1) and made a minister according to the grace of God (Eph. 3:7). His special sphere of action was the gentile world (Rom. 16:16; Gal. 2:7). Since Paul accepted the gospel as a sacred trust (Gal. 2:7), it was necessary that in the discharge of this obligation he speak so as to please God rather than man (I Tim. 2:4). The divine commission had created a sense of urgency that made him cry out, "Woe to me if I do not preach the gospel" (I Cor. 9:16). For the sake of the gospel Paul was willing to become all things to all men (I Cor. 9:22, 23). No sacrifice was too great. Eternal issues were at stake. Those whose minds were blinded and did not obey the gospel were perishing and would ultimately reap the vengeance of divine wrath (II Cor. 4:3; II Thess. 1:9). On the other hand, to those who believed, the gospel had effectively become the power of God unto salvation (Rom. 1:16).

Because Paul, on occasion, speaks of his message as "my gospel" (Rom. 2:16; II Tim. 2:8), and because in his letter to the Galatians he goes to some pains to stress that he did not receive it from man (Gal. 1:11 ff.), it is sometimes maintained that Paul's gospel should be distinguished from that of apostolic Christianity in general.

This does not follow. I Cor. 15:3-5 sets forth with crystal clarity the message of primitive Christianity. Paul, using terms equivalent to the technical rabbinic words for the reception and transmission of tradition (M. Dibelius, *From Tradition to Gospel*, Scribner's, New York, 1935, p. 21), refers to this message as something which he had received and passed on (vs. 3). In verse eleven he can say, "Whether then it was I or they, so we preach and so you believed." In Galatians, Paul tells how he laid before the apostles at Jerusalem the gospel which he had preached. Far from finding fault with the message, they extended to him the right hand of fellowship (Gal. 2:9). What Paul meant by his earlier remarks is that the charges against his gospel as a mere human message were completely fraudulent. The revelation of the full theological impact of the Christ-event was God-given and stemmed from his encounter on the Damascus road. Thus he speaks of "my gospel" meaning his own personal apprehension of the gospel. On other occasions he can speak freely of "our gospel" (II Cor. 4:3; I Thess. 1:5).

For Paul, the *euaggelion* is pre-eminently the "gospel of God" (Rom. 1:1; 15:16; II Cor. 11:7; I Thess. 2:2, 8, 9). It proclaims the redemptive activity of God. This activity is bound up with the person and work of God's Son, Christ Jesus. Thus it is also the "gospel of Christ" (I Cor. 9:12; II Cor. 2:12; 9:13; 10:14; Gal. 1:7; I Thess. 3:2. Verses 16 and 19 of Rom. 15 indicate that these are interchangeable terms). This gospel is variously expressed as "the gospel of our Lord Jesus" (II Thess. 1:8), "the gospel of the glory of the blessed God" (I Tim. 1:11), "the gospel of his Son" (Rom. 1:9), and "the gospel of the glory of Christ" (II Cor. 4:4). It is a gospel of salvation (Eph. 1:13) and peace (Eph. 6:15). It proclaims the hope of eternal life (Col. 1:23). It is "the word of truth" (Col. 1:5; Eph. 1:13). Through this gospel, life and immortality are brought to light (II Tim. 1:10).

IV. THE APOSTOLIC PREACHING. If we wish to investigate more closely the specific content of the primitive gospel, we will do well to adopt the basic approach of C. H. Dodd (*The Apostolic Preaching and its Developments*, Hodder and Stoughton, London, 1936). While Dodd refers to the message as *kērygma*, he is ready to admit that this term is a virtual equivalent of *euaggelion*. (*Kērygma* stresses the manner of delivery: *euaggelion*, the essential nature of the content.)

There are two sources for the determination of the primitive proclamation. Of primary importance are the fragments of pre-Pauline tradition that lie embedded in the writings of the apostle. These segments can be uncovered by the judicious application of certain literary and formal criteria. While at least one purports to be the actual terms in which the gospel was preached (I Cor. 15:3-5), others take the form of early Christian hymns (e.g., Phil. 2:6-11), summaries of the message (e.g., Rom. 10:9), or creedal formulae (I Cor. 12:3; I Tim. 3:16).

A second source is the early Petrine speeches in Acts. These speeches (on the basis of their Aramaic background, freedom from Paulinism, and the general trustworthiness of Luke as a historian) can be shown to give reliably the gist of what Peter actually said and not what a second generation Christian thought he might have said.

These two sources combine to set forth one common apostolic gospel. In briefest outline, this message contained: (1) A historical proclamation of the death, resurrection, and exaltation of Jesus, set forth as the fulfilment of prophecy and involving man's responsibility; (2) A theological evaluation of the person of Jesus as both Lord and Christ; (3) A summons to repent and receive the forgiveness of sins.

It will be noticed that the essential core of this message is not the dawn of the messianic age (as Dodd implies) — although this is most certainly involved — but that sequence of redemptive events which sweeps the hearer along with compelling logic towards the climactic confession that Jesus is Lord.

The gospel is not the product of a bewildered church pondering the theological significance of Good Friday. It is rather the result of a natural development which had its origins in the teachings of Jesus himself. The Passion-sayings of Jesus — far from being "prophecies after the event" (cf. R. Bultmann, *Theology of the NT,* Scribner's, New York, 1951, I, p. 29) — are undeniable evidence that Jesus laid the foundation for a theology of the cross. In his teaching regarding his own person, Jesus furnished what R. H. Fuller has aptly termed "the raw materials of Christology" (*The Mission and Achievement of Jesus,* A. R. Allenson, Chicago, 1954, pp. 79-117). The resurrection was the catalyst which precipitated in the minds of the disciples the total significance of God's redemptive activity. It released the gospel!

This gospel is power (Rom. 1:16). As an instrument of the Holy Spirit it convicts (I Thess. 1:5) and converts (Col. 1:6). It cannot be fettered (II Tim. 2:9). Although it is good news, it is strenuously opposed by a rebellious world (I Thess. 2:2). Opposition to the message takes the form of opposition to the messenger (II Tim. 1:11, 12; Philem. 13). Yet those who proclaim it must do so boldly (Eph. 6:19) and with transparent simplicity (II Cor. 4:2) — not with eloquence lest the cross of Christ be robbed of its power (I Cor. 1:17). To those who refuse the gospel it is both foolishness and a stumbling block (I Cor. 1:18 ff.), but to those who respond in faith it proves itself to be "the power of God unto salvation" (Rom. 1:16).

BIBLIOGRAPHY
G. Friedrich in *TWNT*; R. H. Strachan, "The Gospel in the NT," *IB*, VII, pp. 3 ff; W. Barclay, *NT Wordbook*, pp. 41-46; A. E. J. Rawlinson, *Encyclopedia Britannica*, X, pp. 536 ff; M. Burrows, *JBL*, XLIV, pp. 21-33; W. Milligan, *Thess.*, Note E, pp. 141 ff; Harnack, *Constitution and Law*, Appendix III, pp. 278-331; Lowther Clarke, "What is the Gospel?" in *Divine Humanity*; *RTWB*.

ROBERT H. MOUNCE

GRACE. In the OT many words convey one or more aspects of the doctrine of grace. The two which most comprehensively express the NT word *charis* are *hēn* and *hesed*. The former bears the predominant sense of favor, with an undertone of meaning that the favor is undeserved. Thus Moses said to the Lord: "If I have found *grace* in thy sight, show me now thy ways, that I may know thee, to the end that I may find *grace* in thy sight" (Ex. 33:13). The word *hesed,* most often translated "lovingkindness" or "mercy," has also, though not invariably, the association of the covenant that God makes with his people: "The Lord appeared of old unto me, saying, Yea, I have loved thee with an everlasting love: therefore with lovingkindness have I drawn thee" (Jer. 31:3); "the Lord thy God shall keep with thee the covenant and the mercy which he sware unto thy fathers" (Deut. 7:12). (For the other words forming the nexus of the concept of grace in the OT, see C. Ryder Smith, *The Bible Doctrine of Grace,* Epworth Press, London, 1956, chap. 2).

The most common NT word is *charis*. Its basic significance is to be found in joyfulness, whether in regard to the appreciation of things or of people. But as used by the NT, it conveys the combined meanings of *hēn* and *hesed*: e.g., for the former; "But if it is by grace, it is no more of works: otherwise grace is no more grace" (Rom. 11:6), or: "the exceeding riches of his grace in kindness toward us" (Eph. 2:7); for the latter: "where sin abounded, grace did much more abound" (Rom. 5:20).

The essence of the doctrine of grace is that God is for us. What is more, he is for us who in ourselves are against him. Still more, he is not for us merely in a general attitude, but has effectively acted towards us. Grace is summed up in the name Jesus Christ.

It is quite clear that the NT overwhelmingly associates the word grace with Christ, either directly ("the grace of our Lord Jesus Christ"), or else by implication as the executor of the grace of God. It does this, not in any spirit of

Christomonism, but because it is in his incarnate Son that God puts into effect his being for us, shows us that he is for us and reconciles us to himself, bringing us over to his side, to be for him. Since all this comes to pass only by the incarnate activity of Christ, we may say that grace means Jesus Christ, and Jesus Christ means grace. He is the grace of God towards us.

Jesus Christ is God for us. We may consider this in terms of the covenant (ḥeseḏ). In his Son God binds himself freely to us to be our God, and binds us to himself to be his. By becoming our God he becomes to us what he is in himself — loving, holy, merciful and patient, in a word, gracious. As he is God in himself, so he will be God toward us, for our benefit. He will assume the responsibility for our past, present and future. He, no longer an enemy, stands with us against our real enemies, and that effectively: "If God be for us, who can be against us?" (Rom. 8:31).

But all this is true because Christ has come, died and risen again: "grace . . . came by Christ Jesus" (John 1:17). The incarnation of God's Son, his obedient suffering, his sacrificial death and triumphant resurrection, do not merely show us that God is gracious but is itself God's act of grace, in which he turns to us and effects this relationship. In what Christ does and suffers, God's grace overcomes sin and enmity and sets up the covenant fellowship. We are not to suppose, however, that God began to be gracious to us only when sin had been dealt with, and that previously he had been against us. God is gracious to us because he is gracious in himself first of all. Of his graciousness he is gracious to us in his Son.

Moreover, it is of the essence of grace that it is free. If grace were an obligation on God's part, it would no longer be grace. But it is in his divine freedom that God is gracious to us. He is not forced to show grace; he does so freely. We sinners deserve only to have God against us. God's animosity to sin is plainly revealed in the cross. But we are sinners, irretrievably and inexcusably. Therefore, God should be against us. Yet, wonder of wonders! he sends not a destroyer or a judge, but himself comes to save by letting himself be destroyed and judged. There could be no plainer declaration that God is for us, i.e., declaration of the grace of God. At the same time, the course of Christ into suffering and death forbids us

to regard grace as divine indulgence. Grace does not mean the weak and careless forgiveness of sins; for pardon was effected only by the judgment and condemnation of the innocent and voluntary sacrifice. Grace means God's turning to man by undertaking the responsibility for the enmity against himself. Grace would be an impossibility if Christ had not satisfied the holiness of God in his obedient self-offering.

Because grace is God's free decision upon us in Christ, proceeding from his graciousness, it follows that we have no ability to win his grace or favor. This is why grace is opposed to the works of the law tacitly throughout the NT and expressly in such passages as Rom. 3:19 ff.; John 1:17; Gal. 2:11-21; Eph. 2:8-9. On the contrary, grace must be acknowledged for what it is and accepted with humble and joyful gratitude. This human decision, involving acknowledgment and acceptance, is the faith which corresponds to God's grace. "By grace are ye saved through faith" (Eph. 2:8).

BIBLIOGRAPHY

H. Heppe, *Reformed Dogmatics*, chap. XII, "The Covenant of Grace"; D. Bonhoeffer *The Cost of Discipleship*, chap. 1, "Costly Grace"; C. G. Berkouwer, *The Triumph of Grace in the Theology of Karl Barth*. K. Barth: *Church Dogmatics*, II/1, pp. 351-68; IV/1.

T. H. L. PARKER

GRAVE, THE. The burial of our Lord is typical of the method of burial throughout the Bible. There is also exact equivalence of usage of the Hebrew and Greek words. The OT uses mainly *qeḇer* and *qᵉḇûrâ*, with some assistance from *šaḥaṭ;* the NT uses *mnēma*, *mnēmeion*, and *taphos*. The words chiefly signify the place of burial — grave, tomb, sepulchre; they also have interesting metaphorical sidelights, i.e., human characteristics or occurrences which were thought of as "deadly" in effect (e.g., Ps. 5:9; Jer. 5:16; Luke 11:44; Rom. 3:13). Where *šaḥaṭ* is used (e.g., Ps. 16:10) it signifies the grave as the place where the body corrupts. The references given show that for the OT the grave marked a terminus beyond which faith hardly pressed. On this, and on the occasional use of "the grave" as meaning "the abode of the dead," see HADES, HELL, DEATH.

JOHN ALEXANDER MOTYER

GRECIANS, GREEKS. See HELLENISM.

GREEK ORTHODOX. Greek as distinct from the Latins of the West, and Orthodox as opposed to uniate Romanists and heretical Monophysites or Nestorians, the Eastern Churches comprise a family of independent units which claim to have preserved the original faith intact. They are located in Turkey, Greece, Cyprus, the Balkans, Russia and the Near East, with patriarchates at Constantinople, Alexandria, Antioch and Jerusalem; the first of these was granted a certain preeminence in 451, and a patriarchate of Moscow was added in 1589. In doctrine they adhere to the seven ecumenical councils of undivided Christendom, paying particular honor to the Niceno-Constantinopolitan Creed. Christ is held to be the sole Head of the church, and in 1054 they finally broke with Rome, rejecting papal supremacy, purgatory and the cult of images (though they allow holy pictures called *ikons*), and giving as particular grievances the Latin addition of *filioque* to the Creed (see also PROCESSION OF THE SPIRIT and FILIOQUE) and the Western use of unleavened bread in the Mass. They accept the seven sacraments, baptism being normally by immersion and immediately followed by confirmation, even in the case of infants, while in the Communion, which is administered in both kinds to all, a definite transmutation of the elements is taught. Inferior clergy are allowed to marry, but once only and that before ordination; the bishops are always celibate and usually monks. Worship, conducted in archaic forms of the vernacular, is elaborate and lengthy, but instrumental music is prohibited and preaching occupies a subordinate place, while prayers both to and for the dead are offered. The human will is held to co-operate with divine grace, and predestination to be founded on divine foreknowledge. Scripture and tradition are alike respected, but the ultimate source of authority tends to be found in the unchanging common mind of the churches as guided by the Holy Ghost. Since the time of Constantine, the Eastern churches have always been closely dependent on the state, and this relationship has subsisted even under non-Christian governments. Contact with Western Christians has been increased by groups of exiles in the present century.

BIBLIOGRAPHY

W. F. Adeney, *The Greek and Eastern Churches*; Articles "Eastern Church," "Greek Orthodox Church" and "Russian Church" in *HERE*.

G. S. M. WALKER

GROW, GROWTH. There is a many-sidedness to the concept of growth in Scripture. Vegetable growth is included, caused by the Lord God (Ps. 104:14). Growth is expressed by words signifying "to increase greatly" (Gen. 48:16); "to become firm" (Job 38:38); "to be fruitful" (Gen. 47:27); "to flourish" (Hos. 14:5); "to become great," like a cedar in Lebanon (Ps. 92:12); "to triumph" (Job 8:11); "to go up" (Mark 4:7); "to be nourished" (Ps. 144:12); etc. A people's trespass can be "grown (*gādạl*) up unto the heavens" (Ezra 9:6).

Of most particular interest is the Greek word *auxanō*, "to increase," "grow up." So the "word of God grew and multiplied" (Acts 12:24) and "mightily grew" (Acts 19:20). And so the whole body of Christ "groweth unto an holy temple in the Lord" (Eph. 2:21). Newborn babes, also, are to "desire the sincere milk of the word" that they might "grow thereby" (I Pet. 2:2). The same word is used when Peter urges Christians to "grow in grace, and in the knowledge of our Lord and Saviour Jesus Christ" (II Pet. 3:18). Paul affixes a prepositional prefix to the word, making it *hyperauxanō*, and says: "We . . . thank God . . . that your faith groweth exceedingly" (II Thess. 1:3).

BIBLIOGRAPHY

Geo. A. Coe, *HERE*; E. Stanley Jones, *Growing Spiritually*; Basil Miller, *Growing into Life*.

JOSEPH KENNETH GRIDER

GUILT. Words like "guilty," "guiltless," "guiltiness," occur about thirty times in the Bible. "Guilty" or "guiltiness" usually render the Hebrew *'āšām* which is a common word for "trespass offering" and frequently designates the trespass for which the offering was given. In the NT, "guilty" translates *hypodikos* "under judgment" in Rom 3:19 and *enochos* "worthy of punishment" in the trial of Christ and I Cor. 11:27; James 2:10.

In connection with the sin and trespass offerings, Lev. 4:13; 5:2 say that breaking any of God's commands, ceremonial or moral, brings guilt. James 2:10 emphasizes that to offend in one point of the law makes one guilty of all.

No great progress need be traced in the development of the concept of guilt. Cain was as guilty as David. The early law distinguished motive (Ex. 21:12-14). Guilt was individual (II Kings 14:6) as well as collective (Dan. 9:5). The suffering servant is the prophesied *'āšām*, or offering for guilt (Isa. 53:10).

R. LAIRD HARRIS

H

HADES. Almost without exception the LXX uses *hádēs* to translate *še'ôl*, the OT name for the abode of the departed (see HELL). This background, which commits the Greek word to no doctrine of reward or punishment, shows itself in the majority of the occurrences (e.g., Acts 2:27; Rev. 20:13). Once (Matt. 16:18) Hades signifies the headquarters of opposition to the church. This prepares us for Matt. 11:23 (parallel, Luke 10:15) and Luke 16:23, in which Hades undoubtedly signifies the place of punishment of the wicked. In this connection the above-mentioned equivalence of Hades and Sheol is specially noteworthy. The OT contains only a suggestion of diversity of destiny for the godly and the ungodly, but no sooner does Christ "bring life and immortality to light" than he also reveals eternal loss and death, so that even Hades, otherwise equivalent to Sheol, cannot refuse the further significance. This simultaneous maturing of truth concerning eternal gain and loss is ignored by every attempt to divest the NT of its grim doctrine of eternal punishment (see DESTRUCTION).

JOHN ALEXANDER MOTYER

HAND. The Hebrew *yād* and *kap* and the Greek *cheir* represent the English "hand." Some of the many uses of hand are illustrated in the following examples: supplication (II Chron. 6:12 f.; Ps. 28:2); swearing (Gen. 14:22; 24:2, 9; 47:29; Ezra 10:19); sloth (Prov. 10:4; 19:24); servitude (Judg. 2:14; Jer. 27:6 f.); surety (Prov. 6:1 ff.; 22:26); sealing (Rev. 13:16); silence (Judg. 18:19; Job 40:4); sin (Mic. 7:3; Rev. 9:20); sanctification (Job 17:9; 31:7; Ps. 24:4; I Tim. 2:8; James 4:8).

The "laying on of hands" is associated with blessing (Gen. 48:14 ff.; Matt. 19:13 ff.); succession (Num. 27:18-23); substitution (Ex. 29:10; Lev. 16:21); punishment (Esth. 3:6; 8:7; Acts 5:18); healing (Mark 6:5; 8:23; Acts 9:12; 28:8); baptism (Acts 9:17 f.; 19:5 f.); the Holy Spirit (Deut. 34:9; Acts 9:17); ordination (Acts 6:6; I Tim. 4:14; II Tim. 1:6); a special commission (Acts 13:3).

God's hand is associated with power (II Chron. 20:6; Acts 7:50; Heb. 1:10); prodigies (Ex. 3:20); providence (Ps. 31:15); provision (Ezra 7:6; Ps. 145:16); protection (Ps. 139:10; Isa. 51:16; John 10:28 f.); prediction (Isa. 11:11); punishment (Ps. 75:8; Isa. 40:2; 50:11; Heb. 10:31); pleading (Isa. 65:2; Rom. 10:21).

See also ORDAIN, LAYING ON OF HANDS.

WICK BROOMALL

HARDENING. Passive forms of *pachynō*, "to make fat," "dull" (Matt. 13:15 and Acts 28:27, quoting Isa. 6:10), of *pōroō* and *sklērynō*, "to harden" (Rom. 11:7; II Cor. 3:14; Acts 19:9), the substantives *pōrōsis* and *sklērotēs*, "hardness" (Mark 3:5; Rom. 11:25; 2:5) and the adjective *sklērotrachēlos*, "stiff-necked" (Acts 7:51) designate the condition of the hearts of the Jews (and the Gentiles: Eph. 4:18, using *pōrōsis*); for the OT see *TWNT* V, pp. 1024-32. It is *God's* work to harden (John 12:40; cf. Isa. 6:10; Rom. 9:18: active forms of *pōroō* and *sklērynō*). But this does not exclude man's responsibility: the heart of a disciple who does not yet understand Christ is hardened (*pepōrōmenē*, Mark 6:52; 8:17). Christians are warned not to fall back into the ways of the Old Israel by hardening (*sklērynō*) "themselves" (Heb. 3:8, 13, 15; 4:7, quoting Ps. 95:8). Speaking in Rom. 9-11 of the "unsearchable . . . judgments (11:33) of God, who has mercy on whomever he wills and hardens the heart of whomever he wills" (9:18), Paul (9:17 f.) refers to the hardening of Pharaoh by God *and* by himself (Ex. 4:21; 7:3, 22; 8:15; 9:12, 35; 10:1; 14:4, 8, 17). A final hope remains for the hardened Israel, "if they do not persist in their unbelief . . ." (Rom. 11:23).

BIBLIOGRAPHY
Crem; J. Hastings and J. S. Banks in *HDB*; W. L. Walker in *ISBE*; K. L. and M. A. Schmidt in *TWNT*.

MARTIN ANTON SCHMIDT

HATE, HATRED. The primary meaning of the words *śāṭam, miseō* in the Holy Scriptures is holding in very strong dislike. It includes anger, fear and disgust not just momentarily but as an enduring tendency.

The word *śin'â* for hatred expresses the condition of ill will and aversion toward the object of hatred and fear or anger at his approach, joy when he is injured and anger when he receives favor.

Hate is the opposite of love. It may be between person and person (Gen. 27:41). It is also used of God hating evil (Prov. 6:16), of the righteous hating evil (Ps. 97:10) and of the wicked hating the light (John 3:20). It is one of "the works of the flesh" (Gal. 5:20).

A less strong use of the word hate is observed in regard to God's choice of agents of his purpose. "I loved Jacob and I hated Esau" (Mal. 1:2-3). St. Paul comments on this in Rom. 9:13. Hate here means "not chosen" in the context of the dissertation on predestination and election.

Another usage is in the passage "hate not his father . . . and his own life also" (Luke 14:26). The disciple must be ready to suffer the loss of all things for Christ and the gospel.

ALBERT VICTOR M'CALLIN

HEAD. As the most important physical part of man and the seat of human intelligence, the word head is used to represent man himself, especially as chief, leader, commander, or one in authority. Figuratively it is used of God and of Christ (I Cor. 11:3; cf. Eph. 1:22; Col. 2:19), of human authorities (I Sam. 15:17; Dan. 2:28; Isa. 9:14-15), and of important cities (Isa. 7:8). Blessing or calamity, honor or dishonor, joy or sorrow are often pictured as falling upon the head (Gen. 40:13, 19; 48:14, 17, 18; 49:26; Deut. 33:16; Josh. 7:6; Judg. 9:57; I Sam. 4:12; 25:39; II Sam. 1:2; 13:19; II Chron. 6:23; Ps. 3:3; 23:5; 27:6; 83:2; Lam. 2:10; Ezek. 9:10; Luke 21:28; I Cor. 11:5, 10).

In the NT an important use of the word describes the relation of Christ as Head of the church. As the Head of the church (Eph. 4:15; 5:23) Christ is joined to the church described as his body (Eph. 4:12; Col. 1:24). This relationship is accomplished by the baptism of the Spirit (I Cor. 12:13; cf. Rom. 6:3-4; Gal. 3:27), by which all believers are placed into the body of Christ. The figure speaks of the pre-eminence of Christ, his authority, and his living union with the church. In the same figure the individual believers are described as having spiritual gifts differing as parts of the human body, but combining their varied contribution in one common endeavor directed by the Head (Rom. 12:3-8; I Cor. 12:4-31; Eph. 4:11-16). A similar figure describes Christ as the Head of his church as the bride (Eph. 5:23-33) based on the headship of man over woman, and is prophetic of the future union of Christ and his church in glory.

JOHN F. WALVOORD

HEAL, HEALING. Healing in the NT is of two kinds, (a) physical healing (e.g., Matt. 4:24; 10:8; Luke 5:17; John 4:47) and (b) spiritual healing (e.g., Heb. 12:13). The two main words used are *therapeuō* (which is used ten times in reference to our Lord's miracles) and *iaomai,* and in both of these words is contained the idea of restoration. In most instances of our Lord's healings there was an implicit demand for faith to be exercised by the sufferer (Matt. 9:29; Mark 10:52; Luke 17:19), although there are exceptions (e.g., John 5:1-9). It is important to observe that our Lord's healings are never portrayed as mere wonders. Whereas the Synoptic Gospels bring out the motive of compassion, the Fourth Gospel specifies them as "signs." In the early church this healing ministry was continued by the apostles, while in I Corinthians it is enumerated among the charismatic gifts (12:9, 28, 30).

In both Old and New Testaments the idea of physical healing readily lent itself to an application in a spiritual and therefore a fuller sense (cf. John 12:40; I Pet. 2:24).

See also FAITH-HEALING.

DONALD GUTHRIE

HEAR, HEARKEN. The usual sense of hear, receive sounds, is very frequently found in both Old and New Testaments in the common verbs *šāma',* and *akouō.* When one gives close attention to what he hears, then we use the term listen, or in biblical language hearken. For the latter the RSV uses both listen and hearken. The sense of "response" is conveyed by "hearken," whether in granting a request (I Kings 8:28), following a suggestion (Gen. 3:18), believing a promise (Ex. 4:1), or obeying a command (Neh. 9:16). The word *šāma'* is used for all these senscs, but the OT also frequently has *qāšab,* "give attention" (I Sam. 22:15; Dan. 9:19; Mal. 3:16); also translated "attend" to in Psalms and Proverbs. "Hearken" occurs nine times in the NT (Acts 2:14; 27:21 etc.) but "hear" is used also for close attention (e.g., Matt.

13:9; 17:5). In John 18:37 and I John 4:5-6 "heareth" means personally to accept the speaker, and in I John 5:14-15 it signifies God's acceptance of our prayer.

J. CLEMENT CONNELL

HEART. I. BIBLICAL PSYCHOLOGY. Hebrew and Christian views on the nature of man were developed in a religious setting; there is no systematized or scientific psychology in the Bible. Nevertheless, certain fundamental conceptions are worthy of note: (1) In the OT there is no very marked emphasis on individuality; but, rather, on what is frequently now termed *corporate personality.* Yet (2) A. R. Johnson has shown that a fundamental characteristic of OT anthropology is *the awareness of totality.* Man is not a body plus a soul, but a living unit of vital power, a psycho-physical organism (Aubrey R. Johnson, *The Vitality of the Individual in the Thought of Ancient Israel,* University of Wales Press, 1949). (3) The Hebrews thought of man as influenced from without — by evil spirits, the devil, or the Spirit of God — whereas in modern psychology (*q.v.*) the emphasis has tended to be placed on dynamic factors operating from within (though, at the present time, fresh interest is being evoked in the study of environmental forces as factors influencing human behavior). (4) The study of particular words in the Old and New Testaments affords a comprehensive view of the underlying Hebrew and Christian conceptions of man (*q.v.*). (See John Laidlaw in *HDB,* Articles, "Psychology," "Mind," "Heart," "Soul," "Spirit," "Flesh," "Body").

II. OLD TESTAMENT USAGE. In the English versions several Hebrew expressions are translated "heart," the main words being *leb* and *lebab.* In a general sense, heart means in the midst, the innermost or hidden part of anything (John Laidlaw, *HDB,* II, p. 317). Thus, the midst (or heart) of the sea (Ps. 46:2); of heaven (Deut. 4:11); of the oak (II Sam. 14:18).

In the physiological sense, heart is the central bodily organ, the seat of physical life. Thus, Jacob's heart "fainted" (Gen. 45:26); Eli's heart "trembled" (I Sam. 4:13).

But, like other anthropological terms in the OT, heart is also used very frequently in a psychological sense, as the center or focus of man's inner personal life. The heart is the source, or spring, of motives; the seat of the passions; the center of the thought processes; the spring of conscience. Heart, in fact, is associated with what is now meant by the cognitive, affective and volitional elements of personal life.

The Book of Proverbs is illuminating here: The heart is the seat of wisdom (2:10; etc.); of trust (or confidence) (3:5); diligence (4:23); perverseness (6:14); wicked imaginations (6:18); lust (6:25); subtlety (7:10); understanding (8:5); deceit (12:20); folly (12:23); heaviness (12:25); bitterness (14:10); sorrow (14:13); backsliding (14:14); cheerfulness (15:13); knowledge (15:14); joy (15:30); pride (16:5); haughtiness (18:12); prudence (18:15); fretfulness (19:3); envy (23:17).

III. NEW TESTAMENT USAGE. The NT word is *kardia.* It, too, has a wide psychological and spiritual connotation. Our Lord emphasized the importance of right states of heart. It is the pure in heart who see God (Matt. 5:8); sin is first committed in the heart (Matt. 5:28); out of the heart proceed evil thoughts and acts (Matt. 15:19); forgiveness must come from the heart (Matt. 18:35); men must love God with all their heart (Matt. 22:37); the word of God is sown, and must come to fruition, in the heart (Luke 8:11-15).

Paul's use of *kardia* is on similar lines. According to Dr. Robinson, in 15 cases heart denotes personality, or the inner life, in general (e.g., I Cor. 14:25); in 13 cases, it is the seat of emotional states of consciousness (e.g., Rom. 9:2); in 11 cases, it is the seat of intellectual activities (e.g., Rom. 1:21); in 13 cases, it is the seat of the volition (e.g., Rom. 2:5) (H. Wheeler Robinson, *The Christian Doctrine of Man,* 3rd Edition, T. & T. Clark, Edinburgh, 1926). Paul uses other expressions, such as mind, soul and spirit, to augment the conception of man; but, on the whole, it may be said that the NT word *kardia* reproduces and expands the ideas included in the OT words *leb* and *lebab.*

IV. THE GOSPEL OF THE NEW HEART.

Since the heart is regarded as the center or focus of man's personal life, the spring of all his desires, motives, and moral choices — indeed, of all his behavioral trends — it is not surprising to note that in both Testaments the divine appeal is addressed to the "heart" of man.

The subject is too broad to allow of full treatment here; but the leading ideas may be

outlined thus. The evil imagination, according
to the rabbis, is located in the heart (Gen.
6:5); the heart is engraven with sin; it is de-
ceitful and desperately sick (Jer. 17:1-10);
but it can be cleansed (Ps. 51:10) and renewed (Ezek. 36:26), and can be made to
bear the impress of the divine law (Jer.
31:33). God searches the heart (Rom. 8:27);
he shines in our hearts with the light of the
knowledge of his glory in the face of Jesus
Christ (II Cor. 4:6); it is the pure in heart
who attain to the beatific vision (Matt. 5:8).
The important point is that, whether in Old
or New Testaments, or in rabbinic teaching,
it is in the heart, in the innermost recesses of
his being, that man is illumined, cleansed,
renewed, by attention to the word of God. It
is an inward renewal, a new birth, a regeneration.

V. CONCLUSION. In view of modern trends
in psychology, it is instructive to note this emphasis on the heart in early Hebrew and Christian literature. True, these early writers tended
to think of man as influenced from without;
but they saw clearly that it is in the heart of
man that moral and spiritual battles must be
fought and won. Hence the Psalmist's prayer
(Ps. 19:14): "Who can discern his errors?
Absolve me from faults unknown. . . . May
the words of my mouth and the meditation of
my heart be acceptable in thy sight, O LORD,
my strength and my redeemer."

BIBLIOGRAPHY
Arndt; A-S; Rudolph Bultmann, *Theology of the New Testament*, Vol. I, pp. 220-27; HDB; JewEnc; Aubrey R. Johnson, *The Vitality of the Individual in the Thought of Ancient Israel*; MM; RTWB; H. Wheeler Robinson, *The Christian Doctrine of Man*; W. David Stacey, *The Pauline View of Man*; Thayer-Grimm, *Greek-English Lexicon*; L. S. Thornton, *The Common Life in the Body of Christ*, pp. 103 ff.

OWEN R. BRANDON

HEATHEN, THE FATE OF. By "heathen" in this article we refer to adults who
have not heard the gospel of Christ. Whatever
their culture or country, their unbelief in
Christ is circumstantial; that is, they have had
no opportunity to believe. This fact raises the
question about their "fate." If Christ is the
only way of salvation and these persons do not
so much as know of the existence of Christ,
are we to conclude that they cannot possibly
have salvation, being necessarily lost or
damned? If they are damned, is that not unfair and unjust of God inasmuch as they have
no opportunity to be saved?

Let us meet the question right where it

emerges: Is it not unjust of God to damn a
person who has had no opportunity to be
saved? Why is it? Assuming that God does
damn such persons, why is it unjust of him to
do so simply because they have no opportunity
to be saved? If these persons are damned they
are damned because they are sinners; they are
not damned because they have had opportunity
to be saved and have not utilized it. Their opportunity, or the lack of it, has nothing to do
with their being damned; they are damned
because they are sinners. What is unfair in
God's damning sinners? If God damned them
because they did not believe the gospel, they
could legitimately protest that they had no opportunity to believe the gospel; but, if God
damns them for other sins, what does the fact
that they did not commit this sin of unbelief
in the gospel have to do with it?

Some will say: Granted that God could
damn men for the sins they have committed
even though they did not hear the gospel and
there would be no injustice in that as such.
But, does God not have an obligation to offer
a way of salvation to everyone? But, we ask,
why? Why does God have any obligation to
offer salvation to any sinner? Grace, by definition, is undeserved. If it were deserved, it
would not be a gospel; it would not be grace.
If it is a gospel of grace it must be undeserved. If it is undeserved how can it be said
that God owes it to anyone?

All right, some will reply, but inasmuch as
God (who did not owe the gospel to anyone)
did give it to many, is he not under obligation
to offer it everyone? But why? If a person
who does not deserve it receives a gift, does
another person who does not deserve it thereby gain a right to a gift? If he does gain a
right to it, is it still a "gift" or a "gospel"?
But, it is further urged, this makes God a respecter of persons. Indeed it does; but the respecter of persons which the Bible condemns
is an unfair respecter of persons. God is not
an unfair respecter of persons and this is no
instance of an unfair discrimination. He gives
a gift which he does not owe; that puts him
under no obligation to give a gift, the same
gift, to everyone to whom he does not owe it.
Being a respecter of persons, if it is a fair discrimination, is not evil. Cf. the Parable of The
Laborers, Matt. 20:1 ff., which speaks to this
very point: "Is it not lawful for me to do
what I will with mine own? Is thine eye evil,
because I am good?" (vs. 15).

All of the above is by way of facing the objections which are commonly made to the doctrine that the "heathen" are lost. Such, we believe, is the teaching of the word of God. "Faith cometh by hearing, and hearing by the word of God" is the teaching of Rom. 10:17 in which context the necessity of missionaries is being argued. The world by wisdom knew not God but it pleased God by the foolishness of preaching to make his wisdom known (I Cor. 1:21). The wrath of God is revealed from heaven against all the unrighteousness of men who hold the truth in unrighteousness, but the gospel is the power of God unto salvation to everyone that believeth (Rom. 1:17). Christ is the light of the world. All the world is in darkness until he shines into it (John 8:12; 9:5). There is none other name given under heaven whereby men must be saved but the name of Jesus (Acts 4:12). He is the way, the truth and the life, no man coming to God but by him (John 14:6).

Christ in teaching this doctrine himself, brings out an aspect of the truth which has not yet been mentioned in this article. In Luke 12:47-48 he tells us that the disobedient man who does not know will be beaten with fewer stripes than the disobedient man who does know. That is to say, that those who do not know the gospel are guilty because of the light which they have and which they have transgressed (cf. especially Rom. 1), but they are not so guilty as those who have had the light of the gospel as well as the light of nature and have sinned against that also. Their light having been so much greater their hardness of heart was so much more developed in resisting it and their guilt is much the more grievous. Therefore, according to Matt. 10:15; 11:22, it shall be more tolerable for Sodom and Gomorrah (who are in hell though they sinned only against the light of nature) than for Capernaum and Chorazin (who are in hell with far greater condemnation because they have violated a light so vastly greater than the heathen transgressed).

In conclusion, it may be well to cite the remark of the great Baptist theologian, A. H. Strong: "The question whether the heathen will ever be saved if we do not give them the gospel, is not so serious a one for us as the other question whether we ourselves will ever be saved if we do not give them the gospel." That is to say: Christians have an obligation to evangelize the world. If they do not partici-

pate in that duty, although some persons may be lost through their negligence, they will perish with them and with far greater punishment because they have themselves sinned against the far greater light which they have had. In other words, the "fate" of the "heathen" is inextricably connected with the "fate" of "Christians" in this era.

The view of this article is the general view of the church except that there have always been Christian theologians such as Ulrich Zwingli and John Wesley, who have hoped (more often than they have affirmed) that Christ, the only Saviour of the world, may sometimes, admittedly rarely, work independently of the means of grace. Neo-orthodoxy inclines to a universalistic position which teaches the salvation of the heathen.

BIBLIOGRAPHY
1) Karl Barth, *Christ and Adam*, p. 22 f; 87 f;
2) W. G. T. Shedd, *Sermons to the Natural Man*, pp. 78 ff;
3) John Wesley, *Works*, New York ed., Vol. II, pp. 485 f.

JOHN H. GERSTNER

HEAVEN. The most frequently used Hebrew word for heaven in the OT is *šāmayim*, signifying "heaved up things" or "the heights." In the Greek NT it is *ouranos*, which denotes "sky," or "air." These words refer to the atmosphere just above the earth (Gen. 1:20, etc.); to the firmament in which the sun and moon and stars are located (Gen. 1:17, etc.); to God's abode (Ps. 2:4, etc.); to the abode of the angels (Matt. 22:30). The OT has no word for universe, and to express the idea there is the frequent "heaven and earth." We read of "the heaven and the heaven of heavens" (Deut. 10:14), and of a man's being "caught up into the third heaven" (II Cor. 12:2), but such references are probably to be thought of metaphorically.

What is existence in heaven to be like? Not as for Plato, one in which naked minds will intellectually contemplate the eternal, unchanging Ideas. The whole person survives, in the biblical teaching. Even the body is raised again, so that, if it is no longer flesh and blood (I Cor. 15:50), it nevertheless has a continuity with the present body, a sameness in form if not in material element (see Matt. 5:29, 30; 10:28; Rom. 8:11, 23; I Cor. 15:53). So there is nothing in the Bible (nor in the main creeds of the church) about disembodied spirits in the next world existing *in vacuo*. Yet there is no eating nor drinking

(Rom. 14:17), nor appetite of sex (Matt. 22:30; Mark 12:25; Luke 20:35). Feasting there is evidently to be understood symbolically, according to Matt. 26:29 where Jesus speaks of that day when he will drink the fruit of the vine "new" with the disciples in his Father's kingdom. In heaven the redeemed will be in the immediate presence of God; will forever feed on the splendor of God's majesty, beholding the Father's face. In the present life men "see through a glass, darkly; but then face to face" (I Cor. 13:12). And the sons of God will see Christ "as he is" (I John 3:2). The childlike in faith, even as the angels do now, will "always behold the face" of the Father (Matt. 18:10). They will not so much glory in the presence of Supreme Reason, as the Greeks anticipated, but in the wonder of the All-Holy One (Isa. 6:3; Rev. 4:8). And this God is a Father, in whose house (John 14:2) the redeemed will dwell, where "they shall be his people," and where "God himself shall be with them" (Rev. 21:3).

There will be activities in heaven to engage man's highest faculties. For one thing, there will be governmental ministries. The "spirits of just men made perfect" (Heb. 12:23) will be in the "city of the living God, the heavenly Jerusalem" (Heb. 12:22), and men are to assist in governing the whole. Thus in the parable of the nobleman the good servant, who has been "faithful in a very little" on earth, is in heaven to be given "authority over ten cities" (Luke 19:17). In Matthew the servant who had been given five talents and who had "gained beside them five talents more" is told: "Well done, thou good and faithful servant: . . . I will make thee ruler over many things: enter thou into the joy of thy lord" (25:20-21). Perhaps new songs are to be written and sung (Rev. 5:9). The "redeemed from the earth," too, are to *learn* a "new song" (Rev. 14:3). And the kings of the earth are to "bring their glory and honour into it" (Rev. 21:24). So while there is to be on the part of the redeemed a continuous worship in heaven, it seems to be in the sense that all activities engaged in will be for the sole glory of God and will therefore partake of the nature of worship.

BIBLIOGRAPHY

C. Harris, "State of the Dead (Christian)," *HERE;* W. G. Heslop, *Heaven;* Edwin Lewis, *A New Heaven and a New Earth* (indirectly related); Richard Lewis, *A New Vision of Another Heaven;* D. L. Moody, *Heaven;* K. Schilder, *Heaven: What Is It?*

JOSEPH KENNETH GRIDER

HEILSGESCHICHTE. *Heilsgeschichte* is a German term meaning the "history of salvation." It sees the Bible as essentially such a history. While the Bible says much about other matters, these are merely incidental to its single purpose of unfolding the story of redemption. It traces in history and doctrine the development of the divine purpose in the salvation of men. Considered as a somewhat different approach from the "proof-text" method, which uses the Bible as the raw material for the shaping of a systematic theology, *Heilsgeschichte* stresses a more organic approach.

Johann Albrecht Bengel (1687-1752) is regarded as the father of this approach. However, it is interesting that his contemporary in New England, Jonathan Edwards (1703-58), also conceived of presenting a "Rational Divinity" along these very lines and his posthumously published *History of Redemption* may be considered as the first work of the American *Heilsgeschichte* school. His interest was apparently spontaneous since there is no evidence that Edwards knew of the work of Bengel. If we remember further that John Wesley was influenced by the work of Bengel we can see the significant fact that German, English and American pietism showed a simultaneous concern for our subject. It is not to be supposed, however, that this outflowering of *Heilgeschichte* was from a dry ground, for anticipations of the viewpoint are earlier seen in Irenaeus, Joachim of Flora, Luther, Cocceius and many others. Furthermore, parallel developments appeared in the new science of the History of Doctrine (over against the Roman contention that ecclesiastical dogma was incapable of improvement, being infallible). In the realm of apologetics, to take but one more example, the teleological argument came to be concerned more with the purposive structure of the whole universe than with the marvelous precision of its parts.

While the eighteenth century advocates of *Heilsgeschichte* used this approach as an ally of, rather than as substitute for, systematic theology and had no intention of circumventing the authority of the individual texts by the more general and organic view of Scripture as a whole, some later adherents, especially in this century, have so employed *Heilsgeschichte*. The Roman Church charges Protestantism with teaching that the Bible is authoritative only with respect to "faith and morals" and, by implication, abandoning verbal inspiration. While every Protestant is not guilty as charged there can be no denying that many Protestants defend the Bible in the area of *Heilsgeschichte* alone, not concerned with its accuracy in history, astronomy, geology and the like. This is not an essential of the *Heilsgeschichte* approach but merely a perversion of its original form that has become common today.

Many modern scholars are working in this field. Oscar Cullmann says: ". . . I always come again to the same conclusion, namely, that the real centre of early Christian faith and thought is *redemptive history (Heilsgeschichte)* . . ." W. G. Kuemmel of Marburg, C. H. Dodd, W. Vischer, G. von Rad, W. Zimmerli and others are absorbed with the same subject in terms of promise and fulfilment. On the other hand, Rudolf Bultmann is an implacable foe of *Heilsgeschichte*.

BIBLIOGRAPHY

J. A. Bengel, *Gnomon Novi Testamenti*, Eng. trans. 4 vols., 1859; B. S. Childs, "Prophecy and Fulfillment. A Study of Contemporary Hermeneutics" in *Interp* 12:259-271; O. Cullmann, *The Early Church*; Jonathan Edwards, *A History of the Work of Redemption*; G. Vos, *Biblical Theology*; Gustav Weth, *Die Heilsgeschichte*.

JOHN H. GERSTNER

HEIR, INHERITANCE. The OT terms for heir, inheritance, do not necessarily bear the special sense of hereditary succession and possession, although they are found in laws concerning succession to the headship of the family, with consequent control of the family property (Gen. 15:3 ff.; Num. 27:1-11; 36:1-12; Deut. 21:15-17). The main roots are *nāhal* (the substantival form, *nahălâ*, occurs nearly 200 times) and *yāraš*. Both signify possession in a general sense, though the former means receiving as one's share by lot. *Ḥēleq*, "portion," has the same idea.

A development of thought and spiritualizing of the concept of inheritance is apparent in the OT. From the first, the inheritance promised by Jehovah to Abraham and his descendants was the land of Canaan (Gen. 12:7; 15:18-21; 26:3; 28:13; Ex. 6:8). Israel's possession of the land rested solely on the gift of Jehovah, and, though only entered into with hard fighting, was not hers by self-effort (Josh. 21:43-45; Ps. 44:13). Furthermore, the inheritance had to be divided by lot among the tribes, the allotting having divine sanction (Num. 26:52-56; 33:54; 34:13; Josh. 14:1-5; 18:4-9). The land was to be possessed "for ever" (Gen. 13:15), yet continued enjoyment

and possession was conditional upon faithfulness to God (Deut. 4:26 ff.; 11:8, 9). Although given to Israel, the land also remained the inheritance of Jehovah, his special portion out of all the earth (Ex. 15:17; Lev. 25:23; I Sam. 26:19; II Sam. 21:3; Ps. 79:1; Jer. 2:7).

Alongside and developing from this concept of the land as Jehovah's inheritance is the thought that Israel, whom he has chosen and put in the land, was also his inheritance (Deut. 4:20; 7:6; 32:9). Likewise, Israel, and particularly the faithful of the nation, came to regard Jehovah himself, and not merely the land, as her inheritance (Pss. 16:5; 73:26; Lam. 3:24). Indeed, the Levites never had any inheritance but Jehovah (Num. 18:20-26). However, the earlier thought of the possession of the land was not lost, for in the messianic kingdom such possession is envisaged (Ps. 37:9; Isa. 60:21).

In the NT "heir," "inheritance," represent *klēronomos, klēronomia,* and derivatives (also used in LXX for *nāhal* and *yāraš*). So basic an idea in the Old Covenant as inheritance must have its counterpart in the New Covenant. The Epistle to the Hebrews, particularly, shows that as Israel received her inheritance, so in the New Covenant a better inheritance is to be possessed by the New Israel. Furthermore, as is to be expected, the inheritance is "in Christ." In Mark 12:1-11 Christ claims to be the heir of God. This is confirmed in Heb. 1:2 and implied in Rom. 8:17. Here, more clearly than *nāhal* or *yāraš, klēronomos* conveys the thought of hereditary possession. Rom. 8:17 shows that those "in Christ" are joint-heirs with Christ of the inheritance. Whereas the inheritance is his by right, in that he is the only begotten Son, it is possessed by the believer by grace, as he is adopted as a son in Jesus Christ.

The inheritance is the kingdom of God with all its blessings (Matt. 25:34; I Cor. 6:9; Gal. 5:21). While enjoyment of it begins in this life, in so far as the kingdom is already present, the full possession must be future (Rom. 8:17-23; I Cor. 15:50; Heb. 11:13; I Pet. 1:3, 4).

BIBLIOGRAPHY

W. H. Bennett "Heir" and Alex. Martin "Inheritance" in *HDB*; C. E. B. Cranfield, *RTWB*.

R. COLIN CRASTON

HELL. I. THE OLD TESTAMENT. AV, ERV, translate *šeʾôl* as "hell," whereas ASV,

RSV correctly give "Sheol," the name of the place of the departed (Gen. 37:35). The parallel use of *šaḥaṯ* ("pit," "corruption") as in Job 33:24 and Ps. 30:9, indicates the horror with which men viewed their inescapable (Ps. 89:48) sojourn there. Earthly distinctions survive (Isa. 14:9) but those in Sheol are cut off from God and man (II Sam. 12:23; Job 7:9). God is present in Sheol (Job 26:6; Ps. 139:8) but cannot be contacted (Ps. 6:5). Though the translation "hell" is misleading, there are references connecting Sheol with wickedness of life (Ps. 9:17; Prov. 5:5); Isa. 14:15 and Ezek. 32:23 may indicate special parts of Sheol designed for the wicked (see DESTRUCTION). Similarly, light begins to shine for the righteous (see HADES) (Pss. 16:10; 49:15; Prov. 15:24).

II. THE NEW TESTAMENT. *Geenna* is translated "hell." The Hebrew *gê-hinnōm* ("valley of Hinnom," II Kings 23:10) explains the name, and the use of the place — a common refuse dump, a place of perpetual fire and loathsomeness — explains the usage. The final indignity offered to the executed criminal was that his body was flung into Gehenna (Matt. 5:22). Hence its use of the final spiritual state of the ungodly in Matt. 10:28 and Mark 9:43 (see DESTRUCTION).

JOHN ALEXANDER MOTYER

HELLENIST, HELLENISM. Hellenism may be defined as the culture, language, and philosophy of life prevalent in the Graeco-Roman world during the time of Christ.

The Christian faith owes a great debt to one aspect of Hellenism. Christianity used the Greek language to spread the Christian faith throughout the Mediterranean world — the same language by which Hellenism was spread throughout the same territory. Certain ingredients played strategic roles in Hellenism: common customs, cultural traits, religious ties, free exchange of ideas in philosophy, religion, and politics. Hellenism, though born in Greece, was inherently international in character. The theatre, games or athletic contests, sculpture, architecture, literature — these were all products of Hellenism. Hellenism embodied the individual's spontaneous expression in social, political, economic, or philosophical realms. This freedom to act and to think brought to those who were "Hellenized" a new way of life. Although groups or individuals often refused to accept much that Hellenism brought,

they could not remain untouched by it. Jews who spoke Greek are called Hellenists. Those living outside of Palestine had to speak Greek. On the basic theological truths of the OT they agreed with Palestinian Jews who spoke Aramaic. Yet the Greek language and culture gave them a different outlook.

The noun *Hellas* means Greece. In popular usage it designated the Roman province known officially as Achaia (Arndt, p. 251). This is its meaning in Acts 20:2.

Another noun *Hellēn* (usually found in the plural) occurs twenty-six times. Twice it is used of a man of Greek language and culture. Paul is debtor to the Greeks and to the barbarians (Rom. 1:14). Mankind is here divided between those who speak Greek and those who do not. It is a linguistic-cultural division. The new man is being renewed unto knowledge on the basis of the image of the one who created him. Where such renewal exists there is neither Greek nor Jew — cultural divisions; circumcision or uncircumcision — ceremonial or religious divisions; Barbarian or Scythian — a person of non-Greek culture or a savage; slave or free — social divisions (Col. 3:11). These contexts suggest that a person immersed in Greek culture was an enthusiastic exponent of this way of life.

In a looser sense, *Hellēnes* (Greeks) refers to all those who came under the influence of Greek culture.

The term is used in two places of proselytes (*q.v.*) i.e., God-fearing Gentiles who had turned from paganism to Judaism. Representatives of these sought out Jesus near the end of his ministry (John 12:20-21). Such people were open to the Christian message. Many were persuaded by Paul's preaching to become Christians (Acts 17:4).

In a looser sense the term *Hellēnes* is used of Gentiles (i.e. those who are pagans or heathen), as well as those who speak Greek and thereby exhibit some contact with Greek culture. In certain contexts in Acts referring to Paul's missionary work in cities (Acts 14:1; 18:4; 19:10, 17) and in Romans, men are divided into Jews and Gentiles (Rom. 1:16; 2:9, 10; 3:9; 10:12). Gentile refers to the non-Jew. In such large categories, the cultural denotation of *Hellēnes* is weakened or is lost while the term Jew retains its cultural-religious significance.

In other contexts where *Hellēnes* should be translated "Gentile," the suggestion of Greek culture is clear. The Jews speculated that Jesus would teach the Gentiles (John 7:35). Men of Cyprus and Antioch spoke to Gentiles in Antioch (Acts 11:20). Some texts read "Greek-speaking Jews" in place of Gentiles, but the context certainly favors "Gentiles." Mixed marriages emphasize cultural differences. Timothy's mother was a Jew and his father a Gentile (Acts 16:1, 3), meaning that he spoke Greek and was a representative of Greek culture. This does not necessarily mean he was a Greek national. But to translate *Hellēnos* as "Greek" implies this. On the other hand, when Paul says that the Jews ask for signs and the *Hellēnes* seek after wisdom, the translation "Greek" is as good as "Gentiles" or better. Although the context indicates a two-fold division of mankind, the seeking after wisdom favors the translation "Greeks" (I Cor. 1:22, 24).

The noun *Hellēnistēs* designates a Greek-speaking Jew. Thus all the Jews living in the dispersion were Hellenists. Even in Palestine there were some. The early Christian church made many converts among this group. The murmuring of the Greek-speaking Jews against the Aramaic-speaking Jews threatened to break up the church (Acts 6:1). But the wise appointment of seven Greek-speaking Jews as deacons brought harmony and increased power. Hellenistic Jews who did not respond to the Christian message were very hostile (Acts 9:29-30). Those who did respond made good material for missionaries, especially to the Gentiles (Acts 11:20).

When Paul told the Corinthians to give no offense to the Jews, or to the Gentiles, or to the church of God (I Cor. 10:32) he spoke of the two divisions that existed prior to the incarnation of Christ and of the church as consisting of a third order drawn from the first two categories. In the church the barrier between Jew and Gentile has been broken down forever (Eph. 2:11-22).

BIBLIOGRAPHY

Arndt; H. Windisch, *TWNT*, II, pp. 501-14; W. W. Tarn, *Hellenistic Civilization*. 3rd edition.

A. BERKELEY MICKELSEN

HERESY. The Greek word *hairesis* means: (1) a choice, e.g., Lev. 22:18, 21 (LXX), where "gifts according to their choice" means free-will offering; (2) a chosen opinion, the only NT example being in II Pet. 2:1, where "destructive opinions" are caused by false teaching; (3) a sect or party (holding certain opinions), used in the NT (a) of the Sadducees and Pharisees (Acts 5:17; 15:5), (b) of the Christians (Acts 24:14; 28:22; in 24:14 Paul substitutes "way" for "heresy," possibly because he himself had given the word the bad meaning), and (c) a sect or faction within the Christian body (being synonymous with "schism" in I Cor. 11:19; Gal. 5:20), and resulting not so much from false teaching as from the lack of love and from self-assertiveness, which lead to divisions within the Christian community. It is the meaning given to *hairesis* in II Peter which came to predominate in Christian usage. "Heresy" is a deliberate denial of revealed truth coupled with the acceptance of error (*q.v.*). The creeds were considered to contain the standard of truth and correct belief, and themselves formally contradicted various false teachings, e.g., Arianism, Apollinarianism, Nestorianism and Eutychianism. The union of church and state after Nicaea led in time to legal penalties against heretics. Paul's and Luke's usage (#3 above) survives in, e.g., Eusebius' *HE* X. v. 21-22, where Christianity is "our most sacred heresy," and Augustine *Ep.* 185, a valuable commentary on the early Christian idea of heresy.

The Roman Catholic Church distinguishes heresy from schism (disunity through lack of love) and apostasy (abandonment of Christianity). Heresy may be either "formal" (adherence to false doctrine by a baptized R.C.) or "material" (false doctrine held in ignorance by a non-Roman).

See also SCHISM.

BIBLIOGRAPHY

Augustine, *De Don., Ep.* 185; Cyprian, *De Unitate Eccl.*; Standard histories of the early church; G. L. Prestige, *Fathers and Heretics*; J. V. Bartlet in *HDB*; H. Schlier in *TWNT; ODCC.*

M. R. W. FARRER

HERMENEUTICS. See INTERPRETATION.

HERMETIC LITERATURE. This title designates a body of writings associated with Hermes Trismegistos, whom a popular account quoted by Lactantius equates with the fifth Mercury, called Thoth by the Egyptians. Although a man, he was very ancient, and his vast learning earned him the title Trismegistos (Thrice-great). He wrote many books on the knowledge of divine things, speaking of one God as Father, as Christians do (*Divine Institutes* i. 6). The Greek Hermes was thus assimilated to the Egyptian god Thoth. Hermes was associated with astrology in Alexandrine cults (Clement of Alexandria *Stromateis* vi. 4), and Festugière has shown the place of Hermes Trismegistos in Egyptian magical literature.

Of religious works, a corpus of eighteen Greek tractates, including the notable *Poimandres*, has been preserved; another, *Asclepius*, survives in Latin, while M. Puech announces a Coptic version found with Christian Gnostic works at Chenoboskion, where two more Hermetic opuscula have been found, (*Coptic Studies in Honor of W. E. Crum*, Boston, 1950, pp. 91 ff.); and Stobaeus and others quote fragments of other works.

Most of these writings belong, by common consent, roughly to the second and third centuries A.D. They are mystical, deeply influenced by Platonic and Stoic thought, but not always self-consistent. The use of the LXX seems indubitable, and the cosmogony of *Poimandres* presupposes Gen. 1-2. The Logos (*q.v.*) figures largely, and there are striking parallels of language with John's Gospel: direct borrowing either way is improbable, though Christianity perhaps influenced some Hermetica.

There is no evidence of a Hermetic "church." The literature represents one aspect of the movement of Gnostic personal religion as the Christian mission began. It is therefore essentially syncretistic. Whatever John and Hermes had in common, they could never share the cross of the personal Logos.

BIBLIOGRAPHY

R. Reitzenstein, *Poimandres*; A. D. Nock and A. J. Festugière, *Corpus Hermeticum*, 4 vols. (texts and French translation); A. J. Festugière, *La Révelation d' Hermès Trismégiste*, I; C. H. Dodd; *The Bible and the Greeks; The Fourth Gospel*, pp. 10-53.

ANDREW F. WALLS

HIGH PLACE. See GODS.

HIGH PRIEST. This is an approximate rendering of *ha-kōhēn ha-gādôl*, literally "the great priest," cf. Heb. 10:21 ASV.

Melchizedek, king-priest of Jerusalem (Gen. 14:18), represented the norm for most of Israel's neighbors during the OT period; the king was supreme head of both civil and religious life; other priests held office as his deputies. In Israel religious and civil authority were by God's will separated; in conformity with the established pattern Aaron's sons were purely his deputies. This is shown by the ephod and its breastplate containing the Urim and Thummim (Ex. 28:6-30), by which the high priest alone was able to discover the divine will. The uniqueness of his position is suggested by Num. 35:25 and his inability to delegate his functions for the Day of Atonement. Lack of archaeological information led the Wellhausen school to misinterpret the virtual non-use of the term in pre-exilic history and so to claim that it was an exilic invention. The frequent mention of individuals as "the priest" (e.g., Josh. 19:51; I Sam. 1:9; II Kings 11:9) was sufficient for those living against the pre-exilic cultural background.

The office was apparently strictly hereditary. The problem of two contemporary high priests, Abiathar and Zadok, under David is probably best explained by the Samaritan tradition that Eli stole the office (cf. E. Robertson, *The Old Testament Problem*, p. 176 f.). The opposition of the Qumran Covenanters to the Hasmonean high priests was largely due to Onias III having left a legal heir.

The Melchizedek royal high-priesthood of Christ implies that the ideal of one man as sole representative of God had been realized.

H. L. ELLISON

HOLINESS, HOLY. I. OLD TESTAMENT. From *qāḏōš*, "holy," and *qōḏeš*, "holiness," which occur more than 830 times. Obscure in etymology, the root idea of the Hebrew word, religiously viewed, is that of withdrawal and consecration: withdrawal from what is common or unclean, consecration to what is divine, sacred, pure.

A. *Applied to God.* It signifies (a) his separation from, and transcendency over, all his creation; in fine, his supremacy, majesty, and awesome glory, as in Ex. 3:4, 5; and (b) the ethical spotlessness of his character, as in Lev. 11:44, repeated in I Pet. 1:16.

B. *Applied to objects and institutions.* They are "holy," not in themselves, but in their use as things withdrawn from common employment and dedicated to God's service. Typical is the repeated use of "holy" in Exodus and Leviticus, in reference to such assorted objects as the tabernacle and its furnishings, offerings, water, priestly vestments, and land.

C. *Applied to men.* Their "holiness" is regarded, most frequently, as their *ceremonial* sanctity issuing from appropriate acts of consecration, as in Ex. 29:1 ff., or, occasionally and at a deeper level of significance, their ethical righteousness, as in Ex. 19:2; Ps. 15:1 ff.; Isa. 57:15.

In the main, it is in the Psalms and the Prophets that the ceremonial significance of "holiness" is downgraded and the conception for which it stands is enriched with moral reality.

II. NEW TESTAMENT. Expressed by *hagios,* its derivatives and cognates.

A. *Generally:* a carrying forward and a completing of the spiritual-ethical aspect of sanctity in the OT.

B. *Specifically:* 1. *The status of those who, by faith, have been joined to Christ,* whose perfect righteousness is "made over" to them, so to speak. Cf. I Cor. 1:30. This imputation of righteousness, however, is not regarded as valid except as it is accompanied by that imparted holiness which must result from the believer's union with Christ, who is represented as being himself the negation and destruction of sin. Cf. I John 2:1-6. 2. *The moral quality of the character and actions of those who, through the indwelling of the Holy Spirit, share Christ's nature and consent to be ruled by it.* Cf. Rom. 6:22; II Cor. 7:1; I Thess. 5:23; I John 1:7; 3:6-9. Implicit in the nature of the Christian's relation to Christ is the moral impossibility of a willing continuance in sinning. Christ and sin cannot be at peace in the same heart. Note: The measure of holiness available to the Christian (whether to the extent of partially and progressively extirpating, effectively counteracting, or entirely purging the evil in man's nature) is a question on which theological tradition divides, the principal variant lines being Augustinian-Calvinist and Arminian-Wesleyan. 3. *The ideal and implicit character of the whole body of Christ, the church, wherein the corporate sign of sanctity is seen in the fact of the church's relationship to God through Christ.* Cf. Eph. 1:4; I Pet. 2:9.

III. CHURCH HISTORY. The following are particular emphases to be found in the teaching and practice of Christian groups:

A. *Occult* holiness, as in the instance of early Gnosticism, in which the material order was held to be evil, and holiness lay, therefore, in a certain insight, or *gnosis,* imparted to the initiated, namely, that the soul's sanctification consisted in its exaltation above the world of sense and its immersion in the divine *plēroma,* or fulness.

B. *Mystical* holiness, as in the experiences of those who exalt union with God in pure feeling and vision above the instrumentality of

the word of God or even the mediation of the Son of God.

C. *Sacramental* holiness, as in the case of Roman Catholicism with its teaching of grace as objectively conveyed in the sacraments and meritoriously achieved in the works-process of sanctification.

D. *Ascetic* holiness, as in monasticism where it is held that a life of withdrawal is holier than one of common labor or vocation.

E. *Positional* holiness, where the Christian is seen to be "holy" in virtue of his being "in Christ" while yet inescapably sinful, but still under bonds to Christ to strive for full sanctification through the means of grace and obedience to the commandments.

F. *Experimental* holiness, as in the view of those who, treading a fine line between sinless perfection (which is repudiated as belonging only to Christ) and sinful perfection (which is rejected as not doing justice to the *release* and victory passages of the NT) teach the pure heart as now realizable, through the power of the Holy Spirit, in a communion with God in love.

Note: Those desiring to assess both sides of the question of whether the holiness of the believer, as viewed, for example, in the First Epistle of John, is at best but a religious ideal with exacting implications or is an attainable experience within the limits of human frailty should read R. N. Flew, *The Idea of Perfection in Christian Theology,* Oxford University Press, London, 1934, pp. 92-117; G. G. Findlay, *Fellowship In The Life Eternal,* Hodder and Stoughton, London, 1909, pp. 253-69, and Charles Gore, *The Epistles of St. John,* John Murray, London, 1920.

BIBLIOGRAPHY

HERE, Vol. 6, pp. 731-59; A. Koeberle, *The Quest for Holiness,* pp. 84-136; Harold Lindstrom, *Wesley and Sanctification,* pp. 120-25; W. E. Sangster, *The Path To Perfection,* pp. 113-17, 168-84; George Turner, *The More Excellent Way.*

PAUL S. REES

HOLY COMMUNION. See LORD'S SUPPER.

HOLY OF HOLIES. This, the sanctuary of Jehovah, could be approached only through the holy place, from which it was divided by a curtain. It was a cube (of ten cubits in the tabernacle, of twenty in the temple) and might be entered only by the high priest, and that on the Day of Atonement only. It was apparently completely dark (cf. I Kings 8:12) and its furniture was the Ark overshadowed by the cherubim of the "mercy seat," considered to be the throne of Jehovah. In the second temple it was completely empty. Heb. 9:4 considers that the altar of incense, though outside it, belonged to it. See also TABERNACLE.

H. L. ELLISON

HOLY SPIRIT. See SPIRIT, HOLY.

HONEST, HONESTY. The word *kalos* has various shades of meaning; moral excellence, sincerity and the sense of fairness in moral, social and commercial dealings. *Semnotēs* has the meaning of gravity or venerableness. It occurs three times in the Bible (I Tim. 2:2; 3:4; Titus 2:7). An honest man will automatically be grave in his bearing.

ALBERT VICTOR M'CALLIN

HONOR. The words *doxa* and *timē* express the sense of worth for both God and man. God in his holiness is to be worshiped and so receive the honor due to his name. Man, as a child of God, is precious in his sight and therefore is to be esteemed.

ALBERT VICTOR M'CALLIN

HOPE. *Elpis* (Hebrew *bāṭaḥ*) had in Greek and Roman times a neutral meaning as expectation of good or evil. Some, like Thucydides, treat it cynically, others, like Menander, extol it; Sanskrit poets class it among evils. Paul characterizes the gentile world as *elpida mē echontes*. For OT writers (except Ecclesiastes?) God is "the Hope of Israel," (Jer. 14:8). They trust in him (Jer. 17:7), wait passively upon him, (Ps. 42:5), or actively anticipate his blessing (Ps. 62:5). Some Israelites cherished materialistic hopes for a messianic kingdom; but the Anglican Article VII denies that the old Fathers looked only for transitory promises, since such as Daniel anticipated the resurrection (Dan. 12:2).

Christ himself is described as the Christian hope (I Tim. 1:1), and by his resurrection the specifically Christian virtue of hope is bestowed on the regenerate, who abound in hope through the Spirit (Rom. 15:13). (1) This hope relates to salvation and is an essential grace like faith and love (I Cor. 13:13); but where faith refers to past and present, hope includes the future (Rom. 8:24-25). (2) Its object is the ultimate blessedness of God's kingdom (Acts 2:26; Titus 1:2). (3) It pro-

duces the moral fruits of (a) joyful confidence in God (Rom. 8:28); (b) unashamed patience in tribulation (Rom. 5:3); and (c) perseverance in prayer. (4) It anticipates an actual righteousness (Gal. 5:5) and is thus good (II Thess. 2:16), blessed (Titus 2:13) and glorious (Col. 1:27). (5) It stabilizes the soul like an anchor by linking it to God's steadfastness (Heb. 3:6; 6:18-19). (6) It was generated in the OT fathers by God's promise first given to Abraham (Rom. 4:18), then embraced by Israel (Acts 26:6-7) and proclaimed by Paul as the hope of the gospel.

The one in whom hope is placed is sometimes called *elpis*, e.g., Jesus in I Tim. 1:1; the Thessalonians in I Thess. 2:19; or God in Jer. 17:7. Similarly the thing hoped for is *elpis* (I John 3:3; Col. 1:5), i.e., hope stored up in the heavens, expectation focused on the *parousia* and voiced in the cry Maranatha.

Elpis is a collective hope in the body of Christ. The Thessalonians are exhorted to hope for reunion with their deceased brethren (I Thess. 4:13-18) and ministers hope for their converts (II Cor. 1:7), desiring to present them perfect (Col. 1:28). Christ as the chief Shepherd expresses this hope that his own will together behold his glory (John 17:24), and this consummation is guaranteed by the earnest of the Spirit within Christian hearts and the church (Rom. 8:16-17).

BIBLIOGRAPHY
Arndt; *HDB*; *HERE*; *ICC* on *Romans*; R. Bultmann and K. H. Rengstorf, *TWNT*, II, pp. 515-31.

DENIS H. TONGUE

HOSANNA. The Greek form of the Hebrew salutation meaning, "Save now, we beseech Thee" (see Ps. 118:25). The six occurrences of the word in the NT are all in connection with the triumphal entry of Jesus into Jerusalem. The cry was taken up not only by the multitude that followed our Lord but also by the children in the temple (Matt. 21:9, 15). These Gospel references indicate that the expression, while originally a prayer addressed to God, also assumed the form of a shout of homage or greeting, equivalent to "Hail" or "Glory to."

The word Hosanna early passed into liturgical use in Christian worship as an interjection of joy and praise. It is thus found in the *Didache* (10:6) — "Hosanna to the God of David!" It occurs in the Latin Mass in a form which links it with the Gospel story: "Hosanna in the highest! Blessed is he that cometh in the name of the Lord!" On account of their association with the Roman dogma of transubstantiation, these words were omitted by the English Reformers from the Prayer Book of 1552.

FRANK COLQUHOUN

HOSPITALITY. In part the biblical practice simply reflects proverbial Eastern generosity toward strangers. Abraham (Gen. 18) and Lot (Gen. 19) are early examples. The law made special provision for the stranger (not merely the casual traveler, but the local resident who did not belong to Israel). He was to be treated on an equality with the Hebrew, both because of God's love for him and because of Israel's experience as sojourners in Egypt (Deut. 10:18, 19). He was to be loved in all sincerity (Lev. 19:33, 34). Hospitality could be demanded as a right (I Sam. 25:8). To proffer it freely and fully added to one's reputation for goodness (Job 31:31, 32). Occasional interference by outsiders with the protection offered to strangers brought resentment and punitive action (Judg. 19-20).

Consonant with this historical background, Jesus bade his disciples go forth without special provision, counting on entertainment along the way (Mark 6:7-13). As bringers of good news and of healing for the body, the disciples had the more abundant reason to expect a cordial reception. This precedent doubtless set the pattern for the early church, which depended on hospitality both for its missionary expansion and for the entertainment of its itinerant teachers (Acts 9:43 — 11:18; 16:15; Rom. 16:23; Titus 3:13). The conversions of whole households to the faith is intimately connected with the reception of the servant of God into the home. Apart from the extension of hospitality the local church could not function, for the church in the house was the rule for the first two centuries.

The OT injunction to love the stranger carries over into the life of the church, where the emphasis is not so much on the duty as on the love of hospitality (Heb. 13:1, 2; Rom. 12:13). The word here is *philoxenia*. To be an overseer of the church one must qualify in this respect (I Tim. 3:2; Titus 1:8).

Variations from the norm are indicative of unusual conditions. Hostility to Paul at the time of his last journey to Jerusalem seems to be reflected in the care with which advance provision was made for him and his party, freeing the local church leaders of this responsibility (Acts 21:16). The highhanded conduct of Diotrephes in refusing to receive properly recommended brethren marked him out as a church "boss" (III John 10).

A hint that hospitality might become burdensome lurks in the injunction of I Pet. 4:9 to practice it ungrudgingly. In the second century the church found it necessary to lay down tests to separate true servants of the Lord from those who saw in Christian generosity an opportunity for support without work (*Didache* xi). Yet the church surmounted these irritations and continued to be notable for its benevolence to strangers of all types (Justin Martyr, *Apology* lxvii, 4).

Christian bishops took the lead in establishing hospitals (from the fourth century on), whereas at a later period monks developed the hospice, in connection with the monastery, as a refuge for travelers.

BIBLIOGRAPHY
B. S. Easton in *ISBE;* G. Bonet-Maury in *HERE;* D. W. Riddle in *JBL* 57:141-54.

EVERETT F. HARRISON

HOUR. In the NT the term *hōra* is used of a twelfth part of a day, of the period from sunrise to sunset (John 11:9; Matt. 20:1-12). The night was similarly divided (Luke 12:39; Acts 16:33; 23:23). For references of interest to different hours see Acts 2:15 (the third hour), Acts 10:9 (the sixth hour or noon), and Acts 3:1 (the ninth hour, the hour of prayer). The character of the NT revelation as a revelation in history is clearly indicated by its temporal setting, a setting often expressed by the term *hōra* (cf., e.g., Mark 15:25, 33, 34).

Special interest attaches to the use of *hōra* in connection with our Lord's "hour," the time of his death and the glory that was to follow (John 7:30; 8:20; 13:1; and see also John 2:4; 12:23-27; 17:1; Matt. 26:45; Mark 14:35, 41; and cf. Luke 22:53). The references to Christ's "hour" help to place his whole ministry in right perspective and point to the correct interpretation of his death.

The term hour is also used with important eschatological reference. It is employed, e.g., of the time when the exalted Son of Man will return (Matt. 24:36, 42, 44; 25:13; and see Dan. 7:13, 14).

BIBLIOGRAPHY
Arndt; Robert Law in *HDCG*; MM; Joseph Muir in *HDCG*; H. Porter in *ISBE*; Thayer-Grimm.

JOHN H. SKILTON

HOUSE (HOUSEHOLD). The words house or household usually represent the Hebrew *bayit* and the Greek *oikos* and *oikia*. The biblical usage may be classified as follows:

I. LITERAL. The physical building in which a family dwells is called a house (Gen. 19:2-4). The temple as the abode of God's presence is a house (Matt. 21:13).

II. FIGURATIVE. By extension the terms are applied to those who are united together with some inner bond of unity. A house or household, therefore, may include (1) the members of a family (including servants) who are living together and who recognize one head (Gen. 14:14; Heb. 11:7); (2) the descendants of a man (Gen. 18:19; Luke 2:4); (3) members of the same racial or religious group (Isa. 7:13; Jer. 31:31).

III. SPIRITUAL. The following may be cited as illustrations: (1) believers as "the household of the faith" (Gal. 6:10; cf. Eph. 2:19; I Tim. 3:15; Heb. 3:6; I Pet. 2:5; 4:17); (2) the family of God in heaven (John 14:1); (3) the believer's glorified body (II Cor. 5:1); (4) the whole church (Heb. 10:21).

There are outstanding theological problems involved in these terms, such as the debate as to whether "house" in such passages as Acts 16:31; 18:8 includes infants. The question of infant baptism is involved. Usage would surely seem to indicate that a "house" includes all who are in a family — regardless of their age. There is also the problem regarding the interpretation of "the house of Israel" in Hebrews 8:8 ff. (a quotation from Jer. 31:31 ff.). It would appear that there is reference here to the church, rather than the literal Israel.

WICK BROOMALL

HUMANITY OF CHRIST. The humanity of Christ is clearly taught throughout Scripture. It is *the seed of the woman* who is to bruise Satan's head (Gen. 3:15); in *Abraham's seed* all the nations of the earth are to be blessed (Gen. 22:18), and that seed, as Paul explains, is uniquely Christ (Gal. 3:16); the promised Messiah is to belong to the tribe *of Judah* (Gen. 49:10) and to be *of the royal line of David* (Isa. 11:1, 10; Jer. 23:5). Thus Matthew traces Christ's genealogy forward from Abraham, through David (Matt. 1:1

ff.), and Luke traces it back, through David and Abraham, to Adam, the first man (Luke 3:23 ff.). In accordance with prophecy (Isa. 7:14) Jesus is miraculously born of a human mother who is a virgin (Matt. 1:18 ff.; Luke 1:26 ff.; cf. Gen. 3:15). The incarnate Son does not, indeed cannot, cease to be truly God, but becomes at the same time truly man: he is now both Son of Man and Son of God (Matt. 16:13, 16, etc.). The genuineness of his humanity is further attested by his growth from infancy to manhood (Luke 2:40, 52), by his experience of temptation (Matt. 4:1 ff.; Luke 4:1 ff.; Mark 1:12 f.; Heb. 2:18; 4:15), of hunger (e.g., Matt. 21:18), of thirst (John 4:7; 19:28), of fatigue (John 4:6; Mark 4:38), of grief (John 11:35), of suffering and especially of death (see the accounts of his agony and crucifixion). It is important to notice that our Lord's humanity is retained after his resurrection (cf. Luke 24:38-42). His ascension into heaven is a *bodily* ascension and his return will also be a *bodily* return (Acts 1:1 f., 9 ff.). It is *the Son of Man* whom Stephen sees standing in heaven at God's right hand (Acts 7:55 f.). The famous *Tome of Leo* (fifth century) will repay study.

PHILIP EDGCUMBE HUGHES

HUMILIATION OF CHRIST. Jesus was constantly subjected to humiliation in his earthly life. He was born in a stable to a family in the midst of which he became intimately acquainted with the circumstances of poverty, and he belonged to a village of little note (John 1:46). Throughout his later ministry he was homeless (Matt. 8:20), and dependent on the charity of others (Luke 8:3; 22:11; cf. Matt. 27:59-60).

His acceptance of the call to fulfil his ministry involved him in misunderstanding with his family (John 7:3) and his friends who thought him mad (Mark 3:21), in rejection by his own village (Mark 6:3; Luke 4:28), in being officially regarded as a fanatical and blasphemous impostor (Luke 11:15; 15:2), and finally in desertion by his disciples who had constantly misunderstood him, and in betrayal by one of his intimates for a small sum (Matt. 16:22; 26:14-16, 69-75; Mark 14:50). What success or popularity he had was also humbling, for it ended soon in failure and bitter disappointment (John 6:66; Matt. 27:31). All this culminated in his being reviled, and spat upon and mocked (Matt.

26:67; John 19:1-5) and made to suffer shameful death by being crucified — to which his burial added the final touch.

This earthly career of humiliation (his *tapeinōsis,* Phil. 2:8) is regarded by Paul as the outcome and completion of his self-empty-ing (*kenōsis,* Phil. 2:6-7) as the Son of God in accepting the incarnation and the form of a servant of the flesh. His stooping to give low-ly service to his disciples and all men is a re-flection of his self-humiliation in coming into this world as Redeemer (Matt. 20:28; John 13:1-5). Such humiliation is an aspect of his self-identification with sinners, alongside of whom he had to stand in saving them (*note his baptism*).

His self-emptying involved not the giving up of his deity, but rather the veiling of it so completely that he appeared to many to have nothing divine about him (Matt. 11:25-27). Yet it is within and through this very form of humiliation that his glory is manifested (John 12:23) in such a way as to leave man able to come to faith without being overwhelmed by sight.

BIBLIOGRAPHY

G. Alexander in *HDCG;* A. B. Bruce, *The Humilia-tion of Christ;* K. Barth, *Church Dogmatics,* IV/1, pp. 157-211; H. Heppe, *Reformed Dogmatics,* Chap. XIX.

RONALD S. WALLACE

HUMILITY. In classical writings humility was despised as servile (J. B. Lightfoot, *Com-mentary on Philippians* 2:3), but it is given high place in biblical teaching and example, as in Abraham (Gen. 18:27), Moses (Num. 12:3), the prophets (Mic. 6:8), and John the Baptist (John 3:26-30). The NT brought *tapeinophrosynē* from obscurity (apart from cognates in the LXX Prov. 29:23; Ps. 130:2) into importance. Before God, man is humbled as creature (Gen. 18:27) and sinner (Luke 18:9-14) having nothing to boast in (Rom. 7:18; Gal. 6:3). Corresponding to the humili-ty of Christ in redemption (Phil. 2:8; II Cor. 8:9), humility is the essence of saving faith (Rom. 3:27). The Christian calling by the Holy Spirit (I Cor. 1:29-31) excludes all pride of race or religion (Phil. 3:4-7), social status (Matt. 23:6-11; Mark 10:43-45) or person (I John 2:16). Positively, Christ's teaching gives us a model of unselfconscious humility in the child (Matt. 18:1-4; Mark 9:33-37), and an example of it in selfless serv-ice (John 13:1-17; Luke 22:24-27). Christian stewardship involves taking all opportunities

as God-given (Luke 16:1-12; 19:11-27), and in such ministry for Christ humility is the keynote (I Pet. 5:3-6; I Cor. 15:10; Luke 17:10). Humblemindedness characterizes suf-fering (Job 1:21; Phil. 4:12; I Pet. 3:14, 15; 5:5, 7) and the proper fellowship of the church (Rom. 12:16; Eph. 4:2; Phil. 2:3; Col. 3:12). Only Col. 2:18, 23 alludes to a false humility, a misguided, self-conscious as-ceticism which reappeared in subsequent church history. Calvin (*Institutes* II. ii. 11; III. vii. 4; xii. 6, 7) should be noted for patristic quotations and a Reformed statement.

GEORGE J. C. MARCHANT

HYPOCRISY, HYPOCRITE. The NT concept of hypocrisy has probably been influ-enced by two sources: (1) the Hebrew *ḥānēp,* "polluted," "impious;" (2) the Attic Greek *hypokrisis,* "an actor's response," hence stage-playing or acting. Pedersen lists the root *ḥnp* among words which denote "antagonism to what is sacred" (*Israel,* Oxford University Press, London, 1940, III — IV, p. 271). In Job, where the majority of OT occurrences are found, the word parallels "all who forget God" (Job 8:13), "wicked" (Job 20:5; 27:8), etc. The LXX renders *ḥānēp* with a variety of words meaning lawlessness and impiety: *anomos* (Isa. 9:17), *asebēs* (Job 8:13; 20:5, etc.), *paranomos* (Job 17:8), etc. Occasionally *hypokritēs* is used (Job 34:30; 36:13). The RSV "godless" and "godlessness" convey ac-curately the OT idea that hypocrisy is not so much duplicity or insincerity as impiety and disregard of God's law.

In Christ's stern denunciations of the scribes and Pharisees in the Synoptics (the only NT occurrences of *hypokritēs*), the OT meaning "godless" is strongly felt, e.g., Matt. 22:18; 23:13 — 29, and 24:51, where the parallel (Luke 12:46) has "unfaithful." Furthermore, while Mark 12:15 reads "hypocrisy," Matt. 22:18 and Luke 20:23 have "wickedness" and "craftiness." As A. G. Hebert has noted, Jesus' point is not that the scribes were deliberately acting a part, but that, while outwardly re-ligious, inwardly they were profane and god-less (*RTWB,* p. 109). In Gal. 2:13 it is probably not so much acting a part as un-principled action that Paul condemns.

Elsewhere, the Greek idea of acting appears to be in the forefront. Hypocrite in Matt. 6:2, 5, 16 seems to mean play-actor as does the sole occurrence of the verb *hypokrinesthai* in

Luke 20:20. The adjective *anypokritos,* "genuine," "sincere," "without hypocrisy" (Rom. 12:9; I Tim. 1:5; James 3:17, etc.), also seems to reflect the influence of the Greek drama.

It is not impossible that both NT concepts "godlessness" and "play-acting" may be explained from Hebrew or Aramaic without recourse to Greek thought, for *ḥānēp* in the postbiblical period comes to mean hypocrite, flatterer, or insincere.

BIBLIOGRAPHY

Arndt; W. L. Walker in *ISBE.*

DAVID A. HUBBARD

HYPOSTASIS. The word is a transliteration of the Greek *hypostasis,* "substance," "nature," "essence" (from *hyphistasthai,* "stand under," "subsist," which is from *hypo,* "under," and *histanai,* "cause to stand") and denotes a real personal subsistence or person. In philosophy it signifies the underlying or essential part of anything, as distinguished from attributes which may vary. It developed theologically as the term to describe any one of the three real and distinct subsistences in the one undivided substance or essence of God (*q.v.*), and especially the one unified personality of Christ the Son in his two natures, human and divine. The classic Chalcedonian definition of God, one essence in three hypostases (*mia ousia, treis hypostaseis*), was unfortunately translated into Latin as "one substance (Greek, *hypostasis*) in three persons" (*una substantia, tres personae*). This not only confused threefold substance with the one *ousia* (Latin, *essentia,* "essence"), but the Latin word *persona* ("face" or "mask") sounded like Sabellian modalistic monarchianism to the Greeks! The Council of Alexandria (362) tried unsuccessfully to resolve the conflict by defining *hypostasis* as synonymous with the very different word *persona.* Although much confusion still reigns, orthodoxy has generally held to the one substance of God, known in the three persons of Father, Son, and Holy Spirit.

BIBLIOGRAPHY

H. P. Van Dusen, *Spirit, Son, and Father,* exactly reversing the usual approach to the Trinity; L. Hodgson, *The Doctrine of the Trinity;* C. C. Richardson, *The Doctrine of the Trinity;* C. Welch, *In This Name: The Doctrine of the Trinity in Contemporary Theology.*

WAYNE E. WARD

I

ICONOCLASM. The word, meaning literally "image breaker," was brought into popular use in the eighth century by Leo III. Legal sanction was given to the practice by the Synod of Constantinople (A.D. 745) on the basis of the Decalogue and NT teaching on idolatry. Many in the Eastern Church came to support Iconoclasm when they realized that both the Jews and the Moslems saw them as idolaters because of their use of images. Unfortunately these early Iconoclasts retained superstitious beliefs such as the use of the sign of the cross and intercession through saints. The Reformers were also iconoclastic but in a positive way, replacing the use of images by emphasizing the Scriptures and the doctrine of the priesthood of the believer.

BIBLIOGRAPHY

A. Harnack, *History of Dogma,* Vol. IV, pp. 320-30; E. J. Martin, *A History of the Iconoclastic Controversy;* P. Schaff, *History of the Christian Church,* Vol. IV, pp. 447-65.

WILLIAM NIGEL KERR

IDENTIFICATION WITH CHRIST. The theological doctrine of identification with Christ is derived from various Scriptures which regard Christians as being "in Christ." In a general way Christ is identified with mankind as the second Adam, and identified with Israel as the predicted Son of David. In these cases the identity is a physical fact. In contrast to these relationships the theological concept of identification with Christ relates a Christian to the person and work of Christ by divine reckoning, by the human experience of faith, and by the spiritual union of the believer with Christ effected by the baptism of the Holy Spirit.

Identification with Christ is accomplished by the baptism of the Holy Spirit, an act of divine grace and power sometimes expressed as being baptized into (*eis*) the body of Christ, the church, (I Cor. 12:13), sometimes described as being baptized into Christ (Gal.

3:27). This new relationship of being "in Christ" was first announced by the Lord to his disciples in the Upper Room in the statement, "Ye in me [en emoi], and I in you." (John 14:20). The new relationship of the believer in Christ is defined as a new position, "in Christ," resulting from a work of God. That it is more than merely a position created by divine reckoning is revealed by the companion revelation, "I in you." The resultant doctrine is embraced in the word *union* which is commonly taken as a synonym for identification.

Various figures are employed in Scripture to illustrate this union and identification. The vine and the branches is employed by Christ himself in John 15:1-6. Here the union is manifested by communion, spiritual life, and fruit as a result of the union of branch and vine. The branch is in the vine and the life of the vine is in the branch. Another figure is that of the head and the body (cf. Eph. 1:22-23; 4:12-16; 5:23-32). Here also there is organic union of the body and the head, depicting the living union of Christ and the church. Intrinsic in the figure is the thought that the identification of the body with the head does not imply equality but carries with it the obligation of recognizing the head as the one who directs the body.

Close to the figure of the head and the body is that of the marriage relation of Christ and the church presented in the same section as the figure of the head and the body in Ephesians 5:23-32. Here the relationship is compared to the identification of a wife with her husband stated in the declaration that they are "one flesh."

Various expressions are used to signify this identification. Most frequent is the terminology "in Christ" (en Christō), but others also are used such as "in" or "into Christ" (eis Christon), and "in the Lord" (en kuriō). Though some distinction may be observed between the use of the prepositions en and eis ("in" and "into"), the resultant doctrine is much the same.

Important theological truths are related to the doctrine of identification in Scripture. The believer is identified with Christ in his death (Rom. 6:1-11); his burial (Rom. 6:4); his resurrection (Col. 3:1); his ascension (Eph. 2:6); his reign (II Tim. 2:12); and his glory (Rom. 8:17). Identification with Christ has its limitations, however. Christ is identified with the human race in his incarnation, but only true believers are identified with Christ.

The identification of a believer with Christ results in certain aspects of the person and work of Christ being attributed to the believer, but this does not extend to possession of the attributes of the Second Person, nor are the personal distinctions between Christ and the believer erased. Taken as a whole, however, identification with Christ is a most important doctrine and is essential to the entire program of grace.

See also UNION WITH GOD.

BIBLIOGRAPHY

L. Berkhof, *Systematic Theology*, pp. 447-53; L. S. Chafer, *Systematic Theology*, IV, pp. 54-143; A. H. Strong, *Systematic Theology*, pp. 739-809; H. C. Thiessen, *Lectures in Systematic Theology*, pp. 370-73; J. F. Walvoord, *The Holy Spirit*, pp. 137-50.

JOHN F. WALVOORD

IDOL, IDOLATRY. The Second Commandment seems to be less concerned with man's inability adequately to represent God and more with the implications of his efforts. "Fertile Crescent" religion in the OT period was primarily the worship of the spirits controlling the forces of nature. Their representation, either by symbolic objects, e.g., the *maṣṣēbâ* and *'ăšērâ*, or by images, implied that the spirits were linked to and in measure controlled by the material things they governed. The imageless worship of Jehovah announced not merely that he was greater than nature but also that he was unbound by it. The majority of the Hebrew words used for the symbols of heathen or debased Israelite worship express loathing or contempt, a fact missed in our translations, and serve to condemn the worship behind them. See GODS.

This attitude lies behind the NT usage. Except in Acts 7:41 the stress is seldom, if ever, on the image but on the deity it symbolized. This enabled the writers in large measure to avoid using *theos* of the pagan deities. Eph. 5:5; Col. 3:5 do not suggest that any tangible object had become an object of greater desire than God, but that the creation was usurping the place of the Creator.

H. L. ELLISON

IGNORANCE. This term and its biblical equivalents denote a state of lacking either (1) factual information (e.g., Acts 23:5); or (2) the intention of performing an act having the character and consequences of the act which one actually does perform (as in cases of manslaughter, Num. 35:11, or sins of ignorance, Lev. 4:2; 5:18); or (3) spiritual discernment to "see" and grasp the divine revelation that confronts one (cf. Matt. 13:13-15). The first two sorts of ignorance reduce the wrongdoer's guilt. The third, however, does not, for it is itself culpable, being due to active unwillingness to know God (Rom. 1:28) and wilful suppression of his truth (Rom. 1:18), whether that of general revelation encountered via creation (Rom. 1:19-21) and providence (Acts 14:17), or that of special redemptive revelation given in God's historical dealings with his people (Ps. 95:10), in Christ (John 1:10-11), and in the Gospel message (Rom. 10:3; cf. 16-21). Such ignorance is not an unavoidable natural lack (else it would not be blameworthy: John 9:41a); it is a chosen and induced condition, caused by that hardening (q.v.) of the heart (Eph. 4:18) to which it in turn contributes. Those who perpetuate their ignorance by denying it thereby confirm themselves in the guilt of ignorance (John 9:41b); and the fuller the revelation of which they thus cultivate ignorance, the greater their guilt is (Matt. 10:15; cf. 11:20-24). Since actual light is given to all men, all actual ignorance of God is blameworthy (John 1:5). One way in which God begins to punish such ignorance in reprobates is by so acting as to deepen it (Matt. 13:12-13; Rom. 1:28).

As ignorance in face of an incomplete acquaintance with divine revelation may give way to knowledge (q.v.) and faith (q.v.) under the influence of fuller enlightenment, so sins committed in such ignorance, however grievous, are not unpardonable, but may be forgiven on subsequent repentance (I Tim. 1:13; Acts 17:30; 3:17-19; cf. Luke 23:34).

BIBLIOGRAPHY
James Denney in HDB, C. Harris in HDCG.

JAMES I. PACKER

ILLUMINATION. The word appears in only one instance in the AV (Heb. 10:32). The verb is *phōtizō* and is used of a general enlightening which Christ brings to all men especially through the gospel (John 1:9; II Tim. 1:10). It also describes the enlightening experience of conversion (Heb. 6:4), the understanding of Christian truth (Eph. 1:18; 3:9) and the searching character of future judgment (I Cor. 4:5).

Theologically, the word has been applied to various concepts. In the early church baptism was frequently described as illumination (e.g., Justin, *First Apol.*, chap. 61). A theory of inspiration is called the illumination theory and it regards inspiration "as merely an intensifying and elevating of the religious perceptions of the Christian, the same in kind, though greater in degree, with the illumination of every believer by the Holy Spirit" (A. H. Strong, *Systematic Theology*, the Judson Press, Philadelphia, 1907, p. 204).

Generally the concept of illumination is related to the work of the Holy Spirit making clear the truth of the written revelation. In reference to the Bible, revelation relates to the material, inspiration to the method of recording the revelation, and illumination to the meaning of the record. The unregenerate man cannot experience illumination in this sense for he is blinded to the truth of God (I Cor. 2:14). The believer was promised this ministry of the Spirit by the Lord before his death (John 16:13-16), and he can realize it even to the extent of understanding the deep things of God (I Cor. 2:10). While this illumination is a work of the Spirit it can be hindered by carnality in the life of the Christian, and thus is to a certain extent dependent on the walk of the believer for full realization (I Cor. 3:1-2) (cf. L. S. Chafer, *Systematic Theology*, Dallas Seminary Press, Dallas, Texas, 1947, I, pp. 105-13).

CHARLES C. RYRIE

IMAGE. The image of God is a recurring theme in biblical revelation. The image is man's unique endowment at creation (Gen. 1:26), sullied by the Fall but not destroyed (see MAN for the exposition of man in God's image; this article deals specially with Christ as the image of the invisible God). The Decalogue prohibited making graven images of the Deity. As Spirit, God is invisible and incorporeal, and cannot be localized in space and time; the unique bearer of the divine image, in the creature world, is man himself.

Since the universe was fashioned on redemption lines (Rev. 13:8), the image of God originally created in human nature doubtless anticipated the personal restoration of that image by the incarnate Son. Man as the crown of the universe was called into being by the word of creation, a word not simply instrumental (Gen. 1:3, 6, 9 etc.) but personal (John 1:3). The eternal Son was an active agent in the creation as well as in the redemption of man, and man is himself in some sense a mirror of the Logos (John 1:4, 9a). Yet the

Scripture always speaks of the Godhead, and not of the Son alone, when it specifies the divine image in man.

The eternal Logos unveiled the absolute image of God by himself assuming the form of man (John 1:14, 18). The doctrine of divine incarnation (q.v.) centrally means that Jesus Christ is the supreme revelation of God, the very image of the invisible Father: "He that hath seen me hath seen the Father" (John 14:9). That Jesus of Nazareth is the supreme and express image of God, and not simply a created image, is the clear teaching of Scripture. Older dogmaticians contrasted the divine image in Christ as *Imago substantialis*, with the divine image in man as *Imago accidentalis*. The term *eikōn* is used of Jesus Christ in II Cor. 4:4 and Col. 1:15-17, whereas Heb. 1:2 f. speaks of "the effulgence" of God's glory and the very image or impress of his substance. In context, these passages speak of Christ in his relation to the Father as the eternal Son, more than of his role as incarnate Redeemer; hence they support the doctrine of his essentially divine personality and pre-existent Godhead, being descriptive of the glory of his person. The passage in Hebrews employs the term Image much as John 1:1-3 and Col. 1:15-17 employ the terms Word and Son to designate Christ as the creator, sustainer and governor of all things.

Yet as incarnate Redeemer, and the bearer of a full humanity, Christ is the undistorted image of God in human nature. When the recreation of man is treated in the NT, Jesus Christ is consistently depicted as the prototype of redeemed mankind (cf. Phil. 3:21; Col. 3:10 f.). In and through the Holy Spirit, the risen and exalted Christ indwells regenerate believers, renewing them in truth and righteousness. Since Christ overcame sin in the flesh, and raised human nature to glory in his resurrection and ascension, fallen mankind again has the prospect of spiritual glory through a final and complete conformity to the image of Christ (I John 3:2).

See also CHRISTOLOGY.

CARL F. H. HENRY

IMAGO DEI. See MAN.

IMAGINATION. In contemporary usage this word conjures up visions of children happily transforming cardboard cartons into medieval castles, tree stumps into chargers and broom sticks into lances. Biblical usage conveys a very different type of experience. Of the thirty-six times the word appears in various forms, all but two carry a distinctly negative connotation. The word typically refers to schemes or plots, or some kind of evil intent. In the OT the principal words rendered "imagination" or one of its forms are *yēṣer* (5 times), *šerîrût* (9 times) and the verb *ḥāšaḇ* (8 times). A derivative of the latter, *maḥăšāḇâ*, appears three times. The second word is used mainly by Jeremiah (e.g., 3:17; 7:24). He uses it to convey a stubborn persistence in following one's wicked schemes or inclinations. *Ḥāšaḇ* stresses the idea of malicious plotting or cunning imaginings (Hos. 7:15). *Yēṣer* is a more general word, implying form, conception, imagination or mind. It is used to connote evil attitudes three times (e.g., Gen. 6:5) and is also used simply to refer to one's inner thoughts and motives (I Chron. 28:9; 29:18).

In the NT, the four words translated into some form of imagination are *dialogismos* (Rom. 1:21); *dianoia* (Luke 1:51); *logismos*, (II Cor. 10:5); and *meletaō* (Acts 4:25). These words appear closest in meaning to *yēṣer*, in that they all imply mental activity, such as to turn things over in the mind, meditate, imagine, reason, think, comprehend. As such, the terms in themselves are morally and emotionally neutral. But as they are used they indicate prideful, impenitent self-seeking. In short, "imagination" refers to a spirit of willful, persistent, disobedient self-seeking in the very face of God's expressed will and loving call to repentance and holy living.

LARS I. GRANBERG

IMITATION. The Greek verb *mimeomai* (compare English "mimic") and noun *mimētēs* are translated "follow, follower" in the AV but "imitate, imitators" in the RSV, except I Pet. 3:13 where the textual reading *zēlōtai* is adopted. Although found in pre-Christian writers among the Greeks and in Philo and Josephus, cognate forms occur only eleven times in the NT (all in the Epistles) and in the LXX (Wisdom 4:2; 15:9). The cognate noun *mimēma*, copy or image, not found in the NT (but in Wisdom 9:8, often in Philo and Josephus) expresses the basic biblical notion that man is God's child and reflects his attributes.

Accordingly Christians are to imitate not evil, but good (III John 11), Paul's conduct (II Thess. 3:7, 9; I Cor. 4:16; Phil. 3:17), the apostles, even as they imitate Christ (I Thess.

1:6; I Cor. 11:1), the heroes of faith (Heb. 6:12; 13:7) and God the Father (Eph. 5:1). In I Thess. 2:14 Paul commends the Thessalonian church for imitating the churches of Judea in steadfastness under persecution.

From these passages and more particularly from those indicating that man is made in God's image we derive the popular notion of imitating Christ (see Disciple, Following Christ). The sad facts of sin teach us all that God's image in man is either partially or totally destroyed (see Fall). But the Bible declares that restoration of the image is possible through Christ. Hence the desire to imitate Christ as the only exact and full image (q.v.) of God (Col. 1:15; 2:9). Likeness to Christ is achieved not by legalistically trying to mold one's actions after the divine pattern but by the inward processes of salvation which change heart attitudes, producing good works and Christlike virtues (Rom. 12:2; Phil. 2:12-13; Eph. 2:8-10). The image becomes more like Christ through our attending to him (II Cor. 3:18) but is not finally completed until we see him on the day of resurrection (I John 3:2; Rom. 8:29-30).

From the beginning many desired to imitate the Master, requesting, for example, a model prayer (Luke 11:1-4) which we still repeat today. This ambition prompted the zealous declaration of James and John that they could drink Jesus' cup and undergo his baptism (Mark 10:38-39). It moved Paul, as he sought to let the indwelling Spirit of Christ speak and act through him (Gal. 2:20; Phil. 1:21); so he exhorted others to imitate him even as he imitated Christ (see references above).

In Acts 7:60 we find Stephen imitating the dying words of Jesus (Luke 23:34). In Paul's letters the theme of exhibiting Christ's humility, sufferings and death constantly recurs (e.g., Phil. 1:29-30; 2:5; 3:10 ff.; Rom. 8:17, 18, 36) and Peter says explicitly (I Pet. 2:21 ff.) that we are to follow in Christ's steps in suffering and death.

In the post-apostolic literature there is a conscious effort to point out how the martyrs imitated Christ in their humility, in being betrayed, in their Spirit prompted utterances, and triumphant dying (e.g., Ignatius; Eph. 10:3; Rom. 6:3; Martyrdom of Polycarp 1:1-2; 17:3; 19:1; Diognetus 10:4-5). This literature fortified thousands who nobly imitated their Lord during the terrible Roman persecutions. When Constantine legalized Christianity "sec-ond quality" Christians flooded the churches and the imitation of Christ was confined more and more to the monasteries. Mystical experiences corresponding to those of both Christ and the saints multiplied, culminating in the stigmata of St. Francis of Assisi (d. 1226), a literal physical reproduction of the wounds of Christ. Such mystical experiences continue to our day. (On the subject whether stigmata are self-inflicted or supernatural or psychosomatic, see the discussion of "Stigmata" by H. Cowan in HERE.)

During the fifteenth century and afterward the quiet mysticism of Thomas à Kempis' book, The Imitation of Christ, influenced all branches of the church. In our time James Stalker's Imago Christi (1889) is perhaps the best, although In His Steps by Charles Sheldon (1899) has sold more copies. It is debatable whether John Bunyan's devotional classic, Pilgrim's Progress, should be classified here, but devotion takes many forms; consciously or unconsciously all of them reproduce an image of Christ in the devotee, more or less complete, more or less enlightened.

Modern psychology throws much new light on the perennial desire to imitate Christ by stressing man's need to identify the self with strong personalities (mother figure, father, saint, etc.) in order to build the personality, and by stressing the importance of the subconscious as a reservoir from which our actions rise.

BIBLIOGRAPHY
Arndt; W. Michaelis, TWNT, IV, pp. 661-78.

Terrelle B. Crum

IMMACULATE CONCEPTION. A Roman Catholic tradition that Mary was preserved from original sin. The tradition became a church dogma after protracted theological debate. Mary suffered the temporal penalties of Adam's sin, such as bodily limitation, sorrow, and death. But the active essence of original sin was excluded from the very moment of her conception. Mary was saved by the merits of Jesus. In her case, and in hers alone, the debt of sin was paid in order that the debt might not be incurred. Mary's righteousness consisted in sanctity, innocence, and justice.

When the Council of Trent (1545-63) pronounced on original sin, it added: ". . . it is not its intention to include in this decree on original sin the blessed and immaculate Virgin Mary, Mother of God. . . ."

Pope Pius IX (1846-78) in the bull *Ineffabilis Deus* (Dec. 8, 1854) defined the position as follows: "We declare, pronounce and define: the doctrine that maintains that the most Blessed Virgin Mary in the first instant of her conception, by a unique grace and privilege of the omnipotent God and in consideration of the merits of Christ Jesus the Saviour of the human race, was preserved free from all stain of original sin, is a doctrine revealed by God and therefore must be firmly and constantly held by all the faithful."

The Vatican Council (1869-70) intended to define the immaculate conception as a dogma, but time ran out.

See also MARIOLATRY.

BIBLIOGRAPHY

"Immaculate Conception," in *CE*; Pohle-Preuss, Dogmatic Theology, Vol. VI, Mariology, Chap. I, Sec. 1.

EDWARD JOHN CARNELL

IMMANENCE. Immanence is the counterpart of transcendence. Theologically, the former connotes an indwelling of God within the world and its processes, the latter the superiority of his existence above and beyond the temporal sphere. Pantheism (*q.v.*) which presumes to discover God in all things throughout the natural order, is a familiar form of the theology of immanence. Its effect is to identify God with the universe. In contemporary theology immanentism is most commonly discernible in the writings of those who, while seeking to avoid confusing the Creator with his creation, maintain that God's activity takes place solely within the normal course of nature and that his "creative" operations are discernible in the natural development of new organic forms in the supposed evolutionary process: divine action is viewed as being from within rather than from without, as natural rather than supernatural. The biblical viewpoint combines the concepts of immanence and transcendence: God is immanent in the sense that he is everywhere present (Ps. 139) and that the order of nature unmistakably reveals his handiwork and his eternal power and sovereignty (Ps. 19; Rom. 1:20); God is transcendent in the sense that in being and majesty he is infinitely above all that is human and temporal.

PHILIP EDGCUMBE HUGHES

IMMANUEL. This transliterated Hebrew name means "God with us." It is found first in Isaiah (7:14; cf. 8:8, 10); Matthew (1:23) applies the name to Christ. The name implies deity ("God") and incarnation ("with us").

The views that have been held regarding the prophecy in Isa. 7:14 are numerous. A brief summary must suffice here.

I. NON-MESSIANIC INTERPRETATIONS. These characteristically rule out the predictive element and apply the name to some child already born or about to be born of some Jewish woman. There is no unity of opinion regarding the child or the mother.

II. SEMI-MESSIANIC INTERPRETATIONS. These apply the prophecy to a child of Isaiah's time and also to Jesus Christ.

III. MESSIANIC INTERPRETATIONS. These views center the prediction in Jesus Christ.

Matthew under divine inspiration applies the prophecy to Jesus. The circumstances of the birth ("sign" and "virgin") point unmistakably to Jesus Christ.

BIBLIOGRAPHY

J. G. Machen, *The Virgin Birth of Christ*, pp. 287-316.

WICK BROOMALL

IMMENSITY. See ATTRIBUTES, DIVINE.

IMMORTALITY. The concept of immortality is expressed directly in the Bible only in the NT. The words used are: *athanasia*, *aphtharsia* and its cognate adjective *aphthartos*. *Athanasia* is the exact equivalent of the English immortality and it is used in I Cor. 15:53, 54 where it describes the resurrection body as one which is not subject to death: and in I Tim. 6:16, where God is said to be the one who alone has immortality. He alone in his essence is deathless. *Aphtharsia* has the basic meaning of indestructibility and, by derivation, of incorruption, by which it is rendered in the familiar resurrection paean in I Cor. 15:42 ff. in the AV. The translation *immortality* is used, however, in Rom. 2:7, where the reference is to the life of glory and honor to which the believer aspires: in II Tim. 1:10, where it is said that Christ "abolished death and brought life and *immortality* to light." The adjective *aphthartos* is used to describe God as not being subject to diminution or decay, (Rom. 1:23; I Tim. 1:17); or of things which are not perishable, such as the crown awarded to the successful Christian (I Cor. 9:25), the inheritance which is reserved for the Christian (I Pet. 1:4), the seed of which the Christian is born (I Pet. 1:24).

It may be said, therefore, that immortality

in the biblical sense is a condition in which the individual is not subject to death or to any influence which might lead to death. God is uniquely immortal in that he is without beginning or end of life and is not in any way affected by change or diminution. Man, on the other hand, is immortal only by derivation and when his mortal body has been replaced by one which is immortal. This article is concerned with human immortality.

The biblical idea of immortality thus differs from all others in certain important respects. One of these is that in non-biblical teaching man is inherently immortal. Another is that it is the spiritual aspect of human nature only which is thought to be immortal. The human soul or spirit survives death. A corollary of these two is that the human body is usually thought of as a kind of prison-house of the spirit, or, at best, as a very transitory part of the human personality. In biblical thought man is not inherently immortal; it is the whole man, body and soul, that is immortal even though the body must undergo a transformation in order to achieve immortality.

In the OT as well as in the New, man is a complete being only as his body and spirit are in union. He is then a living soul, or person (Gen. 2:7). While some have understood the Genesis narrative as teaching that man was created immortal and that sin brought mortality, it would seem better to interpret the account as teaching that man would have gained immortality through a period of testing in which he would be obedient to the divine commands. If death was the penalty for sin, life was to be the reward for obedience.

Throughout the OT the dead are described as going down to Sheol, a place of obscurity, forgetfulness and relative inactivity (Job 10:20-22, 14:13 ff.; Ps. 88:10-12 et al.). Sheol, however, was not outside the Lord's purview (Ps. 139:8; Amos 9:2) and it was indicated through some OT writers that there would be a deliverance from it (Ps. 16:10; 49:14 ff., Job 19:25-27). This deliverance would take the form of a resurrection (q.v.), though this climax of OT hope finds expression only in Dan. 12:2.

In the NT it is implied that OT believers did not have a full knowledge of the meaning of immortality, since our Lord Jesus Christ brought life and immortality (aphtharsia) to light through the gospel (II Tim. 1:10). Christians have been begotten in Christ to an immortal (aphtharton) inheritance (I Pet. 1:3, 4). The inheritance is described as one of glory, honor, incorruption (aphtharsia), and eternal life. To be without the life in Christ is not to have immortality, in the biblical sense of the term.

Immortality, for the Christian, involves the resurrection and may be fully attained only after it. While it is said that believers who have died are present with the Lord when they are absent from the body (II Cor. 5:8), they are nevertheless to be changed at Christ's appearing. Both those who have died and those who are alive upon earth will receive a body like the resurrection body of Jesus Christ (Phil. 3:21). Those who are the children of God will be like Christ (I John 3:2), perfected in righteousness (Phil. 1:6), from all sin, sorrow, pain or death (Rev. 22:3 ff.) and they will serve God continually.

BIBLIOGRAPHY

Arndt; S. D. F. Salmond, *Christian Doctrine of Immortality*; Jas. Orr, *Christian View of God and the World*, Lects. iv, v and app.; O. Cullmann, "Immortality of the Soul and the Resurrection of the Dead," *Harvard Divinity School Bulletin*, pp. 7-36; "Immortality and Resurrection," *Christianity Today*, vol. II, Nos. 21 and 22.

DAVID W. KERR

IMMORTALITY, CONDITIONAL. See ANNIHILATIONISM.

IMPUTATION. The doctrine of imputation is an important revelation of divine dealing with man. It is frequently mentioned in the OT (Lev. 7:18; 17:4; II Sam. 19:19; Ps. 32:2) as expressed by the Hebrew ḥāšaḇ, translated variously to impute, reckon, esteem, purpose, account, be counted, devise, think, etc., appearing over one hundred times in the Hebrew text. The doctrine of imputation is an important element in the sacrificial system of the OT. In the NT the doctrine is given extensive revelation in the Epistle to the Romans (Rom. 4:6-25; 5:13) and is mentioned in II Cor. 5:19 and James 2:23, using the verb *logizomai* in all passages except in Rom. 5:13 where *ellogeō* is found. The book of Philemon is a biblical illustration of imputation, "Put that on mine account" (vs. 18), where Paul assumed the debt of Onesimus.

In its principal meaning of "reckoning to the account of another," it is found in three theological connections in Scripture.

I. IMPUTATION OF ADAM'S SIN TO MAN. According to the argument of Rom. 5:12-21, the one sin of Adam was imputed to the race to the extent that "death reigned" (vs. 14), all were condemned in Adam (vs. 18), and all men were made sinners (vs. 19). The judgment "all have sinned" (Greek aorist tense) is based not on the individual experience of sin but on the imputation of Adam's sin to the race. Adam as the fountain of human life was representative of the race and his sin is the basis of divine reckoning of all men as sinning in Adam.

II. IMPUTATION OF THE SIN OF MAN TO CHRIST. In contrast to the imputation of Adam's sin to the race, often considered a *real* imputation, the imputation of the sin of man to Christ is considered *judicial*, and related to the death of Christ on the cross. Christ "hath borne our griefs, and carried our sorrows. . . . But he was wounded for our transgressions . . . the Lord hath laid on him the iniquity of us all" (Isa. 53:4-6). "Him who knew no sin he made to be sin on our behalf; that we might become the righteousness of God in him" (II Cor. 5:21 ASV). "Who his own self bare our sins in his own body on the tree . . ." (I Pet. 2:24). Though the word impute is not actually used to express this idea in the NT, the idea is clearly stated in other words.

III. IMPUTATION OF THE RIGHTEOUSNESS OF GOD TO THE BELIEVER. Embodied in the doctrine of justification by faith is the imputation of the righteousness of God to the believer in Christ (cf. Rom. 3:21 — 5:21). The righteous work of Christ manifested in his death on the cross is reckoned to the account of the believer as a gift of righteousness apart from human merit or works. The imputation of righteousness is a judicial act by which the believer is declared righteous before a holy God. Though this is accompanied by experimental sanctification, conversion, and other spiritual manifestations, in itself it is not an experience but a fact of divine reckoning. Believers are declared "justified by faith" (Rom. 5:1), and Abraham and David are cited as examples in the OT (Rom. 4:1-22).

The imputation of righteousness to believers in Christ is one of the most important doctrines of the NT and rests at the heart of the doctrine of salvation (*q.v.*). It is related to the believer's identification with Christ, his position in Christ, and his participation theologically in the substitutionary work of Christ. Though it is not his antecedently, it is reckoned to the believer at the moment of faith and becomes his forever by judicial declaration

of God. The righteousness thus imputed meets completely the demands of a righteous God, and is the sole basis for our acceptance with God.

BIBLIOGRAPHY

Article on "Imputation," ISBE, Unger's Bible Dictionary; L. Berkhof, Systematic Theology, pp. 237-43, 523; L. S. Chafer, Systematic Theology, II, pp. 296-315; A. H. Strong, Systematic Theology, pp. 593-637, 805, 862.

JOHN F. WALVOORD

INCARNATION. The words incarnation or incarnate do not occur in the Bible. Their two component parts, however, *in carne, (en sarki),* come several times in the NT, with a verb describing either the incarnation in itself or the work of the incarnate Christ. Thus, the Johannine Epistles speak of his "coming in the flesh" (I John 4:2; II John 7), Romans of his being "sent in the flesh" (Rom. 8:3), and the ancient hymn in I Timothy of his "appearing in the flesh" (I Tim. 3:16). On the other hand, the first Petrine Epistle says that he "suffered in the flesh" (I Pet. 4:1), and "died in the flesh" (3:18), Ephesians that he made peace by abolishing "in his flesh the enmity" (Eph. 2:15), and Colossians that "he made reconciliation in the body of his flesh" (Col. 1:21-22). But the central and most comprehensive verse is John 1:14, "And the word became flesh *(kai ho Logos sarx egeneto)."* We will explain *incarnation* by expounding these words.

1. *ho Logos.* The subject of this sentence, *ho Logos* receives its meaning and substance both from its object, *sarx,* and from the preceding verses. To him is ascribed eternity: "In the beginning was the Word"; relationship to the Deity: "And the Word was with God"; and quite bluntly and directly, Deity itself: "And the Word was God." He is described as the maker of all created things: "All things were made by him"; the possessor and imparter of life: "In him was life and the life was the light of men"; and as being the true light." Hence the *Logos* who became flesh was in himself eternal, God, the Creator, life and light. In considering the rest of the verse, we must not forget for one moment the identity and nature of this subject.

The prologue does not make the direct statement: "God became flesh." For although it declares that "the Word was God," it also suggests in the sentence "and the Word was with God," a certain differentiation, which is here only hinted at but will be explained by later references in the Gospel to the Father and the Son, the Son and the Paraclete. Nevertheless, it is perfectly proper and indeed necessary, while bearing such a differentiation in mind, to say with Charles Wesley, "Veiled in flesh the Godhead see! Hail, the Incarnate Deity!"

2. *sarx.* It is not easy to determine the exact significance of "flesh" in this context. In the NT it bears a number of meanings: for example, the actual physical substance comprising the animal body (e.g., I Cor. 15:39), or created life on earth (e.g., I Pet. 1:24, quoting Isa. 40:6 ff.), or man's existence as a sinner (e.g., Rom. 8:3). There is no doubt that *sarx* in John 1:14 includes the first and second meanings. The Word became a man. In other words, he had, as incarnate, the animal body of a man and also a human soul. His incarnate existence was subject to all the needs, limitations and sensations of human life. The humanity of Jesus must be given no less weight than his deity. As to the third sense of the word, the great weight of opinion has been against including sinfulness in the meaning of *flesh* here. The assumption of flesh by the Son of God involved a unity with sinful man sufficient for the bearing and destruction of sin, and able to do justice to such verses as Rom. 8:3 ("sending his own Son in the likeness of sinful flesh"), II Cor. 5:21 ("he hath made him to be sin for us, who knew no sin") and Gal. 3:13 ("Christ . . . being made a curse for us").

3. *egeneto.* This word must be taken in apposition to the four times repeated *ēn* of vss. 1-2. In the beginning the Word *was,* and *was* with God, and *was* God. But now the Word *became* flesh. That is, whereas the earlier verses had spoken of the continued state and activity of the Word, a completely new and different state and activity is now posited. The Word was God; the Word now becomes what he was not — flesh. Yet he became this without ceasing to be what he eternally was — God. Moreover, *egeneto* expresses the activity of the Word; not "was made" as in the AV, but "became." In complete and joyful obedience to the will of the Father, the Word freely became flesh for the sake of his loved creation. No external compulsion moved the Word to become flesh. He took our flesh of his own free will and deliberately, to accomplish our salvation.

BIBLIOGRAPHY

D. M. Baillie, *God was in Christ;* K. Barth, *Church Dogmatics,* I/2, chap. 2; J. Gresham Machen, *The Virgin Birth of Christ;* E. Stauffer, *Theol. d. neuen Testaments,* chap. 3; H. Vogel, *Christologie.*

T. H. L. PARKER

INCENSE. Incense or frankincense is the Hebrew *lᵉḇônâ,* a resin of a shrub about eight feet tall of the genus *Boswellia* growing in South Arabia and Somaliland. From the same area comes myrrh, an aromatic resin from the tree *Balsamodendron* Myrrha.

Frankincense was added to the meal offering and shewbread (Lev. 2:2-16; 24:7), but not to the sin offering or jealousy offering (Lev. 5:11; Num. 5:15). It was one of the precious gifts offered to the infant Saviour.

Frankincense with other spices was the incense (*qᵉṭōreṯ*) burned on the incense altar (Ex. 30:7; I Sam. 2:28). Arabian spice was important in antiquity. The temple incense was a special mixture for holy uses (Ex. 30:37). Its smoke symbolized ascending prayer (Rev. 8:3) and shielded the ark from view (Lev. 16:13). It was not used in the anointing oil (Ex. 30:23-25).

BIBLIOGRAPHY

Gus W. Van Beek, "Frankincense and Myrrh in Ancient South Arabia," *Journal of the American Oriental Society,* 78; 141-52.

R. LAIRD HARRIS

INDULGENCE. An indulgence, from the Latin *indulgentia,* kindness or tenderness, is defined by *The Catholic Encyclopedia,* VII, p. 783, as "a remission of the temporal punishment due to sin, the guilt of which has been forgiven." Whereas in Roman Catholic theology and practice both the eternal and temporal punishment due sin are remitted in baptism, only the eternal punishment is remitted in the sacrament of penance (*q.v.*). An indulgence actually provides for a change in the form of penance, the temporal penalty for sin.

A plenary or full indulgence cancels the accumulated temporal penalty for sin, while a partial indulgence specifies the limits of the remission. Indulgences are granted for many types of good works. In the first undisputed indulgence, Pope Urban II in 1095 promised that all who went to Jerusalem on the first crusade out of pure devotion could "count that journey in lieu of all penance."

By the fifteenth century indulgences were granted for the dead in purgatory by suffrage, and with the rise of the practice of granting them for money payments for worthy causes the immediate cause of the Protestant Reformation emerged. Since the Council of Trent, 1562, money payment for indulgences has been forbidden by the Church, although practice has not always conformed.

DONALD G. DAVIS

INFALLIBILITY. The word infallible occurs in the AV in Acts 1:3 with reference to the resurrection of Christ. There is no corresponding word in the Greek, however, and it is omitted in later versions.

That the revelation of God in Jesus Christ is infallible, in the general sense that it presents mankind with the infallible way of salvation, would be accepted by all Christians; but the seat of infallibility is a matter of controversy. Three main lines of thought may be discerned corresponding to the three main divisions of Christendom. The Eastern Orthodox Church believes that General Councils of the Church are guided by the Holy Spirit so as not to err; the Roman Catholic Church believes that the Pope is personally preserved from error by God; and Protestant thought relies on the sufficiency of Holy Scripture as the guide to God's self-revelation. We can relate these three theories in the following way. Christians of all traditions accord to Holy Scripture a unique place in the determination of the gospel, and there exists an extensive body of common belief derived from it. This common belief is further described and defined by the Councils held in the early centuries, four of which at any rate command universal approval. The Orthodox Church continues to rely on Councils, the Latin Church has finally come to define the seat of infallibility as the Papacy, while Protestants do not place their confidence in Councils as such or in the Papacy but look to the Scriptures as the ultimate source of authority. Particular attention must be given to the doctrine of papal infallibility, and the Protestant doctrine of the sufficiency and supremacy of Scripture.

The doctrine of the infallibility of the pope was defined by the Roman Catholic Church in the year 1870. It declares that the pope is enabled by God to express infallibly what the church should believe concerning questions of faith and morals when he speaks in his official capacity as "Christ's vicar on earth," or *ex cathedra*.

Behind this dogma lie three assumptions which are disputed by other Christians: (1) that Christ established an office of his "vicar" for his church on earth; (2) that this office is held by the bishop of Rome; and (3) that Christ's vicar is infallible in his declarations on faith and morals. The grounds upon which the church of Rome bases these assumptions may be summarized as follows: (1) Our Lord's saying to Peter recorded in Matt. 16:18: "Thou art Peter, and on this rock I will build my church," implies that Christ made Peter the head of the church, or his "vicar on earth." (2) Peter was bishop at Rome, and thereby constituted this see the supreme bishopric over the church, transmitting to his successors the prerogative of being Christ's vicar. (3) The vicar of Christ must be infallible by the very nature of the case. All three arguments are necessary to the doctrine of papal infallibility, and all three display a fallibility which makes it impossible for the Orthodox and Protestant churches to accept them.

When we turn to Protestant or Evangelical thought on this matter, we find that, in so far as it is used at all, infallibility is ascribed to the OT and NT Scriptures as the prophetic and apostolic record. It is so in the fourfold sense (1) that the word of God infallibly achieves its end, (2) that it gives us reliable testimony to the saving revelation and redemption of God in Christ, (3) that it provides us with an authoritative norm of faith and conduct, and (4) that there speaks through it the infallible Spirit of God by whom it is given. In recent years concentration upon historical and scientific questions, and suspicion of the dogmatic infallibility claimed by the Papacy, has led to severe criticism of the whole concept even as applied to the Bible; and it must be conceded that the term itself is not a biblical one and does not play any great part in actual Reformation theology. Yet in the senses indicated it is well adapted to bring out the authority and authenticity of Scripture. The church accepts and preserves the infallible word as the true standard of its apostolicity; for the word itself, i.e., Holy Scripture, owes its infallibility, not to any intrinsic or independent quality, but to the divine Subject and Author to whom the term infallibility may properly be applied.

BIBLIOGRAPHY

W. T. Curtis in *HERE*; G. Salmon, *The Infallibility of the Church*; B. B. Warfield, *The Inspiration and Authority of the Bible*.

W. C. G. PROCTOR

INFANT BAPTISM. See BAPTISM, INFANT.

INFANT SALVATION. The possibility of the salvation of infants was recognized from the earliest times of the NT church, Irenaeus, for instance, includes "infants and children" among those whom Christ came to save. The changing doctrine of the church, whereby the kingdom of God was identified with the external church, and the widespread acceptance of the belief that outside the visible church there could be no salvation, gave rise to the doctrine that baptism, the sacrament of admission to the external church, was necessary to salvation. No unbaptized infant therefore could be saved, although, in the view of medieval churchmen, the sufferings of lost infants are less intense than those of lost adults. Furthermore, Thomas Aquinas and others admitted the possibility that still-born infants of Christian parents might, in the grace of God, be sanctified and saved in a way unknown to us.

The Council of Trent, which defined the position of the papal church as against the Protestant position, committed the Church of Rome to the view that infants dying unbaptized were damned, although it did not express a definite view as of the kind and degree of their punishment. Moreover, the belief was expressed that the desire and intention of godly parents to have their children baptized might be accepted in lieu of actual baptism in the case of still-born babes. Eusebius Amort (1758) taught that God might be moved by prayer to grant salvation to such infants extra-sacramentally. The inconclusiveness of the Tridentine declarations leaves the way open for widely differing conceptions as to what is to be understood by the exclusion of unbaptized children from heaven.

The Augsburg Confession commits Lutheranism to the view that baptism is necessary to salvation, although, in modification of this position, Lutheran theologians have taught that "the necessity of baptism is not intended to be equalized with that of the Holy Ghost." Luther believed that God would accept the intention to baptize the infant in lieu of actual baptism where circumstances made the latter impossible. Later Lutherans adopt the more cautious attitude that it would be wrong to assume that all unbaptized infants, including children of those who are outside the church, are lost. While not committing themselves to a belief in the salvation of all children dying in infancy, they tend to regard it as an uncontradicted hope.

The Reformed doctrine of the church carried with it a distinctive doctrine of infant salvation. The church of Christ being, not an external organization, but the true people of God everywhere, it follows that membership in this community is acquired, not by the external act of baptism, but by the internal action of the Holy Spirit in regenerating the soul. Zwingli took the position that all children of believers dying in infancy are saved, for they were born within the covenant, the promise being to believers and to their children (Acts 2:39). He even inclined to the view that all children dying in infancy are elect and saved. John Owen, a good spokesman of Puritan Calvinism, expresses the belief that infants may have an interest in the covenant even through more remote forebears than parents. And, since the grace of God is free and not tied to any condition, he has no doubt that many infants are saved whose parents are not believers. Whatever differing shades of opinion may be found in Reformed teaching with regard to infant salvation, their Reformed Confessions agree in teaching the possibility of infants being saved "by Christ through the Spirit, who worketh when, and where, and how he pleaseth" (*Westminster Confession*). They do not give confessional authority to the Zwinglian supposition that death in infancy may be taken as a sign of election, and thus of salvation, but with reverent caution assert that only for which they can claim the clear authority of Holy Scripture, namely, that all elect children shall be saved by God's mysterious working in their hearts although they are incapable of the response of faith. They have no claim, in themselves, to salvation, but are, as in the case of saved adults, the subjects of the sovereign election of grace, and the purchase of the redeeming blood of Christ.

BIBLIOGRAPHY

A. A. Hodge, *Class Book on the Confession of Faith*, pp. 174-75; B. B. Warfield, *Studies in Theology*, pp. 411-44; Charles Hodge, *Systematic Theology*, i. pp. 26-27.

GEORGE N. M. COLLINS

INFINITE, INFINITY. See GOD.

INFRALAPSARIANISM. See PREDESTINATION.

INHERITANCE. See Heir.

INIQUITY. See Sin.

INSPIRATION. The theological idea of inspiration, like its correlative revelation, presupposes a personal mind and will — in Hebrew terminology, the "living God" — acting to communicate with other spirits. The Christian belief in inspiration, not alone in revelation, rests both on explicit biblical assertions and on the pervading mood of the scriptural record.

I. Biblical Terminology. Today the English verb and noun inspire and inspiration bear many meanings. This diverse connotation is already present in the Latin *inspiro* and *inspiratio* of the Vulgate Bible. But the technical theological sense of inspiration, largely lost in the secular atmosphere of our time, is clearly asserted by the Scriptures with a special view to the sacred writers and their writings. Defined in this sense, inspiration is a supernatural influence of the Holy Spirit upon divinely chosen men in consequence of which their writings become trustworthy and authoritative.

In the AV the noun appears twice: Job 32:8, "But there is a spirit in man; and the inspiration of the Almighty giveth them understanding"; and II Tim. 3:16, "All scripture is given by inspiration of God, and is profitable for doctrine, for reproof, for correction, for instruction in righteousness." In the former instance, both the ASV and the RSV substitute "breath" for "inspiration," an interchange which serves to remind us of the dramatic fact that the Scriptures refer the creation of the universe (Ps. 33:6), the creation of man for fellowship with God (Gen. 2:7) and the production of the sacred writings (II Tim. 3:16) to the spiration of God. In the latter instance, the ASV renders the text "Every scripture inspired of God is also profitable . . .," a translation abandoned as doubtful by the RSV, "All scripture is inspired by God and profitable. . . ."

II. Biblical Teaching. Although the term "inspiration" is of spotty occurrence in modern versions and paraphrases, the conception itself remains firmly embedded in the scriptural teaching. The word *theopneustos* (II Tim. 3:16), literally God-"spirated" or breathed out, affirms that the living God is the author of Scripture, and that Scripture is the product of his creative breath. The biblical sense, therefore, rises above the modern tendency to assign the term "inspiration" merely a dynamic or functional significance (largely through a critical dependence on Schleiermacher's artificial disjunction that God communicates life, not truths about himself). Geoffrey W. Bromiley, translator of Karl Barth's *Church Dogmatics,* points out that whereas Barth emphasizes the "inspiring" of Scripture, that is, its present use by the Holy Spirit towards hearers and readers, the Bible itself begins further back with the very "inspiredness" of the sacred writings. The writings themselves, as an end-product, are assertedly God-breathed. Precisely this conception of inspired *writings,* and not simply of inspired *men,* sets the biblical conception of inspiration pointedly over against pagan representations of inspiration in which heavy stress is placed on the subjective psychological mood and condition of those individuals overmastered by divine afflatus.

While the Pauline passage already noted lays proximate emphasis on the spiritual value of Scripture, it conditions this unique ministry upon a divine origin, in direct consequence of which the sacred record is profitable (cf. *ōpheleō,* "to advantage") for teaching, reproof, correction, and instruction in righteousness. The apostle Paul does not hestitate to speak of the sacred Hebrew writings as the veritable "oracles of God" (Rom. 3:2). James S. Stewart does not overstate the matter when he asserts that Paul as a Jew and later as a Christian held the high view that "every word" of the OT was "the authentic voice of God" (*A Man in Christ,* Hodder and Stoughton, London, 1935, p. 39).

Emphasis on the divine origin of Scripture is found also in the Petrine writings. The "word of prophecy" is declared to be "more sure" than that even of the eyewitnesses of Christ's glory (II Pet. 1:17 ff.). A supernatural quality all its own, therefore, inheres in Scripture. While involving the instrumentality of "holy men," Scripture is affirmed nonetheless to owe its origin not to human but to divine initiative in a series of statements whose proximate emphasis is the reliability of Scripture: 1. "No prophecy of scripture is of any private interpretation" (RSV, ". . . is a matter of one's own interpretation"). Although the passage is somewhat obscure, it provides no support for the Roman Catholic view that the ordinary believer cannot confidently interpret the Bible but requires a dependence on the teaching ministry of the church. While theologically acceptable, the Scofield Reference Bible comment that no individual verse is self-sufficient but the sense of Scripture as a whole is necessary, is exegetically irrelevant. Everett F. Harrison notes that *ginetai* has the meaning of "emerging," compatibly with 1:21, and that *epilyseōs* may point to origination rather than to interpretation of Scripture. But the emphasis here may fall on divine illumination as the necessary corollary of divine inspiration so that, while the sense of Scripture is objectively given and determinable by exegesis, it must be discriminated nonetheless by the aid of the same Spirit by whom it was first communicated. In any event, the text precludes identifying the content of Scripture as an original product of the human writers. 2. "Prophecy came not in old time by the will of man" (RSV, "no prophecy ever came by the impulse of man"). If the previous passage denies man's ultimate right to interpret Scripture, the present declaration emphatically denies the dependence of Scripture upon human initiative for its origin. 3. "Holy men of God spake . . . moved by the Holy Ghost." The RSV strengthens the divine quality of the sacred words: ". . . men moved by the Holy Spirit spoke from God." Only through a determining and constraining influence of the Holy Spirit did the human agents actualize the divine initiative. The word translated "moved" is *pherō* (literally, "to bear along," "to carry"), and implies an activity more specific than mere guidance or direction.

III. JESUS' VIEW OF SCRIPTURE. If the passages already cited indicate something not only of the nature but of the extent of inspiration ("all scripture"; "the word of prophecy," elsewhere a summary term for the entirety of Scripture), a verse from the Johannine writings indicates something of the intensity of inspiration and at the same time enables us to contemplate Jesus' view of Scripture. In John 10:34 f., Jesus singles out an obscure passage in the Psalms ("ye are gods," Ps. 82:6) to reinforce the point that "the Scripture cannot be broken." The reference is doubly significant because it also discredits the modern bias against identifying Scripture as the word of God, on the ground that this assertedly dishonors the supreme revelation of God in the incarnate Christ. But in John 10:35 Jesus of Nazareth, while speaking of himself as indeed the one "the Father consecrated and sent into the world," nonetheless refers to those in a past dispensation "to whom the word of God

came (and scripture cannot be broken)." The unavoidable implication is that the whole of Scripture is of irrefragable authority.

This is the viewpoint also of the Sermon on the Mount reported in Matthew's Gospel: "Think not that I have come to abolish the law and the prophets; I have come not to abolish them but to fulfill them. For truly, I say to you, till heaven and earth pass away, not an iota, not a dot, will pass from the law until all is accomplished. Whoever then relaxes one of the least of these commandments and teaches men so, shall be called least in the kingdom of heaven. . . ." (Matt. 5:17 ff., RSV). Attempts to turn the repeated declarations, "You have heard that it was said . . . But I say to you" into a sustained criticism of the Mosaic law have not made their case convincingly against the probability that Jesus' protest is leveled rather against traditional reductions of the actual claim and inner intention of that law. Indeed, the necessary fulfillment of all that is written is a frequent theme on our Lord's lips (Matt. 26:31; 26:54; Mark 9:12 f.; 14:19, 27; John 13:18; 17:12). Whoever searches the Gospel narratives faithfully in view of Jesus' attitude toward the sacred writings will be driven again and again to the conclusion of Reinhold Seeberg: "Jesus himself describes and employs the Old Testament as an infallible authority (e.g., Matt. 5:17; Luke 24:44)" (*Text-Book of the History of Doctrine*, Baker Book House, Grand Rapids, 1952, Vol. I, p. 82).

IV. OLD TESTAMENT VIEW. Both in speech and writing the OT prophets are marked off by their unswerving assurance that they were spokesmen for the living God. They believed that the truths they uttered about the Most High and his works and will, and the commands and exhortations they voiced in his name, derived their origin from him and carried his authority. The constantly repeated formula "thus saith the Lord" is so characteristic of the prophets as to leave no doubt that they considered themselves chosen agents of the divine self-communication. Emil Brunner acknowledges that in "the words of God which the Prophets proclaim as those which they have received directly from God, and have been commissioned to repeat, as they have received them . . . perhaps we find the closest analogy to the meaning of the theory of verbal inspiration" (*Revelation and Reason*, tr. by Olive Wyon, Westminster Press, Philadelphia,

1946, p. 122, n. 9). Whoever impugns the confidence of the prophets that they were instruments of the one true God in their disclosure of truths about his nature and dealings with man is driven, consistently if not necessarily, to the only possible alternative of their delusion.

From this same prophetic tradition it is impossible to detach Moses. Himself a prophet, rightly called "the founder of prophetic religion," he mediates the law and the priestly and sacrificial elements of revealed religion in the firm belief that he promulgates the veritable will of Jehovah. God will be the prophet's mouth (Ex. 4:14 ff.); Moses is to be God, as it were, to the prophet (Ex. 7:1).

V. THE OLD AND THE NEW. The NT observations about Scripture apply primarily, of course, to the OT writings, which existed in the form of a unitary canon. But the apostles extended the traditional claim to divine inspiration. Jesus their Lord had not only validated the conception of a unique and authoritative corpus of sacred writings, but spoke of a further ministry of teaching by the Spirit (John 14:26; 16:13). The apostles assert confidently that they thus speak by the Spirit (I Pet. 1:12). They ascribe both the form and matter of their teaching to him (I Cor. 2:13). They not only assume a divine authority (I Thess. 4:2, 14; II Thess. 3:6, 12), but they make acceptance of their written commands a test of spiritual obedience (I Cor. 14:37). They even refer to each other's writings with the same regard as for the OT (cf. the identification in I Tim. 5:18 of a passage from Luke's Gospel, "The labourer is worthy of his hire" [Luke 10:7] as Scripture, and the juxtaposition of the Pauline epistles in II Pet. 3:16 with "the other scriptures").

VI. HISTORICAL VIEW. The traditional theory — that the Bible as a whole and in every part is the word of God written — held currency until the rise of modern critical theories a century ago. W. Sanday, affirming that the high view was the common Christian belief in the middle of the last century, comments that this view is "substantially not very different from that . . . held two centuries after the Birth of Christ," indeed, that "the same attributes" were predicated of the OT before the New (*Inspiration,* Longmans, Green, and Co., London, 1903, pp. 392 f.). Bromiley notes certain rationalizing tendencies that have arisen on the rim of the high view:

the Pharisees' rejection of Jesus of Nazareth as the promised Messiah despite their formal acknowledgment of the divine inspiration of Scripture; the attribution of inspiration to the vowel points and punctuation by 17th century Lutheran dogmaticians; and a depreciation (e.g., in the Middle Ages) of the role of illumination in the interpretation of Scripture ("The Church Doctrine of Inspiration" in *Revelation and the Bible,* Carl F. H. Henry, ed., Baker Book House, Grand Rapids, Michigan, 1959, pp. 213 ff.). The Protestant Reformers guarded their view of the Bible from the errors of rationalism and mysticism. To prevent Christianity's decline to mere metaphysics, they stressed that the Holy Spirit alone gives life. And to prevent decline of the Christian religion to formless mysticism, they emphasized the Scriptures as the only trustworthy source of the knowledge of God and his purposes. The historic evangelical view affirms that alongside the special divine revelation in saving acts, God's disclosure has taken the form also of truths and words. This revelation is communicated in a restricted canon of trustworthy writings, deeding fallen man an authentic exposition of God and his relations with man. Scripture itself is viewed as an integral part of God's redemptive activity, a special form of revelation, a unique mode of divine disclosure. In fact, it becomes a decisive factor in God's redemptive activity, interpreting and unifying the whole series of redemptive deeds, and exhibiting their divine meaning and significance.

VI. CRITICAL THEORIES. The post-evolutionary criticism (*q.v.*) of the Bible carried on by Julius Wellhausen and other modern scholars narrowed the traditional confidence in infallibility by excluding matters of science and history. How much was at stake in a weakening of trust in the historical reliability of Scripture was not at first obvious to those who placed the emphasis on reliability of the Bible in matters of faith and practice. For no distinction between historical and doctrinal matters is set up by the NT view of inspiration. No doubt this is due to the fact that the OT history is viewed as the unfolding of God's saving revelation; the historical elements are a central aspect of the revelation. It was soon apparent that scholars who abandoned the trustworthiness of biblical history had furnished an entering wedge for the abandonment of doctrinal elements. Theoretically such an outcome might perhaps have been avoided by an act of will, but in practice it was not. William Newton Clark's *The Use of the Scriptures in Theology* (1905) yielded biblical theology and ethics to the critics as well as biblical science and history, but reserved the teaching of Jesus Christ as authentic. British scholars went further. Since Jesus' endorsement of creation, the patriarchs, Moses and the giving of the law, involved him in an acceptance of biblical science and history, some influential critics accepted only the theological and moral teaching of Jesus. Contemporaries swiftly erased even this remainder, asserting Jesus' theological fallibility. Actual belief in Satan and demons was insufferable to the critical mind, and must therefore invalidate his theological integrity, while the feigned belief in them (as a concession to the times) would invalidate his moral integrity. Yet Jesus had represented his whole ministry as a conquest of Satan and appealed to his exorcism of demons in proof of his supernatural mission (q.v.). The critics could infer only his limited knowledge even of theological and moral truths. The so-called Chicago school of "empirical theologians" argued that respect for scientific method in theology disallows any defense whatever of Jesus' absoluteness and infallibility. Harry Emerson Fosdick's *The Modern Use of the Bible* (1924) championed only "abidingly valid" *experiences* in Jesus' life that could be normatively relived by us. Gerald Birney Smith went another step in *Current Christian Thinking* (1928); while we may gain inspiration from Jesus, our own experience determines doctrine and a valid outlook on life.

Simultaneously many critical writers sought to discredit the doctrine of an authoritative Scripture as a departure from the view of the biblical writers themselves, or of Jesus of Nazareth before them; or, if admittedly Jesus' view, they sought to dismiss it nonetheless as a theological accommodation, if not an indication of limited knowledge. The internal difficulties of such theories were stated with classic precision by Benjamin B. Warfield ("The Real Problem of Inspiration," in *The Inspiration and Authority of the Bible*, The Presbyterian and Reformed Publishing Company, Philadelphia, 1948, pp. 169-226). This attempt to conform the biblical view of inspiration to the looser modern critical notions may now be said to have failed. The contemporary revolt strikes more deeply. It attacks the historic view of revelation as well as of inspiration, affirming in deference to the dialectical philosophy that divine revelation does not assume the form of concepts and words — a premise that runs directly counter to the biblical witness.

Whatever must be said for the legitimate rights of criticism, it remains a fact that biblical criticism has met the test of objective scholarship with only qualified success. Higher criticism has shown itself far more efficient in creating a naive faith in the existence of manuscripts for which there is no overt evidence (e.g., J, E, P, D, Q, first-century non-supernaturalistic "gospels" and second-century supernaturalistic redactions) than in sustaining the Christian community's confidence in the only manuscripts the church has received as a sacred trust. Perhaps the most significant gain in our generation is the new disposition to approach Scripture in terms of primitive witness instead of remote reconstruction.

While it can shed no additional light on the mode of the Spirit's operation on the chosen writers, biblical criticism may provide a commentary on the nature and extent of that inspiration, and on the range of the trustworthiness of Scripture. The admittedly biblical view has been assailed in our generation especially by an appeal to such textual phenomena of Scripture as the Synoptic problem, and apparent discrepancies in the reporting of events and numbers. Evangelical scholars have recognized the danger of imputing twentieth-century scientific criteria to the biblical writers. They have noted also that the OT canon so unqualifiedly endorsed by Jesus contains many of the difficulties of the Synoptic problem in the features of the books of Kings and Chronicles. And they concede the proper role of an inductive study of the actual phenomena of Scripture in detailing the doctrine of inspiration derived from the teaching of the Bible.

See also REVELATION.

BIBLIOGRAPHY
Karl Barth, *The Doctrine of the Word of God*; Charles Elliott, *A Treatise on the Inspiration of the Holy Scriptures*; Th. Engelder, *Scripture Cannot Be Broken*; L. Gaussen, *Theopneustia. The Plenary Inspiration of the Holy Scriptures*; Carl F. H. Henry, ed., *Revelation and the Bible*; Abraham Kuyper, *Encyclopedia of Sacred Theology*; James Orr, *Revelation and Inspiration*; N. B. Stonehouse and Paul Woolley, eds., *The Infallible Word*; John Urquhart, *The Inspiration and Accuracy of the Holy Scriptures*; John F. Walvoord, ed., *Inspiration and Interpretation*; Benjamin B. Warfield, *The Inspiration and Authority of the Bible*.

CARL F. H. HENRY

INTENTION. The Council of Trent stated the doctrine of intention in relation to the sacraments as follows: "If anyone saith, that, in ministers, when they effect, and confer the sacraments, there is not required the intention at least of doing what the Church does, let him be anathema" (Canon XI, Sess. VII). This was in condemnation of the view of Luther that the validity of the sacrament depends on the faith of the recipient and not on the intention of the minister, and did not touch on the various opinions held in the schools (see James Waterworth, *Canons and Decrees of Trent,* London 1848). After the council, Catharinus defended a view commonly held that, so long as the minister performs the external rite proper to the sacrament, internal dissent cannot invalidate it. The more common doctrine today is that a real internal intention is needed, but discussion of the problem is confined to Roman Catholic and Anglo-Catholic circles. Protestants are content with the very general consideration that ministrations are valid if not performed in obvious play or mockery.

RICHARD J. COATES

INTERCESSION. The Hebrew *pāga',* "to make intercession," originally meant "to strike upon." Later, used in a good sense, it came to mean "to assail anyone with petitions." When this "assailing" was done on behalf of another, its sense was "to intercede." The Greek verb for "to make intercession," *entygchanō,* appears five times in the NT (Acts 25:24; Rom. 8:27, 34; 11:2; Heb. 7:25). The noun, *enteuxis,* is found in I Tim. 2:1 and rendered "intercessions;" and in I Tim. 4:5, where the only possible translation is "prayer" — for one could hardly "intercede" on behalf of "meats" prepared to be eaten (I Tim. 2:3). The English "intercession" is from the Latin *intercedo,* meaning "to go (or pass) between." That "intercession" has a specific meaning is shown when Paul writes, "I exhort therefore, that, first of all, supplications, prayers, intercessions, *and* giving of thanks, be made for all men" (I Tim. 2:1). It does not signify praise or petition in general, but a heart concern for others in which one stands between them and God making request on their behalf. When it is used of Christ's mediation (to be treated presently) there is also the sense of "acting for others."

There is no instance of, nor exhortation to, intercession in the Wisdom literature of the OT, and there are not many examples of it in the poetical books (see Job 1:5; 42:8; Ps. 20; 25:22; 35:13). In the prophets there are numerous instances of intercession, even if those men were primarily spokesmen for the Lord. In Isa. 6; 25; 26; and 37, intercession specially figures. There are such prayers in Jer. 10:23 ff., and 14:7 ff.; in Ezek. 9:8; 11:13; and in Dan. 9:16-19. They are more rare in the Minor Prophets. Jonah makes no plea for Nineveh, although the Lord does spare it (Jonah 4). In Mal. 2:7 it is implied that the priests were failing to intercede. In Joel 2:17 the intercessory character of the priestly office is shown: "Let the priests, the ministers of the Lord, weep between the porch and the altar, and let them say, Spare thy people, O Lord. . . ."

It is in the historical books of the OT that one finds the most frequent instance of intercession. One instance is Abraham's earnest intercession for Sodom (Gen. 18:23-33). Jacob's blessing of Joseph's sons is of this nature (Gen. 48:8-23). Moses had a high view of the social character of faith, and that leader is found in the princely act of go-between numerous times. He prayed for the idolatrous Israel after they had made the golden calf: "Oh, this people have sinned a great sin, and have made them gods of gold. Yet now, if thou wilt forgive their sin —; and if not, blot me, I pray thee, out of thy book which thou hast written" (Ex. 32:31-32). Samuel too, as judge, priest and prophet, is frequently the peoples' advocate. All night he prayed for the sinning Saul, grieved but still tender (I Sam. 15:11).

Throughout the NT intercession is urged and practiced. Christ urged it even for those who "despitefully" use us (Matt. 5:44). He himself said to Peter, "But I have prayed for thee, that thy faith fail not: . . ." (Luke 22:32). His high-priestly prayer for the apostles in John 17 is a lengthy instance. In Acts the young church is frequently so engaged — for Peter (12:5-12), for Barnabas and Saul (13:3), etc. The Epistles are replete with it. In the NT the Holy Spirit also "maketh intercession for us with groanings which cannot be uttered" (Rom. 8:26). And Christ at the present time is in heaven appearing ". . . in the presence of God for us" (Heb. 9:24).

A study of intercession in Scripture specially points up at least a few things about this exalted privilege. One is its naturalness: for to pray for others is to a Christian like breathing. Another is that one really can be baptized into a sense of the plight of those he prays for: wince at the thought of their wounds, twinge with the imagination of their deep hurts. Still another is that one is not to pray for a mass of undifferentiated humanity, not simply for all kinds and conditions of men, but for specific individuals with their fears that taunt and their wounds that drip. Intercessory prayers, surely, have the odor of heaven on them.

BIBLIOGRAPHY

J. B. Bernardin, *The Intercession of our Lord*; Ll. D. Bevan, *ISBE*; G. A. Buttrick, *Prayer*; Madame Chiang Kai-shek, *The Sure Victory*; A. J. Gossip, *In the Secret Place of the Most High*; Georgia Harkness, *Prayer and the Common Life*; J. G. Tasker, *HERE*; A. C. Wieand, *The Gospel of Prayer*.

JOSEPH KENNETH GRIDER

INTERDICT. An interdict is an authoritative prohibition, in the Roman Church, debarring a place or person from divine service, the sacraments, and Christian burial. It was most common in the eleventh and thirteenth centuries under Popes Hildebrand and Innocent III who used it tyrannically. The faithful in the Middle Ages were filled with terror by it. They believed themselves cut off from the grace of God in life and death. Marriages were unblessed. Neither eucharist nor baptism conveyed a blessing. The interdicted regarded it as spiritual death. All this happened because a place or a person had offended the pope. England was interdicted in 1208; France in 1200.

ALEXANDER M. RENWICK

INTERMEDIATE STATE. By the intermediate state is meant that realm or condition in which the soul exists between the death (*q.v.*) of the body and the resurrection (*q.v.*). That such a state is a reality is acknowledged by practically all branches of the Christian church. Differences of opinion regarding it have to do primarily with the nature of the state, as to whether or not it is purgatorial in character, whether or not the soul may reform and repent, and whether or not the soul is conscious or asleep.

The Bible has comparatively little to say about the intermediate state, evidently because it is only a temporary condition. Rather it focuses attention on the return of Christ and the new era that is to follow. There are, however, several passages which teach that it is a state of conscious existence for both the righteous and the wicked. For the righteous

it is a time of rest and of blessedness and joy. And for the wicked it involves suffering. The parable of the rich man and Lazarus represents Lazarus as conscious and blessed in Abraham's bosom, while the rich man is in torment (Luke 16:19-31). While on the cross Christ promised the penitent thief, "Today shalt thou be with me in Paradise" (Luke 23:43). And John says: "Blessed are the dead who die in the Lord from henceforth: yea, saith the Spirit, that they may rest from their labors; for their works follow with them" (Rev. 14:13, ASV). See also II Cor. 5:8 and Phil. 1:23. From these verses we learn that after the death of the body the saints live gloriously in the presence of God and amid the transcendent splendor of Paradise.

That the intermediate state is sometimes characterized as a state of rest does not mean that those who have a part in it are idle or inactive. Rather in Scripture the word "rest" carries with it the idea of satisfaction in labor, or joy in accomplishment. All of the unpleasant features are removed so that the activity of the saints is no longer "toil" or "labor."

But even for the righteous the intermediate state is a time of imperfection, first, because the spirit is without a body, which for human beings is an abnormal condition; and, second, because the rewards promised to the saints are not given in their fulness until the second coming of Christ. See Luke 14:14 and II Tim. 4:8. The blessings of the intermediate state, great as they are, are to be looked upon as only an earnest and foretaste of the good things which are to come.

The life of man is thus represented in Scripture as falling not into two but into three states. First, there is the period from birth until death, which is life in the present world and in the natural body. Second, there is life in the intermediate state, which is life without the body. And third, there is life in the resurrection body and in the fulness of heaven (*q.v.*), which is the final and eternal state.

See also PURGATORY.

BIBLIOGRAPHY

G. Vos in *ISBE*; L. Boettner, *Immortality*.

LORAINE BOETTNER

INTERPRETATION (BIBLICAL). The books of the Bible are ancient books, reflecting social and cultural environments different from ours. In this respect they need to be explained for modern readers like other ancient writings.

I. GENERAL PRINCIPLES. Each biblical document, and each part of a biblical document, must be studied in its context — both its immediate literary context and the wider situation in which it appeared. This requires an understanding of —

(a) the structure and idioms of the biblical languages.

(b) the type of literature represented. Is it prose or poetry, history or allegory, literal or symbolic? Some literary genres found in the Bible have peculiar features (e.g., apocalyptic) which call for special rules of interpretation.

(c) the historical background. A sense of history, such as the biblical writers themselves had, is necessary for the understanding of their writings. The historical background of the biblical record is the whole span of Near Eastern civilization from the early fourth millennium B.C. to *ca.* A.D. 100, the changes within which from time to time were so sweeping that we cannot understand a biblical document if we relate it to the wrong period. An appreciation of this will save us, e.g., from judging actions of the Late Bronze Age by NT ethical principles. Again, the Book of Jeremiah may yield some devotional profit even when one ignores the revolutionary movements which took place during Jeremiah's ministry; but no one could expound the book without appraising those movements and their relation to the prophet's message.

(d) the geographical conditions. The influence of terrain and climate on a population's outlook and behavior patterns is highly important. The religious conflicts of OT times cannot be understood apart from some acquaintance with Palestinian geography. Baal-worship was the consequence of the fact that Palestine depended for its fertility on regular rainfall (cf. Deut. 11:10 ff.; Hos. 2:8; Jer. 14:22). Baal to the Canaanites was the rain god who fertilized the earth, and Baal-worship was a magical ritual designed to make the rain fall and the crops grow. So much, indeed, of the language of the Bible, literal and metaphorical, has direct reference to geographical conditions that an appreciation of these conditions is indispensable for understanding the language (cf. James M. Houston, "The Geographical Background in OT Exegesis," *JTVI* 86, 1954, pp. 62 ff.).

(e) life-setting. What kind of people were those whom we meet in the Bible? The effort to get under their skin and see life through their eyes is difficult, but it is necessary if we are to understand their actions and words, their loves and hates, their motives and aspirations. Here such a book as Ludwig Koehler's *Hebrew Man* (London, 1956) can be very illuminating; cf. also Eric W. Heaton, *Everyday Life in OT Times* (London, 1956); Alan C. Bouquet, *Everyday Life in NT Times* (London, 1953).

II. SPECIAL PRINCIPLES. Biblical interpretation involves not only the interpretation of the separate documents, but their interpretation as parts of the Bible; it involves further the interpretation of the Bible as such, and this involves an appraisal of the Bible. The Bible, the sacred book of the Christian church, records God's self-revelation to men and men's response to that self-revelation; it contains "all things necessary to salvation" and supplies the one trustworthy "rule of faith and life." We therefore expect to find such a unity in the Bible that each part can be interpreted in the light of the whole.

This position was accepted in traditional Jewish interpretation of the OT, where the Prophets and the Writings were understood largely as commentaries on the Torah. Alongside the surface meaning of the text (*pešāṭā'*) was the more extended application (*derāšā'*) which was sometimes rather far-fetched.

The NT regards the OT "oracles" as a unity, teaching the way of salvation and providing the believer with all that he needs for the service of God (II Tim. 3:15 ff.). The basis of this unity is that the men who "moved by the Holy Spirit spoke from God" (II Pet. 1:21) all bear witness to Christ. In the earliest Christian interpretation of the Bible the OT is related to the NT as promise to fulfilment. The promise is found in the histories which lead up to Christ as well as in the prophecies which foretell his coming; the fulfilment is found in Christ. The writer to the Hebrews contrasts the "many and various ways" in which "God spoke of old to our fathers by the prophets" with his perfect and final revelation in Christ (Heb. 1:1 f.). Paul traces God's dealings with the world through successive stages associated with Adam, Abraham, Moses and Christ. This conception of the biblical revelation as historical and progressive is fundamental; it goes back to the creative insight of Christ himself, in which are combined "a profound understanding of the essential teaching of the Hebrew Scriptures and a sure judgment of his own contemporary situation" (T. W. Manson, "The Old Testament in the Teaching of Jesus," *BJRL* 34, 1951-2, 332).

Biblical interpretation in the post-apostolic age is influenced by a Greek theory of inspiration which had as its corollary allegorical exegesis. If a poet like Homer was inspired, then what he said about the gods could be acceptable to thoughtful pagans of that day only if it was treated as a veiled allegorical presentation of truths otherwise perceived by philosophical reasoning. This attitude influenced the OT interpretation of the Alexandrian Jew Philo, and subsequently the biblical interpretation of the Alexandrian Christians Clement and Origen. To them, much in the Bible that was intellectually incredible or morally objectionable, if understood literally, could be made intelligible and acceptable if it was allegorized. By allegorization the intention of the Spirit who controlled the writers could be penetrated. But this approach actually violated the original intention of the Scriptures and almost obliterated the historical character of the biblical revelation. Over against the school of Alexandria (*q.v.*) stood that of Antioch (*q.v.*) which, while it did not completely reject allegorization, paid much more serious attention to the historical sense of the text.

The distinction between the literal and "higher" senses of Scripture developed into the medieval doctrine of the fourfold sense — (a) the literal sense, which related the things done and said in the biblical record, (b) the allegorical sense, which deduced doctrine from the narratives, (c) the moral sense, which extracted lessons for life and conduct, (d) the anagogical sense, which derived heavenly meanings from earthly facts. Water might thus mean (a) literal water, (b) baptism, (c) moral purity, (d) eternal life in the heavenly Jerusalem.

Yet much good work was done on the literal interpretation of the text in the early Middle Ages, notably by the school of St. Victor in France in the twelfth century.

The general effect of the Reformation on biblical interpretation was to emphasize the primacy of the literal sense, as ascertained by grammatico-historical exegesis.

But grammatico-historical exegesis is not sufficient for the interpretation of the biblical documents in relation to their place in the canon. Theological exegesis is also necessary, although it cannot override grammatico-his-

torical findings. Again, the place of the Bible in the life of the church has constantly added to it a wealth of fresh and practical meaning which the interpreter cannot ignore. (Cf., e.g., Rowland Prothero, *The Psalms in Human Life,* London, 1903.) But if such experimental application of any Scripture is to have general validity, it must bear a significant relation to the true sense.

One form of allegorization is typological interpretation, which involves the tracing of correspondences between the OT and NT so as to find the essential meaning of an OT passage in its NT counterpart. The NT writers, for the most part, resort to typology (*q.v.*) to illustrate points already established by more direct means (cf. Paul's treatment of Adam as a "type" of Christ in Rom. 5:12 ff.). The most helpful, and permissible, form of typological interpretation is that which, viewing the Bible as the recital of God's saving acts, discerns a recurrent rhythm in this recital. Israel's deliverance from Egypt, e.g., is regarded as foreshadowing the redemptive work of Christ, and the behavior of the redeemed people on the earlier occasion constitutes a solemn lesson for the redeemed people on the later occasion (cf. I Cor. 5:7; 10:1 ff.). But when one considers the lengths to which allegorization has been carried by Christian interpreters, one may admire the NT writers' restraint.

Our Lord's use of the OT may well serve as our standard and pattern in biblical interpretation; and Christians may further remind themselves that part of the Holy Spirit's present work is to open the Scriptures for them as the risen Christ did for the disciples on the Emmaus road.

See also EXEGESIS.

BIBLIOGRAPHY
 C. W. Dugmore, ed., *The Interpretation of the Bible;* N. H. Snaith, *The Distinctive Ideas of the OT;* B. Ramm, *Protestant Biblical Interpretation;* J. Weingreen, "The Rabbinic Approach to the Study of the OT," *BJRL* 34 (1951-2), pp. 166-90; B. Smalley, *The Study of the Bible in the Middle Ages;* C. H. Dodd, *According to the Scriptures;* H. H. Rowley, *The Unity of the Bible;* E. C. Blackman, *Biblical Interpretation;* L. Berkhof, *Biblical Interpretation;* R. M. Grant, *The Letter and the Spirit;* G. W. H. Lampe and K. J. Woollcombe, *Essays on Typology;* J. F. Walvoord, ed., *Inspiration and Interpretation;* J. D. Wood, *The Interpretation of the Bible.*

FREDERICK FYVIE BRUCE

INVOCATION. Invocation, in general, refers to the religious act of calling upon deity. The opening of many types of service is marked by a prayer of invocation in which God is called upon to bless and guide.

The invocation of the Holy Spirit in the Eucharist involves a difference in practice between the Roman Catholic and the Eastern Orthodox Churches. In the West the church holds that the bread and wine become the very body and blood of Christ at the words of institution, whereas in the eastern liturgies the change takes place after the words of institution when the Holy Spirit is invoked to effect the transubstantiation.

The invocation of saints, praying for the intercession of exemplary Christian dead, sprang up during the early centuries of the church and was sanctioned by the Seventh General Council, 787, and the Council of Trent, 1545-64. All branches of the Reformation rejected the practice in the sixteenth century, as stated, for example, in the Thirty-Nine Articles (XXII), "The Romish doctrine concerning purgatory, pardons, worshipping and adoration as well of images as of relics, and also invocation of saints, is a fond thing vainly invented, and grounded upon no warranty of Scripture, but rather repugnant to the Word of God."

DONALD G. DAVIS

IRRATIONALISM. Irrationalism (better, *non-rationalism*) is the philosophical belief which asserts that reality is contacted non-rationally. The Real is either supra-rational or trans-rational and requires, therefore, a non-rational approach to be contacted. The approach may be by intuition (Bergson), or the will (Schopenhauer), or by emotion (Romanticism), or by mysticism (Plotinus).

Irrationalism in theology is the belief that God is contacted non-rationally. Religious intuitionalism, mysticism, and existentialism are forms of theological irrationalism. Liberalism, rooted in romantic or pantheistic philosophy, has a strong overtone of irrationalism, as does much contemporary theology which has been influenced by Kierkegaard's doctrines of the dialectic and the paradoxical, and by existentialism's separation of existence and essence (also from Kierkegaard).

BERNARD RAMM

ISAAC. Of Abraham's several sons, attention focuses upon Isaac as the prototype of the heirs of the promise made to Abraham. "In the person of Isaac shall there be a posterity to thee [Abraham], which shall pass as such" (paraphrase of Gen. 21:12 in KD). The distinctive circumstances of his birth indicate the sole basis for enjoying the promises made to Abraham. Unlike Ishmael, whose birth was in the usual course of nature, Isaac was born in fulfilment of a specific promise of God (Gen. 17:16) and as the result of the supernatural working of God (Gen. 21:5-7). All the redeemed are likewise "the children of the promise" who accord with Isaac as "born after the Spirit" (Rom. 9:6-9; Gal. 4:28-29), because their position rests not on national standing but on God's gracious working to make them heirs according to the promise made to Abraham.

BIBLIOGRAPHY
HDAC, "Isaac"; P. Jewett, WTJ 17, 1-20.

DANIEL P. FULLER

ISRAEL. The word Israel is derived from the Hebrew root *śārâ*, bearing the intransitive verbal meaning "to strive," "to contend" (Fuerst); also "to wrestle" (Davidson); "to persist," "to persevere," "to struggle" (M. H. Segal, *Hebrew-English Dictionary*, Dvir Publishing Co., Tel-Aviv, 1938); and in Modern Hebrew "to wrestle," "to defeat," "to conquer" (Zevi Scharfstein, *Modern Hebrew Dictionary*, Shilo Publishing House, New York). Scripture unfolds Israel in terms of history rather than definition and employs the word with the following significations: (1) As the name divinely bestowed upon the patriarch Jacob after his striving with the "godlike being" (Hosea 12:4-5, Soncino Press, London) at the crossing of the river Jabbok (Gen. 32:29 [AV 28]; 35:10). The first named Genesis passage marks the initial appearance in Scripture of the word, which is interpreted as meaning "he who strove with God." The AV translation "as a prince hast thou power" is not supported by e.g., Gesenius, Rosenmuller, Soncino Humash. (2) The name applied collectively and nationally to the whole twelve tribes as the descendants of Jacob-Israel (Ex. 3:16), usually called *benê yiśrā'ēl*, "children (or sons) of Israel" and, poetically, Jeshurun (Deut. 32:15; 33:5, 26; Isa. 44:2) derived from a root meaning "to be upright." Jacob was the descendant of Isaac and Abraham, with which latter patriarch Hebrew biblical origins essentially begin (Gen. 11). The descent into Egypt of a group of Hebrews laid the foundation for the subsequent Exodus when the history of Israel as a *people* may be said to have begun. This people merged into nationhood forty years later when they crossed over Jordan under Joshua. An amphictyony of twelve tribes runs through the period of the Judges. The term Israel is used in record of triumphs by Merneptah of Egypt (*ca.* 1230). (3) The united kingdom developed under Saul, David, and Solomon (I Sam. 8 — I Kings 11; I Chron. 10 — II Chron. 9). A representative cross section from Jewish and non-Jewish sources yields the following admittedly approximate chronology: 1095-970 B.C. (Scroggie); 1040-937 B.C. (*JewEnc*); 1020-925 (Orlinsky); 1020-931 B.C. (Francisco); but Acts 13:21 should be a determinative factor in any computation attempted. The period under David and Solomon was Israel's golden era and it saw the erection of the temple at Jerusalem. (4) The name appropriated by the northern Israel kingdom formed by Jeroboam (I Kings 12:25 — 14:20) following the disruption under Solomon's son, Rehoboam. The northern kingdom had nineteen kings through nine dynasties; the bad character and rule of all resulted in the prophesied divine judgment when the kingdom was crushed under the Assyrians in 722 B.C. This narrower usage of the title Israel is found e.g. I Sam. 11:8; II Sam. 20:1; I Kings 12:16. There is no Scripture warrant for views expressed by Anglo-Israel theories. The so-called "Ten Tribes" were not "lost"; they were merely obliterated as a united people. Undoubtedly the majority of Benjamin, probably the entire tribe of Simeon, and that portion of Dan proximate to the Southern Israel kingdom were included in Judah during the currency of the northern kingdom (Duff-Forbes, *The Baleful Bubble of British-Israelism*). Chronology is variously computed as 975-722 B.C. (Scroggie); 937-722 B.C. (*JewEnc*); 922-722 B.C. (Albright); 930-723 (Thiele). The southern kingdom continued for 136 years after the northern kingdom's downfall or until 586 B.C. when the last king, Zedekiah, and the remainder of the people (except a poor remnant) were taken into captivity in Babylon by Nebuchadnezzar (II Kings 25). The southern kingdom had nineteen kings and one queen through a single dynasty. After Zedekiah, Israel had no national king in the Davidic messianic line until Christ's first advent, but he was not then enthroned. (5) The exiles who returned from the Babylonian captivity which commenced 536 B.C. and which would probably include the residue who fled into Egypt but were deported to Babylon when Nebuchadnezzar dethroned Pharaoh Hophra (568 B.C.), resumed the national name Israel and rebuilt the temple destroyed under Nebuchadnezzar. This Second Commonwealth of Israel lasted through many vicissitudes until the destruction of Herod's temple by Titus in A.D. 70, which year witnessed the beginning of the Great Diaspora which persisted until the inauguration of the Third Commonwealth of Israel on May 14, 1948. (6) The name Israel is used with a finer shading to include laymen as distinguished from priests, Levites, and other ministers (Ezra 6:16; 9:1; 10:25; Neh. 11:3; etc.). (7) The spiritual designation bestowed upon Messiah both by application (e.g. Hosea 11:1 with Matt. 2:15) and by implication. (8) Applied figuratively to the children of the promise (Ps. 73:1; Rom. 9:6-13; Gal. 6:16) which term is extended to include gentile believers on equal terms of privilege (Rom. 11:17-32).

BIBLIOGRAPHY

UJE, Vol. V, pp. 613 f.; The Soncino Press Hebrew Bible; H. M. Orlinsky, *Ancient Israel*; W. Chomsky, *Hebrew: The Eternal Language*; L. Duff-Forbes, *Peril from the North*; H. Graetz, *History of the Jews*.

LAWRENCE DUFF-FORBES

J

JACOB. From birth, Jacob (*ya'ăqōb*, "supplanter," *BDB*) resorts to underhanded means to acquire the privileges of the firstborn, which should, according to human reasoning, mean also the enjoyment of Isaac's covenant relations with Jehovah (Gen. 27:33). However, God graciously works out his foreordained purpose to impart this blessing (Gen. 25:23) despite all hindrances and even to the extent of causing Jacob's sins (which are nonetheless punished) to work towards this end. Thus Jacob is evidence that election to enjoy

Abraham's blessing is not by national standing or works, but by grace (Rom. 9:10-13).

Through God's gracious working, Jacob becomes a man of faith whose name is changed to Israel (*yiśrā'ēl*, "God persists," *BDB*). By faith he outlines his sons' futures as heads of Israel's tribes (Gen. 49:3-27; Heb. 11:21). Special notice goes to Judah (Gen. 49:10), which later accounts indicate as the tribe from which Christ came (Matt. 1:2-3).

BIBLIOGRAPHY
Oehler, *Old Testament Theology*, pp. 64-67, 522; G. Vos, *Biblical Theology*, pp. 108-14.

DANIEL P. FULLER

JACOBITES. See MONOPHYSITISM.

JANSENISM. Cornelius Otto Jansen (1585-1638), Bishop of Ypres, with his friend Saint-Cyran, sought to combat the Jesuits' moral laxity by stressing conversion and the necessity and irresistibility of grace; he desired a purification of Romanism on Augustinian lines, but against the Reformers he maintained all of Augustine's ecclesiasticism, accepting the papal church as the extension of the incarnation through which alone salvation is dispensed. Port Royal, a Cistercian convent near Paris, became the center of the movement, and after Jansen's death its chief leader was Antoin Arnauld. Pascal attacked the Jesuits with his *Lettres Provinciales* (1656), and Pasquier Quesnel in his *Réflexions Morales* (1693) encouraged a biblical theology. But five propositions, alleged to be derived from Jansen's posthumously published *Augustinus*, were condemned by the Pope in 1653, and by the Bull *Unigenitus* (1713). Jansenism was driven underground in France. In Holland, it produced the Old Catholics (*q.v.*).

BIBLIOGRAPHY
N. J. Abercrombie, *The Origins of Jansenism*.

G. S. M. WALKER

JEALOUS, JEALOUSY, is used in Scripture of the emotion inspired by the infringing or denial of the right of exclusive possession. It describes the attitude of God toward the infringement of his right to the exclusive worship and service of his people. God is a jealous God (Ex. 20:5); his name is jealous (Ex. 34:14); and he is very jealous for his holy name (Ezek. 39:25) and also for the good name and well-being of his people and of his holy city (Zech. 1:14). Paul speaks of a godly jealousy (II Cor. 11:2) and also of the arous-ing or exciting of the jealousy of the Jews by the calling of the Gentiles (Rom. 10:19, appealing to Deut. 32:21). Elijah pleads in defense of his conduct "I have been very jealous for the Lord God of hosts" (I Kings 19:10). Jealous also describes the attitude of a husband toward a wife suspected of unfaithfulness (Num. 5:14-30; Prov. 6:34; S. of Sol. 8:6). The word jealous is related etymologically to "zealous" (see ZEAL), which renders the same Hebrew and Greek words.

OSWALD T. ALLIS

JEHOVAH. See GOD.

JERUSALEM. In the reign of David, God chose Jerusalem for his temple-habitation (II Chron. 3:1; Ps. 132:13). Zion therefore became "the city of God" (Ps. 46:4), "the joy of the whole earth" (48:2; cf. 97:3), for it signified his presence. Further, "born in Zion" represents the salvation of those who "know God" (87:4; cf. 9:10) and whose names are "written unto life in Jerusalem" (Isa. 4:3 ASV mg.), whether native of Babylon or Ethiopia (Ps. 87:4; *IB*; cf. *ICC*, "religious adoption"). Zion's description as a "mountain of holiness" symbolized Israel's post-exilic reformation (Jer. 31:23); and Isaiah employed "Zion" (54:1), desolate after the captivity of Sennacherib in 701 B.C. (36:1; 49:14; 50:1), symbolically to predict the church as the bride of Christ (54:5), persecuted, but to gain gentile converts (vs. 3) more numerous than Israel had been before (Gal. 4:26-28, G. Douglas Young, Evangelical Theological Society, *Papers*, 1955: pp. 79-80). Jerusalem represents heaven itself (Heb. 16:22). But in biblical eschatology "Written unto life in Jerusalem" means life on earth (WC; cf. Joel 3:17).

The following prophecies have been interpreted both literally and figuratively. Christ and his saints will descend to Olivet (Isa. 35:10; Zech. 14:4-5; Acts 1:11) and unbelievers will ravage Jerusalem (Zech. 12:2; 14:2). Christ, however, rescues the purified Jewish remnant (Isa. 4:3-4; Zech. 12:10; 14:5; Mal. 3:2, 5); and at Zion joins them to his church (Zech. 12:5; Rom. 11:26, Payne, Evangelical Theological Society, *Papers*, 1956: pp. 55-68).

Prophecy, if interpreted literally, describes Jerusalem as Messiah's millennial capital (Jer. 31:40; 33:16; Zech. 8:4-5; 14:20-21), with a temple for sacrifices, not of atonement (Heb. 9:12-28; Ezek. 43:20-21 concerns post-exilic times only, vss. 10-11), but of praise and thanksgiving (Isa. 60:6-7; Jer. 17:20). Christ's peace-making law will go forth from Jerusalem (Mic. 4:1-4), causing submission (Isa. 23:18; 45:14) and worship (60:3; Zech. 14:16-17). At Zion even nature is affected (Isa. 65:25; Ezek. 47:1-12; Zech. 14:10). If interpreted non-literally (amillennialism), these verses symbolize the church.

Attack by Gog and Magog (Ezek. 38-39) against the "beloved city" (Rev. 20:9) brings in God's final judgment; but Jerusalem continues eternally (Isa. 33:20; Mic. 4:7, cf. Heb. 12:27), though now without a temple (Rev. 21:22) because of the perfect holiness (vs. 27) of the new earth (Isa. 65:17-18; Rev. 21:2). In language drawn both from Eden and Zion (cf. Isa. 54:11; Rev. 21:19), the final state of the church is identified as the holy city, new Jerusalem (Rev. 21:9-10).

BIBLIOGRAPHY

"Jerusalem, New," ISBE; MSt; G. F. Oehler, Theology of the Old Testament, pp. 509-21; G. N. H. Peters, Theocratic Kingdom, III, pp. 32-63.

J. Barton Payne

JESUITS. The Jesuits, or Society of Jesus, was founded by Ignatius Loyola, a Spanish aristocrat, in 1534, to combat the Reformation and save his church from ruin. Wounded in battle, Loyola became ascetic, practicing horrible austerities for a time. The Order obeyed the Superior absolutely. The discipline was severe. Every church statement, however unreasonable, was to be believed unquestionably. They considered it permissible "to do evil that good may come." Their activities were boundless. Their intrigues made them hated. The Order was suppressed in most Roman Catholic countries. In 1773, Pope Clement XIV abolished it. Restored in 1814, it remains exceedingly influential.

Alexander M. Renwick

JESUS. The given name of God's incarnate Son — given before birth by divine intimation (Matt. 1:21; Luke 1:31) and then in due course by parental bestowment (Luke 2:21).

Jesus is the Greek form of Jeshua or Joshua (cf. the AV in Acts 7:45; Heb. 4:8) meaning "the Lord is salvation" or "the salvation of the Lord." The name has affinity with that of the great evangelical prophet Isaiah, whose predictions give prominence to the Messiah under various titles. Most important of all, the name was a reminder of the character and purpose of Israel's God as delighting in the salvation (q.v.) of his people, the historic deliverances of the past (Exodus and Restoration from Babylon) serving to underscore his pledge of messianic salvation for the future. Reflection on the meaning of his name must have been a constant reminder to Jesus of his mission (q.v.) in the world as it probably was to his church (I Thess. 1:10).

Since Jesus was a common name, its application to our Lord necessitated mention of lineage and place of residence when full identification was needed — "Jesus, son of Joseph, the one from Nazareth" (John 1:45). During the public ministry "Jesus of Nazareth" was usually sufficient for public use, though it might have further adornment under special circumstances (Matt. 21:11; John 19:19). To his followers the name itself was enough. However, in speaking to him, they seem to have refrained from using it, resorting to Teacher or Lord instead. The penitent thief, in the extremity of his need, did so employ it (Luke 23:42). Variant readings at this point testify to the difficulty created for scribes by this mode of address so lacking in deference. Demons addressed him as Jesus of Nazareth (Mark 1:24) or as Jesus, Son of the Most High God (Mark 5:7). Suppliants used Jesus, Master (Luke 17:13) or Jesus, Son of David (Mark 10:47).

After the resurrection it became common practice to link with the human name the titles Christ and Lord. He could now be confidently proclaimed as the (promised) Christ (Messiah). Before long Christ became so firmly yoked to Jesus, whether as Jesus Christ or Christ Jesus, as to be virtually a part of his name. In this way personal faith approved the identification given long before by divine announcement (Luke 2:11).

Occurrences of the name Jesus are not abundant in the Epistles as compared to the Gospels or even to the Acts. This circumstance makes all the more impressive its use in such a passage as Phil. 2:10 (cf. by contrast vs. 11) where it serves to emphasize the truth that the adoration of which our Lord is worthy in his exaltation must keep in full view the obedience and humiliation experienced in the days of his flesh. The rather generous use of Jesus in Hebrews has the same motivation. Though nearly all the references are to our Lord in his present glorified state (13:12 is an exception), the simple name suits well the stress upon his perfected humanity which was vital to his priesthood.

In keeping with this epistolary usage is Luke's practice of referring to the proclamation of the Christian message as "preaching Jesus" (Acts 8:35; 9:20; 17:18). To preach the gospel and to preach Jesus are convertible terms (cf. Paul's phrase, "preach Christ" I Cor. 1:23; II Cor. 4:5).

The Revelation of John uses the name Jesus several times, especially in the phrase, "the witness of Jesus" (1:9; 12:17; 19:10; 20:4), emphasizing the continuation of Jesus' work as the faithful and true witness as well as his servants' fellowship in his sufferings. The bond between Jesus and his church is firm and enduring (cf. Acts 9:5).

For the bearing of the name upon the question of the historicity of Jesus, see the discussion by Deissmann, cited below.

BIBLIOGRAPHY

A. Deissmann, "The Name 'Jesus'" in *Mysterium Christi*, ed. by G. K. A. Bell and Adolph Deissmann, pp. 3-27; E. Nestle in *HDCG*; Vincent Taylor, *The Names of Jesus*, pp. 5-9.

EVERETT F. HARRISON

JEW, JEWRY. See JUDAISM.

JOHN THE BAPTIST. The son of Zechariah, the priest, and Elizabeth (also of priestly descent and a relative of Mary the mother of Jesus). Born in the hill country of Judah, his birth having been foretold by an angel (Luke 1:11 ff.), he spent his early years in the wilderness of Judea (Luke 1:80). His public ministry began in the fifteenth year of the emperor Tiberius (*ca.* A.D. 27) when he suddenly appeared out of the wilderness.

The Gospels look upon John as the fulfilment of the *Elijah Redivivus* expectation, for both the announcing angel (Luke 1:17) and Jesus (Mark 9:11-13) expressly taught this. Furthermore, John's garb of a "garment of camel's hair, and a leather girdle around his waist" (Matt. 3:4) was similar to the dress of Elijah• (II Kings 1:8). Although John himself denied this identification (John 1:21-25), admitting only to being Isaiah's "voice in the wilderness" (John 1:23), it may be that he was disclaiming the popular hope for the literal resurrection of Elijah, accepting only the fulfilment of his spirit and power. Indeed this was the explicit promise of the angel.

John's message had a twofold emphasis: (1) the imminent appearance of the messianic kingdom, and (2) the urgent need for repentance to prepare for this event (Matt. 3:2). In true prophetic fashion his concept of the nature of the kingdom was not that of the popular mind, and thus was a proper preparation for Christ. The multitudes expected the "day of the Lord" to be happiness for all Israel, basing their hope on racial considerations. John proclaimed that the kingdom was to be a rule of righteousness, inherited only by those who exhibited righteousness by the way they lived. Thus his message of repentance was directed particularly to the Jew, for God was going to purge Israel as well as the world (Matt. 3:7-12). When Jesus appeared on the scene John's role as a forerunner was completed in his personal testimony to the fact of Jesus' Messiahship (John 1:29).

The baptism of John complemented his preparatory task. In its basic sense it was a symbolic act for the cleansing away of sin, and was thus accompanied by repentance. So Matt. 3:6 says, "and they were baptized by him in the river Jordan while confessing fully (*exomologoumenoi*) their sins." But in its fullest sense it was an eschatological act preparing one for admission into the messianic kingdom. Thus when the Pharisees and Sadducees came for baptism, John said, "Who warned you to flee from the wrath to come" (Matt. 3:7). Josephus' account of John's baptism (*Antiquities* xviii. 5. 2) is at variance with this, suggesting that its purpose was to provide a bodily purification to correspond with an already accomplished inward change. The historical background to John's baptism is probably Jewish proselyte baptism, with John emphasizing by this that both Jew and Gentile were ceremonially unclean as far as the true people of God were concerned. The baptism of Jesus by John (Matt. 3:13-15) is to be explained not as a sign that Jesus needed repentance, but rather that by this act he was identifying himself with mankind in the proper approach to God's kingdom.

It has long been felt that John was at one time connected with the Essenes, because of his ascetic habits and his location near the chief settlement of the sect. This has been given greater possibility by the recognized affinities between John and the Dead Sea Scroll (Qumran) sect, an Essenish group which dwelt on the northwest shore of the Dead Sea. This connection is certainly possible, for both John and the Qumran sect resided in the wilderness of Judea, both were of a priestly character, both laid emphasis on baptism as a sign of inward cleansing, both were ascetic, both thought in terms of imminent judgment, and both invoked Isaiah 40:3 as the authority for their mission in life. But although John may have been influenced by the sect in the early stages of his life, his ministry was far greater. John's role was essentially prophetic; the sect's was esoteric. John issued a public call to repentance; the sect withdrew to the desert. John proclaimed an exhibition of repentance in the affairs of ordinary life; the sect required submission to the rigors of its ascetic life. John introduced the Messiah; the sect still waited for his manifestation.

John's denunciation of Herod Antipas for his marriage was the cause of his death by beheading (Matt. 14:1-12). Josephus tells us (loc. cit.) that this took place at the fortress of Machaerus near the Dead Sea. The Mandeans were influenced by John, for he plays a large part in their writings. This connection may have come through John's disciples, who existed for at least twenty-five years after John's death (Acts 18:25; 19:3).

BIBLIOGRAPHY

C. H. Kraeling, *John the Baptist*; Joseph Thomas, *Le mouvement baptiste en Palestine et Syrie*; Kaufmann Kohler in *JewEnc*; R. B. Miller in *ISBE*; W. Brandt, "Mandaeans" in *HERE*; A. Plummer, *Gospel According to St. Matthew*, pp. 30-31; Millar Burrows, *More Light on the Dead Sea Scrolls*, pp. 56-63.

ROBERT B. LAURIN

JOSEPH. The eleventh and favorite son of Jacob, Rachel's first-born. His life story is told in Gen. 30-50, with commentary in Ps. 105:17-22; Acts 7:9-16, and Heb. 11:22. God's providence took him from Mesopotamia to Palestine to Egypt. Sold into slavery by his brothers, falsely accused, imprisoned, he was yet providentially brought to high office and succored his brothers in time of famine.

In Heb. 11, Joseph is an OT example of faith. Apparently he was prospered because he was pure in heart and feared God. He walked with God, and God was with him. His was the first OT record of a choice of God and chastity over lust. His fraternal dealings emphasize the doctrine of forgiveness and suggest that confession of sin must precede true reconciliation. Through him, the sovereign God

caused the wrath of men to effect divine purposes. His life exemplified the communicable attributes of God, the fruit of the Spirit. It is questionable whether the many external similarities in experiences justify his being regarded a type of Christ, but possibly as an OT ideal man he may have prefigured the perfect Man, who lived without sin and by whose active and passive obedience his people were saved.

BIBLIOGRAPHY

C. Fritsch, *Interp*, 9, pp. 21-34; T. Wright, *New-Church Review*, 1, pp. 337-48 and 2, pp. 127-29; W. Taylor, *Joseph the Prime Minister*; H. Tomkins, *Life and Times of Joseph*; A. Kellogg, *Abraham, Joseph and Moses*; G. von Rad in *Copenhagen Congress Volume*, 1, pp. 120-27 and *Die Josephgeschichte* (*Biblische Studien*, heft 5); A. Renou, *En Egypte au temps de Joseph*; Ebers, *Egypten und die Buecher Moses*; H. Heyes, *Biblische Zeitfragen*, 4. folge, heft 9, 341-80; J. Horovitz, *Die Josepherzaehlung*; G. Lawson, *Lectures on the History of Joseph*.

BURTON L. GODDARD

JOY, REJOICE. Scripture abounds with references to joy and rejoicing: natural joy (gladness, contentment, satisfaction, mirth, cheerfulness); moral joy (peace, serenity); and spiritual joy (joy of faith, rejoicing of hope).

In the OT, ten different Hebrew terms express the idea of delight of mind in the good. Kaufmann Kohler (*JewEnc, in loco*) states that no language has as many words for joy and rejoicing as Hebrew. Most common is *simha* ("gladness," "mirth"); then *gûl* or *gîl* ("to spring about," "be joyful"), *māśôś* ("joy," "rejoicing"), and *sāmēah* ("to shine," "be glad"). Shouting was associated with joy (Neh. 12:43). Contrary to paganism, joy is coupled with moral rectitude. Pure joy is joy in God as both its source and object. God is a God of joy (Ps. 104:31); the joy of the Lord is strength (Neh. 8:10); in his presence is fulness of joy (Ps. 16:11). The highest expressions of joy in the OT are found in Psalms.

In the NT, *chara* ("joy") and *chairō* ("to rejoice") are most common. *Agalliasis* ("exultation"), *euphrainō* ("to make glad," "well pleased") and *euphrosynē* ("gladness," "joy"), as well as *kauchaomai* ("to glory") are also used.

The NT regards joy as essentially a divine bestowal: it is the proper response of the soul to the gospel (Luke 2:10); closely related to the work of the Holy Spirit in Acts and the Epistles; listed as one of the fruits of the Spirit (Gal. 5:22); and has an eschatological aspect as a feature of the world to come (e.g., "the joy of thy Lord" in Matt. 25:21, 23, and "my joy" in John 15:11; 17:13).

As a gift of God, joy is unknown to the world (I Cor. 2:14), but paradoxically the believer may rejoice in afflictions and sufferings with joy unspeakable and full of glory (Acts 5:41; II Cor. 6:10; I Pet. 1:6, 8; 4:13). Joy is "not gaiety without gloom, but the victory of faith" (D. M. Edwards, *ISBE*, *in loco*).

BIBLIOGRAPHY
CB; K. Kohler, *JewEnc.*; D. M. Edwards, *ISBE*.

WESTLAKE T. PURKISER

JUDAISM. I. DEFINITION. The term is sometimes used of every form of Jewish religion after the destruction of Solomon's temple in 586 B.C. It seems better to confine it to the period beginning with the destruction of Herod's temple in A.D. 70, except where the phenomena under discussion can be clearly traced back to the intertestamental period. In this article, unless the context clearly demands otherwise, it will be further restricted to that form of Judaism which from the beginning of the third century A.D. to the middle of the nineteenth held the loyalty of all but an insignificant fraction of the Jewish people. Where it is necessary to distinguish it from other forms of Judaism, it is generally called Rabbinic, Traditional or Orthodox.

II. THE BEGINNINGS OF JUDAISM. The restriction of sacrifice to Jerusalem by Josiah, the destruction of the temple in 586 B.C. and the growing dispersion of Jewry both east and west meant a fundamental change in religious outlook. Though theoretically the cultus in Jerusalem remained the center of Jewish religion, at least eighty per cent of the people were not able to make effective use of it. The only one of the many attempted answers to this problem that concerns us here was the making of a strict observance of the law the major concern of all Jews. We may reasonably look on Ezra as the great initiator of this policy. It was greatly strengthened by the discrediting of the hellenized priests in the time of Antiochus Epiphanes and the failure of nationalism under the later Hasmonean priest-kings. In the NT period the Pharisees were the protagonists of the view; though they were only a small group, they had won the respect of the people.

After the destruction of the temple R. Yochanan b. Zakkai set out to make this concept dominant in Jewry. The events of A.D. 70 had deprived the priests of influence and had discredited the apocalyptists like those of Qumran; the Zealot leaders were dead or in hiding; in the Diaspora what sentiment there was was favorable. By A.D. 90 the rabbinic leaders felt strong enough to exclude those they considered heretics (the *mînîm*), including Hebrew Christians, from the synagogue. By 200 they had compelled the ordinary man, without theological learning or interest (the *'am hā-' āreṣ*), to conform.

The struggle must have been very bitter at times and not a few will have preferred to lose their Jewish identity rather than conform. The outcome, however, was that from 200, with the exception of the Karaites, rabbinic Judaism was virtually coextensive with the Jewish people. This lasted until modern rationalism and secularism made rapid inroads into Judaism.

III. THE THEOLOGY OF JUDAISM. It has been denied by many that there has ever been a theology of Judaism, but this is true to a limited extent only. Apart from certain fundamental concepts, Judaism has not been concerned with a detailed and systematic working out of its beliefs; if its members conformed strictly to the rules deduced from these concepts, no question was asked as to whether intellectual assent was being given to them. But these concepts, without which the term rabbinic Judaism has no meaning, are so definite and far-reaching that it is foolish to deny the term theology to them. In the following sketch elements held in common with Christianity are ignored. For clarity a distinction is made between those elements that are clearly pre-Christian and those that arose after A.D. 70.

A. *Pre-Christian Elements in Judaism.*

1. *The Jew.* There is no evidence that the "remnant" teaching of the OT had been understood, that "they are not all Israel, which are of Israel" (Rom. 9:6). While proselytes were welcomed, except when outside pressure made their acceptance undesirable, it is clear that ethnically the Jew was considered as having an abiding, privileged position.

2. *The Torah.* The five books of Moses, or Torah, to be rendered Instruction rather than Law, were regarded as the perfect and final revelation of God. The Prophets were only a commentary on them made necessary by man's sins. Though the whole of the OT is of unquestioned authority, the inspiration of the

Torah has always been placed higher than that of the Prophets or the Writings. Many have regarded it as merely an earthly copy of a heavenly original, antedating creation and an agent in it, for whose sake man was created. These developments were deliberate efforts to make the Torah a counterweight to the person of Jesus.

3. *The Oral Law.* To the written Torah (*tôrâ še-biktāb*) was added the oral Torah (*tôrâ še-be'al-pe*). In its origin this was the rabbinic application of the law of Moses and of some customs of immemorial antiquity (e.g., the washing of hands) to everyday life. Before A.D. 70 this was only one of rival interpretations (cf. that of the Qumran sect), and we can easily understand why the rabbis claimed that it had been handed down from Moses, who was given it on Mt. Sinai. After the triumph of Rabbinism this tradition made any major change impossible, even had it been wished. The underlying concept was that since God had revealed his will in laws, it should be possible from these to deduce a law code covering the whole of life. It followed that the study of Torah was man's *summum bonum.* The process was: (a) the discovery of the commandments given — it is claimed there are 613: 248 positive, 365 negative; (b) the protection of these commandments by the making of new ones that would guarantee their being kept — this is known as "making a hedge about the Torah"; (c) the application of these enlarged laws to all conceivable spheres and possibilities of life.

4. *The Messiah.* Though concepts of the Messiah varied greatly, there was general agreement that his work was above all the setting up of the kingdom of God by the perfect enforcement of the Torah. Earlier it was thought that he would modify it, but this conception was gradually dropped, when the rabbis were faced by Christian teaching on Christ and the law.

5. *The Resurrection.* The teaching of a resurrection of the dead was generally held. A clear distinction was made between the *'ôlām ha-zeh* ("this world") and the *'ôlām ha-bā'* ("the world to come"). The Days of the Messiah were conceived of as limited in length and as connecting the two epochs, there being no agreement as to which they belonged to. In any case the *'ôlām ha-bā'* is earthly, not heavenly. With a few exceptions there was little fear of divine judgment, the aphorism, "All Israel has a share in the world to come," being generally accepted.

B. *Developments After* A.D. *70.* The first efforts of the rabbis were to preserve Judaism by creating a monolithic body. On the one hand they expelled dissident elements, frowned on Gnostic speculation and reduced the area of individual freedom. On the other they so transformed certain basic areas of Jewish thought as to make acceptance of Jesus as Messiah and Saviour virtually impossible.

1. *Uniformity.* The bitter disputes between the schools of Hillel and Shammai were settled and the process of covering the whole of life by deductions from the Torah so expedited that by *ca.* 200 R. Yehuda ha-Nazi was able to codify the oral law and reduce it to writing; this is known as the Mishnah (*q.v.*). The process was carried further in the Gemara — virtually completed by 500 — in which the points left open or undealt with in the Mishnah were discussed and settled. Mishnah and Gemara together form the Talmud (*q.v.*). But it was not only the law controlling life (the *hălākâ*) that was fixed. Also the devotional aspect of Bible study was forced into rigid molds by the authoritative position given to the Midrashim with their edifying exposition (*'aggādâ*) of the various books of the OT.

2. *The Doctrine of God.* Faced with the Christian doctrine of the Trinity, the rabbis transformed the monotheistic doctrine of the OT into a monism that excludes any division in the Godhead and into a transcendentalism that makes the incarnation impossible. Gradually God became a philosophical principle, the unknowable.

3. *The Doctrine of Man.* The Fall was not taken seriously; it marred but did not break the *imago Dei* in man. The giving of the Torah is an act of God's grace, but having received it man can and should use it for his own salvation. Hence the incarnation is unnecessary.

4. *Sin, Sacrifice and Mediation.* Pharisaism had already before A.D. 70, in its stress on the keeping of the Torah by the individual, tended to regard the cultus as being of secondary importance; both the stress on the letter of the law and its exaltation above the cultus led to an underestimate of sin. This tendency became quite understandably dominant once the temple had disappeared. Sin became regarded

as virtually entirely a matter of actions, not of motives. For all that, the synagogue liturgy for the Day of Atonement shows clearly that the sense of the need of God's grace for the forgiveness of sin has never been lost in Judaism. The loss of sacrifice (*q.v.*), the decreasing sense of sin and the Christian stress on Jesus as mediator between God and man has led to a complete denial of the need for a mediator, except perhaps among the Chasidim.

5. *Merit.* For the Pharisees the supreme practical expression of the study of the Torah was the giving of alms. Already in the NT period righteousness (*ṣᵉḏāqâ*; Greek, *dikaiosynē*) had developed the technical meaning of alms (cf. AV and RV in Matt. 6:1). This is equivalent to saying that religion is primarily a question of action, not of a state of mind towards God, and that these actions are directed to man far more than to God. It was taken for granted that these actions would be suitably rewarded by God, either now or in the future. The heaping up of these actions created merit, from which one's children could profit. Similarly the merits of the Fathers were a source of rich help to all generations of Jewry.

IV. CHECKS TO LEGALISM. In spite of the sketch just given Judaism has never been as purely legalistic as is so often believed. For this there are two main reasons.

A. *Motive.* Though the Torah consists of commandments to be kept and God is just in rewarding their keeping, the rabbis constantly stress that our acts must have the right intention (*kawwānâ*) and that they must be done for their own sake (*lišmâ*), not for the reward they might bring. In fact for them the love of God is the true motive, because of the grace he has shown in the choice of Israel and in the giving of the Torah — the latter is regarded as supremely an act of grace.

B. *Mysticism.* Mysticism of a non-pantheistic variety has at every period played a large role in Judaism. Much of it was an effort to know God more closely than was possible through the normal interpretation of the Torah. The best known expression of this movement was Kabbalism with the *Zohar* as its masterpiece. Contrary to widespread ideas Kabbalism has nothing to do with magic, except in as far as the one that knows God better may be expected to have greater power over nature. More important was the eighteenth century Chasidic movement, which was more

concerned with a more inward service of God than knowledge of him. Most of vital modern Orthodox Judaism has been influenced by it.

V. MODERN TRENDS IN JUDAISM. The confining of Jews to special streets and quarters (ghettos) and their exclusion from normal life meant that in Western Europe the influences of the Renaissance and modern thought did not reach them, with few exceptions, until about the time of the French Revolution, and in Eastern Europe and Moslem lands much later. The shock was too great for Orthodox Judaism to be able to adapt itself. Where it has survived as a vital faith and not simply a manner of life, it has been at the price of turning its back on the modern world.

The bulk of religious Jews have accommodated themselves to a greater or less extent to the world in which they live. The Conservative Jew has trimmed away those commandments which seem to have lost their meaning. The Reform Jew ("Liberal" in Britain) places the Prophets before the Torah and retains only those customs of the past which he can rationalize.

It is probable that the majority of Jews are effectively atheist, whether they keep up a link with the synagogue or not. Among them nationalism (Zionism) has been the great substitute for religion, and it has influenced even many who think of themselves as religious.

BIBLIOGRAPHY
JewEnc; G. F. Moore, *Judaism* ('3 vols.); C. G. Montefiore and H. Loewe, *A Rabbinic Anthology*; A. Cohen, *Everyman's Talmud*; A. Lukyn Williams, *The Doctrines of Modern Judaism Considered*; J. Jocz, *The Jewish People and Jesus Christ*; G. G. Schalom, *Major Trends in Jewish Mysticism.*

H. L. ELLISON

JUDAIZE, JUDAIZER. When Paul withstood Peter at Antioch (Gal. 2:11-21), he maintained that Peter's conduct in withdrawing from table companionship with gentile Christians had the force of compelling them to judaize (Gal. 2:14). The implication of Peter's withdrawal was that gentile believers would have to observe Jewish customs, would have to live as Jews, if they were to enjoy again the type of fellowship from which Peter was now excluding them. If they were to regard Jewish practices as binding on them and as essential to justification, they would abandon not only the liberty of the gospel (*q.v.*) but the gospel itself (cf. Gal. 1:6; 2:16; 5:1-3).

A party in the church, originally Pharisees,

which, it is likely, entered after the death of Stephen, did insist that it was necessary for Gentiles to be circumcised and to keep the law of Moses, at least in part, in order to be saved (Acts 15:1; Gal. 5:2; 6:12, 13). From their efforts to induce Gentiles to observe Jewish customs, to judaize, they have been designated Judaizers. They agreed with many points in the apostolic proclamation, but their defection on the matter of salvation by grace alone caused Paul to regard their message as no gospel at all (Gal. 1:6-10). In the Epistle to the Galatians Paul overthrows their attack on his gospel and his apostleship, and exposes their unworthy motives (Gal. 4:17; 6:12, 13). The Jerusalem leaders stood with Paul in the controversy (Acts 15:1-33; Gal. 2:1-10; I Cor. 15:11). The destructive influence of the Judaizers seems to have declined sharply before long. It is indeed reflected in I and II Corinthians, but in the epistles of the first Roman imprisonment it is not noticed, unless perhaps in Phil. 3:2 ff.

BIBLIOGRAPHY

W. Gutbrod in *TWNT*; J. Gresham Machen, *The Origin of Paul's Religion*, pp. 19, 104, 107, 125 f., 128, 129-37; H. N. Ridderbos, *The Epistle of Paul to the Churches of Galatia*, pp. 15 ff.

JOHN H. SKILTON

JUDGE, JUDGMENT. The Hebrew word for "judge," *šōpēṭ*, appears originally to have reference to one who pronounced an oracle, that is, one who spoke for God. This is clear from Ex. 18:13, 15, 16. But in the same chapter, verses 25-26, it is evident that eventually elders were appointed to take care of the many cases that had arisen where counsel was necessary. The word consequently came to have a broader application than it had in the beginning. The regulations of the responsibilities of the judge were quite clear (Ex. 23:6-8; Deut. 16:19). His decisions were to be given without prejudice or partiality. He was to see that absolute justice was done, reject bribes, and guard against the influence of popular opinion upon his judgment. In the period of the Judges justice was administered by leaders in whom the people had confidence (Judg. 4:5). Samuel organized a circuit court for the purpose of judging (I Sam. 7:16). One of the responsibilities of the king was to judge (I Sam. 8:20; II Sam. 15:1-6).

The idea of judgment appears in various contexts in the NT, usually in the ethical sphere: (1) *krinō* means to judge, to give a verdict (Luke 7:43; Acts 15:19), (2) *diakrinō*, to distinguish, to discriminate (I Cor. 11:31; 14:29), (3) *anakrinō*, to investigate, scrutinize (I Cor. 4:3). The Christian conscience makes ethical judgments unavoidable and imperative. "He that is spiritual judgeth all things" (I Cor. 2:15). The NT seems to teach that a Christian should not judge his brother. Jesus gave the command, "Judge not" (Matt. 7:1). Paul says that he that is spiritual is judged of no man (I Cor. 2:15). But an examination of the contexts of these passages shows that what Jesus had in mind was that one must not judge another without first judging oneself, and that Paul means that a spiritual person cannot be judged by a natural man in spiritual things. It is impossible to make an ethical judgment without passing judgment upon the one who performs the act. Jesus made such judgments (Matt. 16:23; John 1:47; 6:70). A Christian's judgment should reflect the mind of Christ and should begin with an examination of self (Matt. 7:3-5).

ARNOLD C. SCHULTZ

JUST, JUSTIFY, JUSTIFICATION. The basic fact of biblical religion is that God pardons and accepts believing sinners (see Pss. 32:1-5; 130; Luke 7:47 ff., 18:9-14; Acts 10:43; I John 1:7—2:2). Paul's doctrine of justification by faith is an analytical exposition of this fact in its full theological connections. As stated by Paul (most fully in Romans and Galatians, though see also II Cor. 5:14 ff.; Eph. 2:1 ff.; Phil. 3:4 ff.), the doctrine of justification determines the whole character of Christianity as a religion of grace and faith. It defines the saving significance of Christ's life and death, by relating both to God's law (Rom. 3:24 ff.; 5:16 ff.). It displays God's justice in condemning and punishing sin, his mercy in pardoning and accepting sinners, and his wisdom in exercising both attributes harmoniously together through Christ (Rom. 3:23 ff.). It makes clear what faith is — belief in Christ's atoning death and justifying resurrection (Rom. 4:23 ff.; 10:8 ff.), and trust in him alone for righteousness (Phil. 3:8 f.). It makes clear what Christian morality is — law-keeping out of gratitude to the Saviour whose gift of righteousness made law-keeping needless for acceptance (Rom. 7:1-6; 12:1 f.). It explains all hints, prophecies and instances of salvation in the OT (Rom. 1:17;

3:21; 4:1 ff.). It overthrows Jewish exclusivism (Gal. 2:15 ff.), and provides the basis on
which Christianity becomes a religion for the
world (Rom. 1:16; 3:29 f.). It is the heart of
the gospel. Luther justly termed it *articulus
stantis vel cadentis ecclesiae;* a church that
lapses from it can scarcely be called Christian.

I. THE MEANING OF JUSTIFICATION. The
biblical meaning of "justify" (Hebrew, *ṣāḏaq;*
Greek, LXX and NT, *dikaioō*) is to pronounce, accept, and treat as just, i.e., as, on
the one hand, not penally liable, and, on the
other, entitled to all the privileges due to
those who have kept the law. It is thus a
forensic term, denoting a judicial act of administering the law — in this case, by declaring a verdict of acquittal, and so excluding all
possibility of condemnation. Justification thus
settles the legal status of the person justified.
(See Deut. 25:1; Prov. 17:15; Rom. 8:33 f.
In Isa. 43:9, 26, "be justified" means "get the
verdict.") The justifying action of the Creator, who is the royal Judge of his world, has
both a sentential and an executive, or declara-
tive, aspect: God justifies, first, by reaching
his verdict, and then by such sovereign action
which makes his verdict known, and secures
to the person justified the rights which are
now his due. What is envisaged in Isa. 45:25
and 50:8, for instance, is specifically a series
of events which will publicly vindicate those
whom God holds to be in the right.

The word is also used in a transferred sense
for ascriptions of righteousness in non-forensic
contexts. Thus, men are said to justify God
when they confess him just (Luke 7:29);
Rom 3:4 = Ps. 51:4), and themselves when
they claim to be just (Job 32:2; Luke 10:29;
16:15). The passive can be used generally of
being vindicated by events against suspicion,
criticism and mistrust (Matt. 11:19; Luke
7:35; I Tim. 3:16). In James 2:21, 24-25,
its reference is to the proof of a man's acceptance with God which is given when his actions show that he has the kind of living,
working faith to which God imputes righteousness.

James' statement that Christians, like Abraham, are justified by works (vs. 24) is thus
not contrary to Paul's insistence that Christians, like Abraham, are justified by faith
(Rom. 3:28; 4:1-5), but is complementary to
it. James himself quotes Gen. 15:6 for exactly
the same purpose as Paul does — to show that

it was faith which secured Abraham's acceptance as righteous (vs. 23; cf. Rom. 4:3 ff.,
Gal. 3:6 ff.). The justification which concerns
James is not the believer's original acceptance
by God, but the subsequent vindication of his
profession of faith by his life. It is in terminology, not thought, that James differs from
Paul.

There is no lexical ground for the view of
Chrysostom, Augustine, the Medievals and
Roman theologians that "justify" means, or
connotes as part of its meaning, *"make* righteous" (sc. by subjective spiritual renewal).
The Tridentine definition of justification as
"not only the remission of sins, but also the
sanctification and renewal of the inward man"
(Sess. VI, ch. vii) is erroneous.

II. PAUL'S DOCTRINE OF JUSTIFICATION.
The background of Paul's doctrine was the
Jewish conviction, universal in his time, that
a day of judgment was coming, in which God
would condemn and punish all who had
broken his laws. That day would terminate
the present world-order and usher in a golden
age for those whom God judged worthy. This
conviction, derived from prophetic expectations
of "the day of the Lord" (Amos 5:19 ff.; Isa.
2:10-22; 13:6-11; Jer. 46:10; Obad. 15;
Zeph. 1:14—2:3, etc.) and developed during
the intertestamental period under the influence of apocalyptic, had been emphatically
confirmed by Christ (Matt. 11:22 ff.; 12:36
f., etc.). Paul affirmed that Christ himself was
the appointed representative through whom
God would "judge the world in righteousness"
in "the day of wrath and revelation of the
righteous judgment of God" (Acts 17:31;
Rom. 2:16). This, indeed, had been Christ's
own claim (John 5:27 ff.).

Paul sets out his doctrine of the judgment-
day in Rom. 2:5-16. The principle of judgment will be exact retribution ("to every man
according to his works," vs. 6). The standard
will be God's law. The evidence will be "the
secrets of men" (vs. 16); the Judge is a
searcher of hearts. Being himself just, he cannot be expected to justify any but the righteous, those who have kept his law (Rom.
2:12-13; cf. Ex. 23:7; I Kings 8:32). But the
class of righteous men has no members. None
is righteous; all have sinned (Rom. 3:9 ff.).
The prospect, therefore, is one of universal
condemnation, for Jew as well as Gentile; for
the Jew who breaks the law is no more accept-

able to God than anyone else (Rom. 2:17-27). All men, it seems, are under God's wrath (Rom. 1:18) and doomed.

Against this black background, comprehensively expounded in Rom. 1:18—3:20, Paul proclaims the present justification of sinners by grace through faith in Jesus Christ, apart from all works and despite all demerit (Rom. 3:21 ff.). This justification, though individually located at the point of time at which a man believes (Rom. 4:2; 5:1), is an eschatological once-for-all divine act, the final judgment brought into the present. The justifying sentence, once passed, is irrevocable. "The wrath" will not touch the justified (Rom. 5:9). Those accepted now are secure for ever. Inquisition before Christ's judgment-seat (Rom. 14:10-12; II Cor. 5:10) may deprive them of certain rewards (I Cor. 3:15), but never of their justified status. Christ will not call in question God's justifying verdict, only declare, endorse and implement it.

Justification has two sides. On the one hand, it means the pardon, remission and non-imputation of all sins, reconciliation to God and the end of his enmity and wrath (Acts 13:39; Rom. 4:6 f.; II Cor. 5:19; Rom. 5:9 ff.). On the other hand, it means the bestowal of a righteous man's status and a title to all the blessings promised to the just: a thought which Paul amplifies by linking justification with the adoption of believers as God's sons and heirs (Rom. 8:14 ff.; Gal. 4:4 ff.). Part of their inheritance they receive at once: through the gift of the Holy Spirit, whereby God "seals" them as his when they believe (Eph. 1:13), they taste that quality of fellowship with God which belongs to the age to come, and is called "eternal life." Here is another eschatological reality brought into the present: having in a real sense passed through the last judgment, the justified enter heaven on earth. Here and now, therefore, justification brings "life" (Rom. 5:18), though this is merely a foretaste of the fulness of life and glory which constitutes the "hope of righteousness" (Gal. 5:5) promised to the just (Rom. 2:7, 10), to which God's justified children may look forward (Rom. 8:18 ff.). Both aspects of justification appear in Rom. 5:1-2, where Paul says that justification brings, on the one hand, peace with God (because sin is pardoned) and, on the other, hope of the glory of God (because the believer is accepted as

righteous). Justification thus means permanent re-instatement to favor and privilege, as well as complete forgiveness of all sins.

III. THE GROUND OF JUSTIFICATION. Paul's deliberately paradoxical reference to God as "justifying the ungodly" (Rom. 4:5) — the same Greek phrase as is used by the LXX in Ex. 23:7; Isa. 5:23, of the corrupt judgment that God will not tolerate — reflects his awareness that this is a startling doctrine. Indeed, it seems flatly at variance with the OT presentation of God's essential righteousness, as revealed in his actions as Legislator and Judge — a presentation which Paul himself assumes in Rom. 1:18—3:20. The OT insists that God is "righteous in all his ways" (Ps. 145:17), "a God . . . without iniquity" (Deut. 32:4; cf. Zeph. 3:5). The law of right and wrong, in conformity to which righteousness consists, has its being and fulfilment in him. His revealed law, "holy, just and good" as it is (Rom. 7:12; cf. Deut. 4:8; Ps. 19:7-9), mirrors his character, for he "loves" the righteousness prescribed (Ps. 11:7; 33:5) and "hates" the unrighteousness forbidden (Ps. 5:4-6; Isa. 61:8; Zech. 8:17). As Judge, he declares his righteousness by "visiting" in retributive judgment idolatry, irreligion, immorality and inhuman conduct throughout the world (Jer. 9:24; Ps. 9:5 ff., 15 ff.; Amos 1:3—3:2, etc.). "God is a righteous judge, yea, a God that hath indignation every day" (Ps. 7:11, ERV). No evildoer goes unnoticed (Ps. 94:7-9); all receive their precise desert (Prov. 24:12). God hates sin, and is impelled by the demands of his own nature to pour out "wrath" and "fury" on those who complacently espouse it (cf. the language of Isa. 1:24; Jer. 6:11; 30:23 f.; Ezek. 5:13 ff.; Deut. 28:63). It is a glorious revelation of his righteousness (cf. Isa. 5:16; 10:22) when he does so; it would be a reflection on his righteousness if he failed to do so. It seems unthinkable that a God who thus reveals just and inflexible wrath against all human ungodliness (Rom. 1:18) should justify the ungodly. Paul, however, takes the bull by the horns and affirms, not merely that God does it, but that he does it in a manner designed "to shew his righteousness, because of the passing over of the sins done aforetime, in the forbearance of God; for the shewing, I say, of his righteousness at this present season: that he might himself be just, and the justifier of him that hath faith in Jesus" (Rom. 3:25 f., ERV). The statement is emphatic, for the point is crucial. Paul is saying that the gospel which proclaims God's apparent violation of his justice is really a revelation of his justice. So far from raising a problem of theodicy, it actually solves one; for it makes explicit, as the OT never did, the just ground on which God pardoned and accepted believers before the time of Christ, as well as since.

Some (e.g., Anderson Scott, Dodd) question this exegesis of Rom. 3:25 f., and construe "righteousness" here as meaning "saving action," on the ground that in Isa. 40-55 "righteousness" and "salvation" are repeatedly used as equivalents (Isa. 45:8, 19-25; 46:13; 51:3-6, etc.). This eliminates the theodicy; all that Paul is saying, on this view, is that God now shows that he saves sinners. The words "just, and" in vs. 26, so far from making the crucial point that God justifies sinners *justly*, would then add nothing to his meaning, and could be deleted without loss. However, quite apart from the specific exegetical embarrassments which it creates (for which see Vincent Taylor, *ExpT* 50, 295 ff.), this hypothesis seems groundless, for (1) OT references to God's righteousness normally denote his retributive justice (the usage adduced from Isaiah is not typical), and (2) these verses are the continuation of a discussion that has been concerned throughout (from 1:18 onward) with God's display of righteousness *in judging and punishing sin*. These considerations decisively fix the forensic reference here. "The main question with which St. Paul is concerned is how God can be recognized as himself righteous and at the same time as one who declares righteous believers in Christ" (Vincent Taylor, *art. cit.*, p. 299). Paul has not (as is suggested) left the forensic sphere behind. The sinner's relation to God as just Lawgiver and Judge is still his subject. What he is saying in this paragraph (Rom. 3:21-26) is that the gospel reveals a way in which sinners can be justified without affront to the divine justice which, as shown (1:18—3:20), condemns all sin.

Paul's thesis is that God justifies sinners on a just ground, namely, that the claims of God's law upon them have been fully satisfied. The law has not been altered, or suspended, or flouted for their justification, but fulfilled — by Jesus Christ, acting in their name. By per-

fectly serving God, Christ perfectly kept the law (cf. Matt. 3:15). His obedience culminated in death (Phil. 2:8); he bore the penalty of the law in men's place (Gal. 3:13), to make propitiation for their sins (Rom. 3:25). On the ground of Christ's obedience, God does not impute sin, but imputes righteousness, to sinners who believe (Rom. 4:2-8; 5:19). "The righteousness of God" (i.e., righteousness *from* God: see Phil. 3:9) is bestowed on them as a free gift (Rom. 1:17; 3:21 f.; 5:17, cf. 9:30; 10:3-10): that is to say, they receive the right to be treated and the promise that they shall be treated, no longer as sinners, but as righteous, by the divine Judge. Thus they become "the righteousness of God" in and through him who "knew no sin" personally, but was representatively "made sin" (treated as a sinner, and punished) in their stead (II Cor. 5:21). This is the thought expressed in classical Protestant theology by the phrase "the imputation of Christ's righteousness," namely, that believers are righteous (Rom. 5:19) and have righteousness (Phil. 3:9) before God for no other reason than that Christ their Head was righteous before God, and they are one with him, sharers of his status and acceptance. God justifies them by passing on them for Christ's sake, the verdict which Christ's obedience merited. God declares them to be righteous, because he reckons them to be righteous; and he reckons righteousness to them, not because he accounts them to have kept his law personally (which would be a false judgment), but because he accounts them to be united to the one who kept it representatively (and that is a true judgment). For Paul union with Christ is not fancy, but fact — the basic fact, indeed, in Christianity; and the doctrine of imputed righteousness is simply Paul's exposition of the forensic aspect of it (see Rom. 5:12 ff.). Covenantal solidarity between Christ and his people is thus the objective basis on which sinners are reckoned righteous and justly justified through the righteousness of their Saviour. Such is Paul's theodicy regarding the ground of justification.

IV. Faith and Justification. Paul says that believers are justified *dia pisteōs* (Rom. 3:25), *pistei* (Rom. 3:28) and *ek pisteōs* (Rom. 3:30). The dative and the preposition *dia* represent faith as the instrumental means whereby Christ and his righteousness are appropriated; the preposition *ek* shows that faith occasions, and logically precedes, our personal justification. That believers are justified *dia pistin*, on account of faith, Paul never says, and would deny. Were faith the ground of justification, faith would be in effect a meritorious work, and the gospel message would, after all, be merely another version of justification by works — a doctrine which Paul opposes in all forms as irreconcilable with grace, and spiritually ruinous (cf. Rom. 4:4; 11:6; Gal. 4:21-5:12). Paul regards faith, not as itself our justifying righteousness, but rather as the outstretched empty hand which receives righteousness by receiving Christ. In Hab. 2:4 (cited Rom. 1:17; Gal. 3:11) Paul finds, implicit in the promise that the godly man ("the just") would enjoy God's continued favour ("live") through his trustful loyalty to God (which is Habakkuk's point in the context), the more fundamental assertion that only through faith does any man ever come to be viewed by God as just, and hence as entitled to life, at all. The Apostle also uses Gen. 15:6 ("Abraham believed God, and it was reckoned unto him for righteousness," ERV) to prove the same point (see Gal. 3:6; Rom. 4:3 ff.). It is clear that when Paul paraphrases this verse as teaching that Abraham's faith was reckoned for righteousness (Rom. 4:5, 9, 22), all he intends us to understand is that faith — decisive, whole-hearted reliance on God's gracious promise (vss. 18 ff.) — was the occasion and means of righteousness being imputed to him. There is no suggestion here that faith is the ground of justification. Paul is not discussing the ground of justification in this context at all, only the method of securing it. Paul's conviction is that no child of Adam ever becomes righteous before God save on account of the righteousness of the last Adam, the second representative man (Rom. 5:12-19); and this righteousness is imputed to men when they believe.

Theologians on the rationalistic and moralistic wing of Protestantism — Socinians, Arminians, and some modern Liberals — have taken Paul to teach that God regards man's faith as righteousness (either because it fulfils a supposed new law, or because, as the seed of all Christian virtue, it contains the germ and potency of an eventual fulfilment of God's original law, or else because it is simply God's sovereign pleasure to treat faith as righteousness, though it is not righteousness; and that God pardons and accepts sinners on the ground of their faith). In consequence, these theologians deny the imputation of Christ's righteousness to believers in the sense explained, and reject the whole covenantal conception of Christ's mediatorial work. The most they can say is that Christ's righteousness was the indirect cause of the acceptance of man's faith as righteousness, in that it created a situation in which this acceptance became possible. (Thinkers in the Socinian tradition, believing that such a situation always existed and that Christ's work had no Godward reference, will not say even this.) Theologically, the fundamental defect of all such views is that they do not make the satisfaction of the law the basis of acceptance. They regard justification, not as a judicial act of executing the law, but as the sovereign act of a God who stands above the law and is free to dispense with it, or change it, at his discretion. The suggestion is that God is not bound by his own law: its preceptive and penal enactments do not express immutable and necessary demands of his own nature, but he may out of benevolence relax and amend them without ceasing to be what he is. This, however, seems a wholly unscriptural conception.

V. The Doctrine in History. Interest in justification varies according to the weight given to the scriptural insistence that man's relation to God is determined by law (*q.v.*), and sinners necessarily stand under his wrath (*q.v.*) and condemnation. The late Medievals took this more seriously than any since apostolic times; they, however, sought acceptance through penances and meritorious good works. The Reformers proclaimed justification by grace alone through faith alone on the ground of Christ's righteousness alone, and embodied Paul's doctrine in full confessional statements. The sixteenth and seventeenth centuries were the doctrine's classical period. Liberalism spread the notion that God's attitude to all men is one of paternal affection, not conditioned by the demands of penal law; hence interest in the sinner's justification by the divine Judge was replaced by the thought of the prodigal's forgiveness and rehabilitation by his divine Father. The validity of forensic categories for expressing man's saving relationship to God has been widely denied. Many Neo-orthodox thinkers seem surer that there is a sense of guilt in man than that there is a penal law in God, and tend to echo this denial, claiming that legal categories obscure the personal quality of this relationship. Consequently, Paul's doctrine of justification has received little stress outside evangelical circles, though a new emphasis is apparent in recent lexical work, the newer Lutheran writers and the *Dogmatics* of Karl Barth.

BIBLIOGRAPHY

(a) *Lexical and exegetical.* Arndt; Quell and Schrenk, *Righteousness* (from *TWNT*); Sanday and Headlam, *Romans*, pp. 24 ff; E. D. Burton, *Galatians*, pp. 460 ff.; C. H. Dodd, *The Bible and the Greeks*, pp. 42-59; L. Morris, *The Apostolic Preaching of the Cross*, pp. 224 ff.; V. Taylor, *Forgiveness and Reconciliation*, pp. 29 ff.
(b) *Historical and systematic.* Luther, *Galatians*; Calvin, *Institutes*, III.xi-xviii; J. Owen, *Justification by Faith*; J. Buchanan, *The Doctrine of Justification*; W. Cunningham, *Historical Theology*, II, pp. 1-120; A. Ritschl, *Critical History of . . . Justification*; C. Hodge, *Systematic Theology*, III. pp. 114-212; L. Berkhof, *Systematic Theology*, pp. 510-26; K. Barth, *Church Dogmatics*, IV, I, Sec. 61.

JAMES I. PACKER

JUSTICE. Justice is a communicable attribute of God, manifesting his holiness. The biblical words thus translated, *ṣᵉdāqâ, ṣedeq,* and *dikaiosynē,* are also rendered as "righteousness." Used of man, justice refers to right rule, right conduct, or to each getting his due, whether good or bad. God's *relative* justice has to do with his rectitude in and of himself; by his *absolute* justice is meant the rectitude by which he upholds himself against violations of his holiness. By *rectoral* justice, he institutes righteous laws and establishes just rewards and penalties, as over against *distributive* justice, whereby he metes out just rewards (*remunerative* justice, expressive of his love) and punishments (*retributive* justice, expressive of his wrath).

God's moral excellence made necessary either the punishment of sinners or expiation whereby their condemnation would be removed. The sinner was without power to offer satisfaction for his sin, but righteousness was provided as Christ, the representative of man, met all the righteous demands of the law and paid the price of sin in the believer's place so that he, trusting only in Christ's righteousness, might be justified by God. The gospel, therefore, is the good news that through the Saviour the requirements of divine justice have been met.

See also JUST, JUSTIFY.

BIBLIOGRAPHY

L. Berkhof, *Reformed Dogmatics*, I, pp. 51-52; S. Charnock, *Existence and Attributes of God*, I, pp. 554-56; II, pp. 181-86; C. Hodge, *Systematic Theology*, I, pp. 416-27; W. Shedd, *Dogmatic Theology*, I, pp. 365-85; T. Dwight, *Theology*, I, pp. 192-201; Crem, pp. 190-93; R. Girdlestone, *Synonyms of OT*, pp. 101, 158-62; G. Quell and G. Schrenk, *Righteousness* (*TWNT* material); E. Brunner, *Justice and the Social Order*, pp. 110-24; N. Snaith, *Distinctive Ideas of OT*, pp. 51-78; H. Cazelles, RB, 58: 169-88.

BURTON L. GODDARD

K

KABBALA. Kabbala, from Hebrew *qābal,* "to receive," is a Jewish theosophy compounded of Platonic, Gnostic and Judaeo-allegorical elements. Tending to be mystical and esoteric, it deals with several basic theological issues such as the nature of God, the destiny of man and the origin of the universe. Answers are developed by appeal to ciphers (*gematria*), magic letters and formulae. Kabbalism flourished in the thirteenth century in Germany, Spain and Italy, chiefly in reaction to the Aristotelianism of Maimonides. Pico di Mirandola (1463-94), an early Christian Kabbalist, held that all Christian doctrine was latent in the Jewish Kabbala. Other Christians in this tradition were Reuchlin (1455-1522) and Fludd (1574-1637). The greatest strength of Kabbalism was in its suppression of rampant Rationalism, and its greatest weakness lay in its reduction of religion to mysticism, magic and superstition.

DAVID H. WALLACE

KENOSIS. The term kenosis is taken from *kenoō* in Phil. 2:7 (AV: "made himself of no reputation"; RSV: "emptied himself"). The rendering "emptied" is a somewhat misleading translation for the following reasons: (1) *kenoō* in the NT is commonly used in the metaphorical rather than the literal meaning

(Rom. 4:14) I Cor. 1:17; 9:15; II Cor. 9:3 (cf. B. B. Warfield in *ISBE*); (2) explicit statements of the NT indicate that Jesus retained his divine nature and attributes (Matt. 1:23; 11:27; Mark 1:1; John 3:13 AV; 14:9; Rom. 1:4); (3) the doctrine of the incarnation requires the continuing divinity of Jesus; (4) the immutability of God (deity is attributed to Jesus in the passage, *morphē theou*) makes an "emptying" inconceivable.

For such reasons as the above, the kenosis has generally been taken to refer not to the subtraction of divinity, but the addition of humanity. "The kenosis is that self-limitation of the logos which was involved in his manifestation in a human form; though at the same time he is not in any way limited as to his cosmic position. This conception of the Kenosis may be regarded as the recognized views of the early church" (F. Loofs in *SHERK*). Likewise, the Reformation saw in Christ's humiliation a veiling (*obscuratio*) of his glory, but not a removal or suspension of his divinity in nature or exercise. Luther, and the Lutherans, because of their doctrine of ubiquity, held the unusual view that the kenosis referred to the incarnate Logos and not the eternal Logos. They agreed, however, with the catholic tradition, that the divine being did not divest himself of any of his divinity.

While the kenotic notion has not been without its representatives in the church from the beginning (though the orthodox tradition has been clearly Chalcedonian), it had a special development in the nineteenth century. Its *raison d'être* seems to have been a desire to emphasize the reality of Jesus' humanity and, possibly, to maintain his ability to err. Thomasius, who was the first to state the doctrine scientifically, held a moderate form of kenoticism (an emptying of certain divine attributes only, and that temporarily). Gess, however, represented the Son of God as losing even his eternal self-consciousness in his descent into human flesh, only gradually to regain it in the course of his ministry. According to Ebrard, the Logos reduced himself to the dimensions of the human soul without ceasing to be the eternal Son. "The same ego exists at once in the eternal and in the temporal form, is both infinite and finite" (L. Berkhof, *The History of Christian Doctrines*, p. 125). Godet, Martensen, William Clarke,

Gore held similar positions. Contemporary kenoticists tend rather to assume than expound their view.

BIBLIOGRAPHY

J. J. Mueller, *The Epistles of Paul to the Philippians and to Philemon*, pp. 82-85, and *Die kenosisleer in die christologie sedert die Reformasie*; L. Boettner, *The Person of Christ*; B. B. Warfield, *Christology and Criticism*; F. J. Hall, *The Kenotic Theory*; W. Sanday, *Christologies Ancient and Modern*; D. M. Baillie, *God Was in Christ*.

JOHN H. GERSTNER

KERYGMA. See GOSPEL.

KEY. See BINDING AND LOOSING.

KIND, KINDNESS. The adjective "kind" translates the Greek *chrēstos*, which is used of God (Luke 6:35; I Pet. 2:30) and men (Eph. 4:32) in the sense of loving, friendly, generous. The expression *to chrēston* is used of God (Rom. 2:4) and the abstract noun "kindness" (*chrēstotēs*) in the sense of goodness or generosity is likewise used of him (e.g., Eph. 2:7). It is used also of men (e.g., II Cor. 6:6; Gal. 5:22). The verb to be kind, loving, merciful (*chrēsteuomai*) occurs in I Cor. 13:4. Outside the NT the word occurs in the LXX and in patristic and secular writers. Often the word Christ was written *Chrēstos* (itacism), "the Friendly."

BIBLIOGRAPHY
Arndt; LC.

J. THEODORE MUELLER

KING. See OFFICES OF CHRIST.

KINGDOM OF GOD. I. TERMINOLOGY. "The kingdom of God" occurs four times in Matthew (12:28; 19:24; 21:31; 21:43), fourteen times in Mark, thirty-two times in Luke, twice in John (3:3, 5), six times in Acts, eight times in Paul, once in Revelation (12:10). "The kingdom of the heavens" occurs thirty-three times in Matthew, once in a variant reading in John 3:5, once in the apocryphal work, The Gospel of the Hebrews 11. "Kingdom" occurs nine times (e.g. Matt. 25:34; Luke 12:32; 22:29; I Cor. 15:24; Rev. 1:9); also "thy kingdom" (Matt. 6:10; Luke 11:10); "his kingdom" (Matt. 6:33; Luke 12:31; I Thess. 2:12), "the kingdom of their (my) Father" (Matt. 13:43; 26:29), "the gospel of the kingdom" (Matt. 4:23; 9:35; 24:14), "the word of the kingdom" (Matt. 13:19), "the sons of the kingdom" (Matt. 8:12; 13:38), "the kingdom of our father

David" (Mark 11:10). Twice "kingdom" is used of the redeemed (Rev. 1:6; 5:9).

"The kingdom of God" and "the kingdom of the heavens" are linguistic variations of the same idea. Jewish idiom often substituted a suitable term for deity (Luke 15:21; Matt. 21:25; Mark 14:61; I Macc. 3:50; Pirke Aboth 1:3). Matthew preserved the semitic idiom while the other Gospels render it into idiomatic Greek. See Matt. 19:23-24 for their identity of meaning.

The kingdom of God is also the kingdom of Christ. Jesus speaks of the kingdom of the Son of Man (Matt. 13:41; 16:28), "my kingdom" (Luke 22:30; John 18:36). See "his kingdom" (Luke 1:33; II Tim. 4:1); "thy kingdom" (Matt. 20:31; Luke 23:42; Heb. 1:8); "the kingdom of his beloved Son" (Col. 1:13); "his heavenly kingdom" (II Tim. 4:18); "the eternal kingdom of our Lord and Saviour Jesus Christ" (II Pet. 1:11). God has given the kingdom to Christ (Luke 22:29), and when the Son has accomplished his rule, he will restore the kingdom to the Father (I Cor. 15:24). Therefore it is, "the kingdom of Christ and of God" (Eph. 5:5). The kingdom of the world is to become "the kingdom of our Lord and of his Christ" (Rev. 11:15). There is no tension between "the power and the kingdom of our God and the authority of his Christ" (Rev. 12:10).

II. THE SECULAR USE. *Basileia* is first the authority to rule as a king, and secondly the realm over which the reign is exercised.

A. *The Abstract Meaning.* In Luke 19:12, 15, a nobleman went into a far country to receive a "kingdom," i.e., authority to rule. Rev. 17:12 speaks of ten kings who have not yet received a "kingdom"; they are to "receive authority as kings" for one hour. These kings give over their "kingdom," their authority, to the Beast (Rev. 17:17). The harlot is the great city which has "kingdom," dominion over the kings of the earth (Rev. 17:18).

B. *The Concrete Meaning.* The kingdom is also a realm over which a reign is exercised. The idea of a realm is found in Matt. 4:8 = Luke 4:5; Matt. 24:7; Mark 6:23; Rev. 16:10.

III. THE KINGDOM IS GOD'S REIGN. The "Kingdom of God" means primarily the rule of God, the divine kingly authority.

A. *The Old Testament Usage.* The Hebrew word *malkût*, like *basileia*, carries primarily

the abstract rather than the concrete meaning. A king's reign is frequently dated by the phrase, "in the . . . year of this *malkût*," i.e., of his reign (I Chron. 26:31; Dan. 1:1). The establishment of Solomon's *malkût* (I Kings 2:12) meant the securing of his reign. The reception of Saul's *malkût* by David (I Chron. 12:23 [Heb., vs. 24]), is the authority to reign as king. The abstract idea is evident when the word is placed in parallelism with such abstract concepts as power, might, glory, dominion (Dan. 2:37, 4:34 [Aram. vs. 31], 7:14).

When *malkût* is used of God, it almost always refers to his authority or his rule as the heavenly King. See Ps. 22:28 (Heb., vs. 29), 103:19; 145:11, 13; Obad. 21; Dan. 6:26.

B. *The New Testament.* The kingdom of God is the divine authority and rule given by the Father to the Son (Luke 22:29). Christ will exercise this rule until he has subdued all that is hostile to God. When he has put all enemies under his feet, he will return the kingdom — his messianic authority — to the Father (I Cor. 15:24-28). The kingdom (not kingdoms) now exercised by men in opposition to God is to become the kingdom of our Lord and of his Christ (Rev. 11:15) and "he shall reign for ever and ever." In Rev. 12:10 the kingdom of God is parallel to the salvation and power of God and the authority of his Christ.

This abstract meaning is apparent in the Gospels. In Luke 1:33 the everlasting kingdom of Christ is synonymous with his rule. When Jesus said that his kingdom was not of this world (John 18:36), he did not refer to his realm; he meant that his rule was not derived from earthly authority but from God and that his kingship would not manifest itself like a human kingdom but in accordance with the divine purpose. The kingdom which men must receive with childlike simplicity (Mark 10:15; Matt. 19:14; Luke 18:17), which men must seek (Matt. 6:33; Luke 12:31), which Christ will give to the disciples (Luke 22:29) is the divine rule.

IV. THE KINGDOM IS SOTERIOLOGICAL. The object of the divine rule is the redemption of men and their deliverance from the powers of evil. I Cor. 15:23-28 is definitive. Christ's reign means the destruction of all hostile powers, the last of which is death. The kingdom of God is the reign of God in Christ destroying all that is hostile to the divine rule.

The NT sees a hostile kingdom standing over against God's kingdom. The "kingdom of the world" is opposed to God's kingdom (Rev. 11:15) and must be conquered. The kingdoms of the world are under satanic control (Matt. 4:8; Luke 4:5). Matt. 12:26 and Luke 11:18 speak of the kingdom of Satan whose power over men is shown in demon possession. This world or age opposes the working of God's kingdom; the cares of the age will choke the word of the kingdom (Matt. 13:22). This opposition between the two kingdoms, of God and of Satan, is summarized in II Cor. 4:4. Satan is called the god of this age and is seen to exercise his rule by holding men in darkness. This statement must be understood in light of the fact that God remains the king of the ages (I Tim. 1:17; Rev. 15:3).

The kingdom of God is the redemptive rule of God in Christ defeating Satan and the powers of evil and delivering men from the sway of evil. It brings to men "righteousness and peace and joy in the Holy Spirit" (Rom. 14:17). Entrance into the kingdom of Christ means deliverance from the power of darkness (Col. 1:13) and is accomplished by the new birth (John 3:3, 5).

V. The Kingdom Is Dynamic. The kingdom is not an abstract principle; the kingdom *comes.* It is God's rule actively invading the kingdom of Satan. The coming of the kingdom, as John the Baptist preached it, would mean a mighty divine act: a baptism of judgment and fire (Matt. 3:11 f.). God was about to manifest his sovereign rule in the Coming One in salvation and judgment.

A. *The Kingdom Comes at the End of the Age.* John looked for a single, though complex, event of salvation — judgment. Jesus separated the present and future visitations of the kingdom. There is a future eschatological coming of the kingdom at the end of the age. Jesus taught the prayer, "Thy kingdom come" (Matt. 6:10). When the Son of Man comes in his glory, he will sit on the throne of judgment. The wicked will suffer the condemnation of fire, the righteous will "inherit the kingdom" (Matt. 25:31-46). The same separation at the end of the age is pictured in Matt. 13:36-43. This eschatological coming of the kingdom will mean the *paliggenesia* (Matt.

19:28), the rebirth or transformation of the material order.

B. *The Kingdom Has Come into History.* Jesus taught that the kingdom, which will come in glory at the end of the age, has come into history in his own person and mission. The redemptive rule of God has now invaded the realm of Satan to deliver men from the power of evil. In the exorcism of demons Jesus asserted the presence and power of the kingdom (Matt. 12:28). While the destruction of Satan awaits the coming of the Son of Man in glory (Matt. 25:41; Rev. 20:10), Jesus has already defeated Satan. The strong man (Satan) is bound by the stronger man (Christ) and men may now experience a new release from evil (Matt. 12:29). The mission of the disciples in the name and power of Christ casting out demons meant the overthrow of Satan's power (Luke 10:18). Thus Jesus could say that the kingdom of God was present in the midst of men (Luke 17:21). In the messianic works of Christ fulfilling Isa. 35:5-6, the kingdom manifested its power (Matt. 11:12. *Biazetai* is best interpreted as a middle form).

C. *The Kingdom Is Supernatural.* As the dynamic activity of God's rule, the kingdom is supernatural. It is God's deed. Only the supernatural act of God can destroy Satan, defeat death (I Cor. 15:26), raise the dead in incorruptible bodies to inherit the blessings of the kingdom (I Cor. 15:50 ff.) and transform the world order (Matt. 19:28). The same supernatural rule of God has invaded the kingdom of Satan to deliver men from bondage to satanic darkness. The parable of the seed growing by itself sets forth this truth (Mark 4:26-29). The ground brings forth fruit *of itself.* Men may sow the seed by preaching the kingdom (Matt. 10:7; Luke 10:9; Acts 8:12; 28:23, 31); they can persuade men concerning the kingdom (Acts 19:8), but they cannot build it. It is God's deed. Men can receive the kingdom (Mark 10:15; Luke 18:17), but they are never said to establish it. Men can reject the kingdom and refuse to receive it or enter it (Matt. 23:13), but they cannot destroy it. They can look for it (Luke 23:51), pray for its coming (Matt. 6:10) and seek it (Matt. 6:33), but they cannot bring it. The kingdom is altogether God's deed although it works in and through men. Men may do things for the sake of the kingdom (Matt. 19:12; Luke 18:29), work for it (Col. 4:11), suffer for it (II Thess. 1:5), but they are not said to act upon the kingdom itself. They can inherit it (Matt. 25:34; I Cor. 6:9 f., 15:50), but they cannot bestow it upon others.

VI. THE MYSTERY OF THE KINGDOM. The presence of the kingdom in history is a mystery (Mark 4:11). A mystery is a divine purpose hidden for long ages but finally revealed (Rom. 16:25 f.). The OT revelation looks forward to a single manifestation of God's kingdom when the glory (q.v.) of God would fill the earth. Dan. 2 sees four human kingdoms, then the kingdom of God.

The mystery of the kingdom is this: Before this eschatological consummation, before the destruction of Satan, before the age to come, the kingdom of God has entered this age and invaded the kingdom of Satan in spiritual power to bring to men in advance the blessings of forgiveness (Mark 2:5), life (John 3:3) and righteousness (Matt. 5:20; Rom. 14:16) which belong to the age to come. The righteousness of the kingdom is an inner, absolute righteousness (Matt. 5:22, 48) which can be realized only as God gives it to men.

The parables of Matt. 13 embody this new revelation. A parable is a story drawn from daily experience illustrating a single, fundamental truth; the details are not to be pressed as in allegory. The kingdom has come among men but not with power which compels every knee to bow before its glory; it is rather like seed cast on the ground which may be fruitful or unfruitful depending on its reception (Matt. 13:3-8). The kingdom has come, but the present order is not disrupted; the sons of the kingdom and the sons of the evil one grow together in the world until the harvest (Matt. 13:24-30, 36-43). The kingdom of God has indeed come to men, not as a new glorious order, but like the proverbial mustard seed. However its insignificance must not be despised. This same kingdom will one day be a great tree (Matt. 13:31-32). Instead of a world transforming power, the kingdom is present in an almost imperceptible form like a bit of leaven hidden in a bowl of dough. However, this same kingdom will yet fill the earth as the leavened dough fills the bowl (Matt. 13:33). In neither of these two parables is the idea of slow growth or gradual permeation important, for our Lord nowhere

else used either idea. In Scripture natural growth can illustrate the supernatural (I Cor. 15:36-37).

The coming of the kingdom of God in humility instead of glory was an utterly new and amazing revelation. Yet, said Jesus, men should not be deceived. Although the present manifestation of the kingdom is in humility — indeed, its Bearer was put to death as a condemned criminal — it is nevertheless the kingdom of God and, like buried treasure or a priceless pearl, its acquisition merits any cost or sacrifice (Matt. 13:44-46). The fact that the present activity of the kingdom in the world will initiate a movement which will include evil men as well as good should not lead to misunderstanding of its true nature. It is the kingdom of God; it will one day divide the good from the evil in eschatological salvation and judgment (Matt. 13:47-50).

VII. THE KINGDOM AS THE REALMS OF REDEMPTIVE BLESSING. A reign must have a realm in which its authority is exercised. Thus the redemptive rule of God creates realms in which the blessings of the divine reign are enjoyed. There is both a future and a present realm of the kingdom.

A. The Future Realm. God calls men to enter his own kingdom and glory (I Thess. 2:12). In this age the sons of the kingdom will experience suffering (II Thess. 1:5) and tribulations (Acts 14:22), but God will rescue them from every evil and save them for his heavenly kingdom (II Tim. 4:18). Men should be careful to assure entrance into the kingdom of Jesus Christ (II Pet. 1:11). Paul frequently speaks of the kingdom as a future inheritance (I Cor. 6:9 f.; I Cor. 15:50; Gal. 5:21; Eph. 5:5).

In the Gospels, the eschatological salvation is described as entrance into the kingdom of God (Mark 9:47; 10:24), into the age to come (Mark 10:30) and into eternal life (Mark 9:45; 10:17, 30; Matt. 25:46). These three idioms are interchangeable. The consummation of the kingdom requires the coming of the Son of Man in glory. Satan will be destroyed (Matt. 25:41), the dead in Christ raised in incorruptible bodies (I Cor. 15:42-50) which are no longer capable of death (Luke 20:35 f.) to inherit the kingdom of God (I Cor. 15:50; Matt. 25:34). Before his death Jesus promised his disciples renewed fellowship in the new order (Matt. 26:29) when they would share both his fellowship and his authority to rule (Luke 22:29-30).

The stages of this consummation is a debated question. The Gospels picture only a single redemptive event at the return of Christ with resurrection (Luke 20:34-36) and judgment (Matt. 25:31-46). Revelation pictures a more detailed consummation. At the return of Christ (Rev. 19), Satan is bound and shut up in a bottomless pit, the first resurrection occurs, and the resurrected saints share Christ's rule for a thousand years (Rev. 20:1-5). In this millennial reign of Christ and his saints is found the fulfilment of such sayings as Rev. 5:10; I Cor. 6:2; Matt. 19:28; Luke 22:30. Only at the end of the millennium (*q.v.*) is Satan cast into the lake of fire (Rev. 20:10) and death finally destroyed (Rev. 20:14).

One interpretation understands this language realistically and looks for two future stages in the accomplishment of God's purpose, one at the beginning and one at the end of the millennium. This view is called premillennialism because it expects a millennial reign of Christ after his Second Coming. It explains the Gospel expectation in terms of progressive revelation. Dan. 2 does not foresee the church age; the Gospels do not foresee the millennial age; only Revelation gives the full outline of the consummation.

Others insist that there is only one stage of consummation and that the coming of Christ will inaugurate the age to come. The binding of Satan is the same as that in Matt. 12:29; the "first" resurrection is not bodily but spiritual (John 5:25; Rom. 6:5) and the reign of Christ and his saints is a present spiritual reality (Rev. 3:21; Heb. 1:3; Eph. 2:5-6). This interpretation is called amillennial because it does not expect a millennial reign after Christ's return. The thousand years is a symbolic number for the entire period of Christ's present reign through the church.

It is often overlooked that in both of these interpretations, the final goal is the same — the consummation of God's kingdom in the age to come. The debate is about the steps by which God will accomplish his redemptive purpose and not about the character of God's redemptive purpose.

B. *A Present Realm*. Because the dynamic power of God's reign has invaded this evil age (*q.v.*), it has created a present spiritual realm in which the blessings of God's reign are experienced. The redeemed have already been delivered from the power of darkness and brought into the kingdom of Christ (Col. 1:13). Jesus said that since the days of John the Baptist the kingdom of God has been preached and men enter it with violent determination (Luke 16:16). The one who is least in the new order of the kingdom is called greater than the greatest of the preceding order (Matt. 11:11) because he enjoys kingdom blessings which John never knew. Other sayings about entering a present realm of blessing are found in Matt. 21:31; 23:13.

The present and future aspects of the kingdom are inseparably tied together in Mark 10:15. The kingdom has come among men and its blessings have been extended in the person of Jesus. Those who now receive this offer of the kingdom with complete childlike trust will enter into the future eschatological kingdom of life.

VIII. THE KINGDOM AND THE CHURCH. The kingdom is not the church. The apostles went about preaching the kingdom of God (Acts 8:12; 19:8; 28:23); it is impossible to substitute "church" for "kingdom" in such passages. However, there is an inseparable relationship. The church is the fellowship of men who have accepted his offer of the kingdom, submitted to its rule, and entered into its blessings. The kingdom was offered to Israel (Matt. 10:5-6), who because of their previous covenantal relationship to God were "sons of the kingdom" (Matt. 8:12) — its natural heirs. However, the offer of the kingdom in Christ was made on an individual basis in terms of personal acceptance (Mark 3:31-35; Matt. 10:35-37) rather than in terms of the family or nation. Because Israel rejected the kingdom, it was taken away from her and given to a different people (Matt. 21:43), the church.

Thus we may say that the kingdom of God creates the church. The redemptive rule of God brings into being a new people who receive the blessings of the divine reign. Furthermore it was the activity of the divine rule which brought judgment upon Israel. Individually, the kingdom means either salvation or judgment (Matt. 3:11); historically, the activity of the kingdom of God effected the creation of the church and the destruction of Israel (Matt. 23:37-38). This is probably the meaning of Mark 9:1. Within the lifetime of the disciples, the kingdom of God would be seen manifesting its power in bringing an historical judgment upon Jerusalem and in creating the new people, the church. Paul announced the rejection of Israel and the salvation of the Gentiles (I Thess. 2:16; Acts 28:26-28). However, the rejection of Israel is not permanent. After God has visited the Gentiles, he will regraft Israel into the people of God and "so all Israel will be saved" (Rom. 11:24-26), receive the kingdom of God and enter into its blessings (see Matt. 23:39; Acts 3:19 f.).

The kingdom also works through the church. The disciples preached the kingdom of God and performed signs of the kingdom (Matt. 10:7-8; Luke 10:9, 17). The powers of the kingdom were operative in and through them. Jesus said that he would give to the church the keys of the kingdom of heaven with power to bind and loose (Matt. 16:18-19). The meaning of the keys is illustrated in Luke 11:52. The scribes had taken away the key of knowledge, i.e., the correct interpretation of the OT. The key of understanding the divine purpose had been entrusted to Israel; but the scribes had so misinterpreted the oracles of God delivered to them (Rom. 3:2) that when Messiah came with a new revelation of God's kingdom, they neither entered themselves nor allowed others to enter. These keys, along with the kingdom blessings, are to be given to the new people who, as they preach the good news of the kingdom, will be the means of binding or loosing men from their sins. In fact, the disciples had already used these keys and exercised this authority, bringing men the gift of peace or pronouncing the divine judgment (Matt. 10:13-15). The kingdom is God's deed. It has come into the world in Christ; it works in the world through the church. When the church has proclaimed the gospel of the kingdom in all the world as witness to all nations, Christ will return (Matt. 24:14) and bring the kingdom in glory.

BIBLIOGRAPHY

K. L. Schmidt, et al., Bible Keywords VII. Basileia (TWNT); G. Dalman, The Words of Jesus, pp. 91-146; G. Vos, The Teaching of Jesus Concerning the Kingdom of God and the Church; G. E. Ladd, Crucial Questions about the Kingdom of God; W. G. Kuemmel, Promise and Fulfillment; C. H. Dodd, The Parables of the Kingdom; R. H. Fuller, The Mission and Achievement of Jesus, pp. 20-49; A. M. Hunter, Introducing New Testament Theology, pp. 13-51.

GEORGE ELDON LADD

KINGDOM OF HEAVEN. See KINGDOM OF GOD.

KINSMAN. See GOEL.

KNOWLEDGE. The problems of knowledge that are raised by the biblical revelation are chiefly two: first, what is the nature of God's knowledge, and, second, what is man's knowledge, particularly man's knowledge of God?

Perhaps the fullest summary of the biblical material on God's knowledge is found in Stephen Charnock's Discourses upon the Existence and Attributes of God, Kregel, Grand Rapids, 1958, chapters VIII and IX, a study of some 200 pages.

The main point in considering God's knowledge is his omniscience: "His understanding is infinite" (Ps. 147:5). The items of God's knowledge are made in the Scripture in great profusion: events past, "God remembered Rachel" (Gen. 30:22), and "a book of remembrance was written before him" (Mal. 3:16); events present, "Doth he not see all my ways and count all my steps" (Job 30:4); events future, "In that day there shall be a fountain opened" (Zech. 13:1), and "He shall reign over the house of Jacob forever" (Luke 1:33); and, as well, hypothetical events contrary to fact, "The Lord said, they will deliver thee up" to Saul if thou stayest in Keilah (I Sam. 23:12).

Not so explicit but more important, God knows himself. When the Apostle says, "The Spirit searches the deep things of God" (I Cor. 2:11), the word search, as is also the case in Rev. 2:23, "I am he which searcheth the reins and heart" (cf. I Chron. 28:9; Rom. 8:27), does not imply that God had been ignorant previous to this search. In these cases, search means to know exactly and completely. Furthermore, that God knows himself may be deduced from his omnipotence, his blessedness, and perfection, all of which are expressed in sundry passages and divers manners.

The idea of omnipotence, perfection, and blessedness requires God to know all things always. His knowledge is eternal. Such an immediate and uninterrupted knowledge has frequently been designated as intuitive. God sees all things at a glance, as it were. He does not learn. He was never ignorant, and he can never come to know more.

This intuitive knowledge is distinguished from both the reasoning and the empirical learning of man. A boy in High School learns the axioms of geometry and painfully deduces the hitherto unknown theorem that triangles contain 180 degrees. God does not reason in this fashion. This is not to say that God is ignorant of the logical relation between axioms and theorems. God's mind, i.e., God himself, is perfectly logical. But he does not reason in the sense of taking time to pass from one idea to another. That is to say, there is no succession of ideas in God's mind. He does not first know one item and then come to know another of which he was previously ignorant. All ideas are always in his mind.

But though there is no succession of ideas in God's mind, it does not follow that there is no idea of succession. The logical succession of conclusion upon premise is a part of omniscience. Similarly the idea of succession in time is known to God. God knows that one event follows another in time. Christ came after David, and David after Moses. But God's ideas do not follow one another in time, for Christ was slain before the foundation of the world. Therefore God did not learn that Christ was crucified or that David came after Moses by waiting for history to show it to him. God does not depend upon experience. His knowledge is entirely a priori. Otherwise prophecy would be impossible.

Charnock says (Vol. I. pp. 456-57, ed. 1873) "As nothing that he wills is the cause of his will, so nothing that he knows is the cause of his knowledge; he did not make things to know them, but he knows them to make them. . . If his knowledge did depend upon the things, then the existence of things did precede God's knowledge of them: to say that they are the cause of God's knowledge is to say that God was not the cause of their being."

Because of God's intuitive omniscience, as well as by reason of his omnipotence and omnipresence, God is incomprehensible. This idea, however, turns the subject from God's knowledge of himself to man's knowledge of God. Of course God comprehends himself. In this respect God is not merely comprehensible but is actually known, understood, and comprehended. But God is incomprehensible to man.

Unfortunately, the term incomprehensible carries undesirable connotations. The word sometimes means irrational, unintelligible, or unknowable. Now, obviously if man could know or understand nothing about God, Christianity would be impossible. It is absolutely essential to maintain that the human mind is capable of grasping truth. Incomprehensible therefore must be taken to mean that man cannot know everything about God. It is necessary to assert that man can know some truths about God without knowing everything that God knows.

In reaction against the optimistic modernism of the nineteenth century, contemporary neo-orthodoxy (q.v.) has insisted on the transcendence of God. But it has distorted the biblical concept of transcendence to the degree of making God completely unknowable. Some of their phraseology may be repeated as examples. God has been called the Wholly-Other. Brunner writes, "God can, when he wants to, speak his word even through false doctrine." Another author denies that a proposition can have the same meaning for man as it does for God. Several theologians collaborated to say that "we dare not maintain that his (God's) knowledge and our knowledge coincide at any single point."

Now, it seems obvious that if a man knows any truth at all, he must know a truth that God knows, for God knows all truths. A sentence must mean to a man who knows its meaning precisely what it means to God; for if the man does not know God's meaning, he does not know the meaning of the sentence. Hence, if man is to know anything, it cannot be denied that there are points of coincidence between human and divine knowledge. Similarly God cannot be Wholly-Other, for this would deny that man was created in the image of God.

The neo-orthodox try to substitute a personal encounter with God for conceptual knowledge of him. Thought, they say, cannot grasp God, or indeed any persons. Persons are met, not thought. But in human relations wordless encounters do not produce friendship. There must be knowledge of character, and this comes mainly through intelligible conversation. Similarly, if God does not give us information about himself, information that is rationally understood, a personal encounter would leave our minds a religious blank.

The intricacies of theology and philosophy are very difficult. Epistemology (q.v.) is terrifyingly technical. Whether we learn by logic

alone as Descartes and Spinoza taught; or
whether we learn by experience alone as
Berkeley and Hume taught; or whether we
need Kant's *a priori* categories; or whether we
can receive truth only by revelation — are
subjects of interesting scholarly discussion. But
however it may be, the Bible does not countenance skepticism. It is not anti-intellectual;
it does not treat doctrine as unimportant, false,
or "incomprehensible." Rather it places considerable emphasis on truth and understanding.

"Grace and truth came through Jesus Christ
. . . And ye shall know the truth . . . I tell you
the truth . . . Sanctify them through thy truth;
thy word is truth" (John 1:17; 8:32; 16:7;
17:17; cf. John 5:53; 8:45; 16:13). In the
face of these utterances it is difficult to understand how anyone can seriously say that we
can be sanctified through false doctrine.

Or, again, "We *know* that the Son of God

is come and hath given us an *understanding*,
that we might *know* him that is *true*" (I John
5:20. Cf. also: I Kings 17:24; Pss. 25:5;
43:3; 86:11; 119:43, 142, 147; Rom. 1:18;
3:7; II Cor. 6:7; 7:14; 11:10; Gal. 2:5, 14;
Eph. 1:13 etc.)

These verses indicate that we can grasp
God's meaning, that the truth can be known,
and that God can be known. Christianity is
the religion of a Book; it is a message of good
news; it is a revelation or communication of
truth from God to man. Only if the propositions of the Bible are rationally comprehensible, only if man's intellect can understand
what God says, only if God's mind and man's
mind have some content in common, only so
can Christianity be true and only so can
Christ mean something to us.

See also EPISTEMOLOGY.

GORDON H. CLARK

L

LABOR. See WORK.

LAITY. From *laos* ("people"), the laity
ought strictly to denote whole people of God.
Historically, however, it has come to be used
of those who are not specifically ordained to
the ministry (clergy). The distinction is particularly marked in the Roman Catholic and
Eastern Orthodox Churches, with a strong emphasis on the fact that the duty of the laity
is to be taught, to obey and to make financial
contribution. The discontent of the laity has
found expression in the various church-state
conflicts and in a deep-seated spirit of anti-
clericalism in many countries. Protestant
churches find the term a convenient one when
it is desired to distinguish between ministers
and non-ministers, but it seems to have no
material validity in view of the fact that all
Christians are priests and all constitute the
real people of God. Hence it is perhaps better avoided in its traditional sense.

GEOFFREY W. BROMILEY

LAMB, LAMB OF GOD. Twice John
pointed Jesus out as the lamb of God (John

1:29, 36). In Acts 8:32 and I Pet. 1:19 he
is compared to the spotless lamb by whose
patient suffering and vicarious dying his people are redeemed. The term roots in the OT,
in the suffering servant of Isa. 53 (cf. Jer.
11:19); in the paschal lamb (cf. I Cor. 5:7;
John 19:36); and in the daily offering of
lambs in the temple. God provides the lamb
(cf. Gen. 22:8), to take upon himself, to
bear in his own body on the tree (I Pet. 2:24;
Isa. 53:4, 6); that is, to make propitiation, to
overcome and to take away the sins of the
world (I John 4:10; 3:5; 1:7). The Lord laid
on him, as the suffering servant, the iniquity
of us all. As the passover lamb, he redeemed
all the Israel of God from the bondage of sin
and Satan. Because he loves us, he gave himself up as a sacrifice to God for us (Eph. 5:2).

Using a variant Greek word, *arnion*, Revelation describes the heavenly Lord twenty-
eight times as the lamb. On the one hand, he
is fully identified with the lamb that was slain
in sacrifice, whose blood expiates the sins of
the redeemed (5:6, 9, 12; 7:14; 12:11; 13:8).
On the other hand, he is also the lamb who

has overcome death and received the horns of power and the eyes of the Spirit (5:6), so that he opens the seals to administer the heavenly counsels (5:7); he brings those written in his book to salvation (7:9, 17; 13:8; 14:1; 21:27); he conquers the powers of Satan (17:14); and he visits upon the impenitent the wrath of the lamb (6:16; 14:10). Triumphantly enthroned with God, he is the Lord of lords and the King of kings (17:14; 19:16), who receives divine worship and reigns forever (22:1, 3; 11:15).

BIBLIOGRAPHY
Arndt; J. Jeremias in *TWNT*; R. H. Lightfoot, C. K. Barrett, C. H. Dodd, W. Bauer, R. Bultmann, W. Hendriksen and E. Hoskyns on John; E. Lohmeyer on Revelation; The Book of Enoch, chaps. 89-90.

WILLIAM CHILDS ROBINSON

LASCIVIOUSNESS. The word *aselgeia* has two shades of meaning. It is used of licentious lechery especially in the AV, also of petulant wantonness as in the RV. The second meaning is the better, as describing conduct that is shameless and shocking to public decency — a "work of the flesh" (Gal. 5:19).

ALBERT VICTOR M'CALLIN

LAST DAYS. See ESCHATOLOGY, AGE.

LATITUDINARIANISM. A name somewhat loosely applied to a trend of thought within the Church of England in the late seventeenth and early eighteenth centuries which tended to reduce to a minimum the doctrinal content of Christianity, passing over in particular the doctrines of sin and grace, and which advocated a broad and generous toleration in religious politics. Though their calm moderation was in part a reaction against the ecclesiastical and theological strife of the earlier part of the century, the elevated but cold moralism which the Latitudinarians preached bore little resemblance to the NT gospel. The state of English society before the Evangelical Revival and the church's reaction to it are sufficient comment on their religion. Merging early with the influential philosophically-minded school of theology known as "Cambridge Platonism," it was the Latitudinarian outlook which formed (though not always consciously) the basis of the "broad" churchmanship and liberal theology of the nineteenth century.

O. RAYMOND JOHNSTON

LAUGH, LAUGHTER. These words are used today, as were their biblical derivatives, to denote: (1) loud laughter showing mirth or gaiety as opposed to sorrow and weeping. Such oriental loud laughter is rarely heard and only upon occasion of the utmost glad surprise. Christ's woe is pronounced on those who laugh now when no such surprise is possible (Luke 6:25); (2) Laughter of wonderment based on something too impossible to believe. The skeptical note is present, as when Abraham and Sarah laughed when they heard the promise of a son. And even when the promise could not be doubted longer by themselves they knew that all who heard would laugh at them for they were so old (Gen. 17:17; 18:12; 21:6); (3) Laughter in derision. In the Hebrew verbs *lā'ag* and *ṣāḥaq* the feeling ranges in expression from that of gentle mocking (Ps. 80:6) to the judicial laughter of him that sitteth in the heavens (Ps. 2:4). *Katagelaō*, the Greek equivalent, occurs only three times in the NT and carries the same thought of "loud and repeated guffaws of scorn."

F. CARLTON BOOTH

LAW. I. TERMS. Scripture is full of judicial terms such as righteousness, transgression, judge, judgment, covenant, condemnation. They define the relationship between God and man as essentially one of Ruler and ruled, King and subject. Hence the importance of the concept of law. The most frequent and characteristic OT word translated "law" is the Hebrew *torah*, which originally signified authoritative instruction (Prov. 1:8); hence it most commonly means an "oracle" or "word" of the Lord, whether delivered through an accredited spokesman such as Moses (Ex. 18:16) or a prophet or priest (Isa. 1:10). Thus *torah* comes to have the wider sense of all "instruction" (so RV margin) from God, e.g., Isa. 8:16-20, Mic. 4:2. It is therefore a synonym for the whole of the revealed will of God — the word, commandments, ways, judgments, precepts, etc., of the Lord, as in Gen. 26:5, and especially throughout Ps. 119.

Following the LXX, the NT uses the Greek *nomos* for *torah* (e.g., Deut. 27:26 in Gal. 3:10). In classical Greek the word meant a legislative code or one legal enactment of such a corpus, but in the NT the thought-content of the OT *torah*, with its emphasis on law as a personal word from God the Lawgiver, is nearly always present. Narrowly, *nomos* can be used to designate the Pentateuch because of its supreme importance as the basic document of God's revelation to his people (Luke 2:23-24; 10:26; John 1:17, 45; Gal. 3:17; James 2:10-11; etc.); or, more narrowly still, the Mosaic legislation, esp. the Decalogue (Ex. 24:12; Rom. 3:20); or, more widely, since all the Scriptures of Israel are the authoritative word of God, *nomos* can refer to the whole of the OT (John 10:34; 12:34; Rom. 3:19; I Cor. 14:21; etc.). The standard description of the OT is "the law and the prophets" (Matt. 5:17; Luke 16:16; cf. 24:27; Rom. 3:21; etc.). The usual Jewish threefold division is used in Luke 24:44. The traditions of rabbinic law are clearly distinguished from the divine statutes in the NT (Mark 7:5-13; Col. 2:8). The constant use of *nomos* in the singular (apart from Heb. 8:10 and 10:16, where the Hebrew OT original was singular) is an impressive testimony to the unity of the OT, viewed as it was by the NT writers as a coherent and completely authoritative expression of the mind and will of God. In Romans the word is occasionally used with other meanings. In Rom. 3:27 and 8:2 the idea of moral code is not present, but rather "rule of procedure" or "principle of working," i.e., a system characterized by the following genitival phrase (as also in James 1:25). A related use of *nomos* is found in Rom. 7:21, though here it means rather "the way things regularly happen," i.e., a law of action. In Rom. 7:23 and 25 "the law of sin" can only refer to a powerful inner principle which controls and determines conduct like a governing authority.

II. MAN, SIN AND THE LAW. From the first, Scripture depicts man as responsible to his Creator and under an obligation to conform to his will; thus he is given a law to live by (Gen. 2:16-17) as a test of obedience and faith. It is the commandment which examines him (Gen. 3:11) and which is the preface to his condemnation (Gen. 3:17). Though the promulgation at Sinai was a restatement within the limited sphere of Israel alone, obedience to the will of God remains binding on all men; the conduct and conscience of the heathen, cut off from any supernatural revelation, bears witness to some apprehension of the content of the law (Rom. 2:14-15). Since the Fall, all men retain some knowledge of the existence of God and the demands of their Creator (Rom. 1:18-32), so that divine punishment is justly meted out to unrighteousness before Moses in the days of the Flood (Gen. 6:5-17) and of Sodom and Gomorrah (Gen. 18-19), and inhumanity among Gentile nations is denounced as an offense later by the prophets (see esp. Amos 1:3—2:3).

To fallen man the law is an instrument of condemnation (Rom. 2:16; 3:19) in that it holds before his largely atrophied moral perception the commands and prohibitions of his Maker and hence gives him a clear knowledge of sin (Rom. 3:20; 7:7). It pronounces wrath on the transgressor (Rom. 4:15) and sentence of death, "slaying" him (Rom. 7:11; cf. Gen. 3); and thus has become a "law of sin and death" (Rom. 8:2) revealing the prospect of the whole race guilty and doomed before the judgment of God (Rom. 3:19). To those who begin to feel their guilt, the law may even become an instrument to goad them further into sin (Rom. 7:11) and hence the strength of sin is the law (I Cor. 15:56). Those who seek to merit divine approval by fulfilling the law's precepts are engaged in a hopeless task, for though eternal life is the reward of complete obedience (Rom. 10:5; Gal. 3:12), such obedience must be perfect (James 2:10), an obedience which only Adam in his innocence could render. This attempt simply confirms man's position as under the curse of God (Gal. 3:10). However, since the law can bring a man to see his own corruption, his need of pardon and gracious reinstatement — in a word, his hopeless condition without a salvation which is completely from God — the law has an essential preparatory work of conviction to perform, and 'it thus becomes a tutor to lead us to Christ (Gal. 3:24).

III. CHRIST, SALVATION AND THE LAW. The Gospels depict the life of Jesus Christ on earth as a fulfilment of the prophecies of the law even in its smallest details (Luke 24: 27, 44). In his teaching Jesus affirmed and upheld the authority of the law (Matt. 5:17-19) and as God Incarnate expounded it, cleared away erroneous interpretations and glosses, brought out its essential spirituality (Matt. 5 *passim;* 7:12) and showed its only proper foundation in love (Matt. 22:34-40). As born under the law (Gal. 4:4) he fulfilled the precepts of both the ceremonial and the moral law throughout his life, "fulfilling all righteousness" in the deepest sense (Matt. 3:15; 5:17). The perfect obedience of Christ to the law of God is not simply an example, but the basis of the redemption of his people who lay condemned by the law (Gal. 4:5). Justification, the central doctrine of the gospel, is nothing but the exposition of salvation in terms of God as King and righteous Lawgiver and man as rebellious subject. False views of justification spring from false views of God's character and God's law. Righteousness must be the basis of justification and righteousness is perfect obedience to the law. Those who are joined to Christ have his righteousness imputed to them. This union and consequent acquittal is obtained by faith when a man acknowledges his own unrighteousness and need of Christ, hence faith is an acknowledgement of the perfection and justice of God's law in both its prescriptive and condemnatory aspects; faith, in fact, establishes the law (Rom. 3:31). This is powerfully argued in Rom. 5:12-21. As Paul states in II Cor. 5:21, justification has two sides, both grounded in the character and law of God. Just as Christ's obedience is reckoned ours, so the condemnation of the law, the curse and wrath of God which our disobedience deserved, fell upon him, freeing us from the obligation of legal obedience as a condition of eternal life (Rom. 7:4-6), from condemnation (Rom. 8:1) and from the curse (Gal. 3:13). In the sense that this righteous status of believers in Christ is not obtainable by obedience to the law, it is "apart from the law" (Rom. 3:21) and its works (Rom. 3:28). Hence the sharp opposition of law and gospel in II Cor. 3 and Gal. 2 and 3, which does not contradict the teaching of Scripture that the law is holy, just and good (Rom. 7:12), but is rather aimed at those who are still attempting to establish their own righteousness (Rom. 10:3).

IV. THE HOLY SPIRIT, SANCTIFICATION AND THE LAW. In Christ the Christian is free from the condemnation of the law and from the necessity of fulfilling its precepts as a condition of eternal life; yet the law is far from irrelevant to Christian living. An outstanding prophecy of the new covenant (Jer. 31:33) emphasized a work God would do within his people, bringing a deeper apprehension and a more inward conformity to the law than was possible (or at least usual) in OT times; thus regeneration is described as a writing of the law on the heart (II Cor. 3:3) and the work of the Spirit through the gospel enables it to be called "the law of the Spirit of life" (Rom. 8:2).

Rightly understood, the law has always demanded a heart conformed to its requirements (Mark 12:28-34). The regenerate are thus commanded and to a large extent enabled to fulfill the law, but at a deeper level by virtue of their new spiritual disposition (Rom. 8:1-9), the motive of their obedience being love (Rom. 13:8-10). The obligation of love to God and man is the "law of Christ" for the Christian's life (I Cor. 9:21; Gal. 6:2 reflecting John 13:34) and it should result in an evident and distinctive life of righteousness (Matt. 5:16, 20). Hence Jesus does not abrogate the law but interprets it for his disciples (Matt. 5) and the apostles can naturally remind Christians of their duty in terms of the law (Eph. 6:2; James 2:8-13; I John 5:3). The Christian is under the evangelical obligation of love and the written law becomes his guide, a rule of gratitude. He may not despise external guidance since, being only partially sanctified, his conscience and good intentions are no infallible safeguard against failures in Christian duty. Indeed, as the law is fundamentally an expression of the perfect character and will of God, it would be impossible for it ever to cease to be the ideal of human morality.

V. HUMAN LAWS. Scripture regards the laws of any community as binding on the people of God unless they command or imply disobedience to God's revealed will (Dan. 1, 6; Acts 4:18-20; 5:27-29; I Pet. 4:15-16). The validity of civil legislation in no way depends on the character of the legislator(s), but rather upon the providential ordering of society, in which all authority is ultimately of God (John 19:10-11; Rom. 13:1-7; I Pet. 2:13-14), despite the fact that the rulers of this world are generally spiritually unenlightened (I Cor. 2:8).

O. RAYMOND JOHNSTON

LAY BAPTISM. The NT affords neither precept nor precedent for the administration of baptism except by an ordained minister. From an early period, however, laymen did give baptism where ministers were not available. The custom was defended by Tertullian and later theologians on the ground that what is received may be passed on, that the sacrament is more important than order, and that the rule of love permits it. Some early authorities insisted on certain qualifications (e.g., monogamy or confirmation), and the medieval church drew up an order of precedence. Luther approved of the practice, seeing in it an exercise of the priesthood of the laity. But the Reformed school rejected and suppressed it on the ground that it is not scriptural, destroys good order, and is linked with the false idea of an absolute necessity of baptism. Baptism by midwives was particularly disliked. The practice was fully debated in the Church of England, and eventually discontinued after the Hampton Court Conference in 1604.

BIBLIOGRAPHY

J. Bingham, *Works*, viii; G. W. Bromiley, *Baptism and the Anglican Reformers*, pp. 80-90.

GEOFFREY W. BROMILEY

LAYING ON OF HANDS. Since the hand is the primary organ of touch, contact with it is often considered a means of transferring powers or qualities from one individual to another. The hand is generally laid upon the head because it is the noblest part of man.

Laying on of hands seems to have played a significant role in the history of religion. For example, by seizing the hands of Marduk, the Babylonian king gained and annually renewed his dominion. Blessing was communicated to an Egyptian king by the deities' laying on of their hands, bestowing long life and a prosperous rule.

It was practiced in the OT for various purposes. The priest laid his hands on the scapegoat ceremonially to transfer to it the sins of the people (Lev. 16:21). Jacob placed his hands upon Joseph's children to convey his blessing (Gen. 48). In ordination Moses conferred a portion of his wisdom and spirit upon Joshua (Num. 27:18-23).

Christ himself employed the laying on of hands in different ways: in healing (Mark 5:23; 7:32) and in benediction (Mark 10:16; Luke 24:50).

Adopted into the life of the church, it was used with healing and blessing (Acts 9:17). It was also employed after baptism with prayer for the reception of the Holy Spirit (Acts 8:14 ff.; 19:1 ff.). And it became of special importance for the conferring of an office or assignment in the service of the church (Acts 6:6; 13:3). Out of this practice arose the rite of ordination in which special grace, *charisma*, accompanied by the gift of the Spirit, was communicated to an individual by the laying on of hands (I Tim. 4:14; II Tim. 1:6) — yet only by one who already possessed the Holy Spirit.

In Christendom today, laying on of hands is also practiced in confirmation, marriage, unction, visitation of the sick and private absolution.

BIBLIOGRAPHY

J. Behm, *Die Handauflegung im Urchristentum;* Hempel, Behm, Glaue in *RGG*, II, 1606-9.

HERMAN C. WAETJEN

LEAVEN. The word leaven represents two Hebrew words, *ḥāmēṣ* and *śe'ōr*, and the Greek word *zumē*. Presumably, leaven was kept as a lump of dough reserved between bakings. The feast of unleavened bread (*maṣṣâ*) at Passover time was instituted because the Israelites, leaving Egypt in haste, would have no time for leavening dough (cf. also I Sam. 28:24). Another word, *ḥōmeṣ*, is translated "vinegar of wine." It was not alcoholic, but acidic, as is shown by its setting the teeth on edge (Prov. 10:26) and its acid-base reaction with nitre (ancient *natron*, an impure soda, Prov. 25:20). It was a true grape vinegar.

Leavened bread was used in sacrifice only in the peace offering, where it was eaten with joy by worshipper and priest (Lev. 7:13) and in the wave loaves of the feast of weeks (Lev. 23:17). No leavened bread was to be burned on the altar or offered with a blood sacrifice (Ex. 23:18; Lev. 2:11).

In the NT it is referred to in the parable of the leaven (Matt. 13:33 ff.); in Jesus' warning of evil doctrine and hypocrisy (Matt. 16:6 ff. and parallels); and in Paul's warning of the leaven of wickedness (I Cor. 5:6 ff.; Gal. 5:9). Many (e.g., Scofield) have held that because leaven undeniably symbolizes evil sometimes, therefore the parable of the leaven signifies the spread of evil in the church. Others (e.g., Alford) hold that the point of this parable is rather the penetrating power of the gospel.

R. LAIRD HARRIS

LENT. The forty days of fasting immediately preceding Easter, beginning on Ash Wednesday (*q.v.*) and concluding on Easter Eve. The forty days do not include the six Sundays, which are feast days. It seems likely that in the early centuries the fast was one of forty *hours,* as part of the preparation of candidates for Easter baptism. Not until much later (*ca.* seventh century) did the forty days' period become universally recognized in honor of our Lord's fast in the wilderness (Matt. 4:2). As a time of abstinence, almsgiving, and acts of devotion, Lent is intended to serve as a preparation for the Easter festival. The name is derived from the old English *lenckten,* meaning the "spring."

FRANK COLQUHOUN

LETTER. In the sense of a missive sent from one party to another, the OT word is usually *sēper* and the NT counterpart *gramma* (in the plural). Examples are found in II Sam. 11:14 and Acts 28:21. The NT has other uses: letters of the alphabet (Gal. 6:11); the elements of education, whether elementary (II Tim 3:15) or advanced (Acts 26:24). In one passage (Luke 16:6-7) *gramma* is used in the sense of bond. The RSV renders it "written code" in Rom. 2:27.

Deissmann insisted that the epistles of Paul are properly letters, in that they are non-literary, personal, and not intended for general publication or permanent use. While substantially valid, this distinction ought not to be unduly pressed, for the NT epistles are of a higher order than private communications, both as to style and content. There is evidence that Ephesians, at least, was intended for a wide circle of readers (cf. Col. 4:16). See also EPISTLE.

Letter is sometimes used in contrast to spirit (*pneuma*), namely, in Rom. 2:29; 7:6; II Cor. 3:6. When allegorical interpretation was in vogue, "letter" was interpreted in these passages as referring to the literal statements of Scripture as opposed to the spiritual sense which one ought to discern. Modern exegesis is quite united in the position that Paul meant the legal code of the Mosaic law in contrast to the present economy of the Holy Spirit. There is some doubt about the first reference, but hardly any concerning the other two.

BIBLIOGRAPHY

Arndt; MM; B. Schneider in *CBQ* 15:163-207.

EVERETT F. HARRISON

LEVITES. (Less frequently, SONS OF LEVI). The three sons of Levi were Gershom, Kohath, and Merari; and they went down to Egypt with their father (Gen. 46:11). After the Exodus, when the terrible apostasy of the golden calf took place, they showed themselves loyal to the covenant (Ex. 32:26-29). This act of obedience is referred to in Moses' blessing of the tribes (Deut. 33:8-11). As a reward Jacob's prophecy concerning them (Gen. 49:7) was fulfilled as a blessing. They were "scattered in Israel," yet not as a punishment, but as an honor. They were set apart for the service of the tabernacle (Num. 1:47-53), being taken by the Lord in the place of the first-born of all the tribes (Num. 3:40-51). The three tribal families had each its special duties in connection with the tabernacle during the period of the wanderings (Num. 3:21-27). But the family of Kohath was especially honored, probably because it was the family to which Moses and Aaron belonged; and Aaron was consecrated high priest and his sons priests (Ex. 28:1). This elevation of Aaron and his sons led to a serious rebellion against the authority of Moses, which was severely punished (Num. 16) and the primacy of Aaron was established by the budding of his rod (Num. 17).

At the conquest the Levites received no tribal inheritance but were given forty-eight cities with their pasturages (Num. 35:1-8; Josh. 21:1-42). They were also allotted a tithe of the income of the tribes (Num. 18:20-25). But since the payment of this tithe was dependent on the good will and faithfulness of the people, the position of the Levite was precarious; and Moses exhorts the people to care for them as for the widow and orphan (Deut. 12:19; 14:27, 29). With the building of the temple, their duty of carrying the tabernacle and its vessels ceased; but David made use of them in instituting the service of song for the temple. He divided the thirty-eight thousand Levites into four classes, four thousand of whom were to be singers and musicians (I Chron. 23). It was also their duty to instruct the people in the law (Deut. 33:10; II Chron. 17:7-9; 35:3; Neh. 8:7).

It is significant of the difference between the status of priest and Levite that while 4289 priests (one-tenth of the entire number of returning exiles) returned from captivity with Zerubbabel, only seventy-four Levites are listed (Ezra 2:40); and when Ezra led back a smaller company to Jerusalem, he succeeded in securing only thirty-eight Levites.

The Levites are rarely mentioned in the NT, but were apparently an important class (John 1:19). Our Lord introduces a Levite in the parable of the Good Samaritan (Luke

10:32); and we are told that Barnabas was
a Levite (Acts 4:36). In view of the teaching function assigned them by the law, it is
quite probable that many of the scribes were
Levites.

BIBLIOGRAPHY
Oehler, *Theology of the Old Testament*, pp. 92-93;
ISBE ("Priests and Levites"). The critical theory is set
forth at great length in von Baudissin's art., "Priests
and Levites" in *HDB*.

OSWALD T. ALLIS

LIBERALISM. Religious liberalism (sometimes called "modernism" but more appropriately "neo-Protestantism") was a post-Enlight-
enment development in German theology
which arose as a protest against the intense rationalism of the Enlightenment and to confessional orthodoxy; and on the positive side was
an attempt to harmonize Christian theology
with the divers elements of the so-called new
learning. It is presumed to have commenced
with Schleiermacher's *Uber die Religion: Reden
an die gebildeten unter ihren Veraechtern*
(Berlin, Realschulbuchhandlung, 1806. First
edition, 1799), and ended with the publication of Barth's *Epistle to the Romans* (Munich,
Chr. Kaiser, 1919).

It spread to France, England, and America,
and then to the mission churches throughout
the world. In each country it took upon itself
a peculiar national impress of that country.
Coleridge's *Aids to Reflection* (American edition; Burlington, Vt., C. Goodrich, 1829. First
edition, 1825) was very influential in introducing neo-Protestantism into both England
and America. It appeared in late nineteenth
century Roman Catholicism as "modernism"
and was efficiently stamped out by the papacy.
In America it became virtually synonymous
with the social gospel.

Liberalism had a fourfold rootage. First,
philosophically it was grounded in some form
of German philosophical idealism (e.g.,
Schleiermacher in Romanticism; Ritschl in
neo-Kantianism; Biedermann in Hegelianism).
Secondly, it placed unreserved trust in the
new critical studies of the Scriptures which
contained implicitly or explicitly a denial of
the historic doctrines of revelation and inspiration. Thirdly, it believed that the developing
science of the times antiquated much of the
Scriptures. Fourthly, it was rooted in the new
learning and believed in a harmony of Christianity with the new learning. In this sense it
is modernistic (preference for the new over

the traditional) and liberal (the right of free
criticism of all theological claims).

Methodologically it first accepted one of the
current philosophies for its conceptual framework, and out of that philosophy developed a
doctrine of religious experience. With this
philosophy and this doctrine of religious experience in hand, it proceeded to Christianity,
wherein it performed a double action: (1) it
gave this philosophy and religious experience
a concrete interpretation in terms of Christianity; and (2) it altered Christianity to suit
this philosophy and this doctrine of religious
experience. Following this it reinterpreted
all the major Christian doctrines in the same
fashion. For example, the traditional doctrine
of the Trinity was rejected and replaced by
some sort of functional Trinity; the transcendence and wrath of God were replaced by overemphasized doctrines of divine immanence
and love. The incarnate Lord of Chalcedon
was replaced by Jesus, the first Christian,
whom God used in an unprecedented way for
an example of unmatched piety. The kingdom
of God was regarded as no longer founded
upon the death and resurrection of a Saviour,
but upon the spiritual and ethical quality of
the life of Jesus. Salvation was seen no longer
as freedom from wrath and sin, but from
sensuousness or a materialistic or selfish ethic.
The kingdom of God was shorn of its transcendental and eschatological elements and
converted into a religious and ethical society.

In that the radical division of saved-or-lost
was denied, and all men held to possess the
same religious potentiality, all men formed
the so-called brotherhood of man whose corollary was the Fatherhood of God. And in
that the purpose of the church was to bring
all men under the Christian ethic in every
aspect of their lives, it preached the so-called
social gospel.

With the coming of neo-orthodox and existential theology neo-Protestantism has lost its
place of theological leadership, a trend more
evident in Europe than America.

Schleiermacher's *The Christian Faith* (Edin-
burgh: T. and T. Clark, 1928), Ritschl's
*The Christian Doctrine of Justification and
Reconciliation* (2nd edition; Edinburgh, T.
and T. Clark, 1902), Harnack's *What Is
Christianity?* (2nd American edition; New
York, G. P. Putnam, 1903), and Fosdick's
The Modern Use of the Bible (New York,

Macmillan, 1925) are regarded as classical expositions of neo-Protestantism.

BIBLIOGRAPHY

H. R. MacIntosh, *Types of Modern Theology;* Karl Barth, *Die protestantische Theologie im 19. Jahrhundert* (2nd edition).

BERNARD RAMM

LIBERALITY. Although no substantive meaning liberality occurs in the OT the bounty of God is often mentioned in the Psalms. On the human side, the contributions for the construction of the tabernacle and temple finely illustrate it. The noun *haplotēs* appears seven times in the Pauline Epistles. It commonly means singleness, simplicity or sincerity, but in II Cor. 8:2; 9:11, 13, and, perhaps, in Rom. 12:8, it is better to render it liberality. The adverb *haplōs* in James 1:5, describes the manner of the divine giving. *Charis* (I Cor. 16:3) stands for a gracious benefaction. Paul attributes Christian liberality to the grace of God and commends systematic giving.

WILLIAM J. CAMERON

LIBERTY. See FREEDOM.

LIE. In Hebrew several words are used for lie, *kāzāb* and *šeqer* being the most common. The underlying thought is that of deceit or emptiness, and this is well brought out by the NT *pseudos.* The lie is primarily a false or pretended message either from or concerning God (Jer. 14:14; Ezek. 13:9; Rom. 1:25). It has its own attractiveness (Ps. 62:4) and creates a false assurance (Isa. 28:15), but its only result is to create error and delusion (Jer. 23:32), to undermine moral standards (Rom. 1:26 ff.), to bring disappointment when its hollowness is exposed (Isa. 28:17) and to incur the judgment of the God who cannot lie (I Sam. 15:29; Titus 1:2) and before whom no lie can stand (Acts 5:3 f.). Yet there can also be lying in the relationships of man and man, as typified in the OT by the false witness (Prov. 6:19). Lying is forbidden by the law (Ex. 20:16; Lev. 19:11), and belongs to the old life which is to be put off by the believer (Col. 3:9). It is a powerful ally of even grosser sins (II Sam. 11:6 ff.; I Kings 21:10), and the liar is warned that he shall not escape (Prov. 19:5, 9). Whether or not there are occasions for innocent or necessary stratagems (cf. I Sam. 16:2 f.) is much argued by casuists. But lying as such is obviously hateful to the God of truth, and

there will be no place for any form of deception, pretense or hypocrisy in the holy Jerusalem (Rev. 21:27; 22:15).

WILLIAM KELLY

LIFE. The OT has two main words for *life,* both very frequent: (1) *hayyîm,* "physical life" (Deut. 28:66), but with special reference to (a) the duration of life (I Kings 4:21); (b) its ethical content, as in Gen. 27:46, "weary of my life," i.e., of the distressing conditions in which he lived. True life was regarded not merely as physical existence but as that in which one enjoyed the favor of God and the consequent spiritual and material well-being. Deut. 30:15-20 plainly sets out the alternatives, "life and good, and death and evil." (cf. Ps. 30:5; 42:8, "the God of my life"). This meaning of *hayyîm* is frequent in Proverbs. (2) *nepeš:* the most frequent translation of *nepeš* in the AV is "soul," but it is not to be regarded as a separate spiritual entity within a man, but rather the individual life belonging to each man and animal; so the AV renders it "life" 119 times. Its root meaning is breath and H. Wheeler Robinson regards it as the breath-soul, dependent on breath for its vitality but not identified with it (*The Christian Doctrine of Man,* T & T Clark, Edinburgh, 3rd Ed., 1926, p. 15). Both men and animals are described as a "living being," *nepeš hayyîm,* in Gen. 2:7, 19, combining these two words for life. This *nepeš* was regarded as having close association with blood as the center of life (Lev. 17:11-14), so that the physical life of man was a union of the immaterial and the corporal. All life was dependent upon God for its initiation and maintenance (Gen. 2:7, 19; Ps. 104:27-30).

"Life" in the NT is designated by *zōē, bios, psychē.* Pagan writers use *zōē* for physical life as opposed to death, but in the NT this physical sense is infrequent (e.g., Rom. 8:38, I Cor. 3:22, Phil. 1:20, Acts 17:25; "lifetime" in Luke 16:25). Mostly *zōē* refers to that quality of life which is derived from God and which characterizes the personality of Jesus Christ and of those who come to God through him. It sets forth "the blessedness of God, and the blessedness of the creature in communion with God" (Trench). This life is derived from Christ (John 1:4), is imparted to those who are united to him by faith (Rom. 6:4; I John

5:12) and reaches through physical death to eternity (II Cor. 5:4; II Tim. 1:10). The emphasis in *zōē* is thus on the spiritual and moral quality of the life given to believers.

Bios on the other hand refers to the conditions of our present earthly life (Luke 8:14; I Tim. 2:2; II Tim. 2:4) or its quality ("the pride of life," I John 2:16), the emphasis, except in I Tim. 2:2, being on its worldly nature.

Psychē, often translated "soul," corresponds to *nepeš* in representing the life belonging to a particular individual, as in Matt. 2:20, 10:39: "He that findeth his life shall lose it," or Mark 10:45: "To give his life a ransom." Even the phrase: "Is not the life more than meat?" (Matt. 6:25), while it contrasts the value of the spiritual and the material, refers to the individual's own life.

See also ETERNAL LIFE.

BIBLIOGRAPHY
Arndt; Trench.

J. CLEMENT CONNELL

LIGHT. To the ancient Hebrew, surrounded by sun worshipers, light was a holy thing, the natural symbol for deity. God is pictured as creating light (Gen. 1:3) and being clothed with light (Ps. 104:2) in the OT; and the term is used in conjunction with life to express that ultimate blessedness which God gives to men (Ps. 36:9). In the NT *phōs* is employed as an expression for the eternally real in contrast to the *skotos* of sin and unreality. Some trace this contrast back to the antithesis between the realms of Ahura-mazda and Angromainyu in Zoroastrianism (*q.v.*); and it certainly colors the doctrine of the Two Spirits in the Dead Sea Scrolls. Plato associated the sun with the idea of the Good, and Philo regarded the Creator as the archetype of light.

In I John 1:5 it is stated absolutely that *ho theos phōs estin*. James calls God, as Creator of heavenly bodies, *patros tōn phōtōn*, (1:17), adding the caveat that he does not change position or suffer eclipse as they do. The Pastorals recall the majesty of God on Sinai by stating that he dwells in *phōs aprositon*. Light in the NT is more often spoken of as residing in the Logos and is described (John 1:3-4) as the life of men. It enters the world, shines in the darkness of error, illumines every man; but only those who receive the Logos become children of light and

ultimately enter the Holy City whose *lychnos* is the lamb (*arnion*, Rev. 21:23).

By becoming incarnate the Logos becomes *phōs tou kosmou* (John 8:12). In rabbinic tradition this phrase had been applied to Torah and temple and did not amount to a claim to deity; but for John it implies that Christ is the *phōs alēthinon*, the ultimate reality. By contrast there are many lesser lights or copies of reality, who derive their transitory flame from the Logos; such a *lychnos* was the Baptist (John 5:35). The true Light bears witness to himself, because light is self-evidencing, and by light we see light. The lesser lights witness to the Logos.

Paul's conversion is essentially an encounter with the *phōs ek tou ouranou* (Acts 9:3). The scales of sinful darkness fall from his eyes, and he is commissioned as a light of the Gentiles (Acts 13:47). He puts on the armor of light to contend with the rulers of world darkness, who are led by Satan, metamorphosed into a parody angel of light (II Cor. 11:14). He exhorts his converts to walk as children of light (Eph. 5:8).

During the Exodus God's light was displayed to Israel as his *shekinah* glory (*q.v.*) in cloud and fire. *Phōs* is also found associated with *doxa* in the LXX of Isa. 60:1-3. The transfiguration accounts contain both themes. Christ's garments become white as *phōs* (Matt. 17:2) and both Peter and John insist that they beheld the *doxa* of God on the mount (John 1:14; II Pet. 1:17). In the Fourth Gospel the light of Christ's glory is manifested not simply on the mount, but by all his signs, and issues in a *krisis* or discrimination by light: evildoers hate the light; truth-seekers come to the light; when light appears all men pass judgment on themselves (John 3:19-21).

BIBLIOGRAPHY
Arndt; C. H. Dodd, *The Interpretation of the Fourth Gospel*, pp. 201-12; *HDB*; Philo *Somn.* I. 75; A. Dupont-Sommer, *The Jewish Sect of Qumran*, 118-30; R. Bultmann, *Zur Geschichte der Lichtsymbolik im Altertum*.

DENIS H. TONGUE

LIKENESS. See FORM.

LIMBO. In Roman Catholic theology the Latin *limbus*, from the Teutonic, hem or border, refers to the abode after death of souls excluded from heaven but not worthy of punishment in hell. The limbo of the fathers, *limbus patrum*, "the bosom of Abraham" (*q.v.*), based on Luke 16:22, served as the temporary habitation of OT saints until "the descent of Christ into hades," when they were removed to heaven.

The limbo of infants, *limbus infantum,* is the permanent place of "natural happiness" for unbaptized children and the mentally incompetent dying "without grievous personal guilt" (*CE,* IX, p. 256). They are denied the beatific vision.

Donald G. Davis

LITURGY. The Greek word *leitourgia* meant originally a public or state duty. In the LXX it is applied particularly to the services of the temple in Jerusalem. As used in the NT it often bears the meaning of priestly service (e.g., Luke 1:23; Phil. 2:17; Heb. 8:6). In ecclesiastical usage, the word is employed (1) in a general sense with reference to any of the prescribed services and offices of the church's worship; (2) in a specific sense with reference to the formularies used at the celebration of the Holy Communion, the eucharistic office being commonly referred to as the liturgy.

The earliest liturgical forms of this latter kind are to be found in the *Didache* (ca. A.D. 100), which prescribes acts of thanksgiving for the cup and the bread, but also gives liberty to the "prophets" to use what words they like in setting apart the elements. The account of the Lord's Supper given by Justin Martyr (mid second century) also contains liturgical teaching, but indicates that at that time a place was still found for extemporaneous prayers and thanksgivings. It seems probable that by the beginning of the third century a set form of prayer was used for the consecration of the bread and wine, though the form varied from place to place. As Canon F. Meyrick has said: "Each congregation at first had its own formula; then each bishop had a special form for his diocese, which the various congregations under his charge were invited, but not compelled, to adopt. When Metropolitans were instituted, it was but natural for the suffragan or provincial bishops to give up their forms for those of the Metropolitan Cathedral, and in like manner the forms used by the Metropolitans were naturally assimilated to those used by primates or patriarchs, when those dignitaries had come into being" (*Protestant Dictionary*).

Around the names of the three great patriarchates, viz., Antioch, Alexandria, and Rome,

may be grouped the principal liturgies of Christendom. With the name of Antioch is associated the fourth century rite found in the *Apostolic Constitutions* and known as the Clementine liturgy. From this in turn was derived the Byzantine rite (Constantinople), including the famous liturgy of St. Chrysostom now in use throughout the Greek Orthodox Church, and also the Syrian and Persian rites. From Alexandria came the liturgy of St. Mark (fourth or fifth century) and various other Egyptian and Ethiopic rites. In the West, Rome developed its own liturgies, employing the Latin language instead of Greek; the earliest extant rite dates from the seventh or eighth century. Alongside the Roman rite until the ninth century there also existed the Gallican, which spread over the rest of Europe (Spain, France, North Italy, British Isles) and exerted a considerable influence on the Roman rite until, with the growing power of the church of Rome, it was finally suppressed under Pepin and Charlemagne.

The liturgies arising from the Reformation in the sixteenth century drew freely upon the ancient forms while introducing drastic and far-reaching changes. The principal schools of liturgical revision were those represented by Luther in Germany, Zwingli at Zurich, Bucer at Strasbourg, Calvin at Geneva, and Cranmer in England.

BIBLIOGRAPHY
W. K. L. Clarke (Ed.), *Liturgy and Worship;* L. Duchesne, *Christian Worship, its Origin and Evolution;* Y. Brilioth, *Eucharistic Faith and Practice;* F. C. Burkitt, *Christian Worship;* Gregory Dix, *The Shape of the Liturgy;* W. D. Maxwell, *An Outline of Christian Worship.*

Frank Colquhoun

LIVING. The Hebrew *hay* (adjective) and the Greek *zōn* (present active participle of *zaō,* "to live") are frequently translated by "living." Both words have practically the same meaning and are used in similar ways. *Hay* is often applied to God (e.g., Deut. 5:26; Josh. 3:10; I Sam. 17:26, 36). *Zōn* is likewise ascribed to God (e.g., Matt. 16:16; 26:63; Acts 14:15).

Hay is posited of such things as soul (Gen. 2:7), man (Lam. 3:39), and animals (Lev. 16:20). In a few places — as applied to water (Jer. 2:13; 17:13; Zech. 14:8) — it is used of spiritual realities.

Zōn is used in a few places to describe the living in contrast to the dead (Matt. 22:32; Acts 10:42; Rom. 14:9; II Tim. 4:1; I Pet.

4:5). Otherwise, in a deeply spiritual sense, *zōn* is ascribed to God (see above), Christ (Matt. 16:16; I Pet. 2:4), the Spirit (John 7:38) and the word of God (Acts 7:38; Heb. 4:12). As regenerated beings (Eph. 2:1; Col. 3:1), believers possess *zōē* in every aspect. They enter by a living way (Heb. 10:20); become living stones (I Pet. 2:5); are made a temple (II Cor. 6:16), church (I Tim. 3:15) and city (Heb. 12:22) of the living God; they trust (I Tim. 4:10) and serve (I Thess. 1:9; Heb. 9:14) the living God, whose children they become (Rom. 9:26); feed upon the living bread (John 6:51), becoming fountains of living water (John 4:10 f.; 7:38); present their bodies as a living sacrifice (Rom. 12:1); and possess a living hope (I Pet. 1:3).

The word "living" sometimes connotes the power to communicate life (John 6:51, 57).

BIBLIOGRAPHY

Arndt; James Donald in *DCG*; J. C. Lambert in *DAC*; W. L. Walker in *ISBE*.

WICK BROOMALL

LIVING CREATURE. "Living creatures" (Heb. *ḥayyôt,* Gk. *zōa* are mentioned in Ezek. 1:5 ff. and in Rev. 4:6 ff. (where AV has "beasts"). Whereas in Heb. 13:11 *zōa* means animals in the ordinary sense, in Revelation the word denotes "beings that are not human and yet not really animals of the usual kind" (Arndt). Both in Ezekiel and Revelation there are four such, but with differences: (1) in Ezekiel, each has "the likeness of a man" but four faces representing man, lion, ox and eagle; in Revelation the four are compared respectively with lion, calf, man and eagle; (2) in Ezekiel, as in subsequent apocalyptic literature, they support or guard the throne of God; in Revelation, they join the twenty-four elders in praising God and sing the Trisagion; (3) in Ezekiel they have four wings; in Revelation, six (cf. the seraphim in Isa. 6:2).

They are usually held to be akin to the two cherubim above the ark (Ex. 37:7-9). To the rabbis they represented four supreme orders of beings in the world. Others have interpreted them astrologically, or in relation to the four Evangelists. It seems best to regard them as portraying creation subject to God's will.

BIBLIOGRAPHY

M. Kiddle in *MNT*, pp. 90-92. P. Carrington, *The Meaning of Revelation*, pp. 115-16.

L. E. H. STEPHENS-HODGE

LOGIA. *Logia* (plural of *logion*) occurs four times in the NT (Acts 7:38; Rom. 3:2; Heb. 5:12; I Pet. 4:11).

The singular and plural forms are common in classical literature for "divine oracle." In LXX readings the singular occurs twenty-five times and the plural fourteen times, and the translators of the Pentateuch, Psalms and Isaiah regularly render *'imrâ* "utterance" by one or the other when God is the subject. Possibly the translator of Psalms equated *'imrâ* with Torah, especially in Ps. 119. *Logia* is used of human speech only in Ps. 19:14, and this was probably understood as a prayer for prophetic, and thus oracular, utterance.

In hellenistic Jewish literature, *logia* designates Scripture (Jos. *Jewish War* vi. 4), or any part of it (*Letter of Aristeas* 158, 177), including narrative. Of Philo's usage, Warfield says: "All that is in Scripture is oracular, every passage is a *logion,* of whatever character or length; and the whole, as constituted by these oracles, is *ta logia,* or even *to logion.*"

These facts fix the meaning in the NT. In Acts 7:38 the living oracles are the law: perhaps the written tablets. Rom. 3:2 refers to the OT as such, not to "those utterances in it which stand out as most unmistakably divine" (Sanday and Headlam), nor to the whole revelation of OT and NT (Kittel). Again, Heb. 5:12 refers most naturally to the OT, as the daily food of Christians. In I Pet. 4:11 alone is there no express relation to the OT. Here the Christian who ministers is to comport himself as the bearer of a "Thus saith the Lord" (although Bigg would paraphrase, "as Scripture speaks").

The Fathers use *logia* for the Scriptures (I Clement liii). The words of the Lord were also *logia* (Justin *Trypho* 18); heretics perverted them (Polycarp *Phil.* vii. 1). Papias wrote an *Exposition of the Lord's Logia,* of which a surviving fragment says: "Matthew wrote the *logia* in Hebrew, and everyone interpreted them as he was able" (Eusebius *HE,* iii. 39). Some refer this to the Gospel source Q or to a collection of OT messianic oracles; but Eusebius clearly understands Papias to refer to the First Gospel. He would call it *logia,* either because the teaching was his main concern, or because "oracles" was already a collective title for a recognized Gospel, as it was for the OT. The latter is clearly the sense in II Clement xiii, and probably in Polycarp vii.

Oxyrhynchus Papyrus I was entitled "Logia of Jesus" by the first editors, Grenfell and Hunt.

BIBLIOGRAPHY
Kittel in *TWNT*; B. B. Warfield, "The Oracles of God" in *Inspiration and Authority of the Bible*, pp. 351-407; J. W. Doeve in *Studia Paulina* (de Zwaan Festschrift) pp. 111-23; B. W. Bacon, *Studies in Matthew*, pp. 443-51.

ANDREW F. WALLS

LOGOS. The most usual Greek term for word (see WORD) in the NT: occasionally with other meanings (e.g., account, reason, motive); specifically in the prologue to the Fourth Gospel (John 1:1, 14) and perhaps in other Johannine writings (I John 1:1; Rev. 19:13) of the second person of the Trinity. In ordinary Greek parlance it also means reason.

I. JOHANNINE USAGE. At the creation, the Logos was already present ("in the beginning" relates to Gen. 1:1), in the closest relationship with God ("with" = *pros*, not *meta* or *syn*). Indeed, the Logos *was* God, (not "divine," as Moffatt — the anarthrous predicate is grammatically required [cf. C. F. D. Moule, *Idiom Book of N.T. Greek*, Cambridge University Press, 1955, *in loco*] but may also indicate a distinction between the persons — see Westcott *in loco*). This relationship with God was effective in the moment of creation (1:2). The entire work of creation was carried out through ("by" = *dia*, vs. 3) the Logos. The source of life (1:4, probable punctuation) and light of the world (cf. 9:5) and of every man (1:9, probable punctuation), and still continuing (present tense in 1:5) this work, the Logos became incarnate, revealing the sign of God's presence and his nature (1:14).

The prologue thus sets out three main facets of the Logos and his activity: his divinity and intimate relationship with the Father; his work as agent of creation; and his incarnation.

In I John 1:1 "the Logos of life," seen, heard and handled, may refer to the personal Christ of the apostolic preaching or impersonally to the message about him (cf. Westcott, *Epistles of John, in loco*). Rev. 19:12 pictures Christ as a conquering general called "The Logos of God." As in Heb. 4:12, it is the OT picture of the shattering effects of God's word (cf. the imagery of vs. 15) which is in mind.

II. BACKGROUND OF THE TERM.

A. *Old Testament*. Diverse factors give some preparation for John's usage. God creates by the word (Gen. 1:3; Ps. 33:9) and his word is sometimes spoken of semi-personally (Ps. 107:20; 147:15, 18) and it is active, dynamic, achieving its intended results (Isa. 50:10-11). The wisdom of God is personified (Prov. 8 — note especially vs. 22 ff. on wisdom's work in creation). The Angel of the Lord is sometimes spoken of as God, sometimes as distinct (cf. Judg. 2:1). God's name is semi-personalized (Ex. 23:21; I Kings 8:29).

B. *Palestinian Judaism*. Besides the personification of wisdom (cf. Ecclus. 24), the rabbis used the word *Memra*, "word," as a periphrasis for "God." This usage occurs in the Targums.

C. *Greek Philosophy*. Among the philosophers, the precise significance of Logos varies, but it stands usually for "reason" and reflects the Greek conviction that divinity cannot come into direct contact with matter. The Logos is a shock absorber between God and the universe, and the manifestation of the divine principle in the world. In the Stoic tradition the Logos is both divine reason, and reason distributed in the world (and thus in the mind).

D. *Hellenistic Judaism*. In Alexandrian Judaism there was full personification of the word in creation (Wisdom of Solomon 9:1; 16:12). In the writings of Philo, who, though a Jew, drank deeply from Platonism and Stoicism, the term appears more than 1300 times. The Logos is "the image" (Col. 1:15); the first form (*prōtogonos*), the representation (*charaktēr*, cf. Heb. 1:3), of God: and even "Second God" (*deuteros theos*) (cf. Eusebius *Prep. Evang.* vii. 13); the means whereby God creates the world from the great waste; and, moreover, the way whereby God is known (i.e., with the mind. Closer knowledge could be received directly, in ecstasy).

E. *Hermetica*. Logos occurs frequently in the Hermetica. Though post-Christian (cf. HERMETIC LITERATURE), these are influenced by hellenistic Judaism. They indicate the Logos doctrine, in something like Philonic terms, in pagan mystical circles.

F. *Sources of John's Doctrine*. John 1 differs radically from philosophic usage. For the Greeks, Logos was essentially reason; for John, essentially word. Language common to Philo and the NT has led many to see John as

Philo's debtor. But one refers naturally to Philo's Logos as "It," to John's as "He." Philo came no nearer than Plato to a Logos who might be incarnate; and he does not identify Logos and Messiah. John's Logos is not only God's agent in creation; He is *God*, and becomes incarnate, revealing and redeeming.

The rabbinic *Memra*, hardly more than a reverent substitution for the divine name, is not sufficiently substantial a concept; nor is direct contact with Hermetic circles likely.

The source of John's Logos doctrine is in the person and work of the historical Christ. "Jesus is not to be interpreted by Logos: Logos is intelligible only as we think of Jesus" (W. F. Howard, *IB* IX, p. 442). Its expression takes its suitability primarily from the OT connotation of "word," and its personification of wisdom. Christ is God's active Word, his saving revelation to fallen man. It is not accidental that both the gospel and Christ who is its subject are called "the word." But the use of "Logos" in the contemporary hellenistic world made it a useful "bridge" word.

In two NT passages where Christ is described in terms recalling Philo's Logos, the word Logos is absent (Col. 1:15-17; Heb. 1:3). Its introduction to Christian speech has been attributed to Apollos (R. L. Archer, *ExpT*, 60, 301).

III. Logos in Early Christian Use. The Apologists found the Logos a convenient term in expounding Christianity to pagans. They used its sense of "reason," and some were thus enabled to see philosophy as a preparation for the gospel. The Hebraic overtones of "word" were underemphasized, though never quite lost. Some theologians distinguished between the *Logos endiathetos*, or Word latent in the Godhead from all eternity, and the *logos prophorikos*, uttered and becoming effective at the creation. Origen seems to have used Philo's language of the *deuteros theos*. In the major Christological controversies, however, the use of the term did not clarify the main issues, and it does not occur in the great creeds.

BIBLIOGRAPHY

TWNT; G. T. Purves in *HDB*; R. G. Bury, *The Logos Doctrine and the Fourth Gospel*; C. H. Dodd, *The Fourth Gospel*; W. F. Howard, *Christianity according to St. John*; Commentaries on John by B. F. Westcott, J. H. Bernard, C. K. Barrett; R. L. Ottley, *Doctrine of the Incarnation*.

ANDREW F. WALLS

LONGSUFFERING. NT words built upon the stem *makrothymia* are generally translated "longsuffering" or "patience." The LXX evidences this Greek stem as equivalent to the OT *he'ĕrîk̲ 'ap* and *'erek̲ 'appîm* ("slow to anger"). *Hypomonē* is the most common NT synonym, pointing to bearing up under suffering or despair, whereas the *makrothymia* word group suggests self-restraint in the face of unsatisfied desire.

Longsuffering, a communicable attribute of God, expresses his goodness and forbearance as he endures the sinner's persistent obstinacy and wickedness and tirelessly calls him to repentance rather than to visit him with immediate judgment (Rom. 2:4; 9:22). In I Cor. 13, longsuffering is a human virtue, received (Gal. 5:22) from the Holy Spirit. God's longsuffering of stiffnecked Israel is mirrored in the one who "opened not his mouth" when oppressed and afflicted.

BIBLIOGRAPHY

Arndt; J. Horst in *TWNT*, IV, pp. 377-90; Vincent, I, pp. 760-61; Trench, pp. 195-200; J. Tasker in *HERE*; H. Lees in *HDCG*; W. Meikle, *Expositor*, 8th series, 19, pp. 219-25, 304-13.

BURTON L. GODDARD

LORD. The usual Greek word for Lord, *kyrios*, is used in a wide variety of ways extending from polite address to a superior, through subjection to the master of a house, the head of a family, or the supreme authority in a state, up to religious obedience to God. In the first century there were "lords many" (I Cor. 8:5), the title being used for each of the cult deities as well as for the Roman emperors. As applied to God in the OT, LORD denotes the active exercise of his power over the world and men, as the Creator and Ruler, the giver of life and death. Thus, LORD is a term expressive not of the metaphysical nature of deity, but of the sovereign authority of the Most High.

In the LXX, *Kyrios* directly translates *Adonai*, "Lord." Moreover, since Adonai was also read by the rabbis for the personal name of God, *Yahweh*, *Kyrios* in the LXX became also the translation for LORD or "Jehovah." In the NT, at times God the Father is addressed as the Lord of heaven and earth (e.g., Matt. 11:25; 9:38; Acts 17:24; Rev. 4:11). Generally, however, Lord is used in the NT of Jesus. And when he is addressed as the exalted Lord, he is so identified with God that there is ambiguity in some passages as to whether the Father or the Son is meant (e.g., Acts 1:24; 2:47; 8:39; 9:31; 11:21; 13:10-12;

16:14; 20:19; 21:14; cf. 18:26; Rom. 14:11). OT texts written of *Adonai* and *Yahweh* are applied to Jesus in the NT (e.g., Isa. 40:3 and Mal. 3:1 in Mark 1:3; Jer. 9:22 f. in I Cor. 1:31 and II Cor. 10:17; Joel 2:28 f. in Acts 2:17-21 and Rom. 10:13; Ps. 102:25 in Heb. 1:10; Ps. 34 in I Pet. 2:3; and Isa. 8:13 in I Pet. 3:15). Moreover, in the OT background of some of the cases there is the identification of *Kyrios* with *ho Theos* (e.g., Isa. 45:22 f. with Phil. 2:9-11; Num. 21:5 f. with I Cor. 10:9; Deut. 6:4-9 with Eph. 6:4; cf. also Ex. 4 with Acts 7). On the road to Damascus the Lord, the God of Saul's fathers, spoke to him in his native "Hebrew dialect" and identified himself as Jesus whom Saul was persecuting (Acts 9:5; 22:8; 26:14-15; 9:17; 22:13). Likewise the term *despotēs*, with its connotation of absolute ownership and unlimited power and its strict correlative *doulos*, "slave," is used both of God (Luke 2:29; Acts 4:24, 29), and of Jesus (II Pet. 2:1; Jude 4; cf. Eusebius, *Ecclesiastical History* I 7:14).

By his resurrection and ascension Jesus is exalted to lordship (Phil. 2:5-11; Acts 2:36; Matt. 28:18; Rom. 1:4). And the invocation of him as Lord is fundamental to the worship of the primitive community (I Cor. 1:2-3; 12:3; 16:22; Rom. 10:9), as it is of the prayers of individuals (Acts 7:59-60; 22:8-10; II Cor. 12:8; I Thess. 3:11 f.; II Thess. 2:16; 3:16).

W. Bousset and R. Bultmann hold that in an atmosphere in which every mystery religion had its cult deity, the Greek-speaking community in Antioch began to worship Christ as Lord in the same fashion as did the mysteries. Against their hypothesis there is evidence of the prior application of Lord to Jesus in the primitive Aramaic speaking community and in the teachings of Jesus. *Maranatha*, "may our Lord come!" (I Cor. 16:22; *Didache* 10:9; cf. Rev. 22:20), testifies to a worship of Jesus as Lord in the Aramaic speaking community which looked for his coming rather than that of the Father (Acts 3:20; I Thess. 4:16; 1:10). Phil. 2:6-11 is now recognized as a part of the primitive *kerygma* taken over by the Apostle from an Aramaic hymn. Jesus used the one hundred and tenth Psalm to describe the Messiah as David's Lord at the right hand of Yahweh and referred thereto in his answer to the high priest. There are a score of references to this passage in the primitive

Christian literature (Mark 12:35 f.; 14:62; 16:19; Matt. 22:44; 26:64; Luke 20:42; 22:39; Rom. 8:34; I Cor. 15:25; Col. 3:1; Eph. 1:20; Heb. 1:3; 8:1; 10:13; I Pet. 3:22; Acts 2:35; 5:31; 7:55; Rev. 3:21; I Clem. 36:5; Barnabas 12:10; James, as reported by Hegesippus in Eusebius, *HE* II 23:13).

The parables speak of a *kyrios*, a *kyrios tēs oikias* and of an *oikodespotēs* to whom the disciples are to give account with implicit reference to Jesus himself (Matt. 24:45-51; 25:13-30; Mark 13:33-37; Luke 12:35-38; 41-46; 13:25-28; cf. Matt. 10:35). The typical Hebrew repetition of *kyrie* in a context of the sovereign lawgiver and the final judge (Luke 6:46; Matt. 7:21-22; cf. also Matt. 25:37, 44) shows the heights of lordship toward which Jesus looked. The appeal of the centurion (Matt. 8:5-10; Luke 7:1-10) is to the *kyrios* to exercise his lordship. In Mark, Jesus is the Lord of the house (13:35); the Lord whose healing power the Syro-phoenician woman invokes (7:28); the Son of Man who is Lord of the sabbath (2:28); and the Christ who is the Lord of David (12:35-37). For this Evangelist, Jesus' advent is the coming of Jehovah prophesied by Isa. 40:3 and by Mal. 3:1 (Mark 1:2-3). For the angels, he is Christ the Lord (Luke 2:11); for Peter, the Lord of all (Acts 10:36); for Paul and for James, the Lord of glory (I Cor. 2:8; James 2:1); for John, the Lord of lords (Rev. 17:14; 19:16); for Thomas, "my Lord and my God" (John 20:28).

If one takes a comprehensive view of the NT, he finds Lord applied to Jesus in a threefold fashion. At times, he is addressed as teacher, rabbi, master or lord by his disciples, for he is their guide and instructor. At other times, he is spoken of as my or our Lord in the sense of the exalted Messiah reigning on his throne at the right hand of Yahweh. In still other cases Lord lacks nothing of the divine glory. Here, if one must distinguish, God is the term of pure exaltation, while Lord carries with it more expressly the idea of sovereign rulership in actual exercise, evoking obedient service.

BIBLIOGRAPHY

Arndt; LSJ; Thayer, K. G. Kuhn, K. L. Rengstorf, G. Quell, W. Foerster in *TWNT*; W. Bousset, *Kyrios Christos*; R. Bultmann, *Theology of the New Testament*; A. E. J. Rawlinson, *The NT Doctrine of the Christ*; V. Taylor, *The Names of Jesus*; R. H. Fuller, *The Mission and Achievement of Jesus*; E. Stauffer, *New Testament Theology*; O. Cullmann, *Christ and Time*; B. B. Warfield, *The Lord of Glory*; *Christology and Criticism*; G. Vos, *The Self-Disclosure of Jesus*; W. C.

Robinson, *Our Lord, An Affirmation of the Deity of Christ*; P. Wernle, *Jesus und Paulus, Antithesen zu Boussets Kyrios*, Z.Th.K., xxv (1915), 1-92; E. Lohmeyer, *Kyrios Jesus, Eine Untersuchung zu Phil.* 2:5-11; W. Lowrie, *The Name which is above Every Name*, ThT, viii (1951), 11-19; G. Vos, *The Continuity of the Kyrios Title in the NT*, PTR, 13 (1915), 161-89.

WILLIAM CHILDS ROBINSON

LORD'S DAY. The scriptural authority for the term is found in Rev. 1:10 — *en tè kuriakê hēmerâ*. The adjective *kuriakos*, "the Lord's," is also found in I Cor. 11:20 in connection with the Lord's Supper. In secular use *kuriakos* signified "imperial" and is extant as early as A.D. 68 (MM 364). The use in I Cor. 11:20 is earlier, and the fact that Paul uses "the first day of the week" in I Cor. 16:2 seems to show that "the Lord's Day" was not yet a widely used expression. In post-apostolic literature there are the following references to the Lord's Day: Ignatius *Ad Mag.* ix. 1; *Ev. Pet.* vss. 35 and 50; Barn. 15:9.

The origin of the Lord's Day must be traced to its association with the day of Christ's resurrection (*q.v.*). Christ sanctified the day by his resurrection and emphasized it by another appearing to the disciples on Sunday (John 20:26) and by sending the Holy Spirit on the first day of the week (Acts 2). Although daily gatherings were held in Jerusalem at the very first (Acts 2:46), gradually Sunday, the Lord's Day, became the distinctive day for worship (Acts 20:7; I Cor. 16:2). The Lord's Day is nowhere present in the NT as a fulfilment of the sabbath, even though other features of Christianity are presented in connection with Jewish ordinances (cf. I Cor. 10:16-21; Col. 2:11; Heb. 10:22). This silence with respect to the Lord's Day is especially marked in the Epistle to the Hebrews, where the sabbath is only mentioned as a type of the believer's rest.

The account in Acts 20:7 shows that the observance of the Lord's Supper was evidently a distinctive feature of Lord's Day worship from the very first. The collection too was a part of the activities of that day (I Cor. 16:2). Justin (A.D. 150) describes other activities (*Apol.* i. 67) as including reading the writings of the apostles and prophets, exhortation, prayer, the Lord's Supper, the collection. Earlier the *agapē* had been a part of the services (I Cor. 11:34) but was evidently discontinued by Justin's time.

See also SUNDAY.

BIBLIOGRAPHY
Deiss LAE, pp. 361-66; HDB, pp. 138-41.

CHARLES C. RYRIE

LORD'S PRAYER. See PRAYER.

LORD'S SUPPER. In each of the four accounts of the Lord's Supper in the NT (Matt. 26:26-30; Mark 14:22-26; Luke 22:14-20; I Cor. 1:23-26) all the main features are included. The accounts of Matthew and Mark have close formal affinities. So have those of Luke and Paul. The main differences between the two groups is that Mark omits the words "This do in remembrance of me" and includes "shed for many" after the reference to the blood of the covenant. Instead of the Lord's reference to his reunion with the disciples in the fulfilled kingdom of God, common to the Synoptic Gospels, Paul has a reference to proclaiming the Lord's death "till he come."

The meaning of Jesus' action can be best understood against its OT background. The meal took place in the context of the Jewish Passover. John says that Jesus died on the afternoon when the passover lamb was slain (John 18:28). In this case the Supper was anticipatory to the Passover meal. But the Synoptic Gospels tell that the meal was prepared for as a Passover, was observed with solemn and joyful Passover ritual, wine was drunk and it was held at night, and the disciples and Jesus reclined instead of sat. All this indicates that it was a true Passover meal. In this the people of God not only remembered, but again lived through the events of their deliverance from Egypt under the sign of the sacrificed Paschal lamb as if they themselves participated in them (See Ex. 12). In this context, giving the bread and wine as his body and blood, with the words, "this do in remembrance of me," Jesus points to himself as the true substitute for the Paschal lamb, and to his death as to the saving event which will deliver the new Israel, represented in his disciples, from all bondage. His blood is to be henceforth the sign under which God will remember his people in himself.

In his words at the table Jesus speaks of himself not only as the Paschal lamb but also as a sacrifice in accordance with other OT analogies. In the sacrificial ritual, the portion of peace-offering not consumed by fire and thus not offered to God as his food (cf. Lev. 3:1-11 and Num. 28:2), was eaten by priest and people (Lev. 19:5-6; I Sam. 9:13) in an act of fellowship with the altar and the sacrifice (Ex. 24:1-11; Deut. 27:7; cf. Num. 25:1-5 and I Cor. 10). Jesus in giving the elements thus gave to his disciples a sign of their own fellowship and participation in the event of his sacrificial death.

Moreover, Jesus included in the Last Supper the ritual not only of the Paschal and sacrificial meal but also of a covenant meal. In the OT the making of a covenant was followed by a meal in which the participants had fellowship and were pledged to loyalty one to another (Gen. 26:30; 31:54; II Sam. 3:20). The covenant between God and Israel at Sinai was likewise followed by a meal in which the people "ate and drank and saw God." The new covenant (Jer. 31:1-34) between the Lord and his people was thus ratified by Jesus in a meal at the Supper.

In celebrating the Supper Jesus emphasized the messianic and eschatological significance of the Passover meal. At this feast, the Jews looked forward to a future deliverance which was foreshadowed in type by that from Egypt. A cup was set aside for the Messiah lest he should come that very night to bring about this deliverance and fulfil the promise of the messianic banquet (cf. Isa. 25-26; 65:13, etc.). It may have been this cup which Jesus took in the institution of the new rite, indicating that even now the Messiah was present to feast with his people.

After the resurrection, in their frequent celebrations of the Supper (Acts 2:42-46; 20:7), the disciples would see in the aspect of the Supper the climax of the table-fellowship which Jesus had had with publicans and sinners (Luke 15:2; Matt. 11:18-19) and of their own day to day meals with him. They would interpret it not only as a bare prophecy but as a real foretaste of the future messianic banquet, and as a sign of the presence of the mystery of the kingdom of God in their midst in the person of Jesus (Matt. 8:11; cf. Mark 10:35 f.; Luke 14:15-24). They would see its meaning in relation to his living presence in the church, brought out fully in the Easter meals they had shared with him (Luke 24:13-35; John 21:1-14; Acts 10:41). It was a supper in the presence of the risen Lord as their Host. They would see in the messianic miracle of his feeding the multitude, his words about himself as the bread of life, a sign of

his continual hidden self-giving in the mystery of the Lord's Supper.

But they would not forget the sacrificial and Paschal aspect of the Supper. The table-fellowship they looked back on was the fellowship of the Messiah with sinners which reached its climax in his self-identification with the sin of the world on Calvary. They had fellowship with the resurrection of Jesus through fellowship with his death. As really as the Lord's Supper related them to the coming kingdom and glory of Christ, so did it also relate them to his once-for-all death.

It is with this background of thought that we should interpret the words of Jesus at the table, and the NT statements about the Supper. There is a real life-giving relationship of communion between the events and realities, past, present and future, symbolized in the Supper and those who participate in it (John 6:51; I Cor. 10:16). This communion is so inseparable from participation in the Supper that we can speak of the bread and the wine as if they were indeed the body and blood of Christ (Mark 14:22 "This is my body," cf. John 6:53). It is by the Holy Spirit alone (John 6:63) that the bread and wine, as they are partaken by faith, convey the realities they represent, and that the Supper gives us participation in the death and resurrection of Christ, and the kingdom of God. It is by faith alone that Christ is received into the heart at the Supper (Eph. 3:17), and as faith is inseparable from the word, the Lord's Supper is nothing without the word. Christ is Lord at his table, the risen and unseen Host (John 14:19). He is not there at the disposal of the church, to be given and received automatically in the mere performance of a ritual. Yet he is there according to his promise to seeking and adoring faith. He is present also in such a way that though the careless and unbelieving cannot receive him, they nevertheless eat and drink judgment to themselves (I Cor. 11:27).

In participating by the Holy Spirit in the body of Christ which was offered once-for-all on the cross, the members of the church are stimulated and enabled by the same Holy Spirit to offer themselves to the Father in eucharistic sacrifice, to serve one another in love within the body, and to fulfil their sacrificial function as the body of Christ in the service of the need of the whole world which

God has reconciled to himself in Christ (I Cor. 10:17; Rom. 12:1).

There is in the Lord's Supper a constant renewal of the covenant between God and the church. The word "remembrance" (*anamnēsis*) refers not simply to man's remembering of the Lord but also to God's remembrance of his Messiah and his covenant, and of his promise to restore the kingdom. At the Supper all this is brought before God in true intercessory prayer.

BIBLIOGRAPHY

E. Schweizer, *RGG*; J. Ramseyer, *CB*, pp. 239-42; J. Jeremias, *The Eucharistic Words of Jesus*; M. Barth, *Das Abendmahl*: T. F. Torrance, *Eschatology and the Eucharist* (in *Intercommunion*, pp. 303-50).

RONALD S. WALLACE

LOST. There are at least six Hebrew words which convey the thought contained in the Greek *apollumi,* which is used throughout the NT and translated variously, e.g., to destroy, to abolish, to ruin, to kill. In the middle voice the word means to perish, denoting irretrievable ruin (John 3:16; 17:12). As a participle used passively, e.g., throughout Luke 15 and in Luke 19:10, it signifies a condition of grave peril yet with the glad prospect of recovery. Christ ate and drank with lost men, sinners; he came to seek and to save that which was lost; and he made conditions of entrance into his kingdom such as were possible for every wandering sheep. He who is lost may be found; he who is perishing may be saved. See PERISH.

F. CARLTON BOOTH

LOT (THE), LOTS. These words usually represent the Hebrew *gôrāl* and *ḥēbel* and the Greek *klēros* and *langchanō.* The lot was an ancient method used to ascertain the divine will. The basic passage is Prov. 16:33.

In the OT we find such uses of this method as the following: (1) the selection of the scapegoat on the Day of Atonement (Lev. 16:8); (2) the division of the promised land (Num. 26:55 f.; Josh. 18:5-10); (3) the detection of a culprit (Josh. 7:14-18; Jonah 1:7); (4) the choice of a punitive expedition (Judg. 1:1-3; 20:9); (5) the choice of Saul as king (I Sam. 10:19-21); (6) the order of priests and their duties (I Chron. 24:5, 31; cf. Luke 1:9).

In the NT the casting of lots for Christ's garments (Matt. 27:35; cf. Ps. 22:18) and the selection of Matthias (Acts 1:24-26) constitute the major uses of this practice.

The Jewish festival Purim (Persian for *lot*), instituted by Mordecai, commemorates this practice (Esth. 3:7; 9:24-32).

WICK BROOMALL

LOVE. Scripture defines love in the only way that it can or ought to be defined; namely, by listing its attributes: "Love is patient and kind; love is not jealous or boastful; it is not arrogant or rude. Love does not insist on its own way; it is not irritable or resentful; it does not rejoice at wrong, but rejoices in the right. Love bears all things, believes all things, hopes all things, endures all things" (I Cor. 13:4-7). Love is fellowship between persons; it is an act of self-surrender.

God is love in his very essence (I John 4:8, 16). The eternal, self-generating nature of God actuates itself in mutual self-surrender between Father, Son, and Holy Spirit. When Christ came to earth, he incarnated perfect love. He bore the very stamp of the divine nature; those who saw him saw the Father. Even Christ's enemies could find no fault in him.

Salvation was conceived by the love of God. The Father planned salvation; the Son executed it; and the Holy Spirit applies it. There is such perfect unity in the Godhead that some acts of redemption are attributed to either a specific person or to the Godhead essentially. The resurrection of Christ is an example of this.

Love is the true point of contact between God and man. Man is made in the image of God, and the image of God is the capacity of self-surrender. The more kind and loving a man is, the more like God he is. A good man prefers others before himself; a bad man is selfish.

Love nullifies law by overcoming law, for love contains its own sense of obligation. If a mother hears the cries of her children, she rushes to their side without the promptings of legal duty. Love needs no law. Therefore, when Christians are commanded to love, the command is as much a judgment against unloveliness as it is a prescription to be lovely.

The first and greatest commandment is, "Hear, O Israel: The Lord our God, the Lord is one; and you shall love the Lord your God with all your heart, and with all your soul, and with all your mind, and with all your strength" (Mark 12:29-30). Since we are totally dependent upon God, we are not rightly related to God unless we are totally surrendered. Love for God issues in worship, and worship issues in fellowship — a fellowship made possible by the life and death of Christ.

The second greatest commandment is, "You shall love your neighbor as yourself" (Mark 12:31). Every normal human being has a sense of his own spiritual dignity written on his heart. He will call no man good who fails to give spontaneous signs of receiving his dignity. Thus, self-love is the basis of love for one's neighbor. We are to love our neighbor with the same degree of zeal and consistency with which we love ourselves. And since there is no practical limit to the claims of self-love, there is no practical limit to our duty toward a neighbor.

As Christ prepared to leave the world, he said to his disciples, "A new commandment I give to you, that you love one another; even as I have loved you, that you also love one another" (John 13:34). Moses gave form to the law of love (Lev. 19:18; Deut. 6:5), but only Christ could give it substance. The life of Christ is the final norm by which a Christian measures virtue in himself and others. Christ perfected human nature by loving God with all his heart and his neighbor as himself.

Love may or may not be accompanied by personal affection. We can be kind and thoughtful to a person, even though we may dislike him. Christ commands us to love even our enemies. "For if you love those who love you, what reward have you? . . . You, therefore, must be perfect, even as your heavenly Father is perfect" (Matt. 5:46-48). Since God loved us while we were yet in our sins (Rom. 5:8), we possess a vital motive for loving those who are unlovely.

Love is the mark of a true disciple. "By this all men will know that you are my disciples, if you have love for one another" (John 13:35). J. C. Ryle observes that humility and love are precisely the graces which the men of the world can understand, if they do not comprehend doctrines. They are the graces about which there is no mystery, and they are within the reach of all classes.

Love is the key to happiness as well as virtue, for without love there is no life. A potential suicide may exist, but he does not have life. Since he does not love, he does not enjoy the release which comes from self-sur-

render. He that saves himself will lose himself.

The Greeks rightly understood that man is not virtuous until he actuates his essence. But the Greeks confused the rational man with the vital man. They thought that man is good when he is subject to the dictates of reason. But this strategy leaves pride and selfishness intact. A rational man may evade the task of self-surrender, but in doing so he falls short of the glory of God.

BIBLIOGRAPHY

S. Kierkegaard, *Works of Love*; Reinhold Niebuhr. "Love and Law in Protestantism and Catholicism" in *Christian Realism and Political Problems*, pp. 147-73; Anders Nygren, *Agape and Eros*.

EDWARD JOHN CARNELL

LOVE FEAST, THE. I. IN THE NT. The brotherly love between Christians which was enjoined by Jesus (John 13:34; Greek *agapē*) found its expression in three practical ways. It was commonly exercised in almsgiving; hence on twenty-six occasions *agapē* is translated in the AV "charity." In the church gatherings and in Christian greetings it was displayed by the kiss (I Pet. 5:14; see also Rom. 16:16; I Cor. 16:20; II Cor. 13:12; I Thess. 5:26). And gradually the term came to be applied to a common meal shared by believers. Although these meals are called *agapae* only in Jude 12 and possibly II Pet. 2:13, where there is a variant reading of *agapais* for *apatais* ("deceivings"), there is a considerable amount of other evidence for their existence in the early church.

In Acts 2:42-47 there is an account of the early form of "communism" practiced by the believers, which includes breaking bread from house to house, and eating their meat (Greek *trophē*) with gladness and singleness of heart. The first phrase may refer to the administration of the Lord's Supper, but the second obviously indicates a full meal. Similar "communistic" behavior is mentioned in Acts 4:32. By the time of Acts 6:1 ff. the increase of disciples in the Jerusalem church led to the appointment of the seven to serve tables, which presumably refers to the responsibility for arranging the common meals. R. L. Cole (*Love-Feasts, A History of the Christian Agape*, Kelly, London, 1916) suggests that this number was selected in order that each one might be responsible for a different day of the week. This arrangement arose from the complaint of the Hellenists (*q.v.*) that their widows were being neglected, and so would indicate that already these common meals were being held for charitable purposes, as was indeed the custom later.

When Paul was at Troas (Acts 20:6-12) there took place on the first day of the week both a "breaking of bread" and a full meal (which idea is contained in the verb *geusamenos*, used here for eating, cf. Acts 10:10). Both here and in 2:42 it is difficult to determine whether the phrase "breaking of bread" denotes a common meal or is a more restricted reference to the Lord's Supper: whenever these words occur together in the Gospels they describe the action of Jesus (Matt. 26:26; Mark 14:22; Luke 22:19; 24:30, 35). Certainly by the time of Paul's writing to the Corinthians (*ca.* A.D. 55) it is evident that that church observed the practice of meeting together for a common meal before partaking of the Lord's Supper (I Cor. 11:17-34). This custom, however, does not appear to have been observed always in the spirit of *agapē*, for the apostle complains that some make it an excuse for gluttony, while others go without: in vs. 21 *to idion deipnon* may refer to the fact that they refused to pool their food, or that from such a pool each took as much as possible for himself. At all events the situation described here is possible only in the context of a meal more substantial than, and preceding, the bread and wine of the Lord's Supper.

Various theories have been put forward suggesting that the *agapē* was a development from pagan guilds or Jewish common meals, or that it was necessitated by the common desire to avoid meats offered to idols. From the fact that most early Christian paintings found in the catacombs depicting the *agapē* show seven persons partaking, Cole argues that the custom developed from the incident on the shore of Tiberias, where Jesus shared the breakfast meal with seven of his disciples (John 21), and that the conversation with Peter on that occasion supplied the title of *agapē* for this meal. It is equally possible that the meal may have arisen from a desire to perpetuate the table-fellowship which the apostles had enjoyed during their Lord's earthly life, and that later as the church grew and communal living became imposs'ble the common meal was continued before the Lord's Supper in an effort to place the receiving of that sacrament in its historical context. The fact that the Johannine account points to the giving of the new commandment of mutual *agapē* at that meal (John 13:34) would be sufficient reason for the application of that name to the rite.

II. IN CHURCH HISTORY. Ignatius (*ad Smyrnaeos* viii. 2) refers to the *agapē*, as does the *Didachē* (x. 1 and xi. 9), the latter suggesting that it still preceded the Eucharist. By the time of Tertullian (*Apology* xxxix; *De Jejuniis* xvii; *De Corona Militis* iii) the Eucharist was celebrated early and the *agapē* later at a separate service, and this may be the practice referred to by Pliny in his letter to Trajan (*Epp.* x. 96), though his information is not altogether clear. Clement of Alexandria (*Paedagogus* ii. 1 and *Stromata* iii. 2) gives evidence also of the separation of the two observances, and Chrysostom (*Homily* xxvii on I Cor. 11:17) agrees with the order mentioned by Tertullian, but while he calls the *agapē* "a custom most beautiful and beneficial; for it was a supporter of love, a solace of poverty, and a discipline of humility," he does add that by his day it had become corrupt. In times of persecution the custom grew up of celebrating *agapae* in prison with condemned martyrs on the eve of their execution (see the *Passion of Perpetua and Felicitas* xvii. 1, and Lucian *De Morte Peregrini* xii), whence developed the practice of holding commemorative *agapae* on the anniversaries of their deaths, and these gave rise to the feasts and vigils which are observed today. *Agapae* also took place on the occasion of weddings (Gregory of Nazianzus *Epp.* i. 14) and funerals (*Apostolic Constitutions* viii. 42).

During the fourth century the *agapē* became increasingly the object of disfavor, apparently because of disorders at the celebration and also because problems were raised by the expanding membership of the church, and an increasing emphasis was being placed on the Eucharist. Augustine mentions its disuse (*Ep. ad Aurelium* xxii. 4; see also *Confessions* vi. 2), and Canons twenty-seven and twenty-eight of the Council of Laodicaea (363) restricted the abuses. The Third Council of Carthage (393) and the Second Council of Orleans (541) reiterated this legislation which prohibited feasting in churches, and the Trullan Council of 692 decreed that honey and milk were not to be offered on the altar (Canon 57), and that those who held love feasts in churches should be excommunicated (Canon 74).

There is evidence that bread and wine

(*Didachē*), vegetables and salt (*Acts of Paul and Thecla* xxv), fishes (Catacomb paintings), meat, poultry, cheese, milk and honey (Augustine *contra Faustum* xx. 20), and *pultes*, "a pottage" (Augustine), were consumed on different occasions at the *agapē*.

III. The Agapē in Modern Times. In the Eastern Church the rite has persisted, and is still observed in sections of the Orthodox Church, where it precedes the Eucharist, and in the Church of St. Thomas in India. From the Eastern Church it was continued through the Church of Bohemia to John Hus and the Unitas Fratrum, whence it was adopted by the Moravians. From them John Wesley introduced the practice within Methodism (see references in his *Journal*), but the only survival of it within that body today is the issue of a quarterly membership ticket which formerly qualified for admission to the love feast. An offshoot of Methodism in England, known as the Peculiar People, still holds the love feast. In the Anglican Prayer Book of 1662 the only survival is probably the collection of alms for the poor during the Communion Service, but the practice of the Sovereign's distribution of Maundy money is a relic of the *agapē*, and in this connection it is interesting that the Epistle appointed for Maundy Thursday is I Cor. 11:17-34. A modern attempt to revive the custom can be seen in the increasing practice of holding a "parish breakfast" following the early Communion service, and experiments at using the *agapē* as an opportunity for interdenominational fellowship are described by Frank Baker in *Methodism and the Love-Feast* (Epworth Press, London, 1957).

BIBLIOGRAPHY
Arndt; Maclean in *HERE; HDAC; ISBE;* Dom Leclerq in *Dictionnaire d'Archéologie Chrétienne;* J. F. Keating, *The Agapē and the Eucharist in the Early Church;* P. Battifol, *Études d'Histoire et de Théologie Positive;* J. C. Lambert, *Sacraments in the New Testament*, pp. 318-45.

                                    David H. Wheaton

LOVING-KINDNESS. The word denotes affectionate kindness produced by deep-felt personal love. Coverdale-coined, it is the AV translation (especially in Pss.) of one out of eight occurrences of the Hebrew *ḥesed*, a communicable attribute of God but not used in that version except for God's love to man. It also stands uniformly for *ḥesed* in the ASV when the reference is to the divine love but is not used in other cases. Other translations of *ḥesed* are merciful kindness, kindness, mercy, pity, favor and goodness. See Mercy and accompanying bibliography.

BIBLIOGRAPHY
R. Bultmann in *TWNT*, II, pp. 475-79; *Oxford English Dictionary;* J. Hastings in *HDB;* W. Walker in *ISBE.*

                                    Burton L. Goddard

LUST. See Desire, Concupiscence.

LUTHERANISM. A term, broadly designating the tenets, principles, and other ecclesiastical characteristics of the Lutheran Church, founded by Luther's Reformation (1483-1546). Lutheranism accepts the canonical Scriptures of the Old and New Testaments as the inspired infallible word of God and the sole source and rule of faith and life (*sola Scriptura*), the ancient Ecumenical Creeds (the Apostles', the Nicene, the Athanasian) and the particular Lutheran confessions (the Unaltered Augsburg Confession, 1530; the Apology, 1531; the Smalcald Articles, 1537; Luther's Small and Large Catechisms, 1529; the Formula of Concord, 1577) as the true declaration of the biblical doctrine. While not all Lutheran communions have officially adopted all these Confessions as binding, the Unaltered Augsburg Confession governs all Lutherans as the creed which seeks to express the continuity of the faith of the Apostles to its own time.

The central teaching of Lutheranism is the doctrine of justification and salvation by grace (*sola gratia*) through faith in the divine-human Christ (*sola fide*) who by his vicarious satisfaction has atoned for the sins of the world (universal grace). It sharply distinguishes between the law and the gospel as God's commanding and promising word, but stresses, above all, the gospel of Christ's free and perfect atonement as the central teaching of Scripture. This, strictly speaking, is the only means of grace, which by its presence in and connection with the sacraments, Baptism and the Lord's Supper, renders also these divinely instituted ordinances efficacious means by which the Holy Spirit offers, conveys, and seals the forgiveness of sins, life, and salvation which the redeeming Christ has secured for all sinners.

Lutheranism teaches the total corruption of human nature since Adam's fall and denies natural man's free will in spiritual matters. It emphasizes pedo-baptism and close communion, separation of church and state in principle, believes in confessionalism and therefore opposes religious unionism as also Freemasonry and lodgery in general as a denial of the gospel way of salvation. It advocates Christian education in parish schools and church schools, favors liturgical services that promote the divine word, and considers confirmation a church rite and not a sacrament. It regards as the true Christian or apostolic church the communion of all believers in Christ, which to men is invisible. Lutheranism repudiates all hierarchical systems of church government and upholds ideally the autonomy of the local congregation, bound, however, in teaching and practice to God's word. Where church and state are joined, the government is by church representation (consistories, etc.), and bishops, though with limited power, are permitted. Under the Lutheran polity, laymen, by virtue of their royal priesthood, take an active part in the government and the work of the church. The pastoral office and the voting membership are ordinarily confined to men. Exceptions to this rule are infrequent. Membership in the Lutheran churches is about 70,000,000.

BIBLIOGRAPHY

Triglot Concordia containing all Lutheran Confessions; Bekenntnisschriften, latest German edition, 1952; John Theodore Mueller, Christian Dogmatics; Erwin Lueker, LC.

J. THEODORE MUELLER

M

MACEDONIANISM. The heretical teaching concerning the Holy Spirit held by the Pneumatomachians ("Fighters against the Spirit") was ascribed by some fourth century historians to Macedonius, Arian Bishop of Constantinople (ca. 362). Denial of the Spirit's divinity was latent in Arian teaching, and under the leadership of Eustathius of Sebaste became explicit ca. 370. The whole sect denied the divinity of the Spirit, some also the consubstantiality of the Son. Pope Damasus and the Cappadocians attacked them, and at the Council of Constantinople their teaching was anathematized while their persons were subject to the anti-heresy laws. It is uncertain how this teaching came to be associated with Macedonius, who was dead before it became prominent, and whose name does not appear in surviving writings which attacked the heresy. Perhaps certain of his influential followers joined the sect and gave his name to it. Nothing written by him survives.

M. R. W. FARRER

MAGIC. Magic is the art of effecting results beyond human power through supernatural agencies or demons. The term in its full meaning comprehends more than clever charlatanry, sleight of hand or jugglery. Often magic is nothing more than these cunning manipulations of natural phenomena. But as it is encountered in ancient history and in the Bible it involves the activity of demons in performing miracles by means of evil supernaturalism.

Divination (q.v.) is a species of magic and bears the same relation to biblical prophecy as heathen magic does to divine miracle. The widespread practice of the magical arts in Bible times may be comprehended from the fact that Scripture alone refers to their being practiced in Egypt (Ex. 7:11), Babylon (Ezek. 21:21), Assyria (II Kings 17:17), Chaldea (Dan. 5:11), Canaan (Deut. 18:14, 21), Proconsular Asia (Acts 19:13, 19) and Macedonia (Acts 16:16).

The Bible just as clearly acknowledges the reality and power of magic as it exposes its illegitimacy and wickedness. The magicians or "sacred scribes," hartummim, of Egypt, who performed miracles before Moses (Ex. 7 — 11), belonged to a priesthood learned in occultism and conversant with demon-controlled religion. Like similar agents of Satan (II Tim. 3:8) in other heathen nations, they practiced the "black arts." Babylon was especially notorious for occult traffic (Dan. 1:20; 2:2, 27; 4:7, 9; 5:11).

Such mighty demonstrations of demon power seem to occur periodically, like religious awakenings, and are found today in the trances, materializations, rappings, clairvoyance, drawings, physical healings, automatic writings, etc. of spiritism.

Occult powers will be revealed in the tremendous latter-day demonic revival under the Antichrist (II Thess. 2:9-12) which will be accompanied by phenomenal signs and miracles (Rev. 13:13-18).

BIBLIOGRAPHY

J. Michelet, *Satanism and Witchcraft*; Edward Langton, *Good and Evil Spirits* and "The Reality of Evil Powers Further Considered" *Hibbert Journal*, (July 1935), pp. 605-15. Merrill F. Unger, *Biblical Demonology*, pp. 107-64; Lynn Thorndike, *A History of Magic and Experimental Science*, I-VI.

MERRILL F. UNGER

MAGNIFICAT. See CANTICLE.

MAGNIFY. The biblical words rendered magnify mean either to make great or to make to appear great. In the latter sense, God is said to magnify himself (Ezek. 38:13), his mercy (Gen. 19:19), his word (Ps. 138:2), his law (Isa. 42:21). Men wickedly magnify themselves at the expense of others (Ps. 35:26; Dan. 8:11; Acts 5:3). Sometimes the reference is to the praise of God. By means of praise the divine greatness, though itself absolute, is brought more impressively before men's minds. Paul earnestly desired that Christ would always be magnified by his conduct, that is, that in all circumstances he might exemplify the power of Christ's grace.

WILLIAM J. CAMERON

MAGOG. *Māgôg* was the name of Japheth's second son (Gen. 10:2; I Chron. 1:5), of his descendants (Ezek. 39:6), and of their land (38:2). Their association with Meshech and Tubal (Assyrian *Mushku* and *Tabal* of NE Turkey, cf. 27:13) under one "chief prince" ("prince of Rosh" 38:2 ASV) indicates Magog as strange northern barbarians (38:15), like the Scythian hords, cf. *Gagaia* of the Amarna letters.

Ezekiel 38-39 predicts that "in the latter years" (38:8) Magog's ruler, Gog, will gather a host from Asia and Africa (38:5-6; "Magog," Rev. 20:8) to attack the messianic kingdom. The motives are satanic self-assertion (Rev. 20:7) and greed (Ezek. 38:12). The results, however, glorify God (38:16, 23; 39:7) as Magog meets civil dissension (38:21), heavenly destruction (vs. 23), and earth's dissolu-

tion (vs. 20, Rev. 20:9-11). Magog figures in later Jewish and Mohammedan speculation.

BIBLIOGRAPHY

IB (Ezek. 38); "Gog," *JewEnc*; J. L. Myers, *Palestine Exploration Fund Quarterly Statement for 1932*, pp. 213-19.

J. BARTON PAYNE

MAJESTY. The term, referring to God, relates (1) to his exaltation (from Hebrew *gā'â*) expressed in overwhelming action (Isa. 2:10, 19, 21) and revealing his royal supremacy (Isa. 24:14; 12:5); or (2) to his magnificent state (Hebrew *hôd; hādār*, I Chron. 29:11; Pss. 96:6; 104:1; 145:5, 12). The king derives his dignity from God (I Chron. 29:25; Pss. 21:5; 45:3-4); and man also (Ps. 8:5). Majesty combines strength, light, exaltation, greatness, magnificence and dignity. Later, in Wisd. 18:24, majesty is the divine name on the high priest's mitre. In the NT *megalōsynē* (Heb. 1:3; 8:1) parallels the rabbinic *gᵉbûrâ* as the name for God in his majesty. Christ's miracles (Luke 9:43) and transfiguration (II Pet. 1:16-17) revealed the objective majesty (*megaleiotēs*) of God (I Tim. 6:15-16). Christ fulfils the dignity of man (Heb. 2:6-9) and the messianic kingship (Matt. 22:42-45), and is exalted to share the divine name and throne (Phil. 2:9; Heb. 1:3-4). See also GLORY.

GEORGE J. C. MARCHANT

MALICE. "Malice" translates *kakia*. But since the seventeenth century malice has acquired the narrower sense of "spitefulness" (cf. *BCP* for the sense of evil generally, e.g., Ps. 94:23). Hence the context of *kakia* decides a modern translation. In I Cor. 5:8 Trench makes *kakia* the vicious principle and *ponēria* its outward exercise. Plummer disagrees, since the LXX uses both indifferently, and Vulgate uses both *malitia* and *nequitia* for both. "Malice" will translate *kakia* tolerably in Eph. 4:31; Col. 3:8; Titus 3:3; and I Pet. 2:1. It must be rendered "trouble" in Matt. 6:34, and "wickedness" in James 1:21. The RSV gives it a wider sense of "evil" in I Cor. 14:20 and I Pet. 2:16. Malice rightly translates *kakoētheia* in Rom. 1:29. The RSV renders *ponērois* "evil" in III John 10.

BIBLIOGRAPHY

Arndt; *HDB*; Robertson and Plummer, *ICC, I Cor.*, pp. 103, 316.

DENIS H. TONGUE

MAMMON. The word mammon represents the Aramaic word for riches or wealth. In pre-

Christian times the expression "the mammon of unrighteousness" (Luke 16:9) had already become synonymous with the evils of money. In the Aramaic Targums mammon is used for wealth or gain. There is no adequate ground for supposing that this term designated a heathen deity in biblical times.

The NT usage of this word is confined to our Lord's teachings (Matt. 6:24; Luke 16:9, 11, 13). In Luke 16:9-13 "mammon" is used three times in a further exposition of the parable of the unrighteous steward (Luke 16:1-13). The parable itself must not be pressed in every detail; it is primarily an illustration with one point. The central theme is that the disciples of Christ should manifest a prudence and foresight in the use of "the mammon of unrighteousness" that is at least comparable, if not superior, to the unrighteous steward's. If worldly possessions are misused, one cannot expect the real and genuine riches to be committed to him. And, of course, it is morally impossible for one to serve God and *mammon* (here and in Matt. 6:24 personified) at the same time.

BIBLIOGRAPHY
J. T. Marshall in *HERE*; James Moffatt in *HDCG*; Eb. Nestle in *EB*.

WICK BROOMALL

MAN. Who is man? This remarkable creature, whose amazing conquest of space and time has yielded unabridged dictionaries indexing the whole of reality, has fallen into frustration — ironically enough — when defining himself.

Is man but a complex animal, as exponents of naturalism have contended in both ancient and modern times? Is he a veritable fragment of divinity — a part of God — as idealists and pantheists would have it? Modern science gives an ambiguous answer, reflecting the divergent philosophies that govern its research. In fact, contemporary science seems less and less sure how to define a species, the human species included (cf. Jan Lever, *Creation and Evolution*, pp. 101-40). Some anthropologists, moreover, currently tend to becloud even the ultimate unity of the human race. In striking contrast with earlier centuries, which debated whether man's nature is trichotomous (divided into body, soul and spirit) or dichotomous (soul and spirit being viewed as functional distinctions within one psychical aspect of man's personality), much recent psychology — biased toward naturalistic evolution — tends to regard

the psychic as merely a differentiation of the physical, or as an emergent from it. Idealistic theories viewing man's mind as the unbroken mirror of Infinite Reason have fallen into discredit through their disregard of man's sin and finitude, their reliance on human speculation having also obscured the contemporary relevance of the biblical revelation of man's nature and destiny. Meanwhile, naturalistic explanations of reflective reason as simply a late evolutionary development all but dominate the academic world.

I. THE IMAGE OF GOD. The Bible answers the question of the nature of man by pointing to the *imago Dei*. That man by creation uniquely bears the divine image is a fundamental biblical doctrine — as also that this image is sullied by sin and that it is restored by divine salvation. Man's nature and destiny are interwoven with this foundational fact, and speculative philosophies inevitably strike at it when they degrade man to animality or otherwise distort his personality (*q.v.*).

The biblical data pertaining to the *imago Dei* in man are found in both New and Old Testaments. Their setting throughout is revealed religion, and not speculative philosophy. Dependence of the Pauline view on the hellenic mystery religions has been asserted by the comparative religions school. Reitzenstein has affirmed (*Die hellenistischen Mysterienreligionen*, pp. 7 ff.) that Paul's teaching on the image is indebted to the private mystery cults in Egypt, Phrygia and Persia, particularly those of Isis, Attis and Cybele, and Mithra, with their goal of salvation secured through personal union with the god or goddess. But H. A. A. Kennedy has argued convincingly in *St. Paul and the Mystery Religions* that the basic NT ideas are forged against the background of Hebrew theology, rather than of the hellenistic cults, and that even in respect to the image the resemblance between the Pauline concepts and the mysteries is superficial. David Cairns also emphasizes that "the New Testament writers make almost no use" — he might properly have deleted the word "almost" — of notions so frequently found in the mystery cults such as the divinization of the believer and human absorption into the Deity (*The Image of God in Man*, p. 56).

Hebrew-Christian theology frames the doctrine of the *imago* in the setting of divine creation (*q.v.*) and redemption (*q.v.*). "The gist of the doctrine of Creation is surely this," Cairns would remind us, in respect to the image, "that man's being, though linked with the divine, is itself essentially not divine, but created, and thus dependent on God, and of a different order from His own being though akin to it" (*op. cit.*, p. 63). Bible doctrine does not, therefore, simply affirm in a religious manner what speculative philosophies express more generally in their emphasis on the inherent dignity and worth of man, or on the infinite value and sacredness of human personality. For Scripture conditions man's dignity and value upon the doctrine of creation, and not upon an intrinsic divinity, and assuredly it does not obscure the fact of man's fall and of his desperate need of redemption. Those who, like Kingsley Martin, profess to find in Stoicism (*q.v.*) a superior and sounder basis for human dignity than that afforded by biblical theology, seem little to realize that in such a transition to pantheism (*q.v.*) the Hebrew-Christian dimensions of the *imago* are actually abandoned.

The biblical discussion turns on the Hebrew words *ṣelem* and *dᵉmût,* and the corresponding Greek terms *eikōn* and *homoiōsis.* Scripture employs these terms to affirm that man was fashioned in the image of God, and that Jesus Christ the divine Son is the essential image (*q.v.*) of the invisible God. The passages expressly affirming the divine image in man are Gen. 1:26, 27; 5:1, 3; and 9:6; I Cor. 11:7; Col. 3:10; and James 3:9. The doctrine is implied also in other passages in which the precise phrase "image of God" does not appear, particularly in Ps. 8, which J. Laidlaw called "a poetic *replica* of the creation-narrative of Genesis 1 as far as it refers to man" ("Image," in *HDB,* II, p. 452a), and in the Pauline reference on Mars Hill to man and his Maker. The terms "image and likeness" in Gen. 1:26 and 5:3 do not distinguish different aspects of the *imago,* but state intensively the fact that man uniquely reflects God. Instead of suggesting distinctions within the image, the juxtaposition vigorously declares that by creation man bears an image actually corresponding to the divine original. In Gen. 1:27 the word "image" alone expresses the complete idea of this correspondence, whereas in Gen. 5:1 the term "likeness" serves the same purpose.

Although man images God by creation — a fact which the divine prohibition of graven images (which obscure the spirituality of God) serves pointedly to reinforce — man's fall precludes all attempts to read off God's nature from man's. To project God in man's image is therefore a heinous form of idolatry confounding the Creator with the creaturely (Rom. 1:23). This confusion reaches its nadir in worship of the beast and his image or statue (Rev. 14:9 ff.).

II. Recent Theological Studies. Granted that the terms "image" and "likeness" denote an exact resemblance, in what respect does man reflect God? What of the vitiating effects of his fall into sin? Is the NT conception of the *imago* in conflict with the OT conception? Is it in conflict with itself? These questions are among those most energetically debated by contemporary theology.

The importance of a proper understanding of the *imago Dei* can hardly be overstated. The answer given to the *imago*-inquiry soon becomes determinative for the entire gamut of doctrinal affirmation. The ramifications are not only theological, but affect every phase of the problem of revelation and reason, including natural and international law, and the cultural enterprise as a whole. Any improper view has consequences the more drastic as its implications are applied to regenerate and to unregenerate man, from primal origin to final destiny.

The new theology supports a "christological" or "eschatological" interpretation of the divine image in man. This orientation is formally commendable, since the God-man assuredly exhibits the divine intention for man, and the glory of redeemed humanity will consist in full conformity to Christ's image. In the past a type of Christian rationalism has sometimes unfortunately emerged, seeking on the basis of anthropology alone, independently of Christology, to delineate man's true nature and destiny. Such expositions, which arbitrarily identify the *imago* in fallen man with that of Christ, blur easily into speculations of a personalistic and idealistic nature.

But there is also need for caution over the new theology, since it often incorporates an evasive turn into its christological appeal. It diverts attention from the important question of man's primal origin — that is, from the creation and fall of the first Adam (*q.v.*) — because of a reluctance to challenge the modern evolutionary philosophy from the standpoint of the Genesis creation account.

By the *imago* the Protestant Reformers had understood especially man's state of original purity, in accord with Gen. 1 and 2, wherein

Adam is depicted as fashioned for rational, moral and spiritual fellowship with his Maker. The existentializing philosophy of our times, however, finding this representation too abruptly contradictory of current scientific views, confers upon the first Adam only a mythical status, regarding him — in respect to deviation from perfection — as simply a type of every man. The *imago* is then no longer conceived as a state, but as a relation — since an original state of Adamic purity is set aside. Hence neo-orthodox theology not only rejects, in common with Protestantism generally, the Roman Catholic exposition of the image in Thomistic terms (of *analogia entis*, a "being" which Creator and creature share in different degrees), but also sets aside the traditional Protestant confidence in the Genesis creation narratives as a scientifically relevant account of origins.

Just because the "christological" or "eschatological" view looks to the end rather than to the beginning, it does not by itself do full justice to the biblical representation. It subordinates the exhibition of the divine image as God's gift in creation, and is vulnerable also to universalistic expositions of redemption. For while the image of the Godhead (Gen. 1:26) on the basis of creation has an anticipatory reference to the God-man, it is not as such the image of Jesus Christ the Redeemer. Although the redemption-image truly presupposes the creation-image, and the creation-image prepares the way for the redemption-image, Karl Barth's emphasis that all divine revelation is redemptive ignores significant considerations. If the original image is in fact a reflex of *grace*, if man *is* God's image only by promise (whereas Jesus Christ is *actually* God's image), can universalism really be avoided? We may note: (1) The creation-image was once-for-all wholly given at the creation of the first Adam; the redemption-image is gradually fashioned. (2) The creation-image is conferred in some respect upon the whole human race; the redemption-image only upon the redeemed. (3) The creation-image distinguishes man from the animals; the redemption-image distinguishes the regenerate family of faith from unregenerate mankind. (4) The creation-image was probationary; the redemption-image is not.

Statements of the *imago Dei* in current theology, while equating the image with those features by which man transcends the animals, often give to the biblical passages a bizarre tone of novelty. Barth has proposed at least two interpretations of the image, and Emil Brunner, three, and their most recent recensions are not devoid of difficulties. The conclusion to be drawn from such adjustment and readjustment is that theologians today seek to comprehend the image within a framework that is unsatisfactorily narrow. While pantheizing liberalism formerly set aside sin and the need for redemption, and mistakenly regarded the natural man as destined for Christ simply on the basis of creation, neo-orthodox writers exaggerate the transcendence of God to the dilution of the *imago* in man both as created and fallen. The recent dialectical reconstructions of the *imago* almost invariably profess to honor the Protestant Reformers, who are credited with first having controlled the *imago* idea in terms of the "true *dialectical* or christological principle." But Calvin's stress on continuity and discontinuity of man's *imago* with his Maker is said to have lacked a proper working balance which the dialectical approach now provides. The new speculation conceives their unity "eschatologically"; that is, neither original righteousness nor the fall are conceded a place in a past empirical time-series, but are held to be known only in faith-response. So it is that the christological and eschatological expositions of the *imago* today are surfeited with dialectical and existential elements.

Recent denials that the *imago* survives in fallen man reflect an extreme point of view. Barth has championed this position at an earlier stage, contending that humanity and personality have no significance for the image. T. F. Torrance has professed to find it in Calvin. Brunner has readily acknowledged that the image formally survives the fall, but has vacillated over the question of its material content. Nonetheless, the divergences of neo-orthodox theologians are not as significant as their agreements, especially their exclusion of the forms of logic and of a conceptual knowledge of God from the *imago*. The result is their depreciation of the rational element in revelation, both general and special. This modern revision of the noetic aspect of the *imago* is tapered to the limitation of human reason in conformity with the dialectical philosophy; the admission of such conceptual knowledge of God would undermine the possibility of and necessity for the dialectic.

Evangelical expositors of the biblical revelation find the created image of God to exist formally in man's personality (moral responsibility and intelligence) and materially in his knowledge of God and of his will for man. Hence the image is not reducible simply to a relation in which man stands to God, but rather is the precondition of such a relationship. The fall of man is not destructive of the formal image (man's personality) although it involves the distortion (though not demolition) of the material content of the image. The biblical view is that man is made to know God as well as to obey him. Even in his revolt man stands condemned by the knowledge he has, and he is proffered God's redemptive revelation in scriptural (that is, in propositional) form. The objections that the admission of such a rational content to the *imago* implies pantheism, or a capacity for self-salvation by reflection through its supposed assertion of an undamaged spot in human nature, loses force when the support for such objections is seen to rest on exaggerations of divine transcendence from which the dialectical view itself arises, rather than on biblical considerations.

Although the Old and New Testaments seem to conflict — since the former reiterates the survival of the image in man after the fall, while the latter stresses the redemptive restoration of the image — there is no real clash. The OT conception is presupposed also in the New, which is a legitimate development. For the NT also speaks of the divine image in the natural man (I Cor. 11:7; James 3:9). But its central message is redeemed man's renewal in the image of Christ.

III. WIDER IMPLICATIONS. The Bible depicts man primarily from the perspective of his relation to God because his nature and destiny can be grasped only from this standpoint. Its interpretation of man is therefore primarily religious. The creation narratives are not written expressly to answer the questions posed by twentieth century science, although attempts to discredit them as unscientific sooner or later are embarrassed by inevitable reversals of scientific opinion. Recent evangelical discussions of the harmony of Scripture and science on such matters as the origin, unity and antiquity of the human race may be found in *Contemporary Evangelical Thought* (C. F. H. Henry, editor; chapter on "Science and Religion") and *Theology and Evolution* (Russell Mixter, editor, sponsored by American Scientific Affiliation). The Bible does not discriminate man from the animals in terms of morphological considerations, but rather in terms of the *imago Dei*. Man is made for personal and endless fellowship with God, involving rational understanding (Gen. 1:28 ff.), moral obedience (2:16 f.) and religious communion (3:3, 16). He is given dominion over the animals and charged to subdue the earth, that is, to consecrate it to the spiritual service of God and man.

Nor does Scripture detail a science of psychology (*q.v.*) in the modern sense, although it presents a consistent view of man's nature. Its emphasis falls on man as a unitary personality of soul and body. Their disjunction is due to sin (2:17); man's reconstitution as a corporeal being in the resurrection is part of his destiny. While the soul survives in the intermediate state between death and resurrection, this is not the ultimate ideal (II Cor. 5:1-4), in sharp contrast to Greek philosophy. The dispute over dichotomy (*q.v.*) or trichotomy (*q.v.*) too often loses sight of the unitary nature of human personality. It is not possible to assert separate distinctions within man's nature simply on the basis of the different scriptural terms for soul, spirit, mind, and so forth. Heb. 4:12, often cited in behalf of trichotomy ("the dividing asunder of soul and spirit, and of the joints and marrow"), does not establish soul and spirit as different entities, but as different functions of the one psychic life of man, as is evident from the parallel phrase "the joints and marrow" in relation to the body.

To the OT picture of man, the NT adds the graphic exposition of his divine sonship through the adoption of grace (John 1:12) and his new role, subsequent to his rescue from an unregenerate race, in the family of redemption. As a member of the church, the body of Christ, whose head has already passed through death and resurrection, the redeemed man already has an existence in the eternal order (Eph. 1:3), so that the sudden end of this world order would disclose the exalted Redeemer as the true center of his life and activity. At the same time, the crowned Christ mediates to the members of the body powers and virtues that belong to the age to come as an earnest of their future inheritance (Eph. 1:14; II Cor. 1:22; Gal. 5:22). Man's destiny is therefore not simply an endless existence, but is moral — either a life redeemed and fit for eternity, or a life under perpetual divine judgment.

BIBLIOGRAPHY

Karl Barth, *Church Dogmatics*, Vol. III/2 (The Doctrine of Man); Emil Brunner, *Man in Revolt*; David Cairns, *The Image of God in Man*; Gordon H. Clark, *A Christian View of Men and Things*; J. Gresham Machen, *The Christian View of Man*; Reinhold Niebuhr, *The Nature and Destiny of Man*; James Orr, *God's Image in Man*; H. Wheeler Robinson, *The Christian Doctrine of Man*; T. F. Torrance, *Calvin's Doctrine of Man*.

CARL F. H. HENRY

MAN OF SIN. See ANTICHRIST.

MANDAEANS. Also known as Nazoraeans, and Christians of St. John, Mandaeans are adherents of Mandaism, which is now confined to a few small communities south of Bagdad. Their sacred writings — chiefly the *Ginza* (Treasure) and *Book of John* — are a strange amalgam of myth, history and ritual where teachings of rabbinic Judaism are mingled inconsistently with Gnostic Manichaeanism and with traces of Christianity. Man's soul, tortured by demons, is imprisoned within the body, from which only a divine being, Manda d'Hayye (Heb. Knowledge of Life) can release him. Frequent baptisms are required to prepare the soul for its ascent. Modern interest in Mandaism centers in the frequent mention of John the Baptist in its literature. Theories have been advanced, notably by Lidzbarski and Bultmann, claiming John as the founder of the sect, whose myths were later interwoven with primitive Christianity, especially by the writer of the Fourth Gospel. Uncertainty in dating the literature, and the intrinsic religious worthlessness of it, suggest that Mandaism borrowed and debased Christian traditions, and vice versa.

BIBLIOGRAPHY

Texts: German translations by M. Lidzbarski; S. A. Pallis, *Essay on Mandaean Bibliography*; C. H. Dodd, *Interpretation of the Fourth Gospel*, pp. 115-30; W.. Brandt in *HERE*; *ODCC*; R. Bultmann in *ZNW*, xxiv.

M. R. W. FARRER

MANICHAEISM. The sources, origins and teachings of Manichaeism are to some extent obscure, though it is obviously connected with the Persian Manes (*ca.* A.D. 215-75) who in the middle of the third century proclaimed himself a prophet, enunciated his new doctrine and was finally executed. So far as they are known to us, his views, which are thought to derive from a certain Terebinthus, are a fusion of different elements in Persian dualism, Gnosticism, Marcionism and Christianity. There are two basic and opposing principles of good and evil, the elements of goodness in the world and man deriving from the former and of badness from the latter. Redemption is liberation of the good elements from the domination of the bad, with which matter seems to be predominantly though not exclusively associated. Christ is one who helped to this end, being now succeeded by Manes. There is a strong docetic element in the picture of Christ, and we are not surprised to learn that the resurrection is denied (though transmigration is the fate of non-Manichaeans) and strictly ascetic practices are enjoined, the civil authorities and physical force being also condemned. The followers of Manes were organized into the two main groups of hearers and elect, with a leader and twelve masters among the elect in imitation of Christ and the apostles. Notwithstanding the decisions and enactments against it, Manichaeism was widely preached and followed, even attracting the young Augustine for a time. Possible traces of its influence may be seen in the medieval and Reformation sects and various modern cults (cf. *HERE*).

WILLIAM KELLY

MANIFESTATION. (1) A predominantly NT word indicating the eternal purpose of God, which had been hidden from human gaze down the ages, but has now been revealed in Jesus Christ. Part of his saving work of redeeming fallen humanity is the revelation of the Father. In a general way this had been done through nature (Rom. 1:19-20). In Jesus Christ revelation becomes personal (Heb. 1:1). Holy Scripture enshrines the permanent record of this saving revelation. The Holy Spirit uses this medium to give fresh revelation to the heart of the believer of his need and God's provision in Christ Jesus (John 14:22; I Cor. 12:7). Another aspect of his saving work is the destruction of the power of the devil (I John 3:8). Eschatological implications are found in Mark 4:22; I Cor. 3:13; Eph. 5:13.

(2) "The Manifestation of Christ to the Gentiles" is the alternative title in the Anglican Prayer Book for the Feast of the Epiphany (*q.v.*), Jan. 6th.

(3) The appearances of the risen Christ to his own are called manifestations (John 21:1).

(4) Christ continues to disclose himself through the life and service of his followers (II Cor. 2:14; 4:10).

(5) At the return of Christ, the glorified

saints will be manifested together with him (I John 3:2).

(6) At the judgment seat of Christ the inner life and motivation of the redeemed will be made known (I Cor. 4:5; II Cor. 5:10; cf. Mark 4:22).

BIBLIOGRAPHY
K. Lake, "Epiphany" in HERE; Neil and Willoughby, The Tutorial Prayer Book; G. H. S. Walpole in HDCG.

RICHARD E. HIGGINSON

MARANATHA. An Aramaic formula found once in the NT in I Cor. 16:22 as part of Paul's concluding greeting, maranatha may be analyzed as an imperative: marana-tha, meaning "Our Lord, come"; or as an indicative: maran-atha, meaning "Our Lord is come." Three interpretations are possible: (1) the prayer for the Lord's return, (2) the confession of the Lord having come, (3) the assertion of the Lord's presence, as it is employed in the Eucharist. Paul most certainly meant to use the formula in the first sense. But it is worthy of note that maranatha appears in the Didache at the end of a series of eucharistic prayers.

Problematic has been the question why Paul, without translation, included an Aramaic formula in a Greek letter to Corinth where Aramaic was not current. To answer that Paul wanted to give the Judaizers a warning is inadequate, for it is not clear whether he had in mind his opponents in I Cor. 16:22a or meant his words to be understood in a general sense. The fact that maran-atha is rendered without translation indicates that it was a fixed and widely circulated formula. As such, however, it could only have originated and received its meaning in an exclusively Aramaic-speaking congregation. Indeed, it is most likely that maranatha was a key expression in the liturgy of the primitive church in Palestine, and that from there it passed into Greek Christendom without translation, in fashion similar to "amen" and "hosanna."

This has meant destruction to the hypothesis posed by Wm. Bousset in his books: Kyrios Christos (1913) and Jesus der Herr (1916). In this "Kyrios" controversy Bousset argued that primitive Christianity in Jerusalem regarded Jesus chiefly as the Son of Man yet to come and usher in God's kingdom. The title "Lord" was only applied later on Greek soil under the influence of hellenistic Christianity. Gentile Christians, familiar with the mystery cults, would interpret the lordship of

Jesus in ways determined by their previous experience.

In later times maranatha became an ecclesiastical device connected with anathema as a reinforcement for the act of solemn cursing.

BIBLIOGRAPHY
K. G. Kuhn in TWNT; O. Cullmann, Early Christian Worship; J. G. Machen, Origin of Paul's Religion, pp. 293-317.

HERMAN C. WAETJEN

MARCIONITES (OR MARCIONISTS). An unorthodox community founded by Marcion in A.D. 144 on his excommunication from the church in Rome. The sect was marked by strict asceticism, distinctive sacramental practices and the use of truncated Scriptures. Despite persecution the Marcionites increased with such rapidity that both Justin (Apol. I, 26, 5) and Tertullian (Adv. Marcion 5, 19) could claim that they permeated the Empire. To what extent they accepted their master's pseudo-Gnostic teaching is uncertain. Apelles, the best known of Marcion's successors (Tertullian, De Praescriptionibus, 30), tempered his radical pessimism and denied the evil origin of the created world. From the third century onwards Western Marcionism declined under Manichaean absorption. It was eventually prohibited by Constantine. It lingered in the East, but had disappeared by the seventh century. The real significance of the movement lay in the stimulus it provided towards the definition of creed and canon.

BIBLIOGRAPHY
A. Harnack, Marcion; E. C. Blackman, Marcion and His Influence.

A. SKEVINGTON WOOD

MARIOLATRY. The worship of Mary. In Latin terminology three words are used to denote "worship" — latria, hyperdulia and dulia. Latria is defined as the worship due to God alone, hyperdulia that due to Mary, and dulia that due to the saints. To speak of Mariolatry, therefore, is not strictly correct according to Roman Catholic theology.

Protestants maintain that the distinction between these terms cannot be properly observed in practice, and accuse Roman Catholics of placing Mary, in their devotional life, in a position akin to, if not equal with, that of Christ, and according to her latria (true worship) rather than merely hyperdulia (extreme honor), as they declare theologically.

The rise of Mary-worship may be traced back to two apocryphal writings — the Protevangelium Jacobi (middle of second century),

and the *Transitus Mariae* (fourth century) —
neither of which can be regarded as consonant
with the Gospel accounts of the NT. An in-
flux into the church of many pagans occurred
when the Emperor Constantine declared himself a Christian, and the thought of a female
element in the divinity, encouraged by pagan
thought generally, Egyptian, Babylonian, Greek
and Latin, began to emerge. A great impetus
to the ascription of divine honors to Mary was
given when the title "Mother of God" was officially bestowed upon her by the Council of
Ephesus in 431, though it is certain that the
object of the Council was not to exalt Mary
but to assert the full deity of Christ from the
very moment of his conception (see Mother
of God). The excesses to which the cult of
Mary has been carried by the Roman Catholic
Church is witnessed to by the dogmas of the
Immaculate Conception of the B.V.M. (defined in 1854), and of the Assumption of the
B.V.M. (defined in 1950). By these dogmas
there are ascribed to Mary ideas parallel to the
facts of our Lord's life. The additional idea
that Mary may also be regarded as Mediatrix
of our redemption is gaining ground, and the
term "Our Lady" (arising in the Middle Ages)
is analogous to "Our Lord" as applied to
Christ.

The references to Mary in Scripture give no
countenance whatever for a cult of Mary. The
following are some of the chief places where
she is mentioned: Matt. 1:16 ff.; Matt. 13:55;
Luke 1:27 ff.; John 2:1 ff.; John 19:25 ff.;
Acts 1:14. Instead of seeing Mary in the light
of these passages as one who submitted herself
to the will of God and faithfully carried out
her ministry, this cult transforms her into a
being who is neither divine nor human. More
dangerous still, from an evangelical point of
view, is the effect of such Mary-worship in
obscuring the person of our Lord in the mind
of the worshiper.

See also ASSUMPTION OF MARY.

W. C. G. PROCTOR

MARONITES. The Maronites are a small
Christian group in Lebanon who take their
name either from St. Maron or from a town
probably named after him. Originally Mono-
thelite (*q.v.*), they entered into communion
with Rome at the time of the Crusades and
were represented at the Lateran Council in
1215. Since 1584 they have had a college at
Rome. Like other uniate churches, they maintain their own liturgy and follow the Eastern
practice in respect of clerical marriage. They
also have their own usage in relation to feasts
and vestments. Although a small church, they
are organized under a patriarch and eight bishops, the former claiming to be the patriarch
of Antioch. There is great veneration for the
bishops, and also a developed monastic life.
Services are read in the vernacular as well as
Latin, and it is to the credit of the church
that it maintained itself in spite of periods of
severe repression under the Turks.

WILLIAM KELLY

MARRIAGE. Biblical teaching on marriage is epitomized in the statement, "Therefore a man leaves his father and his mother
and cleaves to his wife, and they become one
flesh" (Gen. 2:24). This sentence is quoted
by our Lord (Matt. 19:5) and the apostle Paul
(Eph. 5:31) as authority for their teachings
on marriage. The key phrase is the expression
"one flesh" (*bāśār 'eḥād*). "Flesh" here implies
kinship or fellowship, with the body as a medium (Crem. pp. 846-47), thus setting forth
"marriage as the deepest corporeal and spiritual
unity of man and woman . . ." (KD on Gen.
2:24). On the occasion of Eve's creation, God
observes, "It is not good that the man should
be alone" (Gen. 2:18). In this way he indicates the incompleteness of man or woman
apart from one another and sets forth marriage as the means for them to achieve completeness.

Marriage is an *exclusive* relationship. The
total unity of persons — physically, emotionally,
intellectually and spiritually — comprehended
by the concept "one flesh," eliminates polygamy
as an option. One cannot relate wholeheartedly
in this way to more than one person at a time.

It is also plain from the words of our Lord,
"What therefore God has joined together, let
no man put asunder (Matt. 19:6)," that marriage is to *endure* for the lifetime of the two
partners. (For a discussion of the conditions
under which this principle of indissolubility
may be set aside, see DIVORCE.)

Promiscuity is likewise ruled out. Such
unions are neither exclusive nor enduring.
Moreover, they violate the holiness that inheres
in biblical marriage. God instituted marriage
so that men and women might complete one
another and share in his creative work through
the procreation of children. (Celibacy is not
a higher and holier condition — a viewpoint

which finds its roots in Greek dualism rather than in the Bible.) Physical union in marriage has a spiritual significance in that it points beyond itself to the total unity of husband and wife, which is essentially a spiritual union. This is underscored by Paul's use of the conjugal union to symbolize the unity of Christ with his church (Eph. 5:22-33). But to maintain its holiness this union must take place in a relationship committed to enduring exclusiveness. Illicit sexual unions are deemed reprehensible in that they temporarily and superficially establish a *one flesh* relationship (I Cor. 6:16) without proper accompanying intentions and commitments. An act with spiritual significance is made to serve improper ends. Another person is selfishly exploited. What should be a constructive relationship serving as the means to deeper interpersonal communion becomes in promiscuous relationships destructive both to one's capacity for personal unity with a member of the opposite sex and to existing marriage relationships, if any. Hence our Lord made adultery the ground for dissolution of a marriage (Matt. 5:32).

When is a couple married? Of what does marriage ultimately consist? Some, arguing from I Cor. 6:16, maintain that marriage is effected through sexual intercourse. A person is considered in the eyes of God to be married to that member of the opposite sex with whom he first had sex relations (e.g., O. Piper, *The Christian Interpretation of Sex,* Macmillan, New York, 1946). The sex act is viewed as the agent through which God effects marriage in a manner apparently analogous to the way in which adherents of the doctrine of baptismal regeneration see him make the sacrament of baptism the agent in effecting regeneration.

Others consider marriage to be brought about as the result of a declaration of desire to be married accompanied by the expression of mutual intentions of sole and enduring fidelity and responsibility toward the other, preferably undergirded by self-giving love, in the presence of accredited witnesses. This view does not undercut the validity of marriages in which the couple cannot bring about physical consummation. It underscores the fact that marriage never has been regarded as solely the concern of the individual couple. This may be seen, for example, in the prevalence of community laws forbidding incest and regulating the degree of consanguinity permissible for marriage. Since the home is the proper medium for the procreation and nurturing of children, church and community have an important stake in the stability and success of the marriages taking place among their constituents.

Marriage relegates other human ties to a secondary role. Spiritual and emotional satisfactions formerly drawn from the parental relationship, the marriage partners are now to find in one another. To sunder one's parental relationships and join oneself in intimate, lifelong union with a person who hitherto has been a stranger demands a considerable degree of maturity — as expressed in a capacity for self-giving love, emotional stability and the capacity to understand what is involved in committing one's life to another in marriage. Marriage is for those who have grown up. This appears to exclude children, mental defectives, and those who are psychotic or psychopathic at the time of entering into marriage.

The chief contributions of the NT to the biblical view of marriage were to underscore the original principles of the indissolubility of marriage *(supra)* and the equal dignity of women (Gal. 3:38; I Cor. 7:4; 11:11-12). By raising women to a position of equal personal dignity with men, marriage was made truly *one flesh,* for the unity implied in this expression necessarily presupposes that each person be given opportunity to develop his full potentialities. This is not possible in a social system in which either men or women are not accorded full human dignity.

Does not this raise difficulties with the biblical doctrine of subordination of married women (Eph. 5:22-23)? Not at all, for this doctrine refers to a hierarchy of *function* not of dignity or value. There is no inferiority of person implicit in the doctrine. God has designated a hierarchy of responsibility, hence authority, within the family, and he has done so according to the order of creation. But woman's dignity is preserved not only in the fact that she has equal standing in Christ, but also in that the command to submit to her husband's headship is addressed to her. She is told to do this willingly as an act of spiritual devotion (Eph. 5:22) and not in response to external coercion. She is to do this because God rests primary responsibility upon her husband for the welfare of the marriage relationship and for the family as a whole. He, in fact, qualifies for leadership in the church in part through the skill he demonstrates in "pastor-ing" his family (I Tim. 3:4-5).

BIBLIOGRAPHY

D. S. Bailey, *The Mystery of Love and Marriage;* K. E. Kirk, *Marriage and Divorce;* O. Piper *(supra).*

LARS I. GRANBERG

MARTYR. The Greek word *martys* under-lying martyr means "witness" *(q.v.)* and is em-ployed frequently in the LXX with its cus-tomary legal associations, as well as in the ex-tended sense found repeatedly in the NT, of one who testifies to the reality and experience of religious and theological data (Acts 1:6-8, 22, of the apostles; Heb. 12:1, of the gallery of OT saints; Rev. 1:5 and 3:15, of Jesus).

These passages contain the ingredients for the later technical use of martyr denoting one who seals his testimony with blood, but the semantical transition does not appear to be ef-fected in the NT passages usually alleged (Acts 22:20; Rev. 2:13). Both Stephen and Antipas are termed martyrs because of their sterling and selfless testimony, not because they died in giving it. In the latter technical sense the term begins to emerge about A.D. 160 to distinguish one type of confessor from another. Despite detailed monographs the precise evolu-tion is shrouded in mystery, but it is probable that since faithful testimony frequently issued in death and identified the confessor thereby most closely with Jesus, the witness par ex-cellence and faithful to the end, the term *martys* gradually was reserved for one who paid the supreme price. Thus *The Martyrdom of Polycarp* (XVII, 3) states: "(Jesus) being the Son of God we worship, but the martyrs as disciples and imitators of the Lord we right-ly love in view of their unsurpassed devotion toward their own Sovereign and Teacher. May it be granted us to share their company and join them as disciples."

A letter from the Gallic churches (Eus. *HE* 5:2) employs the word *homologoi* to distin-guish confessors who have not yet resisted unto blood from those who have. The techni-cal term which comes into later use for the former is *homologētēs,* and the term *martyr* is reserved exclusively for one who has died for the faith.

BIBLIOGRAPHY

Arndt; P. Kattenbusch, ZNW, 4, pp. 111-27; Ernst Guenther, ZNW, 47, pp. 145-61. R. P. Casey in *The Beginnings of Christianity,* V, Note 5, pp. 30-37.

FREDERICK W. DANKER

MASTER. The word *master* is used in the AV to translate various Hebrew and Greek words. In the NT it is used chiefly for *didaskalos,* "teacher," and directs attention to the prophetic aspect of our Lord's work. It is used also to render "rabbi," a title of honor for teachers (Matt. 23:7 f.), which is applied in the NT only to John the Baptist and, of course, especially, to Christ. On the close re-lationship between *rabbi* (and also the form *rabbouni)* and *didaskalos* see John 1:38; 3:2; and 20:16.

The term *Kyrios,* which is usually translated "Lord" in the AV is also translated "master" a number of times. It is used notably of an own-er of property, a master of a household, a master of slaves, one who controls and dis-poses, a person of exalted rank, a sovereign. The religious use of the term as applied to Christ is accurately reflected in the translation Lord, not by the term Master as it has been used by some persons in modern times.

BIBLIOGRAPHY

Arndt; J. Gresham Machen, *The Origin of Paul's Re-ligion,* pp. 308 f.; Thayer-Grimm.

JOHN H. SKILTON

MEDIATION, MEDIATOR. The word "mediator" is rare in the Bible, being found not at all in the OT (though cf. "umpire" in Job 9:33), and only in Gal. 3:19 f.; I Tim. 2:5; Heb. 8:6; 9:15; 12:24, in the NT. Yet, if the word is infrequent, the idea is one of the dominant conceptions of the Bible. Job recognizes that God "is not a man, as I am, that I should answer him, that we should come together in judgment." He goes on: "There is no umpire betwixt us, that might lay his hand upon us both. Let him take his rod away from me, and let not his terror make me afraid" (Job 9:32-34). It is this inability of man to stand before God that makes mediation necessary.

In the OT this principle is worked out in various ways. Thus when God gave Israel a law he did it not directly, but through a mediator, Moses. Moses might also be thought of as acting in a mediatorial capacity in the de-liverance of the people from the land of Egypt. In the subsequent religion of the people priest-ly activities were prominent, and what is this but another form of mediation? Yet another example is to be seen in the work of the prophets. God did not give his revelation di-rectly to the heart of every man. He spoke through his chosen prophets. In similar fashion the king was thought of as in some sense a mediator when he was referred to as "the Lord's anointed."

In the NT Moses is spoken of as a mediator in Gal. 3:19 f. But the emphasis is not on any merely human mediator but on Christ, so much so that we read "there is one God, one mediator also between God and men, himself man, Christ Jesus, who gave himself a ransom for all" (I Tim. 2:5 f.). In the sense of really bringing God and man together the ministry of Christ is unique. In this sense there is no other mediator. This is implied in the three passages in Hebrews which speak of Christ as Mediator. Each refers to the new covenant, and two of them specifically mention the death of the Saviour. The function of the Mediator, then, is to die for sin, and thus to bring into being that new covenant which truly brings men to God. He interposes in the situation created by man's sin and God's condemnation. He stands between those who are estranged, and makes them one.

But it is not only in these specific texts that we are to see the NT idea of Christ as Mediator. We see it in his nature, as both God and man, wherein he is God's representative to man, and man's representative to God. We see it in his fulfilment of all that is implied in the OT concepts of prophet, priest and king. We see it in the facts that man is totally unable to fit himself for God, and that Jesus perfectly brings him to God.

BIBLIOGRAPHY
Blunt; A. T. Robertson in *HDAC*; F. J. Taylor in *RTWB*.

LEON MORRIS

MEDITATE. So far as the Scripture is concerned this is almost exclusively an OT word. Only twice does the Greek word *meletaō*, translated "meditate," occur in the NT: (1) The form *promeletaō*, "to meditate beforehand," is the classical word for preparing a speech in advance (Luke 21:14); (2) *meletaō*, "to meditate," means to be careful, to take care, to be diligent in these things; from *meletē*, care or practice (I Tim. 4:15). The Latin derivative is *meditare*, "to reflect," "to exercise in," "to practice." In the OT various forms of two Hebrew words *hāgâ* and *śiaḥ* are translated "meditate." They denote "that silent and secret musing in which the children of God are to exercise themselves." Meditation is "talking within the mind and issues in speech. It is the inner whisperings of the

heart." Thus meditation is a form of private devotion or spiritual exercise consisting in deep, continued reflection on some religious theme. St. Teresa, who finally achieved so much in this respect, confessed that when she first made the attempt, she felt the impossibility of collecting her thoughts and fixing her attention; and it was not until more than fourteen years had passed that she was able to practice meditation without the aid of a book.

F. CARLTON BOOTH

MEEKNESS. Meekness closely resembles gentleness, moderation, yet *praotēs* (I Cor. 4:21; II Cor. 10:1; Gal. 5:23; 6:1; Eph. 4:2; Col. 3:12; II Tim. 2:25; Titus 3:2; James 1:21; 3:13; I Pet. 3:15) and *praos* (Matt. 5:5; 11:29; 21:5; I Pet. 3:4) have a distinctive meaning; AV, RV always translating "meekness," "meek." They correspond to *'ănānâ, 'ănî, 'ānāw*, which originally signify distress and helplessness, but acquire a moral significance and denote contrition of spirit before God, becoming synonymous with humility (Pss. 22:24-26; 147:6; Isa. 11:4; 61:1). Meekness in the OT is primarily Godward.

In the NT too, meekness is humility born of trustful submission to God in the first place, but it results in gentle, forgiving unselfishness towards others. Nowhere in Scripture has it an abject, unworthy meaning. The meek are mighty in God's purposes (cf. Moses, Num. 12:3).

Wm. Barclay says *praotēs*, is no "spineless gentleness," and while gentleness is there, behind it is the strength of steel. Moses and, supremely, Christ exhibited it (cf. Mark 10:13-16 and John 2:14-17).

BIBLIOGRAPHY
J. S. Banks in *HDB*; Wm. Barclay, *A New Testament Wordbook*.

R. COLIN CRASTON

MELCHIZEDEK. Historically (in Gen. 14:18-20), Melchizedek was (1) king of Salem (Jerusalem), (2) a priest of God Most High and (3) a bestower of blessing upon Abraham. His identity (various views have been held) is otherwise unknown. Like Abraham, he was a monotheist (Gen. 14:18, 22).

Prophetically (in Ps. 110), Melchizedek becomes the pattern of the Messiah's priesthood. This Davidic Psalm depicts (1) the deity (vs. 1; cf. Matt. 22:41-46), (2) the kingship (vss. 1 ff.; cf. Acts 2:34-36) and (3) the priesthood (vs. 4; cf. below) of the messianic priest-king. This prophecy is a necessary link between Genesis and the NT.

Typically (in Heb. 5:6, 10; 6:20; and particularly chap. 7), Melchizedek illustrates the superiority of Christ's priesthood to Aaron's priesthood. The history (in Genesis) and the prophecy (in Psalms) unitedly demonstrate how Melchizedek's name ("king of righteousness"), residence (Salem, "peace"), life (without birth or death), ordination (with an oath), office (both priest and king) and functions (a bestower of blessings and a receiver of tithes) all surpass Aaron's. Almost incidentally, and yet pregnantly, Christ (in Melchizedek) is likewise superior to Abraham (Heb. 7:4, 6) and Levi (Heb. 7:5, 8).

Hermeneutically, Melchizedek exemplifies (1) the significance of names, (2) the deeper meaning of history, (3) the relationship of history to prophecy and type, (4) the unity of the Testaments, (5) the implicit universality of the messianic mission, (6) the abrogation of ceremonialism and (7) the sanity and mystery of inspiration.

WICK BROOMALL

MERCY. A communicable attribute of God, mercy expresses God's goodness and love for the guilty and miserable. It includes pity, compassion, gentleness, forbearance. It is both free (not required by outward restraint) and absolute (covering all areas of human life). General mercy is best seen in creation and providence. Special mercy, for the elect only, is that which bestows compassion upon the victim of sin. Grace, as distinguished from mercy (which has respect to man's wretchedness), has in view man's culpability. God's mercy to man requires mercy on man's part (Matt. 18:23-35).

The OT word for mercy is *hesed*. NT words are *eleos* and *oiktirmos* ("pity," "mercy," "compassion"). The prevailing LXX rendering of *hesed, eleos,* and a somewhat frequent alternate, *dikaiosynē* ("righteousness") (Ex. 34:7, etc.), suggest an intimate relationship between these two attributes. Apparently no one Greek term was adequate to convey the word's full idea of intertwined righteousness and love. *Hesed* includes the RSV idea of "steadfast love." Many scholars emphasize the close relationship between *hesed* and *berît* (Deut. 7:2; 9:12, etc.) and see in *hesed* the mutual relation of rights and responsibilities. Thus God's mercy is required because of his covenant with his people. See LOVING-KINDNESS.

BIBLIOGRAPHY
T. Torrance, *SJT*, 1, 55-65; BDB; R. Bultmann in *TWNT*, II, 474-82; N. Glueck, *Das Wort Hesed*; W. Lofthouse, *ZAW*, 51, pp. 29-35; Crem, pp. 248-49; H. Mackintosh in *HERE*; L. Berkhof, *Reformed Dogmatics*, I, pp. 48-49; W. Shedd, *Dogmatic Theology*, I, pp. 389-92; T. Dwight, *Theology*, I, pp. 215-25; R. Girdlestone, *Synonyms of OT*, pp. 111-16; N. Snaith, *Distinctive Ideas of OT*, pp. 94-142; W. Robertson Smith, *Prophets*, pp. 160-62, 408-9; T. Cheyne, *Origin of Psalter*, pp. 370-72, 378-79; I. Elbogen in *OS*, 1926, 43-46.

BURTON L. GODDARD

MERCY SEAT. The *kappōreth*, (etymologically, and perhaps literally, "the expiating thing"), which rested on the ark of the covenant, is described in Ex. 25:17-22. It was made of pure gold, two cubits and a half in length and a cubit and a half in breadth, with two cherubim facing each other, their wings overshadowing the mercy seat. On the Day of Atonement the high priest took the blood of a bull and sprinkled it on the front of the *kappōreth* and before it. He did likewise with the blood of a goat.

According to the LXX rendering at Ex. 25:17 the adjective *hilastērion,* ordinarily used to translate *kappōreth,* is followed by *epithema,* for which there is no corresponding word in the Hebrew text. The LXX appears therefore to understand *kappōreth* as an atoning device, and not simply as a cover. Luther's *Gnadenstuhl* (followed by Tyndale: "the seate of grace," then "mercyseate") captures the derivation from the piel of *kapar (kipper),* "to expiate," "to make atonement." Paul's use of the LXX word, Rom. 3:25, conveys this thought of expiatory instrumentality. Whether the OT association is necessarily implied is questionable, but it is difficult to conceive its absence from the Apostle's mind. In any event the substantivized neuter adjective (a simple adjectival use especially in the masculine would be unusual) suggests that Jesus is the expiatory means who through his blood makes atonement. No attempted modification of God's disposition is necessarily implied in the word. Heb. 9:5 clearly refers to the *kappōreth*.

See also PROPITIATION.

BIBLIOGRAPHY
Arndt; A. Deissmann, *ZNW*, 4, 193-212; Herrmann-Buechsel in *TWNT*.

FREDERICK WILLIAM DANKER

MERIT. The word is not found in Scripture, yet the ideas enshrined in it vitally affect the doctrine of salvation. In the time of Christ Judaism had developed a strongly legalistic tinge which is attested for the intertestamental period (e.g., Tob. 12:9) and is reflected in our Lord's exchanges with the scribes. The church in the post-apostolic age was strongly affected by it also, for the Christian faith was thought of primarily as a new law which one must keep in order to gain eternal life.

Even though Augustine magnified divine grace, he retained the position that eternal life comes as a result of merit. He sought to safeguard this teaching by maintaining that grace is essential in order to enable one to do these good works.

The standard position among the Schoolmen was that baptismal grace not only absolved from previous sin but also produced a condition wherein one could win merit. A distinction was made between the merit of congruity and the merit of condignity. The former was connected with general grace. The natural man was regarded as having sufficient virtue to impel him toward the good and therefore toward God. Thus he could merit the second stage, which comes by special grace, the merit of condignity. As the first stage paved the way for justification in the Roman Catholic sense, the second led to eternal life.

Alexander of Hales (d. 1245) advanced the doctrine of the Treasury of Merit. Christ's sufferings were more than enough for the salvation of the race. Also, the sacrificial works of many of the saints exceeded what they themselves required for entrance into heaven. This surplus of merit is thus available to needy, penitent souls. Aquinas endorsed the idea and sought to strengthen it by emphasizing the mystical union which binds the members of the church to one another and to Christ the head. Col. 1:24 has been appealed to as a proof text for the doctrine, which historically was intimately connected with the system of indulgences in the Roman Church against which the Reformation took its stand.

Roman Catholic theology is inextricably tied up with the concept of merit. "Good works are truly and properly meritorious, and that not merely of some particular reward, but of eternal life itself" (Bellarmine).

Scriptural data on this general subject are difficult to systematize. On the one hand recognition is given to the doing of good as leading ultimately to life (Rom. 2:6, 7; Acts 10:35), but this is not recognized as merit. Rather, the desire thus exhibited to please God finds its fulfilment in the divine guarantee to bring those who evidence it to a saving knowledge of the gospel. Certainly the teaching of Paul is clear that no supposed worth of character or amassing of legal works can bring a righteous standing before God.

See also INDULGENCE, SUPEREROGATION, GOOD WORKS.

BIBLIOGRAPHY
CE; Harnack, *History of Dogma*, passim; R. S. Franks in *HERE*; Pohle-Preuss, *Grace Actual and Habitual*, pp. 423-36.

EVERETT F. HARRISON

MESSIAH. The study of the rise and development of the figure of the Messiah is primarily historical, and then theological. Confusion arises when specifically Christian ideas about the Messiah invade the OT data. Jesus' concept of his messianic mission did not accord with contemporary popular Jewish expectation.

"Messiah" is the hellenized transliteration of the Aramaic $m^e\check{s}\bar{\imath}h\bar{a}'$. The underlying Hebrew word is derived from the verb $m\bar{a}\check{s}ah$, to anoint, smear with oil. This title was used sometimes of non-Israelite figures: e.g., Cyrus in Isa. 45:1, sometimes of the altar as in Ex. 29:36, sometimes of the prophet as in I Kings 19:16, but most frequently it referred to the king of Israel as in I Sam. 26:11 and Ps. 89:20. It is noteworthy that the word Messiah does not appear at all in the OT (the AV of Dan. 9:25 is incorrect; it ought to read "an anointed one"), and only rarely in the intertestamental literature. The primary sense of the title is "king," as the anointed man of God, but it also suggests election, i.e., the king was chosen, elect, and therefore honored. It could scarcely be otherwise than that it referred to a political leader, for in its early stages Israel sought only a ruler, visible and powerful, who would reign here and now. But the entire evidence of later Judaism points to a Messiah not only as king, but as eschatological king, a ruler who would appear at the end time. David was the ideal king of Israel, and as such he had a "sacral" character, and this sacral characteristic came to be applied to the eschatological king who was to be like David. How did the national Messiah come to be a future ideal king? After the death of David Israel began to hope for another like him who would maintain the power and prestige of their country. But she came into hard times with the rupture of the kingdom, and with this event there arose a disillusionment concerning the hope for a king like David. Then after the Exile Zerubbabel, a descendant of David, took leadership of Judah, but it developed that he was not another David. Gradually the hope was projected into the future, and eventually into the very remote future so that the Messiah was expected at the end of the age. This is the mood of the messianic expectations in the latter part of the OT. Such prophecies are common. For example, Jer. 33 promises a continuation of the Davidic line; Isa. 9 and 11 foresee the regal splendor of the coming king; Mic. 5:2 looks forward to the birth of the Davidic king in Bethlehem; and Zech. 9 and 12 describe the character of the messianic kingdom and reign.

The Son of Man figure in Daniel is not to be identified with the Messiah; it is later in the history of Judaism that the two figures were seen to be one. The Suffering Servant of Isaiah by reason of his role is yet another figure. So the Messiah, or future ideal king of Israel, the Son of Man and the Suffering Servant were three distinct representations in the OT.

The Apocrypha and Pseudepigrapha are the literary remains of the evolution of messianic hopes within Judah between the testaments. As in the OT, the formal use of "Messiah" is rare. It is well to remember that in this literature there is a distinction between Messiah and messianic; a book may have a messianic theme, but lack a Messiah. The Book of Enoch is best known for its doctrine of the Son of Man which has many messianic overtones. Yet he is not the Messiah, but a person much like Daniel's Son of Man. It remained to the Psalms of Solomon (*ca.* 48 B.C.) to provide the one confirmed and repeated evidence of the technical use of the term in the intertestamental literature. This literature demonstrates, therefore, a diffuse expectation about the Messiah. It speaks of a Messiah of David, of Levi, of Joseph and of Ephraim. The Dead Sea Scrolls add to the confusion by referring to a Messiah of Aaron and Israel. Out of the welter of messianic hopes in this period there emerges a pattern: two kinds of Messiah came to be expected. On the one hand, there arose an expectation of a purely national Messiah, one who would appear as a man and assume the kingship over Judah to deliver her from her oppressors. On the other hand, there was a hope for a transcendent Messiah from heaven, part human, part divine, who would establish the kingdom of God on earth. To the

popular Jewish mind of the first two centuries before and after Christ these two concepts were not mutually hostile, but tended rather to modify each other. It has been argued by some scholars that the conflation of the concepts of Messiah and Suffering Servant took place in the intertestamental period, but the sole evidence for this is from the Targums, which are post-Christian.

It remained for Jesus to fuse the three great eschatological representations of the OT — Messiah, Suffering Servant and Son of Man — into one messianic person. Apart from this truth there is no explanation for the confusion of the disciples when he told them he must suffer and die (Matt. 16:21 ff.). That Christ knew himself to be the Messiah is seen best in his use of the title Son of Man; in Mark 14:61-62 he equates the Christ and the Son of Man. "Christ" is simply the Greek equivalent of the Hebrew "Messiah." John 1:41 and 4:25 preserve the Semitic idea by transliterating the word Messiah. Jesus willingly accepted the appellation Son of David, a distinct messianic title, on several occasions — the cry of blind Bartimaeus (Mark 10:47 ff.), the children in the temple (Matt. 21:15) and the Triumphal Entry (Matt. 21:9), to name but a few. It has long been wondered why Jesus did not appropriate the title Messiah to himself instead of the less clear title of Son of Man. The former was probably avoided out of political considerations, for if Jesus had publicly used "Messiah" of himself it would have ignited political aspirations in his hearers to appoint him as king, principally a nationalistic figure, and to seek to drive out the Roman occupiers. This is precisely the import of the Jews' action at the Triumphal Entry. Jesus seized on the title Son of Man to veil to his hearers his messianic mission, but to reveal that mission to his disciples.

The first generation of the church did not hesitate to refer to Jesus as the Christ, and thereby designate him as the greater Son of David, the King. The word was used first as a title of Jesus (Matt. 16:16), and later as part of the personal name (Eph. 1:1, e.g.). Peter's sermon at Pentecost not only acknowledged Jesus as the Christ, but also as Lord, and so the fulfilment of the messianic office is integrally linked to the essential deity of Jesus. Acts 2:36 affirms that Jesus was "made" Christ, the sense of the verb being that by the resurrection Jesus was confirmed as the Christ, the Messiah of God. Rom. 1:4 and Phil. 2:9-11 contain the same thought. Other messianic titles attributed to Jesus include Servant, Lord, Son of God, the King, the Holy One, the Righteous One and the Judge.

See also CHRISTOLOGY.

BIBLIOGRAPHY
S. Mowinckel, *He That Cometh;* B. B. Warfield, *Christology and Criticism;* V. Taylor, *The Names of Jesus.*

DAVID H. WALLACE

METEMPSYCHOSIS. This is the theory that souls are reincarnate many times. It is an essential part of Buddhism and Hinduism, though the Buddhist conception of the soul is complex. It is also held by Theosophists, Anthroposophists, Rosicrucians, most Occultists, some Spiritualists, and some philosophers. It is often coupled with the theory of *karma,* whereby the present allotment of good and evil is what has been merited in previous lives. "Memories" of earlier lives, sometimes induced under hypnosis, are open to doubt.

Although reincarnation was held by Gnostics and a few early Christians, the Bible lends no support. Heb. 9:27 speaks of "once to die." In John 9:2-3 Christ rejects the theory of sin in a previous life as an explanation of blindness. John the Baptist was not Elijah in person (Matt. 11:14; 17:10-12), but had "the spirit and power of Elijah" (Luke 1:17).

BIBLIOGRAPHY
J. Stafford Wright, "Man in the Process of Time," in *What is Man?,* pp. 138 f.

J. STAFFORD WRIGHT

METROPOLITAN. See OFFICES, ECCLESIASTICAL.

MIDRASH. From the Hebrew *dāraš,* meaning "to examine," a midrash is simultaneously a Jewish-rabbinic commentary and a method of scriptural exposition directed to the activity of penetrating into the meaning of a text. As commentaries, midrashim (plural) are divided into two broad classes.

Of primary importance is the halachic midrash, which is strictly ethical in nature and purposes to expound the deeper meaning of the law. Halachic midrashim originated under the scribes — of which Ezra was the first — when the interpretation of trained scholars was required to make the law applicable to the circumstances of a new environment (e.g., the post-exilic return to Palestine). The oldest extant midrashim are halachic and have their origin in the Tannaitic era (A.D. 1-200): (1)

Mechilta (rule) on a section of Exodus; (2) *Siphra* (book) on Leviticus; and (3) *Siphre* (books) on Numbers and Deuteronomy.

Most of the remaining midrashim are haggadic; that is, they are homiletic in nature and interpret Scripture from the devotional standpoint for purposes of edification. Their origin lies in the homiletic exposition of the sabbath lection in the synagogue. Important haggadic midrashim are the *Tanchuma* (fourth century) and the *Midrash Rabba* (sixth to twelfth centuries).

BIBLIOGRAPHY
H. L. Strack, *Introduction to the Talmud and Midrash;* J. Theodor, *JewEnc,* VIII, pp. 548-80.

HERMAN C. WAETJEN

MIGHT. This word, which signifies ability to enforce one's will, represents a variety of words in Scripture, chiefly *kōah, 'ōz, gᵉbûrâ* and *mᵉōd* in the OT and *dynamis, ischus* and *kratos* in the NT. The AV, ERV, and RSV render variously "might," "power" or "strength."

It is appropriately used of God as Creator and Sustainer of the universe (II Chron. 20:6; Ps. 145:6; Isa. 40:6), and of the ability God gives to men that they may serve him (Judg. 6:14; Dan. 2:23; Col. 1:11). *Dynamis* is actually used as a periphrasis for God in Matt. 26:64 (= Mark 14:62), where the RSV has "Power" (AV and ERV "power"). As strength given to man it is especially associated with the Holy Spirit (Acts 1:8; Eph. 3:16) and is a particular endowment of Messiah (Isa. 11:2).

Never was God's mighty power more clearly seen than in the resurrection of Jesus Christ from the dead (Eph. 1:19-20), and to him finally shall be ascribed all might and majesty in heaven (Rev. 7:12).

L. E. H. STEPHENS-HODGE

MILLENNIUM. The biblical teaching about the millennium is found in Rev. 20:1-10, and the debate on the meaning of this passage has been a long one. The different interpretations of the millennium are distinguished in two ways; sometimes by the relation in which the millennium is thought to stand to the second coming of Christ, and sometimes in terms of the meaning of the millennium itself. The two views to be considered first are those known as pre-millennialism and post-millennialism respectively, views which are distinguished by the relation of the millennium to the Lord's return.

I. PRE-MILLENNIALISM. The view which this term expresses indicates that the Lord will return before the millennium, and it has been presented in two main forms.

A. *Older Form of Pre-millennialism.* This was based upon a correspondence between the six days of creation followed by the one day of rest. It was accordingly conceived that the world's history was to extend over a period of six thousand years and that this in turn was to be followed by a kind of millennial "sabbath" of one thousand years. Very often quite materialistic conceptions were attached to this view, and the term "chiliasm" has been largely employed to indicate this way of conceiving of millennial blessings. It was further held that at the close of the thousand years of sabbath rest there would be the final judgment and the new creation.

B. *Recent Form of Pre-Millennialism.* Under this heading come the views which are sometimes called "Dispensationalist," though there are many expositors who hold to a pre-millennial coming of our Lord but who nevertheless do not subscribe to such dispensationalist views as those of Darby, Bullinger and Scofield. It is impossible to make a brief statement that covers all the varieties of interpretation that are gathered under this heading, but the overall picture may be painted in something like the following terms.

1. Before any of the final events of the *parousia* take place living Christians will be "caught up." This is sometimes called the secret rapture (*q.v.*). There are many pre-millennialists, however, who reject the theory of the secret rapture and hold that the taking up of the saints will occur at the public manifestation of the second coming of Christ. This divergence of opinion is sometimes indicated by the terms pre-tribulation rapture and post-tribulation rapture. The former opinion teaches that the saints do not go through the tribulation, while the latter implies that they do.

2. When Christ returns, the world will be under the sway of evil and Antichrist will be in power.

3. At his coming our Lord will win an outstanding victory in which Antichrist will be destroyed.

4. The resurrection of believers — "the first resurrection" — will occur either before the great tribulation or immediately at the beginning of the millennium.

5. At the inception of the millennium there will be a preliminary judgment of the living nations. The risen saints will reign with Christ one thousand years.

6. At the end of the millennium flagrant wickedness will break out, this being occasioned by the loosing of Satan.

7. After this painful short season the resurrection of the wicked will take place and this will be followed by the last judgment at the great white throne.

One of the main turning points in dispensationalist teaching is the view which is taken of "the kingdom." It is held that the OT prophets predicted the re-establishment of David's kingdom and that Christ himself intended to bring this about. It is alleged, however, that because the Jews refused his person and work he postponed the establishment of his kingdom until the time of his return. Meanwhile, it is argued, the Lord gathered together "the church" as a kind of interim measure.

Some of the objections that are made against pre-millennialism are as follows.

1. It implies an untenable literalism in the interpretation of prophecy.

2. The theory of the "postponed kingdom" is without scriptural support, and there cannot be two gospels, one of "faith" and one of "sight."

3. The view makes a separation of time between the coming of Christ, the resurrection, the judgment and the end of the world. This is considered by many to be contrary to Scripture, which synchronizes these events. Dispensationalism also separates the *parousia* from the *epiphaneia,* the *apocalypsis* and the "day of the Lord" in a manner which Scripture cannot support.

4. The NT does not connect the second coming with an earthly kingdom having its center in an administration from Jerusalem.

5. There is an incongruity in the situation which supposes the risen saints to be living with others in the world who are still in their earthly state.

6. Pre-millennialism is based only on Revelation 20, after having read certain OT prophecies into it. This produces a view which is contradicted by the rest of Scripture.

7. The "first resurrection" may possibly

indicate regeneration by the Holy Spirit, an event which is likened to a resurrection in the writings of Paul and John.

II. POST-MILLENNIALISM. This, as the name suggests, indicates a view which places the coming of Christ after the millennium. Post-millennial theories have been held in two forms which again can be distinguished as older and more recent.

A. *Older Form of Post-millennialism.* Augustine conceived of the thousand years as representing the period that the church was to rule on the earth. According to this, the millennial reign of the saints represented the rule of the kingdom of heaven, while the first resurrection represented the spiritual share which believers had in their Lord's resurrection.

Among other post-millennial thinkers of the older school, some thought the millennium to be a thing of the past, others considered that its blessings were still being experienced, while others regarded it as belonging to some future time, possibly just before the second coming. There are many evangelical believers who hold these post-millennial views and think of the millennium as a period in the later days of the church when, under the special power of the Holy Spirit, the work of God shall be greatly revived and believers shall become so aware of their spiritual strength that to a degree unknown before they shall triumph over the powers of evil. This "golden age" of the church, it is held, will be followed by a brief apostasy — a terrible conflict between the forces of good and evil — and this in turn will be eclipsed by the simultaneous occurrence of the advent of Christ, the general resurrection and the final judgment.

B. *Recent Form of Post-millennialism.* This can be described as, on the whole, humanistic and evolutionary in principle. It is represented in the optimistic and largely secular philosophies of recent years which regard the world as in process of constant amelioration.

Some of the objections to post-millennial views are the following.

1. There is no ground in the Scripture for the hope of unexampled spiritual prosperity just before the coming of the Lord, though there is some suggestion of spiritual revival that is yet to be known before the Lord's return.

2. The idea of an imperceptible passing of the present age into the glorious one of the future is contradicted by the catastrophic representation of the subject in Scripture.

3. The humanistic and evolutionary opinions are contrary to all that the Bible has to say concerning man and his sin.

Before passing on to other aspects of this study, a comment by Gerhardus Vos, which relates both to pre-millennialism and post-millennialism, ought to be heeded. He writes: "In regard to a book [Revelation] so enigmatical, it were presumptuous to speak with any degree of dogmatism, but the uniform absence of the idea of the millennium from the eschatological teaching of the New Testament elsewhere ought to render the exegete cautious before affirming its presence here."

III. THE NATURE OF THE MILLENNIUM. The two views that have been described above have certain conceptions in common in that they both regard the millennium as a period of time in which the kingdom of God, in one form or another, is to prosper. Before considering the third general view of the subject, however, it is necessary to survey the ideas that have been entertained concerning the nature of the millennium. These can be provisionally arranged under the following headings.

A. *Jewish.* This is the view that sees the millennium to be the time of restored national prosperity for Israel. It regards Israel as the center of the divine government of the world and Jerusalem as its glorious capital. Against this, it is asserted that it involves many unwarranted assumptions and violates many of the canons of sound interpretation. It proves too much, and if it were to be carried through consistently it would require the renewal of temple worship, together with the restoration of animal sacrifices and the Aaronic priesthood. Pre-millennialism allies itself with this interpretation.

B. *Ecclesiastical.* By this term is indicated the idea that the millennium is the victorious and successful domination of the church over the world. This domination has been attempted by the Church of Rome and has proved disastrous for both the church and the world. It is a purely external concept of the church's function and in the face of history is unrealistic. Some forms of post-millennialism are associated with this ecclesiastical interpretation.

C. *Eschatological.* Under this view of the nature of the millennium come those conceptions of it which link it with the intermediate state of believers. The millennium might possibly be this, but if it were adopted, very much in the context of Rev. 20 would be left without meaning.

D. *Evangelical.* Under this title may be gathered those views of the millennium which regard it as representing the inward spiritual triumphs which believers in Christ know, both in their own personal lives and in the work of the gospel. This view is reached by an endeavor to recognize the apocalyptic nature of the literature in which the concept of the millennium is presented.

This survey of the views about the millennium itself prepares the way for an examination of what is known as

IV. A-MILLENNIALISM. The negative prefix attached to this word does not deny a millennial idea altogether, as at first it might appear to do. The measure of denial in it, however, is that it holds that there is no sufficient ground for the expectation of a millennium in the sense of a thousand-year period of time, such as pre-millennialism and post-millennialism advocate. A-millennialism cannot find any place in the teaching of the NT for the belief that a millennium will follow the Lord's coming, for the second advent immediately ushers in the last judgment and the eternal state. Similarly, a-millennialism cannot discover any basis in the Bible for the expectation of moral improvement in the world, nor yet of the conversion of the world before the Lord comes.

So far as the eschatological events of time are concerned, the a-millennial understanding of the NT takes the following shape.

1. The end of the age will be marked by increasing lawlessness and godlessness.

2. This godlessness will reach its climax in the appearing of the Antichrist.

3. Christ will return in glory, accompanied by the resurrected saints who have fallen asleep in Jesus, and those who "are alive and remain" will be caught up to join the redeemed host.

4. The second advent of Christ will destroy the evil world.

5. The resurrection of the wicked and the last judgment synchronize with the Lord's return.

6. The present earth will be made to pass away and give place to a new heaven and a new earth.

There have, quite naturally, been a number of differences of detail among a-millennialists.

Some have held that the millennium is a symbol of the completeness of the rest which the Lord gives to his saints, and on this view the millennium has been understood to refer to the intermediate state of believers after death. The more dominant interpretation among a-millennialists of the present day is that the millennium represents the blessedness of Christian experience now. Believers are already in heavenly places in Christ Jesus and reign in life by him; Satan is a destroyed foe, and believers triumph over him in Christ.

A-millennialism rests on a symbolical interpretation of Rev. 20 and gives full value to the apocalyptic nature of the book. The expression "the thousand years" is understood consistently with the symbolic use of numerals in apocalyptic language. In such a context figures represent not arithmetical values but ideas. The figure one thousand is accordingly regarded as symbolical of the idea of fulness and completeness. W. W. Milligan writes, "The thousand years mentioned in the passage express no period of time. They are not a figure for the whole Christian era, now extending to nearly nineteen hundred years, nor do they denote a certain space of time . . . at the close of the present dispensation. . . . They embody an idea; and that idea, whether applied to the subjugation of Satan or to the triumph of the saints is the idea of completeness or perfection. Satan is bound for a thousand years; that is, he is completely bound. The saints reign for a thousand years; that is, they are introduced into a state of perfect and glorious victory" (W. W. Milligan in The Expositor's Bible, *The Book of Revelation*, p. 337). The subsequent events of the "little season" are not a temporal sequence, but indicate merely that even though the decisive blow has been given to the devil, he still has a limited measure of power and in a strictly specified direction. In the Christian era the activity of the devil is but a release from his place of doom: it is a permitted activity and its limitation is symbolized by the reference to "the little season." Says Milligan once again: "Hardly was he conquered for the saints, than he was loosed for the world." So far as the saints are concerned, Satan is completely bound, but his power still operates upon the wicked.

The arguments brought against a-millennialism are many, but they all stem from the same root, that is, the difficulty which some expositors find in accepting the completely symbolical nature of Rev. 20.

See also Eschatology, Kingdom of God.

BIBLIOGRAPHY

W. J. Grier, *The Momentous Event*; Oswald T. Allis, *Prophecy and the Church*; S. Waldegrave, *New Testament Millenarianism*; B. C. Young, *Short Arguments about the Millennium*; Floyd E. Hamilton, *The Basis of Millennial Faith*; Roderick Campbell, *Israel and the New Covenant*; B. W. Newton, *The Millennium and Israel's Future*; The Scofield Bible; W. Adams Brown in *HDB*; W. G. Moorehead in *ISBE*; H. G. Guinness, *The Approaching End of the Age*; Geerhardus Vos, Article, "Eschatology of the New Testament," in *ISBE*; J. A. MacCulloch in *HERE*.

ERNEST FREDERICK KEVAN

MIND. The English versions of the Bible express a variety of emotional, volitional and intellectual movements by the one word mind. The Bible has no word for brain and the exact sense of the several Hebrew or Greek terms is to be determined by the context, for no precise meaning is attached to any of them. To express purpose, desire, memory, feeling, affection Hebrew uses *lēb*, *lēbāb*, "heart"; *nephesh*, "life principle" (often translated "soul"); *rûah*, "spirit"; *yēṣer*, "disposition." The NT presents a fuller account of the activity of the human consciousness. There firstly mind may signify the faculty of thinking or mental apprehension usually rendered "understanding" in the AV (but the RSV has "mind" in Luke 24:45); so in I Cor. 14:14-15, 19, where it is contrasted with a spiritual exercise in which the mind is inactive (see also Rev. 13:18; Phil. 4:7). Secondly, mind represents the intellectual, reflective faculty of man, "the higher, mental part of the natural man, which initiates his thoughts and plans" (Arndt). It is thus the faculty concerned with moral attitudes and activities. If controlled by the Holy Spirit, the mind displays the right attitude to God and to one's fellows (Luke 10:27; Rom. 12:2; I Cor. 1:10) and the mind thus bent on the service of God is contrasted with "the flesh" (Rom. 7:23, 25), the fallen nature still contending within the regenerate man. The mind even of the believer may be controlled by "the flesh" (Col. 2:18) but such perversion of the mind is ascribed more to the unregenerate (Rom. 1:28; II Cor. 3:14; 4:4; II Tim. 3:8). The mind, therefore, is in itself neutral, and its moral quality is determined by the power to which it is subject. Similarly *phronēma* or *phroneō* are used to express the direction of thought, desire and will, whether against God if motivated by "the flesh," or in harmony with God if motivated

by "the spirit," i.e., the renewed nature vitalized by the Holy Spirit (Rom. 8:5-7). The English "minded," expressing a variety of Greek terms, conveys a similar connotation.

BIBLIOGRAPHY

J. Laidlaw in *HDB*; Arndt s.v. *nous*.

J. CLEMENT CONNELL

MINISTER, MINISTRY. It is the consistent NT teaching that the work of ministers is "for the perfecting of the saints . . . for the edifying of the body of Christ" (Eph. 4:12). The minister is called of God to a position of responsibility rather than privilege, as the words for "minister" show (*diakonos*, "table waiter"; *hypēretēs*, "under-rower" in a large ship; *leitourgos*, "servant" usually of the state or a temple).

There are two passages in the NT which are of especial importance in this connection, I Cor. 12:28, and Eph. 4:11 f. From the former we gather that included in the ministries exercised in the early church were those of apostles, prophets, teachers, miracles, gifts of healings, helps, governments, diversities of tongues (possibly also interpretations, vs. 30). The latter adds evangelists and pastors. In every case these appear to be the direct gift of God to the church. Both passages seem to say this and this is confirmed elsewhere in the case of some of the people mentioned. Thus in Gal. 1:1 Paul insists that his apostolate was in no sense from man. He entirely excludes the possibility of his receiving it by ordination. We are to think, then, of a group of men directly inspired by the Holy Spirit to perform various functions within the church by way of building up the saints in the body of Christ.

But there are others also. Thus from early days the apostles made it a habit to appoint elders. Some hold that the seven of Acts 6 were the first elders. This seems very unlikely, but there were certainly elders at the council of Jerusalem (Acts 15). It is very striking that even on their first missionary journey Paul and Barnabas appointed elders "in every church" (Acts 14:23). There is every reason for thinking that these men were ordained with the laying on of hands, as in the case of the elders of the Jewish synagogue. Then there were the deacons of whom we read in Phil. 1:1 and I Tim. 3:8 ff. We know nothing of their method of appointment, but it is likely that it also included the laying on of hands, as it certainly did somewhat later in the history of the church.

It is sometimes said that the first group of ministers is opposed to the second in that they possessed a direct gift from God. This, however, cannot be sustained. In Acts 20:28 we read, "the Holy Ghost has made you bishops," and in I Tim. 4:14 of "the gift that is in thee, which was given thee by prophecy, with the laying on of the hands of the presbytery." It is clear that the act of ordination was not thought of as in opposition to a gift from God, but as itself the means of the gift from God. Indeed the only reason that a man might minister adequately was that God has given him the gift of ministering. The picture we get then is of a group of ministers who had been ordained, men like bishops and deacons, and side by side with them (at times no doubt the same people) those who had a special gift of God in the way of prophecy, apostleship, or the like. The meaning of some of those gifts has long since perished (e.g., helps, governments). But they witness to the gifts that God gave his church in the time of its infancy.

There are some who think of the ministry as constitutive of the church. They emphasize that Christ is the Head of the body, and that he gives it apostles, prophets, etc., that it may be built up. They infer that the ministry is the channel through which life flows from the Head. This does, however, seem to be reading something into the passage. It is better to take realistically the NT picture of the church as the body of Christ, as a body, moreover, with a diversity of function. The life of Christ is in it, and the divine power puts forth whatever is needed. In the Spirit-filled body there will emerge such ministerial and other organs as are necessary. On this view the ministry is essential, but no more essential than any other function of the body. And it preserves the important truth that the body is that of Christ, who does what he wills within it. His blessing is not confined to any particular channel.

BIBLIOGRAPHY

H. B. Swete, *Early History of the Church and Ministry;* J. B. Lightfoot, *Commentary on Philippians,* pp. 181-269; K. E. Kirk, ed., *The Apostolic Ministry;* T. W. Manson, *The Church's Ministry;* S. Neil, ed., *The Ministry of the Church.*

LEON MORRIS

MIRACLE. I. THE BIBLICAL CONCEPT OF MIRACLE. In the NT three terms, miracle, wonder, and sign, occasionally found together (Acts 2:22; II Thess. 2:9; Heb. 2:4), are used to designate the extraordinary events and mighty acts brought to pass in connection with the outworking of redemption whether in its Hebraic or Christian stage. The first of these, *dynamis,* points to the divine power which is operative in the event or act, the invisible, supernatural source of energy which makes the phenomenon possible. The second term, *sēmeion,* points to the teleology of the phenomenon. Far from being a pointless prodigy, it is — at least for the eyes of faith — a work of God which functions as a word of God, a deed simultaneously evidential and revelational. On the one hand, it verifies claims and communications, whether prophetic, messianic, or apostolic (e.g., Ex. 4:1-9, 31; I Kings 18:17-39; Matt. 11:2-8; Acts 13:6-12). On the other hand, it discloses the very nature and purpose of God, and this is especially so in the mighty acts of Jesus Christ (Mark 2:1-11; 7:34; John 2:11; 5:36; 6:30; 7:31; 11:40-42; 14:10; Acts 2:22; 10:38). The last word, *teras,* points to the attention-compelling character of the phenomenon. A striking departure from the normal order of things, it cries out for the reaction of faith and obedience even though it is never performed to coerce such response (Luke 4:9-12; Matt. 12:38-42). Synthesizing the root connotations of these terms, we may define a miracle biblically as an observable phenomenon effected by the direct operation of God's power, an arresting deviation from the ordinary sequences of nature, a deviation calculated to elicit faith-begetting awe, a divine inbreaking which authenticates a revelational agent. In view of Deut. 13:1-4, however, and passages like Ex. 7:10-12; 8:7; Matt. 12:24-27; 24:24; and Rev. 13:15, it must be borne in mind that the mere exercise of preternatural power is insufficient to validate an agent as God-energized. Since preternatural power may be exercised by an agent Satanically-energized, the teaching of the miracle-worker must be congruent with the totality of previous revelation.

II. THE REVELATIONAL POSTULATES OF MIRACLE. The concept of miracle has been attacked historically (e.g., Renan), scientifically (e.g., Huxley) and theologically (e.g., Sabatier); yet as a rule these attacks have been philosophically instigated and controlled (e.g., Hume) even where metaphysical presuppositions have been explicitly disavowed. Within the framework of the biblical *Weltanschauung,* however, miracle is no embarrassing anomaly: it is an inevitable corollary of redemptive theism (q.v.). Granted the postulates of creation, providence, sin, and salvation, miracle becomes a veritable necessity, a necessity of grace.

According to the postulates of creation (q.v.) and providence (q.v.), God in sovereign power and wisdom, having brought the cosmos into existence, now continuously sustains and guides it. Nature therefore cannot be interpreted deistically or pantheistically. Neither, of course, can it be interpreted naturalistically as a self-enclosed, self-explanatory continuum going of its own accord with all events causally interlocked backwards and forwards. Undeniably nature has an order, but, fixed and dependable though it is, the order of nature is not iron-clad, a strait-jacket in which God finds himself helplessly bound. Biblically viewed, nature is plastic in the hands of its sovereign Creator.

Next, according to the postulate of sin (q.v.), nature is now in a state of abnormality. Because of sin (Gen. 3:17-18), the order of nature is shot through with disorder; the entire cosmos, including mankind, is out of line with God's purposes. The biblical teaching with respect to the cause of nature's dysteleological aspects collides head-on with all other philosophies and cosmologies. Creaturely sin, Scripture asserts, sin which the freedom bestowed by creative love permits but does not necessitate, is the fons et origo of natural evil. Hence Scripture opposes any theory which holds that an eternal surd of evil is the ground of creaturely sin. It is creaturely sin, then, which has afflicted the order of nature, human nature not excluded, with disorder and abnormality.

Finally, according to the postulate of salvation, God in his grace has embarked upon a vast program of palingenesis, working abnormally to undo the entail of sin, overcoming the disorder it has introduced and thus bringing his cosmos to the end he has sovereignly ordained. That abnormal mode of the divine working called miracle is therefore not a meaningless, haphazard marvel. It is, rather, that soteriologically motivated deviation from his normal mode of working which the undoing of sin's abnormality requires. As such it appears episodically yet not capriciously. It characterizes the pivotal junctures of Heilsgeschichte (q.v.) — the Exodus, the battle with paganism in the time of Elijah and Elisha, the ministry of Daniel, the life of Jesus, the apostolic era. In the words of Abraham Kuyper, miracle is

"the overcoming, interpenetrating working of the Divine energy by which God breaks all opposition, and in the face of disorder brings His cosmos to realize that end which was determined upon in His counsel. It is from the deeper basis of God's will, on which the whole cosmos rests, that this mysterious power works in the cosmos, breaks the bands of sin and disorder, which hold the cosmos in their embrace; and centrally from man so influences the entire life of the cosmos, that at length it must realize the glory intended for it by God, in order in that glory to render unto God what was the end of the entire creation of the cosmos. Every interpretation of the miracle as a magical incident without connection with the palingenesis of the whole cosmos, which Jesus refers to in Matt. 19:28, and therefore without relation to the entire metamorphosis which awaits the cosmos after the last judgment, does not enhance the glory of God, but debases the Recreator of heaven and earth to a juggler. This entire recreative action of the Divine energy is one continuous miracle, which shows itself in the radical renewal of the life of man by regeneration, in radical renewal of humanity by the new Head which it receives in Christ, and which finally shall bring to pass a similar radical renewal of life in nature. And because these three do not run loosely side by side, but are bound together organically, so that the mystery of regeneration, incarnation, and of the final restitution forms one whole, this wondrous energy of recreation exhibits itself in a broad history, in which what used to be interpreted as incidental miracles, could not be found wanting" (Encyclopedia of Sacred Theology, Scribners, New York, 1898, p. 414).

III. An Apologetic for Miracle. In developing an apologetic for miracle several factors seem to be of primary importance. First, a proper definition must be formulated which sidesteps the mare's-nest of difficulties in Hume's famous assertion that a miracle is "a violation of the laws of nature." Augustine is still a sure-footed guide at this point: "For we say that all portents are contrary to nature, but they are not so. For how is that contrary to nature which happens by the will of God, since the will of so mighty a Creator is certainly the nature of each created thing? A portent, therefore, happens not contrary to nature, but contrary to what we know as nature. . . . There is, however, no impropriety in saying that God does a thing contrary to nature, when it is contrary to what we know of nature. For we give the name nature to the usual common course of nature; and whatever God does contrary to this, we call a prodigy, or a miracle. But against the supreme law of nature, which is beyond the knowledge both of the ungodly and of weak believers, God never acts, any more than He acts against Himself" (*Contra Faustum*, XXVI, 3). Second, in order to achieve a viable definition the concept of natural law, the concept of existential impossibility as distinguished from logical impossibility, and the concept of historical credibility must be searchingly analyzed. Henry Bett has done this very ably in *The Reality of the Religious Life*. Third, the biblical postulates of miracle must be presupposed. Without these no cogent apologetic can be constructed. As J. S. Mill declares, "Once admit a God and the production by His direct volition of an effect, which in any case owed its origin to His creative will, is no longer an arbitrary hypothesis to account for the fact, but must be reckoned with as a serious possibility" (*Three Essays on Religion*, H. Holt and Co., New York, 1874, p. 232). And once admit not alone the postulate of God but also the revelational postulates of sin and salvation, and the acceptance of the biblical signs, an acceptance which never loses its pistic essence, is intellectually compelling.

BIBLIOGRAPHY

Robert Anderson, *The Silence of God*; Henry Bett, *The Reality of the Religious Life*; A. B. Bruce, *The Miraculous Element in the Gospel*; Horace Bushnell, *Nature and the Supernatural*; D. S. Cairns, *The Faith That Rebels*; Robert W. Grant, *Miracle and Natural Law*; Karl Heim, *Christian Faith and Natural Science, the Transformation of the Scientific World View*; Jean Hellé, *Miracles*; Ian Henderson, *Myth in the New Testament*; David Hume, *An Enquiry Concerning Human Understanding*; Karl Jaspers and Rudolf Bultmann, *Myth and Christianity*; T. A. Lacy, *Nature, Miracle, and Sin*; John Laidlaw, *The Miracles of Our Lord*; C. S. Lewis, *Miracles: A Preliminary Study*; S. Vernon McCasland, *By the Finger of God*; Alan Richardson, *The Miracle-Stories of the Gospels*; G. R. H. Shafto, *The Wonders of the Kingdom*; F. R. Tennant, *Miracle and Its Philosophical Presuppositions*; Richard Trench, *Notes on the Parables and Miracles*; B. B. Warfield, *Counterfeit Miracles*; Johannes Wendland, *Miracle and Christianity*; C. J. Wright, *Miracle in History and in Modern Thought*.

VERNON C. GROUNDS

MISHNAH. Hebrew *mišnâ* from *šānâ*, "to repeat," is the term denoting the oral traditions that developed about the law, containing interpretations and applications to specific questions which the law deals with only in principle. Specifically, it is the collection of these traditions made by Rabbi Judah Ha-Nasi (b.

A.D. 135, d. *ca.* 220). Although this collection was made toward the end of the second century A.D., it clearly contains material from several centuries earlier, hence is of value for understanding certain ideas and expressions in the NT. It was written in Hebrew that had developed beyond the latest "biblical" Hebrew, but that this was not merely an academic language we now know from the Dead Sea Scrolls. The Mishnah is divided into six parts (*sᵉdārîm*, "orders"), each of which is further divided into tracts (*massektôt*, "webs") and paragraphs or sentences (*mišnāyôt*). The text of the Mishnah is preserved in three (some scholars say four) recensions.

BIBLIOGRAPHY

H. Danby, *The Mishnah*; H. L. Strack, "Talmud," SHERK 11: pp. 255-60.

WILLIAM SANFORD LASOR

MISSION OF CHRIST. The mission of Christ is a subject of messianic prophecy in the OT. Prediction focused attention on three aspects of his mission in particular. He would have the role of a prophet (Deut. 18:18; Isa. 61:1-3), he would discharge the duties of a king (Ps. 2:7; Isa. 11:1-5), he would perform the functions of a priest (Ps. 110:4; Zech. 6:13). In addition, there is the portrayal of the Suffering Servant, bearing the sin of many, understood in the light of the NT as indicating the manner in which the task of the ideal priest was to be accomplished (Acts 8:35; Heb. 9:12).

During the intertestamental period, political exigencies colored the interpretation of these prophecies. Many assumed that the expected Messiah (*q.v.*) would be primarily a Saviour after the type of the ancient Judges who were raised up to liberate the people in times of emergency; and that, when he achieved victory, he would reign as David's successor with far-extended dominion. The Targum on Isa. 52:13 — 53:12, though of later date, probably represents the erroneous interpretation of this passage current in the time of Jesus. A different kind of expectation found expression in the Dead Sea Scrolls. The Community who produced them seem to have looked for three distinct persons having a messianic mission, an Aaronic priest, a Davidic king and a prophet like Moses.

That Jesus himself had a sense of mission corresponding with prophecy is evident from many of his sayings. When he had read from Isa. 61 in the synagogue at Nazareth, he said it was of him the prophet wrote (Luke 4:16-21). Another aspect of his mission which he often mentioned was its purpose to save from sin (Mark 2:17; Matt. 9:13; Luke 5:32; Matt. 18:11; Luke 19:10). He claimed authority to forgive sin (Mark 2:9; Luke 7:48), but this depended on his sacrificial death for sin, even if exercised before that took place (Mark 10:45; Matt. 26:28; John 10:11-18; Acts 5:31). He described his death to Nicodemus as having in view the eternal salvation of those who trusted him (John 3:15). The prophetic and redemptive functions of his mission, however, though of vast importance, were subordinate to its ultimate aim, the establishment of the kingdom of God among men. To Pilate's question: "Art thou a king then?" he replied: "To this end was I born and for this cause came I into the world, that I might bear witness to the truth" (John 18:37). Because his kingdom was not of this world but spiritual, it attracted only those who recognized the truth and responded to it. Being himself the perfect Exemplar of the kingdom, he engaged in successful conflict on its behalf with the powers of evil, notably in the wilderness (Matt. 4:1-11), in casting out devils (Luke 11:20), and at Calvary (Col. 2:15). For the furtherance of the kingdom he commissioned the apostles and sent forth the Spirit at Pentecost (Acts 1:6-8). Through the witness of the church he continues to extend it; and when he comes to gather all his true servants into the kingdom of glory, it will be abundantly evident that his mission was not in vain (Matt. 13:43; 25:34; Rev. 7:9).

See also OFFICES OF CHRIST.

WILLIAM J. CAMERON

MISSIONS. The primary task of the Christian church from its inception has been the propagation of the gospel of Jesus Christ to the ends of the earth. This call to evangelism springs from the command of the Lord of the church as found in Matthew 28:18-20, Luke 24:46-49, John 20:21, and Acts 1:8. The missionary motive springs from love and obedience for the Redeemer. No one is exempt from the missionary task.

The missionary advance of the early church was dramatic, and there are evidences that the gospel of Christ went far beyond the borders of the Roman Empire even in the first century of the Christian era. In the early period of Christian missions the greatest opposition came from the followers of Mohammed. The church lost North Africa to Mohammedanism and parts of Europe. Charles Martel, in the Battle of Tours, in A.D. 732 stopped the forward movement of Islam.

Roman Catholic missions predominated during the Middle Ages. This church has continued its aggressive missionary program down to the present day. Romanism has emphasized the necessity of baptism for salvation and has majored on the concept of bringing whole groups, rather than individuals, into the church. In order to do this Romanism has often baptized paganism especially in places like South America. The "Malabar rites" (in this instance Jesuit accommodations to Indian customs) are an example of this practice.

The nineteenth century missionary advance represented the greatest forward movement since the days of the apostles. This advance was predicated on a conservative theology which assumed the lostness of men without Christ, the eternity of hell for sinners, and the absolute necessity for the new birth through faith in Jesus Christ. The science of missions was not highly developed during the nineteenth century and the European-American outreach was too often attached to a national imperialism. Despite the lack of an adequate missiology great advances were registered. It was not until the twentieth century that more profound changes occurred.

The twentieth century has been characterized by certain significant modifications. First and foremost has been the shift of the center of missionary gravity from Europe to North America. Whereas the number of missionaries sent from Europe far exceeded those sent from North America, the balance has moved heavily in the direction of North American superiority. At the same time denominational missions have not kept pace with the rising number of non-denominational agencies. In part this new situation derives from changing theological emphases. This in turn was occasioned by the rise of religious liberalism which decried the older theology of the nineteenth century. Liberalism repudiated biblical authority and opposed those who believed the virgin birth, vicarious atonement, the deity of Christ and the bodily resurrection. This same liberalism regarded Christianity as one among many religions and relegated its superiority as relative within the genera and not unique. Liberal penetration in missions resulted in the

view that missionary effort was basically a
sharing with other religions. Hocking's *Rethinking Missions* went so far as to state that
for medical missionaries to try to convert the
nationals to Christianity was ethically wrong.

The rise of liberalism resulted in the creation of competing missionary agencies represented by the Interdenominational Foreign
Mission Association, the Evangelical Foreign
Mission Association of the National Association
of Evangelicals and the missionary arm of
the American Council of Christian Churches.
All of these agencies are theologically conservative.

The rapid advances of Communism have
made difficult further missionary penetration
by western white men. China has become a
closed field to the foreign missionary and
other areas such as Africa and India have been
influenced by Communism in such a way as
to hinder the progress of Christian missions.
The future is obscure but the challenge of
Communism is unmistakable and presents the
church of Jesus Christ with the possibility of
rising to new heights of endeavor and sacrifice
in fulfilling the terms of the Great Commission.

Twentieth century missionary work has
been faced with the problem of vast cultural
advances in every part of the world. New
methods are being developed to meet this challenge and a new missionary orientation is
emerging. There has been a renewed interest
in indigenous church principles. The role of
the missionary is changing to that of a "co-partner in obedience" with the nationals. Missionary strategy now identifies the "foreign"
missionary as a responsible agent, not of the
home church, but of the national church to
which he answers and through whom and for
whom he labors.

The influence of liberalism is easier to assess
than that of neo-orthodoxy (*q.v.*) which is of
more recent vintage. What the impact of this
new theological emphasis will be in missionary
endeavor is not clear as yet. To this date it
has not produced any fresh or dynamic impulses nor has it sparked any new movements
for world evangelism. It has revolted against
the optimistic liberalism of the early twentieth century and has brought fresh eschatological insights from Europe but these have
not become part of the North American tradition which now is the home base for the
bulk of the missionary movement.

See also COMMISSION, THE GREAT.

BIBLIOGRAPHY
K. S. Latourette, *A History of the Expansion of Christianity*, (7 vols.); J. C. Thiessen, *A Survey of World Missions*; C. H. Robinson, *History of Christian Missions*; Reports of the International Missionary Council Conferences at Edinburgh (1910), Jerusalem (1928), Madras (1938), Whitby (1947), Willingen (1952), Ghana (1958). For missionary statistics, see reports of the Missionary Research Library, *Occasional Bulletin*, Reports of the IFMA, EFMA and *World Christian Handbook* (1957).

HAROLD LINDSELL

MOCKERY. The noun "mock" occurs in
Prov. 14:9 AV, "mocking" in Ezek. 22:4; Heb.
11:36, and the verbal forms are found with
the meaning (1) "to ridicule," in e.g., I Kings
18:27; Prov. 1:26, (2) "to deceive," in e.g.,
Judg. 16:10. Almost all the Hebrew words
represented are intensive in form. The Greek
equivalent is *empaizein*, "make fun of," which
bears the meaning "deceive" in Matt. 2:16.
The word is specially associated with the
passion of Christ.

The Evangelists record three occasions when
our Lord endured mockery: (1) immediately
after his condemnation by the Sanhedrin
(Mark 14:65; Matt. 26:67 f.; Luke 23:63 f.),
when he was spat upon, blindfolded, bidden to
prophesy and buffeted; (2) before Herod
Antipas (Luke 23:11), when there were no
blows, but the offering of mock homage by
Herod's men; (3) immediately after his condemnation by Pilate (Mark 15:16-20; Matt.
27:27-31; John 19:2 f.), when clad in purple, and wearing the crown of thorns, he
received the mock obeisance of the Roman
soldiers who smote him with a reed. The
Sanhedrin ridiculed his claim to be a prophet,
the soldiers his claim to be a king. While
mockery is a mark of the ignorant and
foolish (II Kings 2:23; Prov. 14:9; Acts
17:32), patient endurance of it is a mark of
faithful souls (Heb. 11:36; 12:3). God lies
beyond the reach of ridicule (Gal. 6:7).

L. E. H. STEPHENS-HODGE

MODERATION. "Moderation" occurs
once in the AV (Phil. 4:5); the RV has "forbearance," RV mg. "gentleness." It translates
the neuter form of the adjective *epieikēs*,
found also in I Tim. 3:3; Titus 3:2; James
3:17; I Pet. 2:18 ("gentle," in all but the
AV of I Tim. 3:3). The noun *epieikia* occurs
in Acts 24:4 ("clemency"), II Cor. 10:1
("gentleness"). Gentleness (*q.v.*) and forbearance are hardly adequate, and the modern
sense of "moderation" as indicating temperate

indulgence in food, drink, etc. is also misleading.

Wm. Barclay, describing *epieikēs* under the title "More than justice," agrees with Trench in the difficulty of translation. It expresses the quality of considerateness which will not stand for one's own rights, or on the strict letter of the law, but with equity and fairness will consider the well-being of the other. Lack of it can cause strife (Phil. 4:2-5). Christ's *epieikia* (II Cor. 10:1) is seen in John 8:1-11, and supremely in Phil. 2:5-8.

BIBLIOGRAPHY
Trench; J. Hastings in *HDB;* Wm. Barclay, *A New Testament Wordbook.*

R. COLIN CRASTON

MODERATOR. See OFFICES, ECCLESIASTICAL.

MODERNISM. See LIBERALISM.

MONARCHIANISM. This is the term usually applied to the natural concern in the early church to safeguard the unity ("monarchy") of the Godhead. There is, of course, a legitimate monarchianism, for recognition of the Father, Son and Holy Spirit does not involve tritheism. But over-emphasis on this aspect produced two forms of monarchianism which are mutually exclusive but both equally unacceptable. The first is dynamic monarchianism, associated with Theodotus and perhaps Paul of Samosata. Approaching the question from a christological rather than a trinitarian angle, this teaches the inferiority of the Son as a man taken up into the Godhead (see ADOPTIONISM). The second is modal monarchianism, represented by Noetus, Praxeas and Sabellius (see SABELLIANISM). This does not deny the full deity of Christ or the Spirit, but sees them merely as modes or functions of the one God, so that the Father may be said to suffer in the Son (see PATRIPASSIANISM) and indwell us by the Spirit. Hence the crushing remark of Tertullian that Praxeas put to flight the Paraclete and crucified the Father.

WILLIAM KELLY

MONASTICISM, MONACHISM. Derived from Greek *monos,* "alone." It is a general term for the renunciation of life in the world for the ideal of unreserved devotion to God. It is not exclusive to Christianity, but is found in every religious system which has attained an advanced degree of ethical development. Monasticism is commonly extended beyond its strict implication of solitude to embrace the religious communities.

Christian monasticism originated in the latter half of the third century. Its roots have been variously sought in Indian, Greek, Egyptian or Jewish soil, but it would appear that from the outset it has exhibited a marked independence of any other form of asceticism. "It seems probable that the impulse which led to its emergence," writes K. S. Latourette (*A History of Christianity,* Harper, New York, 1953, p. 225), "was predominantly and perhaps entirely from the Gospel." A scriptural basis was, in fact, claimed by appealing to such passages as I John 2:15-17, I Cor. 7:38, 40, Rom. 14:2, 21 and Rev. 14:4 as well as to the precepts of our Lord himself.

The rise of monasticism may be traced in three stages: (1) the hermits, of whom the first was probably Paul of Thebes and the best-known Antony of Egypt; (2) the lauras, or colonies of solitaries under one abbot, developed by Pachomius; and (3) the monasteries. Monasticism was introduced into the West in the fourth century and at first followed Eastern models. Then ca. 525 Benedict founded Monte Cassino and formulated his famous Rule which was eventually to become the single monastic charter of the West for four centuries. This was a turning point in the history of monasticism, marking not only "the transition from the uncertain and vague to the reign of law" (F. A. Gasquet, Preface to Montalembert, *Monks of the West,* Patrick Donahoe, Boston, 1872, I p. 21), but also introducing a completely new conception of the spirituality of toil. But, as H. B. Workman points out (*Evolution of the Monastic Ideal,* London, 1913, p. 220), "this change, invaluable as it was from the standpoint of the history of civilization, proved fatal in the long run to the principles of monasticism," and with the coming of the Friars the movement declined.

BIBLIOGRAPHY
A. Harnack, *Monasticism, its Ideals and History;* C. Butler in Cambridge Medieval History; F. Cabrol in *HERE.*

A. SKEVINGTON WOOD

MONISM. Monism is a doctrine of the unity of things. It may have reference to their origin, to their substance, or to the way by which they are known. The doctrine that all things have but one origin is theism. Although traditional Christianity is in this sense monistic, this is a very rare usage of the term and seldom is in view when monism is mentioned. The doctrine that the nature of all things is one is pantheism. This is the common connotation of monism, and as such is incompatible with theism, although the famous pantheistic monist, Spinoza, was called a "God-intoxicated atheist." Pantheism, which reduces all reality to one substance, may regard this substance as either material (in which case we have the materialism of Haeckel), or spiritual (in which case, we have the Absolute Idealism or philosophical Spiritualism of Hegel). Some present-day philosophers find another type of reality which is neither matter nor spirit but which may manifest itself as either matter or spirit without being identified with either. The doctrine that all things are one as to the way by which they are known is Epistemological Idealism. Advocates of this theory may or may not commit themselves on metaphysics in distinction from epistemology (q.v.).

Christianity is monistic in the first sense of the word, i.e., it holds to one divine origin of all things. It is distinctly hostile to pantheism in any form. This hostility is for several reasons: first, because things change but God remains the same; second, the totality of things includes evil but God is not evil; third, the totality of things is impersonal and involuntary, but self-consciousness testifies indubitably to the reality of personality and freedom.

BIBLIOGRAPHY

P. Carus, (editor) *The Monist;* E. Haeckel, *Der Monismus;* F. Klimke, *Der Monismus und seine philosophische Grundlagen.*

JOHN H. GERSTNER

MONITION. Derived from Latin and French, meaning a reminder or warning. Several words set forth the same idea in Scripture. Warning is given by the divine precepts (Ps. 19:11); by the prophets as divine messengers (Ezek. 33:4; Jer. 6:10); by the apostle Paul to his converts (Acts 20:31; I Cor. 4:14; Col. 1:28; I Thess. 5:14; see fuller references in concordance). It is used of a secret warning (Matt. 3:7), or one received by supernatural means (Matt. 2:12; Acts 10:22; Heb. 11:7). In the Anglican Book of Common Prayer it is used to describe one of the duties of the minister toward his flock (see Ordinal and Commination Services).

RICHARD E. HIGGINSON

MONOPHYSITISM. Derived from *monos* "single" and *physis* "nature," monophysitism is the doctrine which holds that the incarnate Christ had only a single, divine nature, clad in human flesh. Since the Council of Chalcedon (451), which confirmed as orthodox the doctrine of two natures, divine and human, monophysitism has been considered heretical. Its roots probably go back to Apollinaris (*ca.* 370) who laid tremendous stress on the fusion of the divine and human. Alexandria (as opposed to Antioch) became the citadel of this doctrine, and Cyril (*ca.* 430), although deemed orthodox, furnished fuel for the fire kindled by his successor Dioscorus and Eutyches of Constantinople, who denied that Christ's body was the same in essence as the bodies of men. Their chief opponent was Leo I of Rome, whose formulation of the doctrine of two natures in one person triumphed at Chalcedon. Monophysites tended to divide into two main groups: *Julianists,* who held to the immortality and incorruptibility of Christ's incarnate body, and the more orthodox *Severians,* who rejected the Eutychian view that the human and divine were completely mingled in the Incarnation. In the remnant of Syrian Jacobites and in the Coptic and Ethiopian churches (and to a limited extent in the Armenian) it survives to the present day.

BIBLIOGRAPHY

ODCC; J. Lebon, *Le Monophysisme sévérien* (Louvain: 1909); A. A. Luce, *Monophysitism Past and Present;* R. V. Sellers, *Two Ancient Christologies;* ibid., *The Council of Chalcedon;* E. R. Hardy, *Christian Egypt: Church and People.*

DAVID A. HUBBARD

MONOTHEISM. This is the term given to the belief that there is only one God. Monotheism is to be distinguished from atheism (the belief that there is no god) and polytheism (the belief that there are several or many gods); it is further to be distinguished from monolatry (the worship of one god as supreme, without denying the existence of other deities) and from henotheism (which ascribes to one god after another the place of supremacy; henotheism is also used as approximately synonymous with monolatry).

The principal monotheistic religions of the world are Judaism, Christianity, and Islam (Mohammedanism), the latter two of which developed from the first. Sikhism is mystical monotheism, but grew out of polytheistic systems, and Zoroastrianism is limited or eventual monotheism developing out of dualism. According to the school of comparative religion, monotheism was a late development in human thought; this, however, has been denied by W. Schmidt, *Der Ursprung der Gottesidee* (9 vols., 1926-49), S. M. Zwemer, *The Origin of Religion* (1935), and others. It can be demonstrated that in polytheistic religions there is a tendency to multiply deities, possibly as a result of man's attempt to attribute to different gods the individual forces in the complex of life as he becomes aware of them. This would seem to indicate that man could never have developed a monotheistic concept by himself.

There can be no doubt that the Bible presents man as a monotheist at the first. It is further indisputable that Abraham's forebears were polytheists (Josh. 24:2; cf. Gen. 35:2). The Bible does not trace the steps in this development. Nor does the Bible make clear whether Abraham was a monotheist or a monolater. The words of the Decalogue ("Thou shalt have no other gods before me") do not clearly establish monotheism over monolatry — which is in keeping with the principle of progressive revelation, God choosing to reveal to his people the truth step-by-step (cf. Heb. 1:1). Likewise in his contest with the prophets of Baal, Elijah did not clearly enunciate the doctrine of monotheism (I Kings 18:24). With the eighth century prophets, monotheism is more clearly set forth, but at the popular level polytheism continued until the post-exilic period. It is possible that the Jews were cured of their idolatrous practices through their experiences in exile, particularly such events as Nabonidus carrying the gods into the city of Babylon when the Persian army was approaching (cf. Isa. 46:1-7; Ps. 115:4-8), which stood in marked contrast with the account of the mighty deliverance of Israel from Egypt by Yahweh. In the post-exilic period Judaism developed an intransigence in monotheism that made the claims of Jesus difficult if not impossible for many to accept. Mohammedanism absorbed this attitude and made it a principal doctrine in Islam: "Allah is one; . . . he does not beget and he is not begotten."

Monotheism is not denied or distorted, however, by the doctrine of the Trinity (*q.v.*), for the NT clearly holds to the OT revelation of the only true and living God. That this God exists (or subsists) in three persons, Father, Son, and Holy Spirit, was never felt by the apostles to be incompatible with the OT doctrine, for they nowhere challenge the idea. This willingness to accept the trinitarian con-

cept may be explained by the presence in the OT of the "Angel of the Lord" and "Spirit of the Lord" passages, in which we may trace an incipient and progressive revelation to be completed by the teachings of Christ and the apostles.

WILLIAM SANFORD LaSOR

MONOTHELITISM. A heresy especially prevalent in the Eastern Church in the seventh century which said that as Christ had but one nature (Monophysitism) so he had but one will (Greek *monos*, "alone," *thelein*, "to will"). Emperor Heraclius attempted to reconcile the Monophysite bishops, who held that the human and divine natures in Christ were fused together to form a third, by offering in his *ecthesis* the view that Christ worked through a divine-human energy. This compromise was at first accepted by Constantinople and Rome but Sophronius, soon to be Bishop of Jerusalem, organized the orthodox opposition to Monothelitism. A fine defense of the person of Christ as one in two natures with two wills was given by John of Damascus. The Council of Chalcedon (A.D. 451) had declared that "Christ has two natures." This was now amended by the Council of Constantinople (A.D. 680) which declared that Christ had two wills, his human will being subject to his divine will.

BIBLIOGRAPHY

John of Damascus, *Exposition of the Orthodox Faith, Book III*, Chaps. 3-24; A. Harnack, *History of Dogma,* Vol. IV, pp. 252-67; A. A. Luce, *Monophysitism*, pp. 52-87; H. P. Liddon, *The Divinity of Our Lord*, pp. 256-64.

WILLIAM NIGEL KERR

MONTANISM. A second century apocalyptic movement named after its founder Montanus, as in Theodoret (*Haer. fab.* III. 2). Its adherents were formerly known as Phrygians or Kataphrygians (so Eusebius *HE* V. 14 *et. al.*) and sometimes Pepuzians (Epiphanius, *Haer.* 48.14) after Pepuza where Montanus, with his two female associates, Prisca and Maximilla, prophesied. Possibly the whole body were called Priscillianists (Hippolytus, *Ref.* 7.12) unless this title refers to a later subdivision. Hort has summarized the characteristics of Montanism: "First, a strong faith in the Holy Spirit as the promised Paraclete, present as a heavenly power in the Church of the day; secondly, specially a belief that the Holy Spirit was manifesting Himself supernaturally at that day through entranced prophets and prophetesses; and thirdly, an inculcation of a specially stern and exacting standard of Christian morality and discipline" (*The Ante-Nicene Fathers,* Macmillan, London, 1895, p. 100). To these must be added a tendency to set up prophets against bishops and an intense expectation of the imminent return of our Lord.

After the death of Montanus the sect appears to have subsided, but *ca.* 200 it revived and spread over Asia Minor and even into Egypt. In Carthage it captured its outstanding convert in Tertullian. Whether there is such a great gulf fixed between Phrygian and African Montanism as some (e.g., Lawlor) would suggest is debatable.

BIBLIOGRAPHY

G. Bonwetsch, *Die Geschichte des Montanismus;* P. de Labriolle, *La Crise Montaniste; Les Sources de l'histoire du Montanisme;* J. de Soyres, *Montanism and the Primitive Church;* H. J. Lawlor in *HERE.*

A. Skevington Wood

MORTAL. As might be expected, the Greek word for mortal, *thnētos,* is used only by Paul in the NT. It occurs twice each in Romans, I Corinthians, and II Corinthians.

The adjective comes from the verb *thnēskein,* which means "to be dead." Hence it signifies "subject to death." It is used several times in the LXX for man as a mortal being.

In three of its six occurrences Paul applies the term to the physical body (Rom. 6:12; 8:11; II Cor. 4:11). In the first he urges the believer not to let sin reign in his mortal body. In the second he states that the indwelling Holy Spirit will quicken our mortal bodies. In the third he suggests that the life of Jesus should be manifested in our mortal flesh.

The other three passages speak of "this mortal" putting on immortality (I Cor. 15:53, 54) and of "what is mortal" being swallowed up by life (II Cor. 5:4). All these passages indicate that the body, not the spirit, is mortal.

Ralph Earle

MORTIFY, MORTIFICATION. The English term occurs twice in the NT. In Rom. 8:13 it is used for the verb *thanatoō,* suggesting the *action* of killing, while in Col. 3:5 it is a rendering of *nekroō,* suggesting the *result* of killing (to make a corpse). The use is Pauline and derives from his doctrine of the atonement, i.e., that Christ who came "in the likeness of sinful flesh" was so identified with sinners that on the cross he both died for them and their sinful nature was put to death

with him (II Cor. 5:14, 15; Rom. 6:6-8; Col. 2:20; 3:3). In faith the believer is called upon to recognize this as a fact. He has been crucified with Christ (Gal. 2:20), and can thus take up the definite and decisive attitude of crucifying the flesh (Gal. 5:24) and putting to death the sinful members (Col. 3:5). The force of the aorist here is parallel to the "reckoning" of Rom. 6:11. But in Rom. 8:13, the present tense points to continuous action by the power of the Holy Spirit. Constant putting to death is the outcome of the decision of Col. 3:5.

The objects of mortification are sinful habits and the deeds and desires (Col. 3:5-6) of the flesh or sinful nature. But the body and its members are agents of sin, and although Paul has a low estimate of austerities in dealing with the body (Col. 2:23), he shows in I Cor. 9:26-27 that the body must be disciplined in the war against sin. Yet mortifying does not function alone, it is the obverse of living to God by presenting oneself for his service (Rom. 6:12-19; Phil. 1:20).

George J. C. Marchant

MOSES. Moses is pre-eminently the lawgiver. "The law was given by Moses" (John 1:17). In four of the five books which make up the Pentateuch he is the dominant figure, and he casts his shadow over both OT and NT.

Moses' life falls into three periods of forty years each. The first (Ex. 2:1-15a) tells of his birth and adoption by Pharaoh's daughter. If she was the great Hatshepsut, Moses may have played a very prominent role at the Egyptian court (Acts 7:22). But his love for his people led him to imprudent acts which forced him to flee for his life.

The second period (2:15b-25) is almost a blank. It shows us Moses in retirement and eclipse leading the life of a shepherd, apparently a forgotten man.

The third period (Ex. 3:1 – Deut. 34:12) begins with Moses' call. The call is a challenge to Moses' faith in God and love to his people (3:12); and responding to this call he enters upon his life work. The freeing of the people from Egyptian bondage is a task which is achieved by mighty acts of God, who makes Moses his instrument and Moses' rod the symbol of his authority. The proclaiming of the Decalog by the voice of God at Sinai is a tremendous theophany (Ex. 20:1-21); and the covenant (Ex. 21-23) is ratified by sprinkling of blood (Ex. 24:3-8; cf. 19:8). The tabernacle is to be constructed according to the pattern shown to Moses in the mount (25:9; 39:43). All of the laws are given through Moses. The laws for the priests, which are found in Leviticus, are given through Moses and he inducts Aaron and his sons into the priesthood. The journey to Kadesh is briefly described and the sending out of the spies (Num. 13). The refusal to go up to possess the land (Num. 14) receives the punishment of wandering, forty years, a year for a day of the searching of the land (chap. 14). The rebellion of Korah, Dathan and Abiram and the giving of several laws are all that prevents this long interval from being a complete blank. With the beginning of the fortieth year (Num. 20:1) the new generation take up their journey to the land of promise; and under Moses they conquer the kings of the Amorites and of Bashan and are poised to enter the land (Num. 20). The sin of Baal-peor is severely punished and avenged (Num. 25 and 31). The Book of Deuteronomy contains Moses' farewell addresses in which he exhorts and entreats his people to keep the law which is their precious possession and solemnly warns them of the inevitable consequences of disobedience.

In all these great events by virtue of which Israel was molded into a nation Moses is the pre-eminent figure. His place in Israel's history is unique. As lawgiver he had no successor. Joshua followed him as leader. But the vast difference between the authority enjoyed by these two men is shown by comparing Num. 7:89 and 12:6-8 with Num. 27:15-21. Truly, there arose not a prophet like unto Moses whom the Lord knew face to face (Deut. 34:10). The closing word of the last of the OT prophets is this, "Remember the law of my servant Moses" (Mal. 4:4). Despite, yes even because of the singularly exalted position given him by God, Moses is revealed to us as "a man subject to like passions as we are." Like Elijah and Jeremiah the task assigned him, a burden increased tenfold by the murmurings and revoltings of the people, drives him almost to despair (Num. 11:10-15) and leads to outbursts of anger and indignation (Ex. 32:19), one of which had tragic results for himself (Num. 20:7-12), a disappointment which found its rich

compensation on the mount of transfiguration (Matt. 17:1-8).

The supreme tribute to Moses comes to us from the lips of our Lord (Luke 16:31; John 5:46). Moses, the man of God, is the most complete OT type of him who was to come. For he combined in himself in a unique degree the three great offices of Christ — prophet (Deut. 18:15-22; 34:10 f.), priest (he acted as priest and instituted the priestly office, Lev. 8) and king (for forty years he was God's vicegerent over Israel.

In *Moses and His Times* (1887) George Rawlinson made two significant statements: "The materials for the life of Moses are found chiefly in the four later books of the Pentateuch" and "Materials for the description of the 'times' of Moses exist now in enormous quantities through the interpretation of the hierglyphic inscriptions, and of the other native Egyptian documents." This is no less true today. A long list of books on Ancient Egypt might easily be given. It would include such names as Maspero, Petrie, Budge, Steindorff, Baikie, Breasted, Weigall, and J. A. Wilson. But no ancient records have been discovered which mention Moses. How much confidence is to be placed in Josephus and Philo when they enlarge on the biblical account, we do not know. And the same may be said of many of the lives of Moses which have appeared from time to time in recent years. The real Moses cannot be recovered from a vivid sketch of the "times" in which he lived.

OSWALD T. ALLIS

MOST HIGH. See GOD.

MOTHER OF GOD. This title was accorded to Mary, the mother of Jesus, at the Council of Ephesus in 431. A bishop named Nestorius — formerly presbyter at Antioch and then made patriarch of Constantinople, but deposed by the Council — had found it difficult to accept that the infant born of Mary was "God," and his difficulty came to expression in a refusal to describe Mary as the "Mother of God" as she was now commonly styled to emphasize the deity of Christ. The Council decreed that the title could rightly be given to Mary because he who was conceived of her was by the Holy Ghost, and was the Son of God and therefore "God" from the moment of his conception.

Unfortunately, the term soon came to be

regarded as expressing an exaltation of Mary, and by the sixth century false notions about Mary, originally framed by Gnostics and a sect known as Collyridians, were taken up by the church itself, and the way was open for the worship of Mary, which has since grown so greatly, especially in the Roman Catholic Church (see MARIOLATRY).

In the NT Mary is often referred to as the "mother of Jesus" (e.g., John 2:1; Acts 1:14). She was given special grace by God to perform a service to him that was unique. In this regard she stands alone amongst human kind, and is regarded by all generations as "blessed." But Scripture is silent as regards any special standing of Mary herself. The title "Mother of God" (theotokos) is thus to be used with caution as regards its implications for Mary herself, though evangelical theology recognizes its appropriateness when employed, as at Ephesus, to state the true deity of Jesus Christ even in his incarnate life.

W. C. G. PROCTOR

MYSTERY, MYSTERIES. *Mystērion* occurs twenty-seven times in the Received Text of the NT, twenty instances being in the Pauline corpus, and half of these in Ephesians and Colossians.

In most cases the reference is to the plan of salvation or some aspect thereof: the kingdom of God (Matt. 13:11; Mark 4:11; Luke 8:10); the hardening of Israel and admission of the Gentiles (Rom. 11:25), or the fusion of both into one new body (Eph. 3:3-4); the gospel, especially with reference to its ministry (I Cor. 2:7; 4:1; Eph. 6:19; Col. 4:3) and its apprehension (Rom. 16:25; Eph. 1:9; Col. 1:26-27); the whole sweep of God's redemption (Eph. 1:9; 3:9); the event of the resurrection (I Cor. 15:51); the Christian religion or its central verities (I Tim. 3:9, 16); and supremely to Christ himself (Col. 2:2). Once the reference is to marriage (Eph. 5:32); twice to such secrets as prophets might have access to (I Cor. 13:2; 14:2); once to the embodiment of anti-Christian forces (II Thess. 2:3); four times in Revelation to a symbolic figure (Rev. 1:20; 10:7; 17:5, 7).

In the LXX *mystērion* represents "secret": the hidden counsel of God (Ps. 24:14 EVV, Wisd. 2:22), or a general's strategy, hidden until put into operation (Judith 2:2). In classical usage it relates to anything hidden, but predominantly, generally in the plural, to "the mysteries" of a state or religious sect, hidden to the uninitiated.

Mysteries such as the Eleusinian, prominent in the Athenian cultus, sublimated primitive fertility rites. There were also less official mysteries, some crudely orgiastic. Alexander's conquests provided an interaction of Hellenistic and Oriental, of philosophy, mysticism and fertility ritual which gave mysteries far more than local significance. They ministered to the general longing for "salvation" — security, immortality, sacramental comfort — noticeable before the birth of Christ. Cults like those of the Egyptian Isis, the Phrygian Cybele, and especially Mithras (who had a huge following in the Roman army by the third century A.D.), spread throughout the Graeco-Roman world. Great stress was laid on their esoteric nature and on proper initiation: in some rituals the Asian rite of *taurobolium*, or bath in bull's blood, and the formula *renatus in aeternum* were introduced. They had no historical redemption and little moral earnestness.

For NT usage the LXX is more illuminative than the pagan mysteries. *Mystērion* is often associated with God's foreknowledge and inscrutable will (e.g., Rom. 16:25; I Cor. 2:7; Eph. 1:9; 3:9; Col. 1:26). Furthermore, in many contexts, not the hiddenness, but the unveiling of the mystery is stressed. Not only revelation to initiates is in mind: *mystērion* applies to gospel preaching in contexts explicitly mentioning its open character (Eph. 6:19; Col. 4:3). The Christian mystery, hidden from eternity in God's counsel, is now open and can be summarized (I Tim. 3:16) and universally preached (hence Moffatt's translation "open secret" in Eph. 1:9; Col. 1:26; 2:2; 4:3). Whereas classical usage favors the plural, in the NT the singular is usual. The context of I Cor. 2:7 contains several terms redolent of the mysteries: "wisdom," "knowledge," "perfect": but the nature of Paul's argument suggests that it was from the Corinthians themselves that this vocabulary came. Noting reference to the secret counsel of God now revealed, we may conclude that here as in some other places, while there may be undertones of the mysteries many gentile Christians must have known, it is doubtful whether these are ever primary. *Mystērion* is used to indicate climactic points in God's dealings with men. Correspondingly it can be used of the operations of his enemy (II Thess. 2:7).

Few adherents remain of the school which

viewed early Christianity as essentially a salvation-mystery with baptism as initiation, grafted on to the simple teaching of Christ: without explaining how Christianity alone survived the Roman Empire. More frequently it is held that the NT writers are soaked in mystery terminology and are best understood against this background. (Cf. from different standpoints W. L. Knox, *Some Hellenistic Elements in Primitive Christianity*, Oxford 1942, R. Bultmann, *Gnosis* in TWNT; R. Perdelwitz, *Die Mysterienreligionen und das Problem des I Petrusbriefs,* Giessen 1911.) But such cases frequently turn out to be as well or better understood by reference to the OT, LXX or Jewish sources (*mystērion* itself is a loanword in rabbinic Hebrew — SBK, I, pp. 659 ff.) and the parallels often come from times much later than the NT.

Some other uses of *mystērion* remain. In I Cor. 13:2; 14:2, the primary reference is to the hidden, ineffable character of the divine insights which prophets receive, but apparently cannot necessarily communicate. Eph. 5:32 is best explained by the patristic use of the term to mean "symbol." A similar sense is demanded for the instances in Revelation.

The Vulgate rendering of *mystērion* by *sacramentum* was responsible for the later attribution of the title "mysteries" to the sacraments, and to the communion in particular: and this translation at Eph. 5:32 influenced the designation of marriage as a sacrament.

Considering that the mystery religions must have been Christianity's greatest rivals, early Christian writers say surprisingly little about them, probably because they were most concerned with the Gnostic attempt to convert Christianity from within into a mystery cult. Even so, Clement of Alexandria, to demonstrate Christianity as the true Gnosis, can use, with evident rapture, the mystery vocabulary (*Protrepticus CXX. 1*).

BIBLIOGRAPHY
Arndt; G. Bornkamm in TWNT; E. Hatch, *Essays in Biblical Greek*, pp. 57-62; C. L. Mitton, *Epistle to the Ephesians*, pp. 86 ff.; R. Reitzenstein, *Die Hellenistischen Mysterienreligionen*, 3rd edition; H. A. A. Kennedy, *St. Paul and the Mystery Religions*; S. Dill, *Roman Society from Nero to Marcus Aurelius*; F. Cumont, *Les Religions Orientales dans le Paganisme Romain*.

ANDREW F. WALLS

MYSTICISM. The two main elements in mysticism are indicated by the twofold derivation from *myeō* ("initiate" or "consecrate") and *myō* ("close the eyes or mouth"). Mysticism is thus "the higher consecration of man,

which he secures by exercising towards the external world, both passively and actively, the greatest possible reserve. Or it is the passive and active reserve towards the external world, which is at the same time dedicated to a higher consecration of man" (K. Barth, *Church Dogmatics*, I, 2, p. 319).

In accordance with this definition, mysticism presses beyond the external forms of religion to an attempted direct knowledge of God, more especially in prayer and meditation, although sometimes too in trance-like conditions. It is not necessarily hostile to form and tradition. Indeed, it is usually prepared to endorse and use them for their symbolical value. But it finds the core of religion in an inward identity or communion which is ultimately indifferent to and negates the external.

Mysticism is not peculiar to Christianity, but it has found in the latter a long line of representatives including such notable figures as Eckhart, Tauler, Catherine of Siena and John of the Cross. Many of these have obviously attained a high level of Christian faith and fruitage, and in many cases the basic mysticism has not excluded practical interests and gifts.

Yet the question remains whether mysticism is genuinely scriptural, even in its Christian form. To be sure, this avoids the blatant errors of the mysticism which finally identifies God and the soul, or teaches a total absorption rather than a union of love and will. Again, it demands a genuine attempt at identification with Christ in his passion and resurrection. More generally, it can argue from ostensibly mystical elements in Paul and John, and point to the scriptural emphasis upon the inward and spiritual as distinct from the merely external. There is no flagrant or conscious heresy in Christian mysticism, and it is content with accepted forms and formulations.

On the other hand, there are three considerations which suggest that in mysticism, for all the sincerity of faith which may be ascribed to individual mystics, we really have an expression of human religion rather than a true response to the divine revelation.

1. Exegetically, it is begging the question to speak e.g., of the Christ-mysticism of St. Paul when the Bible itself does not use this terminology. Interpreted from within itself, a Pauline statement like Gal. 2:20 has no inherent mystical orientation, though it can obviously be pushed in a mystical direction. It

may be doubted whether there is any direct biblical support for mysticism as distinct from the mystical interpretation of biblical data.

2. Dogmatically, mysticism seems to rest on a false assumption in its search for directness or immediacy of union or communion between the soul and God. The whole point of God's coming and work in Christ, and the present ministry of word and sacrament, is that "no man hath seen God at any time" (John 1:18), and that the eyes of the inward understanding can now be opened by the Holy Spirit only as we look on the incarnate, crucified and risen Son presented to us in the gospel.

3. Practically, mysticism entails an inevitable, if often unwitting and unwilling subjectivization. Even the imitation of Christ is a repetition rather than an entry, and the emphasis falls upon what I do rather than on what Christ has already done wholly and all-sufficiently for me. An ultimate preoccupation with self is the mark even of the denial of self, and it is in the self that truth and salvation are eventually found even though self and God may not ultimately be confused as they may well be even in Christian mysticism.

Mysticism has made its contribution to Christianity, and there is much instruction and inspiration to be gained from its literature. But quite apart from its obvious extravagances it may be doubted whether it is a genuine form of biblical and evangelical Christianity. Open eyes and lips are surely necessary for true initiation into Jesus Christ.

BIBLIOGRAPHY
HERE; K. Barth, *Church Dogmatics*, I, 2, pp. 318-25; E. Brunner, *Die Mystik und das Wort*; F. V. Huegel, *The Mystical Element of Religion*; W. R. Inge, *Christian Mysticism*; E. Underhill, *Mysticism*.

GEOFFREY W. BROMILEY

MYTH. The term *myth* (Greek *mythos*) occurs five times in the NT — four times in the Pastoral Epistles (I Tim. 1:4; 4:7; II Tim. 4:4; Titus 1:14; II Pet. 1:16). In each instance it signifies the fiction of a fable as distinct from the genuineness of the truth (cf. II Tim. 4:4, ". . . turn away their ears from the truth, and turn aside unto myths"). This is in complete harmony with the classical connotation of the term, which from the time of Pindar onwards always bears the sense of what is fictitious, as opposed to the term *logos*, which indicated what was true and historical. (This consideration sheds an interesting ray on John's use of the term *Logos* as a title for Christ, John 1:1, 14, and Paul's frequent use

of it as a synonym for the gospel which he proclaimed.) Thus Socrates describes a particular story as "no fictitious myth but a true logos" (Plato *Timaeus* 26E). It is also the connotation of the term during the period of the NT. Thus Philo speaks of those "who follow after unfeigned truth instead of fictitious myths" (*Exsecr.* 162) and Pseudo-Aristeas, using an adverbial form, affirms that "nothing has been set down in Scripture to no purpose or in a mythical sense" (*mythōdōs, Letter of Aristeas to Philocrates,* 168). In the English language, too, the "mythical" is ordinarily synonymous with the fabulous, the fantastic, and the historically unauthentic.

In contemporary theological discussion the term myth has achieved a special prominence. This is to a considerable degree the result of Rudolf Bultmann's demand for the "demythologization" of the NT, that is, for the excision or expurgation from the biblical presentation of the Christian message of every element of "myth." In Bultmann's judgment, this requires the rejection of the biblical view of the world as belonging to "the cosmology of a pre-scientific age" and as therefore quite unacceptable to modern man (see *Kerygma and Myth*, S. P. C. K., London, 1953). In effect, it amounts to the elimination of the miraculous or supernatural constituents of the scriptural record since these are incompatible with Bultmann's own view of the world as a firmly closed system, governed by fixed natural laws, in which there can be no place for intervention "from outside." John Macquarrie, however, justly criticizes Bultmann for being "still obsessed with the pseudo-scientific view of a closed universe that was popular half a century ago" (*An Existentialist Theology*, S.C.M. Press, London, 1955, p. 168), and Emil Brunner complains that in claiming "that our faith must eliminate everything that suspends the 'interrelatedness of Nature' and is consequently mythical" Bultmann "is using, as a criterion, a concept which has become wholly untenable" (*The Christian Doctrine of Creation and Redemption, Dogmatics,* Vol. II, Lutterworth Press, London, 1952, p. 190).

It is Bultmann's contention that the central message or *kerygma* of Christianity is incredible to modern man so long as it is presented in the mythical setting of the biblical world-view, and that the latter constitutes an offence which is not at all identical with the true and ineradicable offence or *skandalon* of the Christian proclamation. He accordingly finds it necessary to discard such obviously (on his premises) mythical elements as Christ's pre-existence and virgin birth, his deity and sinlessness, the substitutionary nature of his death as meeting the demands of a righteous God, his resurrection and ascension, and his future return in glory, also the final judgment of the world, the existence of spirit-beings, the personality and power of the Holy Spirit, the doctrines of the Trinity, of original sin, and of death as a consequence of sin, and every explanation of events as miraculous. It is self-evident that this process of demythologization, when carried through with the thoroughness Bultmann displays, mutilates the Christianity of the NT in so radical a manner as to leave it unrecognizable. The stature of Jesus is reduced to that of a mere man (cf. *Theology of the New Testament,* Vol. II, S.C.M. Press, London, 1955, pp. 46, 75) and the Christ-event is transformed from an objective divine intervention into "a relative historical phenomenon" (*Kerygma and Myth,* p. 19). And it is in this, according to Bultmann, that the real offence of Christianity lies: the linking of our redemption with God's choice of an ordinary mortal individual, no different from every other man, and of an event, in no way miraculous or supernatural (*Kerygma and Myth,* p. 43), which in its essential relativity belongs to the normal order of all mundane events.

Bultmann's relativism goes hand in hand with subjectivism. The relevance of the Christ-event assumes a merely subjective significance. The incarnation and resurrection of Christ, for example, are not to be understood as datable events of the past, but as "eschatological" events which are to be subjectively experienced through faith in the word of preaching (cf. *Kerygma and Myth,* pp. 41, 209; *Theology of the New Testament,* Vol. I, S.C.M. Press, London, 1952, p. 305). It is, in fact, only *my* experience, here and now, that can have any authenticity for me — not anything that has happened in the past or that will happen in the future. In short, the Christian message is compressed within an existentialist mold. History and eschatology are to be understood in terms of pure subjectivism. Pronouncements about the deity of Jesus are not to be interpreted as dogmatic pronouncements concerning his nature but as existential value-judgments, not as statements about Christ but as pronouncements about me. Thus, for example,

the objective affirmation that Christ helps me because he is God's Son must give place to the subjective value-judgment of the "moment" that he is God's Son because he helps me (*The Christological Confession of the World Council of Churches,* in *Essays,* S.C.M. Press, London, 1955, p. 280). Truth, in a word, is identified with subjectivity.

While the message of Christianity is, beyond doubt, in the truest sense existential and contemporaneous and demands the subjective response of faith, yet the faith it requires is faith in an objective reality. When robbed of its objectivity, the ground of which is God's free and supernatural intervention through Christ in the affairs of our world, Christianity becomes a drifting idea, an abstraction, a rootless idealism, an ungraspable balloon loosed from its moorings. Bultmann's "confusion of the question of the world-view with that of Myth," criticizes Brunner, "and the effort to adapt the Christian Faith to 'modern' views of life, and to the concepts of existential philosophy, comes out continually in the fact that he 'cleanses' the message of the New Testament from ideas which necessarily belong to it, and do not conflict with the modern view of the world at all, but only with the 'self-understanding,' and in particular with the prejudices, of an Idealistic philosophy"; while in his conception of history Bultmann "is lacking in insight into the significance of the New Testament *eph' hapax,* of the 'once-for-all-ness' (or uniqueness) of the Fact of Christ as an Event in the continuum of history" (*Dogmatics,* Vol. I, pp. 267, 268).

Yet, while realizing that in Bultmann's program of demythologization "what is at stake is nothing less than the central theological question of revelation, of 'Saving History,' and the knowledge of God as a 'Living God,' who is the Lord of nature and of history" (*Dogmatics,* Vol. II, p. 186), Brunner refuses to "give up the right to criticize this or that recorded miracle, this or that marvel as due rather to the 'myth-forming imagination' than to the historical fact" (*ibid.,* p. 192). In other words he is prepared to concur with the judgment that in the NT there are mythical elements which require to be eliminated; but as a demythologizer he is unwilling to proceed to such radical lengths as does Bultmann. When, however, we find him repudiating doctrines like the virgin birth of Christ, his bodily resurrection (whence the unbiblical "liberal" distinction between "the historic Jesus" and "the risen Christ"), his bodily ascension, and the general resurrection at the last day, we perceive that he is definitely moving in the same direction as Bultmann, even though, unlike Bultmann, he seeks to defend his procedure by arguing that these doctrines formed no part of the original *kerygma* (*ibid.*, pp. 352 ff.). But nonetheless, despite his criticisms of Bultmann, "modern science" plays a determinative role in Brunner's thinking. Thus Brunner emphasizes that he "cannot say too strongly that the biblical view of the world is absolutely irreconcilable with modern science" (*ibid.*, p. 39); and he assures us that "the position of modern knowledge forces us to abandon" the definite picture of space, of time, and of the origins of life given in the biblical story of creation (*ibid.*, p. 31). And so he rejects as myths the Genesis accounts of creation and Paradise (cf. *ibid.*, p. 74). Likewise he affirms the need for the demythologization of statements concerning the form in which the event of Christ's Parousia will take place on the ground that they are "pronouncements of the New Testament which are clearly mythical, in the sense that they are in fact unacceptable to us who have no longer the world-picture of the ancients and the apostles" (*Eternal Hope*, Lutterworth Press, London, 1954). Again, and inversely (!), new discoveries may reinstate as respectable certain aspects of the biblical world-picture which "modern science" was thought to have exposed as mythical: for example, the doctrine of the sudden end of human history which "until recently seemed to be only the apocalyptic fantasies of the Christian faith has today entered the sphere of the soberest scientific calculations," with the result, says Brunner, that "this thought has ceased to be absurd, i.e., to be such that a man educated in modern scientific knowledge would have to give it up" (*ibid.*, p. 127). And so our modern man so educated must now be invited to de-demythologize at this point where he had so recently and with such approval demythologized!

Karl Barth, whose approach to the question of the authority of Scripture is governed by premises akin to those accepted by Bultmann and Brunner, wishes to establish a distinction between *myth* on the one hand and *saga* or *legend* on the other. By "legend," however, he means what the other two understand by "myth," as Brunner in fact acknowledges

(*Dogmatics*, Vol. II, p. 74, note). Legend, according to Barth, does not necessarily attack the substance of the biblical witness, even though there is uncertainty about what he calls its "general" historicity (i.e., its historical truth as generally conceived), whereas he views myth as belonging to a different category which "necessarily attacks the substance of the biblical witness" inasmuch as it pretends to be history when it is not, and thereby throws doubt on, indeed denies, what he calls the "special" historicity of the biblical narratives (i.e., their special significance as history between God and man), thus relegating them to the realm of a "timeless truth, in other words, a human creation" (*The Doctrine of the Word of God, Church Dogmatics*, Vol. I, part I, T. and T. Clark, Edinburgh, 1936, pp. 375 ff.) This, however, is principally a matter of definition: where Bultmann and Brunner use the term "myth" Barth prefers to use "legend."

There is one further definition of myth to which attention must be drawn, that, namely, which in effect equates it with symbolism, and relates it to the inherent inability of human language to express adequately the things of God. Thus Brunner maintains that "the Christian *kerygma* cannot be separated from Myth" since "the Christian statement is necessarily and consciously 'anthropomorphic' in the sense that it does, and must do, what Bultmann conceives to be characteristic of the mythical — 'it speaks of God in a human way'" (*Dogmatics*, Vol. II, p. 268). And in the same connection Bultmann explains that "mythology is the use of imagery to express the otherworldly in terms of this world and the divine in terms of human life, the other side in terms of this side" (*Kerygma and Myth*, p. 10). To eliminate myth in this sense would mean that it would become impossible for man to say anything about God or for God to say anything intelligible to man, for we have no other medium of expression than the terms of this world. But it certainly does not follow that the terms of this side must always be given a symbolical (= mythological) meaning, or that they are always inadequate for the purpose intended. While there is indeed much symbolism in the NT, it is evident also that many things there are intended in a literal sense, and that events, for example Christ's ascension, are described phenomenally (i.e., from the quite legitimate point of view of the observer).

Finally, it must be stressed that the concept of myth which we have been discussing in this article is incompatible with the Reformed doctrine of Holy Scripture. The Christ of the Bible is *The Logos,* not a *mythos;* he needs no demythologization at the hands of human scholars.

BIBLIOGRAPHY

Major works are mentioned above in the course of the article. The following should also be consulted: P. E. Hughes, *Scripture and Myth;* I. Henderson, *Myth in the New Testament;* F. Gogarten, *Demythologizing and History;* N. B. Stonehouse, "Rudolf Bultmann's Jesus," in *Paul Before the Areopagus.*

PHILIP EDGCUMBE HUGHES

N

NAME. When Scripture employs the term name for God, it follows generally the use of the word as applied to men. "God condescends to us in order that we might ascend to Him" (Augustine). The parallel is not complete, however, because of the difference between sinful and imperfect man and the holy and perfect God (Luke 1:49). A person, for instance, may be called "Mr. Free King," though he may be neither free nor a king, while our Lord is truly and fully what his name denotes, e.g., Jesus, i.e., Saviour. In general, the biblical use of the name for God may be divided into three categories, though there remain some cases that require more special classification.

First, the term name stands for God himself. Thus, "to call on the name of the Lord" (Acts 2:21) means to call on the Lord himself. The same is true of such expressions as "to trust in his name" (Matt. 12:21); "to blaspheme his name" (Rev. 13:6). To bow the knee "at the name of Jesus" means to bow before Jesus himself (Phil. 2:10).

Second, the term name with the preposition *en* or *epi* and the dative means "in the power" or "by the authority of." Thus, "to cast out devils *en tō onomati Iēsou*" means to cast out devils by the power or the authority of Jesus (Mark 9:38). The same is true of such expressions as: "to be baptized *epi tō onomati Iēsou Christou* (Acts 2:38); "to receive such a little one *epi tō onomati mou*" (Matt. 18:6).

Third, the term name with the preposition *eis* and the accusative denotes either "into," so that, for example, one baptized into the name of the triune God has communion with him (Matt. 28:19; I Cor. 1:13, 15); or simply "in": "to believe in the name" (John 1:12).

BIBLIOGRAPHY
Arndt; W. L. Walker in *ISBE.*

J. THEODORE MUELLER

NATION. The descendants of Abraham, according to the divine promise (Gen. 12:2), formed a nation whose God was the Lord. The conditional promise, given through Moses, was that Israel would be God's own possession from among all peoples, a kingdom of priests, and a holy nation (Ex. 19:5-6). It was indeed a nation of exceptional privilege (cf. Rom. 9:3-5), but because of disobedience and unbelief suffered chastisement and judgment. In the time of our Lord, despite Roman rule, there was still a strong national consciousness and a recognition of national identity (cf. Luke 7:5; 23:2; John 11:48, 50-52; 18:35; Acts 10:22; 24:2, 10; 26:4; 28:19). The spiritual descendants of Abraham in NT times were those of faith, whether Jews or Gentiles (Gal. 3:7-9). They received the blessings of the Messiah's day which the Israel after the flesh rejected. They were in truth an elect race, a royal priesthood, a holy nation, a people for God's own possession (I Pet. 2:9).

In both Greek and Hebrew the plural "nations" was used of the nations of the unbelieving world, of pagans, and of Gentiles, and could bear a connotation of reproach. It can at times aptly be translated "heathen" (E. J. Goodspeed, *Problems of New Testament Translation,* University of Chicago Press, Chicago, 1945, pp. 26 f.). In the NT the gospel and its benefits are dramatically and conspicuously extended to all nations, to Gentiles, to heathen. Those who in time past were no people become by faith the people of God (Rom. 9-11; I Pet. 2:10).

BIBLIOGRAPHY
Arndt; G. Bertram and K. L. Schmidt in *TWNT*;
James Donald in *HDAC*; *MM*; A. Norman Rowland in
HDCG; Thayer-Grimm.

JOHN H. SKILTON

NATURALISM. Naturalism is the position which interprets the universe as wholly explanatory in terms of physical and chemical bodies. Proponents of this view, however, do not wish to be classified as materialists, for they admit the existence of much that is of value beside material things; but what is non-material has no "substantial being" in and of itself. Such non-material aspects of the universe are always to be interpreted as *forms* or *functions* of spatially and temporally located "physical" bodies.

Naturalism does not rule out religion, but simply those elements of religion ultimately dependent upon a non-physical structure of the universe (e.g., a divine mind, a teleological interpretation of the universe as a whole, a "soul" existing after the corruption of the body, etc.).

Naturalistic theists (e.g., Julian Huxley, Henry Nelson Wieman, and Bernard Meland) maintain that all true religious values traditionally associated with supernatural theism can be maintained within the framework of pure naturalism.

BIBLIOGRAPHY
Ernest Nagel, "Naturalism Reconsidered" in *Proceedings and Addresses of the American Philosophical Association*, Vol. 28; Henry Nelson Wieman and Bernard Eugene Meland, *Contemporary American Philosophies of Religion*, pp. 211-306; Ralph B. Winn, "Philosophic Naturalism," in Dagobert Runes, ed., *Twentieth Century Philosophy*, pp. 511-37.

KENNETH S. KANTZER

NATURAL LAW. The biblical ground for this notion is found in Romans 2:13-14. This indicates that man knows by creation what is right and wrong, and stands under the guidance and correction of conscience. From this it has been deduced that non-Christian ethics, e.g., as summarized in the cardinal virtues, may be used as a basis for the ethics of revelation, or that the two may be regarded as identical, or even (by Rationalists and Humanists) that the natural law is preferable to the biblical and makes the Christian revelation ethically unnecessary. The argument of Romans, however, is that the natural law, though it is a fact and may find partial fulfilments, is primarily an instrument to condemn the sinner who does not truly perceive or keep it, driving him to Christ as the end of the law for righteousness (Rom. 10:4) and therefore the beginning of real knowledge and observance of the divine will. It cannot, then, be made an independent basis, alternative or substitute for the law of Christ.

See also REVELATION, NATURAL.

GEOFFREY W. BROMILEY

NATURAL REVELATION. See REVELATION, NATURAL.

NATURAL THEOLOGY. *Theologia naturalis* as it is now understood is a theology constructed irrespective of revelation. In its pure form it has never existed within the church, which is clearly committed to revelation in some degree. The role allowed it in Christian theology has therefore been subsidiary, and usually preparatory, to the theology of revelation. This is so whether as "preambles" in Thomas Aquinas (*Summa Theol.*, I, q. 2, art. 2), or as analogy, for example, in Butler (*The Analogy of Religion, Natural and Revealed, to the Constitution and Course of Nature*). From the sixteenth century we see the almost universal use of it as an introduction to dogmatics.

The basis of natural theology in the church is a supposed quality in man that enables him to know God as Creator if not as Redeemer, or at least to know of his existence and in some respects what he is like, or at any rate what he is not like. This rudimentary knowledge will then form the starting point for a fuller understanding of God and hence of the divine-human relationship.

In the twentieth century a radical attack has been directed against natural theology by K. Barth: "I am an avowed opponent of all natural theology" (*The Knowledge of God and the Service of God*, London, 1938, p. 6). This is because it detracts from the comprehensiveness and exclusiveness of Christ as the revelation of God. For Barth there is no other source of the knowledge of God than Jesus Christ as he is witnessed to in the Scriptures.

Natural theology appeals for scriptural support primarily to Rom. 1:18 ff.; Acts 14:15 17 and 17:22 ff. in the NT and certain "nature" psalms (e.g., 19 and 104) and Job in the OT.

See also REVELATION, NATURAL.

BIBLIOGRAPHY
K. Barth, *Church Dogmatics*, II, 1, §23-24; E. Brunner and K. Barth, *Natural Theology*; H. L. Mansel,

The Limits of Religious Thought; C. C. J. Webb, *Studies in the History of Natural Theology.*

T. H. L. PARKER

NATURE. In the NT two Greek words are used: *genesis* as in James 1:23; and 3:6, where the reference is to birth and what man is by origin; and *physis* elsewhere as in Eph. 2:3, where the reference is to the totality of a mode of feeling and acting which by long habit has become nature (Thayer), and as in II Pet. 1:4, where the term means the sum of innate properties and powers (Thayer), in this case with an emphasis on holiness distinctive of divine virtues. Thus the biblical use of the term is in reference to the origin of man and his psycho-physical constitution, indicating a monistic intrinsic structure, and a metaphysical discontinuity, but a moral continuity through divine grace (Eph. 2:3; II Pet. 1:4).

In philosophic discussion "nature" is the Latin equivalent of the Greek *physis*. Different meanings of the term (thirty-seven listed in Baldwin's *Dictionary of Philosophy*) have consolidated into a monistic concept. For Aristotle "nature is the distinctive form or quality of such things as have within themselves a principle of motion, such form or quality not being separable from the things themselves, save conceptually" (Aristotle's *Physics,* II, 193b, Loeb Classical Library edition). For Kant the term signifies the system of all phenomena in the one space and time reality corresponding to our idea of physical or material reality, as contrasted with spirit or mind. Limitation of the term to the system of physical phenomena is seen in some contemporary naturalists (see *Naturalism and the Human Spirit*) for whom the term as an all-inclusive category, corresponding to the role played by "Being" in Greek thought or by "Reality" for idealists. A trend toward a broader concept is seen here because nature includes physical objects and living beings, inclusive of human beings and their ideals. This trend is seen in the religious naturalism of A. N. Whitehead for whom nature is all that there is, but it is dynamic, inclusive of spirit and mind.

See also NATURALISM.

BIBLIOGRAPHY

J. M. Baldwin (ed), *Dictionary of Philosophy and Psychology;* E. S. Brightman, *A Philosophy of Religion,* pp. 210-22; HERE; Y. H. Krikorian (ed), *Naturalism and the Human Spirit,* pp. 357, 121, 243; Thayer's *Greek-English Lexicon.*

E. SIVERTSEN

NATURE, DIVINE. The only biblical use of this phrase is in II Pet. 1:4: "That ye may be partakers of the divine nature *(theias koinōnoi physeōs)*"; and in this case the reference is to our participation rather than to the divine nature as such.

Applied to God, the phrase obviously speaks of the intrinsic being of God in all the plenitude of his perfections. As contrasted with human nature, the divine is self-existent, free, creative, eternal, single, omnipresent, omnipotent, constant, the sum of wisdom, righteousness and love.

In the case of God the Son, it has a more specific reference to the deity united with humanity in the one person of Jesus Christ. But this is simply a particular application of the one sense. In virtue of his deity, Jesus Christ enjoys in the full and strictest sense the being and attributes of the divine nature; though in his incarnation he has also assumed the essence and attributes of human nature. Hence we have the common formulation — one person and two natures, or two natures in one person.

It is in the light of the divine nature of Jesus Christ that we are to understand our own participation in the divine nature. This does not mean deification, but incorporation into Jesus Christ by the Holy Spirit.

See also IDENTIFICATION WITH CHRIST.

RICHARD E. HIGGINSON

NAZARENE. This term is applied in the NT both to Jesus and to his followers. The Jews needed some sobriquet by which to identify disciples of Jesus and they chose "the sect of the Nazarenes" (Acts 24:5; cf. 28:22). Whatever odium adhered to the use of this epithet derived from the crucifixion and the breach within Judaism for which Jesus was held responsible. It is not evident that the general use of the word with reference to Jesus in his lifetime as a means of identification or address carried any adverse connotation. John 1:46 is quite indecisive as affording ground for the opinion that Nazareth had an evil reputation. More likely the passage means that since Galilee as a whole was not expected to produce the Messiah (cf. John 7:41, 52), much less could one of its minor communities do so.

The word occurs in two forms, as *Nazarēnos* (six times) and as *Nazōraios* (thirteen times). But both are probably derived from the place-name Nazareth. The claim that the second word points to a pre-Christian sect to which Jesus belonged is ill-founded. Those who propose it usually doubt the Christian tradition about Nazareth as the boyhood home of Jesus, looking on it as a deliberate attempt to divert attention from Jesus' original connection with the "Nazarenes" by associating him with a place dubbed Nazareth.

Matthew explains the residence at Nazareth as necessitated by prophecy (2:23). A twofold play on words may be involved here. Isa. 11:1 describes Messiah as a *nēṣer* (branch, sprout). In Judg. 13:5 (LXX) *naziraios* (Nazarite) occurs with reference to Samson. Granted that Jesus was not a Nazarite in the strict sense, yet his situation was so akin to that of Samson as the one who would save Israel (Judg. 13:5; Matt. 1:21) that the technicalities of circumstantial description and of philological requirement are brushed aside in the rabbinic word play which relates Jesus to the OT.

BIBLIOGRAPHY
W. F. Albright in *JBL*, 65 (1946), 397-401; J. S. Kennard, Jr. in *JBL*, 65 (1946), 131-41; 66 (1947), 79-81; F. F. Bruce, *The Book of the Acts*, p. 465, f.n. 8, 9; G. F. Moore in *The Beginnings of Christianity* (Jackson and Lake, eds.), Vol. I, pp. 426-32; H. M. Shires in *ATR* 29 (1947) 19-27.

EVERETT F. HARRISON

NAZARITE. *Nāzîr* means "separate," either in dignity (Gen. 49:26; cf. Lam. 4:7 ASV, "nobles") or in holiness, as a Nazarite unto God (Num. 6:2, 8). Most vows concerned property (Gen. 28:20-22); but Nazarites were men or women personally devoted to a priestly life. Nazaritism antedated the Mosaic legislation (Num. 6:2); Num. 6:1-21, however, standardized its requirements. Like certain priests (Ezek. 44:20), Nazarites kept their hair untrimmed; thus unpruned vines are *nāzîr* (Lev. 25:5, 11). Growing hair symbolized unimpaired strength, devoted to God (Jer. 7:29: unshorn hair is *nēzer*, one's "crown"; and Judg. 16:17: Samson's hair [devotion] conditioned his strength). Like officiating priests (Lev. 10:9-10), Nazarites vowed abstinence from wine-products (cf. Judg. 13:4), both to maintain sobriety and to protest Canaanitish luxuriousness with its related Baalism (cf. the extreme Rechabites, Jer. 35:1-11; S. R. Driver on Amos 2:10). Like the high priest (Lev. 21:11-12), the Nazarite preserved separation from dead bodies (cf. unclean food, Judg. 13:7), as symbolical

of sin (Gen. 2:17). Accidental contact required shaving his hair, sacrificing, and recommencing his devotion (with certain freedom, cf. Judg. 14:9, 19; 15:9). Mosaic Nazarites served a stated period and were then released, after sacrifices and the presentation on the altar of the shaven locks and any other items vowed. Samson (Judg. 16:17), Samuel (I Sam. 1:11), and John the Baptist (Luke 1:15), however, were permanent Nazarites.

Like the prophets, God raised up the Nazarites to be devoted leaders (Amos 2:10) and deliver Israel (Judg. 13:5). Nazarites continued (I Macc. 3:49; cf. extensive Talmudic treatment), despite corruption (Amos 2:11). Jesus Christ was not a Nazarite (Matt. 11:19; "Nazarene," 2:23, refers to Isa. 11:1, the Messiah as a *nēṣer*, "sprout," and his home in the new and lightly esteemed village of Nazareth, "sprout-town"). Paul undertook a Nazarite vow (Acts 18:18) and bore release-expenses for others (21:24).

BIBLIOGRAPHY
G. B. Gray, *JTS* 1, 201 ff.; *HERE*; *JewEnc*; *MSt*.

J. BARTON PAYNE

NEIGHBOR. Five Hebrew words are rendered "neighbor" in the AV of the OT, the principal one being *rēaʻ*. The NT words are *geitōn*, "fellow countryman" (Luke 14:12; 15:6, 9; John 9:8), *perioikos* (an adjective used substantively with the definite article), "the one dwelling around" (Luke 1:58), and *plēsion* (an adverb also used substantively with the definite article except as a predicate, cf. Luke 10:29), "the one near or close by."

In the OT one's neighbor is clearly a fellow Israelite as indicated by the statement: "You shall not take vengeance or bear any grudge against the sons of your own people, but you shall love your neighbor as yourself" (Lev. 19:18, RSV). The parallelism of this verse identifies "neighbor" with "sons of your people." A different code of conduct was prescribed towards the foreigner in contrast to one's fellow countryman (Deut. 23:19, 20; cf. Matt. 5:43).

The law of love for one's neighbor is quoted by Jesus (Matt. 5:43; 19:19; 22:39; Mark 12:31; Luke 10:27), by Paul (Rom. 13:9; Gal. 5:14) and by James (2:8), but it is our Lord who gives to it a new and fresh meaning. To the question addressed to him by the lawyer, "Who is my neighbor?" (Luke 10:29), Jesus answered with the parable of the Good Samaritan. One's neighbor is no longer only one's fellow countryman, but anyone in need. Or perhaps even more pertinent, in the parable it is not the priest or the Levite who proves to be neighbor to the destitute man (was he a Jew?), but the despised Samaritan. ". . . the lawyer who wants to justify himself . . . is confronted not by the poor wounded man with his claim for help, but by the . . . Samaritan. . . . This is the neighbor he did not know" (K. Barth, *Church Dogmatics,* Charles Scribner's Sons, New York, 1956, I/2, p. 418).

BIBLIOGRAPHY
    SBK, I, pp. 353-68; Arndt; C. E. B. Cranfield in RTWB.
                            WALTER W. WESSEL

NEO-ORTHODOXY. I. INTRODUCTION. The quandary to which religious liberalism was reduced in the early decades of this century, by the crisis of Western culture, proved the opportunity for a theological renaissance often called Barthianism. This name is sometimes given the movement because the original break-through was most dramatically achieved by a young Swiss pastor, Karl Barth, who had been thoroughly trained in German liberalism. His first published article was a struggle with the problem of relativism. The modern man, he complained, no longer acknowledges any authority outside himself. Both tables of the law slip from the preacher's hands as he approaches the people. From the time of the initial edition of his Commentary on Romans (*Der Roemerbrief*) in 1919, Barth has been a critic of religious liberalism and a champion of a theology which has as its proper subject, the word of God. Some of the leading exponents of this new theology (in this article called neo-orthodoxy) are more "neo" (Tillich, Niebuhr), others are more "orthodox" (Barth, Brunner); but none is consistently liberal and none is consistently orthodox. In an article of brief compass, we cannot pursue the interesting and not insignificant differences between these men; we must simply sketch the general profile of the movement. In so doing we shall state wherein there is a return to the orthodox tradition and look briefly at the distinctive differences.

II. RELIGIOUS AUTHORITY. Like the liberals, the neo-orthodox are theists. But unlike the liberals, they insist on the transcendence of God. God is in heaven and we on earth. There is, as Kierkegaard would say, an absolute qualitative difference between God and man, therefore man can never discover God at the end of a syllogism. The only way God can be known is by revelation, that is, a personal self-disclosure, and this has happened in the person of Jesus Christ.

Since revelation is a "perpendicular from above" (Barth), it is futile to seek to "explain" Jesus. The liberals, assuming the essential continuity between the human and the divine (immanence) made this fatal mistake. The Jesus-event was looked upon by them as a fact of history to be explained according to the analogy of religious experience. Hence the futile quest for the "historical Jesus," who was the great prophet, the religious hero and genius, the holy man, the great example, the lover of the good, the true, and the beautiful, in short, everything but what he really was and is — God. For the neo-orthodox, unlike the liberals, Jesus cannot be understood in terms of history as such. *Finitum non est capax infiniti.* In Jesus, eternity breaks into time, the infinite becomes finite, the divine human, God becomes man. In Jesus and in him only, the true God truly speaks to man.

But since this is so, unlike the orthodox, the neo-orthodox are more or less indifferent to the critical debate over the trustworthiness of the Gospel narratives. Though Christianity can never survive as a "religion independent of all historical foundations" (Schweitzer), it does not rest on history as such, for history is the realm of the relative. The Christ of faith is not the "historical Jesus" of the critics, but he whom the apostles confessed and preached as the Son of the living God, and the only Saviour of men.

To be sure, this witness of prophets and apostles to Jesus as "the Word made flesh," which we have in the Bible, is uniquely inspired. The neo-orthodox do not regard the Bible simply as great religious literature. In this the liberals were egregiously in error. Yet, since this kerygma is a witness *to* the Word, it is a mistake on the part of the orthodox, with the most serious consequences, to identify the words of Scripture with the Word of God. It is human to err and the Bible, though unique, is human and therefore bears the Word of God to us only in a broken and imperfect form. For this reason the neo-orthodox accept, some more, some less, many of the higher critical views of Scripture commonly rejected by the orthodox. Where to draw the line; how to know what can and what cannot become the word of God to the believing individual, remains one of the unresolved problems of the movement. This is why the debate between Barth and Bultmann over the "demythologizing" of the Gospel tradition, has divided the ranks of the neo-orthodox almost from the inception of the movement. See MYTH.

To sum up, the neo-orthodox have reacted against the liberal doctrine of immanence and sought to solve the problem of authority in religion by restoring to theology its proper foundation, namely, revelation, without becoming involved in a view of the Bible which would implicate one in what appears to them to be a hopeless scientific obscurantism.

III. EXISTENTIAL METHOD. As for theological method, the neo-orthodox have been markedly influenced by Soeren Kierkegaard, who revolted against the dead orthodoxism of the Danish State Church, calling the individual to a passionate commitment to the truth, which should change the very form of his existence. Hence the term Existentialism. Such existential (*q.v.*) truth is more than a creed, that is, more than propositions related in a rational pattern so as to be cognizable to the mind. Propositional truth (which is the only sort of truth there can be in science, where reason has its proper sphere) increases one's information, but leaves the man unchanged. Existential truth, on the other hand, is truth which transforms the individual in his concrete, here-and-now *Sitz im Leben*. As an antidote to formal orthodoxy and indifferent liberalism, this emphasis has been most salutary. The best Protestant tradition has always decried both what the Reformers called *fides historica* — mere intellectual assent to the truths of Christianity, and the scientific neutrality of the comparative religion approach. Yet unfortunately, in the writer's opinion, this same emphasis has led, oftentimes, to a depreciation of dogma and creeds, as a forcing of biblical truth into the mold of Greek, rational thought. At best, all creeds and theology books (including those written by neo-orthodox theologians) are an attempt to do the impossible, that is, to express in propositions what cannot be so expressed. This is why all theology, as such, is full of paradoxes. (Hence the name, The Theology of Paradox or Dialectical Theology.) The trouble with orthodoxy, according to the neo-orthodox, is that it tries to dissolve these paradoxes into a rational, logically coherent system, thus doing violence to the biblical asymmetry. Orthodoxy for this reason has become like a frozen waterfall — mighty forms of movement, without movement.

The Bible, on the other hand, is full of paradoxes. God is One and Three; Christ is God and Man; Man is *non posse non peccare*, yet free; faith is an act and a gift, and so on. In the *crisis* of faith (hence the name, Theology of Crisis) the believer rises above these paradoxes to grasp the truth in and beyond them, in a way which cannot be made rationally lucid. If it could, faith would no longer be necessary, according to the neo-orthodox. Having abandoned all cryptic rationalism, having given up the medieval scholastic dream of a perfect system, the neo-orthodox theologian finds the unity of revelation in Jesus Christ. Luther's *Christus dominus et rex scripturae* has been laid under heavy and dubious contribution at this point. All Scripture more or less perfectly bears witness to Christ, who is himself the Word of God. But since the truth of God is a person, (Jesus said, I *am* the truth — which Socrates never could have said), truth, in the biblical sense, can only result in paradoxes for abstract thought.

> Either God has a personal existence or he does not exist at all. One cannot, however, comprehend his personality in a speculative way, but only by relating himself personally to him — that is by making him the thou of his own I — which indeed is required by man's spiritual life and by God himself. And when this happens all speculation and every form of theological and metaphysical erudition *eo impso* ceases. (Ferdinand Ebner, *Das Wort und die geistigen Realitaeten*, *Pneumatologische Fragmente*, Innsbruck, 1921).

In other words, we rationally *analyze* things, we *meet* persons. We can never have an adequate theology, until there has been this "divine-human encounter" (Brunner). In the crisis of faith I become "contemporaneous" with the Christ of history.

IV. THE FALL OF MAN. Probably at no point is this existential method of approaching theological truth illustrated in a more striking way than in the doctrine of man's fall. By one route or another, the neo-orthodox, in abandoning the liberal interpretation of Jesus, have also given up the liberal view of man. This, of course, was inevitable, since any genuine attempt to take the biblical witness to Christ seriously, must carry with it a willingness to accept the biblical testimony concerning man as sinner. In the case of the pioneer thinkers, it was not so much the logic of the thing, as experience and history which drove them to the conclusion that the doctrine of man's inevitable progress was a shallow optimism and an irresponsible complacency. On the continent the World War I did much to foster a pessimistic view of man's innate capabilities for good, and even in America, where the crisis was less acutely felt and less astutely diagnosed, Reinhold Niebuhr began to write "tracts for the times" in the late 20's advocating a return to the biblical doctrine of original sin. The liberal view was most jejune, these thinkers have come to believe, in supposing that the account of the fall in Genesis is simply a composite of primitive stories to explain why snakes have no legs, why weeds grow, why people wear clothes, etc. Though the fall can no longer be conceived as an historical event, it is nonetheless theologically relevant, in fact, indispensable for anyone who is not willfully blind to the flaws in human nature. Of course, in the Pauline-Augustinian-Calvinistic tradition, the doctrine of the fall has always involved an event on the empirical plane. The neo-orthodox considers such a form of the doctrine to invite a conflict with science, which can have only a sorry denouement. (Barth — not the movement as a whole which takes his name — has specialized in ambiguity on the whole matter of the relation of the primal history [Genesis 1-11] to empirical fact. When asked, in Holland, if he believed the serpent really spoke in Eden, he replied that it was more important to pay attention to what the serpent said. Brunner styled this an evasion of a question that could not be evaded, especially in Holland.) Not only should we not insist on a form of the doctrine which has become scientifically obsolete, according to the neo-orthodox, but, as a matter of fact, we owe modern science a debt of thanks for having made the traditional view impossible; for as long as we conceive the fall as an event in the remote past, we fail to think existentially. The fall is something which we all commit. Let us not push the blame off on *Pithecanthropus Adamus*. When God says to Adam, Where art thou? he is speaking to each of us. How it

is possible to existentialize the disobedience of the first Adam out of history, while insisting that the obedience of the second Adam was a fact in history, necessary to all true Christian faith, remains an antinomy in the neo-orthodox approach.

V. INFANT BAPTISM. Another interesting, though not so significant development, which illustrates the existential motive at work in neo-orthodoxy, is the rejection of infant baptism by some of the leaders — notably Barth. In a theology which places the individual at the "crossroads of time and eternity" (Kierkegaard) and stresses the need of passionate appropriation of the truth *(Existenz)*, the rationale of baptismal vows taken by proxy becomes difficult. Barth, who was the first openly to challenge the theology behind the sacrament — judiciously leaving the question of what should be done about the *practice* of the church to those whose feet are on the ground — constantly speaks to this point of the need of a personal acceptance of the relationship into which one is brought by baptism. Others (Brunner) admit it would be difficult to imagine what the apostles would have said of the current practice. Vigorous protests, on the other hand, have been registered from within the movement, by men like Cullmann, and commissions to investigate the practice have been sponsored by some churches, the French Reformed Commission being obviously influenced by Barth in its conclusions, the Scottish Presbyterians rather vehemently reacting against his views.

VI. THE ATONEMENT. Any theology which takes the sinfulness of man seriously, must, of course, be concerned with the death of Christ, as more than an historical fact. In the History of Religion School, the one part of the Apostles' Creed which could be repeated in good conscience was the phrase, ". . . suffered under Pontius Pilate, was crucified, dead and buried." For the neo-orthodox, to stop here, to say that Jesus was simply a victim of circumstances beyond his ken, a noble martyr to a good cause, reflects the same lack of depth that liberalism betrayed in its quest for the "historical Jesus." If we regard Jesus simply as a prophet, if we reduce his life to an event in the time-space continuum, then naturally his death must be placed in the same category with Socrates drinking the hemlock. But the faith which penetrates the veil of Christ "incognito," which sees beyond the human personality to the divine person, also perceives in the cross of Christ the triumph of the Almighty over sin, death and evil, and confesses that "God was in Christ reconciling the world unto himself" (II Cor. 5:19).

Beyond this it is not easy to frame a general statement that will cover all the writers in the neo-orthodox school. There is, for the most part, a tendency to regard all "theories" of the atonement (q.v.) as, at best, human efforts to explain a mystery which is beyond explanation. Some of these theories contain more truth than others, but no one of them is adequate in itself. Gustaf Aulén, whom we might call a neo-Lutheran, in his celebrated study, *Christus Victor,* is critical not only of the Abelardian view and the subsequent development in liberalism along subjectivistic, exemplarist lines, as being too humanistic, but also feels that the orthodox satisfaction theory, stemming from Anselm, though nearer the truth, is too "rational," too exact, too theoretical. He reserves the words "theory" and "doctrine" for medieval and Protestant views, and champions what he calls the *"classic idea"* of the atonement as found in the early fathers, which is the movement of God to deliver man from evil involving theological and psychological antinomies that defy rational systematization. It is the quest for the rainbow's end, therefore, to ask after *the* neo-orthodox theory of the atonement. In the writings which reflect the influence of this point of view, one hears echoes of many theories, without effort at resolution.

VII. SOCIAL THEORY. The doctrine of man as sinner, in neo-orthodoxy, is significant not only as illustrative of the existential method in that theology, but also as a watershed within the movement, from whence two different streams of emphasis have developed. Barth, fearing lest the liberal camel of immanence should thrust its nose in the door of his tent, has tended to stress the infinite gulf between God and man as sinner, and to be more than a little suspicious of Brunner's development of a natural theology. The Holy Ghost needs no point of contact (*Anknuepfungspunkt*) for the gospel other than that which he himself creates. Men like Brunner, Niebuhr and others, however, while sharing Barth's pessimism about human nature, had insisted that inasmuch as fallen man still retains the image of God in some sense and inasmuch as the cross of Christ, the real definition of God's love,

was an event in history, therefore, the grace of God, though it is beyond history, yet has implications for life in its present historical and social forms. Hence these men have wrestled more seriously than any others in our day with the problems attendant upon our Christian duty to seek the highest possible relative justice in this present evil world. In doing this, they have sought to combine the teaching of Scripture with insights derived from anthropology, psychology, sociology, and history.

Here, as in their theological pronouncements, the representative writers differ from one another, yet they all agree that we cannot passively accept the evils in society, but must ever seek for and strive toward the will of God, who is the Redeemer of the social order as well as of the individual believer. Brunner has espoused a reconstructed, controlled capitalism, while Niebuhr has moved further to the socialistic left. Both are committed to a democratic political economy as the most just form of the state (q.v.) in our era, and while espousing agapé love as the ideal for all life, they have rejected the pacifism of the liberals as an unrealistic sentimentalizing of the Christian view, which could only end in the loss of what justice there is in our contemporary society.

VIII. ESCHATOLOGY. Though the leaders of neo-orthodoxy vary in their views on many social issues, even to the extent of questioning in some instances (Barth) whether an answer to such questions as these constitutes the proper task of theology, they all agree that man's sin makes it impossible to find the meaning of history within history. The evolutionary optimism which looks to world renewal ("Christian Americanism") is the bastard offspring of a Christian eschatology (q.v.) and a Renaissance anthropology. To view revelation as a process coterminous with history itself and culminating in some "far off divine event toward which the whole creation moves" was one of the fatal mistakes of modern theology. The kingdom of God is beyond historical analogy and man's ethical attainment. It breaks into history from beyond history. In this regard the neo-orthodox stand essentially on the side of the orthodox, only they would have no sympathy with the literalism prevalent in certain fundamentalists' schemes and patterns of eschatology. They publish no charts and they do not seek to locate contemporary events in the book of Daniel and the Revelation. Faith is not interested in an end-history, but in the end of history. The best composite volume reflecting this renewed interest in a supernaturalistic eschatology is *The Christian Hope and the Task of the Church* (New York, 1954) prepared for the Second Assembly of the World Council of Churches in Evanston, Illinois.

BIBLIOGRAPHY

Karl Barth, *The Doctrine of the Word of God; The Epistle to the Romans; The Word of God and the Word of Man;* Emil Brunner, *Christianity and Civilization; Man in Revolt; Revelation and Reason; The Divine Imperative;* Reinhold Niebuhr, *Moral Man and Immoral Society; The Nature and Destiny of Man; Faith and History;* Paul Tillich, *Systematic Theology.*

PAUL K. JEWETT

NEOPHYTE. In the early church a newly baptized convert who wore the white baptismal robe for eight days. The Greek *neophytos,* newly planted, found but once in the NT (I Tim. 3:6), is closely related in meaning to the Latin *novicius,* "new," from which the English "novice" is derived. In the mystery religions a neophyte was a newly initiated cultist. In Roman Catholicism new converts from other faiths and newly ordained priests and monks are called neophytes.

DONALD G. DAVIS

NESTORIANISM. Appointed Bishop of Constantinople in A.D. 428, Nestorius set out to banish heresy from his diocese, and in so doing attacked the extravagant emphasis on the phrase *theotokos* as applied to the Virgin. This attack was thought to involve a separation between the divine nature of Christ and the human, and Nestorius and his supporters seem to have used incautious terms which suggested that they could not worship the human Jesus, and that the unity of Christ's person is a conjunction of will rather than a genuine hypostatic union. In effect, of course, they were concerned to offset the developing overemphasis of Eutychianism *(q.v.)* in the other direction, but in consequence of the strong opposition of Cyril of Alexandria, supported by Celestine of Rome, Nestorius was deposed at the Council of Ephesus in 431 and banished in 436. Nestorianism, however, maintained a vigorous existence, especially in Persia, and was responsible for missionary work which took the gospel to Arabia, India, Turkestan and China.

GEOFFREY W. BROMILEY

NEW BIRTH. See REGENERATION.

NEW COMMANDMENT. This phrase occurs first at John 13:34 where we would expect mention of the institution of the Lord's Supper. It occurs also in I John 2:8, an echo of the original utterance. I John 2:7 and II John 5 are not directly pertinent.

That we (Christians) should love one another, even as Jesus loved us and laid down his life for us (John 15:13) is the substance of the new commandment. But why did Jesus use the adjective "new" for this obligation when previously he had referred to it in the OT form "thou shalt love thy neighbor as thyself" (Lev. 19:18) on more than one occasion (Luke 10:27 and Matt. 22:39; Mark 12:31), and then had designated it as the second great commandment?

Many have thought that "new" indicates a greater degree of love was intended; not "as thyself" but "more than thyself" (Cyril, Theodore of Mopsuestia, *et al.*). Others believe Jesus meant love one another not as you love yourselves but as I have loved you; that is, replace generalized neighborly love with truly Christlike concern (Grotius, Ebrard, Godet, Hengstenberg, Meyer). Some suggest Jesus intended enlargement of the OT word neighbor (capable of restriction with Israel) to include all men as in the parable of the good Samaritan (so Koestlin, Hilgenfeld).

A second class of interpretations retranslates the word "new" to give such meanings as: a commandment always fresh and never growing old (Olshausen); the old commandment now renewed or repromulgated (Irenaeus, Calvin, Maldonatus); a regenerating command renewing our inner motives (Augustine, Wordsworth); new or unexpected in view of the previous strife regarding rank (Luke 22:24).

Lange ingeniously argues that the new commandment is simply the new covenant, and stands in John's Gospel in place of the Eucharist (whereas some think John intended to substitute here a command to observe the Agape love feast associated with foot washing in place of the Eucharist). The new covenant in Jesus' blood (Eucharist) centers in God's love, and bread and wine signify Jesus' presence among his disciples until he comes again (I Cor. 11:26; cf. Rev. 3:20). The covenant becomes a command through Jesus' words "Do this in remembrance of me." As there is only one new covenant so the one new commandment must coincide with it; the words used here "as I have loved you" point to Jesus' death as unmistakably as do the broken bread and eucharistic cup, says Lange.

Jesus' precepts in general are called commandments in John 14:15, 21; and are called words in vs. 23; 15:10, 12. In the post-apostolic writings this usage is found often (I Clement 13:3; II Clement 3:4; 4:5; 6:7; 8:4; 17:3; Ignatius to Eph. 9:2; Polycarp to the Phil. 2:2).

Paul in I Cor. 14:37 regards his own teachings as commandments of the Lord. However, the "commandments" of Jesus in the Gospels, or of the Lord as they come to us through the Epistles, are basically principles to guide conduct rather than legal regulations, and their appeal is normally to create an attitude rather than to command unquestioning obedience.

BIBLIOGRAPHY

Arndt; Lange, *Commentary on the Holy Scriptures,* vol. 3 at John 13:34.

TERRELLE B. CRUM

NEW CREATION. The phrase "new creation," *kainē ktisis,* appears in II Cor. 5:17 and Gal. 6:15. *Kainē* suggests that the old is discarded and must be replaced by the new, and it follows that the new is superior to the old; cf. the "new covenant" in Luke 22:20. Paul's use of the term expresses the result of the conversion experience, and implies by the adjective that the contrast is radical and transforming. This conversion is not self-generated, but is accomplished by divine grace. It is a spiritual renewal. The need for a new creation is occasioned by the vitiating effect of sin upon the race, for fallen human nature is in such an estate that only a new act of creation will render it fit for devotion and service to God.

Both Pauline occurrences of the term are in contexts which stress the crucial significance of the death of Christ in establishing the new order. It is equally apparent that both passages point to the practical results of participating in the new creation, viz., an unselfish life of dedicated service, and freedom from the "world" and from the moil of Judaistic legalism. New areas of truth and new canons of Christian behavior have superseded the old.

Two parallel expressions are *palingenesia,* "regeneration" (Matt. 19:28, Titus 3:5), and *gennaō anōthen,* "born again" (John 3:3, 7) (RSV reads "born anew," margin "born from above"). That Paul was not averse to using the metaphor of rebirth as well as new creation is demonstrated by I Cor. 4:15, Gal. 4:19 and Philem. 10, all of which refer to birth and travail.

DAVID H. WALLACE

NICENE CREED. See CREEDS.

NONCONFORMITY. Nonconformity indicates a refusal to adhere to the accepted norm. Thus Christians are not to conform to the world, and therefore their beliefs and actions and attitudes should be distinct from those commonly adopted. Yet Christians may also be unwilling to conform to beliefs or practices in the church with which they disagree on various grounds. Thus the term is often used, particularly in British church history, for ecclesiastical dissent. The first Nonconformists in this sense were those Puritans or Separatists who either openly or practically refused to follow the forms of worship laid down by the English Reformation Settlement (Roman Catholics being given the special title of Recusants). Later, the term came to be applied to dissenters of all kinds, e.g., Baptists, Quakers, Congregationalists, Methodists. The issue is a difficult one, since it may be argued on the one side that legitimate majority decisions should be authoritative until legitimately shown to be wrong and reversed, whereas on the other it may be contended that minorities or even individuals should not act against conscience if the purity of evangelical truth or practice seems to be genuinely at stake. Perhaps the attempt at too rigid or detailed a uniformity is the source of inevitable nonconformity.

See also SEPARATION.

GEOFFREY W. BROMILEY

NOVATIANISM. The Novatians were a sect formed by Novatian, a presbyter at Rome. During the persecutions under Decius and Valerian (249 to 260) many thousands of Christians shamefully denied the faith and sacrificed to the heathen gods. When, afterwards, many sought readmission to the church, Novatian insisted that they be rejected permanently no matter how deep their contrition. God might pardon them at death but the church never. It would cease to be a true church if it did so. Bishop Cornelius at Rome, and the renowned Cyprian at Carthage, would receive them back on giving signs of true repentance. Novatus, a presbyter of Carthage, advocated receiving back everyone without question. He suddenly changed completely, departed to Rome, and joined Novatian's party of severity.

A few obscure bishops and presbyters in Italy set up a schismatical church and elected Novatian bishop. It grew rapidly and spread to Gaul, Africa, and Asia.

Constantine dealt severely with the Novatians, but they managed to survive down to the sixth century.

ALEXANDER M. RENWICK

NUMERICS, BIBLE. Numbers are used in the Bible in much the same way as in other books. They are regularly spelled out, despite the fact that numerical signs were early in use. This would favor accuracy of transmission. The use of the letters of the Greek alphabet to represent numbers is late and belongs to the period of Greek influence.

Numbers are used both exactly, e.g., the three hundred eighteen trained servants of Abram (Gen. 14:14) and inexactly, e.g., the forty years of wandering which include the year and a half before the rejection at Kadesh took place.

Some numbers are used much more frequently than others. Seven is the sacred number because it is the number of the sabbath. Ten is a very natural number, since the fingers and thumbs of the two hands count ten. But we cannot be sure that that is the real explanation of the number which appears most conspicuously in the Decalogue. Twelve is the number of the months, of the sons of Jacob, of the apostles of the Lord. Aside from this, no special significance attaches to the number. The fact that it can be regarded as made up of seven and five has no significance. Many elaborate efforts have been made to attach special meanings to numbers. But none is satisfactory. The number forty, for example, is used in both a good sense (Acts 1:3) and a bad sense (Ps. 95:10). The number seventy is used of the sons of Jacob (Ex. 1:5; 24:1), of the sons of Ahab (II Kings 10:1), and of the years of the Babylonian captivity (Jer. 25:11). Cf. also Ezek. 8:11; Luke 10:1. In prophecy numbers are sometimes used in an enigmatical sense, as in the case of the "seventy weeks" of Dan. 9 or the "two thousand and three hundred" evening-mornings of 8:14. But this does not justify us in taking the numbers themselves in anything other than a literal sense. The only number in Scripture which is declared to be symbolic is "666" which is the number of the beast (Rev. 13:18).

In recent years the name of Ivan Panin has been connected with a most elaborate attempt to find numerical significance in every word and letter in the Bible. But his system is far too complicated to commend itself to the careful student. The Bible does not have an intricate numerical pattern which only a mathematical expert can discover. The strict and obvious meaning of words — and this applies to numbers — should be adhered to unless it is quite plain that some further meaning is involved. We know that the souls that were on the ship which was wrecked at Melita numbered two hundred seventy-six (Acts 27:37, 44). Why this was the number we do not know, and it would be idle to try to find a mysterious or mystical meaning in this simple historical fact.

The desire to find symbolic and significant meanings in numbers can be traced back to ancient times, notably to the Pythagoreans. The Babylonian Creation Tablets record the fifty names of Marduk. Contenau has pointed out that Sargon declared that the number of his name was the same as the circuit of the walls of his palace, 16,283 cubits. A familiar modern example is the attempt of Piazzi Smyth (1867) to find an elaborate and mysterious numerical system in the construction of the Great Pyramid at Gizeh. On the assumption that "The Spiritual Significance of numbers is seen in their first occurrence," E. W. Bullinger in *How to Enjoy the Bible* worked out an ingenious system of interpretation of the numbers in Scripture. But a little testing makes it quite clear that the first occurrence theory in the case of numbers as of other words, while ingenious, is quite unworkable. To infer from Gen. 14:4 that the number thirteen in Gen. 17:25 is "associated with rebellion, apostasy, and disintegration" (pp. 311 f.) will hardly commend itself to the sober minded student of Scripture.

OSWALD T. ALLIS

NUMINOUS, THE. Deriving from the Latin *numen* or pl. *numina* (esp. divine pleasure, will, power or majesty), the numinous is a term which has gained currency to describe the mysterious or transcendent element in the Godhead and the feelings of awe or fear or reverence to which it gives rise. To the extent that there is a real transcendence in God, and that this demands a proper fear and humility on the part of man, the word could perhaps be given a Christian sense and usage. Its associations, however, are for the most part with naturalistic or pantheistic notions, e.g., a primitive fear of the unknown, or reverence before the divinity of creation itself, or submission to the absolute and overwhelming inscrutability of God as the so-called "Wholly Other," and the religious emphasis thus comes to be placed upon the sense of the numinous, i.e., the religious feelings of man himself, rather than the numinous as a genuine reality. To mark off the true mystery of the transcendent will and power and majesty of God as self-revealed in Jesus Christ, and to bring the response of man into proper relationship and perspective, it is perhaps better to relegate the term to natural religion and religious anthropology, thus avoiding its corruptive and corrosive influence in Christian theology and piety.

GEOFFREY W. BROMILEY

NUNC DIMITTIS. See CANTICLE.

O

OATH. Scripture ascribes oaths to both God and man. On God's part an oath is his most holy and solemn asseveration of the absolute truth of his divine word (Num. 23:19) in order that his people may trust all the more in his promises (Isa. 45:20-24). Since God cannot swear by anyone greater than himself (Heb. 6:13), as men do (Heb. 6:16), he swears by himself (Heb. 6:13), by his holiness (Ps. 89:13), by his great name (Jer. 44:26), by his life (Ezek. 33:11). The immutable God (Mal. 3:6), however, swears not only to assure men of his fatherly love and mercy, but also to impress upon them as unfailingly sure his chastisements or punishments threatened to those who refuse to obey his divine word and accept his free salvation in Christ (Ps. 110:4-6). In particular, God has confirmed with a most solemn oath the sure hope of man's salvation through faith in Jesus, the Saviour of sinners (Heb. 7:20-28). This anthropomorphic representation of God, swearing an oath on behalf of man's eternal welfare, must be regarded as a most loving condescension on his part which calls for our most unflinching trust in and faithful obedience to his word.

An oath sworn by men is a most solemn appeal to God to confirm the truth of their words with the express implication of his punishment in case they fail to speak the truth.

Oaths in the interest of God's glory and the confirmation of the truth (Deut. 6:13; Isa. 45:23b; Heb. 6:16) are illustrated by the examples of many saints in Scripture (cf. Gen. 24:2-9; 47:31; 50:5, 25; Ex. 13:19; Josh. 2:17; 9:19, 20). We have also the example of Christ himself (Matt. 26:63 f.) and that of his inspired apostle Paul (II Cor. 1:23; Gal. 1:20). Hence the words of our divine Lord: "Swear not at all" (Matt. 5:34) are directed against all false, blasphemous and frivolous swearing as also all swearing in uncertain things. The fact that Christ in Matt. 5:33-37 warned his hearers against the frivolous and sinful swearing of the Jews at his time, is indicated by the special modifiers "by heaven," "by Jerusalem," "by thy head," as also by the command: "Thou shalt not forswear [swear falsely; commit perjury] thyself" (vs. 33). Immediately, however, he adds: "But shalt perform unto the Lord thine oaths," by which he approves all oaths in the interest of God's glory and the truth.

The Scriptures quote a number of grossly sinful oaths. Thus the oath of Peter, when denying the Lord, was blasphemous (Matt. 26:72). King Herod's reckless oath was prompted by passion and immediately led to the murder of John the Baptist (Matt. 14:6-10). The wicked oath by which Paul's enemies bound themselves not to eat till they had killed him was motivated by hatred (Acts 23:12-15). In addition, they did not know whether they would succeed. Equally wrong was Saul's rash oath which endangered Jonathan's life (I Sam. 14:24-45).

BIBLIOGRAPHY
LC; ISBE; NSBD; WDB.

J. THEODORE MUELLER

OBEY, OBEDIENCE. The word "obey," both in the Old and the New Testament, is a contextual rendering of the verb "to hear." So "obedience" in the Bible signifies active response to something one hears, rather than passive listening (cf. Gen. 3:17; Ex. 24:7; Deut. 21:18-21). Thus the OT šama' is the basis for mišma'at, "body-guard, subject," that is, one who hears (and obeys) the commands of another (Isa. 11:14). This is particularly true in respect to the voice or commandments of God. To hear God's word means to obey that word. So the Lord says in Jeremiah 3:13 that the rebellion of Israel means that they have "not obeyed [heard] my voice." Also in Exodus 19:5 God says, "if you will really hear my voice, [that is] keep my commandments. . . ." One cannot truly hear God's word without acting upon it.

This idea is given further emphasis by the fact that on occasion instead of the normal akouō the LXX and the NT use hypakouō, "to hear under [the obligation of compliance]" (Eph. 6:1; Phil. 2:12; Ps. 17:45; cf. Test. Gad 8:3; also eisakouō in I Cor. 14:21; Deut. 1:43). The supreme example of this is Jesus Christ who was "obedient (hypēkoos) unto death" (Phil. 2:8).

"Hearing (obeying)" is also sometimes "believing" in both Testaments. Gen. 15:6 states that Abraham "believed" God, and was accounted righteous. This is defined in Gen. 22:18 as "hearing [obeying]" the voice of God (cf. Rom. 4:3).

Thus "obeying" is intimately linked in Scripture with "hearing" and "believing." When one has indeed heard God's command or promise he believes that it is true, and therefore is under obligation to obey its conditions.

See also HEAR, HEARKEN.

BIBLIOGRAPHY
BDB; Arndt; W. A. Whitehouse in RTWB; G. Kittel in TWNT.

ROBERT B. LAURIN

OFFEND, OFFENSE. These terms translate two groups of Hebrew and Greek words: (1) words which are synonymous with sin, especially viewed as a moral lapse or stumbling; and (2) words meaning causing to stumble, in particular, the Greek skandalon and skandalizō ("snare" RV, "stumblingblock," and "cause to stumble"). This last group is of special importance.

The NT has much to say about offenses in the sense of snares which destroy growing faith.

(a) Jesus' ministry was an offense to his townsfolk (Mark 6:3); to the Pharisees (Matt. 15:12); to the Jews (John 6:61, 66); and to his disciples (Mark 14:27). That is to say, there were elements in the life and teaching of Jesus that were so out of keeping with the preconceived notions of these groups that their faith in Jesus received a check, in some cases a fatal check. John the Baptist was in the same danger. Jesus sent him the message: "Blessed is he whosoever shall not be offended in me" (Matt. 11:6).

In the parable of the sower Jesus foretold that the gospel's consequence of tribulation would prove a snare to destroy the faith of some who at first were attracted (Mark 4:17; cf. Matt. 24:10).

Paul stated that the cross was an offense (Gal. 5:11); by this he meant, not that the cross was an object of distaste, but that the doctrine of a crucified Messiah was a snare or stumblingblock in the path of those otherwise making progress towards a true Christian faith.

That Christ's ministry and gospel would prove a stumbling to those who lacked a true faith in him was foretold in Isa. 8:14 and reiterated in I Pet. 2:8 and Rom. 9:33.

(b) Sternest warnings are uttered against those who provide snares by which the faith of young Christians receive a check (Matt. 18:6; Luke 17:1-2; Rom. 16:17). The exercise of the exquisite gift of Christian liberty must be controlled by consideration for the faith of beginners, lest by misunderstanding Christ's little ones should be injured (Rom. 14:20; II Cor. 6:3; I Cor. 8:13). Christ himself set the example (Matt. 17:27).

(c) In similar manner, Jesus warned his disciples against allowing anything to cause them to stumble. Things in themselves legitimate and gifts of God are to be ruthlessly excised, should they prove snares alienating from Christ (Matt. 18:8; I Cor. 6:12).

Christian liberty is subject to the needs of faith. All things are lawful, but not expedient if they snare the faith of others or ourselves. This is the scriptural basis of what is often condemned as narrow-minded Puritanism.

BIBLIOGRAPHY
HDB; HDCG; MM.
DAVID BROUGHTON KNOX

OFFER, OFFERING, OBLATION. The earliest biblical history records the presentation of sacrificial offerings to God. Offerings were presented by Cain and Abel (Gen. 4:3-4), Noah (Gen. 8:20), Job (1:5), and the patriarchs of Israel (Gen. 12:7; 26:25; 34:20). The term *mizbēaḥ*, "altar," indicates the place of *zebaḥ*, "sacrifice." Pre-Mosaic sacrifices are also known among the Canaanites and other peoples of the ancient world.

The law of the offerings was codified by Moses. In Lev. 1:1—7:38 five offerings were prescribed: (1) *'ōlāh*, "the burnt offering," in which the entire victim was consumed; (2) *minḥâ*, "the meal [AV "meat," RSV "cereal"] offering" of fine flour, a part of which was burned and the remainder eaten by the priests; (3) *š*ᵉ*lāmîm*, "the peace offering," from which the offerer received a portion to use as a thanksgiving meal; (4) *ḥaṭṭā't* "the sin offering," in which the carcass of the sacrificial victim was burned outside the camp; and (5) *'āšam*, "the trespass or guilt offering," in which a ram was prescribed as the required sacrifice and the offender was required to make recompense to the injured party plus a fine of one-fifth the amount of the trespass.

The NT describes the death of Christ as an offering (Eph. 5:2; Heb. 10:10, 14). Believers are exhorted to offer spiritual sacrifices (Rom. 12:1; Heb. 13:15-16; I Pet. 2:5).

See also SACRIFICE.
CHARLES F. PFEIFFER

OFFICES OF CHRIST. Since the days of Eusebius, most theologians have looked upon the mediatorial work of Christ as that of prophet, priest and king. All other christological offices such as advocate or intercessor fall under one of these three heads. Three OT passages point prophetically in this direction, thus assigning to Christ this threefold office, Deut. 18:15; Ps. 110:4; Zech. 6:13. Christ's assumption of this threefold office is to be eternal, since he must reign forever (Isa. 9:6-7) and he is to be priest "forever after the order of Melchisedec" (Heb. 6:20).

As prophet, Christ speaks the truth of God to men. This work includes both prediction and the telling forth of truth in general. Since he is the Truth, he is the infallible prophet. He was conscious of fulfilling this office (Mark 13:57). He has a divine commission in mediating as prophet (Isa. 61:1-3) demonstrated by his manner, message and the results of his teaching.

There is a close connection between Christ's work as prophet and priest. In the prophetic role, he often spoke of what he would accomplish as priest, and as our priest he secures for the believer what he proclaimed as prophet. The priest was one appointed to deal with God in behalf of men and in this work Christ had two chief duties to perform. He must bring a sacrifice and also make intercession. Unlike other priests, he is both the offerer and the offering. Both Leviticus and Hebrews must be studied to learn of Christ as priest.

As king (Ps. 2:6; Isa. 9:6-7; 11:1-9) Christ rules for God. This office relates most directly to Israel, though its exercise affects the world. As Lord, Christ rules his church even now. His kingship is secured and assured by divine covenants with Abraham (Gen. 12 and 17) and with David (II Sam. 7:8-17). His work as prophet is primarily in the past. His role as priest is both past, present and future while his work as king awaits for the most part future fulfilment.

See also CHRISTOLOGY.

BIBLIOGRAPHY
C. Hodge, *Systematic Theology*, Vol. II; L. S. Chafer, *Systematic Theology*, Vol. III; T. Dwight, *Theology*, Vol. II; J. P. Smith, *Atonement and Redemption*; J. J. Van Oosterzee, *Christian Dogmatics*, Vol. II.
HOWARD Z. CLEVELAND

OFFICES, ECCLESIASTICAL. I. ARCHBISHOP. One who presides over a "province" in the Church of England or the Roman Church. A province is a geographical area in which a number of dioceses are grouped together for administrative purposes: the bishop of the chief see or archdiocese is termed the Archbishop or Metropolitan. The term, derived from the Roman Empire, dates from *ca.* A.D. 350. (Derivations: Greek *archi*, "chief," and *episkopos*, "overseer, bishop".)

II. ARCHDEACON. A cleric who exercises

delegated administrative authority under a bishop. The duties are of a general disciplinary character; they also include a particular responsibility for the temporal property of the church. Originally, an archdeacon was the chief of the deacons who assisted the bishop (hence the name *oculus et manus episcopi*). The office has occasionally carried the right of succession.

III. ARCHPRIEST. The term describes a priest who occupies a position of pre-eminence, e.g., the senior priest of a city. An archpriest, in the Early Church, often performed liturgical and administrative duties during the absence of the bishop. At a later date the archdeacon was responsible for administrative functions, and the archpriest for sacerdotal. In the Roman Church and the Eastern the title is essentially an honorific one.

IV. CANON. A member of the chapter of a cathedral. Appointment is either by nomination or election. "Residentiary canons" form part of the salaried staff of a cathedral and have general responsibility for the maintenance of services, the care of the fabric, etc. "Non-residentiary" canons (or honorary canons) are unsalaried, but enjoy certain privileges, including a cathedral stall. The title derives from the fact that in the Middle Ages chapters were usually composed of clergy living under a rule (canon) of life.

V. CARDINAL. In the Roman Church the cardinals rank immediately after the pope, and, when assembled in consistory, act as his immediate counselors. When a vacancy occurs they meet in secret session to elect a pope. There are three ranks: cardinal-priests, cardinal-deacons, and cardinal-bishops. From 1586 to 1958 the number of cardinals was fixed at seventy. In 1958 Pope John XXIII increased the number to seventy-five.

VI. CURATE. Originally a clergyman who had the "cure" of souls; today a clergyman (either deacon or priest) who assists a parochial clergyman. Curate is the term popularly used to describe an assistant or unbeneficed clergyman.

VII. DEAN. The head of a cathedral church ranking immediately after the bishop. He presides over the chapter and is responsible for the ordering and government of the cathedral. The title is also used in a non-ecclesiastical sense, e.g., the dean of a college; the dean of a faculty, etc.

VIII. METROPOLITAN. The title of a bishop exercising provincial, and not merely diocesan, powers. The title first appears in the fourth canon of the Council of Nicaea (325). Metropolitans are commonly called archbishops or primates.

IX. MODERATOR. In the Presbyterian Church the moderator is the presbyter who presides over a presbytery, synod or General Assembly. He has only a casting vote. He is *primus inter pares* and holds office for a limited period (generally one year).

X. PATRIARCH. A title (dating from the sixth century) for the bishops of the five chief sees: Rome, Alexandria, Antioch, Constantinople, and Jerusalem.

XI. PREBENDARY. The occupant of a cathedral benefice. The title dates from the Middle Ages, when "prebends" were usually endowed from the revenue of various cathedral estates. The title has generally been superseded by that of "canon."

XII. RECTOR. Historically, a rector, as distinguished from a vicar, is a parish incumbent whose tithes are not impropriate. With the commutation of tithes this distinction no longer exists. The title is used in Scotland for the head of a school and in Europe for the secular head of a university. It is also the title for the head of a Jesuit house.

XIII. RURAL DEAN. The title for the clergyman who is appointed by a bishop as head of a group of parishes. The rural dean acts as a link between the bishop and the clergy, but his functions have been increasingly overshadowed and superseded by those of the archdeacon.

XIV. SUFFRAGAN BISHOP. The word suffragan derives from the Latin *suffragor* ("to vote for" or "support"), and may be applied to bishops in two main senses. First, all diocesan bishops are suffragans when they join with the archbishop or metropolitan in synod and cast their "suffrage." Second, and more generally, assistants to diocesan bishops are described as suffragans. The use of the term in England dates from the early Middle Ages, but the most striking instance of the creation of assistants is found in the Reformation period (A.D. 1534) when many new suffragans were instituted with definite titles (e.g., Dover).

XV. SUPERINTENDENT. In the Church of Scotland superintendents were first appointed under the *First Book of Discipline* (1560) to oversee various territorial districts. While enjoying a certain measure of superiority, they are subject to the control and censure of the other ministers associated with them. In the Lutheran Church there are also superintendents, but in the Scandinavian churches the title "bishop" is retained. The term is also found in some Methodist churches.

XVI. VICAR. In medieval times, when a church was appropriated to a monastery, the revenue was paid to the monastery, and a monk was employed to perform the duties of the parish. Later, a secular priest, called a vicar (Lat. *vicarius*, "a substitute") was employed. Today, the vicar is simply the incumbent of a parish with the same status and duties as a rector.

STUART BARTON BABBAGE

OLD CATHOLICS. Papal condemnation of Jansenism (*q.v.*) and refusal to let a Dutch archbishop be chosen locally drove some Dutch Catholics from Rome. In 1723 a deposed missionary bishop consecrated Cornelius Steenoven as Archbishop of Utrecht, with suffragans at Haarlem and Deventer. Germans, Austrians and Swiss who repudiated the Vatican Council of 1870, together with small Slavonic groups, augmented this Old Catholic body whose doctrine, formulated in the "Declaration of Utrecht" (1889), accepts the first seven ecumenical councils, but rejects papal infallibility and the immaculate conception. With vernacular services and married clergy, since 1932 they have been in full communion with the Church of England.

BIBLIOGRAPHY
C. B. Moss, *The Old Catholic Movement.*

G. S. M. WALKER

OLD TESTAMENT. See CRITICISM, OLD TESTAMENT.

OMNIPOTENCE. See GOD, ATTRIBUTES.

OMNIPRESENCE. See GOD, ATTRIBUTES.

OMNISCIENCE. See GOD, KNOWLEDGE.

ONENESS. See UNITY.

ONLY BEGOTTEN. The word *monogenēs* occurs nine times in the NT: referring to Isaac (Heb. 11:17), the widow's son (Luke 7:12), Jairus' daughter (Luke 8:42), the

demoniac boy (Luke 9:38), and Jesus Christ (John 1:14, 18; 3:16, 18; I John 4:9). In the LXX it is used to render *yahid*, meaning "only one" (Judg. 11:34, e.g.). Wisdom is *monogenēs* (Wisd. 7:22), having no peer, unique.

The second half of the word is not derived from *gennān*, "to beget," but is an adjectival form derived from *genos*, "origin, race, stock," etc. *Monogenēs*, therefore, could be rendered, "one of a kind." The translation "only" will suffice for the references in Luke and Hebrews. But what about the passages in the Johannine writings? "The adjective 'only begotten' conveys the idea, not of derivation and subordination, but of uniqueness and consubstantiality: Jesus is all that God is, and He alone is this" (B. B. Warfield, *Biblical Doctrines*, Oxford University Press, New York, 1929, p. 194). Cremer finds a parallel in the Pauline *idios huios* (Rom. 8:32). Since the Synoptists use "beloved" (*agapētos*) of the Son, some have concluded that the two words *agapētos* and *monogenēs* are equivalent in force. But "beloved" does not point to the uniqueness of the Son's relation to the Father as *monogenēs* does.

Though the translation "only" is lexically sound for the Johannine passages, since in all strictness "only begotten" would require *monogennētos*, the old rendering "only begotten" is not entirely without justification when the context in 1:14 is considered. The verb *gennāsthai* occurs at the end of 1:13 ("born of God") and *ginesthai* in 1:14. These words ultimately go back to the same root as the second half of *monogenēs*. Especially important is I John 5:18, where the second "born of God" must refer to Christ according to the superior Greek text. As a sample of patristic interpretation, see Justin Martyr, *Dialogue with Trypho* 105. At the very least it is clear that the relationship expressed by *monogenēs* is not confined to the earthly life so as to be adaptable to an adoptionist Christology. The sonship in John is linked to pre-existence (17:5, 24 and the many references to the Son as sent of the Father).

In its significance *monogenēs* relates to the several areas: (1) being or nature (uniquely God's Son), (2) the revelation of God to man (John 1:18), (3) salvation through the Son (John 3:16; I John 4:9).

The Apostles' Creed is content with "only Son," which is the usual form of the Old

Roman Symbol. In the Old Latin Version of the NT *monogenēs* was rendered by *unicus,* but in the Vulgate it became *unigenitus* due to the influence upon Jerome of the Nicene Christological formulation.

BIBLIOGRAPHY

Arndt; W. Bauer, *HZNT* (John 1:14); Buechsel in *TWNT; MM;* Dale Moody, *JBL* 72, 213-19, B. F. Westcott, *Epistles of John,* pp. 169-72; G. Vos, *The Self-Disclosure of Jesus,* pp. 213-27.

EVERETT F. HARRISON

OPHITES. See GNOSTICISM.

OPUS OPERATUM. The term is used in connection with sacramental theology, particularly that of unreformed Christendom. With the cognate term *ex opere operato,* it sums up the view that the benefit of a sacrament avails "by virtue of the work wrought." As first given by Duns Scotus (d. 1308), it was meant to emphasize the grace of God without the deservings of inward goodness in the communicant, so long as no bar was placed within. Gabriel Biel (d. 1495) developed the term to suggest mechanical efficacy of sacraments by virtue of the proper liturgical action by celebrant and receiver. After the Council of Trent incorporated the term into Canon 8 *de Sacramentis* it became authoritative Roman doctrine. There have been admissions made, however, especially after the controversy of Bishop Jewel with Harding (1564-65). Cardinal Bellarmine (d. 1621), for example, accepted the need of faith and repentance instead of a purely passive attitude. Nevertheless, he added that it is "the external act called sacrament, and this is called *opus operatum*" which "actively, proximately, and instrumentally" affects the passive recipient; "it confers grace by virtue of the sacramental act itself, instituted by God for this purpose." The view thus rejects all suggestion of dependence not only on the minister (*ex opere operantis*) but also on the receiver. So much is grace and rite conjoined that the due administration of the latter must necessarily involve the former.

BIBLIOGRAPHY

Duns Scotus; *Quaestiones in Lib. IV. Sententiarum, distinctio i, quaestio vi,* sec. 10; Bellarmine, *De Sacramentis, lib. ii,* chap. 1.

GEORGE J. C. MARCHANT

ORACLES. See LOGIA.

ORDAIN, ORDINATION. The NT has no technical terms which describe admission to ministerial office. Furthermore, office and function are so blurred that it is more correct to speak of acquisition of ministerial function. Three methods of such acquisition are in evidence. First, the Twelve (John 15:16) and Paul (Gal. 1:1) acquire their ministry directly from Jesus Christ. No indication is given of any ceremony. The incident reported in Acts 13 is not Paul's ordination but a commissioning service of men already chosen. Second, there is some evidence of spontaneous assumption of certain functions. The lists of spiritual gifts in I Cor. 12 and Rom. 12 indicate that members of the church are empowered for different tasks without any distinct call or ceremony. Furthermore, Stephanas and his household (I Cor. 16:15, 16) voluntarily assume certain responsibilities. In some communities at least the first converts were active in the leadership of the church. Clement of Rome (I Clement 42) confirms this function of the first fruits, but his statement of a systematic apostolic appointment of such converts goes beyond the evidence of the NT. Third, the Seven (Acts 6:6) and Timothy (I Tim. 4:14; II Tim. 1:6) are admitted to ministerial function by a public ceremony, the chief features of which are prayer and imposition of hands. With reference to the Seven, it is debatable whether anything more than recognition of authority is meant, but the language used in Timothy's case indicates impartation of spiritual power. Through imposition of hands he received a charisma which could fall into disuse. Lohse insists that the key for understanding NT ordination lies in recognition of its prototype, the ordination of scribes by their teachers, in which imposition of hands indicated not only recognition of authority but impartation of a spirit of wisdom. The rite was taken over by the Christian community to denote the same things in relation to the minister of the word. Lohse's view should be balanced by that of Easton who concludes that elders were the only ordained Jewish officials in NT times.

The above picture of admission to ministerial function provides the materials for the modern debate concerning ordination that "begins at the point at which we set about to determine through what precise human channels the Divine sanction and (in a less degree) the Divine enabling should be conveyed" (W. Sanday, *The Conception of Priesthood in the Early Church,* Longmans Green, London, 1899, p. 69).

BIBLIOGRAPHY
B. S. Easton, "Jewish and Early Christian Ordina-
tion," *AThR* 5; 308-19; 6; 285-95; E. Lohse, *Die
Ordination im Spaetjudentum und im Neuen Testament.*

CHARLES A. HODGMAN

ORDERS, HOLY. Holy Orders usually
refers to the major orders of the ministry in
an episcopal church. In the Anglican and the
Orthodox churches these are the bishops,
priests and deacons. In the Roman Church,
where the episcopate and the presbyterate are
counted as one order, the three are bishop-
priests, deacons and subdeacons. The minor
orders are not usually included in the term
"Holy Orders," for they really refer to laymen
set apart for special tasks rather than to clergy
in the proper sense of the term. Admission to
holy orders is by ordination, the important
ceremony being the laying on of hands. It is
this which distinguishes ordination to the
major orders from that to the minor orders. In
the former the minister of ordination is always
the bishop (though certain exceptions appear
to have occurred occasionally), but the minor
orders may sometimes be conveyed by others.
Unlike Roman Catholics and the Orthodox,
Anglicans do not officially regard ordination
as a sacrament (though some Anglicans do in
point of fact hold this view). The official
formularies restrict sacraments (*q.v.*) to ordinances instituted by Christ. Since there is no
conclusive evidence that he enjoined ordination, it is not properly a sacrament. It would
naturally be expected that a man cannot receive orders outside the church; but, especially
in the West, it is usually held that a validly
consecrated bishop conveys valid orders, even
though he be in heresy or schism. On this
principle the Roman Church does not re-
ordain those it receives from Orthodoxy.

LEON MORRIS

ORDERS, MINOR. The minor orders are
those orders of ministry below the major
orders in the Roman and Orthodox churches.
In the former, subdeacons were usually reckoned as a minor order until they were officially classed as a major order in 1207. The
minor orders since then are acolytes, exorcists,
readers and doorkeepers. In the Eastern
Church acolytes, exorcists and doorkeepers
have been merged with the subdiaconate, but
readers and cantors remain. The functions of
the acolyte were lighting the candles, carrying
them in procession, preparing the water and

wine for the Holy Communion, and generally
assisting the higher orders. The exorcist originally was concerned with casting out demons.
Later he looked after the catechumens. The
reader, as his name denotes, read from the
Scriptures. The doorkeeper originally had the
duty of excluding unauthorized persons. Now-
adays practically nothing of the functions of
any of the minor orders survives. They are
little more than a stepping stone to the higher
orders, and are all conferred at the one time.
They are conferred usually by the bishop
(though others on occasion may do so). There
is no laying on of hands, but some symbol of
office is delivered, e.g., a candlestick for the
acolyte, a key for the doorkeeper.

LEON MORRIS

ORDINANCE. In the OT this word generally represents *ḥōq* and *ḥuqqâ*, "something
prescribed." A more frequent alternative translation is "statute." The common application of
these words is the ritual prescribed by God,
but they are also applied to what would now
be called the laws of nature (Jer. 33:25), as
well as to the principles of moral conduct. In
Ps. 2:7 it is the pre-temporal decree of salvation that is referred to. God is thought of as
the One who prescribes the ordinance or
statute.

Another important Hebrew word translated
"ordinance" is *mišpāṭ,* a judgment given as a
precedent to prescribe behavior. Again, it is
God who is thought of as the One ultimately
annunciating the judgment.

In the NT ordinance is used to translate
five different Greek words, *dikaiōma*, "that
which is declared right," especially ceremonial
regulations; *ktisis*, "institution," that which is
set up; *diatagē*, "arrangement"; *dogma*, "an
edict"; *paradosis*, "tradition." Sometimes men
and sometimes God are thought of as the
source of these ordinances.

DAVID BROUGHTON KNOX

ORDO SALUTIS. This phrase appears to
have been brought into theological usage in
1737 by Jakob Karpov, a Lutheran. But the
doctrine of an *ordo salutis* ("order of salvation") is of much greater antiquity. Necessarily, there is a wide divergence between the
Roman Catholic and the Reformed view in
this connection, for although they both agree
that there can be no salvation apart from the
work of Jesus Christ, the Roman Catholic

Church teaches that she herself is the divinely appointed dispenser of saving grace through the sacraments, which, of themselves, convey grace to the recipients. The stages of Rome's *ordo salutis* may be taken as marked by her sacraments of (a) Baptism, in which the soul is regenerated; (b) Confirmation, in which baptized persons receive the gift of the Holy Ghost; (c) the Eucharist, in which they partake of the very body and blood of Christ in the transubstantiated wafer; (d) Penance, by which the benefit of Christ's death is applied to those who have fallen after baptism; and (e) Extreme Unction, which prepares the recipient for death and cleanses him from the remains of sin.

Luther's *ordo salutis* consisted simply in repentance, faith, and good works; but the Lutheran order was elaborated by later theologians into something closely resembling the Reformed order. It rests, however, upon the assumption that Christ's death on the cross was intended to save all men, and that grace is resistible.

The Reformed *ordo salutis* may be found in outline in Calvin's *Institutes*, III; but again, this order has been further elaborated by later Reformed theologians. In the Reformed view, the application of the redemption wrought by Christ on the cross is an activity of the Holy Spirit, and is to be traced in a series of acts and processes until perfect blessedness is reached. The Reformed order may be taken as (a) Effectual Calling, issuing in (b) Regeneration, (c) Faith, leading to (d) Justification, and (e) Sanctification, ultimately resulting in (f) Glorification. Some of these experiences are synchronous, however, and the stages in such cases must be regarded as of logical rather than of chronological sequence.

BIBLIOGRAPHY
    H. Kuiper, *By Grace Alone;* J. Murray, *Redemption Accomplished and Applied.*

GEORGE N. M. COLLINS

ORIGENISM. Origen (A.D. 185-253) was an outstanding Christian teacher. At the age of seventeen he became head of the catechetical school at Alexandria. Here he taught till A.D. 231 when as a result of the displeasure of Demetrius, Bishop of Alexandria, aroused through Origen's ordination in Palestine without Demetrius' permission, he left Egypt for Caesarea, where he taught until his death.

This was hastened through tortures he suffered during the Decian persecution.

Origen was a voluminous writer. He wrote on textual, exegetical, homiletical, theological, devotional and apologetic subjects. Most of his writings have perished on account of synodical condemnation 300 years after his death. The most famous that survives are *On First Principles* and *Against Celsus.*

Along with a strong sense of churchmanship and the authority of church tradition Origen had a profound respect for the authority of Scripture; but he valued the mystical meaning more highly than the literal. By allegorical interpretation he was able to vindicate the OT from the attacks and ridicule of the Gnostics. His historical sense was weak, nor did he use the concept of the progress of revelation to reconcile the Old Testament and the New.

On matters left undecided by Scripture Origen felt free to philosophize. He taught that souls pre-existed, and that the world was created to purge them from sins committed before birth. Our bodies of flesh are part of this purgatory. However, he denied transmigration of souls. Origen believed strongly in the absolute freedom of the will, and without some such theory of pre-existence the inequalities of life seemed to him unfair. He taught also that all souls would ultimately be saved as a result of God's discipline. He believed that Christ's death had a twofold object, victory over the devil and revelation of God's character. Redemption was through education and he drew no distinction between intellectual and moral progress. Substitutionary atonement was alien to his thought.

Origen destroyed Gnosticism and gave philosophy a recognized place in Christian theology.

See also ALEXANDRIA, SCHOOL OF.

BIBLIOGRAPHY
    B. F. Westcott, "Origenes" in *DCB;* W. R. Inge, "Alexandrian Theology" in *HERE;* C. Bigg, *Christian Platonists of Alexandria;* A. Harnack, *History of Dogma;* E. De Faye, *Origen and his Work.*

DAVID BROUGHTON KNOX

ORIGINAL SIN. See SIN.

ORTHODOXY. The English equivalent of Greek *orthodoxia* (from *orthos,* "right," and *doxa,* "opinion"), meaning right belief, as opposed to heresy or heterodoxy. The term is not biblical; no secular or Christian writer uses it before the second century, though the verb *orthodoxein* is in Aristotle (*Eth. Nic.* 1151a19). The word expresses the idea that certain statements accurately embody the revealed truth-content of Christianity, and are therefore in their own nature normative for the universal church. This idea is rooted in the NT insistence that the gospel (*q.v.*) has a specific factual and theological content (I Cor. 15:1-11; Gal. 1:6-9; I Tim. 6:3; II Tim. 4:3-4; etc.), and that no fellowship exists between those who accept the apostolic standard of christological teaching and those who deny it (I John 4:1-3; II John 7-11).

The idea of orthodoxy became important in the church in and after the second century, through conflict first with Gnosticism and then with other trinitarian and christological errors. The preservation of Christianity (*q.v.*) was seen to require the maintenance of orthodoxy in these matters. Strict acceptance of the "rule of faith" (*regula fidei*) was demanded as a condition of communion, and creeds explicating this "rule" were multiplied.

The Eastern Church styles itself "orthodox," and condemns the Western Church as heterodox for (among other things) including the *filioque* clause in its creed.

Seventeenth-century Protestant theologians, especially conservative Lutherans, stressed the importance of orthodoxy in relation to the soteriology of the Reformation creeds. Liberal Protestantism naturally regards any quest for orthodoxy as misguided and deadening.

JAMES I. PACKER

OVERCOME. The Christian idea of overcoming has its basis in the declaration of Jesus that he had overcome the world (John 16:33). The word "world" in this context is to be understood to denote all in the world which is antagonistic to the will of God. A Stronger has come and disarmed these antagonistic forces (Luke 11:22) with the result that the Christian need fear them no longer.

This overcoming is described in two ways in I John. Believers are said to overcome (a) the wicked one (2:13, 14) and those in whom the spirit of antichrist breathes (4:4), and (b) the world (5:4, 5). In the latter sense the "overcomers" show their genuineness by their attitude towards Jesus as Son of God, thus stressing that moral victory is inseparably linked with soundness of doctrine.

The believer must use good as a means of overcoming evil (Rom. 12:21), and his attitude towards his circumstances should be that of a super-conqueror (Rom. 8:37). In the Apocalypse those who endure persecutions and resist false teachers are described as "overcomers" (2:7, 11, 17, 26; 3:5, 12, 21), and the promises of the future are reserved only for these (21:7). The central figure of the book, the slain but royal Lamb, presents the same paradox. As Lion of the tribe of Judah he prevails to open the book (5:5), and as the Lamb he will finally overcome all his enemies (17:14). This power to overcome is in contrast with the temporary power given to the Beast (13:7).

DONALD GUTHRIE

OVERSEER. See MINISTER.

OXFORD MOVEMENT. See TRACTARIANISM.

P

PAGANISM. A term used in several senses with a chronological change of meaning. It has been used to describe the religious and ethical systems of the pre-Christian era, particularly those of classical culture. In this sense it describes the religious and moral aspirations of those who lived before the coming of Jesus Christ into the world and who were not guilty of rejecting him as Lord and Saviour. Thus it concerns the various conceptions of deity and religion, and the general religious outlook found in the philosophies of such Greek and Roman thinkers as Socrates, Plato and Aristotle, Cicero and Seneca.

In a second sense the term paganism is used to describe the religious, moral and philosophical outlook of those who have heard the gospel and who have rejected the biblical offer of salvation in favor of some other form of religious or philosophical system. In this sense it is often used synonymously with materialism, humanism, hedonism, or existentialism. This modern paganism is not the result of an ignorance of the gospel message, but rather of a deep-seated hatred for Christianity (*q.v.*), and it seeks to interpret all of life in terms of non-Christian principles. It is a frank repudiation of the Scriptures and the gospel message and a deliberate attempt to construct a world and life view on some other basis in which man is the focus of attention. In this sense of the term it is often applied to many aspects of American life and western culture in general.

It is used in a third sense to describe the religious and moral state of those civilized and uncivilized people of the present day who have not yet been evangelized and who are living in the darkness of unbelief, superstition and idolatry, and the hardness of their hearts.

BIBLIOGRAPHY
Ralph Stob, *Christianity and Classical Civilization*; Charles Norris Cochrane, *Christianity and Classical Culture*; John Herman Bavinck, *The Impact of Christianity on the Non-Christian World*.

GREGG SINGER

PAIN. A special sense, independent of touch, possessing its own receptors embedded deep in the skin. Its function is protective; owing to its destruction in leprosy, fingers and toes are often lost through accidents.

The quality of pain is profoundly affected by its passage through the brain. Sensitivity to pain depends much on memory and anticipation. Drugs such as morphine function by removing anxiety, not pain. Pain is not felt in times of emotional stress when it would fail to serve a useful purpose.

On relatively very rare occasions pain fails to warn of disease or danger, or is felt acutely when not beneficial. In this as in other ways man's constitution is not perfect; he is subject to "vanity" (i.e., *pointlessness* or *futility*, RSV. See Ecclesiastes and Rom. 8:20).

Pain may ennoble (e.g., Acts 5:41) or embitter. The Christian should think of it, not primarily as the result of sin, but as an opportunity for God to show his power (cf. John 9:2) by giving victory over resentment, frustration, disappointment, etc.

BIBLIOGRAPHY
V. C. Medvei, *The Mental and Physical Effects of Pain*; *Disabilities and how to live with them*; T. J. Hardy, *The Gospel of Pain* and *The Voice from the Valley*.

R. E. D. CLARK

PANTHEISM. The word comes from the Greek *pan*, "all"; *theos*, "god." It denotes the religious belief or philosophical view which identifies the universe with God. The term was first used by the English deist, John Toland (1670-1722), in his tract, "Socinianism Truly Stated" (1705), and developed into his famous statement, "God is the mind or soul of the Universe," in his book, *Pantheism* (1720). The idea goes back to monistic philosophies of India but flows through the Christian writings of Dionysius the Areopagite, John Scotus Erigena, and the German mystics, especially Eckhart.

In contemporary theology it usually takes the form of an attack upon the personality of God, maintaining that God is "supra-personal." Admittedly, God is infinitely beyond any idea or term which men may use of him, but the God of the Bible is not to be identified with his creation — he is the Creator of the ends of the earth. The term "personality" may be inadequate, but it points in the right direction: God is not less than personal.

Under the impact of contemporary science, the most critical point for the Christian theist is the danger of identifying God with some causal process or atomic theory, without maintaining the biblical distinction between the personal Creator-God and the natural orders of creation which he always controls.

See also CREATION, GOD.

BIBLIOGRAPHY
J. Laird, *Mind and Deity*; C. S. Lewis, *Beyond Personality*; C. E. Plumtre, *General Sketch of the History of Pantheism*; Wolf, *Moderner Pantheismus und christliche Theismus*.

WAYNE E. WARD

PAPACY. See POPE.

PARABLE. In the parables of the Bible, the attention of the hearer or observer is drawn to some event or events in the familiar sphere of life in this world, in order that, by taking heed and making comparison and judgment, they may be faced with the reality and challenge of their situation in the face of God's present and coming kingdom.

In the OT this form of utterance is the *māšāl*, frequently translated as *parabolē* in the LXX.

A *māšāl* is the means of drawing men's attention to the presence and purpose of God in their midst and to the critical nature of their situation. A *māšāl* can be given by means of a story (Ezek. 17:2-10) or an action (Ezek. 24:3-14; 20:45-49) or by pointing to some human example (Job 17:6; Ps. 44:14 where *māšāl* is translated "byword"). A *māšāl* can also be a short saying in the form of a popular proverb implying a judgment on a person or situation (I Sam. 10:12; 24:13-14), or a word of wisdom, as in the book of Proverbs, involving a comparison between the familiar in daily life and the decisions men must make before God (Prov. 1:1; 10:1; 25:1). It can also be a prophetic utterance drawing attention to the reversal of human affairs brought about by God's judgment, and inviting men to revise their own judgments (Mic. 2:4; Isa. 14:4; Hab. 2:6; Num. 24:20-24). The stories of II Sam. 12:1-4 and II Kings 14:9, though not called *mešālīm*, have nevertheless the characteristics of the true OT parable.

The utterance of a parable in the OT is linked up with the riddle or "dark saying" indicating that the hidden meaning and intention of the parable can escape the superficial hearer or observer (Pss. 49:4; 78:2; Prov. 1:6 [LXX]; Ezek. 17:2; 20:4-9).

The sayings and stories of Jesus described as his "parables" in the NT likewise vary from the short paradoxical utterance (Mark 7:17), the proverb (Luke 4:23), the allegory with a hidden meaning (Matt. 13:3-9), the elaborate similitude (Mark 4:30-32), the short (Matt. 13:33) or longer story (Matt. 21:33-41), the story with the obvious "moral" (Luke 12:6-21). Many similar short sayings or full length stories are commonly classified as parables without being described as such in the Gospels (e.g., Mark 9:50; Luke 10:30-37).

The contents of the parables are drawn from nature, from the social, political and domestic life of the time, possibly from current stories or contemporary events. Often the parables are true to life. Sometimes there are elements of practical improbability in the story.

The main theme in the parables of Jesus is the significance of his own ministry and work amongst men (Matt. 21:33-41). In the parables Jesus proclaims to his hearers that the kingdom of God is in their midst in his own person, and is sown in the midst of this world's life through his word (Matt. 13:3-9; 18-23) so that men can enter it by receiving his word. Its growth is spontaneous and inevitable (Mark 4:26-29; Matt. 13:24-30). Its final manifestation will be his own coming again in glory (Matt. 25:31-36). But men must decide here and now in face of the hiddenness of the kingdom (*q.v.*). Men can receive it, enter it here and now with joy and repentance, or reject it (Mark 2:19, 21 f.; 3:27; Luke 14:15-24; Matt. 13:44-46, 47-50). Its presence from henceforth will affect the whole of life and history (Matt. 13:24-30, 33). There are also parables dealing with the grace of God manifested in the coming nigh of the kingdom (Matt. 7:9-11; 18:12-14; Luke 15:11-32). Others have reference to the kind of response called for from men (Luke 16:1-8; 17:7-10; 7:36-50; Matt. 5:4-16; 25:14-30, etc.).

Though there are allegorical elements in the parables, they have nevertheless to be distinguished from allegories for the purpose of their interpretation. An allegory is an ingenious and often involved narration of an artificial event or story in which all the individual details and features and the relations between them are determined not so much by what happens in everyday life, but rather by the realities they point to and the detailed message they are meant ultimately to convey (cf. Rom. 11:16-24 and Bunyan's *Pilgrim's Progress*). Thus in an allegory there need be no attempt to be true to life. A parable, however, is constructed so as to present to the hearer a real, familiar life situation in which he can make a judgment often about one main point, and by this judgment on the total impression made by the parable he can be led to understand the one main message which the parable was designed to convey to him (cf. II Sam. 12:1-6). The parables of the Old and New Testaments however (as indeed those of Greece and Judaism) are often mixed with allegorical elements and have features which can legitimately be interpreted allegorically as long as the main message of the parable remains clear. There seems to be no reason, for example, why we should not try to interpret the significance of the lamps and the oil in the parable of the Wise and Foolish Virgins (Matt. 25:1-13), though we must avoid treating the parables as if they were allegories in structure and intention — as has been done too often in the history of the church.

Jesus' teaching in parables is an aspect of the revelation of the "mystery of the kingdom of God" (Mark 4:11). Like the sacraments, and indeed the whole revelation of God in Christ, the parables veil hidden things which are meant to be revealed to those who will penetrate by faith behind the outward form of revelation to grasp the hidden yet present divine reality. Therefore Jesus speaks in parables so that "those within" can know this mystery. The purpose of Jesus in the parables is to reveal and not to hide the mystery (cf. Luke 18:16-18; Mark 4:33). But the mystery is grasped and the kingdom is seen not by the power of human reason but only by the Holy Spirit (John 3:3-6). Therefore the effect of the parables may be to blind the understanding — especially if men go no further than deducing merely a general truth or a moral lesson from a word that is meant to convert their hearts. Thus they may "see" and not "perceive" (Mark 4:12). The possibility of this twofold effect is such an essential part of the revelation of the "mystery" in parable, proclamation, sacrament, and miracle that the revelation may be spoken of as having not only the result, but also the purpose of making blind.

BIBLIOGRAPHY

A. S. Herbert, *The Parable in the Old Testament,* *SJT* 7:180 ff.; T. F. Torrance, "A Study in New Testament Communication," *SJT* 3, 298 ff.; C. H. Dodd, *The Parables of the Kingdom;* J. Jeremias, *The Parables of Jesus;* F. Hauck, *TWNT;* R. C. Trench, *Notes on the Parables;* A. B. Bruce, *The Parabolic Teaching of Christ.*

RONALD S. WALLACE

PARACLETE. See SPIRIT, HOLY.

PARADISE.
A word of Persian origin, probably, appearing as *pardēs* in the OT three times ("orchard," S. of Sol. 4:13, ASV; "forest," Neh. 2:8, ASV; "parks," Eccl. 2:5). The Greek word *paradeisos* is found from the time of Xenophon, appearing in the papyri, inscriptions, LXX (27 occurrences, some of which refer to Eden, e.g., Gen. 2:8, 9, 10, 15, 16), Philo, and Josephus. The NT employs *paradeisos* three times, to denote the place of blessedness promised to the thief (Luke 23:43), the third heaven (II Cor. 12:4), and the location of the promised tree of life (Rev. 2:7).

Since the paradise of Eden was the place of bliss man had lost, rabbinical literature used the term to portray the place of blessedness for the righteous dead, in contrast to Gehenna, the place of torment. Elaborate and highly imaginative descriptions were drawn. See *JewEnc* for examples.

Jesus used the term once (Luke 23:43), and some see here only a reference to heaven. However, Jesus may be exhibiting essential agreement with traditional Jewish opinion by employing "Abraham's bosom" as an alternate term for "paradise" in Luke 16:22. Then paradise as the abode of the righteous is viewed as a separate section of Hades (a term equivalent to Sheol, Ps. 16:10; cf. Acts 2:27, 31). Because the remaining references to paradise in the NT are to heaven, some have concluded that since the resurrection and ascension of Christ, paradise has been removed from Hades to the third heaven, and that the "host of captives" who ascended with Christ were the OT saints (Eph. 4:8, RSV).

If paradise means heaven as the dwelling place of God in all NT instances, then the choice of the term "Abraham's bosom" may have been deliberate. Then Jesus promised to the thief the bliss of heaven on that very day, which prospect belongs to all Christian believers (Luke 23:43; Phil. 1:23; II Cor. 5:8).

See also INTERMEDIATE STATE.

BIBLIOGRAPHY

Alf, I, pp. 661-62; Arndt; Chafer, *Systematic Theology,* VII, pp. 247-48; *HDB; IB; ISBE; JewEnc;* MM.

HOMER A. KENT, JR.

PARADOX.
A paradox is (1) an assertion which is self-contradictory, or (2) two or more assertions which are mutually contradictory, or (3) an assertion which contradicts some very commonly held position on the matter in question.

Paradoxes may be either rhetorical or logical. A rhetorical paradox is a figure used to shed light on a topic by challenging the reason of another and thus startling him. The NT contains many effective examples of this use of the paradox (e.g., Matt. 5:39; 10:39; John 11:24; II Cor. 6:9-10).

Logical paradoxes arise from the attempt by the human mind to unify or to coordinate the multiple facets of experience. Because of the diversity and complexity of reality and also because of the limitations of finite and sinful human reason, man's best efforts to know reality bring him only to the production of equally reasonable (or apparently so) yet unreconcilable truths (or apparently so). In such cases man may be nearer the truth when he espouses both sides of a paradoxical issue rather than when he gives up one side in favor of the other.

Two differing interpretations of the logical paradox have emerged in the history of the church. One asserts actual paradoxes in which what is really true also really contradicts a right application of the laws of human thought. The other holds that paradoxical assertions are only apparent contradictions. Often this difference resolves itself into a mere difference of psychological attitude. He who takes the first interpretation of the paradox is willing to find rest of mind with incoherent elements lying unresolved in his thinking. He who takes the second believes that all truth must make its peace with the laws of human thought such as the law of contradiction and, therefore, does not find mental rest in incoherencies.

Medieval thought was not uniform on the question of paradox but in its ultimate rejection of double truth seemed to veer away from an acceptance of actual paradoxes in favor of apparent paradoxes. Martin Luther's objection to the denial of double truth by the Sorbonne was in reality a defense of actual paradoxes.

In modern theology the concept of paradox has assumed a prominent role in the writing of Soeren Kierkegaard and his twentieth-century followers, Karl Barth, Reinhold Niebuhr, and others. The infinite, timeless, and hidden God can reach into finite time of human history through events which can be discerned only by faith and even then necessarily appear as logical paradoxes.

For theists of any period, of course, a paradoxical "setting aside" of the laws of logic is understood as provisional; a true synthesis is always to be found in the mind of God.

BIBLIOGRAPHY

E. J. Carnell, *A Philosophy of the Christian Religion*, pp. 469, 475; H. De Morgan, *A Budget of Paradoxes*; V. Ferm, ed., *Encyclopedia of Morals*, p. 409; HDB, p. 632; H. R. Mackintosh, *Types of Modern Theology*, pp. 266-68; Dagobert Runes, *Dictionary of Philosophy*.

KENNETH S. KANTZER

PARDON. See FORGIVENESS.

PARONOMASIA. Paronomasia is a type of pun, a rhetorical device whereby similar sounding words are juxtaposed or opposed in a word-play. Among the ancients it was an acceptable practice to arrange words in a clever fashion, but in modern times it has come under faint disapproval. Two kinds of paronomasia predominate: (1) a change in the sense

of a word by alteration of a letter, as in the Jews' nickname Epimanes (Madman) for Antiochus Epiphanes (Illustrious); (2) a play upon words which are similar either in sound or sense, as is seen in the title of J. Sharman's book *A Cursory History of Swearing*. Examples abound in both the Hebrew and Greek Bible. Isa. 5:7 reads:

... and he looked for judgment (mišpaṭ),
But behold, oppression (mišpāḥ);
For righteousness (ṣeḏāqâ),
But behold, a cry of distress (ṣeʿāqâ);

Many of the Psalms contain paronomasia, and Micah is known for them. Matt. 8:26 says "a great calm" *[galēnē megalē]* came over the sea. Paul is especially fond of this device; in Rom. 1:28 he says, "And as they 'refused' *[ouk edokimasan]* to have God in knowledge, God gave them up to a 'refuse' *[adokimon]* mind." And in Rom. 1:29 he speaks of *porneia* ("fornication") and *ponēria* ("wickedness"), *phthonou* ("envy") and *phonou* ("murder"). Often Paul rings the changes by prefixing prepositions to nouns and verbs as in II Cor. 3:2 and II Thess. 3:11. Paronomasia generally does not survive in translation, but Phil. 3:2, 3 preserves it in "concision . . . circumcision."

DAVID H. WALLACE

PAROUSIA. See ESCHATOLOGY, SECOND COMING OF CHRIST.

PASCHAL CONTROVERSY. The observance of Good Friday and Easter was natural in the early church, but the fixing of the date gave rise to many difficulties. Four main disputes may be discerned. First, it was argued by some that the *days* should always be kept, but in Asia Minor there was a strong school which favored the exact *date* (see QUARTO-DECIMANISM). Second, there was a difference between Antioch and Alexandria as to the mode of calculation, the former following the Jewish scheme but the latter working out independent tables. Third, a discrepancy arose between Rome and Alexandria, for, while it was agreed at Nicaea (A.D. 325) that the latter should determine a common rule, divergent cycles were still followed. Fourth, the churches in Gaul and Britain clung to the older Roman cycles when Rome officially adopted the Alexandrian pattern in A.D. 525, and it was only at Whitby that the matter was finally settled in Britain. A difficult point was involved in the first phase of the controversy, but the later stages were merely a matter of calculation and liaison (cf. *JTS*, 25, 254-70).

WILLIAM KELLY

PASSION. (From Latin *passio*, "a suffering," "enduring.") This word is primarily used of the endurance by a submissive victim of afflictions imposed upon him, and is equivalent to the Greek *pathēma*, from *paschō*, "I suffer," which the Vulgate renders by *passio* in Rom. 8:18; II Cor. 1:6-7; II Tim. 3:11; Heb. 10:32, and I Pet. 5:9. It is especially used of the sufferings of Christ. In Acts 1:3 the AV and ERV translate *to pathein* by "passion," and elsewhere (II Cor. 1:5; Phil. 3:10; Heb. 2:9-10; I Pet. 1:11; 4:13; 5:1) the Vulgate translates *pathēma* (and in Col. 1:24 *thlipsis*) by *passio*. This word was used by Latin ecclesiastical writers as early as the Muratorian Fragment, and "passion" appears in the earliest English litanies (1549 Prayer Book) of Christ's sufferings. *Passio* is used by the Vulgate to describe bodily affliction (Lev. 15:13, 25).

Passion also denotes inner emotional experiences; thus the AV translates *homoiopathēs* (Acts 14:15; James 5:17) "of like passions." The root connection here is with *pathos* (used in Rom. 1:26; I Thess. 4:5) which the Vulgate again renders by *passio*, as it also renders *pathēma* in this sense in Rom. 7:5 (see *Trench*, lxxxviii, and Lightfoot on Col. 3:5). Used in these last instances in the bad sense of "lusts," this idea of a strong emotion has become predominant in the modern use of the word.

BIBLIOGRAPHY
RTWB.

DAVID H. WHEATON

PASSOVER. Passover was the first of three annual festivals at which all men were required to appear at the sanctuary (Ex. 23:14-17). The noun *pesah* is derived from the verb *pāsah*, "to pass over," in the sense of "to spare" (Ex. 12:12-13). Passover is associated with the Feast of Unleavened Bread (*hag hammassōt*), the week during which leaven was rigidly excluded from the diet of the Hebrews (Ex. 23:15).

The historical Passover is related to the tenth plague — the death of the firstborn in Egypt. Israel was instructed to prepare a lamb for each household. Blood was to be applied to the lintel and doorpost (Ex. 12:7). The sign of the blood would secure the safety of each house so designated.

On the evening of the 14th of Nisan (Abib) the passover lambs were slain. After being roasted, they were eaten with unleavened bread and bitter herbs (Ex. 12:8), emphasizing the need for a hasty departure and reminiscent of the bitter bondage in Egypt (Deut. 16:3). The Passover was a family observance. In the case of small families, neighbors might be invited to share the paschal meal.

The initial instructions concerned the preparation for the historical exodus (Ex. 12:21-23). Subsequent directions were given for the observance of the seven-day Festival of Unleavened Bread (Ex. 13:3-10). The passover experience was to be repeated each year as a means of instruction to future generations (Ex. 12:24-27).

In subsequent years a passover ritual developed incorporating additional features. Four successive cups of wine mixed with water were used. Psalms 113 to 118 were sung at appropriate places. Fruit, mixed with vinegar to the consistency of mortar, served as a reminder of the mortar used during the bondage.

The first and seventh days of the week were observed as sabbaths. All work ceased and the people met in holy convocation (Ex. 12:16; Num. 28:18, 25). On the second day of the festival a sheaf of first-ripe barley was waved by the priest to consecrate the opening of harvest (Lev. 23:10-14). In addition to the regular sacrifices, two bullocks, one ram, and seven lambs were offered as a burnt offering, and a he-goat as a sin offering each day (Num. 28:19-23; Lev. 23:8).

Passover observances were frequently neglected in OT times. After Sinai (Num. 9:1-14) none took place until after the entrance into Canaan (Josh. 5:10). The reforming kings Hezekiah (II Chron. 30) and Josiah (II Kings 23:21-23; II Chron. 35) gave attention to passover observance. After the dedication of the second temple, a noteworthy Passover was celebrated (Ezra 6:19-22).

The death of Christ at the passover season was deemed significant by the early church. Paul calls Christ, "our passover" (I Cor. 5:7). The command not to break a bone of the paschal lamb (Ex. 12:46) is applied by John to the death of Christ — "A bone of him shall not be broken" (John 19:36). The Christian must put away the "old leaven" of malice and wickedness, and replace it with "the unleavened bread of sincerity and truth" (I Cor. 5:8).

BIBLIOGRAPHY

A. Edersheim, *The Temple: Its Ministry and Services;* W. H. Green, *The Hebrew Feasts in their Relation to Recent Critical Hypotheses;* T. H. Gaster, *Passover: Its History and Traditions;* S. M. Lehrman, *The Jewish Festivals;* John Lightfoot, *The Temple Service;* The Mishna (edited by H. Danby), tractate "Pesahim," pp. 136-51; R. Schaefer, *Das Passah-Mazzoth-Fest;* H. Schauss, *The Jewish Festivals,* pp. 86-95.

CHARLES F. PFEIFFER

PASTOR. See MINISTER, SPIRITUAL GIFTS.

PATIENCE. At least three Greek words must be included under this term, *hypomonē, makrothymia,* and *anochē.* They are biblical words, not found in classical Greek, and specifically Christian in their connotation. Patience is first characteristic of God. It is his longsuffering with evil and wickedness in man (Ex. 34:6; I Pet. 3:20). This quality leads to a quickening of man's own patience in the outworking of God's righteous purposes (Rom. 2:4; II Pet. 3:9, 15). There is sure hope in a future judgment by Christ Jesus. The divine wrath is suspended for a time to give men the opportunity to repent, and to obey the will of God.

Second, patience is cultivated by the saints (Rev. 13:10). The word is both passive and active in meaning. It has varying shades of emphasis. More than mere endurance is implied. It has been described as "masculine constancy under trial" (cf. I Macc. 8:4). It resembles the Roman persistency which would never make peace under defeat. It keeps a man on his feet with his face to the wind. It changes the hardest trial into glory because it enables a Christian to see the goal beyond the pain. He thus faces delay without depression, oppression without retaliation, and suffering without relenting. This virtue he has learned from God, who is patient with him in his weakness, failure, and sin (Col. 1:11).

Third, patience is commended in the Christian minister (cf. II Cor. 6:6; I Tim. 1:16; II Tim. 3:10; Titus 2:2). This grace, so prominent in Christ Jesus, must be reproduced in his servants.

RICHARD E. HIGGINSON

PATRIARCH. The *patriarchēs* is, by derivation, the father or chief of a family or tribe. The term is usually used of the ancestors of the Jewish nation before the time of Moses. It is used in the NT of Abraham (Heb. 7:4), the sons of Jacob (Acts 7:8-9), and David (Acts 2:29).

In contemporary usage the term is usually restricted to the fathers of the Israelite nation, Abraham, Isaac, Jacob, and Jacob's sons, notably Joseph. The patriarchal age of Israel's history is the subject of Gen. 12-50.

Although the patriarchs lived a semi-nomadic life they had a high culture. Abraham was a man of wealth who could muster a private army of 318 men to rescue his nephew Lot (Gen. 14:14) and engage in business transactions with Hittite landowners (Gen. 23:16). Cuneiform tablets discovered at Nuzu (since 1925) and Mari (since 1935) throw light on the social background of the patriarchal age. Biblical references to marriage, adoption, and birthright find their counterpart in the cuneiform literature.

See ABRAHAM, ISAAC, JACOB.

CHARLES F. PFEIFFER

PATRIARCH. See OFFICES, ECCLESIASTICAL.

PATRIARCHATE. The office or see of a Patriarch (a title confined in early Christian usage chiefly to the bishops of Alexandria, Antioch, Constantinople, Jerusalem and Rome), who normally held jurisdiction, defined by a General Council, over neighboring sees. In 1590, the Orthodox Patriarchs consented to the creation of the Patriarchate of Moscow.

M. R. W. FARRER

PATRIPASSIANISM. A form of modalistic monarchianism (*q.v.*) propagated about A.D. 200-50 by Noetus, Praxeas, and Beryllus of Bostra and answered by Hippolytus, Tertullian, and Origen in that order. Praxeas convinced Bishop Victor to outlaw Montanism and accept patripassianism which caused Tertullian to say that Praxeas had "put to flight the Paraclete; and crucified the Father."

Patripassianists (Latin *pater,* "father," and *passus,* from *patior,* "to suffer") with the modalists confused the persons of the Trinity and denied the union of the two natures in the one person of Christ. Defending monotheism they held that since God was one essence there could not be three persons but instead three modes of manifestation. Thus the Son was the Father appearing in human form. Noetus taught that Christ was the Father and so the Father was born, suffered and died upon the cross, hence the name patripassian.

BIBLIOGRAPHY

A. Harnack, *History of Dogma, Vol. III*; A. Harnack, "Monarchianism," in *SHERK*; J. L. Neve, *A History of Christian Thought, Vol. I*, pp. 106-12; J. Orr, *The Progress of Dogma*, pp. 87-98; J. W. C. Wand, *The Four Great Heresies*, pp. 13-38.

WILLIAM NIGEL KERR

PAUL AND PAULINISM. The apostle to the Gentiles appears in the Book of Acts as the founder of churches and in his letters as a devoted pastor, an adroit controversialist, and ardent friend of the saints, revealing a spirit kindled by the love of Christ. It is by means of his letters also that Paul has established himself as the leading theologian of the apostolic age.

I. EXPERIENCE. As a Jew of the Dispersion, born in Tarsus, Paul was unconsciously being prepared by his contacts with the gentile world for his role as a missionary of Christ around the Mediterranean basin. But the largest single influence upon his life in the formative years was his Hebraic environment, including his home training and his education under Gamaliel (Acts 22:3). This is evident from his extensive use of the OT and from his handling of the material, which reflects his rabbinic instruction. As a Pharisee, he strove valiantly to find righteousness through fidelity to the law, but the futility of the effort breathes through his teaching on the subject.

Paul's zeal as a persecutor must be traced to his conviction that the followers of Jesus were mistaken in identifying him with Israel's Messiah. Feelings of humanity were sternly repressed in order to do service to God by stamping out this heresy. But the personal appearance to him of the risen Lord was sufficient to convince him that the claims of the Christians were indeed true. Paul was apprehended by Christ (Phil. 3:12) and became thenceforth his faithful servant. The outward disclosure was followed by an inward revelation of God's Son (Gal. 1:16), wherein the gospel message became luminous (Gal. 1:12). The crucifixion, which was once a stumbling block to Paul, now constituted the ground of his boasting (Gal. 6:14). He was glad to acknowledge that in its essentials this gospel was identical with that of the Jerusalem apostles (I Cor. 15:3-11). Even the truth of the church as the body of Christ shared equally by Jew and Gentile was not disclosed to him alone (Eph. 3:4-6) although it was given special prominence in his teaching.

His mission to the gentile world brought upon him the opprobrium of non-Christian Jews (Acts 22:21-22) and of some Christian Jews as well (Acts 15:2; 21:20-21; Phil. 1:15-17). It is a mark of spiritual greatness that in spite of this opposition the apostle continued to pray and labor incessantly for the conversion of his own people Israel (Rom. 9:1-3; 10:1). In the controversy over the reception of Gentiles into the church, Paul affirmed that faith in Christ was sufficient of itself for their salvation. They must not be burdened with circumcision or the yoke of the Mosaic law. This position was grounded both on revelation and on experience, for Paul had seen many Gentiles saved and sealed with God's Spirit apart from circumcision. On the same twofold basis Peter was able to stand with Paul on this issue (Acts 10; 15:7-11). Paul's refusal to subject Gentiles to circumcision was not motivated by expediency, as though to smooth the way of the Gentiles to Christ by removing something they found objectionable. Rather, circumcision in such cases was a symbol of salvation by human works and therefore a denial of the gospel of grace (Gal. 5:2-4).

The apostle found the purity of the gospel threatened also in Colosse. Although the precise nature of this error is obscure, it seems to have been eclectic; at any rate it was damaging to the pre-eminence of Christ. It was as much a philosophy as a religion.

Other threats to the gospel appeared, such as the denial of the bodily resurrection of the saints (see I Cor. 15) and the tendency to antinomianism. This latter deviation arose from a misunderstanding or misinterpretation of the gospel of grace. Paul combatted the error in Romans and in the Pastoral Epistles (see also Phil. 3:18-19).

II. TEACHING. Considerable attention has been devoted to the effort to discover a central core in the Pauline message. Some have found it in the doctrine of justification (*q.v.*) by faith alone, apart from works. Others have claimed that union with the Lord Jesus, expressed in the oft-recurring phrase, "in Christ," is the very heart of Paul's thinking. Still others have esteemed his teaching on eschatology to be the dominant strain. These three are pivotal because they highlight the past, present, and future aspects of the salvation in Christ. They may be seen together in Phil. 3:9-11, where Paul describes himself as "found" in Christ, possessed of God's righteousness through faith in his Son, and living in anticipation of the resurrection, when every limitation will be removed.

On the practical side, the believer is under obligation to serve the flesh no longer, but in the power of the indwelling Spirit of God to experience that freedom wherein alone the regenerated man may serve God acceptably (Rom. 8:1-14). Through the Spirit the risen Son of God is able to possess each redeemed life and express himself through it (Gal. 2:20; 4:6; Rom. 13:14). Every saint is thus a new creation in which the glorious power of God is to be seen (II Cor. 5:17). The path to spiritual blessing and maturity consists in learning Christ and what belongs to the new nature (Eph. 4:20-24).

III. PAUL IN HISTORY AND CRITICISM. In the post-apostolic age the influence of the apostle waned, probably due to a natural human tendency to find the teaching of grace somewhat hard to believe and to substitute for it a comfortable mixture of faith and works. Marcion was devoted to Paul, but tortured his gospel by cutting its rootage in the OT. The spiritual revival which marked the Reformation was effected in no small degree by the recovery of the Pauline doctrine of justification by faith. Near the middle of the nineteenth century the Tuebingen School, headed by F. C. Baur, professed to find in the apostolic age a conflict between parties represented by Peter and Paul respectively. Baur made the former the spokesman for the legalistic point of view, the latter for the universalistic position. Baur failed to realize that the struggle was between Peter, Paul and other leaders, on the one side, and Judaizing, legalistic teachers, on the other side. At the close of the century the so-called Dutch School brushed Paul aside entirely, denying to him all the epistles which bear his name. The Liberal School of Harnack and others applauded Paul for having grounded his religious experience squarely upon the historical Jesus, but excoriated him for erecting a theology in which Christ became the necessary object of faith instead of being a man who showed the way to the proper realization

of divine sonship by cultivating the filial relation to God. The Apocalyptic School advocated the position that Saul the Pharisee had studied the Jewish apocalypses and had become familiar with the figure of the heavenly Messiah pictured there. Somehow Paul came to identify this exalted figure with Jesus of Nazareth, and in this way developed his emphasis upon pre-existence and incarnation. But the Christ of Paul is a more wonderful person than the Messiah of this literature, which is hard to explain on the theory of borrowing. The Comparative Religion approach sought to find the distinctive elements of Paul's Christology in the mystery religions of the Graeco-Roman world, despite the fact that his Jewish background protests against such borrowing, and his close contact with the Jerusalem church prevents the assigning of his message to any such alien source. A more recent variation of this approach is the position of Bultmann, who posits as the formative influence on Paul's thought the Gnostic speculation about a mythological redeemer who will rescue man from the cosmic powers which threaten him by coming and sharing the agony of his earthly existence. But the Apostle's teaching is too firmly grounded in the historic tradition about Jesus which is reproduced in the Gospels and affirmed by the early church to permit any such extraneous derivation.

Paul remains the unsurpassed interpreter of Christ — the Christ of history, of the NT, of the continuing church.

See also CRITICISM, NEW TESTAMENT.

BIBLIOGRAPHY
W. D. Davies, *Paul and Rabbinic Judaism*; J. Gresham Machen, *The Origin of Paul's Religion*; Olaf Moe, *The Apostle Paul*; H. N. Ridderbos, *Paul and Jesus*; Albert Schweitzer, *The Mysticism of Paul the Apostle*; C. A. A. Scott, *Christianity according to St. Paul*; James S. Stewart, *A Man in Christ*.

EVERETT F. HARRISON

PAULICIANISM. The Paulicians were a highly independent Christian sect which arose in the heart of the Eastern church about A.D. 750. They are frequently interpreted as either "early Protestants" or "radical oriental dualists," neither view giving the entire truth. They were the most influential sect of their time but their formative force on later reform parties is problematical. Though much maligned in contemporary polemical literature they are seen in the ancient Paulician work, *The Key of Truth*, translated by F. C. Conybeare in 1898, as a true reform party.

They were anti-Romanists repudiating mariolatry, intercession of saints and the use of relics and images. They strongly despised the Roman hierarchy, having themselves only one grade of ministry. In rejecting infant baptism they taught that thirty was the age for immersion during which ordinance the Holy Spirit was received. Repentance was also a sacrament and the Agape was practiced with the sacrament of "the body and the blood."

In Christology they were adoptionists but not docetics as often thought. They valued the Pauline writings very highly but made use of other NT and OT books in *The Key of Truth.*

BIBLIOGRAPHY
W. F. Adeney, *The Greek and Eastern Churches*, pp. 216-28; F. C. Conybeare, *The Key of Truth*; R. A. Knox, *Enthusiasm*, pp. 80-91; C. A. Scott in *HERE*.

WILLIAM NIGEL KERR

PEACE. The primary and basic idea of the biblical word "peace" (OT *shalôm*; NT *eirēnē*) is completeness, soundness, wholeness. It is a favorite biblical greeting (Gen. 29:6; Luke 24:36), and is found at the beginning or end of the NT epistles except James and I John. To this day it is one of the commonest words among the Semites. Dismissal is also expressed by the word (I Sam. 1:17). It means cessation from war (Josh. 9:15). Friendship between companions is expressed by it (Gen. 26:29; Ps. 28:3), as well as friendship with God through a covenant (Num. 25:12; Isa. 54:10). Contentment or anything working toward safety, welfare, and happiness is included in the concept (Isa. 32:17-18).

Peace has reference to health, prosperity, well-being, security, as well as quiet from war (Eccl. 3:8; Isa. 45:7). The prophet Isaiah pointed out repeatedly that there will be no peace to the wicked (Isa. 48:22; 57:21), even though many of the wicked continually seek to encourage themselves with a false peace (Jer. 6:14).

Peace is a condition of freedom from strife whether internal or external. Security from outward enemies (Isa. 26:12), as well as calm of heart for those trusting God (Job 22:21; Isa. 26:3), is included. Peace is so pleasing to the Lord that the godly are enjoined to seek it diligently (Ps. 34:14; Zech. 8:16, 19). It is to be a characteristic of the NT believer also (Mark 9:50 and II Cor. 13:11). Peace is a comprehensive and valued gift from God, and the promised and climaxing blessing in mes-sianic times (Isa. 2:4; 9:6-7; 11:6; Mic. 4:1-4; 5:5).

"To hold one's peace" means simply to be silent (Luke 14:4). The words in the OT (*hāraš* as one) and the NT (*siōpaō* among others) have nothing in common with the words now under consideration.

In the NT the word has reference to the peace which is the gift of Christ (John 14:27; 16:33; Rom. 5:1; Phil. 4:7). The word is used many times to express the truths of the mission, character, and gospel of Christ. The purpose of Christ's coming into the world was to bring spiritual peace with God (Luke 1:79; 2:14; Mark 5:34; 9:50; Luke 24:36). There is a sense in which he came not to bring peace, but a sword (Matt. 10:34). This has reference to the struggle with every form of sin. Christ's life depicted in the Gospels is one of majestic calm and serenity (Matt. 11:28; John 14:27). The essence of the gospel may be expressed in the term "peace" (Acts 10:36; Eph. 6:15), including the peace of reconciliation with God (Rom. 5:1; Crem, p. 245), and the peace of fellowship with God (Gal. 5:22 and Phil. 4:7).

The innumerable blessings of the Christian revolve around the concept of peace. The gospel is the gospel of peace (Eph. 6:15). Christ is our peace (Eph. 2:14-15); God the Father is the God of peace (I Thess. 5:23). The inalienable privilege of every Christian is the peace of God (Phil. 4:9) because of the legacy of peace left by Christ in his death (John 14:27; 16:33). These blessings are not benefits laid up in eternal glory only, but are a present possession (Rom. 8:6; Col. 3:15). Thus, peace is "a conception distinctly peculiar to Christianity, the tranquil state of a soul assured of its salvation through Christ, and so fearing nothing from God and content with its earthly lot, of whatever sort that is" (Thayer, *sub voce*).

BIBLIOGRAPHY
Crem, pp. 244 f.; *HDB*, III, pp. 732 f.; *HDCG*, II, pp. 330 f.; *ISBE*, IV, p. 2293; *SBD*, p. 651; Thayer.

CHARLES L. FEINBERG

PELAGIANISM. Pelagius, a monk from Britain, was a popular preacher in Rome A.D. 401-9. He sought to stir to earnest moral endeavor lax Christians who sheltered behind the frailty of the flesh and the apparent impossibility of fulfilling God's commands, by telling them that God commanded nothing that is impossible and that everyone may live free from sin if he will.

Accordingly Pelagius, and his disciples Caelestius and Julian of Eclanum, taught the sufficiency of human nature as created by God. The will was always as free to choose good as evil. There was no inherited inclination to evil in human nature. Neither the fall of Adam, nor the habits of a man's life, ever affected the absolute equipoise of the will.

Caelestius took the lead in denying original sin. Every infant born into the world was in the same condition as Adam was before the fall. This view brought the Pelagians into conflict with the church doctrine that there was "one baptism for the remission of sins."

Pelagians denied the need of internal grace to keep God's commandments. Human nature was created good; and was endowed by its Creator with power to live an upright life easily if a man willed to. In fact, many heathen and Jews had lived a perfect life. In addition to this supreme grace of creation, Pelagius affirmed further grace from God in his provision of the illumination of the law and the example of Christ. Pelagianism knows nothing of redemption.

"By his free will man is emancipated from God." This statement of Julian is the key to Pelagianism, which is rationalized moralism. Man created with free will has no longer to do with God but with himself alone. God only re-enters at the last judgment.

BIBLIOGRAPHY
A. Harnack, History of Dogma; R. S. Moxon, The Doctrine of Sin.

DAVID BROUGHTON KNOX

PENANCE. From the Latin *poena* ("penalty"), the term penance refers to disciplinary measures adopted by the church against offenders. In early days it applied to those guilty of such glaring offences as apostasy, murder, adultery, who were allowed only one chance of restoration after undergoing a course of fastings, etc., on public confession of their sin in renewal of the baptismal profession, and on acceptance of certain lasting prohibitions, e.g., continence in the case of the unmarried. With the barbarian invasions this severe discipline was mitigated, and in the Celtic Penitentials we find that secret confession is allowed and restoration begins to precede the penances, which become much more formal and may be replaced by cash payments according to current notions of satisfaction. Two notable de-

velopments took place in the Middle Ages. First, penance at least once a year was made compulsory from 1215. Second, the whole understanding was developed in a new way which ultimately found codification at the Council of Trent, when penance was officially accepted as a sacrament. It was still agreed that the eternal guilt of mortal sins after baptism could be met only by the atoning work of Christ, true contrition and the word of absolution. From this angle penance properly speaking remained disciplinary. But it was now argued that the temporal guilt of either mortal or venial sin may be met in part by the actual penances, thus mitigating the final expiation demanded in purgatory. In addition, voluntary alms, masses and drawings on the so-called treasury of merit, e.g., by indulgences, could be used for the same purpose, and even take the place of penances. Quite apart from the obviously non-scriptural nature of this whole system, five main evils may be seen in it: (1) it misunderstands the problem of postbaptismal sin; (2) it deflects from the atonement; (3) it promotes related errors such as purgatory (q.v.), masses, indulgences and invocation of saints; (4) it creates legalism and formalism; and (5) it gives rise to the moral evils of the confessional. The Reformers cut through the whole falsification of theory and practice by insisting that what the NT demands is not penance but penitence or repentance, though they saw a real value in the restoring of true discipline and of course the private counseling of those troubled in conscience as individually required.

See also ABSOLUTION.

BIBLIOGRAPHY
HERE; O. D. Watkins, A History of Penance; R. C. Mortimer, The Origins of Private Penance in the Western Church; Canons and Decrees of the Council of Trent; Catechism of Trent.

GEOFFREY W. BROMILEY

PENITENCE. See REPENTANCE.

PENTECOST. A term derived from the Greek *pentekostos*, meaning fiftieth, which was applied to the fiftieth day after the Passover. It was the culmination of the "feast of weeks" (Ex. 34:22; Deut. 16:10), which began on the third day after the Passover with the presentation of the first harvest sheaves to God, and which concluded with the offering of two loaves of unleavened bread, representing the first products of the harvest (Lev.

23:17-20; Deut. 16:9-10). After the Exile it became one of the great pilgrimage feasts of Judaism, at which many of those who lived in remote sections of the Roman world returned to Jerusalem for worship (Acts 20:16). For that reason it served as a bond to unite the Jewish world of the first century and to remind them of their history.

In the Christian church Pentecost is the anniversary of the coming of the Holy Spirit. When Jesus ascended he instructed his disciples to remain in Jerusalem until they should receive power from on high. As a group of 120 were praying in an upper room in Jerusalem fifty days after his death, the Holy Spirit descended upon them with the sound of a great wind and with tongues of fire which settled upon each of them. They began to speak with other languages and to preach boldly in the name of Christ, with the result that three thousand were converted. This tremendous manifestation of divine power marked the beginning of the church which has ever since regarded Pentecost as its birthday.

In the church year Pentecost covered the period from Easter to Pentecost Sunday. The day itself was observed by feasting, and was a favorite occasion for administering baptism. It was the third great Christian feast after Christmas and Easter. In the liturgy of the Anglican church it is called Whitsunday, from the custom of wearing white clothing on that day.

See also CHRISTIAN YEAR.

MERRILL C. TENNEY

PEOPLE. There is a tendency in the OT to describe the "people" of God by *'am,* while reserving *gôy* for the heathen. Indeed in postbiblical Jewish literature *gôy* becomes synonymous with "Gentile." The LXX and the NT also continue this general practice with *laos* and *ethnos.* However the words are sometimes used interchangeably, and the basic difference seems to be that *gôy* and *ethnos* emphasize "people" as a national group (Ex. 19:16; Acts 13:19), while *'am* and *laos* speak of them as similar individuals bound together by certain ties and responsibilities. The "people" in this latter sense may be the members of a family (Gen. 32:8; 35:2), a tribe (Gen. 49:16; Acts 4:27), a city (Gen. 19:4), a nation (I Kings 12:27), or a racial group (Acts 26:17; Rev. 7:9), but they are more than a collection of human beings. They are a psychic community, a unified whole made up of past and future

generations, as well as the present, and existing at any one time in the individual with all their blessings and responsibilities. This is particularly true in the OT with the "people" of Israel. Thus Ahab is punished when his son Joram is killed (I Kings 21:19; II Kings 9:26; cf. Ex. 20:5-6), Gideon profits when his son Abimelech is made king (Judges 9:16, 19; cf. I Sam. 20:16; 24:21-22), and the people of Israel are punished when David sins (II Sam. 24; cf. I Sam. 22:19).

So there is a common bond, a common soul, a common experience, stretching out over past, present, and future, implied in the words *'am* and *laos.* The "people" of Israel are a coherent whole, having a common history and responsibility, while all other peoples have their own unified world as well. This then gives greater meaning to the church as "a people for (God's own) possession" (*laos peripoiēsin;* I Pet. 2:9; cf. Ex. 19:5). The actions of one at any time are the actions of all; the responsibilities of the whole are the responsibilities of the individual.

BIBLIOGRAPHY

BDB; Arndt; J. Pedersen, *Israel Its Life and Culture* I-II, pp. 54-57; 275-79; 475-79; H. Strathmann, R. Meyer in *TWNT.*

ROBERT B. LAURIN

PERDITION. See DESTRUCTION.

PERFECT, PERFECTION. Two OT roots signify ethical or religious perfection: *šlm, tmm.* Both imply completion, wholeness. See Deut. 25:15; 27:6 for the literal force of *šālēm* and Lev. 3:9; 23:15 for *tāmîm.*

In the evaluations of the rulers' spiritual integrity in Kings and Chronicles, *šālēm* occurs frequently, e.g., I Kings 11:4; 15:3: "his heart was not perfect with the Lord. . . ." The restriction of *šālēm,* when used ethically, to such passages suggests that this word, which like the derivatives of *tmm* means integrity of moral and intellectual life (i.e., heart), implies a covenant background. Kings were under special obligation to fulfil the terms of the Davidic covenant and to match David's standard of godly devotion (cf. II Sam. 7:12 ff.; I Kings 11:4).

In contrast, *tāmîm* and cognates — *tām, tōm, tummâ* — occur without the covenant reference, especially in Job (1:1, 8; 2:3; 8:20, etc.) and Psalms (37:37; 64:4; 101:2, etc.). The descriptions of Job's excellence are instructive because they define his perfection as fearing God and avoiding evil (Job 1:1, 8, etc.). Perfection in the OT is maintaining right relationship to God, the standard and judge of perfection, whose ways are perfect (Deut. 32:4; Ps. 18:30).

In the NT several words are translated "perfect." The *artios* Christian (II Tim. 3:17) is described as *exērtismenos* "completely equipped." He is perfect in that he has the necessary spiritual equipment and uses it properly. A *holoklēros* believer lacks nothing which contributes to his completeness (James 1:4); he is whole, sound in every way (I Thess. 5:23).

Katartizō and cognates imply "putting in a proper condition" by equipment or training. Sometimes improvement is involved as in II Cor. 13:9 *(katartisis)* and 13:11, where the passive means "mend your ways." (Cf. Heb. 13:21, equip; I Pet. 5:10, restore in the RSV.)

Teleios and derivatives connote perfect in the sense that the desired purpose *(telos)* is achieved. God, who alone is absolutely perfect, is the standard of perfection (Matt. 5:48, where the context deals with love for enemies). When used of believers, *teleios* apparently has a relative significance. Absolute perfection is not implied, for the sinless Christ was perfected through suffering (Heb. 2:10; 5:9). Paul, though urging his readers to maturity (cf. Eph. 4:13; Col. 1:28; 4:12) and assuming that many were mature (Phil. 3:15), denied that he had attained absolute perfection (Phil. 3:12; cf. I John 1:8—2:1).

Christ's sacrifice is the ground of perfection (Heb. 10:14). His imputed righteousness is the guarantee of ultimate sanctification (II Cor. 5:21; Col. 1:22). Steadfastness in trial (James 1:4), sensitivity to God's will (Col. 4:12), dependence upon the Spirit (Gal. 3:3), assurance of and response to God's perfect love (I John 4:17-18)— these are among the attitudes which aid in the quest for perfection, which culminates in the coming of Christ (Phil. 1:6) or death, when the believer joins the "just men made perfect" (Heb. 12:23) and becomes like Christ (I John 3:2).

These scriptural data have evoked differing interpretations. Lutheran and Reformed traditions reject any view of earthly absolute perfection. The verdict of the *Heidelberg Catechism* that our best works are imperfect and sin-stained is typical. The Reformers defined sanctification as a life-long struggle, in which the Spirit graciously seeks to mortify sinful tendencies and bring to maturity holy dispositions implanted in the believer through regeneration. This process is perfected only when the believer is translated into God's presence.

In contrast, John Wesley and his spiritual heirs maintained the possibility of perfect sanctification, though generally resisting the idea of sinlessness. The crux of these two views is the definition of sin: Wesley distinguished willful breach of God's known law from mistake; the Reformed position brands any transgression of God's law as sin, whether intentional or not.

For Wesley, perfection was attained instantaneously, subsequent to justification, although the believer might not perceive the exact moment. It is not infallibility but salvation from sin, and is best manifested in purity of intention and perfect love for God and man. Reformed theologians reply that Wesleyan perfect love is a fiction: the most ardent Christian love cannot escape sin's taint. B. B. Warfield analyzed historically and critically the Pelagian and Arminian principles in the perfectionism of such diverse figures as Albrecht Ritschl, Charles Finney, and Charles G. Trumbull. The Wesleyan viewpoint still persists within so-called "holiness" movements and among some Methodist theologians like Vincent Taylor, who, denying sinless perfection, holds that fellowship with God expressed in perfect love is sanctification's ideal. In varying degrees of modification the Reformed position continues in the works of Karl Barth and Reinhold Niebuhr.

See also HOLINESS.

BIBLIOGRAPHY

Arndt; O. F. Curtis, *The Christian Faith*, pp. 373-93; R. N. Flew, *The Idea of Perfection in Christian Theology*; C. Hodge, *Systematic Theology*, III, pp. 245-58; F. Platt in *HERE*, IX, pp. 728-37; V. Taylor, *Forgiveness and Reconciliation*, pp. 155-79; Trench, pp. 74-77; B. B. Warfield, *Perfectionism*; J. Wesley, *A Plain Account of Christian Perfection*.

DAVID A. HUBBARD

PERISH. The meaning of "perish" in the Scriptures is explained primarily in three uses of the word. First, purely physical destruction in, or from, this world, without any idea of judgment or punishment. The word *'ābad* used in this way applies mainly to animals and inanimate objects, but may refer to persons (II Sam. 1:27; Job 4:11; so also *apothnēskō*

(Matt. 8:32; John 6:27). Second, much more frequently, the destruction, while purely physical, is regarded as the consequence, or punishment for wrongdoing. This is the typical OT usage (Deut. 4:26). This meaning is also seen in the NT. Luke 15:17 ("I perish with hunger") is an interesting example. The Greek *appollumi* is translated "perish" regarding the son and "lost" as related to the "sheep" and the "coin" (vss. 4, 6, 8, 9). To the son it indicates an attitude of self-will not involved in the others. Yet from the father's standpoint it denotes his own impoverishment (vs. 32). Third, the distinctive NT use is of a "perishing" which is applied to the "soul" as well as the body (Matt. 10:28; Luke 13:3). The antithesis to perishing is "having eternal life." The soul is immaterial and does not suffer annihilation but is separated from life in the spiritual sense. It loses its present status but continues to exist.

See also LOST.

BIBLIOGRAPHY
RTWB.

LEWIS T. CORLETT

PERPETUAL VIRGINITY. A tradition, dating from early church Fathers, that Mary kept her virginity before, during, and after the birth of Jesus. The Fathers contended that for Mary to have had children conceived in sin would be unreasonable and irreverent.

This tradition entered official Romish doctrine. Pope Siricius wrote to Anysius (392): "For the Lord Jesus would not have chosen to be born of a virgin if he had judged that she would be so incontinent as to taint the birthplace of the body of the Lord, the home of the eternal king, with the seed of human intercourse." Many councils referred to "Mary ever Virgin." The Council of Trent (1545-63) declared: "If anyone says that the marriage state is to be preferred to the state of virginity or celibacy and that it is not better and holier to remain in virginity or celibacy than to be joined in marriage: let him be anathema."

EDWARD JOHN CARNELL

PERSECUTION. Persecution (literally, a pursuing), is the systematic attempt to suppress or to exterminate Christianity by social pressure to the point of violence. Persecution of Christians began with the action of the Sanhedrin against Peter and John in reprisal for their proclamation of the resurrection of Jesus (Acts 4:1-3, 5 ff.). Another persecution took place at the time of the stoning of Stephen, when the Christians of Jerusalem were driven out of the city and scattered in every direction (Acts 8:1-4). Organized persecution by the state did not begin until the time of Nero, and was then probably only temporary and local. There were traditionally ten persecutions under the Empire: Nero, A.D. 64; Domitian, A.D. 95; Trajan, A.D. 100; Antoninus Pius, A.D. 161-80; Septimius Severus, A.D. 197; Maximinus, A.D. 235; Decius, A.D. 249; Valerian, A.D. 257; Aurelian, A.D. 274; Diocletian, A.D. 303. The historical evidence for a persecution under Domitian is not clear, and not all of the other persecutions were of long duration. Those under Decius and Diocletian were the most severe.

Diocletian attempted not only to exterminate the Christians, but also to destroy their literature. He confiscated and burned all copies of the Scriptures that he found, and demolished the church buildings. Official persecution ended when Constantine in A.D. 313 by the Edict of Milan declared a policy of toleration for all religions, with a view toward enlisting the public support of Christians for his regime. Ultimately Christianity (*q.v.*) became the official religion of the Roman state.

The causes of persecution were numerous. The Christians were misunderstood by the pagans, who considered them atheists, anti-social, and politically subversive. The decline of the Empire in the third century was attributed to the failure of the people to worship the old gods, and the Christians were consequently blamed. Because worship of the gods was part of the state activity, the Christians, who would not participate in it, were deemed unpatriotic, and consequently a dangerous element in the population. Persecution was the protest of heathenism against the gospel in its spiritual and social manifestations.

BIBLIOGRAPHY
H. B. Workman, *Persecution of the Early Church;* G. Uhlhorn, *The Conflict of Christianity with Heathenism;* W. W. Hyde, *Paganism to Christianity in the Roman Empire,* pp. 168-85; E. T. Merrill, *Essays in Early Church History,* pp. 82-130, 148-201.

MERRILL C. TENNEY

PERSEVERANCE. Perseverance (*hāzaq* in Num. 13:20 and *proskartereō* in Acts 1:14; 2:42; 6:4; Rom. 12:12; Eph. 6:18, as well as in classical Greek and the papyri) means the steadfast continuance in anything. Theologically speaking, it refers to the fifth point of the Calvinistic doctrinal system that true Christians will continue in faith and holiness forever (John 10:28; Phil. 1:6; I Pet. 1:5). Thus Jonathan Edwards finds the very definition of a Christian to be, according to John 8:31, one who continues in the word of Christ.

Against perseverance, the Arminian theologians cite first, the Bible passages which teach the necessity of striving (Luke 13:24; Col. 1:29; II Tim. 2:5), and which warn against falling away (Ezek. 7:20; I Cor. 9:27; Heb. 6:3 f.); second, contend that this doctrine logically leads to antinomianism, for a man's sense of security would incline him to sin boldly; and, third, this doctrine would make all exhortation and command futile. To the first objection, the advocates reply that their doctrine is not inconsistent with striving for this is the very path of perseverance. Warnings against falling away, they say, are not inconsistent for merely professing Christians may fall away from that profession and are warned of the seriousness thereof (Heb. 6:3 f.) while true Christians may test their condition by their resistance to this temptation. Secondly, perseverance not only does not, but cannot, lead to antinomianism because, by definition, it means persevering in holiness and not in unholiness. Actually, the proponents continue, it not only promotes but consists in strenuous and persevering efforts after conformity to Christ. Exhortations, thirdly, are most appropriate for persons who are disposed to the very course exhorted. And, finally, the commands of God could not be improperly addressed to persons whose dominant desire is "speak, Lord, for thy servant heareth."

BIBLIOGRAPHY

Jonathan Edwards, *Works*, III, pp. 509-37; Nash, *Perseverance*; A. H. Strong, *Systematic Theology*, pp. 868 f.

JOHN H. GERSTNER

PERSON OF CHRIST. See CHRISTOLOGY.

PERSONALITY. This word is derived from the Latin word *persona*, with the following psychological meaning: the fluid and changing mental organization within an individual (and as *observable* to others) of all the thinking, emotional, and physical characteristics which have enough consistency to establish him as a unique person.

In common usage personality is a popular and hurried index of character. Very often it is used as a contrast, such as "he has a fine personality, but when you get to know him, he has no depth." By implication, stressing personality implies lack of consistency between the "true" man and the external impression.

The meaning implies a distinctiveness in behavior and reaction to different stimuli — that is, we do not always react in the same way to each person, group or incident, or in the same way to the same person, group or incident at different times, but there is a commonality that forms the basis of an understanding of oneself or others as distinct persons.

There are many definitions of the term, but they generally fall into two classes: external description of behavior or internal description of the true "inner man." The above definition attempts to be complete enough to include both areas.

There is no direct reference to "personality" in the Bible in most translations. However, personality may be substituted for "person" in some passages without doing violence to the meaning.

The commonly accepted concept of "Christian personality" is applied to those who have truly put on the "new" man (that Paul speaks of), or the mind of Christ and who also exhibit the external characteristics which would be considered as "Christ-like." A further extension of the meaning implies a centering of all of the various divergent personality traits in Christ, traits being defined as consistent patterns of action within the individual. In the unorganized person these traits are in conflict with each other. Organization in terms of some central purpose such as selfishness is often achieved, but is ultimately found unsatisfactory. Sometimes the organizing principle is an altruistic one, and a higher level of adjustment is attained.

However, to the Christian, the highest level of adjustment is to center all traits in Christ. Potentially there will be no conflict in such organization. As the spokes of the wheel all center in the hub of the wheel, with no clash among the spokes, so all of the diverse traits of the human personality being centered in Christ avoid inner competition. The result is a strongly integrated, positive Christian personality, which becomes a goal of life.

BIBLIOGRAPHY

G. Allport, *Personality*, pp. 1-48; also *The Individual and His Religion*; D. W. MacKinnon in J. Mc V. Hunt,

Personality, pp. 3-48; E. Ligon, *The Psychology of Christian Personality*, pp. 16-20; 334-71; G. Murphy, *Personality*.

STANLEY E. LINDQUIST

PERSONIFICATION. In heathendom there is much error and variety here: animism (endowing lifeless objects with consciousness); also treating reputedly sacred objects or forces as persons (Asherah, probably sacred pole, Deut. 16:21); eponymous ancestor idea (making personified city, nation, tribe, power, into a god or legendary hero, e.g., the critics' alleged Samson, *sun*-myth). Personification was especially common in Israel, as seen in the anthropomorphism (*q.v.*) of the Bible — human actions or relations transferred to deity or things, e.g., "trees clap hands" (Isa. 55:12); "O death, where . . .?" (Hos. 13:14); "eyes of Jehovah" (Zech. 4:10); Jachin and Boaz (I Kings 7:21). Also, Jotham's fable (Judg. 9); and Proverbs' humorous horse-leech with three daughters (30:15). Similar in principle is the treatment of wisdom (e.g., Prov. 9:1); the name of God (Ex. 23:21); face (presence) of God (Ex. 34:14); the Targum's Memra (word) regarding God (Ex. 19:17); NT Logos or Word (John 1:1) — not derived from Philo and Greek notions. One must distinguish true revelation of God from heathen error, e.g., Tammuz, the personification of agricultural engagement, condemned by Ezekiel (chap. 8).

ROBERT F. GRIBBLE

PETER. Symeon (or Simon) bar-Jonah (Matt. 16:17, John 21:16), though his original name continued in use (Acts 15:14, II Pet. 1:1), was known in the apostolic church principally by the name which Jesus conferred on him, "the Rock," in either its Aramaic form *Kēpha* (Gal. 2:9; I Cor. 1:2; 15:5) or Graecized as *Petros* (Gal. 2:7; I Pet. 1:1; II Pet. 2:1). Matthew associates this with the confession of Caesarea Philippi (Matt. 16:18), but we need not assume that this solemn endowment was the first time the name had been given (cf. Mark 3:16; John 1:42).

He was a fisherman from Bethsaida (John 1:43), but had a home in Capernaum (Mark 1:29 ff.). His brother Andrew, who introduced him to Jesus, had been a disciple of John the Baptist (John 1:35 ff.), and so possibly had he. The seashore call of Jesus (Mark 1:6) was evidently not the first meeting (John 1:41 ff.).

One of the original Twelve, he is depicted by the Synoptic tradition as their leader and natural spokesman (cf. Matt. 15:15; Mark 1:36; 9:5; 10:28; 11:20; Luke 5:5), particularly in crises. He makes the confession at Caesarea Philippi, expresses their revulsion at the idea of the suffering Messiah, and makes the disastrous representative boast (Mark 14:29-31) and denial (Mark 15:66 ff.). Christ chooses him, with James and John, as an inner circle within the Twelve (Mark 5:37; 9:2; 14:32).

The significance of Matt 16:18 ff. is controverted. From early times "this rock" has been identified with Peter's confession of faith in Christ, the archetypal apostolic testimony. The other most common interpretation (especially among Roman Catholic writers) regards the rock as Peter himself, who thus receives special pre-eminence and commission in the founding of the church. The personal reference of vs. 19 may favor this view, but elsewhere in the NT the church's foundation is Christ (I Cor. 3:11) or the apostolic-prophetic witness (Eph. 2:20). Cullmann has urged that the saying has been misplaced from a passion context, but we must recognize that Matthew gives it in a confession context. Note that, even were Peter the rock, there is no hint that his pre-eminence was transferable. Cullmann, who argues that Peter is the rock, shows that only the historic Peter, not any successors, can be in question.

Peter undoubtedly leads the first Jerusalem church. He is the first witness of the resurrection (I Cor. 15:5; cf. Mark 16:7). He leads in the gathered community before Pentecost (Acts 1:15 ff.), and is the first preacher thereafter (Acts 2:14 ff.) and the representative preacher of the early chapters of Acts (3:11 ff; 4:8 ff.). He presides in judgment (Acts 5:1 ff; 8:20 ff.). Paul regards him as a "pillar" of the early church (Gal. 2:9).

In a sense, he is also the first instrument of the gentile mission (Acts 15:7) and his experience is representative of the intellectual revolution involved for Jewish Christians (Acts 10:1 ff.). At the Jerusalem Council he urged the admission of gentile converts without submission to the Mosaic law (Acts 15:7 ff.) and had table-fellowship in the mainly gentile church of Antioch (Gal. 2:12) until, to Paul's disgust, he withdrew in deference to Jewish-Christian opinion. Essentially he was an "apostle of the circumcision" (Gal. 2:7 ff.) but remained, despite obvious difficulties, a warm friend of gentile Christians, whom he addresses in I Peter.

In his lifetime and later, anti-Pauline forces sought to use Peter, without his encouragement. There was a Cephas party at Corinth (I Cor. 1:12), and in the pseudo-Clementine romances, Peter confounds Paul, thinly disguised as Simon Magus. Possibly party strife in Rome over the Jewish question (cf. Phil. 1:15) brought him thither.

There is no evidence that he was bishop of Rome or stayed long in the city. I Peter was written there (so probably I Pet. 5:13), doubtless after Paul's death, for Silvanus and Mark were with him. Probably (cf. Eusebius *HE*, iii:39) Mark's Gospel reflects Peter's preaching (cf. C. H. Turner, *St. Mark*, S.P. C.K., London, 1924). Peter died in Rome in the Neronian persecution (I Clement 5-6), probably by crucifixion (cf. John 21:18). Recent excavations reveal an early cultus of Peter, but the original grave is unlikely ever to be found.

Spurious writings in Peter's name, mainly in heretical interests, caused difficulties in the second century (cf. R. M. Grant and G. Quispel, *Vigiliae Christianae* 2). Canonical works reflecting his teaching (including Mark's Gospel and the Petrine speeches in Acts) unitedly reflect a theology dominated by the concept of Christ as the Suffering Servant and the thought of the ensuing glory. Crises in the life of Christ (e.g., the transfiguration, I Pet. 5:1; II Pet. 1:16 ff.) have made a deep impression.

By the late second century the Roman Church was applying the promise of Matt. 16:18 to Peter and thence to herself, perhaps as possessing Peter's grave; and this was being vigorously resisted by non-Roman churches (Cf. Tertullian, *De Pudicitia* 21). Resistance long continued (e.g. Cyprian, *De Unitate* 4-5; Augustine, *Retractationes* i.21.1). The Middle Ages developed the idea of the transfer of the powers of Matt. 16:18 ff. to the Popes, as Peter's successors. The Reformers support their refutation of this from patristic sources (cf. Calvin, *Institutes* vi. 6).

BIBLIOGRAPHY

O. Cullmann, *Peter* (Eng. Trans.); *Journ. Eccl. Hist.* 8, 238; J. Lowe, *Saint Peter*; F. H. Chase in *HDB*; H. Chadwick, *JTS* (NS) 8, 30 ff.; T. G. Jalland, *The Church and the Papacy.*

ANDREW F. WALLS

PHARISEES. *Pharisaioi* (Hebrew p^erûšîm) = Semitic term for separated one, separatist, though rarely found in sing. (Luke 7:36; Acts 5:34; Phil. 3:5). The Pharisees are usually associated with the Scribes (Matt. 5:20) and Sadducees (Matt. 16:1) or Herodians (Matt 22:15) in opposition to Jesus. Their origin is unknown. Some hold they separated from Judas Maccabeus at the advent of Alcimus 162 B.C. and were the Hasidim, a passive resistance group devoted to the observance of Judaism. Josephus distinguishes them from the Essenes and Sadducees in the days of Jonathan 146 B.C. Others regard them as the Haberim who deserted Hyrcanus 135-104 B.C. and vowed scrupulous observance of the law (Mishna). Under Alexandra (76 B.C.), whose brother was a Pharisee, they were admitted to the Sanhedrin and began to dominate politics; they supported Antipater's pro-Roman policy, and Herod the Great co-operated with their leading rabbis Pollio and Sameas. In the time of Jesus they controlled synagogues and schools and were revered by the masses (Ant. 18:1,3).

Their creed lay midway between the fatalism of the Essenes and the free choice position of the Sadducees (Wars. 2, 8, 14). They believed in the resurrection of the dead, angels and future rewards and punishments, (Acts. 23:8), and quoted the Pentateuch in support (e.g., Num. 18:28) like Jesus (Luke 20:37). They especially reverenced the scribal tradition (Mark 7:9; Ant. 13, 10, 6) which they regarded as binding. While the Sadducees ignored change they tried to fit the law to new environs by practical interpretation. They practiced exorcism (Luke 11:19). Their tithing and fasting (Mon. and Thurs.) was voluntary (Luke 18:9-14). For blasphemy and adultery they prescribed the death penalty. Their messianic hope finds expression in the Psalms of Solomon (*ca.* 50 B.C.), which contrasts the pious (Pharisees) with sinners, denounces the Hasmonaeans and hails Pompey as God's deliverer. The pharisaic Testament of the Twelve Patriarchs (*ca.* 120 B.C.) portrays Messiah binding Beliar, executing judgment and establishing new Jerusalem.

The points of conflict between Jesus and the Pharisees were: (1) their tradition which invalidated the law (Mark 7:12); (2) their rigid sabbatarianism which restricted healing (Matt. 12:12); (3) defilement and moral regeneration (Mark 7:18-23); (4) merit and rewards (Luke 17:10); (5) hypocrisy (Matt. 23:13); (6) the mission to Gentiles and outcasts of society (Luke 7:36-50); and (7) their lack of humility (Luke 18:9-14). Jesus shared some of their more spiritual teaching (Luke 10:27-28) and certain Pharisees like Nicodemus supported him.

BIBLIOGRAPHY

Arndt; F. C. Burkitt, *Jesus and the Pharisees*; M. S. Enslin, *Christian Beginnings*, pp. 112-18; HDB; JTS 28 ('27), 392-97; C. G. Montefiore, *The Synoptic Gospels*; E. Schuerer, Div. II, Vol. II, pp. 2-9 for Josephus and Mishna.

DENIS H. TONGUE

PHILANTHROPY. Though this word is not found in the Bible it is derived from two Greek words, *phileō*, "to love," and *anthrōpos*, "man." The teaching of philanthropy is found in the Bible under the term of "almsgiving" and is found in such passages as Lev. 25:35; Deut. 15:7; Matt. 6:1; 19:21; and Luke 11:41. It is a part of a central notion of Christianity, that of love. It can be conceived as the Christian performance of social duty. It is an antidote to what is signified by the NT term "ungodliness," which Calvin feels is anything that is repugnant to the serious fear of God. Philanthropy on the part of the Christian is an invariable and necessary consequence of saving faith. The summary of the law is that the Christian's love to God is to be expressed by the Christian's rendering of service to man, and to all men whether they be in the faith or not. It has no place for a system of double morality, one for believers and another for unbelievers. Philanthropy is a discipline of the cross in that it is the outworking of man living by the will of God instead of by his own inordinate desires. It finds its expression in the Christian performing acts of love, of helpfulness, of mercy, of kindness to his fellow man. The love of God working in and through the heart of the Christian constrains him to such acts.

LEONARD THOMAS VAN HORN

PHILOSOPHY. The word philosophy is derived from two Greek words, *philein* ("to love") and *sophia* ("wisdom"). The exact origin of the term is somewhat obscure, but through the years it has come to denote several different types of activity all closely related to the original words from which it is derived.

(1) Classical usage applies the term more to the product than to the activity (love of wisdom) which gives rise to it. Philosophy, thus, is the over-all interpretation of the universe from a particular viewpoint. In this sense, philosophy is the equivalent of the German *Weltanschauung*. Augustinian philosophy, for example, is an over-all interpretation of the universe from the viewpoint of St. Augustine; and his philosophy of history is his over-all interpretation of history.

(2) The term philosophy, as used in the phrase "philosophy of life," differs considerably from classical usage. One's philosophy of life consists merely of those beliefs which serve to guide a man's life, however uncritically they may have been adopted or however inconsistent and provincial they may be.

(3) Thomas Aquinas limited philosophy to an over-all interpretation of the universe which can be secured by reason alone apart from special revelation. In this he is followed by Roman Catholics and by many Protestants.

(4) Modern critical philosophers (positivists, analysts, etc.) define philosophy as the attempt to investigate and clarify meanings and relationships rather than an attempt to arrive at any ultimate truth (the latter being a goal of which these thinkers largely despair). For the classicist, critical philosophy represents only the first stage in progress toward the goal of an interpretation of truth (*q.v.*).

The ancients stressed the necessity for disinterestedness in the pursuit of philosophy. Modern thought, to the contrary, stresses that man cannot be neutral when he philosophizes but that personal and social conditioning are largely or wholly determinative of the philosophical process.

The fact that the Scriptures say little about philosophy (the word is used only in Col. 2:8, and that in a somewhat derogatory manner), does not relieve the Christian from the responsibility to engage in this art. Paul's reference to philosophy is against a type of worthless speculation which is not based on scriptural presuppositions and includes mystical pagan elements. Although it presents no formal statement of a world view (with the possible exception of the book of Ecclesiastes), innate within the OT is a philosophy of history and of moral and religious experience (note especially the books of Job and Proverbs). The NT, however, contains passages which are clearly formal attempts at the presentation of broad universal principles in ethics (Rom. 7, 8), in cosmology (Col. 1), and in history (Rom. 9-11).

BIBLIOGRAPHY

C. D. Broad, "Critical and Speculative Philosophy," in *Contemporary British Philosophy*, Series One; Jacques Maritain, *An Introduction to Philosophy*, pp. 102-43; James Orr, *Christian View of God and the World*, pp. 1-36; Bertrand Russell, *The Problems of Philosophy*.

KENNETH S. KANTZER

PIETISM. The origins of Pietism are to be found in seventeenth century Germany, when the after-effects of the Thirty Years War and a hardening of orthodoxy had robbed the church of much of its evangelical vitality. In these circumstances P. J. Spener worked for a spiritual revival through the program announced in his *Pia Desideria,* his emphasis being upon informal gathering for prayer, Bible study and the nurture of the Christian life within the framework of orthodox doctrine and allegiance. He quickly found support among both people and neighboring pastors, and suitable hymns were found for the program in the work of P. Gerhardt. The hostility of the theological world was incurred when Spener's disciple A. H. Francke attacked the teaching methods and curriculum at Leipzig, but a home was found for the Pietists in the newly founded University of Halle. Although Pietism never became an organized school or movement, it exercised an astonishingly varied and widespread influence through the eighteenth and on into the nineteenth century. Even such thinkers as Lessing and Kant were not unaffected by it. It played its part in the awakening of German literature. In addition to its influence upon Lutheranism, it found distinctive expression in the work of the Moravians and Zinzendorf, and thus contributed to the great missionary awakening in the evangelical world. Through John Wesley it came to have a powerful effect upon the English-speaking world, and even today there are many features of Evangelicalism which derive in large part from Pietism. Nor did it fail to influence theological development, although in this respect its contribution was very different from what Spener had envisaged, for Halle became an early center of more critical biblical enquiry and the strong concentration upon individual spiritual life and experience produced in Schleiermacher and his successors the subjectivism or man-centeredness which is the distinctive and persistent mark of liberal Neo-Protestantism.

GEOFFREY W. BROMILEY

PIETY. See GODLINESS.

PILGRIM. See STRANGER.

PIT. See HELL.

PITY, PITIFUL. Pity is an undefinable, almost universal, human passion; in Aristotle, the basis for tragedy; the actuation of Prometheus' self-sacrifice for man's good; initial in God (a counterbalance to justice). Six Hebrew and five Greek roots (*ca.* two hundred times in the OT; eighty in the NT) are translated variously pity, mercy, compassion. The idea is notable in Psalms and Prophets (Pss. 103:13; 136, every verse; Isa. 54:8, 10). Pity is withheld from heretics when true religion is jeopardized (Deut. 13:8; cf. also II John 10; Matt. 23:33). It characterizes God, touching penitents (Isa. 55:7). In man, a signal illustration is the good Samaritan (Luke 10:33, 37). The greatest manifestation is seen in God, through the Saviour (II John 3).

Pitiful is predicate, regarding God (I Pet. 2:8), or man (James 5:4); once attributive (Lam. 4:10). The emotion pity, despised by Stoics, is a "form which love takes," indeed an indication of Godlike strength of character.

ROBERT F. GRIBBLE

PLEASURE, GOOD PLEASURE. The word pleasure and its derivatives represent about eighteen different root-words in Hebrew and Greek. The chief words are *ḥēpeṣ* and *rāṣôn, eudokia* and *hēdonē. Ḥēpeṣ* signifies delight, enjoyment, happiness (Job 22:3; Ps. 111:2; Eccl. 12:1; Jer. 22:28), or that in which delight is taken (Isa. 58:3, 13), and is ascribed to God and man. It can also mean will or purpose, generally of Jehovah (Isa. 44:28; 46:10; 48:14). In this respect *ḥēpeṣ* anticipates *eudokia*, and *thelēma* (Rev. 4:11). *Rāṣôn* also means will or that which is acceptable and pleasing (Ezra 10:11; Neh. 9:37; Esth. 1:8; Pss. 51:18; 103:21), being used of God or man. Other words in the OT translated "pleasure" are *nepeš*, "breath," "soul," "desire" (Deut. 23:24; Ps. 105:22; Jer. 34:16), *reûṭ*, "will," "wish," (Ezra 5:17), and *'awwâ* (Jer. 2:24) and *'ednâ* (Gen. 18:12), both indicating sexual desire.

Eudokia, apparently confined to Jewish and Christian literature, conveys the idea of satisfaction, approval, generally in relation to the divine will, and is sometimes translated "good pleasure" (Eph. 1:5, 9; Phil. 2:13). In II Thess. 1:11 it represents good thought, prompted by good desire and issuing in good resolve. Luke 2:14 with the variant readings brings out different aspects of *eudokia.* The AV renders "goodwill" (i.e., between men), the RV suggests enjoyment of divine favor, while the RV margin leaves both possibilities open (men of good pleasure). The verb *(eudokeō)* means to take pleasure in (II Cor. 12:10; Heb. 10:6, 8, 38). A rare use, of pleasure in evil things, is in II Thess. 2:12. *Hēdonē* refers more specifically to earthly pleasures, sometimes evil in nature (Luke 8:14; Titus 3:3; II Pet. 2:13). Other words with a bad sense are *spatalaō* (I Tim. 5:6) and *tryphaō* (James 5:5).

R. COLIN CRASTON

PLEROMA. See FULNESS.

POLYGAMY. Polygamy, or polygyny, denotes the practice of having more than one wife at one time. It occurs where woman occupies a low station in human society. Islam permits a man four wives, but in recent times, in some Mohammedan countries, notably in Turkey, this practice has been abolished by state law. According to the divine institution, lawful marriage consists of one man and one wife (Gen. 2:18, 24). Christ supported monogamy as the only rightful form of marriage (Matt. 19:4-6). While the Bible does not directly condemn the plural marriages that occurred in the OT, it frankly describes the evil effects of polygyny, as in the families of Jacob (Gen. 35:22; 37:18-28), of David (II Sam. 13:1-29; 15:1 ff.), and especially of Solomon (I Kings 11:1-12). Abraham's marriage with his wife's maid Hagar, upon Sarah's special request (Gen. 16:1-3), is probably not to be regarded as polygamous, but as motivated by the desire to obtain the promised heir in accord with the custom of the land. His wrong consisted in his lack of enduring trust in the divine promise. Scripture therefore depicts the evils that resulted also from this union (Gen. 16:4-16), while Paul rebukes it even as he censures work-righteousness (Gal. 4:21-31).

See also FAMILY, MARRIAGE.

BIBLIOGRAPHY
LC; JewEnc; ISBE.

J. THEODORE MUELLER

POLYTHEISM. See GODS.

POOR, POVERTY. The chief OT words expressing poverty are *'ebyôn, dal, 'ānî,* and *rûš.* The approximate idea is expressed in the NT by *penēs, penichros, endeēs,* and especially *ptōchos* and its cognates.

In the OT the following facts are set forth regarding the poor: (1) Many provisions are prescribed in the Mosaic legislation to safeguard the poor. A slave must be released in the seventh year (Ex. 21:2 ff.). A garment taken in pledge must be returned at sunset (Ex. 22:26 f.). Wages must be paid daily (Lev. 19:13). Essential implements must not be impounded (Deut. 24:6, 12 f., 17). Debts must be released every seven years (Deut. 15:1 f.). Provision was made for the food of the poor (Deut. 24:19-22). (2) The equality of the rich and poor is clearly stated (Prov. 22:2). (3) A man's poverty must not be allowed to pervert justice (Ex. 23:3, 6). (4) Poverty in itself is not a virtue. Many proverbs specify the evil causes of poverty (Prov. 6:10 f.; 10:4; 12:24; 13:4, 18; 14:23; 20:13; 21:17; 23:21; 28:19). (5) The prophets cry vehemently against the mistreatment of the poor (Isa. 3:13-15; 10:1 f.; Ezek. 18:12; 22:29; Amos 8:4). (6) The afflicted and the poor are often represented as the godly and pious (Ps. 35:10; 37:14; 40:17; 68:10; 86:1; Isa. 29:19; 41:17; 49:13; 51:21; 54:11).

The NT speaks of material and figurative poverty. On the material side: (1) Poverty is a permanent characteristic of the present world (Mark 14:7; cf. Deut. 15:11). (2) Christ's Messiahship is evidenced by his preaching to the poor (Luke 4:18; 7:22). (3) Spiritual life is viable in the midst of poverty (Mark 12:42 ff.; James 2:2-5; cf. Luke 16:20-22). (4) Christians are not immune to poverty (Rom. 15:26; Gal. 2:10). (5) Christians should help the poor (Matt. 19:21; II Cor. 8:2 ff.; I John 3:17 f.). (6) Poverty should not be a cause of social discrimination (James 2:5-9).

On the figurative side: (1) True poverty of spirit characterizes the members of Christ's kingdom (Matt. 5:3). (2) A poverty of spiritual life is found among decadent churches (Rev. 2:9; 3:17). (3) Christ's incarnation made him poor so that we through his poverty might become rich (II Cor. 8:9; cf. Phil. 2:5 ff.).

BIBLIOGRAPHY

Arndt; S. R. Driver in *HDB*; W. L. Walker in *ISBE*; W. F. Lofthouse and E. F. Scott in *HDCG*.

WICK BROOMALL

POPE. The term pope is generally understood as referring to the bishop of Rome, but in the early centuries it was used as a form of address in several bishoprics, and is still applied to priests of the Eastern Orthodox Church. It is a corruption of the classical name for "father."

The pope is regarded by Roman Catholics as the head of the church on earth. He is termed the "Vicar of Christ." His prerogatives are said to be derived from Christ's appointment of the apostle Peter to this position, Peter's subsequent bishopric at Rome and the transmission of his authority to his successors. There is, however, no early support for this understanding of Christ's words to Peter recorded in Matt. 16:18, nor is there clear historical evidence that Peter was ever at Rome. But even if exegesis were to establish the first point, and recent archaeological research to confirm the early tradition that Peter was martyred at Rome under Nero, there is still no proof that he passed on his leadership to all subsequent occupants of the Roman see.

The controversy concerning the papacy is one of the oldest in church history. It led, in 1054, to the break away of the Eastern churches from the Western, and, in the sixteenth century to the breakup of the Western church into the Protestant churches and the present Church of Rome. While popes have on occasion been men of outstanding ability, contributing to the well-being of the whole church, others have been men of totally despicable character. Yet the doctrine of the "infallibility" of the Pope has now been defined as an official dogma of the Roman Catholic Church, entailing a total commitment to his *ex cathedra* pronouncements (see INFALLIBILITY). In view of this development, it is inevitable that the pretension of Roman bishops to a universal papacy should constitute one of the most serious obstacles to genuine Christian unity.

BIBLIOGRAPHY

T. G. Talland, *The Church and the Papacy*; J. P. McKnight, *The Papacy*; G. Salmon, *The Infallibility of the Church*.

W. C. G. PROCTOR

PORTION. See LOT.

POSITIVISM. Positivism is that philosophy which limits knowledge claims to mathematics and the empirical sciences. It is "positive" in the sense that it restricts itself to the given, the experimental, the factual, the indubitable. All problems not soluble in principle within these limits are pseudo-problems. In science it is wary of explanations, hypothesis building, the concept of causation, and final causes. It contents itself with the ideal of careful, accurate description. It is intensely hostile to philosophical speculation and metaphysics.

Although in some sense anticipated by such men as Bacon, Hume, and Kant, its first modern advocate was Auguste Comte (1798-1857). He is noted for his division of man's intellectual history into three periods: the theological (explanation in terms of gods or spirits); the metaphysical (explanation in terms of essences, forms); and the positive (explanation in terms of the given, the sensory). Other modifications and refinements of positivism were made by such men (to name only a few) as J. S. Mill, K. Pearson, and Ernst Mach.

In the twentieth century positivism received a new formulation by the Vienna Circle (also known as neo-positivism, logical positivism, or scientific empiricism). It differs from the older positivism in the following: it employs the recent progress in mathematical logic; it has given considerable attention to semantics; and it has worked in closest connection with the discoveries of the new physics and behavioristic psychology.

The neo-positivists declared that all theological sentences (atheistic as well as theistic) were not true or false but meaningless. As a result it has provoked a highly technical literature (especially in England) centering around the logical character of theological language.

In theology positivism has been used in two senses: to denote Ritschl's theology which limits theology to the area of practicable religious evaluation; and to denote a theology of revelation (as a *given*) in contrast to a theology of speculation.

BIBLIOGRAPHY

Julius Weinberg, *An Examination of Logical Positivism*; Alfred J. Ayer, *Language, Truth and Logic*.

BERNARD RAMM

POSSESSION. *Peripoiein* means (1) to save or preserve for oneself, being used of one's life *(psyche)* in Luke 17:33; (2) to acquire for oneself, as God purchased the church with the "blood of his own one" as the ransom price (Acts 20:28; cf. Ps. 74:2; Isa. 43:21 [formed = *peripoiein*, LXX]), or as deacons gain good esteem of the Christian community (I Tim. 3:13 RSV); and (3) to bring about something for someone (II Macc. 15:21).

Peripoiēsis means (1) keeping safe, preserving, saving (Heb. 10:39, with *psyche*); (2) gaining or obtaining, e.g., of salvation (I Thess. 5:9) or glory (II Thess. 2:14); (3) possessing, possession, of property. In this sense it occurs in (a) I Pet. 2:9 (cf. Mal. 3:17, LXX *peripoiēsis*), where Christians are the new Israel, a people for God's special possession, the terms *laos* and *moi* defining *peripoiēsis*; and (b) Eph. 1:14, where *peripoiēseōs* is found by itself, and the context concerns the guarantee of our inheritance. Beza suggests we distinguish two deliverances *(apolytrōseis)*, one past, the other awaited in the future (Rom. 8:23). We best understand *peripoiēseōs* as acquisition at the second deliverance and translate "with a view to a complete redemption, which will give possession" (cf. RSV). Theodore Mopsuestia and Severianus rendered it "with a view to our full recovery of our privileges as sons of God," but this involves reading in *tô theô*. Christ's promise that "by your endurance you will gain your lives" (Luke 21:19) and his references to the heavenly treasure may have prompted the hope of ultimately acquiring possession of the inheritance.

BIBLIOGRAPHY

Arndt; *ICC*, Abbott on Eph. 1:14; K. Lake, *Beginnings of Christianity*, IV, pp. 261-62 on Acts 20:28.

DENIS H. TONGUE

POSTMILLENNIALISM. See MILLENNIUM.

POWER, POWERS. Of the Greek words used in the singular to express the idea of power, *dynamis* describes the general ability to perform, *exousia* the authority of freedom from any inward restraint in the exercise of that ability, and *kratos* the general idea of intensity of power. All three terms are applied to God (I Cor. 1:18; Rom. 13:1; Eph. 1:19), to Christ (Luke 4:36; Matt. 28:18; Rev. 5:13) and to believers (Eph. 1:19 ff.; John 1:12; Eph. 6:10). The plural of both *dynamis* and *exousia* is used of spiritual agencies (e.g., Rom. 8:38; Eph. 6:12), generally of an adverse character, but sometimes neutrally of earthly rulers (as the *exousiai* of Rom. 13:1-3). See also AUTHORITY; MIGHT.

The NT idea of the pre-eminent power of God is a development of the similar OT concept (cf. I Chron. 29:11; Job 26:14; Pss. 66:7; 145:11). The NT, however, is not dominated by an overwhelming display of divine power, but rather a personal manifestation of that power in Jesus Christ. His messianic power was in a direct line with and yet was infinitely greater than the power with which the prophets were endued. It was manifested in two ways, by his life and by his resurrection. His miracles *(q.v.)* were intended as messianic signs to corroborate the powerful effect of his teaching. They were not mere wonders, for there was nothing akin to magic in their form, in the words which commanded them (as contrasted with magical incantations), or in the faith which they required. They reveal a close personal relationship between Christ and the Father as the explanation of their origin. The resurrection of Jesus was the climax of the manifestation of divine power.

The power of the Holy Spirit is seen not only in the commencement of the ministry of Jesus (Luke 4:14, 36), but also in a special manner in the commencement of the church (Acts 2). This power was not an external possession which could be mechanically transferred (cf. Acts 8:19 ff.), but a living presence in the believer (cf. Rom. 15:13; II Cor. 13:3 ff.). Those who possess the Spirit possess power; their words and their works are mighty in proportion as the Spirit controls them.

In the Pauline Epistles much is made of the power of Christ's resurrection (Phil. 3:10), which is the operative principle in the believer (Eph. 1:19-20; cf. II Cor. 13:3-4). The apostle recognized that in preaching the cross he was preaching Christ as the power of God (I Cor. 1:23-24).

The conquest of opposing spiritual powers is well illustrated in the life of Jesus. His power over demonic forces is frequently shown, while Paul declares the overthrow of these powers to have reached its climax in the cross (Col. 2:15). By describing this triumph as a stripping off of the powers of evil the apostle implies a deliberate self-emancipation from all opposing agencies. The same idea is found in I Pet. 3:22, where angels, authorities and powers are grouped as subject to Jesus at the right hand of God, and in the Apocalypse where supreme authority is vested in God (Rev. 19:1) and in the enthroned Lamb (Rev. 5:12). The apostle Paul, on the other hand, vividly describes the Christian's present spiritual struggle against these unseen hostile powers (Eph. 6:12).

BIBLIOGRAPHY

A-S; Arndt; W. H. Dundas, art. "Principality" in *HDAC*; W. Grundmann in *TWNT*; J. B. Lightfoot, *Colossians*; Trench.

DONALD GUTHRIE

PRAGMATIC SANCTION. A pragmatic sanction is strictly a limitation of the sovereign in relation to the succession. Ecclesiastically it is applied to the declaration of A.D. 1438 (the Pragmatic Sanction of Bourges), by which the French clergy restricted the Papacy in relation to the administration of property and nomination to vacancies.

GEOFFREY W. BROMILEY

PRAGMATISM. See GOOD WORKS.

PRAISE. The Bible is full of praise and adoration to God. Praise may be defined as homage rendered to God by his creatures in worship of his person and in thanksgiving for his favors and blessings. Angels that excel in strength render their praise unto the Lord (Ps. 103:20). Their voices were lifted in adoration at the birth of Christ (Luke 2:13-14), and in tribulation days yet to come, they shall join in crying "Worthy is the Lamb that was slain . . ." (Rev. 5:11-12).

Praise is rendered to God by Israel, especially in the "Hallel Psalms" (Pss. 113 – 118). Not only Israel, but all who serve God, both heaven and earth, the seas and all that moves therein – in fact, everything that has breath must rightfully render praise unto the Lord (Pss. 135:1-2; 69:34; 150:6).

God may be praised with musical instruments and with song (Pss. 150:3-5; 104:33). Sacrifice (Lev. 7:13), testimony (Ps. 66:16), and prayer (Col. 1:3) are also activities where praise finds expression. Praise may be public as well as private (Ps. 96:3); may be an inward emotion (Ps. 4:7) or an outward utterance (Ps. 51:15). It is rendered to God for his salvation (Ps. 40:10) as well as for the greatness of all his marvelous works (Rev. 15:3-4). He should be praised for his inherent

qualities, his majesty (Ps. 104:1) and holiness (Isa. 6:3).

Praise occasionally has man as its object, in which case the commendation may be worthy (Prov. 31:28, 31) or unworthy (Matt. 6:2). The apostle Paul sought the glory of God rather than the praise of men (I Thess. 2:6), but recognized a legitimate praise as a tribute for distinguished Christian service (II Cor. 8:18). Such praise may become an incentive to holy living (Phil. 4:8).

It is not good to withhold the glory rightfully due God, for he has said "whoso offereth praise glorifieth me" (Ps. 50:23). Every believing heart which meditates upon his works (Ps. 77:11-14), which recounts his benefits (Ps. 103:2), and which dwells upon his unspeakable gift (II Cor. 9:15) will find the praise of God not only a duty but a delight.

BIBLIOGRAPHY

ISBE; HDB.

GERALD B. STANTON

PRAYER. I. OLD TESTAMENT. (1) The OT's view of prayer stems from a high conception of God. Prayer to God implies that God thinks, wills and feels; yet is omnipotent, omniscient, holy and gracious. Communion between Yahweh and his covenant people was natural, real and intimate. (2) The OT emphasizes the individual aspect of prayer. In Abraham, Moses, Samuel, and Jeremiah religious devotion reached remarkable heights at the individual level. This was especially so in intercession: Abraham interceding for Sodom (Gen. 18), Moses for Israel (Ex. 32:10-13), Job for his friends (42:8-10). The impression is that only outstanding personalities participated in intercession; probably because it was an unusual ministry. At the individual level petitionary prayer is common in the Psalms, however, (e.g., 31, 86, 123, 142); as is also adoration, praise and thanksgiving. (3) But because Israel was a covenant community social prayer is also prominent in the OT. Even some examples of individual prayer had a pronounced social flavor. Moses, Samuel, and Solomon prayed as representatives of the community (Ex. 33:7 ff.; I Sam. 7:2 ff.; I Kings 8:22). The corporate aspect is also prominent where prayer is conjoined with sacrifice: this redeemed the latter from mere slaughter and feasting. In this conjunction of prayer and sacrifice Israel offered her highest service to the Lord. Lawgiver, prophet and psalmist were all concerned to teach Israel that prayer involved giving as well as receiving; the offering of heart and lip as well as of flock and herd.

II. JESUS' TEACHING. (1) The most important factor in Christ's doctrine of prayer is his insistence upon the Fatherhood of God (q.v.). God is essentially *Holy* Father, however, who, while acting in a fatherly manner to all men, is a true father only to those who are his children through his grace and their repentance and faith. (2) Jesus also emphasized the value of the individual before God in prayer. Not only is the individual child of the Heavenly Father assured of a welcome to his presence; he is also assured that the Father had been going out in love toward him, to bring him home to himself. (3) Christ also taught men that true prayer is spiritual, not formal. In Matt. 6:5-8 he exposes the perils of formality in prayer; while his priestly prayer in John 17 emphasizes the inwardness of communion. Spontaneity, therefore, should also characterize true prayer. (4) Arising from its inwardness or spirituality is the Lord's emphasis on the potential of prayer; above all when prayer is the outgoing of the heart toward the Heavenly Father in unclouded faith (Mark 11:20-24). Jesus therefore directs believers to pray with perseverance and importunity (Luke 18:1-8). In addition to faith Christ emphasized two other conditions for success in prayer. Prayer must originate in a loving and forgiving disposition (Matt. 18:21-35), and it must be offered in Christ's own name (John 16:23 f.). (5) But prayer must concern itself with practical things. He directs us to pray for bread, forgiveness, victory in temptation, power over evil spirit forces, the mission field, enemies, the Holy Spirit. Jesus himself petitioned his Father in prayer. For example, in John 17 he requests the Father to keep believers united in truth, and to preserve them from sin. This does not mean, however, that petition is the only, or even the main element in prayer, as is clear from the form of prayer which he taught his disciples to use. (6) Indeed, the Lord's Prayer is a fitting summary of Jesus' teaching on the subject. God, to whom we pray, is a Father who, dwelling in heaven, receives our adoration. The true aim in prayer is not the imposition of our wills upon God but the hallowing of his sacred name, the extension of his kingdom, our submission to his will. Only then does Christ direct us to

petition the Father. Then the prayer ends, not with our needs or desires but with God, with whom it began; with his kingdom, his power, his glory. Truly, "When we pray rightly and properly, we ask for nothing else than what is contained in the Lord's Prayer" (Augustine).

III. PAUL'S TEACHING. The Pauline Epistles were obviously written by a man of prayer. He is constantly breaking forth into thanksgiving, adoration, petition, doxology. I Tim. 2:1-8 is a good summary of Paul's teaching on prayer. The Greek words in verse one provide a rewarding study. (1) Prayer in worship was important for Paul. For example, in Eph. 5:19 f.; Col. 3:16 f., prayer in congregational worship is especially emphasized. In the first Paul stresses orderliness in worship, and has probably the practical aspects of prayer in mind. (2) Rom. 8:26 f., is a classic passage on intercessory prayer. Here the problem is to know what God would have us pray for. Even Jesus faced the problem (Matt. 26:39-44). Under an inner compulsion we may intercede without understanding the petition. We may simply sigh out inarticulate desires. These unspoken aspirations, Paul teaches, are engendered by the Spirit who is, therefore, able to present them to the Father as intercessions. (3) In Rom. 8:34 it is Christ who intercedes for us. See also Heb. 7:25; I John 2:1. This means that the Trinity is involved in Christian prayer. In a word, the indwelling Spirit initiates a Christian's prayers; the Son then supports them as in his name the believer presents them to the Father. (4) It is probably this close connection between the Spirit and prayer that compels Paul to speak of prayer as being very demanding. In Rom. 15:30 he asks his friends to "agonize" with him in prayer. This spiritual "agony" characterized Epaphras' prayers (Col. 4:12). It is in this light that we are to view the Apostle's emphasis upon intercession in prayer (e.g., I Thess. 3:12 f.; II Cor. 13:7-9; Col. 1:9-18; Eph. 1:15-21; 3:14-21). And yet he did not hesitate to ask his converts to engage ceaselessly in intercession. In the NT every believer is an intercessor (Jas. 5:16; I Tim. 2:1), because each is a priest (Rev. 1:6). Yet prayer brought peace to the Christian's heart (Phil. 4:6 f.). Thanksgiving was also an essential part of Paul's prayers (Rom. 1:8; *passim*). When he received something different from his request it deepened his communion with God (II Cor. 12:7 ff.). The Book of Acts emphasizes the corporate nature of prayer; Jas. 5:13-18 bears the same witness.

BIBLIOGRAPHY
H. Trevor Hughes, *Prophetic Prayer;* F. Heiler, *Prayer.*

JAMES G. S. S. THOMSON

PRAYERS FOR THE DEAD. No passage in Old or New Testaments enjoins or even implies this practice. Of the single passage in the Apocrypha which appears to allude to it, it may be said that text, translation and interpretation of II Macc. 12:46 are all uncertain, and that there is considerable evidence that orthodox Jewry of the intertestamental period rejected prayers for the dead. In canonical Scripture, the Christian soul is spoken of as at once "with Christ" (II Cor. 5:6, 8; Phil. 1:23); the Lord promised the penitent thief paradise "today" (Luke 24:43). Scripture everywhere regards death as the end of man's probationary period; after death, even prior to the resurrection of the body and the last judgment, the soul is fixed in a permanent state of bliss or misery (see especially Luke 16:19-31). Hence prayers for the dead are, at best, irrelevant and unnecessary.

The Apostolic Fathers do not mention prayers for the dead. The custom seems to have arisen in the church at the end of the second century. In the Church of Rome the practice is an integral part of an erroneous system of salvation and is particularly connected with Roman teaching on purgatory, indulgences and the mass. The liturgies and confessions of Protestant churches do not countenance prayers for the dead.

O. RAYMOND JOHNSTON

PREACH, PREACHING. Preaching is the proclamation of the word of God to men by men under assignment from God. It is the ordained means for the transmission of the word of God to the world and serves also as an official means of grace for the edification of the church of Christ.

In the patriarchal period and even after Sinai believers were to communicate the promises and commandments of God to their children (Gen. 18:19; Deut. 11:19). In Israel this private instruction was to be supplemented by a public reading of the law every seven years during the Feast of Tabernacles (Deut. 31:9-13). During the revivals in the reigns of Jehoshaphat and Josiah the Levites went from city to city in Judah reading the law publicly

(II Chron. 15:3; 17:7-9; 35:3). Ezra and his assistants probably interpreted the law as it was read publicly after the return from captivity (Neh. 8:7-8). In the synagogues public reading of portions from the law and the prophets was followed by homiletic interpretation.

Prophets were functioning in Israel from the time of Moses to the days of the kings, but prophetism became the outstanding mode of divine revelation in the days of Israel's apostasy. The great prophets were the heralds of God declaring (forms of *nāgad*) judgment and the future hope of salvation, and crying (forms of *qārā'*) against the iniquities of the people and their leaders. The preaching of the prophets was often given by God immediately and transmitted as received, while the preaching of the Levites was based upon the written word, the Torah.

In the NT the preaching of John the Baptist, Jesus, the apostles and others is described by the use of some thirty different terms. The most important are *kēryssein,* "to herald," "to proclaim" (used sixty-one times, *kērygma* about nine times); *euaggelizesthai,* "to publish good news" (used over fifty times, *euaggelion* over seventy times); and *didaskein,* "to teach" (used around ninety times, the nouns *didaskalia* and *didachē* also being used, especially in the Pastoral Epistles). All of these verbs and substantives, following the pattern of extra-biblical usage or OT equivalents, carry a strong note of authority. The preacher has received his assignment and message from God and he comes with the authority of his Sender. The NT terms for preaching cannot be dissociated from the idea of the apostolate and its foundation in the arch-apostolate of Jesus Christ (John 20:21). This is especially true of the word used most often in John, *martyrein,* meaning "to bear testimony judicially as an eye-witness."

The primary message (*kērygma, euaggelion*) of the apostles consists in a declaration of the redemptive-historical facts of Christ's life, death, resurrection, session, and coming again, coupled with the call to repentance (*q.v.*) and faith (*q.v.*). The *kērygma* is fundamental to the life of the church and the apostolic teaching which serves to build up the church (*didachē,* teaching, *paraklēsis,* exhortation, and *nouthesia,* admonition, etc.). "The contents of the 'kerygma' and the *didache* in the New Testament are the same, but the modality is different. . . . [W]hat in the opening of the New Testament is called the 'kerygma' of the Kingdom of Heaven, in the later parts assumes a different shape, that of religious teaching and doctrine" (Herman N. Ridderbos, *When the Time Had Fully Come,* Eerdmans Publishing Company, Grand Rapids, Michigan, 1957, pp. 94 and 95).

Paul's letters to Timothy describe the transitional stage from the apostolate to the pastorate and evangelism. Timothy must hold fast to the apostolic teaching and the OT Scriptures and communicate this teaching in pastoral preaching and evangelism (I Tim. 4:13-14; II Tim. 2:15; 3:14-16; 4:1-5). The transmission of the word is secured for the church in history by the commissioning of faithful men able to teach others (II Tim. 2:2).

Origen's preaching marks the change from the hortatory homily to the expository sermon, but his exposition was clouded by the use of the allegorical method in interpreting Scripture. Through Augustine the defects of this method as reflected in preaching were passed to the Western Church until the time of the Reformation. The Reformers expounded and applied Scripture directly, often preaching in series on entire books of the Bible. Radical re-interpretations of the Bible have influenced preaching for evil but some see encouraging signs in the twentieth century of a return to preaching which aims to be based on an understanding of the Holy Spirit's intended message for the church in Holy Scripture.

BIBLIOGRAPHY
E. C. Dargan, *A History of Preaching;* C. H. Dodd, *The Apostolic Preaching and Its Developments,* pp. 7:13; K. Dijk, *De dienst der prediking,* T. H. L. Parker, *The Oracles of God;* H. N. Ridderbos, *When the Time Had Fully Come;* J. Stewart, *Heralds of God;* J. B. Weatherspoon, *Sent Forth to Preach;* G. Wingren, *Die Predigt.*

CARL G. KROMMINGA

PREBENDARY. See OFFICES, ECCLESIASTICAL.

PRECIOUS. A variety of Hebrew and Greek words underlies the translation "precious," most frequently used to describe objects of fine quality, but extended to define theological concepts. Thus the word *yāqār,* used to express the high regard in which a person or thing is held, is applied in Ps. 116:15 to the death of God's saints. Their death is not something lightly esteemed by God. Wisdom is said to be more precious than rubies, Prov. 3:15, that is, worthy of highest regard. The LXX

rendering of *yāqār* in Isa. 28:16 with *entimos* is followed in I Pet. 2:4. The word expresses the high evaluation to be placed on Jesus as the select cornerstone. In I Pet. 2:7 *timē* (rendered "honor" in I Pet. 1:7) is translated "precious" in the AV (margin, an honor). The point is that Jesus spells eschatological honor for his believers. In a similar vein the adjective *timios* is used to evaluate the blood of Christ (I Pet. 1:19).

FREDERICK WILLIAM DANKER

PREDESTINATION. We define predestination as that theological doctrine, primarily associated with Calvinism, which holds that from eternity God has foreordained all things which come to pass, including the final salvation or reprobation of man.

The doctrine of predestination is contained in the creeds of many evangelical churches, and has had a remarkable influence in both church and state. Probably its fullest expression is found in the Westminster Confession of Faith, which is the authoritative standard for most of the Presbyterian and Reformed churches throughout the world. The Established Church in England and the Episcopal Church in America have a mildly Calvinistic creed in the Thirty-Nine Articles. And while the Baptist and Congregational churches generally have no official creeds, it is expressed in the writings of many of the representative theologians of those churches.

During the first three centuries of the Christian church patristic writers left this doctrine largely undeveloped. It received its first full and positive exposition at the hand of Augustine, who made divine grace the only ground of man's salvation. In the Middle Ages Anselm, Peter Lombard, and Thomas Aquinas followed the Augustinian view to a certain extent, more or less identifying predestination with God's broad providential control over all things. In pre-Reformation times Wycliffe and Huss set forth strict predestinarian views.

At the time of the Protestant Reformation this doctrine was set forth with emphasis by Luther, Calvin, Zwingli, Melanchthon, Knox, and all the outstanding leaders of that period. Melanchthon later modified his views, and under his leadership the Lutheran Church came to oppose the doctrine. Luther's chief works, *The Bondage of the Will,* and his *Commentary on Romans,* show that he went into this doctrine as heartily as did Calvin. It was, however, Calvin who set it forth with such logical clearness and emphasis that it has ever since been designated "Calvinism," and has become an indispensable part of the system of Reformed theology. The Puritans of England and those who early settled in America, as well as the Covenanters in Scotland and the Huguenots in France, were thoroughgoing Calvinists. In more recent times the doctrine has been set forth by Whitefield, Hodge, Dabney, Cunningham, Smith, Shedd, Strong, Kuyper and Warfield.

The Westminster Confession of Faith states the doctrine thus: "God from all eternity did by the most wise and holy counsel of his own will, freely and unchangeably ordain whatsoever comes to pass: yet so as thereby neither is God the author of sin, nor is violence offered to the will of the creatures, nor is the liberty or contingency of second causes taken away, but rather established."

The doctrine of predestination thus represents the purpose of God as absolute and unconditional, independent of the whole finite creation, and as originating solely in the eternal counsel of his will. He appoints the course of nature and directs the course of history down to the minutest details. His decrees therefore are eternal, unchangeable, holy, wise, and sovereign. They are represented as being the basis of the divine foreknowledge (q.v.) of all future events, and not conditioned by that knowledge or by anything originated by the events themselves.

Objections against the doctrine of predestination bear with equal force against the foreknowledge of God, because what God foreknows must be as fixed and certain as that which is predestinated. When we say that we know what we will do, it is evident that we have already determined, and that our foreknowledge does not precede determination, but follows it and is based upon it. God foreknows the future because he has foreordained the future.

Some Scripture references setting forth the doctrine are: ". . . having foreordained us unto adoption as sons through Jesus Christ unto himself, according to the good pleasure of his will" (Eph. 1:5); ". . . in whom also we were made a heritage, having been foreordained according to the purpose of him who worketh all things after the counsel of his will" (Eph. 1:11); ". . . for of a truth in this city against thy holy Servant Jesus, whom thou didst

anoint, both Herod and Pontius Pilate, with the Gentiles and the people of Israel, were gathered together, to do whatsoever thy hand and thy counsel foreordained to come to pass" (Acts 4:27-28); ". . . him (Jesus) being delivered up by the determinate counsel and foreknowledge of God, ye by the hands of lawless men did crucify and slay" (Acts 2:23). See also Acts 13:48; Rom. 8:29-30; 9:11-12, 23; I Cor. 2:7; Eph. 2:10; Ps. 139:16; etc.

Even the sinful acts of men are included in the divine plan. They are foreseen, permitted, and have their exact places. They are controlled and overruled for the divine glory. The crucifixion of Christ, which admittedly was the worst crime in all human history, had, we are expressly told, its exact and necessary place in that plan (Acts 2:23; 4:28).

The doctrine of election (q.v.), which relates to the choice of particular persons, is to be looked upon as a particular application of the general doctrine of predestination as it relates to the salvation of sinners. And since the Scriptures are concerned primarily with the redemption of sinners, this part of the doctrine is naturally thrown up into a place of special prominence, the word election being found some forty-eight times in the NT alone. It sets forth an eternal, divine decree which, antecedently to any difference or desert in men themselves, separates the human race into two portions, one of which is chosen to everlasting life, while the other is left to everlasting death. So far as this decree relates to men it designates the counsel of God concerning those who had a supremely favorable chance in Adam to earn salvation, but who lost that chance. As a result of the fall they are guilty and corrupted; their motives are wrong, and they cannot work out their own salvation. They have forfeited all claim upon God's mercy and might justly have been left to suffer the penalty of their disobedience as all of the fallen angels were left. But instead, a portion of the race, the elect members, are rescued from the state of guilt and sin, and are brought into a state of blessedness and holiness. The non-elect are simply left in their previous state of ruin. They suffer no unmerited punishment, for God is dealing with them not merely as men but as sinners.

In the matter of salvation good works (q.v.) follow, but are not the meritorious cause of salvation. Christ himself says, "Ye did not choose me, but I chose you, and appointed you, that ye should go and bear fruit" (John 15:16). And Paul says, "We are his workmanship, created in Christ Jesus for good works, which God afore prepared that we should walk in them" (Eph. 2:10). Good works are, therefore, the fruits and proof of salvation.

Among Calvinists there has been some difference of opinion as to the order of events in the divine plan. The question here is, Were the objects of the divine decree contemplated as fallen creatures? or were they contemplated merely as men whom God would create, all being equal?

Infralapsarians say that those chosen to salvation were contemplated as members of a fallen race. The order of events then is: God proposed (1) to create; (2) to permit the fall; (3) to elect some out of this fallen mass to be saved, and to leave the others as they were; (4) to provide a redeemer for the elect; and (5) to send the Holy Spirit to apply this redemption to the elect. According to this plan, election follows the fall.

According to the supralapsarian view the order of events is: God proposed (1) to elect some creatable men (that is, men who were to be created) to life and to condemn others to destruction; (2) to create; (3) to permit the fall; (4) to send Christ to redeem the elect; and (5) to send the Holy Spirit to apply this redemption to the elect. According to this plan election precedes the fall.

The infralapsarian order of events seems to be the more scriptural and logical. In matters involving salvation or punishment, sin must at least be assumed as a background for the decree assigning men to different destinies. Discrimination does not in itself necessarily involve sin, but a choice such as is made here, to salvation or punishment, must contemplate men as sinners as its logical basis. God is truly sovereign, but his sovereignty is not exercised in an arbitrary way. Rather it is a sovereignty exercised in harmony with his other attributes, in this case, his justice, holiness and wisdom. It is not in harmony with the scriptural ideas of God that innocent men, i.e., men who are not contemplated as sinners, should be predestinated to eternal misery and death.

The Scriptures are practically infralapsarian — Christians are said to be chosen "out of" the world (John 15:19); and the potter is said to have a right over the clay, "from the same lump," to make one part a vessel unto honor, and another unto dishonor (Rom. 9:21). The elect and the non-elect are regarded as being originally in a common state of misery. Suffering and death are uniformly represented as the wages of sin. No Reformed confession teaches the supralapsarian view. A number do explicitly teach the infralapsarian view, which thus emerges as the typical Reformed view.

BIBLIOGRAPHY
   L. Boettner, *The Reformed Doctrine of Predestination;* C. Hodge, *Systematic Theology* I, pp. 535-49; B. B. Warfield, *Biblical Doctrines,* pp. 3-67; *HERE; ISBE.*

                                    LORAINE BOETTNER

PRE-EMINENCE. Paul's head-on clash with incipient Gnosticism (q.v.) evokes his classic statement concerning the pre-eminence of Christ in Col. 1:13 ff. Gnostic stress on the exaltation of angels and the need for a subdivine mediator in creation to bridge the gap between the perfect God and imperfect matter made it necessary for Paul to highlight the differences between Gnosticism and Christianity with a concise statement of the lordship of Christ. The climax of the passage is the final clause of Col. 1:18: "that in all things he might have the pre-eminence [*prōteuōn,* "be first, have first place"]."

The evidences of Christ's pre-eminence are manifold: (1) he alone is the image of the invisible God (Col. 1:15; John 1:14, 18; Heb. 1:3); (2) he is the pre-existent creator and the perpetual sustainer of the universe, the great Head of creation (Col. 1:15-17; John 1:3; Heb. 1:2-3); (3) he is the triumphant Head of the church, the first conqueror of death (Col. 1:13, 18; Eph. 1:20-23; 4:15-16); (4) he is the possessor of all fulness — whether of virtue or blessing, especially the blessing of reconciliation to God (Col. 1:19-20; 2:9; John 1:16).

Paul leans heavily on the OT and general Semitic background of primogeniture. Twice Christ is called first-born (*prōtotokos,* Col. 1:15, 18). It is as the first-born (q.v.) that he is heir to the Father's authority and inheritance. Here he may be contrasted with Reuben, who, though he was the eldest son, forfeited through incest his rights to pre-eminence (Gen. 49:3-4), i.e., double inheritance (Deut. 21:17) and superior blessing (Gen. 27:35 ff.).

John indicts the ambitious, cantankerous Diotrephes for rejecting apostolic authority and coveting the pre-eminence (*philoprōteuōn*) reserved for Christ and his apostles (III John 9).

BIBLIOGRAPHY
J. Eadie, *Colossians*; J. B. Lightfoot, *Colossians and Philemon*; R. L. Ottley, *The Doctrine of the Incarnation*, pp. 107-10; J. Pedersen, *Israel: Its Life and Culture*, I-II, pp. 258-59.

DAVID A. HUBBARD

PRE-EXISTENCE OF CHRIST. See CHRISTOLOGY.

PRE-EXISTENCE OF SOULS. Three major theories have been advanced concerning the origin of the soul: (1) Pre-existence; (2) Creationism, which holds that each individual soul is a direct creation of God and is placed in the human body, either at birth or some time prior to it; (3) Traducianism, which holds that the soul, as well as the body, is propagated by the parent.

The pre-existence theory holds that all souls, whether they be eternal or created by God in eternity past, exist in an abode or "treasury," from which they are called forth to inhabit men. It does not pretend to be a scriptural doctrine, for the Bible never speaks of a creation of men prior to Adam. Nor is the present condition of the human race ascribed to any higher source than the sin of our first parent.

The idea of pre-existence appears frequently in Talmudic literature, although it has been rejected by the majority of Jewish philosophers. According to Josephus it was held by the Essenes and may reflect the belief of the Jews at the time of Christ.

Among twentieth century religionists, the Mormons are the chief exponents of this theory. They contend that the soul, being synonymous with the spirit, is with God in heaven until sent to indwell the baby. This is essentially a form of reincarnation which has no scriptural foundation. The Bible teaches that souls depart this life, either for eternal punishment or else for the presence of God.

BIBLIOGRAPHY
C. Hodge, *Systematic Theology*, II, pp. 65-67; Scrivner's *Dictionary of the Bible*; *UJE*; J. F. Smith, *Doctrine of Salvation*, I, chap. 4, pp. 56 ff.

GERALD B. STANTON

PRELACY. Prelacy, from the medieval Latin *praelatus*, a high ranking civil or religious official, refers to the type of church government in which the control is vested in bishops, archbishops, metropolitans, and patriarchs. In Roman Catholicism such dignitaries as abbots, provosts, nuncios, and apostolic prefects (see *CE*, XII, pp. 386-7) are included among the prelates. In the Church of England bishops and archbishops are considered prelates.

Among nonepiscopal denominations prelacy and related words have often been used invidiously of the episcopal system. This was especially true of the Puritans and Baptists in England and of Scottish Presbyterians in the seventeenth century, when the Stewarts were attempting to impose episcopacy upon them.

DONALD G. DAVIS

PREMILLENNIALISM. See MILLENNIUM.

PRESBYTER, PRESBYTERY. See ELDER.

PRESENCE, DIVINE. In the Bible the word face or countenance (Heb. *pānîm*; Greek *prosōpon* or *enōpion*, "in the face of") is normally used to indicate presence. As applied to God, there seem to be three main senses. First, there is the general and inescapable presence of God as described in Ps. 139:7 ff. Second, there is the special presence of God among his people or among the nations to save or to judge (cf. Ex. 33:14; Nah. 1:5). This is further expressed by the divine dwelling in the tabernacle and temple (cf. Ps. 48), and especially by the coming of Jesus Christ as Emmanuel (Matt. 1:23; John 1:14), his continued presence in and with his disciples by the Holy Spirit (Matt. 28:20; John 14:16 f.) and his final coming in glory (I Thess. 2:19). Third, there is the presence of God in heaven, before which the angels stand (Luke 1:19), in face of which there can be no self-righteous boasting (I Cor. 1:29), from which the wicked are to be banished with everlasting destruction (II Thess. 1:9), but before which believers will be presented faultless in virtue of the work of Christ (Jude 24), thus enjoying, as the Psalmist dared to hope, the fulness of joy (Ps. 16:11; cf. 73:23 f.). It may be noted that the emphasis of the Bible is not on the divine presence as a general immanence; hence the naturalness with which Jonah can be said to try to flee from God's presence (Jonah 1:3) or worshipers to come before God's presence (Ps. 95:2). For sinful man who cannot see God or abide his presence, the important thing is the special realization of his presence in salvation and the final acceptance of the justified believer in his eternal presence. The presence of God among his people in the new heaven and earth is the goal of the divine work as initiated already by the incarnation and enjoyed in the Holy Spirit but to be consummated only at the last day: "Behold, the tabernacle of God is with men, and he will dwell with them, and they shall be his people, and God himself shall be with them, and be their God" (Rev. 21:3). This ultimate immanence, however, cannot be known and enjoyed by sinners merely in virtue of the divine omnipresence (Rev. 21:8). We are received into God's eternal presence only as we have first received God present to us in Jesus Christ (John 1:12).

GEOFFREY W. BROMILEY

PRIDE. Pride may be defined as "inordinate and unreasonable self-esteem, attended with insolence and rude treatment of others." It is an attempt to appear in a superior light to what we are, with "anxiety to gain applause, and distress and rage when slighted." "Pride is the high opinion that a poor, little, contracted soul entertains of itself" (MSt).

Pride is universal among all nations, being variously attributed in the Bible to Israel, Judah, Moab, Edom, Assyria, Jordan, and the Philistines. It is connected with the sin of Sodom (Ezek. 16:49). Indeed, the ambitious pride of Satan was part of the original sin of the universe (Ezek. 28:17, with I Tim. 3:6). It may well have been the first sin to enter God's universe, and no doubt will be one of the last to be conquered.

The Bible teaches that pride deceives the heart (Jer. 49:16), hardens the mind (Dan. 5:20), brings contention (Prov. 13:10), compasses about like a chain (Ps. 73:6), and brings men to destruction (Prov. 16:18). A proud heart stirs up strife (Prov. 28:25), and is an abomination unto the Lord (Prov. 16:5). A proud look God hates (Prov. 6:17), and those who engage therein shall stumble and fall (Jer. 50:32).

Pride is the parent of discontent, ingratitude, presumption, passion, extravagance, and bigotry. There is hardly an evil committed without pride being connected in some sense. Augustine and Aquinas held that pride was the very essence of sin. Since God resists the proud (James 4:6), the believer must learn to hate pride and to clothe himself with humility.

BIBLIOGRAPHY

Charles Buck, *Theological Dictionary*; L. S. Chafer, *Systematic Theology*, II pp. 63-64; MSt; A. H. Strong, *Systematic Theology*, p. 569.

GERALD B. STANTON

PRIEST, PRIESTHOOD. I. OLD TESTAMENT. In patriarchal times priestly functions were fulfilled by heads of families or tribes (Gen. 8:20; 22:13; 26:25; 33:20). From the Mosaic period a special priestly class existed in Israel. Israelite priests belonged to the family of Aaron, the first high priest in Israel. The priest was mediator between God and men, a minister in holy things on men's behalf, especially in atonement.

Naturally, then, priests were separated unto God. Their consecration to priesthood was a very elaborate piece of ritual (Ex. 29; Lev. 8). They also wore special vestments (Ex. 28). The high priest's main function was to officiate at the Day of Atonement ceremonies (Lev. 16), but he also offered sin offerings (Lev. 4:13-21), and the daily meal offering (Lev. 6:19 f.). The ordinary priests officiated at all sacrifices (Lev. 1-6), declared the unclean clean after examination (Lev. 13-14), and performed other minor duties (Num. 10:10; Lev. 23:24; 25:9). They were supported by the tithes, first fruits, firstlings, and the various sacrifices (Num. 18).

II. NEW TESTAMENT. Aaron and Melchizedek (*q.v.*) form the connection between the Testaments. They are distinctive because they were first in their orders, and because both typified Christ's priesthood: he summed up and completed them. Christ's priesthood is treated only in Hebrews: see especially 2:14-18; 4:14-16; 5:1-10; 7.

As to *order*, Jesus' priesthood is that of Melchizedek (Heb. 7). His qualifications are divine appointment (5:1) and divine preparation (5:2-9). His priesthood is kingly (7:1-3), unique (7:8-12) and indissoluble (7:16-24). As to Christ's priestly *duties*, however, they are after Aaron's priesthood. Having offered himself as a sacrifice for sin (7:27), he presents his blood within the veil (6:20; 8:3; 9:7, 24). Having thereby obtained eternal redemption (9:12), and established the new covenant (9:15-22), cleansing from sin (9:23) is now possible, and sanctification (10:14), free access to the throne of grace (10:19-22), and dedicated service (10:23-25).

Priesthood is also applied to Christians in the NT (I Pet. 2:5, 9; Rev. 1:5 f.). This is natural because our High Priest has given us access to the throne (Heb. 10:19-22). Our priesthood before God is a function of our sonship with God. Since also this access is through Christ (13:15) no priestly ordinance is required.

Four great principles emerge, then, from biblical priesthood: God the Father everywhere takes the initiative in appointing priests (5:4-6); priests were appointed in order to represent sinners to God, and mediate between them and God (5:1); this was effected by atoning sacrifice (8:3); the priests' intercessions are grounded in the priests' atonement.

JAMES G. S. S. THOMSON

PRINCIPALITY. See POWER, POWERS.

PRINCIPLES. The term is derived from the Greek *archē*. Thus the term "first" is basic to the concept and has resulted in the redundant phrase "first principles." Other double terms are "first truths," "basic assumptions" and "basic elements."

The term is used in several disciplines. In metaphysics, where the term is most applicable, it refers to the fundamental truths objectified in reality which determines the order or coherence of fact. Thus, the principle determining the order and coherence of all that is, according to Thales was water, for the atomists, the atom, etc.

Closely related to this use of the term in metaphysics is its use in epistemology where principle means the truths first in the order of explanation. Explaining the concept that water is the principle of things rests upon the principle of the trustworthiness of thought. The "trustworthiness of thought" is, as used here, an epistemological principle since the order of explanation depends on this truth.

Similarly, logic is governed by its principles. They are the basic assumptions upon which the argument rests, upon which the conclusion depends. Or, the term may refer to principles of method; also a reasoner's method or general habit of reasoning may be called his leading principle if he consciously holds that it leads to truth if truth is ascertainable (C. S. Peirce in *Baldwin's Dictionary of Philosophy and Psychology*).

With reference to morals, the term refers to the laws which control the factors of conduct. Closely related are principles of ethics, or the basic assumptions of the good life such as indulgence for the Cyrenaic and control for the Stoic.

BIBLIOGRAPHY
J. M. Baldwin (ed), *Dictionary of Philosophy and*

Psychology, II; E. A. Burtt, *Right Thinking*; HERE; MSt.

E. SIVERTSEN

PRISCILLIANISTS. Followers of Priscillian, a Spaniard (d. A.D. 385), whose teachings were widely accepted for about 150 years in Spain and S. France, especially in Galicia. In origin this teaching was Oriental and Egyptian, and in general terms was a Manichaean dualism, denying the pre-existence and real humanity of Christ, and accepting a modalist Trinitarianism. Their view that the human body was devilish led in practice both to severe asceticism and license. In 380 Priscillianism, which encouraged mixed gatherings for reading and interpreting the Scriptures, was condemned at Saragossa. Priscillian appealed unsuccessfully to the Pope, and eventually, after trial before the Spanish Emperor Maximus he was put to death. This is the first record of capital punishment for heresy. In 400 the Priscillianist bishops who would not abandon the heresy were deposed. In 563, at Braga, Priscillianism was formally condemned, Sulpicius Severus is the chief ancient authority.

M. R. W. FARRER

PRIZE. The word *brabeion* used by Paul to describe the prize awaiting faithful believers is somewhat rare. The LXX instead uses *athlon,* and the association with moral exertion in IV Macc. 9:8 is paralleled in Paul's writings. In Phil. 3:14 Paul speaks of pressing "toward the mark for the *prize* of the high calling of God in Christ Jesus." The prize here is inextricably linked with God's upward call in the gospel. This call involves the ultimate hope of the glorious body fashioned after that of Christ (Phil. 3:21) and rescued from the confining restraints of sin (Gal. 5:5). The prize, then, is the privilege of sharing in this complete eschatological deliverance, and being free to enjoy the untrammeled life of the redeemed in heaven. In similar vein Paul exhorts Christians (I Cor. 9:24-25) to exert every effort to win the prize, as runners do in a race. The point of comparison here is the urgency required. The Christian is to run as though he were in a race in which there could be only one winner. This interpretation finds recent support in a hitherto unknown Orphic writing alluded to in the Demosthenes scholia (cf. A. Ehrhardt in *ZNW*, 48, 101-10).

FREDERICK WILLIAM DANKER

PROBABILISM. In moral theology, Probabilism is the doctrine that where a solid probable opinion favors liberty for a line of action, it may be followed even though a more probable opinion is against it. Originating in the fourteenth century, the view was first developed in the sixteenth under the Dominican Medina. It was adopted by the Jesuits (especially Suarez) and led to considerable laxity where only slight probability was accepted as sufficient. Reaction came in seventeenth century France with Pascal and the Dominicans, the latter favoring Probabiliorism, i.e., that only a more probable opinion is to be followed. However, Probabilism re-established itself under Liguori, was adopted with some safeguards by the restored Jesuits after 1814, and is still the predominant teaching in the Roman Catholic Church.

GEOFFREY W. BROMILEY

PROBATION. Probation denotes the idea that man's life on earth is a period of testing his fitness for fuller life beyond. In this sense, despite its strong appeal to exponents of the reasonableness of Christianity such as Paley and Butler and to Arminian theologians generally, it is only partly biblical. It contains the conviction that this life is incomplete in itself and that man is continually under the eye of the eternal God. Insofar as it expresses the truth that "God will render to every man according to his deeds" as expounded in Rom. 2:6-16, the theory of probation is biblical. But when the Bible speaks specifically of God's probation it is chiefly a testing of his own elect with a view to confirming them in their faith, not a general probation of all men. Thus "God did tempt [ERV prove] Abraham" (Gen. 22:1), his people Israel (Ex. 15:25; 16:4; Deut. 8:16; Judg. 2:22; Ps. 66:10; Zech. 13:9), his servant Job (Job 23:10), and the "righteous one" of the Psalms (Ps. 17:3; 139:23-24).

In the NT it is the Son of God who is tempted, recapitulating in his own person the probation of Israel in the wilderness and exhibiting even to death unswerving faith in his Father. The probation of Christians is viewed consequently as fellowship in the sufferings of Christ to establish their faith (Heb. 12:3-11; I Pet. 4:12-13; cf. I Cor. 10:13; James 1:1-2). See also TEMPTATION.

Far from leading us to suppose that man's destiny depends on his ability to earn God's approbation through the trial to which he is put in life, the Bible indicates that the general probation or "trial which is coming on the whole world" is a probation of condemnation from which only those who are Christ's will be delivered (Rev. 3:10 RSV; cf. Matt. 6:13; 26:41; Luke 21:36; II Pet. 2:9).

Probation is also used of testing the suitability of candidates for office within the church (e.g., I Cor. 16:3; I Tim. 3:10).

BIBLIOGRAPHY
F. R. Shields in HERE; W. Grundmann in TWNT (dokimos).

DONALD W. B. ROBINSON

PROCESSION OF THE SPIRIT. Apart from Matt. 3:11 and Acts 2:33, the definitive texts are found almost exclusively in the Pauline and Johannine writings. The Spirit is "of God" (I Cor. 2:12), but also "of his Son" (Gal. 4:6) and "of Christ" (Rom. 8:9; Phil. 1:19; cf. I Pet. 1:11). The Father gives the Spirit (John 14:16) sent in Christ's name (John 14:26); but Christ himself sends the Comforter (John 15:26; 16:7) who "shall receive of mine" (John 16:14), and in John 20:22 he bestows the Spirit by breathing on his disciples. It is thus clear that both Father and Son are intimately connected in the Spirit's procession, but their precise relationship has been the subject of endless dispute.

Gregory of Nyssa shaped the typically Eastern formula "from the Father through the Son"; but Augustine, to avoid undue subordination, insisted on a double procession from both, maintaining in *De Trin.* v. 14 that the unity of persons obviates any duplicity of source. The Latin addition of *Filioque* ("and from the Son") to the Niceno-Constantinopolitan Creed, noted in 589 and officially sanctioned by 1017, led to the schism between Eastern and Western churches.

BIBLIOGRAPHY
H. B. Swete, *History of the Doctrine of the Procession of the Holy Spirit;* J. N. D. Kelly, *Early Christian Creeds.*

G. S. M. WALKER

PROFANE. In the OT "profane" is a ceremonial word, an antonym of "holy" (cf. I Sam. 21:4; Ezek. 22:26). To profane is to take something out of the sacred sphere into normal life. The Hebrew *hll,* whose original force was apparently to untie, means the removal of a prohibition, either illegitimately as in Lev. 21:4, 9, 15, etc., where prohibitions are imposed upon priests, or legitimately, e.g., in Deut. 20:6 and Jer. 31:5, where *hll* signifies permission to use or enjoy the vineyard; after the first fruits have been given to the Lord, the vineyard is no longer holy but profane or common, i.e., usable by man.

The Lord's name (i.e., person) is the most common object of profanity (Lev. 18:21; 20:3; 21:6; Ezek. 36:21-23; Amos 2:7, etc.); but what God has sanctified by his presence or his word may also be profaned, e.g., the sanctuary with its vessels (Lev. 21:12; 22:15; Ezek. 22:26; 24:21), the sabbath (Ezek. 22:8), and the covenant (Mal. 2:10). Deliberate profanity (godlessness) is expressed by *hnp* as in Jer. 23:11, 15 (see HYPOCRISY).

The NT (like the LXX) employs the verb *bebēloō* to express ceremonial defilement in Matt. 12:5 (sabbath) and Acts 24:6 (sanctuary). The adjective *bebēlos*, "profane," however, takes on a moral or religious tone — "godless" or "irreligious" (I Tim. 1:9; 4:7; 6:20; II Tim. 2:16; Heb. 12:16). Ceremonial profaneness is usually expressed by *koinos*, "common" or *akathartos*, "unclean" (cf. Mark 7:2 ff.; Acts 10:14 ff.).

See also COMMON.

BIBLIOGRAPHY
Arndt; J. Pedersen, *Israel: Its Life and Culture*, III-IV, pp. 270 ff.; N. H. Snaith, *Distinctive Ideas of the OT*, pp. 34-36.

DAVID A. HUBBARD

PROFESSION. The two basic meanings of the word profess as found in the AV are: (1) in the general sense, to make a public declaration about something, and (2) more particularly, to declare (publicly) faith in someone or something. In the former sense *nāgad* (rendered "declare" in the RSV) is used once (Deut. 26:3) in the OT, while *phaskein* (Rom. 1:22), *epaggellesthai* (I Tim. 2:10) and *homologein* (I Tim. 6:21; II Cor. 9:13) are found in the NT. The idea of insincerity or pretense is sometimes found in the word profession, as in Rom. 1:22 and Titus 1:16. In the sense of (2) above, profession is not found in the OT, but the NT has several occurrences (I Tim. 6:12; Heb. 3:1; 4:14; 10:23). In these passages it is invariably a rendering of *homologein* (or the noun form, *homologia*). The RSV, in order to eliminate the overtones of pretense or insincerity often associated with profession, renders *homologia* in the above passages confession.

WALTER W. WESSEL

PROMISE. The English word promise derives directly from the Latin *promissa*, meaning exactly what our word promise means, "a declaration or assurance made to another person with respect to the future stating that one will do or refrain from some specified act, or that one will give or bestow some specified thing, usually in a good sense implying something to the advantage or pleasure of the person concerned" (*Oxford English Dictionary*). Actually, no word in the Hebrew or Greek Scriptures has this exact meaning. The word generally translated promise in the OT writings is *dābar*, rendered speak over eight hundred times, or say more than one hundred times — to talk, to utter, to pronounce. When these pronouncements embrace the idea of something promised, the word is so used, e.g., in the ordinary promises of men to men, and especially the promises of God to the people of Israel (Deut. 1:11; 6:3; 9:28; 15:6; 19:8, etc.) or to one particular individual, as to Solomon (I Kings 5:12).

In the NT Scriptures the word is *epaggelia*, which in the overwhelming number of instances is simply translated promise, as a noun and in its verbal form. The root of this word *aggelia* means something announced; *aggelos*, the announcer or the messenger, and *euaggelia*, a message of good tidings. On rare occasions, the word is used of some incidental promise of man to man, as in Acts 23:21. Its occurrences in the NT may be gathered into three groups. There are, first, the frequent references to God's promises to Abraham concerning an heir (Rom. 4:13-16, 20; 9:8-9; 15:8; Gal. 3:16-22; 4:23; Heb. 6:13-17; 7:6; 11:9, 11, 17). Abraham believed these promises, and they were repeated to his patriarchal descendants Isaac and Jacob, through whom the promised seed should come. The relationship of Christian believers to the promises in Abraham will be considered later.

The second major theme of these promises is David's seed, "a Saviour according to promise" (Acts 13:23). Stephen speaks of the time of the advent as that in which "the time of the promise drew nigh" (Acts 7:17). This promise to David of a Saviour has been confirmed in Christ (Acts 13:32). It is to this group that we must assign Paul's allusion to "the promise by faith in Jesus Christ" (Gal. 3:22). It is probable that this dual grouping of promises, those to Abraham concerning a seed and those to David concerning a king to reign, are united in Paul's references to this subject as "the promises made unto the fathers" (Rom. 15:8); in the familiar discussion of Israel's future, he refers to them as "the children of the promise" (Rom. 9:8-9) and reminds the Israelites that they are the ones who possess the promises of God (Rom. 9:4). Closely associated with this is the gift of God promised to us in Christ, that is, the promise of life in Christ (II Tim. 1:1), or, as elsewhere expressed, "the promise of eternal inheritance" (Heb. 9:15), or, as John wrote, "the promise which he promised us, even the life eternal" (I John 2:29).

The third group of promises concerns the gift of the Holy Spirit after our Lord's ascension, never referred to as a promise until after the resurrection (Luke 24:49; cf. Acts 1:4; 2:33; Eph. 1:13).

Other subjects related to the promises of God are mentioned only incidentally in the NT: the promise of rest (Heb. 4:1); the fulfilment of the promises of a new heaven and a new earth (II Pet. 3:13, from Isa. 52:11 and Hos. 1:4); the promise of the resurrection (Acts 26:6); "the first commandment with promise," regarding obedience of children to their parents (Eph. 6:2, from Ex. 20:12).

There is some similarity between promise and prophecy (q.v.). So, e.g., the frequently-used phrase "the promises to Abraham, and to Israel" for the most part refers to the prophecies given to Abraham and the patriarchs, beginning with Gen. 12:1-3 (see Rom. 9:4, 8; 15:8; Gal. 3:16-22, 29). But there are some notable differences: (1) All promises relate to the desirable, the good, that which blesses and enriches, while some prophecies refer to judgments, destructions, invasions, the appearance of enemies of Christ, such as the little horn, the man of sin, etc. (2) Promises ordinarily have a more general scope than prophecies, often including the entire human race — though we realize that all mankind is involved in some prophecies also — thus, the Fifth Commandment is called "the first commandment with promise" (Eph. 6:2), and would seem to refer to all who obey this command. So likewise the "promise of life" (I Tim. 4:8; II Tim. 1:4). (3) Promises have a more continuous fulfilment, generation by generation, than do most prophecies, as in the often-repeated phrase, "the promise of the Father" or "the promise of the Holy Spirit" (Luke 24:49; Acts 1:4; 2:33, 39; Gal. 3:14; Eph. 1:13).

While there are prophecies relating to Palestine, it is never called "the land of prophecy," but "the land of promise" (Heb. 11:9), and continues to be that down through the ages even though disobedience forfeits for a time the fulfilment of the promise. (4) Many promises are conditional, dependent upon obedience to the word of God, as the Beatitudes, but most prophecies are unconditional, and ultimately will be fulfilled. (5) Generally the concept of promise embraces many utterances of God, as in the phrase "he has granted to us his precious and very great promises" (II Pet. 1:4), whereas prophecies are ordinarily directed to more specific events or individuals.

WILBUR M. SMITH

PROPHET, PROPHECY. The word prophet comes from the Greek *prophētēs*, from *pro* ("before" or "for") and *phēmi* ("to speak"). The prophet is thus the one who speaks before in the sense of proclaim, or the one who speaks for, i.e., in the name of (God).

In the OT there are three terms for the prophet: *rō'eh*, *nābi'* and *ḥōzeh*. The first and last are distinguished by nuances bearing on the habitual or temporary character of the visions. *Nābi'* (he who witnesses or testifies) is best adapted to characterize the prophetic mission.

I. PROPHETIC INSPIRATION. The originality of biblical prophecy derives from the phenomenon of inspiration. As distinct from the sacral figures of pagan antiquity (cf. Frazer, in *Adonis*), the biblical prophet is not a magician. He does not force God. On the contrary, he is under divine constraint. It is God who invites, summons and impels him, e.g., Jer. 20:7 (cf. A. Heschel, *Man is not alone*, pp. 125 ff.; A. Neher, *L'Essence du Prophetisme*, pp. 97 ff.).

By inspiration, God speaks to the *nābi'*, who has to transmit exactly what he receives. The mode of inspiration is verbal. The Bible depicts the mechanism of inspiration as the act by which God puts words (*verba*) in the mouth of the sacred writers. God said to Moses: "I will raise them up a prophet from among their brethren, like unto thee, and will put my words (*verba*) in his mouth" (Deut. 18:18). Similarly to Jeremiah: "I have put my words in thy mouth" (Jer. 1:9). The NT confirms the verbal nature of prophetic inspiration (cf. Gal. 1:11-12; I Cor. 15:1-4; I Thess. 2:13; 4:8).

Yet inspiration does not suppress individuality. It is the miracle of *theopneustia* (II Tim. 3:16). To communicate his thoughts to men, God uses men of different culture, character and status in order that his word might be accessible to all men. Inspiration safeguards individuality (cf. Moses in Ex. 3-4, Jeremiah in Jer. 20:14-18, etc.).

II. THE PROPHETS. The writing prophets of the OT are well known. They are usually divided into the four major (Isaiah, Jeremiah, Ezekiel, and Daniel) and the twelve minor (Hosea, Joel, Amos, Obadiah, Jonah, Micah, Nahum, Habakkuk, Zephaniah, Haggai, Zechariah, and Malachi) according to the length of their writings.

In addition there were many other prophets. Moses, who wrote the law of God, was regarded as a *nābi'* without equal (Deut. 34:10-12). Prophetic voices were also raised in the days of the judges (Judg. 2:1-5; 3:9-11; 4:4; 6:8; I Sam. 3:1). Samuel came as a second Moses (Jer. 15:1; Ps. 99:6), and his work was continued by Gad and Nathan (II Sam. 12 and 24; I Kings 1). After the separation of the ten tribes, Ahijah (I Kings 2), Elijah, and Elisha (I Kings 18-19; II Kings 5 ff.) call for particular mention.

After four centuries of prophetic silence John the Baptist is the last of the prophets of the old covenant and the precursor of Jesus (Matt. 19:1; cf. Matt. 3:7 ff.; Luke 3:16 ff.; John 1:23, 29). In addition to the Baptist, the NT also refers to a prophetic ministry exercised by both men and women. After Pentecost, mention is made of Agabus (Acts 2:28; 21:10), Jude and Silas (Acts 15:32), and the four daughters of Philip (Acts 21:8-10). We might also quote Anna the daughter of Phenuel (Luke 2:36).

III. THE PROPHETIC MESSAGE. The prophecies of the writing prophets of the OT may be divided into three main groups: (1) Prophecies concerning the internal destiny of Israel. These declare the judgment of God on the unbelief and iniquities of the people, but promise restoration after the testing period of the exile. (2) Messianic prophecies. These point to the coming Redeemer of Israel and the world. They attain an astonishing clarity and precision in the case of Micah (5:1) and especially Isaiah. The latter gives us a striking summary of the saving life and work of Christ (52:13 – 53). (3) Eschatological prophecies. These refer to the last days when the kingdom of God will be set up on earth.

From a different standpoint we might adopt the following classification. (1) Prophecies already fulfilled. Two examples are the exile, announced by Hosea, Amos, and Micah in the case of Northern Israel (deported to Assyria in 722 B.C.) and Isaiah, Jeremiah, Ezekiel, Hosea, Amos, and Micah in the case of Judah (exiled in Babylon in 586 B.C.), and of course the coming of Christ himself. (2) Prophecies in process of fulfilment. A good case in point is the restoration of the modern state of Israel. The prophecy of Jeremiah 31:31 (cf. Isa. 27:12-13; Ezek. 37:21) found miraculous fulfilment on May 15, 1948, and the physical resurrection of the Israelite nation, as yet incomplete, is a new and up-to-date guarantee that other prophecies will come to realization. (3) Prophecies not yet fulfilled. We may refer to four. The first is the total recovery of Palestine by all the tribes of Israel (Isa. 27:12-13; Ezek. 37:11-14; Jer. 31:1-5, 31, etc.). The second is the destruction of Israel's enemies (Jer. 30:11; Isa. 17:1-3; Ezek. 38-39). The third is the collective conversion of Israel (Ezek. 37:6b, 10; Zech. 14:4 f.; 12:10). The fourth is the establishment of the kingdom of God on earth. Many prophecies describe the coming of the Messiah, the King of Israel, and the restoration of humanity to righteousness, peace and happiness under his rule (cf. Isa. 2:4; 11:1-10; 65:19-23), the reconstitution of nature (Ezek. 47:13a; 48:1-35, cf. Rom. 8:19-21) and the re-establishment of converted Israel in the prerogatives of its original vocation (cf. Isa. 49:6; Rom. 11:15; Joel 2:28-32; Hab. 2:14; Isa. 55:4-5; Zech. 8:23). Before the kingdom of God is set up, the earth will be the scene of the return and temporary reign of the Messiah (cf. Rev. 20:2b-3, 4b) and Israel will be God's instrument (Zech. 8:13) for the conversion of the nations (cf. on this whole theme, A. Lamorte, *La Vocation d'Israël et la Vocation de l'Eglise*; R. Pache, *Le Retour de Jesus-Christ*; G. N. H. Peters, *The Theocratic Kingdom*).

ANDRÉ LAMORTE

PROPITIATION. Propitiation properly signifies the turning away of wrath by an offering. In the NT this idea is conveyed by the use of *hilaskomai* (Heb. 2:17), *hilastērion*

(Rom. 3:25) and *hilasmos* (I John 2:2; 4:10). In the OT the principal word is *kipper* (see ATONEMENT), usually rendered in the LXX by *exilaskomai*. The word group to which the Greek words belong unquestionably outside the Bible has the significance of averting wrath. But in recent times it has been suggested that the Bible usage is different. C. H. Dodd argues strongly that, when the word group occurs in the LXX and the NT, it denotes expiation (the cancellation of sin), not propitiation (the turning away of the wrath of God). He denies that "the wrath of God" denotes anything more than a process of cause and effect whereby disaster inevitably follows sin.

For a criticism of his arguments see the works by Nicole and Morris in the bibliography. Here it is sufficient to notice that neither Dodd nor others who argue for "expiation" seem to give sufficient attention to the biblical teaching. The idea of the wrath (*q.v.*) of God is stubbornly rooted in the OT, where it is referred to 585 times. The words of the *hilaskomai* group do not denote simple forgiveness or cancellation of sin, but that forgiveness or cancellation of sin which includes the turning away of God's wrath (e.g., Lam. 3:42 f.). This is not a process of celestial bribery, for the removal of the wrath is in the last resort due to God himself. Of the process of atonement by sacrifice, he says: "I have given it to you" (Lev. 17:11). Note also Ps. 78:38: "Many a time turned he his anger away."

While God's wrath is not mentioned as frequently in the NT as the Old, it is there. Man's sin receives its due reward, not because of some impersonal retribution, but because God's wrath is directed against it (Rom. 1:18, 24, 26, 28). The whole of the argument of the opening part of Romans is that all men, Gentiles and Jews alike, are sinners, and that they come under the wrath and the condemnation of God. When Paul turns to salvation, he thinks of Christ's death as *hilastērion* (Rom. 3:25), a means of removing the divine wrath. The paradox of the OT is repeated in the New that God himself provides the means of removing his own wrath. The love of the Father is shown in that he "sent his Son to be the propitiation for our sins" (I John 4:10). The purpose of Christ's becoming "a merciful and faithful high priest" was "to make propitiation for the sins of the people"

(Heb. 2:17). His propitiation is adequate for all (I John 2:2).

The consistent Bible view is that the sin of man has incurred the wrath of God. That wrath is averted only by Christ's atoning offering. From this standpoint his saving work is properly called propitiation.

See also ATONEMENT.

BIBLIOGRAPHY

Arndt; MM; C. H. Dodd, *The Bible and the Greeks*; R. Nicole, *WTJ* 17:117-57; Leon Morris, *NTS* 2:33-43, and *The Apostolic Preaching of the Cross*, chaps. 4-5.

LEON MORRIS

PROPORTION. The only NT occurrence of this term is in Rom. 12:6, "the proportion [*analogia*] of faith," where it is most natural to take it as equivalent to the "measure [*metron*] of faith" in verse 3 preceding. Not pride, but such faith as God has apportioned, must control the exercise of spiritual gifts. If, however, Rom. 12:6 refers to "the faith" (the body of belief), as many take it, the phrase would mean that prophecy must conform to, and not contradict, the gospel (cf. I Cor. 12:3). Another possibility is that "faith" here carries the idea of the Hebrew root *'āman*: "true," "faithful"; "according to the proportion of faith" would then mean truthfully, faithfully, thus combining something of both the above interpretations. Wett aptly quotes Jer. 23:28 (where "faithfully" translates Hebrew *'emet*, LXX *ep' alētheias*) from a passage which may well underlie Paul's teaching here.

BIBLIOGRAPHY

G. Kittel in *TWNT*; C. Hodge on Rom. 12:6.

DONALD W. B. ROBINSON

PROSELYTE, PROSELYTISM. The word proselyte is derived from the Greek *prosēlytos* (lit. "one who has arrived at a place," therefore "a stranger") used in the LXX to identify the resident alien (Hebrew *gēr*) within Israel's borders (Ex. 12:49; Deut. 5:14; 31:12, *et al.*). The *gēr* who did not identify himself with the full religious requirements of Israel was a resident in Israel by sufferance only and without civil rights. The word *gēr*, however, came to be applied to foreigners who became Yahweh's worshipers and adopted Judaism's religious ceremonial, as Nicolaus (Acts 6:5); these converts to Judaism (*q.v.*) were granted full legal and religious, though not necessarily social, equality, and were known technically as proselytes. That they were Jews in every sense of the word is not invalidated by Acts 2:10 which merely distinguishes between born Jews and Gentiles adopting Judaism. Cultural conditions in the last three centuries preceding the Christian era stimulated Judaism to intensive missionary zeal (cf. Matt. 23:15). J. Klausner (*From Jesus to Paul,* New York, 1943, p. 33) estimates more than three million Jews, the majority of whom must have been proselytes, in the Diaspora. Persecutions and legal restrictions after the destruction of Jerusalem initiate a decline in mission effort, or proselytism.

A special problem is raised in the NT by the adherents of Yahweh known as *hoi phoboumenoi* or "God-fearers." They include the centurion of Capernaum (Luke 7:5), the Ethiopian eunuch (Acts 8:27 f.), and Cornelius of Caesarea (Acts 10). These are popularly identified as "proselytes of the gate," or semi-proselytes, in distinction from full proselytes or "proselytes of righteousness," who had become Jews in the full sense of the word. E. Schuerer (*Geschichte des Juedischen Volkes,* 3 ed., Leipzig, 1898, Vol. III, 124 ff.) questions the identification, and many scholars agree that the thought of half-proselytes conflicts with Judaism's basic tenets. As a result of Judaism's increased mission emphasis, the term gēr gradually became associated with converts to Judaism. To avoid confusion between this term as applied to proselytes and the term as applied to resident aliens who had not adopted Judaism, the expression gēr tôšāḇ was adopted. Later Jewish discussions involved the application of technical distinctions occasioned by Jewish mission experience to biblical terminology. Rabbis questioned whether the "proselyte of the gate" (cf. Deut. 5:14) was a gēr haṣṣedeq (proselyte of righteousness) or a gēr tôšāḇ (a resident alien), but the Talmud knows of no half-way condition, nor does it, according to Schuerer (*op. cit.,* III, p. 127), use the term gēr haša'ar. Details on the ceremonial connected with the reception of proselytes are to be found in *The Talmud, Yebamoth* 47a (London, Soncino Press, 1936), I, pp. 310 ff.

BIBLIOGRAPHY

Arndt; E. Schuerer, *Geschichte des Juedischen Volkes,* 3rd ed., III, pp. 102-35; J. Klausner, *From Jesus to Paul,* pp. 31-49; G. F. Moore, *Judaism,* I, pp. 323-53; Tacitus, *History,* V, 5; Juvenal, *Satires,* XIV, pp. 96-104.

FREDERICK W. DANKER

PROTESTANTISM. An inclusive term to indicate that sector of historic Christianity which in seeking to reform the church according to the word of God withdrew from papal obedience in the sixteenth century. Hence, it denotes the system of faith and practice derived from the principles of the Reformation. The name originated in Germany when at the second Diet of Spires in 1529 the supporters of Luther entered their Protestation against the repeal of the previous and more tolerant edict of 1526. A lengthier statement, the *Instrumentum Appellationis,* made it clear that the evangelical minority took their stand, as Luther himself had already done, upon the Word. "This Holy Book is in all things necessary for the Christian . . ." they declared. "This Word alone should be preached, and nothing that is contrary to it. It is the only Truth. It is the sure rule of all Christian doctrine and conduct. It can never fail us nor deceive us."

As R. H. Bainton has pointed out, "the emphasis was less on protest than on witness" (*The Reformation of the Sixteenth Century,* Beacon Press, Boston, 1952, p. 149). That indeed is the primary etymological significance of *protestatio* in post-Augustan Latin, and, according to Dean Inge, "it is ignorance which seeks to restrict the word to the attitude of an objector" (*Protestantism,* E. Benn, London, 1931, p. 1). A positive testimony to the supremacy of the word still remains the distinguishing feature of Protestantism.

BIBLIOGRAPHY

K. von Hase, *Handbook to the Controversy with Rome;* K. Hamilton, *The Protestant Way;* R. N. Flew and R. E. Davies, *The Catholicity of Protestantism.*

A. SKEVINGTON WOOD

PROVIDENCE. Providence is one of the words which do not occur in the Bible, but which nevertheless represent truly a biblical doctrine. There is no Hebrew equivalent for "providence," and the Greek word translated thus, *pronoia,* is used only of human foresight (Acts 24:2; Rom. 13:14). For the verb *pronoeō,* see Rom. 12:17; II Cor. 8:21; I Tim. 5:8. Rather, the Bible uses *ad hoc* words like "he *giveth food* to all flesh" (Ps. 136:25), or "he *sendeth forth springs* into the valleys" (Ps. 104:10), expressing in concrete situations his mighty acts towards the children of men.

We must straightway resist the temptation to think about providence generally and independently of Christ. It would be possible to draw on certain Psalms and the Sermon on the Mount, for example, to make up a doctrine of God's relationship to his creation which had nothing to do with Jesus Christ. But since it is in Christ that this relationship is established, an attempt to understand it apart from him would be a misinterpretation from the start. In Jesus Christ God has set up the relationship between himself and his creature, promising to carry through his purpose in creation to its triumphal conclusion. The primal relationship with Adam, renewed with Noah (Gen. 8:21-22), is no less *in Christo* than is the covenant with Abraham or Moses. The Mediator who is the incarnate Word establishes this relationship, and in him God becomes the God of men and they become his people. (In passing, we should also note that the Mediator must be regarded as setting up the relationship between God and his creatures other than man.) As their God, he will take up the responsibility for their earthly existence.

We may now consider the doctrine of providence from three different aspects.

(1) The creation is the stage on which are enacted God's dealings with mankind. Providence is God's gracious outworking of his purpose in Christ which issues in his dealings with man. We are not at this point slipping over into the doctrine of predestination, but are saying that from the beginning God has ordered the course of events towards Jesus Christ and his incarnation. From the biblical point of view, world history and personal life-stories possess significance only in the light of the incarnation. The squalid little story of lust in Judah's dealings with Tamar (Gen. 38) falls into its place in the genealogy of the Messiah (Matt. 1:3). Caesar Augustus was on the throne in Rome for the sake of the unknown baby in its manger!

(2) According to Acts 14:17, 17:22-30, and Rom. 1:18-23, God's providence served also the purpose of bearing witness to God among the heathen. God's fatherly care was a sign, pointing towards himself. Rom. 1:20 makes it clear that the purpose of this witness of providence was simply to render man inexcusable for not knowing God: *eis to einai autous anapologētous*. At this point also, therefore, providence is included in the doctrine of reconciliation.

(3) The God who gives man life also preserves him while he is on the earth. God is not a God of the soul alone, but of the body also. In Matt. 6:25-34 the disciples are reminded (by their Creator himself!) of their creaturely relationship to God, and are freed from all anxiety about their earthly future. The other creatures (as exemplified by the birds and the wild flowers) have been set in a definite relationship to God which he faithfully maintains by caring for their needs. Will God bestow less care upon man, to whom he has given a higher place in the creation? (cf. Ps. 8:6-8). Men therefore "glorify their Creator . . . by a daily unquestioning acceptance of His gifts" (D. Bonhoeffer, *The Cost of Discipleship*, S. C. M. Press, London, 1948, p. 154). Behind this doctrine lies the almighty and the loving freedom of God.

In sum, the doctrine of providence tells us that the world and our lives are not ruled by chance or by fate but by God, who lays bare his purposes of providence in the incarnation of his Son.

BIBLIOGRAPHY
Art. *"Providence"* in HERE and in HDB; J. Calvin, *Institutio*, I:xvi-xviii; H. Heppe, *Reformed Dogmatics*, chap. XII; K. Barth, *Church Dogmatics*, III/3, §48.

T. H. L. PARKER

PRUDENCE. Several words are rendered "prudence," the same also being translated "understanding," "subtlety." Main Hebrew root-words are *bin* (Isa. 29:14; Jer. 49:7), *'ārōm*, which can express either virtuous prudence (Prov. 8:12; 19:25) or evil guile (Gen. 3:1), *śākal* (Isa. 52:13; Amos 5:13). NT words are *phronēsis* (Eph. 1:8) and *synesis* (I Cor. 1:19), generally and correctly rendered "understanding." Prudence is wisdom issuing in right action.

R. COLIN CRASTON

PSEUDO-ISADORIAN DECRETALS. See FALSE DECRETALS.

PSYCHOLOGY. Psychology is the scientific study of the behavior and experience of living organisms. "Behavior" refers to responses of an organism to its environment observable to an outside person; "experience" refers to inner events which can be fully observed only by the experiencing person — such as memory or perception.

The field consists of two major subdivisions: experimental and applied. Experimental psychology is concerned with basic research. Through empirical techniques it seeks verifiable data which will make possible the prediction and control of human behavior. "Applied psychology" includes a diversity of fields which share the aim of applying psychological principles to human activity. Abnormal psychology, for example, is concerned with understanding the origin and development of pathological behavior; while clinical psychology seeks means for diagnosing and treating emotional disturbances. Both the experimental and applied approaches may be found in all fields of psychology, since these represent attitudes or aims; hence they are not always separable.

In its encounter with theology and the work of the minister both aspects of psychology are present. The experimental or theoretical emphasis is usually classified as the psychology of religion; the applied as pastoral counseling. Recently it has become common practice to subsume both under the term "pastoral psychology."

Systematic work in the psychology of religion began during the last quarter of the nineteenth century and was highlighted by Starbuck's studies of conversion and William James' monumental analysis of religious experience.

Since the rise of the psychoanalytic movement, what is called "depth psychology" has exerted greatest influence upon the psychology of religion. Depth psychology is concerned with the inner urges and strivings of men, especially unconscious strivings.

Depth psychology received its impetus from the work of Sigmund Freud and his associates. Freud took a materialistic view of man, and places his clinical authority behind Feuerbach's "projection theory" of religion, i.e., that religious beliefs stem from man's efforts to objectify some wish — e.g., providence is the desire to believe we are important in the universe; and the idea of God as personal is the effort to establish human personality as the highest form of being. Because, says Freud, life is full of hardships and disappointments, not the least of which is the "painful riddle of death," man feels compelled to "humanize nature" (Freud, *Future of an Illusion*, pp. 28, 32) which enhances the possibility of changing the course of nature through appeasement or bribery (magic). To Freud religious belief is illusion, which he defines as beliefs based on wish, thus neither provable nor unprovable since they do not lend themselves to scientific method. He believed religion to be inherently improbable, the means

for perpetuating infantile and escapist tendencies in human nature, and the most serious enemy of reason and the scientific attitude, in which, he believed, lay the true hope for human progress.

While the influence of these ideas has been widespread, and many have felt that Freud's research and clinical observations undermined current religious belief, this is by no means the case. His conclusions are derived from the uncritical application of nineteenth century rationalism. It is apparent that he never understood mature religious belief, for he drew his major examples of religion from three sources: the primitive, the infantile and the pathological. His greatest error lay in the assumption that religious experience was characterized by beliefs that accorded with convenient wishes. Mature religious experience frequently finds conviction at variance with wishes; pretensions are pricked as the person is enjoined toward deeper self-scrutiny and denial of infantile pleasures in the interests of truth and goodness.

However, the work of Freud has been of great benefit to theology and pastoral care. His systematic exploration of effect of unconscious motives upon perception and behavior have underscored the complexity of behavior, and served as a corrective against the Pelagian view of the will which had insidiously crept into the stream of orthodox theology. This has necessitated a restudy of the nature of freedom, responsibility and guilt. His pessimism about human nature gave pause to those who espoused man's inherent goodness. And his emphasis upon developmental stages taught men to view behavior in the context of the individual's level of development before judging it.

Moreover, many things he said about religious belief are true. People do put their beliefs to psychological uses that foster infantilism and neuroticism. Men do create God in their own image. And it is imperative that resulting behavior be seen for what it is. Moreover, the system of therapy he developed has added to our understanding of the function of confession and forgiveness in spiritual growth. Modifications of this system have been developed as an additional tool for pastoral care.

Jung has often been hailed as deliverer by those who have been disturbed by Freud's comments on religion. He talks positively about religion, setting forth the essential purposiveness of human life and the need to find religious answers to life to attain personal maturity. On closer scrutiny however, he offers little comfort to Christianity. What beckons man forward and provides him with his ultimate purpose is the Self, which seems to mean perfect humanity. He is to achieve Self through individuation, i.e., realizing his unique potential. In the western world individuation is conceived as redemption and Christ is its basic, personalized symbol. The Christ symbol receives validity from the fact that it expresses the Self in symbolic form and is valid to the extent that it does. Jung goes on to assert that in oriental religions other symbols than Christ represent the Self and are no less real. God, to him, is "an obvious psychic and non-physical fact, i.e., a fact that can be established psychically but not physically" (Jung, *Answer to Job*, p. 169). To Jung a psychic fact is real but not objectively verifiable. Nor does he show any great concern about the objective reality of God. He is too concerned with demonstrating the point that "psychic" (subjective) truth is genuine truth. God in this sense is real and necessary, but to press this reality in the objective sense either is a question outside of psychology or it betrays a materialism that regards psychic data as unreal.

While this "two realm" theory of truth is unpalatable, Jung nevertheless has made important contributions to the psychology of religion. Where Freud emphasized the past and instincts, Jung saw the importance of aspirations and the future. Men need to find out the purpose of their lives and allow this to fulfil itself. He also sensed that behind man's irrational gropings was something not irrational; that his search for God is not necessarily a substitute for some frustration.

Alfred Adler's influence has been indirect. The significance of his contribution is increasingly recognized. Like Jung he emphasized the wholeness of man. This is a healthy antidote to Greek dualism and its overtones in Christian theology, for it serves to remind us that man cannot be dealt with solely as body or as spirit, but as an inextricable composite of these in which what affects one component affects the other. Adler also emphasized the acquisition of "social feeling," i.e., a sense of community, as a necessary pre-condition for attaining personal maturity. However he derived this from what he considered to be an inherent unity of the individual psyche with society. Freud, on the other hand, insisted upon a fundamental conflict between individual desires and society's demands. The Christian finds the latter view more in accord with his observations of human life, and considers the Christian gospel to contain both the dynamic for creating a sense of community and the basis for properly defining "community" (I Cor. 12:12-27).

Where Freud's materialistic view of man is sometimes said to have taken man's soul from him, Otto Rank's concept of "will" may be said to have given it back. Rank conceived of "will" as the expression of the person's unconscious potentialities: latent creativity, irrational urges (instincts or purposes), the organizing principle of personality in which resides the source of individuality — an enumeration reminiscent of the Christian view of the person as unique manifestation of the *imago Dei*, by which he is also energized.

Recent contributions, represented by the work of Erich Fromm and Carl Rogers, have reiterated the position that man's basic task is to actualize his potential self. Society is to make it possible for him to do this in his own way, since he alone knows what is best for himself. Both stress the deleterious effect of external authority upon the human personality, and both find hope for human healing and growth in the "accepting" human relationship, a relationship equivalent to the biblical concept of the redemptive relationship, i.e., characterized by *agape*, by seeing the other as subject (Buber's *I-Thou* Relationship) rather than object (Buber's *I-it*).

Today much of the hostility between psychology and religion, which was largely brought about by Freud's onslaughts, is disappearing, with the realm of psychotherapy serving as the basis of rapprochement. Theologians and psychiatrists are thoughtfully reading one another's writings with more openness than has been true for several decades. It is possible that our time will see a resurgence of recognition within psychology that "... the very fact of human personality carries metaphysical overtones. Man's psychological nature suggests something transcendent of which the psyche is but a partial reflection" (Ira Progoff, *The Death and Rebirth of Psychology*, Julian Press, New York, 1956, p. 256). When this takes place psychology can be said to be concerning itself with the totality of man's behavior and experience.

BIBLIOGRAPHY

Erich Fromm, *Psychoanalysis and Religion*; Sigmund Freud, *The Future of an Illusion*; *Civilization and Its Discontents*; *Moses and Monotheism*; C. G. Jung, *Psychology and Religion*; *Answer to Job*; Ira Progoff, *The Death and Rebirth of Psychology*; Otto Rank, *Psychology and the Soul*; *Beyond Psychology*; Carl R. Rogers, *Client-Centered Therapy*; Lionel Trilling, *Freud and the Crisis of Our Culture*.

LARS I. GRANBERG

PUNISHMENT. Throughout the Bible it is insisted that sin is to be punished. In an ultimate sense God will see that this is done, but temporarily the obligation is laid upon those in authority to see that wrongdoers are punished. The *lex talionis* of Ex. 21:23-25 is not the expression of a vindictive spirit. Rather it assures an even justice (the rich and the poor are to be treated alike), and a penalty proportionate to the crime.

Two important points emerge from OT usage. The verb used in the sense of "punish" is *pāqad*, which means "visit." For God to come into contact with sin is for him to punish it. Of the nouns used, most are simply the words for sin. Sin necessarily and inevitably involves punishment.

In the NT "punishment" is not as common as "condemnation," which may be significant. To be condemned is sufficient. Punishment is implied. The removal of punishment is brought about by the atoning death of our Lord. It is not said in so many words that Jesus bore punishment, unless bearing our sins (Heb. 9:28; I Pet. 2:24) be held to mean this. But that his sufferings were penal seems clearly to be the NT teaching.

See also ETERNAL PUNISHMENT.

LEON MORRIS

PURGATORY. The teachings of the Roman Catholic and Greek Orthodox churches set forth a place of temporal punishment in the intermediate realm known as purgatory, in which it is held that all those who die at peace with the church but who are not perfect must undergo penal and purifying suffering. Only those believers who have attained a state of Christian perfection are said to go immediately to heaven. All unbaptized adults and those who after baptism have committed mortal sin go immediately to hell. The great mass of partially sanctified Christians dying in fellowship with the church, but who nevertheless are encumbered with some degree of sin, go to purgatory where, for a longer or shorter time, they suffer until all sin is purged away, after which they are translated to heaven.

The sufferings vary greatly in intensity and duration, being proportioned in general to the guilt and impurity or impenitence of the sufferer. They are described as being in some cases comparatively mild, lasting perhaps only a few hours, while in other cases little if anything short of the torments of hell itself and lasting for thousands of years. But in any event they are to terminate with the last judgment. Gifts or services rendered to the church, prayers by the priests, and masses provided by relatives or friends in behalf of the deceased can shorten, alleviate or eliminate the sojourn of the soul in purgatory.

Protestantism rejects the doctrine since the evidence on which it is based is found not in the Bible but in the Apocrypha, in II Macc. 12:39-45.

BIBLIOGRAPHY
Blunt; CE; SHERK.

LORAINE BOETTNER

PURIFICATION. Israel, chosen by a holy Jehovah to be his people, was required to be holy (Lev. 11:44-45; 19:2; 21:26). Under the Mosaic legislation the holiness of Israel was from the first recognized as moral separation from sin (Lev. 20:22-26); but it was expressed outwardly by separation from objects designated unclean. Uncleanness contracted through contact with such objects required cleansing. Unclean utensils and clothing were washed in running water; but if a porous earthenware vessel became unclean, it had to be destroyed (Lev. 15:12). Metal was sometimes purified by passing it through fire (Num. 31:32-33).

Israelites who had contracted uncleanness had to separate themselves from the congregation, the length of time depending on the nature of the uncleanness (e.g., Num. 5:2-3; Lev. 12; 15:11-13). They were to wash themselves in water and for the more serious forms of uncleanness they were required to offer sacrifice (e.g., Lev. 12:6). For persons unclean through leprosy (Lev. 14) or through touching a corpse (Num. 19) more elaborate cleansing by sprinkling with water mingled with blood or ashes was required in addition. The unclean Israelite who would not purify himself was executed (Num. 19:19).

As revelation progressed, the concept of

holiness deepened. Ps. 51:7 and Ezek. 36:25 both use terms drawn from the purification ritual to describe the cleansing of the heart from sin. In the NT, though ritual purification is referred to (e.g., Luke 2:22; Acts 21:24), our Lord abolished the uncleanness of certain foods (Mark 7:19, cf. Acts 10:15) and Paul affirmed that this abolition extended to every object formerly designated unclean (Rom. 14:14, 20; Titus 1:15; I Tim. 4:4). The NT writers confine purification to cleansing from sin through the blood of Christ (I John 1:7; Heb. 1:3; 9:14) and interpret OT ritual as foreshadowing this cleansing (Heb. 9:13 f., 23).

DAVID BROUGHTON KNOX

PURITAN, PURITANISM. The nickname Puritan was coined about 1564 to denote members of the Church of England who desired a more radical reformation of its worship and order than was prescribed by the Act of Uniformity (1559). These Puritans attacked allegedly superstitious ceremonies and diocesan organization, and campaigned for parity of ministers, parochial discipline, better preaching and more energetic recruitment for the ministry. Elizabethan Puritans were not separatists, nor were Elizabethan separatists called Puritans. In the seventeenth century, however, the name was used loosely and comprehensively for all, episcopalian, presbyterian or independent, who held a Calvinistic creed and practiced serious piety. Puritanism in this broader sense developed a rich, if austere, culture and a noble tradition of moral and pastoral theology, which inspired eighteenth-century Evangelicalism in both Britain and New England. Puritan theology was characteristically Reformed and of a federal cast (witness the Westminster Confession). Two distinctive features were its elaborate treatment of the work of the Holy Spirit and its conception of Sunday as the Christian Sabbath. Notable Puritan theologians were J. Owen, R. Baxter, T. Goodwin, J. Howe, R. Sibbes.

BIBLIOGRAPHY
M. M. Knappen, *Tudor Puritanism;* W. Haller, *The Rise of Puritanism;* H. Martin, *Puritanism and Richard Baxter.*

JAMES I. PACKER

PURPOSE. The English word "purpose" is the translation for a wide variety of Greek and Hebrew words used in the Scriptures. Frequently only the context gives a clue as to the purposeful element in the word (e.g., *'āmar* in I Kings 5:5 and II Chron. 28:10). The word may refer primarily to a goal set up by choice or conceived of as desirable (Dan. 6:17; Prov. 20:18; Acts 27:43; II Tim. 3:10); or it may refer to the mental act of will by which this goal is chosen or decreed (Dan. 1:8; Jer. 4:28; Lam. 2:8).

The purposes of God are eternal (Eph. 3·11), unchanging (Jer. 4:28), and certain of accomplishment (Isa. 14:24). Salvation is the chief concern (Rom. 8:28-30), characterized by grace and centered in Christ (II Tim. 1:9).

KENNETH S. KANTZER

Q

QUARTODECIMANISM. The practice of keeping the Easter festival on the fourteenth Nisan irrespective of the day of the week on which it fell. The main strength of this view was in Asia Minor, where it was said to derive from the Apostle John. On a visit to Rome in A.D. 155 Polycarp tried to persuade Bishop Anicetas to adopt the custom, but they finally agreed to differ. Later in the second century, Victor of Rome attempted to impose the more general observance of the day rather than the date, and in spite of a rebuke by Irenaeus excommunicated the Quartodecimans. His action was both resented and resisted, and although he represented the dominant view Quartodecimanism persisted in a separate communion (cf. *JTS*, xxv, 254-270).

WILLIAM KELLY

QUICK, QUICKEN. Quick (ten times in the AV) never means rapid. Isa. 11:3, *rûah,* "make of *quick* understanding," suggests "acute"; but the verb indicates "delight," ASV. "Quick" generally represents *ḥay*, "alive," ASV, or related forms: Korah went down "alive" to hell, *šeʾôl* (Num. 16:30; cf. Pss. 55:15; 124:3); and "quick," raw (?), flesh distinguished leprosy (Lev. 13:10, 24). In the NT "quick" translates the participle of *zēn*, "living (ones)," ASV. Heb. 4:12 calls the word of God (his spoken promises, *ExpGT*) "quick," active; and the Apostles' Creed describes God's judging "the quick and the dead" (Acts 10:42).

"Quicken" (twenty-five times) translates causative forms of *ḥāyâ* and its Greek equivalent *zōopoiein*, "make alive" or "give life," as in the ASV NT. A planted seed is "quickened" into life (I Cor. 15:36). God "gives breath to all living creatures" (I Tim. 6:13, alternative reading, *zōogonein*) and preserves them alive (MM; I Sam. 2:6; but cf. Crem). Quickening brings life after death. So Abraham, "as good as dead," was quickened to beget Isaac (Rom. 4:17; Alf; cf. Ps. 71:20). Christ's resurrection quickened him from limited fleshly existence into full spiritual life (I Pet. 3:16). Thus the Son, like the Father, "quickens" men (John 5:21; I Cor. 15:45). By regeneration (John 5:24-25) he makes us alive with him, *suzōopoiein* (Eph. 2:5), when we were dead in sin. His Spirit "quickens" by leading men to himself, giving spiritual perception (John 6:63; cf. Ezek. 36:27-28), "quickened in thy way" (Ps. 119:37) from spiritual dullness. Quickening signifies relief from personal troubles (Ps. 143:10), by means of God's written word (Ps. 119:25), or revival from national oppression (Ps. 80:18). John 5:21 climaxes when the Son shall "quicken" men's mortal bodies into resurrection (vss. 28-29, cf. Rom. 8:11).

BIBLIOGRAPHY

Crem; Crem *Supplement, Sunzaō*; E. Hatch, *Essays in Biblical Greek*, 5; HDB; MM; RTWB.

J. BARTON PAYNE

QUIETISM. Although used of earlier movements, this term applies properly to the particular teaching of de Molinos, and to some extent Madame Guyon and Fénelon, in seventeenth century France. The main concern of the Quietists was for a complete passivity in which the will is destroyed, in which there is no desire even for God or for salvation, but the believer is completely filled by God himself. For the attainment of this state, a process of mental prayer was recommended aiming at perfect rest in the presence of God. All forms of works were naturally regarded as futile and even harmful, and the dangerous position was advanced that when complete passivity was attained sin was impossible, since what might seem to be sin if performed in others was merely the devil's work in the Quietist, and preoccupation with it should not be allowed to disturb his mystic death. Molinos himself was condemned by Innocent XI in A.D. 1687, a formidable total of heretical propositions being extracted from his writings. Madame Guyon was protected by Madame de Maintenon and found an able advocate in Fénelon, but the movement in its stricter sense never attained to any strength. Quietistic elements may naturally be found over a much wider field, including many forms of Protestantism which tend to emotionalize or subjectivize the passivity or receptivity of faith. It is to be doubted, however, whether these may be described as Quietism proper, and in most cases there is certainly no wish to maintain its distinctive tenets.

GEOFFREY W. BROMILEY

R

RABBINIC THEOLOGY. See JUDAISM.

RANSOM. Three basic Hebrew words underlie the idea of ransom: (1) *kōper* indicates payment made in substitution for another's life. Ps. 49:7 (a difficult text) appears to suggest that no one can circumvent death through payment of a "ransom," cf. (Isa. 43:3). (2) In contrast with the private nature of the transaction implied in the noun *kōper*, the verb *gāʾal* is primarily associated with family relationships, rooted in the obligations of the kinsman or *gō'ēl* outlined in Lev. 25:25 ff. Thus Isa. 51:10 suggests that God has played the role of a concerned kinsman in ransoming Israel from the sea (cf. Jer. 31:11). (3) The word *pādâ*, used in Isa. 35:10 and Hos. 13:14 of God's gracious salvific activity in general, expresses specifically the redemption of something claimed by God, as in Ex. 13:15, of the first-born.

Through the LXX which renders these concepts in most instances with the verb *lytroun* or the noun *lytron*, the substitutionary note apparent in the OT appears in the NT notably in Mark 10:45 (= Matt. 20:28): "The Son of man came . . . to give his life a ransom for many." No particular OT practice seems emphasized here, but rather the general concept of liberation achieved by the payment of a price, with perhaps accent on hellenistic associations connected with liberation of slaves.

See also REDEMPTION.

BIBLIOGRAPHY
Arndt; F. Buechsel in *TWNT*.

FREDERICK WILLIAM DANKER

RAPTURE. Derived from the Latin *rapio*, "to seize," "to snatch," the word may denote an ecstasy of spirit such as the mystic aspires to enjoy, or it may refer to a removal from one place to another by forcible means. Here it is being considered only in the latter sense, as a phase of the prophetic revelation dealing with the future coming of the Lord for his church. Paul seeks to comfort believers at Thessalonica whose loved ones have recently died, with the assurance that at the return of Christ these shall be given first consideration. When they are raised, the living saints will be "caught up" (*harpagēsometha*) together with them in clouds to meet the Lord in the air, nevermore to be separated from him or from one another (I Thess. 4:17). This will also be the time of the bodily transformation of believers (Phil. 3:20-21; I Cor. 15:51-52).

The verb *harpazō* occurs thirteen times in the NT. We read that the Spirit caught up Philip near Gaza and brought him to Caesarea (Acts 8:39). Paul was caught up into Paradise, where he experienced ineffable things (II Cor. 12:2-4). There can be no doubt that Paul's language in I Thess. 4:17 requires a removal of the saints from earth at the time of the Lord's return. The supposition that the *apostasia* of II Thess. 2:3 is intended to refer back to the rapture is highly improbable, for this term does not indicate mere departure (for which *aphixis*, as used in Acts 20:39, would have been a fitting word) but rather rebellion or apostasy.

Three views are held concerning the relation of this event to the tribulation period which the prophetic Scriptures place immediately before the return of Christ. Pre-tribulationists put the rapture before the tribulation, holding that the tribulation is marked by the pouring out upon a Christ-rejecting society of the divine wrath, which is not intended for the church and is utterly unsuited to her, however much she may profit by the experience of tribulation in the general sense. Advocates of this view believe that God has promised to exempt the church from this whole period of trouble and judgment which is coming upon the world. The rapture is God's way of fulfilling his purpose. The language of Paul requires a removal from the earth scene. There would be little point in a translation into the air to be followed by an immediate return to the earth such as the post-tribulation view demands. In the interval between the rapture and the public appearing of Christ before the world he will reward his people.

Mid-tribulationists hold that it is improper to speak of the great tribulation as coextensive with the seventieth week of Dan. 9:27, for both there and in the Revelation the period is conceived as divided. Only the latter half is to be marked by tribulation. It will be preceded by a period of peace and safety (I Thess. 5:3). Since the saints will be spared the ordeal of tribulation, the rapture will occur approximately at this midway point. In substance, this view does not differ from the preceding, for both maintain the exemption of the church from the tribulation era.

Post-tribulationists maintain that the church will remain on the earth during the predicted time of trouble and wrath, and will experience tribulation but not wrath. The former is visited by man, the latter by God. He will provide protection for his own when his wrath is manifested. There will be no appreciable interval between the rapture and the coming of the Lord with the raptured saints to judge the world and set up the kingdom.

The divergence in viewpoint is due to the fact that nowhere in Scripture is the rapture treated in relation to the coming so as to place it temporally. Post-tribulationists emphasize that their view is the more simple and natural solution. In II Thess. 1:6-10, where the effect of the coming upon both believers and unbelievers is sketched, there is no suggestion that the return has two phases. Pre-tribulationists emphasize the difficulty involved in the exemption of the church from judgments which are represented as poured out on the earth as a whole, though this difficulty is lessened by the fact that the tribulation saints (Rev. 6:14) survive the ordeal. They also feel that, just as the coming of the Lord in the OT was largely undifferentiated in its prophetic portrayal, but turned out to be a double coming, separated by the present age, so the future coming of Christ, though sometimes presented as a single event, may well be effected in two stages, one of which involves the saints only, the other the unbelieving world as well.

BIBLIOGRAPHY
George E. Ladd, *The Blessed Hope*; John F. Walvoord, *The Rapture Question*.

EVERETT F. HARRISON

RATIONALISM. Rationalism (Lat. *rationales,* from *ratio,* "reason") is the assertion by human reason of its own supremacy and sufficiency in all realms of experience. It is the view that human reason alone is sufficient to solve all the problems relating to man's nature and destiny. This does not mean that all questions will be answered and all problems solved, but it does mean that, if a solution is to be found, human reason alone is the instrument of discovery.

In philosophy the term was, for a time, restricted to those who insist that reason by itself (a priori, that is, without the aid of the senses) is the source of all human knowledge. The criterion of truth is not sensory but deductive. Rationalism of this type is rooted in the thought of Plato. The term is often associated with the attempts to introduce mathematical methods into philosophy as in the systems of Descartes, Leibnitz, and Spinoza.

Empirical rationalism (a posteriori, that is, with the aid of sense data) replaced pure rationalism with the development of modern thought. The work of Francis Bacon, John Locke, John Stuart Mill, and many others, is of extreme importance in the development of inductive logic and the empirical or scientific method. The empirical method of verification, as well as of discovery, is claimed as the sole authority by thinkers varying from theists on the one hand to extreme positivists on the other. All rational empiricists emphasize the primacy of sense data in the determination and verification of truth. No other authority is admitted.

In theology rationalism has been present throughout man's history, but it is more evident in modern thought. This means that man's natural abilities are to be used exclusively in the formulation of religious beliefs. There is no reliance on authority or revelation — nothing but man's own reason. Human reason is considered fully competent to discover and to define religious beliefs without any supernatural aid or divine revelation. All religious data are to be found within man's natural or ordinary experience.

In religion rationalism may take the form of liberalism or anti-supernaturalism such as humanism or agnosticism. Generally rationalism emphasizes the development of all modern religions from primitive beliefs and superstitions.

In the eighteenth century the dominant influence and spirit of the Enlightenment was rationalistic. Its religious expression took the form of deism and agnosticism. The *Age of Reason* by Tom Paine probably is the best known American representation.

See also NATURALISM.

BIBLIOGRAPHY
W. Lecky, *History of Rationalism*; Y. Krikorian ed., *Naturalism and the Human Spirit*; E. Brightman, *Nature and Values*; "Rationalism and Supernaturalism," SHERK, IX, pp. 393-402.

WARREN C. YOUNG

READING. There was public reading of the OT Scriptures in the synagogues (Luke 4:16-20; Acts 13:27; 15:21; and see II Cor. 3:14-15), and this practice was continued in the early church (cf. I Tim. 4:13). Writings of the NT were also read in the churches. Paul charged (in the case of I Thess. *adjured*) that certain letters be read in the churches (Col. 4:16; I Thess. 5:27). It is not strange that writings backed by such authority as Paul had been given and which were read along with the OT in the church were at an early time clearly affirmed to be Scripture (II Pet. 3:16). In the second century Justin Martyr mentions the reading of the memoirs of the apostles or the writings of the prophets in services of public worship and says that the reading was followed by admonition and invitation to imitate the good things which they commended (FIRST APOLOGY 67). On the matter of private Bible reading in the early church see Harnack's *Bible Reading in the Early Church* (Eng. tr., New York, 1912).

BIBLIOGRAPHY
W. F. Adeney in *HDCG;* Arndt; R. Bultmann in *TWNT;* D. Miall Edwards in *ISBE;* M. Scott Fletcher in *HDAC;* MM; N. B. Stonehouse, "The Authority of the New Testament" in *The Infallible Word,* especially pp. 116 f., 130 f.

JOHN H. SKILTON

READY. Related words in Greek convey the idea of readiness. The verb *hetoimazō,* the noun *hetoimasia,* the adjective *hetoimos* and the adverb *hetoimōs* all come from the same root. The active aspect emphasizes the act of producing or creating readiness. The passive aspect stresses result — being prepared or being ready (cf. *TWNT,* II, p. 702). In the LXX the verb "to put or keep in readiness" represents eighteen different Hebrew words (cf. *HR,* I, p. 563). However, the verb, noun, and adjective usually represent the Hebrew word *kûn* (*BDB,* pp. 465-67).

The parables teach that God's blessings are ready for those who come to participate (Matt. 22:4, 8; Luke 14:17). Readiness is also related to Christian conduct. We are to be ready to produce good works (Titus 3:1; II Tim. 2:21); to oppose disobedience (II Cor. 10:6); to defend our hope (I Pet. 3:15). Readiness is important in the Christian's expectations: the return of Christ (contrasted with sleep or unpreparedness, Matt. 24:44; 25:10; Luke 12:40); positions in the kingdom and the kingdom itself (Mark 10:40; Matt. 25:34); the salvation to be revealed (I Pet. 1:5); Christ's preparedness to judge (I Pet. 4:5); punishment to be visited upon those banished by the judge (Matt. 25:41).

A. BERKELEY MICKELSEN

REALISM AND NOMINALISM. It is typical of medieval Scholasticism (*q.v.*) that the philosophical question of the reality of universal notions (genus and species, e.g., "man" for several individual men) became important for the discussion of such theological problems as creation, God and man, faith and reason, Trinity, incarnation, etc. Four main solutions were offered: Universals are (1) "before the (individual) things" (*ante rem*), as their transcendent, original forms (ideas) in God's creative mind (view of Augustinian Platonism); (2) "in the things" (*in re*), as their immanent, created forms (Aristotelian Realism in the proper sense); (3) "after the things" (*post rem*), as their concepts in the human mind; (4) only names, words (*nomina, voces*), fictions of our language. Strict Nominalists, as Roscellinus (d. 1123-25) held (4). The classic or moderate Realism of the great scholastics combined (1), (2), and (3). Peter Abelard (d. 1142) emphasized (3) over against (2) and (3). This Conceptualism was revived in the "modern school" of the 14th century (Ockhamism) and then is also called Terminism or Nominalism in the wider sense (since for it there are no universal forms in the reality outside of our mind, as in Realism, but only individuals — although the universal concepts or terms are not merely arbitrary fictions, as in strict Nominalism, but rather our mind's way of conceiving reality and of corresponding to it).

BIBLIOGRAPHY
H. Barth, *Philosophie der Erscheinung,* Vol. I; M. A. Schmidt in *EKL,* Vol. II; A. Carlini and V. Mathieu in *EF,* Vol. III.

MARTIN ANTON SCHMIDT

REAL PRESENCE. The reference in this phrase is to the presence of Christ in the sacrament of Holy Communion. In the more general sense it is not objectionable, for all Christians can agree that Christ is really present by the Holy Spirit when they gather in his name. Theologically, however, the word *real* indicates a particular form or understanding of the presence in terms of Realist philosophy. On this view, the so-called "substance" of Christ's body is a reality apart from its "accidents" or specific physical manifestations. It is this substance which is supposed to be present in or under the accidents of bread and wine and in replacement of (or, as Luther would say, in conjunction with) their own substance (see TRANSUBSTANTIATION). There is, however, no scriptural basis for this interpretation, and in Reformation theology it is rejected and replaced by a more biblical conception of the presence.

GEOFFREY W. BROMILEY

REASON. In accordance with NT psychology which (1) stresses the unity of the psychophysical person, and (2) employs popular, not technical, consistent terminology, the Greek terms for which the most suitable English equivalents are "reason," "reasonable" cover a wide range. Thus *arestos,* which in Acts 6:2 is translated "reason" (AV), means primarily "pleasing," "acceptable." The terms which come closest to our concept of reason are *logos* ("a word, reason, science"); *nous* (mind or understanding); *phrēn* ("understanding"); and their derivatives. *Synesis, from syniēmi (syn* and *hiēmi,* "to send together"), is also translated "understanding."

This phenomenon suggests (and the history of Western thought confirms) that the word reason is employed with widely varying shades of meaning. Common to them all, perhaps, are the concepts of systematic organization in terms, not of particulars, but of universals, and a consequent value or reliability. The term may claim such characteristics for either a view of reality or of some portion thereof, or for a faculty or aspect of the knowing self, or for an activity of the self whereby reality is known.

Thus, when man is defined as "a rational animal," reason is indicated as that characteristic or competence of man wherein he differs from all other animals — a characteristic or competence which consists of man's ability to know reality, not merely in terms of sense-particulars as the other animals do, but in terms of logically organized general propositions. Even so, there may be very great differences as to what reason is. It may be thought of as a mere "logic machine" — individual intellection in its highest form, dear to the eighteenth century thinkers (cf. Thomas Paine, *The Age of Reason.* Note that Arnold Lunn, in complete rejection of this conception, criticizes this whole movement as a *Flight From Reason;* cf. his book by that title). But, when reason is so conceived, it may be regarded as creative of truth, as by the Continental Rationalists (Descartes through Wolff), or as merely a coordinator of the scattered sense-impressions in which truth is thought to lie, as by the English Sensationalists (Locke, through Hume and later English thinkers). On the other hand, reason as a distinguishing characteristic of man may be more broadly conceived. It may be identified with consciousness in its totality, as an "organ" of truth, involving "feeling" (as with Hermann Lotze) and/or "volition" (cf. William James, *The Will to Believe).* Or it may be thought of more broadly still as the total self, including the "subconscious," in one of its characteristic activities.

Reason, as so understood, is attributed primarily to individuals; but romantics and others in the nineteenth century, mainly when engaged in developing a philosophy of history or in certain sociological emphases, represented reason as resident in humanity, or in a smaller human group, regarded as an organic unit, and only reflected in, or partially shared by, individuals. A rationalistic romantic, such as Hegel, went further, as the Stoics had previously done and as science by implication does, identifying Reason with Reality. Hegel thought of Reality as Reason, evolving according to its inherent, dialectical logic of thesis-antithesis-synthesis, towards self-consciousness in philosophy, which received symbolic expression in religion and concrete realization in the state. Marx "stood this Hegelian conception on its head," applying the dialectical process to a materialistic, economic development through class conflict.

In Kant, reason *(Vernunft)* is the power whereby first principles are grasped a priori, as contrasted with understanding *(Verstand)* in which intuitive, valuational processes play a part. But Jacobi exactly reversed this distinction when he identified *Vernunft* with *Glaube,* faith, — an intuitive activity whereby "spiritual" truths are apprehended. In this, he was followed by Schleiermacher, Coleridge, Emerson and others.

Reason may refer to a process — reasoning, ratiocination, more or less broadly conceived. According to Pringle-Pattison *(The Idea of God,* p. 62) this is how A. J. Balfour employed the term. And, again, a reason is a statement of fact whereby a vindication is sought for a belief or an action; cf. giving "a reason for the faith that is in you."

BIBLIOGRAPHY

E. Brunner, *Revelation and Reason;* L. H. DeWolf, *The Religious Revolt Against Reason;* N. F. S. Ferré, *Faith and Reason;* K. Jaspers, *Reason and Anti-Reason in Our Time;* H. R. Niebuhr, *Resurrection and Historical Reason.*

ANDREW KERR RULE

REATUS CULPAE, REATUS POENAE.

Reatus culpae is the state of guilt viewed as blame, *reatus poenae* the state of guilt viewed as penalty. Although this distinction has little force in general jurisprudence, it is essential to the structure of systematic theology. It grew out of the biblical emphasis on federal representation (Rom. 5:12-21; I Cor. 15:45). The first Adam acted in the stead of the human race. While he alone is blamed for his transgression *(reatus culpae),* the penalty of his transgression is imputed to the human race *(reatus poenae).* Christ is the last Adam. He bore the penalty of sin *(reatus poenae),* but not the blame of sin *(reatus cul-*

pae). Only the guilt of punishment, never the guilt of blame, can be imputed to another.

EDWARD JOHN CARNELL

REBAPTISM. During the second century the church in Asia Minor, faced with considerable heresy, refused to recognize the validity of heretical baptism. Converts to the orthodox faith from heretical groups were accordingly rebaptized. The church at Rome, however, took the position that the rite was valid when properly performed, i.e., with the correct formula and with the right intention, despite the erroneous views of its administrator. In North Africa Tertullian, then Cyprian, would not recognize the baptism of heretics. Cyprian carried on a bitter controversy with Stephen, bishop of Rome (253-57) on this issue. An anonymous writing, *de Rebaptismate,* set forth the position of the church at Rome. It made a distinction between water baptism and Spirit baptism. When a heretic was admitted to the church by the laying on of hands, the Spirit was conveyed, making further application of water unnecessary. The Roman position was endorsed by the Council of Arles (314) and was championed by Augustine in his controversy with the Donatists. Its advocates could point to the fact that Scripture contained no instance of rebaptism, that the analogous rite of circumcision was not repeatable, and that the questioning of the legitimacy of heretical baptism made the efficacy of the rite depend upon man rather than God. The Council of Trent, in its fourth canon on baptism, reaffirmed the Catholic position.

In Reformation times the Anabaptists insisted on baptism for those who had been baptized in infancy, and this has continued to be the position of the Baptist churches. The Roman Catholic Church and the Church of England practice what is known as conditional baptism in cases where there is doubt as to the validity of prior baptism. The formula used in the Church of England begins, "If thou art not already baptized, I baptize thee."

BIBLIOGRAPHY

E. W. Benson, *Cyprian,* pp. 331-436; Blunt; H. G. Wood in *HERE.*

EVERETT F. HARRISON

REBUKE. The word describes God's reaction in the face of evil. It is also enjoined on God's people when confronted with wrongdoing in their neighbors (Lev. 19:17; Luke 17:3; I Tim. 5:20). Rebuke involves reproof

and often condemnation. Failure to rebuke makes one a partaker in the wrong. God rebukes the heathen (Ps. 9:5); Israel's enemies (Ps. 76:6); the devourer (Mal. 3:11); the Red Sea (Ps. 106:9); Satan, the accuser of the brethren (Zech. 3:2); even his own people for their chastening (Rev. 3:19). Jesus likewise rebuked demons (Mark 1:25); fever (Luke 4:39); the wind and the sea (Matt. 8:26); and his own disciples when they acted contrary to God's mind (Mark 8:33; Luke 9:55).

DONALD W. B. ROBINSON

RECOMPENSE. See REWARD.

RECONCILIATION. Reconciliation is a change of personal relations between human beings (I Sam. 29:4; Matt. 5:24; I Cor. 7:11); or between God and man (Rom. 5:1-11; II Cor. 5:18 f.; Col. 1:20; Eph. 2:5). By this change a state of enmity and estrangement is replaced by one of peace and fellowship.

"All things are of God" (II Cor. 5:18, cf. Eph. 2:4; John 3:16) in restoring the ruptured relationship between himself and rebellious man. He is the subject of the whole reconciling process, whose gracious love reaches out even for his enemies. Men do not reconcile God, but God so changed the situation between himself and men that he reconciled the world unto himself.

God wrought this reconciliation for us in Christ, so that apart from the Peacemaker and his passion God would not be to us what he is. We were reconciled to God through the death of his Son (Rom. 5:10; Col. 1:22); through the blood of his cross (Col. 1:20; Eph. 2:16). Moreover in Rom. 5 and II Cor. 5, reconciliation so strictly parallels justification *(q.v.)* that they seem to be different descriptions of the same event. As Christ died for the ungodly, so are we reconciled by his death and justified by his blood.

Man's rebellious enmity against God (Col. 1:21; Rom. 8; 7 f.) has called forth his holy enmity against evil (I Cor. 15:25 f.; Rom. 11:28; Jas. 4:4); his wrath (Rom. 1:18; 2:5, 8-9; Eph. 2:3, 5; Col. 3:6); his judgments (Rom. 1:24-32; 2:3, 16; 3:6, 19; II Cor. 5:10); his vengeance (Rom. 12:19; II Thess. 2:8); and the curse of the broken law (Gal. 3:10). The wrath *(q.v.)* of God in the final judgment stands in immediate connection with the enmity which is removed by the reconciliation (Rom. 5:9-10). Thus God so acted in giving his Son to be made sin and a curse for us that his wrath was averted and his righteousness made manifest even in forgiving believers (Rom. 3:25-26). The grace of the Lord Jesus Christ assures them that the sentence of condemnation is no longer against them.

By shedding abroad in our hearts God's love for us, the Holy Spirit makes the reconciliation wrought in Christ effective in us. Thus he brings the prodigal back from self-seeking rebellion into grateful loving obedience in the Father's family. Knowing the fear of the Lord, the believer rejoices in receiving and in proclaiming the word of reconciliation (II Cor. 5:11 f.).

BIBLIOGRAPHY
Arndt; F. Buechsel and W. Foerster in *TWNT*; O. Michel, P. Althaus, M.-J. Lagrange and C. K. Barrett on Romans; K. Barth, *Church Dogmatics*, IV, 1; Leon Morris, *Apostolic Preaching of the Cross*; James Denney, *Reconciliation*; Wm. C. Robinson, *The Word of the Cross*.

WILLIAM CHILDS ROBINSON

RECTOR. See OFFICES, ECCLESIASTICAL.

REDEEMER, REDEMPTION. Though closely allied to salvation, redemption is more specific, for it denotes the means by which salvation is achieved, namely, by the payment of a ransom. As in the case of salvation (q.v.) it may denote temporal, physical deliverance. In the OT the principal words are *pādā* and *gā'al*, which are usually rendered by *lytrousthai* in the LXX, occasionally by *rhyesthai*. In the NT *lytrousthai* is the usual verb form, and nouns are *lytrōsis* and *apolytrōsis*. Occasionally *agorazein* is used, or *exagorazein*, denoting the act of purchase in the market, especially the slave-market. For "ransom" *lytron* and *antilytron* are used.

In ancient Israel both property and life could be redeemed by making the appropriate payment. Since the first-born were spared in the last plague which God visited upon Egypt, he had a special claim on these, so that the first-born thereafter had to be redeemed by a money payment (Ex. 13:13-15). According to the Pentateuchal legislation, if a man lost his inheritance through debt or sold himself into slavery, he and his property could be redeemed if one near of kin came forward to provide the redemption price (Lev. 25:25-27, 47-54; cf. Ruth 4:1-12). The kinsman-redeemer was also the avenger of blood on occasion (see GOEL).

God's deliverance of his people from Egypt is spoken of as a redemption (Ex. 6:6; 15:13), and he as Israel's Redeemer (Ps. 78:35). The emphasis here may well be upon the great output of strength needed to accomplish this objective — strength which itself serves as a kind of ransom price. Once again God's people are found in captivity (Babylon), and again the language of redemption is used in connection with their release (Jer. 31:11; 50:33-34). The probable meaning of Isa. 43:3 is that the conqueror of Babylon and therefore the liberator of Judah, even Cyrus, is being promised a domain in Africa as a compensation for giving up captive Judah and restoring her to her inheritance in the land of Canaan.

The individual also is sometimes the object of God's redemption, as in Job 19:25, where the sufferer expresses his confidence in a living Redeemer who will vindicate him eventually, despite all present appearances to the contrary. Prov. 23:10, 11 presents the same general cast of thought.

It is rather surprising that redemption is verbally so little associated with sin in the OT. Ps. 130:8 contains the promise that Jehovah will redeem Israel from all his iniquities. Isa. 59:20, which Paul quotes in Rom. 11:26, says much the same thing in more general terms (cf. Isa. 44:22). In Ps. 49:7 the impossibility of self-ransom for one's life is emphasized. It is possible that the scarcity of reference to redemption from sin in the OT is due to the ever-present proclamation of redemption through the sacrificial system, making formal statements along this line somewhat superfluous. Furthermore, redemption from the ills of life, such as the Babylonian captivity, would inevitably carry with it the thought that God redeems from sin, for it was sin which brought on the captivity (see Isa. 40:2).

The occurrence of numerous passages in the OT where redemption is stated in terms which do not explicitly include the element of ransom has led some scholars to conclude that redemption came to mean deliverance without any insistence upon a ransom as a condition or basis. The manifestation of the power of God in the deliverance of his people seems at times to be the sole emphasis (see Deut. 9:26). But on the other hand there is no hint in the direction of the exclusion of a ransom. The ransom idea may well be an assumed factor which is kept in the background by the very prominence given to the element of power needed for the deliverance.

This observation affords the necessary bridge

to the NT use of redemption. Certain passages in the Gospels reflect this somewhat vague use of the word as implying divine intervention on behalf of God's people without specific reference to any ransom which shall be paid (Luke 2:38; 24:21).

Mark 10:45, though it does not contain the word redeem, is a crucial passage for the subject, because it opens to us the mind of Christ concerning his mission. His life of ministry would terminate in an act of self-sacrifice which would serve as a ransom for the many who needed it. The largest development of the doctrine in the NT comes in the writings of Paul. Christ has redeemed from the curse of the law (Gal. 3:13; 4:5, *exagorazein* in both cases). In the Apostle's most concentrated section on the work of Christ he couples redemption with justification and propitiation (Rom. 3:24; cf. I Cor. 1:30). One prominent feature of Paul's usage is the double reference to the word — with a present application to the forgiveness of sins based on the ransom price of the shed blood of Christ (Eph. 1:7; cf. I Pet. 1:18, 19), and a future application to the deliverance of the body from its present debility and liability to corruption (Rom. 8:23). This latter event is associated with the day of redemption (Eph. 4:30), not in the sense that redemption will then be operative for the first time, but that the redemption secured by Christ and applied to the soul's forgiveness is then extended to include the body as well, so that salvation is brought to its intended consummation.

Redemption, though it includes the concept of deliverance, is a more precise term. Otherwise it would be expected that biblical writers would make more extensive use of words denoting deliverance per se, such as *lyein* or *rhyesthai*, to the neglect of words for redeem. Yet such is not the case. It is significant that Paul can content himself with the use of *rhyesthai* when setting forth the relation of Christ's saving work for us with respect to hostile angelic powers (Col. 1:13), yet when he passes to a contemplation of the forgiveness of our sins he must change his terminology to that of redemption (Col. 1:14).

No word in the Christian vocabulary deserves to be held more precious than Redeemer, for even more than Saviour it reminds the child of God that his salvation has been purchased at a great and personal cost, for the Lord has given himself for our sins in order to deliver us from them.

BIBLIOGRAPHY
J. Burnier in *CB*; J. Orr in *HDCG*; F. J. Taylor in *RTWB*; B. B. Warfield in *HDAC*; *Biblical Doctrines*, pp. 327-98.

EVERETT F. HARRISON

REFORMATION. In its ecclesiastical connotation, reformation indicates the removal of abuses and the re-ordering of affairs within the church according to the word of God. For scriptural instances, cf. the reformations under Hezekiah (II Kings 18:1-8) and Josiah (II Kings 23:4-20). Historically, reformation refers to the renewal of the church in the sixteenth century by revitalization from its source in the word. Schaff rightly regarded the Reformation as, "next to the introduction of Christianity, the greatest event in history. It marks the end of the Middle Ages and the beginning of modern times. Starting from religion, it gave, directly or indirectly, a mighty impulse to every forward movement, and made Protestantism the chief propelling force in the history of modern civilization" (*History of Christian Church*, Scribners, New York, 2nd ed. 1916, Vol. vi., p. 1).

Although there were advocates of reform prior to the sixteenth century and notable protagonists during the struggle itself, the Reformation nevertheless hinged upon the testimony of a single man. It has been said that Luther apart from the Reformation would cease to be Luther. The reverse is equally true. Luther's spiritual experience was a microcosm. His inward quest for salvation reflected the birthpangs of a new Christian era. His discovery of a gracious God as he confronted the open Bible, unimpeded by sacerdotal intermediation or philosophical presuppositions, represents the essence of the Protestant reform.

It was a reform, not a revolt. Continuity was preserved, so that the Reformers could justifiably claim that what seemed to be the new church was indeed the old church purged of offences and reconstituted according to the scriptural norm. If social, political and intellectual factors were involved, it was basically religious and theological in origin and purpose.

A convenient distinction may be drawn between the magisterial Reformation (Lutheran, Calvinist, Anglican) and the radical Reformation (Anabaptist, Spiritualist).

BIBLIOGRAPHY
T. M. Lindsay, *History of the Reformation*; R. H. Bainton, *The Reformation of the Sixteenth Century*;

W. Pauck, *The Heritage of the Reformation;* H. M. Gwatkin in *HERE.*

A. SKEVINGTON WOOD

REGENERATION. Regeneration, or new birth, is an inner re-creating of fallen human nature by the gracious sovereign action of the Holy Spirit (John 3:5-8). The Bible conceives salvation as the redemptive renewal of man on the basis of a restored relationship with God in Christ, and presents it as involving "a radical and complete transformation wrought in the soul (Rom. 12:2, Eph. 4:23) by God the Holy Spirit (Titus 3:5; Eph. 4:24), by virtue of which we become 'new men' (Eph. 4:24; Col. 3:10), no longer conformed to this world (Rom. 12:2; Eph. 4:22; Col. 3:9), but in knowledge and holiness of the truth created after the image of God (Eph. 4:24; Col. 3:10; Rom. 12:2)" (B. B. Warfield, *Biblical and Theological Studies,* Presbyterian and Reformed Publishing Company, Philadelphia, 1952, p. 351). Regeneration is the "birth" by which this work of new creation is begun, as sanctification is the "growth" whereby it continues (I Pet. 2:2; II Pet. 3:18). Regeneration in Christ changes the disposition from lawless, God-less self-seeking (Rom. 3:9-18; 8:7) which dominates man in Adam into one of trust and love, of repentance for past rebelliousness and unbelief, and loving compliance with God's law henceforth. It enlightens the blinded mind to discern spiritual realities (I Cor. 2:14-15; II Cor. 4:6; Col. 3:10), and liberates and energizes the enslaved will for free obedience to God (Rom. 6:14, 17-22; Phil. 2:13). The use of the figure of new birth to describe this change emphasizes two facts about it. The first is its *decisiveness.* The regenerate man has for ever ceased to be the man he was; his old life is over and a new life has begun; he is a new creature in Christ, buried with him out of reach of condemnation and raised with him into a new life of righteousness (see Rom. 6:3-11; II Cor. 5:17; Col. 3:9-11). The second fact emphasized is the *monergism* of regeneration. Infants do not induce, or co-operate in, their own procreation and birth; no more can those who are "dead in trespasses and sins" prompt the quickening operation of God's Spirit within them (see Eph. 2:1-10). Spiritual vivification is a free, and to man mysterious, exercise of divine power (John 3:8), not explicable in terms of the combination or cultivation of existing human resources (John 3:6), not caused or in-

duced by any human efforts (John 1:12-13) or merits (Titus 3:3-7), and not, therefore, to be equated with, or attributed to, any of the experiences, decisions and acts to which it gives rise and by which it may be known to have taken place.

I. BIBLICAL PRESENTATION. The noun "regeneration" *(palingenesia)* occurs only twice. In Matt. 19:28, it denotes the eschatological "restoration of all things" (Acts 3:21) under the Messiah, for which Israel was waiting. This echo of Jewish usage points to the larger scheme of cosmic renewal within which that of individuals finds its place. In Titus 3:5 the word refers to the renewing of the individual. Elsewhere, the thought of regeneration is differently expressed.

In OT prophecies, regeneration is depicted as the work of God renovating, circumcising and softening Israelite hearts, writing his laws upon them and thereby causing their owners to know, love and obey him as never before (Deut. 30:6; Jer. 31:31-34; 32:39-40; Ezek. 11:19-20; 36:25-27). It is a sovereign work of purification from sin's defilement (Ezek. 36:25; cf. Ps. 51:10), wrought by the personal energy of God's creative outbreathing ("spirit": Ezek. 36:27; 39:29). Jeremiah declares that such renovation on a national scale will introduce and signalize God's new messianic administration of his covenant with his people (Jer. 31:31; 32:40).

In the NT, the thought of regeneration is more fully individualized, and in John's Gospel and First Epistle the figure of new birth — "from above" *(anōthen:* John 3:3, 7, as Moffatt), "of water and the Spirit" (i.e., through a purificatory operation of God's Spirit: see Ezek. 36:25-27; John 3:5; cf. 3:8), or simply "of God" (John 1:13, nine times in I John) — is integral to the presentation of personal salvation. The verb *gennaō* (which means both "beget" and "bear") is used in these passages in the aorist or perfect tense to denote the once-for-all divine work whereby the sinner, who before was only "flesh," and as such, whether he knew it or not, utterly incompetent in spiritual matters (John 3:3-7), is made "spirit" (John 3:6) — i.e., is enabled and caused to receive and respond to the saving revelation of God in Christ. In the Gospel, Christ assures Nicodemus that there are no spiritual activities — no seeing or entering God's kingdom, because no faith in himself

— without regeneration (John 3:1 ff.); and John declares in the prologue that only the regenerate receive Christ and enter into the privileges of God's children (John 1:12-13). Conversely, in the Epistle, John insists that there is no regeneration that does not issue in spiritual activities. The regenerate do righteousness (I John 2:29) and do not live a life of sin (3:9; 5:18: the present tense indicates habitual law-keeping, not absolute sinlessness, cf. 1:8-10); they love Christians (4:7), believe rightly in Christ and experience faith's victory over the world (5:4). Any who do otherwise, whatever they claim, are still unregenerate children of the devil (3:6-10).

Paul specifies the christological dimensions of regeneration by presenting it as (1) a life-giving co-resurrection with Christ (Eph. 2:5; Col. 2:13; cf. I Pet. 1:3); (2) a work of new creation in Christ (II Cor. 5:17; Eph. 2:10; Gal. 6:15). Peter and James make the further point that God "begets anew" (*anagennaō*: I Pet. 1:23) and "brings to birth" (*apokyeō*: James 1:18) by means of the gospel. It is under the impact of the word that God renews the heart, so evoking faith (Acts 16:14 f.; see also CALL).

II. HISTORICAL DISCUSSION. The Fathers did not formulate the concept of regeneration precisely. They equated it, broadly speaking, with baptismal grace, which to them meant primarily (to Pelagius, exclusively) remission of sins. Augustine realized, and vindicated against Pelagianism, the necessity for prevenient grace to make man trust and love God, but he did not precisely equate this grace with regeneration. The Reformers reaffirmed the substance of Augustine's doctrine of prevenient grace, and Reformed theology still maintains it. Calvin used the term "regeneration" to cover man's whole subjective renewal, including conversion and sanctification. Many seventeenth century Reformed theologians equated regeneration with effectual calling, and conversion with regeneration (hence the systematic mistranslation of *epistrephō*, "turn," as a passive, "be converted," in the AV); later Reformed theology has defined regeneration more narrowly, as the implanting of the "seed" from which faith and repentance spring (I John 3:9) in the course of effectual calling. Arminianism constructed the doctrine of regeneration synergistically, making man's renewal dependent on his prior co-operation with grace; liberalism constructed it naturalistically, iden-tifying regeneration with a moral change or a religious experience.

The Fathers lost the biblical understanding of the sacraments as signs to stir up faith and seals to confirm believers in possession of the blessings signified, and so came to regard baptism as conveying the regeneration which it signified (Titus 3:5) *ex opere operato* to those who did not obstruct its working. Since infants could not do this, all baptized infants were accordingly held to be regenerated. This view has persisted in all the non-Reformed churches of Christendom, and among sacramentalists within Protestantism.

BIBLIOGRAPHY

Articles on "Regeneration" by J. Orr (HDB, 1 vol. edit.); J. Denney (HDCG); J. V. Bartlet (HDB); F. Buechsel and K. H. Rengstorf in TWNT, I, pp. 663-74, 685-88; B. B. Warfield, *Biblical and Theological Studies*, pp. 351-74; Systematic theologies of Hodge (III, pp. 1-40); L. Berkhof (IV. vi. 465-79).

JAMES I. PACKER

RELIGION, RELIGIOUS. "Religious" is in general the adjective of the noun, "religion"; but it is also used, without the noun, in a specialized sense, to indicate connection with a monastic order. Thus, a monk may be called "a religious."

The large number, and often contradictory character, of the definitions to be found in modern discussions of religion suggest that scholars find it impossible to formulate a generally acceptable definition. The confusing discussion of this problem in J. H. Leuba's *God or Man?* (Henry Holt and Company, 1933, chap. 2) hardly suggests the amazing variety of the definitions offered. The etymology of the term does not help, both because it is uncertain and because neither *religare* nor *religere* throws much light on the present meaning of religion.

Many of the suggested definitions have been drawn up to serve a particular purpose, e.g., the purpose of psychology, or of sociology, or of some philosophical position such as humanism. Whether they are adequate for such special purpose must be decided by the specialists in that field; but they clearly fail to give a characterization of religion that is useful for more general purposes. This need not cause confusion, provided that their special purpose is noted and that their use is confined to that special purpose. When such a definition is employed as adequate for some other purpose, however, confusion results. Thus F. H. Bradley writes, "I take it to be a fixed feeling of fear, resignation, admiration or approval, no matter what may be the object, provided only that this feeling reaches a certain strength, and is qualified by a certain degree of reflection" (*Appearance and Reality*, p. 438n.). This may or may not be good for the purpose of psychology, but Bradley makes use of it in a discussion that is not confined to psychology. Such confusion is much too common.

The effort to gain a definition by isolating the common characteristics of the recognized religions runs into the following difficulties: (1) there are border-line cases the inclusion or exclusion of which will determine the resulting definition; e.g., including original Buddhism or Marxism in the cases studied will remove from the definition a mention of a supernatural Object. But the decision to include or to exclude must in either case seem arbitrary. (2) The characteristics of the various religions differ so widely that it may be impossible, by this method, to find any common features, or, if any are found, they must be so vague as to be of doubtful value. For example, in Bradley's definition, quoted above, note the indefiniteness of the expressions, "a certain strength" and "a certain degree of reflection." However, those for example who call Marxism a religion in spite of its aggressive repudiation of religion, must feel that a satisfactory definition can be attained in this manner.

Perhaps a satisfactory definition can be attained only by confining attention to one or a few of the "higher" religions, the others being treated as defective and so not normative. This would be to apply to religion the method advocated in philosophy by Bernard Bosanquet, namely that reality can be properly understood only from the standpoint of its highest manifestation. One could not, of course, expect anything like unanimous agreement in the selection on the basis of which such a definition would be reached, but a fairly general agreement might be hoped for if the selection were not too rigid, and the actual selection might be capable of defence. Such a method would yield, as definitive characteristics of religion, the acknowledgment of a higher, unseen power; an attitude of reverent dependence on that power in the conduct of life; and special actions, e.g., rites, prayers, acts of mercy etc., as peculiar expressions, and means of cultivation, of the religious attitude.

BIBLIOGRAPHY
P. A. Bertocci, *Religion as Creative Insecurity*; C. J. Ducasse, *A Philosophical Scrutiny of Religion*; H. H. Farmer, *Revelation and Religion*; W. L. King, *Introduction to Religion*; J. H. Leuba, *God or Man?*; E. C. Moore, *The Nature of Religion*; J. Oman, *The Natural and the Supernatural*; A. Toynbee, *An Historian's Approach to Religion*; A. G. Widgery, *What is Religion?*

ANDREW KERR RULE

REMISSION. See FORGIVENESS.

REMNANT. The translation of several words in the OT, only two of which are of consequence: *yātar* with its noun *yeter* and *šā'ar* with its derivatives *še'ār* and *še'ērît*. The NT equivalents *loipos* and *limma* with its compounds are infrequent. In the majority of cases the words concerned are used in a literal and self-explanatory way. They merely refer to things or people left over after famine, conquest, division, passage of time, etc. In the books of the prophets, however, the hope promised for those of the nation left over after the fall of Jerusalem crystallized into a promise (*q.v.*) not only of preservation for the few people remaining, but a promise for the kernel of the nation which could be kept in all vicissitudes and at length returned to its land and blessed status in messianic times. For this concept, the word *še'ērît* is principally used.

The thought perhaps goes back to Deut. 4:27 where the promise is given to the ones left after dispersal that they will be blessed again if they seek the Lord. Isaiah named one of his sons Shear Jashub, "a Remnant Shall Return" (Isa. 7:3; 8:18). In 10:21 this is interpreted to mean the remnant shall return to God, referring, perhaps, to revival in the days of Hezekiah. Yet in 11:10-16 there is reference to a "second" return from dispersal in which the Gentiles shall join. The quotation in Rom. 15:12 assures us that this refers not to the return from Assyria or Babylon, but a second return at the time of the messianic age.

In Mic. 4:7; 5:7-8; 7:18 the remnant of Jacob is practically a name for Israel in the future days. In Jeremiah, the remnant is used of the return from Babylonian captivity in 50:20; 42:2, etc., but it is also used to refer to Israel in the messianic age in 23:3; 31:7. Zechariah also uses the term for the Jews who came back from Babylon (Zech. 8:6, 11-12), as well as for the residue of the people (*yeter hā'ām*) of the messianic age (14:2). The repentant mourning of the Israelite remnant is detailed in Zech. 12:10 — 13:1 as taking place in the day of Israel's salvation. These verses are quoted in the NT in connection with Christ's second coming (Matt. 24:30; Rev. 1:7).

Much discussed is Amos 9:12, quoted in Acts 15:17. The a-millennial view is defended by O. T. Allis (*Prophecy and the Church*, Presbyterian and Reformed Publishing Co., Philadelphia, 1945, pp. 145-149). In brief, the argument is that the conquest of the "remnant of Edom" in Amos is spiritualized in Acts to refer to the conversion of the Gentiles in this age. An alternative view, presented in Alf and Meyer's Commentary (*in loco*) is that the LXX which Acts 15:17 quotes quite closely had before it a variant Hebrew text. If this be true, the Amos passage prophesied a day when Gentiles and Jews (the remnant of men) would seek the Lord. Heretofore it has often been assumed that when the LXX differed from the Hebrew, the latter was right. Dead Sea Scroll material gives a new perspective on these matters. At least here, where the LXX is supported by the NT, there is good argument that its text is accurate and that it speaks of the promise of salvation for the remnant.

In Rom. 11:5 the remnant of grace appears to be the saved of Israel (*q.v.*) of Paul's day. It seems equally clear that this age, when Jews are cast off and Gentiles grafted into the stock of the people of God (Rom. 11:15-22), will be followed by an age when the Jews will be reintroduced to the privileges of grace (Rom. 11:25-31). Verse 26 then gives the eventual promise for the Jewish remnant of the last days.

BIBLIOGRAPHY
E. G. Hirsch in *JewEnc*; D. Walker in *HDAC*; G. F. Oehler, *Theology of the Old Testament*, 2nd ed. tr. by G. E. Day, pp. 506-8.

R. LAIRD HARRIS

REMONSTRANTS. The Remonstrants, followers of Jacobus Arminius and led by Bisschop and Grotius, presented to Holland and Friesland in 1610 a series of articles known as the Remonstrance. Their positions were: (1) The decree of predestination was conditional; (2) Christ died for all; (3) A man may reject the grace of God; (4) A man may fall from a state of grace.

The Remonstrants were criticized for both theological and political reasons; some were imprisoned and executed by Maurice of Orange. Adjudication came at the Synod of Dort (1618-19); the Calvinistic views prevailed.

However, the Remonstrants in 1630 were granted freedom in Holland. Their theological influence has been great from that time.

See also ARMINIANISM.

SHERMAN RODDY

RENEWAL. This is an integral concept in Christian theology, denoting all those processes of restoration of spiritual strength subsequent to and proceeding from the new birth. It has its roots in the OT (Pss. 5:10; 103:5; Isa. 40:31; 41:1), although it is not predominant in pre-Christian times. The main NT words are *anakainizō* and *ananeoō*. In Rom. 12:2 this renewal (*anakainōsis*) is applied to the mental faculties, and indicates the reinvigorating effect of Christian committal on conduct. This is further illustrated by the apostle's teaching regarding the new man (Col. 3:10), which is represented as in constant need of renewal (II Cor. 4:16). A more specific description is found in Eph. 4:23 where the phrase "renewed in the spirit of your mind" shows the spiritual character of this renewal. "The spiritual principle of the mind must acquire a new youth, susceptible of spiritual impressions" (J. A. Robinson, *ad loc.*, *St. Paul's Epistle to the Ephesians*, Macmillan, London, 1904).

In the sub-apostolic age the idea of renewal tended to become linked with that of baptism (cf. *Barnabas* 6:11, and the apocryphal *Acts of Thomas*, 132). It was not strange that the initiatory rite should mark in Christian thought the commencement of the process of renewal, but there is nothing in the NT teaching to support any notion of baptismal renewal.

Another word, *palingenesia*, is used of the event of rebirth which leads to renewal. The two ideas are linked together in Titus 3:5, where they appear to describe different aspects of one operation. The linking of *palingenesia* in this passage with "washing" suggests the words may have formed part of a baptismal formula, but gives no basis for the later magical estimate of baptism.

BIBLIOGRAPHY
Arndt; J. Behm in *TWNT*; M. Dibelius, *HZNT* (Titus 3:5); Donald Guthrie, *Pastoral Epistles*, pp. 205-6; J. A. Robinson, *Ephesians*; Trench.

DONALD GUTHRIE

REPENTANCE. In the OT the verb "repent" (niph'al of *nāham*) occurs about thirty-five times. It is usually used to signify a contemplated change in God's dealings with men for good or ill according to his just judgment (I Sam. 15:11, 35; Jonah 3:9-10) or, negatively, to certify that God will not swerve from his announced purpose (I Sam. 15:29; Ps. 110:4; Jer. 4:28). In five places *nāham* refers to human repentance or relenting. The LXX translates *nāham* with *metanoeō* and *metamelomai*. Either Greek verb may occur designating either human repentance or divine "relenting" (so the RSV in some places).

However, the background of the NT idea of repentance lies not primarily in forms of *nāham* (except in Job 42:6; Jer. 8:6; 31:19), but rather in forms of *šûb*, meaning "to turn back, away from, or toward" in the religious sense. The LXX consistently translates *šûb* with forms of *epistrephō* and *apostrephō*. Repentance follows a turning about which is a gift of God (Jer. 31:18-20; Ps. 80:3, 7, 19). Isa. 55:6-7 gives the typical OT call to repentance and conversion. Heartfelt sorrow for sin (*q.v.*) and conversion are sometimes placed in an eschatological setting, being linked to the remission of judgment, the return from captivity, the coming of the great time of salvation and the coming of Pentecost (Jer. 31:17-20; 31:31-34; Joel 12:12-32).

In the NT *metanoia* (noun) occurs twenty-three times and *metanoeō* (verb) thirty-four times. *Metamelomai* occurs seldom and is used almost exclusively in the sense of "regretting, having remorse." *Metanoeō* (*metanoia*) is almost always used in a favorable sense.

Repentance is the theme of the preaching of John the Baptist (Matt. 3:1; Mark 1:4; Matt. 3:8). Baptism in water unto repentance is accompanied by confession of sins (Matt. 3:6; cf. I John 1:8-9). Jesus continues John's theme but adds, significantly, "The time is fulfilled" (Mark 1:15). His coming is the coming of the kingdom in person and is decisive (Matt. 11:20-24; Luke 13:1-5). All life-relationships must be radically altered (Matt. 5:17 — 7:27; Luke 14:25-35; 18:18-30). Sinners, not the righteous, are called to *metanoia* (Matt. 9:13; Mark 2:17; Luke 5:32), and heaven rejoices over their repentance (Luke 15). The preaching of repentance and remission of sins must be joined to the proclamation of the cross and the resurrection (Luke 24:44-49). The apostles are true to this commission (Acts 2:38; 3:19; 17:30; 20:21). Unfaithful churches must repent (Rev. 3:5, 16). Apostates crucify to themselves the Son of God afresh and cannot be renewed to repentance (Heb. 6:5-6).

NT writers often distinguish between repentance and conversion (Acts 3:19; 26:20), and between repentance and faith (Mark 1:15; Acts 20:21). "*[Epistrepho]* has a somewhat wider signification than *metanoeō* . . . [and] always includes the element of faith. *Metanoeō* and *pisteuein* can be alongside of each other; not so *epistrephō* and *pisteuein*" (Louis Berkhof, *Systematic Theology*, Eerdmans Publishing Company, Grand Rapids, Michigan, 1946, p. 482). The distinction between *metanoeō* and *epistrephō* should not be pressed. *Metanoia*, at least, is used to signify the whole process of change. God has granted the Gentiles "repentance unto life" (Acts 11:18) and godly sorrow works "repentance unto salvation" (II Cor. 7:10). Generally, however, *metanoia* can be said to denote that inward change of mind, affections, convictions and commitment, rooted in the fear of God and sorrow for offenses committed against him, which, when accompanied by faith in Jesus Christ, results in an outward turning from sin to God and his service in all of life. It is never regretted (*ametamelēton*, II Cor. 7:10) and it is given by God (Acts 11:18). *Metanoeō* points to the inward conscious change while *epistrephō* directs attention particularly to the changed determinative center for all of life (Acts 15:19; I Thess. 1:9).

Calvin taught that repentance stemmed from serious fear of God and consisted in the mortification of the old man and the quickening of the Spirit. Mortification and renovation are obtained by union with Christ in his death and resurrection (*Institutes*, III. iii. 5, 9).

Beza (after Lactantius and Erasmus) objected to the translation of *metanoeō* by "*poenitentiam agite*" but the attempt to replace this with *resipiscentia* ("a coming to one's self") was infelicitous. Luther occasionally used "*Thut Busse!*" but his thesis was that Jesus, in giving this command, meant that all of life was to be penance before God.

Roman Catholicism teaches that the sacrament of penance consists materially of contrition, confession and satisfaction. But the judicial pronouncement of absolution by the church is needed to give these elements real validity.

BIBLIOGRAPHY

Arndt; J. Behm in *TWNT*; L. Berkhof, *Systematic Theology*, pp. 480-92; J. Calvin, *Institutes of the Christian Religion*, III. iii-v; W. D. Chamberlain, *The*

Meaning of Repentance, pp. 1-80; B. H. De Ment in *ISBE*; R. B. Girdlestone, *Synonyms of the Old Testament*, pp. 87-93; HR; O. Michel in *TWNT*; J. Schniewind, *Die Freude der Busse*, pp. 9-33; G. Spykman, *Attrition and Contrition at the Council of Trent*; Trench; E. Wuerthwein in *TWNT*; G. Vos, *The Teaching of Jesus Concerning the Kingdom of God and the Church*, pp. 169-90.

CARL G. KROMMINGA

REPROACH. There are various words used throughout Scripture to convey the idea of reproach, and in all of them the primary meaning is that of shame (*q.v.*) or disgrace or damage, not simply that of rebuke. On occasion the specific sense of "scorn" is in view, that is, something intended to bring shame upon someone else. Thus the punishment of Israel by God for covenant unfaithfulness would merit the scorn (*ḥerpâ*) of the Gentiles (Mic. 6:16), and the failure of Chorazin, Bethsaida, and Capernaum to repent after witnessing the miracles caused Jesus "to reproach (*oneidizein*) the cities" (Matt. 11:20; cf. Mark 15:32; 16:14).

At other times the emphasis is on the "disgrace" or "suffering" which rests upon oneself. So the inability of Israel's armies to cope with Goliath brought humiliation (*ḥerpâ*) to the nation (I Sam. 17:26), and the failure to have children was considered the disgrace (*ḥerpâ*) of Rachel (Gen. 30:23; cf. Job 19:5; Isa. 54:4). Paul challenges Christians to a life of selflessness by invoking the example of Christ, who bore the "sufferings" (*oneidismoi*) due to others (Rom. 15:3; quoted from Ps. 69:9). And when Moses is commended for enduring the "reproach (*oneidismon*) of Christ," that is, shame and suffering for righteousness' sake (Heb. 11:26), the implication is that such undeserved reproach would bring reward in heaven (cf. Matt. 5:11, 12; I Pet. 4:14).

ROBERT B. LAURIN

REPROBATE. The adjective "reprobate" in the sense of disapproved or rejected translates the Hebrew *mā'as*, as reprobate silver, that is, worthless silver (Jer. 6:20) and the Greek *adokimos*, "disqualified," "morally corrupt," "unfit for any good deed" (cf. Rom. 1:28; II Cor. 13:5-7; II Tim. 3:8; Titus 1:6). In all these passages the condition of being reprobate is the result of man's perverse mind which stubbornly refuses to obey God's will. The original meaning of *adokimos* is not to stand the test and therefore to be disqualified. The Greek term appears both in the LXX and in secular Greek. In Isa. 1:22 and Prov. 25:4

(LXX) it is translated "dross," while in I Cor. 9:27 the AV renders it "castaway," the ASV and the ERV "rejected," and the RSV with "disqualified," the last being preferable. In Heb. 6:8 the land, bearing thorns and thistles, does not meet the test and is rejected.

BIBLIOGRAPHY
Arndt; *ISBE*.

J. THEODORE MUELLER

REPROBATION. See ETERNAL PUNISHMENT.

REPROVE, REPROOF. The most frequent significance of these words in the OT is that of rebuke. "Reproof" occurs frequently in this sense in Proverbs, particularly with a view to correction; and "reprove" is found in Job, Psalms and Proverbs. In Isa. 11:3-4, however, it bears the meaning judge, especially in defending the oppressed. In association with the idea of argument at the root of this latter use, HDB gives the meaning disprove, refute, in Job 6:25-26 and Isa. 37:4, but BDB prefers the sense of chide, and thus also the RSV. In the NT "reproof" occurs only in II Tim. 3:16, where it connotes conviction, the negative side of doctrine. The verb "reprove," translating *elegchō*, indicates conviction, whether of persons in proving to them their guilt (John 16:8; II Tim. 4:2), or of their sins in proving them subject to condemnation (John 3:20). The RSV thus rightly uses the verb "expose" in Eph. 5:11, 13 in preference to reprove.

J. CLEMENT CONNELL

RESERVATION. This is the practice of keeping some of the bread and occasionally also the wine consecrated in the sacrament, primarily for the purpose of administering Holy Communion to the sick. Justin Martyr mentions in his *Apology* (chap. 65) the custom of sending a portion of the elements from the Eucharist to the absent. This was hardly reservation, however, but rather extended administration or concurrent communion. Other evidence shows that the practice arose of keeping the elements at home so that communion could be taken constantly before other food (Tertullian, *Ad. uxorem* II. 5). The sacramental species was sent from bishop to bishop as a sign of charity, or from a bishop to the chief churches of his diocese as a sign of unity, or carried as a charm on a journey. Two factors which affected most the practice and theory of reservation were (1) the theory of *viaticum*, that by reception of the Eucharist the dying were prepared for the last journey and assured of resurrection, and (2) the development of the doctrine of transubstantiation and its corollary, concomitance (*q.v.*). Reservation is now usually in the single kind of bread, but in the Eastern Church the bread is dipped in the wine and then dried.

RICHARD J. COATES

RESPECT OF PERSONS. The literal meaning of the Greek *prosōpolēpsia* and cognate terms, "receive the face," is derived from the Hebrew *nāśā' pānîm*, to "raise the face," i.e., to accept favorably. It is confined to biblical and Christian writers. A typical instance of the idea appears in Deut. 10:17: God cannot be bribed to accept favorably those who should be rejected. In the OT the idea may be used in a good sense (e.g., I Sam. 25:35; Mal. 1:8-9) but it frequently means "showing partiality," as in Lev. 19:15, where a guilty man's poverty is no ground for his being accepted favorably. In the NT the good sense disappears and it invariably means to show partiality to a person because of his external possessions, position, or privilege without regard to his true worth. God is no respecter of persons (Acts 10:34), neither accepting the Jew because of his privileges nor rejecting the Gentile because of his lack of them. So also in Rom. 2:11; Gal. 2:6; Eph. 6:9; Col. 3:25. Jesus, while not accepting persons showed that respect must be given where it is due (Luke 20:21-25; cf. Rom. 13:7). James 2:1-9 well illustrates the meaning of the term in Christian conduct.

BIBLIOGRAPHY
Sanday and Headlam, *ICC* (Rom. 2:11); J. B. Lightfoot, *Galatians* (Gal. 2:6); Arndt.

J. CLEMENT CONNELL

REST. The standard rendering of Gen. 2:2, that God "rested" on the seventh day, is seriously misleading. The verb used, *šābaṭ* not *nûaḥ*, means primarily to cease or desist (see Driver *WC* or Skinner *ICC ad loc.*, where it is rightly interpreted as desisting from creative work). These two verbs are brought into juxtaposition in Ex. 23:12 (cf. ASV mg.); there the rest results from desisting from work — *nûaḥ* and its derivatives are always used when relaxation from toil is meant. It is this false shade of meaning in our translations that makes some find a contradiction between Gen.

2:2 and John 5:17. The present continuing work of God is one of preservation and salvation rather than creation. For Israel the sabbath was less a day of rest than of desisting from normal work — in Ex. 23:12 the rest is for the animals.

Rest for "the people of God" should be a "sabbath rest" (Heb. 4:9 ASV — *sabbatismos*), "not an isolated sabbath but a sabbath-life" (Westcott, *The Epistle to the Hebrews*, p. 98), because God's goal for them must be consonant with his nature — his rest (*katapausis*, Hebrew *mᵉnûḥâ*) must be a *sabbatismos*. In spite of the vast majority of commentators and rabbinic analogies quoted by *SBK* III, p. 687, there is no suggestion in Hebrews that this rest is deferred to heaven, though it will not know its perfection until then. When a man is crucified with Christ, he ceases from his own works. It is highly probable that Christ was implying the same truth in Matt. 11:28 ff. *Anapausis* ("rest") is regularly used in the LXX of sabbath rest.

BIBLIOGRAPHY
HDB IV, Articles "Rest" and "Sabbath"; G. H. Lang, *The Epistle to the Hebrews*, pp. 73-80; A. B. Davidson, *Hebrews*, pp. 91-101.

H. L. ELLISON

RESTITUTION. The OT law dealt variously with offences requiring reparation. Ex. 22:1 legislated for stolen goods already disposed of and required a fivefold restitution for oxen and fourfold for sheep. The latter became the normal extreme penalty (II Sam. 12:6; LXX "sevenfold" agrees with Prov. 6:31 where with the parallelism "all the substance of his house" would suggest "full measure" as in Ex. 22:3). Stolen property unconsumed was repayable in double (Ex. 22:4, 7). Gain by fraudulence or oppression and robbery freely confessed involved full repayment plus one fifth (Lev. 6:5; Num. 5:7). The simple restitution of I Sam. 12:3 is too general to serve as legal evidence, especially as Samuel was blameless. The Talmud (*Bab. Metz. 37a*) concluded that penitents against whom robbery could not be proved should restore what strictly they need not. In Luke 19:8, Zacchaeus donated half his goods to the poor, when Jewish precept required only a fifth. He thus accepted the extreme penalty of Ex. 22:1 instead of Lev. 6:5. Christ saw in this evidence of repentance and conversion (Luke 19:9, cf. Luke 7:36-50), not a meritorious work deserving forgiveness. Elsewhere in the NT, apart from civic duties (Matt. 22:21; Rom.

13:7-8), the spirit of the gospel (Matt. 18:23-35) rather than legalism (I Cor. 6:1-8) is to guide on such issues (Philem. 18-19; Gal. 6:1).

GEORGE J. C. MARCHANT

RESTORATION OF ISRAEL. The non-restorationist position seeks to establish its case principally on the following considerations. (1) OT prophecies often appealed to in support of national restoration, such as Isa. 11:11 and Ezek. 37, were fulfilled in the return from Babylonian captivity. (2) What was not thus fulfilled must be regarded as realized in the church of the NT, the new Israel. (3) Jesus frankly told the Jews that the kingdom of God would be taken from them and given to a nation bringing forth its fruits (Matt. 21:43). This emphasizes that the restoration promises regarding Israel in the OT must have a conditional rather than an absolute character. Israel failed to meet the conditions. (4) In the unfolding of the divine purpose the NT church includes both Jews and Gentiles, the middle wall of partition between them being broken down by Christ. A return to special consideration for one nation would seem to be an anachronism once the church is a reality. (5) The return of the Jews to Palestine in considerable numbers in modern times, however interesting as a phenomenon of history, does not in itself guarantee for this nation a spiritual future in terms of national conversion.

The restorationist position emphasizes several factors. (1) The OT prophecies relating to Israel's restoration as a people are too numerous, too emphatic, and too precise to admit of identification with the return from captivity, which did not represent a summit in Israel's history either politically or spiritually. (2) It is poor exegesis to assign to the church what was spoken of Israel. If the curses and judgments pronounced on Israel for disobedience belong to her in a literal sense (which no one denies), then the future blessings ought to belong to her as well. (3) One element in the Annunciation was the declaration that the One to be born would rule over the house of Jacob for ever (Luke 1:33). It seems impossible to assign this reference to the church. (4) Jesus, despite his pronouncements of judgment upon the nation Israel for her sinful condition and especially for her rejection of himself, yet indicated a time of blessing and glory for her in the future (Matt. 19:28;

23:39; Luke 21:24). In answering the query of the disciples about the restoration of the kingdom to Israel, he did not deny the fact, but only the present realization of the hope (Acts 1:6-7). (5) Paul's statement about divine wrath being visited on the Jews of his own time (I Thess. 2:15-16) should not be taken as ruling out a glorious future for Israel, since the latter is suggested so strongly in Rom. 11:26-27.

This latter passage has been the focal point of much discussion. How are we to understand Paul's statement that "all Israel shall be saved"? To hold that all Israel is the totality of the elect, whether Jew or Gentile, on the ground that the reference is to the new Israel, the church, overlooks the fact that from the beginning of this section (Rom. 9-11) Paul is talking about his kinsmen according to the flesh (9:3). Repeatedly in the course of his exposition the apostle contrasts Israel with Gentiles. A second possibility is that "all Israel" signifies the sum total of Jewish believers in Christ. This viewpoint does not grant that there are two stages in Paul's argument, namely, the existence of an election according to grace (Jews now in the church) and secondly, what may be called the promise of a future "comprehensive conversion of Israel" (Vos) mentioned in 11:26-27. The remnant was in existence in Paul's day. He belonged to it himself. Yet the problem of theodicy remained unsolved until the prediction of 11:26-27 reasserted God's pledge to the covenant nation. So it is that the third approach to the passage understands that there will be a national turning of Israel to the Lord at his coming. The principal difficulty inherent in this view is the absence of any teaching in the passage relative to the regathering of Israel into their land and the institution of an earthly kingdom in which Israel fills the leading role.

See also ISRAEL, PROMISE, PROPHECY.

BIBLIOGRAPHY
    Wm. Hendriksen, *And So All Israel Shall Be Saved;* G. N. H. Peters, *The Theocratic Kingdom;* S. H. Wilkinson, *The Israel Promises and Their Fulfilment.*

EVERETT F. HARRISON

RESTORE, RESTORATION. Restoration and restitution refer both to property and to persons. The Mosaic code provided for the return or replacement of property that was stolen (Ex. 22:1-15; Lev. 6:1-7, etc.). In the light of this requirement Zacchaeus offered to restore fourfold (Luke 19:8). The Hebrew *šālam* refers likewise to the reviving and re-covery of those needing comfort (Isa. 57:18).

The Hebrew *šûb* refers to restoration of property (Deut. 22:2); and by David is used to describe his re-animation of soul by the Al-mighty (Ps. 23:3).

Renewal of joy may be expected for the penitent transgressor (Ps. 51:12; Mic. 7:9). For the weary and the infirm there is rehabili-tation (*'ālâ,* Jer. 30:17).

Scripture contains frequent reference to the reclamation of the backslider (Job 22:23; Prov. 24:16; Jer. 3:12). The responsibility and privilege for restoring, *katartizō,* impinges upon spiritually minded Christians (Gal. 6:1); thus becoming "the restorer of paths to dwell in" (Isa. 58:12). There is reconstruction and re-trieval for wasted years "that the locust have eaten" *šālam* (Joel 2:25), with resultant assur-ance of plentiful satisfaction and praise to God (2:26-27).

The re-establishment of the Davidic king-dom is promised in the Scriptures. The apos-tles inquired about the restoration, *apokathis-tēmi,* of the kingdom (Acts 1:6). The risen Lord did not deny the re-establishment of that kingdom; rather, earlier he had told them it would not appear until after his going away and returning again (Luke 19:11-27). He taught them that at his coming would occur the "regeneration" *(palingenesia),* the making new of all things (Matt. 19:28). Peter in his sermon at the Beautiful Gate repeated this truth by referring to "the times of restitution of all things," *apokatastaseōs* (Acts 3:21). Paul spelled out the same truth in Rom. 11:25-26.

BIBLIOGRAPHY
HDAC, II, pp. 321-22; *ISBE,* IV, pp. 2504-61.

V. R. EDMAN

RESURRECTION. When a Christian ut-ters the two theme-related clauses of the Apos-tles' Creed, "I believe in Jesus Christ . . . who . . . the third day rose from the dead," and "I believe in . . . the resurrection of the body," he confesses the absolute uniqueness and the supernaturalness of the person of Jesus Christ, and the particular hope which he has brought to men. No other world religion has framed a confession embracing such clauses as these. Some religions vaguely affirm belief in im-mortality, in one form or another, and Judaism, in its orthodox affirmations, may even creedal-ly give expression to the idea of a future bodily resurrection, but none ever hints that its

founder had, in point of time, on this earth, come forth from a tomb in a resurrection body.

If Jesus of Nazareth actually rose from the dead, in his own body, on the third day, as he predicted, all the other doctrinal affirmations of the Christian faith hold together, including those that pertain to our own ultimate destiny; if such an event did not historically occur, Paul declares, our faith is vain, our preaching is vain, and we are yet in our sins. This fact has been recognized by believers and unbelievers in every age, and accounts for the reiterated denial of the resurrection from the days of the apostles down to this hour.

I. THE NOMENCLATURE OF RESURRECTION. The Greek noun most commonly used to express the idea of resurrection is *anastasis,* derived from the verb *anistēmi.* The verb *egeirō* is used with equal frequency in the NT to con-vey the idea of rising from the dead. It is dif-ficult to detect any specific difference in the connotations of these two words in the minds of the NT writers. In the Gospel records, both are used in parallel accounts; e.g., in Matt. 16:21 and its parallel, Luke 9:22, the word is *egeirō,* but in Mark 8:31, it is *anistēmi;* in Matt. 17:23, it is *egeirō,* but in the parallel in Mark 9:31, it is *anistēmi;* in the account of the raising of Lazarus, *anistēmi* is used ex-clusively. Even in such a definite concept as God raising Christ from the dead, both words are used, e.g., *anistēmi* in Acts 2:24 and 3:26 and *egeirō* in Acts 3:15; 4:10; 5:30, etc.

II. RESURRECTION IN ANCIENT RELIGIONS. Whatever be the rich legacies of the great thinkers and cultures of the ancient world, they have left no contribution to the doctrine of the resurrection of the body. When such an impartial work as the *Oxford English Diction-ary* wholly ignores Osiris rituals, Greek myths, and Zoroastrian speculation, and gives as the first definition of the word resurrection, "the rising again of Christ after his death and burial," it bears witness to the uniqueness of this event in world history. Toynbee's treat-ment of the resurrection of Christ in his epochal *Study of History* is most significant. The chapter, "Christus Patiens" is devoted to the subject of "correspondences between the story of Jesus and the Stories of certain Hel-lenic Saviours with the 'Time-Machine.' " In this attempt at parallel tabulation, Toynbee lists eighty-seven events in and aspects of the life of Christ for which, he says, parallels can be found in the stories of the heroes of antiquity, beginning with "the hero is of royal lineage," and closing with "the executor's conversion." There is no hint, however, that in the ancient world there is a story worth placing at the side of the NT account of the resurrection of Christ. As far as one can tell, Toynbee does not believe in the resurrection of Christ, but it is interesting that he does not care even to consider supposed parallels to this supernatural event.

III. RESURRECTION IN THE OLD TESTAMENT. While it is true that the conception of resurrection was not thoroughly developed in Israel, and the literal resurrection of the body is not frequently referred to in the literature of the OT, the truth is there, and that not only with Israel's prophets. There was surely some idea of the possibility of resurrection even in the days of the patriarchs; for when Abraham offered up Isaac, he was convinced that "God was able to raise him up from the dead, from whence he did also in a figure receive him back" (Heb. 11:19). In that early period the concept was expressed in such a phrase as "to sleep with the fathers" (Gen. 47:39; Deut. 31:16; I Kings 1:29), and as sleep infers an awakening from sleep, such burial would imply a resurrection from the dead.

The writer to the Hebrews (11:35) in speaking of women who received their dead raised to life again was no doubt referring to the three resurrections occurring in the days of the Kings (I Kings 17:17-24; II Kings 4:18-37; 13:20-25). Whatever be the exact translation of the difficult passage in Job 19:26-27, here is deep conviction of the truth of resurrection from the dead (cf. Job 14:13-15). The most important single passage on resurrection in the OT is the conclusion of Isa. 26:16-19. With this must be linked two later declarations of the same truth, Hos. 6:1-2 and the familiar passage on the valley of dry bones, Ezek. 37:1-14. Granted that the primary meaning of these verses is a restoration of Israel, yet there would be no comfort for ancient Israel in such predictions if the Israelites of ancient times were not to be participants in this future restoration; and if so, they will be raised from the dead. The same teaching is set forth in Dan. 12:2, which certainly refers to the end of the age, and whatever its symbolic or typical meaning, it emphatically presents a belief in a resurrection of bodies from the dust of the earth. In addition to these basic

passages, the early church used other OT texts as prophecies or typical foreshadowings of Christ's resurrection, such as Jer. 18:3-6 and Ps. 88:10.

Faith in the resurrection is in the OT, awaiting the advent of the Messiah to whom the OT Scriptures so definitely pointed, he who would indeed bring life and immortality to light through the gospel (II Tim. 1:10). The God of the OT is the eternal, ever-living God, and though death came as a consequence of sin, if redemption is to have complete victory over sin and death, there must ultimately be the sure hope of a resurrection from the dead. (See Edmond Jacob, *Theology of the Old Testament*, London, 1958, pp. 308-15).

As faith in resurrection became increasingly common, more and more frequently expressed during the post-exilic and Maccabean periods, at the time of the advent of Christ it "had become an almost universally accepted dogma of Palestinian Judaism and a test of orthodoxy" (William Fairweather, *The Background of the Gospels*, Edinburgh, 1908, p. 292). The Sadducean denial of the resurrection was an exception, and did not express the common view of first-century Judaism.

IV. RESURRECTION IN THE NEW TESTAMENT. The theme of the resurrection of the body, including the bodily resurrection of Christ, is given more space in the NT than any other one basic Christian truth, with the possible exception of the death of the Lord Jesus. Rarely did Christ speak of his coming death without uttering a prediction of his resurrection within three days following. As an indication of his own power over death, on three occasions he brought back to life those who had died, and he gave his disciples power to raise the dead. All the Gospel writers make the fact of Christ's resurrection the climax and conclusion of their narratives. In his first post-resurrection appearances, the whole emphasis of Christ's discourse and conduct was the fact that he had risen from the dead. Apostles were chosen because they were witnesses to this resurrection. It was the basic theme of apostolic preaching, according to the Book of Acts. By setting forth proofs of this miracle, the church was able to shake the foundations of the ancient religions then predominant in the Mediterranean world.

In the NT Epistles, the deity of Christ, the certainty of his coming to judge the world, and the hope of our resurrection are related exclusively to the fact of Christ's resurrection. The historical resurrection of the Son of God becomes the great type of the spiritual resurrection of all believers passing from death unto life, and these believers are given the assurance that they may live in this present life in the power of that reality. The apostle Paul regarded the truth of the resurrection of such importance that he devoted to it the longest chapter of any epistle of the NT. This age will end in the resurrection from the dead of both the just and the unjust: as resurrection was the marvelous conclusion of our Lord's incarnate life on earth, so it will be of our life in this earthly tabernacle, when we shall be given a body suitable for a heavenly, eternal and glorious life. Remove the truth of resurrection from the NT, and its whole doctrinal structure collapses, and hope vanishes.

A. *Christ's Teaching Concerning Resurrection.* Although there are four different views of John 5:21-29, most interpreters believe that both a spiritual resurrection of the immediate present and an ultimate, final physical resurrection are here involved. On Tuesday of Holy Week, among the many questions asked of Jesus, tempting him, was one proposed by the Sadducees, who denied there was a resurrection (Matt. 22:24-43 and parallels). The Sadducees, accepting the Pentateuch, insisted that one of the reasons they rejected the resurrection was that it was not taught there. Jesus concludes his answer by going back to the great patriarchs of Genesis: when the Sadducees said their God was the God of Abraham, Isaac and Jacob, they were confessing that these patriarchs were living, inasmuch as God is the God of the living (see Gen. 50:24; Ex. 2:24 and 6:8; 3:6 and 15:16; 6:3; Lev. 26:42).

B. *The Three Resurrection Miracles of Christ's Ministry.* On three occasions Jesus himself raised individuals from the dead in, we may say, a progressive order. The first is the son of the widow of Nain (Luke 7:11-18). All the Synoptics record the raising of the daughter of Jairus at Capernaum (Matt. 9:18-19, 23-26; Mark 5:22-24, 35-43; Luke 8:40-42, 49-56). Finally, there is the extended account of the raising of Lazarus, who had died four days before the arrival of Christ in Bethany. Calling this man by name, Jesus commanded, "Lazarus, come forth" (John 11:43). One factor is common to each of these miracles: Christ *spoke* and the dead *heard his*

voice, as though he were extending himself into the other world, and the world the other side of death was accessible and obedient to him.

C. *The Opening of the Graves at the Time of Christ's Resurrection.* Matthew's account of the last week includes an incident not mentioned elsewhere. "Many bodies of the saints that had fallen asleep were raised; and coming forth out of the tombs after his resurrection, they entered into the holy city and appeared unto many" (27:52-53). Note that this took place *after* our Lord's resurrection: it did not precede his. Here, as in other resurrections of the Gospels, it must be assumed that these individuals did not come forth in true resurrection bodies; our Lord is the firstborn from among the dead (Col. 1:18).

D. *Christ's Predictions of His Own Resurrection.* The most daring statement Christ ever made was his prediction that he would rise again from the dead, on the third day after his death. The initial announcement was made at the very beginning of his ministry, at the same time he spoke of his approaching death (John 2:19, 21). Once our Lord identified his resurrection with the experience of Jonah, who was three days and three nights in the belly of the great fish (Matt. 12:40). The principal statements of his coming death and resurrection, with numerous details, were given immediately after Peter's confession (Matt. 16:21; Mark 8:31; Luke 9:22) and at the time of the transfiguration (Matt. 17:9, 23; Mark 9:9, 10, 31). According to the Markan account, the disciples "kept the saying, questioning among themselves what the rising again from the dead should mean." The prediction was repeated as he approached Jerusalem (Matt. 20:19 and parallels).

The time element, "the third day," is drawn from the OT Scriptures (Luke 24:46), as the apostle Paul later said, Christ rose "the third day according to the Scriptures" (I Cor. 15:4, taking us back to such passages as I Sam. 30:12; II Kings 20:5, 8; Lev. 7:17-18 and especially Hos. 6:2 and Jonah 1:17). This explains the amazement of the disciples at finding the tomb of Joseph of Arimathea empty, for "as yet they knew not the scripture that he must rise again from the dead" (John 20:9). If Christ's predictions had not come true, if he had not risen again on the third day, one must believe that confidence in his other utterances would have been shaken, if not destroyed; and surely we would not be reading the NT today, nor worshiping Christ as the Son of God.

V. THE RESURRECTION OF CHRIST.

A. *The Reality of His Death.* It is almost axiomatic, but nevertheless necessary to say that resurrection assumes previous death. Our Lord frequently said he would die (see references for predictions of his resurrection). When the soldiers came to break his legs a few hours after the crucifixion, they said he was already dead (John 19:33-34). It is inconceivable that the Jews, determined to destroy Christ, should have allowed any deception or substitution at this point. The death of Christ is repeatedly referred to in the Book of Acts, by seven different Greek verbs: to crucify (2:36), to slay (2:23, etc.), to kill (3:15), to handle severely (5:30), to hang (5:30), and those who participated in this act are called murderers (7:52). The entire theological system of the Epistles rests upon the fact that it was Christ who was crucified and who died for our sins. The Apostles' Creed affirms the reality in three successive phrases: he was "crucified under Pontius Pilate, dead, and buried." Assuming the reality of Christ's death, the problem is, was his certain death followed by an equally certain resurrection from the dead, a coming forth from the tomb of that which was placed in the tomb? The evidences of the reality of this stupendous event are four: the empty tomb and the testimony of the angels, the post-resurrection appearances of Christ, the transformed apostles through whose witnessing the church was founded, and the institution of the Lord's Day.

B. *The Empty Tomb.* Of the several attempts to explain rationalistically the empty tomb — theft of the body by the disciples, removal by Joseph of Arimathea, the swoon theory, the confusion of Jesus' tomb with one which was empty, the disposal of the body in some other place — it need only be said that none is inherently credible or has commanded general respect. "The empty tomb comes before us only as a fact, not as an argument. . . . The empty grave is not the product of a naive apologetic spirit, a spirit not content with the evidence for the resurrection contained in the fact that the Lord had appeared to his own and had quickened them into new victorious life; it is not the first stage in a process which aims unconsciously as much

as voluntarily at making the evidence palpable, and independent, as far as may be, of the moral qualifications, to which we have already adverted; it is an original, independent and unmotived part of the apostolic testimony" (James Denney, *Jesus and the Gospel,* N. Y., 1909, p. 131). Any theory which attempts to explain how the body was removed from that tomb is confronted with records of Christ's post-resurrection appearances in his own body.

C. *Post-Resurrection Appearances.* These are generally reckoned as ten in number, five occurring on Easter Sunday: the early morning appearance to Simon Peter, the two appearances to the women and Mary Magdalene at the tomb, the afternoon walk with the disciples on the road to Emmaus, and the evening meeting with the ten in the upper room. The following Sunday, Jesus met with the eleven disciples, Thomas being present. There was an appearance to James (I Cor. 15:4), of which we have no details, to several disciples at the Sea of Galilee (John 21:1-23), to the apostles and about five hundred brethren on a mountain in Galilee (Matt. 28:16-20) and finally, at Jerusalem at the time of the ascension (Luke 24:50-52; Acts 1:3-8). Paul was permitted to see the Lord at a later time (I Cor. 15:8). The following basic facts concerning these appearances should be noted: Our Lord appeared only to believers; the appearances were infrequent (only four occasions after Easter Sunday before the ascension, approximately forty days); there is nothing fantastic in the details of these appearances; they were notably different in nature — in the places they occurred, in the length of time involved, in the words spoken, in the mood of the apostles. All, however, were *bodily* appearances, and Christ wanted the disciples to be sure of this fact (see Luke 24:39-40; John 20:27).

Apart from the fantastic assertion, generally rejected today, that all these records are fraudulent, the two theories most often proposed to explain these appearances are the vision theory and the telegraph theory. To account for a visionary experience, there must be, first, a psychological condition for creating such a state — in this case the burning expectation on the part of the disciples that they would behold their Lord again. But such an expectation had not had time to develop in the apostolic company. The women who went to the tomb Easter morning planned to anoint a dead body, not to see a risen Lord. When they did see the Lord, they were frightened, and thought they had seen a spirit, which conclusion Jesus emphatically and immediately destroyed. The disciples on the Emmaus road were depressed, before they realized that it was the Lord who was walking with them. Furthermore, these appearances were solemn, not filled with fantastic accretions so common in abnormal experiences of supposed visions. Though they were to different groups in different places at different times, the vision hypothesis would assume that all these individuals had this vision experience. The ruling temper of the church, moreover, was not one of emotional outbursts, but of work: there is no indication that they gathered together for ecstatic experiences. Finally, the appearances suddenly ceased; they occurred rarely, and only "until that same day that he was taken up from them" (Acts 1:22).

The telegraph theory (Keim, Streeter and others) assumes that the ascended Lord telegraphed back to his followers pictures of himself in bodily form, which convinced the disciples that they had actually seen the risen Lord. This cannot be reconciled with the facts of the records that we have. For example, of the walk to Emmaus, are we to believe that the Lord took a walk in heaven, and telegraphed down his bodily presence as the disciples moved steadily along the road, and then sat down at a table (in heaven) and broke bread, so that these men thought they were eating with him? Did he also telegraph to earth the conversations? That the Lord was in their midst, all records indicate. If, however, these were only his images, the Lord deliberately deceived the apostles.

The principal question related to the appearances involves the nature of Christ's resurrection body, so much like the body of a man that at one time "their eyes were holden that they should not know him" (Luke 24:16), and at the lake "they knew not that it was Jesus" (John 20:14); in fact, Mary Magdalene did not recognize the risen Lord, mistaking him for the gardener, until he called her name. He showed the disciples his hands and feet (Luke 24:20; John 20:20, 27). On one occasion he ate, not of necessity, of course (Luke 24:43), and Milligan's words are wise, "It seems better to say that I neither know nor can offer any satisfactory solution of this act." On the other hand, the body of Christ was able to pass *through* obstructions of matter:

through the grave clothes and through the sepulcher, without the stone having been rolled away, and through the walls of the room in which the disciples were assembled on Easter Sunday night. He was able to vanish from their midst instantly (Luke 24:31, 36). In this body our Lord ascended, and the church has always regarded the ascended Lord as being in the form of a man, the risen Jesus of Nazareth as well as the Lord of glory. Surely the body in which Christ appeared to the disciples is to be identified with the body placed in the tomb of Joseph of Arimathea, but a great change came over that body when Christ rose from the dead, though the exact nature of the change is not revealed. We know more, perhaps, of the risen body of our Lord from Paul's description of our future resurrection bodies than from the Gospel records themselves.

D. *The Angelic Appearances.* All the Gospels record the appearance of angels at one particular hour following the Lord's resurrection, early Sunday morning (Matt. 28:1-8; Mark 16:5-8; Luke 24:3-9, 22-23; John 20:11-13). These give no more difficulty than the presence of angels at the annunciation, temptation, etc.

E. *The Transformed Apostles.* The fourth basic testimony to the fact of Christ's resurrection is the instantaneous, profound and permanent change that came over the apostles when, during the days following Easter morning, they became convinced that Christ had been raised. The cowardice displayed immediately before the crucifixion is gone, never to return, and in its place is a courage that will endure through the remaining years, to the hour of martyrdom. That they went everywhere preaching Christ and the resurrection is commonly acknowledged: their reward was persecution, hardship, imprisonment, and finally martyrdom. Nothing could have driven them, and their successors, to the four corners of the earth, enduring hardness for Christ's sake, but the conviction that this Christ had indeed been raised from the dead by God, and thus declared to be God's Son. Their conviction was honored by the Holy Spirit, and it was "with great power" (Acts 4:33) that they proclaimed this truth. The conviction became contagious, so that Jews and Gentiles alike were convinced that Christ was risen, and churches sprang up throughout the Mediterranean world. The apostles and their associates could preach the resurrection of Christ because they, of that generation, had been witnesses of these things (Luke 24:48; Acts 1:8).

F. *The Observance of the Lord's Day.* One more consequence of the resurrection recorded in the NT and testified to down through subsequent centuries of Christendom is the change in the day of worship from Saturday, the seventh day, so religiously observed by the Jews throughout the world from earliest times, to Sunday. The phrase, "the first day of the week" is not found in Scripture until the dawn of Easter, and is introduced by both the Synoptic writers and the apostle John into their respective narratives of the events of the day of resurrection (Matt. 28:1; Mark 16:2, 9; Luke 24:1; John 20:1, 19) see also Acts 20:7; I Cor. 16:2.

G. *The Preaching of the Resurrection in the Early Church.* The Book of Acts testifies to the fact that it was by the preaching of the resurrection of Christ that the world was turned upside down. The first sermon on the Day of Pentecost was but a proving from the prophetic Scriptures, and from the fact of the empty tomb, and the risen Lord, that God had made this person Jesus, whom the Jews had crucified, both Lord and Christ. The early apostles took seriously the fact that they had been commissioned to be "witnesses of these things" (Luke 24:46-47; for other references to the preaching of the resurrection see Acts 2:32; 3:15; 5:32; 10:39; 13:31-32; 26:16). It was to this fact that Paul constantly alluded in the various defenses he was compelled to make before the rulers of Palestine and Syria: "touching the hope of the resurrection of the dead I am called in question" (Acts 23:6; 24:15; 25:9; 26:8, 23).

VI. THEOLOGICAL IMPLICATIONS OF CHRIST'S RESURRECTION.

A. *Its Confirmation of the Truthfulness of Christ's Teaching.* If Christ said, with definiteness and detail, that after he went up to Jerusalem he would be put to death, and on the third day would rise again, and this prediction came to pass, then, it would seem, everything else he said must also be accepted as truth: that his blood was to be shed for the remission of sins; that he came down from the Father above; that the words he spoke the Father had given him; that he and the Father were one; that he was the Son of God; that whoever would believe on him would have everlasting life, and whoever refused to believe on

him would be eternally condemned. The empty tomb and the fact of the risen Lord should assure us forever that when Jesus said he was going to prepare a place for us, that he would come again and receive us to himself, that when the dead heard the voice of the Son of God, they would come forth from their graves, and that he would be the judge of all mankind, he was speaking the truth. It is impossible to accept the resurrection of Christ and entertain any doubt about the truthfulness of any utterance that proceeded from his lips.

B. *Its Bearing Upon Christ's Person and Work.* In Rom. 1:4, Paul gives a concise statement of the universal belief of the church, even in the generation immediately following our Lord's earthly life — that he must be acknowledged as both Son of David a human being and Son of God a divine being. The text says that the latter fact is *declared* "by the resurrection from the dead."

Paul further asserts that while Christ died for our sins, he was "raised for our justification" (Rom. 4:25), implying that the divine act by which sinners, because of the death of Christ, are justified by a holy and righteous God, is sealed and declared by the resurrection of the one who died for us.

C. *Its Relation to the Resurrection of Believers.* The First Epistle of Peter opens with a doxology the like of which cannot be found in the literature of any other religion or faith in the world: "Blessed be the God and Father of our Lord Jesus Christ, which according to his abundant mercy hath begotten us again unto a lively hope by the resurrection of Jesus Christ from the dead, to an inheritance . . ." (1:3-4). Delete the phrase, "by the resurrection of Jesus Christ from the dead," and the passage falls to pieces. It is faith in the Lord Jesus Christ which gives us this living hope, faith in one who faced death, overcame death, and is now living in the glory of resurrection. But even this would not give us a living hope except that we who believe in him are identified with him. This identification unites us with his death, with his life, and with his resurrection. We are assured "that he who raised up the Lord Jesus shall raise up us also with Jesus" (II Cor. 4:14). The apostle argues that if Christ has not been raised, our faith is vain, and all who have fallen asleep in him have perished; but he affirms positively, "Now hath Christ been raised from the dead, the first fruits of them that are asleep. For since by man came death, by man came also the resurrection of the dead . . . Christ the firstfruits; then they that are Christ's, at his coming" (I Cor. 15:20-21, 23). The Christian lives over again the life of Christ; he is born again by the power of the Holy Spirit; he walks as a pilgrim and sojourner on this earth, going about doing good and living in the will of God; he may expect the opposition and hatred of the world; to the world and to sin he is crucified and dead, and now living in newness of life, he has that hope that he will be like unto Christ in the day of his revelation.

D. *Its Influence Upon the Believer's Present Life.* Both Christ and the apostles emphasized the fact that we are to be living day by day in that power manifested in Christ's resurrection. The relationship of the risen Lord to Christians of every age is the basic theme of Romans 6, the essence of which is contained in vss. 4-5: "We were buried therefore with him through baptism into death: that like as Christ was raised from the dead through the glory of the Father, so we also might walk in newness of life. For if we have become united with him in the likeness of his death, we shall be also in the likeness of his resurrection." The apostle concludes his argument with the words, "Even so reckon ye also yourselves to be dead unto sin, but alive unto God in Christ Jesus . . . Present yourselves unto God, as alive from the dead" (vss. 11, 13; see also 7:4; Rom. 8:11; Eph. 1:18-20; Phil. 3:10-11; Col. 2:13).

VII. THE RESURRECTION OF BELIEVERS.

A. *The Nature of the Resurrection Body.* The Christian believer does not have to ask if there will be a resurrection for him, for this he knows with conviction; but he may often ask the question in the minds of many in the church of Corinth, "How are the dead raised up and with what body do they come?" (I Cor. 15:35). There is no answer to this question apart from the revelation of Holy Scripture, where the most elaborate reply is found in the fifteenth chapter of Paul's first letter to the Corinthians. The first part of the chapter is concerned with the resurrection of Christ, its certainty and importance; the central portion, with the problem of sequence in the resurrections, and the last section, with our resurrection bodies. Paul here sets forth four basic truths regarding the body we will possess in glory: it will be identical with the earthly body, though care must be taken in defining

identical; it will have the qualities of incorruptibility, beauty and power; it will be a spiritual body, in contrast to our present natural bodies, and it will be like unto the body of the Lord Jesus. There will be a similarity between the bodies we now have and those of the resurrection. We will be at home in our resurrection bodies, and will recognize one another. The body that suffered death because of sin will be raised from the dead. Here a mystery arises: around what will this resurrection body be built? If the stalk of wheat, e.g., must come from a living germ buried in the ground, is there some hidden germ of our own being around which Christ will build our resurrection bodies? This was the view of William Milligan (*Resurrection of the Dead,* Edinburgh, 1894, pp. 122-23).

B. *The Time of the Resurrection.* The fifteenth chapter of First Corinthians, especially vss. 20-28, contains more data on the time of the resurrection than any other passage in the NT. Paul gives the following sequence of events: Christ himself is the first fruits, and we are to be raised at his coming; he must reign until he has put all enemies under his feet, the last of which is death; when he has made all things subject to him, he will deliver up the kingdom to God the Father, and he will be subject unto God who put all things under him.

The resurrection is not something that will naturally conclude human history; it is a supernatural achievement. Christ is the first fruits of the resurrection; he is *the* resurrection; our bodies will be like unto his glorious body; it will be at his second coming that the dead will hear the voice of the Son of Man and will be raised. Everything relates to the person and work of the second person of the Godhead. Human history, philosophy and science know nothing of such an event, and, without Christ, no one has any right to hope for such an eternal destiny.

VIII. OPPOSITION TO THE TRUTH OF THE RESURRECTION OF CHRIST AND OF CHRISTIANS.

A. *In the New Testament.* Three different groups mentioned in the NT repudiated the resurrection. First, there were the Sadducees (Matt. 22:23; Acts 23:6-8). Then, some in the Corinthian church were saying that there was no resurrection of the dead, an attitude which may have derived from Sadducean influence, but more likely from the incipient beliefs of Gnosticism (I Cor. 15:12). Finally, Paul refers specifically to two men, Hymenaeus and Philetus, who were teaching that the resurrection was an event of the past (II Tim. 2:17-18). These men, and no doubt others, were insisting that the only resurrection promised in the Scriptures was a spiritual resurrection, or regeneration, which had already taken place with Christians, and no later bodily resurrection need be expected.

B. *In the Early Heresies.* The denial of the resurrection in the gnostic heresies plagued the church for many decades, and references to this heresy are frequent in the writings of the Church Fathers. For references see Irenaeus, *Against the Heresies,* I, 19:3; Basilides, II, 48:2; Justin Martyr, *Dialogue* LXXX; Tertullian, *The Prescription,* VII. That the church successfully met these heretical teachings is generally acknowledged.

C. *Among the Deists.* The initial attack of modern times upon the resurrection narratives of the Gospels was that of the Deists, particularly in the works of John Toland (1670-1722), Anthony Collins (1676-1729), Thomas Woolston (1669-1731) and Matthew Tindal (1656-1733). These men attacked every major aspect of biblical revelation that involved belief in the miraculous and the supernatural, striking principally at the so-called fulfilment of prophecies and the miracles of our Lord, including his bodily resurrection. Deism, however, was smothered by the mass of apologetic literature which it brought forth, some written by men of as great ability in argument as any of the Deists, one of the principal volumes being that of Gilbert West, *Observations on the History and the Evidence of the Resurrection of Christ* (1747).

D. *In French and German Rationalistic Literature.* Deism had not completely died out before another, different approach was made in the assault on the cardinal truth of Christ's resurrection, that known as Gospel criticism. This originated with the German scholar H. S. Reimarus (1694-1768), who left a number of papers attacking the historicity of the Gospels, principally the resurrection, later published by the German writer G. E. Lessing, then librarian of the Wolfenbuettel (1774-78). (See A. S. Farrar, *Critical History of Free Thought,* Bampton Lectures for 1862, London, 1862, pp. 316-19, 602-4.)

E. *In Nineteenth and Twentieth Century Biblical Criticism.* The influence of Reimarus

was still being felt when the most powerful attack of the nineteenth century was launched by David F. Strauss (1808-74), who, in his *Leben Jesu* (1835-36), developed the idea that this was simply an oriental legend or myth constructed from mythological themes current in the first century, a view still found in some extreme liberal works. The mid-twentieth century has seen a new form of attack upon the historicity of Christ's resurrection. This has been promoted most powerfully by Rudolf Bultmann in his scheme for demythologizing the NT. He denies that there was any bodily resurrection, though he does not attempt to account for the empty tomb, and frankly asserts, "The resurrection itself is not an event of past history." The church, however, is not to abandon the theme of the resurrection: "The real Easter faith is faith in the word of preaching. If the event of Easter Day is in any sense an historical event additional to the event of the cross, it is nothing else than the rise of faith in the risen Lord, since it was this faith which led to the apostolic preaching" ("New Testament and Mythology," in *Kerygma and Myth,* ed. by Hans Werner Bartsch, London, 1953, pp. 39-42). In other words, Bultmann argues that we must strip the NT of events that partake of a supernatural aspect because, so he says, supernatural events cannot take place in history. But they do stand for something: they are symbols, and the twentieth century must retain the truth of the symbol even if it forfeits what was once believed to be the historical reality behind the symbol. Faith in a risen Lord was there, but there was no actual rising from the dead.

F. *In the Soviet Encyclopedia.* Russian communistic propaganda rules out the resurrection. The historicity of Christ himself is denied in the large Soviet Encyclopedia. In the article, "The Resurrection of the Dead" (1929, Vol. XIII, p. 196, trans. by D. V. Benson for this article) the doctrine of the resurrection in the Nicene Creed is stated, with the comment, "This dogma is found to be in the most decisive contradiction with scientific natural knowledge which confesses the inescapability of death as the destruction of individuality with its physical and psychical peculiarities." The writer refers to "the dogma about the resurrection of the dead" as "a primitive belief peculiar to all uncultured peoples." The grounds for such a statement are not given, but the article concludes, "Factually speaking, the contemporary church preaches only the immortality of the soul about which the theologians are completely not in a position to reconcile this religious-philosophical spiritualism with the coarse primitive belief in the preserving or possibility of regeneration of life in corpse."

G. *The Disbelief of Modern Science.* The denial of the resurrection in the name of modern science is not exclusive with countries dominated by Marxian materialism, however. In a careful poll of the biological and physical scientists listed in *Who's Who in America* — 228 replying out of 521 inquiries sent — 36 affirmed faith in the resurrection, 142 denied that Christ rose from the dead; 28 indicated they did not wish to express an opinion, and 23 said they did not know. This means that only one out of five of the leading scientists of our country today believes in the resurrection of Christ. Of the 88 who indicated membership in some Protestant church, 41 said they did not believe in the resurrection, 7 did not know and 12 had no opinion. (See my article, "Twentieth Century Scientists and the Resurrection of Christ," in *Christianity Today,* April 15, 1957, pp. 3-6, 22). Unless there is a resurgence of firm belief in the Christian doctrines in our generation, the proportion of negative replies will increase.

In view of the bombardment of the new school of demythologizing, of atheistic education in Russia, and the increasing dominance of a naturalistic science in the Western world, the Christian church must engage in the task of completely re-examining the reason for its belief in the resurrection of the body, or be prepared to see these two great truths (Christ's resurrection and ours) more frequently denied; and with their elimination, many related cardinal truths of the faith vanish. We must affirm, however, that modern thought has not developed any basic incontrovertible reason why men cannot still declare, "I believe in Jesus Christ . . . who . . . the third day rose from the dead," and "I believe in . . . the resurrection of the body."

BIBLIOGRAPHY

From the vast literature on this subject, only a comparatively few titles are listed here. The first three are included because of the reputation they have attained and their extensive influence for many generations: Thomas Sherlock, *The Trial of the Witnesses of the Resurrection of Jesus;* G. West, *Observations on the History and Evidence of the Resurrection of Jesus Christ;* E. M. Goulburn, *The Doctrine of the Resurrection of the Body as Taught in Holy Scripture.* Two books by B. F. Westcott are still worth reading: *The Gospel of the Resurrection* and *Revelation of the Risen Lord.* In the early part of our century, four of the best books on this subject appeared: W. Milligan, *The Resurrection of Our Lord;* W. J. Sparrow-Simpson, *The Resurrection and Modern Thought* (in many ways the most important and comprehensive book on the resurrection in our language); J. Orr, *The Resurrection of Jesus;* H. Latham, *The Risen Master.* T. J. Thorburn, *The Resurrection Narratives and Modern Criticism;* J. M. Shaw, *The Resurrection of Christ;* D. Hayes, *The Resurrection Fact;* C. C. Dobson, *The Empty Tomb and the Risen Lord;* A. M. Ramsey, *The Resurrection of Christ: An Essay in Biblical Theology.*

WILBUR M. SMITH

RETALIATION. See REVENGE.

RETRIBUTION. See ETERNAL PUNISHMENT.

REVELATION, NATURAL. The term natural revelation describes the fact that God the Creator is self-revealed in his work. As Paul tells us in Rom. 1:20, "the invisible things of him from the creation of the world are clearly seen, being understood by the things that are made." The implication is that man, as God created him, may enjoy the knowledge of God without the special revelation attested in Scripture. It is the triune God who is revealed, for both Christ and the Holy Spirit were active in creation as well as the Father. And it is genuine revelation, deriving from God and not from man. In virtue of his sin and fall, however, man is blind to this plain witness of creation (Rom. 1:21). He cannot attain from it to a knowledge of the true God, but only to ignorance or idolatry. If traces of the truth remain in natural religion and philosophy, they do so only in a corrupt or fragmentary form. The revelation itself remains, but sin constitutes a distorting veil which is removed only by the new work of saving grace. For the sinner, therefore, natural revelation serves only to condemnation: "They are without excuse." See also NATURAL LAW.

GEOFFREY W. BROMILEY

REVELATION, SPECIAL. The midtwentieth century's revival of interest in special divine revelation occurs at a significant time in modern history. Naturalism has become a virile cultural force in both East and West. In previous centuries the chief rivals of revealed religion were speculative idealism and philosophical theism; today the leading antagonists are materialistic Communism, logical positivism, atheistic existentialism and variant forms of Anglo-Saxon humanism. Since communist philosophy refers the whole movement of events to economic determinism, the recovery of the Judeo-Christian emphasis on special historical revelation gains pointed relevance.

The term revelation means intrinsically the disclosure of what was previously unknown. In Judeo-Christian theology, the term is used primarily of God's communication to man of divine truth, that is, his manifestation of himself or of his will. The essentials of the biblical view are that the Logos is the divine agent in all revelation, this revelation being further discriminated as *general* or universal (that is, revelation in nature, history and conscience) and *special* or particular (that is, redemptive revelation conveyed by wondrous acts and words). The special revelation in sacred history is crowned by the incarnation of the living Word and the inscripturation of the spoken word. The gospel of redemption is therefore not merely a series of abstract theses unrelated to specific historical events; it is the dramatic news that God has acted in saving history, climaxed by the incarnate person and work of Christ (Heb. 1:2), for the salvation of lost mankind. Yet the redemptive events of biblical history do not stand uninterpreted. Their authentic meaning is given in the sacred writings — sometimes after, sometimes before the events. The series of sacred acts therefore includes the divine provision of an authoritative canon of writings, that is, the sacred Scriptures, providing a trustworthy source of knowledge of God and of his plan.

Despite the distinction of general and special revelation, God's revelation is nonetheless a unity, and it must not be artificially sundered. Even prior to man's fall, Adam in Eden was instructed by specially revealed statutes (e.g., to be fruitful and multiply, to eat and not to eat of certain fruit). In view of man's corruption, after the fall any one-sided reliance simply on general revelation would be all the more arbitrary. Yet we are not on that account to minimize the fact and importance of general revelation, on which the Bible insists (Ps. 19; Rom. 1, 2). But taken alone the so-called theistic proofs have led few men to the living God. The assumption of Thomas Aquinas that God can be known by natural reason apart from a revelation of Jesus Christ may be viewed, in fact, as an unwitting preparation for the revolt of early modern philosophy against special revelation, and its contrary emphasis solely on general revelation. The many types of speculative theism and idealism arising in the wake of this emphasis were only temporarily able to hold a line against the decline to naturalism.

While the Bible indeed affirms God's general revelation, it invariably correlates general revelation with special redemptive revelation. It declares at one and the same time that the Logos is Creator and Redeemer (John 1). It does not present general revelation on the thesis that the true knowledge of God is possible to fallen man through the natural light of reason apart from a revelation of Christ, but rather introduces general revelation alongside special revelation in order to emphasize man's guilt. Thus the Scripture adduces God's unitary revelation, general and special, to display man's true predicament; he is a finite creature with an eternal destiny, made for spiritual fellowship with God, but now separated from his Maker by sin.

Special revelation is redemptive revelation. It publishes the good tidings that the holy and merciful God promises salvation as a divine gift to man who cannot save himself (OT) and that he has now fulfilled that promise in the gift of his Son in whom all men are called to believe (NT). The gospel is news that the incarnate Logos has borne the sins of doomed men, has died in their stead, and has risen for their justification. This is the fixed center of special redemptive revelation.

Christian theology has had to protect the biblical view of special revelation against many perversions. Platonic preoccupation with "eternal ideas" accessible to men by rational contemplation alone, plus the disregard of history as a meaningful arena of events, tended to militate against essential elements of the biblical view, viz., divine *initiative* and *particularity,* and redemptive history as a carrier of *absolute* revelation. The idealistic notion that God's revelation is given only generally, that it is a universally accessible idea, is destructive of biblical emphases such as the particularity of special revelation and a historical sequence of special saving events (climaxed by the incarnation, atonement and resurrection of Christ as the unique center of redemptive revelation). Eighteenth century rationalism revived the notion of pre-Christian Greek idealism that historical facts are necessarily relative and never absolute, and that revelation consequently is to be divorced from historical actualities and identified with ideas alone. While still professing to speak of Christian revelation, this form of rationalism dissolved the essential connection of special revelation with historical disclosure. Moreover, it freely abandoned crucial aspects of redemptive history without protest to the destructive critics. And it surrendered the defense of the uniqueness or once-for-allness of special revelation in deference to the notion that revelation is always and only general. Wherever Christianity has been confronted by idealistic speculations of this kind, it has had to contend against a determination to dissolve the central significance of the virgin birth, unique divinity, atoning death and bodily resurrection of Christ. Since revelation was equated necessarily with a universal manifestation, every historical event was regarded simply as one of many reflections (in lower or higher degree) of this general principle, while an absolute revelation in some particular strand or at some particular point of history was arbitrarily excluded.

Modern evolutionary theory, on the other hand, has attached new importance to the historical process. But this concern for history also has generally been pursued on presuppositions hostile to the biblical view. The tendency to exalt evolution itself into an ultimate principle of explanation works against the recognition of a fixed center or climax of history in the past. While history may be approached with sentimental notions of hidden divinity, and major turning-points in the long sweep of events singled out as providential, the sacred redemptive history of the past is levelled to the plateau of other elements in history, and history as a whole is no longer understood in relation to the unique revelation of God in Christ as its center.

In fact, the tendency to view reason itself only as a late emergent in the evolutionary process suppresses the biblical declaration that reality itself has its ultimate explanation in the Logos (John 1:3), and in effect contravenes the doctrine of rational divine revelation. That is why the question of the nature and significance of mind is one of the crucial problems of contemporary philosophy, in its bearing both upon Christian and Communist philosophy. The modern philosophical revolt against reason, anchored first in skeptical theories about the limitations of human knowledge about the spiritual world, and then in evolutionary dogmas, has an obvious bearing upon the Christian contention that God communicates truths about himself and his purposes.

While it is the case that Christianity in contending for special revelation is concerned for spiritual decision between Jesus Christ and false gods, and not merely for an acceptance of certain revealed truths, yet the Christian movement does not on that account demean the importance of divinely revealed doctrines. Christian experience involves both *assensus* (assent to revealed doctrines) and *fiducia* (personal trust in Christ). Moreover, saving trust is impossible without some authentic knowledge of God (Heb. 11:6, I Cor. 15:1-4, Rom. 10:9).

Since Schleiermacher's day, Protestant theology has been influenced repeatedly by anti-intellectualistic strands in modern philosophy, especially by such thinkers as Kant, James and Dewey. Schleiermacher's formulas, that we know God only in relation to us and not as he is in himself, and that God communicates life and not doctrines, have been influential in encouraging an artificial disjunction in many Protestant expositions of special revelation. Although often striving to advance beyond these restrictions, more recent existential and dialectical expositions nonetheless do not consistently rise above the quicksands of a merely relational theology.

Because of its implications for rational revelation, the traditional identification of the Bible as the word of God written has been especially repugnant to contemporary neo-orthodox (*q.v.*) theology. It is contended that Jesus Christ alone should be identified as the Word of God, and that to speak of Scripture in this way demeans Christ. The evangelical Protestant, however, distinguishes carefully between the *logos theou* and the *rhēma theou*, that is, between the ontological Word incarnate and the epistemological word inscripturate. The motives for the neo-orthodox complaint are, in fact, speculative rather than spiritual. For the witness of Scripture, to which neo-orthodox dogmaticians profess to appeal, is specially damaging to their case here. The OT prophets consistently speak of their words as the words of God, using the formula "Thus saith the Lord" with untiring regularity. The NT apostles, moreover, speak of divine revelation in the form of definite ideas and words (cf. I Thess. 2:13, where the Thessalonians are said to have "received the word of God which you heard from us not as the word of men but as . . . the word of God"; cf. also Rom. 3:2, where Paul characterizes the OT as "the oracles of God"). The disciples also spoke of Scripture as divine revelation and, in fact, had the sacred example and authority of Jesus Christ for so doing. Jesus identified his own words with the word of the Father (John 14:34) and spoke of Scripture as the word of God (John 10:35). The Bible nowhere protests against the identification of Scripture with revelation, but rather supports and approves this identification. The neo-orthodox tendency to look upon Scripture as simply witness to revelation, in fact, contravenes the historic Christian view that the Bible itself is a form of revelation specially provided for man in sin as an authentic disclosure of the nature and will of God.

From all this it is clear how significant is the Christian assertion that the laws of logic and morality belong to the *imago Dei* in man. Christian theology has always been under biblical compulsion to affirm the identity of the Logos with the Godhead, and to find a connection between God as rational and moral and the form and content of the divine image in man. That Jesus Christ is himself the Truth; that man bears the divine image on the basis of creation (*q.v.*), and that this image while distorted by sin is not destroyed; that the Holy Bible is a rational revelation of the nature of God and his will for fallen man; that the Holy Spirit uses truth (*q.v.*) as a means of conviction and conversion — all these facts indicate in some measure the undeniable premium assigned to rationality by the Christian religion. Yet human reason is not viewed as a source of truth; rather, man is to think God's thoughts after him. Revelation is the source of truth, and reason as illuminated by the Spirit, the instrument for comprehending it.

Contemporary theology is marked by its reaffirmation of the priority of revelation to reason. In this respect it is distinguished from the liberal Protestant dogmatics of the nineteenth century, which tended to view human reason as a self-sufficient and independent criterion. Some Neo-Thomistic studies today restate the philosophy even of Thomas Aquinas so as to set the usual summary of his approach, "I understand in order to believe," in a context of faith. The Thomistic hostility to innate ideas, and the Thomistic support for knowledge of God by the way of negation and the way of analogy are, however, firmly reasserted. Protestant theology, heavily influenced by Karl Barth and Emil Brunner, now characteristically reasserts the priority of revelation over reason. Thus the epistemological formulas representative of Augustine ("I believe in order to understand") and of Tertullian ("I believe what is absurd," i.e., to the unregenerate man) are much in the climate of current theological dialogue. But the modern tendency to exaggerate the transcendence of God, by way of revolt against the classic liberal overstatement of divine immanence, subserves the Tertullian more than the Augustinian formula. The historic Christian confidence in a revealed world-and-life view takes its rise from a prior confidence in the reality of rational divine revelation. The modern tendency to veer toward a doctrine of revelation whose locus is to be found in an immediate existential response, rather than in an objectively conveyed Scripture, thwarts the theological interest in biblically revealed doctrines and principles from which an explanatory view of the whole of reality and life may be exposited. Thus it is apparent that a recovery of confidence in the intelligible integration of the whole of life's experiences depends significantly upon a virile sense of the actuality of rational divine revelation.

BIBLIOGRAPHY

John Baillie,* *The Idea of Revelation in Recent Thought*; John Calvin, *Institutes of the Christian Religion*; Bk. I, chaps. VI-IX; Carl F. H. Henry, "Divine Revelation and the Bible," in *Inspiration and Interpretation* (J. F. Walvoord, ed.); Paul K. Jewett, *Emil Brunner's Concept of Revelation*; H. Kraemer, *Religion and the Christian Faith*; B. B. Warfield, *Revelation and Inspiration*, pp. 1-48; Carl F. H. Henry, ed., *Revelation and the Bible*.

CARL F. H. HENRY

REVENGE. *Nāḥam* is the common Hebrew word (cf. Nahum the prophet), cognate with vengeance and avenge. Oddly, four other words have similar translation in the AV (*yāša'*, "save"; *pāqaḏ*, "visit"; *šapaṭ*, "judge"; *pāra'*, "free"; along with *gā'al*, "release"). In the NT, *krinō*, "judge"; *ekdikeō*, "avenge"; *orgē*, "wrath." An improper human passion (Ezek. 25:12) of retaliation for personal satisfaction, from a sense of being galled or mistreated (I Sam. 25:26), revenge is related to egotism. In both Testaments it is forbidden to man (Lev. 19:17 f.; Rom. 12:19a); it pertains only to God (Deut. 32:35; Ps. 94:1; Rom. 12:19b), or to gods (Acts 28:4). God's vengeance, much found in Scripture, is the inexorable execution of eternal right, divine justice. It is only through anthropomorphism confused with man's vengeance; for God, without any passion, vindicates his justice, majesty, world-order, against any assault (Jer. 46:10; Nah. 1:2; II Thess. 1:8), as he also avenges wrong done to his own (Deut. 32:43; Rev. 19:2; Luke 8:7).

There is vast difference and no little confusion between private execution of presumable justice, which is anarchy (Gen. 4:23), and public maintenance of general right, which is obligatory (Josh. 20:5; Luke 18:2 f.). The provision of the *goel* ("revenger of blood") in the Mosaic revelation was ideally the means of effecting theocratic jurisprudence in criminal cases (Num. 35:19, e.g.). *Lex talionis,* so often misunderstood, gives no mandate in Scripture to private or personal procedure, but to the theocratic administration of justice (Ex. 21:23; Lev. 24:19). The Sermon on the Mount is addressed to individuals as (in effect) Christians, who being such, are to take insult or injury, as God's grace may lift them to such a high plane; but our Lord in no sense contradicted the OT theocratic law (*lex talionis,* Deut. 19:21); he endorsed it unequivocally (Matt. 5:17 ff.). To this day the rule, Suit the punishment to the crime, is the state law, never to be abolished as long as there is to be a state.

The futility of revenge is shown in its always provoking reaction in kind (Gen. 4:23). The efficacy of "turning the other cheek" is the resulting end of strife, the disarming of the adversary: "If thine enemy hunger . . ." (Rom. 12:20).

ROBERT F. GRIBBLE

REVIVAL. In many instances the word revive, Hebrew *ḥāyâ,* Greek *anazaō,* means literally to come back to life from the dead: "the soul of the child came into him again and he revived" (I Kings 17:22); "Christ both died and rose and revived" (Rom. 14:9), i.e., "died and lived again," RSV. Even when this is not the meaning, the word carries greater force than it bears to us today, for we have confused revivalism with evangelism. Evangelism is good news; revival is new life. Evangelism is man working for God; revival is God working in a sovereign way on man's behalf. To speak of "holding a revival" is a misnomer. No human being can kindle the interest, quicken the conscience of a people, or generate that intensity of spiritual hunger that signifies revival. All spiritual life, whether in the individual or in the community, in the church or in the nation, is by the Spirit of God. No

man can schedule a revival, for God alone is the giver of life. But when darkness deepens, when moral declension reaches its lowest ebb, when the church becomes cold, lukewarm, dead, when "the fulness of time" is come and the prayer ascends from a few earnest hearts, "Wilt thou not revive us again that thy people may rejoice in thee" (Ps. 85:6), then history teaches it is time for the tide of revival to sweep in once more. Revival always involves the preaching of divine judgment, confession of sin, repentance, acceptance of salvation as a free gift, the authority of the Scriptures and the joy and discipline of the Christian life. While revivals do not last, the effects of revival always endure.

F. CARLTON BOOTH

REWARD. The word reward, if all of its related forms are included, is found one hundred and one times in our English Bible (AV). Four Greek words and several Hebrew words are rendered by this one word.

In present day usage, a reward is a gift given in recognition for some service rendered, either good or evil. Its biblical usage, however, is quite varied, including such ideas as a bribe (Ps. 103:10), punishment (Ps. 91:8), and gift (I Kings 13:7). It includes, therefore, the punishment one experiences in this life for evil deeds (Matt. 6:5) as well as future retribution (Ps. 91:8). Several times the word is used of evil done to a person where good was expected (Gen. 44:4; Ps. 35:12).

Christ often used rewards as an incentive for service. This has been a disturbing thought to some. One need not be troubled by this if he understands the scriptural nature of rewards and dismisses any thought of materialism. Rewards are the result of human effort, to be sure, but as Weiss says: "As the servants of God in the Israelitish theocracy were entitled, by reason of their covenant relationship, to look for the fulfillment of the promise as a reward for their fulfillment of their covenant obligations, so the disciple of Jesus is entitled to look for the completion of salvation as a reward for the fulfillment of the demands which are made upon him in virtue of his being a disciple" (B. Weiss, *Biblical Theology of the New Testament,* Vol. I, T. & T. Clark, Edinburgh, 1885, p. 144).

For the Christian, rewards have an eschatological significance. Paul teaches that every man shall appear before the judgment seat of

Christ for the judgment of his works (Rom. 14:12; II Cor. 5:10). This must be kept distinct in our thinking from judgment for sin, for this, as far as the believer is concerned, is forever past (Rom. 5:1). Salvation is a gift (Eph. 2:8-9) whereas rewards are earned (I Cor. 3:14). The two chief passages of Scripture that discuss rewards at length are I Cor. 3:9-15 and I Cor. 9:16-27. Additional information can be found by studying the various passages where rewards for service are depicted as crowns (I Cor. 9:25; Phil. 4:1; I Thess. 2:19; II Tim. 4:8; James 1:12; I Pet. 5:4; Rev. 2:10; 3:11).

Various types of service merit rewards such as enduring temptation (James 1:12), diligently seeking God (Heb. 11:6), dying for Christ (Rev. 2:10), faithful pastoral work (I Pet. 5:4), faithfully doing God's will and loving his appearing (II Tim. 4:8), soul winning (I Thess. 2:19-20), faithful stewardship (I Cor. 4:1-5), acts of kindness (Gal. 6:10), hospitality (Matt. 10:40-42). Rewards can be lost (Rev. 2:10; II John 8). Then too it is possible to be busy in the Lord's service and receive no rewards at all (I Cor. 3:15; 9:27) or to receive little when one should receive much (II John 8).

See also CROWN.

BIBLIOGRAPHY
D. Walker in *HDAC*; L. S. Chafer, *Systematic Theology*, Vol. IV, pp. 396-405; B. Weiss, *Biblical Theology of the New Testament*, Vol. I, pp. 143-47.

HOWARD Z. CLEVELAND

RICHES. See WEALTH.

RIDDLE. The OT term for an enigmatic or perplexing saying is *hîdâ*, perhaps from the root *'hd*, "hold fast" or "cover" (KB). Translated "riddle," *hîdâ* describes Samson's wager with his Philistine wedding guests (Judg. 14:12-19). Riddles (Prov. 1:6 ASV mg.) were serious matters (cf. possibly Prov. 30:15-16, 24-28); and Solomon profited by answering the *hîdâ*, "hard questions," of the queen of Sheba (I Kings 10:1).

Ezekiel's allegory of the eagles is called a "riddle" (17:2). *Hîdâ* could thus identify any matter needing interpretation (Num. 12:8; cf. I Cor. 13:12 ASV mg.), for example, a predictive "proverb" (Hab. 2:6; ASV mg. "riddle"). It describes a perplexing moral problem (Ps. 49:4), when retribution overtakes the wicked only after death (vs. 15); and Daniel predicted that Antiochus IV would "under-

stand dark sentences" (8:23), that is, be skilled in "double dealing." Ps. 78:2, however, "I will utter dark sayings," is followed by a straightforward historical poem; and this verse is referred by Matt. 13:35 to Christ's parabolic preaching.

BIBLIOGRAPHY
HERE; JewEnc.

J. BARTON PAYNE

RIGHT, RIGHTEOUSNESS. Right is the translation of many Hebrew words. The two most important are *yāšār* and *mišpaṭ*. The former has the sense of "being straight" while the latter is a forensic term meaning "judgment," as in Gen. 18:25. In the NT the chief word is *dikaios*, meaning "equal." It is usually translated "just" or "righteous."

The concept of "right" in the sense of "fair" or "equal" is arrived at early in the developing consciousness of a child and is firmly held. In a community it is the office of a judge to declare what is right. From the beginning in the Hebrew community the judges were regarded as acting on the behalf of God (Deut. 1:17). God is the Judge of all the earth. It was unthinkable that, as such, he should act unfairly. "To slay the righteous with the wicked, that so the righteous should be as the wicked; that be far from thee: shall not the judge of all the earth do right" (Gen. 18:25, RV).

God is the fountain of justice, so that everything which he does may be relied upon as just (Deut. 32:4; Rom. 9:14). God's equity as Judge will be seen most clearly "in the day of the revelation of the righteous judgment of God; who will render to every man according to his works" (Rom. 2:5).

Since God's verdict is absolutely just, man's righteousness may be defined in terms of God's judgment. The righteous is the man whom God's verdict has declared just; the wicked the man whom God has condemned.

Righteousness is the regular translation in the EV of the Hebrew *ṣedeḳ* and *ṣᵉdāqâ* and the Greek *dikaiosynē*. Originally these words signified that which conforms to the norm, and for biblical writers this norm is the character of God himself.

Amos, in particular, emphasizes that God is impartial in his dealings. The prophet called for a similar righteousness in men (Amos 5:15, 24). Inflicting retribution is an element of the righteousness of God (Isa. 61:2; II Thess. 1:6). Moreover, if in a world of unrighteousness and oppression, righteousness is to be established, God himself must become the protector and vindicator of the oppressed. Thus frequently the Bible speaks of God's righteousness as manifested in his defense of those who have no helper, i.e., the poor, the widow, the orphan and the stranger (Pss. 10:14; 72:12). Thus it comes about that righteousness is closely linked with shewing mercy to the poor (cf. Matt. 6:1-2; II Cor. 9:9-10).

Similarly, God is righteous in his protection of his people, and in his rescue of them from the heel of the oppressor. In so doing he vindicates them as his people and shows that they are in the right, that is, he justifies them.

This meaning is clear in each stage of God's dealing with his people:

(1) In his rescue of the chosen nation from the oppression of Pharaoh and his establishment of them in Canaan in the face of their foes. The victories which accomplish this are described as the righteous acts of God (Judg. 5:11; I Sam. 12:7), while Pharaoh himself acknowledged that the ten plagues were evidence of God's righteousness (Ex. 9:27).

(2) In his redemption of his people from the Exile, God showed his righteousness by his deliverance of his own. Righteousness is very closely associated with salvation (Isa. 45:8; 46:13; 51:5-6).

(3) In his redemption of his people from sin, and from bondage to the devil. The Messianic king, foretold in Zech. 9:9, is "just and having salvation." The Gospel is the power of God unto salvation to everyone that believes; in it is revealed the righteousness of God (Rom. 1:16-17).

God's righteousness is shown in his saving of his people from their sins through the cross of Christ. His people are now no longer restricted to the Jewish race but include all who believe on Jesus. "As many as call upon the name of the Lord shall be saved."

God declares righteous those who have faith in Jesus. That is, he justifies them. There can be no doubt that those whom God declares righteous are righteous. It is this righteousness of God with which Paul was anxious to be clothed, rather than with that righteousness which might be thought to be derived from his own partial keeping of the moral law (Phil. 3:9). The former he describes as the righteousness of God, the latter as his own righteousness.

God's declaration of the righteousness of his people is based on the redemption wrought by Christ (Rom. 3:24). In effect, it is a righteousness through complete forgiveness; but this forgiveness is based on an objective fact, the blood of Christ (I John 1:7, 9).

There is no suggestion in Scripture that God's declaration that believers are righteous is in conflict with the sense of right implanted in our heart. Such a conflict is indeed unthinkable, as God is the author of both. Yet Paul recognized that God's passing over of sins done aforetime, rather than the visiting of them with wrath, called for explanation, which he found in the death of Christ for sin (Rom. 3:25-26). It is here that he solved the apparent paradox of a righteous God declaring sinners righteous (Rom. 4:5).

See also JUSTIFICATION.

BIBLIOGRAPHY

HDAC; HDB; TWNT (E.T.); Commentaries on Romans and Galatians; C. H. Dodd, *The Bible and the Greeks*; N. H. Snaith, *Distinctive Ideas of the Old Testament*.

DAVID BROUGHTON KNOX

RITSCHLIANISM. The theology of Albrecht Ritschl, of Goettingen (d. 1889) and of his followers, including such men as A. Harnack, J. Kaftan, F. A. Loofs, and J. Weiss. It was the dominant liberal theology from *ca.* 1875 to 1914. Its influence is still felt in the contemporary "Neo-Orthodoxy" or "New Modernism." (H. R. Mackintosh speaks of Barth as "Ritschl's great successor.")

It is a negative mediating theology, reacting against the speculative rationalism of Hegel and against the subjective mysticism of Schleiermacher. The attempt is made to establish an independent sphere for theology, from which both the intellectual and the emotional are excluded. This is done by maintaining that religious knowledge comes independently of either of these as a result of value judgments. This is a decision that an object is of worth to the individual. Ritschlianism is thus a religious pragmatism.

It is subjective in its emphasis on the value judgment, and yet objective in its insistence upon a return to the historical records about Christ as found in the Bible. To Ritschl Christianity is the highest form of religion, being absolutely ethical as founded upon Christ, the founder of the kingdom of God (*q.v.*). This kingdom is described as "the organization of humanity through action inspired by love." The kingdom or community of believers is a sort of moral collectivism. It is only as the individual identifies himself with the community that he partakes of the religious good of justification and redemption. The example of Jesus inspires us to believe that God is love, and that we are forgiven, and then we become reconciled to God. This, of course, is a reversal of the orthodox order.

BIBLIOGRAPHY

C. Fabricus, *Die Entwicklung in Albrecht Ritschls Theologie;* J. Orr, *The Ritschlian Theology and Evangelical Faith;* A. E. Garvie, *The Ritschlian Theology;* Garvie in HERE; A. T. Swing, *The Theology of Albrecht Ritschl;* J. K. Mozley, *Ritschlianism;* R. Mackintosh, *Albrecht Ritschl and His School;* H. R. Mackintosh, *Types of Modern Theology,* pp. 138-80.

MORTON H. SMITH

RITUAL. More precisely, ritual is the form of words prescribed for a liturgical function. More popularly, however, it is used of the accompanying ceremonial. Thus the so-called Ritualists of nineteenth century England were mainly attacked for their introduction of vestments and ceremonies rather than for verbal alterations.

GEOFFREY W. BROMILEY

ROCK. The principal words are the Hebrew *sela'*, "elevation," and *ṣûr*, "sharpness," and the Greek *petra*. In addition the Hebrew *'eben* and the Greek *lithos* are used for "stone."

Israel had an awareness of Yahweh's dependability and helpfulness early in her history (Gen. 49:24; Ps. 78:35). David put the Lord to the test many times, finding in him his sure defense (Ps. 18:2; 28:1; 62:2). Paul refers to Christ as the Rock of refreshing supply in the wilderness (I Cor. 10:4). On this see H. St. J. Thackeray, *The Relation of St. Paul to Contemporary Jewish Thought,* pp. 204-12.

The OT contains hints (Isa. 28:16) and predictions (Dan. 2:44, 45) of a messianic nature involving one who would be rejected by his own people (Ps. 118:22). That which is spoken of the Lord God, that he would become a stone of stumbling and a rock of offense to Israel (Isa. 8:14), was specifically fulfilled in Christ (Rom. 9:32, 33). Jesus of Nazareth was a stone of stumbling to his own nation because he refused to adopt the role of a political Messiah. Instead he presented himself as the Suffering Servant (I Cor. 1:23). In the resurrection God took the rejected stone — a living stone indeed (I Pet. 2:4) — and made it the foundation (I Cor. 3:11), the chief corner stone (Luke 20:17; Acts 4:11; Eph. 2:20; I Pet. 2:7) of a new edifice, the church of Christ, in which all be-

lievers have their place as living stones (I Pet. 2:5).

The stone appears in a context of judgment as well as salvation (Dan. 2:34, 35; Luke 20:18), depicting by its massiveness and weight the inevitability of crushing destruction for those who repudiate God's Son.

In general the figure of the rock or stone as applied to Christ conveys the thought of permanence (Heb. 13:8) and indispensability as the basis for the redeemed life (I Cor. 3:11). It also betokens the breadth and strength of the future messianic kingdom (Dan. 2:35, 44).

For the allusion in Matt. 16:18, see PETER.

EVERETT F. HARRISON

RUDIMENT. See ELEMENTS OF THE WORLD.

RULE, RULER. In the OT eleven Hebrew words are translated "rule" and "ruler," the most frequent being the verb *māšal,* which appears rather pervasively throughout the OT. It is used of Joseph who was ruler of all Egypt (Gen. 45:8), of David's lineage (II Chron. 7:18), of God's rule over Jacob (Ps. 59:13) and of the Messiah, one of whose titles is ruler (Mic. 5:2).

Of the five NT words for ruler the predominant is *archōn,* a substantival participle of the verb *archō,* "to rule." Rev. 1:5 affirms that Christ is the "ruler of the kings on earth," which is a reflection of the widespread Jewish idea of the character and role of the Messiah. This word is used of Christ only once, but the same thought appears many times, e.g., Rom. 14:9 and Col. 1:18. In the NT *archōn* generally refers to those in positions of religious or political authority. Officers in charge of synagogues were called rulers (Luke 8:41), and members of the Sanhedrin also bore this appellation (John 3:1). Another use of the word applies to evil spirits whose ranks and offices parallel visible organizations. Satan is described as the "prince of demons" (Mark 3:22). Jesus himself calls Satan the "ruler of this world" (John 12:31). Paul alludes to the devil as the "prince of the power of the air" (Eph. 2:2).

DAVID H. WALLACE

RULE OF FAITH. (*Regula Fidei*) D. van den Ende has shown that in Irenaeus and Hippolytus the term refers to "the living doctrine of the churches" and not to any set pattern. For Tertullian it seems to have referred to the settled and unchangeable doctrines of the faith. Many historians believe it to have referred to the baptismal formula, though this has been questioned recently. The term does not seem to have been used in reference to the Bible itself in the Ante-Nicene church.

Today it denotes the source or standard of Christian doctrine. The Roman Church defines the rule of faith as the teaching of the church. Protestants reserve the term for Scripture alone. The Protestant confessions, though serving as secondary norms, are not referred to as "the rule of faith." This is reserved for Scripture alone, which is called "the only rule of faith and practice."

MORTON H. SMITH

RURAL DEAN. See OFFICES, ECCLESIASTICAL.

S

SABBATARIANISM. Christian sabbatarianism, or enforced sabbath-rest, was initiated by Constantine's regulations against Sunday labor, A.D. 321; and with Charlemagne's justification of such from the fourth commandment, 789, sabbatarianism officially prevailed. Luther rejected sabbath-keeping as Romanistic externalism, but the Puritans established England's comprehensive sabbath law of 1677. The Scottish and colonial "blue-laws" are today being increasingly relaxed or eliminated.

Judaistic sabbatarianism has been perpetuated by sectarian attempts to re-establish pre-Christian seventh-day observances. Ignatius, A.D. 107, rejected such "sabbatizing" (Magnesians ix); and the Council of Laodicea condemned it officially, 343. Judaistic sabbatarianism has reappeared among post-reformation groups such as the Seventh-day Baptists, 1671, and the Seventh-day Adventists, 1845.

BIBLIOGRAPHY
"Sunday," HERE; Paul Cotton, *From Sabbath to Sunday.*

J. BARTON PAYNE

SABBATH. The name for the Jewish day of rest and worship. Hebrew: *šabbāt*; Greek: *sabbaton*. It is not used in profane Greek, and is perhaps borrowed from the Aramaic *šabbatā'*. *Subbata* is plural in form in Greek and developed a singular *sabbaton,* but the apparent plural *sabbata* is used also for a single sabbath (W. E. Vine, *Expository Dictionary of New Testament Words,* Oliphants, London, 1940). The word has a cognate in Arabic and Akkadian. Therefore, the root appears to be old Semitic, meaning cease, rest, interrupt.

The sabbath was instituted at creation (Gen. 2:2-3), was next referred to in the giving of manna (Ex. 16:23-30), then at Sinai (Ex. 20:8-11; Deut. 5:12-15). Violation was a capital offense (Ex. 31:14). Leviticus and Numbers give numerous regulations for the sabbath. The individual was to rest. Extra offerings were prescribed at the tabernacle. Other feast days were also called sabbaths (Lev. 16:31, etc.). The seventh year was a sabbatic year and the Hebrews therefore counted years more by sevens than by decades.

The sabbath is mentioned in Kings, Chronicles, Ps. 92:1 (title), Isaiah, Jeremiah, Ezekiel, Hosea, and Amos. The day is to be observed in the messianic age.

Critical students have sought far afield for its origin. J. R. Sampey (*ISBE*) remarks, "The wealth of learning and ingenuity expended in the search for the origin of the Sabbath has up to the present yielded small return." A more recent effort is by S. Langdon (*Babylonian Menologies and the Semitic Calendars,* London, 1935). He finds certain unlucky days, especially in certain months, mentioned in tenth century Assyria: days 1, 7, 9, 14, 19, 21, 28, 29, and 30 were unlucky for any work. Assurbanipal in the seventh century reduced these to days 7, 14, 19, 21, and 28 of which 19 was especially unlucky. Langdon argues that the seven day week began here, based on the phases of the moon. But the lunar month is 29½ days, not 28, and the moon's phases are not exactly seven days apart. Also the unlucky 19th day breaks the sequence. More important, the Hebrew sabbath was clearly far older than this.

The obligation of the Christian for sabbath keeping has been much discussed. The sabbatarian (q.v.) view is ably discussed by Charles Hodge, *Systematic Theology*, Scribners, 1873, Vol. III, pp. 321-48. The Seventhday Adventist view that keeping of the seventh day is an essential moral obligation, is summed up in the *ISBE*. The view that the sabbath is no longer binding is given by Walter R. Martin in *Eternity Magazine*, May 1958, pp. 20-23. An alternative view is that the sabbath was essentially ceremonial and thus was done away in Christ. Ceremonial laws, however, involve basic and eternal principles and have analogies in NT truth and practice. The analogue of the sabbath is the Lord's day, the first day of the week, clearly celebrated by the apostles and the early church.

BIBLIOGRAPHY
Arndt; D. Macmillan, ed., *Sunday the World's Rest Day*; L. S. Chafer, *Systematic Theology*, IV, pp. 102-22; V, pp. 253-60; J. R. Sampey and W. W. Prescott in *ISBE*.

R. LAIRD HARRIS

SABELLIANISM. Taking its name from the third century Sabellius, this is an inadequate conception of the Trinity which in the attempt to guard against tritheism reduced the three persons of Father, Son and Holy Ghost to three characters, modes or relations of the Godhead assumed for the purpose of the divine dealings with man. Thus God is eternally and essentially one, but economically, i.e., for specific purposes, he takes the form of Father, Son and Holy Spirit and may be confessed and worshiped as such. This overfacile solution of the mystery of triunity attracted many followers, but it was quickly realized that, although Jesus Christ is wholly God, he is no mere mode or function but the pre-existent and eternal Son (John 17:3, 5, 24), thus demanding confession of an essential trinity or triunity. In consequence of the opposition of Dionysius of Alexandria, Sabellius and his teaching were condemned at a council at Rome (under Pope Dionysius) in A.D. 263.

WILLIAM KELLY

SACRAMENT. Along with the proclamation (*kērygma*) and teaching (*didachē*), baptism and the Lord's Supper were given a prominent place in the fellowship of the early church (Acts 2:41-42; 20:7, 11; 10:47, etc.). Both these rites were regarded as means appointed by Jesus Christ to bring the members of the church into communion with his death and resurrection and thus with himself through the Holy Spirit (Matt. 28:19-20; I Cor. 11:23-27; Acts 2:38; Rom. 6:3-5; Col. 2:11-12). They were linked together in our Lord's teaching (Mark 10:38-39) and in the mind of the church (I Cor. 10:1-5 ff.) as having such significance. They were the visible enactment of the word proclaimed in the *kērygma* and their significance must be understood as such.

The *kērygma* or proclamation of the gospel in the NT was no mere recital of the events of the life, death, resurrection and ascension of Jesus, the Son of God. It was the representation of these events to the hearers in the power of the Spirit so that through such proclamation they could become related to these events in a living way through faith. In the proclamation of the gospel the once-for-all event continued to be effective for salvation (I Cor. 1:21; II Cor. 5:18-19). The word of the *kērygma* gave men fellowship in the mystery (*mystērion*) of the kingdom of God brought nigh in Jesus (Matt. 13:1-23; Mark 4:11), and the preacher in fulfilling his task was the steward of this mystery (I Cor. 4:1; Col. 1:25; Eph. 3:8-9). The miracles or signs accompanying the *kērygma* in the early church were the visible aspect of the living power which the word derived from its relation to the mystery of the kingdom of God.

It was inevitable, therefore, that baptism and the Lord's Supper, the other visible counterparts of the *kērygma*, should also come to be regarded as giving fellowship in the same *mystērion* of the Word made flesh (I Tim. 3:16), and should be interpreted as themselves partaking in the *mystērion* of the relationship between Christ and his church (Eph. 5:32).

The Greek word *mystērion* was later often given the translation in Latin *sacramentum* and the rites themselves became spoken of as *sacramenta*. The word *sacramentum* meant both "a thing set apart as sacred," and "a military oath of obedience as administered by the commander." The use of this word for baptism and the Lord's Supper affected the thought about these rites, and they tended to be regarded as conveying "grace" in themselves, rather than as relating men through faith to Christ.

A sacrament came later to be defined (following Augustine) as a "visible word" or an "outward and visible sign of an inward and spiritual grace." The similarity between the form of the sacrament and the hidden gift tended to be stressed. Five "lesser" sacraments became traditional in the church: confirmation, penance, extreme unction, order, matrimony. But the church had always a special place for baptism and the Lord's Supper as the chief "mysteries" and at the Reformation these were regarded as the only two which had the authority of our Lord himself, and therefore as the only true sacraments.

Since God in the OT also used visible signs along with the word, these were also regarded as having sacramental significance. Among the OT sacraments the rites of circumcision and the Passover were stressed as being the OT counterparts of baptism (Col. 2:11-12) and the Lord's Supper (I Cor. 5:7).

BIBLIOGRAPHY

Calvin, *Institutes*, IV:14; Robert Bruce, *Sermons upon the Sacraments*; G. Bornkamm in *TWNT*, IV, pp. 809-34; T. F. Torrance, "Eschatology and the Eucharist" in *Intercommunion*, pp. 303-50).

RONALD S. WALLACE

SACRIFICE. The OT provides both for special sacrifices, like covenant sacrifices, and regular sacrifices, which are detailed in Leviticus. Of these there is an offering of cereals, the meal offering (wrongly "meat" offering in AV), one of liquids, the drink offering, and various animal offerings. These last are the most important, and we will concentrate on them. They are four in number, the burnt offering, the peace offering, the sin offering and the guilt or trespass offering. Others like the wave offering and the heave offering refer to parts of the peace offering. See also OFFER, etc.

We may divide the ceremonial of offering into six parts. First, there was the "drawing near." This was so characteristic that the causative of the verb "to draw near" was synonymous with "to sacrifice." It signified the selection of an unblemished victim, chosen from the domestic animals in accordance with the regulations, and the bringing it to the altar. Then came the laying on of hands, a leaning with firm pressure on the animal's head. Thirdly, the worshiper slew the victim. The fourth stage was the first in which the

priest was involved. He caught the blood and disposed of it. In the case of a sin offering for a priest or the whole congregation, he sprinkled it seven times before the veil, put some on the horns of the altar of incense and poured the rest at the base of the altar. If it were for an individual other than a priest, the sevenfold sprinkling was omitted and the blood was put on the altar of burnt offering instead of that of incense. In the case of all the other offerings, the blood was simply poured out at the base of the altar. The fifth stage saw certain prescribed parts, mostly the internal fat (in the burnt offering, the whole animal), burned on the altar. The final stage was the disposal of the remainder of the carcass. In the peace offering certain parts were given to the priest, and the rest was eaten by the worshipers in a meal of fellowship. In the sin and guilt offerings the priests consumed the carcass, unless the offering was for themselves, when it was burned in a clean place outside the camp.

The significance of all this is disputed. W. Robertson Smith held that the basic sacrifice was the peace offering, so that sacrifice was primarily a process of communion between the worshipers and God. G. Buchanan Gray took the burnt sacrifice as primary with the basic idea that of homage, a gift made to God. But theories worked out on the basis of the activity of primitive man will not necessarily apply to the men of the OT who were far from primitive. In the Levitical system there can be no doubt that sacrifice expresses a variety of ideas, among which atonement (*q.v.*) for sin is prominent. The expression "to make atonement" recurs with frequency.

How this is effected is disputed. The most natural view is that the worshiper merits death on account of his sin, a view which is freely expressed in the OT. But God permits him to substitute a spotless victim. So he lays his hands upon the animal and symbolically transfers his sins to it. This is supported by the later practice of making confession of sin at this point. The objection usually raised, that the flesh of the animal would not be described as "most holy" if it were bearing sin, is not really valid. It is "most holy" because it has discharged the holiest of all functions.

In modern times an idea has sprung up that the essential thing in sacrifice is not the infliction of death as sin's penalty, but the presentation of life before God. The worshiper's life may not be thus presented because it is stained with sin. But God graciously permits him to substitute the life of the animal. Thus sacrifice is essentially the collection and presentation of the blood. This view is not adequate. In addition to its faulty exegetical basis (see BLOOD) it does not do justice to such acts as the burning on the altar, nor the confession of sin in later practice. It does not square with the repeated affirmation that sacrifice is "to make atonement." It does not appear how the release or presentation of life makes atonement for sin.

The Bible does not regard sacrifice as having efficacy in itself. It avails only because God has himself given it as the means of effecting atonement (Lev. 17:11). The spirit in which the offering is made is important, and the prophets constantly castigate those who put their emphasis on the outward act and do not offer in penitence and trust. Some have felt that the prophets desired the abolition of sacrifice. But though passages like Isa. 1:11; Jer. 7:22 f.; Hos. 6:6; Amos 5:21 ff.; Mic. 6:6 ff., are forthright, close examination shows that it is not sacrifice as such that is castigated, but sacrifice as the prophets saw it practiced with scant regard for upright living.

In the NT it is recognized that it is not possible for animals to take away men's sin (Heb. 10:4). But what beasts could not do, that Christ did in his death. Sometimes sacrifice in general is used to illustrate his death (Eph. 5:2; I Pet. 1:2); sometimes a particular sacrifice (I Cor. 5:7, or the Day of Atonement sacrifice, Heb. 9 and 10). But throughout Christ is thought of as fully effecting all that the ancient sacrifices dimly foreshadowed. He really took our place. He took our sins upon him. He is the perfect sacrifice. His offering was made willingly (Heb. 10:7), but it was not, as some allege, simply a sacrifice consisting of obedience, for the writer goes on to say that the particular will of God that he obeyed was that requiring "the offering of the body of Jesus Christ once for all" (Heb. 10:10).

BIBLIOGRAPHY

C. R. North in *RTWB*; W. Robertson Smith, *The Religion of the Semites*; G. B. Gray, *Sacrifice in the Old Testament*; Vincent Taylor, *Jesus and His Sacrifice*; B. B. Warfield, *The Person and Work of Christ*, chap. XII; F. D. Kidner, *Sacrifice in the Old Testament*.

LEON MORRIS

SADDUCEES. The term *Saddoukaioi* is confined to the Gospels and Acts. It is taken by some to denote the descendants of Zadok, Solomon's priest (II Sam. 8:17) and therefore the legitimate priesthood (Ezek. 48:11). "Sons of Zadok" is applied to priests of the Dead Sea Sect in the Manual and to all members in the Damascus Document. Others derive the term from the Greek *syndikos*, a name for a member of the supreme council, associated by the party with *ṣaddîq*, "righteous." The Sadducees are often traced back to the party which supported Antiochus Epiphanes in his policy of hellenization.

They are mentioned by Josephus along with the Pharisees and Essenes under Jonathan, 146 B.C. Supreme under Hyrcanus and Jannaeus, they persecuted the Pharisees, 88 B.C., but when the latter recovered under Alexandra, 76 B.C., they associated with them in government. Herod appointed Boethus the Sadducee to be high priest in 26 B.C. In the time of Jesus the Sadducees comprised a small group of wealthy aristocratic families, controlling the temple through the Sagan or Captain (Acts 4:1) and having a majority in the Sanhedrin. They collaborated with the Romans, standing apart from the common people and poorer priests (many of whom were Pharisees). They organized the persecution of the church (Acts 4 and 5) but were restrained by the Pharisees.

They regarded the law (written Scripture) as binding, but rejected the scribal tradition and held the prophets less authoritative. They disliked innovation, hence rejected: (a) the Persian concept of two hierarchies of good and evil spirits (Acts 23:8); (b) the resurrection of the body (cf. Luke 20:27-33, where they argued that the law of levirate marriage disproves it, but were shown from the law that God assumes the continued existence of the patriarchs and that the resurrected are as angels), though Josephus may exaggerate when he says that they denied even the immortality of the soul (Ant. 18.1.4); (c) rewards and punishments in Hades. They asserted human freedom of action against Essene fatalism. Messianic hopes interested them little, and they despised nationalist passions and religious enthusiasm. Preferring indulgence to Pharisaic fasting, they argued that God was not concerned with men's good or evil deeds. Some of their families engaged in feuds with each other (cf. the Baptist's phrase *gennēmata echidnōn,* Matt. 3:7). Some suggest that Ecclesiasticus was composed by a Sadducee *ca.* 200 B.C. D. Sommer thinks that the more spiritual Sadducees left the party to join the Qumran sect.

BIBLIOGRAPHY

For Josephus and Mishna, see Schuerer, *The Jewish People in the Time of Jesus Christ,* Div. II, Vol. II, pp. 29-43; HDB; T. W. Manson, "Sadducee and Pharisee," *BJRL,* 22 (1938) pp. 144 ff.; M. S. Enslin, *Christian Beginnings,* pp. 111-18; A. Dupont-Sommer, *Jewish Sect of Qumran,* pp. 68-74.

DENIS H. TONGUE

SAINT. In the OT this word appears as the rendering of *ḥāsîd* ("pious, godly") and of *qādôš* ("holy"). The basic idea in *qādôš* is separation unto God, whereas *ḥāsîd* stresses godliness grounded on the reception of God's mercy. The NT word is *hagios* ("holy"). It is regularly used in the LXX to render *qādôš.*

From Ps. 85:8, where the saints seem to be synonymous with the people of God, one concludes that the emphasis does not fall on character to an appreciable degree (for all were not godly) but on divine choice and the bestowal of God's favor. In other passages the godly portion of the nation is often singled out by the term. But if the ethical connotation were paramount, the expectation would be that the word should occur regularly in the absolute form — the saints. Yet, ever and again, we read of "thy saints" or "the saints of the Most High" or, as in the NT, of saints in Christ Jesus.

Saints acquire their status by divine call (Rom. 1:7). Doubtless there is latent in the use of this term the idea that relationship to God involves conformity to his will and character (Eph. 5:3). In this way the term becomes linked with the thought of faithfulness (Eph. 1:1; Col. 1:2).

The next stage of development appears in the Book of Revelation, where separation unto the Lord, which characterizes saints, leads to Satan-inspired persecution from the world (Rev. 13:7; 14:12) and even to martyrdom (Rev. 16:6; 17:6). Here are the seeds for the Roman Catholic concept of saint as a peculiarly holy or self-sacrificing person who is worthy of veneration (see CANONIZATION).

In the NT, however, saint is applied to all believers. It is a synonym for Christian brother (Col. 1:2). Except for Phil. 4:21, it is not used in the singular, and even there it reflects the corporate idea — "every saint." The saints are the church (I Cor. 1:2). In Ephesians, where there is strong emphasis on the unity of the church, "all the saints" becomes almost a refrain (1:15; 3:8; 3:18; 6:18). The Apostles' Creed enshrines this significance of the word in the statement, "I believe . . . in the communion of saints."

See also HOLY.

BIBLIOGRAPHY

Blunt; R. H. Strachan in *HDAC;* O. S. Rankin in *RTWB.*

EVERETT F. HARRISON

SALT. Biblical symbolism utilizes salt in four ways. (1) "Seasoned with salt" (Col. 4:6; cf. Job 6:6) describes wise speech, gracious but not insipid. (2) Purity of burnt offerings, like Jericho's water (II Kings 2:20-22), is associated with salt (Ezek. 43:24). (3) Sodom's saltpits (south of the Dead "Salt" Sea? Ezek. 47:11; II Kings 14:7) symbolized perpetual desolation (Zeph. 2:9). So Lot's wife became salt (Gen. 19:26), and destroyed cities were sown with salt (Judg. 9:45). Evil speech, like brackish water, cannot coexist with good (James 3:12), though Ezekiel foresaw an eschatological sweetening of the Dead Sea (47:8-9). (4) Eating a man's salt (Ezra 4:14 ASV) "preserved" his friendship. So salt in meal offerings signified God's redemptive "covenant of salt for ever" (Lev. 2:13; Num. 18:19). By the fire of hell the lost are "salted [preserved]" in never-ending punishment (Mark 9:49), while the saved, thus admonished, "have salt [a peacemaking self-discipline] in themselves," preserving them from hell (vs. 50, *ExpGT;* cf. Isa. 33:14-15) and making them "the salt of the earth" for others' salvation (Matt. 5:13).

BIBLIOGRAPHY

J. Penrose Harland, *BA* 5, 2; MSt.

J. BARTON PAYNE

SALUTATION. This word is used to translate *bārak,* "to bless" (I Sam. 13:10), *šā'al lešālôm* (lit. "to ask for the peace of," I Sam. 10:4) and *aspasmos* ("salutation," Heb. 11:13). Historically in ancient Israel the greeting or salutation was not simply a formality but rather entailed a deep reality (J. Pederson, *Israel,* Oxford University Press, London, 1926, p. 202). Likewise when friends separated they blessed one another in order to confirm their fellowship (Gen. 24:60; 31:28, 55).

The use of "peace" in salutations was no

less meaningful in the beginning. When one granted peace unto another, a real gift was bestowed and this gift added to the blessing of the other (J. Pederson, *op. cit.*, p. 304; cf. *Catholic Bible Encyclopedia*, p. 948). Since *šālôm* included not only peace but prosperity and referred to every kind of material and spiritual well-being, the greeting became actually a prayer (S. Johnson, *IB* Vol. 7, p. 304). Later the salutations became so complicated and tedious and took up so much time that Jesus ordered his disciples to "salute no man by the way" lest they became distracted from their primary task (Luke 10:4).

GLENN W. BARKER

SALVATION, SAVE, SAVIOUR. The Greek NT verb *sōzō*, "to save," its cognate nouns *sōtēr*, "saviour," and *sōtēria*, "salvation," and adjective *sōtērios -on* absorbed Hebrew meaning via the LXX translation which somewhat enlarged and modified the classical idea. *Sōzō* classically meant to make sound, heal, save, preserve, and, in regard to people, to save from death or keep alive in contrast to *apollumi* or *apothnēskō*. These saving acts sometimes were performed by gods, and the participle was sometimes used substantively as their name. (Cf. Deiss *LAE*, p. 179; LSJ, p. 1748, Vol. II for other special uses.) Of 473 uses of *sōzō* and cognates in the LXX (HR), 278 translate *yāša'* and its cognates so that this root supplies the basic meaning in the LXX. The central Hebrew idea of *yāša'*, which in Arabic meant be capacious, is freedom from what restricts and binds. The Hiphil means to deliver, save, liberate, save from moral troubles, give victory, while the Niphal conveys these meanings in passive voice. The cognate nouns crystallize the ideas of the verb (cf. BDB pp. 446-48). Of the other uses of *sōzō*, sixty-eight are translations of *šālôm*, "peace" or "wholeness," and its cognates. However, fifty-five of these are *sōtērios -on* (adj. as subst.) for *šelem*, "a thank-offering for covenant deliverance" which occurs in the Pentateuch, leaving only thirteen other occurrences, and there are other roots which are translated more frequently or nearly as frequently by *sōzō* and its cognates than this. Most LXX uses of *sōzō* and its cognates mean deliverance, escape, or save, and it may conservatively be said that sixty to seventy percent of these relate the deliverance to Jehovah.

Sōtēr, "saviour," was used of philosophers (e.g., Epicurus), of rulers (e.g., Ptolemy IV, Nero), and also widely of gods (e.g., Zeus, Attis). In the LXX, God is declared the only *sōtēr* (Isa. 45:21; 43:11; Ps. 61:2) because salvation of men is vain (Pss. 59[60]:11; 107[108]:12). Only in the sense that men, such as judges (Judg. 3:9, 14; 12:3; Neh. 9:27), and Mordecai (Esth. 8:13), are God's instruments, are they saviours. Although *sōtēr* is used thirty-seven times for God in the LXX, seldom is it a title, because usually it has the pronoun (I Chron. 16:15; Deut. 32:15, *et al.*). But occasionally it was a title (e.g., the LXX gives *sōtēr* in place of Jehovah [Prov. 29:25]) and as an appositive (Isa. 45:15).

God the Father and Christ the Son are both spoken of as Saviours and thus as agents of salvation. In the OT, Messiah receives salvation from God (Pss. 19:6; 20:1-2; II Kings [Sam.] 22:51), but he in turn comes to offer salvation to the ends of the earth (Zech. 9:9; Isa. 49:6, 8; *et al.*). In the NT, God the Father is Saviour in that he provides salvation by sending his Son and through him, the Holy Spirit (Luke 1:47, 67; I Tim. 2:13; 4:10; Titus 3:4-6). The Son was born to save God's people from their sin and their enemies (Matt. 1:21; Luke 1:71, 77) and that was the aim of his ministry (Luke 19:10; John 3:17). As Saviour, Jesus heals (Mark 5:34; 10:52), justifies (Titus 2:13-14; 3:6, 7), heads the church (Eph. 5:23), and gives eschatological deliverance and blessing (Phil. 3:20; Titus 2:13). Although Jesus did not use the noun *sōtēr* of himself, the people of Samaria recognized him as the *Sōtēr* of the world (John 4:42) and Paul freely used that designation (Titus 2:13; 3:6). Most uses of *sōtēr* occur in the Pastoral and General Epistles. In the NT the Hebrew root, *yāša'*, is transliterated in the name Jesus, clearly showing the OT was the source for the NT meaning of Christ's Saviourhood.

It has been shown (Arthur Darby Nock, *Joy of Study,* New York, the Macmillan Company, 1951, pp. 127-48) that the view that the pre-Christian Greek meaning of *sōtēr* implied membership in a hierarchy of beings or implied deity and was the source of NT thought (Deiss *LAE,* pp. 363 ff.; *et al.*) is not correct. Rather, *sōtēr* does no more than crystallize the verb *sōzō* and must always be understood in the light of the function which the context explains. The view that the NT *sōtēr* is derived from mystery religions (Holtzmann, *et al.*), is refuted in that in them salvation is primarily from limitations of earthly life and especially death, and it lacks the ethical note and the emphasis on resurrection of the NT (cf. Albert Schweitzer, *Paul and His Interpreters*, New York, the Macmillan Company, 1951, pp. 182, 193).

The biblical concept of salvation progressively unfolds, but in general may be described as follows. Personal evil power deceives and leads man astray from God and his will. The evil power, Satan (meaning *enemy*), was first the serpent of Eden, later pagan gods and nations against which Israel contended, and finally, evil spiritual forces called demons led by the prince of demons who work in and against the individual, and through unbelievers, against the church as a whole. Because of man's sin or alliance with evil, God often inflicts temporal punishments to encourage man's repentance before the final judgment when God will destroy man along with the evil powers with which he has become allied.

Thus salvation involves three ideas. (1) Justification. Man must be freed from the just punishment which God's judicial sentiment requires so that he may without fear be reconciled to God, but in such a way that God may still be just in his justifying or saving action. Blood sacrifice, which develops its full meaning in Christ's death, is that which propitiates God's wrath and saves (Rom. 5:9). (2) Temporal victory. Victory over evil was promised through the "seed of the woman" (Gen. 3:15). It was accomplished by the Holy Spirit working in OT leaders as they subdued idolatry and evil in Israel and conquered pagan nations and supremely by the victory of the Christ (anointed one) over Satan (Matt. 4:11; 12:26-29). Finally, in the church age, Christ sends the Holy Spirit to work in and through the church so that believers work out their own victory over evil (Luke 10:17-20; 19:9; Phil. 2:12-13; I Tim. 2:15; 4:16). (3) Final deliverance and blessing. Christ will come a second time to deal finally with evil powers and the consequences of sin; he will have complete victory over Satan, destroying him and his allies, while on the other hand he will give immortal bodies to believers and usher them into a new heaven and earth

(Heb. 9:28; John 14:2-3; Rom. 13:11; I Pet. 1:5, 9; etc).

BIBLIOGRAPHY

G. Vos in *HDCG*; Darwell Stone in *HDAC*; B. S. Easton in *ISBE*; Otto Kirn in *SHERK*; F. C. Grant, *An Introduction to New Testament Thought*, pp. 246-67.

CARL W. WILSON

SANCTIFY, SANCTIFICATION. While the etymological origin of the Hebrew root *qāḏaš* is surrounded by obscurity, its fundamental force seems to be to set apart an object from ordinary usage for a special (religious) purpose or function, and in particular to set apart for God. In biblical Greek its equivalent is *hagiazein*, "to sanctify."

I. To SEPARATE FOR A HOLY USE. At God's command Moses sanctifies the people prior to the giving of the law at Sinai (Ex. 19:10, 14); all the first-born, both of man and beast, are sanctified to God (Ex. 13:2; Num. 8:17); Aaron and his sons are sanctified to minister to God in the priest's office (Ex. 28:41); God sanctifies Israel as his own special nation (Ezek. 37:28); in a day of spiritual peril not only is the congregation sanctified, but also a fast, and even war (Joel 1:14; 2:15-16; 3:9); Job sanctifies his sons by offering sacrifices for them (Job 1:5); Samuel sanctifies Jesse and his son prior to offering sacrifice (I Sam. 16:5); even before his birth Jeremiah is sanctified — set apart by the divine will — for the sacred work of a prophet (Jer. 1:5); mount Sinai is sanctified and set out of bounds to the people (Ex. 19:23); the sabbath day (Gen. 2:3; Deut. 5:12; Neh. 13:22), the tabernacle and its vessels (Ex. 30:29; Lev. 8:10; Num. 7:1), the temple in Jerusalem (II Chron. 7:16), and cities of refuge (Josh. 20:7) are sanctified; houses and fields may be sanctified to the Lord (Lev. 27:14 ff.); Jehu traps the worshipers of Baal by sanctifying a solemn assembly for Baal (II Kings 10:20 ff.); Christ is the one whom the Father sanctified and sent into the world (John 10:36); and, finally, every created thing is sanctified through the word of God and prayer (I Tim. 4:4 f.).

II. MAN IS CALLED UPON TO SANCTIFY HIMSELF. Those who have been sanctified, set apart, by God are required to sanctify themselves, that is, to separate themselves from everything that defiles (Lev. 11:44; Josh. 7:13; cf. Ex. 19:22; I Chron. 15:12 ff.; II Chron. 29:15 ff.; 30:3). The significance of this self-sanctification is clearly given in the words of Lev. 20:26: "Ye shall be holy unto me; for I the Lord am holy, and have separated you from the peoples, that ye should be mine." To sanctify oneself for the worship and service of God represents man's responsibility within the covenant of grace. For the same thought carried through to the NT see II Cor. 6:14-18.

III. GOD SANCTIFIES HIMSELF (OR HIS NAME). God sanctifies himself, that is, shows that he is altogether separate, by his mighty works of judgment and salvation, which vindicate to his creatures the uniqueness of his sovereignty and power (cf. Ezek. 36:23; 38:23; and this is also the meaning in Num. 20:26). Christ's sanctifying of himself (John 17:19) has a different sense, namely, that of self-consecration and dedication for the work of his mediatorial office.

IV. MAN SANCTIFIES GOD BY HIS WORSHIP AND OBEDIENCE. Unbelief and disobedience are indicative of failure to sanctify God, that is, to acknowledge his unique lordship and authority (Num. 20:12; 27:14; Deut. 32:51). Justice and righteousness (Isa. 5:16) and reverence of his name (Isa. 8:13; 29:23) are evidence that man is sanctifying God. Christians are exhorted to sanctify Christ as Lord in their hearts (I Pet. 3:15; cf. Lev. 10:3; Ezek. 20:41), that is, to let him, as is his right, exercise his sole lordship in their lives.

V. GOD SANCTIFIES HIS CHURCH AND ITS MEMBERS. As, in the OT, it is the Lord who sanctifies Israel (Ex. 31:13), so, in the NT, it is he who still sanctifies his redeemed (I Thess. 5:23). Christ prays his Father to sanctify them in the truth (John 17:17, 19). God's elect are precisely his sanctified ones (Acts 20:32; I Cor. 1:2). It is the Holy Spirit who sanctifies them (Rom. 15:16). They are living vessels in the new, spiritual temple, "sanctified, meet for the master's use" (II Tim. 2:21 — the NT does not speak of the sanctification of inanimate objects). The effective ground of their sanctification is the blood of the covenant (q.v.) shed by Christ on the cross for his church (Eph. 5:26; Heb. 9:13; 10:10, 14, 29; 13:12). Baptism is the sacramental sign of their being sanctified (I Cor. 6:11) and the symbol of the union, by faith in Christ (Acts 26:18), of both Sanctifier and sanctified (Eph. 5:26; Heb. 2:11).

VI. I COR. 7:14. This verse relates to the problem arising when either a husband or a wife is converted (i.e., from God's side, sanctified) while the spouse remains in pagan unbelief. This does not constitute a ground for disrupting the marriage. By the conversion of husband or wife the whole family, not least the children, are brought within the sphere of God's covenant of grace, which has great respect for the solidarity of the family (already founded on the decree of creation), so that the unbelieving spouse is sanctified (in a formal sense) in the believing spouse and brought into touch with the grace of God (vs. 16).

See also HOLY, HOLINESS.

PHILIP EDGCUMBE HUGHES

SANCTUARY. In the first reference (Moses' song, Ex. 15:17), God's sanctuary is his mount of inheritance (Palestine). His established earthly abode, the tabernacle building (Ex. 25:8) had its forerunner in heaven viewed as a sanctuary (Ps. 102:19). The earthly tabernacle was his own choice for an abode among his people. He is also described as making Judah his sanctuary in a special sense (Ps. 114:2). *Miqdāš* and *qōḏeš*, used interchangeably, are referable to the temple (II Chron. 20:8), and particularly to the holy of holies whether of the tabernacle or temple. The plural (Lev. 21:23; Jer. 51:51) is generally used to denote idolatrous shrines which in heathen practice were the "high places" where the gods (q.v.) had their seat and where they revealed themselves. In such cases high place and sanctuary were synonymous (Amos 7:9). Bethel (king's sanctuary, Amos 7:13), Ramah (where Samuel sacrificed), Shechem, etc., were perhaps former heathen worship-centers. Conversely, God is a sanctuary for his people (Isa. 8:14; Ezek. 11:19). See also the parallel statement in Ps. 90:1. Associated in significance, but not called sanctuaries, though presumably marked by altars, were the places of refuge where unintentional manslayers found temporary asylum (Ex. 21:13). This was anticipatory of cities of refuge in Palestine (Num. 35) whose general idea was widely characteristic of ancient nations (cf. our expression, "to find sanctuary").

ROBERT F. GRIBBLE

SANHEDRIN. The Sanhedrin (Aramaic form of Greek *synedrion*, "council") was the ruling body of ecclesiastics in Judaism who controlled its religious and political life up to the overthrow of the Jewish commonwealth in A.D. 70. Its origin is uncertain. The rabbis held that it began with the seventy elders who advised Moses (Ex. 24:1), but no evidence exists of the persistence of any organized council from the time of the Exodus. In the Persian period the "elders" mentioned in Ezra (Ezra 5:9; 6:7, 14; 10:8) and the "rulers of the people" in the time of Nehemiah (Neh. 2:16; 11:1) may have ruled community affairs. The first clear reference to an organized body is in the time of Antiochus the Great (223-187 B.C.). It had a membership based on age and wealth, over which the high priest presided. After the Maccabean revolt the elders took on new power. With the coming of Pompey in 63 B.C. the Jewish territory was divided into five *synedria*, of which the *synedrion* of Jerusalem, the capital, became the leading factor in forming Jewish policy.

Membership in the Sanhedrin was limited to Israelites of pure blood, and was held for life. Its jurisdiction was limited to Judea. Jesus was brought before the Sanhedrin (Matt. 26:59), and the apostles were examined by it (Acts 4:15-18; 22:30; 23:1 ff.). It made final decisions in cases relating to the interpretation of the law, and acted in criminal cases, subject to the approval of the Roman governor. It served as his advisory council on Jewish affairs, and provided a central government during the years when the nation had been largely stripped of any real independence.

BIBLIOGRAPHY

E. Schuerer, *The Jewish People in the Time of Christ*, II, i, pp. 163-95; S. B. Hoenig, *The Great Sanhedrin*; J. Z. Lauterbach, "Sanhedrin" in *JewEnc*.

MERRILL C. TENNEY

SATAN. Satan (Hebrew *'saṭān*, "an adversary") is a high angelic creature who, before the creation of the human race, rebelled against the Creator and became the chief antagonist of God and man. Theologians to a large extent have refused to apply the far-reaching prophecies of Isa. 14:12-14 and Ezek. 28:12-15 to Satan under the contention that they are addressed solely to the king of Babylon in the first instance and to the king of Tyre in the second. Others contend that this interpretation is unwarranted for two reasons. First, it fails to take into account the fact that these prophecies far transcend any earthly ruler and, second, it ignores the close connec-

tion Satan has in Scripture with the government of the satanic world system (Dan. 10:13; Eph. 6:12) of which both ancient Babylon and Tyre were an inseparable part. In their full scope these passages paint Satan's past career as "Lucifer" and as "The Anointed Cherub" in his pre-fall splendor. They portray as well his apostasy in drawing with him a great multitude of lesser celestial creatures (Rev. 12:4).

These fallen angels (demons) fit into two classes: (1) those that are free and (2) those that are bound. The former roam the heavenlies with their prince-leader Satan (Matt. 12:24) and as his emissaries are so numerous as to make Satan's power practically ubiquitous. The angels (demons) that are bound are evidently guilty of more heinous wickedness and are incarcerated in Tartarus (II Pet. 2:4; Jude 1:6). Many theologians connect these imprisoned demons with fallen angels who cohabited with mortal women (Gen. 6:1-4).

Satan caused the fall of the human race (Gen. 3). His judgment was predicted in Eden (Gen. 3:15) and this was accomplished at the cross (John 12:31-33). As created, his power was second only to God (Ezek. 28:11-16). He is nevertheless only a creature, limited, and his might permitted by divine omnipotence and omniscience.

The Bible doctrine of Satan is not a copying of Persian dualism as some scholars unsoundly allege. Although Satan, even after his judgment in the cross (Col. 2:15), continues to reign as a usurper (II Cor. 4:4), and works in tempting and accusing men (Rev. 12:10), he is to be ousted from the heavenlies (Rev. 12:7-12) as well as the earth (Rev. 5:1—19:16), and is to be confined to the abyss for a thousand years (Rev. 20:1-3).

When released from the abyss at the end of the thousand years, he will make one last mad attempt to lead his armies against God (Rev. 20:8-9). This will eventuate in his final doom when he is cast into the lake of fire (Rev. 20:10), which has been prepared for him and his wicked angelic accomplices (Matt. 25:41). This will be the one place where evil angels and unsaved men will be kept and quarantined so that the rest of God's sinless universe will not be corrupted in the eternal state.

Satan's present work is widespread and destructive. God permits his evil activity for the time being. Demons must do Satan's bidding. The unsaved are largely under Satan's authority, and he rules them through the evil world system over which he is head and of which the unregenerate are a part (Isa. 14:17; II Cor. 4:3-4; Eph. 2:2; Col. 1:13).

As far as the saved are concerned, Satan clashes in conflict with them (Eph. 6:11-18), tempts them and seeks to corrupt and destroy their testimony and even their physical life (I Cor. 5:5; I John 5:16). Satanic and demonic fury were unleashed against the incarnate Christ. The power of a sinless humanity called forth special satanic temptation of our Lord (Matt. 4:1-11). The full glow of light manifested in the earthly life of him who was "the light of the world" (John 8:12) exposed the darkness of the powers of evil. This is the explanation of the unprecedented outburst of demonism that is described in the Gospel narratives. It was because God anointed Jesus of Nazareth "with the Holy Spirit and with power" that he "went about doing good and healing all that were oppressed by the devil" (Acts 10:38).

BIBLIOGRAPHY
L. S. Chafer, *Systematic Theology*, II, pp. 33-98; all standard books on theology and Bible dictionaries; Jules Michelet, *Satanism and Witchcraft*.

MERRILL F. UNGER

SATISFACTION. The word satisfaction occurs only twice in the AV (Num. 35:31-32) as the rendering for the Hebrew *kōper*, literally meaning a price paid as compensation. Theologically the term has played a significant part in the theory of the atonement, especially since the time of Anselm (d. 1109). Prior to his *Cur Deus Homo* the view of Christ's death which prevailed most widely was that it was a ransom paid to the devil in order to deliver the souls of men over whom he had a legal claim. Anselm by contrast stressed the fact that the death of Christ was a satisfaction rendered to God's justice and honor. Since his time this view has become one of the essential ingredients in the orthodox theory of the atonement, both for Roman Catholics and Protestants. In the subsequent Protestant discussion, a distinction has been made between Christ's active and passive obedience. In the former he satisfied the demands of the law by rendering a perfect obedience, and in the latter he satisfied the curse of the law by submitting himself to the ignominious death of the cross. With the rise of liberalism in Prot-

estant theology, the term Satisfaction fell under severe criticism and is still suspect in some circles, as not being a biblical term. The fundamental issue, however, is not whether the term as such occurs in Scripture, but whether or not the idea which it represents is biblical, and this will be decided ultimately by one's view of God. If the love of God be construed in a way that militates against his justice, then there is no divine wrath which needs propitiation (*q.v.*) and there is no guilt in the objective sense which must be expiated. Consequently there is no need that a satisfaction be rendered to appease the judicial sentiment in God which man by his guilt and sin has offended. The Bible, however, plainly teaches that the death of Christ was a sacrifice (*q.v.*). The interpretation of Christ's work as a sacrifice is imbedded in every important type of NT teaching. To ask the question, What according to the NT is the nature of Christ's work? is the same as asking what is the nature of sacrifice. The NT conception of sacrifice, in turn, cannot possibly be understood apart from the OT conception of sacrifice, and in the OT it is very clear that the sacrifice is not simply a gift to God or a mode of communion and fellowship with God. The only explanation which satisfies the OT data is that the sacrifice is propitiatory in character and appeases the wrath of God by removing the guilt of sin through a substitutionary bearing of the penalty. The one who offered the sacrifice placed his hands on the head of the animal victim and thus transferred the guilt to the animal whose blood was shed to satisfy the debt to justice which he owed. Animal sacrifice was only ceremonial or typical, but it is this ceremonial ritual which is transferred in the NT to the work of Christ and is the basis for the theological teaching that the guilt of our sin is removed by the satisfaction which Christ renders to God against whom the sin is committed. Hence Christ is called the Lamb (*q.v.*) of God. When God is propitiated by his blood (*q.v.*) we are redeemed from the curse of the law and reconciled to him. The concept of satisfaction, then, is a theological term which embraces in its connotation all the major categories used in the Scriptures to describe the meaning of Christ's atoning work both as it relates to God and to the sinner. The most crucial passage is Rom. 3:21-26.

See also ATONEMENT.

BIBLIOGRAPHY

Anselm, *Cur Deus Homo?*; C. A. Beckwith in *SHERK*; B. B. Warfield, Studies in Theology, pp. 261-80!

PAUL K. JEWETT

SAVIOUR. See SALVATION.

SCHISM. The Greek word for "schism" (*schisma*) is used eight times in the NT. From this usage the theological meaning of the term can be derived. Immediately one popular misconception can be removed. Schism and heresy (*q.v.*) are two different terms and cannot be used interchangeably, yet they are often so used. Heresy is not schism, for heresy is, at its base, doctrinal, and is opposed to the Christian faith itself. Schism is opposed to charity and is not doctrinal at heart.

Often the departure of Reformers like Martin Luther and John Calvin has been relegated to the area of schism. This is far from the truth. To the Roman Church this was not schism but heresy. To the Reformers it was also heresy, but heresy entertained by Rome which drove them from its fold. Hence John Calvin in his *Institutes of the Christian Religion* argued that the Roman Church was not a true church since it was defective in the true preaching of the gospel and the administration of the sacraments. Therefore he was not leaving the true church. In fact, Calvin argued strongly that whatever the defects of any true church, so long as it continued the marks of a true church, no one should leave its fold.

The Roman Church allowed for the distinction between schism and heresy. A schismatic bishop of that Church could continue to ordain priests, and schismatic priests could continue to celebrate the Eucharist. But heretical bishops and priests could not do so legitimately. Rome recognized that schism is a breach of love, a factious spirit, or a factious division, but not doctrinal divergence. Thus it is that the Roman Church has always recognized the Greek Orthodox Church as essentially orthodox, but schismatic. The Greek Church has sinned against love.

Among the various schisms of the Christian church three can be mentioned briefly: the Donatist schism, the schism of Eastern and Western Churches, and the Great Schism. In the case of the Donatists (*q.v.*) the problem was one of ecclesiastical discipline in which they opposed internal corruption in the church. This party arose during the Diocletian persecution when some Christians surrendered the Scriptures. Augustine wrote against the Donatists because they persistently separated themselves from the fellowship of the church, insisting on rebaptism of Catholics as a condition of communion with them. Narrow and intolerant, the Donatists were nevertheless recognized as connected with the true church, but were regarded as schismatic or sinning against charity.

The second schism relates to the Eastern and Western Churches. This occurred by reason of the growing strength of Rome as against that of Constantinople. Several centuries passed before the church was rent. At last in 1054 the separation was completed. Pope Leo IX was angered by an encyclical of the patriarch of Constantinople. When the patriarch refused to submit the papal legates laid down a sentence of anathema.

The third schism or the Great Schism occurred in the fourteenth and fifteenth centuries and was complicated by strange proceedings. The schism took place shortly after the death of Gregory XI in 1378. There was one pope at Avignon and one at Rome. At the Council of Pisa in 1409 both popes were deposed and a third one elected. Instead of two popes the church now had three. At the Council of Constance the legitimate pope, Gregory XII, resigned with the agreement that his pontificate would be regarded as legal. In 1417 Oddo Colonna was elected pope and reigned as Martin V (1417-31).

Biblically it appears clear that the rending of the body of Christ is sin and that there is no excuse for schism which is related to love and not to doctrine. But when doctrine is involved, it takes on different dimensions and is not so much schism as heresy. Heretics are to be cut off from the church or excommunicated, and this distinction is not one of schism.

In I Cor. 1:10 schism developed from the party spirit or factiousness in which individuals identified themselves as supporters of Paul or Apollos or Cephas. Outwardly the church was one, but internally it was marked by divisiveness. The schismatic tendency noted in I Cor. 11:18 was based largely on social distinctions rather than doctrinal differences. In I Cor. 12 Paul makes the point that the divine wisdom which has established harmony between the members of the human body points to a similar purpose in the body of

Christ (see vs. 25). Diversity of gifts should not invite to envy but to cooperation.

By way of summary it may be said that division based upon primary considerations of essential doctrine is not schism and is not per se wrong. Divisions which are not doctrinal, however, but which yield to other considerations, are reprehensible. They rise from a sin against charity and are contrary to the Spirit of Christ.

BIBLIOGRAPHY
  Blunt; CE; HERE; SHERK.

HAROLD LINDSELL

SCHOLASTICISM. As applied particularly (but not exclusively) to the medieval Christian schools, this word is used for methods in which the doctrines of revealed truth are explained and systematized with the help of philosophical concepts. Although we find throughout the Middle Ages rationalists who criticized the authorities of the faith and anti-rationalists who defended them by attacking the use of "pagan" (especially Aristotelian) philosophy, the general development of Scholasticism was in reconciling rather than in opposing faith to reason. Boethius (d. 525) already had used Aristotelian logic for explaining the creeds. Augustine (d. 431) with his Christian Platonism remained the foremost authority for the medieval thinkers. In his spirit Anselm of Canterbury (d. 1109) said: "I believe that I may understand." Peter Abelard's (d. 1142) dialectical method (using logic in order to harmonize ostensibly contradictory sayings — "sentences" — of the Bible and of the Church Fathers, emphasizing the limits of natural reason) set the pattern of Peter Lombard's (d. ca. 1160) *Four Books of Sentences*, the generally accepted textbook of theological instruction. In the system of Thomas Aquinas (d. 1274), who used the entire work of Aristotle, philosophical (natural) theology, as based upon experience, and Christian theology, as based upon revealed truth, were clearly distinguished but not separated, since "grace does not abolish nature, but presupposes it and perfects it." The later Scholastics, as John Duns Scotus (d. 1308) and particularly William Ockham (d. 1349/50), questioned and criticized Thomas' ways of harmonizing philosophy and theology; but their dialectical play of theses and objections made their method even more "scholastic."

BIBLIOGRAPHY
  E. H. Gilson, *History of Christian Philosophy in the* Middle Ages; M. Grabmann, *Die Geschichte der scholastischen Methode*, 2 vols.; S. Vanni-Rovighi in EF; M. deWulf, *History of Mediaeval Philosophy*, Vol. I.

MARTIN ANTON SCHMIDT

SCHOOLMASTER. *Paidagōgos* occurs once in I Cor. 4:15 and twice in Gal. 3:24-25, where it is rendered by the AV "the law was our schoolmaster to bring us unto Christ." This translation is unfortunate in that it tends to imply that the function of the OT law basically was to educate the Jew in preparation for the Christ (cf. also "tutor" in ASV).

However, *paidagōgos*, formed from *paidos* and *agōgos*, literally means "boy-guider" and in hellenistic society referred to a man, usually a slave, whose duty was to escort his charge back and forth to school and to superintend his activities and associations (see Plato's *Lysis* 208c). The boy was placed in the charge of his *paidagōgos* when he was approximately six years of age and he continued under this protective custody until around sixteen years of age. *Paidagōgos* appears in the Talmud as a loan word and suggests the possibility that wealthy Jews living in gentile cities may have adopted the same custom as a protection for their children (see B. S. Easton, *ISBE*, IV, p. 2702).

By describing the law as *paidagōgos* Paul emphasizes the inferiority of the condition of those who are compelled to remain under its authority as analogous to a child submitting to an irksome but necessary discipline awaiting the opportunity to express the freedom of full maturity.

BIBLIOGRAPHY
  Arndt; TWNT; W. M. Ramsay, *Galatians*, p. 385; *Oxford Classical Dictionary*, pp. 305-306; J. S. Callaway, *JBL* 67, pp. 353-55; H. I. Marron, *A History of Education in Antiquity*, p. 143.

GLENN W. BARKER

SCORN. See MOCKERY.

SCRIBES. A class of professional scholars learned in the law. In the NT they are most frequently called *grammateis*, "learned in the Scriptures" (Matt. 2:4; Mark 1:22, etc.), while the corresponding OT word is *sōp^erim*. Other NT designations are *nomikoi*, "legal experts" (Luke 7:30; 14:3, etc.) and *nomodidaskaloi*, "teachers of the law" (Luke 5:17; Acts 5:34).

Since the law concerns itself to a large degree with the cultus, the earliest Scribes were also priests (e.g., Ezra). However, during the intertestamental period, the growing importance of the law and synagogue produced a separate class of lay biblical scholars. Their function was not only the elaboration of the law, i.e., making explicit what was implicit, but also the teaching of its requirements to the people and the handing down of legal decisions. In later times the Scribes had the additional responsibility of the careful preservation of the sacred text.

In the face of the rising threat of Hellenism, the Scribes became the zealous defenders of the law and increasingly gained popularity and influence among the people. The esteem with which they were held is reflected in the word *rabbi*, "my master," used to address them.

Matt. 23 preserves our Lord's powerful denunciation of their hypocrisy, pride and spiritual obstinacy.

BIBLIOGRAPHY

G. Moore, *Judaism*, I, pp. 37-47; E. Schuerer, *Geschichte des Juedischen Volkes*, 4th ed., II, pp. 372-89.

WALTER W. WESSEL

SCRIPTURE. See BIBLE, INSPIRATION, WRITING.

SEAL. The word seal or signet and related forms are found in the Bible eighty-two times (AV). The noun, "seal," is a translation of the Hebrew *hôtām* and the Greek *sphragis*. This word is very old, being found among the peoples of Egypt, Babylonia, Assyria, and the Hebrews. Its earliest biblical use is recorded in Gen. 38:18, 25. This word is used in two distinct senses in the Bible, literal and figurative.

Literally the seal was a hard substance upon which some sign or figure had been affixed. Carefully engraved seals were usually made on cornaline, jasper, agate, onyx, rock crystal, lapis lazuli, hematite and hard limestone while the poorer type, found in Palestine, were made on soft limestone or steatite (Edith Porada in *TCERK*, Baker Book House, Grand Rapids, Michigan, 1955). The seal was used to make an impression on soft substances such as wax or clay. Some of these seals were cylindrical in shape; some were made in the form of a cone; others were made like the Egyptian beetle and were called scarabs. These were very common in Egypt and those used during the Hyksos period furnish the archaeologist with valuable information about facts of biblical history (J. P. Free, *Archaeology and Biblical History*, Van Kampen Press, Wheaton, Illinois, 1950, p. 85). The small seals, often referred to as stamp seals, are the oldest of the three varieties. They were used for a wide range of purposes such as giving authority or authenticity to letters or commands (I Kings 21:8; Neh. 9:38; Esth. 8:2). Doors in ancient times were frequently closed and sealed in the following manner. Wax was poured on a rope or cord stretched across the door. While it was still soft it was stamped with a seal (Dan. 6:17; Matt. 27:66).

The figurative use of this word sometimes denotes ownership or responsibility (Eph. 1:13; II Tim. 2:19). It might also denote such things as security (Eph. 4:30); authenticity (John 3:33); privacy or secrecy (Dan. 12:4; Rev. 10:4); proof of genuineness (I Cor. 9:2).

BIBLIOGRAPHY

J. P. Free, *Archaeology and Biblical History*, pp. 85-88; Edith Porada in *TCERK*.

HOWARD Z. CLEVELAND

SECOND COMING OF CHRIST. Against the background of his historical appearance in the flesh, Jesus taught that he was coming again. This line of teaching is especially prominent in the parables, and it presupposes the victory of the resurrection (*q.v.*). No sooner had our Lord withdrawn himself into heaven than he confirmed this promise through angelic mediation (Acts 1:11; cf. Rev. 3:11).

It is peculiar that the statements concerning the return should so seldom emphasize that it is a second coming (Heb. 9:28; John 14:3; possibly Heb. 1:6). This circumstance may be explained on the ground that the initial coming is so integral a part of the Christian consciousness as not to require special notice when the return is in view. It is also possible that the two comings are thought of, after the fashion of the OT prophets, as aspects of the one great divine intervention in human life through the person of the Messiah. But the contrast in character between the two comings is so great that this factor is less probable than the former. Perhaps the expectation of the return was so strong that the future coming became thought of as the coming par excellence. At any rate, in passages which have a definite forward look, any description of the event as a second coming would be needless (e.g., James 5:8).

The vividness of the Christian hope is seen in the fact that the ordinary word for a coming (*eleusis*), used once for the first appearing, is not employed for the return, as though it were inadequate to denote so great an event. To be sure, *parousia*, the most frequently used, is an ordinary word indicating arrival or consequent presence (Phil. 1:26), but as applied to Christ it is doubtless intended to have a somewhat technical force such as it has in the hellenistic age for denoting the arrival of a king or a person of prominence (see MM). The other terms are picturesque. Of these *apokalypsis* (II Thess. 1:7) means an unveiling, and thus takes account of Christ's withdrawal to heaven before his final denouement (cf. Col. 3:3-4, where the verb *phaneroō* has much the same force). Similarly, the verb *ophthēsetai* (he shall appear), used in Heb. 9:28, is chosen with the background of the tabernacle and the Day of Atonement ritual in view, when the high priest emerged before the people after being in the most holy place. The word *apokalypsis* connotes more than visibility in contrast to invisibility. It suggests the consummation of God's purpose and the sharing of the saints in it. Then shall we know even as we have been known. Finally, *epiphaneia* (II Tim. 4:1) suggests the public, open character of Christ's appearing. It readily associates with itself the idea of glory (Titus 2:13), and is suitable for suggesting an appearing which is sudden, conspicuous, and overwhelming in its effects on hostile powers (II Thess. 2:8).

As to the purpose of the return, apart from a special significance for Israel (Zech. 12:10; Rom. 11:26), this may be viewed broadly in two aspects. As related to the saints, it will mean their gathering unto Christ, both the dead and the living (I Thess. 4:13-18), together with such transformation as will be necessary to fit the living for glory (Phil. 3:21). The Lord will be admired among those who believe (II Thess. 1:10), and he will reward his servants (I Cor. 4:5; Rev. 22:12). With respect to the world, Christ's coming will bring judgment upon ungodly men and doom upon Satan's kingdom, resulting in the establishment of a reign of righteousness and peace (II Thess. 2:8-10; I Cor. 15:23-26; II Pet. 3:10-13).

See also ESCHATOLOGY, KINGDOM OF GOD, DAY.

BIBLIOGRAPHY
O. Cullmann, *Le Retour du Christ*; C. H. Dodd, *The Coming of Christ*; T. Francis Glasson, *The Second Advent*; René Pache, *The Return of Jesus Christ*; Alexander Reese, *The Approaching Advent of Christ*; John A. T. Robinson, *Jesus and His Coming*.

EVERETT F. HARRISON

SECT. The word is derived from the Latin *secta*, a "faction" or "following." It is applied to bodies of Christians who have separated themselves off from the church, and have their own distinctive doctrinal position, or practices of worship. The term is usually employed not of the great denominations, but of small groups. It is not used by the members of the group themselves, but by their opponents. There is an implied condemnation, the inference being that the separation has been on inadequate grounds. In individualistic Western countries the sects have tended to multiply since the Reformation, and there are now many hundreds.

LEON MORRIS

SECULARISM. The term secularism (Latin *saecula*, "age" or "period") was first applied to a type of utilitarian ethic formulated by G. J. Holyoake (1817-1906) in which he advocated human betterment without reference to religion or theology. His emphasis represented a protest against the dominance and control of human life by ecclesiastical institutions.

Today secularism is the integration of life around the spirit of a specific age rather than around God. It is living as if the material order were supreme and as if God did not exist. While secularism may not indicate theoretical atheism, it certainly does represent practical atheism.

Secularism is deeply in debt to the rise of the so-called scientific world view. The world discovered by the modern empirical method is often accepted as the whole realm of verifiable truth. The world of things is viewed as the whole of existence.

Secularism places the emphasis on temporal social enjoyment rather than on eternal spiritual values. The achievements of modern technological development and cultural advance are considered essential, while the values of religion in general and of the Christian faith in particular are ignored or even denied.

Thus secularism is man living his entire life as if there were no God.

See also POSITIVISM.

BIBLIOGRAPHY
G. Harkness, *The Modern Rival of the Christian Faith;* A. Richardson, *The Gospel and Modern Thought;* H. Kraemer, *The Christian Message in a Non-Christian World.*

WARREN C. YOUNG

SEE. A see is the seat (*sedes*) or so-called throne (*cathedra*) of a bishop, which is usually situated in the main church of the area over which he presides. Hence the term is often used in practice as an alternative for bishopric or diocese, appointment to the diocese of e.g., Canterbury being appointment to occupy this see. The so-called Holy See is the see of Rome, and by extension the papacy.

GEOFFREY W. BROMILEY

SELF. See PERSONALITY.

SELF-CONTROL. The term self-control as such is not given in the Scriptures; but it is taught widely in the OT and the New. Self-restraint, self-mastery (*egkrateia*), is translated temperance. It is a fruit of the Spirit (Gal. 5:23), and is listed among the Christian virtues (II Pet. 1:4-8). The governor Felix trembled when Paul "reasoned of righteousness, temperance, and judgment to come" (Acts 24:25). The notion of sobriety and composure is stressed in Titus 1:8 and 2:2. *Egkrateuomai,* "to be continent" or "to exercise self-government," is enjoined in sexual relations (I Cor. 7:9); and required of "every man that striveth for mastery" (I Cor. 9:25). The exhortation "to abstain," *apechomai,* from sexual vice is stated as "the will of God" (I Thess. 4:3-4); and is enlarged to include "fleshly lusts" (I Pet. 2:11), and abstinence "from all appearance of evil" (I Thess. 5:22). So as not to be a stumbling block to other believers the early gentile Christians were instructed to abstain from immorality and idolatry (Acts 15:20, 29).

The OT placed particular emphasis on the control of the tongue. The true man of God "backbiteth not with his tongue" (Ps. 15:3). "He desires a bridle for his lips" (Ps. 39:1-2), which figure of speech is amplified in James 1:26; 3:2-13. It is the part of wisdom to refrain from speaking (Prov. 17:27-28; James 3:13-18).

Self-control, self-command, temperance and composure are designed for the greater effectiveness of the Christian as a witness and a servant for the Saviour. These characteristics give evidence of consistency between his testimony and his life. It is self-restraint within the freedom of the gospel, imposed upon himself by the individual Christian that he might gain the more to Christ (I Cor. 9:19-23).

Self-control is best evidenced by sobriety and vigilance (I Pet. 5:8). Young men were taught to be "sound in mind" (*sōphroneō*) (Titus 2:6); and the young women to be "prudent" (*sōphronizō*) (Titus 2:5).

See also TEMPERANCE.

BIBLIOGRAPHY
HDAC, II, pp. 553-56; ISBE, V, p. 2929.

V. R. EDMAN

SELF-DENIAL. Self-denial, the forbearance from gratifying one's own desires, is imperative upon the follower of Christ. The Saviour himself set the example of self-abnegation by his *kenōsis* (Phil. 2:7; Heb. 5:8; I Pet. 2:21-24). He taught his disciples "to deny themselves utterly" (*aparneomai*) and to take up daily their cross (Matt. 16:24-26). The believer is identified with Christ in his death (Rom. 6:6-10; Gal. 2:20). The Saviour's death on the cross is efficient and sufficient for the salvation of the sinner; and the cross is likewise the source of his sanctification (Rom. 6:11-13; Gal. 6:14). Therefore, "they that are Christ's have crucified the flesh with the affections and lusts" (Gal. 5:24). The practical application of identification in the Saviour's death is the mortification of one's members (Col. 3:5) by the power of the indwelling Holy Spirit (Rom. 8:13). Our Lord underlined that teaching graphically by declaring that "it is better for thee to enter into life halt or maimed . . . with one eye . . ." than to be lost (Matt. 18:8-9).

The apostle Paul stressed self-denial, declaring that we are to "deny [*arneomai*] ungodliness and worldly lusts" (Titus 2:12). By disowning such conduct the believer can be prepared for the coming of Christ (2:13).

The rewards of self-abnegation are emphasized as much as its necessity. He who leaves all for Christ receives "an hundredfold now in this time . . . with persecutions; and in the world to come eternal life" (Mark 10:28-31). Paul "suffered the loss of all things"; and counted deprivation of position, fame, name, and material substance to be as nothing in contrast with the imputed righteousness of Christ which he had received by faith (Phil. 3:7-11). He therefore could testify that all his glory was in the cross of the Lord Jesus Christ (Gal. 6:14).

The Saviour taught explicitly that to love one's life is to lose it (Matt. 10:39; Mark 8:35; John 12:25); and that "except a corn of wheat fall into the ground and die, it abideth alone; but if it die, it bringeth forth much fruit" (John 12:24). The divine purpose for the self-denial of the Christian is his conformity to the person of his Lord, and his increased effectiveness as a servant of Christ. By ridding himself of "weights" he runs with patience the race of the Christian life (Heb. 12:1-2).

BIBLIOGRAPHY
HDAC, II, pp. 467-68; ISBE, III, pp. 1439-40; SHERK, X, p. 344.

V. R. EDMAN

SELF-EXAMINATION. The scrutiny of one's inner self to determine his spiritual status, motives, attitudes, is largely a NT teaching. In the OT the searching of innermost thoughts and intents was primarily the responsibility of the Almighty (Ex. 20:20; Deut. 8:2, 16; 13:3; Ps. 26:2; which thought is repeated in I Thess. 2:4). The believer is "to examine himself" (dokimazō) to make sure he is in proper relationship to God and to man so that he may partake of the Lord's Supper (I Cor. 11:28). The same verb is translated "to prove" ten times and is rendered "to try" four times, such as: "proving what is acceptable to the Lord" (Eph. 5:10); proving one's work (Gal. 6:4); and proving all things (I Thess. 5:21).

Likewise the Christian is taught "to judge" (diakrinō) himself lest he be judged (I Cor. 11:31-32). In thus judging himself and accepting the correction (chastening) of the Almighty he is not under condemnation. Self-judgment leads to confession and forgiveness.

In borderline practices allowed by some Christians and disallowed by others, the believer is not "to judge" (krinō) his fellow believer; rather, he is to examine himself lest he be a stumbling block (Rom. 14:13). Because one can "believe in vain" (I Cor. 15:2), and thus not have a faith that is "unfeigned" (I Tim. 1:5; II Tim. 1:5), the Christian is "to examine" (peirazō) himself whether he be in the faith (II Cor. 13:5). Thus by careful,

prayerful, self-examination he is to prove himself that the Saviour dwells within.

The lukewarm Laodicean Christian is counseled to judge himself so as to realize his backslidden condition and to prove what values are true and everlasting (Rev. 3:18). The purpose of self-examination is always positive — to know oneself, his weaknesses and frailties, so as to appropriate the grace of God in Christ. Self-examination is a stimulus to faith and holy living (Heb. 12:1-2; I Pet. 2:21-23). It is not morbid introspection for "if our heart condemn us, God is greater than our heart, and knoweth all things" (I John 3:20).

V. R. EDMAN

SEMI-ARIANISM. More generally, Semi-Arianism is often used to describe all who were reluctant to accept the strict definition of Nicaea (namely, that Christ is of one substance with the Father) yet wished to avoid the obvious excesses of the Arians. This might be on solid grounds of tradition, or for ecclesiastical reasons, but there can be no doubt that in the early fourth century there was much orthodox Semi-Arianism of this kind. More strictly, the term is applied to the mediating party which tried to introduce an acceptable alternative in the phrase "of like substance." In spite of the inadequacy of the phrase, the intentions behind it were still mostly conservative, and it is not surprising that the younger generation, e.g., the Cappadocians, finally re-established the full Nicene position when they saw that it was theologically necessary to fulfil these intentions.

See also ARIANISM.

GEOFFREY W. BROMILEY

SEMI-PELAGIANISM. Historically, this term refers to the fifth century reaction against the stricter teaching of Augustine in opposition to Pelagianism (q.v.). The main points which were felt to be objectionable were rigid predestination, the priority and irresistibility of grace, and infallible perseverance. Against these, it was taught that, although grace is essential to salvation, it is added when the first steps are taken by the will of man. Cassian of Marseilles seems to have taken the initiative in this movement, and Lerins became its main center, with Vincent of Lerins (the author of the famous Vincentian canon of catholicity) as one of its leading exponents.

In the more developed theology of the Middle Ages, Augustinianism reasserted itself, yet allowance was almost always made for an element of Semi-Pelagianism, and the teaching has found new champions in the Jesuits and indeed in many schools of Protestant thought.

GEOFFREY W. BROMILEY

SEPARATION. The Scriptures, notwithstanding their affirmation of the fundamental unity of the human race, make room for a lawful and necessary distinction between God's people and those who are not. They also deplore divisions between the saints based on false ideas of presumed superiority or greater holiness.

The data may be classified as follows: (1) Israel, by the choice of God, became his covenant people, thereby separate from all others (Lev. 20:24; I Kings 8:53). The law of the clean and the unclean was a constant reminder of this (Lev. 20:25). At the Restoration, aliens were excluded from the congregation and mixed marriages were broken up in order to safeguard Israel's distinct character (Ezra 10:11; Neh. 13:3). (2) The Levites were separated from the rest of Israel for tabernacle service (Num. 8:14; 16:9). (3) An individual in Israel could take upon himself the Nazarite vow, separating himself thereby unto the Lord and also from wine, the cutting of the hair and from contact with a dead body (Num. 6:1-8). (4) The sins of God's people have the effect of disrupting the fellowship between them and the Lord (Isa. 59:2). (5) Believers are warned against mixed marriages or other close ties which could wean them away from devotion to Christ (II Cor. 6:16-17). (6) By the will of God certain believers are set apart for particular service and witness (Acts 13:2; Rom. 1:1; Gal. 1:15). (7) In the apostolic church certain false teachers brought division by insinuating that they and the group which came under their influence represented a higher type of Christian than the ordinary (Jude 19). (8) The world effects its own separation from those who follow Christ, determined not to be made uncomfortable by the holy life and example of believers (Luke 6:22). (9) There is a separation incident to future judgment, when the righteous are set apart from the unrighteous (Matt. 25:32). (10) No person or power can sunder the saints from the love of God which is in Christ our Lord (Rom. 8:35, 39).

See also SCHISM.

EVERETT F. HARRISON

SERAPH. See ANGEL.

SERVANT. This article deals with the word servant (more properly, slave) in its application to men charged with a specific ministry for the Lord. The Hebrew word is *'ebed,* rendered in the LXX by *pais, therapōn* and *doulos.* As applied to men serving God in a particular capacity, the word denotes (1) submission and (2) the honor of being chosen for service. This latter feature is not clearly seen in the self-designation in prayer (Moses, Num. 11:11; Samson, Judg. 15:18; Samuel, I Sam. 3:10; Saul, I Sam. 14:41; David, II Sam. 7:19 f.; Solomon, I Kings 3:7 f.; Nehemiah, Neh. 1:6; Elijah, I Kings 18:36) which may reflect little more than Semitic etiquette in addressing a superior (see I Kings 1:26-27). However, it is particularly evident in the widespread designation of Moses and David as God's servants (Num. 12:7; II Kings 21:8; Mal. 4:4; II Sam. 7:5; II Kings 19:34; Ps. 89:3). Of special note is the designation, *'ebed YHVH* or *'ebed hā'ĕlôhîm* applied to Moses (Deut. 34:5; Josh. 1:7; I Chron. 6:49; II Chron. 1:3; Neh. 10:29; Dan. 9:11) and his successor, Joshua (Josh. 24:29; Judg. 2:8). Equally significant is the summation of prophetic activity by the phrase "my [his] servants the prophets" (II Kings 17:13, 23; Jer. 7:25; Ezek. 38:17; Amos 3:7; Zech. 1:6). Emphasis here is on faithful proclamation of God's message.

The words with which the LXX renders *'ebed* all occur in the NT. David (Luke 1:69; Acts 4:25) and Jesus (Acts 3:13, 26; 4:27, 30) are each designated as the *pais* of God, and Moses as his *therapōn* (Heb. 3:5). Elsewhere *doulos* is used. The designation of prophets as "slaves of God" is still found, notably in Rev. 1:1; 10:7; 11:18. Perhaps this is the intent of the designation of Paul and Silas as "servants of the Most High God" (Acts 16:17). However, a new development appears in the NT. Men are designated "slaves of Christ": Paul (Rom. 1:1; Gal. 1:10; Phil. 1:1), James (James 1:1), Peter (II Pet. 1:1), Jude (Jude 1) and Epaphras (Col. 4:12). In the case of all but Epaphras, these are self-designations. Rengstorf (*TWNT,* Vol. II, p.

276) affirms that one cannot be certain whether this is a conscious application of the designation prophet or a personal acknowledgment of complete submission to God. Paul's consciousness of being apprehended by Christ (Phil. 3:12) as well as the use of the figure of slaves by Jesus to illustrate the necessity of faithful service (Matt. 24:45 f.; Mark 13:34; Luke 17:7 f.) favors the latter alternative. However, "servant of the Lord" in II Tim. 2:24 is a technical term reminiscent of the title given to Moses.

CHARLES A. HODGMAN

SERVANT OF JEHOVAH. The expression, *'ebed Yahweh*, "servant of Jehovah," designates devoted worshipers, as Abraham (Ps. 105:6), or others who fulfilled God's purposes, as Nebuchadrezzar (Jer. 25:9). But the pre-eminent "servant of Jehovah" appears as Isaiah comforted Israel, ravaged by Sennacherib, 701 B.C. (*ISBE* III: 1497, pp. 1503-8). Twenty times in Isa. 40-53 the *'ebed Yahweh* is prophesied, even as vividly present, spoken to or speaking.

The identity of the servant varies. Sometimes it refers to the whole nation, "Israel, my servant" (41:8), though sinfully deaf and blind (42:19). In Isaiah's "servant-songs" (42:1-7; 49:1-9; 50:4-9; 52:13—53; and probably 61:1-3), however, this national meaning disappears, replaced by a *righteous* servant who restores Jacob (49:5). Superficial criticism has accordingly questioned the Isaianic authenticity of the songs. But Isaiah recognized a pious remnant (10:20-22), which included his prophetic circle (44:26; 8:16). In the songs, however (except for 49:3), the servant cannot be the collective remnant but only an individual. By his objective description, moreover (42:1), he cannot be Isaiah himself. The future reference (52:13) demonstrates that he cannot be Moses, the dying-god Tammuz(!), the king performing ritualistic service, or some other past leader. Finally, his sinless character (53:9) and the magnitude of his work (42:4) forbid his equation with any merely human leader in the future, such as Jehoiachin or Zerubbabel. The NT (John 12:38, 41; Acts 8:32-35) specifies Jesus Christ as the only embodiment of ideal Israel, the final accomplishment of the remnant (Isa. 49:6).

The mission of the Servant is, (1) that of a humanly-born prophet (49:1-2; cf. Jer. 1:5), empowered by God's Holy Spirit (Isa. 42:1; 61:1; Luke 4:21), with a non-self-assertive ministry (Isa. 42:2-3; Matt. 12:18-21). (2) He suffers vicariously, bearing the cares of others (Isa. 53:4; cf. Christ's healings, Matt. 8:17). (3) Meeting disbelief (Isa. 53:1), he becomes subject to reproach (49:7; 50:6; Matt. 26:67; 27:26). (4) Condemned as a criminal, he gives up his life, punished for the sins of others (Isa. 53:5-8; I Pet. 2:22-25), God making his soul a priestly *'āšām*, "guilt offering" (Isa. 53:10). He atoningly "sprinkles many nations" (52:15; Heb. 12:24; I Pet. 1:2). (5) The Servant thereby accomplishes God's pleasure, is buried honorably with the rich (Isa. 53:9-10; Matt. 27:57), and is resurrected in glory (Isa. 53:10, 12). (6) His divine sacrifice justifies many (vs. 11), and avails for Gentiles as well (42:6; Luke 2:32). (7) He establishes ultimate justice in the earth itself (Isa. 42:4; Rom. 15:21). (8) The Servant thus becomes the incarnation of God's redemptive covenant, or testament (Isa. 42:6; 49:8), effectuating it by his death and constituting in his own resurrected life its inheritance for the saints (cf. Col. 1:27).

The servant-songs imply the equation of the Davidic Messiah and the suffering Servant (cf. Gen. 3:15: the messianic seed victorious, but "bruised in the heel"). Both are divinely chosen and uniquely righteous (Isa. 42:1, 6; 9:7; cf. Ps. 89:3-4). The humiliation of the Messiah at his first coming (Isa. 7:15; Dan. 9:25-26; Zech. 9:9) parallels that of the Servant. Isaiah, in contextual proximity, describes both as witnessing to the Gentiles (49:6; 55:4); and the same Holy Spirit of equity who fills the Davidic "Branch" (11:1-4) rests upon the Servant for an identical eschatological function (42:1). The ultimate exaltation of the Servant (49:5, 7; 52:15) requires their equation. Thus Zechariah associates the messianic Branch with the priestly removal of iniquity and combines the two terms: "my Servant, the Branch" (3:8-9; cf. 10:12 with 14:4). Did the prophets understand their own words? Scripture declares, "These things said Isaiah, because he saw his glory and spake of him" (John 12:41), though certain details of Calvary he doubtless described better than he himself knew. John the Baptist identified the Messiah with the sacrificial Lamb of God (1:29-30), but the multitudes failed to grasp this equation

(12:34). Christ conclusively revealed his identity, both as Messiah (4:25-26) and as suffering Servant (Luke 22:37).

BIBLIOGRAPHY

O. T. Allis, *The Unity of Isaiah*, pp. 81-101; I. Engnell, *BJRL*, 31, 54-93; J. Lindblom, *The Servant Songs in Deutero-Isaiah*; S. Mowinckel, *He That Cometh*, pp. 187-257; C. R. North, *The Suffering Servant in Deutero-Isaiah*; H. H. Rowley, *The Servant of the Lord and Other Essays*, pp. 3-88; J. S. Van der Ploeg, *Les Chants du Serviteur de Jahvé*; E. J. Young, *WTJ* 11, 133-55; 13, 19-33.

J. BARTON PAYNE

SERVICE. This word in the OT is usually the rendering of the Hebrew word *'ebôdâ* and bears several connotations. The basic meaning is simply "to work," whether in the field or in the office, or in the work of the ministry and service of God (e.g., Lev. 35:39; I Chron. 9:19).

In the NT several words are usually rendered "to serve" or "to minister." *Diakonos,* whence the word deacon, is a servant or a minister; one who waits on another; one who runs an errand. The AV regularly renders this word either as minister or as servant, except in Phil. 1:1 and I Tim. 3:8, 12 where it is rendered "deacon." The RSV ordinarily renders *diakonos* as servant, though in Matt. 22:13 it is rendered "attendant," while in Eph. 3:7 and Col. 1:23 it is rendered "minister." Where the word occurs in I Tim. it is rendered deacon. *Doulos* is the bond slave and is used to indicate both servile labor and, in a doctrinal sense, to indicate the "bond slave" of Jesus Christ. This word occurs well over a hundred times in the NT; and its significance is particularly rich in the writings of Paul.

Latreia is another word rendered service. This was the old Attic Greek to indicate service to the gods; worship. This aspect is basic in the NT, where the verb form is used about twenty-three times (e.g., Mark 4:10; Luke 1:74; Acts 7:42; Rom. 1:9, 25; II Tim. 1:3; Rev. 7:15); and the noun appears about five times (e.g., John 16:2; Rom. 9:4; 12:1; Heb. 9:1, 6). The Rom. 12 passage is quite significant and probably provides the clue to the real force of the word. Here the word is qualified by the adjectival *logikēn*. This would probably indicate that the "spiritual worship" is "service with a sentiment," i.e., service prompted by genuine love for God as a response to his great love for the sinner. Nor is this the formal worship hour of Sunday morning, but rather the twenty-four hour a day service to God where all of the talent and strength and time is used for him.

ROBERT F. BOYD

SESSION. A sitting (Latin *sessio*). The OT portrays God as seated on the throne of the universe, thereby signifying sovereignty (I Kings 22:19; Pss. 2:4; 99:1), holiness (Ps. 47:8) and majesty (Isa. 6:1-4). In Ps. 110:1 the Messiah is invited to occupy the position of honor at his right hand (Mark 12:36; Acts 2:34; Heb. 1:13). His throne is to be one of sovereignty and priesthood (Ps. 110:1, 4; Zech. 6:12-13) and of judgment (Mal. 3:3). The Hebrew root throughout is *yāšab*.

To this position God exalted Christ at his ascension (Phil. 2:9-11; Eph. 1:20-23, which latter passage alone employs *kathizō*, elsewhere intransitive, transitively). I Pet. 3:22, repeating *poreutheis*, implies a deliberate progress by Christ after his death to the position of sovereignty which he had foretold (Mark 14:62; Matt. 26:64; Luke 22:69, and see Mark 16:19). Heb. 1:3; 10:12; 12:2 describe the session as the sequel to his one complete sacrifice on earth. He sits as High Priest after the order of Melchizedek (Heb. 8:1; 10:12), exercising his priesthood of sympathetic assistance to men and intercession for them (Heb. 4:14-16; 2:17-18; 7:17-27) until all is finally subjected to him (Heb. 10:13). His session also points towards his future judgment (II Cor. 5:10; Matt. 19:28).

Thrice the ascended Christ is depicted as standing: once to succor (Acts 7:55-56); and twice to receive worship (Rev. 5:6; 14:1).

Early creeds (a Roman formula quoted in Greek by Marcellus and one from Jerusalem found in Cyril) mention the Session.

BIBLIOGRAPHY

HDCG; B. F. Westcott, *Epistle to the Hebrews, passim*; W. Milligan, *The Ascension of Our Lord*; H. B. Swete, *The Ascended Christ*; A. J. Tait, *The Heavenly Session of Our Lord*.

DAVID H. WHEATON

SEVEN CARDINAL VIRTUES. The seven cardinal virtues as enunciated by the medieval church are faith, hope, love, justice, prudence, temperance, and fortitude. They are "cardinal" in that all other Christian virtues "hinge" (*cardo*) upon one or another of them.

These virtues are of two kinds. The first three are named "theological" and represent the Pauline triad in I Cor. 13:13 (cf. I Thess. 1:3; Gal. 5:5-6; Col. 1:4-5). The other four are "natural" (or "moral") virtues and find their origin in the philosophical thought of ancient Greece. This four-fold classification of virtue was held by Plato to correspond to the natural constitution of the soul. Prudence corresponded to the intellect, temperance to feeling, and fortitude to will. Justice was a social virtue and regulated the others.

It is understandable that pagan morality could not find a place within Christianity without first undergoing a radical transformation. This process begins in earnest with Augustine who reinterprets the virtues from a Christian perspective and redirects them towards a new object — devotion to God. The three theological virtues are placed alongside as representing the inner disposition in which the external virtues have their source. Thus while the moral ideas of the past are gradually baptized into Christianity they become new creations in the process. Even though the Schoolmen return to Aristotle as a source of moral speculation the end product is always Aristotle read in the light of Augustine (*HERE*, Vol. 11, p. 431).

As the natural virtues can be referred to a psychological basis, so also can the theological. Faith relates to intellect, hope to desire, and love to the will. Thus virtue is that moral excellence in which the whole man (both in inner disposition and external act) is rightly oriented to his Creator.

BIBLIOGRAPHY
HERE, Vol. 11, pp. 430-32; K. E. Kirk, *Some Principles of Moral Theology*, pp. 33-48; J. Stalker, *The Seven Cardinal Virtues*.

ROBERT H. MOUNCE

SEVEN DEADLY SINS.

At an early stage in the life of the church, the influence of Greek thought (with its tendency to view sin as a necessary flaw in human nature) made it necessary for the church to determine the relative seriousness of various moral faults. This ultimately gave rise to what is commonly referred to as the seven deadly sins — a concept which occupies an important place in the order and discipline of the Roman Catholic Church.

These sins are: pride, covetousness, lust, envy, gluttony, anger, sloth. K. E. Kirk (*Some Principles of Moral Theology*, pp. 265-67) stresses that they are to be understood as "capital" or "root" sins rather than "deadly" or "mortal" (viz., sins which cut one off from his true last end). They are the "sinful propensities which reveal themselves in particular sinful acts" (*CE, sub* "Sin"). The list represents an attempt to enumerate the primary instincts which are most likely to give rise to sin (Kirk, *op. cit.,* p. 266).

Even though the original classification may have been monastic in origin (cf. Cassian, *Collationes Patrum,* v. 10), under the influence of Gregory the Great (who has given us the classical exposition on the subject: *Moralia on Job,* esp., xxxi. 45) the scope was widened and along with the seven cardinal virtues they came to constitute the moral standards and tests of the early Catholic Church. In medieval scholasticism they were the subject of considerable attention. Cf. esp. Aquinas, *Summa Theologica,* II. ii.

BIBLIOGRAPHY
Father Connell's *New Baltimore Catechism*; J. Stalker, *The Seven Deadly Sins*; A. B. D. Alexander in *HERE*.

ROBERT H. MOUNCE

SHAME.

Scripture employs more than twelve Hebrew and a half-dozen Greek words for this idea, found more than one hundred times: a painful emotion of misery, reproach, embarrassment, arising from guilt for sin, unworthy act, impropriety. The subject is first mentioned (Gen. 2:25), antecedent to sin, its absence being tacitly approved; there was no cause for shame. Similarly, where sin is forgiven there need be no cause for shame (Isa. 54:4). A number of significant passages fall into line here, expressing the inverse of shame, such as the Apostle Paul's: . . . "not ashamed of the gospel . . ." (II Tim. 1:12); the ideally diligent student of the word, with "no need to be ashamed" (II Tim. 2:15); and similarly in connection with God and his own (Heb. 11:16), with the second coming of the Lord (I John 2:28), and with the Christian as a sufferer (I Pet. 4:16). In contrast, heathen nakedness is shame (Isa. 47:3). Idolatry is a special shame (Isa. 42:17; Jer. 2:26; Hos. 9:10). Wilful sinners of the carnal variety are strongly stigmatized (Phil. 3:19).

Oppositely to Gen. 2:25, the lack of shame, in sinners, is condemned (see especially Jer. 6:15). For shame is the appropriate evidence of conviction touching anything wrong in God's sight, a reaction against sin, which God himself gives (Isa. 61:7; Rom. 6:21). In such connection it is a praiseworthy passion because those who experience it show thereby hope of salvation from sin. It points to real repentance (Ezra 9:6; Ezek. 16:61). Minor uses are:

neglect of propriety, causing discomfort (Judg. 3:25); and reproach for neglect of convention, as regarding woman's hair (I Cor. 11:6). Also shame comes to the Lord's people through taunts of the heathen (Ezek. 36:6).

ROBERT F. GRIBBLE

SHEEP. The Hebrew ṣō'n and the Greek *probaton* are the principal words designating sheep. The children of God are described as sheep in both the Old and New Testaments (Pss. 79:13; 95:7; 100:3; Matt. 10:16; 26:31; John 10:2, 7, 27). Christ is their Shepherd (Ps. 23:1; Ezek. 34:23; John 10:10, 14; Heb. 13:20; I Pet. 5:4; Rev. 7:17).

Believers as sheep are characterized as: (1) audient — they hear the Shepherd's voice (John 10:3, 27); (2) sapient — they know the Shepherd (John 10:4, 14); (3) obedient — they follow the Shepherd (John 10:4 f., 27; Rev. 7:17).

The Good Shepherd (q.v.) confers upon his sheep the following blessings: (1) sacrifice — he gives his life for them (John 10:11, 15, 17; cf. Zech. 13:7); (2) salvation — he saves them (John 10:9 f.); (3) satisfaction — he provides for his sheep now (Ps. 23:1; Ezek. 34:23; John 10:9) and in eternity (Rev. 7:17); (4) separation — he segregates his sheep from the goats at his return in glory (Matt. 25:32 f.); (5) security — he gives them eternal life and "they shall never perish" (John 10:28).

WICK BROOMALL

SHEKINAH. While Scripture denies any permanent localization of God it does describe, simultaneously with his transcendence, his "glory," or apprehensible presence. Glory may be expressed in God's "face," "name" (Ex. 33:18-20), "Angel" — pre-incarnate appearances of Christ — or "cloud" (Ex. 14:19). Shekinah concerns the cloud, which surrounded the glory (40:34), like thunderheads through which lightning flashes (19:9, 16).

The shekinah first appeared when God led Israel from Egypt and protected them by "a pillar of cloud and fire" (13:21; 14:19). The cloud vindicated Moses against "murmurers" (16:10; Num. 16:42) and covered Sinai (Ex. 24:16) as he communed there with God (vs. 18; cf. 33:9). God "dwelt," šākan (25:8), among Israel in the tabernacle, miškān, "place of dwelling" (vs. 9; cf. I Kings 8:13), a type of his dwelling in heaven (I Kings 8:30; Heb.

9:24). The cloud filled the tabernacle (Ex. 40:34-35; cf. Rom. 9:4); and post-biblical usage accordingly designated this permanent, visible manifestation šᵉkinâ, "dwelling [of God's presence]." Shortly thereafter consuming fire twice "came forth from before the LORD" (Lev. 9:23; 10:2). Specifically, God appeared "in the cloud upon the mercy-seat, which is upon the ark" (Lev. 16:2; Ex. 25:22; cf. Heb. 9:5).

The shekinah guided Israel through the wilderness (Ex. 40:36-38); and, though the ark's loss meant "Ichabod [no glory]" (I Sam. 4:21), the cloud again filled Solomon's temple (I Kings 8:11; cf. II Chron. 7:1). Ezekiel visualized its departure because of sin (Ezek. 10:18) before this temple's destruction, and Judaism confessed its absence from the second temple. The shekinah reappeared with Christ (Matt. 17:5; Luke 2:9), true God localized (John 1:14: skēnē, "tabernacle"; cf. Rev. 21:3, = šᵉkinâ?), the glory of the latter temple (Hag. 2:9; Zech. 2:5). Christ ascended in the glory cloud (Acts 1:9) and will some day so return (Mark 14:62; Rev. 14:14; cf. Isa. 24:3; 60:1).

See also GLORY, TRANSFIGURATION.

BIBLIOGRAPHY

HDB; R. E. Hough, *The Ministry of the Glory Cloud.*

J. BARTON PAYNE

SHEOL. The word Sheol is used throughout the OT in two senses: (1) literally, of a place deep under the earth's surface where the dead abide (Deut. 32:22; Isa. 14:9, 15), and (2) figuratively, of grave danger or suffering (Ps. 116:3; Jonah 2:2 ff.). The NT *hādēs* (q.v.), "underworld," carries the same idea (Luke 10:15; Acts 2:27; cf. Wis. Sol. 16:13). Parallel expressions are *bôr*, "pit" (Isa. 14:15; Ps. 88:4), *šahat*, "[place of] corruption" (Ps. 16:10; Ezek. 28:8), and *'ăbaddôn*, "[place of] destruction" (Job 26:6; 28:22).

Sheol is uniformly depicted in the OT as the eternal, amoral abode of both righteous and unrighteous alike. There is neither punishment nor reward in the pit. Death is the entrance into an eternal land of forgetfulness (Ps. 88:13; Job 10:21), darkness (Job 38:17), dust (Dan. 12:2), and sleeping (Job 14:12), where there is "no work or thought or knowledge or wisdom" (Eccl. 9:10; Isa. 38:10-20). This does not imply extinction, for the dead warrior is recognized by his weapon

(Ezek. 32:27), the trappings and thrones of kings are there (Isa. 14:9-11), Samuel retains his robe (I Sam. 28:14), and the dead welcome new arrivals (Isa. 14:9). Men still exist in Sheol, only it is in a form that cannot really be called life. They are $r^e p\bar{a}'\hat{\imath}m$, "sunken, powerless beings," from whom life's vital power (the $nep\bar{e}\check{s}$) is gone (Isa. 14:9-10). They are only shadowy replicas of their former selves.

A development in concept is found in Daniel 12:2, where Sheol is the intermediate dwelling place of certain wicked and righteous (the "many"), while remaining the eternal abode for all the rest. The special class of righteous are given "everlasting life," while the wicked are condemned to "shame and everlasting contempt" (cf. also Isa. 26:19).

BIBLIOGRAPHY

BDB; KB; H. W. Robinson, *Inspiration and Revelation in the Old Testament*, pp. 94-100; W. O. E. Oesterley, *Immortality and the Unseen World*, pp. 63-94.

ROBERT B. LAURIN

SHEPHERD. I. OLD TESTAMENT. Israel was a predominantly pastoral people; its religious concepts were, therefore, colored by the vocabulary and vocational habits current among a pastoral community. This is particularly prominent in the OT use of "shepherd"; but it is the shepherd as *ruler* that is emphasized. (1) The figure is applied to Yahweh (Isa. 40:10). Israel's Shepherd pastors his people from his kingly throne (Pss. 80:1 f.; 95:6 f.). Ps. 23 is an exception. (2) The figure is applied to Israel's national leaders. David is the outstanding example here (II Sam. 5:2; Ps. 78:70 ff.); but Joshua (Num. 27:16 ff.), the Judges (I Chron. 17:6), and the nobility in general (Jer. 2:8; 25:34-36) are also mentioned. Ezekiel condemns the latter for remissness in their pastoral responsibilities (34:2-10). (3) The figure is applied to Messiah. Micah was the first to use the metaphor in this way (5:2-4), but it is prominent in Ezekiel (34:22-24; 37:24 f.).

II. NEW TESTAMENT. The metaphor attains prominence here also. (1) It is applied to Christ (Matt. 2:6, RSV). John 10 explains what this meant. The Good Shepherd leads his sheep (*q.v.*) out (vs. 3), delivers, and provides for, them (vs. 9), gives them "eternal life" (vss. 10, 28) through a voluntary and vicarious self-sacrifice (vss. 11, 15, 18). In Revelation this "great shepherd of the sheep" (Heb. 13:20) continues his ministry in his transcendent life (7:17). (2) The figure is applied to church leaders. The Ephesian presbyters "shepherd" the church (Acts 20:28; cf. Eph. 4:11; I Pet. 5:1 f.), but in exercising pastoral functions church leaders are not to lord it over the flock; and their motives are to be pure (I Pet. 5:2 f.). Alas, the NT churches did not always have such self-dedicated shepherds (Acts 20:29 f.; Jude 12, RSV). (3) The figure is applied to the leaders of the Jews in NT times. The Jews were "lost sheep" (Matt. 15:24) and shepherdless (9:36; Mark 6:34), because their "shepherds" were faithless hirelings (John 10:10-13), unspiritual authoritarians (9:22, 34). Only the Good Shepherd admits to, or excludes from, the true fold.

JAMES G. S. S. THOMSON

SHILOH. As a proper noun Shiloh (Heb. *šilô, šilô* or *šilōh*) refers to the biblical settlement NNE of Bethel, modern Seilûn. The *šilōh* of Gen. 49:10 cannot refer to this. Unless this occurrence be the exception it nowhere refers to an individual. Some take it here as a title of Messiah. Three witnesses to the pre-vocalized Hebrew text, the Septuagint, Syriac and Targum versions, read it *šlh* and vocalized it *šellôh*, meaning "who to him." The relative pronoun *š*, vocalized with the *a* vowel just like the Hebrew article, is used with greater frequency in later books of the OT but is also found in the earlier. It is used with preposition *l* ("to, for") and followed by a pronoun. See II Kings 6:11, Jonah 1:12, and (without preposition) Judg. 6:17. There is a strong likelihood that in Gen. 49:10 we should read "until he come whose it is (who to him)." For the sense of the passage thus rendered cf. Ezek. 21:27.

G. DOUGLAS YOUNG

SIGN. See MIRACLE.

SIMILITUDE. The words "similitude" or "likeness" are used in the AV to translate three Greek NT words: (1) *homoiōsis* (used in the LXX often for Hebrew *d^emût*). This is used in Gen. 1:26 and James 3:9. It implies abstract likeness as distinct from a figure, picture or copy. (2) *homoiotēs*. This is used in Heb. 4:15 and 7:15. It implies likeness of the same order, or equality. (3) *homoiōma* (used most frequently in the LXX for Hebrew *d^emût*,

$tab^e nit$, and $t^e m\hat{u}n\hat{a}$). This word often implies concrete likeness, i.e., "something made like," though it can mean simply "form" or "shape" (Deut. 4:12; Rev. 9:7). As used in its NT contexts by Paul it implies not only likeness in form between two things but similarity in concrete circumstances (Rom. 5:14). In Rom. 8:3 and Phil. 2:7 Christ's assuming the *homoiōma* of our sinful flesh or humanity implies not only likeness of status and form between Christ and ourselves but also his concrete self-identification with us in the flesh in his incarnation. Similarly Rom. 6:5 affirms that we are implanted in baptism into the *homoiōma* of Christ's death and resurrection. The thought is not simply that the experience in the Christian life to which we are pledged through baptism is of the same pattern as Christ's in his dying and rising, but that in baptism there is a "concrete re-presentation" (W. Manson) of the death and resurrection of Christ so that through it we are actually made to grow in living union (*symphytoi*) with Christ himself.

BIBLIOGRAPHY
J. Schneider in *TWNT* V, pp. 186-98; *Church of Scotland Commission on Baptism*, May, 1955, pp. 36-40.

RONALD S. WALLACE

SIMONY. Simony takes its name from the attempt of Simon Magus in Acts 8:18 f. to purchase from Peter the power of mediating the reception of the Holy Spirit through the laying on of hands. It thus refers to the purchase of spiritual office, or to financial agreements with a view to the appointment to a particular sphere of ministry, or by extension to the charging of fees for benefits which may be received through the administration of word and sacrament. The evil seems first to have arisen on any scale during the fourth century. A rule forbidding ordination for money was passed at Chalcedon (A.D. 451), and after this the persistent condemnation of every form of simony points to its widespread existence, more particularly under feudal conditions. In view of the reality of original sin, the particular danger of the love of money (I Tim. 6:10), and the apostolic injunction that honest things should be provided in the sight of both God and man (II Cor. 8:20 f.), it is perhaps as well that there should be careful and forcefully applied safeguards in all churches against the various forms of the evil.

GEOFFREY W. BROMILEY

SIMPLICITY. In the wisdom literature of the OT the "simple" ($p^e t\hat{i}$), as a class, stand between the wise and the foolish. They are the gullible, open to influences both of good and evil. Their need is stability.

The most commonly used NT word (*haplous, haplotēs*) means "without folds." It therefore suggests purity of purpose, a lack of complication in motives. Jesus speaks of the single eye in contrast to that which is evil (Matt. 6:22-23). The man who tries to serve God and mammon lacks singleness of purpose.

Paul speaks of "the simplicity that is in Christ" (II Cor. 11:3). This should be rendered . . . "toward Christ" (RV). The openhearted, undeviating devotion to Christ of believers is quite opposed to the deviousness, the craftiness of the serpent.

The same word, on occasion, means liberality (Rom. 12:8). In giving, one should not hold back by allowing his generous impulse to be thwarted by selfishness or by doubt as to the worthiness of the recipient. Our exemplar here is God (James 1:5), who gives with no subtle intent underneath his ostensible purpose to bless, nor with any pangs of regret at his generosity once it is extended.

The NT pleads for a simple life in the sense of one which is unitary. Its integrating factor is the decision to glorify God. A simple, uncomplicated outlook may yet be profound in its depth of understanding and achievement.

BIBLIOGRAPHY
O. Bauernfeind in *TWNT*; J. H. Farmer in *HDCG*; H. Bulcock in *HDAC*.

EVERETT F. HARRISON

SIN. No single Hebrew word is able to exhibit the OT concept of sin fully. The most common word for sin is $hatt\bar{a}'\hat{a}$ ($hatt\bar{a}'t$) signifying "a missing, a failing, sin." Secular use of its verbal form is illustrated in Judg. 20:16, where it is stated that the tribe of Benjamin had a corps of left-handed warriors who "could sling stones at a hair-breadth and not miss." Other words often used for sin in the OT are $re\check{s}a'$, "wickedness, confusion"; $\bar{a}w\bar{o}n$, "iniquity, perversion, guilt"; $pe\check{s}a'$, "transgression, rebellion"; $\bar{a}wen$, "wrongness, trouble, vanity"; $\check{s}eqer$, "lying, deceit"; ra', "evil" (usually of injurious judicial or natural effects of sin); $ma'al$, "trespass, breach of trust"; $\bar{a}\check{s}\bar{a}m$, "error, negligence, guilt"; $\bar{a}wel$, "injustice"; and the verbs $s\bar{a}rar$, "to disobey," and 'ābar, "to transgress." It is important to note that many of these words are used (in various forms) to denote not only sin but also guilt and even the means by which guilt is removed. Sin, its consequences, and the means for its removal were thus vividly united in the consciousness of Israel.

The LXX *usually* uses hamartia for ḥaṭṭā'â, adikia for 'āwōn (some 53 times), anomia for 'āwōn (about 63 times), paraptōma for ma'al, peša', 'āwel, and parabainein for various words meaning "to transgress," especially when applied to transgression of the covenant. The LXX also translates sōrᵉrîm with ·apeithousin, "disobedient," in Isa. 1:23.

The main NT words for sin are hamartia, "a missing of the mark, sin"; adikia, "unright-eousness"; anomia, "lawlessness"; asebeia, "im-piety"; parabasis, "transgression"; paraptōma, "a fall," indicating disruption of the right rela-tionship to God; ponēria, "depravity"; epithy-mia, "desire, lust"; apeitheia, "disobedience."

The biblical revelation concerning the na-ture of sin lies embedded in sacred history. In Gen. 3 the origin of sin in the human race is attributed to the fall of Adam and Eve in Eden. From the record the following truths are established: (1) that God is not the author of sin, but that sin is suggestively, then overtly proposed by the serpent and freely embraced by Eve (cf. James 1:13-15); (2) that the sin of Eve begins with doubt concerning the rightness of God's command not to eat of the fruit of the tree of the knowledge of good and evil; (3) that the sinful act resulting from rationalized desire was one of direct and will-ful disobedience to the expressed command of God; (4) that the first sinful act by both Adam and Eve resulted in an immediate sense of the shamefulness of nakedness and a con-sequent attempt to hide from God; and (5) that the sin is followed by the divine curse on the serpent, woman, and man, and by expulsion from fellowship with God in the garden. The penalty of death is inflicted on the human race which descends from Adam and Eve (Gen. 4-6).

Mankind corrupts its way upon the earth and its extreme wickedness evokes the judg-ment of the flood (Gen. 6). After the flood the power of the sword is ordained (Gen. 9:5 ff.) for the restraint of sin in human society. God frustrates racial rebellion at Babel and divine special revelation begins to focus on Abraham and his descendants as bearers of the promises of the covenant of grace (q.v.). In this era the destruction of Sodom and Gomorrah serves to remind future generations of the doom which awaits those who live in unbridled sin and corruption (Gen. 13:13; 18:20; 19:1-29). The record of the lives of Jacob and his sons frankly discloses the sins of these men and makes clear to Israel that its national existence as the bearer of the covenant life does not rest on its own good-ness but on the sovereign grace of God (Gen. 34, 37, 38, 49, et al.). Deliverance from Egyptian bondage symbolizes deliverance from the power of sin. But even in the night of deliverance Israel is pointedly reminded of the fact that substitutionary death alone saves Israel from Egypt's fate (Ex. 12). Even after the manifestation of God's saving power at the Red Sea the people rebel (Ex. 17:1-7) and against the background of God's gracious calling of the people to be his peculiar people and the giving of the law at Sinai, Israel's sinfulness comes to ugly manifestation in the worship of the golden calf (Ex. 32). After the people have disobediently tried to force entrance into Canaan in spite of God's pun-ishment of their unbelief a distinction is impressed upon Israel between unwitting sins (in "error") and presumptuous sins, sins "with a high hand" (Num. 14; 15:27-31).

Laws concerning ceremonial uncleanness and unclean diseases and meats are designed to teach Israel vividly the absoluteness of the holiness which is required in those who are called the people of Jehovah (Lev. 11-15; Deut. 14:21). While a distinction is made between sins done wittingly and unwittingly (in "error"), unwitting sin is culpable and in need of expiation (Lev. 5:1-10, 17-19).

From the entrance into Canaan until the time of the Babylonian captivity sin is ex-plicitly described as apostasy from the calling of God for the covenant people (Judg. 2:1-5; I Sam. 2:12 ff., et al.). Even David and his best successors fall from their typical office and show rebelliousness against the God of the covenant (II Sam. 11; 24; I Kings 11:9; et al.). Covenant-breaking increases with but few pauses in the northern and southern king-doms and manifests itself in social oppression (Amos passim; I Kings 21) and idolatry, which is described consistently as spiritual adultery (Hosea; Isa. 1:4, 19-21; Jer. 3:1; Ezek. 16:15, 23). Although Israel is cured of idolatry through the exile the stubbornness of sin comes to expression even after the return (Mal. 1:6—2:17; 3:7-15).

Within this framework a keen sense of sin develops in the godly and comes to expression in the Psalms (Pss. 32, 130). While the total depravity of the ungodly is forcefully proclaimed (Ps. 53), the subtle power of sin in the heart of the believer is confessed (Ps. 139:23-24). In Ps. 51 the presence of sin even at conception is acknowledged (vs. 5).

The consciousness that sin roots in the deepest core of man's being, the heart, is expressed throughout the OT (Jer. 17:9; Gen. 6:5; I Kings 11:9; Prov. 6:14; Eccl. 8:7; 9:3). The hardening of the heart in sin may also be a retributive act of divine justice (Ex. 7:3; 9:12; Isa. 6:10).

The NT contains passages in which sin is defined or described in broad terms. These "definitions" are found especially in the Gospel and First Epistle of John. Jesus says, "Everyone that committeth sin is the bond-servant of sin" (John 8:34; cf. Rom. 6:16, 20, 23). John writes in I John 3:4, "Everyone that doeth sin [hamartian] doeth also lawlessness [anomian]; and sin [hamartia] is lawlessness [anomia]."

The Gospels presuppose and hardly define the sinfulness of men. But the OT conception of sin as rebellion against covenant grace takes on new form. Jesus comes not to call the righteous, but sinners to repentance (Matt. 9:13). The Pharisees, who attribute the mighty acts of Jesus to Satan, come perilously close to blaspheming the Holy Spirit — the unpardonable sin (Matt. 12:22-37). Jesus' sharpest words are reserved for those who "trusted in themselves that they were righteous and set all others at nought . . ." (Luke 18:9; cf. Matt. 23:13-29). The rejection of Jesus as the Messiah is the fearful sin of Israel (Matt. 11:20 ff.; John 9:35-41) and it involves rejection of him as the Son of God (John 10:22-39). The wrath of God abides on those who do not obey the Son (John 3:36). The self-righteous are most sinful because they not only transgress the law but make it void by their traditions (Matt. 15:1-20). Not ceremonial uncleanness, but the evil which proceeds from the heart through the mouth defiles man (Matt. 15:18-20).

The doctrine of sin is most systematically expounded by Paul. In Rom. 1:18—3:19 Paul proves that every Jew and Gentile alike is under divine judgment because of sin. The power of sin is awakened by the law and the observation of sin's reaction to law leads Paul to confess, "I am carnal, sold under sin" (Rom. 7:14). Sin consists not simply in deeds but in a condition, a condition common to all men who are by nature dead in trespasses and sins and are children of wrath (Eph. 2:1-3). Apart from Christ man is in the flesh and from this source come all kinds of actual sins (Gal. 5:19-21). Man, being in the flesh, cannot please God; he is in sin, he is not conformed to the will of God (Rom. 8:5-8). Only divine deliverance can free man from this bondage (Rom. 3:21-26) and, for the saved, the presence or absence of the motive of faith becomes the test of whether or not one is acting in obedience to God (Rom. 14:23).

While the details of the exegesis of Rom. 5:12-21 are disputed, it appears certain that Paul regards all men as sinners in Adam. Not only did Adam introduce sin into the world. The fact is that death exists even where there is no Mosaic law and no imputation of sin in connection with that law. Therefore death must stem from the fact that "through one trespass the judgment came unto all men to condemnation" (vs. 18), and, "by the trespass of the one, death reigned through the one" (vs. 16). The disobedience of one made many sinners (vs. 19). The parallel between condemnation and justification points to imputation as the mode by which each of these judicial sentences is directed to men and to believers, respectively.

In the history of the church fierce controversy has raged about the doctrine of original sin (q.v.). Pelagius and his followers asserted that death is natural, not penal; that good nature created by a good God is not corruptible; that Adam's sin influences the race only as a bad example; that all men are in Adam's state before the fall; and that law and grace are not essentially different. Over against this teaching Augustine asserted that all men inherit natural corruption from Adam and that original sin is sin, punishment and guilt.

Roman Catholicism, by sacramentalizing grace, focused attention on gradations of sin, holding that original sin was eliminated in baptism but that the "fuel" of sin remained, and making a distinction between venial and mortal sin suitable to the sacramental system.

Calvin protested that evil motions and desires in the heart were really accounted as sins by God. While Rome claimed that the remnants of original sin were not "properly" sin in the regenerated, the Reformers maintained that the remaining evil disposition of the heart was sin before God.

The Synod of Dordt (1618-19) firmly maintained the doctrines of total depravity (*q.v.*) and total inability against the weakening of these doctrines by the Arminians. The *Formula Consensus* (1675) of the Swiss Reformed Churches asserted that Adam's sin was immediately imputed to his descendants in virtue of his representative status in the covenant of works. This teaching was directed against the contention of La Place of Saumur that Adam's descendants are guilty mediately, i.e., in virtue of their inherited corruption.

The modern period of church history has also seen the revival of ancient Greek conceptions of sin as ignorance and of sin as the tragic implication of man's finitude. The former is congenial to evolutionism and the latter to existentialism.

BIBLIOGRAPHY

L. Berkhof, *Reformed Dogmatics* (Historical Volume), pp. 131-66; L. Berkhof, *Systematic Theology*, pp. 219-61; P. Y. De Jong, *The Covenant Idea in New England Theology*, pp. 32-49, 138-40; Gesenius; Girdlestone; A. Harnack, *Dogmengeschichte* (Grundriss), pp. 262-71, 361; C. Hodge, *Systematic Theology*, II, pp. 130-277; J. E. Kuizenga in *ISBE*; L. Morris, *The Apostolic Preaching of the Cross*, pp. 125-85; A. Oepke in *TWNT* (III, p. 448); Trench; G. Quell, *et al.* in *TWNT*; G. Vos, *Biblical Theology*.

CARL G. KROMMINGA

SINCERE. The principal Greek words used are *anypokritos* (literally, "without hypocrisy" — originally the hypocrite was one who played a part on the stage) and *eilikrineia* ("sincerity, purity"). Neither of these terms is used in the canonical books of the LXX. *Anypokritos* occurs in Rom. 12:9; II Cor. 6:6; I Tim. 1:5; II Tim. 1:5; James 3:17; I Pet. 1:22. *Eilikrineia* appears in I Cor. 5:8; II Cor. 1:12; 2:17; Phil. 1:10; II Pet. 3:1. Another word, *adolos*, occurs once (I Pet. 2:2) and is used in the old sense of "sincere," meaning unadulterated. There are three other words used which might on occasion be rendered sincere: *gnēsiōs* in Phil. 2:20; *haplotēs* in Eph. 6:5; Col. 3:22; and *hagnōs* in Phil. 1:17.

BIBLIOGRAPHY

RTWB; Trench, pp. 199-200, 304-6.

RALPH A. GWINN

SINLESSNESS OF CHRIST. See CHRISTOLOGY.

SLANDER. See BLASPHEMY.

SLAVE, SLAVERY. Slavery does not occur in the AV and slave occurs only twice (Jer. 2:14 has it in italics as implied and Rev. 18:13 has it for the Greek *sōmatōn*, "bodies"). The RSV has slave, slaves, and slavery a total of 157 times. This is largely due to the fact that the Hebrew '*ebed* and the Greek *doulos*, which may properly be translated servant, may also be rendered slave (Gen. 9:25-27). The basic idea in these words is service and may have reference to service which is freely rendered or to that which is obligatory in the sense of bondage. Among the Hebrews a maidservant or a manservant was the property of his master. He was, in a sense, a slave or chattel. A master could acquire a slave: (1) by purchase (Gen. 17:12; 37:28), (2) by capture in war (Num. 31:9; II Kings 5:2), (3) by birth from slaves already owned (Ex. 21:4), (4) in place of a debt owed by the one enslaved, the debtor thus selling himself into slavery (Lev. 25:39, 47), (5) as a gift (Gen. 29:24).

But the position of the Hebrew slave must not be confused with the lot of a slave in the cruel societies of other nations. Among the Israelites there was no profound difference between the relation of the slave to the master and that of the members of the master's family. The wives and children were just as much under the power of the master as were the slaves. The slaves were not thought of as being inferior, and though they had no civil rights, they were regarded as true members of the family (Gen. 17:23; Ex. 12:44). The Hebrew master was bound by the regulations of the Mosaic law and his responsibility to them was emphasized by such injunctions as those in Deut. 15:15, which reminded him of his own bondage in Egypt. Slaves were protected also by the sabbatical and jubilee regulations (Ex. 21:2-27; Lev. 25:25-55). The disregard of the regulations led to numerous abuses according to Jer. 34:8-22, where the people of Judah are warned against disobeying the Mosaic slave regulations. There are some resemblances but also important differences between the Hebrew slave regulations and those of the Code of Hammurabi. In the NT, the gospel, with its message of love, laid the foundation for the elimination of human slavery (Philem.; Gal. 3:28; Eph. 6:5-9).

See also SERVANT.

BIBLIOGRAPHY
K. Fullerton in *HDB*; I. Benzinger in *EB*, col. 4653.

ARNOLD C. SCHULTZ

SLEEP. (1) Often in both the OT and NT the word is used literally to denote physical sleep (I Sam. 26:7; Judg. 16:14; Matt. 28:13; John 11:12). Peaceful sleep is a good gift of God to his people (Ps. 4:8; cf. 127:2). That too much sleep prevents one from assuming normal responsibilities and leads to poverty is an emphasis peculiar to the Book of Proverbs (Prov. 6:9-10; 20:13; 24:33).

An example of a special type of physical sleep supernaturally induced for a divine purpose is to be found in Gen. 2:21. Deep sleep in the OT is often associated with receiving divine revelation through visions or dreams (Dan. 8:18; 10:9). Abraham (Gen. 15:12) and Jacob (Gen. 28:12) seem to have had experiences of this type.

(2) Sleep, in at least one passage in the NT, metaphorically refers to the spiritual condition of the unsaved (Eph. 5:14). This passage which seems to be a quotation from an early Christian hymn, describes the sleeper as being "dead," a clear indication of its reference to the unconverted.

(3) One of its most frequent metaphorical uses is to inculcate the need for spiritual alertness. Spiritual apathy is likened to sleep by our Lord in the parable of the virgins (Matt. 25:1-13; cf. Mark 13:36). Paul exhorts the Roman Christians to awaken from their sleep in view of the closeness of the *parousia* (Rom. 13:11), and in one of the most significant passages in the NT on this subject, he admonishes the Thessalonians to be spiritually watchful by reminding them that they are not of the night (thus not asleep) but of the day (I Thess. 5:1-9).

(4) Sleep is also used metaphorically of death as is evidenced by the oft recurring phrase in the OT historical books, "he slept with his fathers" (cf. also Job 14:2; Jer. 51:39). In this connection sleep is used more specifically in the NT of the state of the body of the believer between death and the resurrection (I Thess. 4:14; I Cor. 15:51).

WALTER W. WESSEL

SOBER, SOBRIETY. Two groups of Greek words are involved. The adjective *nēphalios* means sober with reference to drink; the verb form (*nēphō*) is used in the NT only in the figurative sense, to be well-balanced, self-controlled, thus almost equivalent to *egkrateia* (self-control, used in Acts 24:25; Gal. 5:23; II Pet. 1:6; I Cor. 7:9; 9:25; Titus 1:8). Accordingly both the AV and the RSV render these words by either temperate or sober in eight of the nine cases where they occur: I Thess. 5:6, 8; I Tim. 3:2, 11; Titus 2:2; I Pet. 1:13; 4:7; 5:8. The one exception is II Tim. 4:5.

The other Greek words (*sōphroneō* and derivatives) occur sixteen times, translated sober twice in the RSV and twelve times in the AV. These words are broader in scope than the former. The meanings range along the lines of sound mind, reasonable, good judgment, moderation, prudence, chastity. The references are: Mark 5:15; Luke 8:35; Rom. 12:3; II Cor. 5:13; Titus 2:6; I Pet. 4:7; Titus 2:4; II Tim. 1:7; Titus 2:12; Acts 26:25; I Tim. 2:9, 15; I Tim. 3:2; Titus 1:8; 2:2, 5.

BIBLIOGRAPHY
Arndt; *HDB*.

RALPH A. GWINN

SOCINIANISM. A deviation from orthodoxy within Protestantism named after Fausto Sozzini (or Socinus, 1539-1604), a product of the radical scepticism of the Italian Renaissance. He denied the full deity of Christ, predestination, original sin, total inability, atonement by penal substitution and justification by faith; the "salvation" he retained was gained by works. The rational theistic morality he asserted bore affinities with Arianism, Pelagianism and the "simple Christianity" of Erasmus. His movement found early support in Poland (where Sozzini ended his days), in the Low Countries and especially in England, where, with the advent of deism in the eighteenth century, Socinian thought became predominant in many circles, both General Baptists and English Presbyterians being widely contaminated. In 1774 the first Unitarian (= Socinian) church as such was formed in London; many — particularly Nonconformists — seceded to join it and the denomination still persists, but is not influential.

See also UNITARIANISM.

O. RAYMOND JOHNSTON

SOLIDARITY. See IMPUTATION.

SON. The sonship of believers is expressed by three Greek words: *teknon* ("child"); *huios* ("son"); *huiothesia* ("adoption").

As to the nature of this sonship, (1) it is restrictive — limited to believers only (I John 3:10-12). Others are children of the devil (John 8:44). (2) It is regenerative — sons have been born by the Spirit (John 3:6-8). The first birth will not suffice (Matt. 3:9; Rom. 2:28 f.). (3) It is restorative — God's image is gradually (Col. 3:10) and, at the Parousia, completely (Rom. 8:29; Phil. 3:20 f.) restored. (4) It is regulative — the norm of the life of sons is determined by divine standards (Matt. 5:44 f.; Phil. 3:14 f.).

Prominent among the blessings of sonship are the following: (1) Adoption (Rom. 8:15; Gal. 4:5; Eph. 1:5). Believers are legally constituted members of God's family. (2) Chastisement (Heb. 12:5-8; cf. Rom. 5:3-11). The Father disciplines his children. (3) Inheritance (Rom. 8:17; Gal. 3:26, 29; 4:7, 30; I Pet. 1:4). God's sons inherit eternal glory.

Our sonship has temporal aspects. (1) Past. Sonship here relates either to the eternal decree (Eph. 1:5) or to the regenerative act in time (James 1:18; I Pet. 1:3, 23). (2) Present. Sonship is reflected in the present world by the changed life (Matt. 5:45; II Cor. 5:17). The regenerate know their sonship by the Spirit's testimony (Rom. 8:14 f.). (3) Future. Glorification is the final display of the believer's sonship (Luke 20:36; Rom. 8:19, 23; Heb. 2:10; I John 3:2).

See also ADOPTION.

WICK BROOMALL

SON OF GOD. See CHRISTOLOGY.

SON OF MAN. See CHRISTOLOGY.

SON OF PERDITION. This expression (*huios tēs apōleias*) appears in John 17:12 and II Thess. 2:3. The word *apōleias* is used in the NT to express: (1) ruin, loss, or waste, as in Mark 14:4, (2) the unbeliever's ultimate destruction (Rom. 9:22). In the phrase son of perdition (after the analogy of such formations as "sons of this aeon" [Luke 16:8]; "sons of disobedience" [Eph. 2:2]), perdition qualifies the subject involved. That is, his life and character are controlled by the forces of destruction and headed towards eternal ruin. The phrase appropriately describes Antichrist, II Thess. 2:3, indicating his demonic charac-

ter and final doom. The application of the term to Judas in John 17:12 suggests a connection in thought with the former passage. Antichrist sits as a traitor in the temple of God, even as Judas in the apostolic circle, but neither circumstance discredits Jesus' saving role.

FREDERICK WILLIAM DANKER

SORROW. The Bible realistically views sorrow as well as joy as intrinsic to present human experience. As joy is the gift of God, so sorrow is immediately or ultimately the effect of sin (Gen. 3:16; Ps. 32:10); although in the mixed moral state of this present life, paradoxically sorrow and joy may characterize the believer's experience at the same time (cf. Rom. 5:2 and 9:2; I Pet. 1:6, 8).

A total of twenty-six Hebrew terms convey the idea of sorrow, including words whose associated meanings are affliction, blinding, fear, grief, labor, lamentation, pain, pang, sadness, vanity, and woe. *Lypeō* ("to grieve" or "to make said") and *odynaomai* ("to be pained") and their derivatives are the NT terms. *Penthos*, translated "sorrow" in the AV of Rev. 18:7 and 21:4, is better rendered "mourning" as by the ASV and RSV.

Familiar causes of sorrow are bereavement (Gen. 42:38; Phil. 2:27; I Thess. 4:13); persecution (Esth. 9:22; Ps. 13:2); the calamities of life (Ps. 116:3); the rebellion of loved ones (Rom. 9:2); and the judgments of God (Lam. 1:12; II Cor. 2:7). An important contrast is made between the "sorrow of the world" which "produces death" and "godly sorrow" which "produces a repentance that leads to salvation and brings no regret" (II Cor. 7:10, RSV).

WESTLAKE T. PURKISER

SOTERIOLOGY. See SALVATION, REDEMPTION.

SOUL. There is a disparity of concept between the OT *nepeš* and the NT *psychē*. The basic difference lies in the fact that the *nepeš*, unlike the *psychē*, is not a spiritual entity which exists apart from the body.

The word *nepeš* is used generally to designate individual men or animals in their total essence (Gen. 1:20; Ex. 1:5). This is made clear in Gen. 2:7 where the divine breath is blown into the body, and so creates "a living *nepeš*," that is, man. "It is not the object of the narrator to analyse the elements of man, but to represent his essential character" (J. Pedersen, *Israel, Its Life and Culture* I-II, Oxford University Press, London, 1926, p. 99). Thus to the Hebrew, man was not a "body" and a "soul," but rather a "body-soul," a unit of vital power. The "soul" is at the same time something visible that can hunger and thirst (Ps. 107:5), and also something invisible that can be distressed (Gen. 42:21), and thus often comes to be used for the ego itself (Job 16:4; Ps. 124:7). It may be used at one extreme to denote the principle of life in man or animal (Gen. 37:21), and at the other to speak of a dead body (Num. 19:11). The *nepeš* is then simply the individual in his totality. After death the *nepeš* ceases to exist, lingering only as long as the body is a body (Job 14:22; cf. II Kings 23:16-18; Amos 2:1). The inhabitants of Sheol are never called "souls."

The NT, although it continues the idea of the soul (*psychē*) as the life-principle (Acts 20:10; Rev. 8:9) which becomes personified (Acts 2:43), yet also views it as a spiritual entity which continues to exist after death. Thus John says that he saw in his vision "the souls of those who had been slain," not "those who had been slain" (Rev. 6:9; cf. 20:4; Matt. 10:28; Luke 21:19; James 1:21; 5:20).

BIBLIOGRAPHY
KB; Arndt; A. R. Johnson, *The Vitality of the Individual in the Thought of Ancient Israel*, pp. 7-26.

ROBERT B. LAURIN

SOUL SLEEP. Psychopannychy, the doctrine that the soul sleeps between death and resurrection, has been held sporadically in the church. It is not a heresy in the narrower sense, due to the paucity of Scripture teaching on the intermediate state (*q.v.*), but it may be called a doctrinal aberration. Some Anabaptists endorsed it. In the Forty-two articles of Edward VI, which preceded the Thirty-nine Articles, the following statement, as the Fortieth Article, was included: "They which say that the souls of those who depart hence do sleep being without all sense, feeling or perceiving till the Day of Judgment, do utterly dissent from the right belief disclosed to us in Holy Scripture."

The case for soul sleep rests principally on these considerations: (1) Human existence demands the unity of soul and body. If the body ceases to function, so must the soul. (2) The use of the term "sleep" in Scripture for death is alleged to point to the cessation of consciousness. (3) A state of consciousness between death and resurrection, characterized by bliss or woe, unwarrantably anticipates the judgment of the last day, when the basis for these experiences is provided.

On the contrary view, while the normal state of man is admittedly a union of soul and body, the possibility of disembodied conscious existence is firmly held, both on the analogy of God's existence as pure spirit (man being made in his image) and on the basis of such passages as Heb. 12:23 and Rev. 6:9-11. As to the word "sleep," it is intended to apply to the body, even though the individual as such may be said to sleep in death. This is clear from Matt. 27:52; John 11:11; Acts 13:36, etc. See Hogg and Vine, *The Epistles to the Thessalonians*, p. 128. On the third point it may be replied that the exclusion of the possibility of bliss or woe from the intermediate state on the ground that the divine judgment which justifies such reactions will not yet have been pronounced, would logically rule out the joyful assurance of salvation in this life as well as the foreboding of judgment to come. But see John 5:24; Phil. 1:28.

Continuing consciousness after death seems to be a necessary (rather than an accidental) element in Jesus' account of the rich man and Lazarus, and also in our Lord's promise to the dying thief. The clearest and strongest passages, however, are in Paul's writings (Phil. 1:23; II Cor. 5:8). If it be contended in the case of the former passage that the sleep of the soul so effectually erases the interval between death and resurrection that the prospect of being with Christ, even though actually long delayed, could produce joyful anticipation, in any event the same thing can hardly be said for the second passage, where not only the resurrection body but the intermediate state is directly contemplated, being a less desirable alternative than the change to the resurrection body without death (vs. 4).

BIBLIOGRAPHY
J. Calvin, *Psychopannychia*; O. Cullmann, *Immortality of the Soul or Resurrection of the Dead?* pp. 48-57; Eric Lewis, *Christ, the First Fruits*; R. Whately, *A View of the Scripture Revelations concerning a Future State*, pp. 27-83.

EVERETT F. HARRISON

SOVEREIGNTY. See GOD.

SPEAKING IN TONGUES. See SPIRITUAL GIFTS.

SPIRIT. There is but one Hebrew word, *rûah,* and one Greek word, *pneuma,* for spirit as understood in the sense of the incorporeal aspect of human nature. *Rûah* is also the only Hebrew word used in the OT for wind. The NT, on the other hand, usually employs *anemos* for wind, *pneuma* having that meaning only in John 3:8.

While in much of Christian thought and writing since the apostolic age soul and spirit are often thought of as being synonymous, in the Bible they are usually distinguished. In the OT the word rendered as soul is *nephesh,* which has the basic meaning of life principle, or individual, animate life. For that reason *nephesh* may also be translated as person or self. Man IS a soul, in OT thought: he does not have a soul. On the other hand, man HAS a spirit but it is never said that he is a spirit. In the NT, however, one may be said to have a soul (Luke 21:19), though in general the two Greek equivalents, *pneuma* and *psyche,* are used in a way very similar to that of the OT. *Psyche* refers to the natural life of man (Matt. 6:25), the human life which Christ laid down (John 10:11, 15) and even the life of beasts (Rev. 8:9).

Where the Bible speaks of the origin of the human spirit, it invariably ascribes it to God, who is the father of the spirits of all flesh (Num. 16:22; Heb. 12:9). Man has no power to retain his spirit (Eccl. 8:8; Ps. 104:29) and when a man dies his spirit returns to God who gave it (Eccl. 12:7). These and similar statements have led some theologians to posit strongly a doctrine of creationism (*q.v.*) with respect to the spirit. This is the view that each spirit is a special creation. Others have held strongly to traducianism (*q.v.*), the view that the spirit as well as the body derives from the procreation of parents, though God must properly be said to be the Creator of both.

In the OT the functions of soul and spirit sometimes coincide, especially where mental or emotional activities are concerned. This is because the soul is the visible life through which spirit expresses itself. The soul, however, may hunger or thirst in a physical sense, the spirit never. NT mention of the spirit is found most frequently in matters which relate to God and the operation of the Holy Spirit upon the human spirit. The spirit, however, grieves (Gen. 26:35), is humble (Matt. 5:3), troubled (John 13:21), thinks (Isa. 27:24;

Job 20:3), remembers (Ps. 77:6). Since the NT has a word for mind, which the Hebrew did not have, there are cognitive functions ascribed to the spirit in the OT which are not in the New. In both Testaments it is man's spirit which is the spring of his inmost thoughts and intents, and the child of God must be renewed in spirit if he is to serve God acceptably (Ps. 51:10 ff.; Gal. 5:22; I John 4:13).

Sometimes the word spirit passes over into a usage which is common in English, where it is the synonym for an attitude or a talent. One may have a jealous spirit (Num. 5:14), a haughty spirit (Prov. 16:18), a contrite spirit (Ps. 34:18). The builders of the tabernacle were given a spirit of wisdom for their task (Ex. 28:3). Ludwig Koehler has very plausibly explained this mode of expression from what he calls the meteorological origin of the word spirit, which referred to the breath or wind, and therefore to the vital force or spirit which enabled men to think and act (*Old Testament Theology,* p. 140).

There are times when it is difficult to tell from the context whether the word spirit as used in a given passage refers to the Spirit of God or to a spirit given man by God, e.g., Ps. 51:11; Rom. 1:4.

BIBLIOGRAPHY
Millar Burrows, *An Outline of Biblical Theology;* Ludwig Koehler, *Old Testament Theology;* Paul Heinisch, *Theology of the Old Testament;* H. Kleinknecht, F. Baumgaertel in *TWNT.*

DAVID W. KERR

SPIRIT, HOLY. There are five main areas in Scripture that yield the material for a summary of the biblical teaching on the Spirit: the OT, the Synoptics, the Fourth Gospel, Acts, the Pauline Epistles.

I. THE OLD TESTAMENT. The OT word for Spirit is *rûah* which is usually rendered *pneuma* in the LXX, though other terms are also used. It is the *activity,* not the nature of the Spirit, that is emphasized in the OT; and it is the Spirit's activity *in man* that is stressed, although the Spirit is described as an agent in creation (Gen. 1:2; Job 26:13; Isa. 32:15), who sustains what has been created (Ps. 104:30; Job 34:14). This creative agent which animates the universe also vitalizes the human organism (Gen. 2:7; Job 33:4). Since this vitalizing *rûah* in man may legitimately be called the spirit of man, the OT feels free to designate the animating principle in human nature both as the Spirit of man (Job 27:3; Ps. 104:29 f.), and the Spirit of God.

The OT conceives that the Spirit could be active at three levels of man's personality.

A. *The Intellectual Level.* The *rûaḥ* is the Spirit of wisdom, understanding and knowledge (Ex. 28:3; 35:3, 31, LXX; Deut. 34:9), and gives men rationality (Job 32:8). Unusual examples of this are Joseph (Gen. 41:38 f.), Moses (Num. 11:17; Ex. 18:22 f.), the seventy elders (Num. 11:16 f.), and Bezaleel (Ex. 31:2 ff.; cf. Ex. 35:3—36:2).

B. *The Moral Level.* The *rûaḥ* of wisdom is also the Spirit of holiness (Ps. 51:11; Isa. 63:10 f.), who begets in man "the moral character of God" (cf. Ps. 143:10; Isa. 30:1; Neh. 9:20). Hence, human morality becomes a necessity. Naturally, then, the divine *rûaḥ* in man is the "lamp" that "searches" man's "innermost parts" (Prov. 20:27), thus keeping man's moral sense alive. The Spirit of God's holiness may be grieved by sin (Isa. 63:10), and may testify against the sinner (Neh. 9:30). In Saul's case this "divine moral witness against sin" is described as "an evil spirit of the Lord" (II Sam. 16:14; 18:10; 19:9), because it tormented his conscience. This is the Spirit that "rules" or "judges" within man (Gen. 6:3; Heb.). In the OT a connection between the spirit of man and his moral attributes, such as pride (Eccl. 7:8; Prov. 16:18), quick temper (Eccl. 7:9), humility (Prov. 16:19), patience (Eccl. 7:8) and fidelity (Prov. 11:13), is also established.

C. *The Religious Level.* This is shown most clearly in the experience of the prophets. The prophet was "the man that hath the Spirit" (Hos. 9:7; cf. Ezek. 2:2; 3:24). Through this *rûaḥ* the prophet received God's word (Zech. 7:12; cf. Amos 3:7), and declared God's word (Mic. 3:8; cf. II Sam. 23:2; and the frequent, "thus saith the Lord"). In other words, the Spirit in prophecy was essentially the Spirit of revelation who made known to the prophet the will of God. But only to this limited extent was God present with his chosen people by his Spirit. Not yet was the prophet's experience of the Spirit shared by all in Israel (Num. 11:29). Not yet was the age of the Spirit; but what would happen when it came was anticipated by Jeremiah (31:32 f.), and Ezekiel (11:19 f.; 39:29; cf. 36:26 f.), and illustrated by the pleroma of the Spirit's gifts received by Messiah (Isa. 11:2), i.e., the Servant of the Lord (Isa. 42:1; 48:16; 61:1

ff.). When Messiah came, all in Israel (Zech. 12:10), and then "all flesh" (Joel 2:28 f.), would have the Spirit poured out upon it, as Pentecost proved.

In the NT the emphasis is again on the Spirit's activity; to such an extent as to justify James Denney's remark, "To the men who wrote the NT, and to those for whom they wrote, the Spirit was not a doctrine but an experience. Their watchword was not, believe in the Holy Ghost, but receive ye the Holy Ghost."

II. THE SYNOPTICS. (1) In our Lord's teaching, only one significant truth concerning the Spirit is underlined, the sin against the Holy Spirit (Mark 3:22-30). The facts of Jesus' ministry signified one thing: he was effecting his miracles through the Spirit of God, and to say that he was casting out demons through collusion with the prince of demons (Matt. 12:24) was to blaspheme the Holy Spirit (vs. 31 f.). We must, then, depend upon what the Synoptics report of our Lord's experience of the Spirit in his life and ministry for their "view" of the Spirit. Several important matters call for notice. (2) The virgin birth (*q.v.*). The Holy Spirit was the active agent in the miraculous conception of Jesus (Luke 1:34 f.; Matt. 1:18). "He was conceived by the Holy Ghost," whereas John the Baptist had been merely "filled with the Holy Ghost from his mother's womb" (Luke 1:15). The Spirit replaced "human paternity" in Jesus' conception (Matt. 1:18-21). It is with Christ's miraculous conception that his sinlessness is connected (Luke 1:35). In Jesus Christ one had been born in whom "the sinful entail" had been broken. (3) In Jesus' baptism the Spirit was also active (Matt. 3:13-17). Under the symbol of a descending dove the Spirit came and abode upon Christ (vs. 16). The divine Prophet, Priest and King had been anointed on assuming his office and ministry. This was a permanent abiding of the Spirit in Christ. Through the Spirit he was consecrating himself to the Father's mission, he was receiving an enduement of power for its accomplishment, and he would later be able to do for his church what the Father was doing for him now (John 1:32 f.). (4) In Jesus' temptation it is the holiness of the Spirit that is emphasized, since it was the Spirit who impelled him to enter into conflict with unclean spirit forces of evil (Mark 1:12). The second Adam went forth to encounter sin, and by triumphing as Man for men undid the tragedy involved in the first Adam's defeat. (5) The Spirit is seen to be the dynamic by which Christ fulfilled the Father's vocation (Acts 10:38). His own testimony was, "The Spirit of the Lord is upon me" (Luke 4:18-21). This was evident from the authority with which he taught and preached (Matt. 7:29), and cast out demons (12:28). God was visiting and redeeming his people.

III. JOHN'S GOSPEL. In contrast to the Synoptics, the Fourth Gospel confines itself principally to the teaching of Christ when referring to the Holy Spirit (1:32 ff. is an exception). (1) The Spirit is the agent who effects the birth from above by which a man enters the kingdom of heaven (3:2 ff.). A man cannot regenerate himself, nor can his parents effect this for him (1:13; 3:6); such is the power of sin. The important factor in the baptismal formula in verse 5 (cf. Matt. 28:19) is not water but Spirit (John 3:8), since only Spirit can communicate spiritual life (vs. 6 f.). (2) In 4:14; 7:37-39, Jesus teaches that the man regenerated by the Spirit finds that the Spirit is an inexhaustible spring of living water welling up within him, and flowing out from him like a river. As in chap. 3, the underlying conviction here is that this life is not native to man but is "from above." The effects of the new birth are the important matters here. The entrance of the life of God into the soul through the Spirit transforms and satisfies, and expresses itself in worship that is sincere and spiritual (4:23). This, of course, was not yet possible (7:39). Christ had to ascend to the Father before the Spirit could be given. Indications of what the Spirit's coming would mean in Christian experience are given in Jesus' farewell discourse in chaps. 13-16. (3) The three names used of the Spirit reveal further the Spirit's nature: Paraclete (14:16) who would protect, sustain and comfort the disciples in difficulty; Spirit of truth (14:17; 15:26; 16:13), a name significant for the Spirit's nature and for Christian ethics; as is also the name, the Holy Spirit (14:26), holiness being the other fundamental element in the Spirit's nature. This recalls the significance of Jesus' temptation for the nature of the Spirit who laid the compulsion upon Christ to engage in conflict with the evil one: it signified that the Spirit with whom Christ had been baptized was the Holy Spirit. Cf. also the virgin birth which is so closely connected with Christ's sinlessness. (4) The Holy Spirit has certain functions to fulfil in his relations with men, but these depend on whether a man is a Christian or a non-Christian. (a) As to the former the Spirit's ministry is to teach (16:12-15). He guides the believer into spiritual truth as revealed in Christ, takes the things of Christ and reveals them. Examples of this ministry are found in 2:2; 12:16; cf. 14:26; Luke 24:8. The Spirit also fosters the Christian's devotional life (cf. John 14:16). He also glorifies Christ by unfolding step by step the significance of Jesus' incarnation, ministry, death, resurrection, ascension and present priestly ministry. (b) The Spirit's function in the non-Christian is described in 16:8-11. He convicts the unbeliever of the sinfulness of not believing on Christ; of righteousness by reminding him of Jesus' triumph over sin, through which God now declares sinners righteous, and enables them to be righteous in reality; and of judgment by showing the relation between Christ's death and resurrection and the judgment of the world. The principal means by which the Spirit effects this is through the Christian's witness to the Lord (15:26 f.; cf. Acts 2:37; 5:33; 7:54). The Spirit witnesses to Christ but media are required to enable the Spirit to fulfil this mission, and these are the witness of individual Christians, and the church. To this end Christ communicates the Spirit still (John 20:21 f.).

IV. ACTS. Naturally the emphasis in Acts concerning the Spirit is on Christian experience, not on Christian doctrine. (1) It is the risen Christ who baptizes the church with the Spirit (1:4, 5, 8; 2:1 ff.). Pentecost was the result of what happened on Good Friday and Easter, and at the ascension (2:33). (2) And what this could mean to the individual appears from the change Pentecost effected in the apostles. Personalities were transformed. Boldness (3:11-15), forbearance (2:37-40) and unity (4:32-35), accompanied by new spiritual insight (2:22-36), and signal success in their witness (2:37-47), showed that "the promise of the Father" had been fulfilled. (3) In accordance with the Lord's teaching on the Spirit in the Fourth Gospel, the Book of Acts shows the Spirit fulfilling his dual mission among Christians and non-Christians. (a) As to his ministry among Christians he was the Paraclete who sustained the church in persecution (4:8 ff.), strengthened it for its daily witness (4:31), preserved its unity (4:31-35), kept it pure (5:3-9), appointed its leaders for "secular" (6:3) and "sacred" (20:28) duties, although the ministry of Philip (6:8; 8:4 ff.) showed that these barriers (6:2) could easily be broken down. In answer to the prayers of the apostles, and in response to the symbolic laying on of their hands, the Spirit came upon new converts (8:14 ff.) who had already been regenerated by the same Spirit. When joined with prayer the laying on of the apostles' hands not only conferred gifts upon the baptized (19:5 f.), but also effected consecration to an office (6:1-6). Alas, reality tends to become symbol when an organism becomes an organization. The Spirit also guided the church (10:19, 44). (b) The Spirit's ministry among non-Christians is best illustrated in the church's missionary ventures. What the Spirit can do with an obedient fearless witnessing church is clear from 11:19 ff. Soon a strong church was formed in Antioch, and through it the Spirit was able to implement plans for evangelizing the Greek and Roman worlds (13:1 ff.). Wherever the missionaries went the Spirit worked through them (13:52), guiding them continually (16:6 f.), communicating himself through them (19:1 ff.), and appointing leaders for the young churches (20:28). Pentecost had been no hallucination. The wind and fire truly proclaimed God's presence in the church; the distribution of tongues proclaimed that his Spirit was with individual Christians and the whole church. The Spirit's gifts and powers (see SPIRITUAL GIFTS) which were new in human experience were now manifesting themselves in the witnessing church in terms of fellowship, worship, obedience, joy, and unity (2:42-47).

V. PAUL'S EPISTLES. So rich is Paul's teaching on the Spirit that selectivity becomes imperative. Only an outline can be offered here. (1) For Paul, one cannot be a Christian without receiving the Spirit (Gal. 3:2). To have Christ's Spirit is to belong to Christ (Rom. 8:9). The Christian life is life in the Holy Ghost (Gal. 5:16), and its characteristics are the result of the Spirit's activity within the Christian (Gal. 5:22). What the law had never been able to do the Spirit now accomplishes from within (Rom. 8:1-4). Indeed, for the Spirit-born Christian the long reign of law is over (7:6). (2) The Holy Spirit is "the Spirit of Christ" (8:9; cf. II Cor. 3:17; I Cor.

6:17; Gal. 4:6; Rom. 8:14 ff.). That is why no man can claim to speak in the Spirit and speak against Christ simultaneously (I Cor. 12:3). To say that the Holy Spirit is the Spirit of Christ does not imply identification of the Son with the Spirit, however, but it does point to the unity of purpose of both. (3) The deity and personality of the Spirit are also prominent in Paul's teaching. The Spirit is the Spirit of God (Rom. 8:9; and cf. I Cor. 3:16 with II Cor. 6:16), and he is one of the persons in the Godhead (II Cor. 13:14; cf. Matt. 28:19). And the personal nature of the Spirit's activity is as prominent in Paul's Epistles as in Acts. Cf., e.g., the Spirit's prerogative in bestowing his gifts (I Cor. 12:4-10) "as he will" (vs. 11), the manner in which he reveals the Father's will (I Cor. 2:10-12), teaches the Christian (vs. 13), and blesses the Christian's witness (vs. 4; I Thess. 1:5). (4) The nature of the Spirit is also emphasized in his relations with believers. The Holy Spirit engages the Christian to war against "the flesh," the sinful nature, that which enables sin to gain a foothold within the Christian. It is the Spirit who enables the believer to do to death the flesh. Failure to do so may "grieve" the Spirit (Eph. 4:30). To "mortify the deeds of the body" through the Spirit (Rom. 8:13) brings the tyrannical reign of sin to an end (6:12-14), and reproduces in the Christian the effects of Christ's death and resurrection (cf. 6:9 f. with 6:1-8, 11; Phil. 3:10 f.). Then it is that "the harvest of the Spirit" (Gal. 5:22) begins to appear, and the Spirit's guidance and witness become clear (Rom. 8:14-17). A moral transformation is effected (II Cor. 3:18), and through the Spirit believers are set free to walk not "after the flesh but after the Spirit" (Rom. 8:5-8), and to become "servants of righteousness" (6:15 ff.). (5) A similar emphasis appears in Paul's Epistles in connection with the Spirit's activity within the community of believers. The Spirit energizes the body of Christ, the church, to such an extent that her worship (Phil. 3:3; I Cor. 14:15), fellowship (Eph. 4:3; Phil. 2:1), gifts (I•Cor. 12:4-11), and her very origin (I Cor. 12:13), are due to the animating presence of the Spirit through whom Christ abides in the church. (6) Paul also connects the Spirit and baptism. Baptism implies Christ's death, burial and resurrection, and parallels the believer's own death to sin, and resurrection to newness of life which the baptism of the Spirit involves (Rom. 6:1-4). The rite becomes efficacious because the Christian believingly participates in it. Concerning infant baptism confirmation is the "effective human act" through which the Spirit acts and speaks.

BIBLIOGRAPHY

H. B. Swete, *The Holy Spirit in the NT;* A. Kuyper, *The Work of the Holy Spirit;* H. Wh. Robinson, *The Christian Experience of the Holy Spirit;* G. Smeaton, *The Doctrine of the Holy Spirit.*

JAMES G. S. S. THOMSON

SPIRITS IN PRISON. The phrase occurs in I Pet. 3:19, and has provoked considerable discussion. Some have held that the reference is to people of Noah's time who heard preaching by the Spirit through his lips but rejected it and now, at the time Peter is writing, are disembodied spirits imprisoned and awaiting final judgment. Against this is the movement of thought, which seems to place the preaching after the death and quickening of Christ and prior to his resurrection. Further, the word spirit is rarely used of the dead, especially in the absolute form of statement.

Some see in the passage a preaching by Christ to the dead between his death and resurrection, whether simply to announce his victory to OT saints or to give further opportunity for people who died unrepentant. It is highly improbable that a doctrine so important as "the larger hope" would be set forth in such enigmatical language, especially when it is tacitly contradicted by statements of Scripture (e.g., Heb. 9:27).

There is much to commend the view that the spirits are the angels who sinned in the time of Noah (Gen. 6:1-5). Not only are good angels called spirits (Heb. 1:14), but demons also (Luke 10:20). Whereas the word prison is hardly a natural term to apply to the state of the human dead, it is appropriate to evil spirits (II Pet. 2:4; Jude 6). To these Christ proclaimed his triumph. The context appears to support this (I Pet. 3:22).

BIBLIOGRAPHY

E. G. Selwyn, *The First Epistle of Peter,* pp. 196-208; 314-62; Bo Reicke, *The Disobedient Spirits and Christian Baptism,* pp. 52-92.

EVERETT F. HARRISON

SPIRITUAL GIFTS. The term *charismata* ("spiritual gifts"), except for I Pet. 4:10, is used only by Paul. *Charisma* (sing.) signifies redemption or salvation as the gift of God's grace (Rom. 5:15; 6:23); a gift enabling the Christian to perform his service in the church (I Cor. 7:7); a special gift enabling a Christian to perform a particular ministry in the church (e.g., 12:28 ff.). The latter use is the subject of this article.

Paul offers instruction on spiritual gifts in Rom. 12:6-8; I Cor. 12:4-11, 28-30; Eph. 4:7-12. Spiritual gifts were unusual manifestations of God's grace (*charis*) under normal and abnormal forms. Not every spiritual gift affected the moral life of him who exercised it, but its purpose was always the edification of believers. The exercise of a spiritual gift implied service in the church. This practical approach is never lost sight of in the NT. The NT spiritual gifts are often divided into miraculous and non-miraculous; but since some are synonymous with specific duties they should be classified according to their significance for preaching the word on the one hand, and exercising practical ministries on the other.

The latter class includes five gifts. (1) "Working of miracles" (I Cor. 12:10, 28-29). "Miracles" is the rendering of *dynameis* (powers). In Acts *dynameis* refers to the casting out of evil spirits and the healing of bodily ailments (8:6 f., 13; 19:11 f.). This may explain "working of powers," but this gift is not synonymous with "gifts of healing." Probably the former was much more spectacular than the latter, and may have signified raising the dead (Acts 9:36 ff.; 20:9 ff.). Paul himself exercised this gift of "working of powers," and was for him proof of his apostleship (II Cor. 12:12), and authenticated both the good news he preached and his right to proclaim it (Rom. 15:18 ff.).

(2) "Gifts of healing" (I Cor. 12:9, 28, 30), as already suggested, resembled "working of miracles" (powers). Witness the ministry of our Lord (Matt. 4:23 f.), of the Twelve (Matt. 10:1), and of the Seventy (Luke 10:8 f.). "Gifts of healing" were also prominent in the church after Pentecost (Acts 5:15 f.; cf. also James 5:14 f.). "Gifts" (plural) indicates the great variety both of the sicknesses healed and the means used in the healings. The person who exercised the gift, and the patient who was healed, had one essential in common — faith in God. The writings of the Church Fathers prove that "the gifts of healings" were exercised in the church centuries after the apostolic period. Since then, this gift has appeared intermittently in the church. For long "gifts of healing" have been in abeyance, but today there are recognized

branches of the church which believe that they are beginning to reappear. Unfortunately the manner in which some act who claim to have received the gift has brought it into disrepute. The kind of ailments that were healed in the NT period, the nature and place of faith, the significance of suffering in God's economy, the importance of the sub-conscious and the nature of its influence upon the body, the relations between "gifts of healings" and medical science (a doctor was numbered among Paul's traveling companions!), have not received the attention they require today. "Gifts of healings" is a permanent gift of the Spirit to the church but it is properly exercised only by men of the Spirit, and of humility and faith.

(3) The gift of "helps" (I Cor. 12:28). What this spiritual gift signified may be gathered from Acts 20:35, where Paul exhorts the Ephesian elders to labor "to help the weak," and constantly to remember the Lord's own words, "It is more blessed to give than to receive." Paul supports this exhortation from his own example. The early church seems to have had a special concern for the needy among her members, and those who helped the indigent were considered to have been endowed by the Spirit for this ministry. It is not impossible that the office of elder originated in the gift of government or rule: by the same token the office or duty of deacon may have originated in this gift of "helps." The deacon was one who ministered to the needy (Acts 6:1).

(4) The gift of "governments" (I Cor. 12:28), or of "rule" (Rom. 12:8). The church's organization was still fluid. Official offices had not been established, nor were duly appointed officials yet ruling the churches. It was necessary, therefore, that certain members should receive and exercise the gift of ruling or governing the local assembly of believers. This gift would take the form of sound advice and wise judgment in directing church affairs. Gradually, of course, this gift of guiding and ruling in church affairs would come to be identified so closely with certain individuals that they would begin to assume responsibilities of a quasi-permanent nature. They would become recognized officials in the church, fulfilling well defined duties in the administration of the Christian community. At the beginning, however, it was acknowledged that some Christians had received the gift of ruling, and

had liberty to exercise it. In addition to administration, practical matters in the conduct of public worship would require wisdom and foresight, and here again those who had recognizably received the gift of ruling would be expected to legislate.

(5) Probably "the gift of faith" (I Cor. 12:9) should also be included among the gifts which were closely related to the practical life and development of the church. These spiritual gifts would naturally strengthen the believers in their faith, and convince the unbelievers of the authenticity of the church's message. The Spirit's gift of faith could effect mighty things (Matt. 17:19 f.)., and keep believers steadfast in persecution. These five spiritual gifts, then, had special reference to the practical aspects of the church's life, the physical well-being of believers, and orderliness of their worship and conduct.

The remainder of the gifts of the Spirit concern the ministry of the word of God. To that extent they were more important than the foregoing; but the latter were, nevertheless, spiritual gifts. In origin and nature they were the result of special endowments of the Spirit.

(6) Concerning the gifts which were especially meaningful for the preaching of the word, Paul gives pride of place to the grace of apostleship: "God hath set some in the church, first apostles" (I Cor. 12:28). The designation "apostle" (*q.v.*) began to be applied to NT personalities other than the Twelve, especially to Paul. So highly did he value the gift of apostleship which the Holy Spirit had conferred upon him that on occasion he was at pains to prove its validity (cf. Gal. 1:12; I Cor. 9:1 ff.). The apostles conceived that they had received this spiritual gift to enable them to fulfil the ministry of the word of God; nothing, therefore, should be allowed to prevent their fulfilling that all-important function (Acts 6:2). We also gather from Paul that the gift of apostleship was to be exercised principally among unbelievers (I Cor. 1:17), while other spiritual gifts were more closely related to the needs of believers. Paul's apostleship was to be fulfilled among Gentiles; Peter's ministry of the word was to be exercised among Jews (Gal. 2:7 f.). Obviously the Spirit's gift of apostleship was not confined to a strictly limited group of men whose gift of apostleship made them *ipso facto* special units of a divine grace or authority. Their function was doubtless conceived to be

the most important so far as the ministry of the word was concerned, but we shall see presently that theirs was only one of a number of such spiritual gifts. The church was built upon prophets as well as apostles (Eph. 2:20), the first ministering in the word to the church, the latter preaching the word to non-Christians. Since, then, the gift of apostleship was spiritual, so also was the authority of the apostles. It remained the prerogative of the Holy Spirit and never became official in the sense that one could communicate it to others of his own volition. The authority exercised by the apostles was exercised democratically, not autocratically (Acts 15:6, 22). They were careful to include "the elders" and "brethren" when substantiating the validity of the directives they were issuing to the church. Even when Paul was asked to legislate for the churches he had founded his authority was not his apostleship but a word from the Lord (I Cor. 7:10).

(7) "Prophets" stand next in importance to "apostles" in Paul's enumeration of the spiritual gifts (I Cor. 12:2 ff.). The gift of prophecy has already been differentiated from the grace of apostleship on the ground of the sphere in which each was exercised. In a sense Moses' desire (Num. 11:29) had been realized in the experience of the church *as a whole* (Acts 2:17 f.; 19:6; I Cor. 11:4 f.), but some individuals seem to have been specially endowed with this grace (Acts 11:28; 15:32; 21:9 f.). These prophets in the NT church seem often to have been itinerant preachers. Moving from church to church they built up believers in the faith by teaching the word. Their ministry would probably be characterized by spontaneity and power, since it seems to have included speaking by revelation (I Cor. 14:6, 26, 30 f.). In these passages, however, the prophet's utterances were clearly understood compared with the utterances in tongues. On occasion God would make his will known through the prophet (Acts 13:1 ff.), or a future event would be foretold (Acts 11:28; 21:10 f.); but the prophet's special gift was the edification, exhortation, consolation and instruction of the local churches (I Cor. 14). In the sub-apostolic period the prophet could still take precedence over the local minister, but the day was not far off when this gift of prophecy passed to the local ministers who preached the word to edify the members of the Christian fellowship.

(8) The nature of this gift of prophecy was such that the danger of false prophets must always have been present. The Spirit, therefore, communicated a gift which enabled some among those who listened to the prophets to recognize the truth or falsity of their utterances. This was not natural insight or shrewd judgment but a supernatural gift. Paul describes this spiritual gift as a "discerning of the spirits." The fact that the prophet spoke by revelation made the appearance of false prophets almost inevitable; while, therefore, Paul urged his converts not to despise prophesyings they were, nevertheless, to prove all things (I Thess. 5:20 f.). The gift of discernment of spirits was an essential. Only then could believers discriminate between the false and the true, when an itinerant prophet claimed to be inspired to speak by revelation (I Cor. 14:29).

(9) Clearly related to, but carefully distinguished from the gift of prophecy is the gift of teaching (I Cor. 12:28 f.; Rom. 12:7). The prophet was a preacher of the word; the teacher explained what the prophet proclaimed, reduced it to statements of doctrine, and applied it to the situation in which the church lived and witnessed. The teacher would offer systematic instruction (II Tim. 2:2) to the local churches.

(10) Next comes the gift of exhortation (Rom. 12:8). The possessor of this gift would fulfil a ministry closely allied with that of the Christian prophet and teacher. The difference between them would be found in the more personal approach of the former. If his exhortations were to succeed they would have to be given in the persuasive power of love, understanding and sympathy. His aim would be to win Christians to a higher way of life and to a deeper self-dedication to Christ. The Spirit, therefore, who bestowed the gift of exhortation (*q.v.*) would with the gift communicate spiritual persuasiveness and winsomeness.

(11) The gift of speaking the word of wisdom (I Cor. 12:8) was also an important part of the Spirit's endowment so far as the Christian community was concerned. This gift would communicate ability to receive and explain "the deep things of God" (Rom. 11:33). In God's dealings with men much is mysterious, and the ordinary Christian is often in need of a word that will throw light upon his situation; and the person fitted by the Spirit

to fulfil this ministry is "through the Spirit" given "the word of wisdom." Because of the strong sense of revelation or insight implied in the phrase perhaps this gift was akin to a revelational utterance by the Christian prophet.

(12) The gift of speaking "the word of knowledge" (I Cor. 12:8) suggests, on the other hand, a word spoken only after long and careful consideration. This would be a word that the Christian teacher would ordinarily speak. Of course, this mental activity would not be entirely unaided; a point being reached when the Spirit would give knowledge, understanding, insight, that might be described as intuition. But since Paul points out that both "the word of wisdom" and "the word of knowledge" are given "through" or "according to" the Spirit, the emphasis is on the reception of the word, not on its interpretation.

(13) Yet another spiritual gift is mentioned by Paul. The Spirit gives "kinds of tongues" (I Cor. 12:10, 28). The nature of this gift is explained in I Cor. 14. (a) The tongue in which the person spoke was unintelligible, and therefore unedifying to the Christian assembly (vss. 2-4); (b) The tongue (*glōssa*) was not a foreign language (*phōnē*, vss. 10-12); (c) The tongue-speaker addressed himself to God to whom he probably offered prayer and praise (vss. 14-17); (d) The tongue edified the speaker (vs. 4); (e) The tongue-speaker lost the control of intellectual faculties (vss. 14-15), the tongue being probably a disjointed, highly pitched, ecstatic series of ejaculations, similar to the tongues spoken in times of spiritual awakening experienced intermittently by the church.

(14) Obviously, then, the gift of "interpretation of tongues" (I Cor. 12:10, 30) was a necessary corollary to speaking in tongues, as was the "discerning of spirits" to the prophet's speaking by revelation. The tongue-speaker might also exercise the gift of interpreting tongues (I Cor. 14:13), but usually others exercised it (vss. 26-28; 12:10); though Paul's advice in I Cor. 14:13 is interesting. This would imply giving meaning to unmeaningful ecstatic ejaculations as an art critic interprets a play, a symphony, or a canvas to the uninitiated; though the tongue-interpreter did not depend on natural knowledge (14:13).

In instructing Christians on the exercise of these gifts Paul is concerned to stress their practical nature. The Spirit bestows his *charismata* for the edification of the church, the formation of Christian character, and the service of the community. The reception of a spiritual gift, therefore, brought serious responsibility, since it was essentially an opportunity for self-giving in sacrificial service for others.

The more spectacular gifts (tongues, healings, miracles) necessitated some degree of order that would prevent their indiscriminate use (I Cor. 14:40). The spirits of the prophets must be subjected to the prophets (vs. 32). Paul clearly insists that spectacular gifts were inferior to those that instructed believers in faith and morals, and evangelized non-Christians. Tongue-speaking was not forbidden (vs. 39), but intelligent exposition of the word, instruction in faith and morals, preaching the gospel, were infinitely superior. The criteria used to judge the relative values of spiritual gifts were doctrinal (I Cor. 12:3), moral (I Cor. 13), and practical (I Cor. 14).

The problem was where to strike the balance. The greatest peril lay in over-emphasizing the gifts which tended to exalt the offices which grew out of them. That led inevitably to institutional ecclesiasticism, and the inevitable corresponding loss of the church's awareness of the Spirit's presence and experience of the Spirit's power.

BIBLIOGRAPHY

T. C. Edwards, *Commentary on I Corinthians;* Robertson and Plummer, *I Corinthians* (ICC); and bibliography for HOLY SPIRIT.

JAMES G. S. S. THOMSON

SPIRITUALISM, SPIRITISM. The doctrine of a religious sect which seeks consolation and spiritual guidance from dead persons, contacted through mediums. The Spiritualist Church denies the fall, the atonement and the resurrection; men earn promotion to higher spheres by good works but "sin is not in itself any offense against the Creator" (Stainton Moses). Christian Spiritualists hold that biblical prophets were mediums, Jesus the greatest. But (1) mediums are controlled by spirits; biblical prophets were in control of their gifts (I Cor. 14:32); (2) all early disciples had spiritual gifts, yet mediums are rare. At best Spiritualism offers no evidence of immortality, though it might be possible to draw the conclusion that there is a temporary continuance after death followed by a slow disintegration of personality.

Most "messages" from spirits arise, probably, from the depths of the unconscious: extra-sensory powers of the mind seem also to be involved. Sometimes the presence of the dead *seems* convincing but the evidence is valueless; all Spiritualists admit widespread impersonation and heartless fraud (e.g., Lord Dowding, *Lychgate*, Rider, London, 1945). The medium Mrs. Blanche Cooler communicated with Gordon Davies, supposedly killed in battle. His voice was imitated, unusual features of a house were described, the future was foreseen, statements, unknown to sitters, were verified. But it transpired that Davies was alive and had no interest in Spiritualism (Soc. Psychical Res., *Proc.*, 1925, 35, 560). The danger of impersonation, even in prophets, is recognized in the NT and a test prescribed (I Tim. 4:1). All Spiritualist writers consulted misunderstand the test, ignore it, or advance reasons for not applying it.

Spiritualism (as *necromancy* or *witchcraft*) is uniformly condemned in the Bible. Saul's crowning sin was the consultation of a witch (I Sam. 28); only those who desert God need solace from the dead (Isa. 8:19); necromancy is a lust of the flesh (Gal. 5:20) and is deserving of hell (Rev. 22:15).

ROBERT E. D. CLARK

SPRINKLE, SPRINKLING. The idea of sprinkling is conveyed in the OT by the verbs *zāraq* ("to hurl in a body" as dust in handfuls, Job 2:12 or blood from a bowl, Ex. 24:8), and *nāzâ* ("sprinkle with the finger" Lev. 4:17), and in the NT by *rhantizō* (once *proschysis*). The blood in sacrifice was carefully collected when the animal was slain and was poured or dashed against the base of the altar (Lev. 1:5; 3:2, etc.). On other occasions it was sprinkled with the finger, e.g., on Aaron's garments (Ex. 29:21); before the veil (Lev. 4:6); on the man being cleansed from his leprosy (Lev. 14:7). Sometimes sprinkling with water is mentioned, as in the cleansing of the Levites (Num. 8:7), or the use of "the water for impurity" (Num. 19:13, 20). Oil is sprinkled "before Jehovah" in the purifying of the leper (Lev. 14:16). From such rites the idea of sprinkling came to be used metaphorically in the sense of "cleansing," as in Ezek. 36:25, "I will sprinkle clean water upon you, and ye shall be clean." In the NT there are references to the sprinkling in the sacrifices. In I Pet. 1:2 the "sprinkling of the blood of Jesus Christ" is at once a reminder

that Christ's death was a sacrifice, and that it cleanses men from sin.

LEON MORRIS

STATE. Modern interest in democratic forms of government, the rise of new totalitarian powers, and recent infatuation with programs for world government are provoking new inquiries into the biblical view of the state.

At man's creation, government was spiritual; Eden was ruled by God's commands. Biblical theology recognizes the state as a divine order of preservation whereby the outward organization of fallen life is maintained. The state is an authority divinely ordained (Rom. 13:1) to promote justice and to preclude fallen man's decline to social chaos. Civil government is therefore not autonomous nor devoid of divine responsibility; all powers are accountable to God revealed in Christ (John 19:20 f.; Matt. 28:18; Col. 1:16). The state is to approve what is good, to rebuke and punish what is evil.

The Middle Ages based the state on the church, thereby giving perverse and sinful empires a divine status. The Reformation, attempting a broad return to the NT, insisted that church and state are distinct spheres. But its doctrine of the state church halted short of separation of church and state championed by founding fathers of the United States. Twentieth century Fascism, Nazism and Communism, extending the Renaissance doctrine of the autonomy of the state, divorced the state entirely from divine responsibility.

While the Bible affirms that the state is a power divinely established because of sin to promote external justice by outer constraints, it recognizes also that the state, vulnerable to sin, may itself gravitate to the borderline of the demonic. The state moves between the poles of the God-state (Rom. 13) and the Beast-state (Rev. 13). Christ's promised judgment of the nations is a reminder that the difference between states, however great, is nonetheless relative; all governments are prone to ordain sinful laws and to interfere with legitimate freedoms.

Scripture affirms that both the state and its citizens are under God. Both have rights and duties which are not to be thwarted. The believer is to be subject to the state not merely by way of resignation, but is bound by conscience to support it (Rom. 13:5 ff.). But the doctrine of the omnipotent state is excluded; the state must not frustrate the obedience man owes to God. The OT prohibited kings from seizing the private property of the people (I Kings 21). The apostles resisted rulers who sought to impede the proclamation of the gospel (Acts 4:19; 5:29).

Oscar Cullmann's attempt to justify the existence and authority of the state exclusively on the ground of its participation in Christ's redemptive triumph over demonic powers seems unconvincing. On Cullmann's view the state has its legitimate foundation and power only in christological redemptive history and not as a divine order of preservation. This theory seems to allow to the state only an unspiritual role previous to Christ's resurrection. Jesus' admonition to "render unto Caesar" (Luke 20:25), however, was not predicated on an assumption that such obligation is mandatory only on the basis of the state's participation in his redemptive triumph. Can it really be thought that Jesus submitted to Pilate because the latter's political power was conformed to divine righteousness with a view to Christ's triumph? Assuredly a christological foundation must be found for the state in the sense that the Logos is the agent in creation and preservation. But this fact does not require a justification of the state only in terms of Christ's redemptive conquest. Significantly, Paul's classic passage on civil obedience was addressed to believers at the heart of the pagan world empire of his day.

BIBLIOGRAPHY

Karl Barth, *Against the Stream*; Oscar Cullmann, *Christ and Time*; *The State in the New Testament*; Jean Hering, *A Good and a Bad Government*; Adolf Keller, *Church and State on the European Continent*.

CARL F. H. HENRY

STATUTE. The word applies to that which is enacted or established and ordained, e.g., statute law. It occurs only in the OT where it usually represents two words derived from a root meaning "to cut in, inscribe or enact." It is used most frequently in Deut. (29 times) and in Ps. 119 (22 times). It is frequently used in connection with other words: "commandments . . . statutes . . . laws" (Gen. 26:5); "statute . . . ordinance" (Ex. 15:25); "statutes . . . judgments" (Deut. 5:1); "commandments . . . testimonies . . . statutes" (I Chron. 29:19). The permanence of the statute is sometimes emphasized as "a statute forever" (Ex. 30:21), "a perpetual statute" (Lev.

24:9). It may concern all the people (Deut. 4:1) or only a special group such as the priests (Lev. 6:18; 7:36).

OSWALD T. ALLIS

STEWARDSHIP. Stewardship (*oikonomia*) is a compound word in the Greek, meaning the management of a household. The person who administers the household is called a steward (*oikonomos*, "law of the house") or an overseer (*epitropos*). The idea has its roots in the institution of slavery. The master appointed a slave to administer his household which might include the teaching and disciplining of the members of the house, especially other slaves and the children. A classic example is the position of Joseph in Potiphar's house (Gen. 39:4-6). The ordinary idea of stewardship is found in several passages in the NT, notably the story of the unjust steward (Luke 16:1-8; cf. Matt. 20:8; Luke 12:42). The guardian of a minor child could also be called a steward (*oikonomos*) (Gal. 4:3). This is a most common use in the papyri (MM). A public official could be called a steward (*oikonomos*) (Rom. 16:23) or an overseer (*epitropos*) (Luke 8:3).

The idea that man is a steward of God in his relation to the world and his own life is inherent in the creation story (Gen. 1-3) in which he is appointed lord of all things except himself. In the NT, the word, when not used in its ordinary sense, refers to the administration of the gifts of God, especially preaching the gospel. By metonymy, stewardship may refer to God's provision for the Christian age (Eph. 1:10; 3:9), the context implying that this plan includes the entrustment of the gospel message to men. This idea is explicit in I Cor. 9:17; Eph. 3:2; Col. 1:25; I Cor. 4:1-2; Titus 1:7. Stewardship is broadened to include all Christians and all the gracious gifts of God in I Pet. 4:10. An unusual use of the word is found in I Tim. 1:4, where it seems to refer to the discipline and training of the Christian in the realm of faith. The requirement of stewards of God, as well as of stewards of men, is faithfulness, i.e., administration of trust according to directions (I Cor. 4:2).

The modern emphasis on the stewardship of possessions, while true, may tend to obscure the fact that the Christian's primary stewardship is that of the gospel and includes the use of his whole life as well as his money.

FRED L. FISHER

STIGMATA. Stigmata, as a phenomenon of mysticism, are reputed to be the reproduction in the body of the wounds of Christ's passion. They occur with varying intensity from actual wounds which bleed to faint red marks beneath the skin. The first well known case is that of St. Francis of Assisi in 1226. It is claimed that many witnesses saw the wounds both before and after his death, and that the likeness of nails, formed of his flesh, protruded from them. Pope Benedict XII instituted a feast (Sept. 17) in honor of the stigmata. Since the time of Francis there have been many examples of the phenomenon. Sometimes the appearance has lasted through many years to the end of life. Sometimes it has occurred periodically on definite days of the week or year. The subjects, who have not all belonged to the Roman Catholic Church, have with two exceptions been women and have usually had a previous history of nervous disorders. Father Thurston (*The Physical Phenomena of Mysticism*, London, 1951) suggests that the signs, which vary according to the suggestibility of the subject, are the result of a pathological condition, and need not have any supernatural character. This does not imply fraud nor cast doubt upon the religious uprightness of the subjects.

RICHARD J. COATES

STOICS. The word is derived from *stoa*, meaning colonnade or colonnaded porch, from which the Stoic philosophers taught in ancient Athens. Stoicism was founded by Zeno, around 308 B.C. and was first systematized into a total world view by Chrysippus (d. 209 B.C.). In its later development Stoicism stressed the practical side of ethical problems and became widely popularized. In Roman times the most famous of its leaders were Seneca (b. 4 B.C., d. A.D. 65 — an almost exact contemporary of Paul), Epictetus (d. A.D. 110) and Emperor Marcus Aurelius.

In pantheistic fashion the Stoics held God, man, animals, plants, and inanimate objects to be "fragments of the divine force." A world-reason or "logos" pervades this universal being, in which all that happens works itself out according to internal necessity. It is futile, therefore, to resist the inevitable. By "right reason" the wise man can discover his proper place in the universe and make such adjustments as are necessary in submitting to this all-determining world order. Passions hinder such resignation and, therefore, are to be suppressed.

Many parallels to Stoic thought have been observed in the Apocrypha (Sirach, IV Maccabees, Wisdom of Solomon, etc.), the Wisdom literature of the OT, the Gospels, and especially Paul and Hebrews. Such parallels do not prove direct borrowing but may indicate only a common habit of thinking and expression held by many individuals.

Major doctrinal likenesses suggested between Paul and the Stoics are the Logos as a principle of reason pervading all, a universal gospel, submission or faith as the criterion for right religious adjustment, and the divine predestination of all things.

The differences between Stoicism and the NT are, however, far more significant than the likenesses. Stoicism is pantheistic, whereas the whole of the NT is based on the essential otherness of God and man. Stoic fatalism, in which not even God is free, is opposed in Paul by the doctrine of divine providence and the sovereign care of a loving Father. The Stoics were optimistic about man's capacity in and of himself to attain the good life; basic to Paul's thought was his radical view of man's sin and ultimate helplessness with a corresponding emphasis upon divine grace. The Stoic lack of a clear-cut future life is replaced in Paul and in the NT by a vivid hope of a life to come lived in fellowship of love with the Father and Jesus Christ. In ethics, the passionless existence of the ideal Stoic aimed to crush down all emotional reaction. For Paul and the whole of the NT, however, God created the whole man. The whole man as man is good, including his emotional nature. Emotions and passions, therefore, are not to be annihilated, but are to be brought into proper focus.

The only direct NT reference to Stoics occurs in Acts 17:18, which notes that on Mars Hill Paul addressed himself to Epicureans and Stoic philosophers, some of whom (the Epicureans?) mocked him, and others (the Stoic?) did not. Heb. 4:12 likewise recalls a hymn of Cleanthes and the wording of Heb. 2:10 is similar to that prevalent in Stoic writings. An unsubstantiated tradition in the Christian church states that the Stoic philosopher, Seneca, under the teaching of the apostle Paul, became a Christian.

BIBLIOGRAPHY
F. Jackson and K. Lake, *Beginnings of Christianity*,

I, pp. 239-48; E. V. Arnold, *HERE*, XI, pp. 860-64;
J. B. Lightfoot, "St. Paul and Seneca," *Philippians*,
pp. 270-331.

KENNETH S. KANTZER

STONE. See ROCK.

STRANGER. The Hebrew word *gēr* (synonym of *tôšaḇ*) designated a non-Israelite who
placed himself under Israel's protection and
who thereby had certain rights, privileges and
responsibilities denied to the *zār* ("foreigner")
and *nēkār* ("alien").

Gēr is applied to Israel in Egypt (Gen.
15:13; Ex. 22:21), to Abraham in Canaan
(Gen. 23:4), to Moses in Midian (Ex. 2:22),
to Israel as a chosen people (Lev. 25:23; I
Chron. 29:15), to David (Pss. 39:12;
119:19) and to Jehovah (Jer. 14:8).

The *gēr* is classified with the widows, fa-
therless and needy (Deut. 14:29; Ps. 146:9;
Ezek. 22:29). He shared in covenant obligations (Deut. 29:11 f.; 31:12 f.; Josh. 8:33,
35). He could eat the Passover if circumcised
(Ex. 12:48). He participated equally with
native Israelites in rites and ceremonies (Num.
15:14 f.; Deut. 26:11; Josh. 20:9; II Chron.
30:25; Ezek. 14:7; 47:22 f.). He must share
punishment for disobedience to divine legislation (Lev. 17:8-16; 18:26 ff.).

The *gēr* should be loved (Lev. 19:34) and
helped (Lev. 25:35). He must not be oppressed (Ex. 22:21; 23:9). Provision was
made for his physical needs (Deut. 24:19 ff.).

This class of people came largely from three
sources: (1) the "mixed multitude" (Ex.
12:38); (2) the unexterminated Canaanites
(Josh. 9:3-27); (3) captives in war (Num.
31:12). In Solomon's time their number was
153,600 (II Chron. 2:17).

In the NT gentile believers, once "alienated
from the commonwealth of Israel, and strangers from the covenants of the promise," are
now "fellow-citizens with the saints, and of
the household of God" (Eph. 2:12, 19, ASV).
While in this world, believers are sojourners
(I Pet. 1:1, 17; 2:10 f.). Their real citizenship is in heaven (Phil. 3:20; Heb. 11:13-16;
13:14).

BIBLIOGRAPHY

W. H. Bennett in *EB*; H. M. Wiener in *ISBE*;
James Donald in *HDAC*.

WICK BROOMALL

STUMBLING BLOCK. Greek words so
translated in the NT are: *proskomma* and
skandalon. *Skandalon* is properly the piece of

wood that trips a trap. Used metaphorically,
it carries the idea of deliberate enticement to
sin. This meaning is clear in several passages
(Matt. 18:7 = Luke 17:1; Rom. 16:17; Rev.
2:14). In other passages, it becomes a synonym for *proskomma*, literally an obstacle on
a rough road. In such cases, the idea of intent
to harm is absent (cf. Matt. 16:23, Peter said
to be a hindrance to Christ).

A common use of both words is to indicate
the antagonism of the Jews to Jesus (Rom.
9:32-33 = I Pet. 2:8). Jesus' cross is identified as the particular cause of stumbling in
I Cor. 1:23 and Gal. 5:11. The Jews' own
religion is said to be a trap and stumbling
block (Rom. 11:9).

Christians are warned against putting a
stumbling block in the way of others (Rom.
14:13, 20; I Cor. 8:9). Christian love guards
one against this sin (I John 2:10; II Cor.
6:3).

Those who entice to sin, warned (Matt.
18:7), are to be watched (Rom. 16:17) and
will be expelled from God's kingdom at the
judgment (Matt. 13:41).

FRED L. FISHER

SUBDEACON. See OFFICES, ECCLESIAS-
TICAL.

SUBSTANCE. The Hebrew words *hôn*,
"wealth"; *hayil*, "might"; *qinyān*, "possession";
and *rᵉkûš*, "property," are the principal terms
designating substance. Corresponding words in
Greek include *ousia*, "being"; *hyparxis*, "possession"; *hyparchonta*, "things that exist"; and
hypostasis, "substance."

With the exception of *hypostasis*, these
terms usually designate material possessions
(e.g., Gen. 15:14; Prov. 28:8; Luke 15:12 f.).

Because of its theological significance,
hypostasis warrants special attention. The ASV
renders it as "confidence" (II Cor. 9:4; 11:17;
Heb. 3:14), "substance" (Heb. 1:3) and
"assurance" (Heb. 11:1). Etymologically,
hypostasis, like the Latin *substantia* and the
English substance, denominates the "thing"
that lies under something, that is, the internal
and invisible substratum that gives form and
expression to the external and visible manifestation.

In Heb. 1:3 Christ is described as "the
very image of his [God's] substance" (ASV).
Here *hypostasis* is equivalent to "nature"
(RSV) rather than "person" (AV). Subsisting

in the "form" (*morphē*) of God, Christ became visible in his incarnation so that man might "see" God (John 1:14, 18; 14:9-11; Phil. 2:6). "God was in Christ" (II Cor. 5:19).

In Heb. 3:14 *hypostasis* probably expresses the substantiality of the Christian faith in contrast to the "shadows" of the old covenant (Heb. 8:5; 10:1).

In Heb. 11:1 faith is defined as *"hypostasis* of things hoped for."* Here the word represents the unseen reality that constitutes the essence of faith (I Cor. 2:9-16; II Cor. 4:18). Even in the present life the believer possesses by faith the substance (the essential equivalence) of that which will be fully revealed in his glorification (I Cor. 13:12; I John 3:1 f.).

See also HYPOSTASIS.

BIBLIOGRAPHY

Arndt; M. S. Fletcher in *HDAC*; James Lindsay in *HERE*; C. Hodge, *Systematic Theology*, I, pp. 376 ff., 605 f.; W. G. T. Shedd, *Dogmatic Theology*, I, pp. 151-70, 270 f.; R. E. Witt in "Amicitiae Corolla" (R. Harris *Festschrift*), pp. 319-43.

WICK BROOMALL

SUFFER, SUFFERING. The fact of suffering is conveyed by a number of words in the Hebrew language. Some of the most significant are the following: (a) *yāsar*, suggests a purpose in suffering, namely, that it serves "to discipline" (Hos. 10:10), "to instruct" (Ps. 2:10), and "to chasten" (Jer. 6:8); (b) *'ānâ* denotes "doing violence to another" (Gen. 15:13), "to humiliate" (Num. 24:24), and "to be afflicted" (Ps. 107:17); (c) *sārar* primarily means "to bind" or "to press hard" and then moves on to the meaning "to be in straits, to distress" (Jer. 10:18).

In the AV, "suffer" frequently appears with the meaning of "permit," "bear with," or "endure." It is the current meaning of the word, however, *viz.*, to undergo an unpleasant experience or affliction, which will be dealt with here.

The common verb meaning "to suffer" in the NT is *paschō*, which occurs forty-two times in the NT and *ca.* twenty times in the LXX including Apocrypha. Its basic meaning is to experience, but in Greek literature it has come to be used almost exclusively of unpleasant experiences and afflictions.

The problem of pain and suffering in all ages, has stood as a paramount challenge in the thinking of men. The challenge which the age-old problem presents is expressed in these words: "The dilemma of Epicurus is still with us: if God wishes to prevent evil but cannot, then he is impotent; if he could, but will not, he is malevolent; if he has both the power and the will, whence then is evil?" (*The Elements of Pain and Conflict in Human Life*, by W. R. Sorley and others, p. 48. *HERE* Vol. XII:1).

Some of the questions raised by the problem of suffering are: Is moral goodness being wrought out by means of suffering as is found in the whole of human life? If so, is there a remaining margin of suffering which bears no relation at all to character and cannot be related to the chief purpose of creation?

The philosophical answers to the problem have centered in hedonism, with resultant disappointment and pessimism; stoical defiance without victory over pain; meliorism proclaiming progress with suffering being eliminated and its ultimate banishment as a reasonable certainty; optimism proclaiming the highest good as moral good which can be attained by man only through a process of discipline which includes work, suffering, and temptation.

The philosophical solutions of suffering are no more than speculations, however attractive they may be.

Jesus presented no formula relative to the why and the origin of suffering. He presented a way of victory in the face of suffering. He lived in triumph in the midst of it. The secret of his triumph was his identification with the will of the Father in suffering. His submissive identification with the will of the Father enables him to handle the thorn of life in triumph rather than extract it. Jesus imparts his triumph in handling the thorn of life to those who identify themselves with him in submission to the will of the Father.

The problem of pain cannot be divorced from the wider and deeper problem of moral evil (*q.v.*). The fact of physical evil in the world, as appalling as it is, is incidental and secondary to the graver problem of sin (*q.v.*). If the breach with God can be healed, no other discord can remain finally unresolved. The final solution of a mystery of pain (*q.v.*) which reverberates along every rim of the universe, is reconciliation (*q.v.*) with God. The triumph of this reconciliation brings the realization: "All things work together for good to them that love God."

In the Christian message we find the unveiling of a suffering God. The cross is the

Christian apologetic, the sublime and majestic vision (Heb. 12:2).

In reconciliation men become identified with a suffering God, whereby there is a transmutation of their own sufferings (Rom. 8:15-17 RSV), from pessimism to optimism, from confusion and uncertainty to immortal hope for the banishment of suffering (Rev. 21:4).

BIBLIOGRAPHY

E. Stanley Jones, *Suffering, Punishment, and Atonement; an Essay in Constructive Interpretation of Experience;* C. S. Lewis, *The Problem of Pain;* E. F. Sutcliffe, *Providence and Suffering in the Old and New Testaments;* HERE, Vol. XII, pp. 1-9; I. J. Gerber, *The Psychology of the Suffering Mind.*

JULIAN C. McPHEETERS

SUFFRAGAN. See OFFICES, ECCLESIASTICAL.

SUICIDE. Widely varying and sharply conflicting attitudes have been entertained towards *felo de se* in different times and cultures (cf. *in loco HERE*). While there is no explicit prohibition of suicide in either the OT (cf. the cases of Ahithophel, Zimri, Samson, Saul, and Abimelech) or the NT (prohibitory implications have been drawn, however, from Rom. 14:7-9; I Cor. 6:19; Eph. 5:29), both Judaism and Christianity have strongly opposed the practice. The early Church Fathers allowed the taking of one's own life under very stringent circumstances, but Augustine denied its legitimacy no matter what the situation, arguing that it precludes the possibility of repentance and that, as a species of murder, it violates the sixth commandment. His position was adopted by Thomas Aquinas, who held that suicide is (1) "unnatural, being contrary to the charity which every man bears towards himself; (2) an offense against the community; (3) an usurpation of God's power to kill and make alive." Traditionally, therefore, Roman Catholic and Protestant theologians have agreed that God has "fixed his cannon 'gainst self-slaughter," though today greater stress is laid upon the mitigating factor of possible psychopathy.

Today, moreover, voluntary euthanasia, which is plainly a form of suicide, finds supporters among the Protestant clergy. The moral issues at stake are discussed by Willard L. Sperry, *The Ethical Basis of Medical Practice.* A vigorous defense of voluntary euthanasia is made by Joseph Fletcher, *Morals and Medicine.*

VERNON C. GROUNDS

SUNDAY. Sunday, the first day of the week, is observed as the Christian day of worship in remembrance of Christ's resurrection. Sunday worship became the custom early in the life of the church (Acts 20:7), although it was not the only day on which services were held at the very first (Acts 2:46). Since the Jewish day began with sundown, early Christian worship apparently began Saturday evening and continued throughout the night, climaxing in the observance of the Lord's Supper (Acts 20:7, 11). This practice may have been related to the early believers' desire to be worshiping when their Lord returned, on the basis of a warning recorded in Luke 12:35-40. Again, there may have been the practical necessity of meeting at a time when slave members could be present (cf. John Wordsworth, *The Ministry of Grace,* Longmans, Green and Co., London, 1903, pp. 312-18). The collection and the Eucharist regularly characterized these early services from the first (Acts 20:7; I Cor. 16:2).

Sunday was also called the Lord's Day or the eighth day in honor of the resurrection (Ignatius *Ad. Mag.* ix. 1; Barnabas 15:9; Justin *First Apol.*, ch. 67; Rev. 1:10). "Opposed to the claim that the Christians in celebrating Sunday had indirectly appropriated a day already observed in honor of a heathen deity, it is to be considered that in addition to the motive for observing that day assigned by Justin Martyr and Barnabas, the great aversion of the early Christians to idolatry would preclude the possibility of such appropriation" (Ralph E. Prime, "Sunday," *SHERK* XI, p. 145). Roman Catholics claim that they were responsible for changing the sabbath to Sunday; and Seventh-day Adventists, assuming that this claim is true, assert that all who worship on Sunday are followers of Rome and have thereby received the mark of the Beast. The apostolic church failed to name a particular day of rest among the necessary things of Acts 15:28-29, and clearly taught that the fact that worship was held on Sunday did not sanctify the day any more than any other day (Rom. 14:5-6). Alcuin (733?-804) was the first to claim that the Roman Church had transferred the rules for the sabbath to Sunday. The Reformers stoutly rejected this claim, Calvin even proposing to observe Thursday instead of Sunday. The strict sabbath laws of English Puritanism and Scottish Presbyterianism are to be explained as a reaction to the extreme laxity of the times.

See also LORD'S DAY.

CHARLES C. RYRIE

SUPEREROGATION. Works of supererogation, according to Roman Catholic moral theology, are voluntary works besides, over and above those which God commands. *Supererogare* means "to pay out more than is necessary." In ecclesiastical matters *supererogatio* means doing more than God requires. The term goes back to the Vulgate of Luke 10:35 (*quodcumque supererogaveris*), but was not used in its present technical sense until the Middle Ages. The conception is based upon a distinction between works which are necessary and those which are voluntary. In doing the latter (such as accepting vows of poverty, celibacy and obedience), we can do more than God requires. Such works of supererogation are meritorious and can avail for the benefit of others. Hence the so-called treasury of merit and the possibility of indulgences.

RICHARD J. COATES

SUPERNATURAL, SUPERNATURALISM. The supernatural (Latin *super natura*, "supernature") refers to the realm existing above and beyond the realm of sense experience; the belief that behind the world of ordinary, everyday experience is the world of the spiritual or divine. It is often that which transcends the powers of nature or what natural causes cannot produce.

In dealing with primitive religions the term is used to mean the realm of spirits, both good and evil, who animate both objects and persons (animism). Such spirits are believed to control both human activities and natural forces.

In philosophy the term refers to the realm or being which transcends the realm of nature. It is denoted by philosophers as Being, God, Spirit, etc. The distinction between natural and supernatural should not be confused with the distinction between natural and spiritual. Belief in man as spiritual as well as material does not necessarily require the affirmation of the supernatural.

In Christian theology the supernatural is the realm of the infinite, eternal Spirit, God. Traditionally Christian thought has emphasized strongly a reliance on revealed knowledge

rather than natural theology. God cannot be grasped by human reason alone, but he must reveal his nature and purpose to man in a special manner.

BIBLIOGRAPHY
J. Orr, *The Christian View of God and the World*; Carl F. H. Henry, *Notes on the Doctrine of God*; W. Hordern, *A Layman's Guide to Modern Theology*.

WARREN C. YOUNG

SUPERSTITION. From the Latin *super*, meaning "over," "above," and *stare*, meaning "to stand." A superstition is thus a belief, practice or attitude which is judged to "stand above" or go beyond an acceptable norm, and thus to be unworthy of acceptance. Commonly, a superstition lies in the area of religion (*q.v.*); it is a religious belief or practice which is thought to be irrational. But the term is sometimes used more broadly. Thus Spencer wrote of a *political* superstition, and in contemporary usage anything that is not *scientifically* acceptable is likely to be classified as superstition. Any such judgment involves an evaluation, depending on the prior acceptance of some truth as normative. The norm may be merely an unreflective prejudice or a carefully reasoned view. It may be science, or some special science, or a philosophical position, or a religion, such as Christianity as understood in some one theological tradition; or it may be a view within any one of these broader areas. For example, when L. T. More, a laboratory physicist, characterizes the picture of reality derived from relativity and the quantum physics as "a phantasmagoria instead of a world," he is really calling it a superstition, or when a liberal theologian confronts some of the beliefs of a conservative or a fundamentalist he is apt to call them superstitions.

In Acts 25:19 the Greek term *deisidaimonia* (from *deidō*, "to fear," and *daimōn*) is probably to be translated "superstition." Whether the comparative of that term in Acts 17:22 also bears that connotation may be doubted (compare the AV with more modern translations).

ANDREW KERR RULE

SUPRALAPSARIANISM. See PREDESTINATION.

SURE, SURETY. Faith is justified because the truth of Christianity is sure, guaranteed. It is the realization of the "sure" *(pistos)* mercies of David (Acts 13:34), God's promise to Abraham (Heb. 6:13-19) and the prophetic word (II Pet. 1:19). Hence, the gospel *(q.v.)* is not based on cunningly devised myths (II Pet. 1:16). Coming from God, the gospel is the climax of God's redemptive movement in history (cf. Heb. 2:2-3; Rom. 15:8; I Cor. 1:6).

Further assurance is based on the resurrection of Jesus (Acts 13:34), eyewitness testimony to his majesty (II Pet. 1:19) and the knowledge of God (II Tim. 2:19). Because faith is the way of salvation, God's promises are made sure *(bebaios)* to all men (Rom. 4:16). Thus, in Christ we have a "sure" *(asphalēs)* and "steadfast" *(bebaia)* anchor for our soul (Heb. 6:19). Faith is not a blind leap but an intelligent choice, the commitment of self to a guaranteed way of salvation.

The individual may make his calling and election "sure" *(bebaios)*, i.e., assure himself of the reality of his salvation, by supplementing his faith in Christ with the characteristics of Christlikeness (II Pet. 1:5-10).

"Surety" *(eggyos)* was commonly used in legal and business documents to indicate the guarantee of a contract (MM). In the OT, Judah made himself a surety for Benjamin (Gen. 43:9; 44:32). In the NT, *eggyos* is found only in Heb. 7:22. Jesus, as our eternal high priest, is surety that the new covenant will not be superseded as was the old. We can believe in the finality of Christianity *(q.v.)*; our belief is based on the solid reality of Christ's unchanging position as the mediator between God and man.

FRED L. FISHER

SWEAR. See OATH.

SWEDENBORGIANISM. Emanuel Swedenborg (1688-1772) had clairvoyant faculties. His main theological teachings were: (1) God is not three persons, but in Jesus Christ is the divine (Father), the divine human (Son), the divine power (Spirit); (2) Jesus Christ had a human state and a divine state; (3) by victories over temptations Christ overcame the hells, and so men can forsake evil; (4) only parts of the Bible are accepted (e.g., in NT the Gospels and Revelation), interpretation being by *correspondences*, a form of allegory; and (5) the Last Judgment on the Christian church was in

1757, after which Swedenborg's teachings were adopted by the New Church.

J. STAFFORD WRIGHT

SYMBOLISM, SYMBOLICS. The words *symbolism* and *symbolics* are derived from the Greek *symballein*, meaning to make a comparison. When two parties made a contract, it was customary to break an object. Each party kept a piece (a *symbolon*, or *symbol*) as proof of identity when one or the other presented his piece. In ecclesiastical usage the word easily adapted itself to denominate an identifying confession, whereby a person's confessional position could be ascertained. Thus the Apostles' Creed was called a symbol from the fourth century onward. The scientific study of the distinctive doctrinal characteristics of church bodies is called symbolics.

More generally the word is applied to a familiar object which serves as a mark of identification. Symbols, like the barber's striped pole and the pawnbroker's three gilt balls, form a significant element in every culture and help transcend language barriers. In religious circles symbols are employed to express significant theological truths. The earliest symbols employed in the Christian church dealt with our Lord. Most often he is represented as the Good Shepherd or as the Lamb of God. The names of our Lord also suggested symbols, such as the well-known *chirho* for *Christos* and IHC (not IHS), for *Iēsous*. The function of symbols is to communicate meaning, but they may also be used to conceal the truth. Thus the sign of the fish was used very early to communicate in the presence of hostile elements. Eventually a rebus was made of the Greek word for fish *(ichthys)*, forming the statement: Jesus Christ, Son of God, Saviour.

In the Middle Ages symbolism grew apace with scholastic love for allegory. One of the most articulate symbolists, Durandus, even found a spiritual significance in the cement used in the churches. Many *ex post facto* explanations were made. Thus the amice was used to protect the celebrant's costly raiments from touching the skin. This collar-like piece was then later regarded as a "helmet of salvation, to meet the assaults of the wicked one." In general, however, medieval art gave purposeful profound expression to spiritual truths, as a cathedral like that of Chartres testifies, and continues to inspire modern church art and architecture.

Since the symbol, to serve its purpose must be recognizable, bizarre inventions and clever originality in geometric design are to be avoided.

BIBLIOGRAPHY
F. R. Webber, *Church Symbolism*, 2nd rev. ed.; SHERK, IX, pp. 203-12; CE, XIV, pp. 373-77.

FREDERICK W. DANKER

SYMPATHY. The English term represents (Latin, *sympathia*) the Greek *sympatheia* from *syn* meaning "with" and *paschō* meaning "to suffer." Sympathy therefore is basically a suffering in unison, or specifically the suffering incurred by a person because of the suffering of another with whom he feels an affinity.

The word does not occur in the AV but is found twice in the RSV. The Greek *sympatheō* occurs twice: translated "sympathize with" (Heb. 4:15), "had compassion" (Heb. 10:34). The form *sympatheis* ("sympathetic") occurs in I Pet. 3:8.

While sympathy is the quality of being affected by another's affection, it was originally like pity and compassion, signifying fellow feeling with the sorrows of others, but now it is used to denote our fellow feeling with any passion whatever. Sympathy with sorrow or suffering is compassion, with joy or prosperity is congratulation.

The meaning of sympathy goes beyond the "feeling with" stage at times as two persons feeling alike do not make a true sympathetic couple unless the feeling of one has partly caused or is reinforcing the feeling of the other. Ferm calls it the emotional and imaginative experience of entering into and sharing the mind, particularly the thought and sentiment, of someone else. As a "feeling with" others it is experienced at non-reflective levels and makes for social solidarity. At higher levels it involves mental assimilation, communion, and personal insight. It is the main root of altruism.

BIBLIOGRAPHY
Andrew K. Rule in *TCERK*; *MSt* X, p. 70; S. Bryant in *HERE*, XII, p. 152; R. W. Frank in *ER*, p. 755.

LEWIS T. CORLETT

SYNAGOGUE. The term *synagōgē* designates a Jewish house of worship. Tradition suggests that the first synagogues were established during the Babylonian exile. In the disruption which followed the destruction of the Jerusalem temple (587 B.C.), local assemblages for prayer and the study of Scripture became the focal point of Jewish life. Such gatherings doubtless first took place in private homes (cf. Ezek. 8:1; 20:1-3).

Subsequent to the decree of Cyrus, exiles returned to Jerusalem and rebuilt their temple. The synagogue continued as an institution of Palestinian Judaism, however, and synagogues were built wherever groups of Jews settled.

The earliest synagogue worship included prayer and the reading and explanation of a portion of Scripture. By the time of the Mishna (2nd and 3rd centuries after Christ), a more elaborate pattern of service had developed. This included five parts. (1) The *šema'* consisted of the reading of Deut. 6:4-9; 11:13-21; Num. 15:37-41. (2) Prayer embraced "the eighteen (benedictions)." For the text of these, see E. Schuerer, *The Jewish People in the Time of Jesus Christ*, Div. II, Vol. II, pp. 85-87. (3) There was also the reading of the law (i.e., the Pentateuch). Various reading cycles were used. In Palestine the reading of the Hebrew portion was followed by an Aramaic translation, or Targum. (4) In the reading of the prophets selections were chosen with a view to the explanation and illustration of the law. (5) The sermon developed from the translation and explanation of the Scripture lesson. In earliest times it seems to have been connected with the reading from the prophets. It formed a part of the sabbath afternoon service. The preacher spoke from a sitting position on an elevated place (Luke 4:20). Any competent teacher might be asked to speak (cf. Acts 13:15).

The supervision of synagogue services was entrusted to the "Ruler of the Synagogue" (*archisynagōgos*). The "minister" (*hazzān*) brought the Scriptures to the reader and replaced them after the lesson was read.

Associated with the synagogue was a court known as the Sanhedrin (*q.v.*). In large communities the Sanhedrin consisted of twenty-three "elders" (*presbyteroi*), in smaller localities, seven. One of these elders was the "chief ruler" (*gerousiarchēs*). In Palestine the Sanhedrin represented the civil as well as the religious government. Punishment by scourging, excommunication, and, in extreme cases, death might be decreed. The Jerusalem Sanhedrin was associated with the temple and served as the highest court among the Jews (cf. Acts 9:2).

In the center of the synagogue was a platform on which a lectern was placed. The "ark" containing the biblical scrolls was the chief article of furniture. Wooden seats surrounded the platform. The chief seats were those nearest the ark.

A white limestone synagogue, dated in the third century A.D., has been discovered at the site of ancient Capernaum. A synagogue with elaborate murals depicting OT scenes was discovered at Dura Europus in Syria. Ancient synagogues generally faced Jerusalem. When possible they were built on the highest spot of the city and close to water, which was used for ceremonial ablutions.

The synagogue proved to be a fruitful field for evangelism by early Christian missionaries, and its service greatly influenced Christian worship.

BIBLIOGRAPHY

F. V. Filson, *BA*, VII, p. 4; M. Friedlander, *Synagoge und Kirche in ihren Anfaengen*; H. G. May, *BA*, VII, p. 1; E. L. Sukenik, *Ancient Synagogues in Palestine and Greece*.

CHARLES F. PFEIFFER

SYNCRETISM. This word is derived from the Greek *synkrētizein*, "to combine." Plutarch used the term to refer to the uniting of quarreling brothers in the face of a common enemy. Bessarion revived the term in reference to a proposed reunion of the Western and Eastern Churches. It was used in the early Reformation concerning attempts to maintain the unity of the church. In this connection it was used with praise, but by the middle of the seventeenth century, when the dogmas of the various branches of Protestantism became settled, it became a term of censure to describe those who would minimize doctrinal standards for the sake of unity.

The controversies arising in the latter part of the seventeenth century concerning the efforts to unite various parties of Protestants in Germany have been called the "Syncretistic Controversies."

It is a term currently used to describe both efforts to unite branches of Christianity, and attempts to harmonize Christianity with non-Christian thought.

MORTON H. SMITH

SYNERGISM. The term synergism means literally "working together" and is associated with the view that in the work of individual salvation both man and God cooperate. Pelagius (*ca.* A.D. 400) affirmed the complete competence of man's will for the keeping of God's law. His teaching was vigorously opposed by Augustine, who maintained that apart from the grace of God man is powerless to contribute anything to his salvation. Augustine's doctrine is that of monergism, according to which God is the sole agent in man's salvation. This doctrine was reaffirmed by the Reformers in the sixteenth century. The mediating view of synergism is found (1) in semi-Pelagianism (*q.v.*) which teaches that man must first worthily dispose himself for the reception of divine grace by showing faith, hope, and love, and which was prevalent in the Middle Ages and is still so in Roman Catholic theology; and (2) in Arminianism (*q.v.*), which asserts man's freedom either to accept or to reject the regenerating grace of God in Christ, and, in the event of his accepting it, the possibility of his failing of final perseverance. While the NT undoubtedly teaches that man's salvation is attributable entirely to God's grace (cf. Eph. 2:4-10), this truth in no way diminishes man's responsibility when confronted with the gospel or the relevance of the church's missionary task (cf. Rom. 9 with Rom. 10).

PHILIP EDGCUMBE HUGHES

SYNOD. See COUNCIL.

T

TABERNACLE. The tabernacle as a whole expressed two facts in Israel's religion. (1) Standing in the center of the camp it symbolized the presence of God in Israel. (2) It symbolized the divinely appointed means by which sinful man could approach God, of otherwise unapproachable holiness, ineffable majesty, perfect unity.

This structure, referred to chiefly in Ex. 25-27, 30-31, 35-40; Num. 3:25 ff.; 4:4 ff.; 7:1 ff., had two main parts.

(1) The outer court (Ex. 27:9), entered from the east and formed by curtains suspended from pillars which stood in bronze bases. In the court were two objects. (a) The altar of burnt offering (Ex. 27:1-8). This stood as a perpetual reminder to the worshiper that as he drew near to the Lord sacrifice was essential. (b) The bronze laver (Ex. 30:17-21). Here the priests serving the altar washed hands and feet before performing priestly functions. It stood between the altar and the holy place (Ex. 40:30), and taught the worshiper that to draw near to God one must be pure (cf. Titus 3:5).

(2) The tabernacle, standing within the court (Ex. 26:1 ff.). It consisted of curtains laid upon a framework. The tabernacle was divided into two parts, the holy place and the holy of holies, by a veil (Ex. 26:31 ff.). This veil symbolized the barrier separating sinful man from a holy God (Heb. 9:8). All three Synoptics report the rending of the veil when Christ died, signifying that the way into the holiest of all was now open (cf. Heb. 10:19 ff.).

The holy place, entered only by the priests, contained three objects. (a) A table on which was placed the shewbread, the bread of the presence (Ex. 25:23-30; 37:10-16). Placing the bread upon the table was an act of thanksgiving for the sustenance of life, the dedication of the life so sustained, and the acknowledgment that man does not live by bread alone. (b) A golden lampstand (Ex. 25:31-40; 37:17-24) which provided stands for seven golden lamps. As it shone in the darkness of the holy place so Israel was to shine in the world. Now the church fulfils that function (Matt. 5:14-16; Luke 12:35; Phil. 2:15). (c) An altar of incense (Ex. 30:1-7; 27:25-28) which stood before the dividing veil. Upon this altar was offered the morning and evening incense offering (Ex. 30:7 ff.). This symbolized the worshiper's life of devotion and aspiration after God. The rising incense was a symbol of ascending prayer at the beginning and the close of each day. At the time of incense the people engaged in prayer (Luke 1:10; and cf. Rev. 5:8; 8:3).

The holy of holies where God's glory was, entered only by the high priest once a year, contained two objects. (a) The ark of the covenant. The ark symbolized God's meeting with his people in grace and on the ground of atonement. The ark contained the Decalogue (Ex. 25:16), meaning that God who thus met with his people had revealed his will and his ethical nature, which represented his demands upon his people. (b) The mercy seat or propitiatory (Ex. 25:17 ff.), a slab of gold resting upon the ark and overshadowed by the winged cherubim. Blood was sprinkled upon it on the Day of Atonement, teaching that salvation is by the blood of sacrifice, the blood covering or atoning for sin.

The tabernacle symbolism found its fulfilment in Christ. He was tabernacle, priest, altar and sacrifice. He is our High Priest who has passed into the heavens now to appear for us, and to give us access to the holiest by his blood, the blood of the everlasting covenant. God who tabernacled with Israel, and with men in the Word incarnate (John 1:14), does so still in the body of Christ (Eph. 2:21 f.) and in the believer (I Cor. 6:19).

BIBLIOGRAPHY

Wm. Brown, *The Tabernacle*; James Strong, *The Tabernacle of Israel*; B. F. Westcott, *Hebrews*, pp. 233 ff., 240 ff.

JAMES G. S. S. THOMSON

TALMUD. Hebrew *talmûḏ*, often derived from a hypothetical four-consonant root *tlmd*, but probably developed from *lāmaḏ*, "to study," from which also *limmēḏ*, "to teach." The word specifically designates the Mishnah (*q.v.*) together with the Halakic and Haggadic discussions. This second part of the Talmud, namely, the discussions by the Amoraim (literally, "speakers," referring to the Jewish scholars concerned) is known as the Gemara (from Aramaic *gᵉmar*, "to complete, to master completely by study," whence *gᵉmârâ*, "that which has been learned by thorough study"). The Amoraim were active from the time of the conclusion of the Mishnah to the end of the fifth century A.D. The Halakah (pl. Halakoth, from Heb. *hālaḵ*, "to go, walk") is the teaching to be followed, the categorical law derived from the Scriptures and taught by prevailing authority. The Scriptures deal with principles but usually do not govern specific cases. But life is complex and ever changing, and law needs to be specific. The Halakoth deal with the specific situations and give authoritative regulations. One cannot help but feel that this is the "law" to which Jesus and Paul sometimes referred, rather than the principal law of the Scriptures. The Haggada (from Heb.

nāgaḏ, "to be prominent," Hiphil *higgîḏ*, "to declare, proclaim, publish") is the non-Halakic material derived from searching the Scriptures, usually in the form of proverbs, parables, and the like. Frequently Haggada conveys an idea not suggested immediately by Scripture and at times becomes fanciful or allegorical. The Talmud exists in two forms, the Babylonian Talmud and the Palestinian (or Jerusalem) Talmud, the principal difference being that the discussions following the Mishnah are by Babylonian or Palestinian Amoraim as the case may be.

BIBLIOGRAPHY

H. L. Strack, *Introduction to the Talmud and Midrash*.

WILLIAM SANFORD LASOR

TARES. *Zizanion* (Arabic *Zuwan*), a Semitic word for bearded darnel or cheat, occurs only in Matt. 13:25-40. It closely resembles wheat, until it heads out to form dark grain erect on stalk. Trench regards it as degenerate wheat and quotes the Talmud; Thomson denies this and says the light grain is carried by wind and flourishes when autumn rains drown wheat. The bitter tasting seeds act as a violent emetic and cause dizziness; hence it is called by Vergil *Infelix Lolium*. Tares are weeded out by women at harvest, before men reap wheat. The seeds are sold as chicken food; they are winnowed out of wheat before grinding, being a strong soporific poison.

In our Lord's teaching the tares appear to denote the cunning work of the evil one which at times can so resemble what is of God (cf. II Cor. 11:14).

BIBLIOGRAPHY

Arndt; W. M. Thomson, *The Land and the Book*, pp. 420-22; Trench's *Parables*, pp. 90-91.

DENIS H. TONGUE

TARGUM. Although, strictly speaking, any translation may be called a targum, the term is used in biblical studies to designate a particular type of translation of the Hebrew Scriptures into Aramaic.

When Hebrew ceased to be understood, translations into the colloquial Aramaic became a practical necessity. Neh. 8:8 appears to be a reference to such translations. After the Scripture was read in Hebrew, an interpreter would give its sense in Aramaic. In the reading of the law this was done verse by verse. Three verses of the prophets might be rendered at once. It was required that the rendition be oral. Some targums were quite literal, others were free and interspersed with illustrative material.

By the fifth century A.D. two authorized targums had been written and circulated, that of Onkelos, a literal rendition of the Pentateuch, and that of Jonathan, a freer version of the prophets. Other targums were reduced to writing at an early date. Some have affinities with the Peshitta and the LXX.

CHARLES F. PFEIFFER

TEACH, TEACHING, TEACHER. The Bible uses many words to describe teaching or the role of the teacher. A teacher is presented as one having service to render, although it could be interpreted to indicate an office.

Some important OT words, and a description of each, are as follows: (1) *bîn*, "to separate." This word often is used to mean "teach." It suggests the teacher's ability to distinguish the necessary from the unimportant, in which the teacher solves difficult problems, both spiritual and otherwise. (Used in Dan. 8:16; Ps. 119:34.) (2) *zāhar*, "to shine." This word is used when Moses enlightens the people about the principles sent by God (Ex. 18:20). The teacher illuminates for the student. (3) *lāmaḏ*, "to beat." Used many times in the OT, this word denotes discipline in teaching, as found in Hos. 10:11; Isa. 2:3. Obedience was the greatest result expected from this type of instruction, along with consistency with the will of God. (4) *rā'â*, "to feed a flock." This term expresses the sense of responsibility the teacher should feel for his learners (Prov. 10:21; Eccl. 12:11). (5) *yārâ*, "to cast." This indicates the teacher's responsibility to cast out or to present new ideas to the pupils. From this word came the usual word for "law" (*torah*) as used in such passages as Ps. 19:8; II Kings 14:6. Other OT words are *sākal*, "to be wise"; *yāḏa'*, "to see"; (hiphil, "cause to know"); *nāḇa'*, "to boil" (pour forth words).

In the NT, some of the important words are as follows: (1) *didaskō*, "to teach," which conveys both lecture and discussion teaching. Emphasis is on the instructor and implies fitness for the task. The word is used in such passages as Matt. 28:19; Eph. 4:11. (2) *diermēneuō*, "to interpret." The teacher explains the lesson, as in Luke 24:27; I Cor. 14:5. (3) *paratithēmi*, "to place beside." This technique adapts the lesson to the existing situation. Christ used this method in the parables. (4) *ektithēmi*, "to place out." This implies responsibility to uncover hidden meanings of passages or method of living. Paul's exposition in Acts 11:4 demonstrates the idea. (5) *manthanō*, "to learn," which conveys the important principle of causing one to learn. It recognizes that there will be a personal relationship, as in Matt. 28:19. Other NT words used are *prophētēs*, "one who speaks for"; *poimēn*, "a shepherd"; and *episkopos*, "an overseer."

The great responsibilities of the teacher are clearly evident in the foregoing survey of biblical terms for teaching. The teacher can fulfil this responsibility only when he understands the basis of true teaching, a basis which can come only from the word of God.

With this as a foundation, the teaching philosophy and method must agree. If either of these is inconsistent with the final authority — the Scriptures — it will not be true teaching. The pragmatic and humanistic tenets of modern education develop no criterion for deciding what should and what should not be taught. Therefore, they present a vacuum-like system of thought. The Christian educator, on the other hand, starts with, "In the beginning, God . . ." and means by this the sovereign God of the Scriptures. This continues as his point of reference all through the educative process.

Further, the Christian teacher should realize the purpose of teaching: forming man into an independent personality serving God according to his word. This purpose can be achieved only by fostering obedient submission to the word of God by both teacher and learner.

Teaching, according to the Bible, is simply the meeting of a divinely ordained need (the reforming of fallen and redeemed man into what God meant him to be), in a divinely ordained way (the use of methods consistent with the highest authority, the Scriptures).

BIBLIOGRAPHY
ISBE; KB; C. Van Til, *The Dilemma of Education*, pp. 33-44; J. Waterink, *Basic Concepts in Christian Pedagogy*, pp. 34-51.

LEONARD T. VAN HORN

TELEOLOGY. (Greek *telos*, "end" and *logos* "word" or "discourse.") In opposition to mechanism, which explains present and future in terms of the past, teleology explains all in terms of the future. It is the theory that everything has a final cause. Aristotle used both the mechanistic (first cause) and the teleologic (final cause) arguments to "prove" the existence of God. The former was subordinate to the latter.

Augustine developed a teleological theory of history in his *City of God*. Following Aquinas, Paley's *Natural Theology* and the famous *Bridgewater Treatises* use the teleological argument as a "theistic proof." The difficulty with the teleological argument for reasoning from the finite to the infinite is that it presents only a possible, or, at best, a probable God, unless it is based on presuppositional reasoning, whereby it becomes a definite finger pointing to the living and true God.

See also GOD.

MORTON H. SMITH

TEMPERANCE. A NT term, although the idea of temperance as a prudential virtue is frequently found in the OT, particularly Proverbs. Temperance stands for the mastery of desires in the interests of higher ends and ideals. The Greek term, *egkrateia*, is derived from *egkrateuomai*, "to hold oneself in," "to have inward power"; hence, self-controlled.

Temperance was preached by Paul to Felix, along with righteousness and judgment to come (Acts 24:25), a trilogy well calculated to bring conviction of sin.

Temperance is a part of the fruit of the Spirit (Gal. 5:23). It is the third virtue to be added to faith in the list given in II Pet. 1:5-7, and contributes to fruitfulness, vision, steadfastness, and an abundant entrance into the everlasting kingdom of Christ (vss. 8-11). It is one of the essential characteristics of bishops or elders, who in addition are to be lovers of hospitality (*q.v.*) and goodness, sober, just, and holy (Titus 1:7-8).

Paul lays special stress on temperance as essential to success in Christian service (I Cor. 9:25-27), using the analogy of those who strive for athletic proficiency. He gives it clear definition in the statement: "But I pommel my body and subdue it, lest after preaching to others I myself should be disqualified" (vs. 27, RSV).

It should be clearly seen that temperance applies only in the area of the legitimate. There is no temperance in that which is inherently wrong. No one may be temperate in doing evil. Complete abstinence is the Christian rule in acts or practices contrary to the known will of God (II Cor. 6:17).

WESTLAKE T. PURKISER

TEMPLE. The basic concept of the temple in Hebrew thought was that it was the house of God, and hence it was usually termed "the house of Yahweh" *(bēth Yahweh)*. This did not mean that Jehovah's proper home was in any structure fashioned with men's hands (cf. Solomon's remark in I Kings 8:27), but rather that his divine presence abode there, symbolized by the dazzling "glory-cloud" which settled down over the holy of holies (both at the dedication of the tabernacle in Ex. 40:34-35, and at the dedication of Solomon's temple in I Kings 8:10-11). The most sacred spot in the temple was the inner chamber where rested the "ark of the covenant" with its golden lid or cover known as the "propitiatory" *(kappōreth)*, a term related to *kippēr* — "to make atonement or propitiation." Here the Spirit of God rested in the midst of his covenant people Israel (cf. Ps. 46:5; Isa. 12:6), in anticipation of that final state of blessedness promised in Rev. 21:3 when God will dwell in the midst in his redeemed in the heavenly Jerusalem. Access to the holy of holies was forbidden to all but the high priest himself, and even he might enter it only once a year, on the Day of Atonement, to sprinkle the blood of the sin offering upon the propitiatory (Lev. 16:2, 14).

After the crucifixion and resurrection of Christ the physical temple became obsolete in God's economy, for Christ and his church became the antitypical fulfilment (Heb. 9:11-14) of all that which it foreshadowed and symbolically presented. "Know ye not that your body is the temple of the Holy Ghost which is in you, which ye have of God . . .?" (I Cor. 6:19). Because Christ's Spirit dwells within the genuine believer, therefore his body is a "house of God" or a true temple. On the other hand the whole aggregate of believers constitute "living stones, built up as a spiritual house" (I Pet. 2:5), and are in Christ "builded together for an habitation of God through the Spirit" (Eph. 2:22).

GLEASON L. ARCHER, JR.

TEMPTATION. In the OT the specific verb indicating the act of tempting is the Pi'el form *nissâ*. In I Sam. 17:39 the word is used of proving or testing armor. In Gen. 22:1 *nissâ* characterizes God's command to Abraham to offer Isaac as a burnt offering in the land of Moriah. A similar use of the term in application to God's testing of men is found in Ex. 16:4; 20:20; Deut. 8:2, 16; 13:3; Ps. 26:2; II Chron. 32:31; *et al.* Related to this

sense of the term is that which is given to it when it is applied to the terrible and wonderful acts of God against Egypt (Deut. 4:34).

The same technical term is applied to those acts of men which challenge God to demonstrate his veracity and justice. It describes the iniquitous imaginations and acts by which men through doubt, disobedience and unbelief oppose God's revealed will, thus putting his perfections to the test. The outstanding instance of this type of sinful tempting of God occurs when Israel murmurs against Jehovah at Rephidim. One of the names which Moses subsequently applies to the place is "Massah," a tempting (Ex. 17:2, 7; Deut. 6:16; cf. Pss. 78:18, 41, 56; 95:9; 106:14).

The term *nissâ* is rarely, if ever, applied in the OT to Satan's act of enticing men to sin. Nevertheless, the essence of temptation in this sense is clearly revealed in the account of the fall and in the record of Satan's role in the affliction of Job (Gen. 3:1-13; Job 1 — 2:10). Eve tells God, "The serpent beguiled me *(hiśśî'anî)*, and I did eat" (Gen. 3:13; cf. *exapataō* in II Cor. 11:3; I Tim. 2:14). Deception plays an important part in satanic temptation. Satan avoids making a frontal attack immediately on God's probationary command and its threatened penalties. Instead, he sows the seeds of doubt, unbelief, and rebellion. The temptation of Eve is typical. She is made to feel that God has unwisely and unfairly withheld a legitimate objective good from man. Thus Satan tempts, i.e., entices Eve to tempt, i.e., to test the veracity, goodness, and justice of God. In Job's trials the strategy is different but the end sought is the same — the rejection of God's will and way as just and good.

The NT reflects the translation of *nissâ* with *ekpeirazō*, etc., in the LXX (Matt. 4:7; Heb. 3:8-9; I Cor. 10:9). In these passages the sinful tempting of God is referred to by way of quotation of, or reference to, the OT. However, the same sense is employed by Peter in connection with the sin of Ananias and Sapphira (Acts 5:9) and the prescriptions to be given to gentile Christians (Acts 15:10).

The additional use of *peirazō* and related forms is complex. The words may refer to exterior circumstances which try the believer's faith and are designed to strengthen that faith (James 1:2; I Pet. 1:6). Although these circumstances are held to be under the absolute control of God, the explicit causal ascription of them to God is not prominent. Perhaps some reasoning by analogy is permissible here. Paul, for instance, recognizes that his "thorn in the flesh" is under God's sovereign control (II Cor. 12:8-9). But the "thorn" is "a messenger of Satan" (II Cor. 12:7). The same phenomenon may be viewed from two aspects. The *peirasmon* is a trial of one's faith controlled and, even in some sense, sent by God. But God is not the author of the prompting to sin which such trial seems to bring with it. The believer may rejoice in trial because he detects God's good purpose in it (James 1:2-4, 12). But the subjective use of trying situations, the internal incitement to sin in connection with trials and testings, is not and cannot be the work of God. Here temptation in the strict sense of the term comes to manifestation. Enticement to sin and to impatient rebellion is the work of Satan (Rev. 2:9; I Pet. 5:8-9; cf. I Thess. 3:5). In this he is immensely aided by the deceptive power of *epithymia*, lust, in the old nature (James 1:14-15). While Satan's role in temptation is usually assumed rather than stated, in I Cor. 7:5 Paul explicitly warns Christians to observe his charge with respect to marital relationships, "that Satan tempt you not because of your incontinency" (cf. Matt. 4:1; Luke 4:2; Mark 1:13).

Jesus teaches the disciples to pray, "And bring us not into temptation, but deliver us from the evil one" (Matt. 6:13), and the Bible is replete with warnings to be watchful because of the ever-present danger of falling into temptation (Luke 22:40; Gal. 6:1; I Pet. 5:8-9). But the Bible assures the believer that God will make a way of escape from temptation (I Cor. 10:13), and that "the Lord knoweth how to deliver the godly out of temptation . . ." (II Pet. 2:9a).

Jesus was repeatedly "tempted" by the Jewish leaders (Mark 8:11; *et al.*). But these temptations were designed either to force Jesus to prove his Messiahship in terms of the preconceptions of his enemies, or to compel him to show himself incapable of being a true rabbi (Luke 10:25), or to cause him to make self-incriminating statements (Mark 12:15; cf. Luke 23:2).

Very likely Jesus was subject to temptation throughout his ministry (cf. Luke 4:13; 22:28). But the great temptation is the crucial temptation in redemptive history (Matt. 4:1 and parallels). This temptation confronts one with the question, "How could the sinless Son of God be really tempted?" Granted that appeal could be made to legitimate desires in his human nature, what force could temptation have on a divine person who cannot be tempted? Efforts to solve the problem run the risk either of impairing the "without sin" of Heb. 4:15 or of making the temptation unreal. Our understanding of the matter is beclouded by the fact that our awareness of being tempted immediately involves us in at least a momentary inclination to yield to the temptation. This was not true of Jesus, and yet the temptation was real, so that he is able to "succor them that are tempted" (Heb. 2:18).

M. G. Kyle relates the great temptation by way of I John 2:15-17 to the temptation of Eve in Eden (Art. "Temptation, Psychology of," *ISBE*). Although the details of this connection may be disputed, the necessity of the temptation in view of Adam's fall is evident. Jesus *triumphed* over Satan with his immediate and obedient use of the word of God. He thereby proved that he was qualified to be the "last Adam." At the beginning of his ministry he demonstrated the truth of I John 3:8b, "To this end was the Son of God manifested, that he might destroy the works of the devil."

BIBLIOGRAPHY
F. L. Anderson in *ISBE*; L. Berkhof, *Systematic Theology*, pp. 219-26; Gesenius; Grimm-Thayer; M. G. Kyle in *ISBE*; H. Seeseman in *TWNT*; C. M. Stuart in *ISBE*.

CARL G. KROMMINGA

TESTAMENT. This biblical term is derived from the Latin *testamentum*, which was used in Jerome's Vulgate to render the Hebrew *bᵉrit*, covenant, in a few instances, as in Num. 14:44, and the Greek *diathēkē*, as in II Cor. 3:14. Since Tertullian's time it has been used to designate the two main divisions of Holy Scripture — the Old Testament and the New. This represents the literary use of the word.

As used in biblical theology, the term may denote the era from the arrangement given through Moses (Ex. 19:5-8; Jer. 31:32; Heb. 8:9) to the death of Christ. This is the old testament or covenant in contrast to the new, which began legally with the death of Christ, as may be inferred from Luke 22:20 and I Cor. 11:25.

The AV uses the term testament as well as covenant for the Hebrew and Greek originals *bᵉrit* and *diathēkē*, but the ASV uses the word covenant regularly, apart from the exceptional use of testament in Heb. 9:16-17. The

Roman testament, in order to go into effect, required "the death of the testator" (Heb. 9:16), but this was not necessarily so in Semitic practice, as is illustrated in the parable of the prodigal son and elsewhere.

The old testament or covenant had its tabernacle or temple and its ceremonial and civil laws, but when the death of Jesus introduced the new testament or covenant, these provisions of the old order became antiquated and were "nigh unto vanishing away." In fact, in A.D. 70 the temple did vanish away with the destruction of Jerusalem. Meanwhile, the moral law of the ten commandments, written "in tables of stone" (II Cor. 3:3) but in the new testament written "in fleshy tables of the heart" (II Cor. 3:3; cf. vs. 6) still stands and abides. For the elaboration of the various views on this matter, see especially Berkhof and Chafer in the literature cited below.

See also COVENANT.

BIBLIOGRAPHY

Systematic Theologies of L. Berkhof and L. S. Chafer; G. Vos, *Biblical Theology*, especially pp. 32-36; M. J. Wyngaarden, *The Future of the Kingdom*, chap. VIII.

MARTIN J. WYNGAARDEN

TESTIMONY. See WITNESS.

THANKSGIVING. Two Hebrew words (*yādâ* and *tôdâ*) and two Greek words (*eucharisteuō* and *eucharistia*) are the principal terms expressing "thanksgiving." In addition, *exomologeō* is used in Matt. 11:25. The presentation here will deal with the NT words exclusively.

Our Lord expressed thanks for physical food (John 6:11, 23), for answered prayer (John 11:41), and for the bread of the Lord's Supper (Luke 22:17, 19; cf. I Cor. 11:24).

Among the physical blessings calling for thanksgiving, the following are mentioned: (1) healing (Luke 17:16); (2) food (John 6:11, 23; Acts 27:35; Rom. 14:6; I Cor. 10:30; I Tim. 4:3 f.); (3) peace (Acts 24:2 f.); (4) deliverance from dangers (Acts 27:35; 28:15).

Paul frequently expressed thanks for blessings bestowed on the churches. We note here the following: (1) proclamation of the faith (Rom. 1:8; Col. 1:3 f.; I Thess. 1:2; cf. Eph. 1:15 f.); (2) grace bestowed (I Cor. 1:4; II Cor. 1:11; 4:15); (3) acceptance of the word preached (I Thess. 2:13); (4) fellowship in the gospel's progress (Phil. 1:3-5); (5) growth in grace (II Thess. 1:3); (6) knowledge of election (II Thess. 2:13); (7) spiritual blessings (Col. 1:12); (8) liberality in giving (II Cor. 9:11 f.); (9) joy over converts (I Thess. 3:9).

The Apostle also gave thanks for personal benefits such as: (1) deliverance from bondage (Rom. 7:25); (2) the sacrificial labor of others (Rom. 16:4); (3) the non-commission of certain acts (I Cor. 1:14); (4) gifts bestowed upon him (I Cor. 14:18); (5) a friend's spiritual growth (Philem. 4 f.).

As to its characteristics, thanksgiving is acceptable according to God's will (I Thess. 5:18); its neglect is always sinful (Luke 17:16; Rom. 1:21); it will always be a dominant feature of heaven's praise (Rev. 4:9; 7:12; 11:17). Christians should render it continually (I Cor. 1:4; Col. 4:2), under every circumstance (Phil. 4:6), to God through Christ (Col. 3:17), and as an antidote to sin (Eph. 5:4).

WICK BROOMALL

THEISM. The term theism might be defined as belief in a god or gods of any kind. Deism (*q.v.*), pantheism, henotheism, monolatry, polytheism, animism, and even the personification of values by some of the anti-supernaturalists, would all be included in theism under such a definition. For the purposes of the present article, the definition will be limited to Christian theism, or belief in the God of the Judeo-Christian tradition as contained in the Bible. The biblical view of God is precisely summarized in the words of the Westminster Shorter Catechism: "God is a Spirit, infinite, eternal, and unchangeable in his being, wisdom, power, holiness, justice, goodness, and truth" (Q.4. See also qq. 5 and 6).

Excluded by definition are certain views which would properly be investigated under a more general definition of theism, such as the absentee God of deism, the supreme god or the unmoved mover of Aristotle; the unknowable, unrelated, indescribable God of Barth, of certain parts of Thomas' Summae, of Daniel Lamont, Karl Heim and many devout souls; and the finite (not omnipotent) God of John Stuart Mill, H. G. Wells, Brightman, and Bertocci.

The attributes of the God of the Judeo-Christian tradition, succinctly given in the definition quoted above, have sometimes been misunderstood. "Spirit" (John 4:24) means self-conscious, self-determining non-material person. "Infinite" is an adjective modifying the nouns which specify attributes. "Infinite . . . in his being," in its historical context does not imply pantheism, but omnipresence. God is everywhere, not as embodying all things, not as a fluid which is partly here and partly there, but as a personal presence. Everything is immediately in his presence. "Unchangeable" indicates a dynamic, not static, immutability, except in certain philosophical back eddies (Aristotle *Metaphysics,* Book Lambda, as reflected in Thomas's "fully realized," in whom there is no potential). The God of the Bible is immutable, not that he cannot do anything in time and space, but that his character is perfectly consistent in all his works.

The doctrine of creation (Gen. 1 and 2; John 1:3; Heb. 11:3) does not postulate an infinite Subject, with no object, eternally existing before the finite creation (Eddington's objection). According to the doctrine of the Trinity, infinite subjectivity subsists eternally with infinite objectivity in God.

The theistic arguments (see Buswell's *What is God,* Zondervan 1937, pp. 109-57; *Thomas and the Bible* privately printed 1953) answer the following questions. (1) What is the explanation of the cosmos? If anything now exists, something must be eternal (*ewig,* not *notwendig,* Kant), unless something comes from nothing (emergentism, Fred Hoyle). God is the most probable answer (Rom. 1:19-21). (2) What is the explanation of purposiveness, *Zweckmaessigkeit?* God is the most probable answer (Ps. 19; Rom. 10:18; F. R. Tennant, *Philosophical Theology,* Cambridge 1937, Vol. II Ch. IV). (3) What is the explanation of the Judeo-Christian concept of God? The answer is not Anselm's deductive idealistic ontological argument, but Descartes' inductive (*Meditations.* Reply 2nd Objection, Proposition II; see discussion in Buswell's *Philosophies of F. R. Tennant and John Dewey,* Philosophical Library, 1950, pp. 181 ff.).

See also GOD.

J. OLIVER BUSWELL, JR.

THEOCRACY. The word is derived from the Greek *theos,* "God," and from *kratein,* "to rule." Hence it denotes the rule of God. Josephus apparently coined the word, according to Thackeray, and gave it a political connotation (*Against Apion* II, 165). But the idea goes back to the OT (Ex. 19:4-9; Deut. 33:4-5).

The law of the king (Deut. 17:14-20) recognizes the ultimate control of the Lord God. Saul's trend was antitheocratic, but David's was theocratic, and to him was given the promise of the great Son of David (II Sam. 7:13-16).

Although the political sense is essential to the word theocracy, as coined by Josephus, a broader meaning is usually implied, to include every sphere and relationship of life as governed in OT times by the contemporaneous and continuing special revelation of God. The human agencies provided to enable Israel to carry out Jehovah's will included not only kings but also a succession of prophets, culminating in the great prophet like Moses (Deut. 18:14-15). Priests and Levites were included also, to whom God gave the duties of presenting the typically redemptive sacrificial blood to the Lord, pointing forward to the blood of Christ, and the duty of teaching the people the moral law, the statutes, the judgments, the sacred history, prophecy, and poetry of the OT (Lev. 10:8-11; Deut. 31:9-11).

BIBLIOGRAPHY

M. G. Kyle, *The Problem of the Pentateuch,* chap. I; M. J. Wyngaarden, *The Future of the Kingdom,* chap. III.

MARTIN J. WYNGAARDEN

THEODICY. (Greek *theos,* "God" and *dikē,* "justice"). A term taken from the title of a work of Leibnitz entitled: *Essais de Théodicée sur la bonté de Dieu, la liberté de l'homme, et l' origine du mal.* It is the realm of theology or philosophy devoted to the vindication of God's goodness and justice despite the existence of evil.

Leibnitz set forth the optimistic view. It is assumed that this is the best of all possible worlds. God as good cannot will to bring to being a universe less beneficent than any other possible universe. The error of this view is twofold: (1) it assumes, without warrant, that the greatest natural good of the creation is God's highest end in creating; (2) it limits the power of God.

This optimistic view has been abandoned by philosophers for far more skeptical views, either that evil is itself good, or that evil comes from something within God that he is unable to overcome. None of these theodicies is satisfactory.

The Bible makes no attempt to justify God. It is clear that he is absolutely sovereign, and that he has willed the existence of both good and evil, and that all of this is for his own glory. The sacrifice of Christ gives the hum-

ble believer not a solution but a satisfying
reply. There must have been some good reason for allowing evil, but this does not imply
a defect in God or in his benevolence. If there
had been any defect in him, he would hardly
have sent his holy Only Begotten Son, who
was worth more than all worlds, to save one
(R. L. Dabney, *Theology*, Presbyterian Committee of Publication, Richmond, Va., 1927).

MORTON H. SMITH

THEOLOGY. Strictly, theology is that
which is thought and said concerning God.
True theology is thus given by the Bible itself
as the revelation of God in human terms. But
the Bible gives rise to exposition, reflection
and presentation. Hence there is a theology
of the church as well as the Bible, though not
in addition or opposition to it. It is this
theology that we must briefly review, assessing it always by its fidelity to the scriptural
norm. In so doing we follow the four main
historical groupings — patristic, scholastic, reformed and modern.

I. PATRISTIC. The reference here is to the
movement of Christian thought which began
with the post-apostolic writers, culminated in
the great age of trinitarian and christological
reflection and declined with the disruption of
the Roman Empire. To follow the complicated
course of this movement is hardly possible, but
some of the leading features may be indicated.

After the first and fragmentary period, the
initial task was that of practical and philosophical apologetics as seen in Justin Martyr.
But reckoning with the pagan world carried
the dangers of Gnosticism and speculative if
brilliant theorising such as that of Origen. It
was in perception of this threat, and resistance
to it, that there grew up especially in the west
a strong traditional movement represented by
Irenaeus and Tertullian and associated with
the acceptance of the canon and appeal to the
historic church and ministry.

This was followed by an age of preoccupation with the great problem posed by confession of Jesus as Lord, namely, the understanding of the trinity and the incarnation. Every
conceivable over-emphasis or deviation emerged
during the prolonged theological discussion,
but the result was general agreement on such
great confessions as the Nicene Creed and the
Chalcedonian Definition, and we owe some
of the best patristic work (e.g., of Athanasius,

the Cappadocians, Augustine and Jerome) to
these and related debates.

Nor were the problems of man neglected,
for in defense against Pelagius there was the
development of a powerful doctrine of original
sin and predestination, while the doctrine of
the church was formulated in answer to the
Donatist challenge. At the same time a good
deal of direct work was done on the Bible itself, both in the form of textual study and
catechetical and homiletic exposition. And it
must not be forgotten that concern for the
atonement was a cardinal issue in what seem
to be the abstruse discussions of the incarnation.

The patristic age is so varied that it is hard
to assess it in general terms. In the main, it
remains faithful to the Bible, and we are permanently indebted to it for securing a biblical
statement of many of the basic themes. Yet it
was obviously susceptible to pagan influences
militating against a truly biblical understanding. In particular, it had a constant impulse
towards a new legalism on the one side and
a new rationalism on the other which involved
a serious distortion of biblical teaching and
practice and underlay many of the later evils
of the church.

II. SCHOLASTIC. The patristic age was followed by a comparatively sterile period when
the East hardened into orthodoxy, the West
was overshadowed by barbarian incursions, and
East and West were separated by dissension.
Even in the Dark Ages there were many fine
scholars such as Bede and Alcuin to pass on
the learning of the past into the future, and
many later developments arose out of the
thinking of this period. Yet it was not until
the medieval period that there came a new
outburst of formative theology, stimulated to
some extent by the rediscovery of the thought
of the Greeks.

The outstanding feature of Scholasticism is
its deliberately attempted synthesis of philosophy and biblical theology in which the former
provides the basis and the latter the superstructure. If Abelard represents a movement towards
greater rationalism and Anselm towards a more
biblical conception of reason learning from
faith, Thomas Aquinas gives us the impressive
norm which dominates all subsequent development and is still a potent influence today.

In the light of this synthesis it is not unnatural that Scholasticism should be semi-
pelagian in its doctrine of grace, codifying the

legalistic developments of an early time within an Augustinian framework. It is to this period that we owe the detailed outworking of such distortions as the doctrines of baptismal regeneration, purgatory, penance, infused grace, implicit faith and transubstantiation, which is only possible or intelligible in terms of philosophical realism.

There are, of course, many satisfactory features which we must not fail to note. The traditional patristic doctrines were carefully maintained. Anselm gives us a finely objective doctrine of the atonement in the light of current views of satisfaction. Biblical material is used even though it often appears in distorted form. There is a good spirit of inquiry and disputation which allows of the development of a conflicting trend like Nominalism and thus prepares the way in some sense for the Reformation. But these virtues cannot offset the fact that Scholasticism was mistaken in its general enterprise and achievement, and must bear responsibility for the disastrous corruption which follows.

III. REFORMED. By the middle of the fifteenth century Scholasticism had lost its first impulse and was degenerating into subtle but futile disputation. But new influences were at work, notably the fresh investigation of the Greek and Hebrew Scriptures, the rediscovery of the Fathers and more straightforward methods of exegesis. It was out of this that there arose the new and more biblical theology of the Reformation in opposition to the dominant rationalism and legalism. In spite of the acute division into Lutheran on the one side and Reformed in the more technical sense on the other (with sectarianism on the outer edge as an unorthodox extreme), this is sufficiently unified in its main features to enable us to speak of a Reformation theology.

Primarily, this is a biblical theology in the direct sense. It does not take philosophy as a basis, or framework, or ally. Its first business is to know and· expound the Bible. It realizes that to talk of God it must be taught by God. Its positive theological work is preceded, accompanied, informed and corrected by biblical study. It does not claim Aristotle and Plato as friends or forerunners. It uses reason, but reason informed by the Bible and put to a biblical use. The root of scholastic and a good deal of patristic distortion is thus exposed and cut.

But this means that it is a christological the-

ology, not merely accepting the early christological formulations but making Christ the sum and center of exposition. In the great doctrines of the trinity and incarnation and atonement it has little to add except perhaps in the restatement of Anselm's doctrine of satisfaction. But whether we turn to Luther, Zwingli, Calvin or any of the great Reformers, we see always the perception that no man comes to the Father except by Christ, and therefore that Christ is the beginning and center and end of all true theology.

Again, it is a theology of faith in Christ as our righteousness no less than our wisdom, the moral synthesis of medieval theology being thus opposed as well as the intellectual. Led by the Bible, it goes to Christ himself for salvation. This means that Christianity is really understood as gospel and not as a new law. It means a new apprehension of justification in relation to sanctification, as well brought out by Calvin. It means a new emphasis on the place and importance of faith, as so finely seen by Luther. It means a biblical understanding of grace and the means of grace. It means a strong doctrine of election, and the corresponding impotence of the sinner. It means a necessary and uncompromising rejection of the complicated pseudo-doctrines which had invaded and corrupted the church. It means a total reconstruction of theology, not in the sense of innovation, but in the sense of genuine reformation according to the biblical and to some extent patristic norm.

The Reformers are not infallible. They do not escape the influences of their age. They differ in points of detail. But they stand for true biblical theology as opposed to Tridentine dogma on the one side and the well-meaning but not so well-informed teaching of the sects on the other. Of all theological movements, they come closest to the Bible in method, in understanding, in content, and in the distinctive combination of intellectual and spiritual power. Quite apart from their lasting insights, they teach us what is the proper work of theology, and bring us constantly under the correcting and purifying scrutiny of the written word.

IV. MODERN. Unfortunately a large part of the church refused to accept the Reformed correction. This means that in the modern period we have to reckon with two independent if interacting forces in the West. More recently there has also been renewed contact with the East, which has pursued its own autonomous course and has much that is strange but fruitful to offer in biblical understanding. But this belongs more particularly to the future.

When we consider Roman Catholicism, we see a church fettered by the rigid formulations of Trent but unable to suppress completely the stirring of theological life. A possibility of renewal was offered by the revived Augustinianism of Jansenism (q.v.), but the imposing of Dominican orthodoxy closed this hopeful door. Liberalism was firmly resisted, but Ultramontanism (q.v.) has brought new dogmatic definition more particularly in relation to the Papacy and the Virgin Mary. Yet in spite of this disastrous trend, the outlook is not as gloomy as might appear, for the last decades have seen a vigorous resurgence of biblical scholarship in Roman Catholic circles, with all the possibilities which this involves.

In the Protestant field we may ignore confessional disputes and concentrate on more general aspects. In this respect three main developments demand our attention. The first was the detailed formulation of Protestant orthodoxy in answer to the attacks of Romanists, Socinians and Arminians, this being the work of the seventeenth century. The second was the ensuing deviation into liberal Protestantism, when an attempt was made to restate Christian doctrine, first in terms of the rationalism already used as well as resisted by the orthodox, then more originally and powerfully by Schleiermacher in terms of subjective experience (as required by Kant's critique of reason and suggested by Pietism). The third is a strong biblical and theological reaction against every form of liberalism, deriving from many sources, combining various strands, involving the danger of reversion as in Bultmann, but aiming in Barth and others at a genuine if not uniformly successful reconstruction of theology on a biblical and Reformation basis.

The story thus breaks off at a critical but not unpromising juncture. There are many hostile forces, from entrenched Romanism on the one side to persistent liberalism on the other. But there are hopeful factors too, the climate of the age, the richer ecumenical discussion, the desire for real theology and above all the intensifying and fructifying study of the Bible itself. The battle has thus been joined again for a true theology distorted neither by legalism nor rationalism; and it is not impossible that it should be won if we can teach and learn from one another to be more genuinely biblical and therefore to think and speak of God himself as self-revealed in Jesus Christ.

See also BIBLICAL THEOLOGY.

GEOFFREY W. BROMILEY

THEOPHANY. A theophany may be defined as a visible manifestation of God. Usage restricts the term mainly to the theophanic manifestations during the OT period. Such manifestations may be loosely classified as (1) a direct message (Ex. 19:9-25), (2) a message in a dream (Gen. 20:3-7; 28:12-17), (3) a message in a vision (Gen. 15:1-21; Isa. 6:1-13; Ezek. 1:1-3; 8:1-4), (4) a message by an angel (Gen. 16:7-13; 18:1-33; 22:11-18; 32:24-30; Ex. 3:2 – 4:17; Josh. 5:13-15; Judg. 2:1-5; 6:11-24; 13:2-25), and (5) a message in a dream by an angel (Gen. 31:11-13).

These theophanies may be characterized as (1) often introducing momentous events (Ex. 3:1-12), (2) further revealing God's plan (Gen. 15:1-17; 28:12-17), (3) always manifesting the supernatural (Ex. 3:2 f.; Josh. 5:13-15), (4) designedly supporting the wavering (Ex. 3:2 – 4:17; Judg. 6:11-24), and (5) invariably restricted to God's people except where non-Israelites are specifically involved (Gen. 20:3-7; Num. 22:20-35).

"The angel of the Lord" (or "of God" – cf. Judg. 6:20 f.), though occasionally designating an angel (e.g., II Sam. 24:16; I Kings 19:5, 7; Matt. 2:13, 19; Luke 1:11), often describes a person whose characteristics seem to fit Christ only.

The deity of this unique angel is proved by the facts that he (1) is identified as God (Gen. 16:7 f., 13; 18:2, 10, 13; 22:10-12, 15-18; Ex. 3:2-6, 14, 18; Judg. 2:1, 5; 6:11, 14, 16), (2) is recognized as God (Gen. 16:9-13; Judg. 6:22-24; 13:21-23; cf. Gen. 32:24-30 with Hos. 12:4 f.), (3) is described in terms befitting the Deity alone (Ex. 3:5 f., 14; Josh. 5:15), (4) calls himself God (Gen. 31:11, 13; Ex. 3:2, 6, 14), (4) receives worship (Josh. 5:14; Judg. 2:4 f.), and (5) speaks with divine authority (Judg. 2:1-5).

The identification of this angel with Jesus Christ is confirmed by the facts that he (1) is distinguished personally from God the Father (Gen. 21:17-20; 48:16; Ex. 23:20 f.),

(2) is differentiated from angels in his acceptance of worship (Judg. 5:14 f.; cf. Rev. 19:10; 22:8 f.), (3) is called by a messianic title (Judg. 13:18; cf. Isa. 9:6; also cf. Ex. 3:14 with John 8:58), (4) is described as Redeemer (Gen. 48:15 f.; Isa. 63:9), (5) is predicted as the angel (messenger) of the new covenant (Mal. 3:1 [Heb.]; cf. also Ex. 14:19; 23:20 ff.; 32:34; 33:2, 14 f. with I Cor. 10:4), and (6) is equated with Christ's kingship (Josh. 5:13-15; cf. Rev. 19:11-16).

Theologically, the theophanies (1) corroborate the OT doctrine of the Trinity (Isa. 6:1-3, 8), (2) anticipate the NT doctrine of Christ's incarnation (John 1:14; 8:56), and (3) typify the biblical doctrine of God's eternal dwelling among the redeemed (cf. Ex. 25:8; 29:45 f.; Lev. 37:27 f. with Rev. 21:3, 22; 22:3-5).

See also ANGEL.

WICK BROOMALL

THEOPHOROI. From *theophoros* (God-bearing or God-borne), this term seems sometimes to have been used of early Christians as those who are indwelt by Christ or his Spirit. Thus Ignatius of Antioch (martyred *ca.* A.D. 110) bore the title or name Theophoros, although this was explained by some to be due to the fact that he was one of the infants carried and blessed by Jesus. In the Middle Ages an adjectival form (theophoric) was sometimes used of those who in processions carried the monstrance containing the sacred host and therefore, as it was supposed, the substance of the body of the divine Son.

GEOFFREY W. BROMILEY

THEOSOPHY. Simply construed, the term means God-wisdom, but since the theosophist does not lay claim to knowledge that is a revelation from God, but knowledge that is attained (through astral faculties) the term can at best mean divine wisdom.

In a more accurate way the term is construed as extra-temporal wisdom because its attainment depends on the theosophist's experience of withdrawing into the mental body, there to find the answers to life's secrets from spirits or to be taught by re-incarnated teachers.

Theosophy, then, is a kind of religion propagated by the American Theosophical Society and those of like mind. The term stands for an autosoteriological religious system. The experiences of salvation are dependent on knowledge attained in a special way from the world of spirit either directly or through teachers reincarnated. The incarnation of the supreme teacher is a Christ.

BIBLIOGRAPHY
Wm. O. Judge, *The Ocean of Theosophy;* J. K. Van Baalen, *The Chaos of the Cults.*

E. SIVERTSEN

THEOTOKOS. See MOTHER OF GOD.

THERAPEUTAE. A monastic sect which maintained an establishment at Lake Mareotis in Egypt around the beginning of the Christian era. The name probably denotes worshipers rather than healers. Philo's treatise, *The Contemplative Life,* is the one source of information about them. He describes the community as containing both men and women who devoted themselves to a studious and prayerful life. To this end they gave up their worldly possessions and lived on a simple diet with fastings. In their studies they made use of the OT and writings of ancient men. Their method of interpretation was allegorical. Not only did they observe the sabbath, but every fifty days they had a night-long convocation marked by an edifying discourse followed by a meal of leavened bread and water and hyssop, then singing and a choral dance. This group, highly praised by Philo for having attained the true excellence of life, belongs to hellenistic Judaism. No connection with the Essenes is apparent.

Eusebius, however, claimed them as early Christian converts, prototypes of the strong monastic movement which flourished in Egypt. His arguments are entirely inconclusive, but his opinion prevailed until modern times. Lucius (1879) questioned the authenticity of *The Contemplative Life,* assigning it to a date shortly before Eusebius' time and regarding it as a writing intended to exalt asceticism. Modern research, by Conybeare and by Wendland in particular, has tended to demonstrate its Philonic character.

BIBLIOGRAPHY
Philo, *The Contemplative Life;* Eusebius, *HE,* II. xvii. pp. 1-24; J. Moffatt in *HERE.*

EVERETT F. HARRISON

THINK, THOUGHT. Only the more important terms can be noted here. In the OT *ḥāšaḇ* is the most frequently used and the most varied in meaning — to reckon, impute, suppose, devise, reflect on, plan (Mal. 3:16; Jer.

29:11). Its corresponding noun, *maḥăšebeṭ*, is the most commonly used word for thought. Other verbs are *'āmar*, to say (to oneself), as in II Kings 5:11, and *dāmâ*, to liken, to devise (Esth. 4:13).

Among the NT verbs are *dokeō*, to suppose, to have an opinion (Luke 24:37); *enthymeomai*, to reflect on (Matt. 1:20); *hēgeomai*, to consider, regard, esteem (II Pet. 1:13; I Thess. 5:13); *logizomai*, to reckon, estimate, consider (Rom. 2:3; Phil. 4:8); *nomizō*, to account, suppose (Matt. 5:17; Acts 16:13); *noeō*, to perceive, understand, consider (I Tim. 1:7; II Tim. 2:7); *phroneō*, to take a viewpoint (I Cor. 13:11), to set the mind upon (Col. 3:2), to be earnestly disposed (Phil. 2:5), to be concerned (Phil. 4:10). Somewhat apart from these is *merimnaō*, to have anxious thought (Luke 10:41).

The principal Greek nouns are *dialogismos*, reasoning, usually with a bad connotation (Matt. 15:19); *dianoia*, understanding, thought, attitude (Eph. 4:18; Col. 1:21); *enthymēsis*, reflection, idea (Acts 17:29; Heb. 4:12); *ennoia*, insight (I Pet. 4:1); *vous*, which may indicate the content of the mind as well as the mind itself (Rom. 11:34), and *phronēma*, way of thinking, bent of thought (Rom. 8:6).

A few observations may be made upon the place given to thought in the Bible. There is little emphasis upon pure intellection of the Greek philosophical sort. The reason for this is that in the biblical setting thought moves in dependence upon God and his revelation. To think God's thoughts after him is the highest exercise of the mind. To think in independence of God is to think contrary to his will and purpose. The thoughts of the wicked are vain.

Scripture insists on the connection between thought and deed and between thought and character. The inner life must be kept with all diligence, for out of it are the issues of life. Injunctions to hear the word of God are admonitions to hear it with thoughtfulness, to heed its teaching. In the area of sanctification, pivotal importance is assigned to the process of reckoning oneself dead unto sin and alive unto God (Rom. 6:11).

The communication of revelation to the writers of the Bible raises problems incident to the degree and nature of human participation. However much it may be felt necessary to emphasize the passivity of the writers in order to safeguard the purity of the truth communicated through them, this need not mean that their mental faculties were dormant during the process. Rather, it would seem that they must have been stimulated. We have clear testimony, at any rate, that the prophets gave themselves to reflection and industrious research into the meaning of the messages given to them (I Pet. 1:10-11).

See also MIND.

EVERETT F. HARRISON

THOMISM. The world view of Thomas Aquinas (1225-74). Thomistic theology deals with truth on the authority of revelation, Thomistic philosophy with truth accessible to unaided reason. God is the unifying element in theology and philosophy, for the source of all truth must at the same time be the source of all being. Revelation and reason, thus, cannot be in contradiction.

By-passing Plato and reviving Aristotle, Aquinas denies that man enjoys an innate knowledge of God's existence. Reason must infer the existence of God from the effects of God in nature. Aquinas defended five proofs for God's existence: from motion, efficient cause, potentiality, degrees of being, and teleology. These arguments reduce to one, namely, that the sufficient reason for any existing thing necessarily implies the being of God. If anything exists, something necessarily exists; for from nothing, nothing can come.

Since the essence of God exceeds the capacity of the human mind, reason can only enumerate the divine attributes. God is known by what he is not. He is not in time; he has neither matter nor potency. In sum, God is simple being. This simplicity excludes everything not reducible to being as such. God is being in itself, whereas everything else derives its being from God. Created being is good, for it resembles God's inherent goodness.

Creation can only be dimly grasped by reason. Creation is not logical sequence, for the world would then have come of necessity. It is not temporal, for there was no time till creation. It is not motion, for in motion something changes while something remains unchanged. The world could never be discovered by examining God. Creation is an act, though reason imagines it under the form of change. God could have created an infinite number of worlds. The actual world is the best there is, though not necessarily the best there might be.

Angels (*q.v.*) are pure spirits; they enjoy the highest degree of created perfection. Angels are demonstrated on the assumption that God willed a plenitude of being. Since God created higher creatures in greater abundance, the number of angels is enormous. Angels differ from God because their essence is not identical with their existence.

Aquinas followed Aristotle in conceiving the world as a series of seven concentric planetary spheres. These spheres are contained within an eighth sphere, forming the fixed stars and having the earth as their physical center.

Man is a composite of body and soul. His body is not evil, for matter is good in itself. The soul is the intellectual principle, the form of the body. Matter is the passive agent in individuation, while form is the active agent.

Thomism marks the highest point in medieval scholasticism.

BIBLIOGRAPHY
Thomas Aquinas, *Summa Theologica* and *Summa Contra Gentiles*; Étienne Gilson, *The Philosophy of St. Thomas Aquinas*.

EDWARD JOHN CARNELL

THRONE. Both literal and symbolic uses are found in Scripture. The Hebrew *kissē'* signifies any elevated seat occupied by a person of honor. In a country where people usually squatted or reclined, the use of a chair was already a token of dignity (cf. II Kings 4:10; Prov. 9:14). In order to specify a throne in our sense of the term, it was necessary to add to *kissē'* the idea of royalty or some office such as that of the high priest (I Sam. 1:9), a judge (Ps. 122:5), or a military leader (Jer. 1:15). Royalty is reflected in the phrase "the throne of the kingdom" (Deut. 17:18; I Kings 1:46; II Chron. 7:18).

The characteristic feature of the royal throne was its elevation — Solomon's throne was approached by six steps (I Kings 10:19; II Chron. 9:18), and Jehovah's throne is described as "high and lifted up" (Isa. 6:1). The material and workmanship were costly — that of Solomon is described as a throne of ivory (i.e., inlaid with ivory) and overlaid with pure gold in all parts except the ivory in-lay. The king sat on his throne on state occasions, as when granting audience (I Kings 2:19; 22:10; Esth. 5:1), receiving homage (II Kings 11:19), or administering justice (Prov. 20:8). At such times. he appeared in his royal robes (I Kings 22:10; Jonah 3:6; Acts 12:21).

Symbolically, the throne was emblematic of supreme power and dignity (Gen. 41:40), and hence was attributed to Jehovah both in respect to his heavenly abode (Pss. 11:4; 103:19; Isa. 66:1; Acts 7:49; Rev. 4:2), or to his earthly abode at Jerusalem (Jer. 3:17), and more particularly in the temple (Jer. 17:12; Ezek. 43:7). Similarly, "to sit upon the throne" implied the exercise of regal power (Deut. 17:18; I Kings 16:11; II Kings 10:30; Esth. 1:2), and "to sit upon the throne of another person" means succession to the royal dignity (I Kings 1:13). In Col. 1:16 "thrones" apparently designates celestial beings rather than earthly potentates.

Of special importance in messianic prophecy is the right to occupy "the throne of David" (II Sam. 7:13, 16; Luke 1:32).

D. H. WALTERS

TIME. The definition of time (*chronos*) is one of the most vexing problems of philosophy. The Bible presents a distinctive conception of time, reflected especially by its peculiar use of the terms *kairos* and *aiōn*. Instead of viewing time abstractly as a problem, it regards time as a created sphere in which God's redemptive plan is actualized.

In the usual secular sense, *kairos* refers to a definite point of time especially appropriate for a given undertaking (Acts 24:25), *aiōn* to an extent of time (stipulated or unstipulated). The NT builds on this usage with a special eye to redemptive history (John 7:6), in which divine determination (Acts 1:7), not human deliberation, constitutes a given moment or age the appropriate time of God's working. "Because . . . the divine plan of salvation is bound to such time points or *kairoi* chosen by God, . . . it is . . . redemptive *history*. Not all fragments of ongoing time constitute redemptive history in the narrower sense, but rather . . . these *kairoi* singled out from time as a whole" (Oscar Cullmann, *Christ and Time*, pp. 40 f.).

While the NT gives prominent scope to the future *kairoi* associated with the eschatological drama, its central *kairos* is the life and death and resurrection of the incarnate Christ, which is decisively significant for the kingdom of God. The terms "day (of the Lord)" and "hour," "now" and "today" likewise gain dramatic significance in the NT context whenever the eternal order and redemptive history impinges upon the sweep of ordinary events.

The interconnected redemptive *kairoi* supply the threadline of salvation history. Yet the divine *kairoi* at the same time secretly enfold the entire secular movement of time (Acts 17:26) for the fulfilment, often unwittingly, of God's ultimate purposes.

As the *kairos* is a decisive momentary unveiling of the eternal, so the *aiōn* discloses the Lord of ages who divides the long sweep of time according to his own purposes. The *kairoi* are decisive turning points within the larger *aiōna*, The Bible brackets history with an eye on the age of promise, the age of fulfilment, and the age to come.

Man's transition to the eternal order will not involve him in the supersession of temporal experience since, although redeemed, he remains a creature (Rev. 10:6, "there will be no more time," teaches not the cessation of time, but the expiration of opportunity. The word here means "delay").

Modern philosophy characteristically affirms that it takes time more seriously than did ancient or medieval philosophy. Classic Greek thought dissolved the significance of the temporal world, depicting it as illusory shadow alongside the eternal ideas and forms (cf. ETERNITY). The influence of Platonic and Aristotelian thought upon medieval scholars served to divert attention from the unique biblical view of history to the revealed truths of Judeo-Christian religion, although the importance of historical revelation and redemption remained central in the great creeds. Modern idealistic philosophy shunned the historical and temporal as bearing eternal meaning and significance at any point and therefore was hostile, even if often in a concealed manner, to the doctrines of Christ's unique incarnation and atonement. Led by Hegel, however, modern idealism placed time and history in the very nature of the Absolute. Thus it simultaneously minimized the uniqueness of biblical history and exaggerated the spirituality of history in general by viewing all as divine process. In two ways this profoundly unbiblical speculation retained nonetheless a debt to the biblical view. Against the depreciation of the temporal by classic ancient philosophy, it stressed God's aggressive interest in history; and against cyclical views of history as a process of recurring ages, it emphasized that the time process moves towards a perfect goal.

Equally significant, evolutionary naturalism, returning to the Greek cosmocentric outlook at the expense of theistic interpretations of reality, appealed to modern evolutionary views as lifting time to decisive importance. Its notion that time itself actualizes new forms of life was more popularly held in the first half century after Darwin than today, when speculative interest in emergent evolution is enlarging. Both approaches usually retain the expectation of a higher goal to which the temporal process moves, thus reflecting a secret indebtedness of modern theories of progress to the biblical doctrine of the kingdom of God, which speculative expositions strip of its supernatural features.

Outside the stream of biblical theology, virtually the whole movement of ancient religion and philosophy depreciated the significance of the temporal order. Not all religions of the Orient indeed shared the notion of nirvana, peculiar to Buddhism, with its emphasis on history and personal existence as evil and its expectation of bliss through annihilation or by absorption into the divine rather than through historical redemption, but none of them rose to the biblical emphasis that history displays a purposive movement to an intelligent, moral goal. The non-biblical religions and speculations of antiquity did not escape the cycle theory of history as a series of recurring ages; in fact, this conception was sometimes spiritualized by designating the process "God" along pantheistic lines. While Zoroastrianism (*q.v.*) made more room for ethical teleology through its insistence on two eternal principles, Good and Evil, its unrelieved dualism excluded an abiding significance for history. In fact, while shunning the notion of eternal recurrence, Zoroastrianism nonetheless divided the world movement into four ages.

Nowhere does the importance of time come into view as in biblical teaching. While time is not ultimate, it is the divinely created sphere of God's preserving and redemptive work, and the arena of man's decision on his way to an eternal destiny. History moves toward a divine goal involving the redemption of the elect by the Creator and Lord of the universe. Within this historical matrix, every thought, word and deed has repercussions in the eternal moral order. Richard Kroner aptly summarizes the biblical philosophy: "History has a beginning in God, it has its center in Christ and its end in the final consummation and the Last Judgment" (*ER*: "Philosophy of History," p. 582. New York: The Philosophical Library, 1945).

Oscar Cullmann emphasizes that, as against the Jewish conception of a linear history still awaiting its climax (the Christ-event coinciding with the Parousia), in the Christian view the center of history lies in a past event rather than in the eschatological future (the death and resurrection of Jesus of Nazareth decisively controls the time-line thereafter).

Cullmann properly warns against excessive disjunctions of time and eternity by Kierkegaard, Barth, Brunner and Bultmann. But his own alternative impairs the unique eternity of God (see ETERNITY). Moreover, Cullmann's biblical realism is threatened by concessions to the notion of "temporal, non-historical myth" to which he reduces much in the biblical narratives of the beginning and the end. If such myth actually preserves the continuity of the temporal line, why may not all biblical events be reduced to this status, and the second Adam be dismissed on the same pattern as the first Adam?

BIBLIOGRAPHY
K. Barth, *Church Dogmatics*, III, 2 §47; O. Cullmann, *Christ and Time*; J. Marsh, "Time," in *RTWB*; E. Trocmé, "Time," *CB*.

CARL F. H. HENRY

TITHES. The following words express the concept of a tithe:'āśar (Gen. 28:22 bis; Deut. 14:22 bis; 26:12; I Sam. 8:15, 17; Neh. 10:37-38); ma'ăśēr (Gen. 14:20; Lev. 27:30, 31, 32; Num. 18:21, 24, 26 bis, 28; Deut. 12:6, 11, 17; 14:23, 28; 26:12 bis; II Chron. 31:5-6 bis, 12; Neh. 10:37-38 bis; 12:44; 13:5, 12; Ezek. 45:11, 14; Amos 4:4; Mal. 3:8, 10); dekatoō (Heb. 7:6, 9); apodekatoō (Matt. 23:23; Luke 11:42; Heb. 7:5); apodekateuō (Luke 18:12); and dekatē (Heb. 7:2, 4, 8-9).

The basic OT facts may be summarized thus: (1) The tithe was recognized in patriarchal times (Gen. 14:20; 28:22). (2) In the Mosaic legislation the tithe, belonging essentially to the Lord (Lev. 27:30-33), was given to the Levites because of their priestly service and because of their non-inheritance in Israel (Num. 18:21-32). Modifications — but not contradictions — of the law appear in the legislation (Deut. 12:5-19; 14:22-29; 26:12-15) designed for the settlement in Palestine. (3) In subsequent history the tithe is recognized (II Chron. 31:5 f., 12; Neh. 10:37 f.; 12:44; 13:5, 12); however, it appears that this law was either perverted into legalism (Amos 4:4) or diverted into oblivion

(Mal. 3:7-12). (4) Significantly, the tithe is not introduced as a part of the restored temple and priesthood in Ezekiel's vision (Ezek. 40 — 48).

The NT is all but silent on the tithe. Christ rebuked the Pharisees for their legalistic observance of it (Luke 18:9-14) and for their placing it above justice and the love of God (Matt. 23:23). A final reference in Hebrews 7:2-9 (citing Abraham's tithe to Melchizedek) concludes what the NT says on the subject.

The silence of the NT writers, particularly Paul, regarding the present validity of the tithe can be explained only on the ground that the dispensation of grace has no more place for a law on tithing than it has for a law on circumcision. The principles of Christian giving are clearly set forth in Paul's letters to the Corinthian church (I Cor. 16:1 f.; II Cor. 8-9). These do not exclude the tithe as a convenient basis for proportionate giving, nor do they limit one to the tithe.

BIBLIOGRAPHY
Blunt; *HDAC*; *HDB*; *HERE*; *ISBE*.

WICK BROOMALL

TOLERATION. From the Latin *tolerare*, meaning "to endure." When the term is used strictly, the acceptance of something not regarded as ideal is indicated. It may be used to refer to an allowable inaccuracy in the dimensions and operation of the parts of a machine, or to the ability of an organism to function acceptably despite the presence in it of poisons or drugs. More commonly, it indicates the permission of, or patience in the presence of, opinions or practices that are not regarded as really good or of persons identified with such opinions or practices. In this stricter sense of the term, the superiority of those who extend toleration is clearly implied or asserted. Thus the Act of William and Mary, 1689, (cf. Gee and Hardy, *Documents Illustrative of the History of the English Church*, pp. 654 ff.) which legally establishes one church but permits, under specific restrictions, the existence of "dissenting" religious bodies, is properly called The Toleration Act. To receive toleration in this sense is scarcely flattering, but it may be demanded and accepted as the best obtainable.

When, however, general appeals for "toleration" are issued, as has become common since, for example, John Locke's "Letter on Toleration," 1685, the judgment that one opinion, or one group, is superior, though still implied, is not emphasized. They are usually contentions that other opinions than one's own, and the people holding them, are to be treated with respect. A typical modern example is Roland H. Bainton's, *The Travail of Religious Liberty* (obtainable as a Harper Torchbook).

ANDREW KERR RULE

TONGUES, GIFT OF. See SPIRITUAL GIFTS.

TOTAL DEPRAVITY. See DEPRAVITY, TOTAL.

TRACTARIANISM. A movement launched in 1833 through a series of *Tracts for the Times* by a group of Anglican clergymen at Oxford (hence also called The Oxford Movement). Prominent were the poet John Keble, R. Hurrell Froude, John Henry Newman, leader of the movement, and Dr. E. B. Pusey. Stimulated by the new Romantic interest in the (idealized) Middle Ages and the Catholic Revival in France, alarmed by the rising political power of the largely irreligious lower classes, Nonconformists and Roman Catholics (now emancipated from legal disablements), dissatisfied with the rationalism, worldliness and ineffectiveness of most of the clergy except the Evangelicals, the Tractarians asserted the doctrine of Apostolic Succession of the Anglican clergy and the independence and supremacy of the Church of England *vis-à-vis* the state. These views culminated in Tract 90, written by Newman in 1841, with its proposal that the Anglican formularies should all be interpreted in a Roman Catholic sense. A complete return to all the main pre-Reformation beliefs and practices was clearly implied. Newman followed these convictions to their logical conclusion, being received into the Church of Rome in 1845 and becoming a cardinal in 1879. Many Anglo-Catholics (the modern name) have followed him since. Nevertheless, moderate Anglo-Catholic influences have increased to a position of dominance in the Church of England, particularly among the bishops. Anglo-Catholics have revived monasticism and are noted for their insistence on ritual and some devoted work in slum parishes. The movement has never commanded the allegiance of a large section of the laity.

O. RAYMOND JOHNSTON

TRADITION. I. DEFINITION. "In the early Christian Fathers, tradition (*paradosis, traditio*) means the revelation made by God and delivered to his faithful people through the mouth of his prophets and apostles. It does not mean something 'handed down' but something 'handed over.'" (*Oxford Dictionary of the Christian Church,* Oxford University Press, London, 1957, p. 1369). *HERE* (xii, p. 411) is nearer popular usage when it says, "The word 'tradition' means, etymologically, 'handing over.' The conception of 'tradition,' therefore, implies (a) a 'deposit' which is handed over, and (b) 'depositaries,' i.e., persons who are in possession of the deposit, and are commissioned to preserve it and transmit it to successors." Popular usage, even among theologians, stresses, however, the unwritten aspect of tradition, which is therefore normally regarded as less reliable than written documents. *JewEnc* (xii, p. 213) defines tradition as "doctrines and sayings transmitted from father to son by word of mouth, and thus preserved among the people." In our understanding of tradition we must distinguish clearly between that which is handed down officially as a "deposit," memories of the past of uncertain antiquity, and customs which by virtue of long usage have come by some to be regarded as of binding force.

II. ORAL TRADITION. The scholar is rightly sceptical of information based on a long period of popular memory. Recent research has established that where such tradition existed in a stable society, was publicly recited at major religious or secular festivals and was checkable by written records (all of which conditions existed in early Israel), it may be regarded as fundamentally reliable (cf. Albright: *From the Stone Age to Christianity,* pp. 33 ff., 40-43). Nyberg (*Studien zum Hoseabuch*) argued that the oral transmission of at least some of the earlier OT books is in fact a better guarantee of their accuracy than the writing of the time.

III. TRADITION AND SCRIPTURE. Without entering into the difficult and controversial question of the formation of the canon of Scripture it is clear that considerable portions of the information in it must for longer or shorter time have been passed down orally (cf. II Tim. 1:13; 2:2; I Cor. 15:13; 11:23 (*paralambanō apo,* cf. Arndt p. 87b), etc.). Few would question K. Barth's dictum, "It is, of course, obvious that there is a tradition which is older than Holy Scripture and on which Holy Scripture as such is founded: it is the way from revelation as such to its scriptural attestation" (*Church Dogmatics*, E.T. T. & T. Clark, Edinburgh, 1956, I, 2, p. 552).

This does not give tradition any authoritative coexistence with Scripture. As soon as Holy Scripture has come into existence by divine inspiration, all tradition left outside it, even if it could be proved to be factually true, has to bow to the authority of Scripture and be interpreted by it. It could, theoretically, illustrate the truth; it cannot interpret it.

It is entirely illegitimate to try to penetrate from Scripture to the tradition behind it, as is done especially by Form Criticism (*q.v.*), in the hope of reaching more objective truth. This is a denial of the reality of inspiration and ignores that in both OT and NT we are dealing with a tradition carefully fixed and handed down from the first, not with random memories that might be embroidered in the telling.

IV. THE VALUE OF TRADITION. Where there is evidence that tradition has been carefully preserved, we value its historical testimony, though we subordinate it to the illumination of the Spirit in the interpretation of Scripture. The most striking example of this is the Masoretic Text of the OT. Though this did not take its present definitive form till the sixth to ninth centuries A.D. — the consonantal text is attested by the Qumran discoveries as existing essentially in its present form in the first century B.C. — increasingly modern scholars are loath to leave it unless the clear sense and divergent traditions of the versions demand it. In the RSV probably 98 per cent of the translation remains true to the Masoretic tradition.

V. THE LIMITATIONS OF TRADITION. It is a striking fact that whenever we turn to Ante-Nicene exegesis for light on more difficult NT passages, we find the most divergent views. There is clearly no authoritative theological tradition linking the apostles with the second century. This is confirmed by the writings of the sub-apostolic fathers, all of whom deviate from the standard of the NT in some respect. It is clear that the only tradition that has any real claim to link with the apostolic church is the type of anecdote that Papias collected.

We find much the same position in Jewish tradition. Josephus, as priest and Pharisee, had access to the two main sources of tradition of his time. Yet few would attribute value to most of the few additions he can make to the biblical account in his *Antiquities*. Even for the Post-Exilic and Intertestamental periods he tells us little that is new until he can base himself on the work of Nicholas of Damascus, Herod the Great's historian. There is adequate evidence of a priestly, cultic tradition, in part of great antiquity, some of which is preserved in the Mishnah, but while it enables us to reconstruct the cult background of the life of Christ (e.g., Edersheim: *The Temple*), it is too uncertain to be authoritative in the interpretation of the OT. The rabbinic tradition found in the Talmud and Midrashim, with the exception of a few older portions of the Mishnah, cannot be used without great care for the period before A.D. 70, and the nearer it comes to the Maccabean period — it may be ignored for almost everything earlier — the less valuable it becomes. Nor has Qumran revealed the Essenes as possessors of a valid tradition. In other words there is no valid tradition extant, Jewish or Christian, that would enable us to supplement or give an authoritative interpretation to Scripture.

BIBLIOGRAPHY

HERE; E. Nielsen, *Oral Tradition*; C. Salmon, *The Infallibility of the Church*, chap. V; Karl Barth, *Church Dogmatics*, E.T. I, 2, pp. 547-72, II, 2, pp. 458 ff.

H. L. ELLISON

TRADUCIANISM. This is one of four theories of the origin of the individual soul, i.e., that the soul, as well as the body, comes from the parents. Alternatives are: (1) Pre-existence of all souls; held by e.g., Origen and Mormons; (2) Reincarnation (see METEMPSYCHOSIS); (3) Creationism (*q.v.*), whereby God creates a fresh soul for each body.

Direct biblical evidence is non-existent, and conclusions must be based on deductions. In favor of traducianism: (1) God's breathing into man the breath of life is not said to be repeated after Adam (Gen. 2:7); (2) Adam begat a son in his own likeness (Gen. 5:3); (3) God's resting (Gen. 2:2-3) suggests no fresh acts of creation *ex nihilo*; and (4) original sin affects the whole man, including the soul; this is simply accounted for by traducianism.

Traducianism was held by Tertullian and many Westerns; since the Reformation by Lutherans; also by the Eastern Church. Roman Catholics and most Reformed theologians are creationists, though Shedd and Strong favor traducianism. Modern studies in heredity and psychosomatic unity are indecisive, but can easily be interpreted on the traducianist side.

BIBLIOGRAPHY

A. H. Strong, *Systematic Theology*, V. I. iv.

J. STAFFORD WRIGHT

TRANSCENDENCE. A theological term, referring to the relation of God to creation. It may mean (1) difference or "otherness"; (2) distance or remoteness. In the OT Ex. 24; Isa. 6:1; 40:12-26; Ezek. 1 might seem to imply remoteness. But in Isa. 57:15; Ezek. 11:22-23 God's transcendent holiness and glory is compatible with his gracious presence. He is the holy one in the midst (Hos. 11:9), independent and different from his creatures (Isa. 55:8-9), yet near in providence and grace (Ps. 139). During the intertestamental period the remoteness of divine transcendence was overemphasized e.g., in not using the divine name. The incarnation and the coming of the Holy Spirit fulfils the OT revelation in the New (Matt. 1:23; John 14:14-15, 23). In highest glory Christ is above his church, yet as the Head who is also one with it (Col. 1:18; 2:9-10; Heb. 4:14-15; Rev. 1:10-20). The Colossian heresy overemphasized remoteness (Col. 2:18-23) and its repetition is evident later in Arianism, Socinianism and Deism.

See also ATTRIBUTES, DIVINE.

GEORGE J. C. MARCHANT

TRANSCENDENTALISM. The term transcendental was used by the Scholastics to designate properties of objects that transcend the ten Aristotelian categories. It was after Kant applied it to those elements that were constituents of experience but which did not come through sense-perception, that it began to assume its distinctive meaning. With further impetus from Schelling, "Transcendentalism" came to designate German idealism in general. Through the influence of Coleridge its ideas passed into English thought to take unique form in New England after 1836. Here it was used to designate the varied eclectic circles in which Emerson, Margaret Fuller, Theodore Parker, and other kindred spirits moved. The group represented a reaction against materialism and Unitarianism, while at the same time stressing intuitive knowledge — the inspiration of the individual soul — and optimism concerning human nature. The best literary expression of the movement came through a quarterly publication, *The Dial*, 1840-44, while its ideals of social brotherhood were tried unsuccessfully at the Brook Farm community, led by George Ripley.

Transcendentalism is more widely used to designate all objective idealists, regardless of individual differences, often carrying an implication of unwarranted idealism.

BIBLIOGRAPHY

O. B. Frothingham, *Transcendentalism in New England*; C. L. F. Gohdes, *The Periodicals of American Transcendentalism*; P. Miller, *The Transcendentalists*; *The American Transcendentalists*; H. Walsh, *EncyBrit*, 12, pp. 399-400; D. MacKenzie, *HERE*, 12, pp. 419-25.

JACK P. LEWIS

TRANSFIGURATION. The verb *metamorphoō* is found in three connections in the NT, first and foremost of that mysterious change which came over the appearance of Jesus on the mount (Matt. 17:2; Mark 9:2), then of the growing moral likeness to Christ which believers experience in this life (II Cor. 3:18), an experience quite in contrast to conformity to the present age (Rom. 12:2).

Clearly the transfiguration incident is intended to be understood as a turning point in Jesus' ministry. From this time on he gave himself less to instruction of the multitudes and more to the training of the Twelve. From this time on he was mastered by the necessity of going to Jerusalem to die. The story is told naturally, despite its unusual features. But it is not accompanied by interpretation. So the reader must look to the broad context, and there he finds a logical connection in the Caesarea-Philippi episode one week earlier. The announcement of Jesus that he must go to Jerusalem to die and then be raised from the dead shocked the disciples beyond measure. Of the week which followed nothing is recorded. Tension was high. Some new disclosure was called for. This time it was given to the select circle of Peter, James and John, and it did not come merely from Jesus' lips; but it was confirmed out of the lips of two representatives of the old covenant, Moses and Elijah. Furthermore, it received the endorsement of God himself, who instructed the three to listen to his Son, with obvious reference to the very matter which had proved a stumbling block to their faith, namely, the necessity that the Messiah should suffer death.

There is no suggestion that this experience came to Jesus to sharpen his convictions or bolster a wavering determination to fulfil God's purpose. Emphasis falls on the value of the experience for the disciples. Christ was transfigured before them, and the Father's voice was directed to them rather than to the Son.

The connection with OT revelation is established by means of the glory-light and the cloud, which had previously been united in the shekinah, as well as by the divine voice and the presence of leading saints of olden days. Revelation which was then incomplete comes to fulness now (cf. Heb. 1:1-3). The connection with the baptism is made by the Father's voice, the title Son, and by the very significance of the baptism as pointing ahead to the cross. The connection with the temptation appears in the acceptance of the path of suffering rather than a grasping after immediate glory. The transfiguration has its proper sequel in Gethsemane, for there the commission which Christ accepted at the baptism and shared with the disciples as a fixed purpose at Caesarea-Philippi is accepted afresh in its terrifying reality. The connection with the resurrection is apparent from Jesus' caution to the three disciples to maintain silence about what they had seen on the mount until the Son of Man should rise from the dead (Mark 9:9). The connection with the future glory of the messianic kingdom is suggested by the words of Jesus about some of his company being privileged to see the kingdom in its manifested power (Mark 9:1). A similar use is made of the transfiguration in II Pet. 1:16-18.

Critical attempts to make this incident a throwback from the post-resurrection appearances have failed. Nowhere in the appearances does Jesus possess the dazzling brilliance described here. Uniformly he is represented as speaking to the disciples when he manifested himself to them. This is not true here; he merely converses with Moses and Elijah. Further, Christ always shows himself in solitary fashion after his resurrection, but here he is accompanied by the men from the past. The divine voice is not a feature of the resurrection appearances, but it has a prominent role in the incident before us.

The lesson to be gleaned from the transfiguration for Saviour and disciple alike is the inseparable yoking of suffering and glory. The cross is the will of God. It is the path to the splendor of rewarding bliss. There is a further lesson, perhaps. The place of prayer is the place of transfiguration (Luke 9:29).

A. M. Ramsey has well summarized the value of the transfiguration for the church. "It is a mirror in which the Christian mystery is seen in its unity. Here we perceive that the living and the dead are one in Christ, that the old covenant and the new are inseparable, that the cross and the glory are of one, that the age to come is already here, that our human nature has a destiny of glory, that in Christ the final word is uttered and in Him alone the Father is well pleased. Here the diverse elements in the theology of the New Testament meet" (*The Glory of God and the Transfiguration of Christ,* Longmans, Green and Co., London, 1949, p. 144).

See also GLORY.

BIBLIOGRAPHY
P. Bonnard in *CB*; G. H. Boobyer, *St. Mark and the Transfiguration Story;* W. M. Clow, *The Secret of the Lord,* pp. 165-254; A. S. Martin in *HDCG*; Harald Riesenfeld, *Jésus Transfiguré;* W. M. Smith, *The Supernaturalness of Christ,* pp. 165-85.

EVERETT F. HARRISON

TRANSGRESSION. See SIN.

TRANSLATION. The translation of Enoch and Elijah and the future translation of the saints at the second advent constitute the scope of the present article.

Enoch was a godly man whose life was pleasing to the Lord (Gen. 5:22 ff.). Like Noah, he was a preacher of righteousness to an ungodly generation (Jude 14 f.). His translation was (1) accomplished by God (Gen. 5:24); (2) prompted by faith (Heb. 11:5) and (3) rewarded by heaven (Heb. 11:5).

Elijah also was a godly man. His translation was (1) announced (II Kings 2:1); (2) known by others (II Kings 2:2-9); (3) accomplished by God (II Kings 2:1, 9); (4) plainly visible (II Kings 2:11) and (5) permanent (II Kings 2:12). On the mount of transfiguration Elijah appeared with the glorified Lord (Matt. 17:3).

There are two translations of the saints. The first is primarily spiritual and is synonymous with regeneration. This translation, initiated by God (Col. 1:13) and prompted by faith (John 5:24), transfers believers from Satan's kingdom to Christ's kingdom (Col. 1:13) and issues in the forgiveness of their sins (Acts 26:18). By this spiritual translation their real citizenship is in heaven (Phil. 3:20, ASV).

The second and final translation of believers is primarily physical and is synonymous with the rapture (*q.v.*) (I Thess. 4:13-18). This translation is (1) contingent on the Lord's return (I Cor. 15:51 f.); (2) completely transforming (Phil. 3:21); (3) instantaneous (I

Cor. 15:52); (4) unannounced (I Cor. 15:53); (5) permanent (I Cor. 15:53); and (6) subsequent to the resurrection of dead believers (I Thess. 4:16). By this translation the bodies of believers are transformed so they may live as citizens in the new Jerusalem (Phil. 3:20 f.; I John 3:2 f.; Rev. 21:1-7, 9-11).

WICK BROOMALL

TRANSMIGRATION OF SOULS. See METEMPSYCHOSIS.

TRANSUBSTANTIATION. The theory of transubstantiation, accepted by Rome as a dogma in 1215, is an attempt to explain the statements of Christ: "This is my body," and "This is my blood" (Mark 14:22, 24) as applied to the bread and wine of the Lord's Supper. It is insisted that the "is" must be taken with the strictest literalism. But to our senses the bread and wine seem to remain exactly as they were even when consecrated. There is no perceptible miracle of transformation. The explanation is found in terms of a distinction between the so-called "substance" (or true reality) and the "accidents" (the specific, perceptible characteristics). The latter remain, but the former, i.e., the substance of bread and wine, is changed into that of the body and blood of Christ. This carries with it many serious consequences. If Christ is substantially present, it is natural that the elements should be adored. It can also be claimed that he is received by all who communicate, whether rightly to salvation or wrongly to perdition. There also arises the idea of a propitiatory immolation of Christ for the temporal penalties of sin, with all the associated scandals of private masses. The weaknesses of the theory are obvious. It is not scriptural. On sharper analysis it does not even explain the dominical statements. It contradicts the true biblical account of Christ's presence. It has no secure patristic backing. It stands or falls with a particular philosophical understanding. It destroys the true nature of a sacrament. And it certainly perverts its proper use and gives rise to dangerous superstitions inimical to evangelical faith.

BIBLIOGRAPHY
J. Calvin, *Institutes*, IV, 18; T. Cranmer, *The True and Catholic Doctrine of the Lord's Supper*; N. Dimock, *Doctrine of the Lord's Supper*; W. H. Griffith Thomas, *The Principles of Theology*, pp. 388-410.

GEOFFREY W. BROMILEY

TRIBULATION. The word "tribulation" is derived from the Latin *tribulum*, an agricultural implement employed for separating the husks from the corn by a rigorous process known as *tribulatio*, and which readily suggests a usage illustrative of human experience. Apocalyptical, eschatological, and predictive considerations lend the English word "tribulation" its major biblical interest centered in the great apocalypse of Matthew 24 (cf. Mark 13 and Luke 21) where the Greek word is *thlipsis* which means literally "a pressing together." The word is translated variously in the AV by tribulation, afflicted, affliction, anguish, burdened, persecution, trouble. Together with the verb *thlibō* the following groupings are suggested: (1) Parable (Matt. 13:21; Mark 4:17; John 16:21). (2) Retribution (Rom. 2:9; II Thess. 1:6; Rev. 2:22). (3) Discourse (Acts 7:10; 7:11; II Cor. 8:13; Acts 11:19; I Cor. 7:28). (4) Apocalypse (Matt. 24:7, 21, 29; Mark 13:19, 24). (5) Disciples and discipline (appointed to — I Thess. 3:3 and eighteen other references; secure in — Rom. 8:35; Rev. 7:14; refined by — Rom. 5:3(2); 12:12; II Cor. 7:4; 1:6; comforted in — II Cor. 1:4; 4:17; Phil. 4:14; I Thess. 3:7; succor enjoined — James 1:27; II Cor. 1:4; I Tim. 5:10). The thought contained in the Greek word *thlipsis* is best represented in the Hebrew by words derived from the related roots *sûq*, which in the hiphil means "to straiten," "to distress" (Deut. 28:53, 55, 57); *sûr*, "to bind up," "to press upon," "to beset"; and *sarar*, "to oppress," "to persecute" (Num. 10:9). Derivatives from the last named root are found in Deut. 4:30, a passage which became contributory to Jewish eschatological and apocalyptic concepts by association with the biblical term "end of days," found in the same verse, and always connected with the advent of the messianic age which was to be ushered in by "birth-pangs" (Sota IX, 15; Enoch XCIX, 4; C,1).

BIBLIOGRAPHY
Mishnah; R. C. Trench, *Study in Words*; M. Buber, *For the Sake of Heaven*.

LAWRENCE DUFF-FORBES

TRICHOTOMY. This term, which signifies a division into three parts (Greek *tricha*, "in three parts"; *temnein*, "cut"), is applied in theology to the tripartite division of human nature into body, soul, and spirit. This view developed from Plato's twofold division, body and soul, through Aristotle's further division of the soul into an (1) animal soul, the breathing, organic aspect of man's being and a (2) rational soul, the intellectual aspect.

Early Christian writers, influenced by this Greek philosophy, found confirmation of their view in I Thess. 5:23, "And the very God of peace sanctify you wholly; and . . . your whole spirit and soul and body be preserved blameless unto the coming of our Lord Jesus Christ." Origen even took the words *soma* ("body"), *psyche* ("soul"), and *pneuma* ("spirit") as clues to the proper method of interpreting all Scripture, suggesting that each Scripture should be interpreted (1) in its natural or somatic meaning, (2) its symbolic or psychical meaning, and finally (3) in its spiritual or pneumatic meaning. Such piecemeal interpretation of Scripture or of human nature is likely to miss the tremendous biblical emphasis upon wholeness and unity, where even in the Thessalonian proof-text Paul prays that they may be sanctified *wholly* and that their *whole* spirit, soul, and body may be preserved blameless.

Both Tertullian and Augustine held to the dichotomy (*q.v.*) of body and soul but leaned almost to the threefold analysis of man by making the Aristotelian distinction between the animal and rational soul. Present theological and psychological emphasis is almost altogether upon the fundamental wholeness or unity of man's being as against all philosophical attempts to divide it.

BIBLIOGRAPHY

The classic work, without parallel, is J. B. Heard, *The Tripartite Nature of Man.* For the scholastic, Roman Catholic treatment see R. E. Brennan, *History of Psychology, from the Standpoint of a Thomist.* For the contemporary psychological approach to Christian anthropology see D. E. Roberts, *Psychotherapy and a Christian View of Man;* W. M. Horton, *A Psychological Approach to Theology.*

WAYNE E. WARD

TRINITY, THE. Although not itself a biblical term, the trinity has been found a convenient designation for the one God self-revealed in Scripture as Father, Son and Holy Spirit. It signifies that within the one essence of the Godhead we have to distinguish three "persons" who are neither three gods on the one side, not three parts or modes of God on the other, but coequally and coeternally God.

The main contribution of the OT to the doctrine is to emphasize the unity of God. God is not himself a plurality, nor is he one among many others. He is single and unique: "The Lord our God is one Lord" (Deut. 6:4), and he demands the exclusion of all pretended rivals (Deut. 5:7 ff.). Hence there can be no question of tritheism.

Yet even in the OT we have clear intimations of the trinity. The frequent mention of the Spirit of God (Gen. 1:2 and *passim*) may be mentioned, as also, perhaps, the angel of the Lord in Exodus (23:23). Again, the plural in Gen. 1:26 and 11:7 is to be noted, as also the plural form of the divine name and the nature of the divine appearance to Abraham in Genesis 18. The importance of the word (Ps. 33:6) and especially the wisdom of God (Prov. 8:12 ff.) is a further pointer, and in a mysterious verse like Isa. 48:16, in a strongly monotheistic context, we have a very close approach to trinitarian formulation.

In the NT there is no explicit statement of the doctrine, (apart from the rejected I John 5:7), but the trinitarian evidence is overwhelming. God is still preached as the one God (Gal. 3:20). Yet Jesus proclaims his own deity (John 8:58) and evokes and accepts the faith and worship of his disciples (Matt. 16:16; John 20:28). As the Son or Word, he can thus be equated with God (John 1:1) and associated with the Father, e.g., in the Pauline salutations (I Cor. 1:3, etc.). But the Spirit or Comforter is also brought into the same interrelationship (cf. John 14-16).

It is not surprising, therefore, that while we have no dogmatic statement there are clear references to the three persons of the Godhead in the NT. All three are mentioned at the baptism of Jesus (Matt. 3:16 f.). The disciples are to baptize in the name of Father, Son, and Holy Ghost (Matt. 28:19). The developed Pauline blessing includes the grace of the Son, the love of God and the communion of the Holy Ghost (II Cor. 13:14). Reference is made to the election of the Father, the sanctification of the Spirit and the sprinkling of the blood of Jesus Christ (I Peter 1:2) in relation to the salvation of believers.

The fact that Christian faith involves acceptance of Jesus as Saviour and Lord meant that the Trinity quickly found its way into the creeds of the church as the confession of faith in God the Father, Jesus Christ his only Son, and the Holy Ghost. The implications of this confession, especially in the context of monotheism, naturally became one of the first concerns of patristic theology, the main aim being to secure the doctrine against tritheism on the one side and monarchianism on the other.

In the fully developed doctrine the unity of

God is safeguarded by insisting that there is only one essence or substance of God. Yet the deity of Jesus Christ is fully asserted against those who would think of him as merely adopted to divine sonship, or pre-existent but in the last resort created. The individuality of Father, Son and Holy Spirit is also preserved against the notion that these are only modes of God for the various purposes of dealing with man in creation or salvation. God is one, yet in himself and from all eternity he is Father, Son and Holy Ghost, the triune God.

Trinitarian analogies have been found by many apologists both in nature generally and in the constitution of man. These are interesting, but are not to be thought of as providing a rationale of the divine being. More pregnant is the suggestion of Augustine that without the trinity there could be no fellowship or love in God, the divine triunity involving an inter-relationship in which the divine perfections find eternal exercise and expression independent of the creation of the world and man.

Rationalist objections to the Trinity break down on the fact that they insist on interpreting the Creator in terms of the creature, i.e., the unity of God in terms of mathematical unity. More scientifically, the Christian learns to know God from God himself as he has acted for us and attested his action in Holy Scripture. He is not surprised if an element of mystery remains which defies ultimate analysis or understanding, for he is only man and God is God. But in the divine work as recorded in the Bible the one God is self-revealed as Father, Son and Holy Ghost, and therefore in true faith he must "acknowledge the glory of the eternal Trinity."

BIBLIOGRAPHY

HDB; K. Barth, *Church Dogmatics,* I, 1, §8-11; J. F. Bethune-Baker, *An Introduction to the Early History of Christian Doctrine,* pp. 139 ff.; W. H. Griffith Thomas, *The Principles of Theology,* pp. 20-31.

GEOFFREY W. BROMILEY

TRISAGION. This name (*trisagion,* "thrice holy") was originally applied to a liturgical hymn based on Isa. 6:3. Later, probably during the patriarchate of Proclus (434-46), it assumed the following form: "Holy God, Holy and Mighty, Holy and Immortal, have mercy upon us." The *Trisagion* entered into the Monophysite controversy when the clause "who was crucified for us" was inserted after the word "Immortal." Neither this nor later modifications found favor except among the Monophysites and Monothelites. The apostolic origin of the *Trisagion* cannot be maintained. Its liturgical use is almost exclusively confined to the Greek and Roman churches.

BIBLIOGRAPHY

Blunt; P. Drews in *SHERK;* J. Bingham, *Origines,* XIV, ii, p. 3; XV, iii, p. 10.

WICK BROOMALL

TRITHEISM. See TRINITY.

TRUST. See FAITH.

TRUTH. The first Christian theologian to attempt any systematic exposition of the concept of truth was Augustine. His immediate aim was to refute skepticism. If man's mind is incapable of grasping truth, particularly if man is incapable of grasping the truth about God, then morality and theology are impossible. (See KNOWLEDGE. For an account of Augustine's epistemology, see B. B. Warfield, *Studies in Tertullian and Augustine.*) Augustine distinguished four senses of the term truth. First, truth is the affirmation of what is; e.g., three times three is nine, and David was king of Israel. Second, every reality (particularly the immutable, supersensible ideas) can be considered as an affirmation of itself: it is true when it merits the name it claims. In this sense beauty and wisdom are truth. Third, the Word of God, Jesus Christ, is the Truth because he expresses the Father. And fourth, in the realm of sensible objects, such as plants and animals, there is a resemblance, but only a resemblance, to the primary realities of point two above. Strictly speaking, a visible tree is not a true tree. But as the resemblance is real, even sensible objects have a degree of truth.

Many contemporary students of the Bible, fearing that Augustine or others are too deeply influenced by Greek philosophy, attempt to specify the several senses in which truth is used in the Scripture. Hoskyns and Davey, *The Riddle of the New Testament* (Rev. ed. pp. 33 ff.), after quoting Eph. 4:20-24, seek for a conception of truth that will have "not an intellectual but a moral and spiritual effect upon them." The common conception of truth as "a fact" or "what is real," so they assert, "has no moral or spiritual significance." The Hebrew notion of truth, with its close relation to God, is considered un-Greek. So also Gerhard Kittel (*TWNT,* Vol. I, pp. 240 ff.) distinguishes, more cautiously perhaps, between Hebrew and Greek usage, citing several passages in the Platonic dialogues.

One should, however, bear in mind that the technical concepts of the philosophers are hardly ever used by the majority of the population, whether in ancient Greece or modern America. The Bible, too, is written in colloquial language, and the senses in which it uses the term truth are not so different from colloquial usage anywhere.

One should also bear in mind that moral and spiritual truth is as much truth as mathematical, scientific, and historical truth. It is all equally "intellectual." Non-intellectual truth is unthinkable. It is not true that the common conception of truth as a fact or what is real "has no moral or spiritual significance." We need only to recall that God gave the Ten Commandments.

Furthermore, the Greek philosophers did not divorce truth from moral and spiritual values. Plato went so far as to teach, to the consternation of many readers, that a knowledge of the truth automatically guarantees a moral life. Both Pythagoreanism and Neoplatonism were systems of salvation; and even the Stoics and Epicureans made ethics the culmination of philosophy.

The differences between the Hebrew Scriptures and the Greek philosophies are rather to be sought in the nature and the method of the salvation proclaimed, in the concepts of sin, of redemption, and the specific norms of morality; and not in the usage of the word truth. The relation between God and truth in the Scriptures is indisputably quite different from anything found in Greek philosophy, mainly because the concept of God is so different. It is in such theological content, not in philological usage, that the important distinctions are to be found.

The usage of the words in the Scripture supports this conclusion. Plain, ordinary, factual truth is the point of Gen. 42:16, "Ye shall be kept in prison, that your words may be proved, whether there be any truth in you" (Cf. Deut. 13:14; 17:4; 22:20; Prov. 12:19; Jer. 9:3). Esth. 9:30 concerns legally certified information, and Josh. 2:12 points to a private oath.

It is not a different meaning but precisely the same meaning when the veracity of divine revelation is asserted. God tells the truth; he tells what is so; his assertions are correct. Cf. Dan. 8:26; 10:1; 21; Pss. 19:9; 119:160.

For the NT Kittel lists six different meanings of the word truth, but adds that "in many individual cases the distinction is not certain." One of the six meanings is "that which has existence or duration." It is true that truth exists or endures, but it is not in this sense that Eph. 4:21 and Gal. 2:5, 14 define truth.

Similarly one can rely on the truth without defining truth as "that on which man can rely." Rom. 15:8 is not thus to be pressed; nor with the connotation of "sincerity" can II Cor. 7:14, 11:10; and Phil. 1:18 be used for this purpose.

Rather, all these usages are derivative from the basic meaning of "the actual fact" or "the truth of an assertion." Cf. Mark 12:14, 32; Luke 4:25; Acts 26:25; Rom. 1:18, 25. It is not another and different meaning of the term, but exactly the same meaning, in the NT as in the OT, when it is applied to correct doctrine or right belief. Cf. II Cor. 4:2; 6:7; 13:8; I Tim. 2:4; II Tim. 3:7.

Like other words, truth too can be used figuratively, by metonymy, in which the effect is substituted for the cause. Thus when Christ says, "I am the Way, the Truth, and the Life," the word truth is just as figurative as the word life. As Christ is the cause of life, so is he the cause of truth. That water freezes and that a sinner may be justified by faith are true because Christ creatively said, Let it be so.

GORDON H. CLARK

TWELVE, THE. See APOSTLE.

TYPE, TYPOLOGY. Such terms as *typos*, "type" (Rom. 5:14; I Cor. 10:6, 11); *skia*, "shadow" (Col. 2:17; Heb. 8:5; 10:1); *hypodeigma*, "copy" (Heb. 8:5; 9:23); *sēmeion*, "sign" (Matt. 12:39); *parabolē*, "figure" (Heb. 9:9; 11:19); and *antitypos*, "antitype" (Heb. 9:24; I Pet. 3:21) are involved in the study of biblical typology.

A type is a shadow cast on the pages of OT history by a truth whose full embodiment or antitype is found in the NT revelation. Our survey is limited to a few aspects of this important subject.

That typology is a legitimate part of theological study is proved by the following considerations: (1) the word *typos* and its synonyms (see above) are used in such a way as to justify this approach to OT history. (2) The "as . . . so" construction (e.g., Matt. 12:40; Luke 17:26; John 3:14) indicates a close spiritual affinity between an OT fact and its NT counterpart. (3) In many places (e.g.,

I Cor. 15:22; II Cor. 3:7 ff.; Gal. 4:22 ff.; Heb. 3:1 — 10:18) an obvious parallel is drawn between OT history and its NT interpretation.

Types have the following characteristics: (1) They are thoroughly rooted in history. Jonah's experience is just as credible as the momentous event which it adumbrates (Matt. 12:40). The serpent episode belongs to the same historical category as the event which it graphically prefigures (John 3:14). (2) They are prophetic in nature. Their *terminus ad quem* is always in messianic times. Melchizedek, the historical figure (Gen. 14), becomes the spiritual prefiguration of Christ's eternal priesthood (Ps. 110; Heb. 7). (3) They are definitely designed as an integral part of redemptive history. Types are not afterthoughts cabalistically read back into the OT story. They retain their typical significance even after the antitype has appeared (cf. I Cor. 10:1-11). (4) They are Christocentric. They all point to Christ in one way or another. If the OT as a whole centers in Christ (Luke 24:24, 44; Acts 3:24 ff.), surely the types anticipate his redemption of fallen mankind. (5) They are edificatory — having spiritual meaning for God's people in both dispensations. The OT saint was undoubtedly edified by the typical significance of such things as circumcision (Deut. 30:6), the sacrifices (Hos. 14:2) and the coronation of Joshua (Zech. 6:9-15). Much of the OT (e.g., Ex. 25 — 40) would have only antiquarian value today if it were not for types embedded in the text.

Widely divergent views are held by expositors regarding the scope of typology. Some have so embellished the OT history with types that the simple history is all but ignored. At the other extreme are found those who refuse to see in OT history any typical meaning. The true view is found between these extremes.

A few simple distinctions will safeguard the student of typology. (1) One must distinguish between the type backed by NT authority and the type based on the speculation of the modern interpreter. It is not to be inferred, however, that no type is valid unless supported by specific NT authority. Sober exegesis must prevail over wild fancies. (2) One must distinguish between the type that definitely corroborates a doctrine and the type that has no relevance to a supposed doctrine. Jonah's expulsion from the great fish typifies Christ's resurrection (Matt. 12:40); but Jonah's restoration to the land does not necessarily typify Israel's restoration to Palestine. (3) One must distinguish between what is essential in a type and what is peripheral in the same type. Some typologists have become so bogged down in details that absurdities and puerilities have swallowed up the essential truth. (4) One must distinguish between the type that is completely fulfilled in the antitype and the type, though partly fulfilled, that still retains its typical significance for the future world. The Book of Revelation affords many illustrations of this feature of typology (e.g., 14:1).

BIBLIOGRAPHY

C. T. Fritsch, BS 104, pp. 87-100; 214-22; J. C. Lambert in HDAC; J. R. Darbyshire in HERE; P. Fairbairn, *Typology of Scripture*; B. Keach, *Tropologia*, pp. 225-37.

WICK BROOMALL

U

UBIQUITY. See GOD.

ULTRAMONTANISM. Though Ultramontanism existed in the eleventh century, the term refers to the policy of the papal party within the Roman Church in the nineteenth century. Its adherents looked to the papacy, rather than the bishops, to formulate policy. Ultramontanism supports the notion that political, intellectual, and religious attitudes of all Catholics are determined by Rome. It is intolerant toward any other creed. National Catholic sentiment finds in Ultramontanism a ready enemy.

Ultramontanism arose with the post-revolutionary generation of France. It gathered strength as the papacy recovered its power and influence until finally its policy became regnant as a result of the Vatican Council of 1870.

SHERMAN RODDY

UNBELIEF. Although there are many references in the OT (Num. 20:10; Isa. 9:30 f.) to the phenomenon of unbelief, no single word is employed for it. In the NT on the other hand, the writers use *apeitheia* and *apistia*, both of which imply a certain obstinacy and resistance to truth (Rom. 11:20, 23; Eph. 2:2; 5:6; I Tim. 1:13; Heb. 3:12). The truth which the unbeliever refuses to accept is never a general philosophical category or an abstract idea, but is God's self-revelation (a) in nature, and (b) in redemption. Thus unbelief is fundamentally a rejection of the offer of the gospel of God's grace (Matt. 13:58; Mark 16:16; Acts 7:51 f.; 14:2; Rom. 2:8; 11:30 f.). It is the ground-motive of sin (Rom. 14:23; I John 5:10), causing man's disobedience to God's law. So it is unbelief which brings upon him, unless there is a Mediator, God's wrath and judgment (Rom. 11:20-24; Eph. 2:2; 5:6).

Unbelief in the Christian sense is caused neither by merely intellectual doubts of, nor by emotional opposition to the truth. It finds its origin in what the Bible calls "the heart," and is the outgrowth of a basic characteristic of the corruption of the man's personality, the desire for human autonomy over against the sovereignty of God. This comes out clearly in the account of the fall contained in Gen. 3 and in Paul's exposition of this theme in Rom. 1:20-25. (cf. also Ps. 14:1; Isa. 6:9-12; Jer. 17:9.) Unbelief thus dominates the whole man so that he needs to be reborn spiritually by the grace of God (John 3:3-13; I Cor. 1:22-24; 2:12-16).

There are, of course, instances of unbelief on the part of Christians, as in the case of the disciples, particularly of Thomas, after the resurrection of Christ (Mark 16:11; Luke 24:41; John 20:27). Such unbelief was but temporary, however, whereas the non-Christian's unbelief according to the usual Christian view is his total rejection of God's self-revelation. The Christian's doubt is the result of a temporary weakening of faith, while that of the non-Christian is much deeper and more fundamental as shown in the ultimate differ-

ence between Peter and Judas (Luke 22:32; Matt. 27:3 f.; Acts 1:16 f.).

W. STANFORD REID

UNBLAMEABLE. In the AV this concept is translated by such words as blameless, guiltless, innocent, clean, acquitted, and to be unpunished. The Hebrew verbs *nāḳâ, zāḳâ,* and *zāḳak,* with their derivatives, primarily carry this meaning. The basic idea of *nāḳâ* is probably to empty out and moves on to be free of guilt (Num. 5:31), exempt from punishment or an oath (Gen. 24:8). The word *zāḳâ* carried the sense of cleanness, of being justified before God (Isa. 1:16) whereas *zāḳak* puts the stress on brightness or purity (Lam. 4:7).

At least eleven adjectives, representing ten roots, are used in the NT (and in the LXX), as follows: *amemptos* (and the adverb *amemptōs*), from *memphomai,* "to blame"; *amōmētos* and *amōmos,* from *mōmos,* "a blemish"; *anaitios,* from *aitia,* "cause," "responsibility," "accusation"; *anegklētos,* from *egkaleō,* "to call in," "to accuse," "to prosecute; *anepilēmptos,* from *epilambanomai,* "to lay hold of"; *athôos,* from *thōē,* "penalty"; *aspilos,* from *spilos,* "spot," "blemish," "stain"; *aproskopos* from *proskoptō,* "to stumble," "to strike against"; *akakos,* from *kakos,* "evil," "pernicious"; *akeraios,* from *kerannymi,* "to mix," "to mingle"; the *a-* or *an-* in each instance being a negating prefix.

The state of the natural man is portrayed in the Scriptures as one of guilt, condemnation, reproach, impurity, and justly deserving punishment. The wretchedness of the guilt and the severity of the condemnation can be removed only through the atoning merits of the shed blood of Christ (Col. 1:21-22).

JULIAN C. MCPHEETERS

UNCIRCUMCISION, UNCIRCUMCISED. The Hebrew adjective *'ārēl,* the noun *'orlâ,* and the verb *'āral* represent this condition. Similarly, the Greek adjective *aperitmētos,* the noun *akrobystia,* and the verb *epispaomai* describe the same condition. The presentation here is based on these terms.

In the OT the uncircumcised are those — whether Israelites (Josh. 5:7) or non-Israelites (Judg. 14:3; 15:18; I Sam. 17:26) — upon whom the act of circumcision had not been performed. As circumcision represented obedience to God's covenant (Gen. 17:9-14; Ex. 4:24-26), so uncircumcision represented rebellion and unbelief (Jer. 6:10; 9:25 f.). Spiritually, the uncircumcised were the unregenerated (Lev. 26:41; cf. Deut. 10:16; 30:6; Jer. 4:4). The uncircumcised were excluded from the covenant (Gen. 17:14), from the Passover (Ex. 12:48), from the land (Josh. 5:7), from the sanctuary (Ezek. 44:9), and from the holy city (Isa. 52:1). The occupants of hell are described as uncircumcised (Ezek. 32:19-32). Figuratively, Moses called himself a man of "uncircumcised lips" (Ex. 6:12, 30) — that is, slow of speech (Ex. 4:10).

The following truths summarize the NT teaching: (1) All Gentiles are uncircumcised (Acts 11:3; Rom. 3:30; I Cor. 7:18; Gal. 2:7; Eph. 2:11). (2) Uncircumcision is equated with the unregenerated state (Acts 7:51; Col. 2:13). (3) The unbelieving Jew, though physically circumcised, is spiritually uncircumcised (Rom. 2:28 f.; cf. Phil. 3:2 ff.). (4) A Gentile who in physical uncircumcision keeps the righteousness of the law is accounted spiritually circumcised; but a Jew, obversely, though physically circumcised, becomes uncircumcised by his disobedience (Rom. 2:25-27). (5) Thus in Christ neither circumcision nor uncircumcision has any spiritual value (I Cor. 7:19; Gal. 5:6; 6:15; Col. 3:11). (6) Uncircumcision in heart (that is, unregeneracy) is infinitely worse than uncircumcision in the flesh (Acts 7:51; cf. Jer. 9:25 f.). (7) Jews and Gentiles, the circumcised and the uncircumcised, are united in one body of believers (Eph. 2:11-22). This spiritual union is illustrated by the fact that Abraham, their common father, was justified (Gen. 15:5 f.) while still uncircumcised (Rom. 4:9-12).

WICK BROOMALL

UNCLEAN. See CLEAN, UNCLEAN.

UNCTION. See ANOINTING.

UNDERSTANDING. A biblical term used to refer to the comprehension of meanings, as distinguished from the bare apprehension of facts or data (Dan. 12:8; Matt. 13:13-14). It is the most frequent rendering of the Hebrew *bîn*, *bînâ* ("understanding, wisdom, knowledge, meaning"), from a root meaning to separate (mentally), to distinguish. The OT speaks of understanding as the gift of God (I Kings 3:9), through the word (Ps. 119:104). In the parallelism of Prov. 4:5, it is synonymous with wisdom, an intellectual virtue highly extolled in Proverbs. It is associated with discrimination between good and evil in I Kings 3:9, a usage which comes very close to its essential significance.

The most frequent NT terms are *noeō* ("to ponder, think, understand"), *ginōskō* ("to know, be cognizant of"), and *suniēmi* ("to send or put together, to understand, comprehend thoroughly, to perceive clearly") and their derivatives.

The repeated contrast between "hearing" and "understanding" in the Scriptures (Neh. 8:8; Isa. 6:9-10; Mark 4:12; 7:14; Acts 28:27, etc.) is the best clue to the meaning of the concept. To understand implies to grasp the significance of, in addition to a mere apprehension of the given datum. Thus, in spiritual things particularly, understanding is a divine gift (Ps. 119:34, 73; II Tim. 2:7; I John 5:20); one's understanding may be "opened" (Luke 24:45); "enlightened" (Eph. 1:18) or, conversely, "darkened" (Eph. 4:18). It results from faith (Heb. 11:3); is essential to the knowledge of God's will (Col. 1:9); is spiritual riches (Col. 2:2); but may surpass a person's attainments in love (I Cor. 13:2).

The frequent NT citation of Isa. 6:9 ff. (e.g., Mark 4:12; Matt. 13:13-14; John 12:40; Acts 28:26, 27) indicates the close connection between understanding of the things of God and obedient surrender to the will of God (cf. I Cor., chaps. 1-2).

WESTLAKE T. PURKISER

UNGODLINESS. The word *asebeia* in its various forms occurs seventeen times in the NT. The translation "ungodly" or "ungodliness" occurs in every instance in the AV and, excepting Titus 2:12 ("irreligion") and I Pet. 4:18 ("impious"), in the RSV. Ungodliness is not merely another evil in a catalog of sins but is the root out of which other sins grow. Thus in Rom. 1:18 *asebeia* is distinguished from *adikia* ("unrighteousness, wickedness"). The works of *adikia*, whose range is very broad, of which Paul speaks in 1:24-32, spring out of the *asebeia* of which he speaks in 1:19-23 (Gerhard Kittel, *TWNT*, Verlag von W. Kohlhammer, Stuttgart, 1949, Bd. I, s. 156). This same idea is present in other passages also. The grace of God that accomplishes salvation also disciplines us to renounce ungodliness and worldly desires — the order is significant (Titus 2:12). The flood was a judgment upon ungodliness (II Pet. 2:5). The result of that ungodliness is indicated in Gen. 6:5. Seemingly, the sins of Sodom and Gomorrah which brought those cities into judgment resulted from ungodliness (II Pet. 2:6). In Jude 4 ungodliness perverts God's grace into licentiousness. Rom. 4:5 and 5:6 might also be mentioned, though the connection is perhaps not as clear. Rom. 11:26 is a quotation from the OT in which banishing ungodliness is equivalent to taking away sins. In every case in the NT the word occurs in connection with various sins; in several cases, as shown, the connection is casual. The other NT references are I Tim. 1:9; II Tim. 2:16; I Pet. 4:18; II Pet. 3:7; Jude 15 (four times); Jude 18.

The word is used frequently in the LXX. Though not as predominant, one can say that the same idea is at least present when the LXX uses *asebeia* to render such Hebrew words as *sārâ* ("apostasy, revolt") and *pešaʿ* ("transgression," especially against God's law, "revolt, rebellion").

BIBLIOGRAPHY

Arndt; Schrenk in *TWNT* (on *adikia*).

RALPH A. GWINN

UNION WITH GOD. Belief in a religious devotee's ability to unite himself with his god is very ancient. Much ethnic religion is based upon this concept, whether it be the idea of the believer's becoming physically one with his god as in Mithraism, or of his being absorbed spiritually into his god as in Buddhism. This type of thinking has also appeared frequently in the Christian church since the days of Neo-Platonism in the teachings of such men as Meister Eckhart (1327) and other mystics. It would seem to be basic to the Roman Catholic idea of the "stigmata" of Christ's passion which are said to appear in those who have given themselves wholly to him, and it probably also exercised an early influence on the doctrine of the Mass.

The biblical point of view is radically different, since it takes seriously two fundamental facts: creation and fall. Man is the creature of God, which means that while made in God's image, he is never eternal, autonomous nor self-sufficient as is God (John 5:26; Acts 7:25; Rom. 9:19; 11:33-34), but is mortal,

spacially and temporally conditioned and dependent (Gen. 1:26-27; Job 33:4; Ps. 8:5; Isa. 64:8). There is thus a qualitative metaphysical difference between God and man. At the same time there is also an ethical separation, for although made in God's own image, man by attempting to elevate himself to equality with God broke with him ethically by disobeying him (Gen. 3:5; Eccl. 7:29; Rom. 5:12). Thus man is now not only different, but also in conflict with God.

The only unity, therefore, which man may have with God is through God's action in reconciling man to himself through Christ (see IDENTIFICATION WITH CHRIST). The elect from all eternity are by the divine will united with Christ in whom they died on Calvary (John 6:32-58; Gal. 2:20), and by whom they now live through the indwelling presence of the Holy Spirit (John 15:1 ff.; 16:7-15; 16:21-23; Rom. 8:5-17; Col. 1:27). This becomes concrete in the symbolism of the Lord's Supper (Matt. 26:26-28; I Cor. 11:23-26; Gal. 2:20). In principle, therefore, during this life they are united to God in Christ so that ethically they strive to be one with him, but metaphysically they still remain creatures who even in eternity will never become divine.

BIBLIOGRAPHY

J. Calvin, *Institutes of the Christian Religion*, Bk. III, chap. i; L. Berkhof, *Systematic Theology*, pp. 447 ff.; A. Kuyper, *The Work of the Holy Spirit*, pp. 203-33; A. Schlemmer, "Y a-t-il un Mysticism Réformé?" *Philosophia Reformata*, XXII, pp. 149 ff.

W. STANFORD REID

UNION, HYPOSTATIC. See CHRISTOLOGY.

UNITARIANISM. The origin of this ancient heresy is to be found in the Arian controversy of the early fourth century when Arius, presbyter in the church at Alexandria, set forth the system of thought which bears his name. He denied the orthodox doctrine of the Trinity and asserted that there was a time when God was not the Father and Jesus Christ was not the Son. Because God foresaw the merit of Jesus the man, Christ was accorded a kind of divinity, but he was never of the same substance as the Father although he is worthy of worship. This early and rather high form of Unitarianism was condemned by the Council of Nicaea in 325 and by the Council of Constantinople in 381. Throughout the Middle Ages Unitarianism in any form was regarded as heretical. It reappeared in a somewhat different guise in the writings of Michael Servetus and was accepted by some of the more radical of the Anabaptist groups.

It received a new impetus and theological foundation in the Socinianism (*q.v.*) of Laelius and Faustus Socinus and in the Racovian Catechism of 1605. Although they rejected the deity of Christ and the orthodox doctrine of the Trinity, the Socinians held to a kind of supernaturalism and even insisted on the worship of Jesus Christ as a divine person, believing in his resurrection from the dead and his ascension. But his divine nature was the result of his perfect obedience. They denied the orthodox position on the fall of man and held that he still possesses a full freedom of the will. Thus the redeeming work of Christ is to be found in his life and teachings rather than in his vicarious death upon the cross.

With the coming of the Enlightenment and the appearance of deism (*q.v.*) Unitarianism in the hands of Joseph Priestly and others became more rationalistic and less supernaturalistic in its outlook. Nature and right reason replaced the NT as the primary sources of religious authority, and what authority the Scriptures retained was the result of their agreement with the findings of reason.

Unitarianism came to New England as early as 1710 and by 1750 most of the Congregational ministers in and around Boston had ceased to regard the doctrine of the Trinity as an essential Christian belief. In 1788 King's Chapel, the first Anglican church in New England, became definitely Unitarian when its rector, with the consent of the congregation, deleted from the liturgy all mention of the Trinity. The triumph of Unitarianism in New England Congregationalism seemed complete with the election of Henry Ware, an avowed opponent of the trinitarian position, to the Hollis chair of divinity at Harvard.

In the nineteenth century, under the impact of Transcendentalism (*q.v.*), Unitarianism became steadily more radical. Its later leaders such as Ralph Waldo Emerson and Theodore Parker rejected those remaining supernatural elements which William Ellery Channing had seen fit to retain. Modern Unitarianism has become increasingly humanistic. Many members of the American Unitarian Association, founded in 1825, have come to the conclusion that their movement is not a part of the Christian church. In 1959 they voted to merge with the Universalists.

BIBLIOGRAPHY
S. H. Fritchman, *Together We Advance*; J. Orr, *English Deism: Its Roots and Fruits*; E. M. Wilbur, *History of Unitarianism*, 2 vols.; C. Wright, *Beginnings of Unitarianism in America*.

C. GREGG SINGER

UNITY. The word unity is as such very rare in the Bible, but the thought behind the term, that of the one people of God, is extremely prominent. Already in the OT Israel is descended from the one father, and although the tribes are later divided the Psalmist commends unity (Ps. 133:1) and Ezekiel looks to the time when there shall be "one stick" (Ezek. 37:17). Nor is this merely a political or natural unity, for Abraham is divinely elected, and Isaac is the child of special promise and miracle.

In the NT this unity is expanded in accordance with the original promise. The wall of partition between Jew and Gentile, and indeed between Greeks and barbarians, bond and slave, male and female, is broken down. There is now the one people of God embracing men of all nations (Eph. 2:12 f.; Gal. 3:28).

But this new unity is not one of mere good will, or common interests, or ecclesiastical organization. It is a unity of expansion because of contraction. It is a unity in the one seed (Gal. 3:16) who has come as the true Israelite and indeed the second Adam (Rom. 5:12 f.). The old and estranged men are made one in Jesus Christ (Eph. 2:15). The one Jesus Christ is the basis of the unity of his people.

But they are one in Jesus Christ as the one who reconciled them by dying and rising again in their stead. As divided men they first meet in his crucified body, in which their old life is put to death and destroyed. They are reconciled in one body by the cross (Eph. 2:16). "We thus judge, that if one died for all, then were all dead" (II Cor. 5:14). But Jesus Christ rose as well as died, and as the Resurrected he is the one true life of his people (Col. 3:3-4). They thus meet in his risen body, in which they are the one new man. See also NEW CREATION.

Yet if this unity is centered in Jesus Christ, it is necessarily a unity of the Holy Spirit. Believers have their new life in Christ as they are all born of the one Spirit (John 3:5; Eph. 4:4). But this means that they are brothers of Jesus Christ and of one another in the one family of God. They have the one God and Father of all (Eph. 4:4). They not only have a common birth, but a common mind which is the mind of Christ (Phil. 2:5). They are led by the one Spirit, being built up an habitation of God through the Spirit (Eph. 2:22).

How full and real this unity is emerges in the fact that the church (q.v.) is called the bride of Christ, and is therefore one body and one spirit with him (cf. I Cor. 6:17; Eph. 5:30). It can thus be described quite simply as his body, of which Christians are the different members (Rom. 12:4). Since it is by faith that Christians belong to Christ, their unity is a unity of faith (Eph. 4:13). It is expressed in the two sacraments, for as there is only one baptism (Eph. 4:5), so there is only one loaf and cup (I Cor. 10:17).

Since unity belongs so essentially to the people of God, it is right that it should find expression in the creed (one church), and that in all ages there should be a concern for Christian unity according to the prayer of Christ himself (John 17:21). For the attainment of genuine unity, however, it is necessary that the following points should be observed.

Christian unity is a given fact of the new life to be believed and accepted in faith in Christ. It is not the unity first created, safeguarded or enforced by a human institution or association. Nor can it be simply equated with a particular structure of the church or form of ministry, practice or dogma. Like the righteousness of the Christian, it is found first and primarily and exclusively in Christ.

Again, Christian unity is not identical with uniformity. It does not allow division. But it does not exclude variety. The one Spirit gives different gifts (I Cor. 12:4 f.). In the one body of Christ there are many members (ibid., 14 f.). The unity grounded in Christ leaves scope for diversity of action and function, the only conformity being to the mind of Christ and direction of the Spirit.

Finally, the unity received in faith must find expression in historical life and action. There must be no antinomian acquiescence in divided or competitive Christian bodies. To this extent, it is right and necessary that there should be an active pursuit of practical unity, but only on the basis of the unity already given, and therefore with a fuller looking to Christ and readier subjection to his Spirit.

GEOFFREY W. BROMILEY

UNIVERSALISM. Universalism is the doctrine of the ultimate well-being of every person. The doctrine has a pagan and a Christian form. According to the former, all will ultimately be happy because all are, by nature, the creatures and children of God. The universalistic heresy (it is rejected by the general tradition of the church — Eastern, Roman and Protestant) in Christianity teaches that although all of the human creatures of God have fallen into sin and are lost, all will be saved through the universal redemption of Christ.

Christian universalism has existed in two historical forms: restoration at death and restoration after future punishment. The latter may be said to be the classical theory of Christian universalism taught by some from the time of Clement of Alexandria to the Universalist denomination of today. Probably the most celebrated adherent of this position was Origen (d. 254). He rejected the notion of endless punishment, teaching that the wicked, including the devil, after enduring the pains of hell for a season would come forth purified for heaven (Peri Archōn i, 18 f.). This is the doctrine of the apokatastasis pantōn. The Universalist movement in America was torn asunder by the appearance of those who affirmed perfection of all at death without further purgatorial punishment, but a declaration adopting the "orthodox" view of punishment before perfection was made in 1878, at Winchester, N. H. After insisting on the possibility of repentance and salvation in the next world, the conciliatory statement goes on to affirm that, "Whatever differences in regard to the future may exist among us, none of us believe that the horizon of eternity will be relatively either largely or for a long time overcast by the clouds of sin and punishment, and in coming into the enjoyment of salvation, whenever that may be, all the elements of penitence, forgiveness, and regeneration are involved. Justice and mercy will then be seen to be entirely at one, and God be all in all."

James Edwin Odgers notes that the scriptural arguments of Universalism turn on three points: (1) The purpose of God: the restoration of all things to their original excellence (Acts 3:21); (2) The means of restoration: through Christ (Rom. 5:18; Heb. 2:9); (3) The nature of the restoration: union of every soul with God (I Cor. 15:24-28). The church catholic construes these verses as referring not to every man, but to every man who is united with Christ, and she feels that only such an interpretation is compatible with the biblical teaching of the diverse destinies of the righteous and the wicked (Matt. 25:46; John 3:16; 5:29; Rom. 2:8-10; 9:22-23).

The Unitarian denomination has, from early times in this country, been close to the Universalists in sentiment and action. The other denominations of Christendom have stood for the doctrine of future, endless and irremediable punishment of the wicked. Nevertheless, the Universalist leaven has been mightily at work especially among Protestants. Edwyn Bevan (*Christianity*, H. Holt & Co., New York, 1932, p. 224) says of modern Roman Catholics — and it is truer of Protestants — "Some . . . teach that the punishment involves real pain, but that it is not torment as pictured in the old view."

BIBLIOGRAPHY
R. Eddy, *History of Universalism;* H. Ballou, *The Ancient History of Universalism;* J. E. Odgers, article in *HERE.*

JOHN H. GERSTNER

UNKNOWN GOD. (Greek *agnōstos theos*). This phrase is found only once in the NT, at Acts 17:23. As there is no definite article in the Greek, the translation "to an unknown god" is somewhat better than "to the unknown god" of the AV. Much debate has raged concerning the exact source from which Paul took the phrase. Pausanias (i. 1, 4 and v. 14, 8) of the second century A.D. and others after him mentioned altars "to unknown gods" in and around Athens. Deissmann argues rather convincingly that a mutilated inscription found at Pergamum, probably to be dated in the second century A.D., ought to be read "to unknown gods." Diogenes Laertius (I. 110) tells the story of how a plague in Athens was brought to an end by following the advice of Epimenides, who told the Athenians to release sheep on the Areopagus, and wherever they lay down, to sacrifice "to the appropriate god," evidently to whatever unknown god was responsible for sending the plague. Paul may have seen an actual altar inscribed "to an unknown god," though he may have adapted a plural to a singular for the purpose of his Areopagus address. At any rate he made the concept of a god who was unknown to the Greeks a most

effective point of contact to introduce them to the true and living God.

BIBLIOGRAPHY
A. Deissmann, *St. Paul,* Appendix II; Arndt, under *agnōstos;* G. H. C. Macgregor in *IB* on Acts 17:23.

SAMUEL A. CARTLEDGE

UNLEARNED. This word is used to render (1) *amathēs,* in the sense of "ignorant" or "unteachable" in its only occurrence (II Pet. 3:16); (2) *apaideutos,* an "uninstructed," "boorish" or "foolish person" (occurs in the NT only in II Tim. 2:23, but sixteen times in the LXX); (3) *idiōtēs,* a non-professional who does not have the benefit of special training, an uninitiated person, an outsider (I Cor. 14:16, 23-24; Acts 4:13 *et al.*); (4) *agrammatos,* to describe "a totally illiterate individual" (Arndt; A-S). This last word is used by the Jerusalem authorities to refer to Peter and John in Acts 4:13. In this context it is either deliberately intended as a vicious insult (MM) or (and this is more likely) it is used in a more moderate sense to describe men who were without the benefit of technical training in the Jewish professional schools.

GLENN W. BARKER

UNPARDONABLE SIN. See BLASPHEMY.

UNRIGHTEOUSNESS. The term *adikia* occurs twenty-six times in the NT. The word is rendered by four different terms in the AV: "iniquity" (seven times), "unjust" (twice), "unrighteousness" (sixteen times), and "wrong" (once). The RSV translates *adikia* as "wickedness" (seven times), "iniquity" (four times), "unrighteous" and "wrongdoing" (three times each), "unrighteousness" and "wrong" (twice each), and "dishonest," "falsehood," "injustice," "wicked" (once each). In Heb. 1:9 the RSV reads *anomia* ("lawlessness") instead of *adikia.*

In the LXX *adikia* occurs some 190 times as the translation of no less than thirty-six Hebrew forms. It is used most frequently in Ezekiel (forty-eight times) and in Psalms (thirty-three times). The AV uses "unrighteousness" only four times in the OT.

Adikia means either "wrongdoing" or "unrighteousness, wickedness, injustice" (Arndt-Gingrich, *A Greek-English Lexicon of the NT,* University of Chicago Press, Chicago, 1957). One must be careful not to think of unrighteousness as the opposite of the distinctively Pauline emphasis on the righteousness that comes *from God (dikaiosynē ek theou)*. In Paul's thought righteousness stands opposed to wrath *(orgē)*. At the same time it is not without significance that *adikia* and *dikaiosynē* are formed from the same root.

See also UNGODLINESS.

BIBLIOGRAPHY
Arndt; Schrenk in *TWNT; RTWB.*

RALPH A. GWINN

UPRIGHT, UPRIGHTNESS. These are predominantly OT terms. The Greek word *orthos* "upright" occurs only twice in the NT: "Stand upright" (Acts 14:10) and "make straight paths" (Heb. 12:13).

The Hebrew verb *yāšar* (occurring 27 times), the adjective *yāšār* (119), and the nouns *yōšer* (14), *mēšar* (19, always plural), and *mišôr* (23) are employed with three areas of meaning: (1) the literal "upright, erect" or derivative "straight, smooth, level, even" (I Sam. 6:12; I Kings 6:35; Ps. 26:12; Prov. 2:13; Isa. 26:7; 40:3; Jer. 31:9); (2) the figurative "straight, upward in the eyes of = pleasing, agreeable to" (Ex. 15:26; Deut. 6:18; 12:8; Judg. 14:3; I Sam. 18:20; Jer. 27:5); and (3) the ethical "just, upright, straightforward" (Deut. 32:4; II Kings 10:15; Job 1:1; Ps. 67:4; Prov. 8:6; Hab. 2:4).

Scholars differ as to the original meaning of the root *yšr*. Some consider it to be the literal Hebrew meaning "upright" while others hold that the Arabic meaning "be gentle, easy, tractable" is original. In either case the ethical meaning is a later development. Just when it came into being in Israel is difficult to determine, but it is possible that it was in use by the time of Moses (Deut. 32:4). Be that as it may, this moral, ethical usage is clearly illustrated by the following examples: the adjective appears with *tôb*, "good" (Deut. 6:18), *ṣaddiq*, "righteous, just" (Deut. 32:4), and *tām*, "complete, blameless, perfect" (Job 1:1); the plural adjective *yešārîm* (32 times) designates "the upright" = "the righteous" as distinguished from "the wicked" (Prov. 14:11); and with *ṣedeq*, "righteousness," are found the nouns *mēšar* (Prov. 1:3; 2:9) and *mišôr* (Isa. 11:4).

BIBLIOGRAPHY
KB; RTWB, p. 273.

DEWEY M. BEEGLE

V

VAIN, VANITY. The basic meaning of the Hebrew words translated by "vain, vanity," revolves about the ideas of emptiness, worthlessness, and purposelessness: (a) *hebel*, which concretely means "vapor" or "breath," but figuratively that which is evanescent, and without purpose (Ps. 94:11), it also means: "to act without meaning," "to become worthless" (Jer. 2:5 and Job 27:12); (b) *hinnām*, that which "costs nothing," that which has "no purpose," that which is "done without cause" (Ps. 35:19); (c) *šāw'*, that which has "no good purpose" (Ex. 20:7) or has been "done to no avail" (Jer. 4:30), "emptiness of speech" (Job 35:13), a "worthless character" (Ps. 26:4) or "worthless motives" (Isa. 5:18); (d) *rîq* or *rîqām*, "being a worthless person" (Jer. 9:4), "efforts which have not effect or success" (Ps. 7:5); (e) *tōhû*, "formlessness" (Gen. 1:2), or "empty space" (Job 26:7), that which is unreal (I Sam. 12:21).

The idea is expressed in the NT and in the LXX by the following: *dōrean*, "undeservedly, to no purpose," from *dōrea*, "a gift"; *eikē*, "without cause," "to no purpose"; *kenos*, "empty"; *mataios*, "in vain, futile," from *matēn*, "folly." All of these words carry the idea of useless, empty, to no purpose, etc., in a generally neutral sense morally. The idea of vanity in the sense of conceited, proud, etc., is not expressed by these words.

Life is empty, useless, to no purpose, worthless and without meaning, when lived upon the human plane, without recognition of the claims of God on the whole of life.

JULIAN C. MCPHEETERS

VAINGLORY. *Kenodoxos* or *kenodoxia* is a Pauline term used only in Gal. 5:26 and Phil. 2:3. It is compounded from *kenos* ("empty, vain") and *doxa* ("glory"). The RSV translates the words with "self-conceit" and "conceit" respectively. The best insight into the meaning of the term is found in its consequences and contrasts. In Gal. 5:26, vainglory results in provoking and envying others. In Phil. 2:3, Paul contrasts lowliness of mind or humility with vainglory. F. Davidson says of the latter usage, "Vainglory means the ambition of any member of the church to gain position, so as to create a following and to minister to his personal vanity." (*NBC, in loco*).

WESTLAKE T. PURKISER

VENGEANCE. See REVENGE.

VICAR. See OFFICES, ECCLESIASTICAL.

VICARIOUS. See BLOOD, SACRIFICE.

VICE. The Greek term *kakia* occurs eleven times in the NT. In Matt. 6:34, and only here in the NT, it has the idea of "trouble." It is used in the general sense of depravity, wickedness, vice, though the translation vice does not occur in either AV or RSV. The word vice in the broad sense of that which corrupts or degrades might well be used in I Cor. 14:20; James 1:21; I Pet. 2:16. In Acts 8:22 the Greek word is used in the general sense but without the connotation of our word vice. Most often the word represents a specific type of wickedness. In this latter sense perhaps the best translation would be "malice" (Rom. 1:29; Eph. 4:31; Col. 3:8; Titus 3:3; I Pet. 2:1). In I Cor. 5:8 the word might be rendered either malice or vice, depending on whether one thinks Paul is referring to the divisions in the church at Corinth or to the case of immorality of which he speaks in the immediate context.

See also MALICE.

BIBLIOGRAPHY
Arndt.

RALPH A. GWINN

VICTORY. Victory is above all a religiously conditioned concept in Scripture. This is rooted in the basic biblical principle that God is just, punishing sin and rewarding righteousness (cf. Deut. 11:26-28). Victory always connotes some basis in religious or divine action. Thus II Sam. 23:10 reads, "the Lord wrought a great victory [literally, salvation] that day" (cf. Pss. 20:5-6; 106:47). Victory is for the vindication of God's purposes, or because of righteous living on the part of God's people. So it is that in many passages "righteousness" becomes equivalent to "victory," and thus victory is the result or vindication of that righteousness. Isaiah says, "Can the prey be taken from the warrior, or can the captive of the victor [literally, righteous man] be rescued?" (Isa. 49:24; cf. 41:2, 10; 54:17; Mal. 4:2).

In the OT victory is almost exclusively over external foes and issues in physical peace and security (cf. Josh. 1:15; Jer. 23:6; Ps. 69:14). But in the NT victory is expressed mainly in terms of spiritual forces and blessings. It is not triumph over social or economic difficulties that is the concern of the NT; it is mastery over temptation and the powers of evil. To be sure, the ultimate issue of this age will be Christ's victory over physical forces (Rev. 5:5; 6:2) and over Satan himself (Rev. 19:11—20:3). In this the Christian will share (Rev. 3:21). But the NT gives greater emphasis to a victory that the Christian can enjoy in his present daily life, a victory over the enticements and assaults of the world. This is made possible when one appropriates by faith the power of Christ's victory on the cross (I John 5:4-5; John 16:33; Rom. 8:37; Eph. 6:10), which is made manifest through Christ's indwelling presence (I John 4:4), and when the word of God rules in one's life (I John 2:14).

Thus victory is both present and eschatological. It is now that a Christian enters into the power and blessings of a triumph yet to find its complete realization in the future (cf. I Cor. 15:24-28, 54-57).

BIBLIOGRAPHY
N. H. Snaith, *The Distinctive Ideas of the Old Testament*, pp. 90-92; Arndt; O. Bauernfeind in *TWNT*.

ROBERT B. LAURIN

VINE. The word occurs many times in the Scriptures as the Hebrew people were vinedressers and vineyards were plentiful in the land.

The theological meaning of the word emerges in its figurative use. Israel is referred to as the choice "vine," *śōrēq*, which the master had planted (Isa. 5). It should have produced the finest of grapes but instead the harvest was wild grapes. This symbolic language pictures the disobedience of Israel to God and the disappointment of God over their actions. The tenderness, care and wise planning ends in disappointment and a prediction of the punishment which God would send upon Israel for her disobedience.

Jesus referred to himself as the true vine and the disciples as the branches (John 15). This figurative use of the word "vine" is one of the most striking references to the intimate relationship of the child of God to the Saviour. Paul referred to this fellowship as being "in Christ." The disciple is spiritually alive only as he remains in Christ and receives life and strength from the living Christ. Through him the child of God is able not only to be a dynamic Christian but also to bear fruit for the Master.

See also FRUIT.

BIBLIOGRAPHY
KD; IB.

LEWIS T. CORLETT

VIRGIN, VIRGINITY. Scripture uses three sets of terms for virginity. *Bᵉṯûlâ,* "virgin, maid(en)," AV, from the root "separated," unambiguously designates a woman withheld at home from sexual relations (Judg. 21:12). *Bᵉṯûlâ* thus contrasts with widow or divorcee (Lev. 21:14). *Bᵉṯûlîm* (pl.), "stage of virginity," signifies concretely the evidence of chastity from the wedding bed (Deut. 22:17, ICC). The term *'almâ,* "virgin, maid, damsel," AV, possibly from the root "concealed," stems more likely from "vigorous, mature," cf. its masculine, "youth" (Job 33:25). While less specific than *bᵉṯûlâ, 'almâ* in the OT never signifies a married woman but rather "maiden," for whom virginity is presumed, as Rebekah (Gen. 24:43), Miriam (Ex. 2:3), and the maiden Mary (Isa. 7:14). The word *'almâ* is therefore never defined by the addition of *bᵉṯûlâ,* contrast *na'ărā bᵉṯûlâ,* "a damsel that is a virgin" (Deut. 22:23). The NT term *parthenos,* "one put aside," specifies virginity, *partheneia,* as Mary's (Matt. 1:23; Luke 1:27) prior to her relations with Joseph (Matt. 1:18, 25; Luke 1:34), or even of chaste men (Rev. 14:4). In the LXX *parthenos* renders *bᵉṯûlâ,* but also *na'ărā* when a virgin is intended (Gen. 24:14; cf. *'almâ,* vs. 43; Isa. 7:14).

Pre-marital virginity is prized in Scripture (Gen. 24:16; Lev. 21:13-14; Esth. 2:2).

Chastity is assumed for reputable maidens (Lev. 21:3; Luke 2:36) and seems generally to have been maintained (Judg. 21:12), except in dire straits (19:24). Virgins were guarded (II Sam. 13:2) and violation brought shame (vss. 12-13; Deut. 22:14). The lustful look is itself sin (Job 31:1; Matt. 5:28). Absence of virginity implied harlotry, which required stoning (Deut. 22:21); false accusation was thus criminally serious (vss. 18-19). In the event of rape, marriage must follow (vss. 28-29), unless the seduced virgin is refused to the man, when he must still pay the "bride-price" (Ex. 22:16-17). Fornication with an engaged virgin (cf. Joel 1:8) equaled adultery and carried the death penalty (Deut. 22:23-27).

In Israelitish society (cf. Deut. 32:25) virgins sometimes wore distinctively long garments (II Sam. 13:18-19). They received special consideration (cf. Amos 8:13) and were so characterized by ornaments (Jer. 2:32) and joyful dancing (31:13) that their sorrow represented calamity (Lam. 1:4, 18). Virgins rejoiced as brides' companions (Ps. 45:14; Matt. 25:1; cf. S. of Sol. 1:3; and 6:8), though in times of distress (I Cor. 7:26) or for religious service (vs. 32) a virgin might not be given in marriage (vss. 36-37) or might remain single (vs. 28; though cf. Judg. 11:38-39).

"Virgin" symbolized Israel's political inviolability (Isa. 37:22; contrast Jer. 14:17; 31:4) or Babylon's protected luxury, until suffering violence (Isa. 47:1; cf. Egypt, Jer. 42:6). Virginity also symbolizes God's people as sincerely betrothed to himself (Isa. 62:4-5; II Cor. 11:2; contrast Ezek. 23:3, 8; Jer. 18:13).

BIBLIOGRAPHY
ISBE; John Murray, *Principles of Conduct,* pp. 45-81; R. D. Wilson, *PTR* 24, pp. 308-16.

J. BARTON PAYNE

VIRGIN BIRTH OF JESUS, THE.
I. DEFINITION. The virgin birth of Jesus, as presented in the Bible, was a birth in normal human flesh from a normal human mother who was a virgin in the strictest sense of the word. That is, not only did Jesus have no human father, but no coitus of any kind, natural or supernatural, took place. The virgin birth was a special miracle wrought by the Third Person of the Trinity, whereby the Second Person of the Trinity, the eternal Son of God, took to himself a genuine and com-

plete human nature, and was born as a man, without surrendering in any way his complete divine nature.

The kind of miracle involved is made clear by the fact that no branch of the Christian church, no sect or heresy within the historical Christian movement has ever regarded the Holy Spirit as the father of Jesus.

The statement that the scriptural phrase, "Son of God," never alludes to the virgin birth may be disputed. See Luke 1:35. However, even here the words "Son of God" need not be based upon the virgin birth. It is reasonable to paraphrase as follows: "Because of the overshadowing protection of the Holy Spirit and the power of the Highest, the child when born will be called *holy*. He is God's [eternal] Son." But however one may interpret this and other passages, it is clear that Jesus is presented in the Scriptures as the Son of God primarily because of his eternal pre-existent relationship to the Father, and not chiefly, if at all, because of the virgin birth.

II. SCRIPTURE REFERENCES. The virgin birth is explicitly taught in the first two chapters of Matthew and the first three chapters of Luke. Matthew's account is given entirely from the point of view of Joseph, the husband of Mary. The facts may have been given to Matthew by Joseph himself. The genealogy in Matt. 1:1-16 may well be that of Joseph, for Jesus, born and reared in his household was legally his son. This fact does not in the slightest degree constitute an argument against the virgin birth. Contrary to the RSV footnote to Matt. 1:16, "Other ancient authorities read *Joseph, to whom was betrothed the virgin Mary, was the father of Jesus who is called Christ*," there is only one Greek manuscript which contains this reading, and there is no textual evidence that this is anything but a scribal error.

Luke's account is given from Mary's point of view. Mary herself may have been one of the "eyewitnesses" (Luke 1:2) from whom Luke says he gathered data. The genealogy of Luke 3:23-38 may be taken as Mary's genealogy.

The alleged discrepancies between the two accounts are, for the most part, resolved by careful study. Mention may be made of the fact that in Luke 2:27 the plural pronoun is supported by sound evidence, — "the days of *their* purification." This is alleged to constitute

evidence that Joseph was the physical father of Jesus. However, the ceremony, as commanded in Lev. 12, has reference to the mother and the child, not the father in any sense. Therefore the plural pronoun in Luke 2:22 refers, not to Joseph and Mary, but to Mary and Jesus. From the initiatory rite, circumcision and presentation with a blood offering, throughout his life, Jesus conformed to the Jewish ritual in every respect.

Aside from the accounts in Matthew and Luke, the doctrine of the pre-existence of Jesus as the eternal Son of God, as taught by John and Paul, requires the presupposition of the virgin birth. See especially Gal. 4:4 and John 1:14.

The prophecy of Isa. 7:14 has been much discussed. The argument that the "Son" born of the "Virgin" there referred to is Jesus, does not depend on the technicalities of the study of the Hebrew word *'almâ* or the Greek word *parthenos*. (1) The fact is plain that the birth of the Son was to be a "sign," *'ôt*. (2) The prophecy is addressed to the "house of David" as a whole, and the "sign" is for "you" (plural) not for "thee" Ahaz (singular). (3) The name of the "Son" was to be "Immanuel," "God with us." (4) Before the "Son" would pass his infancy, the political issues of the time of Ahaz would be a matter of the past.

III. UNIQUENESS. The biblical doctrine of the virgin birth is unique in human culture. Attempts have been made to argue that the virgin birth is just another legend, like the pagan stories of heroes who were half god and half man. On the contrary, the biblical doctrine is that of a virgin birth in the strictest sense. See the "Definition" above. Without exception the pagan stories with which comparison has been attempted, involve the cohabitation of a god with a human being. Moreover, it is essential to the biblical doctrine that Jesus is not half god and half man, but that he is "God manifest in the flesh." "Retaining all the essential attributes of God [en morphē theou hyparchōn] . . . he humbled himself by taking the essential attributes of a servant" (Phil. 2:6-7).

IV. IMPORTANCE. It is sometimes alleged that the doctrine of the virgin birth is of relatively little importance to the Christian church.

On the contrary, if the biblical doctrine of the virgin birth is not historically true, there is no reason or basis for holding the other evangelical doctrines, for the Bible must then be rejected as an authority for faith and life. Furthermore, there can be no honest doubt that the Bible presents the incarnation as having taken place by means of the virgin birth, and that not mythically as is so widely claimed and held today. In fact, we cannot conceive of the eternal pre-existent Son of God becoming man by means of ordinary generation without ceasing to be God. In ordinary generation a new "person" begins to exist.

BIBLIOGRAPHY

In all the mass of literature two books must be mentioned as outstanding: (1) *The Virgin Birth of Christ* by James Orr, Scribners, 1907. From this the answer to alleged discrepancies, especially the two genealogies, mentioned above, is taken. (2) *The Virgin Birth of Christ* by J. Gresham Machen, Harper, 1930. This is a masterful treatment of the subject, noteworthy, among other features, for the handling of the alleged similarities in pagan mythology.

J. OLIVER BUSWELL, JR.

VIRTUE. The word *aretē* occurs five times in the NT: Phil. 4:8; I Pet. 2:9; II Pet. 1:3; twice in II Pet. 1:5. In the AV the word is translated "virtue" in each reference with the exception of I Pet. 2:9 where the AV has "praises." The RSV renders *aretē* as "excellence" in Phil. 4:8 and II Pet. 1:3, as "wonderful deeds" in I Pet. 2:9, and as "virtue" both times in II Pet. 1:5. All of these translations are properly within the scope of *aretē* but interpreters will differ as to which meaning belongs in any particular case.

The LXX translates *hôd* ("splendor, majesty, vigor") as *aretē* in Hab. 3:3 and Zech. 6:13, and *tᵉhillâ* ("praise, adoration, thanksgiving") as *aretē* in Isa. 42:8, 12; 43:21; 63:7. Under the influence of *aretē* for *tᵉhillâ*, a good case can be made for rendering *aretē* as praise(s) in both I Pet. 2:9 and II Pet. 1:3.

The AV also translates *dynamis* ("power") as "virtue" in Mark 5:30 (and the parallel account in Luke 8:46) and Luke 6:19. The word virtue may be used properly in this sense (see e.g., Webster's *New Collegiate Dictionary*), though the word power is the more natural translation of *dynamis*. The idea of virtue as a translation for *dynamis* in these passages is no doubt due to the derivation of our English word. It comes from the Latin *virtus,* meaning strength or courage, and *virtus* is derived from *vir,* "man." (A very good discussion of virtue as power or energy may be found in *IB*, Vol. XII, pp. 172-73).

MM makes the interesting observation that the infrequent use of *aretē,* a word which might be expected to occur more frequently, is due to the breadth of meaning of the word in non-Christian ethics. The thought is that the word is not sufficiently precise for a Christian ethical term.

BIBLIOGRAPHY

Arndt; reference given above to IB; MM.

RALPH A. GWINN

VISION. The revelation of the word and will of God to man by the inspiration of the Holy Spirit involves besides the dream (*q.v.*) the phenomenon of supernatural vision. Whereas the dream occurs only during sleep, the vision is more vividly perceived by the physical sense of sight and occurs more normally when one is awake (Gen. 46:2; Num. 24:4, 16; Dan. 10:7; Acts 9:7; 10:9). However, the human agent of the vision, under the overpowering influence of the divine presence, frequently oscillates between the sleeping and the wakening state (Zech. 4:1-2; Luke 9:32; Rev. 1:17).

Behind the biblical term "vision" lies some derivative of Hebrew *hāzâ* or *rā'â,* "to see," or Greek *optomai, horaomai,* "to envision." From the nature of the vision as an instrument of divine communication, this phenomenon is associated with spiritual revivals (Ezek. 12:21-25; Joel 2:28; Acts 2:17) and the absence of such divine manifestations with periods of religious decline (Isa. 29:11-12; Lam. 2:9; Mic. 3:6; Ezek. 7:26). In the time of Eli such declension is thus described: "And the word of the Lord was precious [i.e. rare] in those days; there was no open [diffused, or widespread] vision" (I Sam. 3:1).

The visions vouchsafed in the Bible were often given for the purpose of guiding the recipient in an immediate situation, as in the case of Abram (Gen. 15:2), Lot (Gen. 19:15), Balaam (Num. 22:22) and Peter (Acts 12:7). Often they were predictive, and in many instances messianic, as the visions of Isaiah, Jeremiah, Ezekiel, Hosea, Micah, Daniel, and John the Revelator. As genuine visions were granted the true prophets of the Lord by means of the Holy Spirit, so false visions were promulgated by demon powers working in false prophets. These impostors were denounced and their destruction foretold (Deut. 18:20-22; Jer. 14:14; 23:16; Ezek. 13:7-10).

BIBLIOGRAPHY

Standard Bible Encyclopaedias.

MERRILL F. UNGER

VISITATION. The use of *episkopē* as "visitation" (Luke 19:44; I Pet. 2:12) signifies a demonstration of God's power. Its OT background reveals that this may be one of blessing or punishment. The phrase *hēmera episkopēs* (I Pet. 2:12) is a verbal repetition of Isa. 10:3 as *kairos episkopēs* (Luke 19:44) is of Jer. 6:15; 10:15; 11:23. In all of these OT passages punishment is the purpose of the visitation. However, the verb *pāqaḏ*, often rendered by *episkeptesthai*, describes both God's visitation for blessing (Gen. 50:24; Jer. 29:10; Ruth 1:6, etc.) and for punishment (Hos. 8:13; Jer. 5:9; Lam. 4:22, etc.). Closely allied with the actual outcome is the idea of judicial investigation (Job 7:18; 31:14; Ps. 17:3).

The context of Luke 19:44 indicates a gracious visitation. In the person and work of Jesus, God was making available salvation to his people. That Jesus' ministry was regarded as a gracious visitation of God is corroborated by Luke 1:67, 78; 7:16; Acts 15:14.

The interpretation of I Peter 2:12 offers some difficulty. The context reveals that in this visitation (either a final or intermediate one, probably the latter) the pagans will gain clear insight into Christian conduct. The question is: Does this insight proceed from God's gracious dealing and issue in conversion or from God's judgment and result in condemnation? Critical opinion is divided, but the majority prefer the former alternative.

CHARLES A. HODGMAN

VOCATION. See CALL.

VOICE. The words for "voice" in the original languages, the Hebrew *qōl*, and the Greek *phōnē*, have a wide area of use. They are used to express (1) the tone of musical instruments (II Sam. 15:10; Matt. 24:31); (2) the sound of water (Ezek. 1:24; Rev. 1:5); (3) the noise of a multitude (Isa. 13:4; Rev. 19:1); (4) the clap of thunder (Ps. 68:34; Rev. 19:6); (5) the whir of wings (Ezek. 1:24); (6) the clatter of horses and chariots (Rev. 9:9); (7) the grinding of a millstone (Rev. 18:22); (8) the song of a bird (Eccl. 12:4); (9) the crackling of thorns (Eccl. 7:6); (10) the cry or voice of animals (Job 4:10); (11) the spread of rumor or fame (Gen. 45:16).

But these words express also not only the voice of man but of God. The Scriptures represent God as using his voice as a means of self-communication and revelation. It is represented as an outwardly audible voice which constitutes the material substratum of the theophany, as in I Sam. 3:4-21, where the boy Samuel is at first mistaken in believing that the voice was that of Eli. In Deut. 4:12 special importance is placed upon this method of revelation: "The Lord spoke to you out of the midst of the fire; you heard the voice of the words but you saw no form; there was only a voice." Here voice is placed in opposition to form. Revelation by the voice of God spans the gamut from communication by the nearly inarticulate utterance (I Kings 19:12), to the clear declaration of the entire law of conduct (Deut. 5:22-24).

Later Jewish theology developed the doctrine of the *bath qōl* (Bath Kol), which means literally, daughter of the voice. It means that God's voice itself was not heard, but only an echo or its working. The voice was audible to man but not accompanied by a visible manifestation of God. Jewish writers are not agreed as to the precise meaning of *bath qōl*, but they agree it was inferior to the biblical idea of revelation. In the OT the notion is found in Dan. 4:31 (4:28 in MT). In the NT one finds the idea in the divine voice at the baptism of Jesus (Matt. 3:17), and the voice from heaven heard by Paul (Acts 9:4).

ARNOLD C. SCHULTZ

VOW. By a vow is meant a voluntary obligation or promise made to God. It is generally taken on condition of receiving special favors from God. Often during sickness or other kinds of affliction the vow is made to God. It is then to be carried out when the calamity is over or the desire is granted (Gen. 28:20-22; Num. 21:2; I Sam. 1:11; II Sam. 15:8). The conditions of the vow are the following: (1) a consciousness of entire dependence upon the will of God and of obligation of gratitude; (2) that it is something which in itself is lawful; (3) that it is something which is acceptable to God; (4) that it is something which tends to the spiritual edification of the one who makes the vow.

Who may take such a vow? (1) The person assuming the vow must be competent, that is, having sufficient intelligence. A child or a person with an unbalanced mind may not take it. (2) The vow may be assumed only after due deliberation. Being an act of worship, it may not be taken rashly. (3) It must be voluntary and be taken cheerfully.

Is the vow lawful? On this subject there is little or no diversity of opinion. That the vow is lawful appears from the following considerations. First, from the nature of a vow, being a promise made to God. It may be an expression of gratitude for some favor already granted or a pledge to manifest gratitude for some blessings desired, should God see fit to grant them. Jacob vowed that if God would bring him back to his father's house he would consecrate one-tenth of all he possessed to Jehovah. Various parts of the Bible, the Psalms especially, abound with such vows to God (Ps. 65:1; 76:11). These are expressions of thanks to God. Second, the vow is lawful because the Bible contains many examples and many injunctions to their faithful observance. This is sufficient proof that on proper occa-

sions vows are acceptable in the sight of God (Deut. 12:6; Eccl. 5:4; Gen. 28:20). Third, the lawfulness of the vow is also evident from the fact that the baptismal covenant is in the nature of a vow. An element of vow is also clearly implied in the celebration of the Lord's Supper. In both sacraments there is a consecration to Christ and a vow to be faithful to him. The same is true of the marriage covenant, because the promises therein made are not merely promises made between two parties, but an oath and a vow taken before God.

Vows may never be taken rashly. This principle was enforced by the example of Jephthah and clearly stated in Prov. 20:25.

BIBLIOGRAPHY

C. Hodge, *Systematic Theology*, III (on the Third Commandment); *DDB*, art. on "Vow"; *Christelijke Encyclopaedie* on "Gelofte."

WILLIAM MASSELINK

W

WAGES. The word wages as used in the English Bible is the translation of two Greek words and five Hebrew words. Since it is found only eighteen times in the Bible (AV) one is surprised to find it occurring forty-two times in the RSV. This is due to the fact that the translators of the RSV have adopted a freer rendering of various words and phrases.

The earliest biblical reference to wages is in Gen. 29:15. The OT law demanded the payment of daily wages (Lev. 19:13) and judged severely anyone withholding wages (Jer. 22:13).

This word occurs only five times in the NT (AV) conveying the general idea of compensation for work done. It may be the allowance given to soldiers (Luke 3:14) or the penalty one suffers from sin (Rom. 6:23). The Greek word, *misthos*, more frequently rendered "reward" (*q.v.*), in the NT is only twice translated in the AV "wages" (John 4:36; II Pet. 2:15). Thayer's lexicon notes that the other Greek word, *opsōnion*, originally meant anything bought to be eaten with bread. Later on it came to be a general term for remuneration

for any service given, which seems to be its main biblical meaning.

HOWARD Z. CLEVELAND

WAIT. The word appears in the Scriptures as both a substantive and a verb. There are various words used in the original languages for this idea but the most frequent one is the Hebrew root *'ārab,* which means to lurk, to ambush, etc. It is the root also of wake, watch, and Arab. As a substantive the word means an ambush, a plot, or a watch, and is used in three different ways. (1) Lie in wait (Deut. 19:11; Josh. 8:4). In Judg. 9:25 the AV has, "And the men of Shechem set liers in wait for him . . ." while the RSV has, "And the men of Shechem put men in ambush against him . . .," (2) lay wait, Judg. 16:2, "and they compassed him in, and laid wait for him all night." The RSV has here "lay in wait for him all night" (cf. Jer. 9:8). (3) Laying of wait, as in Numbers 35:20, "But if he thrust him of hatred, or hurl at him by laying of wait. . . ." The RSV has here, "lying in wait." When wait is used as a verb it is used in different ways. It is used (1) of God's long-suffering towards men (Isa. 30:18; I Pet. 3:20), (2) to express expectation (Luke 12:36; Acts 10:24; II Thess. 3:5), (3) in the sense of serving or ministering to someone (II Chron. 13:10; I Cor. 9:13), (4) to refer to the faith of the believer who is ready to listen to God and who is confident that God will speak to him, and that he will see a demonstration of God's power (Pss. 33:20; 37:7; Isa. 40:31; Rom. 8:19).

ARNOLD C. SCHULTZ

WALDENSES. Peter Waldo was a rich merchant of Lyons who, concerned with life's brevity, sought counsel from a priest. Since the priest suggested that Waldo should sell his goods and give them to the poor, he did so in 1176. He turned his attention to the Scriptures and decided to follow the example of Christ.

Followers were attracted to Waldo, choosing to call themselves the "Poor in Spirit" or the "Poor Men of Lyons." Dressed in simple garb they went around preaching, only to be forbidden by the archbishop of Lyons. The pope allowed them to preach where the local bishop gave permission. However, the Waldenses disregarded this restriction and then sought authority from the Third Lateran Council (1179). The council denied them, but they went on preaching despite the church's restriction. In 1184 they were declared heretics by the pope. They spread up the Rhone, the Rhine, into the Netherlands, Germany, and Bohemia, as well as Spain and Italy.

The Waldenses sought to conform to the apostolic church. They used the vernacular Scriptures, went about two by two in simple clothes, and preached. They denied the efficacy of the mass and the existence of purgatory. They revived the Donatist attitude and adopted a pietistic view of life.

The Waldenses of the Piedmont valley have persisted to the present and make up the oldest Protestant church.

BIBLIOGRAPHY
E. Comba, trans. T. E. Comba, *Waldo and the Waldensians Before the Reformation;* J. J. Doelinger, *Beitraege zur Secktengeschichte des Mittelalters.*

SHERMAN RODDY

WALK. A familiar word in the NT, and possibly misunderstood because of having several meanings: (1) commonly to go about, (2) to walk with someone, to walk alone, (3) a symbolic and nonliteral meaning, (4) figurative, as conduct, to live, walk of life. This latter meaning is frequently found in Pauline literature.

Figuratively, *peripateō* is a Hebraism. The word ". . . self-evident as it seems to us, seems never to have been used by the Greeks uninfluenced by Semitic thought" (A. L. Williams, Ed. *Col. and Philem.*). Walk as conduct rests upon the OT as used in both Pauline and Johannine passages (Rom. 13:13; Eph. 4:1; Col. 1:10; I John 1:7; III John 4). In the NT the metaphor *peripateō* is found in Paul thirty-three times, elsewhere sixteen times. Arndt notes its common use "to walk" with its many shades of meaning; also the metaphorical use with emphasis on conduct. In this sense there are numerous grammatical combinations in the Greek NT.

Chrysostom, *Homilies,* writes, "As to walk is necessary for us, so also is to live rightly." The classic NT passage is probably Col. 1:10. Eadie comments: "It describes the general tenor of one's life, his peculiar gait and progress in his spiritual journey, . . . to be good and to do good." An interaction of right thinking and right conduct is involved leading to a worthy walk.

In the NT there are several related words: *stoichos, stoicheō,* from "a row"; so to walk in a line; *poreuomai,* "to journey, to pass from one place to another"; *anastrophē,* "conduct, deportment." As a metaphor, *peripateō* is akin to all of these.

BIBLIOGRAPHY
Arndt; John Eadie, *Colossians; ExpB; ExpGT;* J. B. Lightfoot, *Colossians and Philemon;* Moule, *Romans;* J. H. Moulton, *Grammar, Prolegomena;* MM; *Nicene Fathers,* XIII; Sanday and Headlam, *Romans,* ICC; B. F. Westcott, *St. John, Greek Text and Notes;* A. L. Williams, *Colossians and Philemon,* CGT.

ROBERT WINSTON ROSS

WARFARE, WAR. Several Hebrew words are involved, as *ṣābā',* "a mass of persons," then campaign and thus warfare; *milhāmâ,* "fight," or "a battle"; *qᵉrāḇ,* "encounter, battle, war"; and others. Greek words are *stratia,* and *polemos,* "warfare" and "fighting," also "war." The term war or warfare is generally applied to armed conflict between groups as organic units; i.e., tribes, races, states or geographic units either religious or political (see *EncSoc Sci*).

Early references to war in the OT were tribal raids (Gen. 14). Whether to plunder, to attack, to repel attack or to avenge, the tribe or group gathered around its champion (Judg. 7). The spoil from such warfare was shared. Warfare depended in part upon the season of the year (II Sam. 11:1), taking place in the spring and summer. The soldiers were placed in a battle order depending upon army size and number and the size of the enemy forces. Night watches were kept because of night attack, ambush and attack from hiding.

Warfare exhibited cruelty. The victor often proved unmerciful, putting kings and leaders to death and enslaving prisoners (I Kings 20:30 ff.). Spies were regularly used (Josh. 2:1; I Sam. 26:4) and the simile of the strong arm was correct because the battle was hand to hand combat. Victory was celebrated by war songs (Num. 21:27-30; Ex. 15:21; Judg. 15:16) and heroes were often military men. Four of those in Heb. 11 are mentioned solely because of war heroism. Warriors returning home were welcomed with victory celebrations (Judg. 11:34; I Sam. 18:6 ff.), memorials were set up, and gold, silver, and trophies were placed in the sanctuary.

Jehovah was a God of war. Israel sought the will of God before engaging in warfare (Josh. 1:1; 20-23) and priests accompanied the army as did the ark. Eli died upon hearing that the ark was captured in battle (I Sam. 6:12-18). Jehovah used war to punish Israel and also to judge Israel's enemies (I Sam. 15:1-3). The soldiers joined in the sacrifice before the battle, kept themselves pure (II Sam. 11:1) and sought the blessing of Jehovah actively. To sanctify war was a common simile (Jer. 6:4; Mic. 3:5).

The early Christians used the language of war metaphorically. "More than conquerors," "good soldier," "trumpet-sound," were all common. As the trumpet sounded the charge, so the trumpet will signal the return of Christ. This with other similes gives chiliasm a military sound and a martial setting, and Satan will be set down in final conquest, or war. Jehovah as a God of war is pictured as a conqueror, as a shield and fortress, as shooting his arrows at his enemies, and as championing the defenseless.

The Christian life was also seen as a spiritual warfare (II Cor. 10:3-4), therefore the soldier must have spiritual weapons (Eph. 6:11-17). James and I Peter speak of "war in the soul" and "warfare in your members." In the spiritual warfare the Christian has a trustworthy Captain, a good cause and tried weapons. He fights the good fight of faith.

The Christian ethics of war poses immense problems. A theodicy of history must consider the ramifications of God's sovereign purpose in relation to the nations of the earth.

BIBLIOGRAPHY

S. J. Case, "Religion and War," *AJT*, XIX (1915); Calvin, *II Corinthians*; *HDAC*; *HERE*; *EncSocSci*; P. T. Forsyth, *The Justification of God*; John Gill, *Body of Divinity*; *SHERK*.

ROBERT WINSTON ROSS

WATCH. Six or more words are translated "watch" in the NT. Four are used in relation to Christ's return and are always used metaphorically in these contexts as well as in passages dealing with ethical conduct. *Agrypneo* and *gregoreo* mean "to keep oneself awake," or "to be on the alert, be wide awake spiritually." While *nepho* literally means "to be sober" (antonym of to be drunk), only the metaphorical meaning "to be well-balanced, self-controlled" is found in the NT. *Blepo* has the idea of "watch out, look to yourselves, beware of." These four words imply that we are to be mentally and spiritually ready for the coming of Christ. Such readiness comes from dedication to him. Two other words for watch are: *tereo*, "to keep watch over, guard, to keep in the sense of preserve, protect, observe"; *paratereo*, "watch someone to see what he does, watch, guard, and observe."

The NT stresses attentiveness regarding Christian life and conduct. This includes alertness in prayer (Eph. 6:18; Col. 4:2; Matt. 26:41; Mark 14:38); watchfulness for false teaching (Mark 8:15; 12:38; Acts 20:31); being well-balanced and alert because of the devil's activity (I Pet. 5:8); taking care not to fall from the position one has reached spiritually (I Cor. 10:12; II John 8); watchfulness for souls and self-control under all circumstances as characteristics of Christian leaders (Heb. 13:17; II Tim. 4:5); alertness in spiritual defeat (Rev. 3:2-3).

In eschatological passages, "watch" points up the urgency of the situation. In the Olivet discourse the alertness is for the coming of Christ which is to occur after the tribulation of those days (Matt. 24:4, 29, 42; 25:13; Mark 13:5, 9, 33, 35, 37; Luke 21:8, 36). Christians in Thessalonica, although they are sons of light so that the day of the Lord Jesus will not overtake them as a thief, are yet to be on the alert and well-balanced (I Thess. 5:6, 8). Prepared for action and exercising self-control, the believer looks to the grace to be brought to him at the revelation of Christ (I Pet. 1:13).

BIBLIOGRAPHY

Arndt; G. E. Ladd, *The Blessed Hope*, pp. 105-19; A. Oepke in *TWNT*, II, p. 337; O. Bauernfeind, *TWNT*, IV, pp. 935-40.

A. BERKELEY MICHELSEN

WATER. The present survey attempts to classify some of the literal and some of the symbolic uses of water in the Bible. In some cases the line of demarcation between these uses is thinly drawn.

The literal uses of water are seen in the following instances: (1) the water of creation (Gen. 1:2, 6-10, 20-23; Pss. 18:15; 33:6 f.; 104:2-9); (2) the water of ordinary providence (Job 5:10; 36:27-29; 37:6-13; 38:25-30, 34-38; Ps. 65:9; Jer. 10:13; 51:16); (3) the water of extraordinary providence — miracles (Ex. 7:14-25; 14:21-31; Josh. 3:13-17; 4:15-18; I Kings 18:33-38; II Kings 2:8; Jonah 1:12-17; Matt. 14:28 f.; Luke 8:24; John 2:7); (4) the water of judgment — the flood (Gen. 6 — 8; Isa. 54:9; I Pet. 3:20; II Pet. 3:5 f.).

The symbolic uses of water are illustrated in the following examples: (1) symbolizing the Trinity — the Father (Jer. 2:13), the Son (John 7:37; Rev. 1:15), the Holy Spirit (Isa. 32:15; Ezek. 36:25-27; John 3:5; 7:38 f.); (2) symbolizing man's state of sin — sinfulness (Isa. 57:20), apostasy (Jer. 2:13), self-will (Isa. 8:6), punishment (Isa. 1:30; 8:7; Jer. 8:14; 23:15), death (Job 24:19; 26:5; 27:20); (3) symbolizing man's state of grace — the gospel invitation (Isa. 55:1; Rev. 21:6; 22:17), sorrow for sin (Jer. 9:1; Lam. 2:19), regeneration (Ezek. 47:1-12; Joel 3:18; John 3:5; Titus 3:5 f.; Heb. 10:22), the Spirit's baptism and indwelling (Isa. 32:15; 44:3; Ezek. 36:25-27; Joel 2:28; John 7:37 f.; I John 5:6-8), eternal life (John 4:14), sanctification (John 13:5, 10; Eph. 5:26), trials (Isa. 30:20; 43:2), fruitfulness (Ps. 1:3; Jer. 17:8; Ezek. 47:12), perseverance (Isa. 58:11; Jer. 31:9); (4) symbolizing man's eternal state — the lost, without water (Luke 16:24); the saved, with the water of life (Rev. 7:17; 22:1 f.).

The use of water in the OT ceremonial system (e.g., Ex. 29:4; 40:7, 12, 30) undoubtedly has symbolical significance.

BIBLIOGRAPHY

James Patrick in *HDB*; John Reid in *DCG*; James Strahan in *HDAC*.

WICK BROOMALL

WAY. One of the earliest designations for the Christian faith was *hē hodos*, "the Way." All six references are found in Acts and in connection with the apostle Paul. The word occurs twice in reference to his pre-conversion persecution of Christians (9:2; 22:14), twice in connection with the opposition to his ministry in Ephesus (19:9, 23), and twice in his defense before Felix (24:14, 22). These settings of hostility suggest that for the non-Christian world the term *hē hodos* — like the uncomplimentary *christianos* — was decidedly derogatory. The expression may well mark a significant crisis in the growth of primitive Christianity. In the eyes of the priesthood at Jerusalem the ever-expanding band of disciples were becoming a distinct and heretical sect within Judaism (cf. esp. 24:14).

The background of the term is to be found in the teaching of Jesus concerning the two ways — the easy way that leads to destruction as opposed to the hard way that leads to life (Matt. 7:13-14). Jesus also spoke of himself as "the way . . . unto the Father" (John 14:6). The author of Hebrews reflects that through his flesh Jesus had opened up the "new and living way" into the heavenly sanctuary (Heb. 10:20). Back of all this lies the wealth of teaching in the OT — especially in the Psalms — concerning "the way of the righteous" and "the way of the wicked" (Ps. 1:6; cf. also Isa. 30:21 and Jer. 21:8).

The concept of the two ways formed the pattern for a good deal of the catechetical instruction in the early church. The *Didache* begins, "There are two Ways, one of Life and one of Death," and then follows six chapters of commentary on these two ways. Closely connected are the last chapters of *Barnabas* (xviii-xx) which treat the "two Ways . . . one of Light and one of Darkness."

BIBLIOGRAPHY

ISBE; Commentaries *sub* Acts 9:2; *HDB*.

ROBERT H. MOUNCE

WEALTH. The word generally used for "wealth" in the OT is *ḥayil* (Gen. 34:29), and in the NT *euporia* (Acts 19:25). The idea expressed by wealth is sometimes that of a feeling of well-being but usually it means to possess riches. The possession of wealth is in Scripture frequently looked upon as an indication of God's blessing (I Sam. 2:7; Eccl. 5:19). Wealth, even though given by God, was not to dominate a man's life. In fact, its limitations are seen in such passages as Ps.

49:6-7, and its transitory character in Job 21 and Jer. 12. Although it is recognized in Scripture that poverty may bring sorrow, it is also emphasized that wealth has its dangers. Jesus condemned the man whose main interest was in building larger barns (Luke 12:16-21).

Wealth may even imperil one's salvation (Matt. 19:23). Consequently there are many warnings in the Scriptures directed at the rich (I Tim. 6:17; James 5:1-3). The Scriptures also make clear that the wealthy are subject to specific sins. Wealth may result in trusting too much in self, and in conceit (Prov 18:11; 28:11). It may result in highmindedness (I Tim. 6:17) and selfishness (Luke 12:19). Jesus made it clear that all would be held accountable for the use made of their riches.

ARNOLD C. SCHULTZ

WHITSUNDAY. The Christian feast of Pentecost, celebrating the descent of the Holy Spirit on the apostles (Acts 2:1-4). It falls on the fiftieth day after Easter; hence the date of Whitsunday is governed by the date of Easter. In the early centuries of the church the vigil of the feast was, like Easter eve, a day specially set apart for baptism, and the title "White Sunday" almost certainly owes its origin to the white garments worn by the newly baptized. The celebration of the festival is of great antiquity, dating possibly from apostolic times (cf. Acts 20:16).

See also CHRISTIAN YEAR.

FRANK COLQUHOUN

WHOLE. In the Bible, the English word "whole" is a translation of ten different Hebrew words and twelve Greek. The basic OT word is *kōl* which means the whole, totality. The basic NT word is *holos* and means whole, entire, complete. In Hebrew as well as Greek, without the article the word refers to the whole collection without concern for the intensive quality. With the article it means that the integral parts are complete as well. The adjective almost always stands in the predicate position. The articular phrase "in the whole world" (Rom. 1:8) shows the intensive idea. In the expression "the whole city" (Acts 21:20) the adjective is used after the noun and also shows intensity.

The most distinctive special use occurs in the Gospels and the Book of Acts where the word rather often denotes a sound, healthy condition as a result of cures effected by Christ or the apostles. For this purpose the verb *sōzō* and the adjective *hygiēs* are employed.

ROBERT V. UNMACK

WICKED, WICKEDNESS. Since the first and all-important demand which God makes upon man is perfect obedience to his revealed will (Gen. 2:16 f.), it follows that any want of conformity to or transgression of the law of God is sin. In the OT as in the NT a number of different words are used to describe the sinful condition of fallen man. They are rendered by such English words as evil, sin, iniquity, transgression, and wickedness. "Wicked" (wickedness) is the rendering of more than a dozen Hebrew words and of five Greek words. Of the former, it most frequently renders *rāšā'* (252 times). Wicked apparently always involves a moral state, unlike *ra'* (usually rendered by "evil") which may describe misfortunes and distresses resulting from sin as well as sin itself. Wicked is contrasted with "righteous" (*ṣaddiq*), especially in Proverbs (e.g., 12:5; 13:5; 29:2) and in Ps. 37. Wickedness is an active, destructive principle (Prov. 21:10; 29:16). This active opposition to God and his people causes suffering and distress (Ps. 10). But it is vain; the wicked shall perish in his wickedness (Ps. 9:16). It is the confident prayer and expectation of the righteous that this may be true (Ps. 11; 68:13). The prosperity of the wicked tries and tests the faith of the righteous (Ps. 73). "Wicked" is used less frequently in the NT where it usually renders the strong word *ponēros* (e.g., Matt. 13:19, 38, 49). But the word "sinner" (*hamartōlos*), which frequently renders *rāšā'* in the LXX, is also frequently used in the NT.

OSWALD T. ALLIS

WIDOW. The widow in the OT is primarily a figure of helplessness or neediness, that is, one unable to protect or provide for herself. For this reason the Mosaic law enjoins special consideration and justice for her, along with orphans and strangers, and threatens punishment by God upon those who do otherwise (Ex. 22:22-24; Deut. 10:18; 24:17-21; cf. Mal. 3:5). So the widow is an apt symbol for destroyed Jerusalem, that is, a city bereft of people and goods, helpless and unprotected (Lam. 1:1; cf. Isa. 47:8; Rev. 18:7), and severity of judgment can be expressed when even the widow is destroyed (Isa. 9:17).

The NT continues the idea of special concern for the widow (James 1:27) and of judgment upon those who oppress (Mark 12:40), but makes more explicit the OT idea of neediness by drawing a distinction between widows and "real widows" (I Tim. 5:3-8). The latter are those without children or grandchildren to care for them, and thus are to be provided for by the church. If anyone neglects a relative who is a widow he has disowned his faith, for this is contrary to the will of Christ. He is worse than an unbeliever, for even the heathen care for parents (I Tim. 5:8).

There is also an indication of a special class of widows who, according to patristic sources, had certain charitable and overseeing duties. It was required that they be at least sixty years of age, married only once, and well-known for good works. Younger widows were refused admission to the order because of lack of maturity and self-control (I Tim. 5:9-16).

ROBERT B. LAURIN

WILL. The Scriptures manifest greater interest in the will of God (q.v.) than in the will of man. The latter is not treated in analytic fashion any more than heart or other psychological terms. Yet the material warrants consideration. The notion of inclination is expressed in the OT by *'āḇâ*, nearly always in negative form, whereas the other leading words for will, *rāṣôn* and *ḥāp̄ēṣ*, emphasize the element of good pleasure. In the NT the chief verbs are *thelō* and *boulomai*, which mean to wish or to will according to the demands of the context. The noun *thelēma* is used mainly of God. Decision or plan is the force of the rarely used *boulē* (Luke 24:51; Acts 5:38). To will in the sense of coming to a decision is sometimes expressed by *krinō* (I Cor. 5:3). Among the more striking passages in which *thelēma* is used of man are Eph. 2:3, where the word has the force of desire, and II Pet. 1:21, where it denotes an act of the will. Of supreme import is Luke 22:42, the Gethsemane declaration of Jesus' submission to the will of the Father. Here is the pattern for the capitulation of the will of the believer to God. But this does not mean the adoption of an attitude of passivity such as may be suggested by the motto: "Let go . . . let God." It means rather the determination that the individual shall actively cooperate with the revealed purpose of God for him. The power of the flesh is so great that even in the Christian the will

to do the will of God may be largely immobilized (Rom. 7:15 ff.). The aid of the Holy Spirit is needed (Rom. 8:4). Continued dependence on the Spirit results in the strengthening of the will so that the meeting of the divine requirement becomes more constant.

The present trend in psychology is away from the notion of will as a faculty and toward the viewpoint that it is an expression of the total self or personality (q.v.). Normal life includes the capacity for making decisions, and one is responsible for his choices. That choice which makes all others the more meaningful is commitment to Christ.

See also FREEDOM.

EVERETT F. HARRISON

WILL OF GOD. In the OT the Hebrew *ḥāp̄ēṣ* designates God's "counsel" or "good pleasure" (Isa. 44:28; 46:10; 48:10; 53:10); *rāṣôn*, his "goodwill" and "favor" (Ezra 10:11; Pss. 40:9; 103:21; 143:10); *'ēṣâ*, "his counsel," in the sense of that which has been planned by deliberation (Pss. 33:11; 73:24; Prov. 19:21; Isa. 5:19; 46:10). In the Aramaic of Daniel the usual term employed is the verb *ṣᵉḇā'*, signifying God's "will" and "desire" (Dan. 4:17, 25, 32; 5:21). The NT makes use of three principal words: *boulē*, God's "eternal plan and purpose based on his deliberation" (Luke 7:30; Acts 2:23; 4:28; 20:27; Eph. 1:11); *thelēma*, his "will according to his inclination" (Acts 22:14; Rom. 12:2; Eph. 1:9; 5:17; Col. 1:9); and *eudokia*, his "good pleasure" and "delight" (Luke 2:14; Eph. 1:5, 9; Phil. 2:13).

Although God's will is absolute, i.e., unconditioned by anything outside himself, it is not distinct from his divine nature, that is, *absolutely* arbitrary, but is in complete harmony with his holiness, righteousness, goodness and truth. Thus there are those things which God cannot do (Num. 23:19; I Sam. 15:29; Heb. 6:18; James 1:13; II Tim. 2:13), because they are contrary to his essential character. The highest end of God's will is himself.

All that which is not God exists by his sovereign will, which is therefore the basis of all existence. God is under no obligation to will that which is, and he rules over all according to his free counsel and determination (Ps. 115:3; Prov. 21:1; Job 10:9; Isa. 29:16; Rom. 9:15-18; I Cor. 12:11; Rev. 4:11).

God's decretive will determines whatsoever comes to pass (Ps. 115:31; Dan. 4:17, 25,

32, 35; Acts 2:23; Eph. 1:5, 9, 11), while his perceptive will declares how man *should* live (Matt. 7:21; John 4:34; 7:17; Rom. 12:2). He does not cause sin (*q.v.*), but it exists in accordance with his purpose and he controls and punishes it (Ex. 4:21; Josh. 11:20; I Sam. 2:25; Acts 2:23; 4:28; II Thess. 2:11). He is under no obligation to save sinners, but he wills so to do and chooses whom he will (Ezek. 18:23; I Tim. 2:4; II Pet. 3:9; Rom. 9:11, 18).

God's will is inscrutable, for no man may understand it, any more than he may comprehend the being of God himself (Job 9:10; Rom. 11:33). Therefore, one must submit to God in reverent obedience, knowing that he does all things well (Isa. 45:12, 13; Rom. 9:16-23).

BIBLIOGRAPHY
H. Bavinck, *The Doctrine of God*, pp. 223-41; L. Berkhof, *Systematic Theology*, pp. 76-78; H. Heppe, *Reformed Dogmatics*, pp. 83 ff.

W. STANFORD REID

WILL-WORSHIP. This is the rendering of the Greek *ethelothrēskeia* (Col. 2:23) in the AV, ASV, ERV (RSV "rigor of devotion"). *Ethelothrēskeia* is not attested elsewhere; it may have been coined by Paul himself, on the analogy of words like *ethelodouleia* (a compound used by Plato and other Greek writers in the sense of "voluntary subjection"). Deissmann renders it a "self-made cult" and contrasts it with the "spiritual service" (*logikē latreia*) of Rom. 12:1 (*Paul*, London, 1926, p. 118). H. N. Bate renders it a "faked-religion" (*A Guide to the Epistles of St. Paul*, London, 1926, p. 143), as though the element *ethelo-* implied pretense, like English "would-be" (so J. H. Moulton and W. F. Howard, *Grammar of NT Greek*, Vol. II, Edinburgh, 1929, p. 290). But Paul uses it in order to suggest that the heretical teachers at Colossae thought that by initiation into their higher "mysteries" they could offer God a voluntary addition to his basic requirements — a supererogatory devotion by which they hoped to acquire superior merit in his sight. In this sense "will-worship" has come to be used of "worship according to one's own will or fancy, or imposed by human will, without divine authority" (*New English Dictionary* X. ii, Oxford, 1928, *s.v.*).

BIBLIOGRAPHY
Arndt; K. L. Schmidt in *TWNT*; MM; J. B. Lightfoot, *Colossians, ad loc.*

FREDERICK FYVIE BRUCE

WINE. Among the words used for "wine" is the Hebrew *yayin* for which the Greek NT has *oinos* and the Latin *vinum*. *Yayin* apparently is a loan word from a non-Semitic root. It is the usual word in the OT for the fermented juice of the grape (Gen. 9:21, etc.), and appears in our traditional Hebrew text 141 times. It is uniformly rendered "wine." *Oinos* is found over thirty times in the NT, not including its use in compounds, as in *oinopotēs*, "winebibber" (Matt. 11:16; Luke 7:34). *Yayin* was used as a family beverage as well as at special dinners and was included in some of the offerings (Ex. 29:40). The wine of the drink offerings is consistently designated as *yayin* (Num. 15:5, 10, etc.). In the OT period *yayin* is limited in its use to the juice of the grape but in later Hebrew it includes the fermented juice of different kinds of fruit, such as apple wine and date wine.

Another important term for wine in the OT is *tîrōš*. It occurs thirty-eight times in the OT and is sometimes translated "wine" and sometimes "new wine." It was considered a staple along with corn and fresh oil (Gen. 27:28; Deut. 7:13, etc). As such it is mentioned with corn and fresh oil as subject to tithe (Deut. 12:17), and the payment of first fruits (Deut. 18:4). Thus in some cases *tîrōš* has reference to fresh grape juice, before and during fermentation. The word is also used of the juice while still in the grape as "the new wine is found in the cluster" (Isa. 65:8). However, in some passages it clearly denotes the fermented juice of the grape (Hos. 4:11), where it has intoxicating properties. The *tîrōš* that is drunk in the courts of the sanctuary (Isa. 62:8-9) is fermented wine. This is supported by the evidence that *yayin* was used in the offerings.

A third important word used for wine is *šēkār*. It occurs twenty-two times in the OT and is rendered "strong drink." Its root is the basis for the Hebrew for drunk, drunkard, and drunkenness. The etymology of the word justifies the conclusion that *šēkār* may designate any intoxicating drink regardless of its source. It should be pointed out, however, that the Targumim and the Peshitta sometimes translate *šēkār* as "old wine." Added to this is the fact that Num. 28:7 designates the drink offering as being of *šēkār*, which is rendered in this passage by some versions as "strong wine." No beverage other than the juice of the grape would be accepted for this purpose. The word also appears in parallelism to *yayin* (Isa. 5:11, 22; 28:7; Prov. 20:1; 31:6).

More infrequently used words are: (1) *hemer* (Deut. 32:14 where the AV renders "grape," and the RSV has "wine"; Isa. 27:2, AV has "red wine," RSV, "a pleasant vineyard"), (2) *'āsîs* (Isa. 49:26, AV has "sweet wine," RSV, "wine"; Amos 9:13, AV, RSV, have "sweet wine"; Joel 1:5, AV, "wine," RSV, "sweet wine"; Joel 3:18, AV, "new wine," RSV, "sweet wine"; S. of Sol. 8:2, AV, RSV, have "juice"), (3) *sōbe'* (Isa. 1:22, AV, RSV, have "wine"; Hos. 4:18, AV, "drink," RSV, "drunkard"; Nah. 1:10, AV, "drunkards," RSV footnote has, "drunken as with their drink," (4) related terms derived from the verbal root *māsak*, "to mix [wine] with spices" (Ps. 75:8; Prov. 23:30; Isa. 65:11; S. of Sol. 7:2; 8:2).

BIBLIOGRAPHY
S. R. Driver, *The Books of Joel and Amos*, p. 79; B. S. Easton in *ISBE*; A. R. S. Kennedy in *HDB*; *EB*, col. 5307 f.; H. Seesemann in *TWNT*.

ARNOLD C. SCHULTZ

WISDOM. In the OT the English word wisdom represents the translation of many Hebrew words, but by far the most common is *hokmâ* (150 times). More than half of these references are found in the so-called Wisdom literature (Job, Proverbs, and Ecclesiastes).

Outside this Wisdom literature, the word seldom refers to God or even purely "spiritual" wisdom but to human skills or abilities which may or may not be God-given. Such skills were involved in the tabernacle preparation (Ex. 28:3; 31:3, 6), in warfare (Isa. 10:13), in sailing (Ps. 107:27), and in ruling (Deut. 34:9; Ezek. 28:4; I Kings 2:6 and very frequently with reference to Solomon). Wisdom (skill) may be bad and condemned by God (Ezek. 28:17; Isa. 29:14; Jer. 8:9; II Sam. 20:22; Isa. 47:10).

In the Wisdom literature, the word often refers to a mere humanly derived knowledge (Eccl. 1:13; Job 4:21), which brings only grief and frustration (Eccl. 1:12; 2:9-11). In contrast with this human wisdom, however, there is a divine wisdom, given by God, which enables man to lead a good and true and satisfying life. Such divine wisdom keeps the commandments of God (Prov. 4:11), is characterized by prudence (Prov. 8:12), discernment (Prov. 14:8), humility (Prov. 10:8), is based on the fear of the Lord (Job 28:28; Prov. 9:10), and is of inestimable value (Job 28:13 ff.). Only God, of course, possesses this wisdom in the absolute sense (Job 12:13). It cannot be derived by human intelligence (Job 28:12; Eccl. 7:23; Job 2:21). The scoffer will never find it (Prov. 14:6); but God, whose attribute it is (I Kings 3:28; Dan. 2:20), freely gives it to those who seek it (Prov. 2:6; Eccl. 2:26).

The controversial passage in Proverbs (8:22-31) has often been interpreted as a proof of the Trinity in the OT. In its context, however, it is better taken as a personification of the divine attribute which God exercised in the creation of all things and which also he wishes to impart to men in order to lead them into a righteous life.

In the OT the concept of divine wisdom must not be abstracted from its practical implications for men. The truly wise man is the good man, and the truly good man is he who at the very beginning wisely chooses to give God his proper place in his life.

In the OT Apocrypha three books, the Wisdom of Solomon, Ecclesiasticus, and Baruch, are also to be included in the "Wisdom" literature. In post-biblical times, the Jews developed this type of literature still further. Its culmination is to be found in the works of the Jewish philosopher Philo (d. A.D. 50).

In the NT, the Greek word *sophia* occurs frequently and repeats most of the OT usages supplemented by the relation which Christ bears to the divine wisdom. Wisdom is an attribute of God (Luke 11:49), the revelation of the divine will to man (I Cor. 2:4-7), a religious and spiritual understanding of the will of God on man's part (Matt. 13:54; James 1:5; and often ascribed to Christ in an absolute sense as perfect humanity), and the human intellectual capacity (Matt. 12:42 and 11:25). There is also a proud human wisdom which spurns the divine wisdom and which leads only to destruction (I Cor. 1:19-20).

The distinctive element in NT wisdom is its identification of Jesus Christ as the wisdom of God (I Cor. 1:24), who becomes the ultimate source of all the Christian's wisdom (I Cor. 1:30).

BIBLIOGRAPHY
W. R. Harvey-Jellie, *The Wisdom of God and the Word of God*; H. A. Wolfson, *Philo*.

KENNETH S. KANTZER

WITCHCRAFT. The term witch is popularly used of one who uses black magic, a process of working harm through a compact with an evil spirit or, more particularly, the devil. For temporal possessions or power the witch was thought to have sold her soul to the devil, as in the Faust legend.

The biblical witch is entirely different from this medieval concept. She is more properly the sorceress, $m^e\underline{k}a\check{s}\check{s}ep\hat{a}$ (Ex. 22:17). The sorcerer and the sorceress used magical formulae, incantations, or mutterings to exercise control over the unseen world.

Sorcery, or witchcraft, was common in the ancient Near East. The term is used of the "wise men" of Egypt during the time of Moses (Ex. 7:11) and their Babylonian counterparts during the exile (Dan. 2:2). Nahum (3:4) calls Babylon "the mistress of witchcrafts," $ba'\bar{a}la\underline{t}$ $k^es\bar{a}p\hat{i}m$. Jezebel and her Baalist compatriots were accused of resorting to "whoredoms and witchcraft" (II Kings 9:22). All forms of sorcery and witchcraft were strictly forbidden in Israel (Ex. 22:18; Lev. 20:27; Deut. 18:10-12).

The so-called "witch of Endor" (I Sam. 28:3 ff.) is called $'\bar{e}\check{s}e\underline{t}$ $ba'\bar{a}la\underline{t}$ $'\hat{o}\underline{b}$ "a woman who is mistress of necromancy." She was a member of a class of people who sought to communicate with the dead. Saul sought her services as a move of desperation. Although God used this interview to bring a message of judgment upon Saul there is no hint that the woman had supernatural power. She appeared terrified at the sight of Samuel.

Samuel declared, "Rebellion is as the sin of witchcraft $(qesem)$" (I Sam. 15:23). Balaam (Josh. 13:22) and the Philistines (I Sam. 6:2) were "diviners." The "witchcraft" or $pharmakeia$ of Gal. 5:20 in the first instance referred to drugs or potions. It came to be associated with poisoning and witchcraft.

CHARLES F. PFEIFFER

WITNESS, TESTIMONY. Properly, "a witness" $(martys)$ is "one who testifies" $(martyre\bar{o})$ by act or word his "testimony" $(martyrion)$ to the truth. This act of testifying is called his "testimony" $(martyria)$. In ancient days, as at the present, this was a legal term designating the testimony given for or against one on trial before a court of law. In Christian usage, the term came to mean the testimony given by Christian witnesses to Christ and his saving power. Because such testimony often meant arrest and scourging (cf. Matt. 10:18; Mark 13:9), exile (Rev. 1:9), or death (cf. Acts 22:20; Rev. 2:13; 17:6) the Greek was

transliterated to form the English word $martyr$ $(q.v.)$, meaning one who suffers or dies rather than give up his faith. However, in the NT, suffering was an incidental factor in the word.

A thorough study of witnessing would necessitate a study of the whole Bible. Such words as preaching, teaching, and confessing would have to be included. Greek words (fifteen in number) stemming from "witness" $(martys)$ are used over two hundred times in the NT. The most common usage is found in the Johannine writings in which seventy-six instances are found. Acts has thirty-nine instances and the Pauline writings thirty-five.

Leaving aside those uses of the word which refer to man's witness to men (cf. III John 12, et $al.$), God's witness to men (cf. Acts 13:22, et $al.$), man's witness against men (cf. Matt. 18:16, et $al.$) and miscellaneous uses (cf. John 2:25, et $al.$), we will consider the distinctively Christian use of the words.

First, there are those testimonies which are meant to establish the incarnation and the truth of Christianity. In John's Gospel, where this is primary, we find instances of all the main witnesses. John the Baptist "bears testimony" $(martyre\bar{o})$ to Jesus as the coming Saviour of the world (John 1:7, 8, 15, 32, 34; 3:26; 5:32). The works that Jesus did were a testimony that he came from the Father (John 5:36); this explains why John called the miracles "signs" $(s\bar{e}meion)$. The OT Scriptures are a testimony to Jesus (John 5:39) — this thought is behind most of the NT quotations from the OT. After the resurrection, the main evidences of the truth of Christianity are: the ministry of the Holy Spirit (John 15:26), the witness of the disciples to the resurrection (Acts 1:22, et $al.$) and the signs and wonders by which God attested the ministry of the apostles and the churches (Heb. 2:4).

The pattern of Christian missionary and evangelistic activity is set in the NT. Several principles emerge. (1) Witnessing is the universal obligation of all Christians (Luke 24:48; Acts 1:8). That the act of witnessing was not restricted to the apostles or ministers is shown by those references in Acts which speak of all the disciples giving testimony (cf. Acts 2:4). This is one of the most needed emphases for modern Christianity. (2) The testimony to be given centered in the facts and the meaning of the earthly ministry of Jesus (Acts 10:39-41) and to his saving power (Acts 10:43). The primary witnesses were the apostles who had personal knowledge of this ministry from its beginning (Acts 1:22). This knowledge they delivered to others who gave testimony to it also (Heb. 2:3-4). They, in turn, were to entrust this message to others who would continue to give witness to it (II Tim. 2:2). The primary message was this Christian "tradition" (*paradosis*) (I Cor. 15:1-3). (3) Christian witnesses were to be faithful without regard to their personal safety or comfort (Matt. 10:48, *et al.*). (4) Christian testimony was attended by the ministry of the Holy Spirit and the manifestation of God's presence and power (Heb. 2:3-4).

BIBLIOGRAPHY
Arndt; MM.

FRED L. FISHER

WOE, WOES. The Hebrew uses two main terms for "woe," *hōwy* and *'ōwy*, while the Greek uses *ouai*. The word sometimes signifies a feeling of sympathy or compassion (Matt. 24:19) or an expression of despair or lamentation, as, "Woe is me . . . !" (Ps. 120:5). In other places it has an oracular significance and is a form of anathema, curse, or warning of punishment.

The Hebrew prophets frequently used oracles beginning "Woe unto . . ." concerning a wide area of Israelite life. For example, "Woe unto thee, O Jerusalem!" (Jer. 13:27). "Woe be unto the pastors that destroy and scatter the sheep of my pasture!" (Jer. 23:1). "Woe unto the foolish prophets . . ." (Ezek. 13:3). "Woe unto them that are at ease in Zion . . ." (Amos 6:1). The seven woes of Isaiah (Isa. 5:8, 11, 18 f., 20, 21, 22, 23; cf. 10:1) may be compared with the seven woes pronounced against the religious leaders of his day by Jesus (Matt. 23:13, 15, 16, 23, 25, 27, 29).

ARNOLD C. SCHULTZ

WOMAN. The generic term man includes woman, but as an individual creation of God she was formed out of the man (Gen. 2:21-24). Because of this creative order the Bible assigns headship (I Cor. 11:7-9) and authority (I Tim. 3:12-13) to the man. Rulership is also delegated to the man as a result of the fall (Gen. 3:16).

In Judaism the position of woman was markedly better than it was in Greek or Roman civilization. In the ancient Greek world women were considered inferior to men. Wives led lives of seclusion and practical slavery. The *hetairai* enjoyed more freedom of movement

but did not have the rights or status of men. Greater freedom came to women in Macedonia, but it was enjoyed only by a minority. In Roman society women enjoyed greater practical, though not legal, freedom than in Greece, but licentiousness and moral laxity was rampant. In the Hebrew society the woman had little position legally (cf. Gen. 31:14-15; Num. 27:1-8), but her practical status was one of dignity, particularly in the home. Children were the special charge of the mother (Ex. 20:12; 21:15; Lev. 19:3; Prov. 1:8; 6:20; 20:20; 30:11, 17). God included "all the people" (including women, Ex. 19:11) in the covenant relationship with himself. Women were expected to share in religious ceremonies (Deut. 12:12, 18; 14:26; 16:11, 14); they could take part in the offerings (Lev. 6:29; 10:14); and they may have formed a kind of "temple choir" (Ezra 2:65; Neh. 7:67; cf. Heinrich Ewald, *The History of Israel*, Longmans, Green, and Co., London, 1878, p. 285).

Christianity brought a revolution in the status of women, the Virgin Mary being the turning point (Luke 1:48). Jesus taught women and received their ministrations and financial support (Matt. 28:1; Luke 8:3; 10:38-42; 23:56; John 4). In the life of the early church women were among the first believers (Acts 12:12; Phil. 4:2). Some, like Priscilla and Phoebe, were outstanding leaders. However, the NT does not allow them leadership in public worship and assigns subordination, dependence, and difference of nature as reasons for this restriction (I Cor. 14:34; I Tim. 2:13-14). Deaconesses are not unequivocally attested as a recognized group until the third century and probably grew out of the order of widows which was prominent in the first two centuries (I Tim. 5). Throughout this period the emphasis was still on the dignity of woman in the home (Eph. 5).

BIBLIOGRAPHY
The Ministry of Women (SPCK, London, 1919); C. C. Ryrie, *The Place of Women in the Church*; F. Zerbst, *The Office of Woman in the Church*; L. Zscharnack, *Der Dienst der Frau in den ersten Jahrhunderten der christlichen Kirche*.

CHARLES C. RYRIE

WOMEN, ORDINATION OF. There being no clear scriptural statements on the question of women's ordination, consideration of the question should include the following related biblical teachings: (1) Although the Bible emphasizes equality in spiritual capacity and worth of both sexes before God (Gen.

1:26-29; Ex. 15:20 ff.; Luke 10:39-42; 24:5-8; John 11:21-27; Acts 17:4), consistently from the Adamic sin until the end of the present order, woman's function is designated as helpmeet and mother (Gen. 3:16; 18:11 ff.; Judg. 13:3 ff.; Luke 1:26 ff.; I Tim. 2:15), while that of man is to provide for and govern the family, this latter requiring teaching, judging, and disciplining (Gen. 3:16; 18:19; Eph. 5:22 ff.; I Tim. 4:13-16). In Christ the wife's subjection to the husband is changed from the OT motivation of outward conformity to law to heart devotion to Christ (Eph. 5:22, 33). Government of higher institutions grew out of OT patriarchal family structure, and male family government is a basis for choosing church leaders (I Tim. 3:4-5). As in OT, all appointments to NT offices are men (Mark 3:13 ff.; Acts 1:26; 6:5 ff.; etc.). Paul's prohibitions of women's speaking in the church have in view preserving male authority in the home (I Cor. 14:34, 35; I Tim. 2:11-12). Thus, the important reason against women's ordination is that it offers a logical and psychological inconsistency to clear Bible teaching concerning home government and its relationship to higher institutions, and therefore strikes at the root of government and law and order.

(2) The normal relationship of the sexes as a basis for society during fleshly life, which is marriage ("one flesh" Matt. 19:5), will give way *after* the resurrection to an eternal status in which men and women are as angels (Matt. 22:30). Both men and women are "heirs" to this future state in Christ, and concerning it Paul teaches there is "neither male nor female" (Gal. 3:28-29; cf. Eph. 5:22; 6:5; etc.). Peter teaches that now wives should be subject to their husbands and appeals in the same passage to women's equal heirship as reason why men should treat them with careful consideration (I Pet. 3:5-7).

(3) The prophetic gift involves having a *direct objective message* from God so that the man or woman acts simply as God's mouth and does not convey his or her own message, but God's (Ex. 7:1; 4:15-16; Jer. 1:9; Ezek. 3:27; I Cor. 14:30; II Pet. 1:20-21). False prophets or prophetesses give their view of God's will out of their own heart (Ezek. 13:2, 17; Jer. 23:16, etc.). On the other hand, the gifts of government and teaching involve the individual's giving *subjective judgment* under guidance of the Holy Spirit and are always differentiated in Scripture from prophecy (Mal.

2:4-8; 3:11; Jer. 18:18; I Cor. 12:28; Eph. 4:11-12). Hence, to prophesy is not the same as to preach. Prophecy was the gift par excellence which indicated God's presence, approval, and *sometimes* choice for leadership in government. But from the outset women were warned that for them it did not include governing (Num. 19, cf. Judg. 4:8-9 concerning the only exception). Since prophecy showed God's presence, in the NT where the Holy Spirit's presence becomes the earnest of heirship (Eph. 1:13-14), it was essential that many women have that gift (Acts 2:17, etc.).

See also WOMAN.

BIBLIOGRAPHY
  R. C. Prohl, *Woman in the Church;* F. Zerbst, *The Office of Women in the Church: A Study in Practical Theology;* C. C. Ryrie, *The Place of Women in the Church.*

CARL W. WILSON

WONDER. See MIRACLE.

WORD. I. THE VOCABULARY. The principal Hebrew expression is *dābār,* which also means "subject" (cf. Judg. 3:20), but can equally mean an act or deed. Sometimes, as in I Kings 11:41, it is difficult to decide which is intended.

In the LXX *dābār* is usually represented by *logos* or *rhēma.* This passes into the NT, where *logos* occurs more than 300 times and *rhēma* more than 70. The two are not always easy to distinguish though *rhēma* relates strictly to "that which was said." It has also preserved, especially in Luke-Acts, something of the sense in which *dābār* is used for deed.

II. THE ACTIVE WORD. Allied with the ambivalence between word and act in the meaning of *dābār* is the dynamic Hebrew conception of word. Evil words are tantamount to evil deeds (Ps. 35:20 — "matters" — in the AV is *dᵉbārîm*). A word solemnly given carries its own potency, and cannot be recalled (cf. the whole story in Gen. 27). In this God's word is archetypal. God speaks, the universe comes into being (Gen. 1:3 ff.), and, despite the necessity of anthropomorphic language (e.g., Ps. 8:3), the OT insists on the active word as the means of creation (cf. Ps. 33:6), and this is a cardinal Christian understanding (Heb. 11:3). God's word will effect its purpose as surely as snow and rain effect theirs (Isa. 55:10-12). The miraculous birth of Jesus is certain because God's word is self-fulfilling (Luke 1:37 ASV, which echoes the LXX of Gen. 18:14, on the miraculous birth of Isaac).

God, when he fulfills a promise, "performs his word" (Deut. 9:5).

III. WORD AS REVELATION. Such is the background of the use of *dābār* to designate the prophetic message. The word of the Lord had not been revealed to Samuel at the time of his call (I Sam. 3:7). The word "comes" to a prophet (Jer. 1:2, 4 and *passim*). It may be an object of vision to the prophet (Jer. 38:21). But the word is so inseparably linked with God's acts of mercy and judgment in history that, in the light of recent sad events and his own message, Jeremiah entreats the nation to *see* the word of Jehovah (Jer. 2:31). When the prophets cry, "Hear this word" (e.g., Amos 4:1; 5:1), they are declaring a revelation which must have a historic fulfilment; for God's word is settled in heaven (Ps. 119:89). The covenant-loving Israelite is guided by God's revelatory word (Pss. 119:105, 130, etc.). *Dābār* occurs nearly 400 times in the OT to express divine communication to God's people.

The OT viewed as a whole is described by Christ as God's word (Matt. 15:6). The same term applies to the Christian revelation as a whole (cf. Col. 3:16). It is used, moreover, of Christ himself (John 1:1, 14), God's personal word of revelation (see LOGOS). In the OT, and, completely and perfectly, in Christ, God has spoken (Heb. 1:1): in different degrees, but the same word. Christ himself keeps God's word of commandment (John 8:55). Those who reject Christ do not possess God's words (John 5:38); his disciples are marked by their possession of Christ's words (John 15:7). And this active word can strip a man of his pretensions, and convict him (Heb. 4:13).

IV. WORD AS GOSPEL. God's word of revelation has reference to salvation, and itself effects that salvation. The context of Isa. 55:10 ff. relates to pardon for the penitent. The prophetic word speaks of grace and mercy as well as of wrath and judgment. The saving word may even be personified, and spoken of as sent by God to heal his people (Ps. 107:20). The word of our God which endures for ever (Isa. 40:8) is explicitly called the gospel (I Pet. 1:25). The word is still self-fulfilling; for in the same context it is "by the word of God" that Christians are born again (I Pet. 1:23; cf. James 1:18). The disciples are clean through the word spoken by Jesus (John 15:3).

The message spoken by Jesus is the word of God (Luke 5:1 etc.); so too is the message of which he is the subject, preached by the apostles and the early Christians (Acts 4:29, and frequently). It may be particularized by a distinctive feature, e.g., the word of the *kingdom* (Matt. 13:19), or of the cross (I Cor. 1:18).

V. WORD AS SCRIPTURE. Ps. 119 presupposes a written revelation which the Psalmist can describe as laws, precepts, statutes, judgments — or as God's word (vs. 105) or words (vs. 130).

This usage is adopted by our Lord, who distinguishes between the word of God and the human tradition confused with it (Matt. 15:6), and who correlates the original revelation and its written form (John 10:35). Paul refers to the teaching of the OT as the word of God (Rom. 9:6 ff.), and to an individual passage as a "word" (Rom. 13:9; Gal. 5:14). The difficult I Tim. 4:5 probably relates to scriptural prayers (the *active* word once more).

Biblical usage thus appears under several forms, yet with an overall consistency. The word of God is his self-communication. He spoke by the prophets. He has spoken by Scripture: Scripture is his word. He has spoken by a Son: Christ is his Word. The gospel, the doctrine of Scripture, and the preaching of Christ are his word. In each case the word is active, saving and judging.

VI. WORD AND SPIRIT. This implies neither a mechanical nor a magical view of the word of God. The key is in the concomitance of word and Spirit. The revelation to the prophets (and in NT days to the apostles also, Eph. 3:5) is regularly associated with the Holy Spirit. Functions predicated of the Spirit are predicated also of the word (cf. John 16:8 f. with Heb. 4:12 f., John 14:16 with Rom. 15:4, John 5:39 with John 15:26). In some of these instances there is explicit reference to Scripture; elsewhere "the word" in the wider sense is in view.

This lies behind the confidence of the Reformers in their appeal to Scripture. They appeal to the text, rightly understood; but they recognize also that the word carries its own enlightenment (that of the Spirit) to those who approach it in penitence and faith. The word acts because of the Holy Spirit speaking in Scripture. The word read, like the word preached, profits when it is "mixed with faith in them that hear it" (cf. Heb. 4:2).

BIBLIOGRAPHY
BDB; Arndt, s.v. *logos, rhema*; *TWNT*, s.v. *logos, rhema*. Representative Reformation texts are Calvin, "On Scripture," in *The Mystery of Godliness* (republished Eerdmans 1950), and Zwingli, "On the Certainty and Clarity of the Word of God," in *Zwingli and Bullinger*, edited by G. W. Bromiley.

ANDREW F. WALLS

WORK. Throughout the Bible there are many references to work, the words used to designate it being divided into two classes. There is the term which has no moral or physical implications as, for instance, when God works in creation, or when reference is made generally to man's works in this life. Mᵉlā́ḵâ (Gen. 2:2; Ex. 20:9; I Chron. 4:23; Hag. 1:14), *ma'ăśeh* (Gen. 5:29; Ex. 5:13; Prov. 16:3; Eccl. 1:14) in the Hebrew, and *ergon* in the Greek are the usual words employed for this purpose. There are, however, other words, *yᵉğî'â* (Gen. 35:42; Deut. 28:33; Ps. 128:2; Isa. 55:2; Ezek. 23:29) and *'āmāl* (Ps. 90:10; Eccl. 1:3; 2:10 *et seq.*; Jer. 20:18) in the OT, and *kopos* in the NT (Matt. 11:28; John 4:38; I Cor. 4:12; 15:58; I Thess. 1:3; II Thess. 3:8), which imply weariness, trouble and sorrow.

Work and labor of themselves are never held to be evil, but rather are thought of as man's natural occupation in the world. Even in the state of innocency man as the apex of creation, the representative of all creation before God (Gen. 2:15 ff.), was given work to perform as part of his normal existence. This is contrary to much modern thinking which adopts the attitude that man should avoid work as something evil and to be avoided if at all possible.

That man's sin has corrupted and degraded work is at the same time continually repeated in the Bible. Gen. 3:17 f. specifically states that work will, because of sin, change its character to become the cause of man's ultimate physical disintegration. This would seem to be the reason for work in subsequent portions of the Bible frequently embodying the idea of weariness. Indeed, this is the theme of the Book of Ecclesiastes in which the Preacher states that all man's labor that he does under the sun is vanity. Man as a sinner works solely with worldly ends in view, the outcome being a sense of frustration and hopelessness, for ultimately he will disappear from this earth and his works with him (Eccl. 2). Only as he interprets his work in the light of eternity will his understanding of it change.

Yet even sinful man possesses great gifts and abilities with which to subdue and use the physical world. In Exodus 31:1 ff., Judges 3:10 (cf. also Isa. 45) and many other places it is stated that it is the Holy Spirit who gives man these endowments. Certain OT characters are also said to have received special gifts from God which would enable them to do their work: the Judges, Saul, and even the heathen king Cyrus (Judg. 3:10; I Sam. 10:6 f.; Isa. 45). The NT writers assume the point of view of the OT, but stress it particularly in connection with gifts and abilities possessed by members of the church (I Cor. 12; Eph. 4:11 ff.). Moreover, they continually emphasize that God calls all men to work and positions in life in which they are to serve him. While this appears in the OT as in the case of Esther (Esth. 4:13-14), the apostle Paul repeats it with great frequency in his writings (Eph. 6:5 ff.; I Tim. 6:1-2; Philem.).

Work, however, even though a man may be richly endowed with gifts, cannot be anything but ultimately empty unless man realizes that its true purpose is to glorify God. Paul makes this very plain in speaking to both servants and masters (Eph. 6:5 ff.; I Tim. 6:1-2) summing it all up in his instruction to Christians to be not "slothful in business, but fervent in spirit serving the Lord" (Rom. 12:11), and in his exhortation to do all things to the glory of God (I Cor. 10:31).

In practice, such a view of work means that the Christian must always regard his work as a divinely appointed task in which, as he fulfills his calling, he is serving God. This requires him to be honest and diligent in all that he does, whether as employee or employer. Such, for instance, is the central point in the parable of the talents (Matt. 25:15). If he is a servant, he is to be faithful and obedient, doing all things as in God's sight (Eph. 6:5 ff.), while if he is an employer God lays upon him the responsibility of fair dealing and consideration towards his employees. He is to pay them adequately and not to defraud them of their wages, "for the laborer is worthy of his hire" (Lev. 19:13; Deut. 24:14; Amos 5:8 ff.; Luke 10:7; Col. 4:1; James 5:4 f.). Thus all honest work is honorable and to be performed as a divinely given commission to God's eternal glory (Rev. 14:13).

BIBLIOGRAPHY
J. Calvin, *Institutes of the Christian Religion*, bk. III, chap. vii; A. Kuyper, *The Work of the Holy Spirit*, pp. 32-43; J. Murray, *Principles of Conduct*, chap. iv.

W. STANFORD REID

WORKS. See GOOD WORKS.

WORLD, WORLDLINESS. In the OT, *'ereṣ*, which is properly earth in contrast to heaven (Gen. 1:1), is occasionally rendered world, but the more usual term is *tēḇēl*, which signifies the planet as having topographical features, as habitable and fruitful (Pss. 19:4; 90:2). The NT words are *oikoumenē*, denoting the populated world (Luke 4:5); *aiōn*, which is usually rendered age (*q.v.*), but which occasionally combines with the concept of time that of space (Heb. 1:2; 11:3); and *kosmos*, which contains the thought of order or system. The latter word may denote the material world (Rom. 1:20), or even the totality of heaven and earth (Acts 17:24); the sphere of intelligent life (I Cor. 4:9); the place of human habitation (I Cor. 5:10, l.c.); mankind as a whole (John 3:16); society as alienated from God and under the sway of Satan (I John 5:19); and the complex of ideas and ideals which govern men who belong to the world in this ethical sense (I John 2:15-17; James 4:4).

Since *kosmos* is the leading term involved, it calls for further consideration. Among the Greeks, *kosmos* became used for the universe, since it suitably expressed the order noted there. The Hebrews, on the other hand, were not hospitable to the concept of universe, but thought in terms of the heavens (the abode of God) and the earth (the realm of human existence). God was the author of both, and the regularity of the movements of the heavenly bodies and the rhythm of the seasons bore witness to his creative wisdom and the power of his sustaining control. NT writers follow this pattern of OT thought, avoiding, with rare exceptions, the use of the word *kosmos* for the heavens and the earth combined (Acts 17:24 is explicable as an adaptation of the message in terms congenial to the hearers, who were Greeks). The word *kosmos*, then, in the NT, prevailingly denotes the earth, and by an extension of thought is used for mankind which dwells on the earth. Perhaps this process was assisted by the fact that, owing to human intelligence and the drive for social integration, man's life presents considerable order.

But the most striking fact about the NT use of *kosmos* is the readiness with which the term is employed in an evil sense. Again and again, especially in the Johannine writings, the world is presented as something hostile to God. This seems to spell disorder. How, then, can *kosmos*

be used to describe such a state of affairs? The answer is likely to be found in the fact that the powers of spiritual evil, which have Satan as their head and appear to be organized on a vast scale and with great efficiency (Eph. 6:12), dominate the life of unredeemed humanity. Satan rules a kingdom which is opposed to the kingdom of God (Luke 11:18).

We are not dropped into the depths of a hopeless dualism by reason of this opposition, for the word teaches that the sphere of divine control embraces "all things." Therefore, even over the world which is marred by the love of evil and by the sinister hold of the devil, God is still sovereign. Satan's kingdom exists by permission, not by reason of divine helplessness. Reconciliation has been provided for the world (II Cor. 5:19), whereby men may leave the realm of darkness and be transferred into the kingdom of the Son of God's love. Those who will not do so must share the fate of Satan.

Worldliness, though not a scriptural term, is certainly a scriptural concept. It is an affection for that which is unlike God and contrary to his will (James 4:4; I John 2:15-16). The refusal to live an ascetic life is not a proof of worldliness, nor is the love of the beautiful. The determination of what is worldly should not rest solely upon the nature of an activity or habit viewed as a thing-in-itself, but also upon the spirit of the one who indulges himself. If one is actuated by selfishness or neglect of God, he may be more worldly in God's sight than another whose outward acts are more questionable, but whose heart does not condemn him, because he is not consciously disobeying his Lord.

BIBLIOGRAPHY

CB; HDCG; V. H. Stanton in HDB; G. Kittel, *Die Religionsgeschichte und das Urchristentum*, pp. 88-92; Art. "kosmos" in *TWNT*.

EVERETT F. HARRISON

WORSHIP. Our English word means "worthship," denoting the worthiness of an individual to receive special honor in accordance with that worth. The principal biblical terms, the Hebrew *šāḥâ* and the Greek *proskyneō*, emphasize the act of prostration, the doing of obeisance. This may be done out of regard for the dignity of personality and influenced somewhat by custom (Gen. 18:2), or may be based on family relationship (Gen. 49:8) or on station in life (I Kings 1:31).

On a higher plane the same terms are used

of divine honors rendered to a deity, whether to the gods of the nations (e.g., Ex. 20:5) or to the one true and living God who reveals himself in Scripture and in his Son (Ex. 24:1). The tutelage of Israel in the wilderness laid great stress on the sinfulness of idolatrous worship and its dire consequences (e.g., Deut. 8:19). No injury to God compares with the denial of his uniqueness and the transfer to another of the recognition due to him. In this light must be understood his references to himself as a jealous God (Ex. 20:5).

Perversion of worship is seen in Satan's avid effort to secure for himself what belongs properly to God alone (Matt. 4:9), as well as in the blasphemous figure of the beast (Rev. 13:4). Undue deference paid to men verges at times on worship and is resisted by the godly (Acts 10:25, 26). Barnabas and Paul protested the attempt to worship them at Lystra based on the impression that they were gods who had come down to men (Acts 14:11-14). Loyal angels refuse veneration (Rev. 22:9).

It is useful to distinguish between a broad and a restricted meaning of worship as applied to God. In general he may be honored with prayer and praise and the bringing of sacrificial gifts (I Sam. 1:3). This cultic worship is especially appropriate in the house of God (Ps. 138:2) and when it is carried on with a desire to be clothed in his holiness (Ps. 29:2). In a still broader sense the service which issues from worship and derives therefrom its inspiration may be included (Matt. 4:10).

In the narrower sense worship is pure adoration, the lifting up of the redeemed spirit toward God in contemplation of his holy perfection. Matthew distinguishes between the presentation of gifts by the Magi to the Christ child and their worship of him (Matt. 2:11).

Jesus made an epochal statement on this subject (John 4:24). To worship God in spirit involves a contrast with worship in the letter, in the legalistic encumbrance so characteristic of the Jew; to worship him in truth contrasts with the Samaritan and all other worship which is false to a greater or lesser extent.

Our Lord made possible a more intelligent worship of God by revealing the Father in his own person. As the incarnate Son, he himself is deserving of the same veneration (John 9:38; 20:28; Heb. 1:6; Rev. 5:6-14).

BIBLIOGRAPHY

R. Abba, *Principles of Christian Worship*; R. Martin-Achard in *CB*; A. B. Macdonald, *Christian Worship in the Primitive Church*; J. S. McEwen in *RTWB*.

EVERETT F. HARRISON

WRATH. Wrath, anger, and indignation are integral to the biblical proclamation of the living God in his opposition to sin. While God's love is spontaneous to his own being, his wrath is called forth by the wickedness of his creatures. Thus it is the wounding of his gracious love, the rejection of his proffered mercy, which evokes his holy wrath. God's act of wrath is his strange work (Isa. 28:21). C. H. Dodd has well observed, "Wrath is the effect of human sin: mercy is not the effect of human goodness, but is inherent in the character of God."

On the other hand, the exhaustive studies of Fichtner in the OT and of Staehlin in the NT (see BIBLIOGRAPHY) do not sustain the thesis that wrath is an impersonal retribution, an automatic, causal working out of an abstract law. In the OT wrath is the expression of the personal, subjective free will of Yahweh who actively punishes sin, as in the NT it is the personal reaction of God, not an independent hypostasis. In the face of evil, the Holy One of Israel does not dodge the responsibility of executing judgment. He demonstrates his anger at times in the most personal way possible. "I the LORD do smite" (Ezek. 7:8 f.). In such NT passages as John 3:36; Rom. 1:18; Eph. 5:6; Col. 3:6; Rev. 19:15; 11:18; 14:10; 16:19; 6:16; cf. Rom. 9:22, wrath is specifically described as God's wrath, his wrath, thy wrath, or the wrath of the Lamb. The wrath of God is being continually revealed from heaven, actively giving the wicked up to uncleanness, to vile passions, to reprobate minds, and punishing them in the day of wrath and revelation of the just judgment (q.v.) of God (Rom. 1:18 — 2:6). In II Thess. 1:7-9 Paul writes as personal a description of the Lord Jesus' action in directly punishing the disobedient as can be penned.

In the total biblical portrayal, the wrath of God is not so much an emotion or an angry frame of mind as it is the settled opposition of his holiness to evil. Accordingly, the wrath of God is seen in its effects, in God's punishment of sin in this life and in the next. These inflictions include pestilence, death, exile, destruction of wicked cities and nations, hardening of hearts, and the cutting off of the people of God for idolatry or unbelief. They reach into the life to come in Jesus' descriptions of everlasting punishment, of a hell of fire, where their worm dieth not and the flame is not quenched. The day of wrath is God's final judgment against sin, his irrevocable condemnation of impenitent sinners.

The OT description of God as "slow to anger and plenteous in mercy" is best understood as a blessed revelation full of wonder and awe. For only he who apprehends the reality of God's wrath is overpowered by the magnitude of his mercy, as it is declared in Isa. 54:7-10 or in the ASV reading of Ps. 30:5, "His anger is but for a moment, his favor is for a lifetime." As mercy gets the upper hand in these OT passages, so the ultimate NT word is the grace of our Lord Jesus Christ, the love of God the Father made ours in the fellowship of the Holy Spirit.

Accordingly, the way of escape from the wrath of the Almighty is abundantly presented in both testaments. While man's puny efforts are insufficient, God's own heart of love provides a way of salvation. He calls men to repent, to return unto himself, to receive his forgiveness and renewal. He receives the intercession of his servants — Abraham, Moses, Eleazar, and Jeremiah — for his people; and himself provides the OT sacrificial system by which his wrath may be averted.

In the NT the call is to faith, to repentance, to baptism in the name of the Lord Jesus who saves us from the wrath to come (I Thess. 1:9-10). For when we are justified by his blood and reconciled by his death we shall be saved from the wrath by his life (Rom. 5:9-10). The most poignant word about God's punishment is that it is the wrath of the Lamb (q.v.) who took upon himself and bore the sins of the world.

BIBLIOGRAPHY

F. Buechsel, J. Fichtner, and G. Staehlin in *TWNT*; commentaries on Romans, especially those by C. H. Dodd and O. Michel; L. Morris, *The Apostolic Preaching of the Cross*; H. N. Snaith in *RTWB*; R. V. G. Tasker, *The Biblical Doctrine of the Wrath of God*.

WILLIAM CHILDS ROBINSON

WRITE, WRITING, WRITTEN. The significance of writing is incalculable: its invention may well act as the dividing point between primitive and civilized peoples — prehistoric and historic times. Writing first appears in pictographic script somewhere around 3200 B.C. and is found among the Sumerians (believed to be the inventors of writing), the Egyptians, and the Canaanites. From their pictographic script, the Sumerians soon developed the cuneiform system of writing and their documents dating from as early as 2900 B.C. can be read by means of these wedge shaped characters. The cuneiform system spread rapidly to the Semitic Babylonians, Assyrians, Hittites, and many others.

In Egypt writing developed according to a hieroglyphic system which can be traced back to as early as 2900 B.C. This system passed through its own series of independent modifications and developments.

The alphabetic system appears to have originated around 1800 B.C. in Canaan. It is not altogether certain how this system related to the older systems of writing, but since all alphabets can be traced back to an original type, it is believed by many that the alphabet was invented in a single place by one or a group of individuals who had enjoyed a familiarity with Egyptian hieroglyphics, cuneiform, and other styles of writing (see F. Cross, Jr., "Writing", *TCERK*, pp. 1191-92). In any event this Canaanite (Phoenician) system of writing became in time the basis for all alphabetic scripts and from this source the Hebrew alphabet took its origin. To date the earliest samples of classical Hebrew script are the Moabite stone *ca.* 850 B.C. and the more recently discovered Gezer Calendar *ca.* 925 B.C., but the antecedents of classical Hebrew are much earlier than this.

Writing is frequently mentioned in the OT, particularly in regard to various historic and sacred events (Ex. 17:14; 28:11; 31:18; 32:15). Kings, priests, prophets, professional scribes, and people in superior position were expected to be able to read and write (Deut. 17:18; 24:1, 3; Isa. 29:11-12).

Various writing materials are also mentioned in Scripture such as stone covered with plaster (Deut. 27:2-3), as well as stones engraved with iron pen or chisel (Josh. 8:32; Ex. 34:28; Deut. 4:13). Although leather or papyrus are not mentioned in the OT, they are presumed known and used (Jer. 36:2-4, 18, 23; Ezra 4:7-11). Other writing materials used by OT people were potsherds, wooden tablets, metals, and precious stones. In NT times parchment and papyrus became the dominant writing materials.

The word written, *gegraptai*, is used more than fifty times in the NT with reference to quotations from the OT. (John uses *gegrammenon estin*). It is derived from *graphō*, "to write," and is related to *hē graphē* which is used of individual scripture passages or in the plural of Scripture as a whole. *Gegraptai* is used widely in the papyri with reference to the regulative and authoritative character of the document referred to. In the sphere of divine revelation *gegraptai* "always implies an appeal to the indisputable and normative authority of the passage quoted" (Crem p. 165). Consequently when the sacred writers referred to Holy Scripture in these terms it meant they did so as an appeal to absolute authority (*DeissBS*, T & T Clark, Edinburgh, 1901, pp. 112-14).

It has been a problem to some today to acknowledge that a written word could rightly be described as the authoritative revelation of God. It is not to be understood, of course, that the writers of Scripture believed that because they wrote their words down they thereby possessed some magical authority, but rather that the sacred writers, having received the word of revelation from God, recorded these words that they might constitute an objective standard against the fluctuations of time and history. So God spoke to Moses, "write this for a memorial" (Ex. 17:14). It must also be remembered that it is only the written word which is entitled "to claim the four characteristics of durability, catholicity, fixedness and purity, — four attributes, the first two of which impart something of the divine stamp to our human word, and the last two of which form a corrective against the imperfection of our sinful condition" (A. Kuyper, *Principles of Sacred Theology*, Eerdmans Publishing Co., Grand Rapids, Michigan, 1954, pp. 405 f.).

BIBLIOGRAPHY

G. Bonfante, "Alphabet," *Colliers Encyclopedia*, 1955, I, pp. 408-12; B. F. C. Atkinson, "Alphabet," *Ency Brit* 1957, I pp. 677-85; A. C. Moorhouse, *The Triumph of the Alphabet*; B. B. Warfied, *PTR*, 8:560 f.; D. Diringer, *The Alphabet*.

GLENN W. BARKER

Y

YOKE. Widely used in the Bible, yoke has several meanings. It may refer to a piece of curved timber fitted with bows for the necks of draft animals to serve as an instrument in pulling a cart or plow. It is also a symbol of slavery. In I Tim. 6:1 Paul employs the Greek counterpart, *zygos*, in this sense when he admonishes all under "the yoke of slavery" to respect their masters regardless of the treatment they receive.

More important, however, is the theological significance of the word in its connection with the idea of slavery. The slavery here is not physical but spiritual; and the yoke is a picture of the law as the people's taskmaster. In this respect Paul warns the Galatians not to resubmit to the "yoke of slavery" because they have been freed by Christ from servitude to the law (5:1). The same idea is expressed in Acts 15:10.

A paradox presents itself in the use of yoke in Matt. 11:29 f. How can a yoke be easy? But Jesus is addressing those who already bear a yoke, the "yoke of the law," the *'ôl tôrâ*, which is a vital concept in rabbinic piety. Bearing the *'ôl tôrâ* along with the *'ôl malkût š*e*mayim*, "the yoke of the kingdom," will eventually inaugurate the messianic age. Not so for Jesus; for the yoke of the Pharisees produces slavery; but his, freedom and direct access to the Father.

BIBLIOGRAPHY

SBK; K. H. Rengstorf in *TWNT*.

HERMAN C. WAETJEN

YOUNG, YOUNG MEN. Young men are conspicuous on the pages of both the OT and NT. Samuel, Saul, David and Daniel were all young men when they came into prominence. Jesus began his ministry as a young man and revealed a genuine concern for youth (cf. Matt. 19:16-22 and parallels; Luke 7:11-17). Paul was a young man when he was converted (Acts 7:58), and he and Barnabas chose a young companion, John Mark, to accompany them on their first Gentile mission. Timothy also was relatively young (I Tim. 4:12) when he assumed the responsibility of the Ephesian church — an indication that positions of leadership were sometimes entrusted to the young.

There is evidence, however, that there were well marked distinctions between the young and the old in the early church. I John 2:13 — 14 indicates that only two special age groups, "fathers" and "young men" were recognized in the church. ("Children" is probably an in-clusive designation, cf. 2:18.) Age was revered and received due respect (I Tim. 5:1-2; I Pet. 5:5) while youth was exhorted to self-control and godly living (Titus 2:6).

WALTER W. WESSEL

Z

ZEAL. The Hebrew noun *qin'â* "zeal, ardor, jealousy" (occurring 43 times) has its counterpart in the Greek *zēlos* (16 times in the NT), while the denominative verb *qānā'* (= to have *qin'â*) "be zealous, jealous" (34) is equivalent to the Greek verb *zēloō* (11). Being equivocal terms, *qin'â* and *zēlos* can be either *good* "zeal, ardor, jealousy for" (Ps. 69:9; II Cor. 7:7) or *bad* "envy, jealousy of" (Num. 5:14; Acts 5:17), depending on the motive. At times, however, even zeal with a sincere motive is improper (Rom. 10:2; Phil. 3:6). Paul, sensing the dual function of these terms, made himself explicit in II Cor. 11:2: "For I am jealous for you with a godly jealousy."

The qualification "godly" hearkens back to the OT usage of *qannā'* (Ex. 20:5 = Deut. 5:9; Ex. 34:14; Deut. 4:24; 6:15) and *qannô'* (Josh. 24:19; Nah. 1:2), always of God, in the striking anthropomorphic expression "jealous God." God is jealous for Israel, as a husband for his wife, because by choice and covenant they are peculiarly his own. He is zealous for their protection and salvation, but at the same time he is a "consuming fire" (Deut. 4:24) when evil is in their midst. God's jealousy is as much a part of his righteous, holy character and being as is his love.

The NT does not speak of God being jealous. Rather, it is God's Son (John 2:17) and God's spiritual sons (II Cor. 7:11; 11:2), who exhibit this "divine zeal" in behalf of God's holiness and kingdom, and so it must be in the church today.

BIBLIOGRAPHY
Arndt; KB; *RTWB*; *SHERK*.

DEWEY M. BEEGLE

ZEALOT. The Zealots were a party of militant Jewish patriots of the first century.

Their movement began with Judas of Galilee in the days of Quirinius as an underground opposition to the Roman power. They held that violence was justified if it would free the nation from its foreign oppressors. Josephus (BJ IV, iii. 9; VII, viii. 1) described them as fanatics whose extravagant claims and untempered rashness made them a hindrance to their own cause. He identified them with the extremists who provoked the war with Rome in A.D. 66, and he intimated that the internal strife that weakened the defense of Jerusalem and ultimately contributed to the fall of the city in A.D. 70 was partially attributable to them. Toward the last of this period they seem to have become a group of political assassins with no constructive program, but with a mania for overturning all government and order. Josephus' estimate may have been biased, but it is the best primary source available.

In doctrine they were closely akin to the Pharisees because of their extreme nationalistic interpretation of the OT, and in spirit they were like the Maccabees. Their intense desire for an independent kingdom may have drawn some of them into the company of Jesus' disciples. At least one of them, Simon, is distinguished from Simon Peter by being called "the Zealot" (Luke 6:15; Acts 1:13).

BIBLIOGRAPHY
W. R. Farmer, *Maccabees, Zealots, and Josephus*; E. Schuerer, *The Jewish People in the Time of Christ*, I, ii, 80, 177; Josephus, *Wars of the Jews*, IV. iii. 9. 12-14.

MERRILL C. TENNEY

ZION. Geographically, Zion designates, as is now generally held, the lower eastern hill or ridge of Jerusalem. Modern excavations have confirmed this location.

Historically, Zion began, as far as biblical history is concerned, when David captured the

Jebusite fortress and made it, as enlarged, into "the city of David" — the capitol of his kingdom (II Sam. 5:6-10). Three geographical factors enhanced its historical significance: (1) its strong position; (2) its central location; (3) its being outside the territory of the twelve tribes. Zion came to its predicted end (Jer. 26:18; Mic. 3:12) when Jerusalem was destroyed (A.D. 70).

Figuratively, Zion — under such descriptions as "daughters of Zion" (Isa. 3:16 f.), "children of Zion" (Joel 2:23), etc. — represents, by a figure called synecdoche, the city of Jerusalem or the entire Hebrew nation.

Typically and spiritually, Zion (gathering significance from its geographical, historical and figurative background) becomes, in the Psalms and in the prophets, the spiritual counterpart of the literal city. The theology of the "spiritualization" of Zion has hardly yet been explored by expositors. A few gems from this rich territory must suffice: (1) The literal Zion was a strong fortress (II Sam. 5:7); the spiritual Zion is immovable (Ps. 125:1). (2) The literal Zion became the seat of David's throne (II Sam. 5:9, 12); the spiritual Zion is the place of the messianic throne (Ps. 2:6). (3) The literal Zion became the birthplace of David's children (II Sam. 5:13); the spiritual Zion is the birthplace of God's elect (Ps. 87:5 f.; Isa. 66:8). (4) The literal Zion was the place where David received the promise of an eternal house and throne (II Sam. 7); the spiritual Zion is the place where "the everlasting covenant" is established (Jer. 50:5; cf. Heb. 8:6-10). (5) The literal Zion, in contrast to the ceremonialism of Sinai, housed the ark in a single form of worship (I Kings 8:1 ff.); the spiritual Zion becomes the eternal embodiment of the true worship of God "in spirit and truth" (John 4:23 f.; cf. Amos 9:11 f.; Acts 15:15 ff.; Heb. 12:22 ff.).

WICK BROOMALL

ZOROASTRIANISM. A religion that developed in Iran from about the sixth century B.C., generally ascribed to Zoroaster (Zarathustra) who was born in Iran "258 years before Alexander." The date of Zoroaster's birth has been given variously at 6000 B.C., 1400 B.C., and 1000 B.C., but Herzfeld accepts the traditional date, approximately, as now confirmed (Herzfeld, 570-500 B.C.; Jackson, 660-583 B.C.). Accordingly, Zoroaster was contemporary with other great religious personages, including

Buddha, Confucius, Lao Tze, and several Hebrew prophets. That Zoroaster used Vedic materials found in early Hinduism can hardly be denied; that he was a polytheist like Darius, Xerxes, and others who were probably Zoroastrians (at least, their inscriptions pay homage to Ahura Mazda), seems most likely. But Zoroaster was protesting against the false and cruel in religion, and followed the principle, "if the gods do aught shameful, they are not gods." Accordingly, he exalted Ahura Mazda ("wise Lord," often improperly translated "Lord of light") as supreme among the gods or spirits, and viewed the world as an age-long struggle between Ahura Mazda and Angra Mainyu (or Ahramanyuš, Ahriman, "Spirit of evil"), both of whom came into existence independently in the distant past. Zoroastrianism is therefore called a Dualism — but it is a limited Dualism. Zoroaster calls upon men to join in this conflict on the side of Ahura Mazda, the key words of such religion being "good thoughts, good words, good deeds." The ultimate victory of Ahura Mazda, however, was not to be accomplished by human assistance but by the advent of a messiah-like figure, the Saoshyant. The duration of the struggle was to be 6,000 years (3,000 had already passed when Zoroaster was born), following which was to be the resurrection and judgment. Many of the details of Zoroastrianism are later developments, some post-Christian and even post-Mohammedan, and scholars are divided on what elements are to be traced to Zoroaster's own teaching.

Because of the fact that the revelation of the doctrines of resurrection, angels, Satan, and the Messiah comes late in the OT or even in the intertestamental period in early Judaism (q.v.), scholars have frequently traced these ideas to Zoroastrian influence exerted upon the Jewish people after the Babylonian exile. Moulton examined these points in detail and concluded that they were "not proven." The discovery of the Dead Sea Scrolls has reopened the discussion, due to the presence of marked "Zoroastrian" influences in the Qumran literature. Some of the most striking parallels to Jewish-Christian eschatology can be shown to be very late developments in Zoroastrianism. On the other hand, it would not do violence to a high view of inspiration to admit that God could have used Zoroastrianism as a means of stimulating the Jewish mind to think on these subjects even as he used Hellenism to prepare the Jewish mind for the Christian revelation (witness Saul of Tarsus). The Magi ("Wise Men") of the birth-narrative may have been Zoroastrian priests.

BIBLIOGRAPHY

J. H. Moulton, "Zoroastrianism," *HDB* 4, pp. 988-94; A. V. W. Jackson, "Zoroastrianism," *JewEnc* 12, pp. 695-97; E. Herzfeld, *Zoroaster and His World*, 2 vols.

WILLIAM SANFORD LASOR